D1716222

Handbook of Urban Educational Leadership

Handbook of Urban Educational Leadership

Edited by Muhammad Khalifa, Noelle Witherspoon Arnold,
Azadeh F. Osanloo, and Cosette M. Grant

ROWMAN & LITTLEFIELD
Lanham • Boulder • New York • London

Published by Rowman & Littlefield
A wholly owned subsidiary of The Rowman & Littlefield Publishing Group, Inc.
4501 Forbes Boulevard, Suite 200, Lanham, Maryland 20706
www.rowman.com

Unit A, Whitacre Mews, 26-34 Stannary Street, London SE11 4AB

Copyright © 2015 by Rowman & Littlefield Publishers

All rights reserved. No part of this book may be reproduced in any form or by
any electronic or mechanical means, including information storage and retrieval
systems, without written permission from the publisher, except by a reviewer who
may quote passages in a review.

British Library Cataloguing in Publication Information Available

Library of Congress Cataloging-in-Publication Data

Khalifa, Muhammad A., 1975–
  Handbook of urban educational leadership / Muhammad Khalifa,
Noelle Witherspoon Arnold, Azadeh F. Osanloo , and Cosette M. Grant.
      pages cm
  Includes bibliographical references and index.
  ISBN 978-1-4422-2084-3 (cloth : alk. paper)— ISBN 978-1-4422-2085-0 (electronic)
1. Education, Urban—United States. 2. Education, Urban—United States—
Administration. 3. Educational leadership—United States. I. Title.
  LC5131.K55 2015
  370.9173'2—dc23
                                                                          2014050039

♾️™ The paper used in this publication meets the minimum requirements of
American National Standard for Information Sciences—Permanence of Paper
for Printed Library Materials, ANSI/NISO Z39.48-1992.

Printed in the United States of America

Muhummad Khalifa

I dedicate this work to my mother, Faith; my pop, Aziz; my loving wife, Nimo; and my sons, Ibrahim, Adam, and Zack. Thank you for your patience with me, and for bearing my absence as I push for this work for the voiceless and oppressed.

Noelle Witherspoon Arnold

I dedicate this to my colleagues, Muhummad, Azadeh, and Cosette, and other scholars who share my commitment to urban communities and to the educators, children, and families in them. And as always, I dedicate this to my husband, who supports me in my "anger" and helps me channel it for advocacy and activism.

Azadeh F. Osanloo

To my mother—unequivocally, irrefutably, and unapologetically the strongest and most badass woman I know.

Cosette M. Grant

I dedicate this masterpiece handbook to my son, Jameson, our next-generation doctor, lawyer, inventor, president, educator, or entrepreneur. Paving the way for you to bear the torch as you emerge and hoping you will be a force one day for equity and access to high-quality education for all. I also celebrate this timely work with my colleagues, who are trailblazers—Muhammad, Noelle, and Azadeh. May our individual and collective voices on urban educational leadership for the sake of advancing education, opportunities, and hence a better quality of life for our children, continue to magnify and make a longstanding impact!

Contents

In this country, one of the most challenging dilemmas of the twentieth and now the twenty-first centuries has been our horrendous and continuous failure to adequately educate the large numbers of students in urban schools (Barton and Coley, 2010; Delpit, 2012; Hrabowski, 2004; Krueger and Whitmore, 2001; Lee, 2002; National Commission of Teaching and America's Future, 2007; Paige and Witty, 2010; U.S. Department of Education, 2009). These schools have changed substantially in a number of ways, including their structure, emphasis, and student characteristics. In the face of these and many other changes, urban schools continue to fail the large majority of children in their charge.

The structure of inner city schools today varies significantly from the way they were structured twenty-five years ago. For one thing, we have magnet schools and charter schools. While magnet schools have been around since the 1960s (largely unsuccessful in their efforts to attract white families to inner city schools), twenty-five years ago urban schools were primarily neighborhood schools.

Charter schools (on the whole, another failed reform effort) did not come about until the early part of the 1990s. They now seem to have taken on the business model. They have become an investment product that is not evaluated in terms of how well they serve families; instead the focus is on the profit margin. Indeed the public/private partnership in education seems well on the road to privatization.

DEMOGRAPHICS

The student population in U.S. urban public schools has significantly changed in many ways over the past twenty-five years. Racially, the percentage of Hispanic students in these schools has substantially increased, the percentage of students who are white has drastically declined, and the percentage of black students has remained virtually static (National Center for Education Statistics, 1996, 2013). (See table 0.1.)

Table 0.1.   Racial Composition of Students in Urban Public Schools in the U.S. (1990, 2004 & 2010)

	Whites (%)	Blacks (%)	Hispanics (%)	Other (%)
1990	43	32	19	6
2004	na	28	29	Na
2010	20	33	38	9

Never before have we experienced the level of student diversity that we currently see in U.S. urban public schools. (See the Sleeter chapter in this volume.) From 2000 to 2010, the percentage of English as a second language (ESL) learners increased by nearly 54 percent and is considerably higher in urban schools than it is in rural or suburban schools (Quartz, 2012). (See table 0.2.)

Table 0.2.   ESL Learners in U.S. Schools (2004 & 2009)

	Urban (%)	Suburban (%)	Rural (%)	All (%)
2004	17	8	na	11
2009	19	10	6	na

By 2007, more than a third of the teachers in U.S. public schools were in urban centers, as were nearly a third of the schools. In addition, as of 2011, almost 30 percent of the students in U.S. public schools were in urban districts (National Center for Education Statistics, 2013; National Commission on Teaching and America's Future, 2007). (See table 0.3.)

Table 0.3.   Selected Demographics in U.S. Urban and Non-Urban Public Schools (2007)

	Total	Urban	Non-Urban
Teachers	3,447,000	1,229,398 (36%)	2,217,602 (64%)
Districts	14,383	850 (6%)	13,533 (94%)
Schools	95,726	29,886 (31%)	65,840 (69%)
Students	49,000,000	14,000,000 (29%)	35,000,000 (71%)

STATE OF URBAN SCHOOLS

Glaringly, several negative sets of circumstances continue to be reflected in urban public schools in the United States. These include:

- Underachievement
- Institutionalized white racism
- Segregation
- Poverty
- Teacher flight
- Poor teacher quality
- Inadequate material resources (e.g., buildings, science labs, textbooks, physical education equipment)
- Failed reform efforts
- Pre-school to prison pipeline
- High student dropout rate

Underachievement

We continue to fail students in U.S. urban public schools—particularly those who are poor and so-called minority—at astronomically high rates (Ahram, Stembridge, Fergus, and Noguera, 2011; Theoharis, 2009; Wright, 2012). (See the Sleeter chapter in this volume.) While researchers have identified a plethora of explanations for this quandary—and posed solutions—rarely has their evidence-based research become effective funded policy.

Institutionalized White Racism

We live in a society—in a world—wherein people continue to be discriminated against, based upon the color of their skin (and other illegitimate forms of exclusion). (See the Hopson, Whitaker, Sakho, and Wilkins; and King and McTier chapters in this volume.)

Segregation

Sixty-one years after Brown I (and sixty years after Brown II), black and Hispanic children continue to go to school in largely segregated settings (Wright, 2012). Most black and Hispanic children in urban communities attend public schools where the minority population exceeds 75 percent (Krauser, 2012). Indeed, in 2009 the twenty largest urban school districts each had minority student enrollments of 80 percent or more (Quartz, 2012). While segregation in and of itself is not necessarily problematic, more often than not, there is attendant inequity in human and material resources that lead to disparate educational outcomes.

Poverty

Poverty continues to raise its ugly head in U.S. urban public schools as another major source of the challenges therein. It is massive and increasing in urban schools. Fifty-six percent of urban school students qualify for free lunch programs and 40 percent are eligible for Title I programs. In suburban communities, the comparable percentages are 32 percent and 20 percent respectively (Jacob, 2007). Poverty, unfortunately, is reflected in a lack of educational resources in the home, increased crime, and many other less-than-desirable circumstances that are not conducive to educational success.

Teacher Flight

With increased diversity of the student population in U.S. urban public schools, we have seen a remarkable increase in the percentage of teachers leaving these schools. By 2005, 20 percent of teachers were leaving urban schools each year. This was up by 50 percent from 1990 (National Commission on Teaching and America's Future, 2007). By 2007, this mass exodus had led to what has become a $7 billion problem. The inconsistency associated with high teacher turnover contributes to low student achievement.

Poor Teacher Quality

Teachers in urban schools—when compared to other teachers—generally have less teaching experience, lower standardized achievement test scores, an inferior educational background, and are less likely to have appropriate teacher certification. This is the case because the teachers with the best qualifications have the most options and generally prefer to work in the "better" schools. Moreover, urban schools have the most difficulty attracting STEM teachers. For example, 35 percent of urban schools have difficulty recruiting math teachers. In suburban schools, the comparable statistic is 25 percent (Jacob, 2007).

Inadequate Material Resources

Still, in 2014, public schools in U.S. urban centers significantly lag behind in the quality and quantity of material resources. The books used in the classroom are insufficient and older, the computers are substantially more aged, and the science laboratory equipment is significantly outdated or nonexistent. Moreover, there is a lesser emphasis on college preparation in the curriculum in part because of the relatively low teacher quality and the inadequate material resources (Hudley, 2013). (See the Granger and Noguera chapter in this volume.)

Failed Reform Efforts

There have been few—if any—large-scale, national reform efforts in the history of U.S. education that have benefitted the majority of students in urban public schools. I would agree with others who have argued that the failures include—but are not limited to—charter schools, magnet schools, No Child Left Behind (Kozol, 2006;

Wright, 2012), Race to the Top, The Elementary and Secondary Education Act (Wright, 2012), desegregation, and so on. Most successful reforms have been brought about through relatively small-scale, localized efforts. (See, for example, the Baete, Burks, Pollio, and Hochbein; Diem and Carpenter; and Peters, Liang, and Finklin chapters in this volume.)

Pre-school to Prison Pipeline

Some states and/or municipalities are predicting future prison needs based upon third grade student success or lack thereof. Related data are being accumulated by the U.S. Department of Education in concert with the U.S. Department of Labor—*as early as pre-school*. (See the Cole, Heilig, Fernandez, Clifford, and Garcia chapter in this volume.)

Let me take one Southern state to give an illustration of the current state of the penal system in the United States—Louisiana. Here are a few highlights of the infamous Louisiana penal system.

Louisiana has more prisoners per capita than any state in the union. It has three times the incarceration rate of Iran, seven times the rate of China, and ten times the rate of Germany. From 1992 to 2012, its prison population doubled; it now totals more than forty thousand. One in eighty-six adults in Louisiana is doing time. In New Orleans, one out of every fourteen black men is in prison, and one out of every seven black men is in prison, on probation, or on parole.

In that city, five thousand black men and four hundred white men are incarcerated. Most prison entrepreneurs in Louisiana are sheriffs. Think about that. Sheriffs build the prisons, sheriffs are responsible for filling them, and when they get filled, sheriffs get paid—and their lobby prevents prison reform efforts from succeeding in Louisiana. Also in Louisiana, if one is convicted of murder, they are *automatically* sentenced to life without parole. This law has also made Louisiana the state with the highest percentage of inmates with life sentences without parole. While a "poor" state, it spends $663 million a year on its inmates, and it rewards sheriffs, as $183 million of that goes to for-profit prisons that they fill.

High Student Dropout Rate

Perhaps the most glaring comparison of urban and surrounding suburban nonurban public schools in the United States is in the dropout rates. Nationally, in 2005, 47 percent of the students in urban schools dropped out of school; for their adjacent non-urban schools, the percentage was 29. Some big cities showed significantly larger gaps (Dillon, 2009). (See table 0.4.)

Table 0.4.   Selected Urban and Non-Urban Public School Dropout Rates in the U.S. (2005)

	New York City	Cleveland	Baltimore
Urban	46	62	59
Suburban	17	20	19

SCHOLARSHIP ON URBAN SCHOOLS

Over the past fifty years, quite a bit of writing has been done about urban public schools in the United States. However, little success in improving these schools has occurred; indeed, some argue that these schools may now be worse.

I edited the journal *Urban Education* for nearly twenty years (1992–2011). During that time I read, on average, more than two hundred manuscripts a year on various aspects of urban education, broadly defined. Some of them were the best of the best; some were not so good. In the final analysis I learned quite a bit about inner city schools and about the work of many of the scholars who conduct research on those schools. Contributors to the journal wrote—and continue to write—about the importance of various factors in improving the academic success of students in urban schools. They wrote/write about characteristics associated with:

- teachers (experience, quality, attitudes and beliefs, etc.)
- principals (leadership, management, experience, commitment, etc.)
- parents/families/communities (socioeconomic status, attitudes, etc.) (See, for example, the Fields-Smith, Williams, and Shoemaker; Khalifa, Gil, Marshall, and White; and Loder-Jackson, McKnight, Brooks, and Perry chapters in this volume.)
- students (background, attitudes, abilities, etc.)
- schools and school districts (funding, class size, academic orientation, school size, etc.).

While much has been written on the various factors associated with urban school success, and while it is true that there is enough responsibility to be spread around, I continue to believe in the unique importance of school leadership in bringing about significant sustained improvement in the success of students in (urban) schools. (See the Jackson, McDermott, Simmons, and McDermott chapter in this volume.) Certainly for African-American, Hispanic, Native American, and Asian students—and indeed for all students—a culturally responsive learning environment is critical. (See, for example, the Brown and Williams; Lomotey and Lowery; and Santamaría, Santamaría, Webber, and Pearson chapters in this volume.) In earlier work, along with Lowery, I discussed the importance of the principal in bringing about a culturally responsive learning environment (Lomotey and Lowery, 2014).

There is a plethora of research illustrating the importance of several key characteristics of school leaders in bringing about student success, including goal development, energy harnessing, communication facilitation, and instructional leadership.

THIS VOLUME

Khalifa, Witherspoon Arnold, Osanloo, and Grant have put together a volume that is important for several reasons. First, it focuses on school leadership and its importance in urban schools. And the concept of leadership is defined broadly herein to include the leadership provided not only by administrators, but also by teachers, counselors, and parents and community people. (See, for example, the Furtado; Milner, Laughter, and Childs; Reddick, Smith, and Bukoski; and West-Olatunji chapters in this volume.) The authors do a good job of describing the previous work in their respective areas, and they build on that work in a useful way.

This volume is important because it provides a vision for the future with regard to the education of students in urban public schools. (See, for example, the Price; May and Sanders; Watkins, Anthony, Shaffer, and Smith; and Whiteman, Scribner, and Crow chapters in this volume.) More particularly, the authors in this volume provide an analysis of best practices in urban public schools. (See, for example, the Baete; Burks, Pollio, and Hochbein; Garza; Gutelius; Osanloo and Schwartz; and Young, Gooden, and O'Doherty chapters in this volume.)

In fact, the historical perspectives offered in this volume are invaluable. (See, for example, the May and Sanders; Alston; Xia, Gao, and Shen; and Boggs and Dunbar chapters in this volume.) For if we are unable to understand where we have been, we will have difficulty planning our way forward. This has been a problem thus far with national educational policy initiatives (e.g., magnet schools, No Child Left Behind, charter schools, Race to the Top).

A critical part of the discussion in this volume focuses on the many dimensions of the politics of education. (See the Gaines, Bogotch, and Salaam chapter in this volume.)

The volume also focuses on the importance of social justice, equity, and ethics. (See, for example, the Barnett and Stevenson; Jean-Marie, Normore, and Brooks; Rigby and Tredway; and Roegman and Hatch chapters in this volume.)

There is no doubt that research and publications on urban schools and on how to make them work better will continue to appear in *Urban Education* and other leading journals on urban schools. It is also likely that—in part because of the contributions in this volume—we will become better at educating the students who attend these schools. This is true because we are getting better at this work; the current volume is a testament to this fact—as well as a wake-up call.

Leadership, broadly defined, must continue to be a focus of our exploration. Leaders have the potential to influence community people, parents, teachers, and, most importantly, students in fundamentally enlightening ways. This volume reinforces this truism.

What is also made clear through this volume is that when leadership is broadly defined, there is hope of improving the circumstances of students in urban public schools in the United States in a more comprehensive way. In all schools and in all communities there are leaders (and potential leaders) who do not sit in the principal's office; these leaders must be allowed to shine.

REFERENCES

Ahram, R., Stembridge, A., Fergus, E., and Noguera, P. (2011). Framing urban school challenges: The problems to examine when implementing response to intervention. Washington, DC: RTI Action Network. http://www.rtinetwork.org/learn/diversity/urban-school-challenges

Barton, P. E. and Coley, R. J (2010). *The black-white achievement gap: When progress stopped.* Policy Information Report. Princeton, NJ: Educational Testing Service.

Cohen, S. (2010). A $5 children's book vs. a $47,000 jail cell—choose one. http://www.forbes.com/sites/stevecohen/2010/12/25/a-5-childrens-book-vs-a-47000-jail-cell-choose-one/

Delpit, L. (2012). *"Multiplication is for white people": Raising expectations for other people's children.* New York: The New Press.

Hrabowski, F. (2004). Leadership for a new age: Higher education's role in producing minority leaders. *Liberal Education* 90(2), n.p.

Hudley, C. (2013). *Education and urban schools.* Washington, DC: American Psychological Association.

Jacob, B. A. (2007). The challenges of staffing urban schools with effective teachers. *The Future of Children, 17*(1), 129–153.

Kozol. J. (2006). *The shame of the nation: The restoration of apartheid schooling in America.* New York: Crown Publishing.

Krauser, M. (2012). Segregation continues in urban schools. *Next American City.* http://www.salon.com/2012/07/11/segregation_in_urban_schools_salpart/

Krueger, A. B. and Whitmore, D. M. (2001). *Would smaller classes help close the black-white achievement gap?* Working Paper, Princeton University, Industrial Relations Section. http://www.irs.princeton.edu/pubs/working_papers.html.

Lee, J. (2002). Racial and ethnic achievement gap trends: Reversing the progress toward equity? *Educational Researcher 31*(1), 3–12.

Lomotey, K. and Lowery, K. (2014). Black students, urban schools, and black principals: Leadership practices that reduce disenfranchisement. In H. Richard Milner IV and Kofi Lomotey (Eds.), *Handbook of urban education* (pp. 325–349). New York: Routledge.

National Center for Education Statistics. (1996). *Urban schools: The challenge of location and poverty.* Washington, DC: U.S. Department of Education, Office of Educational Research and Improvement.

National Center for Education Statistics. (2013). *The Condition of education.* Washington, DC: US Department of Education, Office of Educational Research and Improvement.

National Commission on Teaching and America's Future. (2007). *Policy brief: The high cost of teacher turnover.* Washington, DC: Author.

Paige, R. and Witty, E. (2010). The black-white achievement gap: Why closing it is the greatest civil rights issue of our time. New York: American Management Association.

Quartz, K. H. (2012) Urban schools, teacher preparation for diversity. In James A. Banks (Ed.), *Encyclopedia of diversity in education.* Thousand Oaks: CA: Sage.

Ravitch, D. (1998). *A new era in urban education?* Brookings Policy Brief Series. Washington, DC: The Brookings Institute.

U.S. Department of Education, National Center for Education Statistics. (2009). *Characteristics of public, private, and Bureau of Indian Education elementary and secondary schools in the United States: Results from the 2007–08 Schools and Staffing Survey (NCES 2009-321).* nces.ed.gov/FastFacts/display.asp?id=55-22k

Wright, W. (March 29–31, 2012). *The disparities between urban and suburban American educational systems: A comparative analysis using social closure theory.* Proceedings of the National Conference on Undergraduate Research HUSL(NCUR). Weber State University, Ogden, Utah.

The Editors first of all thank former Rowman & Littlefield acquisitions editor Nancy Evans, for offering the first contract and for being so enthusiastic and supportive about the project. We could not have done this without you. We miss you.

Sarah Kendall, our new R&L editor, you did not skip a beat when this project was turned over to you, and we thank you so much for helping guide us to the home stretch. You were the right editor at the right time. Carlie Wall—what can we say? You are amazing.

Thank you to all the amazing scholars and contributors to this Handbook. Your inclusion makes this a premier reference for scholars and practitioners. We are so honored to have you. Moreover, this was quite a task to undertake as mid-career professionals, and we have benefited greatly from all your knowledge, expertise, and suggestions.

Thank you to Rhodesia McMillian, University of Missouri graduate assistant, for all your work on this. We thank you for keeping us organized. We appreciate all your hard work, but mostly your kind spirit. Thank you also to Laurita Mendez, New Mexico State University graduate assistant, for being our eleventh-hour savior. And lastly, we thank Elizabeth Gil, Michigan State University graduate assistant, for organizing us early on in the project.

Finally we thank our own personal circle of friend-scholars who have supported us, served as sounding boards, and made the work fun.

URBAN EDUCATIONAL LEADERSHIP

A Historical Perspective

In this section we examine the history of urban communities and educational leadership. While this section cannot explore all of history, we do examine critical periods and incidents that impact modern urban education and leadership. In chapter 1, "Urban Education and Leadership: A Historical Perspective," Judy Jackson May and Eugene Sanders examine the nexus between urban culture and communities, and significant educational policy decisions from post-World War II through contemporary reform and transformation.

Judy A. Alston builds on concepts in May and Sanders's work in chapter 2, "Sankofa: Leadership and the Twenty-First Century Black Female School Superintendents," by discussing the historic *Brown* decision of 1954 the loss of black teachers and administrators in public schools. Ten years after the ruling, the number of black principals in the eleven southern border states (Virginia, North Carolina, South Carolina, Florida, Kentucky, Tennessee, Georgia, Alabama, Mississippi, Louisiana, and Arkansas) dropped by 95 percent (Coursen, 1989). Alston focuses her chapter by reflecting on the legacy of the Jeanes supervisors to provide lessons for the twenty-first-century African-American female superintendent.

The authors of chapter 3, "Demographic and Professional Characteristics of Urban School Principals in the United States: A 20-Year Trend Study," examine the historic trends of urban school principals' demographic and professional characteristics over the last twenty years. Jiangang Xia, Xingyuan Gao, and Jianping Shen give an important look at various issues impacting urban school principals, such as race, gender, and principal preparation. The section ends with chapter 4, "An Interpretive History of Urban Education and Leadership in Age of Perceived Racial Invisibility" by Brian J. Boggs and Chris Dunbar. The authors offer a fitting ending to this section as they unpack the social and political review of the history or evolution of urban education through a policy lens-the creation of urban communities and subsequent urban schools pre-and post-*Brown*.

CHAPTER 1

Urban Education and Leadership

A Historical Perspective

Judy Jackson May and Eugene Sanders

This chapter explores the relationship between urban culture, communities, and educational policy from an organizational transformation perspective. The authors focus on the span between post–World War II and significant contemporary initiatives such as No Child Left Behind and school transformation efforts. Captured in the discussion is the persistent impact of urbanization and industrialization on our current educational challenges. The decades of school reform in American education are framed by chronicling early school improvement efforts, beginning with the release of *A Nation At Risk* and concluding with our current quest for global competitiveness. Reflecting on the nexus between urban culture, communities, and educational leadership, the authors posit five significant lessons learned from the last fifty years of American education.

Lesson One: The economic and political survival of the United States of America is 100 percent contingent upon the creation of a national wholesale transformation plan for public schools.

Lesson Two: Comprehensive school reform will be difficult, disruptive, emotional, and volatile. Be prepared for community unrest when implementing a transformation plan.

Lesson Three: Money, in and of itself, is not the total solution to successful school transformation.

Lesson Four: Failure to successfully accomplish the goals of a national transformation plan must have consequences for all groups within the educational organization.

Lesson Five: Ensure sustainability of the transformation plan by institutionalizing and creating what has been coined as a "sense of urgency" for implementation.

INDUSTRIALIZATION, URBANIZATION, AND BUREAUCRACY IN THE POST–WORLD WAR II ERA

Urban school transformation in the twenty-first century is complex and contextual. Examination of the current efforts to improve the quality of schools and communities in urban centers requires a perspective of the historical role of political, economic, and social forces. To explore the evolution of urban culture, communities, and educational leadership, it is important to recognize the persistent and inescapable impact of industrialization on urban centers and, subsequently, urban education. While the nineteenth century is characterized as a period of institution building in America, the twentieth century is characterized by urbanization and a growing bureaucracy within educational institutions (Kanter and Lowe, 1995).

As cities began to grow in size and complexity, public funding for urban schools grew out of a need to create social stability (Payne, 2008). The educational goal was to ensure that all newcomers (immigrants) were trained to become responsible citizens and able to meet the demands of the burgeoning industrialization complex. Growing urban centers and the economic viability of the nation became increasingly more dependent on expanding the skilled labor force needed to maintain a vibrant country. With an expanding economy and plentiful jobs, the consequences for dropping out of school were negligible (Cuban, 1989). Rumberger (1987) cites that in 1940 "more than 60 percent of all persons 25–29 years old had not completed high school" (p. 101). By 1980, however, the national dropout rate of whites and African Americans, aged 16–19, improved significantly to 12 percent and 14 percent respectively, but Latinos lagged markedly behind at 28 percent

(Rumberger, 1987). In spite of the 1980s dropout rate decline nationally, urban school centers continue to battle rates of 50 percent among African-American and Latino populations (Nogura and Wells, 2011).

The cost of urbanization and industrialization include a boundless spectrum of social, political, and economic challenges that continue to haunt our societal consciousness. Over fifty years ago, Leo F. Schnore wrote, "the vast majority of social phenomena identified as problematic are they themselves correlates, concomitants, or consequences of urban industrialism" (1962, p. 228). Many of our societal and educational challenges, whether direct or indirect, regardless of the origins, are most noticeable in urban settings (Schnore, 1962). While issues such as poverty, joblessness, homelessness, crime, low academic achievement, and systemic racial injustices are found in nearly every corner of the nation, they are exacerbated and magnified in densely populated areas (Ahram, Stembridge, Fergus, and Nogura, 2012).

As post–World War II urban centers continued to grow, negative perceptions relative to living conditions and academic quality began to typify urban communities (Rury and Saatcioglu, 2011). In contrast, "the rapidly growing suburbs exhibited higher income, less racial and ethnic diversity, and lower population density" (Rury and Saatcioglu, 2011, p. 308), and significant numbers of Americans viewed suburban communities as representing a more desirable standard of living. As a result, "white flight," or the move of more affluent whites from urban to suburban communities, economic, political, and educational deterioration began to occur.

Describing the role of "white flight" on the loss of financial and social capital, West (1994) describes,

> the exodus of stable industrial jobs from urban centers to cheaper labor markets here and abroad, housing policies that created "chocolate cities and vanilla suburbs," and White fear of Black crime . . . .as helping to erode the tax base of American cities just as the federal government has cut its support and programs. The result is unemployment, hunger, homelessness, and sickness for millions. (p. 9)

Squires and Kubrin (2006) describe the ensuing urban and suburban disparities with clarity, writing, "the linkages among place, race, and privilege are shaped by dominant social forces that play out in response to public policy decisions and practices of powerful private institutions" (para. 5). Consequently, inner-city urban communities continue to serve families who are unable to migrate to suburban communities, and often present layers of challenges for urban school and community leaders (Kruse, 2005).

Hunter and Bartee cite extensive research illustrating that social and environmental contexts have a significant impact on the development of children (as cited in May, 2006). This is particularly distressing for youth of color because schools are perceived as the gateway to economic prosperity through the creation of a competitive workforce (Lytle, 1992). Students who are not successful are blamed, either as a family or individual, for their perceived lack of ability, character, or motivation, or for parents failing to prepare children for school (Cuban, 1989; O'Connor and Fernandez, 2006). Others argue that the plight of the urban poor is an individual choice based on financial capacity (Squires and Kubrin, 2006) and again focuses on the individuals' failure as the cause of the problems (Blanchett, Mumford, and Beachum, 2005). According to May (2006),

> the academic failure of urban children provides validation to the meritocracy ethos that undergirds the belief system of many Americans. Meritocracy refers to a social system where people achieve success proportionate to their talents and abilities, as opposed to one in which social class, or wealth play a significant role. If we, as a nation, overtly acknowledge that wealth, or lack thereof, plays a role in the success one is able to obtain, we also have to acknowledge that some individuals are privileged by wealth and may even be bestowed with such at birth. This suggests that some individuals may not have a fair or equal opportunity for economic or academic success. (p. 44)

Many factors contribute to urban school failure, but most pervasive is the inability to overcome the institutional, social, political, and economic forces that "undermine the educational progress and economic mobility of non-white poor students" (Kincheloe, as cited in Blanchett, Mumford, and Beachum, 2005, p. 74). Many urban schools represent a small-scale version of the societal, economic, and political aura (Blanchett, Mumford, and Beachum, 2005) and are plagued by high unemployment rates, a lack of economic progress, and the exclusion of minorities from the fiscal picture (Urban Economic Working Group, 1990). In actuality, the genesis of urban deterioration is largely based on racial bias in policy and practices emanating from powerful economic, political, and social institutional structures (Squires and Kubrin, 2006). Economic, political, and institutional practices include the Federal Housing Administration's discriminatory practices to racially and financially restrict mortgage loans based on race by withholding mortgage capital for those who could purchase homes (commonly called redlining) (Wilson, 2011); urban zoning policies excluding single-family dwellings, while incorporating concentrations of public housing; federal tax incentives and infrastructure investments for suburban communities, encouraging business and jobs to vacate urban centers; and the use of public funds to build highways separating urban neighborhoods from business and white areas (Wilson, 2011). Racial and economic disparities continue as tenacious forces yet to be overcome, and even with similar education, blacks earn 60 percent of what whites earn, contributing to communal wealth disparities. Squires and Kubrin (2006) cite that "as of the year 2000 no group is more physically isolated from jobs than Blacks" (para. 18).

Neighborhoods of highly concentrated poverty are seen as dangerous, and therefore become more socially and economically isolated as they are avoided for being such (Jargowsky, 1994). Over time, the word "urban" has become synonymous with negative connotations, and Buendia (2011) notes that the word "engages" a discussion of the poor and racial other, as well as the location, or place, in which these populations reside (p. 2). Further, Buendia describes terms often associated with urban such as "dysfunctional family, zones of blight, the diseased center, violent, and at-risk" (p. 3).

As presented, much research show that the forces surrounding industrialization create a "domino effect," adversely affecting economic and political structures that, in turn, have devastating effects on urban communities and schools. These stubborn trends are entrenched in our urban centers and will remain significant components shaping the twenty-first-century educational landscape.

KEY POST–WORLD WAR II EDUCATIONAL POLICIES IMPACTING URBAN COMMUNITIES

In the post–World War II era, a number of key measures serve to shape the evolution of the American educational agenda. These key actions are significant because they undergird the path of educational policy. While any number of significant movements can be illuminated, four are selected for review including (a) the Truman Commission, (b) the *Brown v. Board of Education of Topeka* Supreme Court decision, (c) President Johnson's 1964 War on Poverty and the Elementary and Secondary Act of 1965, and (d) *A Nation at Risk* and the Standards-Based Reform Movement of the 1980s.

President Truman's Commission on Higher Education. Immediately following World War II in 1946, President Harry Truman (the only president in the twentieth century to not graduate from college) appoints a higher education commission to examine the role of higher education in our democracy. The findings of the Commission highlight that post–World War II access to higher education is inequitable and far too dependent on the circumstances surrounding an individual's community, race, family, gender, and religion (Gilbert and Heller, 2010). "The Truman Report" acknowledges that economic factors serve as a major obstacle for individuals from low economic environments. Further, the report asserts that discrimination should not occur based on one's background skills and abilities, but in fact should illuminate the need for a variety of available post-secondary opportunities (Gilbert and Heller, 2010). Hutchinson (2002) notes the significance of the Truman Report as the first national dialogue relative to opportunities for higher education, noting that access was contingent on the influences of social and economic factors on the individual (as cited in Gilbert and Heller, 2010).

Brown v. Board of Education **Decision of 1954.** Historians view the *Brown v. Board of Education* Supreme Court decision as the most significant event in the history of American education (Blanchett, Mumford, and Beachum, 2005). By overturning the separate but equal clause established in the 1896 landmark *Plessy v. Ferguson* Supreme Court decision (Paris, 1994), the courts assert that segregated schools deny black students their constitutional right to equal protection under the law for all citizens as guaranteed by the Fourteenth Amendment. This reform measure shook the foundation upon which public schools had been built for over one hundred years (Garrison, 2009).

THE EFFECT OF *BROWN* ON URBAN CULTURE, COMMUNITIES, AND EDUCATIONAL LEADERSHIP

Considerable literature exists reflecting the significant dynamics between culture, community, and education in urban environments (Delpit, 1995; Goodlad, 1984; Lytle, 1992; Sheldon 2003; Warren, 2005). Researchers find that positive school–community relationships assist in creating learning environments that foster the academic, emotional, and social development of black and minority children. A school community refers to the familial, socio-economic, experiential, and civic attachments that are vested in its well-being and growth (Great Schools Partnerships, 2013). Peterson (1994) describes culture as a "complex web of norms, values, beliefs, assumptions, traditions, and rituals that are built up over time as teachers, parents, and administrators work together, deal with crises, and develop unstated expectations for interacting and working together" (para. 5). The positive interaction among these community and cultural variables promotes schools reflecting the child's values, and are more likely to engage parents naturally in the educational process.

Parental engagement and involvement in the educational process is a significant contributor to student success, and studies point to a positive relationship between parent involvement and academic achievement (Arnold, Zeljo, Doctoroff, and Ortiz, 2008; Barnard, 2004; Marcon, 1999). Further, decades of research show that positive parental involvement in urban communities is a result of familial values and active school connections (Clark 1983; Hoover-Dempsey and Sandler, 1997; Sheldon, 2003) between the school and school leaders.

Prior to the Brown decision African-American students attended neighborhood schools with African-American teachers and administrators who generally held high expectations for achievement. Through the seminal work of renowned researchers such as Ron Edmonds and James Comer, we understand that "all children are eminently educable and that the behavior of the school is critical in determining the quality of that education" (Edmonds as cited in Lytle, 1992, p. 122), and schools are "strategically located in the life of a child . . . a critical societal institution" (Comer as cited in Lytle, 1992, p. 122). Historically, the strong cultural link between urban schools and the community allows the school to serve as a focal point of a child's development (Woodruff, 1997). From the classroom to the grocery store, teachers, administrators, and staff are community centerpieces, affording informal parental access to student progress as well as demonstrating positive teacher parent interactions (Woodruff, 1997). Classrooms that reflect a child's experiences, values, community, and culture make a child feel "significant and cared for," and elimination of this dynamic creates barriers between the school's goals and the child's innate abilities (Woodruff, 1997; para. 3). Woodruff further claims that school "loses its relevance as a valid source of knowledge" with staff that cannot identify with the child's life (Woodruff, 1997; para. 3). Meier, Stewart, and England (1989) reference that "black teachers are more likely to identify black students as gifted and less likely to refer them for special education, expulsion, and suspension . . . Black teachers are without a doubt the key to student academic success" (p. 6). Irvine and Irvine (1983) surmise that the effects of Brown "significantly altered the pupil-teacher relationship, which has historically been the foundation for black student achievement" (p. 415). Reflecting on the work of Billingsley, Irvine (2007) postulates that Brown essentially dismantled the collective support of the black community structure, "diluting its collective whole, collective struggle, and collective will" (p. 301).

In the wake of desegregation, the unintended consequences on home–school relationships in the urban community remain (Woodruff, 1997). In the eleven years post *Brown*, the number of African-American teachers and administrators, providing instruction for two million minority children, dwindled by 46 percent from 82,000 to 44,000 (Toppo, 2004). Additionally, Toppo (2004) reports that in states such as Arkansas and Texas, 90 percent of the African-American principals lost their leadership posts, no African-American educators were hired in desegregated districts for a decade beginning in 1958, and inferior white teachers were hired in the place of qualified African-American educators. The loss of the leadership of the teachers and principals in the wake of *Brown* is significant. Leadership is a critical component in urban schools because "teachers, principals, and superintendents all function daily as group leaders" (Lytle, 1992, p. 117). Literature continues to emphasize that the role of the school leader is key in creating effective schools. Many scholars assert that the leader's impact on student scholarship cannot be overstressed and the principal maintains a significant effect on the effectiveness of the school and the academic success of the students (Halawah, 2005; Hallinger and Heck, 1998; Murphy, 2010).

President Lyndon Johnson's 1964 War on Poverty and the Elementary and Secondary Education Act of 1965. In 1964 President Johnson, a former teacher, introduced the Economic Opportunity Act, officially initiating his "War on Poverty." The Act created the Office of Economic Opportunity where initiatives such as Head Start, Job Corps, and the Office of Child Development began (Hanna, 2005).

While the Truman Report marks the first higher education dialogue, the Elementary and Secondary Education Act (ESEA) marks the first national conversation relative to additional funding for K–12 education (Sunderman, 2009). This comprehensive legislation is the most extensive federal education bill in history and provides funds for primary and secondary education while explicitly forbidding the establishment of a national curriculum. According to the National Education Association, central to ESEA legislation is providing large financial resources, known as Title I funds, to "bridge the gap between hopelessness and hope for more than five million educationally deprived children" (Jehlen, n.d, para. 2). The legislation focuses on policies to equalize educational opportunity through the redistribution of resources to promote attention to educational issues not adequately addressed at the local level (Sunderman, 2009). The four major components of the ESEA legislation include (1) professional development, (2) instructional materials, (3) educational programs, and (4) promotion of parent involvement. The significance of this legislation is the national and concerted attention drawn to more effectively meeting the needs of the nation's impoverished youth. As a result of Johnson's War on Poverty, funding to school districts soared from $1.5 billion to $4 billion, signaling

the federal government's absolute entrance into the realm of public education (Hanna, 2005).

A Nation at Risk and the Standards Movement. The decade of the 1980s is characterized by the release of several pieces of powerful literature on the challenges facing public schools and the initiation of a national standards movement. In addition to reporting on the deeply inadequate state of the nation's educational system, these publications provide the impetus for decades of sweeping reform measures attempting to address student failure.

In 1983 the National Commission on Excellence in Education released *A Nation at Risk: The Imperative for Educational Reform*. This pivotal document draws grim attention to America's pervasive failure to adequately educate its youth and is credited with initiating the decades of reform movements to follow. In 1986, on the not-yet-cooled heels of *A Nation at Risk*, came two more critical publications: *A Nation Prepared: Teachers for the Twenty-first Century*, a publication sponsored by the Carnegie Task Force on Teaching as a Profession, and *Tomorrow's Teachers* published by the Holmes Group. According to the Carnegie Task Force on Teaching (as cited in Labaree, 1992), "the key to success lies in creating a profession equal to the task—a profession of well-educated teachers prepared to assume new powers and responsibilities to redesign schools for the future" (p. 124). While the focus of the Holmes Group was the improvement of teacher preparation institutions, both the Carnegie and Holmes groups support the elimination of undergraduate degrees in favor of requiring a graduate degree (Labaree, 1992; Wiggins, 1986). Additionally, the two groups promote the reduction of bureaucratic authority and the increase of teacher autonomy with stratified levels of professionalism and compensation (Labaree, 1992; Wiggins, 1986).

A Nation at Risk provides the impetus for a national agenda to create curricular standards identifying what students need to know and what students should be expected to do to be successful in life. Silver (2004) describes the nation's reform movements in three basic trends, namely: (a) standards-based reform (improving student learning through the provision of clear goals and assessments), (b) comprehensive school reform (improving student learning through whole school efforts focusing on the use of research-based practices), and (c) student-centered reform (improving student learning by focusing on caring teachers, positive culture, and relationships). The combination of clear goals and assessments are to ensure the academic success of all students, and the National Council of Teachers of Mathematics and the National Board for Professional Teaching Standards are two of the first groups to publish national curriculum standards (Silver, 2004). Lee and Ready (2009) also provide three stages for conceptualizing the standards-based movement for high schools. The first phase, initiated during the 1980s, introduces broad reform pushing for more courses in core subjects. The second phase moves the focus from how many courses students should take to what courses students should take. And the third phase focuses on college preparation. Our current reform agenda centers on outlining common core standards to create high school graduates ready for college, career, and life.

A FRAMEWORK FOR CONTEXTUALIZING DECADES OF REFORM

As the chapter highlights, the release of *A Nation at Risk* (National Commission on Education, 1983) essentially marks the contemporary (1983–current) beginning of school reform efforts in American schools. The impact of this pivotal document is explored in three major eras:

1. Early Stage of Reform Awareness from 1983 to 1993.
2. Stage of Pseudo Accountability from 1993 to 2003.
3. Stage of Testing, Economic Reinvestment, and Globalization from 2003 to Current.

In addition to discussing the three major reform eras, characteristics describing a fourth stage are explored. This emerging and dynamically evolving fourth period is the Transformation and Innovation Stage.

The Early Stage of Reform Awareness, 1983–1993

The Early Stage of Reform Awareness begins in 1983 with the official release of *A Nation at Risk: The Imperative for Educational Reform* (National Commission on Excellence, 1983). This important document is the beginning of the call for major systemic public school reform. Commissioned by President Ronald Reagan's Secretary of Education Terrell H. Bell, the report criticizes the nation for failing to adequately educate its youth. The report calls for sweeping reform in student achievement and teacher training. A notable phrase of the report reads: "if an unfriendly foreign power had attempted to impose on America the mediocre educational performance the commission found, that nation might have viewed it as an act of war" (National Commission on Excellence 1983, para. 2). The report identifies eight risk factors in contemporary school reform. The risk factors include (a) poor academic performance compared to international students, (b) high levels of illiteracy among seventeen-year-olds, (c) declining achievement scores, (d) increased enrollment in collegiate remedial courses, (e) diluted curriculum in schools, (f) low expectations for student performance, (g) less time devoted to instruction and homework, and (h) poor quality teachers (National Commission on Excellence 1983, para. 12). What scholars and educators remember about *A Nation at Risk* is that it concludes with the notion that "for the first time in history, the educational skills of one generation will not surpass, will not equal, will not even approach that of their parents" (National Commission on Excellence 1983, para. 17).

Following the release of *A Nation at Risk*, the next two decades resulted in a significant focus on school improvement efforts at the local, state, and federal levels. The state of California is one of the first states to pass legislation after the release of the report, resulting in the adoption of an education reform bill raising expectations for homework, student conduct, testing, graduation requirements, length of the school day and year, and funding (Cohen and Hill, 2000).

The mid-1980s became a period of a growing awareness of the lack of confidence in American schools, as well as more fully acknowledging the connection between economic stability, graduation rates, and general school achievement (Chubb and Moe, 1990). Economists Richard Murnane and Frank Levy (1996) summarize the education and economic correlation by identifying three comprehensive or basic skills that American students need to enhance business and economic stability: (a) basic mathematics including problem solving and reading abilities, (b) the ability to work in groups and make effective oral and written presentations, and (c) the ability to use personal computers. This era increases critical attention on teachers, teacher unions, and the state of teacher professionalism development. Labaree (1992) elaborates on two significant reports that address a central theme of the Early Stage of Reform Awareness, namely the Carnegie Task Force on Teaching as a Profession (1986) and the Holmes Group, which published *Tomorrow's Teachers* (1986). Labaree notes that "both of these reports argue the quality of public education can only improve if teaching is transformed into a full fledge profession" (p. 124).

The awareness period also put more emphasis on state education agencies and heightened the debate about local versus state control (Holmes Group, 1986). Conversations among scholars and practitioners relative to "unfunded mandates," local funding sources, and the role of teachers in the reform process began to unfold, and the National Board of Professional Standards establishes certification for the teaching profession (National Board of Professional Teaching Standards, 1989). The Awareness Stage brought additional upheaval around the discussion of who the significant players should be in the national debate about school reform. Cherryholmes (1987) notes that prior to the early 1980s, much of the school reform debate was restricted to circles of teachers and education interest groups. Following the release of *A Nation at Risk* and subsequent analysis of the report, state policymakers, business leaders, mayors, and activist parent groups demanded inclusion in the debate and more accountability of results. In sum, the Early Stage of Reform Awareness signals the importance of public schools to both the economy and the overall stability of the nation (Wiggins, 1986). The period also calls attention to the notion that critical steps are necessary to move America off the track of mediocrity and the inability to compete internationally. The Early Stage of Reform Awareness puts the discussion of schools front and center for many Americans, and the stage that follows, the Pseudo Accountability Stage, characterizes the need to determine who would indeed be accountable for results.

The Stage of Pseudo Accountability, 1993–2003

The Awareness Stages closes with public debate on what is wrong with education, offering little in the way of practical steps to improve the academic achievement of the nation's children. In addition to the lack of grassroots efforts to improvement, there is a serious lack of accountability. Federal education agencies become experts at pushing policy decisions down to the state level, and the state departments of education establish a reputation for pushing unpopular decisions down to the local level. Community members want to know *who is in charge* and *who is accountable for the improvement*. The period of 1992–2002 is referred to as the Stage of Pseudo Accountability because it ushers in an era of educational reform where stakeholders attempt to identify the parties accountable for national school improvement (Beyer and Zeichner, 1987). The term "pseudo" is used because calls for greater accountability reflect increases in standards and financial investment, but fail to show academic growth.

In early 1990s a considerable amount of energy is devoted to establishing standards by which both states and local districts could be measured (Elmore and Associates, 1990) as well as consequences for not measuring up. This period focuses on establishing content and performance standards and creating a culture to govern conditions for learning (Gage and Needels, 1989). The standards period has the sound of true accountability, but ultimately is again void of measurable results. The focus on systemic educational change in the Pseudo Accountability Stage proves problematic as leaders question where to concentrate their efforts (Wilson, 1987). Target areas for consideration include coherent learning goals, curriculum changes, and educator professional development. Additionally, the decade of the 1990s is witness to fourteen state supreme court decisions surrounding school finance relating to "how much does it cost to educate a child?" and the constitutionality and equity of using property taxes as a means to determine school funding.

Perhaps the most significant educational activity of the Pseudo Accountability Stage is the Educate America Act of 1994 or Goals 2000 (Paris, 1994). This legislation provides $105 million for a broad list of academic goals designed to be achieved by the year 2000. The Educate America Act of 1994 presents six broad educational goals: (a) school readiness, (b) school completion, (c) student academic achievement, (d) leadership in math and science, (e) adult literacy, and (f) drug-free schools (Federal Education Policy

History, 2011). This most recent accountability design spells disaster from the beginning. Under the plan, individual states submit applications to the Department of Education depicting how their goals are to be reached. Eager to gain national education funding, state boards of education develop elaborate plans but lack appropriate accountability measures. A review of the goals below reveals little progress in accomplishing the mission. The goals from The Educate America Act of 1994 include:

1. All children in America will start the day ready to learn.
2. High school graduation rate will be at least 90 percent.
3. Grades 4, 8, and 12 will demonstrate competency in content areas such as English, math, science, foreign language, government, economics, arts history, and geography.
4. U.S. students will be first in the world in math and science.
5. Every adult will be literate.
6. Every school will be free of drugs, alcohol, and violence.
7. Teachers will have access to professional development.

While commendable goals, questions arose about their feasibility and the degree to which the goals were achievable by the year 2000. The comprehensive nature of the goals pleased educators, but again lacked a connection to accountability. The passing of the No Child Left Behind Act of 2002 (U.S. Department of Education, 2012) brings the era of Pseudo Accountability to a close.

The Stage of Testing, Economic Reinvestment, and Globalization, 2003–2014

The Stage of Testing, Economic Reinvestment, and Globalization provides an analysis of the last ten years of policy development and the implications of those policies on urban communities and leadership. Consistent with the previous two stages, the period covering 2003 through 2014 is characterized by the influence of federal education policy on local and urban communities (Darling-Hammond, 2010). This section addresses the increase in testing by state and local educational organizations, and the relationship between educational attainment and the economic viability of the nation. The section also provides a perspective on the globalization factors that impact the quality of schools in urban communities.

When President George W. Bush secures support from a Democratic Congress to pass No Child Left Behind (NCLB) in early 2002, waves of reform occur at every level of governance. NCLB, a reauthorization of the Elementary and Secondary Education Act of 1965, rests on high standards, accountability, and the notion that all students must succeed. One of the most significant differences between NCLB and other legislation is the inclusion of consequences or penalties for unsuccessful schools. Central to NCLB legislation requires states expand the scope of testing in reading and math. Additionally, states must establish proficiency tests to show yearly progress. The passing of NCLB is nationally polarizing. NCLB supporters hail the law as the high point for the Bush administration, while opponents argue the accountability measures of NCLB reinforce the perception that children in poor urban communities are not able to achieve at the same levels as suburban students.

This stage of the reform era also ties educational attainment to economic recovery (Chubb and Moe, 1990; Payne, 2008; Rothstein, 2004). Ormell (2012) provides an argument that educational attainment throughout the world has an impact on the global economy. He notes that "Education, properly conceived, can do a lot to put the economy back on its feet, to rebalance it, and to rebuild confidence in the future" (p. 21). In previous decades, whenever the economy experienced a negative downturn, a fairly sustainable recovery followed. Recovery efforts from previous decades relied heavily on manufacturing and labor-intensive work. Over the last five decades jobs becoming increasingly more technical requiring more advanced education, magnify the correlation between education and job attainment. Leaders in urban communities know that job creation is an essential key to social, emotional, economic, and educational growth.

In addition to the responsibility of educating, training, and producing workers for the American economy, educational institutions must now engage the importance of retraining the adult workforce to meet the demands of shifting skill requirements. Zakaria (2011) believes that most of the high paying jobs associated with industries like automobile parts will not likely return, and this certainly presents a different scenario from previous decades. Residents of urban communities in the past could secure reasonably comfortable lifestyles through the automobile and related industries. The increase in educational requirements combined with the reduction in inner-city economic reinvestment means that urban communities also require stronger emphasis on retraining of older work forces.

Impact of globalization

Another key element of the Stage of Testing, Economic Reinvestment, and Globalization centers on the impact of globalization on urban communities and leaders (Greene and Symonds, 2006). The connection between increased accountability, economic reinvestment, and globalization factors requires educational leaders to address educational management and strategic planning with a more integrated approach. Semary, Khaja, and Hamidou (2012) describe the context of the global challenge in a dual manner, citing that educational systems have to meet the challenge of ensuring that students have new knowledge relating to required skills and values, as well as creating responsible adults, who are good citizens both in their native country and throughout the world.

The harsh reality is that globalization has a dramatic impact on the quality of experiences for urban communities, their schools, and leaders (Gertz, 2010; Tyack and Cuban, 1995). "Over the past ten to fifteen years, about four hundred million people from China, India, South Africa, Indonesia, and elsewhere have entered the global labor force, offering services to make the same products Americans make for a tenth of the price" (Zakaria, 2011, p. 2). The global impact also applies to the knowledge economy of the twenty-first century. Hargreaves (2003) describes the knowledge economy as one "stimulated and driven by creativity and ingenuity" (p. 1). The participation of urban communities and schools in the knowledge economy will be critical and vital to any long-term academic, educational, and economic outcome.

LEADERSHIP LESSONS LEARNED OVER THE LAST FIFTY YEARS OF SCHOOL REFORM

Reflecting on the research on the evolution of American education over the last fifty years, there are lessons that may assist in creating a more successful path into the future. These lessons come from a unique intersection of the authors' experiences as academics and school leaders. As academics we hold great deference to research and how it informs practice. As practiced urban school leaders there is also great deference for on the job trial and error and seasoned intuition. Krajewski (2005) explains that seasoned urban leaders understand the tough path to effective school leadership, but in spite of the challenges they find ways to lead—all of it done from the heart (para. 2). Outlined below are five overarching lessons from an experiential perspective. It is the hope that these lessons learned will provide *food for thought* in the development of transformation plans to address urban district and community educational needs.

Lesson One: The Economic and Political Survival of the United States of America Is 100 Percent Contingent Upon the Creation of a National Wholesale Transformation Plan for Public Schools

Welcome to the Knowledge Economy. Public schools are entering a phase of engaging in a global marketplace where the new economy is the ability to analyze, compute, synthesize, and provide technology-based decisions in a fast-paced environment. It is crystal clear that America is not the nation of a generation ago, and that globalization and technology now require educators to teach, instruct, and manage curriculum in a much different manner. The emphasis on Science, Technology, Engineering, and Math (STEM) makes it apparent that school leaders now must focus on their direct role in the maintaining and improving of the American economy. In the twenty-first-century knowledge economy, educators must continue to internalize understand the direct correlation between classroom instruction and achievement. While the connection between teaching and the economy may not have dominated the periphery of educators in the past, the twenty-first-century knowledge economy requires a heightened degree of engagement on the part of school leaders. Educational leaders and policy makers must accept this new challenge, thereby ensuring the survival of American society as we know it.

Transformation and reform is a learning process. The last fifty years of reform efforts in America failed to effectively communicate that the learning process is extensive, and once a corrective effort is under way, "blood sweat, and tears" will be shed to stay the course. Federal and state policymakers are typically adept at presenting charts and graphs that describe "what" the problem is, but all too often, there is little to no detail about "how" it will be addressed and "who" is ultimately responsible. And the ultimate question of reform complexity is what happens if the effort is not successful? How can accountability be assured across the spectrum? The learning process has to be free of political and stakeholder priority. It requires the leadership team to create a culture of comfort from which to continually communicate the priorities of the reform effort. Michael Fullan, an educational researcher and noted author on educational reform, has written extensively about the time and the change process (Fullan, 2009; Hargreaves and Fullan, 2012). Fullan and Hargreaves (2012) assert that effective management and at least five years are necessary for true comprehensive reform. This means that the local politicians and community members looking for overnight success need to understand that time and measurable benchmarks are key steps in the transformation process. The last thirty years of reform efforts in America have been a series of stops and starts based upon variables as basic as a change in leadership. Authentic transformation will require patience in the improvement process, but America is capable of redirecting the current education disposition and regaining the role as leader of the free world.

The federal government cannot be the singular leader in wholesale school transformation. Over the last thirty years of school reform, there is an ongoing debate about the role of the federal government in our daily lives. The Democratic Party has historically taken the position that there is a significant role for government in the social, economic, and governance of our lives. The Republican Party has historically taken a position that there is little to no role the government should play in our daily decision making, whether it be schools or other institutional decision making. As is the case with most political debates, the true answer

lies somewhere in the middle. However, in the case of public education, it is clear that since *A Nation at Risk*, there is a role the federal government can play, but if this effort is to be successful, it cannot be the singular leader in school transformation. Real and sustained transformation must occur at the local level and have federal financial and facilitation oversight. This difficult balance must be achieved, and the coordination of this effort will require a central emphasis on ensuring America's greatness. We must view a national school transformation effort in the way in which we would view a national crisis. One of the enduring visual messages of World War II is the notion that everyone was involved in the war effort. The classic picture of "Rosie the Riveter" defines the collective approach the entire nation took toward the threat to our national security. The same kind of threat is upon us now, and it will require the same spirit toward its resolution.

Political ideology cannot be the tail that wags the dog in the discussion of school transformation. Every political official is elected on some change platform or promise of delivering some citizen-based reform. These officials then spend the majority of their term attempting to either introduce the change that distinguishes them from their predecessors or trying to get reelected. Reviewing thirty years of school reform in America leads to at least one clear conclusion: political ideology cannot be the cornerstone of decision making about our children and their success. If there is any issue that should require a bipartisan approach regarding the overall well-being of our nation, it should be education. If we take the collective approach that our nation has gone from being "at risk" to being "at crisis," it would at least allow the dialogue focusing on students and the survival of our nation. The reality is that for far too long politicians have used all of the appropriate verbiage about the importance of education, but have been all too willing to compromise in the backroom for a deal that has a higher personal political value. There can be no more important or significant value to America than its children and the success of our nation. Addressing political maneuvering means that elected officials will often have to risk angering a constituency that demands a different set of priorities.

The last three and a half years of politics in Washington yields some of the most divisive and partisan bickering in recent memory. One need not look further than the debate on the income debt ceiling to see that there is enough "my way or the highway" thinking leading us down the wrong path. While our elected representative government structure is the best in the world, we must also understand, appreciate, and value our children and their education as a key element of our national agenda. There can be no higher priority than educating the next generation of Americans.

Utilizing technology must be a required component of all transformation plans. One of the ugly truths about the role of technology in schools is that teachers are lagging behind in terms of knowledge and competence about technology as compared to the students they teach. As a result, a significant portion of our students are not being exposed to the power of technology, which in turn means we run the risk of being left behind by students of higher skill levels than those in other countries. A powerful transformation plan must include equal access to technology taught by educators who can connect the relevance of contemporary technology with classroom instructional models that meet or exceed national and international standards.

Select a transformation strategy that yields results and don't change it. Transformation suggests a degree of systemic redesign. The authors of this chapter bring a unique perspective on this issue, because both have experience as central office urban school leaders and higher education faculty members (superintendent, director of curriculum, and tenured professors). The goal is to merge both theory and practice in the leadership of urban schools and communities.

After thoughtful and community-based involvement, a leader will want to launch a new plan. One of the difficulties of this participative approach is that the new leader is faced with questions such as: (a) why are we using a new plan and what happened to the old plan? (b) how much will the new plan cost and who will pay for it? (c) how collaborative will the board of education be in the process? and (d) does this plan have buy-in from the community? As you may imagine, these questions are followed by more questions that can often delay the introduction and implementation of a transformation effort.

One consistent theme of reform plans over the last thirty years is that as soon as a strategy is unveiled, there is often opposition to the plan components. The recommendation here is that all school plans should be properly vetted with as much community feedback as possible, but there is a point where the debate stops and the plan starts. The question is often more about who is doing the work than the work itself. School boards and political personalities spend an enormous amount of time on the "who" of the work instead of the "results" and "outcomes" of the work. When a transformation plan is selected, stick with it. If new leadership is hired, the core elements of the transformation plan must be in place. New leadership can adjust and modify the plan as appropriate, but the anticipated outcomes of the plan should not change.

The Department of Education must be a facilitator of transformation and not the enforcer of rules that don't determine measurable outcomes. The Department of Education and the majority of state education agencies may interpret their role in the transformation process as the enforcer of rules. The compliance role of agencies is important and needed to ensure consistency within the rules of engagement. This is not an argument for a no-holds-barred kind of approach to school management and change, but a call for redefining the role of the U.S. Federal Government. The first U.S. Department of Education was created in 1867 to gather data to create an effective school system (U.S. Department of Education, 2012). The current U.S. Department of Education, since its inception in 1979 under the Carter Administration (U.S. Department of Education, 2012), spends too much time checking to see if the form is completed in triplicate and not enough time providing flexibility to states to determine what works best in their community. Local education agencies often desire a hands-off type of approach with access to funds without scrutinizing oversight. From a federal perspective, the role should be to facilitate and monitor progress. The agreed-upon rules of engagement should not change, and the department's role should be to help facilitate the local transformation effort.

Lesson Two: Comprehensive School Transformation Will Be Difficult, Disruptive, Emotional, and Volatile. Be Prepared for Community Unrest When Implementing the Transformation Plan

One of the areas that bring out an emotional reaction from parents, students, alumni, and the larger community is a local school decision being made where there is widespread disagreement. The reality is that most local communities become fairly effective at organizing neighborhood events. There are even local block leaders who are responsible for keeping the block or area informed about key decisions impacting the community. These communities also understand that if they raise enough of a fight, and enlist some local politicians, school decisions are often reversed, put on hold, or ultimately passed on to the next administration or completely shelved. The leadership team should prepare for negative reaction to the transformation plan and have a set of strategies in place to address unrest. Being prepared for community unrest is an important take-away from thirty years of school reform. Leaders should certainly not be callous in their public responses or written communication, but should be consistent with their plan, and all members of the school community should be able to speak to why the plan is being implemented and what the benefits will be for each stakeholder group.

Listen and modify transformation plans based on input from the local community that fits the rubric for decision-making framework. A national transformation plan that impacts a local community must be flexible enough to include ongoing feedback by community members. A high level of transparency is required at all times. In most communities, there will be a significant debate or differences based on philosophy, background, and experiences, or disagreements over research-based strategies. Regardless of the degree of differences about the key elements of the transformation plan, school and community leaders must be willing to listen and modify when it is necessary. A "rubric for decision-making" must be established, even in the midst of dissent, to ensure that all the key requirements and guidelines for the transformation plan are maintained. While you can bet on spirited debate and a degree of political leveraging, the ultimate decision must require the input of all groups and citizens and be in the best interest of the children.

Lesson Three: Money, In and By Itself, Is Not the Total Solution to Successful School Transformation

Let's be very clear on this point. Wholesale school transformation will not be successful without a signifi-

cant financial investment by federal, state, and local entities and citizens. Expecting students and school districts to work miracles without sufficient funding is ludicrous at best and uninformed at least. However, the other side of the argument is abundantly clear from thirty years of school reform, that supplying unprecedented funds at the school challenge without proper authorization and oversight is a big mistake.

Economic Impact. The combination of persistent and pervasive poverty and neighborhood decline leads to what Cuban (1989) defines as "the corrosive effects of long-term poverty that has splintered families" (p. 780). Sanders (1999) proposes a theory called circular hopelessness and poverty. This theory suggests that underrepresented populations experience severe and consistently negative social interaction with the unspoken and unwritten social norms associated with business and career opportunities, and the (a) legal system, (b) financial system, (c) political system, (d) health care system, and (e) social services system, that ultimately results in a severe feeling of hopelessness that becomes cyclical" (p. 7). Consistent and persistent negative interaction and discrimination within the societal systems in which one is dependent for life causes stress leading to other chronic issues. Devine, Plunkett, and Wright (1992) suggest that chronic stress caused by economic deprivation has a significant impact on urban communities and the children of poverty. "Poverty in and of itself does not lead to poor cognitive ability, but rather causes the stressful reaction that accompanies it" (Neel, 2013, p. 42). Moreover, Neel describes a "feedback loop" where the deeper the family poverty, the more chronically ill the members become, and the more chronically ill the members become, the more likely the children are to perform poorly in school and also grow up in poverty (p. 43).

An economic-based incentive for parents must be a part of a federal effort toward wholesale school reform. It's time to start compensating parents for the academic achievement of their children. This idea is controversial, and some critics will consider it yet another form of social welfare. The critics should look at compensating parents for ensuring high achievement for their children similar to the way we look at farm subsidies, Wall Street buyouts, incentives for first-time homeowners, the alternative minimum tax, and

National Science Foundation Grants. There is a need for a national effort focusing on educating our children and placing a financial priority on that challenge. This effort should either be a direct pay to parents or a key school agency of which the child directly benefits. This finance-based support to parents for achievement should be a national priority, especially if we are serious about education and ensuring that America competes in the twenty-first century.

Make investments in targeted communities where the need is the greatest and reward success nationwide regardless of socio-economic condition. There is always a debate in schools concerning whether all students should receive the same economic support regardless of their socio-economic status. The investment component of a national transformation plan should include an emphasis on those schools and communities that are uniquely disadvantaged by poverty, poor medical care, and difficult socio-economic factors. As a result, economic investment should be increased to students and communities based on their need. A national transformation plan should be comprehensive enough to include all students and place the onus of responsibility on students and families to succeed.

Lesson Four: Failure to Successfully Accomplish the Goals of a National Transformation Plan Must Have Consequences for All Groups Within the Educational Organization

Whether you are an athletic coach, a financial advisor, a parent, a CEO, or the factory worker in a unionized auto shop, there is a common thread that will lead to success for all individuals and people working or being served by the organization. The commonly shared variable is that ALL members of the organization believe that the success of the group is contingent upon each member being totally vested in the attainment of the group.

David Matthews (2006) indicates that one of the reasons reform efforts fail is because there is no public clarity on who is responsible for ensuring that the initiative is carried out. This essentially summarizes the majority of the last thirty years of school reform. While more recent efforts under the American Reinvestment Recovery Act (2009) initiates stronger levels of collective accountability, it is clear that the essence of the work over the thirty-year period of school reform fails to identify, not just accountability, but the need to have all stakeholders vested in the outcome. There have been discussions about merit pay, closing low performing buildings, differentiated compensation, and other innovative approaches to reward educators, but the true call for authentic transformation of schools is the collective buy-in as well as the collective accountability for the group. Previous reform efforts include many key variables that can lead to success, but one of the reasons the overall achievement level of students is not successful is that there was not sufficient buy-in and accountability. A national transformation plan requires not just buy-in, but individual accountability as well. If the individual building does not meet their goal, then all members of the school are held accountable, not just the school administration and/or union leadership.

Lesson Five: Ensure Sustainability of the Transformation Plan by Institutionalizing and Creating a "Sense of Urgency" for Implementation

While the federal government can provide financial support for transformation plans, the ultimate cost must be placed upon the local community. Financial provisions must be included for solid sustainability of a transformation plan. Educators often talk about how to sustain state and federal grant supported programs and refer to it as the "funding cliff," meaning the money will run out, and there are often few strategies in place for the eventuality of the funding loss. There has be a relationship between funding, institutionalizing, and creating what Kotter (1996) refers to as "establishing a sense of urgency" for sustaining the success that will occur (p.35). It is not the government's role to pay for all of our educational needs. The local community must embrace both the need for financial support and the urgency for implementing a transformation plan.

URBAN SCHOOL LEADERSHIP

Effective urban school leadership is a critical component of a successful school–community environment. Academic achievement of all students is the *ultimate goal*, but the pervasive impact of poverty and institutional structures creates steadfast barriers proven difficult to overcome. Wilson (2011) notes that impoverished and underrepresented populations often look to school leaders to provide support well beyond the traditional educational responsibilities. Peterson (1994) writes that "for many students, schools provide the strongest, most enduring, and most systematic part of their educational world" (para. 4). As a result, there is a unique relationship that exists between the urban leader and the community. As the nation moves into the age of globalization, we realize that we have not yet measured up to ensuring even an adequate education for our most underprivileged youth. Urban school leaders, and the nation as a whole, understand that they must improve their efforts, but Warren (2005) cites the work of Rothstein, asserting that "it is patently unreasonable to expect that they alone can compensate for the effects of poverty and racism" (p. 134).

History tells us that the advent of desegregation resulted in the loss of the cultural support structures present in urban communities and neighborhood schools. Loss of significant school–community relationships creates additional burdens on the urban school leader to foster school climates supportive of student growth. Unlike other school leaders, urban leaders must ensure the creation of "authentic, contextually sensitive school communities that welcome students and parents as equal participants into the broader goal of learning and school success" (Woodruff, 1997, para. 8). Fostering culturally sensitive practices on the part of educators who may not value their students' cultural background is a challenge. Many educators regard low-income minority students as "deficient" and their perceptions limit academic and social expectations that ultimately limits achievement (O'Connor and Fernandez, 2006). Addressing and eradicating these historical perceptual trends is essential and requires dedicated leadership focusing student abilities and potential. Kasinitz, Mollenkopf, Waters, and Holdaway (2008) note that developing and maintaining a positive school culture require sustained and intentional strategies. According to Peterson (1994), the foundation for change includes a supportive professional culture promoting continuous renewal of instructional methods and curricular offerings in an atmosphere of collegiality, trust, and a shared mission (para. 1).

The initial introduction of the urban leader was born out of the need to address the growing political, social, economic, and economic context of a growing industrialized America (Garrison, 2009). Globalization has taken the place of industrialization, but the needs remain unchanged with the goal of sustaining a globally competitive society.

SUMMARY

An important component of the urban community is defined by the unique interrelationships between the culture, community, and schools. Strong and effective leadership within these settings is paramount and requires an understanding of the cultural and social variables impacting the environment, and ultimately academic achievement. At the heart of urban school leadership is gaining validation for and creating avenues to overcome the fact that poverty and institutional racism do indeed influence academic performance and the path to success in our democratic society (Irvine, 2007; Rothstein, 2004; Squires and Kubrin, 2006; Wilson, 2011). Neither poverty nor racism should serve as the parameters by which we define the potential of a child, family, community, or race. Our "barometer" for success, writes Morris (1999), in light of desegregation, is the "quality of education received by low-income African-American and minority students who remain behind in predominantly African-American schools in the inner cities" (p. 316). The Urban Economic Development Working Group (1990) surmises four conditions are necessary for the nation to remain globally competitive: (1) an educated workforce, (2) the availability of financial capital, (3) technological innovation and entrepreneurial talent, and (4) public infrastructure (1990). Success depends on urban school leaders' ability to simultaneously managed these four conditions, while ensuring that society is not permitted to shape student expectations based on the influences of dominant social forces.

Despite the pressure of the position, the Wallace Foundation reports that school leaders treat the larger environment as a source of opportunities as opposed to roadblocks and unreachable requirements (p. iv, n.d.). This type of enthused, dedicated, and positive leadership will continue to be the hope for the future.

REFERENCES

Ahram, R., Stembridge, A., Fergus, E., and Nogura, P. (2012). Framing urban school challenges: The problems to examine when implementing response to intervention. Retrieved from www.rtinetwork.org/learn/diversity/urban-school-challenges.

American Reinvestment Recovery Act. (2009). Retrieved from www.ed.gov/recovery.

Arnold, D. H., Zeljo, A., Doctoroff, G. L., and Ortiz, C. (2008). Parent involvement in preschools: Predictors and relation of involvement to pre-literacy development. *School Psychology Review, 37*, 74–91.

Barnard, W. M. (2004). Parental involvement in elementary school and educational attainment. *Children and Youth Services Review, 26*, 39–62.

Beyer, L. E. and Zeichner, K. (1987). Teacher education in cultural context: Beyond reproduction. In T. Popkewitz (Ed.), Critical studies in teacher education (pp. 298–334). Philadelphia: Fulmer Press.

Billingsley, A. (1968). *Black Families in America*. Englewood Cliffs, NJ: Prentice Hall.

Blanchett, W. J., Mumford, V., and Beachum, F. (2005). Urban school failure and disproportionality in a post Brown era: Benign neglect of the Constitutional rights of students of color. *Remedial and Special Education, 26*, pp. 70–81. DOI: 10.1177/07419325050260020201.

Buendia, E. (2011). Reconsidering the urban education: Interdisciplinary conversations. *Urban Review, 43*, 1–21.

Carnegie Task Force on Teaching as a Profession. (1986). *A nation prepared: Teachers for the 21*st *century*. Washington, DC: Carnegie Forum on Education and the Economy.

Cherryholmes, C. H. (1987). The political project of Tomorrow's Teachers. *Social Education 51*(7), 501–505.

Chubb, J. E. and Moe, T. M. (1990). Politics, markets, and American schools. Washington DC: Brookings Institute.

Clark, R. M. (1983). *Family life and school achievement: Why poor Black children succeed or fail*. Chicago: University of Chicago Press.

Cohen, D. K. and Hill, H. C. (2000). Instructional policy and classroom performance: The mathematics reform in California. *Teachers College Record, 102*(2), 294–343.

Comer, J. P. (1984). Home-school relationships as they affect the academic success of children. *Education and Urban Society, 16*, 323–337.

Cuban, L. (1989, June). The "At-Risk" label and the problem with urban reform. *Phi Delta Kappan, 70*(10), 780–784, 799–801.

Darling-Hammond, L. (2010). *The flat world and education: How America's commitment to equity will determine our future*. New York: Teachers College Press.

Delpit, L. (1995). *Other people's children*. New York: New Press.

Devine, J. A., Plunkett, M., and Wright, J. D. (1992). The chronicity of poverty: Evidence from the PSID, 1968–1987. *Social Forces, 70*(3): 787–812.

Edmonds, R. (1979). Effective schools for the urban poor. *Education Leadership*, 37(1), 15–24.

Elmore, R. F. and Associates (1990). *Restructuring schools: The next generation of educational reform*. San Francisco: Jossey-Bass.

Federal Education Policy History. (2011). Retrieved from federaleducationpolicy.wordpress.com/2011/06/15/goals-2000-educate-america-act/.

Fullan M. (2009, April). Large scale reform comes of age. *Journal of Educational Change, 10*, 101–113.

Gage, N. L. and Needels, M. C. (1989). Process-product research on teaching: A review of the criticisms. *Elementary School Journal, 89*, 253–300.

Garrison, M. J. (2009). *The measure of failure: The political origins of educational testing*. Albany: State University of New York Press.

Gertz, C. (2010, December 23). A nation at risk 25 years later. *Education Week*. Retrieved from www.edweek.org.

Gilbert, C. and Heller, D. E. (2010, November). *The Truman Commission and its impact on federal higher education policy from 1947 to 2010*. Paper presented at the Association for the Study of Higher Education Annual Conference, Indianapolis, Indiana. Retrieved from www.personal.psu.edu/deh29/papers/ASHE_2010_Gilbert_Heller.pdf.

Goodlad, J. I. (1984). *A place called school: Prospects for the future*. New York: McGraw-Hill Book Company.

Great Schools Partnership. (2013). Retrieved from edglossary.org/school-community/.

Greene, J. and Symonds, W. C. (2006, June 26). Bill Gates gets schooled. *Business Week*, 3990, 64–70. Retrieved from www.businessweek.com/stories/2006-06-25/bill-gates-gets-Schooled.

Halawah, I. (2005). The relationship between effective communication of high school principals and school climate. *Education, 126*(2), 334–345.

Hallinger, P. and Heck, R.H. (1998). Exploring the principal's contribution to school effectiveness: 1980–1985. *School Effectiveness and School Improvement 9*(2), 157–191.

Hanna, J. (2005, June). The Elementary and Secondary Education Act 40 years later. *Harvard Graduate School of Education*. Retrieved from www.gse.harvard.edu/news/2005/0819_esea.html.

Hargreaves, A. (2003). *Teaching in the knowledge society: Education in the age of insecurity*. New York: Teachers College Press.

Hargreaves, A. and Fullan, M. (2012). Professional capital: Transforming teaching in every school. New York: Teachers College Press.

Holmes Group (1986). *Tomorrow's Teachers*. East Lansing, Michigan.

Hoover-Dempsey, K. V. and Sandler, H. M. (1997). Why do parents become involved in their children's education. *Review of Educational Research, 67*, 3–42.

Hunter, R. & Bartee, R. (2003). The achievement gap: Issues of competition, class, and race. *Education and Urban Society, 35*(2), 151–160.

Hutchinson, P. (2002). The 1947 president's commission on higher education and the national rhetoric on higher education policy. *History of Higher Education Annual, 22*, 91–109.

Irvine, J. J. (2007, Summer). The impact of the desegregation process on the education of Black students: A retrospective analysis. *Journal of Negro Education, 76*(3), 297–305. Retrieved from www.jstor.org/discover/10.23 07/40034572?uid=2129&uid=2134&uid=2&uid=70&uid =4&sid=21104232591827.

Irvine, R. W. and Irvine, J. J. (1983). The impact of the desegregation on the education of Black students: Key variables. *The Journal of Negro Education 5*(2), 410–422.

Jargowsky, P. A. (1994, Spring). Ghetto poverty among Blacks in the 1980s. *Journal of Policy Analysis and Management, 13*(2), 288–310.

Jehlen, A. (n.d). ESEA at 45: From help to hurt . . . and back to help. National Educational Association. Retrieved from www.nea.org/home/38860.htm.

Kanter, H. and Lowe, R. (1995). Class, race, and the emergence of federal education policy: From the New Deal to the Great Society. *Educational Researcher, 24*, 4–11.

Kasinitz, P., Mollenkopf, J. H., Waters, M. C., and Holdaway, J. (2008). *Inheriting the city, The children of immigrants come of age*. New York: Russell Sage Foundation.

Kincheloe, J. (1999). *How do we tell the workers? The socioeconomic foundations of work and vocational education*. Boulder, CO: Westview.

Kotter, J. (1996). *Leading change*. Boston: Harvard Business School Press.

Krajewski, B. (2005, March). In their own words. *Educational Leadership, 62*(6), 14–18. Retrieved from www.ascd.org/publications/educational-leadership/mar05/vol62/num06/In-TheirOwn-Words.aspx.

Kruse, K. M. (2005). *White flight: Atlanta and the making of the modern conservatism*. Princeton, NJ: Princeton University Press.

Labaree, D. F. (1992, Summer). Power, knowledge, and the rationalization of teaching: A genealogy of the movement of professional teaching. *Harvard Educational Review 62*(2), 123–154.

Lee, V. E. and Ready, D. D. (2009, Spring). U.S. High school curriculum: Three phases of contemporary research and reform. *The Future of Children, 19*(1), 135–156.

Lytle, J.H. (1992, July). Prospects for reforming urban schools. *Urban Education, 27*(2), 109–131.

Marcon, R. A. (1999). Positive relationships between parent school involvement and public school inner-city preschoolers' development and academic performance. *School Psychology Review, 28*, 395–412.

Mathews, D. (2006). *Is there a public for public schools?* Dayton, OH: Kettering Foundation.

May, J. J. (2006). The role of money, race, and politics in the accountability challenge. *Journal of Urban Learning, Teaching, and Research, 2*, 39–47.

Meier, K. J., Stewart, J., and England, R. E. (1989). *Race, Class, and Education: The Politics of Second Generation Discrimination*. Madison: University of Wisconsin Press.

Morris, J. E. (1999). What is the future of predominantly Black urban schools?: The politics of race in urban policy. *Phi Delta Kappan, 81*(4), 316–319.

Murnane, R. J. and Levy, F. (1996). *Teaching the new basic skills: Principles of educating children to thrive in a changing economy*. New York: Free Press.

Murphy, J. (2010, May). Nine lessons for turning around failing schools. *Phi Delta Kappan, 91*(8), 93–97.

NASULGC Urban Economic Working Group. (1990). Urban Economic Development. *Journal of Planning Literature, 5*(1), 6–11.

National Board of Professional Teaching Standards. (1989). *Toward high and rigorous standard for the teaching profession: Initial policies and perspectives on the National Board for the Professional Teaching Standards*. Detroit: Author.

National Commission on Excellence in Education. (1983, April). *A Nation at Risk: The imperative for educational reform*. Retrieved from www2.ed.gov/pubs/NatAtRisk/risk.html.

Neel, J. (2013). Poverty and stress. *Berkeley Scientific Journal, 1*(1), 42–45.

Nogura, P. A. and Wells, L. (2011). The politics of school reform: A broader and bolder approach for Newark. *Berkeley Review of Education, 2*(1), 5–25.

O'Connor, C. and Fernandez, S. D. (2006, Aug/Sep). Race, class, and disproportionality: Reevaluating the relationships between poverty and special education placement. *Educational Researcher, 35*(6), 6–11.

Ormell, C. (2012, September). The economy and education. *Prospero 18* (3), 14–24.

Paris, K. (1994). *A leadership model for planning and implementing change for school-to-work transition.* Madison: University of Wisconsin-Madison, Center on Education and Work.

Payne, C. M. (2008). So much reform; so little change: The persistence of failure in urban schools. Cambridge, MA: Harvard Education Press.

Peterson, K. (1994). *Building collaborative cultures: Seeking ways to reshape urban schools.* Retrieved from www.ncrel.org/sdrs/areas/issues/educatrs/leadrshp/le0pet.htm.

Plessy v. Ferguson. (2013, September). Landmark case of the U.S. Supreme Court. Retrieved from www.streetlaw.org/en/landmark/cases/plessy_v_ferguson.

Rothstein, R. (2004). *Class and schools: Using social, economic, and educational reform to close the black-white achievement gap.* Washington, DC: Economic Policy Institute.

Rumberger, R. W. (1987, Summer). High school dropouts: A review of issues and evidence. *Review of Educational Research, 57*(2), 101–121.

Rury, J. L. and Saatcioglu, A. (2011, May). Suburban advantage: Opportunity hoarding and secondary attainment in the postwar metropolitan north. *American Journal of Education, 177,* 307–342.

Sanders, E. T. W. (1999). *Urban school leadership: Issues and strategies.* Larchmont, NY: Eye on Education.

Semary, H. E., Khaja, M. A., and Hamidou, K. (2012). The interaction between education and globalization: A comparative study of four GCC countries. *Cross Cultural Communication, 8*(4), 58–69.

Schnore, L. F. (1962, Winter). Social problems in an urban-industrial context. Social Problems, 9(3), 228–240.

Sheldon, S. B. (2003, June). Linking school-family-community partnerships in urban elementary schools to student achievement on state tests. *The Urban Review, 35*(2), 149–165.

Silver, M. (2004, March). New horizons for learning. Retrieved from education.jhu.edu/PD/newhorizons/Transforming%20Education/Articles/Trends%20in%20School%20Reform/.

The Social Welfare History Project. (n.d.). Retrieved from www.socialwelfarehistory.com/events/elementary-and-secondary-education-act-of-1965/.

Squires, G. D. and Kubrin, C. E. (2006, Fall). Privileged Places: Race, opportunity, and uneven development in urban America. *Shelterforce Online,* 147. Retrieved from nhi.org/online/issues/147/privilegedplaces.html.

Sunderman, G. L. (2009). The federal role in education: From the Reagan to the Obama administration. vue.annenberginstitute.org/sites/default/files/issuePDF/VUE24.pdf.

Toppo, G. (2004, April). Thousands of Black teachers lose jobs. Retrieved from usatoday30.usatoday.com/news/nation/2004-04-28-brown-side2_x.htm#.

Tyack, D. B. and Cuban, L. (1995). *Tinkering toward Utopia: A century of public school reform.* Cambridge, MA: Harvard University Press.

U.S. Department of Education. (2012, February). The federal role of education. Retrieved from www2.ed.gov/about/overview/fed/role.html.

Wallace Foundation. (n.d.). Leadership for Learning Improvement in Urban Schools. Retrieved from www.wallacefoundation.org/knowledge-center/school-leadership/district-policy-and-practice/Pages/Leadership-for-Learning-Improvement-in-Urban-Schools.aspx.

Warren, M. R. (2005, Summer). Communities and schools: A new view of urban education reform. *Harvard Educational Review, 75*(2), 133–173.

West, C. (1994). *Race matters.* New York: Vintage.

Wiggins, S. P. (1986, October). Revolution in the teaching profession: A comparative review of two reform reports. *Educational Leadership,* 56–59.

Wilson, W. J. (1987). *The truly disadvantaged: The inner-city, the underclass, and public policy:* Chicago, IL: University of Chicago Press.

Wilson, W. J. (2011, Spring). Being poor, Black, and American: The impact of political, economic, and cultural forces. *American Educator, 35*(1), 10–23, 46.

Woodruff, D. W. (1997). Keep community "real" for urban school success. *Education Digest, 62*(9), 8, 23.

Zakaria, F. (2011). A flight plan for the American economy. *Time, 177*(22), 1–5.

CHAPTER 2

Sankofa

Leadership and the Twenty-First-Century Black Female School Superintendents

Judy A. Alston

INTRODUCTION

A by-product of the historic *Brown* decision of 1954 was the decimation of the number of Black teachers and administrators in public schools. Ten years after the ruling, the number of Black principals in the eleven Southern border states (Virginia, North Carolina, South Carolina, Florida, Kentucky, Tennessee, Georgia, Alabama, Mississippi, Louisiana, and Arkansas) dropped by 95 percent (Coursen, 1989). Now more than fifty years after *Brown*, there continues to be an ever-shrinking number of African-American women in the superintendency (Alston, 1999). In 1954, Toppo (2004) noted that about 82,000 Black teachers were responsible for teaching as many as two million Black children, and in the eleven years following *Brown*, more than 38,000 Black teachers and administrators in seventeen Southern and border states lost their jobs. Many of these black teachers and administrators worked as Jeanes supervisors. For over sixty years, these master teachers traveled throughout the South to provide education and other related services to poor black children. Eighty percent of these supervisors were Black women who were the precursors to the modern-day black female superintendent. The purpose of this chapter is to celebrate and reflect on the legacy of the Jeanes supervisors and provide lessons for the twenty-first-century African-American female superintendent.

Throughout history it has been evident that the black female has pioneered new frontiers in education as leaders as well as participants (Rusher, 1996). In forging new paths, the modern-day twenty-first-century African-American female school superintendent faces extraordinary challenges as a leader and a role model. This small cadre of black women educational leaders

(Alston, 1999, 2000; Jackson, 1999) faces the challenge of an outmoded, stymied system that while the student body is diversifying, the teaching force continues to be very white and female and the administrative force white and male. Furthermore, Brunner and Grogan (2007) stated, "the superintendency is one of the most heavily white and masculine roles in our society" (12). In the midst of this educational quagmire and with her feet firmly planted in the present, she has not forgotten her historical past as she endeavors to be a spirited tempered radical (Ngunjiri, 2006) embodying *Sankofa*—an Akan word meaning, "We must go back and reclaim our past so we can move forward; so we understand why and how we came to be who we are."

Prior to the 1954 *Brown* decision, approximately eighty-two thousand Black teachers taught two million Black children who attended mostly segregated schools (Hudson and Holmes, 1994; Toppo, 2004). An unfortunate by-product of the historic *Brown* decision was the decimation of the number of Black teachers and administrators in public schools. In the segregated Black schools of the South before the decision, Henig, Hula, Orr, and Pedescleaux (1999) noted that Black teachers and principals were important role models and respected leaders in their communities. Tillman (2004) furthered that teaching was a noteworthy and important profession in the Black community and served as a primary leadership role, particularly for Black women (Ethridge, 1979; Foster, 1997; Yeakey, Johnston, and Adkison, 1986). Even more pointedly, Foster (1997) stated, "Of the 63,697 black teachers in the United States in 1940, 46,381 were employed in the South" (p. xxv). Ten years after the 1954 ruling, the number of Black principals in the thirteen Southern and border states dropped by 95 percent (Coursen,

Mazzarella, Jeffress, and Hadderman, 1989). Additionally, more than thirty-eight thousand Black teachers and administrators in seventeen Southern and border states lost their jobs.

Many of these black teachers and administrators were Jeanes supervisors. For over sixty years, these master teachers traveled throughout the South to provide education and other related services to poor Black children. Eighty percent of these supervisors were Black women who were the precursors to the modern-day Black female superintendent. The purpose of this article is to celebrate and reflect on the legacy of the Jeanes supervisors as well as to provide lessons for the twenty-first-century African-American female superintendent.

HISTORICAL VIEW

Today's black educators stand on the shoulders of these master teachers and supervisors of the twentieth century. Before there was a black female superintendent, there were the Jeanes teachers. When the Civil War ended, some provisions were made for educating the children of freed slaves, as many white Northerners who viewed education as the vehicle for not only industrial development, but also as a reuniting tool for our country (Southern Education Foundation, 1998). In the late nineteenth and early twentieth centuries, funds were established to provide money for the education of destitute children (*Peabody Education Fund, 1867*), African-American children (*John F. Slater Fund, 1882*), and African-American teachers. For the establishment and future direction of black education, the latter were the most significant funds: *The Negro Rural School Fund* and *The Virginia Randolph Fund* (Alston and Jones, 2002).

Anna T. Jeanes, a Philadelphia Quaker philanthropist, sought to improve community and school conditions for rural African Americans. As one of ten children in a wealthy family, she was a well-to-do single woman in the 1800s interested in the causes of her day. Since none of her brothers and sisters left heirs, over time, she inherited a great deal of money. She donated her monies to charitable endeavors, and in 1907, shortly before she died, she gave one $1 million for the creation of *The Negro Rural School Fund (a.k.a. the Anna T. Jeanes fund)* to hire black teachers as supervisors in black schools and to improve black communities. These teachers became known as Jeanes supervisors. According to Botsch (1998), in a fateful meeting with Booker T. Washington, she asked Mr. Washington and a colleague from Hampton Institute to put together a board of trustees and to spend her money in the rural areas where most African Americans lived. She wanted to provide supervisors for rural schools where they would serve as consultants and assistants to the teachers, most of whom had little training. Many of the Jeanes supervisors themselves attended Tuskegee and Hampton Institutes for in-service training for their jobs (Botsch, 1998).

To further the philosophy and work of the initial Jeanes fund, *The Virginia Randolph Fund* was created in 1937 to honor the first "Jeanes Teacher." Born on June 8, 1874, in Richmond, Virginia, Miss Randolph began teaching at the Old Mountain Road School in Henrico County, Virginia, at the age of eighteen. She initially became a teacher by the time she was sixteen years old and taught in Goochland County, Virginia. Because of Randolph's young age, her uncle had to sign for her employment before she was given her school in Goochland (Jones, 1937). On October 26, 1908, after having taught for eighteen years (sixteen at Mountain Road Schools), Randolph was appointed the first Jeanes Supervisor Industrial Teacher, providing the first formal in-service teacher training anywhere in Virginia for rural Black teachers. Her accomplishments included improving industrial skills, education in general, in every one of the county's rural schools for Blacks. With no outline, formal plan, or curriculum guide, she designed and fashioned industrial work and community self-help programs to meet specific needs of schools. In Randolph's *A Brief Report of the Manual Training Work Done in the Colored Schools of Henrico County, Virginia for Session 1908–1909* (Jensen, 1981), she documented reports for each of the twenty-three schools she visited, including the amount of industrial work done and in the general improvements accomplished. One thousand copies of the report were printed and mailed to county superintendents throughout the South. It was authorized for use in other Virginia counties, and county superintendents from all over the South requested additional information regarding the Henrico Plan. Randolph's teaching techniques and philosophy were later adopted in Britain's African colonies (Bude, 1983; Wallbank, 1938).

Soon, an influx of these supervising teachers became prominent throughout the South. They were known as "supervising industrial teachers," "Jeanes supervising industrial teachers," "Jeanes supervisors," "Jeanes agents," or "Jeanes teachers." By the 1950s, their titles changed to Jeanes curriculum directors. Some of them were supervisors for an entire county; others were supervisors for only a part. Several county school boards began to assist in the teachers' efforts by providing small grants to aid transportation. By 1909–1910, 129 Jeanes teachers were working in 130 counties of thirteen states (Jones, 1937). The Jeanes teacher movement was so popular and successful with the African-American schools and communities that it remained in place until 1968.

For sixty years, Jeanes teachers traveled to rural areas in the South that had high populations of minorities to provide education and other related services. Botsch (1998) notes that they were also active in other parts of the nation and even beyond national borders, because of the success of the Jeanes model. Additionally, an early experiment with Jeanes supervision in Liberia in the late 1920s but had to be terminated due to a yellow fever epidemic. Later, however, the program would be used as a model overseas with teachers who supervised schools in Asia, Africa, the Virgin Islands, and Latin America (Botsch, 1998).

Eighty percent of Jeanes supervisors were women (Guthrie-Jordan, 1990). African-American females were chosen during this time because they were "self-effacing, stimulating others to put forth their best effort rather than making . . . [themselves] too active or too prominent" (Brawley, 1971, 62); i.e., they were perceived to be less threatening. However, female Jeanes supervisors did face similar problems that working women have always faced and that African-American women often face in their relationships with white men—those being issues of power, gender, and race (Botsch, 1996; Smith, 1997).

With no set guidelines for them and numerous obstacles placed before them, these supervisors, themselves former teachers, did any and all things needed as they sought to improve education for Blacks during turbulent times (Dale, 1998; Kridel, 1992). These supervisors were initially hired to supervise African-American teachers in the small rural schools for blacks; however, they also spent a great deal of time on improving home conditions and other community organizations (Kridel, 1992). Later the Jeanes supervisors placed more emphasis on improvement of instruction, introducing new teaching methods and curricula, and organizing in-service teacher training workshops at African-American colleges. The Jeanes supervisors were increasingly called upon to serve in administrative capacities as assistants to the County Superintendent of Schools (who were White males); they became essentially de facto superintendents (Dale, 1998; Jones, 1937). Like modern-day superintendents, the Jeanes supervisors served as negotiator, crisis-handler, resource allocation specialist, disseminator of information, staff developer, and personnel specialist (Cuban, 1988; Hallinger and Murphy, 1987). These Jeanes supervisors also undertook the role of attendance officer, enrollment manager, record-keeper, and organizer of the countywide events for the counties to which they were assigned. This involved regular visits to all schools and homes (Dale, 1998; Jones, 1937). African-American female leaders were "helpful as teachers . . . not simply in the public schools . . . but in classes formed in neighborhoods that sorely need[ed] this knowledge" (Loewenberg and Bogin, 1976, 300).

BROWN DECISION: LIBERATION AND LIABILITY

According to the Southern Education Foundation (SEF) (1998), when Brown was decided in 1954, there were more than five hundred Jeanes supervisors working in the South. However, due to the landmark decision, many of these teachers/supervisors lost their jobs because of the closing of schools and the reassigning and outright firing of black teachers and principals. Moving up the educational organizational hierarchy, we find that there was only one Black woman superintendent in 1954. Revere (1986) shares that Velma Ashley, an African-American woman, served as superintendent in Oklahoma from 1944 to 1956. Also, there were fewer than a dozen Blacks classified as assistant superintendents (Ethridge, 1979). To further illuminate this unfortunate result, Karpinski (2006) states:

Desegregation resulted in the closing and consolidation of schools that created a job crisis that undermined the status of Black educators who traditionally had occupied a valued position in their communities and who were often the bulwark of the middle class. In particular, African-American principals were role models and community leaders. Their removal from the educational landscape or demotion from an esteemed position affected not only these leaders as individuals but also the children and the communities they served. More than two generations of African-American students have borne the consequences of this employment crisis, deprived of their example, and subjected to treatment and policies that inadequately embodied the principle of *Brown*. (238–239)

Furthermore, with the desegregation came federally funded programs that supplied schools with educational specialists, such as directors of special programs, reading consultants, and instructional assistants—most of whom were White and not African American. There was no longer a proper "fit" or a proper place for the Jeanes teachers, the supervisors of African-American schools and communities who were once perceived as being the influential and powerful personalities in the local schools and communities. The majority of them returned to classrooms as teachers. The mass firings of Black educators were made easier because during desegregation all-Black schools were usually closed down, making Black educators expendable even when their credentials surpassed their White peers. The National Education Association's figures from this period show that 85 percent of minority teachers had college degrees compared with 75 percent of White teachers (Echols, 2006).

In October 1956 the NEA ATA Joint Committee *The New York Times* (Fine, 1956) documented the dismissal of Black educators in several states. Karpinksi (2006) notes that in Texas, five thousand substandard White teachers were employed although certified Black educators were told to find other lines of work. This practice continued, and the more Black administrators were removed, they were replaced with uncertified and/or inexperienced White candidates in the newly integrated schools (Bell, 1976; *Displacement*, 1971).

The years between 1954 and 1965 were the most devastating for Black teachers and principals for it was during this time that more than six thousand teachers in the Southern and border states lost their positions (Ethridge, 1979). *The Status of School Desegregation in the South—1970* reported that demotions were far more common. The majority (63 percent) of the moni-

tored districts demoted at least 386 black principals, wherein half of these individuals were made assistant principals, though they were more qualified than their White counterparts. Tillman (2004) noted that post-*Brown* job losses for Black educators can be attributed to five factors:

1. Judges were confronted with the question of inferior schools, and thus Black teachers were perceived to be inferior;
2. Judges were reluctant to interfere with the segregated policies and practices of local school boards;
3. The courts had no experience responding to the kind of massive resistance to the *Brown* mandate to desegregate elementary and secondary schools;
4. There was a lack of monitoring and a lack of effective data collection after the court orders; and
5. *Brown* was more of a civil rights decision than an education decision (Etheridge, 1979).

Additionally between 1970 and 1971, $240,564,911 in salaries was lost after Black teachers in Southern states were dismissed from their positions.

TODAY'S BLACK FEMALE SCHOOL SUPERINTENDENTS

Unfortunately in 2015, Black female superintendent is more of an oxymoron than ever. Arnez (1981) and Revere (1986) noted that in 1978 the number of African-American female superintendents was five. In 1982, there were eleven African-American female superintendents, sixteen in 1983, twenty-nine in 1984, and twenty-five in 1985. Fast forward to 2010: the American Association of School Administrator's *2010 Study of the American Superintendency* reported that 24 percent of superintendents nationwide are women, yet only 2 percent of these superintendencies were held by African Americans (Kowalski, McCord, Petersen, Young, and Ellerson, 2010). There was no reporting of the percentages of Black females holding the position of superintendent. A previous survey in 2003 (Brunner, Grogan, and Prince, 2003) reported that Black women held 4.4 percent of the superintendencies. The more things change, the more they remain the same.

While there are still few black women educational CEOs, those who do attain these positions are determined to succeed not only for themselves, but also for the children whom they serve. While they have been viewed historically as the "messiah or scapegoat" for a school district (Scott, 1980), these spirited tempered radical servant leaders (Alston 2005; Alston and McClellan, 2011; Ngunjiri, 2006) stand tall as they endeavor to make a better way for those whom they serve. They remain dogged in their quest regarding the education of children of color. As one Black female superintendent in Jackson's 1996 study stated, "I have to remain focused on the kids . . . " (151). They may be radical in their ideals (Alston, 2005) and sometimes action; yet they are tempered and becoming more refined as they work within the system of education that we have in place—working to change it slowly from the inside.

LESSONS LEARNED

As a part of their survival instinct, many of these women have an unyielding faith and sense of spirituality that enables them to always strive toward excellence. Like her Jeanes predecessors, today's Black female superintendent has a strong sense of spirituality as her foundation. For many, this spirituality is the foundation from which they mount daily struggles (Reid-Merritt, 1996). From this underpinning they learned pivotal lessons of servant leadership and social activism, which have aided them along their journey.

Servant Leadership

Equipped with a strong sense of efficacy, these "Sister Servant Superintendents" are empowered and deeply caring about their mission—to serve, lead, and educate children. Service is the greatest lesson learned from the Jeanes supervisors. Black female school superintendents desire to serve and serve first and then lead (Greenleaf, 1991). As true servant leaders, they follow the Jeanes design to " . . . make(s) sure that other people's highest priority needs are being served" (7). They also act on what they truly believe versus being under the influence of whatever the current culture may be. As reflective practitioners, they also regulate themselves via the Greenleaf's servant leader litmus test:

- Do those served grow as people?
- Do they, while being served, become healthier, wiser, freer, more autonomous, more likely to become servants?
- And what is the effect on the least privileged in society; will he or she benefit, or at least will he or she not be further deprived?

Social Activism

Miss Randolph and the Jeanes supervisors and another also set a blueprint of social action for future educational leaders. As vocational educators, they taught simple industrial skills such as sewing, canning, basketry, and woodworking. As development officers, they raised money for numerous building needs, school materials, and salary supplements. As community activists, they held meetings, distributed supplies, and generally promoted the welfare of the African Americans in the school and in their larger communities. As building architects and planners, they promoted schemes for the building or renovating of schools. As social workers, they visited homes in order to enlist help from parents and to increase school attendance, fostered health talks to promote good hygiene and cleanliness. And as professional development experts, they introduced more effective ways of teaching school subjects.

Like another "Social Activist Servant Leader Mother," Fannie Lou Hamer, today's Black female superintendent fuels her work and passion by recognizing what Williams (1998) lays as foundation for the work:

- Selfless devotion to a task garners results.
- Intelligence is more than knowledge learned in school.
- Faith sustains hope in uncertain times.
- Inspiration should precede aspiration.
- Smart leaders trust their inner voices.
- Loyalty to the lowliest of followers is often most rewarding. (196–197)

From this example of social action, today's "Sister Servant Superintendent" is a culturally responsive leader. She impacts the lives of those she leads by truly making a difference for the culturally diverse students and families they serve (Johnson, 2006).

CONCLUSION

As practitioners and personifiers of the ethic of care and justice, the twenty-first-century African-American female school superintendent stands firmly in a space that does not easily welcome her—an organization that was not created with her or her children in mind. As the purveyor of care, she reflects the presence of benevolence and compassion (Gilligan, 1982) that her Jeanes mother laid as the foundation for the work that must be done to see that students of color have an opportunity to succeed in life, keeping and honoring education at their nucleus. As proponents for justice, these women seek and practice fairness and impartiality (Kohlberg, 1984). They seek to provide a space of democratic practice to combat the injustices of an unequal and unleveled educational field. As spirited tempered radical servant leaders, their use of prophetic pragmatism (Dantley, 2005; West, 1982) fuels them to move forward and themselves provide the shoulders for which the next generation will stand and realize *Sankofa*.

REFERENCES

Alston, J. A. (2005). Tempered radicals and servant leaders: Black females persevering in the superintendency. *Educational Administration Quarterly 41*(4), 675–688.

Alston, J. A. (2000). Missing in action: Where are the black female school superintendents? *Urban Education 35*, 525–531.

Alston, J. A. (1999). Climbing hills and mountains: Black females making it to the superintendency. In *Sacred dreams: Women and the superintendency*, edited by C. Cryss Brunner, (pages 79–90). Albany: State University of New York Press.

Alston, J. A. and Jones, S. N. (2002). Carrying the torch of the Jeanes supervisors: 21st century African American female superintendents and servant leadership. In *The promises and perils facing today's school superintendents*, edited by Bruce S. Cooper and Lance D. Fusarelli, (pages 65–75). Lanham, MD: Scarecrow Press.

Alston, J. A. and McClellan, P. A. (2011). *Herstories: Leading With the Lessons of the Lives of Black Women Activists*. New York: Peter Lang Publishers.

Arnez, N. (1981). *The besieged school superintendent: A case study of school superintendent-school board relations in Washington D.C., 1973–74*. Lanham, MD: University Press of America.

Bell, Jr., D. A. (1976). Serving two masters: Integration ideals and client interests in school desegregation litigation. *The Yale Law Journal, 85*(4), 470–516

Botsch, C. S. (1998). The Jeanes supervisors. www.usca.edu/aasc/jeanes.htm.

Brawley, B. G. (1971). *Dr. Dillard of the Jeanes fund*. Freeport, NY: Books for Library Press.

Brunner, C. C. and Grogan, M. (2007). *Women leading school systems: Uncommon roads to fulfillment*. Lanham, MD: Rowman & Littlefield.

Brunner, C. C., Grogan, M., and Prince, C. (2003). *AASA national survey of women in the superintendency and central office: Preliminary results*. Paper presented at the annual conference of the American Educational Research Association, Chicago, IL.

Bude, U. (1983). The adaptation concept in British colonial education. *Comparative Education, 19*(3), 341–355.

Coursen, D., Mazzarella, J. A., Jeffress, L., and Hadderman, M. (1989). Two special cases: Women and Blacks. In *School leadership: Handbook for excellence*, edited by Stuart C. Smith and Philip K. Piele (pages 84–106). Eugene, OR: ERIC Clearinghouse on Educational Management.

Cuban, L., (1988). *The managerial imperative and the practice of leadership in schools*. Albany: State University of New York Press.

Dale, L. F. R., (1998). The Jeanes supervisors in Alabama, 1909–1963. *Dissertation Abstracts International* (UMI Microform No. 9835325).

Dantley, M. E. (2005). African American spirituality and Cornel Wests' notions of prophetic pragmatism: Restructuring educational leadership in American urban schools. *Educational Administration Quarterly 41*(4), 651–674.

Displacement and present status of black school principals in desegregated school districts: Hearings before the Select Committee on Equal Educational Opportunity of the U.S. Senate, 92nd Congress. 1971.

Echols, C. (2006). Challenges facing Black American principals: A conversation about coping. cnx.org/content/m13821/latest/.

Ethridge, S. B. (1979). Impact of the 1954 *Brown vs. Topeka Board of Education* decision on Black educators. *The Negro Educational Review, 30*(4), 217–232.

Fine, B. (1956, October 14). 450 Negroes lose jobs in integration. *The New York Times*, 1, 50.

Foster, M. (1997). *Black teachers on teaching*. New York: The New Press.

Gilligan, C. (1982). *In a different voice: Psychological theory and women's development*. Cambridge, MA: Harvard University Press.

Glass, T. E., Björk, L., and Brunner. C. C. (2000). *2000 Study of the American School Superintendency*. Arlington, VA: AASA.

Greenleaf, R. K. (1991). *The servant as leader*. Indianapolis, IN: Robert K. Greenleaf Center for Servant-Leadership.

Guthrie-Jordan, M. J. (1990). *A descriptive study of Black public school administrators in Ohio who hold the positions of superintendent, assistant superintendent, or high school principal*. Unpublished doctoral dissertation. Oxford, OH: Miami University of Ohio.

Hallinger, P. and Murphy, J. (1987). *Approaches to administrative training in education*. Albany: State University New York Press.

Henig, J., Hula, R. C., Orr, M., and Pedescleaux. D. S. (1999). *The color of school reform: Race, politics, and the challenge of urban education*. Princeton, NJ: Princeton University Press.

Hudson, M. J. and Holmes, B. J. (1994). Missing teachers, Impaired Communities: The Unanticipated Consequences of *Brown v. Board of Education* on the African American Teaching Force at the Pre-collegiate Level. *The Journal of Negro Education 63*, 388–393.

Jackson, B. L. (1999). Getting inside history—against all odds. African American women superintendents. In *Sacred dreams: Women and the superintendency*, edited by C. Cryss Brunner (pages 141–160). Albany: State University of New York Press.

Jensen, J. M. (1981). *With these hands: Women working on the land*. New York: McGraw-Hill.

Johnson, L. (2006). Making her community a better place to live: Culturally responsive urban school leadership in historical context. *Leadership and Policy in Schools, 5*, 19–36.

Jones, L. G. (1937). *The Jeanes teacher in the United States 1908–1933*. Chapel Hill: The University of North Carolina Press.

Karpinski, C. F. (2006). Bearing the burden of desegregation: Black principals and *Brown*. *Urban Education 41*(3), 237–276.

Kohlberg, L. (1984). *The psychology of moral development. The nature of validity of moral stages. (Essays on moral development*, Vol. 2). San Francisco: Harper & Row.

Kridel, C. (1992). The Jeanes teacher of South Carolina: The emergence, existence, and significance of their work. *Dissertation Abstracts International, 53* (08), (UMI Microform No. 9239100).

Lewin, K. (1951). *Field theory in social science*. New York: Harper & Brothers Publishers.

Loewenberg, B. J. and Bogin, R. (Eds.). (1976). *Black women in 19th-century American life*. University Park: The Pennsylvania State University Press.

Ngunjiri, F. W. (2006). *Tempered radicals and servant leaders: Portraits of spirited leadership amongst African women leaders*. Unpublished doctoral dissertation. Bowling Green, OH: Bowling Green State University.

Pincham, L. B. (2005). A league of willing workers: The impact of northern philanthropy, Virginia Estelle Randolph and the Jeanes Teachers in early twentieth-century Virginia. *The Journal of Negro Education, 74*(2), 112–123.

Reid-Merritt, P. (1996). *Sister power: How phenomenal Black women are rising to the top*. New York: John Wiley & Sons, Inc.

Revere, A. B. (1986). *A description of Black female superintendents*. Unpublished doctoral dissertation. Oxford: Miami University of Ohio.

Rusher, A. W. (1996). *African American women administrators*. Lanham, MD: University Press of America.

Scott, H. J. (1980). *The Black superintendent: Messiah or scapegoat?* Washington, DC: Howard University Press.

Smith, A. B. (1997). *Forgotten foundations: The role of Jeanes teachers in Black education*. New York: Vantage Books.

Southern Education Foundation. 1998. Our Heritage. www.sefatl.org/heritage.htm.

The Status of School Desegregation in the South—1970. A Report. 1970. American Friends Service Committee.

Tillman, L. C. (2004). (Un)intended Consequences? The Impact of the *Brown v. Board of Education* Decision on the Employment Status of Black Educators. *Education and Urban Society 36*(3), 280–303.

Toppo, G. (2004). Thousands of Black teachers lost jobs. www.usatoday.com/news/nation/2004-04-28-brown-side2_x.htm.

Wallbank, T. W. (1938). British colonial policy and native education in Kenya. *The Journal of Negro Education 7*(4), 521–532.

West, C. (1982). *Prophesy deliverance: An Afro-American revolutionary Christianity*. Philadelphia: Westminster Press.

Williams, L. E. (1998). *Servants of the people: The 1960s legacy of African American leadership*. New York: St. Martin's.

Yeakey, C. C., Adkison, J. A., and Johnston, G. S. (1986). In pursuit of equity: a review of research on minorities and women in educational administration. *Educational Administration Quarterly 22*, 110–149.

CHAPTER 3

Demographic and Professional Characteristics of Urban School Principals in the United States

A Twenty-Year Trend Study

Jiangang Xia, Xingyuan Gao, and Jianping Shen

INTRODUCTION

This chapter examines the historic trends of urban school principals' demographic and professional characteristics. We inquired into that, during the past twenty years, (a) how the diversity of urban principalship has evolved with respect to principals' gender and race/ethnicity, (b) how principals have been prepared with respect to their participation in the aspiring program, (c) how principals' perspective of most important educational goals has evolved, and (d) how principals' teaching experience before principalship has evolved. Four sections were developed below, which include (a) background, which is a brief review around the four research questions above, (b) methodology, which is an explanation of the data source and analysis approach, (c) findings, and (d) conclusions and discussions.

BACKGROUND

Diversity of Urban School Principals

During the past twenty years, student demographics have changed rapidly. According to Hernandez (2008), the changes "are manifesting themselves in the classroom in unexpected ways and with breathtaking speed." For instance, Maryland's state population was still majority white (58.2 percent) in 2010, but its public schools were not—only 43 percent of students were white (Maryland State Department of Education, 2010). The changes are nationwide, and by 2020 half of K–12 students will be minority. These demographic changes of student population continue to challenge school principals with respect to their leadership capability as related to diversity.

This challenge could be labeled as "leadership *with* diversity" (Coleman, 2012, p. 592), meaning that leadership should meet all individuals' needs and benefit every individual and the organization as well. Ayman and Korabik (2010) suggested leaders should learn how their own leadership behaviors or leadership styles are different from others, so that misunderstandings in interacting could be avoided. Howard (2007, p. 17) suggested five steps for principals to transform themselves and their schools for the growing diversity of students as well as parents, including: (a) building trust, (b) engaging personal culture, (c) confronting issues of social dominance and social justice, (d) transforming instructional practices, and (e) engaging the entire school community.

Another aspect of the challenge of growing diversity could be labeled as "leadership *for* diversity" (Coleman, 2012, p. 592), implying that the range of school leaders should be increased in terms of race, ethnicity, gender, and so on. Wegenke and Shen (2005) conducted a twelve-year trend study and more diversity was found in the public school principalship in terms of gender, race, and ethnicity, particularly for urban schools.

Having more minority or female principals clearly brought changes to the leadership in schools as well as relationship in the communities. A study on Latino parental involvement argued that the minorities at school administrative levels would have positive impact on minority parents' attitudes as well as parental involvements; the study suggested that Latino parents would be 38 percent more involved if they think a Latino teacher or principal is important for the child's education (Shah, 2009).

Although women are traditionally considered less effective leaders by society given the gender stereotype and prejudice toward female leaders (e.g., Eagly and Karau, 2002; Rudman and Fairchild, 2004), studies found that females can outperform males in instructional and administrative roles (Guramatunhu-Mudiwa and Bolt, 2012). Carless (1998) reported that female leaders practice more transformational leadership behaviors in teamwork, participatory decision-making, and interpersonal relationships. A meta-analysis of forty-five studies on leadership style conducted by Eagly, Johannesen-Schmidt, and van Engen (2003) confirmed that women outperform their male counterparts in some areas of leadership, because women leaders can better encourage effective performance through transformational leadership as well as transactional aspects of leadership in terms of rewarding subordinates. Nevertheless, a fact noteworthy is that while the majority of the teaching profession are women, men still have been the prevalent gender in school administrative positions (Baker, Punswick, and Belt, 2010; Nogay and Beebe, 1997).

Urban School Principals' Teaching Experience

Principals' traditional role is the manager of school operations. However, since the 1980s the role of instructional leadership has been added to principals' responsibility (e.g., Cross and Rice, 2000; Crow, Matthews, and McCleary, 1996; Shen, Rodriguez, and Rincones, 2000; Shen et al., 2005; Stronge, 1993), and principals are expected to be "instructional leaders" (Beck and Murphy, 1993; Hallinger, 2005; Robinson, Lloyd, and Rowe, 2008). As a result, what could contribute to principals' instructional leadership attracts more and more attention of both researchers and practitioners. As noticed by Hallinger, Bickman, and Davis (1996), many researchers believed that principals' teaching experience prior to becoming a principal has a positive association with principals' instructional leadership capacity (see Eberts and Stone, 1988; Glasman, 1984; Hallinger, 1983; Leithwood et al., 1990). For instance, principals' teaching experience, along with leadership experience, were found among the most important in explaining student achievement (Eberts and Stone, 1988).

Many countries require a certain amount of teaching experience before a person becomes a principal. For instance, in the United Kingdom, according to Weindling (1990), the new secondary school headteachers' (as principals) average teaching experience is twenty years. However, U.S. principals seem to have less teaching experience: elementary school principals were found having an average teaching experience of eleven years (Eberts and Stone, 1988), while high school principals were found having an average teaching experience of 14.2 years (Brewer, 1993).

Researchers have noticed that principals' average teaching experience before being a principal is changing. For instance, Rodriguez-Campos, Rincones-Gomez, and Shen (2005) noticed that public school principals' teaching experience had slightly increased between 1990–91 and 1999–2000, and they also noticed that during 1999–2000 the new principals tend to have more teaching experience than that of experienced principals when they started principalship. However, the trend may have changed due to the federal regulation of school performance. Since the NCLB act was initiated in 2001, schools not meeting adequate yearly progress were required to be restructured in various ways—replacing the principals and teachers, or reopening the school as charter schools, or closing the schools (see Maxwell, 2009; Mead, 2007), both the leadership teams and teaching forces for underperforming schools may be radically changed (see Maxwell, 2009). As a result, the average teaching experience before principalship would probably have a drop due to NCLB.

Urban School Principals and the Aspiring Principal Program

Despite traditional university degree-granting programs for principalship, in the past two decades, the aspiring principal training program has emerged as an alternative for schools and districts to resolve the shortage of qualified principals (Educational Research Service, 1998, 2000; Tracy and Weaver, 2000; Wegenke, 2000). A survey by Tracy and Weaver (2000) indicated that participants had valuable experience through the aspiring program. In New York City, Corcoran, Schwartz, and Weinstein (2009) compared principals who were from the aspiring program with principals who were from traditional university programs; they found that principals who went through the aspiring program outperformed their counterparts who graduated from traditional university programs as far as student achievement was concerned. Darling-Hammond and her colleagues (2007) also noticed that graduates from aspiring principal programs "felt significantly better prepared for nearly every aspect of leadership practice" (p. 10).

Daresh (1994) noticed aspiring principals tended to emphasize the demonstration of technical skills, while experienced principals regarded those skills as least important, and socialization skills as most important from their points of view. A longitudinal study by Fisher (2011) on self-efficacy of aspiring principals from a two-year training program provided two interesting findings: first, before being principals themselves, teachers used to hold an assumption that instead of pedagogical tasks, principals put most of their work on general managerial tasks or tasks pertaining to emotion and interpersonal relationships. However, as they practiced with their coaches (i.e., actual principals in real school contexts), they realized that the main role of principals is associated with pedagogy. Second, the aspiring training program helped aspiring principals change their understanding of "the tasks they are free to carry out based solely on their decision and the tasks that depend on external and distant factors" (p. 116). For example, they realized that they could greatly influence most pedagogy-related tasks, but for many general managerial tasks, they cannot fully control and need support from the school staff and the community.

Rodriguez-Campos, Rincones-Gomez, and Shen (2005) reported that an increasing trend for principals to take part in the aspiring programs based on Schools and Staffing Survey public principal data from 1990–91 to 1999–2000. It will be interesting to see whether the trend continues since 1999–2000.

Principals' Perception on Educational Goals

Researchers have already noticed that one dimension of principal leadership, principals' role in framing school goals, has indirect but significant effects on student achievement (see Robinson, Lloyd, and Rowe, 2008), and has more influence on school effectiveness than the emphases of traditional areas do (Goldring and Pasternack, 1994). As reviewed by Robinson et al. (2008), researchers found that leadership made a difference in student achievements through setting clear academic and learning goals, among others (Bamburg and Andrews, 1991; Brewer, 1993; Heck, Marcoulides, and Lang, 1991).

Goodlad (1979, 1994, 2006) suggested three possible lenses that might be used to determine school goals: (a) what schools are asked to do; (b) what schools actually do; or (c) what schools ought to do. Based on a review of the goals put forth by various state and local boards of education and special commissions, Goodlad (1979) recommended twelve goals for U.S. schools, and further, Goodlad (1979, 1984, 1994a, 2006) categorized these twelve goals into four broad categories: (a) academic goals, (b) vocational goals, (c) social goals, and (d) personal goals. Shen's (1997) empirical study using structural equation modeling confirmed these four dimensions.

John Dewey (1916) believed that social goals and personal goals could exist harmoniously, while Shen (1997) noticed that during the twentieth century, there was a tension between academic goals and vocational goals. Although in the history the educational goals tend to swing between academic and vocational, and between social and personal goals (Cuban, 1990; Goodlad, 1994b), the situation may have been changed during the past twenty years. Since some important educational reforms were initiated at both federal level (e.g., Goals 2000: Educate America Act passed in 1994 and No Child Left Behind Act passed in 2001) and state level (e.g., all states have established accountability systems since the 1990s), emphasis on academic goals has become a predominant phenomenon since the 1990s (Shen, Palmer, and Crawford, 2005).

No Child Left Behind Act (NCLB), passed by Congress in 2001, has brought new dynamics to educational goals. NCLB's dominant goals are to improve "academic proficiency" and reduce "achievement gap" (see Ratner, 2007), toward which federal government and states hold districts and schools accountable for Adequate Yearly Progress (AYP) with standardized tests. This results in more and more emphasis on students' academic achievements. For example, researchers found that NCLB shifted the allocation of instructional time toward math and reading (Dee and Jacob, 2010). The shift of school goals toward academic was also observed. Based on Goodlad's twelve proposed educational goals, Potthoff and Walker (2009) surveyed five groups of individuals including

(a) K–12 educators, (b) teaching candidates, (c) university faculty, (d) K–12 parents, and (e) local K–12 school board members. Their study confirmed Goodlad's categorization of school goals, and also found that overall the two most highly rated and ranked goals were "mastery of basic skills/fundamental processes" and "intellectual development." It is interesting to examine whether and how school principals' perception of most important educational goals changed during the past twenty years.

Focused Inquiries

In this chapter we inquired into urban school principalship from five aspects:

Over the last twenty years,

a. Whether urban school principalship has become more diversified in terms of race and ethnicity given the predominance of the minority student body in urban schools?

b. Whether urban school principalship has become more diversified in terms of the gender given the rhetoric on gender equity?

c. Whether urban school principals' average teaching experience before principalship has increased, remained the same, or decreased?

d. Whether more and more urban school principals have participated in the aspiring program?

e. Whether urban school principals' perception of educational goals has changed?

METHODOLOGY

Data Source

The data we used for the book chapter are from the nationally representative Schools and Staffing Survey (SASS), which is the largest survey of K–12 education collected by the National Center for Educational Statistics (NCES). SASS data have four essential components: teacher data, principal data, school data, and district data. Until 2012, NCES has already conducted seven cycles of surveys: 1987–1988, 1990–1991, 1993–1994, 1999–2000, 2003–2004, 2007–2008, and 2011–2012. However, data of SASS 2011–2012 are still not available at this point. As a result, this chapter uses the data from 1987–1988 to 2007–2008 and, thus, it is a twenty-year trend study. Specifically, the public principal data are used for the purpose of inquiring into urban school principals' demographic and professional characteristics.

Sample

NCES applied stratified probability sampling design to collect SASS data and ensure that the samples contain sufficient numbers for reliable estimates. Thus a set of sampling weights were included in each data set. The actual achieved sample sizes and weighted sample sizes for each of the six SASS principal data sets were presented in Table 3.1. The sample sizes for all national public schools principals were also included for the purpose of possible comparisons.

Data Analysis Approach

In order to investigate the trend of urban school principals' demographic and professional characteristics, the analysis of descriptive statistics is applied to all six cycles of SASS public principal data, and the sampling weights are utilized as well. The SASS data are national representative. Through using the sampling weights the results could be generalized to either the state or national level.

Table 3.1.   Actual and Weighted Sample Sizes of Urban and All Public Schools*

		1987–88	1990–91	1993–94	1999–2000	2003–4	2007–8
Actual	Urban	2,050	1,980	2,060	1,870	1,920	1,670
	All	8,170	9,050	9,100	8,520	8,140	7,460
Weighted	Urban	18,410	18,450	19,030	19,580	21,850	22,150
	All	74,590	78,890	79,620	82,800	87,620	90,470

*All sample sizes are rounded to the nearest 10 per rules of using restricted data from National Center for Education Statistics.

Specifically, concerning urban school principals' race and ethnicity, we (a) computed urban schools' average percentages of minority principals, Hispanic principals, and African-American principals in different school years; (b) compared them to that of all public schools; and (c) did a state-by-state comparison of the change of urban schools' average percentages of minority principals between 1987–88 and 2007–08. We applied a similar approach to all other characteristics: (a) the gender diversity—we focused on the percentages of female principals; (b) urban school principals' average teaching experience before being principals; (c) participation in aspiring principal programs; and (d) principals' perception of most important educational goals. For the last characteristics, based on Goodlad's categorization, before applying the analysis approach, the original eight educational goals were condensed into four educational goals.

FINDINGS

Race/Ethnicity

As to race and ethnicity, the results in figure 3.1 show that over the past twenty years, compared to all public schools, urban schools held consistently higher percentages of minority principals, with both having an upward trend. Further examination of the composi-

tion of minority principals showed that compared to all public schools, urban schools had consistently higher percentages and more notable increase of Hispanic principals (see figure 3.2); compared to all public schools, urban schools also presented consistently higher percentages of African-American principals (see figure 3.3), and a similar but more marked trend of changes—first an increase between 1987–1988 and 1999–2000, and a decrease thereafter.

Over the same twenty years, the change in percentage of principals who were minority varied greatly across states, with a majority of states having a higher percentage of minority principals and surprisingly a few states (including New Mexico, New Hampshire, etc.) having a lower percentage of minority principals (see figure 3.4).

Gender Diversity

As to gender, the percentages of female principals were 35.3 percent in 1987–1988 and 60.9 percent in 2007–2008 for urban schools and 24.6 percent and 50.3 percent for all schools (figure 3.5). Therefore, there has been a dramatic increase of female principals for both urban and all schools over the twenty years, and the percentage of female principals has been consistently, significantly higher for urban schools than for all schools. Over the same twenty years, the change

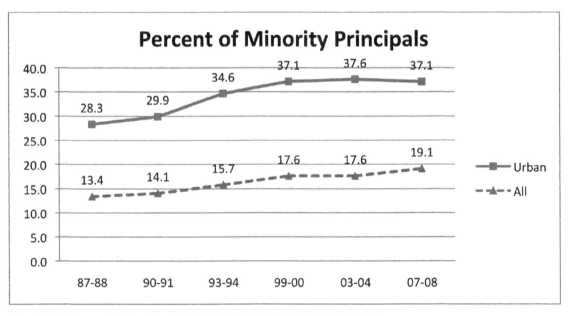

Figure 3.1. Percent of minority principals between 1987–1988 and 2007–2008

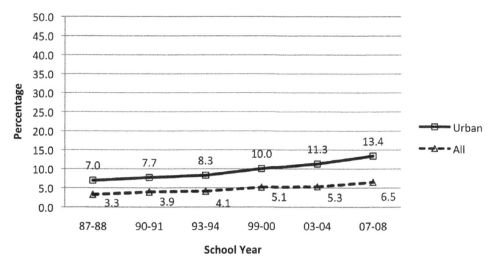

Figure 3.2. Percent of Hispanic principals between 1987–1988 and 2007–2008

in percentage of principals who were female varied greatly across states; all states, except for Maryland, having a higher percentage of female principals (with Kansas demonstrating an increase of more than 60 percentage points) (figure 3.6).

Teaching Experience Before Principalship

As far as teaching experience before principalship is concerned, the average years of teaching that principals had were 10.48 in 1987–1988 and 12.48 in 2007–2008 for urban schools and 9.77 and 12.65

for all schools (figure 3.7). Therefore, there has been an increase of average years of teaching for principals in both urban and all schools over the twenty years. For the five time points between 1987–1988 and 2003–2004, urban principals consistently had a higher average of years of teaching than all principals, a trend that was reversed in 2007–2008. Over the same twenty years, all states, except for Michigan, Mississippi, and Rhode Island, had a higher average of teaching experience for urban principals, and the variation across the states for the change in the average was significant (figure 3.8).

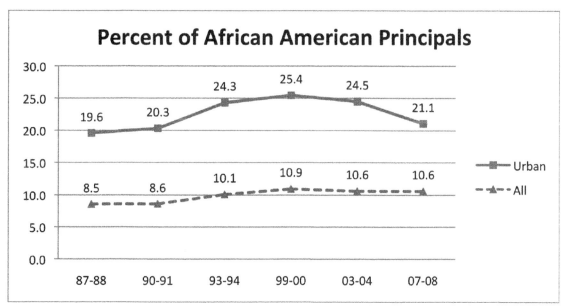

Figure 3.3. Percent of African-American principals between 1987–1988 and 2007–2008

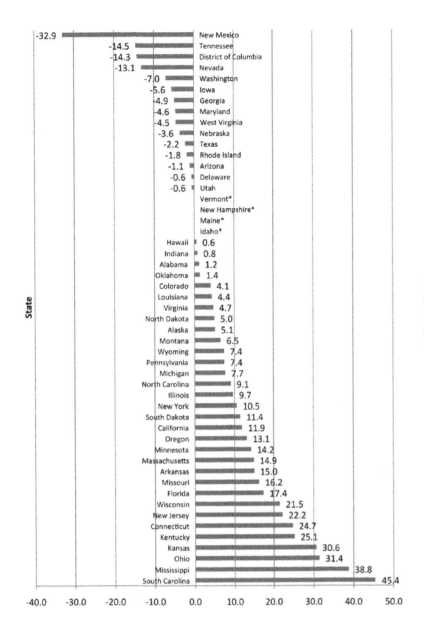

Figure 3.4. The change in percentages of minority principals in urban schools between 1987–1988 and 2007–2008 by state. *Note: These four states had 100 percent of white principals for both 1987–1988 and 2007–2008 school year.

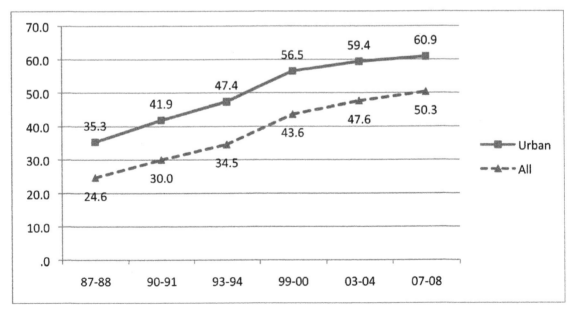

Figure 3.5. Percentage of female principals between 1987–88 and 2007–2008

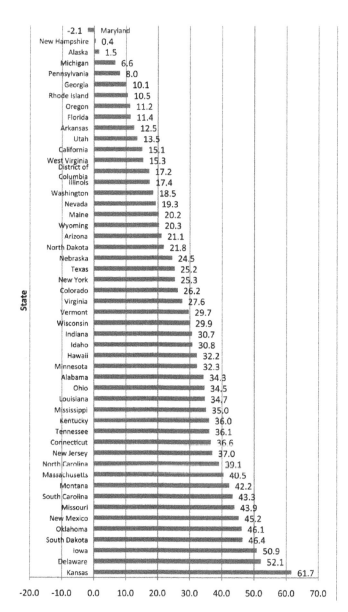

State	
Maryland	-2.1
New Hampshire	0.4
Alaska	1.5
Michigan	6.6
Pennsylvania	8.0
Georgia	10.1
Rhode Island	10.5
Oregon	11.2
Florida	11.4
Arkansas	12.5
Utah	13.5
California	15.1
West Virginia	15.3
District of Columbia	17.2
Illinois	17.4
Washington	18.5
Nevada	19.3
Maine	20.2
Wyoming	20.3
Arizona	21.1
North Dakota	21.8
Nebraska	24.5
Texas	25.2
New York	25.3
Colorado	26.2
Virginia	27.6
Vermont	29.7
Wisconsin	29.9
Indiana	30.7
Idaho	30.8
Hawaii	32.2
Minnesota	32.3
Alabama	34.3
Ohio	34.5
Louisiana	34.7
Mississippi	35.0
Kentucky	36.0
Tennessee	36.1
Connecticut	36.6
New Jersey	37.0
North Carolina	39.1
Massachusetts	40.5
Montana	42.2
South Carolina	43.3
Missouri	43.9
New Mexico	45.2
Oklahoma	46.1
South Dakota	46.4
Iowa	50.9
Delaware	52.1
Kansas	61.7

Figure 3.6. The change in percentages of female principals in urban schools between 1987–88 and 2007–08 by state

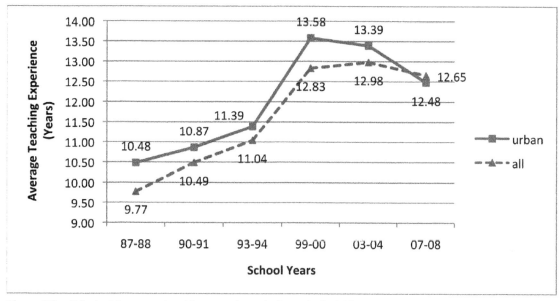

Figure 3.7. Principals' average teaching experience before principalship

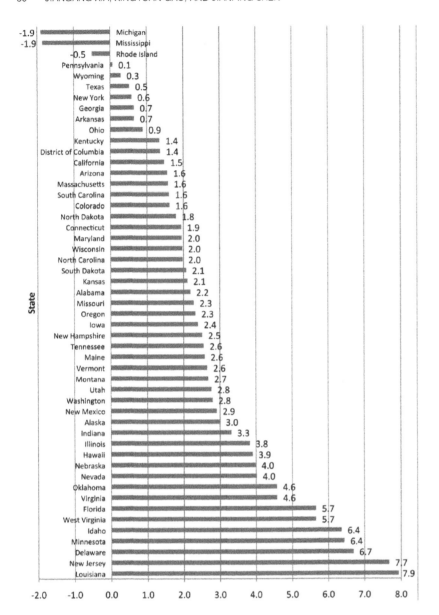

Figure 3.8. *The change in average years of teaching before principalship for principals in urban schools between 1987–1988 and 2007–2008 by state*

Participation in the Aspiring Program

As to participation in the aspiring program for principals, percentages of principals who participated in the aspiring program were 44.6 percent in 1987–1988 and 61.6 percent in 2007–8 for urban schools and 35.8 percent and 56.0 percent for all schools (figure 3.9). Therefore, there has been an increase of principals who went through the aspiring program for both urban and all schools over the twenty years, and the percentage of principals who joined the aspiring program has been consistently, significantly higher for urban schools than for all schools. Over the same twenty years, the change in percentage of principals who participated in the aspiring program varied greatly across states;

most states had a higher percentage of principals who participated in the aspiring program (with Minnesota demonstrating an increase of nearly 60 percentage points) (figure 3.10). It appears that both state policies played a role.

Educational Goals

As to most important educational goals, the patterns were similar for urban principals and all principals. Over the twenty years, academic goals (based on original "building basic literacy skills" and "encouraging academic excellent") had seen an increase while personal goals ("promoting personal growth" as phrased

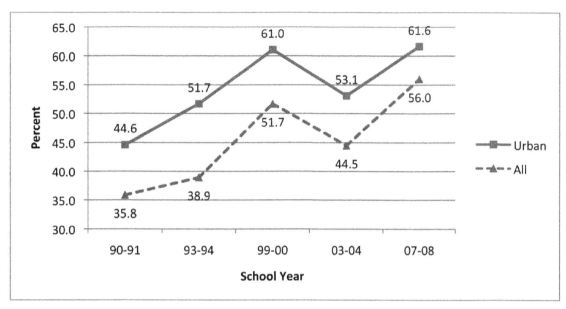

Figure 3.9. *Percent of principals who participated in aspiring principal programs*

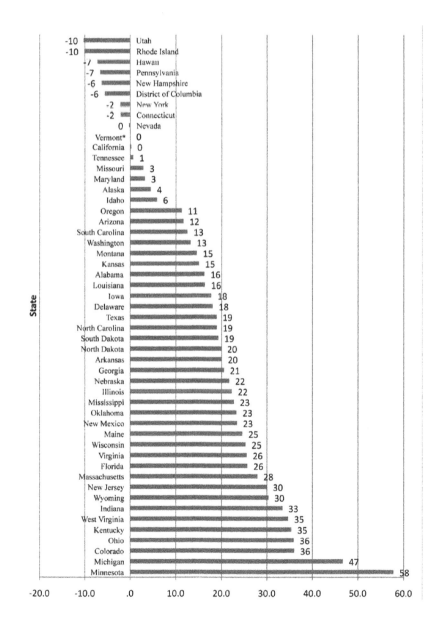

Figure 3.10. *The change in percentages of urban school principals who participated in aspiring principal programs between 1987–1988 and 2007–2008 by state. *Note: There were no data for Vermont State for both 1987–1988 and 2007–2008.*

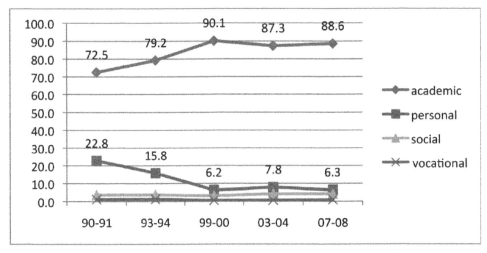

Figure 3.11. *Principals' perception of the most important educational goal (urban)*

on the survey) had witnessed a precipitous drop (figures 3.11 and 3.12). Furthermore, academic goals had been consistently rated as the most important educational goals. The changes were consistent with the recent educational policies which emphasize accountability primarily based on academic achievement.

SUMMARY AND CONCLUSIONS

This chapter explores the historical trend of urban school principals' demographic and professional characteristics. Based on the evidence from nationally representative SASS data, some patterns emerged with respect to principals' diversity (race/ethnicity and gender), principals' professional preparation (teaching experience before principalship and participating in the aspiring program), and their perception of educational goals. In this section we summarize the findings first, and then present conclusions.

Summary

Race/ethnicity diversity. The data indicate that although the public urban schools were still dominated by white principals, principals' race/ethnicity diversity has been enhanced over the years. Although the same trend exists as well for all public schools, urban schools consistently doubled the percentages of minority principals in all schools across the six surveys. Roza (2003) suggested that principals stay in the

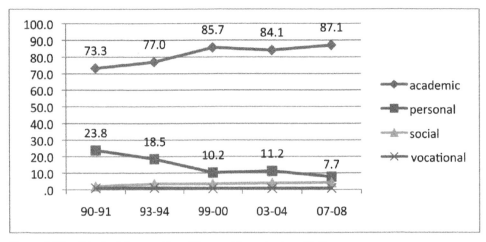

Figure 3.12. *Principals' perception of the most important goal (all)*

position longer when the majority of students in their schools are of principals' own ethnic group—which probably imply a situation that principals would have higher job satisfaction in a school of predominantly same ethnicity—and given the general trend of continuing diversity along race/ethnicity at both national level and urban level, we predict that the upward trajectory for the percentage of minority principals would remain unchanged in the near future.

As for the state-by-state comparison of the change of percentage of minority principals between 1987–88 and 2007–08, thirty-two states presented higher percentages of minority principals. Although some states indicated lower percentages of minority principals, many of them had already had a very high percentage of minority principals—close or over 50 percent. In places such as the District of Columbia, actually white principals were the "minority" (98.4 percent minority principals during 1987–88 and 84.2 percent during 2007–08 were minority).

Gender diversity. For urban schools, the percentages of female principals increased across the six surveys. The percentage of female principals was consistently higher than that of all public schools for all six surveys. The principal teaching force has become more diversified over the years. Female principals are found to have overall better campus accountability ratings than those of male principals (Roser, Brown, and Kelsey, 2009). The trend that more and more females became principals could be related to the increasing pressure for accountability, particularly for urban schools, where accountability is regarded as the centerpiece of school reform and restructuring (Darling-Hammond and Ascher, 1991; Hess, 1999).

As for the state-by-state comparison of the change of percentage of female principals between 1987–1988 and 2007–2008, all states except Maryland presented increased percentages. Although Maryland presented a decreased percentage of female principals, it only dropped 2.1 percent from 60.4 percent during 1987–1988 to 58.3 percent during 2007–2008.

Teaching experience before principalship. The data showed that there has been an increase of average years of teaching for principals in both urban and all schools over the twenty years. However, the increase was observed primarily between 1987–1988 and 1999–2000 for urban schools, and between 1987–

1988 and 2003–2004 for all public schools. A decrease of teaching experience before principalship between 1999–2000 and 2007–2008 was observed for urban schools and between 2003–2004 and 2007–2008 for all public schools as well. For the five time points between 1987–1988 and 2003–2004, urban principals consistently had a higher average of years of teaching than all principals, a trend that was reversed in 2007–2008. Given the fact that urban schools confront more issues such as student poverty, behavior, and achievement, on the one hand, and the fact that the federal NCLB regulation sets the AYP requirements, on the other hand, urban schools face more challenges and urban school principals could be more likely to leave or be replaced. As long as the accountability requirement still exists, this trend might continue.

Over the same twenty years, all states, except for Michigan, Mississippi, and Rhode Island, had a higher average of teaching experience for urban principals; and the variation across the state for the change in the average was significant.

Participation in the aspiring program. There has been an increase of principals who went through the aspiring program for both urban and all schools across the five surveys, and the percentage of principals who participated in the aspiring program has been consistently, significantly higher for urban schools than for all schools. The increasing participation in the aspiring principalship program might be related to the lament that traditional university principal preparation programs are not adequate to prepare school principals, particularly in terms of the new challenges posed by an era of accountability (Hess and Kelly, 2005).

Over the same seventeen years, the change in percentage of principals who participated in the aspiring program varied greatly across states; most states had a higher percentage of principals who participated in the aspiring program, with examples including Minnesota (with an increase of nearly 60 percentage points) and Michigan (with an increase of nearly 50 percentage points).

Perception of educational goals. As to most important educational goals, the patterns were similar for urban principals and all principals. Over the seventeen years, academic goals (originally including "building basic literacy skills" and "encouraging academic excellent" in the survey questionnaire) had seen an increase while personal goals (originally including "promoting personal growth" and "promoting good work habits" in the survey questionnaire) had witnessed a precipitous drop. Furthermore, academic goals had been consistently rated as the most important educational goals. As a result, the dynamics between academic and vocational goals, and between social and personal goals, as have been observed in the history (Cuban, 1990; Goodlad, 1994b; Shen, 1997), seems to have changed. Given the high pressure of accountability requirement from both the federal and state levels, the finding is not surprising.

CONCLUSION

Based on the longitudinal and rich SASS data, in this chapter we inquired into the evolution of urban school principals' demographic and professional characteristics. The longitudinal analyses showed that over the past twenty years, urban school principals' race/ethnicity and gender diversity was notably enhanced. Urban school principals' average teaching experience before being principal presented an increase between 1987–1988 and 1999–2000, and a slight decrease thereafter. A higher percentage of urban school principals participated in aspiring principal programs between 1990–1991 and 2007–2008. In terms of the most important educational goal, at urban schools, more principals chose academic goals, and fewer selected personal goals, while very low percentages of principals chose social goals and vocational goals as the most important goals. The urban principalship has been evolving, indeed.

REFERENCES

Ayman, R. and Korabik, K. (2010). Leadership: Why gender and culture matter. *American Psychologist, 65,* 157–170. doi:10.1037/a0018806

Baker, B. D., Punswick, E., and Belt, C. (2010). School leadership stability, principal moves, and departures: Evidence from Missouri. *Educational Administration Quarterly, 46*(4), 523–557.

Bamburg, J. D. and Andrews, R. L. (1991). School goals, principals, and achievement. *School Effectiveness and School Improvement, 2,* 175–191.

Banks, J. A. (1999). Multicultural education in the new century. *School Administrator, 56*(5), 8–10.

Beck, L. G. and Murphy, J. (1993). *Understanding the principalship: Metaphorical themes, 1920s–1990s.* New York: Teachers College Press.

Brewer, D. J. (1993). Principals and student outcomes: Evidence from US high schools. *Economics of Education Review, 12*(4), 281–292.

Carless, S. A. (1998). Gender differences in transformational leadership: An examination of superior, leader, and subordinate perspectives. *Sex Roles, 39,* 887–902.

Coleman, M. (2012). Leadership and diversity. *Educational Management Administration & Leadership, 40*(5), 592–609.

Corcoran, S., Schwartz, A., and Weinstein, M. (2009). *The New York City aspiring principals program: A school level evaluation.* Retrieved from the New York University Steinhart School of Culture, Education and Human Development website at steinhardt.nyu.edu/scmsAdmin/uploads/003/852/APP.pdf.

Cross, C. T. and Rice, R. C. (2000). The role of the principal as instructional leader in a standards-driven system. *NASSP Bulletin, 84*(620), 61–65.

Crow, G. M., Matthews, L. J., and McCleary, L. E. (1996). *Leadership: A relevant and realistic role for principals.* Princeton, NJ: Eye on Education.

Cuban, L. (1990). Reforming again, again, and again. *Educational Researcher, 19*(1), 3–13.

Daresh, J. C. (1994). Aspiring and practising principals' perceptions of critical skills for beginning leaders. *Journal of Educational Administration, 32*(3), 35. doi:10.1108/09578239410063102.

Darling-Hammond, L. and Ascher, C., Columbia Univ., New York, NY. Teachers Coll. National Center for Restructuring Education, Schools and Teaching, & ERIC Clearinghouse on Urban Education, New York, NY (1991). *Creating accountability in big city school systems.* Urban diversity series no. 102 ERIC Clearinghouse on Urban Education, Teachers College, Box 40, Columbia University, New York.

Darling-Hammond, L., LaPointe, M., Meyerson, D., and Orr, M. (2007). *Preparing school leaders for a changing world: Executive summary.* Stanford, CA: Stanford University, Stanford Educational Leadership Institute.

Dee, T. S. and Jacob, B. A. (2010). The impact of no child left behind on students, teachers, and schools. *Brookings Papers on Economic Activity, 2010*(2), 149–194.

Dewey, J. (1916). *Democracy and education.* New York: Macmillan.

Eagly, A. H., Johannesen-Schmidt, M. C., and van Engen, M. L. (2003). Transformational, transactional, and laissez-faire leadership styles: A meta-analysis comparing women and men. *Psychological Bulletin, 129,* 569–591. doi:10.1037/0033-2909.129.4.569.

Eagly, A. H., and Karau, S. J. (2002). Role congruity theory of prejudice toward female leaders. *Psychological Review, 109,* 573–598.

Eberts, R. W. and Stone, J. A. (1988). Student achievement in public schools: Do principals make a difference? *Economics of Education Review, 7*(3), 291–299.

Educational Research Service (ERS). (1998). *Is there a shortage of qualified candidates for openings in the principalship? An exploratory study.* Arlington, VA: ERS.

Eiseman, J. W. (2008). Increasing aspiring principals' readiness to serve: Knowledge and skill application laboratories. *Journal of Research on Leadership Education, 3*(2), 1.

Fisher, Y. (2011). The sense of self-efficacy of aspiring principals: Exploration in a dynamic concept. *Social Psychology of Education: An International Journal, 14*(1), 93–117. doi:http://dx.doi.org/10.1007/s11218-010-9136-9.

Glasman, N. S. (1984). Student achievement and the school principal. *Educational Evaluation and Policy Analysis, 6*(3), 283–296.

Goldring, E. B. and Pasternack, R. (1994). Principals' coordinating strategies and school effectiveness. *School Effectiveness and School Improvement, 5*(3), 239–253.

Goodlad, J. (1979). *What schools are for.* Los Angeles, CA: Phi Delta Kappan.

Goodlad, J. I. (1984). *A place called school: Prospects for the future.* New York: McGraw-Hill.

Goodlad, J. I. (1994a). *Educational renewal: Better teachers, better schools.* San Francisco: Jossey-Bass Publishers.

Goodlad, J. I. (1994b). *What schools are for (2nd ed.).* Bloomington, IN: Phi Delta Kappa Educational Foundation.

Goodlad, J. I. (2006). *What schools are for (Signature ed.).* Bloomington, IN: Phi Delta Kappa International.

Guramatunhu-Mudiwa, P. and Bolt, L. L. (2012). Does the gender of school personnel influence perceptions of leadership? *School Leadership & Management, 32*(3), 261–277.

Hallinger, P. (1983). *Assessing the instructional management behavior of principals.* Unpublished doctoral dissertation, Stanford University, Stanford, CA.

Hallinger, P. (2005). Instructional leadership and the school principal: A passing fancy that refuses to fade away. *Leadership and Policy in Schools, 4*(3), 221–239.

Hallinger, P., Bickman, L., and Davis, K. (1996). School context, principal leadership, and student reading achievement. *The Elementary School Journal,* 527–549.

Heck, R. H., Marcoulides, G. A., and Lang, P. (1991). Principal instructional leadership and school achievement: The application of discriminant techniques. *School Effectiveness and School Improvement, 2*(2), 115–135.

Hernandez, N (2008, January 22). Minority students become the majority: Area's schools adapt to serve rapidly diversifying populations. *Washington Post.* Retrieved from www.washingtonpost.com/wp-dyn/content/article/2008/01/21/AR2008012101974.html.

Hess, F. M. (1999). *Spinning wheels: The politics of urban school reform.* Washington, D.C: Brookings Institution Press.

Hess, F. and Kelly, A. P. (2007). Learning to lead: What gets taught in principal-preparation programs. *Teachers College Record, 109*(1), 244–274.

Howard, G. R. (2007). As diversity grows, so must we. *Educational Leadership,64*(6), 16.

Leithwood, K. A., Begley, P. T., and Cousins, J. B. (1990). The nature, causes, and consequences of principals' practices: an agenda for future research. *Journal of Educational Administration, 28*(4).

Maxwell, L. A. (2009). Stimulus Rules on "Turnarounds" Shift: Stimulus Guidelines Changed for Turning around Schools. *Education Week, 29*(13), 1–19.

Mead, S. (2007). The Easy Way Out: "Restructured" usually means little has changed. *Education Next, 7*(1), 52.

Nogay, K. and Beebe, R. J. (1997). Gender and perceptions: Females as secondary principals. *Journal of School Leadership, 7,* 246–265.

Potthoff, D., and Walker E. (2009). School goals in an era of accountability: Getting back to the basics of educating for democracy. *Education in a Democracy: A Journal of the NNER, 1,* 65–84.

Ratner, G. M. (2007). Why the No Child Left Behind Act needs to be restructured to accomplish its goals and how to do it. *DCL Review, 9,* 1.

Robinson, V. M. J., Lloyd, C. A., and Rowe, K. J. (2008). The impact of leadership on school outcomes: An analysis of the differential effects of leadership types. *Educational Administration Quarterly, 44*(5), 635–674.

Rodriguez-Campos, L., Rincones-Gomez, R., and Shen, J. (2005). Principal's educational attainment, experience, and professional development. In J. Shen, and Associates, *School principals.* New York: P. Lang.

Roser, V., Brown, M., and Kelsey, C. (2009). Principal gender as related to campus size, level, and academic rating. *Advancing women in leadership journal, 29*(10). Retrieved from www.advancingwomen.com/awl/Vol29_2009/Valer_Rosser.pdf.

Roza, M. and Washington Univ., Seattle. Center on Reinventing Public Education. (2003). *A matter of definition:*

Is there truly a shortage of school principals? Center on Reinventing Public Education.

Rudman, L. A. and Fairchild, K. (2004). Reactions to counter stereotypic behavior: the role of backlash in cultural stereotype maintenance. *Journal of personality and social psychology, 87*(2), 157–176.

Shah, P. (2009). Motivating participation: The symbolic effects of Latino representation on parent school involvement. *Social Science Quarterly, 90*(1), 212–230. doi:10.1111/j.1540-6237.2009.00612.x

Shen, J. (1997). Structure of the theoretical concept of educational goals: A test of factorial validity. *The Journal of Experimental Education, 65*(4), 342–342.

Shen, J. and Associates (2005). *School principals.* New York: Peter Lang Publishing.

Shen, J., Palmer, L. B., and Crawford, C. (2005). The importance of educational goals as perceived by principals. In J. Shen and Associates. *School principals.* New York: Peter Lang Publishing.

Shen, J., Rodriguez-Campos, L., and Rincones-Gomez, R. (2000). Characteristics of urban principalship: A national trend study. *Education and Urban Society, 32*(4), 481–491.

Stronge, J. H. (1993). Defining the principalship: Instructional leader or middle manager. *NASSP Bulletin, 77*(553), 1–7.

Tracy, G. and Weaver, C. (2000). Aspiring leaders academy: Responding to the principal shortage. *NASSP Bulletin, 84*(618), 75–83.

Wegenke, G. L. and Shen, J. (2005). Gender, racial, and ethnic diversity among principals. In J. Shen and Associates, *School principals.* New York: Peter Lang Publishing.

Weindling, D. (1990). The secondary school headteacher: New principals in the United Kingdom. *NASSP Bulletin, 74*(526), 40–45.

CHAPTER 4

An Interpretive History of Urban Education and Leadership in Age of Perceived Racial Invisibility

Brian J. Boggs and Chris Dunbar

INTRODUCTION

Wallace Stevens poses an interesting question in his poem, "The Man on the Dump." He asks, "Where was it one first heard of the truth?" He argues that it is, "The the." He means this in terms of the use of the definite article, "the." It seems that when we use the word "the" we are signaling the definiteness, the certainty of a statement or fact—its truth, as it were. However, that is not the purpose of this chapter. This is not "The History of Urban Education," but rather, "An History of Urban Education"—in other words, it only highlights major turning points, but the story is never fully complete. It cannot be the ultimate truth, if there even is such a thing, but rather a connection of ideas and events that have had the appearance of leading to the current state of existence. The story of humanity is often one-sided and written by the powerful (hence having the ability to portray themselves as the victors). And this one-sidedness is no longer an acceptable practice in this century. In our effort to shed light on the influences of the human condition that has led us to our current reality, what follows is a social and political review of the history or evolution of urban education through a policy lens. We provide a brief overview of the literature that illuminates the creation of urban communities and subsequent urban schools pre-*Brown*. We also examine the development of urban schools post-*Brown*, which will provide an overview of the multiple policies that have been imposed/implemented to address the educational disparities that in many any instance, continue to exist today. In this effort, we also discuss the perils and strengths urban leaders have and continue to face. In particular, we focus on the formation of ghetto areas, civil rights and issues of poverty, the rise of school choice, and racial invisibility.

To begin, it is almost impossible to firmly separate the influences of history on education from that of the influences of events on society at large. Often what happens in our schools is the result of various societal events. Rarely do schools produce an event that comes to shape society first. Bowels and Gintis (1976) acknowledge this phenomenon and discuss this in terms of social reproduction theory. Specifically, that schooling reinforce and reproduce already existing social structures, which means that the history of education can be thought of as a result of societal movements. Bowles and Gintis state that, "Beneath the façade of meritocracy lies a reality of an educational system geared toward the reproduction of economic relations only partially explicable in terms of technical requirements and efficiency standards" (1976, pg. 103). In other words, it is about race and class. Bowels and Gintis (1976) argue that the experience of schooling is about socialization that reproduces class structures. An example of this occurs in teaching practices. Lower-class students receive more basic instructional skills, and discipline is more of a focus. While upper-class students are thought to think critically and question assumptions. However, these instances could not occur if the students were not already grouped by class and race. Staffing of schools also occurs in the same way. Various positions need to appear "egalitarian in process and just in outcome," but are only such in appearance (Bowels and Gintis, 1976, pg. 104). There are different rules and standards for different groups of society, but the current manifestation of events just did not happen. Rather it is the result of a series of socially engineered events designed to control where people lived, how they were educated, and what they were destined to do in society. All of this leads to the lens with which we examine the events of urban history.

FRAMEWORKS FOR HISTORICAL EXPLORATION: CRITICAL RACE THEORY AND POLICY

In looking at the United States's historical context of urban areas, we used critical race theory coupled with policy analysis. Critical race theory "seeks to decloak the seemingly race-neutral, and color-blind ways . . . of constructing and administering race-based appraisals . . . of law, administrative policy, electoral politics . . . political discourse [and education]" (Denzin and Lincoln, 2000, pg. 159). This lens "enacts an ethnic epistemology, arguing that ways of knowing and being are shaped by the individual's standpoint, or position in the world" (Denzin and Lincoln, 2000, pg. 159).

In other words, it acknowledges the fact that we cannot divorce ourselves from ourselves to remove bias and become completely objective. It is impossible to walk away from the experiences that have shaped our view of and relationship to what we know. However, it is more than just realizing absolute objectivity does not exist; it is also about being able to "disrupt and challenge the status quo" (Kincheloe and McLaren, 2000, pg. 279) and realizing that the west, in all of its outwardly democratic ways, is not free of problems that marginalize, dehumanize, and de-democratize citizens.

The world is not as simple as blaming or crediting fate for the turn of events. Instead, critical race theory "rejects economic determinism and focuses on the media, culture, language, power, desire, critical enlightenment, and critical emancipation" to examine why the world exists as it does (Denzin and Lincoln, 2000, pg 160). Critical race theory makes us ask the question of how we look at race. As Dunbar et al. state, "being 'white' is the unreflected-upon standard from which all other racial identities vary" (2001, pg. 280). In other words, white is normalized and is the backdrop to which all other races and cultures are juxtaposed. This normalized white has affected all levels of society, including the interpretation of history, especially for minorities and urban populations.

This normalization of whiteness leads us to the role of policy. When thinking of policy, whether retrospectively or in the present context, we should consider what is the purpose of the policy? Keeping in mind that history of urban areas are filled with policy decisions, and policies can have multiple perspectives and

multiple goals and, as Deborah Stone demonstrates, are fraught with ambiguity (2002). This occurs when groups unite behind particular goals or agendas that are unclear and they each construct their own understanding of what the policy means (2002). However, what has happened in urban areas is not the result of a series of unfortunate accidents, but rather carefully planned political, isolated maneuvers—a form of social engineering. Even if there was a great deal of ambiguity around urban policies, there still had to be someone who knew that certain policy actions could result in awful consequences to urban populations.

Building on the idea of unintended consequences of policy, it is important to note that influence is often transmitted through the environment in the form of policy. Noted sociologist Alejandro Portes explains that it is because of our complex social relationships that any kind of policy implementation is difficult (2000). So, where policy begins is not always representative of where it ends or evidenced by its outward stated purpose. This is often because policy is thought of in linear and rational relationships. However, history has shown a consistent gap between reality and theory, especially as it pertains to enacting policy. However, it is important not to overlook the intentionality of evil. There have been generally unpleasant people, and will continue to be, throughout history, who set out to marginalize and isolate groups and succeed at their mission. There is also another element, instead of having good intentions and having unforeseen results (that could result in either positive or negative social change), or groups that set out to intentionally inflect harm, there is a final group—a group encompassed with indifference; people who are apathetic to the plight of others and what they perceive as not affecting them directly. All of these groups and more come to influence relationships of power and policy. As a result, there is a link between critical race theory and policy formation in the urban historical context, which could be thought of as critical policy analysis.

FORMATION OF URBAN AREAS TO 1950S GHETTOS

When thinking about how we have reached this point in our society's development (the location of homes, businesses, and the distribution of people), it is important to reflect upon the history of events and the movements (and restrictions) of people that have led to this point. This is especially important as we think about how various races and classes of society have effectively controlled the development of other groups, including creating locations in large urban areas where African Americans and people of lower socioeconomic class are isolated from other parts of society. However, this did not just happen. There was a several-decade process that occurred to create ghettos. In point of fact, this is very timely as we reflect on the sesquicentennial of the Civil War (1861–1865) because the roots of ghetto creation in urban areas as we know it can be traced back to then. However, to understand ghetto formation, we must first ask ourselves what is a ghetto?

Defining Ghettos

We always hear the term *ghetto* thrown about on television and popular culture references in a variety of different ways—usually in the negative. However, we never stop to think exactly about what the term means and whom it directly affects. What is a ghetto? Who lives there and why? Defining it is not an essay task and explaining its significance is even more daunting. Originally, the term *ghetto* was used to describe an area in a community where Jews were restricted and segregated. Today, ghettos are more often described as a large, continuous area that, as Foner and Garrity call it, is "almost exclusively [comprised of] black residences and institutional life" (1991). Unpacking this statement further, we realize that this is a form of isolation, especially given the use of the word *institutional*. In sociology, there is a term to describe such as a phenomenon—a total institution. However, when a sociologist uses these terms, they are generally referring to one of two distinct institutions: schools or prisons. That is because both of these institutions encompass your entire being and it is very hard to remove yourself from these collectives that isolate you from the rest of world. When you go to school, you leave your family behind and you are at school with others of your determined group (usually by age or grades in school), and in prison there is absolutely no way out except death or release, and maybe the occasional breakout. Both are systems based on rules and order—marches, lines, and endless population counting.

Well, a ghetto could also be classified as a total institution. It is cut off from the rest of the known world through a variety of ways. Cut off in so many respects that it is its own world and way of life. There is also almost always some form of barrier to maintain containment of African Americans in these ghettos. In schools, it is the walls of the school, the location of the institutions, and the societal values of said school and community. In prisons, it is also the walls, but also the guards, the guns, and we would be remiss if we did not also point out the societal values that keep people in prison through various power and authority relationships. Considering these elements of institutional life, the ghetto is not different from these other institutions. One could argue that there is the absence of an organizing system to a ghetto, which would disqualify it from being a total institution. However, despite the seemingly non-system that guides a ghetto, there are rules of interaction and rules of association for its inhabitants, they are just not always formalized or written. The system of the ghetto does not become apparent with the rules of the outside world until we look at what binds the ghetto into a system. Oftentimes there are many physical barriers that separate the urban ghettos from the rest of the world.

One such example is how Hirsch describes the separation of Chicago. Many parts of the ghetto were separated from other parts of the city through large tracks of industrial areas or railroad tracks (1998). While this is not a brick wall or iron gate, it is hard and dangerous to pass through busy factory and foundry areas to connect back to the rest of society—it is a spatial and social barrier. Also, the train tracks created massive obstructions because these were not just single railed areas where a train may or may not pass by during the day, but multiple tracks with many rail yards that connected to the industrial areas. That being said, trains do two things really well. The first of which is they sit and do not move—forming a wall that is not really a permanent structure, but one that serves the same purpose to isolate and block without the directness and political incorrectness of building a wall. The second is that trains move, which means they create an impassable and lethal obstacle course to prevent certain races and classes of people from interacting with the rest of society.

In some cases, barriers were actual walls constructed to keep people separate. However, the municipal term for such obstructions is brumes. In Detroit, Sugrue describes the construction of the expressway system as a method of isolation (2005). However, further isolation was not the only effect, but rather neighborhood devastation. Sugrue states that,

Postwar highway and urban redevelopment projects further exacerbated Detroit's housing crisis, especially for blacks. Detroit's city planners promised that the proposed system of cross-city expressways would dramatically improve the city's residential areas, as well as bolster the city's economy. For the thousands of blacks who lived in the path of Detroit's first expressways, both promises were false. (2005, pg. 47)

These expressways further isolated the residents of black communities and left behind a "'no-man's land' of deterioration and abandonment" (Sugrue, 2005, pg. 47). However, these expressways allowed for middle-class working people to enter and leave the city with ease; they never had to traverse the ghetto on their way to the office or their way back to suburbia.

Aside from actual barriers, there are also many social barriers that keep African Americans in these total institutions of ghettos. The creation of the ghetto was also very much political. There were various forces at work, several of which were city governments that were only representative to a very select few. They believed that progress was good, but it had to be for the middle, voting class. Massive industrial projects and residential building projects to separate classes would both keep their people at work and allow the elected officials to maintain their position of power and authority. Along with local government, various businesses and businessmen have certain vested interests both in real estate and other holdings to control urban growth and the movements of people. Their goal is keep their workforce and maintain their business clientele, which means changes in demographics threaten their bottom line.

Massey and Denton explain that it is about tolerances (1993). They state that, "When a black family moves into a formerly all-white neighborhood, at least one white family's tolerance threshold is exceeded, causing it to leave" (Massey and Denton, 1993, pg. 96). In the chaos that the authors state exists, there is money to be made. Groups can inflate real-estate prices to keep African Americans out, but also direct them to certain neighborhoods to live, but the agents can also make a profit out of white flight by selling white homes to other black families. In essence, there were groups taking advantage of the situation, but at the same time systematically maintaining the status quo of segregation. Where you live matters.

Historical and Economic Development of Racism

It can be very difficult to ever pinpoint where or when something began to take shape because everything is a result of a complex series of events and relationships that build upon each other over time. That being said, historian Kenneth Kusmer seems to place special emphasis on the time period between 1870–1915 (1978). He calls this the formative years of the black ghetto. However, while this was a very key moment that has shaped segregation and urban areas today, Kusmer paints a rosy picture of life before the Civil War for African Americans in the North. One could get the impression that things were not that bad, but we truly doubt that was ever the case. The mounds of historical evidence that have poured forth about living conditions and societal status of African Americans and the condition of the modern day do not seem to support the idea that the races were ever treated equally even in the antebellum North.

In looking at the era between 1870–1915, it is important to frame it within the historical events of the United States. The Civil War would be a very recent memory by 1870, having only ended in 1865. This means much of the country would still be in political, social, and economic upheaval and we would begin the era of Reconstruction, which would formally lasts until the election of 1876. From this point on, the Civil War became romanticized as veterans and Civil War politicians began to pass away and the country began to move toward industrialization. The industrialization was as much a sign of the times in technological development as it was about putting the nation back together after the Civil War. However, Kusmer argues that during this period something happened in societal tensions. Specifically, he states this was a "period of growing racial hostility [that] coincided with an era of dramatic change in the patterns of urban life" (Kusmer, 1978, pg. 35).

In reading Kenneth Kusmer (1978), he takes us back to the antebellum era with an opening reflection on John Brown. Part of this is to frame the mood of Clevelanders at the time; and, secondly to frame his book: *A Ghetto Takes Shape: Black Cleveland, 1870–1930*. Both of which can be described as showing a Cleveland that is not racist, but just has a series of unfortunate racist events. However, we cannot have a place that is only anti-black when it suits them and one that is progressive at other times. During this period of time, there were sharply divided social conflicts at work deep beneath the city's surface. One such example is the conviction of two men for kidnapping because they were returning two fugitive slaves and movements by Ohioans to allow slavery throughout the state (Kusmer, 1978). Both are critical to the development of the era, especially both happening in 1819.

However, a "chief hallmark of white opinion in Cleveland was the desire to avoid sectional conflict" (1978, pg. 6). To a large degree, Kusmer frames Clevelanders as pacifists. For example, it is expressed that Cleveland had an "ambivalent attitude [that] prevailed on the subject of slavery" (Kusmer, 1978, pg. 5). Then within the next breath, Kusmer also points out that despite ambivalence, the supporters of the "antislavery cause did not necessarily also favor racial equality" (1978, pg. 7). So, while most were ambivalent, there were those that did care about abolition but did not favor equal rights. However, he then continues that, "In Cleveland, however, the two ideas were frequently conjoined [meaning antislavery and equal rights], and militant abolitionists were almost always in the forefront of the struggle for equal rights" (Kusmer, 1978, pg. 7). Kusmer argues that this ambivalence made Cleveland different from other northern cities. He states that,

> The posture of the white press on the race issue, though far from ideal, also helped keep down racial tensions in Cleveland. The progressive era was a period of widespread and sometimes violent Negrophobia among white journalist. But while other white newspapers in the northern and border . . . inflamed racial hatreds with lurid stories of lynchings and black criminal activity, Cleveland's two major dailies for the most part adopted a policy of ignoring the Negro. (Kusmer, 1978, pg. 56)

Again, Clevelanders return to a policy of passive avoidance. We are reminded of the quote by Edmund Burke, who said something along the lines of all it takes for evil to prevail is for good men to do nothing, which is exactly what we see being demonstrated by the newspapers of Cleveland in 1915. Well, this comment adds a new spin to the interpretation of the average Clevelander in the antebellum era, the water is still very muddy.

As late as 1915 Cleveland, ghettos had not yet formed. One newspaper article of the time argued, "'We have no "Little Africa" in Cleveland,' Robert Drake, a Negro Clerk, boasted in 1915. . . . 'There is not a single street in this city that is inhabited by nothing but Negroes'" (Kusmer, 1978, pg. 42). However, African Americans were being pushed in certain directions of the city. Specially "spread throughout the eastern part of the city"; but that "does not mean that a black ghetto existed in Cleveland" (Kusmer, 1978, pg. 42). By 1915, there was a push toward the eastside, which began a process of isolation.

However, we can deduce from Kusmer that these urban ghettos, like Cleveland's, started out as mostly downtowns or central city areas of what were in the beginning very small and new settlements. That means that these cities developed over decades, and in some cases a century or more, into large metropolitan areas and are effectively the older cities relative to the major regions of the country they are in today. More importantly, it demonstrates that like the long-term development and redevelopment of these cities, the ghettos were not just created overnight, but are the product of lengthy movements to control African-American populations in both where they live and interact and through socioeconomic class. James Scott would call this a high modernist social engineering strategy to control people through "urban planning." However, we must also ask ourselves, for whom was it planned?

However, why was there such growing racial hostility? We argue that there always was—nothing really changed, except the way people were now living with one another and where they lived. In the years after the Civil War, African Americans were free to move about the country, and with little holding them in the Old South, there was opportunity in the North because of industrial expansion. Thus began what many historians term the Great Migration during the early 1900s. However, we maintain that this term has a major definitional flaw. The Great Migration looks at the movement of African Americans only as they headed to the North for work; it does not examine the fact that former poor Confederate whites, whose previous generation fought in the Civil War, moved to the North also. This moved much of the poor and resentful Southern white class into large urban areas with large numbers of African Americans. On top of this, the North could not get enough workers to fill the demand for manufacturing and also hired many European immigrants. Large urban areas became a crucible of races and classes that previously had not lived together in such close quarters.

Several authors argue that the new immigrants were very territorial and formed "enclaves," or neighborhoods of their own (Hirch, 1998; Kusmer, 1978; and Sugrue, 2005), which meant they excluded other races. However, one of the areas that the literature does not seem to cover is how race relations were in Europe with African Americans before the immigrants arrived here. We know race relations could not be great because the etymology of "ghetto" is European in origin and is where Jewish families were forced to live, but that says nothing of African Americans. There is also something problematic about the use of this terminology in describing urban areas. One example is the term "enclaves" used by Hirsch (1998). He states that the "evolution of West Side black colony, from enclave to ghetto, was a post-World War II development" (Hirsch, 1998, pg. 3). As modern researchers describe it, as a neighborhood becomes black, it becomes a ghetto. Massey and Denton also state something similar, by stating that "European . . . immigrant enclaves . . . were in no way comparable to the black ghetto" (1993, pg. 32). The term "enclaves" was used to describe neighborhoods where white immigrants (many of whom were poor) lived and that were homogeneous by European ethnicity. However, whenever a black neighborhood is discussed, it is always discussed in terms of being a ghetto.

By 1915, the new industrialized North was heavily comprised of both Southern blacks and whites, making very much the Old South in a new location with confined urban quarters. By 1917, the United States was deeply embroiled in World War I, which allowed many women and African Americans to work in in-

dustries previously closed to them while white men were at war. However, soon after the war ended, many African Americans found themselves without jobs again, and matters only became worse as the county faced the Great Depression. Massey and Denton argue that "The Great Depression of the 1930s ravaged the black communities of the north and quickly wiped out gains of prior decades" (1993, pg. 116). With that in mind, several authors (Massey and Denton, 1993; and Sugrue, 2005) point out a relationship between hard economic times and an increase in racism and racial tensions. Part of this is because of white pushback against other groups in an effort to maintain their position. However, another part of the equation is that,

> If racial segregation concentrates poverty in space, it also focuses and amplifies any change in the economic situation of blacks. In a segregated environment, any economic shock that causes a downward shift in the distribution of black income will not only bring about an increase in the poverty rate for the groups as a whole; it will also cause an increase in the geographic concentration of poverty. (Massey and Denton, 1993, pg. 126)

So, in essence, because African Americans are confined as an underclass in a segregated location, then small problems have vastly devastating effects. This means that it only would amplify the effects of the Great Depression on the urban underclass.

Before the dawn of World War II, the ghetto had reached an institutional point in American culture and was here to stay. Massey and Denton state, "Throughout the United States—in both southern and northern cities—the ghetto had become an enduring, permanent feature of the residential structure of black community life by 1940, and over the next thirty years the spatial isolation of African Americans only increased" (1993, pg. 49). Looking back on what Kusmer stated about the formative years of the black ghetto being between 1870–1915, it only took twenty-five years to move the ghetto and urban segregation from being formed to being an enduring part of urban life.

Following World War II, the United States experienced a postwar economic boom (Sugrue, 2005). This led to a Second Great Migration, especially to Detroit—as a result of the military-industrial complex; however, the situation was different from the first

Great Migration in the early 1900s. First, the attraction to the cities pulled in a different crowd. There were not as many immigrants, but "Thousands of newcomers flooded the city, coming from places as diverse as rural Appalachia, depressed farm counties in central Michigan, Ohio, and Indiana, and the declining Black Belt regions of the Deep South" (Sugrue, 2005, pg. 19). Second, any African Americans who moved to northern cities during this postwar economic boom were already moving into a segregated system of housing and ghettos. Those who arrived and who were born after 1945 only knew of the ghetto and did not watch it form.

Many northern cities continued to grow until the 1970s. During this time, there was increased interest put on urban planning and designing high modernist systems that favored business and white middle-class workers, such as the expressway systems and new subdivisions that were constructed (Sugrue, 2005; Massey and Denton, 1993). However, in 1973, there was an economic recession, which caused black income levels to fall. As the recession increased in severity, the worse racial relations became. There was much hostility from lower- and middle-class whites, who were "afraid of falling," to use a sociologist's term, into poverty. Much resentment developed when African Americans were still working and whites were laid off. This coupled with already strong segregation practices meant, "By 1970, racial segregation in U.S. urban areas was characterized [as] a largely black central city surrounded by predominantly white suburbs" (Massey and Denton, 1993, pg. 61). However, the Civil Rights Movement will come to define urban areas and African Americans in ways not expected of that policy.

EDUCATIONAL POLICY AND THE CREATION OF SEPARATE AND UNEQUAL URBAN SCHOOLS

As expounded upon earlier, separate black and white communities necessarily (in most instances) create separate and unequal education institutions. Ghetto communities created ghetto schools. The Supreme Court sanctioned this separation in its *Plessy v. Ferguson* decision in 1896, which held that separate but equal facilities did not violate the Fourteenth Amendment. For the next fifty plus years, racial segregation was a sanctioned and inextricable part of the American

fabric. With this decision, the direction of educational policy for African Americans was set.

During this era, schools for African Americans were substandard, overcrowded, and primarily geared toward vocational training. African Americans were thought to be incapable of doing work beyond servitude and manual labor. Nancy Neckerman (2009) points out that recent immigrants of that period—many of whom spoke little English—were afforded opportunities to enroll in courses that taught them English and that prepared them to work in roles not afforded to blacks. Frequently, classes for blacks were overcrowded due to a lack of space, and in many instances, there was a shortage of teachers because some white teachers refused to teach black students. As a result, classes were offered in shifts to accommodate black students. The facilities were separate but obviously not equal.

BROWN V. BOARD OF EDUCATION: TURNING POINT FOR EDUCATION OR SIMPLY AN ILLUSION?

There were several court cases that challenged the separate but equal doctrine (*Hocutt v. Wilson, Henderson v. the United States, Murray v. Maryland*), but it was *Brown v. the Board of Education* that struck it down. Essentially, as Church and Sedlak argue, the "*Plessy* doctrine as it applied to schools by arguing that separate schools were inherently unequal. Segregation in and of itself had a 'detrimental effect' on black children, the Court held, 'for the policy of separating the races is usually interpreted as denoting the inferiority of the Negro group'" (1997, pg. 444). A new educational policy was set with the hope of providing equal opportunities for all Americans, particularly black Americans.

However, it was far from being that simple. After multiple court cases to thwart the new policy, desegregation was slowly implemented in school districts across the country but not without violence and the need for the National Guard to escort children and adults to elementary, high school, and universities. Unfortunately, death was also a part of this history. According to Hirsch, "As civil rights forces mobilized in the South and as the *Brown v. the Board of Education of Topeka, Kansas* decision of 1954 was hailed as a new beginning in race relations, Chicago moved in the opposite direct by institutionalizing a greatly enlarged black ghetto and turning away from the ideals that seemed so compelling during the fight against Nazism" (1998, pg. 215). Chicago was not the only one. As Kentor and Brenzel observe, "as the Supreme Court was mandating the dismantling of the old dual system of schooling, the transformation of space was creating two new separate and unequal systems of schooling in many metropolitan areas: one mainly for low-income children of color in the cities, the other largely for middle-class children in the suburbs" (1992, pg. 284).

There were undoubtedly successes with efforts to desegregate schools; however, integration for the most part was an illusion for many children. As Church and Sedlak argue, "the *Brown* decision should have been a climax to decades of educational aspirations among American blacks, proof that their tenacity had paid off and that they had achieved parity. Instead, it turned out to be but another source of frustration for the black community and the beginning of a startling rapid deterioration of the blacks' faith in education's power to improve their lot" (1976, pg. 445). However, this change did not occur for several reasons, but probably the most disturbing had to do will, or lack thereof. It was clear that the "nation's unwillingness to implement the Court's demand for integration deeply disappointed the blacks" and progressive Americans. As a result, "public schools in the northern cities grew more segregated, rather than less, as urban whites fled to the suburbs just as fast as, if not faster than, blacks migrated to and within the cities" (Church and Sedlak, 1976, pg. 446). This led to several conclusions about the power of schools and court cases to make a difference. Church and Sedlak summarize the aftermath of the Brown decision (before the civil rights movement) best. They argue "the *Brown* decision did not lead to widespread integration of white and black children; rather, it precipitated a reaction that starkly revealed white revulsion at the prospect of sending their children to school with blacks. Such revulsion suggested that revisions in the statute books and in educational organization were unlikely to alter racial injustice as much as blacks had hoped" (1976, pg. 448).

EQUATING POORNESS AND BLACKNESS: CIVIL RIGHTS AND THE GREAT SOCIETY

The quest for civil rights changed the entire direction of society and education. However, the policy inten-tion also had unforeseen ramifications in desegregation, such as African-American teachers and principals losing their positions as black schools merged with white schools. Policy, as Portes argues, can start off with one goal, but the intervention of outside forces transforms it mid-course into a different one (2000).

A prime example comes from the writings of Church and Sedlak on "Changing Definitions of Equality of Educational Opportunity" (1976). As they outline the changes in education from the 1950s to mid-1970s as a result of the Civil Rights Movement, we can see over the course of time, various interventions—in the form of accountability and assessment—were placed on schools. Part of this, especially during the War on Poverty in the 1960s, is when assessments were used to see where students would be placed and then develop plans for their improvement. However, partway into the War on Poverty, the emphasis began to shift (Church and Sedlak, 1976). It started out to help the invisible poor, which existed all through the country in various forms, including both urban poor (mostly minorities in large cities) and rural poor (mostly poor whites of Appalachian areas). However, many of the rural areas were forgotten about in large-scale accountability pushes. Perhaps this is because large populations were easier to reform and implement accountability standards with because disadvantaged individuals were already grouped in the same area, which meant easier access, rather than all across rural regions.

Many "public leaders and opinion makers demanded schools take a major part in achieving justice for the poor" (Church and Sedlak, 1976, pg. 433). This is because "schooling in American has always attracted those concerned with social problems because it promised to relieve the situation without in any way threatening to upset the current social structure"—promoting gradual change (Church and Sedlak, 1976, pg. 433). It was believed that education could be provided cheaply for the disadvantaged without reducing the amount offered to everyone else, which could create an equality of opportunity and shift the outcomes of economically disadvantaged groups.

However, the War on Poverty slowly left Appalachia behind, and at some point, reforms began to confuse poverty with blackness (Church and Sedlak, 1976). Part of this was because of the focus on urban areas where the poor were mostly African American. Thus, outside forces transformed the goal mid-course from a War on Poverty to a battle for racial equality between poor minorities in urban areas and the rest of the country. At a certain point, even support from liberals for racial equality began to erode because large sections of urban districts wanted more local control and a less centralized system, especially after books like *110 Livingston Street* came out in 1968, which outlined problems of bureaucracy within large districts that made them inaccessible to parents. However, this put liberals at odds with local urban leaders because liberals saw large systems as the only way to get at universality (Church and Sedlak, 1976). It can be argued that as the goal of improving education for the poor moved through the political and educational environment, shifts and divergences occurred, equating poorness with blackness and a focus on urban areas.

THE RISE OF CHOICE: FREIDMAN TO REAGAN

The various educational policies prompting the idea of market-based choice and competition have steered much of the discussion in educational reform for the last several years. Many supporters of choice reforms hope that a market-driven education will give our children a competitive edge by better educating students based on their needs, especially in urban areas (Hess, 2010). After the 1960s, choice and competition in education made relatively little progress until Reagan's bid for president and the 1980s.

It is problematic to argue with any certainty that education is completely a competitive market because it has not been historically. We also know that the current educational arena is codependent on governmental regulation. It is important to understand the historical aspect of choice and competition. However, as Maris Vinovskis would suggest, this is an examination to understand how we got to where we are, "rather than directly trying to inform current policymaking" on a course of action (2009, pg. 17). By understanding the past we can make informed decisions, but at the same time not making the error of assuming the future will be representative of the past (Floden, 2007).

That being said, it is difficult to pinpoint exactly where and when the ideas of choice and competition became the normal mantra in education because they have so long been part of human society. After all, Fredrick Hess, educator and political scientist, argues that choice and competition are as old as civilization

itself (2010). He points to ancient Athens as a starting point, where there were marketplaces of sophists and philosophers, and each person who came into the marketplace was able to choose their school of thought.

For the American context, it can really be traced back to the eighteenth century with the writings of Thomas Paine and the nineteenth century with the writings of John Stuart Mills (Hess, 2010). To summarize, both of these influential individuals felt that the state should ensure that young people be given a basic education, but at the same time that this goal should be advance through private arrangements. Arrangements that would meet the ends of the individuals whom they served while at the same time satisfying the state's aim of providing a basic education, which many have agreed is necessary in creating citizens who know their rights and how government functions (Hess, 2010; Jacobsen, 2009).

However, until the progressive era and the emergence of administrative progressives, there was relatively autonomy in schools (Chubb and Moe, 1990), which did not hinder their functionality. The overly formal bureaucracy had not yet taken such hold as to hinder schools' effectiveness to the degree of present day, which is one of the main problems choice advocates hope to correct. The autonomy in this era provided the funds for schools to operate and local control provided the ability to operate within the community. However, this does not mean that everyone was served equally, but it did provide greater access from the community and a greater ability for the community to impact what took place in the daily operations of their schools.

Continuing in that same vein, choice today can really be traced back to the writings of economist Milton Friedman from the 1950s. He argued for a voucher system in education, a system that would limit the role of government to one of providing funds and setting basic standards for approved educational institutions. He stated that, "A stable and democratic society is impossible without a minimum degree of literacy and knowledge on the part of most citizens and without widespread acceptance of some common set of values" (Friedman, 1962, pg. 86). However, at the same time he would allow parents the right to choose which institutions would best serve the needs of their children (Hess, 2010; Friedman, 1962). As Cusick would argue, this allows the parents to have a greater capacity in the educational arena to have their voices heard because as it stands currently, they can be drowned out by unequal footing among other competing interests for the school's attention, such as unions, textbook companies, and other professional organizations, not to mention local and national politics, which are not always sympatric to concerns of parents (Cusick, 1991).

Friedman's hope was that this form of education would promote equitable and efficient schooling, with the hope that it would also eliminate class differences, which currently keep repeating themselves. By this, we are referencing hegemonic reproduction theory, which holds that government is deeply involved in the socializing of education and is controlled by the dominant group, the group in power, which can hold other groups in place. In essence, the group in control could keep lower classes and those who struggle in a constant cycle of reaping the same setbacks or allow the up-and-coming powerful to reach the potential of where their groups places them. Choice and market competition Friedman was hoping would break this cycle by giving everyone a variety of different options not controled for by the state.

Friedman went on to argue that the desire for government funding for education is not a desire for government ran education. In addition to freeing the students, it would also free up resources by allowing student demand to control the educational landscape, instead of neighborhood effects and tying education to the housing market. After all, before choice, one went to school where one lived and to change schools one had to sell one's house and move. Better schools have almost universally held higher property values over lower performing schools (Hess, 2010). However, that is not to say that schools are the only element that contributes to reality markets. Reality markets, emblematic of who lives where, can also be related to the type of schools available to residents.

Moving forward in time, the Johnson administration tried to implement a test case of Friedman's idea with a voucher program in Rock, California. It was run by the newly created Office of Economic Opportunity and failed wholeheartedly (Hess, 2010). Chubb and Moe would argue that its main reason for failure was the excessive bureaucracy created by trying to manage the system. It is hard to free school from the political

system because they are in fact created in the shadows of that system and have adopted the same political process (Chubb and Moe, 1990).

After the 1960s, choice and competition in education made relatively little progress until Reagan's bid for president and the 1980s. Reagan looked for support from four distinct, and some could argue incompatible, groups to promote educational marketplace competition. The first of these groups were disenfranchised Catholics, who had recently been dismayed by judicial assaults on school prayer (Hess, 2010). In addition, because of shifting resources, having less religious (people becoming priests, nuns, and brothers), Catholic schools were beginning to use laypeople (non-religious) to run schools. This meant they had to pay them a living wage, as opposed to what they paid religious orders to run schools. In essence, the cost was going up and they needed more funds to run their schools. They hoped for financial assistance with parochial education.

The second group was really the major players of the Republican Party. They wanted to promote a market-friendly agenda, especially for business, and many felt that schools should also be part of this reform. To some degree, this group felt that market forces should be part of all institutions, public and private. The third group was the American Federation of Teachers and especially their leader, Al Shanker. He had been pushing that charter schools would allow teachers to establish schools with her autonomy and would allow schools to isolate themselves from district bureaucracy. The final group was frustrated African-American leaders who were looking for good and safe schools. They had for sometime been stuck in horrible mismanaged schools, especially urban districts. More specifically, these four groups could agree with Reagan because of ambiguity of concept (Stone, 2002). They all saw something in his pro-choice agenda from which they could benefit, while at the same time having varying degrees of understanding of what choice and competition meant for them.

However, of these four groups, Hess would argue that the most politically viable were the black urban leaders. The argument of pro-competition then became not about markets, economic theories, and data, but a political and moral imperative. It became a political charge to help poor, black parents in urban areas experience the choice that suburban, mostly white, homeowners took for granted. Choice advocates began to push morality and choice as a venue for achieving social justice, not deregulation and efficiency, which are at the heart of market reforms (Hess, 2010).

For the public, this new view had profound effects on the direction the choice movement would take. Being that educational competition began arguing morality, its advocates spent substantially less time looking at the market-based aspect of education as opposed to deregulators of energy, transportation, telecommunications, and even cable television (Hess, 2010). In essence, competition in education, at least as it exists since the 1980s, really has its foundations not in market data like every other form of deregulation, but is founded on the idea of being a moral crusade. It has only more recently with popular new approaches, like the film *Waiting for Superman*, been using more social science research to argue for educational choice and competition.

However, we must give a word of caution as we move toward the future. An unchecked faith in open markets can have devastating effects if it does not work as the advocates predict it will. Historian Diane Ravitch states that schools embrace reforms, like choice and competition, all too quickly (2010). She goes on to state the "lure of the market is the idea that freedom from government regulations is the solution all by itself . . . this is very appealing, . . . [but] . . . education is too important to relinquish to vagaries of markets and the good intention of armatures" (2010, pg. 11).

RESULTS OF URBAN EDUCATION POLICY

Today, many black students continue to struggle despite nearly sixty years post-Brown. The struggle continues for equal educational opportunities, which many believed would be addressed with desegregation of schools. However, segregated classrooms in desegregated schools was not the solution. Scholars argue that there was a period when school integration was at its highest point in the 1970s, but has steadily retreated to its pre-Brown conditions (Crain et al., 1997).

A recent civil rights project at UCLA (2012) reports that school segregation is sharply increasing not only by race but also around economics and class. Deseg-

regation, a fleeting moment soon dissipated. When the dust settled, the following data surfaced:

- The most extreme levels of black-white school dissimilarity exist in the Chicago, New York, Detroit, Boston, St. Louis, and Pittsburgh metropolitan areas.
- The nation's largest metropolitan areas report severe school racial concentration. Half of the black students in the Chicago metro area, and one third of black students in New York, attend apartheid schools.

Desegregation to address education inequality doesn't seem to have made an indelible imprint on the lives of children most disenfranchised. Education in our nation also began to come under scrutiny. Our educational system began to fall behind other nations, which soon prompted elected officials to create policy to improve education outcomes for the nation's children.

In 1983, *A Nation at Risk* was introduced to improve the quality of education in the wake of the Cold War and U.S.–Soviet space race. It proposed to challenge students by raising standards and expectations. It also sought to promote a "free (education) market system." Goals 2000, another of several education policies, proposed that states be held accountable for education outcomes; high stakes testing was implemented and again called for higher standards. Clearly, this was an educational movement that caught the attention of supporters who decided that education had to improve for the nation's children.

Oddly enough, there was not a great deal of attention placed on educational outcomes for minority students in particular until No Child Left Behind and, subsequently, Race to the Top when national attention was drawn to the racial achievement gap. The gap did not simply appear out of thin air, but the persistent gap had garnered public attention. Teachers are being held accountable for student academic growth, rewards and other incentives are being dangled at districts and teachers, as well as threats to dismantle schools and districts that do not make adequate yearly progress with particular emphasis placed on low-achieving minority students. District takeovers, emergency managers, and pink slips distributed to teachers have become a significant part of the landscape for urban school districts and the children who attend these schools.

THE GHOSTLY HAND OF SOCIAL ENGINEERING—CREATING AN AMERICAN UNDERCLASS

In thinking about the history of urbanization and ghetto formation, several trends seem to develop across history. Most important is to think of it in the terms that Massey and Denton use—an American apartheid. However, in the text, they never really give a complete definition of what an apartheid is. So, with that in mind, an apartheid by law is, "Defined by the 2002 Rome Statute of the International Criminal Court as inhumane acts of a character similar to other crimes against humanity 'committed in the context of an institutionalized regime of systematic oppression and domination by one racial group over any other racial group or groups and committed with the intention of maintaining that regime.'"

While we think that truly applies to American society in terms of African Americans, we are not sure it is that organized. We do not think that there is a formal organization, as the definition would imply, in American society that is systematically oppressing people, but rather it is a series of informal relationships situated in a loosely coupled system. By this we mean the system is driven by irrational hate in rational ways through informal alliances to keep certain people in certain places while at the same time what these power players are doing is both increasing racism, creating an urban underclass, and in some ways profiting from it. After all, rational systems that carry out tasks by definition function in a logical and hierarchical way, but that does not mean that the motives and reasons for the rational system, in this case hatred, have to be logical or sane.

Looking at Hirsch and forming the second ghetto, he describes it as a "sequence of events [that] clearly demonstrated the combination of forces that produced" it (1998, pg. 213). Specifically, he states that the major forces included large "downtown interests and . . . powerful institutions . . . found themselves confronted, after the war, with threats to their survival that were beyond even their considerable means of control" (Hirsch, 1998, pg. 213). These interests were in fear of the white clientele reaching tolerance levels, or intolerance levels, of African Americans and leaving. However, these organizations could not leave the city: "They realized that the power of the state—not

as it then existed but in a greatly augmented form—would have to be enlisted in their aid" (Hirsch, 1998, pg. 213). This means that those with power, money, and resources had to affect the political system and control it to oppress African Americans. Beyond governmental control, there was always the looming and often actual use of violence to effectuate change that government manipulation could not accomplish.

While all these items added to creating ghettos, Massey and Denton present a more abstract, but very exact and systematic, method of how to create an urban underclass. They state that the creators, whoever they may be, must start by choosing "a minority group whose members are somehow identifiably different from the majority" (1993, pg. 182). By doing this, the oppressors can always find them anywhere and anytime to control the group's movements. From here it is necessary to separate the members, in this case African Americans, from everyone else by forcing them into select areas and any "attempt to leave the enclave is systematically steered away from majority neighborhoods and back to minority or racially mixed areas" (Massey and Denton, 1993, pg. 182). This means there must be informal alliances in the case of the United States, where such practices are illegal, to steer people in the segregated direction. To aid in this, it is necessary to also control the movement and lending of money. It is important to remember the golden rule—he who has the gold makes the rules. However, there are always those who will resist, perhaps on both sides, and for them, it is necessary to harass them and, if that does not work, then it is necessary to escalate to violence. After all, those who are in charge have the ability to do violence to maintain their order.

From here, "Once a group's segregation in society has been ensured, the next step in building an underclass is to drive up the rate of poverty" (Massey and Denton, 1993, pg. 183). However, this poverty and segregation then becomes political power. Massey and Denton go on to state that, "Geographic isolation translates into political isolation, making it difficult for segregated groups to form political coalitions with others to end policies inimical to their self-interests or to promote policies that might advance their welfare" (1993, pg. 183). The final tactic to create an urban underclass is "to set off a spiral of decay within the ghetto . . . [with] . . . a first-class economic disaster that removed the means of subsistence from a large share of the population" (1993, pg. 183). As we discussed before, economic recessions are always worse in poor, isolated areas. This then creates a circular and repetitive system from which the urban underclass cannot escape until it becomes part of institutional life, and after a generation or so, it is just accepted as how things are. All this means that, "Given the lack of opportunity, pervasive poverty, and increasing hopelessness of life in the ghetto, a social-psychological dynamic is set in motion to produce a culture of segregation . . . [and] . . . as new generation are born into conditions of increasing deprivation and deepening racial isolation" (Massey and Denton, 1993, pg. 184). Once this happens, it becomes hard to leave because a different culture and even language can be created that separates the urban underclass from the rest of humanity.

However, the goal has not been to create ghettos; they are a by-product, a side effect of the treatment. So, what is the treatment? Many would argue that it is segregation and racism, but again, these are mere tools to achieve the goal. The end goal is really to create an urban underclass that is isolated and subjugated by higher classes. However, the purpose of that goal is not clear. Unless it is solely to have a group of people to lord over and have do the remedial tasks the other classes wish not to do—a form of institutional and societal slavery.

The Next Big Thing in Organized Racism

We are standing on a great precipice in the next re-creation of racism and segregation and it has already begun to take shape. Major proportions of society have worked to make racism invisible, but yet enduring, and now they will work to make us forget that it exists altogether. All of the events and history of segregation, racism, and ghetto creation have been leading to a point, this point. While we do not believe there was (or is) a great plan, at least not one written, the stars have aligned for racists. We are at the point that segregation has become institutionalized and part of American life, which means the next evolution is to say there is no problem—that it does not exist—that it never existed because it has become part of the landscape.

The focus has become on individuals and economics and not race, which has purposely been the direct shift.

However, what started this shift? Many of these arguments are a result of the election of President Obama. A recent issue of the *Peabody Journal of Education* stated in the introduction to their post-racialism edition that,

> Many presupposed that the mere election of the first president of color erased the pervasive and institutionalized racism that has historically oppressed Americans of color since the creation of the nation. This framing has resulted in the solidification of a de-contextualized and de-raced analysis of some of the most important economic and social issues and policies of the last several generations (Aleman, Salazar, Rorrer, and Parker, 2011)

We would agree with these authors and argue the inverse of what many people, especially the media who championed America to be post-racial on election night, are saying about the election of President Obama. While it was historical that he was elected, it did not solve anything. This type of "post-racial" rhetoric has lauded parts of society into a false sense of complacency; this "rhetoric of color-blindness presents a façade of individualism, it ignores the social conditions that affect achievement gaps in education, graduation rates, underrepresentation in higher education (particularly prestigious institutions), and employment disparities remain" (Aleman et al., 2011, pg. 485). There is an overdrive whose goal is to spin his election to say that everything is solved, and at the same time these groups are convincing the world there is no problem while systematically oppressing African Americans more so, or to a fuller extent, than before Obama was elected to compensate for the election of a black president (Aleman et al., 2011). Coupled with the economic woes of late, race relations are on a decline in present-day America, not nonexistent. It is one thing to argue with someone and the other person take the opposing view, but it is much harder to argue with people who say that the problem does not exist, in this case inequality.

If we say a problem is nonexistent, then there is a lack of urgency to do anything about it. From an economic point of view, why should we, as a society, spend money on fixing something that people say does not exist? After all, it would be cheaper, as money continues to get tighter, to divert those funds to other "real" problems. It is a difficult logic to argue with when people keep saying that a problem has been abated by a mere election. However, we all know that harsh reality—that a single election and change in the guard in Washington has not resulted in direct changes in the day-to-day operations in urban cities or urban schools.

As we move to focusing on the individual in this "post-racism era," we can forget about groups of people and say they are not important and we will obliterate racial identity. We can pretend that racism never existed because it has both become institutionalized and invisible in this capitalist society. In a society that David Labaree says is fraught with social mobility, it is about everyone for themselves and the best deal they can get in a market-based approach to life (1997). Race becomes "obscured by economic individualism . . . Individuals are linked to their economic viability and stripped of their individual components, like race, furthering the myth of a color-blind society" (Aleman et al., 2011, pg. 483–84). This is especially the case because economics looks at everyone as individual utility maximizers, which means one person will leverage what they can to do the best for themselves and completely ignore society in favor of an animal spirit as economist Keynes would note. The final move will be to convince the world that it is about a single person that cannot get ahead, not a race of people, and if humanity is not careful, it will happen—total isolation at the most personal level.

RECOMMENDATIONS FOR FUTURE RESEARCH

Future research will need to take into consideration this idea of perceived racial invisibility. Where exactly did this start? It did not just occur with the election of Obama. Does its roots align with those of indifference as Kusmer (1978) points out in post–Civil War Cleveland, or are these a more recent result of the push for educational choice in the marketplace? Tracing the roots of this concept and its manifestations over time could shed light on where this has come from and its anticipated trajectory. Whatever any of us do, as we move forward, we should think about what has happened before us and take the advice of educational philosopher Thomas Green and approach future educational policy with a quite sense of tragedy (1983).

REFERENCES

Aleman, E., Salazar, T., Rorrer, A., and Parker, L. (2011) "Introduction to Postracialism in U.S. Public School and Higher Education Setting: The Politics of Education in the Age of Obama." *Peabody Journal of Education* 86, 479–487.

Bowles, S. and Gintis, H. (1976) "Education and Personal Development: The Long Shadow of Work," In Bowles and Gintis, *Schooling in Capitalist America: Educational Reform and the Contradictions of Economic Life,* pp. 125–148. New York: Basic Books.

Chubb, J., and Moe, T. (1990). *Politics, Markets, & America's School.* Washington, DC: The Brookings Institution.

Church, R. and Sedlak, M. (1976). Changing Definitions of Equality of Educational Opportunity, 1960–1975. In *Education in the United States: An Interpretive History.* New York: Free Press.

Cusick, P. (1991). *The Education System: Its Nature and Logic.* Columbus, OH: McGraw-Hill.

Denzin, N. and Lincoln, Y. (2000). *Handbook of Qualitative Research.* 2nd edition. Thousand Oaks, CA: Sage Publications.

Floden, R. (2007). Philosophical Issues in Education Policy Research. In S. H. Fuhrman, D. K. Cohen and F. Mosher (Eds.), *The State of Education Policy Research* (3–15). Mahwah, NJ: Lawrence Erlbaum Associates.

Foner, E. and Garraty, J. (1991). *The Reader's Companion to American History.* Chicago: Houghton Mifflin.

Friedman, M. (1962). *The Role of Government in Education. Capitalism and Freedom.* Chicago: University of Chicago Press.

Green, T. F. (1983). Excellence, equity, and equality. In L. Shulman and G. Sykes (Eds.), *Handbook of Teaching and Policy* (pp. 318–341). New York: Longman.

Hess, F. (2010). Does School Choice "Work"? *National Affairs,* Fall (5), 35–55.

Hirsch, A. R. (1998*). Making the Second Ghetto: Race and Housing in Chicago 1940–1960.* Chicago: University of Chicago Press.

Jacobsen, R. (2009). The Voice of the People in Educational Policy. In G. Sykes, B. Schneider, and D. Plank. *Handbook of Educational Policy Research* (pp. 307–318). New York: Rutledge.

Kantor, H. and Brenzel, B. (1992). Urban Education and the "Truly Disadvantage": The Historical Roots of the Contemporary Crisis, 1945–1990. *Teachers College Record,* 94, 278–313.

Kincheloe, J., and McLaren, P. (2000). Rethinking Critical Theory and Qualitative Research. In Denzin, N. and Lincoln, Y. *Handbook of Qualitative Research* (pp. 279–313). 2nd edition. Thousand Oaks, CA: Sage Publications.

Kusmer, K. L. (1978). *A Ghetto Takes Shape: Black Cleveland, 1870–1930*. Champaign: University of Illinois Press.

Labaree, F. (1997). Public Goods, Private Goods: The American Struggle Over Educational Goals. *American Educational Research Journal* 34, 39–81.

Massey, D. and Denton, N. (1993). *American Apartheid: Segregation and the Making of the Underclass*. Cambridge, MA: Harvard University Press.

Portes, A. (2000). The Hidden Abode: Sociology as Analysis of the *Unexpected. American Sociological Review* 65, 1–18.

Ravitch, D. (2010). *The Death and Life of the Great American School System: How Testing and Choice are Undermining Education*. New York: Basic Books.

Reardon, S. (2011). The Widening Academic Achievement Gap Between the Rich and Poor: New Evidence and Possible Explanations. In R. Murnane and G. Duncan (Eds.), *Whither Opportunity? Rising Inequality, Schools, and Children's Life Chances*. New York: Russell Sage Foundation Press.

Stone, D. (2002). *Policy Paradox: The Art of Political Decision Making*. New York: W.W. Norton & Co.

Sugrue, T. (2005). *The Origins of the Urban Crisis: Race and Inequality in Postwar Detroit*. Princeton, NJ: Princeton University Press.

Vinovskis, M. (2009). Historians and Educational Policy Research in the United States. In G. Sykes, B. Schneider, and D. Plank (Eds.), *Handbook of Education Policy Research* (pp. 17–26). New York: Routledge.

TEACHING, LEARNING, CURRICULUM, AND EDUCATIONAL OUTCOMES

In this section we explore the urban educational leader's role in curriculum, instruction, and educational outcomes. However, we also explore key policy changes that impact teaching and learning in urban schools such as NCLB and the student achievement gap, and the urban charter schools movement.

Chapter 5, "Creating a Culture of Confidence: Re-Conceptualizing Urban Educational Leadership" by Yvette Jackson, Veronica McDermott, Marlon Simmons, and Mairi McDermott present their groundbreaking theory grounded in their work with urban communities. Their concept of *fearless leadership* is presented as an alternative frame to examine the realities faced by urban educators and students. Authors Glenn Baete, Joe Burks, Marty Pollio, and Craig Hochbein present chapter 6, "Bringing Urban High School Reform to Scale: Rapidly Moving Dramatic Numbers of Students to Proficient Performance" by summarizing the effects of Project Proficiency (PP), a high school scale-up effort implemented in a large urban school district. The chapter ultimately suggests that PP is a viable and scalable urban high school reform based on its elements of depth, spread, shift of ownership, and sustainability.

In chapter 7, "Developing Teacher Leadership for Equity in Urban Schools," authors H. Richard Milner IV, Judson Laughter, and Joshua Childs argue for the necessity of teacher leadership—in, from, and beyond the classroom—to cultivate practices that support equity in urban schools. In this chapter, they suggest that teacher leadership be a central goal of teacher preparation programs and professional development opportunities in order to prepare them to teach and lead in urban classrooms. This section is anchored by chapter 8, "Teachers Learning to Lead: An Action Research Process Model," in which author Leena Furtado focuses on the importance of pedagogy in teacher preparation programs to build enhanced professional and leadership skills.

CHAPTER 5

Creating a Culture of Confidence

Re-Conceptualizing Urban Educational Leadership

Yvette Jackson, Veronica McDermott, Marlon Simmons, Mairi McDermott

INTRODUCTION

What does it mean to destabilize the taken-for-granted received narratives of what is possible in urban educational spaces? What does it mean to re-imagine urban educational leadership as something other than the conventional hierarchical leader/follower relationship? In this chapter, we seek to address these questions as they come to be framed in the present epoch of neoliberalism in education. Neoliberalism has had a particularly pernicious role in urban education, saturating many urban schools with fear and uncertainty. Among the tough questions urban educational leaders cope with daily in this epoch are: Will their schools be closed, re-constituted, or otherwise punished because their students and teachers do not "measure up" to increasingly more punitive standards imposed without considering the historical ways in which various identity locations—race, class, gender, sexuality, language, ability, and religion—have hierarchized access to power and privilege? Will they be able to find, cultivate, and retain committed, confident, and competent teachers critical enough to withstand the constant pressures of a system designed to drive them, and many of their students, into "educational exile" (Dei, et al., 2000; Fine, 1991; Jackson and McDermott, 2012)? Will they be able to rewrite the cultural script and counter the deficit model narrative that has been written about their schools, their teachers, and especially their students, in order to reveal the often under-recognized, under-cultivated, under-promoted, and under-demonstrated potentials in their schools (Delpit, 1995; Duncan-Andrade and Morrell, 2008; Dweck, 2000; Jackson, 2011)?

We suggest that in order to do so, leaders must cultivate a culture of confidence, by way of critical values, support systems, resources, and gumption to holistically understand, challenge, and disrupt the variant threats including misguided punitive public policies, purposeful media misrepresentations, and private-sector interests that have usurped the conversation about public education for their own means as well as to maintain the status quo. These leaders must have a germane knowledge base and volition to respond to the contingencies of an imposed system that devalues the work of their teachers and the lives of their students, an imperial system that simultaneously masks its oppressive effects on the lives of their students. These leaders must have the will to respond to the needs of historically marginalized students. In other words, they must have the epistemological framework and resiliency to counter fixed essentialist categories, which discursively organize and inscribe their experiences within institutional schooling and education settings.

We suggest that leaders who work to address these concerns ought to be fearless, that fearless leaders comprehensively understand the landscape of urban education, including the socio-historical contexts that have led to contemporary conditions. Fearless leaders consider the possibilities and limitations of pedagogy, striving to find transformative approaches that foster distinctive, productive ways of being, living, and knowing for students, pedagogues, and leaders that cultivate their strengths, as well as their competence and confidence for academic thriving and self-actualization.

The chapter considers what fearless leadership involves, the manner in which it comes to be particularly needed in urban schools, and how fearless leadership can transform urban schools into oases of learning and being. This is done by considering, rethinking each of the ideas outlined above: the socio-historical context of urban education, the production and dissemination of learning and teaching through a critical pedagogy imbued with belief and confidence, and a reconceptualization of leadership in urban education.

SOCIO-HISTORICAL CONTEXT OF URBAN EDUCATION

Urban Education and the "Grammar of Schooling"

Re-conceptualizing urban educational leadership begins by fearlessly asking questions about what could be. How might we imagine schooling and education differently? How might we go about transforming urban education so that students, teachers, and leaders can actualize their full potential and beyond? Simultaneously, re-conceptualizing urban educational leadership requires fearlessly asking questions about how we got where we are. We believe that a critical engagement with the historical, colonial ways in which education broadly conceptualized, and urban education in particular, have been constituted is necessary in order to burst open the taken-for-grantedness of the way schooling is done. As such, we believe this critical engagement must destabilize that which has been deemed immutable through policy, media, and public discourses in an effort to imagine something different for urban education. In other words, we work with a "theory of mediation [that] highlights the ideological interests and contradictions inherent in cultural texts and social processes . . . by subjecting them to a mode of critical reflection that exposes the social function of those meanings and ideas legitimated by the dominant culture" (Giroux, 2001, p. 65). To situate the politics of education we query, which students, teachers, and administrators are located where and by what means? Furthermore, some of the questions we think through in this section are: How do we come to locate the particular knowledges, bodies, and geographies that constitute urban education? What is the relation of urban education, as it is presently conceptualized and lived, to standardized education as imbued through a neoliberal schooling framework? This discussion will provide a backdrop for our suggestions of re-conceptualizing urban leadership by way of critical pedagogy.

In situating the socio-historical context of urban education, we would like to address what David Tyack and Larry Cuban have termed "the grammar of schooling," which "include[s] such familiar practices as the age-grading of students, the division of knowledge into separate subjects, and the self-contained classroom with one teacher" (1995, p. 9, quoted in Albrecht-Crane, 2005, p. 495). In an era when students, teachers, and education broadly speaking are suffering from the onslaught of reform efforts, we know that we can count on schools remaining recognizable. Despite the reforms, schools remain recognizable even in terms of what knowledges and pedagogical approaches are engaged depending upon the type of schooling site. Albrecht-Crane continues, "Coupled with other binary segmentations in terms of gender, class, race, and sexuality, which are operative in Western societies, the school becomes a place in which individuals are folded into a distinct system of classification and ordering. As Tyack and Cuban put it, the school provides 'a place for every child and every child in his or her place' (1995, p. 20)" (ibid.).

The "grammar of schooling" in Western society is decidedly familiar. What does this familiar grammar look like in urban education? There is largely no consensus as to what counts as "urban education" (Milner, 2012); however, it is increasingly conjured up as a descriptor for schooling sites embodied by historically marginalized youth, regardless of the particular geography of the school. Urban, as a term, has come to be codified through various means (which are outside the scope of this paper) to signify racialized, impoverished students and communities. This contention alone has significant implications for re-conceptualizing urban leadership, not the least of which speaks to the reification of what "places" historically marginalized youth can take up in contemporary society.

If we were to trace the history of marginalization in institutionalized schooling and education in relation to the roles made available for which groups in contemporary society, we would confront the history of subjugation and be forced to contend with the issue that schools were historically designed with particular groups in mind. Linda Darling-Hammond (2010) (among others) traces the opportunity gap for minoritized students to the history of subjugation and the system of colonial education. With this history in mind, in what follows we focus on the contemporary situation in which neoliberal discourses and policies have exacerbated the marginalization of particular youth by way of intensification of impossible standardizations within schooling practices. Since the 1800s, particularly since Horace Mann, common schooling has been heralded as the great equalizer, and while we believe in the critical democratic possibilities of education (as will be explicated in the next two sections), we believe there is an urgency to unmasking the insidious character of contemporary education. In this discussion, we focus on the role of neoliberalism in urban education that has given rise to the current roles and embodiments made available.

Neoliberalism and Urban Education

Historically, schooling formed hegemonic relations with the capitalist market in which particular bodies were excluded from education. Colonial schooling formed hegemonic relations with educational delivery, curricula, and schooling practices. Dominant perspectives on education institutionalized curricula in ways that organized knowledge dissemination within multiple and distinct spheres of schooling. At the same time conservative manifestations of schooling imbued parochial forms of curricula that centered particular underlying assumptions of knowledge, which imposed rote procedures, standardized testing, and evaluative measures of assessment (Apple, 1995; Giroux, 2001; Kincheloe, 2010; Marcuse, 2009a; 2009b; Stanley, 1992). These practices culminated in the production and reproduction of inequalities within the governing socio-cultural public sphere. Students tangentialized by race, class, gender, sexuality, religion, language, and ableism were historically excluded from classroom discussions that spoke to their lived experiences and pedagogical articulations, which shaped and characterized their day-to-day lives through these processes of standardization, banking models of pedagogy, outcomes based assessment, and universalized knowledge (Freire, 1970, 1985; Ladson-Billings, 2000; Steinberg, 2012).

Many of these historical colonial practices that previously informed educational goals and schooling relationships have given way to another equally limiting approach in the form of neoliberal articulations through universalized methods of teaching and learning, which, in the process, silences questions about power, privilege, and the relevance of embodied cultural knowledge as a means to come to understand the world we live in (Apple, 2001; Giroux, 2005; Harvey, 2005; McDermott and Simmons, 2013; McMahon and Portelli, 2012; Simmons, 2011). Even though schools are political spaces embodied through cultures of difference—cultures of difference that have historically resisted dominant narratives of understanding the socio-cultural environment—these bodies of cultural difference have been ignored. Particular accounts of schooling and education have emerged that ultimately delineate the way in which educational resources are organized, inscribed, and disseminated within schools. This delineation works to produce, reproduce, and maintain existing hegemonic relations of power and privilege (Davies, 2000; Dehli, 2003; McDermott and Madan, 2012; Popkewitz, 1997). Many of these hegemonic practices are experienced, and even exacerbated, under the trope of urban education.

Over the past decades neoliberalism has emerged as the dominant discourse that frames curricula initiatives and pedagogical practices. David Harvey (2005), in his important work on neoliberalism, notes that neoliberalism consists of particular institutionalized discursive practices, which promulgate that the human condition can be improved by way of entrepreneurship, free market, and free trade. And the role of the state is to organize and inscribe institutional methods to meet those market needs. Institutions of the state such as schools and universities have become saturated with neoliberal modes of thought resulting in curricula practices such as standardized testing, overdependence on questionable evaluative measures of learning, and banking concepts of education. The banking concept emanates from the notion that knowledge is to be deposited, repeated, and memorized (Freire, 1970). In a sense then, emphasis on knowledge that is deposited, standardized, and measurable reduces learning and understanding to something tangible. Student success becomes determined through this singular measurable relationship with the texts and curricula.

We want to be explicit that we start with the notion of neoliberalism as a re-inscription of colonial dominance over knowledge production and educational space, while also obfuscatory in a manner privileging of particular bodies—Euro, white males, for example. To quote Coleman (2006):

> Since the categories of privilege attempt to secure their privilege by rendering their preferential status as natural and therefore as immutable and irresistible, it is important that we remind ourselves that they are in fact projects. Deeply invested in maintaining, if not increasing, their social status, they are passively dynamic, always

engaged in the activities of self-invention, reinvention, self-maintenance, and adaptation, even as they try to avoid observation or detection as anything but fixed. (p. 10)

Our examination of neoliberalism in urban education has led us to identify five key features of the neoliberal agenda:

1. Market Rationale—Choice, Competition, and Consumption
2. Privatization and De-Regulation
3. Excellence, Effort, and Meritocracy
4. Universalism, Standardization, and Performance Outcomes
5. Deficit Thinking and Stop-Gap Policies

While each of these features is fraught with contradictions, both within each category as well as across the features, they are organized around a certain logic, a logic that seeks to maintain status quo relations to power and privilege for limited bodies. One assumption of the Market Rationale is that competition will create more choice and innovation; however, the patterns show that competition has actually created more similarity. As Michael Apple (2001) describes it, with the neoliberal agenda, "More time and energy is spent maintaining public image of a 'good school' and less time and energy is spent on pedagogic and curricular substance." As a result, "schools themselves become more similar and more committed, to standard, traditional, whole class methods of teaching, and a standard and traditional (and often mono-cultural) curriculum" (p. 416). Ironically, this is especially true in urban educational spaces where it is particularly harmful and dehumanizing.

Privatization and De-Regulation speaks to the notions that less government is inevitably more efficient and that the market is the great equalizer. However, as Larner (2000) points out, "while neoliberalism may mean less government, it does not follow that there is less governance. . . . It [neoliberalism] involves forms of governance that encourage both institutions and individuals to conform to the norms of the market" (p. 12). In this frame, only some institutions and individuals, even if they "conform to the norms," are viewed as "legitimate" while too many others, particularly those in urban education, are made expendable. Simultaneously, this pressure to "conform to the norms of the market"

obscures the historical injustices that shape those very norms. To uphold the rationale for privatization and de-regulation, the third feature, Excellence, Effort, and Meritocracy, plays an important role. Success becomes dehistoricized and is de-linked from its social context by way of individualization. To "make it," one must merely "pull themselves up by the bootstraps." In other words, through excellence and effort one will be rewarded in the market. The message is that those who have "made it" did so through merit.

Contradicting the emphasis on individualization is the emphasis on Universalism, Standardization, and Performance Outcomes, which are rationalized due to their measurability. First of all it must be asked, how are the universals and standards conceptualized? Who is doing the defining? What is being done when only outcomes are measured and not processes? "Those who do not fit the productivity profile along the lines of gender, race, first-third world situatedness, or educated-illiterate are likely to be marginalized, for example, by way of surveillance and disciplining through the criminal justice system" (Essed and Goldberg, 2002, p. 1075). In other words, what happens to those who do not or cannot meet the standards-market norms based on how the standards are defined? In our different experiences, we have all been confronted with various renditions of the following: data being collected on the "success" (both past, present, and projected) of students in urban schools informing the decisions for building and/or maintaining jail capacity in the community. Finally, Deficit Thinking, where the emphasis is placed on "fixing" the deficient student, rather than the system or structures. To address these deficiencies, Stop-Gap Policies, quick "fixes" often focused on the individual students (or their communities), are implemented in the mistaken belief that if we add a course here, or change something over there, we can somehow mend the fragile foundation filled with gaping holes. Stop-Gap Policies are nothing more than manifestations of the seduction of simple solutions and do little by way of transforming a system that is invested in upholding the status quo.

Since the 1983 Reagan-era report, *A Nation At Risk*, we have witnessed increasingly pejorative representations of education in society. In that report, we were told that where the United States was once a leader, we were now fast falling behind other Westernized nations. This was the catalyst (or perhaps the scapegoat) to dramatically change government funding schemes for education and other social supports and opened the door for neoliberal rationality. Klaf and Kwan (2010) refer to this as the neoliberal straitjacket, "This 'one-size-fits-all' garment [which] has 'pinched' spaces of education (although differentially), pressuring schools to improve their students' performances or face sanctions" (p. 195). We want to be clear that we too believe there is much room for improvement in contemporary schooling and education; however, we will be making different suggestions to move us there.

RETHINKING KNOWLEDGE THROUGH PEDAGOGY OF CONFIDENCE™

While neoliberal educational policies may have had a long and deep, hegemonic and marginalizing hold on the experiences of many students, we must remember that they make up a project that is actively being constructed, and it is not, in fact, natural or inevitable (Coleman, 2006) as proponents of the current policies would have you believe. In other words, schooling-as-usual, or "the grammar of schooling," can be challenged and transformed. Indeed, it requires rethinking knowledge, the subject of the next section, which, we suggest, can happen with re-conceptualizing and re-valuing leadership dedicated to fostering cultures of confidence.

What is needed to counter the "grammar of schooling" is an alternative orientation of thought, a critical pedagogy, such as the *Pedagogy of Confidence* (Jackson, 2011), as a way to address the "crime of squandered potential" (Jackson and McDermott, 2012) in urban education framed by neoliberalism. Pedagogy of Confidence amplifies the possibilities of ways of believing and being that are different from the limiting historical relationships shaped in and through hegemonic meta-narratives, the media, and educational policies. This alternative way of knowing, which dialogues with what students bring to school—their cultures, knowledges, and ways of being—provides teachers with seven operational practices for engaging and motivating students to demonstrate critical intellectual performances, and aims to build a community of learners which works to disrupt historical hierarchical configurations—to nurture a mediative learning community (Jackson, 2011) in which students, teachers, and leaders—through communal spaces, mediational practices, and reciprocal relationships—come to know, learn, and understand differently.

The Pedagogy of Confidence, as an alternative orientation of thought, is purposefully counter-hegemonic. Rather than focusing on and/or lamenting the perceived deficits of urban students, teachers, schools, and communities, the Pedagogy of Confidence is grounded in mining for strengths and challenging the conventional notion of "gifted." How could education be different, it asks, if learning is embodied in the lived experiences of urban students, rather than denigrating or disacknowledging them? What are the possibilities if we challenged the notion of the ways in which some students are "gift-ed"—that is, how some students continually receive gifts while others are systematically ignored in education—by providing urban students with the same approaches to learning that encourage students marked as "gifted" to pursue their interests, challenge their intelligence, follow their creative instincts, develop leadership skills, improve their self-esteem and social skills, and do all of this in an environment framed by trust and modified to accommodate individual needs through self-directed learning supported by a full range of enriching experiences and fueled by a belief in their ability and potential? The Pedagogy of Confidence shatters the delimiting current level of expectations for urban students and simultaneously acknowledges that supports need to be in place to cultivate cultures of confidence in urban schools. Several counter-hegemonic beliefs underpin this critical pedagogy: both students and teachers are viewed as capable; pedagogical and cultural orientation matters; and confidence is an important ingredient in learning and teaching. Furthermore, the Pedagogy of Confidence is based upon three transformative beliefs: intelligence is modifiable; all students benefit from a focus on critical intellectual performances; and learning is influenced by the interaction of culture, language, and cognition (for a more thorough discussion of these points, see Jackson, 2011).

Building from this understanding, the Pedagogy of Confidence engages particular practices that dramatically alter what is happening in classroom spaces in ways that transform expectations and relationships, and that question existing structures and practices. The focus of the Pedagogy of Confidence is on how teachers orient themselves to learning and teaching, rather than the neoliberal approach, which prescribes what is taught and how it is taught. The seven practices grounding the Pedagogy of Confidence are: identifying and activating student strengths, building relationships, eliciting high intellectual performance, providing enrichment, integrating prerequisites for academic learning, situating learning in the lives of students, and amplifying student voice.

Our goal, here, in thinking through the beliefs and practices outlined in the Pedagogy of Confidence is to attempt to articulate an embodiment of knowledge that diverges from rote procedures of curricula, standardized testing, and evaluative measures of assessment in order to foster cultures of confidence and rehumanize education. Like the Brazilian educator Paulo Freire, we posit a critical pedagogy that is ecologically concerned with questions of transformative education, social change and justice in the urban context, one that is counter-hegemonic, political, and involves the lived experiences of students. In this way students can think through lessons, reflecting on their lived experiences, make connections to the broader socio-cultural and political issues governing urban societies, and the possibilities for their contributions for transformative actions. Such lessons would speak to a range of conversations involving teachers and students about the complexities of power, privilege, and knowledge production as installed through the configurations of urban education. It would allow students to be the center of their knowledge production rather than passive depositories. It allows students to engage in political dialogues with the classroom pedagogue to hone critical interpretive, dialogic, communicative, civic, and analytical tools. In the urban context, such a framework allows students to come into an understanding of dominant/colonial forms of knowledge embedded within curricula; what constitutes emancipatory ways of knowing; how they come to be located through these paradigms within their everyday world; and the particular ways of leading the self through these hegemonic epistemological terrains. This provides space for students and teachers to co-create cultures of confidence, cultures of support, cultures of alternative ways of being.

A critical pedagogy, then, works to rupture hegemonic relationships of students, teachers, administrators, and communities. The Pedagogy of Confidence allows space for teachers to learn from students and community members as much as students and community members learn from teachers. One of the hallmarks of the Pedagogy

of Confidence is Student Voice/NUA (National Urban Alliance), where, among other things, students become co-learners with their teachers in professional learning sessions. Students learn about learning as a way to empower them. They co-design lessons as a way to dialogically engage with teachers around teaching.

They present lessons to other students and to teachers as a way to transform pedagogy throughout the school. The Pedagogy of Confidence is not, therefore, content with simply changing what happens in a classroom or multiple classrooms. Instead, it is meant to be a culture-shifting mechanism designed to topple hegemonic relationships, ways of being, and definitions of learning. It is designed to transform schools into mediative learning communities. As Jackson (2011) indicates:

> Mediative learning communities are communities in which all participants (teachers, principals, and students) are emancipated and empowered to share their voices to transform the school into an oasis of success where strengths are valued and self-directed learning is enabled. (p. 4)

FEARLESS LEADING: RE-CONCEPTUALIZING AND RE-VALUING LEADERSHIP IN THE URBAN LANDSCAPE

As we come to conclude, we draw on *Aim High, Achieve More: How to Transform Urban Schools Through Fearless Leadership* (Jackson and McDermott, 2012), which conceptualizes fearless leadership by addressing a set of corresponding values that come to inform urban educational leadership for transformational schooling and education. These values are affirmation, inspiration, and mediation, which, taken holistically, re-value the ways in which schools respond to historical and contemporary issues of marginalization.

By thinking through questions of leadership in urban education, we ask, how do we come to re-conceptualize the notion of leadership as a model of leading the self? In other words, what does it mean to think of self-actualization by way of leadership in urban education? What do urban leaders need to be fearless about and what are the ways in which they can come to lead fearlessly in schooling and education?

Our work is based upon three key assumptions about transforming leading and learning.

- Transforming urban schools to disrupt their histories and current state is too complicated to be the work of an individual. It requires a purposeful toppling of the hegemonic ordering of leader-follower relationships, universalized standards and individualized meritocracy by way of competition.

- All constituents (students, teachers, leaders, and community) need to be leaders in the transformation of themselves, which leads to the co-transformation of the culture of the school and uncovers cultures of confidence that can undo hegemonic forces toward market-driven goals and banking models of learning.

- How participants in this process of transformation understand themselves in relation to social spaces and histories matters, so that they can rewrite the narrative that too often marks them as deficient. Transformative critical leadership necessitates asking tough questions of stopgap policies such as who does the policy benefit, who produced the policy, and what is the policy productive of?

Our position is that through re-conceptualizing leadership, urban schools can be transformed from within in ways that create a culture that is purposefully made different than what is proposed by the neoliberal educational agenda, a culture that has the ability to stoke potential; to disrupt existing conceptions of learning, power, and privilege; and to lead to equitable practices for achievement and self-actualization. We encourage critical engagement amongst official leaders—leaders who possess titles—and unofficial leaders—those who come into leadership by way of community membership, race, class, gender, and language—to name and mark power and privilege. In other words, leaders must be prepared to destabilize their position by asking what conditions make their power and privilege possible and how can we re-conceptualize leadership to be more inclusive? The re-conceptualization of leadership is multifold. It requires dismantling *who* is made recognizable as a "leader," as well as what metaphors are engaged to inform models of leadership. In neoliberal approaches, leaders are often conceptualized as "all-knowing," charismatic individuals who both define the ultimate goals and impose the methods to attain those goals. Instead, as reframed by Jackson and McDermott (2009, 2012), leadership should engage different metaphors—those of

architect, soul-friend, muse, and minister (for detailed discussion on how these metaphors have been framed, see Jackson and McDermott, 2012)—to reflect the values for transformative education by way of critical pedagogy. We suggest, then, that leaders who conceptualize themselves differently position themselves differently and perform differently.

Time and again we have seen schools transformed when leaders respond to a call to action and open up the spaces for shared re-conceptualization of leadership that enables a process that is organic to students' lived experiences. For educational leadership to rupture hegemonic conceptions of schooling, hierarchical notions of leadership must be ruptured. Leaders capable of challenging the dominant system do so from a confident sense of self, a critical moral compass, and a sense of urgency. They are radically confident, radically present, and radically strategic. They are radical in the sense that they get to the *root* of what really matters, they understand and unmask the socio-historical and current conditions that drain the energy from urban education, and they ignite and sustain a mutually shared transformational process (Jackson and McDermott, 2012).

Getting to the root of what matters involves urban leaders collectively building confidence of students and teachers, as well as entire communities who may be worn down by the narratives others have written about their lives, their worth, and their potential. Fearless leadership, then, involves leaders throwing off the "neoliberal straitjacket" by uncovering, asserting, recognizing, and valuing their lives, worth, and potential. When school communities look at the contemporary situation through the lens of the "crime of squandered potential" (Jackson and McDermott, 2012), they discard the notion that school failure lies within them, and instead they amplify that failure lies within the ways urban schools have been conceptualized. This alternative frame of reference enables them to find ways to cultivate their strengths and critically question key aspects of the neoliberal agenda.

To garner the strength and vision to engage communities in a shared, countercultural re-imagining of educational spaces requires a different kind of leadership. We are suggesting that fearless leadership involves acts of mediation through the Pedagogy of Confidence which dialogues with the production, dissemination, and reception of knowledge within schooling practices.

It involves drawing from the varied representations of the classroom as a *text* that constitute different teachers and learners, to come to make possible a critical theoretical framework that disentangles the historical tensions of curricula as governed through schooling practices. Thus fearless leadership inculcates a mode of thinking that self-reflexively considers how different ways of making meaning come to wittingly or unwittingly inform one's thoughts and resultant actions. In so doing, fearless leaders come into a critical conceptual map that amplifies oppressive and subordinate spaces, at the same time enabling themselves with the praxis to transcend their lived sociocultural experiences under the governing hegemonic nexus of schooling and society.

The production of fearless leaders also involves the cultural embodiment of the self. Part and parcel of leadership of the self is with decoding the ways in which meaning comes to be made through culture and how this meaning comes to be valued and devalued within schools. Yet these culturally inscribed ways of knowing one's sociocultural environment are filled with discontinuities, contradictions, and encumberings. If our collective goal is with cultivating critically fearless leaders of the self in urban education through mediative learning communities that uncover cultures of confidence, we propose a particular leadership of the self which dialogues with these discontinuities, contradictions, and encumberings immanent to everyday social processes to build communal spaces for transformative education, social change, and social justice.

REFERENCES

Albrecht-Crane, C. (2005). Pedagogy as friendship: Identity and affect in the conservative classroom. *Cultural Studies*, 19(4), 491–514.

Apple, M. (1995). *Education and power*. New York: Routledge.

Apple, M. (2001). Comparing neo-liberal projects and inequality in education. *Comparative Education*, 37(4), 409–423.

Coleman, D. (2006). *White civility: The literary project of English Canada*. Toronto: University of Toronto Press.

Darling-Hammond, L. (2010). *The flat worlds and education: How America's commitment to equity will determine our future*. New York: Teachers College Press.

Davies, B. (2000). *A body of writing: 1990–1999*. Walnut Creek, CA: AltaMira Press.

Dehli, K. (2003). Making the parent and the researcher: Genealogy meets ethnography in research on contemporary school reforms. In M. Tamboukou & S. J. Ball (Eds.), *Dangerous encounters: Genealogy and ethnography* (pp. 133–151). New York: Peter Lang.

Dei, G. J. S., I. M. James, S. James-Wilson, L. L. Karumanchery, and J. Zine. (2000). *Removing the Margins: The challenges and possibilities of inclusive schooling*. Toronto: Canadian Scholars' Press.

Delpit, L. (1995). *Other people's children: Cultural conflict in the classroom*. New York: The New Press.

Duncan-Andrade, J. M. R. and E. Morrell. (2008). *The art of critical pedagogy: Possibilities for moving from theory to practice in urban schools*. New York: Peter Lang.

Dweck, C. (2000). *Self theories: Their role in motivation, personality, and development*. New York: Psychology Press.

Essed, P. and D. T. Goldberg. (2002). Cloning cultures: The social injustice of sameness. *Ethnic and Racial Studies*, 25(6), 1066–1082.

Fine, M. (1991). *Framing dropouts: Notes on the politics of an urban public high school*. Albany: State University of New York Press.

Freire, P. (1970). *Pedagogy of the Oppressed*. New York: Continuum.

Freire, P. (1985). *The Politics of Education: Culture, Power and Liberation*. Westport CT: Bergin & Garvey.

Giroux, A. H. (2005). The Terror of Neoliberalism: Rethinking the Significance of Cultural Politics. *College Literature, 32*(1), 1–19.

Giroux, A. H. (2001). *Theory and resistance in education: Towards a pedagogy for the opposition*. Connecticut: Bergin & Garvey.

Harvey, D. (2005). *A Brief History of Neoliberalism*. Oxford: University Press.

Jackson, Y. (2011). *The Pedagogy of Confidence: Inspiring high intellectual performance in urban schools*. New York: Teachers College Press.

Jackson, Y. and V. McDermott. (2009). Fearless leading. *Educational Leadership*, 67(2), 34–39.

Jackson, Y. and V. McDermott. (2012). *Aim high, achieve more: How to transform urban schools through fearless leadership*. Alexandria, VA: ASCD.

Kincheloe, J. (2010). *Knowledge and Critical Pedagogy: An Introduction*. New York: Springer.

Klaf, S. and M. P. Kwan. (2010). The neoliberal straitjacket and public education in the United States: Understanding contemporary education reform and its urban implications. *Urban Geography*, 31(2), 194–210.

Ladson-Billings, G. (2000). Racialized discourses and ethnic epistemologies. In N. K. Denzin & Y. S. Lincoln (Eds.),

Handbook of qualitative research (pp. 257–277). Thousand Oaks, CA: Sage Publications.

Larner, W. (2000). Neoliberalism: Policy, ideology, governmentality. *Studies in Policy Economy*, 63, 5–25.

Marcuse, H. (2009a). Lecture on education, Brooklyn College, 1968. In D. Kellner, T. Lewis, C. Pierce, and K. D. Cho (Eds.), *Marcuse's challenge to education* (pp. 33–38). New York: Rowman & Littlefield Publishers, Inc.

Marcuse, H. (2009b). Lecture on higher education, and politics, Berkeley, 1975. In D. Kellner, T. Lewis, C. Pierce, and K. D. Cho (Eds.), *Marcuse's challenge to education* (pp. 39–43). New York: Rowman & Littlefield Publishers, Inc.

McDermott, M. and A. Madan. (2012). Avoiding the Missionary (Dis)Position: Research Relations and (Re)Presentation. In Cannella, G. S. and S. R. Steinberg (Eds.) *Critical qualitative research reader* (pp. 235–245). New York: Peter Lang.

McDermott, M. and M. Simmons. (2013). Embodiment and the Spatialization of Race. In G. J. S. Dei, and M. Lordan, *Contemporary issues in the sociology of race and ethnicity: A critical reader* (pp. 153–168). New York: Peter Lang.

McMahon, B. J. and J. P. Portelli. (2012). The Challenges of Neoliberalism in Education: Implications for Student Engagement. In B. J. McMahon and J. P. Portelli (Eds.), *Student Engagement in Urban Schools: Beyond Neoliberal Discourses* (pp. 1–9). Charlotte, NC: Information Age Publishing, Inc.

Milner, H. (2012). But what is Urban Education? *Urban Education* 47(3), 556–561.

National Commission on Education (1983). A nation at risk. Washington, DC: U.S. Government Printing Office.

Popkewitz, T. (1997). The production of reason and power: Curriculum history and intellectual traditions. *Journal of Curriculum Studies*, 29(2), 131–164.

Simmons, M. (2011). The race to modernity: Understanding culture through the Diasporic-self. In Wane, N., A. Kempf, and M. Simmons (Eds.), *The Politics of Cultural Knowledge* (pp. 37–50). Rotterdam: Sense Publishers.

Stanley, W. B. (1992). *Curriculum for Utopia: Social Reconstruction and Critical Pedagogy in the Postmodern Era*. Albany: State University of New York Press.

Steinberg, S. (2012). It's all just Smoke and Mirrors: Isn't there more than one way to be diverse. In H. K. Wright, M. Singh and R. Race (Eds.), *Precarious International Multicultural Education: Hegemony, Dissent and Rising Alternatives* (pp. 347–370). Rotterdam: Sense Publishers.

CHAPTER 6

Bringing Urban High School Reform to Scale

Rapidly Moving Dramatic Numbers of Students to Proficient Performance

Glenn Baete, Joe Burks, Marty Pollio, and Craig Hochbein

INTRODUCTION

The purpose of this paper is to provide urban practitioners hope for the increased probability of effective, scalable, and sustainable high school reform. After articulating the requirements and challenges of taking high school reform to scale, the paper describes the significant success of Project Proficiency (PP), a large urban district's high school reform effort. The next part outlines the results of three empirical studies of the impact of PP across eleven high schools, followed by a detailed description of PP's overarching strategy of "guaranteeing competency" and its four organizing components. The paper finally argues that PP meets a scalability litmus test and merits further research for PP's potential to establish high school reform to scale in an urban district.

HIGH SCHOOL REFORM

In 1932 a group of over three hundred colleges and universities partnered with thirty high schools in one of the twenty-first century's first high school reform projects. In what was later called the 8-Year Study, a cross section of American high schools had the freedom to redesign their curriculum without the fear of graduates denied admittance to college for lacking traditional entrance requirements (Aiken, 1942). Given the charge to redefine the purpose of their high schools, 8-Year participants connected teaching and learning to emerging knowledge of human growth and development, experimented with longer class periods, eliminated divisions between curricular and extracurricular activities, and modified graduation requirements. In turn, the participating colleges unconditionally admitted project

high school graduates who secured the principal's recommendation and submitted a record of their involvement in activities, interests, and academic work. The study revealed that students from 8-Year Schools were neither ill-prepared for college work, nor displayed negative differences in college performance than their non-8-Year counterparts (Aiken, 1942). Subsequent analysis revealed that secondary schools with the most progressive reform strategies produced gains that exceeded non-participating schools.

Seven decades after Aiken (1942) reported the findings of the 8-Year Study, educators continue to grapple with high school reform. The desire for educators to make significant and lasting instructional improvements is high as public confidence in public schools is at record-low levels (Gallup, 2011). Modern policymakers seek to create a twenty-first-century workforce with globally competitive skills, improve American productivity and economic growth, and continue the United States' role as world power (National Center on Education and the Economy, 2008). National leaders have asserted that education, particularly at the high school level, will stem the tide of mediocrity that threatens America's prosperity (Obama, 2011; U.S. Department of Education, 1983). Since the work of Aiken (1942), a plethora of studies over the past half-century have investigated the efforts taken by districts and high schools to implement large-scale reforms (Berends, Bodilly, and Kirby, 2002; Bryk, 2010; Consortium on Chicago School Research, 2010; Crandall et al., 1982; Cuban, 1984; Darling-Hammond, 2006; Datnow, 2005; Datnow and Stringfield, 2000; Fullan, 2000; Fullan, Bertani, and Quinn, 2004; Fullan and Pomfret, 1977; Holdzkom, 2002; McLaughlin, 1990; Oxley and Kassissieh, 2008; Oxley and Luers, 2010; Quint, 2006; Rorrer, Skrla, and Schuerich, 2008; Stringfield, Reynolds, and Schaffer, 2008). These researchers identified successes and challenges with implementing high school reform and cited key considerations, which included identifying the purpose of the reform, creating structures necessary for successful implementation, and providing effective internal and external supports to scale up those reforms.

ELEMENTS OF SUCCESSFUL REFORMS

Definition of Purpose

For the past twenty years, the desire of school and district leaders to meet state and federal accountability measures and avoid sanctions has driven American high school reform (Datnow, 2005; Fullan, 2000, 2011; No Child Left Behind, 2001; Race to the Top, 2010). While such mandates often did not require a school to identify a specific reform initiative, three of the four current federal turnaround models require high schools to redesign structures and use frequent benchmarking to measure progress (School Improvement Fund, 2010). Coexistent with meeting accountability requirements, many reform efforts sought to assist students who enter high schools ill-prepared for the rigor necessary to succeed (Datnow, 2005; Holdzkom, 2002; Quint, 2006). Thirty years before Race to the Top (RTTT), Fullan and Pomfret (1977) discussed the moral imperative for schools to raise student achievement levels and close achievement gaps for all individuals and schools. Federal legislation supported this trend, as No Child Left Behind (NCLB) guidelines required schools to show achievement gains for traditionally disadvantaged student populations and other groups. School, district, and state accountability has remained as a subject of debate on the local, state, and federal levels serving as a call for schools to adopt reform efforts.

A great deal of scrutiny regarding high-stakes accountability systems and their counterproductive effects exists. Fullan (2011) asserted that such accountability produces a negative attitude in teachers and schools and creates a destructive effect on a school culture, "assuming that educators will respond to these prods by putting the effort to make the necessary change" (p. 8). In contrast to the negative impact that high-stakes accountability has on reform, Fullan identified four drivers of change necessary to judge the effectiveness and sustainability of reform efforts: fostering intrinsic motivation of teachers, engaging educators and students in continuous instructional improvement efforts, inspiring collective teamwork, and affecting 100 percent of students in the effort.

In her identification of NCLB accountability as an impediment to high school reform efforts, Darling-Hammond (2006) identified four elements present in high-performing urban schools: program personalization, well-qualified teachers, use of a common set of core academic standards, and targeted supports for struggling students. She noted that "complicated rules that accompany NCLB have unintentionally made it more difficult for many heroic high schools in low-income neighborhoods to do their work well and keep the neediest students in school and moving to productive futures" (Darling-Hammond, 2006, p. 646). Darling-Hammond suggested five problems with current NCLB legislation and called for repealing NCLB and identifying ways in which to support instructional innovation for America's neediest students.

Cultivation of Support

To ensure that schools meet accountability benchmarks and have implemented structures that foster and sustain high school reform, district leaders must utilize a wide variety of internal and external supports. Internal supports include actions taken by an individual school or district to promote the reform effort and implementation. Fullan et al. (2004) called for school districts to build coalitions of leaders who have the ability to engineer reform and increase engagement with stakeholders through effective two-way communication. Datnow (2005) cited the importance of institutionalizing reform and the multiple factors that lead to the stability of the effort, noting that, "forces at the state, district, design team, school, and classroom level all interacted to shape the longevity of the reform" (p. 145). Full and sustained reform requires district stewardship that promotes a strong vision of instruction, focuses on a strong instructional core, shifts resources to support change, and ensures swift implementation (Oxley and Luers, 2010). The internal capacity of a school district to build, support, and sustain reform efforts is key to its ultimate success (Bryk, 2010; Datnow, 2005; Fullan, 2000; Fullan et al., 2004; Holdzkom, 2002; McLaughlin, 1990).

In a narrative synthesis of eighty-one peer-reviewed research articles on district reform, Rorrer et al. (2008) identified four essential roles of school districts to support school reform. First, the authors found that districts provide instructional leadership that generates the will and capacity of reform for all schools in a district. As a second function, school districts reoriented the organization, refined organizational structures and processes, and made changes to district culture. Establishing policy coherence is a third function of school districts that involves managing federal, state, and local policies in addition to aligning district resources. A fourth role, maintaining an equity focus, involves a district's work to own and identify inequities within a district and establishing practices that promote accessibility and transparency for all schools within a district.

In addition to cultivating internal partnerships, collaborating with external partners assists with the development of strategies, procurement of resources, collection of feedback, and dissemination of professional development (American Institutes for Research 1999, 2006; Fullan et al., 2004; Fullan and Pomphret, 1977). However, in their review of scale-up reform efforts, Bodily, Glennan, Kerr, and Galegher (2004) noted that technical assistance providers were often relatively young and "provide only limited evidence of their value and have only limited capacity to deliver high quality services" (p. 2). While the supports received through partnerships with technical assistance providers was a popular means to accomplish whole school or district reform, the ability of a reform effort to adapt to the unique context of the schools served was equally important.

A delicate balance between reform fidelity and sensitivity to the individual context of a school makes full redesign effort implementation a challenge. Datnow (2005) noted that successful reform designs institutionalize reform involving "a multilevel process of embedding an innovation in the structure and norms of the organization" (p. 123). The ability of a school or district to operationalize the key elements of a reform effort while adapting to the unique context in which a school operates was critical to the success of a reform (Aiken, 1942; Datnow, 2005; Datnow and Stringfield, 2000; Fullan and Pomphret, 1977; Holdzkom, 2002; Stringfield et al., 2008). In addition to a school district's adaptability and flexibility, their ability to manage the supports and

activities from a variety of stakeholders was critical for scale-up success. Bodily et al. (2004) noted that, "if scale-up is to succeed, the actors involved—including developers, district officials, school leaders, and teachers—must jointly address a set of known, interconnected tasks, especially aligning policies and infrastructure in coherent ways to sustain practice" (p. 648).

Alignment of Structures

To make reform successful amidst the turmoil and politically charged NCLB landscape and take reform efforts to scale, interdependence is necessary between school structures and instructional practices (McLaughlin, 1990; Oxley and Kassissieh, 2008; Quint, 2006). Although reform efforts that target students most in need experience relatively few hurdles to implementation, similar reforms focused on comprehensive changes to a school tend to encounter many more difficulties. Reorganization status may debase not only the school and staff, but also the reforms applied to it. Oxley and Luers (2010) studied the progress of the federal Small Learning Communities (SLC) program and noted that districts that proactively launched reform initiatives across all high schools, regardless of their accountability status, conveyed the message that reform initiatives are a set of best practices for all schools as opposed to interventions suitable only for low performers, thereby generating more favorable prospects for implementation.

Researchers have noted that structural considerations are necessary at the school, district, and legislative levels to create and sustain innovation. For instance, Stringfield et al. (2008) described how leaders and educators in high reliability schools established finite goals, standardized operating procedures, and utilized data and data analysis to create a context in which failure is unacceptable. Fullan et al. (2004) identified the importance of finding appropriate structures that give districts a common direction and collective purpose, focusing on improving teaching and learning for both adults and students, and providing role clarity. McLaughlin (1990) called for revisions in existing federally funded reform programs in order to "provide resources and support professional growth" (p. 13). However, the challenge for reformers is to move quickly from the development of structures to close examination and refinement of such structures, so as to influence instructional practices and raise student achievement (Bryk, 2010; Datnow, 2005; Fullan, 2000; Fullan and Pomfret, 1977; Quint, 2006).

PROBLEMS TAKING REFORM TO SCALE

Sustaining high school redesign efforts in a politically charged and turbulent context is difficult for districts wishing to improve schools and maintain public confidence. Current NCLB and School Improvement Grant (SIG) guidelines require quick improvements in order to avoid sanctions that remove principals and teachers, relinquish control of the school to an external management organization, adopt a performance-based transformation model, or even close a persistently low-achieving school. The disconnect between the time required to implement a reform at scale and the time mandated to improve remains a key factor in failed efforts. In his review of Comprehensive School Reform (CSR) projects, Holdzkom (2002) observed that gains following a school reform effort became evident after three years of implementation. Fullan (2000) noted that high school reform success requires five to six years and district-wide efforts need six to eight years. High stakes accountability systems that require quick gains hinder schools implementing reforms by forcing schools to put reform aside for test preparation, placing a premium on instructional strategies versus deep reform models, eliminating programs that may be of great benefit to students but not measured on accountability tests, and creating rules and policies that stymie innovation (Darling-Hammond, 2006; Datnow, 2005; Holdzkom, 2002).

Elements of school reform driven by purpose, implementation structures, and effective internal and external supports have been necessary and at times successful, but not reliably sufficient to move significant numbers of students to proficient performance in urban school districts (Earl, Torrance, and Sutherland, 2006; Payne, 2008; Stringfield and Datnow, 1998). Districts fall into a "fragmented circuit of school improvement activity" (Newman et al., p. 298). Instead of a variety of programmatic changes, schools need instructional program coherence to coordinate structures, staff working conditions, and resources uniformly aimed at improving student achievement (Honig and Hatch, 2004; Kedro,

2004; Newmann et al., 2001; Oxley, 2008). Genuine and sustainable reform may require coherence of the elements of reform through an overarching strategy (Childress, Elmore, Grossman, and Akinola, 2004).

Newmann et al. (2001) defined instructional program coherence as "a set of interrelated programs for students and staff that are guided by a common framework for curriculum, instruction, assessment, and learning climate and are pursued over a sustained period" (p. 299). Through teacher surveys, student test scores, and field studies within 222 Chicago elementary schools, Newmann et al. found schools that improved instructional coherence also improved student achievement. From their study, three conditions surfaced as evidence for improved instructional coherence: a common instructional framework for guiding teaching and learning, staff working conditions to support implementation of the common framework, and coordinated resources to support the framework.

PROJECT PROFICIENCY

The Jefferson County Public Schools (JCPS), a large urban district of approximately 100,000 students in Louisville, Kentucky, has created a system, Project Proficiency (PP), that is designed to meet the Newmann et al. (2001) litmus test for robust, instructional program coherence. Results from the 2010–2011 school year indicated that all twenty-one JCPS high schools gained in reading and math proficiency, with the eleven persistently low-achieving (PLA) and near-PLA schools averaged a 14 percent gain in reading and a 17 percent gain in math, tripling state gains (Kentucky Department of Education, 2011).

To connect practitioners and coordinate reform efforts amid the landscape of NCLB sanctions and challenges of advancing disadvantaged high school students inherent with large urban districts, PP boldly established an overarching strategy of "guaranteed competency," or the goal of ensuring learning of key reading and math standards by each student. Through the "strategic function" (Childress, Elmore, and Grossman, 2006, p. 59) of guaranteed competency, JCPS created district-wide instructional program coherence evidenced by a common instructional framework, complementary staff working conditions, and supportive resources.

Common instructional framework. Through a narrow curriculum, balanced assessment system, and purpose-driven instructional principles, PP enabled teachers to guarantee student competency of three key standards each grading period and leverage a coherent common instructional framework. First, each six weeks, the district established three priority standards with corresponding curriculum maps for core high school English and math courses, providing clear learning targets and expectations for staff and students. Unifying schools and the district around a reduced and nonnegotiable set of content standards provided a common direction for students, school staff, and district administrators. These goals resembled the set of goals that characterized highly reliable organizations (HRO) (Datnow and Stringfield, 2000; Stringfield et al., 2008).

Second, guaranteeing competency produced a "balanced assessment system" (Stiggins, 2008, p. 3) to track student progress. PP included a district diagnostic assessment to determine early levels of student understanding of each standard, a summative proficiency assessment for an end-of-grading-period measure, and frequent teacher-designed formative assessments to evaluate student improvement toward competency. Basing student grades on demonstrations of competency unified teachers around standards-based instruction and assessment. Teachers reinforced their standards-based approach with opportunities for students to reflect on their own progress, cited by Stiggins (2008) to positively impact student achievement. To ensure learning, teachers were required to guide each student to demonstrate competency for each of the three key standards by the time the proficiency assessment was administered, and those scoring below 80 percent on the proficiency assessment were guided to recover or correct their work until they met the threshold target. Through a balance of diagnostic, formative, and summative assessments designed to guarantee student competency of clear standards, PP converted high school assignments, tests, and grades into a coherent system to ensure learning.

Third, similar to the Coalition of Essential Schools design to improve teaching and learning through guiding principles rather than a packaged program (Coalition of Essential Schools, 2011), PP coalesced instructors around the precepts of shared accountability for high-level, standards-based teaching, and ownership of student results. To guarantee competency, teachers

needed to create tasks through which students could demonstrate understanding, develop lessons with focused learning targets aligned with those tasks, and ensure each student demonstrated understanding of each key standard. With instruction tied to required outcomes, teachers regularly adjusted how they delivered instruction, assessed, and intervened for struggling and reluctant learners. Guaranteeing competency transformed teachers from "directors into diagnosticians" (Kedro, 2004, p. 32), shifted their mission from ownership of teaching to ownership of learning, and merged curriculum, assessment, and instructional systems into a seamless, coherent, and common instructional framework.

Working conditions. Complementing a common instructional framework, PP fostered working conditions characterized by collective teacher efficacy (DuFour, DuFour, Eaker, and Karhanek, 2004; Newmann et al., 2001). Establishing the goal of guaranteed student competency generated levels of collaborative practice, decision-making, and professional development not previously experienced by teachers. Due to the goal of moving each student to levels of competency by the end of each six weeks, teachers of common courses met weekly and sometimes daily to diagnose learning gaps and exchange updates on the numbers of students meeting competency. Drawing ideas from one another, instructors collectively designed new lessons, tasks, and interventions to address student deficiencies. District resource teachers provided recommendations for adjustments and ideas from other teacher teams. School-based administrators promptly responded to teacher requests for time, resources, and support. Collaborative reflection, collective action, and collegial "expertise development" (Bryk, 2009, p. 599) produced a coherent learning climate for practitioners through their "agency that produced the texts, rules, and guidelines of their school change process" (Stringfield and Datnow, 2002, p. 282).

Coordinated resources. JCPS completed its coherent instructional program design with unprecedented support resources of curricular materials, data management, and principal leadership. Childress, Elmore, and Grossman (2006) asserted, "Only the district office can create such a plan, identify and spread best practices, develop leadership capabilities at all levels, build information systems to monitor student improvement, and hold people accountable for results" (p. 55). With input from local school practitioners, district curriculum specialists identified the key standards for each core course from state-mandated content, developed curriculum pacing guides for each grading period, and designed corresponding diagnostic and proficiency assessments.

To provide effective and timely student performance information and positively impact interventions at the classroom, school, and district levels (Stiggins and DuFour, 2009), JCPS designed a web-based data entry system for diagnostic, formative, and summative assessment results that provided teachers with details for tracking student demonstration of competency, diagnosing possible content misunderstandings, and converting standards-based evaluation of student competency into grades (Jefferson County Public Schools, 2011a). Leadership made the ultimate difference for effective supervision and support. Principals provided common planning and facilitated teacher learning team protocols to foster collective efficacy; district and state improvement funding afforded additional materials, staff, and stipends; and district leaders organized principals into accountability teams for comparing school data trends, exchanging leadership innovations, and assessing district instructional needs.

Promoting coherence through a district-wide strategy of guaranteeing student competency of key standards, JCPS implemented PP to move dramatic numbers of high school students to proficient performance in one school year. However, institutionalizing this reform across its urban high schools confronted JCPS with a formidable challenge. Fullan (2001) asserted, "25 percent of the solution is having good directional ideas; 75 percent is figuring out how to get there in one local context after another" (p. 268). Having met the criteria for instructional program coherence, JCPS needed to move its PP reform to scale at the district level.

PROJECT PROFICIENCY'S IMPACT ON STUDENT ACHIEVEMENT

To demonstrate the effect of PP on student achievement, we conducted three empirical studies that utilized similar quasi-experimental non-equivalent control group designs (Shadish, Cook, and Campbell, 2002). We compared the performance of students who received PP against two control groups. The first control group consisted of students enrolled in Algebra II from the year prior, not receiving the PP treatment. This comparison evaluated the performance of different students in the same subject area. The second control group consisted of the same students who received PP in Algebra II, but utilized their state assessment performance in another subject area, such as social studies or science. This comparison evaluated the performance of the same students in different subject areas. Together, these comparisons reduced the threats to validity and isolated the impact of PP on student performance on state assessments in Algebra II. In the tables and figures below we demonstrated the mean differences between groups; however, quantitative analysis using ordinary least squares regression, hierarchical linear modeling (HLM), and analysis of variance (ANOVA) determined that PP strengthened the relationship between grades and performance on state mathematics assessments, improved student achievement on a state mathematics assessment, and provided an effective support to students most at-risk for failure and subsequent drop out.

First, our studies revealed that PP accentuated the association between classroom grades and academic achievement. Within both the PP cohort and the non-PP cohort, grades had a low-positive association with state test scores. For students evaluated on a standards-based grading approach, the association between grades and test scores was stronger than those students evaluated on a traditional grading model (Table 6.1). In addition, all students, minority students, and at-risk students had stronger correlations between grades and state assessments when experiencing standards-based grading.

Most importantly for the research on standards-based grading within PP, grades became much more of a valid indicator of achievement as measured by success on the state assessment. Students who experienced traditional grading methods in both cohorts scored below proficient nearly 75 percent of the time even though they received an A or a B in the specific content class. For students experiencing standards-based grading, over 55 percent of students scored above proficient when they received an A or a B in the content course. As a result, over twice as many students scored proficient or above on the state assessment when successfully scoring above average on a standards-based grading approach as opposed to a traditional grading model. We determined that standards-based grades were a more valid and reliable predictor of student achievement than traditional-based grades.

Table 6.1.   Mean State Scores of Cohorts by Classroom Grade

Grade	PP-Math[a]	Non-PP-Math[b]	PP-Science[c]
A	47.31	35.40	34.26
B	37.48	28.69	29.50
C	31.18	23.34	24.69
D	26.93	19.96	23.29
U	22.34	16.59	22.04

Note. [a]State mean = 37.00. [b]State mean = 36.00. [c]State mean = 36.00.

Second, through HLM models controlling for prior achievement and SES at the student level and SES and PP implementation at the classroom level, we determined that PP increased mathematics achievement and decreased variation between classrooms. In PP classrooms, mathematics scores increased nearly one-half of a performance level on the state assessment and yielded a 22 percent increase in students reaching state-established proficiency benchmarks (table 6.2). We found a statistically significant decrease in between-classroom variation in PP classrooms, with estimates diminishing from 31 percent to 14 percent under PP. We concluded that PP ameliorated the negative effect of classroom SES on student achievement, and the combination of improved mean achievement and decreased variation between classes implied that instructional practices changed with large numbers of teachers across PP schools.

Third, empirical evidence suggested that PP impacted the math achievement of students most at risk of dropping out of school. We found statistically significant increases in mathematics achievement for at-risk PP students who met dropout-predictive criteria (Balfanz et al., 2007). The study revealed that 14 percent of PP students who scored below proficient on the eighth grade state assessment met the proficiency benchmark in the eleventh grade, as opposed to 6 percent in the non-PP group (figure 6.1). In addition, 77 percent of PP students with proficient or higher eighth grade results scored proficient in eleventh grade, as opposed to only 33 percent in the non-PP group. Finally, statistically significant gains were revealed in state assessment scores from the eighth grade to the eleventh grade.

PROJECT PROFICIENCY AS A SCALABLE INSTRUCTIONAL DESIGN

Faced with external demands to rival international academic standards, produce a globally competitive workforce, and rapidly move dramatic numbers of students to levels of proficiency, educational practitioners, policymakers, and researchers continue to search for effective urban high school reform scalable at the district level. Results of these three empirical studies of the impact of PP across eleven high schools in a large urban district indicated that teachers more accurately evaluated student work, classrooms more equally provided instructional quality, and at-risk students significantly increased their achievement in mathematics. We suggest that the PP design not only reached every persistently low-achieving high school in JCPS, but also exhibited the "multidimensional nature" (Coburn, 2003, p. 3) of authentic scalability through its "depth, spread, shift of ownership, and sustainability" (p. 4).

Table 6.2.   Students Meeting Grade 11 Proficiency Benchmarks Based on Prior Achievement and Project Proficiency Implementation

	Cohort	Non-Proficient Grade 11		Proficient Grade 11	
		N	%	N	%
Non-Proficient Grade 8	NPP	812	69.82	54	4.64
	PP	723	56.13	216	16.77
Proficient Grade 8	NPP	161	13.84	136	11.69
	PP	71	5.51	278	21.60

Note. NPP = Non-Project Proficiency (N = 1,163). PP = Project Proficiency (N = 1,288).

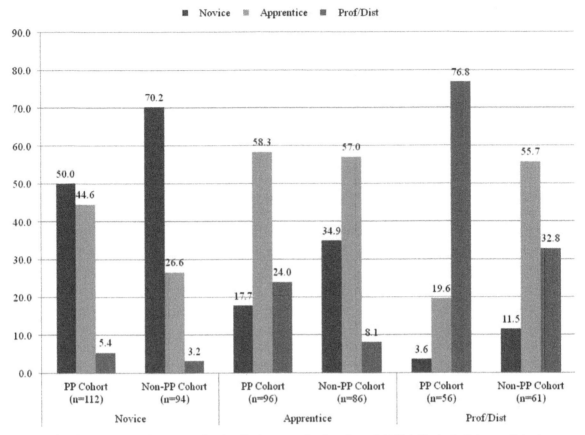

Figure 6.1. *Comparison of Changes in Student Performance Designations of At-Risk Students Between Cohorts*

PP consisted of four facets. First, the district provided a curriculum map, diagnostic assessment, and end-of-six-weeks summative proficiency assessment for each grading period based on three key standards or content categories. Second, teachers were asked to create tasks and assignments through which students could demonstrate competency for each key standard. Competency was not proficiency or mastery, but a level of understanding that a teacher respected. Teachers evaluated student work with standards-based grading, evaluating student understanding rather than simply averaging numbers. Third, with the help of district resource teachers, curriculum specialists, and local administrators, teachers collaboratively and collectively sought to guide 100 percent of their students to demonstrate competency for each of the three key standards by the time the proficiency assessment was administered. The district provided a web-based, electronic system for teachers to collect and track results of diagnostic, formative, and summative assessments. Fourth, students scoring below 80 percent on a six-weeks proficiency assessment were guided to recover missed content until they scored 80 percent or higher.

Depth. The results of these studies revealed that the interrelated dimensions of scale (Coburn, 2003) were evident in each of the four facets of the PP reform. The author noted that a depth in the change of classroom practice is necessary to bring substantial educational reform to scale. According to Coburn (2003), "Because teachers draw on their prior knowledge, beliefs, and experiences to interpret and enact reforms, they are likely to gravitate toward approaches that are congruent with their prior practices, focus on surface manifestations, rather than deep pedagogical principles" (Coburn, 2003, p. 4). The change to a standards-based grading approach within PP forced teachers to make profound changes to pedagogical principles that had dominated their classroom practice for decades. The four main tenets of PP aided teachers in their transition to a standards-based grading approach and led to "deep and consequential change in classroom practice" (Coburn, 2003, p. 4).

Based on the data from this research, the depth of instructional change caused by a move to standards-based grading led to an increased association between grades and achievement scores. The four main tenets of PP created conditions for depth in instructional change. First, math curriculum was condensed to three key standards for each six weeks. Prior to PP, the math curriculum was driven by state core content and district pacing guides that led to coverage of many topics with little emphasis on mastery of key standards. In order to implement a standards-based grading approach, PP established three key standards for each grading period. PP enabled teachers to evaluate students on their attainment of the three key standards for each six weeks.

Second, teachers created tasks that would demonstrate competency of the three key standards. Teachers could no longer use a hodgepodge of factors to determine a student's grade for the six-week period. Every task or assignment given to students directly measured their competency in one of the key standards for the six weeks. At the conclusion of each grading period, students were evaluated solely on their attainment of the three key standards established by PP. This move to standards-based grading was the change in pedagogical principles that established the depth required to move educational reform to scale.

Third, and possibly most important, teachers guaranteed the competency of every student in the three key standards. Teachers had to collaboratively find ways to establish interventions for students who did not attain proficiency in any of the key standards. Diagnostic and formative assessments provided data for teachers on student mastery of the three key standards for the grading period. Without the pedagogical change to standards-based grading, guaranteed competency of the standards would be impossible. Teachers had to evaluate the achievement level of students through standards-based grading in order to guarantee their competency in the key standards.

Fourth, PP provided a fail-safe opportunity for students to recover any standard that they had not mastered at the conclusion of the grading period. If the student still had not met proficiency standards by this time, teachers would provide remediation opportunities in order to guarantee competency. By establishing a depth of instructional change within all schools through implementation of standards-based grading, teachers were able

to evaluate student progress on the three key standards, grade students on their attainment of those standards, and provide opportunities after the grading period to recover missed standards and improve student grades. Through the implementation of standards-based grading in these schools, the four facets of PP provided the depth necessary to bring this instructional reform to scale.

Spread. PP created conditions for spread between classrooms and across eleven high schools in JCPS. Coburn's (2003) scalability framework identified the need for schools to "move beyond the spread of activities, materials, and structures to the propagation of 'beliefs, norms, and principles'" (p. 7). Through guaranteeing competency in three key standards, PP challenged teachers and school leaders to change existing beliefs about teaching and learning. In the new context, all students were required to reach a degree of competency prior to taking an end-of-unit proficiency assessment, thus requiring teachers to own the achievement results for each of their students. As opposed to prior practices that assigned low grades for students not demonstrating competency and the continuing with course content, PP required teachers and their professional learning communities to create instructional activities and targeted interventions to ensure competency prior to the end of a six-week grading period. The shared responsibility for students learning created conditions for substantive collaboration among teachers.

The combination of new instructional practices and supporting structures reflected a change in beliefs in PP schools. Professional collaboration became a new and highly valued norm for PP teachers. During formal and structured PLC meetings, teams of teachers met to review learning targets and plan instructional activities; examine student work to identify trends, needs, and instructional strategies; review diagnostic, formative, and proficiency data; and plan for school-wide student interventions. This increase in collective efficacy represents the spread of deep changes in instructional practices across classrooms and schools in Jefferson County. We find additional support for this finding. After controlling for prior achievement and individual and classroom SES, PP implementation decreased variation among classrooms by approximately 55 percent. Given that PP was implemented in 110 classrooms in eleven schools, reductions in between-classroom variation from 31 percent to 14 percent suggested that PP's changes in instruction, norms, beliefs, and principles created conditions for the spread of depth across JCPS classrooms. Carroll (2009) observed the futility of individual teachers working alone and their inability to "know and do everything to meet the needs of thirty diverse students every day throughout the school year" (p. 10). The author called for schools to become places that value and take full advantage of teamwork that is part of high-performance organizations across the world. Through implementing the four key elements of PP, strong collaboration created spread among teachers, ensured competency for all students, and deepened the instructional knowledge base.

In addition to identified increases in the number of schools implementing a reform, Coburn (2003) identified spread as to what extent district policies, procedures, and professional development reflect a reform effort. Leaders in JCPS challenged schools to examine traditional approaches to teaching and create a new instructional approach that "guarantees competency" for all students through an emphasis on key standards and changes in assessments, interventions, and support mechanisms. As opposed to the traditional instructional planning activities where individual teachers and schools review core content curriculum documents and create learning objectives and supporting activities, PP shifted the curriculum alignment responsibilities to the district and gave teachers a clearly articulated and aligned set of learning standard categories for each grading period. District leaders promoted the spread of the PP design across schools by creating diagnostic and proficiency assessments aligned to three key standards in the PP design and creating district-wide professional development on formative assessment, instructional strategies, and professional collaboration.

PP was a unified approach to learning that changed pedagogical and philosophical beliefs and reflected the "normative coherence" that Coburn (2003) identified as a necessary element to reach scale. With eleven schools and 110 classrooms participating in PP, district officials operated as a strategic agent charged with creating curriculum and support materials for teachers in addition to allocating existing technological and technical assistance resources to support the effort. Furthermore, by providing opportunities for teachers and school leaders to participate in PP-specific professional development, district leaders deepened an individual school's capacity to implement the reform design. With results from the study reporting that PP increased mean achievement, strengthened the association between classroom grades and achievement, reduced variation between classrooms across the district, and improved achievement for the districts most at-risk students, we propose that the elements of PP spread across classrooms and schools in JCPS.

Shift of ownership. By bringing coherence to the four facets of PP, JCPS created conditions for the shift of ownership of reform from the district to teachers and students. To genuinely move to scale, Coburn (2003) asserted that a reform must shift from external to internal "authority for the reform held by those who have the capacity to sustain, spread, and deepen reform principles" (p. 7). Although a literature review revealed that effective urban high school reform for at-risk students included early middle school intervention, whole-school high school reform, and a supportive learning environment for the current generation of students in the desks in front of us, these reforms were too late, too slow, or too little to immediately impact significant numbers of at-risk students. However, without the luxury of previous interventions or a prescribed reform provided by the district, JCPS teachers in eleven PLA high schools significantly increased math achievement by at-risk students who experienced PP.

Through a "reconceptualization of proprietorship" (McLaughlin and Mitra, 2001, p. 317), PP shifted from an external to an internal reform by narrowing the state's growing number of content standards to three key standards each grading period, providing corresponding diagnostic and summative assessments, and holding schools accountable for results rather than activity. Teachers were recruited to help identify the standards, create the assessments, and own the design. Once schools received the key standards and assessments, local administrators and teachers determined the sub-content and learning targets they believed best prepared students to understand each key standard and aligned lessons with the learning targets. Each school was allowed the flexibility to determine its own learning targets and was accountable for summative assessment results rather than adherence to prescribed sub-content. When principals led course-common learning teams of teachers to compare assessment results, and district officials guided teams of principals to collaboratively examine summative test scores, practitioners borrowed and exchanged lessons and learning targets and increasingly constructed, owned, and helped spread the most effective curriculum.

PP shifted ownership of instructional development by creating conditions for teachers to evaluate student competency using standards-based grading of assignments and tasks. "Adapting to local contextual needs" (Datnow and Stringfield, 2000, p. 195), teachers were free to define what competency looked like in student work and the district provided a web-based system for recording individual student competency for each key standard. The web-based program lifted the burden of grading from teachers by ultimately converting competencies into daily grades for students. The knowledge required for PP reform rested with the practitioners who were allowed to create student work through which students demonstrated understanding, design lessons that prepared students for those tasks, and evaluate whether students met a level of acceptable competency through the tasks. Scoring student work and averaging grades using a point system require a good calculator and at least a teacher's aide, but evaluating student understanding for competency demanded decision-making and ownership by the instructor.

By establishing the PP goal of guaranteed competency of key standards each grading period, JCPS shifted ownership of assessment to practitioners and students. In addition to acquiring responsibility for establishing learning targets, designing lessons, and evaluating student tasks for understanding, teachers assumed responsibility for student learning and demonstration of competency before the end-of-six-weeks summative assessment. Teachers moved from independence and isolation in their classrooms to dependence on one another and eventual interdependence to collectively reinvent their instruction, assessment, and intervention practices (Allensworth and Easton, 2007). Administrators provided and facilitated learning team opportunities for teachers through creating common planning time and "mechanisms for ongoing learning" (Coburn, 2003, p. 8) as opposed to the usual checklists, required meetings, and completion of compliance documents. Teachers owned student results, relied on one another's expertise, and developed an unprecedented collective efficacy in JCPS high schools.

In addition, the PP goal of guaranteed competency elicited student ownership of learning. The district

strongly suggested that student reflection count for 20 percent of the final grade each grading period. Teachers were allowed to collaboratively design means for students to reflect about progress toward competency and misunderstandings of standards. Although reflection designs varied across the PP schools, after the diagnostic assessments and daily formative assignments, students were guided at every site to own their own learning by describing where they were on learning continua toward competencies, requesting assistance by specific standard, and realizing that below standard work meant "not yet" instead of failure. In fact, due to the PP fail-safe requirement that students must eventually score 80 percent or higher on each six-weeks summative assessment, teachers and students collaboratively discussed ways to move from remediation to recovery of competency for each key standard, building a "sense of community that empowered students" (Wilkins, 2008). PP shifted ownership of assessment to teachers and students and created conditions for expected, possible, probable, and inevitable learning for students most at-risk of dropping out.

Sustainability. Although we examined the impact of PP after only one year of reform, educational practitioners, policymakers, and researchers should consider the parallels of PP with HRO principles as evidence for the sustainability of PP. Hargreaves and Fink (2006) concluded that secondary school reforms were typically unsustainable. However, since 1996, the Neath-Port Talbot (NTE) Local Education Authority in an economically disadvantaged area in southern Wales, Great Britain, has sustained its implementation of HRO principles, and after equaling the Welsh national average in 2000, moved its test scores in 2007 considerably above the national average (Stringfield et al., 2010). Confidence for the sustainability of PP lies in its alignment with many of the customized and sustained HRO principles implemented by NTE including the urgency to succeed, a finite set of shared goals, powerful databases, a balance of tight and loose standard operation procedures (SOP), and collegial decision making (Stringfield et al., 2008; Stringfield et al., 2010).

The PP goal to guarantee competency of key standards by each student produced an HRO-like urgency unlike previously implemented high school reforms in JCPS, and aligning district curriculum maps, common assessments, and intervention supports with three key standards each grading period matched the HRO principle of establishing a clear and finite set of goals. The JCPS web-based tool for tracking diagnostic, formative, and summative assessment data corresponded to the HRO practice of gathering and effectively using data. The JCPS tight expectations for common key standards, standards-based grading, and ensured learning, balanced by looseness of demands for processes and local implementation details, reflected the HRO recommendations for complementary district-school SOP. Finally, the PP shift of ownership for decision-making about processes to improve curriculum, instruction, assessment, resources, and SOP affirm the most convincing parallel with HRO principles, allowing for continuous improvements from practitioners who are "flaw finders and process/program improvers" (Stringfield et al., 2010, p. 15).

Results of this study of PLA high schools in a large urban district indicated a strong relationship between PP and teacher grading practices, classroom impact, and student achievement of students at-risk of dropping out. We found significant results across all eleven high schools that implemented PP, and the reform meets the scalability litmus test for depth, spread, shift of ownership, and sustainability. PP principles required no additional money, staff, or purchased programs and relied on "strong systems rather than strong or unusually effective people" (Reynolds, Creemers, Stringfield, Teddlie, and Schaffer, 2002, p. 289), increasing its probability for scalability and sustainability. Although a combination of factors influenced the achievement gains associated with PP, the results of this study provide hope and demand for further research for PP's potential to establish high school reform to scale in an urban district.

REFERENCES

Aiken, W. M. (1942). *The story of the eight year study*. New York: Harper.

Allensworth, E. M. and Easton, J. Q. (2007). *What matters for staying on-track indicator and graduating in Chicago public high schools*. Chicago: Consortium on Chicago School Research at the University of Chicago. Retrieved from ccsr.uchicago.edu/publications/0%20What%20Matters%20Final.pdf?q=graduating-students-research-ready.

American Institutes for Research. (1999). *An educator's guide to school-wide reform*. Washington, DC: Author.

American Institutes for Research. (2006). *CSCQ center on middle and high school comprehensive school reform models*. Washington, DC: Author.

Berends, M., Bodilly, S., and Kirby, S. N. (2002). Looking back over a decade of whole-school reform: The experience of new American schools. *Phi Delta Kappan, 84*(2), 168–175.

Bodilly, S. J., Glennan, T. K., Kerr, K. A., and Galegher, J. R. (2004). *Expanding the reach of education reforms: Perspectives from leaders in the scale-up of educational interventions*. Santa Monica, CA: Rand Corporation.

Bryk, A. S. (2009). Support a science of performance improvement. *Phi Delta Kappan, 90*(8), 597–600.

Bryk, A. S. (2010). Organizing schools for improvement. *Phi Delta Kappan, 91*(7), 23–28.

Carroll, T. (2009). The next generation of learning teams. *Phi Delta Kappan, 91*(2), 8–13.

Childress, S., Elmore, R., and Grossman, A. (2006). How to manage urban school districts. *Harvard Business Review, 84*(11), 55–68.

Childress, S., Elmore, R., Grossman, A., and Akinola, M. (2004). Note on the PELP coherence framework. Public Education Leadership Project at Harvard University. Retrieved from www.kasa.org/professionaldevelopment / documents/PELPFramework.pdf.

Coalition of Essential Schools. (2011). *The CES Common Principles*. Retrieved from www.essentialschools.org/items/4.

Coburn, C. E. (2003). Rethinking scale: Moving beyond numbers to deep and lasting change. *Educational Researcher, 32*(6), 3–12.

Consortium on Chicago School Research (2010). *Chicago high school redesign initiative: Schools, students, and outcomes*. Chicago, IL: Author.

Crandall, D. P., Loucks-Horsley, S., Bauchner, J.E., Schmidt, W.B., Eiseman, J.W., and Cox, P. L. (1982). *People, policies and practices: Examining the chain of school improvement* (Vols. 1–10). Andover, MA: The Network.

Cuban, L. (1984). *How teachers taught: Constancy and change in American classrooms, 1890–1980*. New York: Longman.

Darling-Hammond, L. (2006). No Child Left Behind and high school reform. *Harvard Educational Review, 76*(4), 642–667.

Datnow, A. (2005). The sustainability of comprehensive school reform models in changing district and state contexts. *Educational Administration Quarterly, 41*(1), 121–153.

Datnow, A. and Stringfield, S. (2000). Working together for reliable school reform. *Journal of Education for Students Placed at Risk, 5*(1), 183–204.

DuFour, R. P., DuFour, R. B., Eaker, R. E., and Karhanek, G. (2004). *Whatever it takes: How professional learning communities respond when kids don't learn.* Bloomington, IN: National Educational Service.

Earl, L., Torrance, N., and Sutherland, S. (2006). Changing secondary schools is hard: Lessons from 10 years of school improvement in the Manitoba school improvement program. In A. Harris and J. Chrispeels (Eds.), *Improving schools and educational systems.* London, GB: Routledge.

Fullan, M. (2000). The return of large-scale reform. *Journal of Educational Change, 1*(1), 5–28.

Fullan, M. (2001). *The new meaning of educational change* (3rd ed.). New York: Teachers College Press.

Fullan, M. (2011). *Choosing the wrong drivers for whole system reform* (Report 204). Victoria, Australia: Centre for Strategic Education.

Fullan, M., Bertani, A., and Quinn, J. (2004). New lessons for districtwide reform: Effective lessons for change at the district level has 10 crucial components. *Educational Leadership, 61*(7), 42–46.

Fullan, M. and Pomfret, A. (1977). Research on curriculum and instruction implementation. *Review of Educational Research, 47*(2), 335–397

Gallup (2011). In *New Record-Low Confidence in US Public Schools.* Retrieved from www.gallup.com/poll/148724/near-record-low-confidence-public-schools.aspx.

Hargreaves, A. and Fink, D. (2006). *Sustainable leadership.* San Francisco, CA: Jossey-Bass/Wiley.

Holdzkom, D. (2002). *Effects of comprehensive school reform in 12 schools: Results of a three-year study.* Appalachian Educational Laboratory: Author.

Honig, M. I. and Hatch, T. C. (2004). Crafting coherence: How schools strategically manage multiple, external demands. *Educational Researcher, 33*(8), 16–30.

Jefferson County Public Schools. (2011). *Project proficiency guide.* Unpublished manuscript: Author.

Kedro, M. J. (2004). Coherence: When the puzzle is complete. *Principal Leadership, 4*(8), 28–32.

Kentucky Department of Education. (2011). *Kentucky Department of Education Open House.* Retrieved from openhouse.education.ky.gov/.

McLaughlin, M. W. (1990). The RAND change agent study revisited: Macro perspectives and micro realities. *Educational Researcher, 19*(9), 11–16.

McLaughlin, M. and Mitra, D. (2001). Theory-based change and change-based theory: going deeper, going broader. *Journal of Educational Change, 2*(4), 301–323.

National Center on Education and the Economy (2008). *Tough choices or tough times: The report on the new commission on the skills of the American workforce, revised and expanded.* San Francisco, CA: Jossey-Bass.

Newmann, F. M., Smith, B., Allensworth, E., and Bryk, A. S. (2001). Instructional program coherence: What it is and why it should guide school improvement policy. *Educational Evaluation and Policy Analysis, 23*(4), 297–321.

No Child Left Behind Act, 20 U.S.C. § 6319 (2001).

Obama, B. (2011, January 25). *State of the Union Address.* Copy of text downloaded on July 5, 2011 from www.whitehouse.gov/the-press-office/2011/01/25/remarks-president-state-union-address.

Oxley, D. (2008). Creating instructional program coherence. *Principal's Research Review, 3*(5), 1–7.

Oxley, D. and Kassissieh, J. (2008). From comprehensive high schools to small learning communities: Accomplishments and challenges. *Forum, 50*(2), 199–206.

Oxley, D. and Luers, K. W. (2011). How small schools grew up and got serious (but did not lose their spunk). *Phi Delta Kappan, 92*(4), 62–66.

Payne, C. M. (2008). *So much reform, so little change: The persistence of failure in urban schools.* Cambridge, MA: Harvard Education Press.

Quint, J. (2006). *Meeting five challenges of high school reform: Lessons from research on three reform models.* Manpower Demonstration Research Corporation: Author.

Race to the Top Act, 75. Fed Reg. 19496 (2010).

Reynolds, D., Creemers, B., Stringfield, S., Teddlie, C., and Schaffer, G. (Eds.). (2002). *World class schools: International perspectives on school effectiveness.* London: Routledge Falmer.

Rorrer, A. K., Skrla, L., and Schuerich, J. J. (2008). Districts as institutional actors in educational reform. *Educational Research Quarterly, 44*(3), 307–358.

School Improvement Fund (2010). *School Improvement Grants; American Recovery and Reinvestment Act of 2009 (ARRA); Title I of the Elementary and Secondary Education Act of 1965, as Amended (ESEA).* Retrieved from www2.ed.gov/programs/sif/legislation.html.

Shadish, W. R., Cook, T. D., and Campbell, D. T. (2002). *Experimental and quasi-experimental designs for generalized causal inference.* Boston, MA: Houghton-Mifflin.

Stiggins, R. J. (2008). *Assessment Manifesto: A Call for the Development of Balanced Assessment Systems.* Princeton, NJ: Educational Testing Service.

Stiggins, R. J. and DuFour, R. (2009). Maximizing the power of formative assessments. *Phi Delta Kappan, 90*(9), 640–644.

Stringfield, S. and Datnow, A. (1998). Scaling up school restructuring designs in urban schools. *Education and Urban Society, 30*(3), 269–276.

Stringfield, S. and Datnow, A. (2002). Systemic supports for schools serving students placed at risk. In S. Stringfield and D. Land (Eds.), *Educating at-risk students* (pp. 269–285). Chicago, IL: National Society for the Study of Education.

Stringfield, S., Reynolds, D., and Schaffer, E. C. (2008). Improving secondary students' academic achievement through a focus on reform reliability: 4- and 9-year findings from the high reliability schools project. *School Effectiveness and School Improvement, 19*(4), 409–428.

Stringfield, S., Reynolds, D., and Schaffer, E. C. (2010, October). *Toward highly reliable, high-quality public schooling.* Paper presented at the McREL Best in the World Consortium Meeting, Denver, CO.

United States Department of Education, National Commission on Excellence in Education. (1983). *A nation at risk: The imperative for educational reform.* A report to the Nation and the Secretary of Education. Washington, D.C.

Wilkins, J. (2008). School characteristics that influence student attendance: Experiences of students in a school avoidance program. *The High School Journal, 91*(3), 12–24.

CHAPTER 7

Developing Teacher Leadership for Equity in Urban Schools

H. Richard Milner IV, Judson Laughter, and Joshua Childs

When thinking about leadership in education, we typically think about principals, superintendents, or even coaches as those who lead; teachers and teaching are not who and what come to mind. However, the authors of this chapter have observed in our work in many schools that those in traditional *leadership* positions can be so detached from the realities of what happens inside the classroom, especially urban[1] classrooms, that they are not well equipped to support teacher practices that shape students' learning opportunities; this leadership detachment has only become increasingly the case as outside pressures related to accountability further remove administrative attention away from the classroom. For instance, principals can be so inundated with handling bureaucratic expectations, pressures, and paperwork that it can be difficult for them to support teacher development in instruction or even discipline practices.

In this chapter, we argue for the necessity of teacher leadership—in, from, and beyond the classroom—to cultivate practices that support equity in urban schools. To be clear, we are suggesting that teacher leadership should be a central goal of teacher preparation programs and professional development opportunities in order to prepare teachers to teach and lead in urban classrooms. We explore what teacher leadership means, how it can be cultivated in social contexts, and how *equity* in particular should be the guiding ideal of teacher leaders in urban classrooms. To build our argument, in the next sections, we define educational equity and then lay out a synthesized definition of teacher leadership.

DEFINING EQUITY

Secada (1989) pointed to a major difference between *equality* and *equity* despite a history of being used interchangeably: "Though these constructs are related, equality is group-based and quantitative. Equity can be applied to groups or to individuals; it is qualitative in that equity is tied to notions of justice" (p. 23). Equality means the same thing for every person in a particular place at a particular time. Equity, on the other hand, requires judgments about whether a given state of affairs is just.

For instance, equity in education may mean that we are attempting to provide students, regardless of their racial, ethnic, linguistic, cultural, or SES background, with what they need to succeed—not necessarily the exact same goals and visions across different environments. Secada further explained,

> The essence of equity lies in our ability to acknowledge that even though our actions are in accord with a set of rules, the results of those actions may still be unjust. Equity goes beyond following the rules . . . equity gauges the results of actions directly against standards of justice. (p. 23)

In this sense, although related equity and equality do not have the same meaning; equity specifically addresses how what is necessary for success in one school or district or with one student may be meaningfully different from the next.

This is particularly important in the context of urban classrooms that include wide ranges of diversity among the 6.9 million students, as well as in the context of urban schools that are often under-resourced. We press the need for teacher leadership related to equity because it allows teacher leaders to focus on specific aspects of P-12 student development and learning; it provides an ideal toward which teachers might lead others.

A LOOK AT TEACHER LEADERSHIP

There is an important body of conceptual and empirical literature concerning teacher learning and practices with a focus on equity (Brown, 2012; Ladson-Billings, 1999; Milner, 2008; Sleeter, 2008), but little established research or conceptual literature concerns teacher leadership with an equity focus. Indeed, there are several practitioner-oriented guides describing teachers as leaders, but they often focus on teachers stepping into leadership roles, such as *team leaders* or *department heads* (e.g., Pellicer and Anderson, 1995); even at the university level, departments of educational leadership are associated more with policy and administration than classroom practice. We found it difficult to locate an agreed-upon and/or coherent definition of teacher leadership with an equity focus within education.

The research literature addressing educational leadership with a focus on equity (often labeled *social justice*) tends to consider only those members of a school in *leadership* positions, not teachers. While *social justice* takes on numerous interpretations (Shoho, Merchant, and Lugg, 2005) especially in practice, it has become a focus for educational researchers, practitioners, and policymakers (Jean-Marie, Normore, and Brooks, 2009). However, research has shown that too many school leaders are not exposed to social justice issues, training, or approaches in leadership development and preparation programs (Jean-Marie et al., 2009; Pohland and Carlson, 1993; Shoho, 2006).

If preparation programs, both teacher and leadership, devalue social justice and diversity among their course content, faculty, and students, then leaders will be less prepared to confront and address equity in schools and communities (Rusch, 2004). Theoharis (2007) argued that good leadership, with equity-minded principles, focused on creating successful schools that improve the educational and human condition of marginalized students. Addressing the needs of racially and socioeconomically diverse student populations requires school leaders to develop professional identities that support diversity, equality (when appropriate), equity, and inclusiveness (Evans, 2007).

Drawing from research in business, Bowman (2004), building on Bennis and Thomas's (2002) list of qualities shared by leaders emerging from a study of multiple generations focused on what a leader can do to develop an effective community; however, this research did not necessarily focus on a more distributive understanding of leadership. Similarly, Bowman (2004) built on Bennis and Nanus's (1997) list of key leadership abilities, but these are cast only as management skills: management of attention, meaning, trust, and self. From these, Bowman (2004) developed his own conceptualization, addressing teachers as leaders (see table 7.1):

> Education leaders guide their colleagues by engaging in collective conversations, invoking symbolic gestures that reveal relationship, modeling professionalism beyond the label of one's role, championing evocative ideas in both the classroom and the workplace, and being "in influence" as opposed to being "in control." (p. 188)

This definition of how teacher leaders lead is mirrored across several other conceptualizations of teacher leader roles, responsibilities, and realities (e.g., Lieberman and Miller, 2005). In fact, James (1997) even reversed the process and developed a definition of a quality teacher to support a definition of quality leadership.

The commonality across all these definitions is the focus on community and relationship (Fullan, 1994; Lambert, 2003; Little, 1990). It is here, we argue, that teacher leadership must be grounded, particularly if it seeks to be applicable to teaching for equity in urban schools. Urban classrooms and schools require specific attention and intention toward developing and maintaining relationships in a society that understands education as a competitive field following business models of investment and return. The recent onslaught of school "reform" literature and programs from outside education has attempted to forego this focus on community and relationship, which is grounded in the socio-political

Table 7.1. Teacher Leadership Characteristics

Bowman (2004)	Crowther, Kaagan, Ferguson, & Hann (2002)
• Collective conversations • Symbolic gestures → Relationship Professionalism beyond role • Evocative ideas • "In influence"	• Convey convictions about a better world • Authenticity • Facilitate communities of learning • Confront barriers • Translate ideas into sustainable systems of action • Nurture culture of success

context of schools and education, in favour of standardization, neoliberal approaches, and business models of education.

For example, in citing a Carnegie Foundation study, Barth (2007) outlined ten areas where teacher leadership was most needed and concurrently most lacking. We provide a complete list here to then address how each area can be undermined by recent "educational reforms":

1. Choosing textbooks and instructional materials
2. Shaping the curriculum
3. Setting standards for student behavior
4. Deciding whether students are tracked into special classes
5. Designing staff development and in-service programs
6. Setting promotion and retention policies
7. Deciding school budgets
8. Evaluating teacher performance
9. Selecting new teachers
10. Selecting new administrators (p. 10)

The tri-partite "reforms" in standards, teacher evaluation, and politics we are currently experiencing only provides stronger barriers to teacher leaders in every one of these areas.

It can be argued that Common Core State Standards and associated assessments hinders teacher leadership in numbers 1, 2, and 4 by removing planning, instruction, and assessment possibilities and de-professionalizing teachers who were once trusted to make decisions in these areas. The arrival of new evaluation models for teachers (like TEAM or TIGER) can hinder teacher leadership in numbers 3, 5, 6, 8, and 9 by expecting "effective teaching" to look like, and be graded by, the same set of *a priori* designed rubrics.

Likewise, increasing political pressure placed on schools at local, state, and federal levels perhaps hinders teacher leadership in numbers 7 and 10 by making funding reliant on formulae and requirements having little to do with actual education. Moreover, we do not see strong links to equity, diversity, or urban education well-articulated in these reforms.

In response, some exploring leadership within education see teacher leadership as a viable space to address reform, especially in practices. In particular, Crowther,

Kaagan, Ferguson, and Hann (2002) heralded the emergence of a new paradigm with their *Teachers as Leaders* Framework. Although somewhat philosophical, by building on Katzenmeyer and Moller's (1996) metaphor of *Awakening the Sleeping Giant*, Crowther and colleagues (2002, pp. 4–5) presented six activities for teacher leaders that might achieve real education reform (see table 7.1). These activities specifically address diversity in urban classrooms, the inequitable funding of urban schools, and need for relationships in dense urban environments.

While we believe the *Teachers as Leaders* framework offers a strong response to issues that plague urban schools in particular, we recognize that institutionalized structures can work to reject principles of leadership:

> Teacher leadership still faces heavy odds today. It must compete not only with vested interests in traditional assumptions about leadership but also with schools that are still a bit uncomfortable with the idea of teacher leaders. (Ackerman and Mackenzie, 2007, p. x)

Both within and beyond the urban school, teacher leadership is needed now more than ever with the emergence of non-educational entities vying for control of schools. In the next section of this chapter, we outline several specific areas related to equity that we believe are essential for teacher leadership in urban schools.

TEACHER LEADERSHIP FOR EQUITY

Teachers need to know a range of information—from how to best organize their classroom to maximize student learning to how to best handle discipline issues when they present themselves in the classroom. In addition, teachers must know their subject matter and understand contextual idiosyncrasies as they teach that content. However, teacher education programs have struggled to develop the multiple layers of knowledge essential for teacher learning, although these areas have been recognized as essential for teacher learning and effectiveness in practice.

In addition to the points made above, some believe and would argue that teacher leadership is only needed to enhance teachers' subject matter knowledge such as mathematics, science, or language arts. Shulman's (1987) work pointed to the necessity of teachers' development of content knowledge and pedagogical knowledge, but also stressed the convergence of the two: pedagogical content knowledge, knowledge of how to teach specific content. Clearly, teachers' knowledge about and ability to teach their particular subject matter is necessary for student success in any classroom.

The point that subject matter knowledge is necessary but insufficient is perhaps even more essential in urban learning environments. For instance, Haberman (1995), building from forty years of research of teachers of urban and high poverty students, explained that while it is essential for teachers to know their subject matter, this is insufficient for the kind of work necessary to be successful in urban and high poverty schools. He maintained that many teachers fail in high poverty environments because they do not have the ability to connect with students and build relationships with them. In the simplest form, an essential element of teaching is learning about students teachers are teaching, and it is not easy to develop the skill and knowledge to engage this learning about students.

Moreover, with particular attention to support the development and learning of students in urban schools, teacher learning for leadership can be enhanced to address the many complex areas involved in the teaching and learning exchange. For instance, teachers need to be equipped to address the following in urban environments:

- build relationships with students;
- develop classroom management strategies and skills;
- understand and build on the historical context of a community and school;
- understand and negotiate the sociopolitical landscape of an environment;
- develop partnerships with family members of their students, the community, and other stakeholders;
- work collaboratively with their colleagues and administrators for student success;
- develop culturally relevant and responsive instructional materials and instructional practices;
- understand psychological and socio-emotional needs of students;
- determine and address basic needs of students such as hunger and health of students;
- gauge and address socioeconomic and language development needs of students;

- understand racism, sexism, homophobia, and other forms of discrimination;
- understand the role of popular culture in the lives of students;
- understand and negotiate policy and reform movements both on local and national levels;
- build on and from interests of students and the community;
- develop professional identities to make appropriate decisions for student learning;
- identify and build on assets of all students, the community, their colleagues, and themselves (as teachers); and
- know how to contextualize and transform standards in ways that are instructionally innovative.

Surely, teacher leadership can be essential in building a school community that allows and supports the ideas above.

In addition to the issues outlined above, a teacher can lead beyond the classroom and the community and engage larger oppressive forces in education, both the long-standing hegemonies of discrimination and the newer, business-based intrusions of "education reform." Each of these forces has a particularly detrimental effect on urban classrooms and schools. Admittedly, this is the hardest area in which a teacher can lead because it moves beyond the immediate sphere of influence; however, it is only through organization of individual teacher leaders into a more powerful voice that any of these forces will be faced and defeated.

CONCLUSION

A common theme present across the literature on teacher leadership is the warning that both teacher leadership and teacher leadership development are not easy (Barth, 2007). However, developing teacher leadership is essential in the face of structural and practical challenges teachers face, as well as the need for teachers to take ownership of the work they do to promote student learning in an entire school. Barth described several potential benefits that support our push for an increase in teacher leadership. Teacher leaders "offer valuable assistance to the overworked and overwhelmed principal" (p. 12); they "enlist student leadership to amplify their own" (p. 12); they make "better decisions . . . about curriculum, professional development, faculty meetings, scheduling, and discipline" (p. 13); and they "are enriched and ennobled in many significant ways" (p. 14).

NOTE

1. The adjective *urban* when used in education is an oft-contested term. Our definition of urban education includes (1) *the size* of the city in which schools are located: dense, large, metropolitan areas; (2) *the students* in the schools: a wide range of student diversity, including racial, ethnic, language, and socioeconomic demographics; and (3) *the resources*: the amount and number of resources available in a school, such as technology and financial structures through federal programs as well as property taxes. For deeper exploration of *urban*, please see Milner (2012) and Milner and Lomotey (2014).

REFERENCES

Ackerman, R. H. and Mackenzie, S. V. (2007). Preface. In R. H. Ackerman and S. V. Mackenzie (Eds.), *Uncovering teacher leadership: Essays and voices from the field* (pp. ix–xii). Thousand Oaks, CA: Corwin Press.

Barth, R. S. (2007). The teacher leader. In R. H. Ackerman and S. V. Mackenzie (Eds.), *Uncovering teacher leadership: Essays and voices from the field* (pp. 9–36). Thousand Oaks, CA: Corwin Press.

Bennis, W. and Nanus, B. (1997). *Leaders: Strategies for taking charge* (2nd ed.). New York: Harper Business.

Bennis, W. and Thomas, R. (2002). *Geeks and geezers: How era, values, and defining moments shape leaders.* Boston: Harvard Business School Press.

Bowman, R. F. (2004). Teachers as leaders. *The Clearing House: A Journal of Educational Strategies, Issues, and Ideas, 77*(5), 187–189.

Brown, K. D. (2012). Trouble on my mind: Toward a framework of humanizing critical sociocultural knowledge for teaching and teacher education. *Race Ethnicity and Education, 16*(3), 316–338.

Crowther, F., Kaagan, S. S., Ferguson, M., and Hann, L. (2002). *Developing teacher leaders: How teacher leadership enhances school success.* Thousand Oaks, CA: Corwin Press.

Evans, A. E. (2007). School leaders and their sensemaking about race and demographic change. *Educational Administration Quarterly, 43*(2), 159–188.

Fullan, M. (1994). Teacher leadership: A failure to conceptualize. In D. R. Walling (Ed.), *Teachers as leaders: Perspectives on the professional development of teachers* (pp. 241–253). Bloomington, IN: Phi Delta Kappa.

Haberman, M. (1995). *Star teachers of children in poverty.* West Lafayette, IN: Kappa Delta Pi.

James, D. (1997). Teachers and leaders. *The Journal of Leadership Studies, 4*(4), 141–144.

Jean-Marie, G., Normore, A., and Brooks, J. S. (2009). Leadership for social justice: Preparing 21st-century school leaders for a new social order. *Journal of Research on Leadership in Education, 4*(1), 1–31.

Katzenmeyer, M. and Moller, G. (1996). *Awakening the sleeping giant: Leadership development for teachers.* Thousand Oaks, CA: Corwin Press.

Ladson-Billings, G. (1999). Preparing teachers for diverse student populations: A Critical RaceTheory Perspective. *Review of Research in Education, 24*, 211–247.

Lambert, L. (2003). Shifting conceptions of leadership: Towards a redefinition of leadership for the twenty-first century. In B. Davies and J. West-Burnham (Eds.), *Handbook of educational leadership and management* (pp. 5–15). London: Pearson Education.

Lieberman, A. and Miller, L. (2005). Teachers as leaders. *The Educational Forum, 69*(2), 151–162.

Little, J. W. (1990). Teachers as colleagues. In A. Lieberman (Ed.), *Schools as collaborative cultures* (pp. 165–193). New York: Falmer Press.

Milner, H. R. (2008). Critical race theory and interest convergence as analytic tools in teacher education policies and practices. *Journal of Teacher Education 59*(4), 332–346.

Milner, H. R. (2012). But what is urban education? *Urban Education, 47*(3), 556–561.

Milner, H.R. and Lomotey, K. (2014). Introduction. In H.R. Milner and K. Lomotey (Eds.), *Handbook of urban education* (pp. xv–xxiv). New York: Routledge Press.

Pellicer, L. O. and Anderson, L. W. (1995). *A handbook for teacher leaders.* Thousand Oaks, CA: Corwin Press.

Pohland, P. and Carlson, L. T. (1993). Program reform in educational administration. *University Council for Educational Administration, 34*(3), 4–9.

Rusch, E. A. (2004). Gender and race in leadership preparation: A constrained discourse. *Educational Administration Quarterly, 40*(1), 14–46.

Secada, W.G. (1989). Agenda setting, enlightened self-interest, and equity in mathematics education. *Peabody Journal of Education, 66*(2), 22–56.

Shulman, L.S. (1987). Knowledge and teaching: Foundations of the new reform. *Harvard Educational Review, 19*(2), 4–14.

Shoho, A.R. (2006). Dare professors of educational administration build a new social order: Social justice within an American perspective. *Journal of Educational Administration, 44*(3).

Shoho, A. R., Merchant, B. M., and Lugg, C. A. (2005). Social justice: Seeking a common language. In F. W. English

(Ed.), *The Sage handbook of educational leadership: Advances in theory, research, and practice*, pp. 47–67. Thousand Oaks, CA: Sage.

Sleeter, C. E. (2008). Preparing white teachers for diverse students. In M. Cochran-Smith, S. Feiman-Nemser, and J. McIntyre (Eds.), *Handbook of Research in Teacher Education: Enduring Issues in Changing Contexts*, 3rd ed. (pp. 559–582). New York: Routledge.

Theoharis, G. (2007). Social justice educational leaders and resistance: Toward a theory of social justice leadership. *Educational Administration Quarterly, 43*(2), 221–258.

CHAPTER 8

Teachers Learning to Lead

An Action Research Process Model

Leena Furtado

INTRODUCTION

In the twenty-first century, the call has risen in importance for both teachers to successfully create learning environments for diverse children (Davis, Darling-Hammond, LaPointe, and Meyerson, 2005) and for teacher educators to be more mindful to develop teacher education programs that equip teachers with the enhanced pedagogical knowledge, skills, and dispositions to effectively teach urban students (Corbett and Wilson, 2002; Darling-Hammond, Bullmaster, and Cobb, 1995; Junor Clarke and Fournillier, 2012; York-Barr and Duke, 2004). Similarly, there is also a growing consensus for school leaders to create school contexts where teachers can cultivate the knowledge (Leithwood, Louis, Anderson, and Wahlstrom, 2004) of "their students—their distinct cultures, their languages, their home lives, their perceptions of the world and their place in it" (Schulte, 2004, p. 1). There is evidence that teachers who are nurtured to reach such "cultural competence" acquire the dispositions, beliefs, and expectations to address the needs of inner-city schoolchildren and lead in classroom instruction (Corbett and Wilson, 2002; Ladson-Billings, 2001).

The present descriptive study describes the professional development of teachers learning to lead in urban classrooms through action-oriented research and iterative reflections as a deliberate and organic approach to instructional changes (Furtado, 2012; Hagevik, Aydeniz, and Rowell, 2012). Most importantly, when teachers engage in reflection before, during, and after research intervention, they are able to better understand their own actions as well as the thought processes behind those actions, and are better able to communicate these reflections to others, empowering them as leaders in educational practice (Dick, 2007;

Postholm, 2008; Watts and Lawson, 2009). This review will describe the implementation, development, and overall characteristics of reflections, both personal and professional, from five purposive selection of instructional interventions based on a theoretical model of action-oriented research conducted during a capstone study for a Masters in Education program. The teacher participants, their classrooms, and the mentor/instructor all operate within a diverse urban educational setting.[1]

REVIEW OF LITERATURE

This chapter begins with a review of literature on urban teachers who can lead and the concept of what leadership looks like among educators (Danielson, 2006; Darling-Hammond, 2007; Fullan, 1994; Lieberman and Miller, 2005; Ross, Adams, Bondy, Dana, Dodman, and Swain, 2011; Snell and Swanson, 2000). This follows with teacher leadership initiated by school principals as a whole school reform effort, the complex issues encountered by leadership among teachers (Brooks et al., 2004; Ovando, 1996; Phelps, 2008), as well as best practices of teacher leadership (Fullan, 1994; Katzenmeyer and Moller, 2009; Phelps, 2008; Pounder, 2006). Then, research examines the more critical and active engagement in the fulfillment of leadership roles though action research (Carr and Kemmis, 1986; Furtado, 2012; Hagevik et al., 2012; Hendricks, 2009). Finally, the recommended educational program model of Action Research draws heavily on the reflective and action-oriented theories of (Dewey, 1993; Dick, 2007; Freire, 1970; Schon, 1987; Wellington, 1991) leading to transformational teacher leadership dispositions as conveyed by current research.

Teacher Leadership

Literature typifies teachers who lead as those who are, or have been, teachers with significant teaching experience, a repertoire of teaching expertise, and have the respect of their colleagues and peers through formal and informal roles, such as peer-coach and professional team leaders (Liston et al., 2008). York-Barr and Duke (2004) established that teacher leadership enhances teachers' status, builds their leadership skills, improves and corroborates their professional knowledge, and enhances their motivation and intellectual stimulation. Snell and Swanson (2000) concluded that because teachers demonstrated high levels of instructional expertise, collaboration, reflection, and sense of empowerment, they became leaders or, more precisely, were permitted by peers to lead. Issues can arise when this permission is not received.

Wasley's (1991) longitudinal case study chronicled the complicated issues that three teacher leaders encountered when working within their schools after assuming innovative leadership roles. The teachers faced resistance from peer teachers and a lack of support for their initiatives. The study conducted by Lieberman and Miller (2005) described the leadership styles of two teachers using different strategies in order to gain support from their colleagues. One learned to lead from the classroom through "demonstrations rather than remonstrations" (p. 157), whereas the other led from a "middle space" (p. 158), or a space between teachers and administrators, to act as a bridge when leading peer teachers and adult learners (Lieberman and Miller, 2005). For example, Teacher 1 identified leadership through courage and willingness to share classroom teaching through videos, question answer relationship during instruction, and strategies to promote open discourse among students. Teacher 2, after ten years of classroom teaching, accepted the role as the school's coordinator for curriculum, instruction, and assessment and soon found out that he had become a teacher for adults. As a paraprofessional the teacher conducted professional development services for teachers to make the transition of integrating student work and teacher practices to curriculum and textbooks.

Effective teacher leadership requires high-level attainment in several teaching roles. According to Fullan (1994), teachers demonstrate competency in leadership along multiple levels of disposition as follows: 1) knowledge of teaching and learning pedagogy; 2) collegiality; 3) engagement in lifelong learning and growth; 4) awareness of change processes within the educational context and the larger community; and, 5) a moral perspective toward the profession. Danielson (2006) calls for delineation of teacher dispositions and required models for leadership in the profession where teachers not only do things differently, but do them *better* (italics, author) as a standard of professional practice.

The impact of teacher leadership on teacher quality for urban school teaching has yielded books to guide educators about how to develop teacher leaders (e.g., Hendricks, 2009; Katzenmeyer and Moller, 2009). However, there has been less guidance related to the development of teacher leadership within graduate programs for practicing teachers and their professional leadership roles within school reform programs. Ovington, Diamantes, and Roby's (2002) study established that graduates in a university-directed leader program enhanced their confidence and demonstrated their willingness to engage in school-related professional development activities. Current research documents the impact of university-based graduate teacher leadership program models where teachers gain empowerment and confidence to lead within a capstone course designed for teacher leadership (Furtado, 2012), while Ross et al.'s, (2011) study establishes on the perspectives of classroom practice and student achievement through studies from a sample of teachers and school principals about program impact.

In a conceptual model of leadership, Liebermann and Miller (2005) describe three major concepts of leadership roles to be undertaken by teachers in leadership positions. They are: *advocators*, who articulate desirable teacher dispositions effective for student learning and offer alternatives to the existing model of efficiency and accountability; *innovators*, who design models of effective instruction and professional leadership to propel the school to become a community; and *stewards*, who actively model teacher leadership and raise the status of teaching to a profession in which teachers engage in continual professional development and receive acceptance of their peers in all three leadership roles (italics, p. 153).[2] This is a conceptual model of leadership; other studies provide more specific prescriptions for best practices.

Furthermore, Dozier (2007) states that in order to lead and bring about effective change teachers need to:

1) be actively involved with peers and professionals; 2) utilize data-driven evidence to garner support and discussion about proposed changes; 3) get to know their environment, including identification of those who can be approached for the smooth and efficient acceptance of proposals and curricular modifications; 4) be at the right time and the right place to give advice when opportunities arise; 5) learn the language of etiquette, deliberations, and consensus, and become familiar with educational policies and mandates; and 6) take ownership, and exhibit the courage, vision, and passion to change (adapted from Dozier). Whether reaching high-level attainment, taking on multiple teaching roles, or enacting change through engaging best practices, it is clear that much is required of teachers taking on leadership positions. In order to support these efforts and affect positive changes in classrooms and school communities, teachers need the support of their administrations.

Teacher Leadership Through School-Wide Initiative

Efforts toward partnership between teachers and principals through collaboration, collegiality, and commitment to teacher leadership within the context of school-wide reform are well-documented by scholars (Blase and Blase 2006; Fullan and Hargreaves, 1996; Lieberman, Saxl, and Miles, 2000; York-Barr and Duke, 2004). At times, such enterprises become entangled by difficulties emerging out of the complex relationships among teachers, and between teachers and administrators. Empowered leadership can lead to conflicts, challenges (Brooks, Scribner, and Eferakorho, 2004), and teacher disequilibrium, especially when teachers in leadership positions are required to teach as well as lead other professionals. The dual assignment of teaching and leading aptly coined and explained by Little and Bartlett (2002) as the "Huberman Paradox" can result in teacher burnout, alienation, and disillusion; these issues make up part of larger arguments against school reform and teacher leadership (Ovando, 1996).

Some studies indicate that teachers often encounter obstacles from non-collegial, peer teachers when assigned leadership tasks (Wasley, 1991; Yoder, 1994), while some opine that all teachers may not be equipped with dispositions to lead or be willing to accept the additional work and demand on time associated with lead-

ership (Phelps, 2008; Teitel, 1996). But others suggest that issues encountered by teachers taking on leadership roles are related to lack of preparation. Katzenmeyer and Moller (2001) explain that, at times, "we ask teachers to assume leadership roles without any preparation or coaching because [we assume] they appear to intuitively know how to work with colleagues" (p. 47) and suggests the need for explicit attention to the training of teachers for leadership. The solution offered by Katzenmeyer and Moller (2001) indicates a larger issue, which, when addressed, could also help to alleviate disputes between faculty members and the disinclination of teachers to take leadership positions: that is, the need to take teachers' needs and concerns into account when enacting school reform. This proposition is supported by High and Ovando (2004), who suggest that "resistance to change may also be created by ignoring the voices of those who will actually be in charge of change implementation, namely teachers" (p. 6).

Best Practices of Teacher Leadership

Research calls for more examination of collaborative efforts between principals and teachers, which entail an adjustment of leadership roles from hierarchical to more interactive models (Hart, 1994; Little, 2003; Smylie and Denny, 1990). When principals make intentional, deliberative efforts to collaborate with teachers, effective school reform becomes possible. Fullan (1994) pronounces "neither top-down nor bottom-up strategies for educational reform work. What is needed is a more sophisticated blend of the two" (p. 1). Phelps (2008) agrees that leadership needs to emerge as a shared paradigm in order to stimulate school reform, and stresses the need to nurture this relationship with strong conceptual and operational definitions of each role founded on notions of shared or participatory leadership.

Bennett (1993) invites school administrators and district officials to provide a "supportive context" where "teacher-researchers have the potential to enhance the professional image of educators" to leadership (p. 70). In other words, administration can affect positive change by fostering an environment that supports professional development, which demonstrates itself through "processes by which an individual selectively acquires the knowledge, skills, and dispositions needed to perform a social role effectively" (Normore, 2004, p.

111). Normore further posits that this social role necessitates "dialogue, collaboration, and mentoring by an experienced professional . . ." (p. 112) and exploration of the themes of learning and partnerships (Junor Clarke and Fournillier, 2012). Schoen (2007) also espouses that leadership is developed through the process of "professional socialization" where teachers at all levels and positions are encouraged to engage in "collaborative inquiry, reflection, and dialogue" (p. 211) and to take action to improve instructional practices and educational outcomes. While outcomes in individual schools and districts have been reviewed thus far, initiatives for inclusion of teachers in leadership positions, and the actions taken by administration to support them, are also being enacted on a national and global scale.

Globally the focus of school improvement owes its initiatives mainly to the publicly funded systems of education in the United States (U.S. Department of Education, 2011), Canada, UK (Frost and Harris, 2003), and Australia (Crowther, Kagan, Ferguson, and Hann, 2002) and the gradual progression of teacher leadership (Pounder, 2006). A study conducted by Barnett, Johnson, and Montgomery (2005) examined the idea of teacher empowerment and the success to which it can lead through National Board (NB) certification in the United States.[3] This national certification recognizes the nation's most exemplary teachers. By receiving the NB certification, teachers are potentially less confined to standard curriculum and are more enabled by administrators to design lessons specifically for their classrooms. Certifications of this type are achieved through engagement in leadership development by teachers through continued learning, such as pursuit of a masters-level education.

Empirical literature beckons for more formal preparation and support of teachers taking on leadership positions. These teacher-leaders collaborate, create community, foster ownership, empower themselves and others, and most importantly, learn to lead by researching and improving their instructional expertise in the classroom (Fullan, 1994; Lieberman and Miller, 2005). The action research program described below is designed to empower teachers in these tasks by facilitating further research and helping them to sharpen their skills through reflection.[4]

Action Research

Since its inception, literature abounds in a number of definitions for action research (AR) or teacher re-

search (e.g., Carr and Kemmis, 1986; Cochran-Smith and Lytle, 1993) with Rearick and Feldman (1999) harnessing its complexities of action research along three dimensions: of theoretical orientation, purpose, and an array of reflective processes. The scholar's theoretical dimension defines AR by interest of particular persons and their worlds, or why teachers and other practitioners ask questions during reflection, and the critical perspective of some to uncover societal structures that limit freedom and justice by practitioners. Action research is a cyclical system of inquiry that educators and administrators alike can use to study their own situations in order to improve their work with students and in schools (Hendricks, 2009). "Action research is something we've done for years in our classrooms, schools," says [one participant] in a study by Schmuck (2006), and continues "what we lacked was the formal structure to work methodologically through issues" (p. 12).

An expanding body of literature attests to the merits of teacher action research endeavors when engaging methodology through qualitative research. According to Denzin and Lincoln (1994), "qualitative researchers study things in their natural settings, attempting to make sense of, or interpret, phenomenon in terms of the meanings people bring to them" (p. 10). Through qualitative research, teachers training to be leaders engage in real-life classroom phenomena on a larger scale. It includes describing a problem, seeking knowledge from research-based investigations, collecting data, devising and implementing both highly organized and creative problem-solving strategies with clearly stated results and implications for change, evaluating the results, and planning for another cycle of improvement (Furtado, 2012). Through this process, educators are able to generate knowledge and then disseminate what they have learned to their colleagues by creating lasting and sustainable improvements in schools (Fullan, 2002; Hagevik et al., 2012).

Under the umbrella of qualitative research, Dick (2007) describes action research to be an extension of a natural approach to problem-solving entailing "*review→plan→act→review→* . . . and so on" (p. 150). The iterative cycles of action and research require an individual to engage in a systematic exploration of an issue to determine potential resolutions. This leads teachers to fulfill the "dual aims of action (or change) and research (or theory, or understanding)" (Dick, 2007, p. 150), which "incorporates questioning, assessing, investigating, collaborating, analyzing, and refining" the problem (Schoen, 2007, p. 211). McKay and Marshall (2001) attest that AR is more than just problem solving. The processes require educators to delve farther into the results found through reflective inquiry and then apply their personal knowledge to form questions in need of researching. When teachers engage in action research, it leads them to better understand and therefore improve upon their instructional practice and educational outcomes (Schoen, 2007).

Teacher Reflection in Action Research

The origins of teacher inquiry can be traced to Dewey's (1933) philosophy of progressive education. He viewed inquiry as a process of pragmatic problem-solving and nurturing of reflective skills that is an essential ingredient to improve the practice of teaching (Emerling, 2010). Dewey (1980) articulates the process of sound, experiential "reflective inquiry" as having five phases: 1) dissonance, confusion, and ambiguity in response to a situation; 2) a tentative interpretation of the given elements; 3) a careful survey of all attainable consideration that will define and clarify the problem at hand; 4) an elaboration of the tentative hypothesis; and 5) the development of a formal hypothesis upon which to act (and which itself remains open to further testing and revision). Although articulated as a process, or model for inquiry, entering into inquiry is an intentional choice or commitment. In defining his key term, praxis or "action-reflection," Freire (1970) articulates the connection between action and analysis as an essential component of pedagogical practice. He explains that praxis must be a concurrent, recursive, and an ongoing process of action-reflection. Foundational texts, Dewey and Freire set a foundation for later pedagogical practices.

The benefits of applying pedagogical practices of inquiry in the continued education of teachers are well documented, and can be wielded to transform teachers into innovators and leaders. Rearick and Feldman's (1999) and Hendrick's (2009) research indicates three types of reflection that can occur during AR. They are: autobiographical, where the researcher tries to understand the purpose of their research and then explain it; collaborative is when the action researcher abstracts principles or propositions and tries to seek answers beyond oneself and through analysis and interpretation

finds a new kind of clarity; and communal reflection is on one's self in communication with others and larger contexts such as cultural, historical, and institutional. They involve dialogues about actions, ideologies, and development of society.

Wellington (1991) states, "reflection practice calls for personal and professional transformation" (p. 5) where teachers ponder actions and initiatives. The process of reflection, Canning (1991) adds, can lead the teacher to explore alternatives that eventually lead to "Aha!" (p. 20) moments associated with participating in systematic research. One method utilized to initiate reflection is posing questions to teachers at each stage of continued learning, questions that demand answers such as, *"What do I do? . . . Ask yourself, what does this mean? . . . Ask, How did I come to be this way? . . . And lastly, how might I do things differently?"* and which effectively "[result] in the call to action" (Wellington, 1991, p. 5). These kinds of reflective questions are "intended to raise consciousness, to challenge complacency, and to engender a higher order of professional practice" in educators (p. 5). Surbeck, Han, and Moyer (1991) suggest that another method for initiating this process that "encourages thinking" is asking teachers to keep journals (p. 25).

The act of journal writing initiates several levels of reflective thought. Surbeck, Han, and Moyer (1991) comment, "taking the time to write in a journal means also taking time to reflect" upon one's profession (p. 27). In other words, the time taken to complete the actual kinetic activity of writing a journal produces a kind of automatic space for engagement. In this contemplative moment, teachers engage in "integrating course content, self-knowledge, and practical experiences with teaching and learning situations" (p. 25).

Schon (1987) describes two activities in journal writing that can be used to help develop a reflective thought process: "Reflection-*in*-Action" involves reflecting "on phenomena and on one's spontaneous ways of thinking and acting in the midst of the action," and "Reflection-*on*-Action" is to reflect "on one's actions and thoughts, undertaken after the process is completed" (as cited in Killion and Todnem, 1991, p. 15). Killion and Todnem (1991) encourage teachers to view reflection as "a gift we give ourselves, not passive thought . . . but an effort we approach with rigor, some purpose . . . and in a formal way . . . to reveal the wisdom embedded in our experience" (p. 14). In a longitudinal study of teachers learning from self-reflection and the reflections of other participants in the study, Systma (2007) documents positive experiences of personal and professional transformation. The element of continuous reflection-*in*-action and reflection-*on*-action leads a teacher to acquire knowledge in understanding classroom events. And these learning moments blossom into unexpected realizations and solutions to problems, marking significant growth in the professional and leadership development of teachers.

Teachers learning to solve problems through the practice of AR and systematic reflections are better orientated to effectively teach in urban environments. Blumenreich and Falk's (2006) study states "learning to solve problems through the study of practice has a special significance in the context of the culturally, socioeconomically, and linguistically diverse communities that increasingly make up the population of today's American schools" (p. 871). This echoes similar calls to improve traditional teacher education programs (Carr and Kemmis, 1986; Darling-Hammond, 2006; Lumpe, 2006; U.S. Department of Education, 2003).

METHODOLOGY

This descriptive study documents a university-based graduate capstone course for teacher practitioners to generate action-oriented research supported with systematic reflective writing. The teacher educator/researcher acted as a facilitator, mentor, and guide to teacher practitioners who participated in a collaborative approach to construct understandings about teaching and learning that are uniquely applicable to their own settings. A spiral rather than a linear approach of action research was conducted by the researcher for teachers to: examine and discourse traditional and contemporary philosophies of teaching and learning; design action research as a way to solve problems; and improve practice by following a series of steps that is similar to the traditional scientific method (Hendricks, 2009). All teachers were required to have two groups of subjects (experimental and control groups) and to start the AR intervention with a baseline assessment data (pre-test) and conclude with (post-test) assessment data for analysis. Teachers were permitted additional inter-

mediate tests, quizzes, et cetera, as deemed necessary during their two to three weeks of AR study. The study appropriated concepts of the "activity-theory" (Lave and Wenger, 1991; Wenger, 1998) within Vygotsky's (1978) "sociocultural" context of social and cultural urban school situations to nurture leadership styles (Lieberman and Miller, 2005) and formalize the recursive cycles of reflections throughout the AP process (Dick, 2007; Schoen, 2007; Schon, 1987).

Context of Study and Research Questions

The literature overwhelmingly supports the call for training of teacher leaders both in the K–12 schools and teacher education programs. Three essential concepts flow through the theory of action research seeking to develop a reflective teacher learning to lead from the classroom. First, action research is developed by exploring uncharted territory through an "iterative cycle" where the process involves "*review→plan→act→review*" (Dick, 2007; Schoen, 2007; Swanson, et al., 1997). Systma (2007) calls this the "search in re-search." Second, "reflective-practice" leads to teacher enlightenment and revelation, resulting in professional transformation (Canning, 1991; Schon, 1987; Wellington, 1991). Third, teacher leadership is nurtured through dialogue and collaboration with an experienced professional[4] (Normore, 2004). This mentor relationship acts as a formal way to "reveal the wisdom embedded in our experience" and culminates in ownership and empowerment of teacher participants (Killion and Todnem, 1991).

With the goal of empowering teachers to lead from the classroom, this illustrative study is directed by three research questions to ensure success in the formal preparation in and guidance through the iterative cycles of action research (AR) and systematic reflection. The AR questions supporting this study are:

1. In what ways does a formal preparation and instructor mentorship guide teachers to conduct Action Research Projects (ARP)?
2. In what ways do teachers reflect to learn from innovative teaching experiences?
3. How does systematic reflection affect self-perceptions of teachers and how does this perception influence their leadership in the classroom?

Participant Characteristics

Several preparatory requirements preceded the action research intervention in the capstone class. Detailed profiles of select case studies are provided later in the chapter. The characteristics of the participants are as follows:

- All twenty-six participants were teacher practitioners from urban schools of Southern California enrolled in a fifteen-week capstone course (last three units of coursework) while pursuing a master's degree in curriculum and instruction at a Southern California university.
- There were twenty-five female and one male teacher in this graduate class with full-time teaching experience ranging from three to seven years; one student was a long-term substitute teacher.
- The participants comprised seven African Americans, one Asian, five Hispanics, two Pacific Islanders, and eleven Whites.
- Teachers attended five discourse sessions with exposure to scholarly readings, reflections, and a variety of ARPs done by earlier students in previous years.
- Concurrently, for a period of seven weeks, students received direct instruction in the theory and practice of action research as described in the assigned textbook *Improving Schools through Action Research* (Hendricks, 2009) and engaged students to think, share, and design AR inquiry questions and hypotheses.
- The culmination of weekly discourses, in-depth review of curricular issues, interpretation of related research findings, and reflections consolidates teacher preparation to begin the journey to lead through action-oriented reflective research projects.

Sources of Data

Weekly discussions in preparation for AR. By engaging in open and flexible dialogue each week, teachers have the opportunity to build rapport, modify personal philosophy of teaching and learning, receive inspiration and guidance from classical and contemporary curricular specialists and education scholars (e.g., Confucius, Plato, Burber, Dewey, Freire, Goodlad, Fullan, Schon), and consciously engage new ways to increase student learning. Within the contemporary K–12 professional world of mandates, curriculum standards, and school hierarchy, the weekly dialogues broke the routine, as they tended to originate within the Freire paradigm of "critical pedagogy," where dialogue is honest, horizontal, fluid, and based on the complex and "generative themes" of education (Freire, 1970, p. 154).

Weekly discussions on assigned readings related to scholarly research and best practices were designed to encourage both independent and collaborative inquiry. The readings were mainly peer-reviewed research articles encompassing critical pedagogy of teaching and learning, contemporary and classical philosophical suppositions, the importance and art of reflection, and teacher leadership. Teachers worked in groups of four to read the assigned texts and prepare to engage with the whole class in weekly dialectical discourse. Teachers supplemented their scholarly readings with bibliographic searches. Searches were conducted on the assigned author(s) and/or comparative research on alternative ideas. Larger classroom discussions often focused on the concerns and issues experienced by teacher participants. Small and larger group discourse helped to develop the critical reasoning skills of participants, which affected professional development.

Weekly readings and reflections in preparation for AR. After discussion with the entire class, teachers were asked to reflect in weekly written exercises in order to prepare them for AR. The following examples of weekly teacher reflections from select and expanded readings provide a panoramic view of reflections written by the twenty-six teachers. Figures 8.1 to 8.4 and weekly readings (see Appendix) show how teacher perceptions, experiences, and beliefs are prefaced, deliberated, and modified as their awareness of their role in an AR develops. The reflections were written directly after discourse with the whole class in order to capture views shared by teachers and analyzed in class. The instructor then read teacher reflections and provided constructive feedback to encourage students, build their confidence, and evoke a genuine desire to improve student learning.

Examples of instructor's questions helped guide teacher reflections. Such as:

- How does the author's scholarship and philosophy help to enrich, grow, and modify your philosophy of teaching and learning?

Week 1 Reflections Prior to AR

"I do have to admit the way the articles are connected make the class discussion very rich. The expertise and opinions of the group are so varied that each article was made to fold into each other so that it would seem to belong together. Hearing the group discuss Friere was extremely valuable because I think it was one of the most valuable conversations and learning experiences about him."

"My biggest take away is that teachers want to be involved. However, I notice that their efforts are very rarely materialized. As a result, their motivation to participate in new initiatives diminishes.

"Teaching of historical philosophers and educators.......the discussion that followed....that as educators there are many lessons that can be taken from wise words of these philosophers.... Their ideas and values are still pertinent today.....teaching and learning are reciprocal that students must be motivated by their own desire to learn which happens through teachers taking interest and getting to know their students. ...teaching moral character...and setting examples for our students ... to develop their own sense of responsibility and ethics... teachers need to treat their student with respect and need to be understanding while maintaining their position as the educational leader of the classroom and their high expectations for all students."

Figure 8.1.   *Week 1 Reflections Prior to AR*

- How do the dialectical discourses on the philosophy and practice of critical pedagogy support your values, beliefs, and principles of transformative leadership?
- Does the message and actions differ from the dominant paradigm in most schools?
- How would you engage in personal, professional, and analytical reflections to examine best practices that testify to transformative teacher leadership?

Overall, teacher reflections indicate a positive response to readings and discussion. Teachers valued the readings by classical and contemporary philosophers. Some expressed inspiration, sharing intentions to renew their ethical commitment to students, while others noted the continuity between readings, their thoughts, and class discussions. Reflections were also an opportunity for teachers to express concerns from their professional experiences. Teachers invested in school reform expressed desire for unity, a shared vision and voice, but felt excluded by their administrations. A common theme, collaboration for school-wide reform is often mired with conflicts and challenges as addressed in Brooks, et al. (2004), High and Ovando (2004), Ovando (1996), and York-Barr and Duke (2004), which undercuts commitment to enacting change. Reflections from week one indicate enthusiasm and a hesitant, or qualified, interest in school reform.

By the second week teachers felt safe to share personal experiences of teaching: their practice in classrooms and the views they held. Danielson (2006) describes this process as a professional exploration

Week 2 Reflections Prior to AR

"I realize that I am weak in leadership skills because I give student more kindness and leniency rather than structure, rules, and demands. I need to deliver a stronger personality and develop better leadership skills."

"I really appreciated this article as well as the discussion that followed the group's synopsis of the reading. I strongly believe that the most effective teachers are those that partake in ongoing research that develops their effectiveness in the classroom and allows them to evaluate their own teaching..."

"Teachers must remind themselves that they are a service to children, not a service to educational systems."

Many parents believe, and with good reason, that teachers continue to teach the same way year after year. This type of research invigorates the learning community at a school."

Figure 8.2.   *Week 2 Reflections Prior to AR*

Week 3 Reflections Prior to AR

"The reflection practice discussion brought to light aspects that I had not thought of before. Discussion of action research results at staff meetings and PLC meeting would be helpful because of the relevance to the student population."

"In my experience, I have found that even small actions taken in my class or with other teachers helps to keep us active in improving ourselves."

"Without reflection it makes it very difficult for research to be meaningful and to create change in the classroom. Reflecting on our research as educators pushes us to think critically about our practices and to evaluate how new findings can help to increase our effectiveness."
"Most importantly, I now know that reflection is the method by which I deeply evaluate the effectiveness of all the decisions that I make."

"When teachers reflect critically they take into consideration the moral and ethical aspects of their decisions
...... When we reflect we start to see things differently, which leads to thinking differently, and ultimately acting differently."

Figure 8.3. Week 3 Reflections Prior to AR

of practice. Statements made by teachers reflect a conscious awareness of social justice, and the equity of learning opportunities for all as echoed by Dewey (1993) and Freire (1970). They also comprehended the challenge to complacency in the profession (Canning, 1991). Ermeling (2010) and Schon (1987) suggest that taking time to think about one's teaching indicates a desire to improve in one's profession and gain acceptance by the community, including parents and other major stakeholders of a child's education.

In week three, teachers expressed understanding of how and why reflection improves teaching, or what Barth (2006), Dewey (1993), and Phelps (2008) characterize as call to and catalyst of effective teaching. Teachers also shared their personal and professional challenges and concerns through reflections (Dozier, 2007; Hendricks, 2009). The desire to reflect even in incremental steps indicates a positive increase in the teachers' self-efficacy to improve student learning. Benefits of reflection in learning are well documented: Wellington (1991) argues that a contemplative process

helps improve efficiency in the profession. Surbeck et al. (1991) suggested that teaching improves when supplemented with student reflections about learning. And finally, teaching warrants all teachers to have high expectations of student performance (Dewey, 1993; Dozier, 2007; Fullan, 1994; and Phelps, 2008). The information assimilated in this section promoted agency because participants had a fully transparent understanding of why reflections were assigned and what benefits might result. The information also affects the teachers' understanding of teaching in classrooms, generating a willingness to ask for reflection from their own students.

In the fourth week, teacher progress through discourse and deliberations indicates the growth in self-efficacy and the power of action research supporting effective teaching practices. Teachers accept the ethical and personal ownership to be accountable and the best they can be in the profession.

For this chapter the researcher selected five purposive AR participants to describe the case studies as a manageable group for in-depth AR analysis and reporting

Week 4 Reflections Prior to AR
"The teacher as a researcher is interesting to me because I have always thought elementary teachers do not conduct research in their classroom unless they are in a program that requires it. I am hoping that I will be able to influence a teacher in my school who has good teaching practices to conduct research with me."

"AR Is not only a good idea, it becomes an ethical responsibility for monitoring the effectiveness of one's practice and improves competency of one's teaching. It engages in a process of observing-doing-observing-adjusting and doing again."

Figure 8.4. Week 4 Reflections Prior to AR

process. The five reflection journals illustrate the three theoretical and practical components of exploring an "iterative cycle" of reflections; always recursive, these reflections were also, at times, in disarray, but did not require a neat and linear process to benefit teachers in their AR endeavors. The selected journals reflect efforts of teachers from public schools across Los Angeles, California. The action research projects were conducted in classrooms by teachers (using pen names) in K–12 grade classrooms over a time period of four to five weeks. Several of the participants used the Question Answer Relationships[5] (QAR) (explicit or implicit) as a tool for conceptualizing and developing comprehension skills within the grade level content and student needs. All five teachers were able to develop a quasi-experimental ARP design with control and intervention student groups to assess differences in the student learning outcomes.

Participants' Profiles and ARPs

This segment provides a brief description of the individual teacher's design and execution of the ARP following the research guidelines delineated by the teacher-educator/researcher.

Ms. Patty—ARP Title: *"Cooperative learning opportunities within the classroom to improve students' unit test scores."*

Ms. Patty is a ninth grade history teacher in Los Angeles, California, with five years of teaching experience. Ms. Patty introduced cooperative learning opportunities to scaffold her direct instruction. The hypothesis of her action research was that students placed in mixed-ability cooperative learning groups comprised of students with varied academic abilities would be able to learn from each other and perform better in world history lesson unit tests. Ms. Patty did a purposive sampling of mixed-ability and cross-cultural group learning for the quasi-experimental intervention study comprising (N = 35, control group, period 2) and (N = 33, experimental group, period 1).

All students took a unit test, which served as a baseline for measuring outcomes of the study. After this test, the experimental group, which had more low-performing students, participated in cooperative lessons. Students cooperatively worked through lesson activities, discussing and sharing tools such as graphs, conceptual

mapping, cause-and-effect charts, note-taking, multiple choice questions, and homework assigned from the textbook. Students in the experimental group also validated each other's work. The control group, consisting of more advanced student performers, was given activities already familiar to all of the students in the class: that is, Cornell notes, KWL charts, and Teacher Generated *Close Question* handouts. Both groups were assigned informal reflective journals, which helped the teacher to get a sense of what interested and engaged students in either group. Data analysis recorded better scores on tests, on quizzes, and on the unit test for the weaker students of the experimental group versus the modest improvement of scores in the more advanced students of the control group. Teacher acknowledges increased student success in tests when students learn and acquire knowledge with other students, in activities where they can use what they have learned.

Ms. Nettie—ARP Title: *"Success with Foldable Graphic Organizers in Teaching Math Concepts"*

Ms. Nettie is a seventh grade math teacher with three years' experience in teaching mathematics in Los Angeles, California. Her ARP hypothesis was to determine if the use of foldable graphic organizers would increase student performance and engagement in the learning process of math concepts. The control group (N = 25) was comprised of students with academic abilities ranging from basic to proficient. The academic ability of students in the experimental group (N = 22) ranged from far below basic to basic. Over the course of three weeks, both groups took a series of pre- and post-tests in order to assess their knowledge of adding and subtracting integers, and calculating the mean, median, and mode of a set of data. The experimental group, with teacher modeling, created three-dimensional, foldable graphic organizers. The goal was to increase understanding of the concepts students were learning by having them build and utilize an interactive educational aid.

Analysis of the assessment data showed that there was a significant difference between the two groups from the very beginning of the study: In the control group (CG), the average score for all three post-tests was higher than that of the experimental group (EG). The post-test scores from the CG were also higher than the EG's scores despite educational intervention. Rather than simply comparing the average pre/post-test scores, the teacher compared the level of growth each group experienced from pre-test to post-test. In general, the data showed that the difference between the average pre- and post-test scores of the EG was 19.6 points, in comparison to a general increase of 16.8 points displayed by the control group. The teacher concluded that foldable graphic organizers increased student engagement with and attainment of math concepts.

Ms. Maddi—ARP Title: *"The Effect of Implementing the QAR model on 7th Grade Science Student's Content Mastery."*

Ms. Maddi, a seventh grade science teacher, divided four sections of students (all taught in the morning) into two groups of control and experimental students. Her AR research hypothesis was that students receiving science content instruction using the QAR techniques following each lesson will achieve higher-than-average gains from pre-test to post-test on teacher-created, criterion-referenced tests. The baseline was determined using a pre-test, and after QAR treatment a post-test was given. Three assessments were given throughout the study to determine the differences in the rate of reading and content comprehension between the control and experimental groups. The students in the experimental group were instructed in comprehension and questioning hierarchy–factual to more open-ended question and answers using the QAR strategy. The results of the study showed an overall improvement in the test scores of students instructed using QAR strategies. When assessed with open-ended questions, these students were also better able to synthesize concepts and use learned information in written responses. Beyond content mastery, the QAR strategy helped students to feel more confident in their abilities and produced a sense of confidence and ownership in learning. The teacher expressed interest in using the QAR approach for math instruction.

Ms. Trish—ARP Title: *"The Agile Learner, Action Research Project"*

Ms. Trish, a ninth grade math teacher, divided her two sections of geometry class students into control and experimental study groups. Ms. Trish's action research hypothesis was that the Agile Mind (www.agilemind.com) learner program instruction would help improve the exploration of quadrilaterals. The data used in this study was collected from student discussion, quiz results, surveys, and individual tasks. A pre-test and post-test was administered to both groups to determine results of the treatment. Students in the experimental group (N = 20) were exposed to animations that explained and posed math problems on content such as quadrilaterals, charts, activities, and graphic organizers. The control group (N = 22) received regular geometry instruction by the teacher. Analysis of the data showed no evidence that the program had an impact on test scores of students. The three-week time for ARP study was not adequate for students and the teacher to become familiar with all functions and procedures of the Agile Mind learner program. It was suggested that more time was needed to see a significant impact with the program.

Mr. Hal—ARP Title: *"Question and Answer strategies used to improve summarization skills."*

Mr. Hal, a grade six teacher, divided students from his two Earth science classes into equally sized (N = 27) experimental and control groups. His action research hypothesis was that students receiving direct/explicit instruction in QAR questioning strategies along with teacher "metacognition modeling" of questioning text material will show improvement in summarization skills. The experimental group was instructed with sample questions in the text along with additional assistance on how to ask critical thinking questions to scaffold comprehension. The teacher hoped for more meaningful interactions with assigned texts, reflecting increased comprehension, summarization, and recall of concepts. The control group did not receive any additional instruction. The compared pre- and post-test scores showed that students in the experimental group experienced modest increase in content comprehension skills. The teacher noted that additional time was required for the students and teacher to better familiarize themselves with this new method of thinking and responding to contextual questions, and for the explicit adoption of the QAR techniques.

FINDINGS

The teacher practitioner's preparatory and action-oriented reflective journals and APR project guided the report of the findings within the three research questions. The selected reflective journal writing excerpts are paralleled with teacher leadership concepts, iterative reflections, and the advocacy to mentor teachers to lead in the urban classroom.

In what ways does a formal mentorship and guidance to conduct Action Research Projects (ARP) support teachers learning to lead in the classroom?

The preliminary weeks of instruction were dedicated to interactive pedagogical discourse between teachers on best teaching practices, systematic reflection, the natural approach to innovative problem solving (Swanson et al., 1997; Systma, 2007). AR Teaching interventions were also planned and proposed to instructors for review and approval. During this time, teacher participants expressed both reservations and enthusiasm for their proposed interventions.

For example,

Sixth Grade teacher, Mr. Hal, expresses confidence in the material he teaches, stating that he can rely on his competence in the content of the lesson, while he focuses on implementing new pedagogy:

> Starting an action research project in my classroom has been exciting and stimulating task as well as a complex and daunting one. I am very comfortable and familiar with the content that I teach as well as the delivery of it . . . This will allow me to focus my efforts on the thrust of the research that I am doing and that is to be able to model, scaffold, display, motivate, explain, and reinforce high quality literature summarization along with questioning skills, and conceptual understanding of content on a daily basis.

Ninth grade teacher Ms. Trish, reflects on the way her original apprehension gradually became optimism and enthusiasm to commence the ARP:

> I was a little nervous going into this research because I was not sure about how I would approach it. I struggled with the QAR and different comprehension strategies. I could not figure out how to relate them to a mathematics class.
>
> Deciding the topic for my action research did not come about until I knew what I wanted to change within my classrooms . . . I went to one workshop . . . and I was interested in this new program called Agile Mind and its impact on student achievement. From that point, I knew that I wanted to integrate this program into my instruction to see whether there was an impact or *not*.

Seventh grade teacher Ms. Maddie, expresses her eagerness to embark upon her study while anxiously anticipating student behavioral outcomes:

> I am excited to begin this process because I think that this project will offer me a lot of insight into how students learn . . . I am a little concerned . . . I think that some of my students will resist because reflecting can be a very challenging task.

Seventh grade math teacher Ms. Nettie experiences the process of implementing an ARP as a professional challenge:

> I am preparing to engage in an Action Research project like no other. I can't remember the last time I had to do research that actually required me to follow the scientific method . . . to create a hypothesis and establish a research design in order to test a theory. This is a very difficult task that I am about to undertake. Quite frankly, I feel a little bit overwhelmed.

This fundamental awareness of growth as a continual process unleashed an introspective dialogue among teachers. They simultaneously experienced and implemented a philosophy of teaching, which helped them to relate to their students, and therefore improve their understanding of how their students learn (Shim, 2008). Hereafter, teachers participated in teaching challenges required for action research.

In discussions, teacher participants shared their views and deliberated over several fundamental teaching concepts. They reached a consensus over integrated learning: that is, that effective learning among children comes through integration of skills rather than isolated and fragmented learning opportunities. And through meaningful engagement with subsequent, scholarly readings they came to understand that knowledge of course content goes beyond the realm of a prescribed curriculum; it can also come from the rigor of selecting research-based instructional approaches. This understanding of theory through selective design and application led to a conscious ownership of the curriculum and instructional practices among teachers and their students as advocated by Schoen (2007).

In what ways do teachers reflect to learn from innovative teaching experiences?

A critical and systematic approach to successfully evaluate teaching innovations is through the practice of "reflection-*in*-action" and "reflection-*on*-action" (Schon, 1987). This approach requires teachers to note discrepancies in student learning and to design creative solutions. The following reflections provide a window into the reflection-*in*-action taking place in the teachers' reflective journals:

Sixth grade teacher Mr. Hal reflects on how he restructured his instruction of summarization to maximize students' receptivity to learning,

> I feel as though I differentiated the instruction sufficiently well as to create a possibly measureable difference in the summarization skills of the two classes. The class receiving treatment was far more engaged.

> I also have found that in preparing for this actions research it has Focused MY attention more on what I am doing in the classroom (both for science and math) in that I am forced to 'extra' prepare for the two groups and think more deeply about the strategies that will be useful or non-useful and why I would want to use them.

Ninth grade teacher Ms. Trisha expresses doubt in implementing changes:

> Throughout this process, I was skeptical about the research. I was not sure everything would work out. I had thought that the program was too complex for the students to understand . . . The guided quizzes on the program were a great help to introduce the students to the self-tests.

> I think that my instructional practices will improve because I am adding something that can potentially increase students learning.

Seventh grade teacher Ms. Nettie's reflection illustrates how a teacher acclimates to the program, and shows optimism over changes in learning behaviors of students:

> In order to get a better understanding of what this unique organizer was, I discussed the concept with a teacher who has utilized the organizer. Based on their demonstration I selected the four door-foldable . . . As I showed students a sample of a foldable, they got really excited. They made comments like, "Wow, Ms. This is cool!" or "Why didn't we make these before!"

> During a few seconds of down time . . . I could hear pairs of students giving each other problems and asking them to locate the part of the foldable that would help them derive a solution. Their action indicated to me that they liked using the foldable.

The study is about to come to a close. However, what I have learned over the last few weeks is that my students like fun and creative ways to record information and to organize their thoughts. I relied so heavily on Cornell note taking because that was what was required/suggested of me by my school administrator.

Seventh grade teacher Ms. Maddie shares concerns that her students will not respond well to changes in the classroom:

> I am a little concerned with how my students will react to the implementation of this new strategy initially. I think that some of my students will resist because reflecting can be a very challenging task.

Ninth grade teacher Ms. Patty reflects[6] upon positive changes in her classroom environment through application of learning theory:

> I teach teenagers, and I believe Albert Bandura's 'social learning theory' applies to my students . . . I often model the behavior . . . particularly politeness and sharing. My efforts have met with success with parents partnering to model positive behaviors . . . showing respect to all students allows learning from others to be smoothly exchanged.

After ARPs were completed, teachers exercised reflection-*on*-action. Many were able to acknowledge their accomplishments in the study and identify professional growth (Canning, 1991). From the several reflections noted, it becomes apparent that reflecting-*in*-action and *on*-action is conducive to teacher growth and positive engagement (Wellington, 1991). Participants experienced emotions that ranged from anxiety to exultation; as they implemented changes, they identified a need for flexibility and came to accept the benefits of having a flexible approach to teaching. These varied reflections document teacher behavior that is indicative of an iterative process of action built through dialogue and mentoring, which oftentimes follows a nonlinear approach in achieving the best from teachers and students (Barnett et al., 2005; Dozier, 2007).

How does systematic reflection affect self-perceptions of teachers and how does this perception influence their leadership in the classroom?

Corresponding to well-known educational practices and concepts such as the need for leadership opportunities

(Isaacson, 2007; Wasley, 1991), Killion and Todnem's (1991) leadership transformation, and Normore's (2004) and Schoen's (2007) "professional socialization," reflection and action research can be a fulfilling and successful avenue to teacher empowerment and leadership. The following provide examples of teacher participants experiencing moments of empowerment and self-actualization, as expressed in teacher reflection journals. Some identified the practices used in implementing an ARP as useful, sharable tools, while others were motivated to continue with self-reflection and study of teaching practices.

Seventh grade teacher Ms. Maddie reflects:

I find that this strategy is useful . . . this is something that I would be more than willing to share with other teachers.

Ninth grade teacher Ms. Trisha reflects:

My experience with this research project overall has been very positive and is a tool that I believe other teachers should be utilizing in order to develop and refine their own teaching practices. Giving teachers the opportunity to be leaders in their classroom and to learn from and with their students is an experience that can, in no way, be replaced. This is an experience that is important for not only educators but students as well who are able to see that their teachers are learning along with them and are working to be more effective leaders in their classroom.

Seventh grade teacher Ms. Nettie reflects:

I plan on expanding my study. Over time, I would like to examine how the uses of foldables impact the comprehension and performance of male and female students . . . I may want to conduct may be comparison of multiple foldable and their usefulness in teaching specific topics . . . One thing is for sure, I plan on sharing the knowledge I have gained from my study with other educators.

Sixth grade teacher Mr. Hal reflects:

There is no doubt that the amount of work (planning, organizing, implementing, analyzing, and reflecting) in carrying out an action research project in the middle-school classroom is enormous, time consuming, and exhausting. However, I have found that it is always useful for me to get myself out of my comfort zone and pursue something that is important, professional, and worthwhile. Doing something of this magnitude and scope is the only way can I grow and develop as a professional and, more importantly, as a teacher. I have high standards for myself, personally and professionally.

These moments of realization are milestones that mark significant growth in the process of reflection. Methodical reflection and action research can lead to positive outcomes such as confidence, personal empowerment, enhanced professionalism, and improved student learning (Lieberman and Miller, 2005; Phelps, 2008). In order to grow through the process of reflection and action research, teachers must be receptive to trial and error; testing and experimenting with research-based methods; and voluntarily aspire to master their craft. The following excerpts were recognized as teachers reaching moments of self-actualization or belief in the self, and taking ownership of change—an essential growth attribute marking the transformation of a teacher to a leader (Canning, 1991).

DISCUSSION

The researcher's descriptive analysis of the case studies in this study are analogous to leadership studies reported by Lieberman and Miller (2005), with teacher leaders' roles identified as "*advocator, innovator, and steward*"; to Phelps's (2008) case studies illuminating upon the three roles; and to Wasley's (1991) report on teachers' "attempted techniques and methods" based on what Goodlad (1987) called an "authorized opinion" (cited by Wasley, 1991, p. 171). The empowering responsibilities for teachers witnessed in this study correspond to: "1. The autonomy to decide which strategies they will work with; and 2. The freedom to experiment with those techniques with students and other teachers" (Wasley, 1991, p. 171).

Structure-Based Action Research Development

In order to cultivate teaching dispositions capable of leading other teachers, the teacher educator/researcher focused on building skills with a foundation "in research and strong undergirding instructional philosophies" (Wasley, 1991, p. 171). Using the three questions posed above, the teacher educator/researcher developed an accessible theoretical framework from which teacher participants drew; and the reflections show a high absorption level when translating theory to experiential practice (Dewey, 1993; Freire, 1970). In order to execute an ARP that would improve student learning (Danielson, 2006), students were encouraged to base their projects on evidence-based teacher theory and practices (Dick, 2007; Swanson et al., 1997; Systma, 2007). These interventions required constant reflection, as well as regular adaptation to thoughts and procedures necessary to leading (and taking ownership in) an ARP. In order to facilitate this reflection, teacher participants received continual instruction and mentoring on how to design and execute an AR throughout the semester.

The professional skills development of each participant, while different, is made clear in attitudes and actions described in journal reflections. Consider the following examples from the reflections: Ms. Patti directly acknowledged the way her cognitive and reflective pedagogical thinking was influenced by the scholarly readings, while Mr. Hal expressed his eagerness to embrace challenges to enhance his research and teaching repertoire. Ms. Trisha hoped to improve student learning through practical application: integration of software program applications that she acquired at the school workshop into the instruction of geometry concepts. Her reflections accompanying her data analysis express a desire, despite having experienced difficulty executing the intervention, to make another attempt and perform well. Ms. Nettie received assistance of peer-teachers in confidently demonstrating three-dimensional foldable graphic organizers, which scaffold learning experiences, and had a positive impact in her classroom   increasing motivation among her low-performing students. Ms. Maddi, after gaining success with QAR comprehension strategies in science, was motivated to do the same in her math class. Scholarly readings prior to execution of the AR, discourse and reflection with other students throughout, direct instruction, and journal reflections written before, during, and after each step of the AR helped guide teacher participants and cultivate positive and motivated teaching dispositions.

Importance of Mentorship and Guidance

The mentorship and nurturing support provided by teacher educator/researcher was central to the preparatory stages of action research. Teacher participants needed guidance in understanding the potential impact of action research, as both a source of personal growth and new knowledge in the field of education (Barth, 2006; Danielson, 2006; Lieberman and Miller, 2005) before they could "adopt leadership as a possibility" (Phelps, 2008, p. 119). This reassurance or confidence building through consistent feedback and discourse throughout several weeks of instruction manifested itself through the process by which the individual teachers selectively acquired "the knowledge, skills, and dispositions needed to perform a social role effectively" (Normore, 2004, p. 111); and instructors ensured that the processes were founded upon "collaborative inquiry, reflection, and dialogue" (Schoen, 2007, p. 211). The researcher created an environment that encouraged growth in teacher participants parallel to Bennett's (1993) solicitations for school administrators to provide a "supportive context" where "teacher-researchers have the potential to enhance the professional image of educators" (p. 70) through "professional socialization" (Schoen, 2007, p. 211). In other words, educational support has reciprocal benefit: in addition to supporting the growth of teachers hoping to lead in the field, instructors were themselves invested in the process, which, through the contribution of their leadership, becomes mutually beneficial.

Reflective Inquiry Influences the Process

Reflective practice (Schon, 1987; Wellington, 1991) was initiated in the first week of the course and included weekly submission of written reflections. Responses from individuals and from class discussions helped both teacher mentor/researcher and teacher-participants make adjustments each week (Issacson, 2007; Normore, 2004). This continual reflection allowed for cross-sectional feedback to be incorporated into the design and implementation of the classroom interventions. During follow-up discussions, teacher participants were also able to find commonality amongst fellow teachers in their experiences, which gave credence to progressive changes that initially seemed daunting and challenging. Finally, reflection generated the cognitive acts of learning between teacher and student (Freire, 1970).

Self-Perceptions of Learning to Lead

Teachers learned to lead in their classrooms within the four processes of learning, meaning, community, and identity grounded in Lave and Wenger's (1991) and Wenger's (1998) "social theory of learning." Teachers learned from active "re-search" (Systma, 2007), shifting from teaching only in individual classrooms toward a potential to reshape learning and instruction on a larger scale. They positioned themselves to assume the many roles and responsibilities of leading as advocates, innovators, and stewards of their profession (Lieberman and Miller, 2005; Phelps, 2008). Reflections from participants indicate positive outcomes in leadership development, with participants showing increased confidence in and enthusiasm for executing educational interventions. For example, Ms. Trisha expressed a conviction that action and reflection through an ARP was not only important for her, but for all teachers so that they can become effective leaders in the classroom. Ms. Nettie was so confident after reporting her AR outcomes that she proposed to expand the study from incorporating gender-differentiated student learning and student learning opportunities in her mathematics instruction to instruction of science content. Mr. Hal, after confidently executing an ARP using science content, proposed to go further, stating that he wanted to "get out of his comfort zone" and expressed that in "doing something of this magnitude . . . I can grow as a professional and a teacher"; he was strongly motivated to perfect his pedagogy. Ms. Maddi's demonstration of peer-learning and mutual respect met "success with parents partnering to model positive behaviors." The reflective action research experiences of the five teacher illustrations indicate that teachers who "formally or informally acquire leadership positions can make change happen" (Lieberman and Miller, 2005, p. 155). Each of these responses reflects positive outcomes in AR, and are representative of the outcomes for the overall group in gains to confidence and enthusiasm for further leadership activities.

CONCLUSION

The five case studies underscore several general features about teachers constructing understandings about teaching and learning that are uniquely applicable to their own context in Los Angeles, California, urban schools following a model of action research accompanied with systematic reflective inquiry. Teachers enrolled in a Masters of Education program have taken a major step toward enhancing their professional skills to qualify and

act as part of a highly vibrant and intellectual professional community. Such teachers embrace leadership emanating from best teaching practices; utilize their wisdom of practice to develop a body of knowledge about the challenges of urban schools; become lifelong learners, thereby influencing other teachers to do the same; bring about a positive change and demonstrate the belief that leading and learning are interrelated; and showcase student performance outcomes at the classroom level of practice to complement success at the organizational level.

The conceptual design and analysis of this action research and teacher reflection model ensures a pathway for a nascent and organic teacher leadership where teachers can renew the ownership of practice, increase confidence, and enhance student performance when equipped with the necessary professional exploration of practice. Future studies in professional teacher leadership and whole school instructional reform will encourage the collaboration and commitment of school administrators and educators in applying systematic reflection and action research to educational programs. And it will indicate the extent to which teachers can gain the knowledge, skills, and dispositions to lead in the profession.

NOTES

1. In this study Action Research (AR) and Action Research Project (ARP) are used synonymously.

2. Additional examples of teacher leaders in York-Barr and Duke (2004), and Lieberman and Miller (2005).

3. According to Barnett et al. (2005), "today more than 40 thousand teachers in the U.S. have a NB certification, as research has shown students of NB certified teachers have performed better on standardized tests, especially students in low income communities with low performing schools" (p. 56).

4. Isaacson's (2007) "leadership opportunities for teachers" encourages requisitioning a "master" teacher to act as "mentor" to "novice" teachers.

5. *Question answer relationships now*, written by the creators of QAR, extensively outlines the QAR strategy, provides a framework for organizing instruction, and offers many classroom examples across grade levels. The book contains lesson plans and activities that teachers can utilize when implementing the strategy. See Raphael, Highfield, and Au (2006).

6. Ms. Patty bases her ARP intervention on Bandura's (1977) pioneering study that behavior is learned from the environment through the process of observational learning.

REFERENCES

Bandura, A. (1977). *Social Learning Theory*. Englewood Cliffs, NJ: Prentice Hall.

Barnett, B., Johnson, D., and Montgomery, D. (2005). The power of teacher leadership. *Educational Leadership, 62*(5), 56.

Barth, R. (2006). Improving relationships within the schoolhouse. *Educational Leadership 63*(6), 8–13.

Bennett, C.K. (1993). Teacher-researchers: All dressed up and no place to go? *Educational Leadership, 51*(2), 69–70.

Blase, J. and Blase, J.J. (2006). *Teachers Bringing Out the Best in Teachers: A Guide to Peer Consultation for Administrators and Teachers*. Thousand Oaks, CA: Corwin Press.

Blumenreich, M. and Falk, B. (2006) Trying on a new pair of shoes: Urban teacher-learners conduct research and construct knowledge in their own classrooms. *Teaching and Teacher Education 22*, 864–873

Brooks, J.S., Scribner, J.P., and Eferakorho, T. (2004). Teacher leadership in the context of whole school reform. *Journal of School Leadership,14*(3), 242–265.

Canning, C. (1991). What teachers say about reflection? *Educational Leadership, 48*(6), 18–21.

Carr, K. and Kemmis, S. (1986). *Becoming Critical: Education, Knowledge, and Action Research*. Philadelphia: Falmer.

Cochran-Smith, M. and Lytle, S. (1993). *Inside Outside: Teacher Research and Knowledge*. New York: Teachers College Press.

Corbett, D. and Wilson, B. (2002). What urban teachers say about good teaching. *Educational Leadership, 60*(1), 18–22.

Crowther, F., Kagan, S., Ferguson, M., and Hann, L. (2002). *Developing Teacher Leaders: How Teacher Leadership Enhances School Success*. Thousand Oaks, CA: Corwin Press.

Danielson, C. (2006). *Teacher Leadership That Strengthens Professional Practice*. VA: Association for Supervision and Curriculum Development.

Darling-Hammond, L. (2000). Teacher quality and student achievement: A review of state policy evidence. *Educational Policy Analysis Archives 8*(1), 1–50.

Darling-Hammond, L. (2006). Constructing 21st century of teacher education. *Journal of Teacher Education 57*(3), 300–314.

Darling-Hammond, L. (2007). The flat earth and education: How America's commitment to equity will determine our future. *Educational Researcher 36*(6), 318–324.

Darling-Hammond, L., Bullmaster, M.L., and Cobb, V.L. (1995). Rethinking teacher leadership through professional development schools. *The Elementary School Journal 96*(1), 86–106.

Davis, S., Darling-Hammond, L., LaPointe, M., and Meyerson, D. (2005). School leadership study: Developing successful principals. *Stanford Educational Leadership Institute*. Commissioned by the Wallace Foundation 1–27.

Deans, T. (1999). Service-Learning in two keys: Paulo Freire's Critical Pedagogy in relation to John Dewey's Pragmatism. *Michigan Journal of Community Service-Learning 6*(1), 15–29.

Denzin, N.A. and Lincoln, Y.S. (1994). Introduction: Entering the field of qualitative research. In N. A. Denzin and Y.S. Lincoln (Eds.) *Handbook of Qualitative Research* (1–17). Thousand Oaks, CA: Sage.

Dewey, J. (1964). The need for a philosophy of education. In R. Archambault (Ed.), *John Dewey on Education: Selected Writings* (3–14). New York: Random House.

Dewey, J. (1980). *The middle works, 1899–1924*. Volume 9: 1916. Jo Ann Boydston (Ed.). Carbondale, IL: Southern Illinois University Press.

Dewey, J. (1993). *How We Think*. New York: Dover.

Dick, B. (2007). Action research as an enhancement of natural problem solving. *International Journal of Action Research 3*(1+2), 149–167.

Dozier, T.K. (2007). Turning good teachers into great leaders. *Educational Leadership, 65*(1), 54–59.

Ermeling, B.A. (2010). Tracing the effects of teacher inquiry on classroom practice. *Teaching and Teacher Education 26*, 377–388.

Freire, P. (1970, rpt. 1985). *Pedagogy of the Oppressed*. Trans. Ramos, M. Bergman. New York: Continuum.

Frost, D. and Harris, A. (2003). Teacher leadership: towards a research agenda. *Cambridge Journal of Education 33*(3), 479–498

Fullan, M.G. (1993). Why teachers must become change agents. *Educational Leadership 50*(6), 12–17.

Fullan, M. (1994). Teacher leadership: A failure to conceptualize. In *Teachers as Leaders: Perspectives on the Professional Development of Teachers*, ed., D.R. Walling, 241–53. Bloomington, IN: Phi Delta Kappa.

Fullan, M. (2002). The change leader. *Educational Leadership 59*(8), 16–20.

Fullan, M. and Hargreaves, A. (1996). *What's Worth Fighting for in Your School?* New York: Teachers College Columbia University.

Furtado, L. (2010). Enhancing summarization skills using twin tests: Instruction in narrative and expository text structures. *The Reading Matrix: An International Online Journal 10*(2), 271–281.

Furtado, L. (2012). The Reflective teacher leader: An action research model. *Journal of School Leadership 22*(3), 531–568.

Goodlad, J. (Ed.). (1987). *The Ecology of School Improvement.* Chicago: University of Chicago Press.

Hagevik, R., Aydeniz, M., and Rowell, C. G. (2012). Using action research in middle level teacher education to evaluate and deepen reflective practice. *Teaching and Teacher Education 28*, 675–684.

Hart, A.W. (1994). Creating teacher leadership roles. *Educational Administration Quarterly 30*, 472–497.

Hendricks, C. (2009). *Improving Schools Through Action Research: A Comprehensive Guide for Educators.* Saddlebrook, NJ: Pearson Education, Inc.

High, C.S. and Ovando, M.N. (2004). *Teachers' voices in constructing leadership to enhance student success.* Paper presented at the University Council of Administration, Pittsburgh, November 1–3, 2004.

Isaacson, L.E. (2007). *The Principal's Purpose: A Practical Guide to Moral and Ethical School Leadership.* Larchmont: Eye on Education.

Junor Clarke, P. A. and Fournillier, J. (2012). Action research, pedagogy, and activity theory: Tools facilitating two instructors' interpretations of the professional development of four preservice teachers. *Teaching and Teacher Education 28*, 649–660.

Katzenmeyer, M. and Moller, G. (2001). *Awakening the Sleeping Giant: Helping Teachers Develop as Leaders* (2nd edn). Thousand Oaks, CA: Corwin Press.

Killion, J.P. and Todnem, G.R. (1991). A process for personal theory building. *Educational Leadership 48*(6), 14–16.

Ladson-Billings, G. (2001). *Crossing Over to Canaan: The Journey of New Teachers in Diverse Classrooms.* San Francisco: Jossey-Bass, Inc.

Lave, J. and Wenger, E. (1991). *Situated Learning: Legitimate Peripheral Participation.* Cambridge, UK: Cambridge University Press.

Leithwood, K., Louis, K., Anderson, S., and Wahlstrom, K. (2004). *How leadership influences student learning.* New York: The Wallace Foundation.

Lieberman, A. and Miller, L. (2005). Teachers as leaders. *The Educational Forum 69* (Winter), 151–162.

Lieberman, A., Saxl, E.R., and Miles, M.B. (2000). *Teacher Leadership: Ideology and Practice.* In *The Jossey-Bass Reader on Educational Leadership* (348–365). San Francisco: Jossey-Bass.

Liston, D., Borko, H., and Whitcomb, J. (2008). The teacher educator's role in enhancing teacher quality. *Journal of Teacher Education 59*(2), 111–116.

Little, J.W. (2003). Construction of teacher leadership in three periods of policy and reform activism. *School Leadership and Management 23*(2), 401–419.

Little, J.W. and Bartlett, L. (2002). Career and commitment in the context of comprehensive school reform. *Theory and Practice 8*(3), 345–354.

Lumpe, A. (2005). Toward needed reforms in science teacher education. *Journal of Science Teacher Education 16*(2), 89–93.

McKay, J. and Marshall, P. (2001). The dual imperatives of action research. *Information Technology and People 14*(1), 46–59.

Normore, A.H. (2004). Socializing school administrators to meet leadership challenges that doom all but the most heroic and talented leaders to failure. *International Journal of Leadership in Education: Theory and Practice 7*(2), 107–125.

Ovando, M.N. (1996). Teacher leadership: Opportunities and challenges. *Planning and Change: An Educational Leadership and Policy Journal 27*(1/2), 30–44.

Ovington, J., Diamantes, T., and Roby, D. (2002). Early distance learning success story: The teacher leader program. *College Student Journal 36*(3), 387–398.

Phelps, P.H. (2008). Helping teachers become leaders. *The Clearing House 1/2*, 119–122 .

Postholm, M. B. (2008). Teachers developing practice: Reflection as a key activity. *Teaching and Teacher Education 24*, 1718–1728.

Pounder, J.S. (2006). Transformational classroom leadership. The fourth wave of teacher leadership? *Educational Management Administration and Leadership 34*(4), 533–545.

Raphael, T., Highfield, K., and Au, K. (2006). *Question Answer Relationships Now.* New York: Scholastic.

Rearick, M. and Feldman, A. (1999). Orientations, purposes and reflection: A framework for understanding action research. *Teaching and Teacher Education 15*, 333–349.

Ross, D., Adams, A., Bondy, E., Dana, N., Dodman, S., and Swain, C. (2011). Preparing teacher leaders: Perceptions of the impact of a cohort-based, job-embedded, blended teacher leadership program. *Teaching and Teacher Education 27*, 1213–1222.

Schoen, S. (2007). Action research: A developmental model of professional socialization. *The Clearing House 80*(5), 211–216.

Schon, D.A. (1987). *Educating the Reflective Practitioner.* San Francisco: Jossey-Bass.

Schmuck, R.A. (2006). *Practical Action Research for Change* (2nd edn.). Thousand Oaks, CA: Corwin Press.

Schulte, B. (2004). Teaching teachers how to connect with urban students. Workshops at University Policies "Cultural Competency." *Washington Post*, July 26.

Shim, S.H. (2008). A philosophical investigation of the role of teachers: A synthesis of Plato, Confucius, Buber, and Freire. *Teaching and Teacher Education 24*, 515–535.

Smylie, M.A. and Denny, J.W. (1990). Teacher leadership: Tensions and ambiguities in organizational perspective. *Educational Administration Quarterly 26*(3), 235–259.

Snell, J. and Swanson, J. (2000). *The essential knowledge and skills of teacher leaders: A search for a conceptual framework*. A paper presented at the Annual American Education Research Association, New Orleans, LA.

Sparks-Langer, G.M. and Colton, B. (1991). Synthesis of research on Teachers' reflective thinking. *Educational Leadership 15*(1), 37–44.

Surbeck, E., Han E.P., and Moyer, J.E. (1991). Assessing reflective responses in journals. *Educational Leadership 48*(6), 25–27.

Swanson, B.L., Watkins, K.E., and Marsick, V.J. (1997). Qualitative research methods. In R.A. Swanson and E.F. Holton (Eds.), *Human Resource Development Research Handbook: Linking Research and Practice* (88–113). San Francisco: Berrett-Koehler.

Systma, S. (2007). *The Leading Way of Changing Meaning*. Teneriffe: Post Pressed.

Tietel, L. (1996). Finding common ground: Teacher leaders and principals. In G. Moller and M. Katzenmeyer (Eds.), *Every Teacher as a Leader: Realizing the Potential of Teacher Leadership* (139–154). San Francisco: Jossey-Bass.

U.S. Department of Education. (2003). *Meeting the Highly Qualified Teachers Challenge: The Secretary's Second Annual Report on Teacher Quality*. Washington, DC: U.S. Department of Education.

U.S. Department of Education. (2011). *No Child Left Behind*. Retrieved February 26, 2011, from www2.ed.gov/policy/elsec/leg/blueprint/index.html.

Vygotsky, L. (1978). *Mind in Society: The Development of Higher Psychological Processes*. Cambridge, MA: Harvard University Press.

Wasley, P.A. (1991). *Teachers Who Lead: The Rhetoric of Reform and the Realities of Practice*. New York: Teachers College Press.

Wasley, P.A. (1994). *Stirring the Chalkdust: Tales of Teachers Changing Classroom Practices*. New York: Teachers College Press.

Watts, M. and Lawson, M. (2009). Using a meta-analysis activity to make critical reflection explicit in teacher education. *Teaching and Teacher Education 24*, 609–616.

Wellington, B. (1991). The promise of reflective practice. *Educational Leadership 48*(6), 4–5.

Wenger, E. (1998). *Communities of Practice: Learning, Meaning, and Identity*. Cambridge, UK: Cambridge University Press.

Yoder, N. (1994). *Teacher Leadership: An Annotated Bibliography*. St Louis, MO: Danforth Foundation and Washington, DC: National Foundation for Improvement of Education (ERIC Document Reproduction Service, No. ED374081).

Yogev, S. and Yogev A. (2006). Teacher educators as researchers: A profile of research in Israeli teacher colleges versus university departments of education. *Teaching and Teacher Education 22*, 32–41.

York-Barr, J. and Duke, K. (2004). What do we know about teacher leadership? Findings from two decades of scholarship. *Review of Educational Research 74*(3), 255–316.

APPENDIX

The following peer-reviewed journal articles were read and discoursed as a preparation to Action Research Projects.

Week 1 Readings: Pedagogy of Critical Thinking in the Profession of Teaching

1. Shim, S. H. (2008). A philosophical investigation of the role of teachers: A synthesis of Plato, Confucius, Buber, and Freire. *Teacher and Teacher Education* 24(3), 515–535.

2. Deans, T. (1999). Service-Learning in two keys: Paulo Freire's Critical Pedagogy in relation to John Dewey's Pragmatism. *Michigan Journal of Community Service-Learning* 6(1), 15–29.

3. Pounder, J.S. (2006). Transformational classroom leadership: The fourth wave of teacher leadership? *Educational Management Administration and Leadership* 34(4), 533–545.

4. Freire, P (1970). Pedagogy of the oppressed. From Paulo Freire, *Pedagogy of the Oppressed*. New York: Continuum, 75–86, 95–100. Reprinted by permission.

Week 2 Readings: The Philosophical Constructs of Teaching and Learning

1. Killion, J.P. and Todnem, G.R. (1991). A process of personal theory building. *Educational Leadership* 15(1), 14–16.

2. Schoen, S. (2007). Action research: A developmental model of professional socialization. *The Clearing House* 80(5), 211–215.

3. Author (2012). The reflective teacher leader: An action research model. *Journal of School Leadership* 22 (3), 531–568.

Week 3 Readings: Systematic Practice of Teacher Reflections

1. Canning, C. (1991). What teachers say about reflection? *Educational Leadership* 15(1), 16–25.

2. Sparks-Langer, G.M. and Colton, B. (1991). Synthesis of research on teachers' reflective thinking. *Educational Leadership* 15(1), 37–44.

3. Surbeck, E., Han, E.P., and Moyer, J.E. (1991). Assessing reflective responses in journals. *Educational Leadership* 15(1), 25–27.

4. Wellington, B. (1991). The Promise of reflective practice. *Educational Leadership* 15(1), 4–5.

Week 4 Readings: Peer-Teacher Collaborations for Action Research Innovations

1. Furtado, L. (2010). Enhancing summarization skills using twin tests: Instruction in narrative and expository text structures. *The Reading Matrix: An International Online Journal* 10(2), 271–281.

2. Lieberman, A. and Miller, L. (2005). Teachers as leaders. *Educational Forum 69* (Winter), 151–162.

3. High, C.S. and Ovando, M.N. (2004). *Teachers' voices in constructing leadership to enhance student success.* Paper presented at the University Council of Administration, Pittsburgh.

GENDER, RACE, CLASS, AND CULTURE

This section focuses on contemporary approaches regarding the intricacy of education within an urban context. This section begins with a Voice from the Field by Camille Wilson titled, "Critical Care, Collaborative Activism, and Professional Risk: Unsung Yet Essential Aspects of Urban Educational Leadership." In chapter 9, "Urban Schools, Black Principals, and Black Students: Culturally Responsive Education and The Ethno-Humanist Role Identity," authors Kofi Lomotey and Kendra Lowery examines the quality of education that Black students receive in urban public schools in the United States and identify factors that exacerbate the disenfranchisement of Black students. This chapter focuses on the significance of the leadership of Black principals for Black students. Chapter 10, "Equity and Race-Visible Urban School Reform," written by Christine Sleeter, purports that the lack of academic achievement can be attributed to the absence of attention to race, equity, and culture—all of which thwarts the ability of education leaders to make substantial research-supported changes that actually reach students. Sleeter constructs three areas for change, offering examples and implications for education leaders in each: (1) Race-visible pedagogy (2) Race-visible teachers and (3) Race and class-visible equity. In chapter 11, "Culturally Responsive Leadership Preparation and Practices," authors Monica Wills Brown and Frankie K. Williams extend the achievement gap conversation by exploring culturally responsive leadership preparation and practices as a means to developing leaders who embrace and practice cultural responsiveness. Brown and Williams places an emphasis on the emergence of culturally responsive

education and tenets of principal preparation programs and practices related to cultural responsiveness focused on African American students within urban settings. Chapter 12, "From Dysconsciousness to Consciousness of Stereotypes that Disparage Black Youth: Calling for Transformative School Leadership," authored by Joyce E. King and Syreeta A. McTier, address critical habits of mind that urban school leaders and teachers need to develop regarding disparaging corporate controlled media (mis)representation of Black students and how negative portrayals influence their own perceptions and practices toward these students and their families. This chapter confronts dysconscious racism in relation to selected research and theoretical explanations regarding the impact of media stereotypes on the perceptions and practices of teachers, school leaders, and school polices (e.g. discipline). King and McTier conclude this chapter by providing recommendations for the transformative education of teachers and school leaders and suggestions for future research. Lastly, this section is finalized by chapter 13, "Tempered Radicalism in the Ivory Tower: Black Urban Educational Leaders Negotiating Lives in a Creative Class City." Authors, Richard J. Reddick, Stella L. Smith, and Beth Bukoski extend the definition of urban education leadership to encompass faculty charged with the responsibility of mentoring, nurturing and developing those who eventually will lead classrooms, schools, and districts. The findings within this chapter illustrate how Black faculty in the study enacted a tempered radical stance in their work on campus and in their communities. Taken together, these chapters highlight the importance of urban school reform but also a recommitment to the communities around our schools. This section demonstrate the possibilities for linking school change to policymaking strategies that confront normed practices in urban schools. The new approach to urban educational change must link this change to theory and practice.

Critical Care, Collaborative Activism, and Professional Risk

Unsung Yet Essential Aspects of Urban Educational Leadership

Camille M. Wilson

In writing this reflective essay, I was asked to consider: "What would you like urban educational leaders and educational administration/leadership professors to know or think about?" During my reflection, I contemplated the dire state of large inner-city schools dramatically affected by poverty and entrenched in failing organizational infrastructures. Most importantly, I thought of the many students who are languishing in such schools desperate for increased safety, nurturing, and educational opportunity as they live and learn amidst educational conditions and sociopolitical contexts that sometimes feel hopeless. Soon a few striking remarks I have heard from such youth came to mind, as noted below.

> "I must create my own growth through the oblivion of darkness."[1]
>   "I am my brother's shooter."
>   "I am scared more by what I have to face on my walk to school than I am at school."
>   "They (teachers) don't care."

These remarks, which come from public high school students in Detroit, convey a combination of resiliency, determination, disappointment in their harsh realities, and a sense that they may ultimately have to fend for themselves and their loved ones, even if—as in the case of one—it means "shooting" anyone who would harm his or her family. These youth, as others in large urban centers like Chicago, Philadelphia, and Cleveland, can feel like the weight of their unjust circumstances rest solely on their shoulders. It is morally imperative, however, that we as educators and preparers of educational leaders cultivate a greater sense of urgency to enact transformative practices that lessen their plight. Three particular aspects of urban educational leadership worthy of more wide-scale theorizing, strategizing,

and practice are critical care, collaborative activism, and professional risk. These behaviors are interrelated and signify the notion that educational leadership is a political act that should be undertaken with ideological clarity and social justice intent. In the remaining text, I overview the significance of these acts given the endangered state of urban public education and assert a call to action that is informed by my own efforts to critically care, "act up," and risk.

COUNTERING DOMINANT LEADERSHIP NORMS

Critical care moves beyond one exuding sentimental and altruistic concern toward others at the individual level. It, instead, involves one demonstrating empathy, having political consciousness about various forms of social oppression, and advocating to help redress inequities faced by oppressed peoples (Cooper, 2009a;[2] Wilson, in press). Collaborative activism connects critical care to a group effort and refers to members of groups, communities, and/or institutions partnering to rupture "the status quo in order to socially deconstruct, politically transform, and share sense of hope" (Cooper and Gause, 2007, p. 214). Such care and activism can require educators to take significant risks and sometimes challenge the constraining systems that employ and/or benefit them.

Critical care, collaborative activism, and professional risk-taking are unsung yet essential aspects enacting transformative educational leadership. These acts politically counter dominant and regulatory leadership norms that: proliferate preoccupation with school management technicalities; confine instructional leadership to the walls of schools while excluding community-based connections; and concentrate on raising the test scores of student "subgroups" at the expense of holistically addressing students' educational and developmental needs (Dantley, 2003; Simmonds, 2007; Wilson, in press). Such preoccupation is too often reaffirmed rather than interrogated and critiqued within educational leadership programs. Programs that groom educational leaders to treat urban schools and youth as though they are not nested in and co-shaped by broader cultural and sociopolitical contexts do all students a disservice.

Typically missing from educational leadership programs are teaching approaches and the use of scholarship that enable current and future educational leaders to understand the damage being done by neoliberal politics that negate the needs of urban youth and support the privatization and commodification of public schooling. Giroux (2006) and Means (2008) have referred to such phenomena as the "politics of disposability," which encompasses the devaluing and discarding of urban public spaces, institutions, and communities (p. 11; para. 1). This has led to public disinvestment and the erosion of funding, safety nets, and civic concern for urban schools and communities that are predominantly populated with people of color and low-income or working-class residents. Public investment has been increasingly replaced by for-profit educational entrepreneurialism that targets these same residents.

Of course many urban educators detect the daily consequences of oppressive dynamics in their schools but may not be equipped or encouraged to name or resist the racist, classist, and xenophobic ideologies and practices that too many students of nondominant cultural, social, and economic backgrounds endure. Moreover, dominant, Westernized conceptions of leadership are still individualistically framed as work of lone, charismatic authority figures, though civil rights struggles and seminal works by Freire (1998), Hooks (1989), Payne (1995), Watkins (2005), Warren (2011), and many others remind us that positive educational transformation has only come in marginalized communities via collaboration and political resistance from those visible and those unseen.

Defiance and dissent of course are not rewarded, though they are seminal democratic acts. Instead, cooperation, compliance, polite civility, and even silence in the face of systemic injustice is frequently a prevailing and rewarded cultural response within many educational bureaucracies and failing schools. Such contexts

place equity-oriented public educators in a precarious position of having to strategize about what, when, and how to challenge the systems and authority figures that affect one's livelihood and status. Still, it is key to recognize political conscientiousness and risk-taking as leadership necessities. As Simmonds (2007) suggests, educational leaders must be supported in their "strategic risk-taking" (p. 81) and their efforts to exude "critical vulnerability" so they can lead with "a conscious recognition and willingness to transform society, and its institutions, into places where equity is experienced rather than considered" (p. 84). This aligns with the enactment of critical care, collaborative activism, and professional risks.

A PERSONAL CALL TO ACTION

Recently, I was asked to boldly engage in the types of care, activism, and risk that I recommend. A civil rights law firm requested my involvement in a lawsuit against a for-profit charter school company. The company took over a once-beloved and successful inner-city public high school that served mainly African-American students highly impacted by poverty. Current and former students and families from the school alleged that the charter school management team implemented improper and inequitable procedures upon assuming its leadership role. The company was also affiliated with the city's urban school district and another public education agency. These were two public entities in which I would have ordinarily wished to conduct research and with which my then employer was vested in building positive relations.

My involvement in the case would require me to write an evidentiary report, undergo a deposition in which I was warned that the opposing team would aggressively assault my judgment and work, and then testify for the public record. It would further require me to risk public scrutiny, research access, and potentially displease administrative officials within my institution. These were prospects over which I lost a couple nights of sleep. I imagined distressing worst-case scenarios; yet, the circumstances of the case were compelling. They pertained to equity issues directly related to my teaching, research, and political agendas. When I contemplated the decision from a moral and spiritual place, I gained the clarity and courage to accept the law firm's invitation. I did so after consulting with my university administrators and university legal policies. I was also mindful of the privilege I had as a tenured faculty member. Nevertheless, consciously choosing to put myself in a position where I could have to rely on tenure's protection was not easy. Ultimately, my choice to participate in the case was emblematic of my critical care and social justice commitments.

To date, I am still involved in the lawsuit and unsure of its outcome. I have worked hard to arrive at a place where my expertise is valued and influential, so I have decided to have faith in the risk-taking process and proceed with savvy. I am moving forward in collaboration with a pro bono legal team that is advocating for urban youth who otherwise could not afford to challenge a complex bureaucracy. Regardless of the case's outcome, I know I will learn from this risk experience and demonstrate to youth who feel victimized that educators indeed care.

FINAL THOUGHTS

In all, demonstrating critical care and collaborative activism is severely needed within the educational leadership field along with strong efforts to prepare leaders to ally and take calculated risks with teachers, families, staff, and advocates of marginalized communities. Within higher education, this work should be more centered in curriculum, teaching, program coordination, and field placement efforts. Education faculties should revisit programs to assess how well they integrate attention to school-family-community engagement, the sociopolitical contexts of cities and economies, urban public policy, and diversity and structural inequality. Individually, we must increase our willingness to educate ourselves about such matters to be better teachers even if that means exiting our comfort zone to pursue critical pedagogical and political practices that fall outside our honed skill sets. Ultimately, for those of us in the academy, modeling critical care, collaborative activism, and risk-taking is the most effective way we can simultaneously teach, learn, and spark educational transformation.

NOTES

1. These quotes are from different students. The first comes from a member of the InsideOut poetry troupe associated with the InsideOut Literary Arts Project based in Detroit, Michigan. The quote is excerpted from the InsideOut poet's January 22, 2013 performance at Wayne State University that I attended. Retrieved from www.youtube.com/watch?v=JVp1Z9wPCXs. The other comments are not related to the poetry troupe and come from informal conversations and presentations I have been involved in with Detroit youth.

2. Prior to 2012 I published under the name Camille Wilson Cooper. I authored works referenced as Cooper, C. W.

REFERENCES

Cooper, C. W. (2009). Parent involvement, African American mothers, and the politics of educational care. *Equity and Excellence in Education 42*(4), 379–394.

Cooper, C. W. and Gause, C. P. (2007). Who's afraid of the big bad wolf? Confronting identity politics and student resistance when teaching for social justice. In D. Carlson and C. P. Gause (Eds.), *Keeping the promise: Essays on leadership, democracy and education* (pp. 197–216). New York: Peter Lang.

Dantley, M. (2003). Purpose-driven leadership: The spiritual imperative to guiding schools beyond high-stakes testing and minimum proficiency. *Education and Urban Society 35*(3), 273–291.

Freire, P. (1998). *Pedagogy of freedom: Ethics, democracy and civic courage.* Lanham, MD: Rowman and Littlefield.

Giroux, H. (2006). *Stormy weather: Katrina and the politics of disposability.* Boulder: Paradigm.

hooks, b. (1989). Talking back: Thinking feminist, thinking black. Boston: South End Press.

Means, A. (2008). Neoliberalism and the Politics of disposability: Education, urbanization, and displacement in the new Chicago. *Journal for Critical Education Policy Studies 6*(1). Available online at www.jceps.com/archives/565.

Payne, C. M. (1995). *I've got the light of freedom: The organizing tradition and the Mississippi freedom struggle.* Berkeley: University of California Press.

Simmonds, M.R. (2007, Spring–Summer). Critical vulnerability: An imperative approach to educational leadership. *Journal of Thought,* 79–97.

Warren, M. R. and Mapp, K. L. (2011). *A match on dry grass: Community organizing as a catalyst for school reform.* Oxford: Oxford University Press.

Watkins, H. H. (Ed.). *Black protest thought and education.* New York: Peter Lang.

Wilson, C. M. (in press). Enacting critical care and transformative leadership in schools highly impacted by poverty: An African-American principal's counter narrative. *International Journal of Leadership in Education: Theory and Practice.*

CHAPTER 9

Urban Schools, Black Principals, and Black Students

Culturally Responsive Education and the Ethno-Humanist Role Identity

Kofi Lomotey and Kendra Lowery

The quality of education that black students receive in urban public schools in the United States is poor. The data clearly illustrate this fact (Barton and Coley, 2010; Delpit, 2012; Hrabowski, 2004; Krueger and Whitmore, 2001; Lee, 2002; Paige and Witty, 2010; U.S. Department of Education, 2009). Reasons for the low achievement of black students range from low teacher expectations to racist standard operating procedures, including disproportionate representation of black children in special education programs, systematic tracking into the least challenging courses, and disproportionally high numbers of office discipline referrals and suspensions (Gay, 2010; Kunjufu, 2005; Ladson-Billings, 1994; Skiba, Horner, Chung, Rausch, May, and Tobin, 2011; Talbert-Johnson, 2006; Ware, 2006; Weinstein et al., 2004).

More than two decades ago, Lomotey (1990) said that the underachievement of black students has been persistent, pervasive, and disproportionate. We argue that this is a direct result of their *disenfranchisement* in U.S. public schools. This is, indeed, discrimination of the highest order. It is the epitome of what Pettigrew and Taylor (1990) describe as "a complex system of social relations" which "may be direct or indirect, and may have both short- and long-term consequences" (p. 688). Frederickson and Knobel (1982) characterize this system of disenfranchisement as one that involves "actions, subtle or covert, that serve to limit the social, political, or economic opportunities of particular groups" (p. 31).

In schooling, this severe discrimination or disenfranchisement is the historic, unrelenting, systematic, and systemic deprivation of access to quality education. The focus on disenfranchisement highlights the fact that these students are not primarily responsible for their status. Rather, forces beyond their control have foisted it upon them (Harris and Davis, 2012; Noguera, 2003).

While it is accurate to say that black students underachieve in urban schools, it is important to acknowledge that their wide scale underachievement is *primarily* the result of intentional and systematic societal and institutional factors and not something intrinsic in black students. We seek to avoid directly, inadvertently, or inaccurately blaming the victim (Ryan, 1976). Societal and institutional concerted efforts have brought about the disenfranchisement of black students. It is the very nature of the *schooling* experience of these students that perpetuates this condition.

In distinguishing education from schooling, Shujaa (1993) says schooling extends prevailing power relationships and perpetuates the existing politically controlling cultural orientation. That is, schooling occurs when one group has power over another. Through schooling, the culture of a dominant group is imposed upon another. The group that is imposed upon adjusts and adapts in response to contact with the dominant group.

Education, on the other hand, according to Shujaa (1993), is learning and internalizing one's own cultural norms. It occurs in informal and formal settings. Education, Shujaa contends, provides the wherewithal for members of a group to effectively function within their family, community, and race and to retain the integrity of their own culture in social contexts where unequal power relations exist among cultures.

Because of the power relationships that exist in the United States, black students experience more schooling (as defined by Shujaa) than education. Nobles (1978) argues that power is the capacity to interpret reality and to persuade others that it is their reality. Relatedly, Spring (1991) defines power as the capacity to control others as well as the capacity to avoid being controlled by others. The disenfranchisement of black students, which is based on a system of the deprivation of power of black people, is a longstanding truism. It cannot be fully overcome in the absence of changes in power relations in U.S. society.

There is, however, evidence that some factors may contribute to mediating this disenfranchisement—particularly in urban public schools in the United States. In this chapter, we explore two of these factors: culturally responsive education and the importance of black principals. The first—the presence of culturally responsive education—is similar to Lomotey's (1993) concept of the ethno-humanist role identity.

CULTURALLY RESPONSIVE EDUCATION

We posit that it may be possible to partially address the underachievement of black students in urban public schools in the United States through the provision of culturally responsive education. We define culturally responsive education as an effective teaching/learning experience facilitated by educators who draw upon the culture of the student/learner, enabling them to "see themselves" in the curriculum (Gay, 2010; Lomotey, 1989a). The most commonly cited definition of culturally responsive education, also known as culturally relevant education, is from Ladson-Billings (1994): "Culturally relevant teaching is a pedagogy that empowers students intellectually, socially, emotionally, and politically by using cultural referents to impart knowledge, skills, and attitudes" (p. 18). There are many synonyms and various definitions used in the literature about cultural responsiveness including cultural competence, cultural relevance, cultural responsiveness, cultural proficiency, multicultural education, and cultural synchronization (Howard, 2010). All of the descriptions focus on methods used for the purpose of creating classrooms and whole school environments in which instruction and engagement "are more consistent with the cultural orientations" (Gay, 2010, p. 29) of students (Robins et al., 2002).

In culturally responsive education, students are active participants in the teaching/learning process. Culturally responsive teaching rests on a set of generally agreed-upon core beliefs and practices of educators. They include:

- acknowledging that race exists and openly discussing how race impacts educators' and students' interactions with others in the institution (Davis, 2007; Landsman, 2001; Robins et al., 2002; Singleton and Linton, 2006)
- creating and affirming identities of academic success through a culture of caring (Gay, 2010; Ladson-Billings, 1994; Perry, Steele, and Hilliard, 2003; Talbert-Johnson, 2006; Tatum, 2007; Ware, 2006)
- an examination of the teacher's and the school's cultural norms and how they may contribute to cultural incongruence for students and families (Gay, 2010; Howard, 2010)
- understanding the importance of diverse cultural imaging throughout the building and curriculum (Davis, 2007; Tatum, 2007)
- examining the significance of language development and communication in order to increase positive student and family engagement in school (Dandy, 1991; Delpit, 2001; Wheeler and Swords, 2006) and
- creating content and instruction that incorporates the teacher's understanding of cultural diversity and builds sociopolitical awareness and analysis (Gay, 2010; Grant, 2009; Hollins and Oliver, 1999; Ladson-Billings, 1994; Tatum, 2007)

A second factor that may contribute to mitigating the disenfranchisement of black students in urban schools and their resultant underachievement is principal leadership. In particular, some evidence suggests that black principals, due to a shared cultural understanding of black students, may make a positive difference for black students in urban schools.

While our focus in this chapter is on the significance of the leadership of black principals for black students, we believe that there is relevance herein for all principals who work with black students. That is, we believe it is possible for principals who are not black to embrace many—if not all—of the qualities discussed herein. Again, our focus is specifically on the importance of black principals for black students in urban schools in the United States.

BLACK PRINCIPALS

Positive role models are important for students at all levels. Black students may benefit from having black principals. For many years, researchers have argued that black students may experience increased academic success in the presence of black teachers. Similarly—and more recently—some research has indicated that there may be a benefit accrued to black students when a black principal is present. That is, in part because of a shared culture and common experiences, black principals may serve effectively as role models for black students in urban schools (Henderson, 2008; Kelley, 2005; Reitzug and Patterson, 1998; Tillman, 2004; Williams, 2012).

In political science, the notion of bonding social capital refers to establishing ties to people who are like you in some important way. This idea, akin to conflict theory, assumes increased ethnocentrism and dictates that diversity fosters distrust of those who are dissimilar and solidarity with those who are similar. Indeed, many people in the United States are uncomfortable with diversity (Putnam, 2007).

In Lomotey's earlier work (1987, 1989b, 1993), he discussed a similar concept borrowed from sociology, *homophily*: the proclivity of people to fraternize and connect with others like themselves. That is, "love of the same" or "birds of a feather flock together." This phenomenon is at play, we argue, in the relationships established between black educators—teachers and principals—and black students in urban public schools in the United States.

CULTURALLY RESPONSIVE EDUCATION AND BLACK PRINCIPALS

Recent research identifies the ways in which principals can play a role in facilitating a culturally responsive education. Some characteristics of this type of leader include

- involving parents and community members in the educational process (Johnson, 2007)
- employing culturally relevant activities (Lee, 2007)
- utilizing one-on-one and group activities for immigrant and refugee students (Gardiner and Enomoto, 2006)
- being a public intellectual, a curriculum innovator, and a social activist (Johnson, 2006)
- culturally uplifting and caring for students (Foster, 2005)
- having high expectations and developing a sense of community (Kelley, 2012) and

- using data-driven decision making and providing professional development around cultural diversity issues (Kelley, 2012).

Lomotey's concept of *ethno-humanism* (1993) shares many of the characteristics identified in principals who exhibit this more recent concept of culturally responsive education.

ETHNO-HUMANISM

In 1993, Lomotey coined the term ethno-humanist to describe one predominant role identity of black principals. The ethno-humanist role identity encompasses "commitment to the education of all students; confidence in the ability of all students to do well; and compassion for, and understanding of, all students and the communities in which they live" (p. 396). More recently other researchers have employed this ethno-humanist role identity framework as an analytical tool in assessing the leadership of black principals (e.g., Gooden, 2005; Nicotera, Clinkscales, and Walker, 2003; Tillman, 2009).

Educators—regardless of their own background—provide a lens through which students see the world and see themselves in the world. For black students it is important for their lens, at the core, to be African-centered. The goal is an environment in which these students see themselves as world citizens who have a vested interest in the evolution of civil society. In discussing the ethno-humanist role identity, Lomotey said:

> In this role, principals identify with African-American students as a member of their culture. They argue that academic success is not enough. What is needed, these principals contend, is an education about one's culture, about life, and about where these African-American students fit in the society and in the world. In essence, these leaders encourage African-American students to look at the world through an African-centered set of lenses that provides them with vision that is more focused, has a wider periphery, and more depth. (p. 397)

This ethno-humanist role identity is comprised of characteristics similar to those that researchers have more recently argued are important in facilitating culturally responsive educational experiences, such as creating content and instruction that builds sociopolitical awareness and analysis (Gay, 2010; Ladson-Billings, 1994). Because of the similarities of these concepts, understanding the extent to which this role identity still exists—and the form(s) in which it exists—can increase our understanding of what is entailed in culturally responsive education, particularly as it relates to black students in urban schools in the United States.

THE REVIEW

The characteristics associated with culturally responsive education are similar to the characteristics embodied in the ethno-humanist role identity of black principals. That is, *by exhibiting the ethno-humanist role identity, black principals may, in fact, be contributing to the provision of culturally responsive education.* While we recognize that black principals are not the only principals who can embody both ethno-humanist and culturally responsive characteristics, our review focuses on the significance of black principals, the ethno-humanist role identity, and culturally responsive education.

We analyzed data from studies of "successful" black principals in urban public schools in the United States to determine if and how these leaders exhibit the ethno-humanist role identity and, accordingly, how, if at all, they assist in facilitating a culturally responsive education for black students. That is, we sought to determine if these principals displayed the three aspects of the ethno-humanist role identity—confidence, commitment, and compassion. If they do, we argue that they are facilitating a culturally responsive education and thereby contributing to improved academic success. This approach is consistent with the work of Foster (2005), who indicated that understanding the types of leadership characteristics displayed by successful black principals will help researchers and leaders predict what experiences will lead to higher black student achievement.

Our point, again, is that black students underperform in urban public schools in the United States because of their historic disenfranchisement. This disenfranchisement, as opposed to innate racial factors, brings about their underachievement. In other words, we are significantly challenged in our attempts to effectively educate black students in urban schools when multiple longstanding societal and institutional barriers continue to be present—and are reinforced by existing power relationships in society. We posit that the underachievement of black students can be mitigated, in part, through the provision of a culturally responsive educational experience facilitated by black principals. Further, we argue that by displaying the ethno-humanist role identity, black principals are, in effect, helping to facilitate culturally responsive education.

Given that the characteristics associated with the ethno-humanist role identity are similar to those associated with facilitating culturally responsive education, ascertaining whether successful black principals exhibit the ethno-humanist role identity in urban schools could give us insights into whether they, in fact, are contributing to providing a culturally responsive education for black students. The specific question with which we were concerned in this review was:

To what extent do successful black principals display the characteristics associated with the ethno-humanist role identity—and in what ways?

The overwhelmingly large majority of the research on black principal leadership has been done in the past twenty-five years. Consequently, in our review, we focused on research published during the period from 1987 through 2013. Most of the research on principal leadership appears in dissertations and journals, and we focused our search on these two sources. We sought to uncover studies of individual black principals or groups of black principals who were leading in urban schools with black students and who were viewed as successful in that—by some measure—their students were doing well academically or their performance was improving significantly.

We only included studies that explored aspects of the relationship between successful black principals and black students. We included one literature review (Foster, 2005) that focused on research on effective leadership practices of black principals working with black students and did not include other literature reviews (e.g., Tillman, 2004) that did not focus solely on the leadership characteristics of successful black principals in predominantly black urban schools. We uncovered a total of sixteen studies: seven emerged from journals and nine were dissertations. All of the studies except three were qualitative, utilizing one or more of the following methods: interviews, case studies, focus groups, document review, and observations. One study was of an historical nature, one used a mixed-methods

Table 9.1. Overview of Reviewed Studies

Author (Yr)	Source	Data	Sample	Findings	Additional Information
Banks-Thompson (2006)	Dissertation	Case Study: observations, interviews, student focus groups and document review	Two black elementary school principals	Belief that all students can learn; relationship building focus; purpose and passion	Improving low performing schools
Berry (2008)	Dissertation	Qualitative: interviews, observations, and focus group	Three black female elementary school principals	God, data, student needs, teacher needs, parent needs, communication; church involvement	Critical spirituality
Byrd (2009)	Dissertation	Case studies: interviews and focus group	Four (elementary, middle, high and K–8) black female principals	Mission-like responsibility to self, community and children; community servants; Black female identity	Framework: Cross' four-stage theory of identity development: Nigrescense;
Dillard (1995)	Journal Article	Case study: observations and interviews	One black female high school principal	Keys for transformative leadership: leadership as interpretation and leadership as authentication (nurturing/protecting)	Critical feminist theories of leadership; focus: effective schools and Black female principals' leadership; men's realities are not necessarily women's realities; understanding of leadership effectiveness necessitates inclusion of culture
Foster (2005)	Journal Article	Review of 13 studies	"Numerous"	Recognition of cultural norms, tying leaders to communities; recognition of race; help imperative	Interpersonal caring and institutional caring framework
Henderson (2008)	Dissertation	Survey, interviews and focus group	Six black male high school principals	Focus on culture of inclusion; love and support focus; self-respect and student-centeredness; commitment to academic success and life of students; community involvement; importance of inclusive and caring experience; belief that students can achieve; paternalistic role models; consistent and fair; concern for students' lives	Black principals develop extensive skills to deal with urban student academic success
Khalifa (2008)	Dissertation	Qualitative: observation, field notes, interviews and document review	One black male high school principal	Student and community relationships; earned trust and credibility and had rapport; challenged teachers	At-risk alternative school student success
Lee (2007)	Dissertation	Qualitative case study: interviews and observations	Three black female elementary school principals	Promoted cultural responsiveness at classroom level only	Using culturally responsive learning experiences to improve academic achievement: more of a focus on school wide and district wide cultural relevant curriculum is needed

Author (Yr)	Source	Data	Sample	Findings	Additional Information
Lomotey (1987)	Journal Article	Principal and teacher interviews	Three black (one female and two male) elementary school principals	Deep compassion for students; principals impact behavior of teachers	Premises: (1) Black principals positively impact Black student achievement; (2) homophily at play
Miller (2011)	Dissertation	Interviews	One black male high school principal	Autocratic, dogmatic, immoral, directive, intimidating charismatic and caring.	Exploration of one principal's leadership style; controversial but successful
Morris (2004)	Journal Article	Qualitative: interviews, observations and document analysis	Two black elementary school principals (one male and one female)	Building cultural bridges between school and community; cultural and academic leaders; setting high academic standards	Schools that are successful in educating Black students; strong academic schools connected to families
Randolph (2004)	Journal Article	Historical analysis of primary and secondary sources, oral histories and Interviews	Two black elementary school principals: one male and one female	Confidence; role model, approachable; high expectations; community support and participation	All-Black school in Columbus, OH; historical leadership
Reitzug & Patterson (1998)	Journal Article	Observations, shadowing, interviews	One black middle school female principal	(1) personal connection, (2) honor voice, (3) concern, (4) connecting to community, (5) seeing alternatives	Caring, empowering practices; empowerment through caring; (1) Students a priority, (2) caring interactions and (3) empowering students
Reynolds (2009)	Dissertation	Mixed methods	Four black female principals in elementary schools	Five themes: (1) work relations, (2) taking charge, (3) acceptance and challenge, (4) empowering others, and (5) achievement focus	
Sawyer (2010)	Dissertation	Case study (survey, document analysis, observations and interviews)	One black female principal	Visionary, community and culture builder, promoter of student learning, developer of teacher leadership, facilitator of shared decision making	Student-centeredness
Walker & Byas (2003)	Journal Article	Interviews, speeches and document review	One black male high school principal	Focus on achievement; community support; public communication/marketing; community leader; exemplary leader; sought tight-knit community	

approach and, as indicated earlier, there was one literature review. (See table 9.1.)

We sought to explore the ethno-humanist role identity characteristics of black principals who were successful in positively affecting the achievement of black students in urban schools. Given the long-standing concern with regard to black student underachievement and knowing that the principal does make a difference (Sanchez, Thornton, and Usinger, 2009; Williams, 2012), it seemed clear that understanding the characteristics of successful black principals would offer valuable insights.

Using the ethno-humanist role identity typology, we analyzed the studies to see if this role identity emerged and, if so, to determine the way(s) that it emerged. *The purpose of our analysis was to explore the leadership of the principals in these studies to see if they exhibited the ethno-humanist role identity.* Given the similarities between this role identity and the characteristics associated with culturally responsive education, positive results would suggest that these principals do, in fact, exhibit characteristics associated with culturally responsive education. Again, while this review focuses on black principals, we do not claim that only black principals have the capacity to exhibit the ethno-humanist role identity—or to facilitate a culturally responsive education. Rather, the characteristics common between the ethno-humanist role identity and cultural responsiveness are ones that can and must be developed among all principals in order to successfully educate black students—and other historically less successful students. If we can learn more about this role identity, we may learn more about the function of black principals in facilitat-

ing culturally responsive education, and consequently, we would have information necessary to address the underachievement of black students in urban schools which may be generalizable to principals of all races. We now move to our findings.

FINDINGS

These sixteen studies each focused specifically on an individual black principal or a group of black principals who were considered to be successful. The three most common characteristics of these successful principals were (1) a commitment to the education of all students, (2) confidence in the abilities of all students, and (3) compassion for all students and their communities. (See table 9.2.)

Table 9.2.   Summary of Studies Reviewed: By Ethno-Humanist Role Identity Characteristic

Study	Commitment to Education	Confidence in Students' Ability	Compassion for Students & Communities
Banks-Thompson (2006)	Relationship building focus; improving low performance schools	Belief that all students can learn	—
Berry (2008)	Student needs	—	—
Byrd (2009)	Mission-like responsibility	—	Community servant;
Dillard (1995)	Seeing the principalship as a moral obligation	—	Leadership and culture linked; leadership is nurturing and protecting
Foster (2005)	Help imperative	—	Institutional & interpersonal caring framework; leadership linked to communities;
Henderson (2008)	Culture of inclusion; commitment to academic success	Belief that students can achieve	Love and support focus; importance of inclusion and caring experience; concern for students' lives
Khalifa (2008)	Earned trust & credibility; challenging teachers	—	Focus on student and community relationships;
Lee (2007)	-----	—	Promoted cultural responsiveness at classroom level
Lomotey (1987)	Principals influencing teacher interactions with students	—	Deep compassion for students; homophily at play
Miller (2011)	Autocratic, dogmatic and directive	—	Charismatic & caring
Morris (2004)	Setting high academic standards;	—	Building cultural bridges between school & community; connections to families
Randolph (2004)	High expectations	Confidence stressed	Community support & participation stressed;
Reitzug & Patterson (1998)	Students are the priority	—	Personal connections stressed; concern; connecting to community; caring empowering practices; caring interactions; empowering students
Reynolds (2009)	Emphasis on academic achievement	Attitude of acceptance and challenge	Work relations
Sawyer (2010)	Promoted student learning	Student-centered visionary	Community and culture builder
Walker & Byas (2003)	Focus on achievement	—	Community support stressed; sought tight-knit community

Commitment. Banks-Thompson (2006), in her study of two black elementary school principals, identified ways that the principals stressed relationship-building and improved their low-performing schools. These principals embodied a commitment to the education of all students. Berry (2008), in her study of three black women elementary school principals, talked about the importance these women placed on student needs. They created "level playing fields so that children of color [could] secure educational and social capital with the end goal being that of college readiness" (p. 200).

Byrd (2009), in a study of four black female principals, described the mission-like sense of responsibility that these principals had. The commitment of the principals in this study was "characterized by each participant's sense of responsibility to their jobs as service to others as well as an answer to the calling of their lives" (p. 312). Gloria Nathan, the black woman high school principal in the Dillard (1995) study, saw her principalship as a moral obligation enabling her to help black students succeed; she constantly stressed the importance of school with her students. She also intervened when she believed that teachers were not putting forth adequate effort with students. This is consistent with Lomotey's (1987) observations of how the three black elementary school principals in his study influenced the behavior of teachers as they interacted with students.

Foster (2005) spoke of the moral imperative to help black students that the principals in the thirteen studies she reviewed felt with regard to their commitment to education. Henderson (2008) referred to the notion of a culture of inclusion and a commitment to academic success that the six black male high school principals in his study demonstrated. These principals also indicated that their passion to improve their students' quality of life and academic achievement served as their motivation for being principals. Henderson pointed out that these leaders developed skills far beyond those associated with the traditional administrator role—such as developing meaningful relationships with families who face poverty, safety, and health risks—in order to ensure that their students achieved academic success.

Khalifa (2008), in a qualitative study of one black male high school principal, spoke of how this principal earned the trust and credibility of students and, in demonstrating his commitment to education, challenged teachers accordingly. Miller (2011) talked about the

black male high school principal in her study as autocratic, dogmatic, and directive—yet successful. These characteristics, Miller argued, reflected the principal's commitment to education. Morris (2004) stressed how the two principals in his study always focused on setting high academic standards for students. One of the two principals in the Randolph (2004) study, Maud C. Baker, believed that she had a responsibility to "lift the African-American race through educational means" (p. 599).

The black female middle school principal in the Reitzug and Patterson study (1998) indicated unequivocally that, for her, students were the priority. Walker and Byas (2003) described the focus on achievement that was displayed by Byas—the principal in their qualitative study of his leadership. According to the teachers who were surveyed in the Reynolds study (2009), the four black female principals each placed a strong emphasis on academic achievement in their high-achieving elementary schools. In the Sawyer case study (2010) of one black principal, there was strong evidence of a conscious effort by the principal to promote student learning.

Confidence. Black principals also demonstrated and articulated confidence in the abilities of their students. Banks-Thompson (2006) spoke of the principals in her study demonstrating a belief that all students can learn. The same was true for Henderson (2008). The following excerpts illustrate the focus on confidence by the six male principals in the Henderson study.

"The participant began by asserting his belief that all students can learn." (p. 100)

"Participant 3 discussed his belief that everyone is capable of learning . . . he stated his belief that every student is educable in something, everyone has a talent, and everyone is able to successfully be a good citizen and a contributing citizen to this democracy . . ." (p. 101)

"The belief system that Participant 4 (Luther) shared included every child's ability to learn and desire to be told what to do in a positive way." (p. 101)

Randolph (2004) pointed out how the principals in her historical study had high expectations for their students and teachers and they also stressed confidence in the abilities of their students. Randolph looked at all-black Champion High School in Columbus, Ohio. From interviews, she learned that the principal, Dr. Mitchell:

began his career at Champion with the intent of making it an exemplary school to affirm that black youth can learn a classical curriculum and achieve and that all-black did not mean inferior . . . Mitchell set out to prove that blacks could learn as well as whites given the proper environment . . . Mitchell and his cadre of hand-picked teachers expected respect, order, and success . . . He was determined to make the best of the students at Champion despite segregation and poverty. (pp. 601, 604)

The principals in the Reynolds study (2009) displayed confidence in students' abilities. This was illustrated in their focus on acceptance of all students and constantly challenging them academically. Also, the Sawyer dissertation (2010) found that the principal under study was a student-centered visionary, always focusing on the capacity of students to excel.

Compassion. Compassion was the third characteristic exhibited by the principals in these studies. Byrd (2009) talked about the principals in his study as community servants. Dillard (1995) talked about how, for the black female high school principal in her case study, leadership and culture were linked and leadership meant nurturing and protecting students. This principal's "everyday work include[d] seeking out and nurturing this capacity through personal contact with students" (p. 551).

Foster (2005) discussed the longstanding institutional and interpersonal caring style of successful black principals that she contended came about shortly after the end of the enslavement of blacks in the United States. This style, she argued, included identifying student needs, addressing those needs, and involving parents in the educational enterprise. She stressed the linkage between leadership and community for the principals in her literature review and talked about the importance of principals consciously recognizing the significance of race.

Henderson (2008) described the love and support focus of the principals in his study as well as a culture of self-respect and student-centeredness that they fostered. The principals facilitated a caring experience and stressed concern for their students' lives. They recognized the importance of acknowledging aspects of the personal lives of students, such as health concerns, poverty issues, family matters, and safety concerns, all of which impact educational achievement.

Khalifa (2008) identified the ways that the principal in his study focused on relationships with students and with members of the larger community. Strategies included holding rap sessions with students and hosting breakfasts for parents. According to Khalifa, "two of the most remarkable differences between [what occurred at the school that I studied] and traditional approaches to leadership are the close relationships that the school leader ha[d] with the community, and the close relationships he had directly with students" (p. 193).

Lee (2007) talked about the emphasis of the three black female elementary school principals in her study on promoting cultural responsiveness at the classroom level. In Lomotey's study (1987) of three black elementary school principals, he described their deep compassion for students and the significance of homophily in their relationships with their students. Miller (2011) identified the charisma and caring characteristics of the principal in her study. Morris (2004) discussed the efforts of the two principals in his study at building cultural bridges between the school and community and connecting with families. They exhibited these traits through attending community events, caring about students, and providing educational resources for teachers and parents.

Reynolds (2009) illustrated the compassionate behavior of the principals in her study, exhibited by their focus on strong community and campus relationships. Similarly, Sawyer (2010) found that the principal in her case study exhibited compassion through a focus on community building and school culture development—on and off campus.

Randolph (2004) described how the principals in her study stressed the importance of parent and community participation. Reitzug and Patterson (1998) talked about the principal in their study stressing personal connections and relating to communities. The principal also focused on caring interactions and student empowering practices. Walker and Byas (2003) talked about how the principal in their study (1) stressed the importance of community support, (2) discussed how he was a community leader, and (3) described how he sought to create a tight-knit community.

The principals in each of these studies of effective leadership employed characteristics of the ethno-humanist role identity. They exhibited and articulated (1) a commitment to the education of their students, (2) confidence in the abilities of their students, and (3) compassion for their students and their communities.

CONCLUSION

In describing the *commitment* to education displayed by these successful principals, the authors of these studies noted their:

- focus on student needs (Berry, 2008; Reynolds, 2009),
- concentration on the cultural requirements of black students (Berry, 2008; Dillard, 1995; Henderson, 2008; Randolph, 2004),
- mission-like focus/moral obligation to the education of their students (Byrd Sr., 2009; Henderson, 2008; Foster, 2005; Reitzug and Patterson, 1998; Reynolds 2009),
- guidance of teachers to ensure the provision of a culturally responsive education (Dillard, 1995; Khalifa, 2008; Lomotey, 1987) an stressing to students the importance of education (Dillard, 1995).

In enumerating illustrations of the confidence in the abilities of their students that these principals displayed, the authors mentioned:

- certainty with regard to their students' ability (Randolph, 2004; Reynolds, 2009; Sawyer, 2010), and
- a belief that all students can learn (Banks-Thompson, 2006; Henderson, 2008).

It is evident that there were significantly less clearly articulated examples of principals' confidence in students' ability in these studies. Yet, it seems unlikely that principals would commit themselves to such mission-like work without a belief that the students they serve were capable of academic success. One explanation for the lack of evidence in this area may be that while the principals have confidence in students' ability, they may not clearly articulate it because it is a given guiding principle of their work. Additionally, it is possible that the research we reviewed was not designed to highlight statements of principals' confidence, so the findings did not identify this area.

The third area of focus for these successful principals was compassion for their students and for their communities. This was displayed by:

- establishing relationships within the larger community (Sawyer, 2010; Reynolds, 2009; Byrd Sr., 2009; Khalifa, 2008; Randolph, 2004; Morris,

2004; Walker and Byas, 2003; Reitzug and Patterson, 1998),
- offering a nurturing experience (Dillard, 1995),
- providing a caring atmosphere (Miller, 2011; Henderson, 2008; Foster, 2005; Reitzug and Patterson, 1998), and
- stressing the importance of race in the educational process (Lee, 2007; Lomotey, 1987).

DISCUSSION

We began with the premise that black students in urban public schools—as a group—receive a poor education. We posited that their underachievement is a result of historic disenfranchisement. And we argued that the inequities in the power of black people prevent black students from completely overcoming this disenfranchisement. Further, we contended that schooling (as opposed to education) reinforces this unequal power relationship.

We mentioned that culturally responsive education might mediate this disenfranchisement and that principal leadership particularly that of black principals—may also play a mediating role. Next, we argued that black principals may help facilitate culturally responsive education, through the exhibiting of what Lomotey (1993) has called the ethno-humanist role identity, a construct that is not dissimilar from culturally responsive education. Our study focus, then, was on how (if at all) successful black principals display the ethno-humanist role identity with black students in urban schools in the United States.

The results indicate that successful black principals do exhibit the characteristics associated with the ethno-humanist role identity: (1) commitment to the education of their students, (2) confidence in the ability of their students, and (3) compassion for their students and for the communities from which they come. Given that the attributes of the ethno-humanist role identity are similar to those associated with culturally responsive education, we would postulate that these successful black principals are also contributing to the provision of culturally responsive education.

We do not want to lose sight of our earlier discussion of power relations in U.S. society. As long as the relationships remain as they are, the disenfranchisement of black students will continue. However, as we have suggested, there are significant mitigating strategies that can have a positive impact on the achievement of black and other underserved students, including the provision of a culturally responsive education and the support of black principals. In the next section, we describe selected opportunities to pursue strategies associated with the implications of our findings.

IMPLICATIONS

Implications for Practice

The foci—commitment, confidence, and compassion—in the present review are of particular relevance for educational practice. That is, these characteristics appear to be very important for successful black principals in their interactions with black students in urban public schools in the United States. Noddings (1992) discussed the importance of compassionate relationships between educators and students in bringing about trust, increased effort, and, ultimately, student success. Indeed, the nature of the increasing challenges within urban schools are such that perhaps black principals are most often forced to focus on the ethno-humanist or caring and nurturing aspects of their leadership that are consistent with the characteristics of culturally responsive education.

Professional development programs for principals could increase the focus on these characteristics. Literature on culturally responsive education exists wherein researchers have identified essential elements of culturally responsive education for teachers and leaders. For example, these programs could stress the importance of:

- guiding teachers to ensure the provision of culturally responsive education (compassion for students and communities)
- stressing the importance of education to students (commitment to education/confidence in students' ability)
- working closely with and establishing relationships with the communities surrounding their schools (compassion for students and communities)
- employing a nurturing/caring disposition (compassion for students and communities)
- acknowledging and demonstrating that racial understanding is important in creating culturally responsive education (commitment to education)

We now discuss each of these suggestions in greater detail.

Guiding teachers to ensure the provision of a culturally responsive education. Culturally relevant education does not take place outside of a political analysis of our society. Therefore, the ultimate aim of professional development, as well as the implementation of culturally relevant education, focuses on the analysis of power dynamics between students, educators, and political organizations in society (Gay, 2010; Grant, 2009; Tatum, 2007; Ladson-Billings, 1994). For example, Howard (2010) highlights a teacher who, when assigning a speech-writing activity, told students they must write about topics they were passionate about and would "fight for the right to believe" (p. 80). As evidence of this teacher's ability to connect classroom learning to students' sociopolitical consciousness, the topics students chose to write on included why the government does not care about poor people, why city leaders should listen to student ideas, and why the neighborhood center should not have been closed (p. 81).

In order to make the tenets of culturally relevant education clear, scholars have identified key characteristics of culturally relevant education that are applicable to educators, regardless of the grade level or subject taught. They include: building meaning between school curriculum and students' home lives—in short, being able to answer the question, Why are we learning this?—and empowering students by making connections between their personal, national, and global identities (Gay, 2010; Grant, 2009; Tatum, 2005; Ladson-Billings, 1994).

Students of all backgrounds need to see representation of the diversity of our society in imaging around the school as well as in the curriculum (Tatum, 2007; Lomotey, 1989a). Visual representations of diverse representations of students in successful roles reinforce an inclusive culture where the success of all students is the norm (Davis, 2007). This diverse representation should extend beyond posters and other images in the hallways throughout the school. The curriculum should also be inclusive of the racial and cultural diversity of the student body. Lastly, diverse cultural imaging and curriculum is important even in culturally homogeneous schools because all students need to be exposed to the diversity of humankind (Tatum, 2005).

Gay (2010) points out the significance of showing teachers "how to become cognizant of their habits of using examples and how to modify them to be more culturally diverse" (p. 147). Through her research, she suggests several ways to teach this through professional development including:

- analyzing how teachers reference culturally diverse examples
- developing protocols that characterize specific examples and then replicating them from diverse cultural perspectives
- collecting teaching examples from culturally diverse classrooms
- habitually using multiple examples from culturally diverse contexts

In order to expand the knowledge base of prospective teachers, Gay assigns her students the task of including less known activists in their lessons in lieu of teaching about the "standard" racial or ethnic role models such as Cesar Chavez for Mexican Americans or Martin Luther King Jr. for blacks.

Additionally, teachers must ensure that their assessments are performance-based and take into account the multiple ways students from various cultures can demonstrate their knowledge of information and analytical application of themes (Lee, 1998).

Stressing the importance of education to students. Educators must affirm all students' sense of academic inclusion and challenge them to "assume a culture of achievement" (Ware, 2006, p. 443). Tatum (2007) captures the meaning of identity: "Identities are the stories we tell ourselves and the world about who we are, and our attempt to act in accordance with these stories" (p. 24). Educators need to be aware of the messages or stories they are sending about which students are expected to be successful through their curriculum and engagement of students. These stories of success must be inclusive of all students (Talbert-Johnson, 2006).

Ladson-Billings (1994) calls the creation of a dialogue for success creating a "relevant black personality" (p. 17) that allows black students to choose both academic success and identification with their black culture. Black students often enter schools with a sense that they are not considered intellectually equal, and that they do not have to perform to high expectations or standards. Perry (2003) argues that educators must rely on a history of the "task of achievement" of black edu-

cators and community members as models for creating a counter-narrative to the typical messages black students receive about failing. The role of the principal as a professional development facilitator is to coach teachers to think about how they can individually develop identities of academic success for black students and move beyond deficit ways of thinking about students and families who have not been successful in school (Howard, 2010; Nieto, 2000).

Working closely with and establishing relationships with the communities surrounding their schools. Culturally responsive school leaders value the communities in which they teach by incorporating "the history, values, and cultural knowledge of students' home communities in the school curriculum" (Johnson, 2007, p. 51). Those leaders also advocate for social change for their communities (Johnson, 2006).

Educators who identify the assumptions or stereotypes they have about different cultural expressions and communication styles of the students and families in their communities will most likely decrease discipline problems and referrals in their classrooms because they will approach students seeking to understand and explain the rules in their classroom, rather than to only punish students who do not behave as expected (Bireda, 2002). Attention to the cultural aspects of communication will also ease tensions that result from judgmentalism between families and educators when communicating is difficult. Although certain norms for communication and respect must be established in schools, educators who are culturally responsive operate out of an understanding that all adults in the school community do not communicate according to the same cultural norms (Grant, 2009; Ware, 2009). Understanding how various cultural groups communicate must be at the root of professional development in this area, and principals must model this characteristic for the staff in their buildings.

Lopez (2001) stressed that culturally responsive leaders must understand there are different ways for parents to be involved in their children's schooling. While traditional norms for parental involvement include "specific practices such as bake sales, fundraisers, PTA/PTO, and 'back to school' nights" (p. 416), Lopez cautioned against deeming non-white families "uninvolved" because they are not visible at school functions or in activities that the school acknowledges as important. For instance, he asserted that "marginalized groups from immigrant backgrounds are *already* involved in the lives of their children, though they may not be 'involved' in traditionally sanctioned ways" (p. 420) such as the Padilla family, whose parents' idea of family involvement "was seen as teaching their children to appreciate the value of their education through the medium of hard work" (p. 422).

Employing a nurturing/caring disposition. Gay (2010) articulates the creation of a counter-narrative of success (Perry, 2003a, 2003b) among black students as caring. She explains that culturally responsive educators care about their students as people and as academic performers. One element of caring is not more important than the other. These teachers have high expectations that prompt students to put effort into academics. Both Gay (2010) and Ware (2006) have identified the essential characteristics of what Gay calls caring teachers and what Ware refers to as warm demanders. They include teachers who:

- care about the complete development of the student
- demand accountability for high expectations for students to be the best they can be seek to learn about students and families from various cultures

Ware (2006) identified specific attributes of *warm demanders* who specifically identify the culture of success for students. These include:

- clearly stating the purpose of homework and requiring a note of explanation if it is not turned in
- teaching with authority in a no-nonsense style
- establishing expectations for classroom behavior
- teaching families how to navigate school culture

Acknowledging and demonstrating that racial understanding is important in creating a culturally responsive education. In order for educators to address the role that race and culture play in the interpretation of curriculum and assessment for their students, they must be willing to talk openly and honestly about race and its impact on people's lives. This is also true for white educators because they, too, must understand their position in relation to their students in our racialized society. Their raised sense of critical consciousness (Freire, 1973 from McDonough, 2009) that heightens

their understanding of their position will inform their analysis of the similarities and differences that exist between educator and student as a starting point to address how to teach students who are different from themselves (Davis, 2007). In order to teach students who are different, one must first acknowledge and talk openly about those differences (Davis, 2007). Because talking about whiteness and race is so difficult, Buehler, Gere, Dallavis, and Haviland (2009) suggest that leaders who train educators to be culturally responsive are "wise to focus not on the achievement of cultural competence, but rather on the struggle involved in enacting it" (p. 416), because talking about race is a never-ending, complex process (McDonough, 2009).

While this core belief does not suggest that educators should ignore common human experiences, it underscores the necessity of avoiding a "color-blind" philosophy that ultimately seeks to "treat all children the same." Robins et al. (2002) point out that although educators often seek to be color-blind out of goodwill, this philosophy does not allow them to see the effect they have on students who are different. Another negative result of a presumed color-blind philosophy is the inability of educators to recognize how they render people who are different as invisible. Often, educators who want to treat everyone the same, regardless of differences, treat people as if they are the same as the educator— disallowing a discussion or realization of how people do not have the same cultural norms (Robins et al., 2002). Treating all students the same is, by definition, treating some students unfairly.

Although the reflection on the significance of race is a continual process, several scholars have designed specific activities that engage educators in discussions about race in professional development settings. Ethno-humanist/culturally responsive principals must either recognize the importance of building their capacity to reflect on race by participating in sessions, being leaders by modeling and facilitating discussions/activities about race, or both. An example of such activities includes writing racial autobiographies wherein people are asked to describe:

- their first recognition of race
- how race has influenced their interactions in society (Davis, 2007; Singleton and Linton, 2006)
- the privileges white people have by using a series of statements about what they can or cannot do in

society (McIntosh, 1988 from Singleton and Linton, 2006)

Landsman (2001) required new teachers to think about how they would teach students from various backgrounds and urged them to resist making students of color the spokespeople for their race.

Buehler et al. (2009) highlight the importance of white teachers struggling with race whether it is guilt or uncertainty, as they teach students from various races. In a study of the development of critical consciousness in a first-year teacher, McDonough (2009) found that the teacher was challenged by her own feelings of guilt about racism as well as the persistent negative comments about students by some staff in her school. The challenge to stay focused on developing a racial consciousness is especially real if the teachers use race as part of their lessons. In their examination of a first-year teacher who used race as the focal point of her role play about McCarthyism, Buehler et al. (2009) found that the teacher was paralyzed when confronted with "actual moments and interactions that were racially charged," prompting the researchers to conclude that there was a gap between "her stated ideals and training" and "her ability to enact those ideals in practice" (p. 413).

An essential part of discussing race is creating an environment in which participants can engage in "reflexive dialogue" (McDonough, 2009, p. 530) or critical reflection (Howard, 2003). In order for this to occur, it is crucial that principals establish norms for honest conversation because most people do not have experience talking about race either at all, or in inter-racial settings (Landsman, 2001). For professional development about race and achievement to be effective, establishing norms based on Singleton and Linton's (2006) norms for discussions is critical. They include staying engaged, speaking one's truth, expecting to experience discomfort, and expecting and accepting non-closure (p. 17).

Ladson-Billings (2001) demonstrated that a crucial part of analyzing the effect of professional development for student achievement includes empowering teachers to examine achievement data that are disaggregated by race. In her work with early literacy teachers, she found that prior to a meeting wherein district data were shared, teachers had not looked at standardized test scores and had not considered how to use those scores to examine

weaknesses and to "develop appropriate curriculum and instructional strategies to improve achievement" (p. 678). As a result of her professional development with the teachers, they were able to look at data and identify students about whom they were the most concerned.

Implications for research. We now turn to implications for research. As this is an exploratory review of the relevant literature, there is a plethora of additional exploratory and theory-testing studies that can be done by way of follow-up. The following questions are suggested for interested investigators.

- How do successful (black) principals focus on student needs?
- In what ways do successful (black) principals guide teachers in providing a culturally responsive education?
- How do successful (black) principals stress education with their students?
- How do successful (black) principals display confidence in the ability of all students to be successful?
- How do successful (black) principals work with communities to improve schools?
- What are the characteristics of successful (black) principals who show a nurturing/caring disposition?

FINAL REMARKS

Black students underachieve academically on multiple measures. We contend that their underachievement is a result of their historic, unrelenting, systematic, and systemic disenfranchisement brought about by uneven power relationships in U.S. society. Many have argued that culturally responsive educational experiences can, to some extent, mitigate the effects of this disenfranchisement and partially address the underachievement of black students. Many have also stressed the importance of the principal in bringing about a culturally responsive education. We have posited that the ethno-humanist role identity closely mirrors the characteristics needed by principals to facilitate a culturally responsive educational experience. It is important to restate that principals who are not black have the ability to be culturally responsive to black students in urban schools. However, in this study, we have explored the existence of this role identity in successful black principals. The evidence indicates that black principals who are successful with black students do employ the traits associated with the ethno-humanist role identity and do, in fact, we argue, help to facilitate a culturally responsive education. Johnson (2007) also noted the connections between a culturally responsive framework and Lomotey's ethno-humanist role identity after reviewing three of the studies that are included in this review.

There have been few attempts to apply this culturally responsive framework to the study of leadership practice in urban, high poverty, challenging schools. Those efforts that come closest have been a series of recent case studies of black women principals in urban schools (e.g., Dillard, 1995; Reitzug and Patterson, 1998). Collectively, the women leaders profiled in these studies emphasize high expectations for student academic achievement, an ethic of care (or what Reitzug and Patterson, 1998, term "empowerment through care"), and a commitment to the larger community. Lomotey (1989) also found that the three black principals he studied in the 1980s had a deep compassion for their students and a commitment to the educability of black children in general (p. 50).

These truisms present challenges for the field. In order to improve the achievement of black students—and all underachieving student groups—we must provide culturally responsive education. For black students, black principals who demonstrate the ethno-humanist role identity have a role to play in that process. We need more black principals who demonstrate compassion for, commitment to, and confidence in black student achievement. Finally, we need to provide increased support and professional development for those who are currently leading urban schools.

REFERENCES

Banks-Thompson, J. E. (2006). *The impact of African American principal leadership on African American student achievement in low-performing elementary schools: A case study*. Unpublished doctoral dissertation. University of San Francisco, San Francisco, CA.

Barton, P. E. and Coley, R. J. (2010). *The black-white achievement gap: When progress stopped*. Policy Information Report. Princeton, NJ: Educational Testing Service.

Berry, S. D. (2008). *Principals of critical spirituality: African American females in elementary urban schools*. Unpublished doctoral dissertation. College Station: Texas A & M University.

Bireda, M.R. (2002). *Eliminating racial profiling in school discipline: Cultures in conflict*. Lanham, MD: Scarecrow Education.

Buehler, J., Gere, A.R., Dallavis, C., and Haviland, V.S. (2009). Normalizing the fraughtness: How emotion, race, and school context complicate cultural competence. *Journal of Teacher Education 60*(4), 408–418.

Byrd Sr., C. (2009). *Voices of identity and responsibility: A description of the development of identity, using Cross' theory of Nigrescence, and the manifestation of responsibility among African American urban school principals*. Unpublished doctoral dissertation. Milwaukee, WI: Cardinal Stritch University.

Dandy, E. (1991). *Black communications: Breaking down the barriers*. Chicago, IL: African American Images.

Davis, B. (2007). *How to teach students who don't look like you: Culturally relevant teaching strategies*. Thousand Oaks, CA: Corwin Press.

Delpit, L. (2012). *"Multiplication is for white people": Raising expectations for other people's children*. New York: The New Press.

Delpit, L. and Dowdy, J. K., eds. (2001). *The skin that we speak: Thoughts on language and culture in the classroom*. New York: The New Press.

Dillard, C. B. (1995). Leading with her life: An African American feminist (re)interpretation of leadership for an urban high school principal. *Educational Administration Quarterly 31*(4), 539–563.

Foster, L. (2005). The practice of educational leadership in African American communities of learning: Context, scope, and meaning. *Educational Administration Quarterly 41*(4), 689–700.

Frederickson, G. M. and Knobel, D. J. (1982). A history of discrimination. In S. Thernstrom, A. Orlov, and O. Handlin (Eds.), *Prejudice: Dimensions of ethnicity* (pp. 30–87). Cambridge, MA: Harvard University Press.

Gardiner, M. E. and Enomoto, E. K. (2006). Urban school principals and their role as multicultural leaders. *Urban Education 41*(6), 560–584.

Gay, G. (2010). *Culturally responsive teaching: Theory, research, and practice*. New York: Teachers College Press.

Gooden, M. A. (2005). The role of an African American principal in an urban information technology high school. *Educational Administration Quarterly 41*(4), 630–650.

Grant, C.A. (2009). *Teach! Change! Empower! Solutions for closing the achievement gaps*. Thousand Oaks, CA: Corwin.

Harper, S. R. and Davis, C. H. F. III (2012). They (don't) care about education: A counternarrative on black male students' responses to inequitable schooling. *Educational Foundations*, Winter–Spring, 103–120.

Henderson, G. (2008). *Leadership experiences of male African-American secondary urban principals: The impact of beliefs, values and experiences on school leadership practices*. Unpublished doctoral dissertation. Cleveland, OH: Cleveland State University.

Hollins, E. R. and Oliver, E. I., eds. (1999). *Pathways to success in school: Culturally responsive teaching*. Mahwah, NJ: Lawrence Erlbaum Associates.

Howard, T. (2010). *Why race and culture matter in schools: Closing the achievement gap in America's classrooms*. New York: Teachers College Press.

Howard, T. C. (2003). Culturally relevant pedagogy: Ingredients for critical teacher reflection. *Theory Into Practice* 42(3), 195–202.

Hrabowski, F. (2004). Leadership for a new age: Higher education's role in producing minority leaders. *Liberal Education* 90(2), n.p.

Johnson, L. (2007). Rethinking successful school leadership in challenging U.S. schools: Culturally responsive practices in school-community relationships. *International Studies in Educational Administration* 35(3), 49–57.

Johnson, L. (2006). "Making her community a better place to live": Culturally responsive urban school leadership in historical context. *Leadership and Policy in Schools* 5(1), 19–36.

Kelley, G. J. (2012). *How do principals' behaviors facilitate or inhibit the development of a culturally relevant learning community?* Unpublished doctoral dissertation. Terre Haute: Indiana State University.

Khalifa, M. A. (2008). *"Give me the worst of them, and I'll make them the best": An ethnographic study of a successful alternative school for at-risk African American children*. Unpublished doctoral dissertation. East Lansing: Michigan State University.

Krueger, A. B. and Whitmore, D. M. (2001). *Would smaller classes help close the black-white achievement gap?* Working Paper, Princeton University, Industrial Relations Section. www.irs.princeton.edu/pubs/working_papers.html.

Kunjufu, J. (2005). *Keeping black boys out of special education*. Chicago: African American Images.

Ladson-Billings, G. (2001). Just showing up: Supporting early literacy through teachers' professional communities. *Phi Delta Kappan* 82(9), 675–679.

Ladson-Billings, G. (1994). The dreamkeepers: Successful teachers of African American children. San Francisco, CA: John Wiley and Sons, Inc.

Landsman, J. (2001). *A white teacher talks about race*. Lanham, MD: Rowman and Littlefield Education.

Lee, C. (1998). Culturally responsive pedagogy and performance-based assessment. *The Journal of Negro Education* 67(3), 268–279.

Lee, J. (2002). Racial and ethnic achievement gap trends: Reversing the progress toward equity? *Educational Researcher* 31(1), 3–12.

Lee, R. (2007). *How principals promote a culturally relevant learning experience to improve black student achievement in urban elementary schools*. Unpublished doctoral dissertation. Statesboro: Georgia Southern University.

Lomotey, K. (1993). African American principals: Bureaucrat/administrators and ethno-humanists. *Urban Education* 27(4), 395–412.

Lomotey, K. (1990). *Going to school: The African American experience*. Albany: State University of New York Press.

Lomotey, K. (1989a). Cultural diversity in the urban school: Implications for principals. *NASSP Bulletin* 73(521), 81–85.

Lomotey, K. (1989b). *African American principals: School leadership and success*. Westport, CT: Greenwood Press.

Lomotey, K. (1987). Black principals for Black students: Some preliminary observations. *Urban Education* 22(2), 173–181.

Lopez, G. R. (2001). The value of hard work: Lessons on parent involvement from an (im)migrant household. *Harvard Educational Review* 71(3), 416–437.

McDonough, K. (2009). Pathways to critical consciousness: A first-year teacher's engagement with issues of race and equity. *Journal of Teacher Education* 60(5), 528–537.

McInerney, D. M. and Van Etta, S. (Eds.). (2002). *Research in sociocultural influences on motivation and learning*. New York: Information Age Publishing.

Miller, O. P. (2011). *A phenomenological case study of a principal leadership: The influence of Mr. Clark's leadership on students, teachers, and administrators at Eastside High School*. Unpublished doctoral dissertation. Atlanta: Georgia State University.

Morris, J. E. (2004). Can anything good come from Nazareth? Race, class, and African American schooling and community in the urban south and Midwest. *American Educational Research Journal* 41(1), 69–112.

Nicotera, A. M., Clinkscales, M. J., and Walker, F. R. (2003). Understanding organization through culture and structure: Relational and other lessons from the African-American organization. Mahwah, NJ: Lawrence Erlbaum Associates.

Nieto, S. (2000). Placing equity front and center: Some thoughts on transforming teacher education for a new century. *Journal of Teacher Education* May/June, 1–17.

Nobles, W. W. (1978). *African consciousness and liberation struggles: Implications for the development and construction of scientific paradigms.* (unpublished).

Noddings, N. (1992). *The challenge to care in schools: An alternative approach to education.* New York: Teachers College Press.

Paige, R. and Witty, E. (2010). The black-white achievement gap: Why closing it is the greatest civil rights issue of our time. New York: American Management Association.

Perry, T. (2003a). Freedom for literacy and literacy for freedom: The African-American philosophy of education. In T. Perry, C. Steele, and A.G. Hilliard III, *Young, gifted and black: Promoting high achievement among African-American students* (pp. 11–51). Boston: Beacon Press.

Perry, T. (2003b). Up from the parched earth: Toward a theory of African-American achievement. In T. Perry, C. Steele, and A. G. Hilliard III, *Young, gifted and black: promoting high achievement among African-American students* (pp. 1–10). Boston: Beacon Press.

Pettigrew, T. F. and Taylor, M. C. (1990). Discrimination. In E. F. Borgatta and M. L. Borgatta (Eds.), *Encyclopedia of Sociology*, Vol 1. (pp. 498–503). New York: Macmillan.

Putnam, R. D. (2007). E pluribus unum: Diversity and community in the twenty-first century. The 2006 Johan Skytte Prize Lecture. *Scandinavian Political Studies 30*(2), 137–174.

Randolph, A. W. (2004). The memories of an all-Black northern urban school: Good memories of leadership, teachers, and the curriculum. *Urban Education 39*(6), 596–620.

Reitzug, U. C. and Patterson, J. (1998). "I'm not going to lose you!" Empowerment through caring in an urban principal's practice with students. *Urban Education 33*(2), 150–181.

Robins, K.N., Lindsey, R.B., Lindsey, D.B., and Terrell, R.D. (2002). *Culturally proficient instruction: A guide for people who teach.* Thousand Oaks, CA: Corwin Press, Inc.

Ryan, W. (1973). *Blaming the victim.* New York: Random House, Inc.

Sanchez, J. E., Thornton, B. and Usinger, J. (2009). Increasing the ranks of minority principals. *Educational Leadership 67*(2), n.p.

Shujaa, M. J. (1993). Education and schooling: You can have one without the other. *Urban Education 27*(4), 328–351.

Singleton, G. L. and Linton, C. (2006). *Courageous conversations about race: A field guide for achieving equity in schools.* Thousand Oaks, CA: Corwin Press.

Skiba, R. J., Horner, R. H., Chung, C., Rausch, M. K., May, S. L., and Tobin, S. L. (2011). Race is not neutral: A national investigation of African American and Latino disproportionality in school discipline. *School Psychology Review 40*(1), 85–107.

Spring, J. (1991). Knowledge and power in research into the politics of urban education. In J. G. Cibulka, R. J. Reed, and K. K. Wong (Eds.), *The politics of urban education in the United States* (pp. 45–56). Bristol, PA: Taylor and Francis, Inc.

Talbert-Johnson, C. (2006). Preparing highly-qualified teacher candidates for urban schools: The importance of dispositions. *Education and Urban Society 39*(1), 147–160.

Tatum, A. (2005). *Teaching reading to black adolescent males: Closing the achievement gap.* Portland, ME: Stenhouse Publishers.

Tatum, B. D. (2007). *Can we talk about race? And other conversations in an era of school resegregation.* Boston: Beacon Press.

Tillman, L. C. (Ed.). (2009). *SAGE Handbook of African American education.* Thousand Oaks, CA: Sage Publications.

Tillman, L. C. (2004). African American principals and the legacy of Brown. *Review of Research in Education 28*(1), 101–146.

U.S. Department of Education, National Center for Education Statistics. (2009). *Characteristics of public, private, and Bureau of Indian Education elementary and secondary schools in the United States: Results from the 2007–08 Schools and Staffing Survey (NCES 2009-321).* nces.ed.gov/FastFacts/display.asp?id=55-22k.

Walker, V. S. and Byas, U. (2003). The architects of black schooling in the segregated south: The case of one principal leader. *Journal of Curriculum and Supervision 19*(1), 54–72.

Ware, F. (2006). Warm demander pedagogy: Culturally responsive teaching that supports a culture of achievement for African American students. *Urban Education 41(4)*, 427–456.

Weinstein, C. S., Tomlinson-Clarke, S., and Curran, M. (2004). Toward a conception of culturally responsive classroom management. *Journal of Teacher Education 55*(1), 25–38.

Wheeler, R. S. and Swords, R. (2006). *Code-switching: Teaching standard English in urban classrooms.* Urbana, IL: National Council of Teachers of English.

Williams, I. (2012). Race and the principal pipeline: The prevalence of minority principals in light of a largely white teacher workforce. Unpublished paper.

CHAPTER 10

Equity and Race-Visible Urban School Reform

Christine E. Sleeter

In U.S. schools, it is no secret that student achievement is less than stellar, and that racial achievement gaps persist. On the Trends in International Mathematics and Science Study (TIMSS) in 2011, U.S. fourth graders ranked internationally "among the top fifteen" in mathematics and "among the top ten" in science. U.S. eighth graders ranked "among the top twenty-four" in mathematics and "among the top twenty-three" in science (Aud et al., 2013). On the Program for International Student Assessment (PISA) in 2009, U.S. students ranked seventeenth in reading, twenty-third in science, and thirty-first in mathematics.

Increasingly, these patterns are due to persistent under-teaching, with resulting under-achievement, of students of color in U.S. schools. On the National Assessment for Education Progress, between 1971 and 2012, reading scores for white nine-year-olds climbed about fifteen points, and for black and Hispanic nine-year-olds by thirty-six and twenty-five points respectively. But among thirteen-year-olds, while white students' reading scores over the same forty-year period climbed only nine points, scores of black students climbed dramatically until 1988, after which they dropped and have only partially recovered, leaving a wide achievement gap intact. Scores of Hispanic students followed a similar, although less dramatic, pattern, in 2012 the achievement gap between white and Hispanic thirteen-year-olds was the same as it had been in 1988, and wider between white and black thirteen-year-olds than in 1988. Among seventeen-year-olds, while white students' reading scores largely stagnated over the forty-year period, scores of black and Hispanic students jumped markedly until 1988, then declined, resulting in 2012 in a wider achievement gap between white and black students than in 1988, and between white and Hispanic students, about the same as in 1988. In mathemat-

ics, while achievement scores for all three groups have improved among fourth and eighth graders more than in reading, the pattern of persistent racial achievement gaps is much the same (National Center for Education Statistics, 2013). These data illustrate a general stagnation in achievement of students as they mature, and a drop over the last twenty-five years in schools' ability to reach and teach students of color.

What has changed is the proportion of students of color in schools. White students now make up only slightly under half of the enrollment in U.S. public schools; black and Hispanic students are about 45 percent of the enrollment (National Center for Education Statistics, 2011a). In urban schools, students of color and from poverty backgrounds commonly are the majority. Thus, improving overall student achievement in the United States hinges on improving achievement of students of color, an imperative that has not been addressed well, particularly since the late 1980s.

THE PROBLEM WITH COLOR-BLIND SOLUTIONS TO URBAN SCHOOL CHALLENGES

The main approaches to improving student achievement U.S. educators have used for the past twenty-five years are market-based reforms derived from business and heavily promoted by venture philanthropists: raising academic standards (previously state standards, now Common Core Standards), testing students regularly, testing teachers, eliminating teacher tenure, and expanding charter schools. For example, Scott (2009) notes that curriculum standards, longer school days, and teacher quality were policy areas that billionaire venture philanthropists Eli Broad and Bill Gates pushed during the 2008 presidential election. Venture philanthropists have had a huge impact on the current popularity of charter schools. Scott points out that urban school districts, desperate for economic resources, are often quick to embrace market-based reforms that have dollars attached to them.

Direct attention to race, equity, and culture are conspicuously absent, however, in these market-based reform efforts. Yet, as Gooden (2012) clearly points out, the work of urban school leaders takes place in contexts that are structured by racism. To ignore racism only exacerbates leadership challenges. Persistent color blindness and equity-blindness thwart the ability of education leaders to make substantial and lasting, research-supported changes that actually reach students, especially students of color.

For example, Ares and Buendía (2007) investigated what happened in a Utah school district when individually focused, color-blind policy purporting to improve education for an increasingly diverse student population was implemented. The school district, having received a school reform grant, developed five policy areas: accountability, teaching practice, community involvement, student achievement, and advocacy. The researchers explained that what initially caught their attention was the district's proclamation that: "Each student will be known as an individual and their individual needs will be easily met" (p. 563). Over their two-year study, the researchers found that the way teachers and principals interpreted the policy precluded substantive and constructive change. The problem was that the policy directed attention to individuals, which most teachers interpreted through intact deficit ("at risk") and assimilationist perspectives, rather than through an analysis of impacts of systemic racism, and recognition of cultural resources students of color and their families bring. As a result, the educators were unable to transcend how they already understood students of color, resulting in little change. Ares and Buendía concluded that,

> a color-blind focus on students as individuals constrains educators' abilities to respond to students' experiences as members of social, cultural, and linguistic groups, ignoring their differential treatment in schools and in the larger world. Translation of such policies sets in motion a process that moves from color-blind policy to deficit-based color-conscious talk to unintended reproduction of the very problems many reforms seek to remedy. (p. 583)

Color-blind and equity-blind approaches to improving student learning ignore race- and class-based access to resources and the centrality of race and ethnicity to how students, teachers, administrators, and families view their world. Such approaches keep giving the same results. For example, Trujillo and Renee (2012) analyzed the U.S. education system's forty-year history with "turnarounds" as a way to improve schools, particularly those in urban areas. They argue that short-term school improvement grants divert attention from adequate funding of public schools as a whole, and that research does not find that urban students benefit when their education is disrupted by reconstituting school staffs, or closing schools and moving the students to other schools. Yet, the "turnaround" model continues to be pushed, rather than other approaches that might actually make a powerful difference in student learning. Negative impacts on students of color of such market-based, color-blind policies of the past twenty-five years can be critiqued on numerous levels, including how they assign students to schools and how they define and measure school success (Wells, 2014).

While I see public education mainly as a resource for our collective well-being rather than a tool for international competition, the test data point toward problems schools have in connecting with students as they mature, and especially students of color. As someone who has been long engaged with teacher preparation and research focusing on race, ethnicity, and culture, I have witnessed many white educators downplay or ignore the significance of race and culture, interpret equity as meaning treating everyone the same, and express skepticism toward school practices that center on cultural communities rather than individuals. In this chapter I will explore in some detail school-based practices that center race and culture, and by doing so, help dismantle institutional racism in ways that positively impact on students of color.

Before exploring such practices, I offer international examples to substantiate the relationship between equity, culture-based solutions, and academic achievement. Based on international test results, Finland is often regarded as having reformed its education system exceptionally well. Although a small Nordic country with a somewhat ethnically homogeneous population may seem irrelevant to U.S. urban schools, I believe its core approach is highly relevant. Finnish educator and policy advisor Pasi Sahlberg (2012) explains that Finland's excellence is a result of its commitment to equity. In brief, forty years ago Finnish leaders decided Finland needed a well-educated population, which meant educating "all of its youth equally well" (p. 28). This goal required that differences in educational outcomes not be "the result of differences in wealth, income, power, or possessions" (p. 28). Finland built an equitable education system in two phases: centralization in order to instantiate equal opportunity (including a nationwide curriculum) and support (including health services and meals) for all children; then decentralization of curriculum planning, student assessment, and school improvement plans so teachers would be able to connect these with local community contexts where children and youth live. Rather than sorting students by level of academic achievement, Finnish schools mix them, then use pedagogy that activates their learning. But while Sahlberg has spoken extensively in the United States about Finnish school reform, Americans seem not to hear his message about the centrality of equity rather than test- and market-based reforms (Partanen, 2011)

New Zealand, where Māori initiatives drive some school transformation, receives much less attention than Finland, except within indigenous communities. One such initiative, Te Kotahitanga, I know quite well, having been a member of a team that evaluated it for the Ministry of Education (Meyer et al., 2010). In essence, Te Kotahitanga is based on the premise that what works for indigenous students works for everyone, but what works for "everyone" does not necessarily work for indigenous students. It turns out that, by focusing on the minoritized group least-well taught and deliberately seeking solutions from that group, the initiative has improved achievement of Māori students as well as that of students as a whole in the secondary schools engaged in the project. Further, Māori student achievement is directly related to educators learning to learn from and co-construct teaching with their indigenous students (Sleeter, 2011).

Three central ideas emerge as highly relevant to improving urban education in the United States: a deep focus on equity of opportunity that directly addresses inequalities across communities and families, localization of curriculum and pedagogy so that schooling is contextually relevant, and basing reform on the insights of students and educators from racial/ethnic groups in

schools currently least well served. In neither country have these efforts been speedy: Finland has been at it for decades, and Te Kotahitanga, for about twelve years. These international examples converge with research on smaller projects within the United States that involve education of urban students of color, suggesting a way forward that is of use to education leaders.

RACE-VISIBLE PEDAGOGY IN THE CLASSROOM

Frequently, school leaders attempt to improve achievement of students of color through pedagogical interventions that ignore students' racial identities and cultural experiences. Examples include shifting from state standards to Common Core Standards, adopting particular curriculum packages such as America's Choice, or training teachers to use frameworks such as Backward Design (Wiggins and McTighe, 2005). While such efforts may (or may not) have value, color-blind solutions do not solve racialized problems. Curriculum, teaching processes, relationships within the classroom, and academic expectations all embody cultural judgments about what is worthwhile, appropriate, or possible. Crucial is the realization that such judgments are made within cultural and racialized contexts, most commonly by white professionals whose view of reality, even with good intentions, may not recognize or support students of color.

For example, while attempts to raise standards have implications for curriculum, mainstream curricula and standards still only minimally engage the experiences and knowledge of communities of color. Content related to African Americans, Latinos, and Native Americans has been added to textbooks and, to a lesser degree, state standards, but the deeper patterns and narratives that reflect Euro-American experiences and worldviews that have traditionally structured K–12 textbooks—particularly in history and social studies—remain intact (Brown and Brown, 2010; Clawson, 2002; Foster, 1999; Gordy and Pritchard, 1995; Loewen, 1995; Noboa, 2012; Sanchez, 2007; Sleeter, 2002). Beginning as early as elementary school, students of color notice absences of people like themselves, and gaps between curriculum and what they know from home and community (El-Haj, 2006; Epstein, 2001, 2009; Ford and Harris, 2000). By the time they reach high school, many students of color are not only aware of a Euro-American bias in curriculum, but they can describe it in some detail, and have begun to distrust school knowledge, which contributes to their disengagement (Epstein, 2009; Wiggan, 2007).

Research documents a link between racial/ethnic identity of students of color and their academic achievement. For example, Chavous and colleagues (2003) surveyed 606 African-American students from four predominantly black high schools during twelfth grade, then again two years later. The students most likely to graduate and go on to college expressed high awareness of race and racism and high regard for being black. Those least likely to stay in school expressed low awareness of race and racism, low personal regard for being black, and a perception that other people do not value blacks. They had internalized society's negative images of blacks. Similarly, Altschul, Oyserman, and Bybee (2008) surveyed 185 Latino/a eighth graders in three low-income middle schools where students ranged from being recent immigrants to second- and third-generation; most were of Mexican descent. Students with higher grades tended to have bicultural identities, identifying with their ethnic origin as well as focusing on overcoming obstacles within mainstream society. Students who identified little with their ethnic origin tended to achieve poorly, as did the relatively fewer students who identified exclusively with their ethnic origin and not at all with the mainstream society. Studies such as these show that students who are secure in their racial/ethnic identities, especially if their identity is affirmed at school, are more likely to take school seriously, believe in themselves, and achieve than students who are not secure in their own identity. Students of color who recognize how racism works are more likely to learn to navigate around it, while those who have only a vague idea of how it works, especially if they have internalized negative images of their own racial/ethnic group, are likely to see themselves as academically incapable.

Jupp (2013) explains that race-visible teaching "recognizes race as fact or issue" rather than ignoring it, attempting not to see it, or focusing on other issues (that may also be relevant) such as poverty. Drawing from a teacher interview, he explains that once one recognizes race as a fact, one can begin to recognize "what kids bring to the classroom" as resources (p. 31). Culturally responsive pedagogy, which has a significant presence in the literature but a lesser presence in professional development for teachers, is race-visible.

Ladson-Billings (1995) identified three broad dimensions of culturally responsive pedagogy: holding high academic expectations and offering appropriate support such as scaffolding; acting on cultural competence by reshaping curriculum, building on students' funds of knowledge, and establishing relationships with students and their homes; and cultivating students' critical consciousness regarding power relations. Gay (2010) points out that, "Students of color come to school having already mastered many cultural skills and ways of knowing. To the extent that teaching builds on these capabilities, academic success will result" (p. 213). In other words, culturally responsive pedagogy is a process of academically rigorous teaching that builds explicitly on what students of color know and how they approach learning, in a way that specifically engages their cultural identities and community-based knowledge.

Many case studies show what culturally responsive pedagogy looks like in the classroom. For example, Mitchell (2010) analyzed the teaching practice of three African-American professors to illustrate its key dimensions in relationship to how they taught their black students: 1) situating black life in the United States within a history of white supremacy that has ongoing effects that must be named and challenged; 2) recognizing black students' experiences with racism as well as students' cultural assets; and 3) specifically seeking out students' "inherent brilliance" (p. 626). He noted that culturally responsive teachers are "students of their pupils' communities" (p. 626). His study suggests that teachers who are of the same racial or ethnic background of their students may be better able to use culturally responsive pedagogy with them, but perhaps more important is the teacher's willingness to learn where their students are coming from. The issue of who teaches and how teachers might be helped through professional development is addressed later in this chapter.

Case studies show a positive relationship between culturally responsive pedagogy/curriculum and student engagement (e.g., Copenhaver, 2001; Hill, 2009; Nykiel-Herbert, 2010; Rodriguez, Jones, Pang, and Park, 2004; Thomas and Williams, 2008). For example, using observations and interviews, Howard (2001) studied the impact on African-American students of four elementary teachers who used culturally responsive pedagogy. The students described the teachers as caring about them, creating community and family-like environments in the classroom, and making learning fun. As a result, they wanted to participate.

Research that directly connects culturally responsive pedagogy with student academic learning consists largely of small-scale case studies (e.g., Camangian, 2010; Krater and Zeni, 1995; Lipka et al., 2005; Rickford, 2001; Sheets, 2005), which may be why so many school leaders are unaware of its power. Nonetheless, the research shows considerable promise. Consider Lee's (2006) Cultural Modeling Project, which "is a framework for the design of curriculum and learning environments that links everyday knowledge with learning academic subject matter, with a particular focus on racial/ethnic minority groups, especially youth of African descent" (p. 308). The project, which she developed through her work in English classes in predominantly black high schools, involves helping students learn literary analysis by starting with cultural forms that reflect black urban life, such as music lyrics or black films. As the students develop competence in analyzing cultural forms they can relate to, the teacher gradually shifts them toward analyzing literature they are unfamiliar with. Lee has assessed the model's impact on learning, for example by having students write an analysis of a short story they have not seen before. In a study comparing four English classes taught through Cultural Modeling with two taught traditionally, she found that, from pre-test to post-test, the Cultural Modeling students gained over twice as much as the traditionally taught students (Lee, 1995, 2007).

Another excellent example of highly impactful culturally responsive curriculum and pedagogy is the Social Justice Education Project (SJEP) in Tucson's former Mexican-American program.[1] SJEP, which was designed on a model of "critically conscious intellectualism" for strengthening teaching and learning of Chicano students, comprised a four-semester high school social studies curriculum (Cammarota and Romero, 2009). It included critical pedagogy in which students created knowledge in addition to consuming it, authentic caring in which educators demonstrated deep respect for students as full human beings with an ethnic identity, and social justice content based on Chicano studies intellectual frameworks that connected directly with students' lived experience. The curriculum, which taught about racial and economic inequalities, included a community-based research project in which students gathered data about manifestations of racism in their school and community and used advanced-level social science theory to analyze why patterns in the data exist and how they can be challenged. Over a six-year period, participating Mexican-American students outscored Anglo students on the state's reading, writing, and math exams, and their graduation rates exceeded those of Anglo students in the site(s) where the program was offered (Cambium Learning, 2011; Cabrera et al., 2014). Importantly, the students came to see themselves as intellectually capable. This program's approach to curriculum and pedagogy had such a powerful impact on the academic achievement of Mexican-American students that, as part of its ongoing desegregation plan, Tucson Unified School District has agreed to incorporate perspectives of Mexican Americans and African Americans into curriculum and to train its teachers in culturally responsive pedagogy.

For school leaders, research on race-visible pedagogy suggests at least two implications. First, students benefit when teachers have leaders who understand it and can support them in working with it in their classrooms. For example, a follow-up of the Māori reform project in New Zealand mentioned earlier found that in schools that sustained student achievement gains, the principals not only understood the pedagogic reform and supported their teachers, but also connected classroom pedagogy with equity in the school as a whole (Bishop, Berryman, and Wearmouth, 2014). In other words, the school leader's knowledge about and support for the pedagogic reform was key to what the school was able to do with it. Second, leaders can learn to enact race-visible leadership, which is based on the same principles as race-visible pedagogy. For example, Khalifa (2012) found that urban principals who engaged in community-centered leadership improved student academic outcomes more than those who used school-centered leadership. Like teachers who directly address systemic racism as it is manifest in the classroom, race-visible leaders do so at the level of the school and its relationships with the communities of color it serves.

RACE-VISIBLE TEACHERS

Teachers with capacity to recognize and work constructively with race, racism, and students of color in the classroom—whether teachers of color or white teachers—have developed race-visible identifications (Jupp, 2013; Tintiangco-Cubales, Kholi, Sacramento, Henning, Agarwal-Rangnath, and Sleeter, 2015). For urban school leaders, however, hiring and supporting such teachers is very often eclipsed by the more basic problem of simply finding enough teachers to fill classrooms (Jacob, 2007). Shortage of urban teachers is one reason many urban school districts collaborate with Teach for America, even though evidence does not bear out its graduates producing better student learning than traditionally prepared teachers, and its graduates are likely to leave teaching after a few years, exacerbating the problem of teacher turnover (Heilig and Jez, 2010).

A long-term approach to staffing urban schools that takes account of the importance of race involves collaboration with communities and local universities to grow local urban teachers, with a focus on teachers of color (see Sleeter, Kumashiro, and Neal, 2015). This approach turns the preference of most teachers to remain close to home (Boyd, Lankford, Loeb, and Wyckoff, 2005) from a liability into an asset.

It also helps to close the cultural gap between teachers and students. While students who are culturally and linguistically diverse comprise 45 percent of the nation's K–12 students (National Center for Education Statistics, 2011a), white people comprise 83 percent of the teaching force (National Center for Education Statistics, 2011b). This skewed racial gap means that students of color are disproportionately unlikely to have teachers they can relate to, while decisions about curriculum, disciplinary actions, special education referrals, appropriate pedagogy, and so forth, are made through overwhelmingly white perspectives that generally minimize attention to racism, and reflect far less knowledge of cultural assets of communities of color than of white communities. According to Villegas, Strom, and Lucas (2012), "The notion that people of color are well suited to teach students of color not only is consistent with theories of learning but also receives support from a large body of qualitative research that illustrates numerous ways in which competent teachers of color draw on the cultural backgrounds of students of color to facilitate their learning" (p. 287).

In a research review, Sleeter and Milner (2011) examined programs that recruit and prepare teachers of color, identifying two types: programs that bring candidates of color into and through existing teacher education programs, and those that involve redesign or alternative versions of existing teacher education programs. Programs that bring potential teachers of color into and through existing programs build pipelines and support systems that may start as early as elementary or middle school. For example, Tandon, Bianco, and Zion (2015) describe Pathways2Teaching in Denver, offered to students of color in several high schools. Participating students earn college credit at the University of Colorado at Denver. Through the program, students learn about critical theories of education, as well as about how teaching can be an act of social justice. Pipeline programs attempt to demystify higher education and support academic preparation of young people, while also engaging them in experiences that may attract them into teaching.

Programs that encourage university students of color on predominantly white campuses to go into teaching typically offer financial aid such as scholarships, academic support, and social and cultural support to combat alienation. Programs aimed toward working adults—paraprofessionals, emergency certified teachers, and career-changers—take into account not only ethnic identity and cultural support but also pragmatic concerns associated with adults' need to continue to work and barriers adults may experience in higher education institutions. The DeWitt Wallace–Reader's Digest Fund's Pathways into Teaching Careers, a large cluster of programs in the 1990s for working adults of color, had forty-one sites around the United States. Partnering districts actively helped to recruit and select participants, using a selection process that included nontraditional criteria such as commitment to teaching in urban schools. University teacher education curricula were modified to meet participants' needs, and programs offered a system of academic support, social support, and financial support (Clewell and Villegas, 1999). Grow Your Own Teachers in Illinois is a current example involving a partnership among community organizations and a university to build a pipeline into teaching for paraprofessionals and parents from communities of color who are committed to teaching in their local schools (Bartow et al., 2015). Teach Tomorrow in Oakland offers support for adults of color who wish to become teachers, but cannot stop working to enroll as full-time university students (Rogers-Ard and Mayfield-Lynch, 2015).

While these kinds of efforts benefit from (and usually need) financial support, probably more significant is leadership that recognizes that the disparity between who populates classrooms and who populates the teaching force is a problem, and is determined to do something about it. In a discussion of the University of Missouri-Kansas City's relatively recent collaboration with the Kansas City Missouri School District, Ukpokodu (2015) explains that little would have happened without bold, aggressive leadership willing to take "out of the box" action.

Concurrent with efforts to diversify the teaching force should be efforts to help teachers who are already in the classroom learn to teach their students of color more effectively. A workshop will not do it. For one thing, teachers rarely change what they do in the classroom on the basis of one workshop. For another, grappling with race is tricky, since white teachers often feel that efforts to make race visible imply they are overtly racist, which is insulting to how they see themselves.

There has been very little research on effective teacher professional development for culturally responsive pedagogy. Professional development in general that is most likely to impact on classroom teaching is sustained over time, focuses on specific instructional strategies or content areas, involves teachers collectively rather than individually, is coherent, and engages teachers actively (Penuel, Fishman, Yamaguchi, and Gallagher, 2007; Snow-Runner and Lauer, 2005). It usually also includes classroom-based coaching (Cornett and Knight, 2009; Teemant, Wink, and Tyra, 2011; Zozakiewicz and Rodriguez, 2007). For example, Teemant et al. (2011) evaluated a thirty-hour workshop connected with seven individual coaching sessions across an academic year, designed to improve teacher pedagogy and classroom organization in elementary classrooms serving culturally diverse students. Researchers found coaching associated with statistically significant improvements in teacher pedagogy, teacher growth, and classroom organization.

The New Zealand reform project mentioned earlier, which is not well-known in the United States, has developed a very effective teacher professional development process for culturally responsive pedagogy in secondary schools. The process helps teachers learn to enact an "effective teaching profile" derived from interviews with Māori students regarding what would work for them in the classroom. The school-based process, which includes classroom coaching, helps teachers learn to form constructive pedagogical relationships with their Māori students, then work with their students to co-construct pedagogy. Research on the impact of the professional development program has found shifts in teachers' classroom pedagogy that is sustained over time, and is associated with gains in Māori student achievement and schools' retention of Māori (e.g., Bishop, Berryman, Wearmouth, Peter, and Clapham, 2012; Meyer et al., 2010).

For urban school leaders, perhaps the greatest implication of this discussion of growing, supporting, and developing race-visible teachers is that many solutions can be found in collaboration with the local community. For example, Ellis and Epstein (2015) worked successfully to develop grow-your-own teacher projects in Oakland, California, by beginning with meetings of community residents, publicized through local ethnic presses. Local universities were brought in as collaborators, but conversations with the community drove the reform effort. While community members may know little or nothing about how to organize teacher certification and professional learning, students and their parents know what does and does not work for students in the classroom. Framing school staffing and teacher professional development in terms of connecting the school with the community, and helping teachers learn to access and use community knowledge, is perhaps the best place to start (see Khalifa, 2012).

RACE AND CLASS VISIBLE EQUITY IN ACCESS

Several years ago, a conversation with a former student who is now an elementary teacher pinpointed an enormous equity issue that is common in U.S. schools. At the time of our conversation, she was teaching in a predominantly white affluent school district, but she had previously taught in a racially diverse, low-income district. She explained to me she did not find teaching satisfying in the racially diverse district because the curriculum, narrowed to reading and math in order to prepare students for standardized tests, was very prescribed and taught largely through drill. In the white affluent district, in contrast, since the students routinely scored well on tests, teachers were encouraged to teach through interdisciplinary projects that were much more interesting.

She observed that both teachers and students were much more intellectually engaged in the latter context.

Her story of glaringly inequitable access to high-quality, interesting teaching and a full curriculum has become common throughout the United States as attention over the past twenty-five years has narrowed to how students do on tests (Valli, Croninger, Chambliss, Graeber, and Buese, 2008). Turning our attention back to Finland, it is instructive that strong achievement outcomes are supported by equity in opportunities to learn. For example, Sahlberg (2011) explains that after tracking was abolished in the 1980s, "the achievement gap between low and high achievers began to decrease" and overall student achievement began to rise (p. 45). Special education support is used intensively at the primary grade level, then scaled back as students become competent in higher-level learning. Teacher education and professional development include considerable attention to teaching heterogeneous groups of students well through cooperative learning and project-based learning. Education itself occurs within a state system that provides "all children and their families with equitable conditions for starting a successful educational path" (p. 48); very few families live in poverty because of state welfare policies supported by a public value for equity.

School leaders in the United States can learn from the example of Finland not to equate equity with sameness, but rather to build differentiated supportive systems for diverse students so that opportunities to learn will be equitable. The effectiveness of such work can be monitored through "equity audits." Scott (2001) defines systemic equity as

> the transformed ways in which systems and individuals habitually operate to ensure that every learner—in whatever learning environment that learner is found—has the greatest opportunity to learn enhanced by the resources and supports necessary to achieve competence, excellence, independence, responsibility, and self-sufficiency. (p. 6)

Equity audits are tools for identifying inequities in outcomes and opportunities to learn, so inequitable systems can be made more equitable.

Skrla, Scheurich, Garcia, and Nolly (2004) developed a fairly simple formula for equity audits. The formula proposes that equity in teacher quality plus programmatic equity will lead to achievement equity. Here, I will provide only a few examples of how they unpack this formula, from a much larger body of highly accessible and useful work (Bell McKenzie and Skrla, 2011; Skrla, Bell McKenzie, and Scheurich, 2009).

Skrla, Scheurich, Garcia, and Nolly (2004) begin examining teacher quality with its well-substantiated link to student learning. A school district question can then be: which racial/ethnic and social class groups of students have greatest access to the highest quality teachers? To operationalize this question, one can examine teacher quality in terms of factors like academic degrees teachers hold, years of teaching experience, teacher mobility, and whether teachers are teaching within their area of certification. This list of criteria, while obviously not exhaustive, nonetheless can produce a useful analysis. Commonly districts find, for example, that lower SES students are taught by less-experienced teachers who are highly mobile, while high SES students have more-experienced teachers who tend to remain in the same school year after year. Such findings should prompt the question of whether this pattern produces inequity in the quality of teaching students have access to and, if so, what solutions would address the problem. The U.S. Department of Education, finally recognizing the inequitable distribution of excellent teachers as a problem, is beginning to look into how to tackle the problem (McNeil, 2014).

Programmatic inequities include factors like access to programs for Gifted and Talented, access to college preparation, access to the arts, racial disparities in school disciplinary infractions, and so forth. Skrla, Scheurich, Garcia, and Nolly (2004) explain that in their work with schools and school districts, they pull together committees of relevant and diverse stakeholder groups such as teacher unions, the PTA or PTO, and the NAACP, so that solutions actually address and transform rather than simply reconstitute the identified inequities.

The main implication for urban school leaders is to learn to use equity audits, in collaboration with diverse local stakeholders, to identify changes that can be made, and that would benefit students. At the same time, addressing inequities within schools and school systems, while highly important, still does not address larger inequities in families' lives. Berliner (2014) argues that factors outside schools may well account for disparities in school achievement more than factors within schools. Poverty and income inequality have a negative impact on the well-being of children, the mental health of children and their families, incidents of illegal drug use, infant and maternal mortality, rates of imprisonment, teen pregnancy, and so forth; and these factors all impact negatively on students' achievement, school attendance, and graduation. Berliner argues that in addition to working toward equity within schools and school systems, leaders of urban schools must advocate actively for public policies that support equity in the lives of children and their families. This is, after-all, part of the bigger picture of equity that has produced Finland's excellent student achievement.

CONCLUSION

"Racism is a social problem that often hides in plain sight" (Gooden and Dantley, 2012, p. 250). In this chapter, I have argued that color- and equity-blind approaches to improving student learning simply fail to address the systemic racism and cultural identity that are inextricably part of the education process. In contrast, race-visible pedagogy, in schools staffed by race-visible teachers, led by leaders who do the courageous work that race-visible equity demands, will serve not only our urban students of color but also the nation as a whole.

This argument has important implications for the preparation of school leaders. Gooden and Dantley (2012) point out that the main way leadership preparation programs currently address race is to concentrate racial awareness into one diversity course, as though the rest of the program adequately addresses leadership that is unrelated to race. The problem is that urban students and their communities do not experience race and culture as add-ons to an otherwise nonracial existence. Rather, race, racism, and culture are fundamental to how everyone experiences education, all the time. Understanding this and its implications for teaching and leading requires a profound shift in thinking, yet one that it is possible to make. Perhaps the most important place to start is to acknowledge that the well-publicized achievement gap contains a message about systemic racism, the failure of color- and equity-blind approaches to addressing it, and the promise of work that places addressing racism front and center.

NOTE

1. In 2010, the Arizona state legislature took aim directly at this program, and through Arizona Revised Statue 15-111 and 15-112, criminalized ethnic studies. January 2012, the Tucson Unified School District shut down the Mexican American Studies program and reassigned the teachers to other courses.

REFERENCES

Altschul, I., Oyserman, D., and Bybee, D. (2008). Racial-ethnic self-schemas and segmented assimilation: Identity and the academic achievement of Hispanic youth. *Social Psychology Quarterly 71*(3), 302–320.

Ares, N. and Buendía, E. (2007). Opportunities lost: Local translations of advocacy policy conversations. *Teachers College Record 109*(3), 561–589.

Aud, S., Wilkinson-Flicker, S., Kristapovich, P., Rathbun, A., Wang, X., and Zhang, J. (2013). *The Condition of Education 2013* (NCES 2013–037). U.S. Department of Education, National Center for Education Statistics. Washington, DC. Retrieved February 15, 2014 from nces.ed.gov/pubsearch.

Bartow J., Gillette, M., Hallett, A., Johnson, K., Madda, C. L., Salazar, I., and Valle, V. M. (2015). Growing your own teachers in Illinois: Promising practice for urban and rural "high need" schools (99–110). In Sleeter, C. E., Neal, L. I., and Kumashiro, K. K. (Eds.), *Diversifying the teacher workforce*. New York: Routledge.

Bell McKenzie, K. and Skrla, L. (2011). *Using equity audits in the classroom to reach and teach all students*. Thousand Oaks, CA: Corwin Press.

Berliner, D. C. (2014). Effects of inequality and poverty vs. teachers and schooling on America's youth. *Teachers College Record 116*(1). Retrieved at www.tcrecord.org.

Bishop, R., Berryman, M., and Wearmouth, J. (2014). Te Kotahitanga: *Towards effective education reform for Indigenous and other minoritized students*. Wellington, New Zealand: NZCER.

Bishop, R., Berryman, M., Wearmouth, J., Peter, M., and Clapham, S. (2012). Professional development, changes in teacher practice and improvements in Indigenous students' educational performance: A Case study from New Zealand. *Teaching and Teacher Education 28*, 694–705.

Brown, K. D. and Brown, A. L. (2010). Silenced memories: An Examination of the sociocultural knowledge on race and racial violence in official school curriculum. *Equity and Excellence in Education 43*(2), 139–154.

Boyd, D., Lankford, H., Loeb, S., and Wyckoff, J. (2005). The Draw of home: How teachers' preferences for proximity disadvantage urban schools. *Journal of Policy Analysis and Management 24*(1), 113–132.

Cabrera, N. L., Milem, J. F., Jaquette, O., and Marx, R. D. (2015). Missing the (student achievement) forest for all the (political) trees: Empiricism and the Mexican American student controversy in Tucson. *American Educational Research Journal 51*(6): 1084–1118.

Cambium Learning and National Academic Educational Partner. (2011). *Curriculum audit of the Mexican American Studies Department, Tucson Unified School District.* Retrieved from saveethnicstudies.org/state_audit.shtml.

Camangian, P. (2010). Starting with self: Teaching autoethnography to foster critically caring literacies. *Research in the Teaching of English 45*, 179–204.

Cammarota, J. and Romero, A. (2009). The Social Justice Education Project: A critically compassionate intellectualism for Chicana/o students. In W. Ayers, T. Quinn, and D. Stovall (Eds.), *Handbook for social justice education* (pp. 465–476). New York: Lawrence Erlbaum.

Chavous, T., Hilkene, D., Schmeelk, Cone, K., Caldwell, C. H., Kohn-Wood, L., and Zimmerman, M. A. (2003). Racial identity and academic attainment among African American adolescents. *Child Development 74*(4), 1076–1090.

Clawson, R.A. (2002). Poor people, Black faces: The portrayal of poverty in economics textbooks. *Journal of Black Studies 32*(3): 352–361.

Clewell, B. C. and Villegas, A. M. (1999). Creating a non-traditional pipeline for urban teachers: The Pathways to Teaching Careers Model. *Journal of Negro Education 68*(3), 306–317.

Copenhaver, J. (2001). Listening to their voices connect literary and cultural understandings: Responses to small group read-alouds of *Malcolm X: A Fire. New Advocate 14*, 343–359.

Cornett, J. and Knight, J. (2009). Research on coaching. In J. Knight (Ed.), *Coaching: Approaches and perspectives* (pp. 192–216). Thousand Oaks, CA: Corwin Press.

El-Haj, T. R. A. (2006). *Elusive justice: Wrestling with difference and educational equity in everyday practice.* New York: Routledge.

Ellis, W. F. and Epstein, K. K. (2015). Tactics and strategies for breaking the barriers to a diverse teaching force (pp. 139–149). In Sleeter, C. E., Neal, L. I., and Kumashiro, K. K. (Eds.). *Diversifying the teacher workforce.* New York: Routledge.

Epstein, T. (2001). Racial identity and young people's perspectives on social education. *Theory Into Practice 40*(1), 42–47.

Epstein, T. (2009). *Interpreting national history.* New York: Routledge.

Ford, D. Y. and Harris III, J. J. (2000).A Framework for infusing multicultural curriculum into gifted education. *Roeper Review 23*(1), 4–10.

Foster, S. J. (1999). The Struggle for American identity: Treatment of ethnic groups in United States history textbooks. *History of Education 28*(3): 251–278.

Gooden, M. A. (2012). What does racism have to do with leadership? *Educational Foundations 26*(1), 67–85.

Gooden, M. A. and Dantley, M. (2012). Centering race in a framework for leadership preparation. *Journal of Research on Leadership Education 7*(2), 237–253.

Gordy, L. L. and Pritchard, A. M. (1995). Redirecting our voyage: A Content analysis of social studies textbooks. *Urban Education 30*(2), 195–218.

Heilig, J. V. and Jez, S. J. (2010). *Teach for America: A Review of the evidence.* Arizona State University, Tempe, AZ: Educational Policy Research Unit.

Hill, M. L. (2009). Wounded healing: Forming a storytelling community in hip-hop lit. *Teachers College Record 111*, 248–293.

Howard, T. C. (2001). Telling their side of the story: African American students' perceptions of culturally relevant teaching. *Urban Review 33*(2), 131–149.

Jacob, B. A. (2007). The Challenges of staffing urban schools with effective teachers. *Future of Children 17*(1), 129–153.

Jupp, J. C. (2013). *Becoming teachers of inner-city students.* Boston: Sense Publishers.

Khalifa, M. (2012). A Re-New-ed paradigm in successful urban school leadership: Principal as community leader. *Educational Administration Quarterly 48*(3), 424–467.

Krater, J. and Zeni, J. (1995). Seeing students, seeing culture, seeing ourselves. *Voices from the Middle 3*(3), 32–38.

Ladson-Billings, G. (1995). Toward a theory of culturally relevant pedagogy. *American Educational Research Journal 47*, 465–491.

Lee, C. D. (1995). A Culturally based cognitive apprenticeship: Teaching African American high school students skills in literary interpretation. *Reading Research Quarterly 30*, 608–630.

Lee, C. D. (2006). "Every good-bye ain't gone": Analyzing the cultural underpinnings of classroom talk. *International Journal of Qualitative Studies in Education 19*, 305–327.

Lee, C. D. (2007). *Culture, literacy and learning: Taking bloom in the midst of the whirlwind.* New York: Teachers College Press.

Lipka, J., Hogan, M. P., Webster, J. P., Yanez, E., Adams, B., Clark, S., and Lacy, D. (2005). Math in a Cultural Context: Two case studies of a successful culturally based math project. *Anthropology & Education Quarterly 36* (4), 367–385.

Loewen, J. W. (1995). *Lies my teacher told me.* New York: New Press.

McNeil, M. (2014). Scrutiny rises on placement of best teachers. *Education Week*, February 19. Retrieved from www.edweek.org/ew/articles/2014/02/19/21equity_ep.h33.html?cmp=ENL-EU-NEWS1.

Meyer, L. H., Penetito, W., Hynds, A., Savage, C., Hindle, R., and Sleeter, C. E. (2010). *Evaluation of the Te Kotahitanga programme, Final Report*. Wellington, NZ: Ministry of Education.

Mitchell, R. (2010). Cultural aesthetics and teacher improvisation: An epistemology of providing culturally responsive service by African American professors. *Urban Education 45*, 604–629.

National Center for Education Statistics (2011a). Public elementary and secondary enrollment, student race/ethnicity, schools, school size, and pupil/teacher ratios, by type of locale: 2008–09 and 2009–10. *Digest of Education Statistics*. Retrieved from nces.ed.gov/programs/digest/d11/tables/dt11_094.asp.

National Center for Education Statistics (2011b). Teacher trends. *Fast Facts*. Retrieved from nces.ed.gov/fastfacts/display.asp?id=28.

National Center for Education Statistics (2012). *The nation's report card: Trends in academic progress 2012*. Washington, DC: Institute for Education Sciences, U.S. Department of Education.

Noboa, J. (2012). Missing pages from the human story: World History according to Texas standards. *Journal of Latinos and Education 11*, 47–62.

Nykiel-Herbert, B. (2010). Iraqi refugee students: From a collection of aliens to a community of learners. *Multicultural Education 17*(30), 2–14.

Partanen, U. (2011, December 29). What Americans keep ignoring about Finland's school success. *The Atlantic*. Retrieved from www.theatlantic.com/national/archive/2011/12/what-americans-keep-ignoring-about-finlands-school-success/250564/.

Penuel, W. R., Fishman, B. J., Yamaguchi, R., and Gallagher, L. P. (2007). What makes professional development effective? Strategies that foster curriculum implementation. *American Educational Research Journal 44*(4), 921–958.

Rickford, A. (2001). The effect of cultural congruence and higher order questioning on the reading enjoyment and comprehension of ethnic minority students. *Journal of Education for Students Placed at Risk 6*(4), 357–387.

Rodriguez, J. L., Jones, E. B,, Pang, V. O., and Park, C. D. (2004). Promoting academic achievement and identity development among diverse high school students. *High School Journal 87*, 44–53.

Rogers-Ard, R. and Mayfield-Lynch, K. (2015). Teach Tomorrow in Oakland: History, teacher profiles and lessons learned (pp. 32–45). In Sleeter, C. E., Neal, L. I., and Kumashiro, K. K. (Eds.), *Diversifying the teacher workforce*. New York: Routledge.

Sahlberg, P. (2011). *Finnish lessons*. New York: Teachers College Press.

Sahlberg, P. (2012). Quality and equity in Finnish schools. *School Administrator*, 27–30.

Sanchez, T. R. (2007). The depiction of Native Americans in recent (1991–2004) secondary American history textbooks: How far have we come? *Equity & Excellence in Education 40*, 311–320.

Scott, B. (2001). Coming of age. *IDRA Newsletter*, March. Retrieved from www.idra.org/IDRA_Newsletter/March_2001_Self_Renewing_Schools_Access_Equity_and_Excellence/Coming_of_Age/.

Scott, J. (2009). The Politics of venture philanthropy in charter school policy and advocacy. *Educational Policy 23*(1), 106–136.

Sheets, R. H. (1995). From remedial to gifted: Effects of culturally centered pedagogy. *Theory Into Practice, 34*, 186–193.

Skrla, L., Bell McKenzie, K., and Scheurich, J. J. (2009). *Using equity audits to create equitable and excellent schools*. Thousand Oaks, CA: Corwin Press.

Skrla, L., Scheurich, J.J., Garcia, J., and Nolly, G. (2004). Equity audits: A Practical leadership tool for developing equitable and excellent schools. *Educational Administration Quarterly 40*(1), 135–163.

Sleeter, C. E. (2002). State curriculum standards and the shaping of student consciousness. *Social Justice 29*(4), 8–25.

Sleeter, C. E. (2011). *The Academic and social value of ethnic studies*. Washington, DC: National Education Association.

Sleeter, C. E., Neal, L. I., and Kumashiro, K. K., Eds. (2015). *Diversifying the teacher workforce*. New York: Routledge.

Snow-Runner, R. and Lauer, P. A. (2005). *Professional development analysis*. Denver, CO: Mid-continent Research for Education and Learning.

Tandon, M., Bianco, M., and Zion, S. (2015). Pathways2Teaching: Being and becoming a "rida" (pp. 111–125). In Sleeter, C. E., Neal, L. I., and Kumashiro, K. K. (Eds.), *Diversifying the teacher workforce*. New York: Routledge.

Teemant, A., Wink, J., and Tyra, S. (2011). Effects of coaching on teacher use of sociocultural instructional practices. *Teaching and Teacher Education 27*, 683–693.

Thomas, C. D. and Williams, D. L. (2008). An Analysis of teacher defined mathematical tasks: Engaging urban learners in performance-based instruction. *Journal of Urban Teaching and Research 4*, 109–121.

Tintiangco-Cubales, A., Kohli, R., Sacramento, J., Henning, N., Agarwal-Rangnath, R., and Sleeter, C. (2015). Toward an ethnic studies pedagogy: Implications for K–12 schools from the research. *Urban Review 47*(1): 204–225.

Trujillo, T. and Renee, M. (2012). *Democratic school turnarounds: Pursuing equity and learning from evidence*. Boulder, CO: National Education Policy Center.

Ukpokodu, O. N. (2015). The turning point of one teacher education program: Recruitment, preparation, and retention of diverse teacher candidates (pp. 71–84). In Sleeter,

C. E., Neal, L. I., and Kumashiro, K. K. (Eds.), *Diversifying the teacher workforce*. New York: Routledge.

Valli, L., Croninger, R. G., Chambliss, M. H., Graeber, A. O., and Buese, D. (2008). *Test-driven: High stakes accountability in elementary schools*. New York: Teachers College Press.

Villegas, A. M., Strom, K., and Lucas, T. (2012). Closing the racial/ethnic gap between students of color and their teachers: An elusive goal. *Equity & Excellence in Education 45*(2), 283–301.

Wells, A. S. (2014). *Seeing past the "colorblind" myth: Why education policymakers should address racial and ethnic inequality and support culturally diverse schools*. Boulder, CO: National Education Policy Center. Retrieved March 15, 2014 from nepc.colorado.edu/publication/seeing-past-the-colorblind-myth.

Wiggan, G. (2007). From opposition to engagement: Lessons from high achieving African American students. *The Urban Review 40*(4), 317–349.

Wiggins, G. and McTighe, J. (2005). *Understanding by design*, 2nd ed. New York: Pearson.

Zozakiewicz, C. and Rodriguez, A. J. (2007). Using socio-transformative constructivism to create multicultural and gender-inclusive classrooms: An intervention project for teacher professional development. *Educational Policy 21*, 397–425.

CHAPTER 11

Culturally Responsive Leadership Preparation and Practices

Monica Wills Brown and Frankie K. Williams

Emerging evidence has found that preparation programs influence the efficacy of future school leaders (Darling-Hammond, LaPointe, Meyerson, and Orr, 2007; Jackson and Kelly, 2002), and demands are prevalent that school leadership preparation attend to issues of cultural competence (Dantley, 2005; Evans, 2007; Lopez, Magdaleno, and Reis, 2006; Shields, 2004; Young and Brooks, 2008; Young and Laible, 2000). The changing demographics of schools requires instructional leadership skills, advocacy skills, and specialized knowledge in what works best for students from culturally and linguistically diverse backgrounds (Johnson, 2006; Ladson-Billings, 2001). Further, a large body of literature points to persistent achievement gaps for children of color and especially for African-American males, particularly in urban school settings. Despite the rise in concern about cultural diversity in leadership preparation programs, the research base about such programs is thin (Gooden and Dantley, 2012).

The research on teaching and learning offers resources and tools that can be utilized by individuals developing leaders who embrace and practice cultural responsiveness (Delpit, 1995; Gay, 1979, 1994, 2000; Giroux, 2001; Ladson-Billings, 1995a, 2000; Nieto, 2009). Through culturally responsive or culturally relevant teaching and learning, the tenets of social justice that seek to provide educational equity, tolerance, and cultural respect are transmitted to school leadership candidates (Brown, 2013; Gay, 2000; Gooden and Dantley, 2012; Ladson-Billings, 2000).

The relationship between culture and the academic achievement of the African-American school-age population advances the argument that a set of authentic culture-based values is supported by behavioral, thought, and interactional patterns of African Americans (Boykin, 1983). African-American students' academic performance is optimal when the cultural values of their behavioral, thought, and interactional patterns are a part of the instructional practices utilized in schools (Boykin, 1983; Boykin and Cunningham, 2001). This chapter provides a synthesis of the literature and related research regarding principals' experiences within the context of culturally responsive leadership preparation and practices that promote academic achievement of African-American students.

DIVERSITY IN SCHOOLS

Schools reflect the society in which they are situated. As changes in society take place, schools reflect similar transformations. In the sweeping case of society's changing racial and cultural demographics, schools must respond to efficiently meet the needs of the various races and cultures that permeate schools. Challenges have emerged on the status quo of school leadership, curriculum, and pedagogy (Anyon, 1997; Carlson and Apple, 1998; Darling-Hammond, 1997; Delpit, 1995; Dimitriadis and Carlson, 2003). As open systems, schools in racially diverse societies require leaders and models of leadership that address the racial, cultural, and ethnic makeup of the school community (Brown, 2005; Murtadha and Watts, 2005). By 2020, students of color are most likely to constitute 50 percent of the total school population (Marshall, 2004). A focus on cultural responsiveness is particularly important in educational leadership given the rapidly increasing number of students of color in prekindergarten through twelfth grade (Brown, 2005). The academic achievement of African Americans particularly in urban settings is a concern for principals, especially in the increasing call for higher and more stringent accountability (Beachum,

Denith, McCray, and Boyle, 2008; Scheurich and Skrla, 2003). The excessive job demand placed on school principals makes it difficult for them to focus solely on teaching and learning. In addition, there appears to be a growing shortage of people who are qualified and willing to assume principal positions that are committed to instructional improvement, especially in culturally diverse schools in urban settings (Darling-Hammond et al., 2007).

Despite a half century following the desegregation of America's schools mandated by *Brown v. Board of Education*, the proper and appropriate education of African-American students in U.S. schools remains ever more problematic and more troubled than in pre-Civil Rights days (Foster, 2005). The overpopulation of black males in special education, the tremendous disparities between black and white student achievement, and the fact that African Americans' rate of suspension is higher than any other ethnic group gives reason to pause and reflect (Dantley, 2005). Ladson-Billings (2000) argued that the educational literature was silent on the issue of teaching African-American students because much of the educational research relied on generic models of pedagogy positioned as culturally neutral and actually supporting the learning of mainstream students (Shulman, 1987).

EMERGENCE OF CULTURALLY RESPONSIVE EDUCATION

Culture is conceptualized and defined differently depending on one's worldview and one's particular needs as a researcher and scholar (Tillman, 2002, 2005). Culture continues to be viewed as a major influence in cognitive development (Sue, 2004). The attribution of culturally relevant educational practices can be connected to Vygotsky's (1978) genetic law of cultural development and further with his sociocultural theory that "emphasizes social activity and cultural practice as sources of thinking, the importance of mediation in human psychological functioning, and the inseparability of the individual from the social context" (Moll, 1990, p. 15). Vygotsky's (1978) student-centered learning approaches are aligned with how educators can address the cultural diversity issues that exist in American society.

MULTICULTURAL EDUCATION

In the early 1970s, concerns for the racial and ethnic inequities that were apparent in learning opportunities and outcomes began to evolve in a myriad of multicultural educational reform approaches by scholars (Abrahams and Troike, 1972; Banks, 1974; Carlson, 1976; Gay, 1979, 2002; Howard, 2010). The beginning of the educational multicultural movement provided guidance for how educators should respond to the multicultural needs of students (and sometimes of educators themselves). The works of Abrahams and Troike (1972) suggested that teachers must learn the cultural differences of their students as well as be able to analyze their own cultural attitudes and assumptions. Carlson (1976) advised educators to embrace the realities of ethnic differences among students and the roles those differences play in U.S. education. Banks (1974) admonished teachers of racial minority students to stop the use of "traditional" instructional conventions. Banks stated that educators should respect the cultures of students and revise curriculum so that it is reflective of students' learning and cultural styles that enhance student achievement.

CULTURE, RACE, AND AFRICAN AMERICANS

Drawing from King (1995), Hilliard (2001), and McCarthy (1998), Tillman (2002) defined culture as a group's individual and collective way of thinking, believing, and knowing. This definition includes the group's shared experiences, consciousness, skills, values, and forms of expression, social institutions, and behaviors. Culturally responsive educational practices are not solely identified with race, but may include economic differences, geographic differences, gender, sexual orientation, and religion. Culturally relevant educational responses and culturally responsive practices help educational systems that have been dominated by a particular group of individuals. Darder (1991) defined this as "cultural invasion." Cultural invasion is a way majority groups maintain continuous economic, political, social, and cultural power over minority groups. Structural inequalities in public education are attributed to Darder's (1991) "cultural invasion." Darling-Hammond and Orphanos (2006) stated that access to resources and high-stakes assessment practices contribute largely to the structural inequities that maintain unequal opportunity among racial groups. They further found that because the minority racial groups are not being given equal access to high-quality education, the achievement of students from minority backgrounds is far lower than nonminority students (Darling-Hammond and Orphanos, 2006).

AFRICAN-AMERICAN STUDENTS AND EDUCATION

The early works of scholars such as W. E. B. Dubois (1903) and Carter G. Woodson (1968) defined the history of social inequities and educational opportunities afforded to African Americans in the United States. Although DuBois (1903) and Woodson (1968) were speaking from an early to mid-twentieth-century perspective, it is evident from twentieth-century achievement gaps and disciplinary infractions within schools that "race matters," as incited by Cornel West (1994). Groups, particularly African Americans, who have been excluded from educational opportunities over the past centuries represent those who now in the twenty-first century, continue to be at or near the bottom of the achievement hierarchy (Howard, 2010). Educators attempting to cross the intersection of race and culture while attempting to identify methods to eradicate achievement gaps must include a historical understanding of African Americans. While disparity was more political and class driven in the early 1900s, the "eagerness to learn" by blacks during the pre–Civil War era was observed by Northerners as well as by those who attributed negative values to blacks (Anderson, 1988). In addition, a perplexing component of the current poor performance of African-American students and poor parent participation are inconsistent with the educational attainment of blacks following the Civil War. Anderson's summation of African Americans' acquisition of education in America from slavery to the modern Civil Rights movement argued that African Americans pursued learning because it established freedom and humanity, it contributed to the racial uplifting and liberation of their people, and it prepared one to be a leader (Perry, 2003). Those attempting to understand the history of African Americans for the sake of mitigating academic disparity must examine the correlation between their systemic exclusion from educational opportunities and their current state of educational progress (Howard, 2010).

When scholars begin discussing the needs of African-American students, the argument is that their performance is related to their having a poor or lower socioeconomic status. However, a startling discovery of African-American achievement finds that African-American students who have middle-class backgrounds exhibit lower academic performance than white students from low socioeconomic standings (Gay, 2010; Howard, 2010).

URBAN EDUCATION AND AFRICAN-AMERICAN STUDENTS

The concept of African-American performance being linked to varied societal and educational ills is a segue to understand the link between African-American students and urban education. Because African-American students are generally found in predominately urban areas, studies have replicated how African-American students are alienated and marginalized in urban educational settings (Lewis, James, Hancock, and Hill-Jackson, 2008). However, there is a discrepancy among researchers, policy makers, and practitioners with how urban education is defined (Milner, 2012). Thompson, Ransdell, and Rousseau (2005) attributed the tenets of urban education to the actual students. Students in these settings have substandard academic performance, increased volumes of student disciplinary infractions, and poor resources. Tatum and Muhammad (2012) referred to urban education as to where the schools are located.

EDUCATIONAL LEADERSHIP PREPARATION PROGRAMS

Changes in accountability structure, demographics, and overall educational needs require quality principals who are equipped with the tools needed to meet the numerous needs and functions of schools (Levine, 2005). Among the challenges in leadership preparation programs for meeting the new demands of school leaders are the limits of educational leadership curricula for adequately addressing issues of how race, sexual orientation, ethnicity, and other cultural characteristics that create a climate that places some students at an educational disadvantage (Furman and Starratt, 2002). Another challenge is the need to adequately prepare educational leaders with experiences that increase their desire to promote and practice social justice (Scheurich and Laible, 1999). There is also the misconception that pre-service training or professional development will provide aspiring school leaders with all the knowledge needed to be an effective leader (Daresh and Playco, 1995).

Preparation programs are responsible for developing principals who have the knowledge, skills, and attributes of instructional leaders that have the capacity to galvanize increased student achievement and learning (Barth, 2001). Gurr, Drysdale, and Mulford (2007) stated that "educational leadership makes a difference in different ways" and causes a critical analysis in understanding the complexity of leadership and the importance of avoiding one-size-fits-all preparation approaches. Rather than using outmoded and failed educational methods from the past to prepare school leaders, universities are now called upon to create a new type of program of study that is embedded in a social, cultural, and moral leadership based in democratic authority that is committed to a just and equitable school (Allen, 2006).

Historical Snapshot of Educational Leadership Programs

A large number of changes have taken place that modify how educational leaders are prepared (Levine, 2005). Tucker and Codding's (2002) assessment of "elite" educational administration programs observed that there is little connection between what is being taught and the existing demands of today's educational landscape (Hess and Kelly, 2005). The traditional process of preparing leaders in many programs was not meeting the need of school leaders. The role of principal is essential to school reform, yet problems occur when the inadequacies of preparation programs cannot meet the current needs of schools (Crowther, 2002; Foster, 1989: Hallinger and Heck, 1996).

In the late 1980s, the National Commission on Excellence in Education and the National Policy Board for Educational Administration called for educational preparatory programs to institute change by increasing the sequencing of program content and aligning programs to meet the job demands of a school administrator (Jackson and Kelly, 2002; Levine, 2005). In 1996, the Council of Chief State School Officers advanced a set of standards through the Interstate School Leaders Licensure Consortium (ISLLC) that established a framework for administrator preparation in approximately forty states. In 2002, the National Council for Accreditation of Teacher Education (NCATE) adopted the standards for accreditation of school administration programs (Cambron-McCabe, 2010). While ISLLC standards received acclaim for focusing attention on leadership practices and student learning, the standards received intense criticism. There was concern that the standards inadequately addressed social justice concerns or did very little to bring about significant shifts in leadership practices (Achilles and Price, 2001; English, 2000). In 2008, the National Policy Board for Educational Administration released updated standards, called Educational Leadership Policy Standards: ISLLC 2008. These standards gave attention to and were specifically directed toward social justice and making shifts in leadership practices (Cambron-McCabe, 2010).

Preparing School Leaders

The process of training and preparing school leaders is paramount to address the criticism of reform (including the need to clarify accountability measures and standards of effective leadership). Leaders should not only understand how to perform as effective instructional leaders, but to be effective, they need training that prepares them to become culturally responsive leaders. These school leaders should enable learning by all student populations. Preparation should make school leaders cognizant about their personal dispositions that may impact their leadership performance.

State accountability measures have focused educators' attention on student learning as well as on the development of curriculum and pedagogy to ensure that students meet high academic standards (Cambron-McCabe, 2010). The accountability standards place student achievement at the center of the programs of study of preparation programs and licensure requirements. The route to ensuring that administrators receive adequate content related to cultural responsiveness is embedded in one's requirement for licensure to practice (Hale, 2003). Typically, applicants must pass an examination that connects the leadership preparation programs to the applicants' performance on a state assessment test (McCarthy and Murtadha, 2001). A correlation to the quality of leadership preparation program is made on how leadership practices taught in preparation programs influence the overall school-learning climate (Orr and Orphanos, 2011).

Programs that are considered exemplary in the current accountability climate have similar constructs and features. These programs have a well-defined and comprehended theory of leadership for school improvement; a coherent curriculum that addresses effective instructional leadership, organizational development, and change management that aligns with state and professional standards; active learning strategies that simultaneously integrate theory and practice and stimulate reflection; internships with a myriad of opportunities to apply leadership knowledge and skills under the auspices of an exemplary principal; knowledgeable faculty; support that organizes students into cohorts that take common courses together in a prescribed sequence with advising from expert principals; and use of standards-based assessments for candidate and program feedback with continuous improvement that is tied to the program vision and objectives (Davis, Darling-Hammond, LaPointe, and Myerson, 2005; Jackson and Kelly, 2002, Orr and Orphanos, 2011; Young, Crow, Ogaway, and Murphy, 2009). The quality of preparation influences what graduates learn, which ultimately leads to how they lead schools (Orr and Orphanos, 2011). Therefore, in addition to the themes that an exemplary preparation program must possess, programs committed to preparing culturally responsive leaders should provide a necessary prerequisite in building cultural proficiency for educational leaders. These proficiencies involve the process of self-evaluation to identify personal beliefs about ethnicity, race, class, gender, ability, and other cultural elements, including unearned privileges afforded to members of dominant cultures (Abbate-Vaughn, 2006; Lindsey, Roberts, and Campbell-Jones, 2005; Ponterotto, Utsey, and Pedersen, 2006).

Culturally Responsive Leadership Preparation

Educational leaders are challenged to promote greater cultural competence among school personnel and create school climates where all students have equitable opportunities to learn (Lindsey et al., 2005). The focus on culture and climate promoting social justice as both object and subject of individual and group learning serves as a way of breaking the destructive cycle of racial, gender,

and ethnic oppression (Guy, 1999). There are examples of how leadership preparation programs make social justice the focus of their programs. In these preparation programs, universities generally form collaborative efforts with surrounding school districts. The collaboration includes, but is not limited to, customizing the preparation programs to meet the needs of the surrounding districts; sharing the responsibility of planning the program; selecting the program candidates; teaching the classes; evaluating the program; and receiving professional development as new school leaders. The goal of some initiatives is to prepare leaders for a particular student population (i.e., African-American students in urban settings). Others are guided by a commitment to social justice while simultaneously placing a strong emphasis on the role of principal as instructional leader. Some programs ensure that the content includes moral and ethical leadership, power and politics, change and diversity, and teaching and learning (Cambron-McCabe, 2010).

Theoharis (2007) and Bogotch (2002) argued that social justice cannot be separated from the practices of educational leadership. While scholars agree that social justice is difficult to define (Dantley and Tillman, 2010), there are characteristics that help connect social justice with educational leadership preparation programs (Cambron-McCabe, 2010). McKenzie et al. (2008) linked social justice to student achievement, critical consciousness, and inclusive practices. Feldman and Tyson (2007) stated that in order for preparation programs to address leadership for social justice, there must be a framework to which programs adhere. Such a framework should include antibias education, critical pedagogy, multicultural education, and whiteness studies. The collaboration of the work by McKenzie et al. (2008) and that of Feldman and Tyson (2007) greatly assists faculty in preparing social justice leaders. However, without assessing this framework, professors responsible for preparing future school administrators subject them to the same kind of hidden curriculum that has the opportunity to exacerbate racism, classism, sexism, conditions of hierarchy, and oppression (Riehl, 2000).

CULTURALLY RESPONSIVE LEADERSHIP PRACTICES

Effective school leaders take responsibility of leading their schools in rethinking of goals, priorities, curriculum, pedagogies, learning resources, and assessment methods (Levine, 2005). Effective leaders must design environments that allow people to learn the appropriate skills needed in order to address the critical challenges they encounter in daily practice (Senge et al., 2000). Lomotey (1993) indicated that principals who lead in effective urban school settings exhibit culturally responsive traits in that they believe their students have the necessary abilities to learn and are sensitive to their students' backgrounds. Lomotey (1993) asserted that strong leaders also make a concerted effort to become involved in the community as well as in the lives of the parents.

Instructional Leadership Practices

Instructional leadership is conceived as a curriculum-oriented role carried out by the school principal (Dwyer, 1986; Glassman, 1984; Hallinger and Murphy, 1985). Daresh and Playko (1995) defined instructional leadership as the direct or indirect behaviors that significantly affect teacher instruction and, as a result, student learning. This definition identifies a connection between leadership, teaching, and student learning. Cumulative research conducted by Leithwood, Louis, Anderson, and Wahlstrom (2005) found that there are two important claims regarding a link between successful leadership on student learning. The first is that leadership is second to classroom instruction in terms of impact on student learning. The second claim states that the greater the need, the greater the impact leaders' actions have on learning.

As instructional leaders, principals are concerned with ensuring that teachers are equipped with meaningful pedagogical practices (Senge et al., 2000). Therefore, principals who are committed to ensuring that students have an equitable opportunity to learn are also committed to social justice. They realize that the tenets of social justice leadership complement those of culturally responsive pedagogy.

Instructional leadership traditionally assumed a focus by the principal on teacher instructional behaviors that affected student outcomes; such leadership consisted of a blending of supervision, staff development, and curriculum development (Blasé and Blasé, 1998; Hallinger and Heck, 1996; McKenzie et al., 2008). The instructional role of principals is paramount in increas-

ing academic achievement. Principals who are willing and able to reach outside the traditional standards of leadership understand that there is a moral responsibility connected to leadership (Murphy, 2002). These principals recognize that the avoidance of issues of culture and race further perpetuate the status quo (Larson and Murtadha, 2002). However, leadership for social justice requires that leaders identify good teacher instructional behaviors and ensure that these behaviors daily meet the learning needs of every child (Frattura and Capper, 2007; Larson and Murtadha, 2002). More specifically, instructional leadership that utilizes culturally responsive pedagogy acknowledges what "good" instruction looks like especially for African-American students (Gupton, 2003; Ladson-Billings, 1994).

Culturally Responsive Practices

Culturally responsive educational practices have ties with how teachers effectively and efficiently deliver instruction to culturally diverse students. Teachers who have proven to be successful have shared three propositions that constitute culturally relevant pedagogy: (1) students must experience academic success; (2) cultural competence must be developed and maintained by students; and (3) students understand the ways that social structures and practices help reproduce inequities (Ladson-Billings, 1995b). In addition to culturally relevant pedagogy, the term *cultural responsiveness* expresses how teachers can address the myriad academic needs of students from diverse backgrounds. Culturally responsive educational systems use cultural characteristics, experiences, and perspectives of ethnically diverse students as conduits to teaching them more effectively (Gay, 2000). Villegas and Lucas (2002) advanced the conversation on cultural responsiveness by applying the term to teachers who have a sociopolitical consciousness and affirmed views of students from diverse backgrounds. These teachers are responsible for and capable of bringing about educational change, embracing constructivist teaching and learning, and building on the prior knowledge and beliefs of students while challenging and expanding familiar knowledge sets.

While the term *culturally relevant* or *responsive* has traditionally appeared in the literature focusing on teacher practices, the concept of principals applying culturally responsive leadership practices can be found in Lomotey's (1989) research on the compassionate and caring attitudes of African-American principals as well as in Dillard's (1995) research on African-American women principals. The vitality of these research studies examined how all races of principals can be prepared to eradicate personal biases and deficit thinking and replace those mind-sets to that of being caring and committed and empowering marginalized students to attain high levels of academic achievement.

Instructional Leadership Practices and African-American Students

School leaders who have come to realize that schools are situated in a broader social and political context can see how the systemic practices and policies of racism are often part of the educational process and can hinder the academic and self-esteem of African-American children (Dantley, 2005). Good instruction that addresses the needs of some or even most students does exist, but rarely does good instruction meet the needs of every child in the classroom (McKenzie, 2008). Teaching and learning describe a common set of strategies that greatly increase the effectiveness of teachers in meeting the needs of students (Delpit, 1995; Ladson-Billings, 1995a; McKenzie, Skrla, and Scheurich, 2006). However, rarely are those strategies applied consistently with all students (McKenzie et al., 2008).

Although political, social, and economic contexts of schools impact student achievement, the correlation of school leader practices to student achievement cannot be underestimated (Marzano, 2003). Teacher quality plays a large role in student achievement; however, research has shown that school leaders play an additionally integral role in influencing student achievement in the school learning environment (Darling-Hammond, 2002, 2007; Hallinger and Heck, 1996; Marzano, 2003). Principals are at the nexus of accountability and school improvement with the definitive expectation that they will function as "instructional leaders" (Hallinger, 2005). Not surprisingly, the need for instructional leadership is greatest where there are acute learning needs. The greater the challenge (i.e., societal inequities and achievement gap), the greater the impact of actions leaders make toward learning (Leithwood et al., 2005).

Principals who are strong instructional leaders define the instructional climate and exhibit particular instruc-

tional actions. In a review of research, Leithwood et al. (2004) concluded that the leadership practices that contribute most to student achievement include (1) principals must have a vision and believe that all students can achieve at high levels; (2) principals are focused on providing high-quality programs; (3) principals are committed to their students until they achieve high levels of performance; (4) principals emphasize the value of research-based strategies; and, (5) principals are highly involved with providing instructional support to assist teacher performance.

SIGNIFICANT CONTEXT FOR CULTURALLY RESPONSIVE LEADERSHIP PROGRAMS AND PRACTICES

Culturally responsive educational leadership programs have a distinct program structure and a commitment to diversity. The program structure includes the tenets of an effective leadership program (Davis, Darling-Hammond et al., 2007; Jackson and Kelly, 2002). Such programs have measures in place that ensure faculty develop a culturally relevant knowledge base, design culturally relevant curricula, demonstrate cultural care, build a learning community, and deliver culturally responsive instruction (Gay, 2002).

Culturally responsive principals have characteristics unique to specific leadership styles. These principals demonstrate a commitment to diversity and encourage themselves as well as their teachers to recognize the belief systems of students and parents. As instructional leaders, they utilize leadership practices aligned with the tenets of Gay's (2002) culturally responsive theory. Culturally responsive leadership preparation programs influence culturally responsive principal practices that, in turn, produce successful student outcomes.

Brown (2013) advocated that university faculty members must consider several issues as they design and deliver the curriculum to ensure candidates receive culturally responsive instruction. Principal preparation programs must ensure that those preparing principals follow tenets of cultural responsiveness to mitigate the achievement gap. This is first accomplished by responding to one's own attitudes and practices of different cultures (Montgomery, 2001). Culturally responsive leaders understand the cultural characteristics and learning needs of different cultures (DeCuir-Gunby, Taliaferro, and Greenfield, 2010). Preparation programs must be committed to and believe the principles of cultural responsiveness by ensuring candidates develop culturally diverse knowledge (Gay, 2002). Preparation programs must ensure that the assessments of the preparation program curricula are culturally relevant (Gay, 2010). This begins with being cognizant that curricula assessments are a powerful means to convey the extent to which principals are culturally responsive. Candidates must be properly assessed to determine that they are sound culturally responsive leaders who will be able to transform what they have learned to the schools that they lead. Internships should include culturally responsive activities and assignments. This allows aspiring principals to learn how to supervise instruction to recognize academic models that are built on the cultures and experiences of students to make learning more meaningful (Brown, 2013). The faculty of principal preparation programs must incorporate curriculum focused on data decision making related to cultural responsiveness. Once the design is in place, the subsequent consideration is to deliver culturally responsive instruction (Gay, 2002).

Aspiring principals should thoroughly investigate the structure of principal preparation programs prior to enrollment in university programs. They should consider how to apply culturally responsive leadership behaviors as they learn the content related to school administration and move into their internship practices. Foremost, aspiring principals must carefully consider their biases prior to accepting positions in culturally diverse schools.

Practicing principals must hire and/or train teachers to support and promote culturally responsive teaching. Practicing principals must also build culturally responsive assessment measures in classroom observations.

RECOMMENDATIONS FOR FUTURE RESEARCH

The following recommendations are for further research regarding educational leadership preparation programs and culturally responsive leadership.

1. There is a definite need to explore the effectiveness of "culturally responsive leadership preparation" programs to help foster a culture that focuses on meeting the needs of culturally diverse groups. Further research could explore how preparation programs construct culturally responsive pro-

grams as well as assess the cultural responsiveness of faculty.
2. Further research could explore how culturally responsive leadership preparation programs assess candidates' levels of cultural responsiveness. The assessment should take place prior to program entrance, throughout coursework, and as candidates exit programs.
3. Further research could measure the effectiveness of culturally responsive preparation programs' influence on leadership efficacy (which is measured by student achievement).
4. An exploration of the policies that relate to cultural responsive leadership preparation programs would enhance the current literature.

Practicing Principals

1. Additional research is needed to measure the level of cultural responsiveness of an administrator influences the outcomes of culturally diverse students.
2. More research is needed to study how and what principals utilize to measure teachers' cultural responsiveness.
3. An investigation should be conducted that measures how culturally responsive administrators move culturally diverse schools from low-performing to high-performing schools.

REFERENCES

Abbate-Vaughn, J. (2006). Multiculturalism in teacher education: What to assess, for how long, with what expected outcomes? *Electronic Magazine of Multicultural Education* *8*(2) 1–12. Retrieved September 3, 2007, from www.eastern.edu/publications/emme/2006fall/abbate-vaughn.pdf.

Abrahams, R. D. and Troike, R. C. (1972). *Language and cultural diversity in American education.* Englewood Cliffs, NJ: Prentice Hall.

Achilles, C. M. and Price, W. J. (2001).What is missing in the current debate about education administration standards? *AASA Professor 24*(2), 8–13.

Allen, L. A. (2006) The moral life of schools revisited: Preparing educational leaders to "build a new social order" for social justice and democratic community. *International Journal of Urban Educational Leadership 1*, 1–13.

Anderson, J. D. (1988). The education of Blacks in the South, 1860–1935. Chapel Hill: University of North Carolina Press.

Anyon, J. (1997). *Ghetto schooling: A political economy of urban educational reform.* New York: Teachers College Press.

Banks, J. A. (1974). Cultural pluralism and the schools. *Educational Leadership 32*(3), 163–166.

Barth, R. S. (2001). Principal centered professional development. *Theory Into Practice 25*(3), 156–160.

Beachum, F. D., Denith, A. M., McCray, C. R., and Boyle, T. M. (2008). Havens of hope or the killings fields: The paradox of leadership, pedagogy, and relationships in an urban middle school. *Urban Education 43*(2), 189–215.

Blasé, J. and Blasé, J. (1998). *Handbook of instructional leadership.* Thousand Oaks, CA: Corwin Press.

Bogotch, I. (2002). Educational leadership and social justice: Practice into theory. *Journal of School Leadership 12*(2), 138–156.

Boykin, A. W. (1983). The academic performance of Afro-American children. In J. Spence (Ed.), *Achievement and achievement motives* (pp. 221–271). San Francisco: W. Freeman.

Boykin, A. W. and Cunningham, R. (2001). The effects of movement expressiveness in story content and learning context on the analogical reasoning performance of African American children. *Journal of Negro Education 70*(1–2), 72–83.

Brown, F. (2005). African Americans and school leadership: An introduction. *Educational Administration Quarterly 41*(4), 585–590.

Brown, M. W. (2013). Principals' experiences regarding culturally responsive leadership preparation and practices that promote academic achievement of African American students. (Doctoral Dissertation). Retrieved from UMI ProQuest database. (3550200).

Cambron-McCabe, N. (2010). Preparation and development of school leaders: Implications for social justice policies. In C. Marshall and M. Oliva (Eds.), *Leadership for social justice: making revolutions in education* (pp. 35–54). Boston: Pearson.

Carlson, P.E. (1976). Toward a definition of local-level multicultural education. *Anthropology and Education Quarterly, 7*(4), 28–29.

Carlson, D. and Apple, M. W. (1998). *Power/knowledge/pedagogy: The meaning of democratic education in unsettling times.* Boulder, CO: Westview.

Crowther, F. (2002). Big change question: Is the role of the principal in creating school improvement over-rated? *Journal of Educational Change, 3,* 167–173.

Dantley, M. (2005). African American spirituality and Cornel West's Notions of Prophetic Pragmatism: Restructuring educational leadership in American urban schools. *Educational Administration Quarterly, 41*(4), 651–674.

Dantley, M. and Tillman, L. (2010).Social justice and moral transformative leadership. In C. Marshall and M. Oliva (Eds.), *Leadership for social justice: Making revolutions in education* (pp. 19–34). Boston: Pearson.

Darder, A. (1991). *Culture and Power in the Classroom. A critical foundation for bicultural education.* Westport, CT: Bergin and Garvey.

Daresh, J. C. and Playko, M. A. (1995). *Supervision as a proactive process: Concepts and cases.* Prospect Heights, IL: Waveland Press.

Darling-Hammond, L. (2002). Learning to teach for social justice. In L. Darling-Hammond, J. French., and S. P. Garcia-Lopez (Eds.), *Learning to teach for social justice.* New York: Teachers College Press.

Darling-Hammond, L. (2007). The flat earth and education: How America's commitment to equity will determine our future. *Educational Researcher, 36*(6), 318–334.

Darling-Hammond, L., LaPointe, M., Meyerson, D., and Orr, M. (2007). *Preparing school leaders for a changing world: Executive summary.* Stanford, CA: Stanford University, Stanford Educational Leadership Institute.

Darling-Hammond, L. and Orphanos, S. (2006). *Leadership development in California. (Getting down to facts: Effectiveness studies series).* Stanford, CA: Stanford University, Institute for Research on Education Policy and Practice and the School Redesign Network.

Davis, S., Darling-Hammond, L., LaPointe, M., and Meyerson, D. (2005). *School leadership study: Preparing successful principals.* Palo Alto, CA: Stanford University, Stanford Educational Leadership Institute.

DeCuir-Gunby, J. T., Taliaferro, J. D., and Greenfield, D. (2010). Educators' perspectives on culturally relevant programs for academic success: The American Excellence Association. *Education and Urban Society, 42*(2), 182–204.

Delpit, L. (1995). *Other people's children: Cultural conflict in the classroom.* New York: The New Press.

Dillard, C. B. (1995). Leading with her life: An African American feminist (re)interpretation of leadership for an urban high school principal. *Educational Administration Quarterly, 31*(4), 539–563.

Dimitriadis, G. and Carlson, D. (2003). *Promises to keep: Cultural studies, democratic education, and public life.* New York: Routledge Falmer.

Dubois, W. E. B. (1903). *Souls of Black folk.* New York: Heron Press.

Dwyer, D. (1986). Understanding the principal's contribution to instruction. *Peabody Journal of Education, 63*(1), 3–18.

English, F. W. (2000, April). *The ghostbusters search for Frederick Taylor in the ISLLC standards.* Paper presented at the annual meeting of the American Educational Research Association, New Orleans, LA.

Evans, A. E. (2007). School leaders and their sensemaking about race and demographic change. *Educational Administration Quarterly, 43*(2), 159–188.

Feldman, S. and Tyson, K. (2007). *Preparing school leaders to work for social justice in education: Clarifying conceptual foundations.* Paper presented at the American Education Research Association Conference, Chicago, IL.

Foster, M. (1989). "It's cooking now": A performance analysis of the speech events of a Black teacher in an urban community college. *Language in Society, 18*(1), 1–29.

Foster, L. (2005). The practice of educational leadership in African American communities in learning: Context, scope, and meaning. *Educational Administration Quarterly, 41*(4), 689–700.

Frattura, E. and Capper, C. A. (2007). *Leading for social justice: Transforming schools for all learners.* Newbury Park, CA: Corwin.

Furman, G. C. and Starratt, R. J. (2002). Leadership for democratic community in schools. In J. Murphy (Ed.), *The educational leadership challenge: Redefining leadership for the 21st century* (pp. 105–133). Chicago: National Society for the Study of Education.

Gay, G. (1979). Changing conceptions of multicultural education. In H. P. Baptiste, *Developing multicultural process in the classroom* (pp. 18–27). Washington, DC: University Press of America.

Gay, G. (1994). *At the essence of learning: Multicultural education.* West Lafayette, IN: Kappa Delta Pi.

Gay, G. (2000). *Culturally responsive teaching: Theory, research, and practice.* New York: Teachers College Press.

Gay, G. (2002). Preparing for culturally responsive teaching. *Journal of Teacher Education, 53*(2), 106–116.

Gay, G. (2010). *Culturally responsive teaching: Theory, research, and practice.* New York: Teachers College Press.

Giroux, H. (2001). *Public spaces, private lives: Beyond the culture of cynicism.* New York: Rowman and Littlefield.

Glassman, N. (1984). Student achievement and the school principal. *Educational Evaluation and Policy Analysis, 6*(3), 283–296.

Gooden, M. A. and Dantley, M. (2012). Centering race in a framework for leadership preparation. *Journal of Research on Leadership in Education 7*(2), 235–251.

Gupton, S. L. (2003). *The instructional leadership toolbox: A handbook for improving practice.* Thousand Oaks, CA: Corwin.

Gurr, D., Drysdale, L., and Mulford, B. (2007). Instructional Leadership in Three Australian Schools, *International Studies in Educational Administration, 35*(3), 20–29.

Guy, T. C. (Ed.). (1999). Providing culturally relevant adult education: A challenge for the twenty-first century. *New Directions for Adult and Continuing Education, 82,* 5–18. San Francisco: Jossey-Bass.

Hale, J. (2003). *National school reform and partnership initiative: Preparing a new generation of leaders.* Madison, WI: Thurgood Marshall College Fund.

Hallinger, P. (2005). Instructional leadership and the school principal: A passing fancy that refuses to fade away. *Leadership and Policy in Schools, 4*(1), 1–20.

Hallinger, P. and Heck, R. (1996). Reassessing the principal's role in school effectiveness: A review of empirical research, 1980–1995. *Educational Administration Quarterly, 32*(1), 5–44.

Hallinger, P. and Murphy, J. (1985). Assessing the instructional management behavior of principals. *Elementary School Journal, 86*(2), 217–247.

Hess, F. M. and Kelly, A. P. (2005). An innovative look, a recalcitrant reality: The politics of principal preparation reform. *Educational Policy, 19* (1), 1–26.

Hilliard, A. (2001). Race, identity, hegemony, and education: What do we need to know now? In W. Watkins, J. Lewis, and V. Chou (Eds.), *Race and education: The role of history and society in educating African American students* (pp.7–33). Washington, DC: National Alliance of Black School Educators.

Howard, T. (2010). *Why race and culture matter in schools: Closing the achievement gap in America's classrooms.* New York: Teachers College Press.

Jackson, B. L. and Kelley, C. (2002). Exceptional and innovative programs in educational leadership. *Educational Administration Quarterly, 38*(2), 192–212.

Johnson, L. S. (2006). "Making her community a better place to live": Culturally responsive urban school leadership in historical context. *Leadership and Policy in Schools, 5*(1), 19–36.

King, J. E. (1995). Culture-centered knowledge: Black studies, curriculum transformation, and social action. In J. A. Banks and C. M. Banks (Eds.), *Handbook of research on multicultural education* (pp. 265–290). New York: Macmillan.

Ladson-Billings, G. (1994). *The dreamkeepers: Successful teachers of African American children.* San Francisco: Jossey-Bass.

Ladson-Billings, G. (1995a). Toward a theory of culturally relevant pedagogy. *American Educational Research Journal, 32*(3), 465–491.

Ladson-Billings, G. (1995b). But that's just good teaching! The case for culturally relevant pedagogy. *American Educational Research Journal, 32,* 159–165.

Ladson-Billings, G. (2000). Fighting for our lives: Preparing teachers to teach African American students. *Journal of Teacher Education, 51*(3), 206–214.

Ladson-Billings, G. (2001). *Crossing over into Canaan. The journey of new teachers into diverse classrooms.* San Francisco: Jossey-Bass.

Larson, C. L. and Murtadha, K. (2002). Leadership for social justice. *Yearbook of the National Society for the Study of Education, 101*(1), 134–161.

Leithwood, K., Louis, K. S., Anderson, S., and Wahlstrom, K. (2005). *How leadership influences student learning.* Toronto, Canada: Center for Applied Research and Educational Improvement and Ontario Institute for Studies in Education.

Levine, Arthur. (2005). *Educating School Leaders.* New York: Teachers College, The Education Schools Project.

Lewis, C. W., James, M., Hancock, S., and Hill-Jackson, V. (2008). Framing African American students' success and failures in urban settings: A typology for change. *Urban Education, 43(2),* 127–153.

Lindsey, R., Roberts, L. M., and Campbell Jones, F. (2005). *The culturally proficient school: An implementation guide for school leaders.* Thousand Oaks, CA: Corwin.

Lomotey, K. (1989). *African-American principals: School leadership and success.* New York: Greenwood Press.

Lomotey, K. (1993). African-American principals: Bureaucrat, administrators and ethnohumanists. *Urban Education, 27*(3), 395–412.

López, J. A., Magdaleno, K. R., and Reis, N. M. (2006). Developing Leadership for Equity: What Is the Role of Leadership Preparation Programs? *Educational Leadership and Administration: Teaching and Program Development, 18,* 11–19.

Marshall, C. (2004). Social justice challenges to educational administration. *Educational Administration Quarterly, 40*(1), 3–13.

Marshall, C. and Oliva, M. (2010). *Leadership for social justice: Making revolutions in education.* Boston: Pearson.

Marzano, R. J. (2003). *What works in schools: Translating research into action.* Alexandria, VA: Association for Supervision and Curriculum Development.

McCarthy, C. (1998). *The uses of culture: Education and the limits of ethnic affiliation.* New York: Routledge.

McCarthy, M. and Murtadha, K. (2001, April). *Standards-based certification for Indiana school leaders and social justice concerns.* Paper presented at the annual meeting of the American Educational Research Association, Seattle, WA.

McKenzie, K. B., Christman, D. E., Hernandez, F., Fierro, E., Capper, C. A., Dantley, M., Gonzalen, M.L, Cambron-McCabe, N., and Scheurich, J.J. (2008). From the field: A proposal for education leaders for social justice. *Educational Administration Quarterly, 44,* 111–138.

McKenzie, K., Skrla, L., and Scheurich, J. (2006). Preparing instructional leaders for social justice. *Journal of School Leadership, 16*(2), 158–170.

Milner, H. R. (2012). But what is urban education? *Urban Education, 47(3),* 556–561.

Moll, L. C. (Ed.). (1990). *Vygotsky and education: Instructional implications and applications of sociohistorical psychology.* Cambridge: Cambridge University Press.

Montgomery, W. (2001). Creating culturally responsive, inclusive classrooms. *Teaching Exceptional Children, 33(4),* 4–9.

Murphy, J. (2002). Recapturing the profession of educational leadership: New blueprints. *Educational Administration Quarterly, 38*(2), 176–191.

Murtadha, K., and Watts, D. M. (2005). Linking the struggle for education and social justice: Historical perspectives of African American leadership in schools, *Educational Administration Quarterly, 41*(4), 591–608.

Nieto, S. (2009). *Affirming diversity: The sociopolitical context of multicultural education.* White Plains, NY: Longman.

Orr, M. T. and Orphanos, S. (2011). How graduate level preparation influences the effectiveness of school leaders: A comparison of the outcomes of exemplary and conventional leadership preparation programs for principals. *Educational Administration Quarterly, 47*(1), 18–70.

Perry, T. (2003). Up from the parched earth: Toward a theory of African-American achievement. In T. Perry, C. Steel, and A. G. Hilliard (Eds.), *Young gifted and Black: Promoting high achieving among African-American students* (pp. 1–108). Boston: Beacon.

Ponterotto, J. G., Utsey, S. O., and Pedersen, P. B. (2006). *Preventing prejudice: A guide for counselors, educators, and parents* (2nd ed.). Thousand Oaks: Sage.

Riehl, C. J. (2000). The principal's role in creating inclusive schools for diverse students: A review of normative, empirical, and critical literature on the practice of educational administration. *Review of Educational Research, 70,* 55–81.

Scheurich, J. J. and Laible, J. (1999). The buck stops here in our preparation programs: Educational leadership for all children (no exceptions allowed). *Educational Administration Quarterly, 31*(2), 313–322.

Scheurich, J. J. and Skrla, L. (2003). *Educational Equity and Accountability: Paradigms, Policies, and Politics.* London: Routledge.

Senge, P., Cambron-McCabe, N., Lucas, T., Smith, B., Dutton, J., and Kleiner, A. (2000). *Schools that learn: A fifth discipline field book for educators, parents, and everyone who cares about education.* New York: Doubleday.

Shields, C. (2004). Dialogic leadership for social justice: Overcoming pathologies of silence. *Educational Administration Quarterly, 40*(1), 111–134.

Shulman, L. (1987). Knowledge and teaching: Foundations of the new reform. *Harvard Educational Review, 57*, 1–22.

Sue, D. W. (2004). Whiteness and ethnocentric monoculturalism: Malting the "invisible" visible. *American Psychologist*, 761–769.

Sue, D. W. and Sue, D. (2003). *Counseling the culturally diverse: Theory and practice* (4th ed.). New York: Wiley.

Tatum, A. W. and Muhammad, G. E. (2012). African American males and literacy development in contexts that are characteristically urban. *Urban Education, 47(2)*, 434–463.

Theoharis, G. T. (2007). Social justice educational leaders and resistance: Toward a theory of social justice leadership. *Educational Administration Quarterly, 43*, 221–258.

Tillman, L. (2002). Culturally sensitive research approaches: An African-American perspective. *Educational Researcher, 31*(9), 3–12.

Tillman, L. C. (2005). Mentoring new teachers: Implications for leadership practice in an urban school. *Educational Administration Quarterly, 41*, 609–629.

Thompson, S., Ransdell, M., and Rousseau, C. (2005). Effective teachers in urban school settings: Linking teacher dispositions and student performance on standardized tests. *Journal of Authentic Learning, 2*, 22–34.

Tucker, M. S. and Codding, J. B. (Eds.). (2002). *The principal challenge: Leading and managing schools in an era of accountability*. San Francisco: Jossey-Bass.

Villegas, A. M. and Lucas, T. (2002). Preparing culturally responsive teachers: Rethinking the curriculum. *Journal of Teacher Education, 53*(1), 20–32.

Vygotsky, L. (1978). *Mind in society: The development of higher psychological processes* (M. Cole, V. John-Steiner, S. Scribner, and E. Souboerman, Eds.). Cambridge, MA: Harvard University Press.

West, C. (1994). *Race matters*. New York: Vintage Books.

Woodson, C. G. (1968). *The education of the Negro prior to 1861*. New York: Arno Press. (Original work published 1919.)

Young, M. D. and Brooks, J. (2008). Supporting graduate students of color in educational administration preparation programs: Faculty perspectives on best practices possibilities, and problems. *Educational Administration Quarterly, 44*(3), 391–423.

Young, M. D., Crow, G., Ogawa, R., and Murphy, J. (2009). *The handbook of research on leadership preparation*. New York: Routledge.

CHAPTER 12

From Dysconsciousness to Consciousness of Stereotypes That Disparage Black Youth

Calling for Transformative School Leadership

Joyce E. King and Syreeta A. McTier

Urban leader, what do you see?
Urban leader, what do you read?
Urban leader, what do you teach?
Urban leader, how do you lead?
Urban leader, what do you think?
Urban leader, who or what do you critique?
Urban leader, please dedicate time
to the active struggle against miseducation and dysconscious minds

DYSCONSCIOUS RACISM

King (1991) coined the term dysconscious racism when studying pre-service teachers' explanations of societal inequity (King and Akua, 2012). Defined as an "uncritical habit of mind (including perceptions, attitudes, assumptions, and beliefs) that justifies inequity and exploitation by accepting the existing order of things as given," dysconscious racism represents an impaired way of thinking that "tacitly accepts white norms and privileges as given" (p. 135). The uncritical ways of thinking about racial inequity associated with dysconsciousness accept "culturally sanctioned assumptions, myths, and beliefs that justify the social and economic advantages white people have as a result of subordinating diverse others" (p. 137). Dysconsciousness, therefore, reflects a lack of analysis of social reality and an acceptance of inequity without questioning the status quo. King notes that dysconsciousness stems from miseducation, and encourages teacher education programs to provide a space for teachers to think critically, become conscious, and reconstruct their social knowledge and self-identities. Moving from dysconsciousness to consciousness includes the ability to recognize systemic forces that oppress and other minorities and reaffirm white privilege.

Systemic forces consistently oppress black students, parents, and communities through institutionalized racism in education, poverty, criminal justice, housing, and media. Educators of black students must think critically about the assumptions, myths, and beliefs that subordinate minorities and socially and economically advantage white people. This chapter will examine negative images about black youth communicated in news and network media and educational literature as a form of taken for granted, yet systematic oppression with the intention to inspire a critical habit of mind in urban educators about the images they consume and the thoughts and perceptions they have about the children and families they serve in urban schools. The chapter will conclude with a discussion of research-based strategies urban leaders can use in professional learning with teachers that target deficit-based thinking and to support antiracist education as a part of transformative school leadership.

STEREOTYPES AND SYSTEMIC RACISM

Tan et al. (2009) credit Lippman (1922) for first defining stereotypes as "pictures in our heads" (Tan, 2009, p. 262). These pictures or images serve as social categories to organize information about people, including overgeneralized beliefs about society and others, to make sense of and simplify the world. Similarly, Devine and Elliott (1995) assert that a stereotype is a "well-learned set of associations that link a set of characteristics with a group label" (p. 1140), and a stereotype remains as an active organizational structure even if the individual does not personally believe the stereotype.

Stereotypes about black youth are prevalent in politics, media, and education literature. Black youth are associated with being "lazy, ignorant, athletic, rhythmical, low in intelligence, poor, criminal, hostile, and loud" (Devine and Elliott, 1995, p. 1144). In education literature, black youth are presented as low performing, in crisis, and at risk for being pushed out of school through suspension and expulsion (Brown, 2011; Losen and Gillepsie, 2012; Losen and Martinez, 2013; Schott Foundation for Public Education, 2012).

Wynter's (2000a, 2000b) theory of biocentrism, race and ethno-class "Man" provides a broad lens through which to view the social construction of blackness and stereotypes communicated about black students in news and network media as well as in educational literature. Wynter (2000a, 2000b) defines biocentrism as a belief system that conceptualizes the human as a biological being who creates culture and reproduces conceptions of humanity through both nature-culture dynamics (both ontogeny and sociogeny). Wynter uses the term ethno-class "Man" to describe the secular conception of what it means to be human within our present Western bourgeois or white and middle-class cultural model. Wynter notes that this Western bourgeois cultural model offers us only one conception of what it means to be human; however, within the order of knowledge arising from the modern European state (and by extension U.S. society as well), this Western bourgeois notion of modern "Man" has been represented as the ultimate indicator of humanity, as if any deviation from it amounts to being subhuman. Furthermore, Wynter asserts that in every order, a liminal category exists to denote deviation from the "law-like" norm. Wynter asserts that in the United States of America, the normative model of being human is this Western bourgeois or white middle-class ideal, whereas black (blackness) constitutes a liminal category as conceptual blackness, as the alter ego of conceptual whiteness, is the deviation from the norm. Crediting Fanon's (1967) assertion that within this cultural model of the West, in order to be human "you must be anti-Black," Wynter states that blackness is degraded so that whiteness can be celebrated (Wynter, 2003). As Wynter (2000b) has noted:

> For example, America is held together on the basis of Whiteness. The middle class has been able to "sucker" the lower-middle class by bonding it to itself on the fact that "We are all White." So trans-gender, trans-race, trans-everything, they are held together by the concept of White. But "White" is a cultural conception that is only possible as an opiate-triggering reward conception by means of the degradation of the "Black." (p. 363)

In a similar vein Collins's (1999) theory of controlling images is also relevant to the discussion of the role of negative stereotypes about black youth in the corporate-controlled media and education literature as a form of systematic racism. Collins asserts that the "intersecting oppressions of race, class, gender, and sexuality could not continue without powerful ideological justifications for their existence . . . controlling images are designed to make racism, sexism, poverty, and other forms of social injustice appear to be natural, normal, and inevitable parts of everyday life" (pp. 76–77). As Collins further notes, controlling images of black males and black females exist to represent blacks as the "other" or as the inherent opposite to whites in order to justify oppression (1999, 2004). Controlling images of black females as mammies, matriarchs, welfare queens, and Jezebels (1999), and black males as bucks, brutes, athletes, criminals, thugs, hustlers, sidekicks, and emasculated are used to objectify black men and women as the "others" of society who do not belong. However, at the same time, these oppressive images are needed in society governed by the rules of white supremacy racism in order to demarcate those who do belong from those who do not (1999, 2006). Controlling images extend beyond news and network media into the urban film genre, further reinforcing the stereotypical image of black youth as gang members and thugs (Yosso and Garcia, 2010). Furthermore, the urban education film genre presents black youth as "others" in need of saving by white teachers. This trope of the white teacher versus black students presents a visual dichotomy of good versus evil in which the good white teacher wins the struggle.

Moreover, Delgado and Stefancic (2000) assert, "Racism is normal, not aberrant in American society. Because racism is an ingrained feature of our landscape, it looks ordinary and natural to persons in the culture" (p. xvi). That is to say, racism is pervasive in institutional structures and schooling practices on the macro-level as well as in the daily interactions of individuals and groups of people on the micro-level (Davis, 1989; Ladson-Billings and Tate, 1995; Taylor, 2009). Subordinated groups confront racism in daily interactions with others and with print, television, and electronic media. Media stereotypes that disparage these groups constitute a form of business-as-usual racism (Delgado and Stefancic, 2000) that protects white privilege and the white reputation by othering "minorities" as inferior. Further, Solórzano and Yosso (2009) have noted, "The majoritarian story distorts and silences experiences of people of color. Using 'standard formulae,' majoritarian methods purport to be neutral and objective yet implicitly make assumptions according to negative stereotypes about people of color" (Solórzano and Yossop, 2009, p. 136; Ikemoto, 1997). Specifically, the majoritarian story communicates and reinforces stereotypes that correlate blackness with poverty and violence and overtly and covertly associate blackness with whatever is presumed to be bad and whiteness with what is thought to be good. Negative media stereotypes serve a macro-level function of institutionalized racism contributing to this majoritarian narrative of natural black inferiority and natural white superiority (Solórzano and Yosso, 2009).

The remainder of the chapter will review selected examples from the empirical literature detailing prevalent stereotypes in the popular media and education literature that disparage black youth; the discussion will relate media stereotypes and stereotypes in education literature to disproportionate discipline practices and stereotypes held by pre-service and in-service teachers in schools; detail implications and strategies for professional learning for urban school leaders and other educators and provide suggestions for future research.

MEDIA STEREOTYPES AND VIEWER PERCEPTIONS OF BLACK YOUTH

Bogle (1994) noted a long history of recurring negative stereotypic representations of black people in film and television media beginning in the early 1900s and extending to the twenty-first century. In other words, black Americans have historically been represented as morally and intellectually inferior through characterizations as Uncle Toms, Coons, Tragic Mulattos, Mammies, Jezebels, Sapphires, or Brute Bucks, while the related contemporary categories include assimilationists, entertainers, angry divas, criminals, or the sources of societal problems. Historically and contemporarily, black characters are stereotyped as those who are:

Preoccupied with simple ideas, employ inferior strategy in warfare or conflict situations, express low or nonexis-

tent occupational status, exhibit poor speech patterns or dialect, and participate in comedic foil . . . display a low regard for human life, participate in criminal activity, exhibit sexual promiscuity, abuse drugs and alcohol, and exhibit dishonesty. (Wilson and Gutierrez, 1985, p. 79)

Additionally, Entman and Rojecki (2000) explored portrayals of blacks on network and local news, and conducted interviews with white Americans to address how mass media shapes the attitudes of white Americans toward black Americans. The authors report that network television programming portrayals of black Americans are associated with poverty, drugs, crime, and noisy communicators of special interest politics, supporting the idea that blacks are criminals and problems for society. Similarly, Greenberg, Mastero, and Brand's (2002) comprehensive analysis of black portrayals in the media also suggests that blacks went from servants, buffoons, and mammies to poor, lazy, aggressive entertainers and athletes. The authors specifically noted that black Americans are overrepresented as criminals and suspects.

Furthermore, Dixon and Linz (2000) analyzed the portrayals of African Americans, Latinos, and whites in television news as lawbreakers and law defenders. The authors randomly sampled local television programs airing in Los Angeles and Orange County, California, including 118 thirty-minute programs across local news channels over a period of twenty weeks. Inter-group and inter-role comparisons analyzing the roles of lawbreaker versus law defender found that blacks and Latinos are more likely to be portrayed as lawbreakers than defenders, and whites are significantly more likely to be portrayed as law defenders than lawbreakers. The authors compared the portrayals of lawbreakers and defenders on television news with official crime reports from the California Department of Justice and determined that blacks are overrepresented as lawbreakers on television, while Latinos and whites are underrepresented as lawbreakers on television compared to actual crime rates. The authors conclude that blacks are inaccurately and overly portrayed as criminals in news media.

Lee et al. (2009) further examined the role of media in shaping viewers' perceptions of others by analyzing the influence of television on viewers' perceptions of ethnic groups. The authors investigated the amount of television, the genre of television programming watched, and viewers' subsequent stereotypes held about Caucasians, African Americans, Asians, Latinos/Hispanics, and Native Americans as related to Goldberg's (1992) Big-Five personality traits of extroversion (energetic, sociable, assertive), agreeableness (cooperative, polite, trustful, fair), conscientiousness (organized, responsible, cautious), neuroticism (angry, nervous, secure, moody), and openness (intelligent, perceptive, curious, creative, sophisticated). Research participants included 450 undergraduate students from universities in the northwest and southwest regions of the United States of America, of whom 58 percent were female, 39 percent male, 79 percent Caucasian, 4 percent African American, 5 percent Asian, 4 percent Latino, 1 percent Native American, 0.4 percent Middle Eastern, and 6.6 percent Other. The participants completed a survey detailing their viewing patterns of television and then rated their personal perceptions of the ethnic groups. Specific genres of television watched included entertainment, drama, informational, educational, reality, soap opera, and sports. The authors found that heavy television viewing was related to perceiving ethnic minorities negatively. Heavy television viewers of all genres rated Caucasians positively as being dependable, stable, and less angry. Heavy television viewers perceived African Americans negatively, and the traits varied by genre watched. That is, heavy viewers of entertainment perceived African Americans as less agreeable and less extroverted consistent with stereotypes of being uncooperative and antagonistic; however, heavy viewers of drama, informational, and reality programming rated African Americans positively as more open and less neurotic. Heavy television viewers perceived Asians negatively as less extroverted, less conscientious, and more neurotic, while Latinos/ Hispanics were perceived as less extroverted, but more agreeable describing Latinos as cooperative and fair, but not assertive. Native Americans were also perceived negatively as less open, less conscientious, and less extroverted. The authors conclude that heavy television viewing is related to stereotyping ethnic minorities with special emphasis on information programming as it is related to positive perceptions of ethnic groups; however, entertainment, educational, and sports programs were related to more negative ethnic perceptions.

MEDIA FOCUSING ON URBAN EDUCATION

Wells and Serman (1998) describe films depicting urban schools as the "Great White Hope Phenomenon"

in that a white teacher in these films usually rescues impoverished and unmotivated African-American and Latino students. In these portrayals of urban schools as sites where gangs, violence, and drugs are present, the brave white teachers possess saving power in their influence over African-American and Latino students by motivating the students to achieve. The authors assert the "Great White Hope Phenomenon" suggests that these students "cannot or will not be saved by people of color" (p. 186).

Furthermore, Yosso and Garcia (2010) assert that films about public education in urban schools portray students of color as delinquents embedded in a culture of poverty. The films "echo disproven social science theories and demean students of color with subtle, stunning, and derogatory messages-racial microaggressions" (p. 86). The racial micro-aggressions "communicate that people of color are unintelligent, foreign, criminally prone, and deserving of socially marginal status" (p. 86). The authors note that Hollywood uses the urban schooling film genre, including movies such as *Blackboard Jungle* (1955), *The Principal* (1987), *Stand and Deliver* (1988), *Lean on Me* (1989), *Dangerous Minds* (1995), and *Freedom Writers* (2007), to exploit race and reinforce white privilege and that this exploitation is massive as the films are viewed by mass audiences over generations. Indeed, as Yosso and Garcia (2010) stated:

> Establishing shots most often introduce the optimistic, naive novice (white) teacher as he/she navigates a chaotic school hallway, only to be disrespected and overwhelmed by a classroom of predominately black and Latina/o students shooting spit wads, dancing, and fighting with one another. A male student usually brutalizes and/or sexually threatens a female teacher in the first act. Deflated faculty work in misery to collect a paycheck and seek refuge in the teacher's lounge, having lost their belief in the sense of service or mission. Administrators perpetuate the system with cynical, authoritative, and often hostile management. The protagonist teacher distinguishes him/herself from these pessimists, determined to make a difference. Delinquent and remedial Students of Color eventually become inspired to learn academic basics, build up self-respect, and to pursue their education. (p. 87)

Urban education films reinforce white privilege by celebrating the white teacher who saves the delinquent students from their lack of motivation and their behavioral defects. The white teacher is viewed as the savior and the black and Latino/a students are viewed as the deviants.

The depiction of black youth in urban education films is a subject of concern as these films may influence teachers' perceptions of black students. Hampton, Peng, and Ann (2008) examined pre-service teachers' perceptions of urban schools and found that pre-service teachers indicated that media informed their perceptions of urban schools. The authors recorded the response of one pre-service teacher who stated:

"Most of my perceptions about urban schools come from T.V. and movies and how they portray urban schools, and it usually is not good. It always seems more dangerous and underfunded. I remember seeing a movie about an urban school and it had no windows because they were all broken and none of the students ever listened to their teacher. Also, all the girls had babies and all the males were drug dealers." (Subject 35) (Hampton, Peng, and Ann, 2008, p. 287)

STEREOTYPES IN EDUCATION LITERATURE: THE ACHIEVEMENT GAP AND DISCIPLINE GAP

Negative stereotypes about blacks not only exist in film and media but also exist historically in social science and educational research literature. The stereotypes of black youth as low performing and as "at-risk" for academic failure centers on education research that highlights the black-white achievement gap (Ladson-Billings, 2006). Indeed, many studies have documented that black students perform lower than white students on standardized tests, are underrepresented in gifted education and advanced placement classes, and are over-represented in special education (Barton and Coley, 2010; Chubb and Loveless, 2002; Ladson-Billings, 2006; Losen and Orfield, 2002; Milner, 2012; Schott Foundation for Public Education, 2012; Vanneman, Hamilton, Baldwin, and Rahman, 2009). In exploring reasons to explain the black-white achievement gap, education research has focused on factors that promote deficit- based thinking as many scholars have sought out to determine what is wrong with black students and their families as opposed to what is wrong with systemic structures of schooling including the low expectations for learning (Hilliard, 1991; Ladson-Billings, 2006; Milner, 2012; Perry, Steele, and Hilliard, 2003). It is also worth noting that scholars have called conceptualization of the "gap" into question (King et al., 2014).

Ladson-Billings, for example, conceptualized the problem as the "education debt." Hilliard (2003) stressed the emphasis should be placed not on comparisons with the achievement of white students (whose performance is below par when assessed using international metrics) but African-American students' potential for excellence in education should be the standard.

Education research that blames minority students, parents, and families for their school failure is driven by the deficit-thinking model, which asserts that a student fails in school due to his/her own internal deficiencies, including "limited intellectual abilities, linguistic shortcomings, lack of motivation to learn, and immoral behavior" (Valencia, 2010, p. 7) transmitted by genetics, culture and class, and/or familial socialization. Valencia (2010) asserts that blaming the victim is one characteristic of deficit thinking. Victim blaming identifies individuals and racial groups as the source of their own problems and failures, and in response, social programs are instituted to change the individual or the behavior of the target group such as compensatory education as opposed to structural changes in schools (Valencia, 2010)

Ladson-Billings (2006) specifically highlights the Coleman Report (1966) as a key piece of education literature that fostered deficit thinking about the academic achievement of black students and their families. While the Coleman report indicated that a variety of factors influence achievement including "composition of a school (who attends it), the students' sense of control of the environment and their futures, teachers' verbal skills, and students' family background" (Ladson-Billings, 2006, p. 4), family background became the subject of many subsequent studies on black student achievement. In an attempt to determine whether compensatory education or racial integration would be most beneficial in raising academic achievement, the researchers reported that the students' family background impacted student achievement more than school resources (Gamoran and Long, 2006; New York State Archives, 2012).

Brown (2011) has pointed out that education research has a long history of associating educational achievement with the behavior and poor socialization of black youth with a particular emphasis on negative stereotypes about the behavior of black males. To be more precise, in his analysis of the depictions of black males in social science and education literature from the 1920s to the present, Brown (2011) identified stereotypical themes of black male behavior presented in the literature that have created and supported a historical and universal (deficit) narrative about black male behavior. Consistent with themes of deficit discourse, Brown determined that the narratives about black male behavior are composed of recurring themes such as "absent and footloose" from 1920s–1950s, impotent, powerless, ineffective and effeminate in the 1960s, soulful and culturally adaptive in the 1970s, and endangered and in crisis from the 1980s to the present. The themes of absent, footloose, powerless, and impotent resonate with the language of the Moynihan Report (1965) detailing absent fathers, overbearing mothers, and poorly socialized and underperforming students. The themes of soulful and culturally adaptive reflect education research focusing on the unique speech patterns of black youth (Anderson, 1978; Abrahams and Gay, 1972, as cited in Brown, 2011). The current theme of "at risk" aligns with black students' dropout rates, special education rates, suspension/expulsion rates, and incarceration rates (Gregory and Mosley, 2004; Losen and Martinez, 2013; Losen and Orfield, 2002; Skiba et al., 2002, 2011). These recurrent themes are publicized and are part of a general narrative about black youth. For example, Brown (2011) noted that these narratives "exist in the news media, popular culture, policy, reports, educational conferences, special education meetings, and everyday language" (p. 4).

STEREOTYPES IN THE EDUCATION RESEARCH LITERATURE: THE DISCIPLINE GAP

On the opposite side of the black-white achievement gap is education research focusing on the black-white discipline gap that takes note of disproportionate school exclusion practices that black students experience (Gregory and Mosley, 2004; Losen and Gillepsie, 2012; Losen and Martinez, 2013; Skiba et al., 2002). Gregory and Mosely (2004) observed that the discipline gap is the "reverse image of the achievement gap for African-American, white, and Asian students" (p. 19). While the high school dropout and graduation rates for black students are 8 percent and 66.1 percent, respectively (U.S. Department of Education NCES, 2012), scholars assert that black students are being pushed out of school through practices such as disproportionate suspension and expulsion (Losen and Gillepsie, 2012; Losen and Martinez; 2013; Schott Foundation for Public Education, 2012). It is in the context of the black-white disci-

pline gap that we situate the discussion of teacher perceptions and stereotypes of black students. In particular, the chapter will detail key findings regarding the black-white discipline gap and relate these findings to relevant research with regard to stereotypes teachers hold.

Disproportionate Suspension/Expulsion of Black Students

Losen and Gillepsie (2012) report that 17 percent of black students enrolled in kindergarten through twelfth grades were suspended at least one time during the 2009–2010 school year, amounting to one in every six black students. Analysis of suspension rates by race and ethnicity indicate disproportionate suspension in that 17 percent of black students were suspended, while 8 percent of Native Americans, 7 percent of Latinos, 5 percent of whites, and 2 percent of Asian-American students were suspended. Further analysis indicates the risk of suspension increases in secondary school, including middle and high school. Specifically, 24 percent of black students, 12 percent of Latino students, 8.4 percent of American Indian students, 7.1 percent of white students, and 2.3 percent of Asian-American students were suspended from secondary school in 2009–2010 (Losen and Martinez, 2013). Furthermore, 25 percent of black children with disabilities enrolled in grades K–12 were suspended and were more likely than students without disabilities to be suspended more than once during the 2009–2010 school year. Researchers correlate suspension with high school dropout rates, noting that 32 percent of students who drop out have been suspended at least once from high school (Losen and Martinez, 2013).

School exclusion practices, including suspension and expulsion, are used to enforce school rules by removing students who challenge school safety (Vavrus and Cole, 2002). However, Losen and Gillepsie (2012) assert that in response to zero tolerance policies and get-tough discipline, suspension is often used as a consequence for black male students for non-violent and minor offenses. Researchers have observed that "the vast majority of suspensions were for minor infractions of school rules such as disruptions, tardiness, and dress code violations rather than for serious violent or criminal behavior" (Losen and Gillepsie, 2012, p. 1). School disciplinary practices of suspension and exclusion disproportionately affect black male and female students and reinforce negative stereotypic representations of blacks as criminal and dangerous. Being that black students are two to three times more likely to be suspended than their white counterparts for similar infractions (Gregory and Mosely, 2004), disproportionate school exclusion practices should be examined as a consequence of stereotypic teacher perceptions about black students and deficit thinking.

Wallace, Goodkind, and Wallace's (2008) examination of racial, ethnic, and gender differences in school discipline among a national sample of U.S. high school students between 1991 and 2005 indicated "56 percent of black boys have been suspended or expelled compared to 19–43 percent of non-black boys" (Wallace, Goodkind, and Wallace, 2008, p. 54). Similarly, "black girls are approximately twice as likely as white girls to be sent to the office or detained, but they are more than five times more likely than white girls to be suspended or expelled, in that 43 percent of black girls have been suspended or expelled compared to 7 percent to 26 percent of girls in the other racial and ethnic subgroups" (Wallace, Goodkind, and Wallace, 2008, p. 54). The authors conclude that suspension and expulsion rates are highest among black boys, followed by American Indian boys, Hispanic boys, and black girls. Therefore, black girls and black boys are both suspended more often than white boys.

Nicholson-Crotty, Birchmeier, and Valentine (2009) explored the impact of racial disproportionality in school discipline with racial disproportionality in the juvenile justice system. The authors found that "jurisdictions in which schools disproportionately target African-American students for exclusionary sanctions also experience higher relative rates of juvenile court referrals for black youth" (p. 1015). Multivariate analysis of offense type also indicated that black youth had higher rates of out-of-school suspension and referrals to juvenile court than white youth who committed the same offenses in objective categories such weapons, violence, and tobacco. For instance, 95 percent of black students committing weapon offenses were suspended; however, only 85 percent of white students committing weapon offenses were suspended. Additionally, black students committing violent acts were suspended 88 percent of the time, but white students committing violent acts were suspended 72 percent of the time. Finally, black students were

suspended 55 percent of the time for tobacco-related offenses, whereas white students were suspended only 37 percent of the time for tobacco, making black students one-and-a-half times more likely than white students to receive an out-of-school suspension for tobacco-related offenses. The authors concluded, "even when they commit the same offenses as white students, black students are significantly more likely to receive the type of exclusionary discipline that contributes to increased contact with the justice system" (Nicholson-Crotty, Birchmeir, and Valentine, 2009, p. 1015).

Mendez and Knoff (2003) also analyzed the suspension data by infraction and found that 90 percent of school suspensions were for infractions including disobedience/insubordination (20 percent), disruption (13 percent), fighting (13 percent), inappropriate behavior (11 percent), noncompliance with assigned discipline (7 percent), profanity (7 percent), disrespect (6 percent), tobacco possession (4 percent), battery (3 percent), threat/intimidation (2 percent), leaving class without permission (2 percent), weapons (0.7 percent), narcotics (0.7 percent), sexual harassment (0.6 percent), and alcohol (0.3 percent). The researchers note that though black male students make up 12 percent of the population, they accounted for one-third of suspensions for "disruptive behavior, fighting, inappropriate behavior, battery, intimidation, leaving class without permission, and sexual harassment" (p. 40). Disobedience, disruption, and inappropriate behavior are subjective categories. Teacher referrals and subsequent suspension by administrators for subjective behaviors may be influenced by a lack of understanding of students, and teachers' and administrators' perceptions about black students' behaviors. Skiba et al. (2011) also analyzed a national sample of office discipline referrals by school level, infraction type, race, and gender and found that African-American students are twice as likely as white students to be referred to the office during elementary school and four times as likely as white students to be referred to the office in middle school. Furthermore, the researchers note that administrators treat black and white students differently for minor infractions noting that administrators suspended African-American students for truancy, disrespect, and disruption twice as often as they suspended white students for the same behaviors noting that African-American students receive more severe punishment for minor behaviors.

Furthermore, Gregory and Mosely (2004) explored teacher processes that affect the over-representation of black students referred for school discipline. The authors recognize the power of teachers to interpret student behavior and refer students to the administrators for disciplinary consequences, so the authors interviewed teachers in an urban high school with more than 3,300 students to determine implicit racial beliefs and theories of discipline that might guide teachers' decisions to refer students for punishment. Disproportionality in discipline was present in the school such that African-American and white students each represented 37 percent of the student population, but 80 percent of students serving out of class suspension (OCS) were African American, and only 9 percent were white. After interviewing the teachers about their techniques for handling discipline problems and disproportionate discipline in their school, the researchers found that 80 percent of teachers attributed discipline problems to adolescent development in that high school students fight for autonomy and rebel against authority, 50 percent of teachers attributed student misbehavior to acting out as a result of frustration from low academic achievement, 50 percent of the teachers attributed misbehavior to African-American youth culture and factors related to poverty, 50 percent of the teachers mentioned organizational problems in the school, 70 percent of the teachers also mentioned problems with the school culture; however, less than 50 percent of teachers attributed student misbehavior to teacher beliefs or teacher practices. The teachers attributed misbehavior to theories that did not include race and culture, despite the disproportionality of discipline by race. When race was explicitly questioned in the interview, teachers emphasized the problems that low-income African-American students bring with them to school and did not address the under-representation of white and Asian students in discipline. The authors note a disconnect between teachers' articulation of beliefs about race and student behavior and their actions in referring students for disciplinary consequences (Gregory and Mosely, 2004).

As the above research indicates, teachers and administrators play a critical role in school discipline in that teachers are directly responsible for interpreting student behavior and referring students to the office, while administrators are directly responsible for as-

signing disciplinary consequences. Discipline referrals for disrespectful behavior and classroom disruption are subjective, therefore it is important to account for the perceptions of teachers and administrators, including stereotypes teachers and administrators hold about black students. The discussion will now focus on research detailing stereotypes held by teachers about black students in education and conclude with examples of studies of strategies used in teacher education programs that target deficit thinking, teacher awareness of stereotypes, and anti-racist teaching.

STEREOTYPES AND TEACHER PERCEPTIONS OF BLACK STUDENTS

Negative stereotypes about black youth carry over into school settings by potentially influencing the perceptions of teachers and administrators about student achievement and interpretations of student behavior. Davis (2003) has noted that the media communicates cultural messages about black male behavior through the portrayal of blacks in negative stereotypic roles and that stereotypic roles carry over into school settings. According to Davis:

> "These images portray the black male as violent, disrespectful, unintelligent, hyper- sexualized, and threatening. These cultural messages, without a doubt, carry over into schools and negatively influence the ways young black male students are treated, positioned, and distributed opportunities to learn . . . Black boys' demeanors are misunderstood by white middle-class teachers and seen as defiant, aggressive, and intimidating." (pp. 520–521)

Furthermore, Aggrey (2007) investigated pre-service teachers' perspectives on race and key experiences that influenced their racial perceptions. In this study, thirteen white pre-service teachers were interviewed before they enrolled in a multicultural education class at a large research university in the Midwest in order to determine the racial knowledge they bring with them to the classroom, key events that shaped their attitudes about race, and concerns about their ability to teach students who are racially different from them in the future. The participants confirmed a fear that their lack of racial knowledge would lead to misunderstanding and misperceptions about students of a different race. The author found that the pre-service teachers admitted to feelings of prejudice and bigotry about people of different racial backgrounds and highlight early experiences with family and media as sources influencing their prejudiced feelings. The participants credited "early media experiences with sitcoms as contributing to positive feelings about African Americans, their families, and college life. At the same time, some participants reported feelings of increased prejudice with exposure to news reports that they said presented an unrelentingly unbalanced view of African Americans" (p. 128). The participants reported complex emotions and feelings about racial dialogue, but were also hopeful in their ability to teacher children of diverse backgrounds.

Chang and Demyan (2007) also investigated contemporary and specific stereotypes teachers held about Asian, black, and white students. The researchers assessed stereotypes through free response of personal beliefs as well as rating of traits for each race. A sample of 188 teachers enrolled in continuing education courses at the University of California, including 153 women and 33 men of whom 139 were white, 20 Latino, 7 African American, 5 Asian/Pacific Islander, thirteen of mixed race, and 4 other, completed a free response activity listing up to six traits to describe their thoughts about black, Asian, and white schoolchildren in general after viewing a behavior profile of an Asian, black, or white student. The participants then rated the percentage of Asian, black, and white students possessing fifteen stereotypical traits, and then rated the percentage of people in the world possessing the fifteen stereotypical traits. The participants attributed more favorable characteristics to Asians than blacks or whites, and attributed both positive and negative characteristics to black students and white students. The teachers consistently rated Asian students as industrious, introverted, intelligent, and compliant. Black students were rated as sociable, friendly, athletic, disobedient, intelligent, active, and aggressive. White students were rated as sociable, friendly, industrious, intelligent, compliant, materialistic, privileged, and athletic. Teachers also endorsed cultural stereotypes in that:

> Asians were perceived as 57 percent more gentle, 34 percent more passive, and 31 percent more intelligent and industrious compared to the general population . . .

Whites were 31 percent more athletic, 23 percent more materialistic, and 21 percent more lazy and selfish compared to the general population . . . Blacks were viewed as 60 percent more athletic, 65 percent more rhythmic, 31 percent more aggressive, and 23 percent more stubborn than other groups. (p. 105)

Similarly, DeCastro-Ambrosetti and Cho (2011) analyzed teacher expectations of students based on student appearance including race, gender, and social class by addressing a particular form of prejudice known as lookism. Lookism is defined as "prejudice or discrimination on the grounds of appearance" (p. 52). Two hundred twenty-six secondary teacher candidates enrolled in education classes in Southern California completed an anonymous attitudinal survey. The survey included eight photos of black, white, Asian, and Hispanic adolescent males and females ages fifteen to seventeen in stylish clothing, along with ten inflammatory statements to elicit perceptions. The participants matched the photos with the statements that they felt best represented the students. The themes of the responses were academic success, athletic success, perceived as outsiders, academic adversity, and challenging classroom authority. The researchers found that 70 percent of the participants designated Asian males and females as most likely to be academically successful, while 66 percent of the respondents rated the black male as likely to excel in athletics even though none of the photos displayed students in athletic attire. Furthermore, 39 percent of the respondents perceived the black male as likely to be affiliated with a gang even though the students wore academic attire, while 21 percent of participants stated the black male would be involved in drugs. Similarly, 48 percent of the participants identified the black male as most likely to commit a crime before graduating from high school and 29 percent of participants selected the black male as likely to challenge classroom authority. Additionally, 53 percent of the participants identified the Hispanic female and 25 percent identified the black female as most likely to become pregnant before high school graduation. The authors conclude that teacher candidates held preconceived notions about the adolescents along racial lines and that stereotypical perceptions of students can lead to unequal access to educational opportunities with the teachers serving as gatekeepers.

IMPLICATIONS FOR URBAN SCHOOL LEADERS AND TEACHERS: TRANSFORMATIVE LEADERSHIP

The literature indicates that pre-service and in-service teachers hold deficit perceptions of black students. The messages about urban students, including the perpetual black-white achievement gap (Ladson-Billings, 2006), black-white discipline gap (Gregory and Mosely, 2004), and black students and minorities as people with deficit cultural values (Solórzano and Yosso, 2001) are communicated and reinforced in network and news media that synonymously portray black people as violent, aggressive, poor, lazy, and criminal. A missing factor, however, is the awareness of how negative stereotypes in media and education literature concurrently reaffirm white privilege by normalizing whiteness and othering or criminalizing blackness (Alexander, 2010; Muhammad, 2010). Educational leaders and teachers must consider who benefits from (mis)representations of black youth as violent, criminal, or athletic, whose interests are served when black students drop out of high school and suffer disproportionate disciplinary consequences of suspension and expulsion (Ferguson, 2001; Mendez and Knoff, 2003; Skiba et al., 2002, 2011), and how such (mis)representations reaffirm white privilege and reinforce structures of institutional racism.

Urban leaders and teachers must become active resisters to the transmission of deficit- based stereotypes about black students as normal, truthful, and taken-for-granted assumptions and address the disparities as a form of structural racism. Valencia (2010) suggests teacher education as a primary space for deconstructing deficit thinking and racist practices, noting that teacher education is racialized, consisting of primarily white teachers who will be employed in urban schools teaching minority students. The American Association of Colleges for Teacher Education reports "82 percent of candidates who received bachelor's degrees in education in 2009–10 and 2010–11 were white. By contrast, census figures show that close to half of all children under five in 2008 were members of a racial or ethnic minority" (Rich, 2013, p. 1). The requirements for teacher certification vary by state; however, the Interstate Teacher Assessment and Support Consortium (InTASC) Standards developed by the Council of Chief State School Officers (CCSSO, 2013) guide expectations for teacher preparation in terms of learner development, learning differences, learning environments, content knowledge, application of content, assessment, planning for instruction, instructional strategies, professional learning, and ethical practice as well as leadership and collaboration with an emphasis on personalized learning for diverse learners. Furthermore, the Council for Accreditation of Educator Preparation (CAEP), a council that evaluates teacher certification programs, calls for a focus on student diversity as a critical component of teacher certification programs. In fact, the CAEP noted that teacher competency in addressing diversity should be embedded in all aspects of teacher preparation suggesting that teachers examine "their own frames of reference (e.g., culture, gender, language, abilities, ways of knowing), the potential biases in these frames, the relationship of privilege and power in schools, and the impact of these frames on educators' expectations for and relationships with learners and their families" (CAEP, 2013, p. 21).

Similarly, the requirements for education leadership certification vary by state; however, the Interstate School Leaders Licensure Consortium (ISLLC) standards developed by the Council of Chief State School Officers (CCSSO, 2008) outline expectations for educational leaders to promote success for every student through a collaborative vision for learning, a school culture conducive to student learning and staff professional growth, a safe, efficient, and effective learning environment, responding to diverse community needs and interests, acting with integrity, fairness, and in an ethical manner, and understanding and responding to political, social, economic, legal, and cultural contexts. ISLLC Standard Five is particularly relevant to leaders' awareness and understanding of systemic racism as well as how racism affects their own leadership practices in that Standard Five expects education leaders to act with integrity, fairness, and in an ethical manner. Leaders are specifically expected to "model principles of self-awareness, reflective practice, transparency, and ethical behavior" (ISLLC, 2008, as cited in CCSSO, 2008, p. 15).

In order to lead with integrity, fairness, and in an ethical manner, education leaders must prioritize ongoing professional learning that addresses stereotypes, deficit-based thinking, disproportionate discipline, and antiracist education practices in particular. In addition, a strengths-based model of cultural diversity and community-centered teaching, learning, and assessment are needed to counter deficit-based thinking about black students and their cultural heritage and alienating school practices (King, 2008; King, Akua, and Russell, 2014; King, Goss, and McArthur, 2014). The remainder of the chapter will therefore highlight the strategies of scholars using teacher and leader education programs as spaces to target deficit-based thinking and practices and to promote antiracist education that is culturally inclusive. These strategies can be used as a part of ongoing professional learning for leaders and teachers in urban schools as a part of transformative school leadership.

PROFESSIONAL LEARNING FOR TRANSFORMATIVE LEADERSHIP AND ANTIRACIST EDUCATION

King (1991) described the liberatory pedagogy for the elite as a strategy that she used to challenge the dysconscious racism of teacher education students that King argued is a result of their mis-education. This pedagogical approach provided opportunities for students to challenge taken-for-granted assumptions about racial inequity and provided an intellectual context for self-reflective experiences needed for critical consciousness and emotional growth. For instance, King found that pre-service teachers explained racial inequality in limited ways tied to their beliefs (and what they have learned or not learned) about slavery, prejudice, and discrimination and without linking their explanations of racial inequity to ways that exploitation and structural societal oppression are connected. For example, only student in the study made a connection between inequity and the way the society normalizes racism and discrimination. The students' responses focused on negative characteristics of black people without accounting for either certain beliefs of white people that justified slavery or discrimination in society and the racial privileges white people enjoy. King's pedagogy challenged her students' mis-education by focusing on ways schooling "contributes to unequal educational outcomes that reinforce societal inequity and oppression" (p. 134). In this Social Foundations of Education course, students "examine[d] what they know and believe about society, about diverse others, and about their own actions" (p. 134).

Specifically, King's (1991) pedagogy addressed ideology, identity, and indoctrination using counter-knowledge grounded in the discipline of black studies to

enable these pre-service teachers to decipher how ideology shapes the way people think about power and privilege and "what race does" in society (King, 2005). The course material, including readings, class discussions, media, and lectures, support students' understanding that education is not neutral, but serves various political and social interests. Students examined the social purposes of schooling and "alternative explanations of poverty and joblessness, competing viewpoints regarding the significance of cultural differences, and discussions of education as a remedy for societal inequity" (p. 140). Students also examined connections between societal issues with classroom issues addressing the socialization of teachers, teacher expectations, tracking, and the hidden curriculum. Students reflected on their own knowledge and experiences, critiqued ideologies, and made decisions about their own identities as teachers. That King's study continues to be cited in the research literature in education (Gillborn and Ladson-Billings, 2004; McIntyre, 2002) suggests that teacher education programs should provide a space for teachers to recognize systemic forces that subordinate people of color and reaffirm white privilege in order to be able to choose whether they want to learn in more liberating ways and to reconstruct their social knowledge and self-identities.

Lee (1998) identifies as an antiracist educator and provides professional development to teachers, administrators, and school districts. Lee's antiracist framework focuses on closing not only the racial gap in academic performance but also the individual gap among students who are deskilled because their language, culture, and curiosity are devalued through subtle racism and low expectations. Lee asserts, "Racism is systemic, not episodic, and must be addressed as such. But every episode of racism must and can be confronted and interrupted at every turn as a means of reaching back to its systemic roots" (p. 6). In addition to confronting situational and systemic racism, Lee's work with teachers includes an examination of the history of race and racism in education, the history of relationships between and among racial groups, the advantages and disadvantages racial groups have, and an analysis of their practices as teachers within this institutional framework. Lee also addresses teachers' misguided attempts at color-blindness as opposed to color consciousness. Lee asserts that racism in education will not be addressed without examining "how skin color plays a part in what people do or do not receive or experience in the educational process" (p. 10). Finally, Lee emphasizes obtaining educational equality, not by treating everyone the same but through "equity measures or extra measures" (p. 10) to fill gaps created by a racist system in "representation, respect, rights, and resources" (p. 11).

Lawrence and Tatum (1998) address white racial identity as a key component of antiracist pedagogy aimed at changing teachers' beliefs about race and education. The authors note that it is important for teachers to systematically explore the impact of race on classroom practices and student development and for white teachers to develop an awareness of their own whiteness that is socially meaningful but not based on superiority. Lawrence and Tatum used a combination of required readings and films addressing race, racism, and white privilege, as well as discussions and reflection on subtle and overt racist behaviors and attitudes that influence children daily at school and away from school. Teachers also participated in taped self-interviews at the beginning of the course discussing their "prior experience and contact with people of color, their attitudes about race and racial issues, their images of people color, and their personal identity in racial terms" (p. 5). Teachers then listened to their interviews at the end of the course and reflected on their interviews with awareness of their own racial attitudes and behaviors. Teachers also created action plans to challenge racist behaviors and thoughts in their pedagogy as well as in their personal and professional lives.

Likewise, Sleeter (2004) argued that teachers need opportunities to engage in systemic analysis of structures that provide privileges to whites and denies privileges to people of color.. In her research on how white teachers participating in a two-year staff development project on multicultural education construct race, she found that teachers either denied race, stating they did not see color, or viewed students of color as immigrants. Sleeter notes that teachers asserted they were color-blind in an effort to "suppress negative images they attach to people of color, given the significance of color in the United States, the dominant ideology of equal opportunity, and the relationship between race and observable measures of success" (p. 168). Though the teachers denied seeing color, the researchers note that when the white teachers in the study discussed their students and parents,

the white teachers associated African Americans and Latinos with "dysfunctional families and communities, and lack of ability and motivation" (p. 168). Teachers who did not claim to be color-blind viewed students of color as immigrants and acknowledged that cultural differences can interfere with students' assimilation into schools and sought to adjust their teaching methods to include strategies such as cooperative learning and parent communication in order to assist in the home-to-school transition. Some teachers also began to "reinterpret students' behavior as cultural rather than as simply 'wrong'" (p. 170). Sleeter noted that few teachers began to connect racism to white supremacist institutions that privilege whites and deny privileges to people of color. The teachers viewed multicultural education as discussing and celebrating other groups, not as discussing the social structure that benefits whites. Sleeter notes that the teachers wanted to help their students of color but also have an interest in maintaining the educational system that benefits their own children. Sleeter asserts that an educator must "directly confront the vested interest white people have in maintaining the status quo, force them to grapple with the ethics of privilege, and refuse to allow them to rest comfortably in apolitical interpretations of race and multicultural teaching" (p. 177).

In their research and theorizing, Solórzano and Yosso (2001) also seek to identify, analyze, and transform the use of racial stereotypes and deficit-based theories in education that assist in the subordination of students of color. These scholars state that racial stereotypes in the media and professional environments are based on genetic and cultural deficit models and are used to justify certain attitudes toward students of color. They argue that stereotypes of black people as stupid, violent, and unclean justify claims for segregated schools and communities and dumbing down the curriculum. Solórzano and Yosso suggest addressing racial stereotypes in teacher education programs. According to Solórzano and Yosso:

> In dealing with racial stereotypes in our teacher education classrooms, we need to hear about, discuss, and analyze those racial experiences that people of color and whites encounter in their public and private worlds. Not only do we need to discuss overt or blatant racial stereotypes, attitudes, and behaviors, but we also need to listen, understand, and analyze racial microaggressions." (Solórzano and Yosso, 2001, p. 6)

These scholars suggest that teacher education classrooms become a space to define and analyze racial stereotypes as well as "identify racial stereotypes in film, television, and print forms of media, which are used to justify attitudes and behavior toward students of color" (Solórzano and Yosso, 2001, p. 7).

With respect to educational leaders, the University Council for Educational Administration (UCEA), a consortium of higher education institutions focused on educational leadership preparation, specifically provides curriculum modules addressing advocacy, learning environment, instructional leadership, family and community engagement, racial awareness, and using resources to prepare leaders to support diverse learners (UCEA, 2013). The racial awareness module, developed by Mark A. Gooden and Ann O'Doherty, is based on the assumption that racism permeates all aspects of life, including educational practices, educational leadership, and achievement. The learning module uses dialogue, reflection, and key readings to guide educational leaders as they "compare and contrast the definitions of race, racism, and white privilege/advantage, investigate whiteness and privilege and the impact that each has on education, analyze the social/political construction of race for people of color and whites in the United States, and interrogate racial awareness of self and others" (UCEA, 2013, p. 1). The goal of the racial awareness module is to develop the leader's understanding of how race impacts the leader's thoughts, actions, and leadership decisions in order to equip the educational leader to fight institutional racism in schools and society.

The scholars highlighted above all indicate the importance of addressing systemic and institutional forms of racism in education, white privilege, and educators' personal and professional attitudes and practices as strategies to combat deficit-based mis-education (King, 1991; Lawrence and Tatum, 1998; Lee, 1998; Solórzano and Yosso, 2001; Sleeter, 2004; Valencia, 2010; Young, 2011). Emphasizing systemic racism and confronting situational racism in order to relate it back to the systemic roots is critical in targeting deficit thinking because the emphasis is placed on systemic forces and not individual or group deficiencies (King, 1991; Lee, 1998; Valencia, 2010). It is important for urban leaders and teachers to develop awareness of the link between situational racist acts and systemic racism in education. Educators rest between situational and systemic forces of racism including racist stereotypes communicated about black students in media and professional environments (Brown, 2011; Davis, 2003; Solórzano and Yosso, 2001), inequitable teaching and disciplinary practices in schools as noted by the black-white achievement gap (Ladson-Billings, 2006; Perry, Steele, and Hilliard, 2003) and discipline gap (Gregory and Mosley, 2004; Losen and Martinez, 2013; Skiba et al., 2002, 2011), as well as educators' personal racial attitudes (DeCastro-Ambrosetti and Cho, 2011; Chang and Demyan, 2007), deficit thinking practices (Brown, 2011; Ladson-Billings, 2006; Valencia, 2010), and professional assessments about students (Ferguson, 2001; Sleeter, 2004) that can perpetuate racism. Urban leaders must play an active role in prioritizing ongoing professional development that targets systemic and situational attitudes, beliefs, and practices that discriminate against students as a form of transformative school leadership (King, 1991; Lawrence and Tatum, 1998; Lee, 1998; Sleeter, 2004; Solórzano and Yosso, 2001; Valencia, 2010; Young, 2011).

SUGGESTIONS FOR FUTURE RESEARCH

Future research should examine specific education leadership preparation programs to determine the required knowledge and skills of educational leaders and the extent in which recognizing and addressing racist attitudes, perceptions, and beliefs are intensively addressed as a part of leader preparation and certification programs. Future research should also focus on urban educational leaders' and teachers' awareness of negative media stereotypes and deficit educational thinking, assessing levels of dysconsciousness and critical consciousness, in particular. Additional research should also be conducted on school leaders who already engage teachers in critical dialogue and professional learning that resists images of black inferiority and deficit thinking. Furthermore, urban educators will also benefit from research on the process of becoming critically conscious leaders and teachers experience as they dialogue and learn more about systemic forces such as media discrimination that affect the way they relate to their students, parents, and the community they serve in urban settings.

Finally, King (2006) has consistently emphasized the importance of curriculum content and policy-making with respect to school knowledge that is emancipatory.

Thus, following Wynter (2005a, 2005b) and Woodson (1933), King's approach underscores the problem of knowledge, that is to say, racism is a form of knowledge that has to be replaced in order to undo the belief structures upon which white supremacy racism rests. Therefore, education leaders and teacher educators need opportunities to explore the under-theorized and under-utilized power of partnerships and collaborative arrangements with black studies departments and ethnic studies programs to support culturally informed teacher development and the professional learning of school leaders (King, 2008). Such strategic partnering, however, will require practice-based research in partnership with communities to challenge the dominant paradigm in which urban schools, their teachers, and school leaders are currently under siege.

REFERENCES

Abrahams, R. and Gay, G. (1972). Talking Black in the classroom. In R. Abrahams and R. Troike (Eds.), *Language and cultural diversity in American education* (pp. 158–167). Englewood Cliffs, NJ: Prentice Hall.

Aggrey, L. K. (2007). *Pre-service teachers' perspectives on race. The impact of key experiences*. Doctoral dissertation. Retrieved from ProQuest Information and Learning Company. (UMI Microform 3297858).

Alexander, M. (2010). *The new Jim Crow: Mass incarceration in the age of color blindness*. New York: The New Press.

Anderson, E. (1978). *A place on the corner*. Chicago: University of Chicago Press.

Barton, P. E. and Coley, R. J. (2010). *The Black-White achievement gap: When progress stopped*. Princeton, NJ: Educational Testing Services.

Bogle, D. (1994). *Toms, coons, mulattoes, mammies, and bucks: An interpretive history of Blacks in American film*. New York: Continuum Publishing.

Brown, A. (2011). "Same old stories": The black male in social science and educational literature, 1930s to the present. *Teachers College Record, 113*(9), 1–27.

Chang, D. and Demyan, A. (2007). Teachers' stereotypes of Asian, Black, and White students. *School Psychology Quarterly, 22*(2), 91–114.

Chubb, J. E. and Loveless, T. (Eds.). (2002). *Bridging the achievement gap*. Washington, DC: Brookings Institution Press.

Coleman, J., Campbell, E., Hobson, C., McPartland, J., Mood, A., Weinfeld, F. D. et al. (1966). Equality of educational opportunity. Washington, DC: Department of Health, Education, and Welfare.

Collins, P. H. (1999). Mammies, matriarchs, and other controlling images. In J. Kournay, J. Sterba and R. Tong (Eds.), *Feminist philosophies* (2nd ed., pp. 142–152). Upper Saddle River: Prentice Hall.

Collins, P. H. (2004). Booty call: Sex, violence, and images of black masculinity. In *Black sexual politics: African Americans, gender, and the new racism* (pp. 149–180). New York: Routledge.

Council for the Accreditation of Educator Preparation. (2013). CAEP accreditation standards. Retrieved from caepnet.files.wordpress.com/2013/09/final_board_approved.pdf.

Council of Chief State School Officers. (2008). *Educational leadership policy standards: ISLLC 2008: As adopted by the National Policy Board for Educational Administration*. Retrieved from www.ccsso.org/documents/2008/educational_leadership_policy_standards_2008.pdf.

Council of Chief State School Officers. (2013). *Interstate Teacher Assessment and Support Consortium InTASC model core teaching standards and learning progressions for teachers 1.0: A resource for ongoing teacher development*. Washington, DC: Author. Retrieved from www.ccsso.org/Documents/2013/2013_INTASC_Learning_Progressions_for_Teachers.

Davis, J. (2003). Early schooling and academic achievement of African American males. *Urban Education, 38*, 515–537.

Davis, P. (1989). Law as microaggression. *Yale Law Journal, 98*, 1559–1577.

DeCastro-Ambrosetti, D. and Cho, G. (2011). A look at "Lookism": A critical analysis of teachers' expectations based on student appearance. *Multicultural Education*, 51–54.

Delgado, R. and Stefancic, J. (Eds.). (2000). *Critical race theory: The cutting edge*. Philadelphia: Temple University Press.

Devine, P. and Elliot, A. (1995). Are racial stereotypes really fading? The Princeton trilogy revisited. *Personality and Social Psychology Bulletin, 21*(11), 1139–1150.

Dixon, T. L. and Linz, D. (2000). Overrepresentation and underrepresentation of African Americans and Latinos as lawbreakers on television news. *Journal of Communication, 50*(2), 131–154.

Entman, R. and Rojecki, A. (2000). *The Black image in the White mind: Media and race in America*. Chicago: University of Chicago Press.

Fanon, F. (1967). *Black skins white masks. The experiences of a Black man in a White world*. New York: Grove Press.

Ferguson, A. A. (2001). *Bad boys: Public schools and the making of black masculinity*. Ann Arbor: University of Michigan Press.

Gamoran, A. and Long, D. A. (2006). *Equality of Educational Opportunity: A 40-year retrospective* (WCER Working Paper No. 2006-9). Madison: University of Wisconsin–Madison, Wisconsin Center for Education Research. Retrieved from www.wcer.wisc.edu/publications/workingPapers/papers.php.

Goldberg, L. R. (1992). The development of markers for the big five factor structure. *Psychological Assessment, 4,* 29–42.

Greenberg, B. S., Mastero, D., and Brand, J. E. (2002). Minorities and the mass media: Television into the 21st century. In J. Bryant and D. Zillmann (Eds.), *Media effects: Advances in theory and research* (pp. 333–352). Mahwah, NJ: Lawrence Erlbaum Associates.

Gregory, A. and Mosely, P. M. (2004). The discipline gap: Teachers' views on the over-representation of Black students in the discipline system. *Equity and Excellence in Education, 37,* 18–30.

Hampton, B., Peng, L., and Ann, J. (2008). Pre-service teachers' perceptions of urban schools. *Urban Review, 40*(1), 268–295.

Hilliard, Asa G. III. (2003). No mystery: Closing the achievement gap between Africans and excellence. In T. Perry, C. Steele, and A. G. Hilliard (Eds.), *To be young, gifted and Black: Promoting high achievement among African-American students* (pp. 131–166). Boston: Beacon Press.

Hilliard, A. G. III. (1991). Do we have the will to educate all children? *Educational Leadership, 49*(1), 31–36.

Ikemoto, L. (1997). Furthering the inquiry: Race, class, and culture in the forced medical treatment of pregnant women. In A. Wing (Ed.), *Critical race feminism: A reader* (pp. 136–143). New York: New York University Press.

King, J. E. (1991). Dysconscious racism: Ideology, identity, and the miseducation of teachers. *Journal of Negro Education, 60*(2), 133–146.

King, J. E. (2005). Rethinking the Black/White duality of our times. In A. Bogues (Ed.), *Caribbean reasonings: After man, toward the human—Critical essays on Sylvia Wynter* (pp. 25–56). Kingston, Jamaica: Ian Randle Publishers.

King, J. E. (2008). Critical and qualitative research in teacher education: A blues epistemology for cultural well-being and a reason for knowing. In M. Cochran-Smith et al., (Eds.), *Handbook of research on teacher education: Enduring questions in changing contexts* (3rd ed., pp. 1094–1136). New York: Routledge.

King, J. E. (2011, Summer). "Who dat say (we) too depraved to be saved?" Remembering Katrina/Haiti (and beyond): Critical studyin' for human freedom. *Harvard Educational Review, 81*(2), 343–370.

King, J. E. and Akua, C. (2012). Dysconscious racism and teacher education. In J. A. Banks (Ed.). *Encyclopedia of diversity in education* (pp. 724–727).Thousand Oaks, CA: Sage.

King, J. E., Akua, C., and Russell, L. (2014). Liberating urban education for human freedom. In H. R. Milner and K. Lomotey (Eds.), *Handbook for research on urban education* (pp. 52–107). New York: Routledge.

Ladson-Billings, G. (2006). From the achievement gap to the education debt: Understanding achievement in U.S. schools. *Educational Researcher, 35,* 3–12.

Ladson-Billings, G. and Gillborn, D. (Eds.). (2004). *The Routledge Falmer reader in multicultural education.* New York: Routledge.

Ladson-Billings, G. and Grant, C. A. (1997). *Dictionary of multicultural education.* Phoenix, AZ: Oryx Press.

Lawrence, S. and Tatum, B. (1998). White racial identify and anti-racist education: A catalyst for change. In Lee, E., Mekart, D., and Okazawa-Rey, M. (Eds.), *Beyond heroes and holidays: A practical guide to K–12 anti-racist, multicultural education and staff development.* Washington, DC: Network of Educators in the Americas.

Lee, E. (1998). Anti-racist education: Pulling together to close the gaps. *Beyond Heroes and Holidays: A Practical Guide to K–12 Anti-Racist. Multicultural Education and Staff Development.* Washington DC: Network of Educators on the Americas. Retrieved from people.ucsc.edu/~marches/PDFs/Anti-racist%20Education%20Pulling%20Together%20to%20Clsoe%20the%20Gaps,%20Lee.pdf.

Lee, M., Bichard, S., Irey, M., Walt, H., and Carlson, A. (2009). Television viewing and ethnic stereotypes: Do college students form stereotypical perceptions of ethnic groups as a result of heavy television consumption? *The Howard Journal of Communications, 20*(1), 95–110.

Lippman, W. (1922). *Public opinion.* New York: Harcourt Brace.

Losen, D. and Gillespie, J. (2012). *Opportunities suspended: The disparate impact of disciplinary exclusion from school.* Retrieved from civilrightsproject.ucla.edu/resources/projects/center-for-civil-rights-remedies/school-to-prison-folder/federal-reports/upcoming-ccrr-research/losen-gillespie-opportunity-suspended-2012.pdf.

Losen, D. and Martinez, T. (2013). Out of school and off track: The overuse of suspensions in American middle and high schools. Retrieved from civilrightsproject.ucla.edu/resources/projects/center-for-civil-rights-remedies/school-to-prison-folder/federal-reports/out-of-school-and-off-track-the-overuse-of-suspensions-in-american-middle-and-high-schools/Exec_Sum_OutofSchool_OffTrack_UCLA.pdf.

Losen, D. and Orfield, G. (2002). *Racial inequity in special education.* Cambridge: Harvard Education Publishing Group.

MacIntyre, A. (2002). Exploring whiteness and multicultural education with prospective teachers. *Curriculum Inquiry, 32*(1), 31–49.

Mendez, L. and Knoff, H. (2003). Who gets suspended from school and why: A demographic analysis of schools and disciplinary infractions in a large school district. *Education and Treatment of Children, 26*(1), 30–51.

Milner, H. (2012). Beyond a test score: Explaining opportunity gaps in educational practice. *Journal of Black Studies, 43*(6), 693–718.

The Moynihan Report, U.S. Department of Labor (1965). *The Negro family: The case for national action.*, Office of Planning and Research, U.S. Department of Labor. Retrieved from www.dol.gov/oasam/programs/history/webid-meynihan.htm.

Muhammad, K. G. (2010). *The condemnation of blackness: Race, crime and the making of modern urban America.* Cambridge: Harvard University Press.

New York State Archives U.S. Department of Education. (2012). Federal Education Policy and the States, 1945–2009: The Johnson Years: The Coleman Report – Equal Educational Opportunity. NYSED.gov. Retrieved from www.archives.nysed.gov/edpolicy/research/res_essay_johnson_cole.shtml.

Nicholson-Crotty, S., Birchmeier, Z., and Valentine, D. (2009). Exploring the impact of school discipline on racial disproportion in the juvenile justice system. *Social Science Quarterly, 90*(4), 1003–1018.

Perry, T., Steele, C., and Hilliard, A. (2003). *Young, gifted, and black: Promoting high achievement among African-American students.* Boston: Beacon Press.

Rich, M. (2013). Minority groups remain outnumbered at teaching programs, study reports. *New York Times.* Retrieved from www.nytimes.com/2013/03/20/education/teaching-degree-minority-enrollment-lags-study-shows.html?ref=educationand_r=1and.

Schott Foundation for Public Education. (2012). The urgency of now: The Schott 50 state report on public education and black males. Retrieved from blackboysreport.org/urgency-of-now.pdf.

Skiba, R., Horner, R., Chung, C., Rausch, M., May, S., and Tobin, T. (2011). Race is not neutral: A national investigation of African American and Latino disproportionality in school discipline. *School Psychology Review, 40*(1), 85–107.

Skiba, R., Michael, R., Nardo, A., and Peterson, R. (2002). The color of discipline: Sources of racial and gender disproportionality in school punishment. *Urban Review, 34*, 317–342.

Sleeter, C. E. (2004). How white teachers construct race. In G. Ladson-Billings and D. Gillborn (Eds.), *Routledge Falmer reader in multicultural education* (pp. 163–178). New York: Routledge.

Solórzano, D. G. and Yosso, T. J. (2001). From racial stereotyping and deficit discourse. *Multicultural Education, 9*(1), 1–8.

Solórzano, D. G. and Yosso, T. J. (2009). Critical race methodology: Counter-storytelling as an analytical framework for educational research (pp. 131–147). In E. Taylor, D. Gillborn, and G. Ladson-Billings (Eds.), *Foundations of critical race theory in education* (pp. 1–13). New York: Routledge.

Tan, A., Zhang, Y., Zhang, L., and Dalisay, F. (2009). Stereotypes of African Americans and media use among Chinese high school students. *The Howard Journal of Communications, 20*(1), 260–275.

Taylor, E. (2009). The foundations of critical race theory in education: An introduction. In E. Taylor, D. Gillborn, and G. Ladson-Billings (Eds.), *Foundations of critical race theory in education* (pp. 1–13). New York: Routledge.

University Council for Educational Administration. (2013). *Curriculum modules for leadership preparation: Building a community of trust through racial awareness of self.* Retrieved from ucea.org/building-a-community-of-trust/.

U.S. Department of Education, National Center for Education Statistics. (2012). *The Condition of Education 2012* (NCES 2012-045), Indicator 33. Retrieved from nces.ed.gov/fastfacts/display.asp?id=16.

Valencia, R. (2010). *Dismantling contemporary deficit thinking: Educational thought and practice.* New York: Routledge.

Vanneman, A., Hamilton, L., Baldwin Anderson, J., and Rahman, T. (2009). *Achievement gaps: How Black and White students in public schools perform in mathematics and reading on the National Assessment of Educational Progress* (NCES 2009-455). National Center for Education Statistics, Institute of Education Sciences, U.S. Department of Education, Washington, DC. Retrieved from nces.ed.gov/nationsreportcard/pubs/studies/2009455.aspx.

Vavrus, F. and Cole, K. (2002). "I didn't do nothing": The discursive construction of school suspension. *The Urban Review, 34*(2), 87–111.

Wallace, J., Goodkind, S., and Wallace, C. (2008). Racial, ethnic, and gender differences in school discipline among U.S. high school students: 1991–2005. *The Negro Educational Review, 59*(2), 47–62.

Wells, A. and Serman, T. (1998). Education against all odds: What films teach us about schools. In G. Maeroff (Ed.), *Imaging education: The media and schools in America.* New York: Columbia University Press.

Wilson, C. and Gutierrez, F. (1985). *Minorities and media: Diversity and the end of mass communication.* Beverly Hills, CA: Sage Publications.

Woodson, C. G. (1933). The mis-education of the Negro. Washington, DC: Associated Publishers.

Wynter, S. (2005a). Appendix B-1. Black education, toward the human, after "Man": In the manner of a manifesto. In J. E. King (Ed.), *Black education: A transformative research and action agenda for the new century* (pp. 357–359). Mahwah, NJ: Lawrence Erlbaum.

Wynter, S. (2005b). Appendix B-2. Race and our biocentric belief system: An interview with Sylvia Wynter. In J. E. King (Ed.), *Black education: A transformative research and action agenda for the new century* (pp. 361–366). Mahwah, NJ: Lawrence Erlbaum.

Wynter, S. (2003, Fall). Unsettling the coloniality of our being/power/truth/freedom: Towards the human after man, its overrepresentation—An argument. *The New Centennial Review, 3*(3), 257–357.

Yosso, T. J. and García, D.G. (2010). "From Ms. J. to Ms. G.: Analyzing racial microaggressions in Hollywood's urban school genre." In B. Frymer, T. Kashani, A.J. Nocella II, and R. Van Heertum (Eds.), *Hollywood's exploited: Public pedagogy, corporate movies, and cultural crisis* (pp. 85–103). New York: Palgrave Macmillan.

Young, E. (2011). The four personae of racism: Educators' (mis)understanding of individual vs. systemic racism. *Urban Education, 46*(6), 1433–1460.

CHAPTER 13

Tempered Radicalism in the Ivory Tower

Black Urban Educational Leaders Negotiating Lives in a Creative Class City

Richard J. Reddick, Beth E. Bukoski, and Stella L. Smith

Urban education is often construed as a scholarly focus on "critical concerns facing inner-city schools" (*Urban Education*, 2014)—therefore, a volume on urban educational leadership might focus expressly on PK–12 schooling dynamics and the actors within. As scholar-practitioners engaged at preschool, elementary, secondary, undergraduate, and graduate levels, we would like to extend the conceptualization of urban education leadership to the scholars charged with the responsibility of nurturing and developing those who eventually will lead classrooms, schools, and districts. These faculty are essential educators and supporters of urban educational leaders, and additionally lead as mentors, intellects, and role models.

A further aspect of urban education leadership can be applied to the lived experience of black scholars engaged in civic life in an urban setting. Professionally—through their research and writing, service activities, and teaching—these faculty members are directly influencing policymaking and practice in the urban context. Personally, via their own engagement as parents, caretakers, mentors, volunteers, board members, and as public intellectuals, black faculty bring a fuller dimension of themselves to the community, and are leaders not simply in the hierarchical sense but also as thought leaders. They also bridge a large, bureaucratic institution and a historically neglected and exploited community. We posit that they navigate this space as tempered radicals (Meyerson, 2003)—"people who operate on the fault line . . . organizational insiders who contribute and succeed in their jobs . . . treated as outsiders because they represent ideals or agendas that are somehow at odds with the dominant culture" (p. 5).

These perspectives are particularly salient in the context of a rapidly changing urban context, where demographics, economic development, and structural inequities in educational settings are at the core of every public policy concern. Perhaps this is nowhere more evident than in the category of urban areas termed "creative class cities" by urban theorist Richard Florida: populated by "a fast-growing, highly educated, and well-paid segment of the workforce on whose efforts corporate profits and economic growth increasingly depend" (2002); journalist David Brooks (2001) uses the term "latte towns" to describe similar patterns of economic and cultural development. No urban area is more emblematic of this development than Austin, Texas, the very city that Florida (2002) uses as a vignette to describe the creative class. The subtext to these exemplars of a new economy and culture is the vestiges of historical exclusion and structural inequities.

As a city established in the postbellum South in the Jim Crow era, Austin is a fascinating mixture of progressivism and inequality. The University of Texas at Austin (UT-Austin) has reflected these dichotomies through its 131-year history. The following examination of black faculty at UT-Austin who engage in forms of activism supporting the lives of black citizens in this creative class city postulates how urban educational leadership is exhibited not only through direct action in schools but also in community engagement experiences where black intellectual leaders must contend as tempered radicals with individual and structural impediments to the quality of life for black citizens.

Since the 1960s, predominantly white institutions (PWIs) such as UT-Austin and its peers have continued to make incremental changes toward creating a more diverse faculty (Turner, Myers, and Creswell, 1999); however, the percentage of black faculty at PWIs remains low (*Journal of Blacks in Higher Education* [JBHE], 2005). Differential outcomes in job satisfaction persist among black faculty compared to their peers and faculty at historically black colleges (Allen, Epps, Guillory, Suh, and Bonous-Hammarth, 2000). Higher education institutions, however, are nested within communities; therefore, research on black faculty experiences must encompass institutional as well as civic contexts. Racism is a daily, lived experience for people of color, challenging black faculty to respond productively to racism both within and outside the academy. A vivid example lies in the experience of Henry "Skip" Gates, who was arrested, in essence, for housing while black (Stripling, 2009). In addition, privileges conferred by education, class, and professional identity do not inoculate black faculty from garden-variety racism still present in many communities (Dyson, 2009).

Understanding the experiences of black academics requires contextual approaches centered on the lived experiences of those often (and sometimes not by choice) on the front lines of social change. In our other work (Reddick, Bukoski, Smith, Valdez, and Wasielewski, in press) we have focused on black academics' community engagement and cultural taxation in the creative class city Austin, Texas, however, when viewed from an organizational and community change perspective, we believe these data have further contributions to make. In this chapter, we aim to use previously collected data to examine the ways black academics at a PWI (The University of Texas at Austin [UT-Austin]) in a creative class city—many of whom identify as urban educators and mentor aspiring urban educators at the undergraduate and graduate level—enact change and to extend the tempered radicals framework to account for the necessity of authenticity.

LITERATURE REVIEW

Black Faculty and Faculty of Color: The PWI Context

It is undeniable that race plays a key role in creating differential experiences for many faculty, with black faculty tending to be less satisfied than their white peers at PWIs due to institutional and community demands (Aguirre, Martinez, and Hernandez, 1993; Cohen, 1988; Turner, 2003; Turner, Gonzalez, and Wood, 2008). Such demands are often experienced by all faculty of color and include increased advising burdens (Gay, 2004; Murakami-Ramalho, Nuñez, and Cuero, 2010). Moreover, promotion and tenure decisions do not recog-

nize or reward "diversity work" (Fogg, 2003; Sámano, 2005). Indeed, at PWIs, scholars have identified additional service obligations as central to the lived experiences of minority faculty (Baez, 2000; Brayboy, 2003; Griffin and Reddick, 2011; Trower and Chait, 2002).

The literature reveals that PWIs are often stressful and challenging environs for faculty of color. For instance, one area of research discusses how faculty must cope with "racial battle fatigue" at PWIs (Smith, Allen, and Danley, 2007) as well as racial microaggressions (Solórzano, Ceja, and Yosso, 2000). In addition, a study conducted at six PWIs in the Midwest found black faculty were employed at less prestigious institutions, held lower rank, were less likely to be tenured, earned less, and held less academic stature in comparison to their white peers (Allen et al., 2000). PWIs and their latent hegemonic structures, therefore, have been shown to have an adverse impact on the lives and careers of black faculty.

There is also a developing body of research documenting the tenure and promotion process for faculty of color. Researchers have found that black academics struggle to maintain a sense of identity while progressing toward tenure (Butner, Burley, and Marbley, 2000). In addition, while mentorship both on and off campus has been identified as a key ingredient to faculty success (Stanley, 2006) and black faculty embrace opportunities to be mentor or mentee (Turner, 2003), there are also critiques of the structure and scope of academic mentoring (Tillman, 2001). Furthermore, black female academics have received some focus in the literature, with studies commenting on the importance of mentorship in career advancement as well as the dearth of mentoring relating to navigating challenges in obtaining tenure, career development, and family balance (Gregory, 2001; Thompson and Louque, 2005). Black male faculty have also garnered recent attention in the areas such as institutional fit and job satisfaction (Hooker and Johnson, 2011) as well as the importance of social, political, and financial capital in achieving tenure (Williams and Williams, 2006).

This work, like an emerging vein of research, examines black faculty engaged in urban education at different levels (Grant-Overton, Reddick, and Burbanks, 2013). Certainly gender and race interact meaningfully for black faculty, particularly on PWI campuses. However, race, gender, and other dimensions are not identities shed when leaving campus. Therefore, understanding the communities in which black faculty reside may have an important influence on the daily lived experiences of faculty at PWIs.

Black Faculty: The Progressive Community Context

We have chosen to describe the progressive urban context through the work of urban theorist Richard Florida (2002a, 2002b). Florida argues post-industrial cities must use the growth of the "the creative class" to spur economic development, describing such a class as "people in design, education, arts, music, and entertainment, whose economic function is to create new ideas, new technology, and/or creative content" (Florida, 2002a, p. 8). This definition bears similarity to more pop cultural references such as "latte towns," or "upscale liberal communities, often in magnificent natural settings, often university based, that have become crucial gestation centers for America's new upscale culture" (Brooks, 2001, p. 104). Brooks describes "latte" towns as being inhabited by "bobos," or creative *bo*hemians in the ambition and success-driven *bo*urgeois environment. Such citizens are also well-educated, bringing independent entrepreneurial energy to bear on their communities, and their work is in evidence in locales such as the Boston-Cambridge metroplex, Silicon Valley, the North Carolina Research Triangle, and Austin, Texas. In addition to their creativity and entrepreneurial spirit, such citizens also carry a degree of social awareness to their lives and work (Florida, 2002b): "Creative-minded people enjoy a mix of influences. They want to hear different kinds of music and try different kinds of food. They want to meet and socialize with people unlike themselves, trade views and spar over issues." While Florida's theory places "diversity" centrally, it avoids "political hot buttons" on purpose and contains no explicit mention of racial diversity. Instead, the creative class ostensibly fosters post-racial harmonious acceptance and tolerance. This focus on music, food, and thought as key indicators of diversity noticeably diminishes the recognition of the lived experiences of people of color. The absence of explicit discussion of race does not, however, make racial bias and racism disappear from communities, experience, or memory.

In the Boston-Cambridge metroplex, the reality of racism in creative class cities is most aptly illustrated by the 2009 arrest of Henry Louis "Skip" Gates for housing while black, an event that has had a chilling effect on black academics who must navigate campus and community tensions simultaneously (Allen et al., 2000; Dyson, 2009; Reddick, 2011; Turner and Myers, 2000).

Austin Texas: The creative class context. Gates's arrest serves as an apt illustration of the reality of racism in the lives of black faculty. Racism is, however, also ubiquitous, with racial profiling and high-profile crimes in Denver and Portland causing community tension (Salzman, 2009; Yardley, 2008). These kinds of incidents require renewed energy to understand the experiences of black faculty. Creative class cities are often viewed as "cool places to live" (Dougherty, 2009), yet professionals of color often experience this seemingly welcoming environment in incongruous ways. For example, while Austin tops multiple lists of "Best Places [to live and work]" (Austin Convention Center Department, 2009), a local black business advocacy organization posts the following on their website: "There is a general perception in Austin's black community that this town is a less than ideal city to live in" (Austin Blackpages, 2006). This perception is backed by the work of UT-Austin researcher Eric Tang (2012), who connects societal inequities to the lives of blacks in measures of poverty, infant mortality, and HIV infection rates in comparison to whites. Tang (2012) further states, "That this should take place in a city consistently noted for being among the nation's 'healthiest,' 'most liberal,' 'best places to raise kids,' and 'most sustainable' cities makes the situation all the more disturbing."

This chapter centers on the experiences of black faculty as they traverse the permeable contexts of campus and community life at UT-Austin. However, Austin shares characteristics of other "mind magnet" cities, such as Raleigh-Durham and Portland, which are attractive to educated, social, and environmentally progressive youth. Brooks's prototypical "latte towns" include Boulder, Colorado, and Seattle, Washington (Breen, 2000); based on its demography and history, Austin also fits this mold. In addition, while work exists focusing on the experiences of black faculty in specific locales, research has rarely examined a specific community and engagement context within the framework of the urban, creative class (Alexander and Moore, 2007; Butner, Burley, and Marbley, 2000; Few, Piercy, and Stremmel, 2007; Turner and Myers, 2000). Furthermore, while the (re)election of President Barack Obama is often tied to claims of a post-racial America, the continued persistent racism and racial bias paint a clear picture of the need for this research.

Theoretical Framework: Tempered Radicals

In the initial study from which these data are drawn, we were not looking at dimensions of leadership among social change agents. Rather, we were conducting an exploratory analysis of the experiences of black faculty in a creative class city (Reddick, Bukoski, Jimenez, Smith, and Wasielewski, in press). In that study, we used Florida's (2002a, 2002b) theory of the creative class and intersectionality (Collins, 2000; Crenshaw, 1991; Dill and Zambrana, 2009, hooks, 1994) as conceptual frameworks. However, as we explored the data and discussed our findings, we came to the realization that many of the black academics in our study were enacting a tempered radical stance (Meyerson, 2001b), a finding of significance when we consider the PWI and urban contexts. This chapter, therefore, extends our prior work to explicitly interrogate this idea.

Meyerson (2001a) describes a tempered radical as "an informal leader who quietly challenges prevailing wisdom and provokes cultural transformation" (p. 1).Tempered radicals often disagree with organizational actions and processes but nonetheless choose loyalty over leaving. Individuals with this orientation may or may not see themselves as tempered radicals but are unwilling to compromise values and identities in order to "fit in"; instead, they work quietly to simultaneously incite change and remain loyal to the organization (Meyerson 2001a, 2001b). Tempered radicals are leaders who tend to be "less visible, less coordinated, and less vested with formal authority; it is also more local, more diffuse, more opportunistic, and more humble than the activity attributed to the modern-day hero" (Kezar, Gallant, and Lester, 2011, p. 171).

Meyerson (2001a, 2001b) delineates five ways tempered radicals work to make change in their organizations and communities: (a) disruptive self-expression, (b) verbal jujitsu, (c) broadening impact through negotiation, (d) leveraging small wins, and (e) strategic alliance building. All of these techniques assist tempered radicals in transforming threats into opportunities (Meyerson, 2001b).

The first tactic, disruptive self-expression, occurs when a tempered radical proclaims resistance in small ways—via the expression of identity and values through dress, scheduling, office décor, leadership behaviors, and language. According to Meyerson (2001a), the second strategy, verbal jujitsu, entails turning personal threats into opportunities by redirecting or obliquely challenging negative statements, thus creating opportunities for positive change. The third tactic entails broadening impact through negotiation (Meyerson, 2001b). This requires seeking the broader issues to which localized encounters are attached. Fourth, tempered radicals leverage small wins, requiring blurring the lines of organizational culture and language; this technique highlights the importance of appropriately framing the meaning of small wins. The final mechanism by which radicals create change is strategic alliance building, which can organize a response to a shared threat or opportunity, or organize for personal and professional support. This technique develops a collective framing of an issue among diverse stakeholders through either formal or informal group mechanisms (Meyerson, 2001b). The tolls of tempered radicalism can be steep psychologically and emotionally, depending on the degree to which the radicalism is enacted. Despite myriad challenges, tempered radicals tend to persist, working quietly to incite change in their environments.

Methods and Data

This chapter encompasses newly derived findings culled from three rounds of data collection investigating community engagement experiences of black faculty. The researchers distributed a brief survey to the 104 tenured and tenure-track black faculty at UT-Austin. This confidential survey asked faculty about their perceptions of the community context and captured basic demographic information. Of the faculty who responded (fifty-five black tenure/tenure-track faculty), thirty-one replied with a willingness to engage in the next phase of the study, a semi-structured, one-on-one interview. Research team members responded to each participant and were able to conduct eighteen phenomenological interviews. The team followed up with all respondents, but participants who could lend diversity to the sample were prioritized to capture diverse experiences along several axes of difference, including (but not limited to) gender, field, rank, partnered/marital status, and sexual orientation (Patton, 1990).

As in any mode of qualitative inquiry, the researchers themselves are an integral part of the study design. The research team consisted of seven members: the principal investigator and lead author, a black male junior professor (now tenured); a white female graduate assistant (now a professor); and a black female graduate assistant (now a postdoctoral fellow). These three researchers also analyzed the data and wrote this article in conjunction with two Latino graduate students (both of whom are PhD graduates). In addition, three others participated in interviewing and preliminary data analysis: a white male graduate assistant (now a professor) and a Latina graduate of the master's program in higher education. All of the research team members brought personal and professional commitments to social justice, as well as significant qualitative research experience to the project, including experiences building rapport and interviewing across cultural and racial boundaries.

The researchers utilized the literature on experiences of black faculty at predominantly white institutions (PWIs) and community engagement to craft the protocol, which was designed to capture professorial pathways to the institution and glean how faculty make meaning of their community experiences through their teaching, research, service, and social interactions. Each interviewer also wrote analytic memos immediately following each interview to capture impressions as well as query themes and concepts shared with other interviews and unique to each. The researchers' memos were an organizational tool and recursive outlet for clarification of concepts, thoughts, themes, and approaches. The researchers addressed trustworthiness concerns through audiotaped recording, professional transcription services, and sharing coding and memos with an interpretive community (Kvale, 1996; Maxwell, 1996; Seidman, 1998).

After we collected data through one-on-one interviews, we arranged a focus group to continue the discussion. This structure allowed participants to build meaning together via the sharing of anecdotes and each other's perspectives (Kitzinger, 1994). Focus groups can be "particularly useful for exploring people's knowledge and experiences" (Kitzinger, 1995, p. 299). In addition, the homogeneity of our participants on the axes of race and profession was advantageous to this approach since they shared a common experience. The analysis echoed our prior, self-reported approach

(Kreuger, 1988; Mays and Pope, 1995; Morgan, 1988). We relied on themes from the analysis of the individual interviews, coded the data—noting unique interactions in the group such as participants asking questions, changing perspectives, or sharing anecdotes (Kitzinger, 1995). We also paid close attention to incongruous data, or "opinions and examples that do not fit with the researcher's overall theory" (Kitzinger, 1995, p. 301). Trustworthiness concerns were addressed selecting a diverse group of participants (Groenewald, 2004), audiotaping the focus group, and professional transcription services to provide a verbatim record of the discussion (Kvale, 1996; Maxwell, 1996; Seidman, 1998).

Like all forms of qualitative inquiry, there were limitations in the study design. The study relied exclusively on self-reported data, thus subject to bias such as selective memory and "telescoping" (inaccurately recalling the timing and sequencing of events) (USC Libraries, 2014). However, the focus group allowed for triangulation of some of the data. Additionally, the salience of the vignettes shared by the participants suggested that their accounts of experiences were reasonably accurate.

Secondary Analysis

For this chapter we utilized secondary analysis with the one-on-one interview and focus group data to query a new idea appropriate for this volume, given that a large number of participants were engaged in urban education research and practice, and impacted students engaged in the same work. Since we address new, unique research questions through the analysis of previously collected data, secondary data analysis is suited to our endeavor (Heaton, 1998; Lewis, 2011). In addition, the possibility of misinterpretation is minimized since all of the authors were involved in the original study from conceptualization through data collection, analysis, and writing (Long-Sutehall, Sque, and Addington-Hall, 2010). Thus, we incorporated interviews from eleven of the original eighteen interviews and the focus group discussion for this secondary analysis (see Appendix A for a listing of participants). This chapter, therefore, is not separate from, but rather an extension of the original study (Long-Sutehall, Sque, and Addington-Hall, 2010). Furthermore, the broad aims of the original study—to understand the lived experiences of black faculty at a PWI in a creative class city—remain consistent; therefore, we had no ethical concerns in writing this chapter.

FINDINGS

Our analysis can be categorized in two major areas. First we discuss how black faculty in the study enacted a tempered radical stance in their work on campus and in their communities. Second, we offer a critical extension of the tempered radicals framework—the necessity of authenticity for black faculty. Although staying true to one's self is a component of the tempered radical's framework, we found authenticity to be particularly critical for black faculty in urban PWI contexts; in addition, the unique ways faculty performed their tempered radical stance is a nuanced and important extension of Meyerson's work. The following section reflects the analysis of these findings.

The Campus Tempered Radical

In this study, we saw that generally the life experiences and philosophy of black faculty were challenged by the "status quo" culture of the predominantly white institution. Consistent with a tempered radical approach to change, those faculty recognized that in order to make lasting change at the institution, they needed to create a tension within the system challenging the status quo. In addition, faculty felt a responsibility to the campus community to use their position within the system to advocate for change, as Horace shared in this reflection:

> In other words, to feel responsible to the community it means there is a community to feel responsible to. That's important, because there is some kind of expectation and reciprocity one way or the other. The things that you are doing for others, there is some notion that some of those things can happen for you in a generally hostile atmosphere.

Although Horace recognized the duality of his situation, he accepted ambiguity in his identity as related to the institution to make a positive change. Moreover, Horace also recognized the power of acting as a critic of the status quo. The black faculty in the study were savvy enough to recognize the political forces at play and, therefore, advocated for tempered change, evident in this exchange between Tiffany and Horace:

> *Tiffany:* Also because there are a fair number of us in a place to be advocating for that, the tension is there be-

cause we are there to push back. You know? Same with American Studies. I think that there are five or six out of eleven or twelve faculty of color in our department. Some of the conversations that happen in the faculty meetings are a lot more contentious because we're there to voice that side of it. Sort of push for graduate students or whatever.

> *Horace:* I think that is true on campus. As our numbers do increase, but as we keep pushing, and especially at a time when reactions are up on it and resources are scarce, things are really getting tense.

> *Tiffany:* Because for the moment, we do have a fair number of resources.

In this exchange, Tiffany and Horace shared how faculty of color are able to advocate for change as they have the numbers and resources to make a more diverse agenda the priority in their department. However, they also recognized how easily resources can shift; this understanding of the politics of resource allocation connected to their ability to make change and to continue to increase their numbers. In recognizing the importance of strategic alliance building, Tiffany and Horace were able to leverage small wins—tactics that must be used in unison to maintain movement.

The data reveal that although activism and radicalism were exercised in the community, faculty in this study saw their radical role more solidly situated and rooted on campus. In Horace's view, for instance, black faculty are able to challenge the status quo while also being a part of the status quo:

> At this point in my life I don't feel like I have to be an activist outside of the university because there is a community here at the university I can be an activist in, and the things that I'm doing are ethically correct, but they are also, hopefully have some kind of impact.

Horace understood the value of the tempered approach and chose to advocate from within, rather than outside, the organization. This quote also reveals an example of verbal jujitsu—Horace turned the threat of the PWI environment to solidify his nonnegotiables—his ethical center—and turned that into an opportunity in an otherwise threatening campus environment.

Participants enacted their tempered radical identities on campus in multiple ways. Examples included advocating for admission of nontraditional students to undergraduate and graduate programs; sharing information with tenure-track black faculty to demystify the process of promotion and tenure; and mentoring and sponsoring black students who have been failed by their assigned advisers and who are at risk of leaving the institution without graduating.

Moreover, participants positioned themselves in administrative positions where they could provide more opportunities for diverse candidates who might be overlooked otherwise, as exemplified in Cliff's statement:

I think when you add some kind of service like being a director, I know in many ways that enables me to do some things in my program to provide opportunities . . . for people of color, which tends to be a challenge . . . I also know that if I didn't do that tomorrow, those opportunities would be there for some other folks, or I wouldn't be able to hire black folks to teach certain courses.

By taking a tempered but radical stand, Cliff demonstrated how he was slowly changing the organization from the within. He aligned his personal conventions and credo with the institution by creating opportunities for people he believes can improve the institution and, by acting as an "outsider within," he makes those changes. Admittedly, these are small wins, but wins nonetheless, upon which he and his colleagues can build.

It is important to note the level of awareness black faculty in this study brought to their work supporting and assisting students. Alvin reflected on this experience:

There is a way, I think, to do a lot of things on campus that will get the job done with competence and to the level that meets the expectations and basic needs of the university, but don't move the ball forward in ways that are important to you. Folks will say, "Shoot, I did that. What's the big deal?" The big deal is your five hours took me fifteen, and there is a dramatic impact in terms of how many more of this student is there. Or how many students have chosen to stay instead of dropping out, or what the students would even say about the quality of life at the end of the program because of the way you took responsibility? I bet some of us take on these jobs with a little more gusto in these ways.

Alvin's quote exemplified the personal cost that tempered radicals pay to make change. Their work is

often neither seen during the day-to-day nor rewarded in tenure and promotion policies, but over time the impact is felt. In addition, black faculty felt a substantial investment on campus, which affected their activism outside the institution. Horace noted that:

I guess for me those boundaries in between community and job have slowly eroded over the years . . . There are critical certain constituency of community members, of people, of black folk, who can benefit from our experience and expertise and just the relationship of us as teacher-student.

Horace's quote highlights the importance of understanding both campus and community environs in the lives of black faculty. Many black faculty are tempered radicals both on campus and in their communities—it is an identity and activist stance they carry with them. And while the activist might be situated on campus through advocacy for a student, this activism is also felt in the impact the faculty and graduate students make in the greater community.

The Community Tempered Radical

Participants also stated they bring a tempered radical approach to work they do off campus. Many saw a connection between the educational work performed on campus and their community work, either because the community work focused on their own graduate students or because the community work focused on educational opportunities for students in P-20 urban educational systems. Noting her work advising graduate and undergraduate students as a form of community engagement, Tiffany said, "It just feels a lot more organic to me that this sort of separate distinction between community and job on campus." Tiffany's words illustrate the synergy between on-campus and off-campus engagement for black faculty in the study. Moreover, some black faculty participated in community activism by serving as advisors for community educational institutions, as Gail shared:

What I do partners well with thing[s] that people ask me to do on occasion; it makes sense to me because I know something about that. I feel really uncomfortable, like I serve on a school board for a little small private school and these sorts of things, you know what I mean? Those are the things that I know how to do. I don't know what I would if I was in a field that didn't translate well to the community.

Gail's comments reflect how community activism in urban education is a natural extension of the role of black faculty, particularly those in social science disciplines, at predominantly white institutions. Their tempered radical approach to problem solving made positive changes in the larger community as well. For several faculty in the sample, however, there was another "pull" toward community activism due to their children. Gail described how she felt the need to bring her professional identity into her community interactions because of negative stereotypes about black parents in educational settings:

Now, I do talk about my professional life when I'm in the context of schools, particularly for my son. And I think some of that really has to do with just being an African-American person and I know how parents of color are often read when they walk into school settings and how children of color are read. And so, in some cases I think it is important for me to talk about or to at least acknowledge—I don't talk about it a lot—but to acknowledge what I do, and how important I and my husband, who's also a faculty member here, who's also African American, views education.

Gail's comment suggested that her professional identity of professor served as a defense for her son and other families of color. This became a leveraging point for creating small wins because her positionality helped her translate threats into opportunities for herself, her son, and other marginalized communities. Often, educators assume black parents are disengaged or uninformed concerning their children's progress. Gail refuted this stereotype by making sure she was visibly involved in schools. Through her example, she hoped to change how the teachers in her son's school view African-American parents. Performing her professional identity as a university professor is a key part of this activism.

Authenticity as a Cornerstone of Tempered Radicalism

An extension of tempered radicalism for black academics is the centrality and importance of authenticity.

To negotiate tensions between a prevailing cultural context that demands surrender of one's identity and values, participants in the study discussed their efforts to maintain authenticity, a commitment to their own values in spite of the various pressures to conform and abandon their deeply held convictions. These expressions of authenticity can be categorized as a component of faculty recruitment to Austin; finding one's place as a member of the community; as an anchor to build relationships with students with social justice orientations (particularly students of color and specifically, black students); and last, as a valid expression of faculty identities in predominantly white spaces in the academy. This section presents these expressions of authenticity in greater detail.

Authenticity as a Component of Recruitment to Austin

From the outset, the faculty interviewed discussed how essential it was that they themselves take responsibility and ensure that newly recruited faculty got the "whole picture" about life in the city. Lawrence recounted an experience where a senior black professor sent a message to a group of faculty from the Center of African American Studies:

[The senior black professor] sends out an email the other day, saying there's a faculty member coming in, looking for this type of housing . . . Who are the realtors we need to connect them to, because we *know* we've got to be careful about which realtors you work with because of the way in which the realtors have different ideas.

The "different ideas" Lawrence refers to are the myriad examples of realtor discrimination, such as directing black professionals away from predominantly white communities, which has been discussed in the literature (Brown, 2014). Lawrence went further, noting the wrong realtor experience "can send somebody packing, right . . . if they have a bad experience with their realtor, that just kicked it off wrong." Taking the concept further, Lawrence termed this work as being similar to the work of a chamber of commerce: "Man, we do a lot of 'chamber.' Whenever somebody comes in and I really like them, I throw them in my pickup and we drive all over. We eat the foods that they want to eat. You sell the place." This sort of honest assessment of the community experience equated to a greater sense of satisfaction for some of the participants in the study such as Derek, who relocated to Austin from an East Coast city:

> As a result of visiting here . . . Austin fit pretty close to what my expectations of it were going to be. It was, I think, a little larger and a little more active than I thought . . . Austin I was surprised that, being a state capital, the university doesn't actually drive everything. It drives a lot but there's a lot more going on . . . There was nothing that really put me off in the recruiting process.

The "largeness" that Derek refers to can be interpreted as providing enough social spaces in which he and his partner felt they could "fit"—in their case, a community of martial artists. Because Derek was exposed to these diverse communities, he reported a positive experience finding an environment that welcomed his authentic self: "If anything, I think I came back from the visits being more optimistic."

Authenticity as a Member of the Community

Once faculty arrive on campus, there exists the challenge of maintaining authenticity. Gail discussed how the multiple roles she occupies—academic, mother, spouse, and education expert—are negotiated and dealt with:

> It's interesting. When I'm out in the community I'm not Dr. Gail, I'm not Professor Gail . . . unless someone has asked me specifically to come and talk about my work . . . But in most instances I don't really talk about being a professor because I find that that can sometimes create a distance between other people in the community that you're wanting to just connect with . . .

Gail further expressed that she did not shy away from expressing her expertise in urban education when the situation warranted such an approach. Even balancing and representing these multiple roles, Gail added: "I try to be authentically whatever I'm supposed to be in that space," further commenting, "Whatever I'm there to do I try to be that, because it's schizophrenic not to." This challenge of navigating multiple spaces authentically resonated with other participants who found themselves interacting in schools. Erica noted, "A lot of what I do, even socially, is because of the kids. We get together with people who have kids at their school, and we do

things with the parents of soccer players." Danielle additionally stated, "[Who] I mostly interact with are other parents; you go to the playground and talk to your neighbors and things like that." These women participants shared experiences where they found it necessary and important to interact with school professionals and parents, yet did so in a way that did not compromise their values, culture, or ways of being.

Authenticity as an Anchor to (Mostly) Students of Color with Social Justice Orientations

The participants in the study shared that authenticity is a character trait particularly valued by social justice oriented students, many of whom are black. By expressing their tempered radical identities via authentic expressions of themselves, they not only assisted their students but also attracted others sharing similar values. Cliff expressed how authenticity led to a more supportive relationship between his students and him, especially juxtaposed with faculty attempting to fit students in methodological or epistemological molds:

> So [students] know that [some faculty expect adherence to their way of thinking]. What they may find in you, on the other hand, might be somebody who will allow them to be who they are, research what they want to, who will help develop them as a scholar who will be supported by you. They ask, "Who will understand that I have a life? I'm trying to do all these things." So it's more of a humane approach.

Unsurprisingly, this care manifested in authenticity is noticed and sought out by students. As Karl commented, "We all have heard graduate students in our department say, 'Oh yeah, I've heard about you,' 'So-and-so said I should talk to you,' or here's a student you don't even know, 'I was told to come to you.'" Students share information about those faculty members who influence and support them in a positive manner. Furthermore, it was evident to the participants that students knew which faculty fit this mold by reputation, as Francis related: "Students will say, 'When we go to dissertation defenses, you ask questions. I already know so-and-so didn't read it. I couldn't believe he was asking these kinds of questions.' They already know that." He continued, "They already know who is going to read their dissertation; they already know who is not going to support them. They already know who is going to be a hard-ass just because. They already know that."

As essential as this assistance is to students, faculty also expressed that being known for authenticity can be burdensome. Cliff endorsed this point: "You find your roster is stacking up. What happened to me in my department, I got the, I guess, students who were challenged. Nobody tells me 'til a year later, 'Oh, you're working with so-and-so? Geez, I can't believe they are still in the program.'" Other faculty related similar concerns, such as Alvin's investment in assisting a student in another department. After helping to keep the student at the university and securing funding for her studies, Alvin's student returned to her dissertation chair, leading Alvin to lament, "She wasn't even in my department." Clearly, the support that authentic tempered radicals extended to students exacted a toll on an already overly taxed faculty. Faculty found that they often had a disproportionate load of students who struggled in their academic programs, their advising load (formal and informal) was heavier, and that their efforts to assist students were rarely acknowledged or rewarded by departmental or university leadership when compared to colleagues who did not embrace tempered radical approaches.

Authenticity as Validation of One's Place in the Academy

A particularly interesting finding related to participants expressing that adhering to their authentic selves brought them into a community context that blurred the lines between "campus" and "community." Rather than seeing these constructs as separate, the participating faculty viewed these two spheres as integrated. Horace, who had taught at the university for over three decades, commented on this integrated view of his role in the campus and community:

> I've sort of looked at students, colleagues, staff and realized the community is here, on campus as well, like what we think of as community. There are students who are floating around out there who are clueless, who don't have a sense of direction or where to go to get direction . . . who are thinking about all these things they might want to do with their lives and how that kind of fits into their family's expectations.

Horace's recognition of students attempting to find a role to serve the community in their lives spoke powerfully to the false dichotomy of campus/community. Indeed, he felt that the unique journeys of black academics who managed to maintain their integrity were instructive and helpful to black students: "Maybe this is the first time in their lives a professor or teacher is working with them has taken an interest in them intellectually, and that means something."

Tiffany similarly discussed how her authentic journey had eradicated the divide between community and campus when she related her developmental relationships with students. Tiffany noted, "I think to the extent that I consider myself a teacher and mentor to graduate students and undergraduates, I find that I'm engaged in the black community in Austin and Texas."

Perhaps the most forceful expression of the value of an authentic presence in the academy came from Horace, who artfully expressed how his anger related to his perceptions of inequity and injustice, which in fact motivated his investment in working with the black community at the university. As several participants discussed their frustration dealing with the "Obama backlash," a seeming retrenchment from active pursuit of civil rights goals due to the emergence of a "postracial" reality, Horace brought forth this perspective regarding how he channeled his ire: "I'm angry too, but that anger really feeds me. Maybe it doesn't feed other folks, but it makes me feel vindicated. It makes me feel like I'm actively doing things that are important." Linking his passion to feeling vindicated—and an ethical stance—Horace's response is an impactful commentary to those who might claim that urban educators in the academy are not present in some iteration of the community. He further commented, "I'm doing what I should be doing. I don't have to seek outside the university for these kinds of morally redeeming practices. They are possible for me right here, because there is a struggle here."

DISCUSSION AND IMPLICATIONS

The findings of this study revealed the presence of a tempered radical stance as a mechanism for change in the campus and community lives of black faculty at a PWI situated in a creative class city, a population that we suggest also fall under the definition of urban educational leaders. Many of the participants (six) maintained research and teaching in domains of urban educational leadership, and all through teaching, research, and mentoring were responsible for teaching and mentoring a new generation of urban educators. Indeed, our findings point to the fact that the campus and community lives of many tenured and tenure-track black faculty at the flagship state institution in Austin, Texas were quite permeable. Faculty leveraged their professional identity off campus and turned threats into opportunities through advocacy and taking prominent positions to influence the community and particularly, urban education, in positive ways. In their roles off campus, the participating faculty may not have been completely satisfied with the diversity, politics, or cultural opportunities, but they saw their communities as intrinsically connected to their sense of self and, indeed, being a part of a community where they saw change as possible served to reenergize faculty around their community efforts.

Likewise, on campus, black faculty found there was plenty to be involved in—to the point they expressed awareness that they were doing more and accomplishing multiple small wins through their extended efforts. They also expressed their sense of self, in articulating their ethical and moral centers, and were motivated by their work on campus with other faculty and students, many of whom aspired to careers as urban educational leaders. Furthermore, the participants had a degree of awareness of their tempered radical stance—they recognized the importance of building alliances, turning challenges into opportunities, and remaining savvy in a politically charged and somewhat regressive sociopolitical climate. These faculty exhibited urban educational leadership through their navigation of these issues, and served as exemplars for the next generation of educational leaders and the community. Indeed, the study highlights the importance of sharing the experiences of black faculty in particularized contexts. Specifically, the urban, creative class context of this study revealed many nuances pertaining to the personal and professional lives of black faculty, which higher education institutions should be aware of and responsive to.

Black faculty, like all faculty, do not and, to an extent, cannot separate their work and home lives. Both must be fulfilling in some way. For black faculty, their tempered radical identity was carried with them from work to home and back—suggesting the effort to distinguish between research and engagement, for instance,

is less applicable to the work of black academics, particularly those in the social sciences. Indeed, it is well-documented faculty of color face additional challenges on the way to promotion and tenure (Brayboy, 2003; Fogg, 2003; Griffin and Reddick, 2011; Sámano, 2005; Trower and Chait, 2002), perhaps in part because their sense of self is so tied to work as tempered radicals on and off campus. This is particularly true of those scholars working in urban education, given that their values, beliefs, and research converge in very public ways. At the heart of the work of these black academic tempered radicals is authenticity and dedication to make the academy a better place.

Higher education is under fire for many reasons—a perceived lack of public value, an alleged failure to hold itself accountable, increasing disparities in both access and attainment, all wrapped in an ever-shrinking box of financial viability. Urban educators are at the nexus of these battles, often posing counterpoints to the prevailing political environment that promotes standardization and disdains cultural relevance, especially in the statewide Texas context (Vasquez Heilig, Brown, and Brown, 2012). This crucible in which higher education finds itself calls for change, yet the very faculty working to make that change—in tempered, savvy, strategic ways—are not rewarded for their work. If we can leave the reader with one core question for future consideration, it is this: how can we value both change *and* the change agents? We therefore posit that perhaps what the literature says about faculty of color *not* being rewarded in promotion and tenure is closely entwined with the notion of a tempered radical stance. In other words, we recognize there is a certain internal logic in not rewarding behaviors seeking to change the status quo—indeed, the academy is notoriously resistant to change. However, given current crises in higher education, institutions now more than ever should reconsider rewarding behaviors seeking to change the status quo—systems that more and more are perceived as unresponsive, irrelevant, and not creating public value.

This point is all the more important considering the urban environment—often a code phrase for high-minority and high-poverty areas. Faculty such as the participants in this study are engaged actively with the community in multiple ways, including personally working to improve urban education as well as shaping and directing students who are on the path to becoming urban educators themselves. If the work faculty perform is not rewarded, they will leave (voluntarily or involuntarily), leaving a shrinking cadre of dedicated radicals to continue the fight on and off campus. In addition, this study should also serve to help inform urban institutions of how they can better leverage faculty work to create partnerships with the community, and (re)gain relevance and impact in their surrounding communities. The days when higher education was seen as valuable by all has passed, and institutions could learn well from the work of tempered radicals like those in this study, faculty whose authenticity and high ethical conviction radiate into tangible change for fellow faculty, students, and community.

REFERENCES

Aguirre, A., Martinez, R., and Hernandez, A. (1993). Majority and minority faculty perceptions in academe. *Research in Higher Education, 34*(3), 371–385.

Alexander, R. and Moore, S. (2007). Benefits and challenges of working at predominantly White institutions: Strategies for thriving. *Journal of African American Studies, 12*, 1–3.

Allen, W. R., Epps, E. G., Guillory, E. A., Suh, S. A., and Bonous-Hammarth, M. (2000). The Black academic: Faculty status among African Americans in U.S. higher education. *Journal of Negro Education, 69*(1–2), 112–127.

Austin Blackpages. (2006). Guide to Austin. Retrieved from www.austinblackpages.com/guide-to-austin.asp.

Austin Convention Center Department. (2009). Austin rankings. Austin, TX: City of Austin.

Baez, B. (2000). Race-related service and faculty of color: Conceptualizing critical agency in academe. *Higher Education, 39*(3), 363–391.

Brayboy, B. M. J. (2003). The implementation of diversity in predominantly White colleges and universities. *Journal of Black Studies, 34*(1), 72–86. doi: 10.1177/0021934703253679.

Breen, B. (2000, December 31). Where are you on the talent map? *Fast Company, 42*, 102. Retrieved from www.fastcompany.com/42105/where-are-you-talent-map.

Brooks, D. (2001). *Bobos in paradise: The new upper class and how they got there.* New York: Simon and Schuster.

Brown, E. S. (2014). *The Black professional middle class: Race, class, and community in the post-civil rights era.* New York: Routledge.

Butner, B. K., Burley, H., and Marbley, A. F. (2000). Coping with the unexpected: Black faculty at predominately White institutions. *Journal of Black Studies, 30*(3), 453–462.

Cohen, J. J. (1998). Time to shatter the glass ceiling for minority faculty. *The Journal of the American Medical Association, 280*(9), 821–822. doi: 10.1001/5jama.280.9.821.

Collins, P. H. (2000). *Black feminist thought: Knowledge, consciousness, and the politics of empowerment* (2nd ed.). New York: Routledge.

Crenshaw, K. W. (1991). Mapping the margins: Intersectionality, identity politics, and violence against women of color. *Stanford Law Review, 43*(6), 1241–1299.

Dill, B. T. and Zambrana, R. E. (Eds.). (2009). *Emerging intersections: Race, class, and gender in theory, policy, and practice.* New Brunswick, NJ: Rutgers University Press.

Dougherty, C. (2009, May 16). "Youth magnet" cities hit midlife crisis: Few jobs in places like Portland and Austin, but the hipsters just keep on coming. *Wall Street Journal.* Retrieved from online.wsj.com/article/SB124242099361525009.html.

Dyson, M. E. (2009). Commentary: Professor arrested for "housing while Black." Retrieved from www.cnn.com/2009/LIVING/07/22/dyson.police/index.html.

Few, A. L., Piercy, F. P., and Stremmel, A. (2007). Balancing the passion for activism with the demands of tenure: One professional's story from three perspectives. *National Women's Studies Association Journal, 19*(3), 47–66.

Florida, R. (2002a). The rise of the creative class and how it's transforming work, leisure, community, and everyday life. New York: Perseus Book Group.

Florida, R. (2002b, May). The rise of the creative class: Why cities without gays and rock bands are losing the economic development race. *Washington Monthly.* Retrieved from www.washingtonmonthly.com/features/2001/0205.florida.html.

Fogg, P. (December, 2003). So many committees, so little time: Professors' growing service obligations make advancement tougher for many of them, particularly women and minority-group members. *The Chronicle of Higher Education, L(17)*, A14–17.

Gay, G. (2004). Navigating marginality en route to the professoriate: Graduate students of color learning and living in academia. *International Journal of Qualitative Studies in Education, 17*(2), 265–288.

Grant-Overton, C. M., Reddick, R. J., and Burbanks, S. (2013, November). Creating social justice curricula and praxis in P-20 educational settings through quality leadership preparation. Paper presented at the annual University Council for Educational Administration (UCEA) Convention, Indianapolis, IN.

Gregory, S. T. (2001). Black faculty women in the academy: History, status, and future. *Journal of Negro Education, 70*(3), 124–138.

Griffin, K. A. and Reddick, R. J. (2011). Surveillance and sacrifice: Gender differences in the mentoring patterns of Black professors at predominantly White research universities. *American Educational Research Journal, 48*(5), 1032–1057. doi: 10.3102/0002831211405025.

Groenewald, T. (2004). A phenomenological research design illustrated. *International Journal of Qualitative Methods, 3*(1). Article 4. Retrieved from www.ualberta.ca/~iiqm/backissues/3_1/html/groenewald.html.

Heaton, J. (1998). Secondary analysis of qualitative data. *Social Research Update, 22.* Retrieved from www.soc.surrey.ac.uk/sru/SRU22.html.

Hooker, K. and Johnson, B. J. (2011). African American male faculty satisfaction: Does institutional type make a difference? *Journal of African American Males in Education, 2*(2), 168–187.

hooks, b. (1994). *Teaching to transgress: Education as the practice of freedom.* New York: Routledge.

Journal of Blacks in Higher Education. It's time to do better: JBHE counts of Black students and faculty at the nation's 50 flagship state universities. (2001). *Journal of Blacks in Higher Education, 32,* 86–92.

Kezar, A., Gallant, T. B., and Lester, J. (2011). Everyday people making a difference on college campuses: The tempered grassroots leadership tactics of faculty and staff. *Studies in Higher Education, 36*(2), 129–151.

Kitzinger, J. (1994). The methodology of focus groups: The importance of interactions between research participants. *Sociology of Health and Illness, 16,* 103–121.

Kreuger, R. (1988). *Focus groups: A practical guide for applied research.* London, UK: Sage.

Kvale, S. (1996). *Interviews: An introduction to qualitative research interviewing.* Thousand Oaks, CA: Sage Publications, Inc.

Lewis, J. (2011). Design issues. In J. Ritchie and J. Lewis (Eds.), *Qualitative research practice: A guide for social science students and researchers* (pp. 47–76). London: Sage Publications.

Long-Sutehall, T., Sque, M., and Addington-Hall, J. (2010). Secondary analysis of qualitative data: A valuable method for exploring sensitive issues with an elusive population? *Journal of Research in Nursing, 16*(4), 335–344.

Maxwell, J. (1992). Understanding and validity in qualitative research. *Harvard Educational Review, 62,* 279–300.

Mays, N. and Pope, C. (1995). Rigour and qualitative research. *British Medical Journal, 311,* 109–112.

Meyerson, D. E. (2001a). Radical change, the quiet way. *Harvard Business Review, October,* 1–10.

Meyerson, D. E. (2001b). *Tempered radicals: How people use difference to inspire change at work.* Cambridge, MA: Harvard Business School Press.

Meyerson, D. E. (2003). Tempered radicals: How everyday leaders inspire change at work. Cambridge, MA: Harvard Business School Press.

Morgan, D. (1988). *Focus groups as qualitative research.* London, UK: Sage.

Murakami-Ramalho, E., Nuñez, A., and Cuero, K. K. (2010). Latin@ advocacy in the hyphen: Faculty identity and commitment in a Hispanic-serving institution. *International Journal of Qualitative Studies in Education, 23*(6), 699–717.

Patton, M. Q. (2002). *Qualitative research and evaluation methods* (3rd ed.). Thousand Oaks, CA: Sage Publications.

Reddick, R. J. (2011). Intersecting identities: Mentoring contributions and challenges for Black faculty mentoring Black undergraduates. *Mentoring and Tutoring, 19*(3), 319–346.

Reddick, R. J., Bukoski, B. E., Jimenez, J. M., Smith, S. L., and Wasielewski, M. V. (in press). A hole in the soul of Austin: Black faculty community engagement experiences in a creative class city. *Journal of Negro Education.*

Reddick, R. J., Bukoski, B. E., and Smith, S. (2012, April). *Taxed for the public good: Black faculty, agents of change in a creative class city.* Paper presented at the AERA 2012 Annual Conference, Vancouver, BC.

Salzman, J. (2009). Fox 31 in Denver promotes Rush-like scare tactics. *Huffington Post.* Retrieved from www.huffingtonpost.com/jason-salzman/fox-31-in-denver-promotes_b_374036.html.

Sámano, A. (2005). Cultural taxation: Workload issues for faculty of color in predominantly White institutions. Retrieved from lanecc.edu/fpd/grants/sabbatical/paid/sabbreports05/CCMomentPaper.htm.

Seidman, I. (1998). *Interviewing as qualitative research: A guide for researchers in education and the social sciences* (2nd ed.). New York: Teachers College Press.

Smith, W. A., Allen, W. R., and Danley, L. L. (2007). "Assume the position . . . you fit the description": Psychosocial experiences and racial battle fatigue among African American male college students. *American Behavioral Scientist, 51*(4), 551–578.

Solórzano, D., Ceja, M., and Yosso, T. (2000). Critical Race Theory, racial microaggressions, and campus racial climate: The experiences of African American college students. *Journal of Negro Education, 69*(1/2), 60–73.

Stanley, C. A. (2006). Coloring the academic landscape: Faculty of color breaking the silence in predominantly White colleges and universities. *American Educational Research Journal, 43*(4), 701–736.

Stripling, J. (2009). News: If it can happen to him . . . Retrieved from www.insidehighered.com/news/2009/07/22/gates.

Tang, E. (2012, June 18). Austin has taken great leap backward in racial equality. *Austin American-Statesman*. Retrieved from www.statesman.com/opinion/austin-has-taken-great-leap-backward-in-racial-2401413.html.

Thompson, G. L. and Louque, A. (2005). *Exposing the "culture of arrogance" in the academy: A blueprint for increasing Black faculty satisfaction*. Sterling, VA: Stylus.

Tillman, L. C. (2001). Mentoring African American faculty in predominantly White institutions. *Research in Higher Education, 42*(3), 295–325.

Trower, C. and Chait, R. (2002, March–April). Faculty diversity: Too little for too long. *Harvard Magazine*, 33–37.

Turner, C. S. V. (2003). Incorporation and marginalization in the academy: From border toward center for faculty of color? *Journal of Black Studies, 34*(1), 112–125.

Turner, C. S. V., Gonzalez, J. C., and Wood, J. L. (2008). Faculty of color in academe: What 20 years of literature tells us. *Journal of Diversity in Higher Education, 1*(3), 139–168.

Turner, C. S. V. and Myers, S. L. (2000). *Faculty of color in academe: Bittersweet success*. Boston: Allyn and Bacon.

Turner, C. S. V., Myers, S., and Creswell, J. (1999). Exploring underrepresentation: The case of faculty in the Midwest. *Journal of Higher Education, 10*, 27–44.

USC Libraries. (2014). Limitations of the study: Organizing your social sciences research paper. Retrieved from libguides.usc.edu/content.php?pid=83009andsid=616083.

Vasquez Heilig, J., Brown, K. D., and Brown, A. L. (2012). The illusion of inclusion: A Critical Race Theory textual analysis of race and standards. *Harvard Educational Review, 82*(3), 403–424.

Williams, B. N. and Williams, S. M. (2006). Perceptions of African American male junior faculty on promotion and tenure: Implications for community building and social capital. *Teachers College Record, 108*(2), 287–315.

Yardley, W. (2009, May 29). Racial shift in a progressive city spurs talks. *New York Times*. Retrieved from www.nytimes.com/2008/05/29/world/americas/29iht-29portland.13302483.html.

APPENDIX A

Participants Included in Secondary Analysis of Original Study

Table 13.1.   Participants Included in Secondary Analysis of Original Study

Pseudonym	Gender	Rank	Area	Former city/region	Years at UT	Partner status
Derek	Male	Untenured	Liberal Arts	Capital City, Midatlantic	0–5	Partnered
Horace	Male	Tenured	Liberal Arts	Central America	15+	Partnered
Alvin	Male	Tenured	Communication	Midwest	15+	Partnered
Francis	Male	Untenured	Education	College Town, West Coast	0–5	Partnered
Erica	Female	Untenured	Education	Metropolis, Northeast	0–5	Single
Gail	Female	Untenured	Education	College Town, Midwest	0–5	Partnered
Cliff	Male	Tenured	Education	College Town, Midwest	0–5	Partnered
Lawrence	Male	Untenured	Education	College Town, Midwest	0–5	Partnered
Karl	Male	Untenured	Education	College Town, Northeast	0–5	Partnered
Danielle	Female	Tenured	Law	Midatlantic	0–5	Single
Tiffany	Female	Tenured	Liberal Arts	College Town, Northeast	6–10	Partnered

THEORY AND RESEARCH METHODOLOGY

There are exciting new ways individuals are conducting research in urban districts and schools, and the theories they use are just as interesting. This section highlights promising approaches to the complex issues of urban schools. This section begins with a Voice from the Field by Ty-Ron M. O. Douglas titled, "Sound the 'Bell': Seeing Space, Seeing Color in Urban School Leadership Discourses."

In chapter 14, "Using Social Norming and Ecological Theories and Diversity-Based Strategies for Bullying Interventions in Urban Areas: A Mixed-Methods Research Study," authors Azadeh F. Osanloo and Jonathan P. Schwartz explore best practices in the field and current research trends related to bullying interventions in urban areas, examine a mixed-methods bullying study based in the Southwest, and assist school leaders and teachers to develop individualized intervention plans based on the unique needs of their schools. Chapter 15, "Toward Community-Centric Educational Leadership in Addressing the School Discipline Disparity" Jacqueline Roebuck Sakho, Ronald W. Whitaker, Rodney Hopson, and Tiffany Wilkins challenge our current notions of urban education and how these certain constructions fail to account for the complexity of urbanity.

Their chapter problematizes urban education and schooling and the type of leader that seeks to address the myriad of challenges and interest convergences faced in the context of schools, communities, and higher education institutions. In chapter 16, "Revisiting Black Feminist Thought and Home-School Relations in the U.S. South," authors Tondra L. Loder-Jackson, Andrew N. McKnight, Michael Brooks, and Tonya B. Perry address relationships between predominantly African-American mothers and women school personnel in an urban school district in the Southeast.

Their chapter is framed conceptually by Patricia Hill Collins' (2000) classic Black Feminist Thought (BFT) perspective on black women's work, family, and oppression, along with a critical review of empirical studies on home-school relations. The chapter's three key themes highlight urban parents' and school personnel's sometimes divergent perspectives on: (1) the conceptualization of parent involvement; (2) urban parents' capacity for constructive involvement in their children's lives; and (3) appropriate strategies for enhancing home-school relations.

Sound the "Bell"

Seeing Space, Seeing Color in Urban School Leadership Discourses

Ty-Ron M. O. Douglas

"To see what is in front of one's nose needs a constant struggle."

—George Orwell

It appears that discourses related to urban education and urban educational leadership are occurring with greater regularity inside and outside the academy. Yet, despite the growing chorus of voices on these vogue topics and scholarly platitudes at educational conferences, there seems to be an unwillingness to acknowledge the numbing capacity of the very language being used to engage these discussions. Terms like *multicultural leadership* and *social justice leadership*, which have become hallmarks of urban educational leadership discourses and reform, are often difficult to define and even more difficult to operationalize. As such, I draw on the work of the late Derrick Bell and a few tenets of Critical Race Theory in an effort to (re)contextualize urban school leadership discourses.

Language and labels are indissoluble aspects of any discourse. In fact, how individuals, ideologies, and institutions are described have significant ramifications for educational reform, and the discourses and distributions of power that greatly determine how and why issues are addressed, and by whom. Ironically, language and labels also have a way of cloaking these tensions, while simultaneously shrouding the waning criticality of terms, ideologies, and theorizations that were once used to disrupt hegemonic manifestations. The work of Professor Derrick Bell is particularly relevant here. Bell (2002) speaks to these tensions between our language, our motivations, and our actions:

> I cannot emphasize enough what I see as the potentially dangerous and destructive consequences of words and actions intended to do good. Medicine has long had the term "iatrogenic" to describe conditions accidentally caused by the doctor, whether through treatment, diagnosis, or even manner. We might say that, as with the healing arts, so with the practice of those of us who seek to heal the bodies politic, social, and economic. It is the most frequently ignored pitfall of those motivated by good intentions, particularly those involved in social change and progressive politics. (pp. 160–161)

Breaches between language and lived experience exemplify the "abstraction[s]" Professor Bell saw as the "decontextualization . . . [that] too often masks unregulated—even unrecognized—power" (Bell 1995b, p. 901). In this sense, language and labels can exemplify and reflect "standards and institutions created by and fortifying white power," which must be "resisted" (Bell 1995b, p. 901) and (re)contextualized. Much like laws and reforms are not written from a neutral perspective, language is neither neutral nor benign. Bell's (2002) work reminds me that we must be sufficiently courageous and honest to acknowledge these biases if we seek to engage in authentic and ethical reform efforts.

Language and labels often become tools for the systematic and systemic perpetuation of racism. Drawing on the work of Marable (1983), Bell declares (1985), "all of our institutions of education and information—political and civic, religious and creative—either knowingly or unknowingly provide the public rationale to justify, explain, legitimize, or tolerate racism" (p. 399). Thus, scholars and practitioners who authentically desire to engage in effective urban educational leadership must be challenged to wrestle with the realities of race and racism and the inequities that are rampant, reified, and recursive in schools. Bell (2002) asserts and I concur:

> Without a willingness to continually critique our own policies, question our own motivations, and admit our

own mistakes, it is virtually impossible to maintain programs and practices that are truly ethically related to the real needs of those we wish to serve. (p. 161)

Notably, within the context of urban education, little has changed since Kantor and Brenzel (1992) made this disturbing observation:

> After two and a half decades of federal, state, and local efforts to improve urban education for low-income and minority children, achievement in inner-city schools continues to lag behind national norms, and dropout rates in inner-city high schools (especially among African-American and Hispanic youth) remain distressingly high, while many of those who do graduate are often so poorly prepared they cannot compete successfully in the labor market (p. 279)

In this light, it's necessary that we acknowledge and address the reality that black and brown children are most vulnerable to hegemonic, Eurocentric norms and paradigms (Howard, 2010); black and brown children are most often on the short end of social justice (Cooper and Gause, 2007); and black and brown children are the subject (and victims) of most urban education discourses and reforms (Giroux and Giroux, 2008).

CRT, which emerged out of Critical Legal Studies and the work of scholars like Derrick Bell, has been a centralized framework in the explication of U.S. educational discourses, leadership, and reform (Decuir and Dixon, 2004; Ladson-Billings, 1998; Ladson-Billings and Tate, 1995; Lopez, 2003; Solorzano and Yosso, 2001). CRT is characterized, in part, by attentiveness to the dangers of color-blind stances and similar ideologies that have led many educational leaders to do great damage to students with seemingly good intentions (Bell, 2002). Specifically, CRT discourses have rightly problematized the privileged "I don't see color" stance of some school leaders, since not seeing color is to miss key aspects of identity (Bonilla-Silva, 2006; Crenshaw, 1997), which lead to normative presumptions and oppressive readings of the Other. Still, the work of Professor Bell reminds us that CRT is not a static construction, but is, instead, a transgressive and transformative mechanism for resisting and rupturing standards and institutions created or used for "fortifying white power" (Bell, 1995, p. 901).

One of the fundamental tenets of CRT is the acknowledgment of the historical and contemporary linkages between racism and U.S. property rights (for example, the Constitutional and exclusive rights of wealthy, white males to own property—in the form of land and the bodies of African-American slaves). While CRT scholars have contended that vestiges of this oppressive arrangement are evident today (for example, black students being treated as property in schools), CRT can also be employed and extended to consider how the property and community spaces of black people are ignored and rendered invisible. In essence, attempting to or claiming to not see color can also be applied to space—in this context, urban or minority space. Many school leaders do not see urban communities, in part because they drive into them from their homes in the suburbs without ever engaging in or with the community. Ideologically, culturally, and educationally, these spaces are invisible to many school leaders. Bell's (2002) work is informative in this regard. He notes: "Humility gives us space to see that we do not have all the answers, even in our so-called areas of expertise; it lets us listen and respond to what is actually happening, being said, being felt" (p. 165). Sadly, too few school leaders have the time, interest, or humility to visit and appreciate the cultural capital of urban communities, and even fewer see potential solutions that can emerge *from* urban communities. This is why CRT's focus on the dangers of color-blind ideologies and the significance of racism within the context of U.S. property (space) rights are vital to discourses on urban education and leadership. In essence, Bell helps us understand that color-blind leaders have no need (and likely lack the ability) to see the value in community spaces that define and are defined by minoritized students. A large part of the problem within educational leadership discourses has been the obfuscation of languages that could actually better serve children of color. Notably, within academic discourse there seems to be a blurring between terms like *multicultural leadership* and *social justice leadership*.

Bell's contribution to educational leadership in this regard is in his ability to poignantly argue that discourses around race must not be diluted to the extent that they become ineffectual. Rather, they should be constantly centered and dynamically addressed. Though it is sometimes difficult to differentiate between these terms, scholars who have articulated key components of multicultural leadership (for example, Gardiner and Enomoto, 2006) and those who have helped characterize key aspects of social justice leadership (see, for example, Theoharis, 2007) consistently acknowledge the centrality of community engagement. For example, Theoharis (2007) rightly asserts that one characteristic of a social justice leader is that she or he "becomes intertwined with the life, community, and soul of the school" (p. 252). Similarly, Gardiner and Enomoto (2006) declare that a task of a multicultural leader is "building connections between school and communities" (p. 575), while the third cog in Riehl's (2000) vision for multicultural leadership is "fostering strong relationships between schools and the community" (p. 3). Clearly, there is a community emphasis that runs through social justice leadership and multicultural leadership discourses. Still, there has to be investment in the urban and community-based spaces surrounding the schoolhouse (Douglas and Peck, 2013) if we are to apply CRT in a manner that is congruent with the ethos of Professor Bell's work. Bell (1995b) asserts, "Critical race theorists strive for a specific, more egalitarian, state of affairs. We seek to empower and include traditionally excluded views and see all-inclusiveness as the ideal because of our belief in collective wisdom" (p. 901). For this to occur, there must be a rupturing of constructs that not only marginalized black and brown bodies but also those that ignore black and brown space.

Ideologically and culturally, the schoolhouse is reflective of white, middle-class standards (Howard, 2010). As a result, K–12 students of color and students from low socioeconomic backgrounds often feel like "strangers in a strange land" (Bell, 1970, p. 540) as they seek to navigate the schoolhouse norms that are often different from the cultural norms of their home environments and communities (Baldridge, Hill, and Davis, 2011; Douglas and Peck, 2013). Still, the value of collective wisdom and community-based pedagogical spaces (Douglas 2012a) is not a novel concept for people of color—a people who have consistently drawn on extended kin constructs and community-orientated learning environments to buttress the miseducation of and alienation from mainstream schools (Douglas and Peck, 2013; Williams, 2005). Clearly, there is much wisdom that school leaders can draw from educative spaces outside the schoolhouse where traditionally marginalized groups have consistently created educative networks in non-school-based contexts (Douglas and

Peck, 2013; Williams, 2005). This reality is consistent with Kantor and Brenzel (1992), who opine:

> Restructuring efforts and reform within urban schools must come from within schools themselves and the communities they serve so that principals, teachers, and parents can envision fresh approaches to teaching and learning that build on the contextual knowledge and experiences in communities. (p. 297)

Heeding Bell's (1995) counsel to "include traditionally excluded views" not only means hearing the voices of leaders in community-based spaces, but seeing these community-based spaces, perhaps for the first time, as existent, relevant, and resources for potential solutions. Specifically, color-blind ideologies have not just blinded school leaders to the identities of individuals but this problematic approach has also blinded school leaders to the relevance of ideologies and community-based spaces like black barbershops and black churches (Douglas 2012a, 2012b; Douglas and Peck, 2013; Harris-Lacewell and Mills, 2004; Mills, 2006), which must be considered in urban educational leadership discourses and reform efforts. Discourses of educational reform have not addressed issues such as community impact and school-community relationships in a manner that systematically attaches incentives or sanctions to what it means to be a successful school leader. This reality must change. Much like CRT has been the impetus for asking different questions about the significance of race and racism in past policy decisions, I believe that interest convergence ideals can be leveraged to help shift the educational marketplace so that the relationships between schools and community spaces are not only encouraged but these relationships can also lead to tangible investment in the community-based educative settings that serve school constituents.

Additionally, urban school leaders, in preparation programs and those in practice, must spend time in the community-based settings that serve their students. School practitioners must explore how their leadership practices can be enhanced by observing and learning from the formal and informal pedagogical and leadership strategies employed in spaces outside of schools (Douglas 2012a, 2012b, 2013; Khalifa, 2012). Educational leaders, along with their faculty and staff members, must be proactive in visiting, embracing, and creating partnerships with the communities and non-school educative spaces that surround and impact their schools and students (Wilson, Ek, and Douglas, 2013). I concur with Dantley (2005), who asserts that "what happens in the schoolhouse is inextricably linked to what is going on in the local and wider community" (p. 653). Thus, school leaders who avoid or are afraid of the urban community spaces that surround their schools will struggle to see and appreciate the cultural contexts that invariably affect their schools. It takes courage to see and address that which we would prefer to avoid. Bell (2002) puts it this way:

> Courage is our tool in vanquishing fear, but it's not always an easy tool to use, truth be told, it's rarely glamorous. It's a daily decision to wake up and try to do the right thing, no matter how big the reward or how great the fear. (p. 43)

Professor Bell lived this experience. His activism costs him something, real activism always does. Bell not only fought with his pen, but he also put his livelihood and career on the line through protests, resigning from positions, public critiques, and boycotts to make others aware that racism continues to be a part of the fabric that makes up this country. We need urban school leaders of similar ilk and commitment today: urban school leaders who have the courage to *see* spaces and communities of color, the willingness to *challenge* injustice everywhere, and the capacity to *engage* in honest and critical discourses that problematize benign language and labels toward more thoughtful and incisive action. Urban educational leaders must sound the bell and answer the call for a balanced and engaged approach to urban educational leadership that is both inclusive of localized voices and grassroots expertise, and informed by larger, critical discourses and understandings of the geopolitical dynamics of urban space and racial identity.

REFERENCES

Baldridge, B. J., M. L. Hill, and J. E. Davis. (2011). "New possibilities: (Re)engaging Black Male Youth Within Community-Based Educational Spaces." *Race Ethnicity and Education 14*, 121–136.

Bell, D. A. Jr. (1970). "Black Students in White Law Schools: The Ordeal and the Opportunity." *University of Toledo Law Review 2*, 539.

Bell, D. (1987). *And We Are Not Saved: The Elusive Quest for Racial Justice.* New York: Basic Books.

Bell, D. (1993). *Faces at the Bottom of the Well. The Permanence of Racism.* New York: Basic Books.

Bell, D. (1995a). "Property Rights in Whiteness—Their Legal Legacy, Their Economic Costs." *Critical Race Theory: The Cutting Edge*, edited by R. Delgado, pp. 75–83. Philadelphia: Temple University Press.

Bell, D. (1995b). "Serving Two Masters: Integration Ideals and Client Interests in School Desegregation Litigation." In *Critical Race Theory: The Key Writings That Formed the Movement*, edited by K. Crenshaw, N. Gotanda, G. Peller, and K. Thomas, 5–20. New York: The New Press.

Bell, D. (2002). *Ethical Ambition.* New York: Bloomsbury.

Bonilla-Silva, E. (2006). *Racism without Racists: Colorblind Racism and the Persistence of Racial Inequality in the United States.* 2nd ed. Lanham, MD: Rowman and Littlefield.

Cooper, C. W., and C. P. Gause. (2007). "Who's Afraid of the Big Bad Wolf? Facing Identity Politics and Resistance When Teaching for Social Justice." In *Keeping the Promise*, edited by D. Carlson and C. P. Gause, 197–216. New York: Peter Lang.

Dantley, M. E. (2005). "African American Spirituality and Cornell West's Notions of Prophetic Pragmatism: Restructuring Educational Leadership in American Urban Schools." *Educational Administration Quarterly* 41: 651–674.

DeCuir, J. T. and A. D. Dixson. (2004). "'So When It Comes Out, They Aren't That Surprised That It Is There': Using Critical Race Theory as a Tool of Analysis of Race and Racism in Education." *Educational Researcher* 33: 26–31.

Douglas, T. M. O. (2012a). "'Border Crossing Brothas': A Study of Black Bermudian Masculinity, Success, and the Role of Community-Based Pedagogical Spaces." Unpublished doctoral dissertation, The University of North Carolina at Greensboro, North Carolina.

Douglas, T. M. O. (2012b). "Resisting Idol Worship at HBCUs: The Malignity of Materialism, Western Masculinity, and Spiritual Malefaction." *The Urban Review* 44 (3): 378–400.

Douglas, T. M. O. and C. M. Peck. (2013). "Education by Any Means Necessary: An Historical Exploration of Community-Based Pedagogical Spaces for Peoples of African Descent." *Educational Studies* 49 (1): 67–91.

Gardiner, M. E. and E. K. Enomoto. (2006). "Urban School Principals and Their Role as Multicultural Leaders." *Urban Education* 41 (6): 560–584.

Giroux, H., and S. Giroux. (2008). "Challenging Neoliberalism's New World Order: The Promise of Critical Pedagogy." In *Handbook of Critical and Indigenous Method-*

ologies, edited by N. Denzin, Y. Lincoln, and L. Tuhiwai Smith, 181–189. Thousand Oaks: Sage.

Harris-Lacewell, M. and Q. T. Mills. (2004). "Truth and Soul: Black Talk in the Barbershop." In *Barbershops, Bibles, and BET*, edited by M. Harris-Lacewell. Princeton, NJ: Princeton University Press.

Howard, T. C. (2010). *Why Race and Culture Matter in Schools: Closing the Achievement Gap in America's Classrooms*. New York: Teachers College Press.

Kantor, H. and B. Brenzel. (1992). "Urban Education and the 'Truly Disadvantaged': The Historical Roots of the Contemporary Crisis, 1945–1990." *Teachers College Record* 94 (2): 278–314.

Khalifa, M. (2012). "A Re-New-Ed Paradigm in Successful Urban School Leadership: Principal as Community Leader." *Educational Administration Quarterly* 48 (3): 424–467.

Ladson-Billings, G. (1998). "Just What Is Critical Race Theory and What's It Doing In a Nice Field like Education?" *International Journal of Qualitative Studies in Education* 11 (1): 7–24.

Lopez, G. (2003). "The (Racially Neutral) Politics of Education: A Critical Race Theory Perspective." *Educational Administration Quarterly* 39 (1): 68–94.

Mills, Q. T. (2006). "Color-Line' Barbers and the Emergence of a Black Counterpublic: A Social and Political History of Black Barbers and Barbershops, 1850–1970." Unpublished doctoral dissertation, University of Chicago, Chicago.

Riehl, C. (2000). "The Principal's Role in Creating Inclusive Schools for Diverse Students: A Review of Normative, Empirical, and Critical Literature on the Practice of Educational Administration." *Review of Educational Research* 70 (1): 55–81.

Solorzano, D. and T. Yosso. (2001). "From Racial Stereotyping and Deficit Discourse Toward a Critical Race Theory in Teacher Education." *Multicultural Education* 9 (1): 2–8.

Theoharis, G. (2007). "Social Justice Educational Leaders and Resistance: Towards a Theory of Social Justice Leadership." *Educational Administration Quarterly* 43 (2): 221–258.

Williams, H. A. (2005). *Self-Taught: African American Education in Slavery and Freedom*. Chapel Hill: University of North Carolina Press.

Williams, P. (1991). *The Alchemy of Race and Fights; The Diary of a Law Professor*. Cambridge, MA: Harvard University Press.

Wilson, C. M., L. Ek, and T. M. O. Douglas. (2013). "Recasting Border Crossing Politics and Pedagogies to Combat Educational Inequity: Experiences, Identities, and Perceptions of Latina/o Youth." *The Urban Review* 46 (1).

CHAPTER 14

Using Social Norming and Ecological Theories and Diversity-Based Strategies for Bullying Interventions in Urban Areas

A Mixed-Methods Research Study

Azadeh F. Osanloo and Jonathan P. Schwartz

INTRODUCTION

Bullying is a prevalent and destructive problem in our schools. Bullying is considered an act where aggressive behavior is used that is "intentional and involves an imbalance of power or strength" (Olweus, 1993, p. 24). Bullying has been identified as the most prevalent form of school violence (Batsche and Porter, 2006). Studies have found that 75 percent of students have been bullied at some point during their school experience and 17 percent to 25 percent of students are bullied regularly (Espelage and Holt, 2001; Nansel et al., 2001). Unfortunately there are long-term outcomes related to bullying behavior including depression and anxiety for the victim (Bond et al., 2008) and future convictions for violent crimes and future drug use for the bullies (Bender and Lösel, 2011; Farrington and Ttofi, 2011).

Although there is increasing attention to bullying in the literature, our understanding of the context of bullying is unclear. A social ecological model of bullying (Bronfenbrenner, 1979) has been commonly applied to bullying prevention, yet each school context is unique. It is important to understand how bullying occurs within each school, family, and community context in order to effectively prevent it. Bullying is often based on perceived differences; however, what frequently is not accounted for in bullying research are issues of diversity. In this chapter proposal aspects of diversity will be discussed in the context of bullying at specific middle-size urban intermediary schools in the Southwest. In addition, the prevalence, grade level, gender, race, and class differences, and correlates with family culture and urban community issues will be discussed.

Over the past five years a resurgence of bullying incidents have permeated print and media news as well as the educational arena. According to Cohn and Can-

tor, bullying is the most common form of violence; 3.7 million youth engage in it, while more than 3.2 million are victims of bullying annually (2003). These bullying incidents and related events resulted in a resounding call to action for educators, clinicians, medical professionals, and policymakers with regards to prevention and intervention as it relates to anti-bullying measures. This call to action was further promulgated by a 2008 study in the *Journal of the American Academy of Pediatrics*, which demonstrated the association between bullying and health problems and concluded that bullying should be considered a significant international public health issue (Gini and Pizzoli, 2009). These educational and public health issues are evidenced by the negative socio-emotional impacts of bullying, which include, but are not limited to, more bullying, retaliation, depression, excessive school absence, dropping out of school, and in some extreme cases, suicide (Boyle, 2005). For example, it is estimated 160,000 students miss school for fear of being attacked or intimidated by other students; it is the main reason students miss school (National Education Association, 2003).

This systemized and reinvigorated bullying pandemic has long-lasting and widespread impacts, which affect multiple stakeholders including students, parents, educators, medical professionals, and the community. It is incumbent upon educators to not only address bullying from a systemic manner but also attend to the needs of both bullies and victims. Indicative of the unparalleled need to address bullying in schools is that over two thirds of students believe that schools respond poorly to bullying. The majority of students believe that adult help is infrequent and ineffective (Cohn and Cantor, 2003).

This research is significant because although there are a plethora of programs designed to prevent and intervene in school bullying (Farrington and Ttofi, 2009), no known program directly focuses on diversity as a target to prevent and intervene in bullying. Moreover, although homophobia/heterosexism has gained attention as a causative factor in bullying (Kimmer and Mahler, 2003), few bullying programs directly intervene to prevent or intervene homophobia, sexism, racism, anti-Semitism, or other discriminatory bullying practices. This is in spite of specific guidance from the U.S. Department of Education's Office of Civil Rights (2011) to have school-wide systemic responses to discriminatory bullying behavior.

Previous research has found that approximately 75–83 percent of gay and lesbian youth reported some form of verbal or physical abuse during because of their sexual orientation (D'Augelli, 2003; Pilkington and D'Augelli, 1995). Additionally, two studies by the American Association of University Women (1993, 2001) found that 81 percent of women reported experiencing some form of sexual harassment at some point during their school experience. Thus there is a need to examine bullying from a diversity-based perspective, in both the reason for and solution to the problem. This study presents preliminary data on the prevalence of diversity-based bullying in the schools and explores the impact and social influence of diversity as it relates to bullying prevention and intervention. Finally, systemic intervention ideas are presented that address diversity-based bullying.

The main objectives of this study were to examine the dynamics of bullying at two large-size Southwestern middle schools. Specifically, we were interested in the role of diversity and student experiences in the understanding of bullying and being bullied. The research questions that guided this work were: How do middle school students at two large middle schools in the urban Southwest understand and experience bullying? And, how are issues of diversity integrated with these student perceptions?

DEFINITION OF BULLYING

For the purposes of this research, the term *bullying* is defined as "the mistreatment of an individual or group characterized by a willful intent to cause harm and a perceived advantage of power. These acts can be socially, emotionally, and physically damaging in nature" (Garrity, Jens, Porter, Sager, and Short-Camilli, 2000).

Moreover, victims can experience acts of bullying physically (for example, hitting, shoving), verbally (for example, name-calling, teasing, threats), and psychologically (for example, public humiliation, shunning, and manipulation) (Garrity et al., 2000; Olweus, 1993). It is important to note, physical bullying peaks in middle school and declines in high school; however, verbal abuse remains constant in secondary education (Cohn and Cantor, 2003). In order to help better understand the student needs, educators need to become aware of the differences between normal conflict and bullying. Students in K–12 schooling will experience normal conflict throughout their education. Normal conflict is when two peers of equal power, who may even be friends, clash or have a one-time disagreement. Often these conflicts are resolved with each person taking responsibility for what happened.

Whereas, the concept of bullying underscores three integral components described as intentional, imbalanced, and repeated. Meaning, the behavior is *intended* to cause harm; there is an *imbalance* of physical or psychological power or strength among the parties, and the behavior occurs *repeatedly* over time (Garrity et al., 2000; Olweus, 1993). Bullying is purposeful and aimed at hurting the other person or to earn (negative) praise from peers. Bullying behavior is exemplified by a power differential between the bully and the person being bullied. This imbalance could be based on physical strength or relational power, such as when someone who is popular uses that popularity to bully someone who is less popular. Finally, bullying is rarely a one-time incident. It occurs repeatedly and is typically targeted toward a "favorite" victim (Garrity et al., 2000; Olweus, 1993).

Lastly, and apropos to this research, bullying can also include racial, religious, ethnic, language, and sexual orientation harassment, or bullying based on difference. For example, a 2001 study reported that 84.6 percent of GLBTQ students heard homophobic remarks from other students *frequently* and 24 percent heard these homophobic remarks at least some of the time from school faculty and staff (GLSEN, 2010).

Data on Diversity and Bullying

To assess the relationship between diversity and bullying, we surveyed two large middle schools in the

Southwest. We gathered descriptive data on issues of perceived safety, bullying experiences, school belongingness, strategies to deal with bullying, and experience with diversity-based bullying. The two middle schools consisted of approximately fourteen hundred children, equal rates of males and females. Overall, both schools had a higher rate of bullying (34 percent) then the national average (15–25 percent). The majority of the children at the two schools were Hispanic (58 percent) followed by white (40 percent) followed by equally small numbers of African Americans, Native Americans, and Asian Americans. *School Site One:* Have you ever witnessed bullying related to: (1) Race/Ethnicity—46.7 percent; (2) Family Income/Wealth—22 percent; (3) Sexual Orientation—31 percent; (4) Appearance—49 percent; (5) Religion—23 percent; (6) Disability—26 percent; and (7) Other—12 percent. *School Site Two:* Have you ever witnessed bullying related to: (1) Race/Ethnicity—37.7 percent; (2) Family Income/Wealth—16.7 percent; (3) Sexual Orientation—24.2 percent; (4) Appearance—40.3 percent; (5) Religion—17.7 percent; (6) Disability—24 percent; and (7) Other—6.3 percent. Although there were notable differences between the two schools, overall this data demonstrates a high rate of witnessing bullying based on perceived differences. The majority of bullying programs that views all types of bullying as the same miss the nuances of power and oppression that led to specific hate crimes laws. There needs to be specific interventions that address diversity-based bullying.

In this same vein, there is currently no federal law that directly addresses bullying, it often overlaps with discriminatory harassment, which is covered under federal civil rights laws enforced by the U.S. Department of Education and Department of Justice. Federal anti-bullying legislation and policy is under works via the Office of Safe and Drug Free Schools. In fact, President Obama held the first-ever anti-bullying conference in 2011. At this event, he stated:

> If there's one goal of this conference, it's to dispel the myth that bullying is just a harmless rite of passage or an inevitable part of growing up. It's not. Bullying can have destructive consequences for our young people. And it's not something we have to accept. As parents and students, as teachers and members of the community, we can take steps—all of us—to help prevent bullying and create a climate in our schools in which all

of our children can feel safe; a climate in which they all can feel like they belong.

The Anti-Defamation League sent the President many recommendations regarding establishing guidelines to address bullying. Three of the seven recommendations, most connected to this research, were: (1) establishing a comprehensive anti-bullying policy for all schools; (2) providing training and technical support for school administrators on anti-bullying programs; and (3) analyzing the impact of bullying on social and emotional health and academic achievement. Obama strongly advocated for a federal anti-bullying policy to ensure effective anti-bullying and cyber bullying programs ("United Effort to Address Bullying," 2011).

Lastly, an interagency collaboration was developed to further conversation and policy initiatives in the area of bullying. The Departments of Education, Health and Human Services, Justice, Defense, Agriculture, and Interior banded to establish the Federal Partners in Bullying Prevention Steering Committee. This steering committee is charged with ways to explore and provide guidance for individuals and organizations in combating bullying ("United Effort to Address Bullying," 2011).

SOCIAL ECOLOGICAL AND SOCIAL NORMING THEORIES

To best understand the interconnectedness of diversity and bullying, it is important to underscore the interplay of social ecological framework and social norming theories. This understanding is grounded in an assets-based approach to promulgating diversity as a community strength as well as source for inclusivity and connectivity.

Social Ecological Framework for Bullying

A number of bullying intervention programs have utilized a social ecological approach to bullying (i.e., Olweus, Limber and Mihalic, 2000; Orpinas and Horne, 2006; Swearer and Espelage, 2004), which provides guidance on addressing bullying as an interaction of the many contexts that children interact in. The ecological system (Bronfenbrenner, 1979) is important for understanding the behavior of both the bully and victim. As we know, behavior is a combination of traits of the person and their environment (school, family, community, and culture).

Bronfenbrenner's Ecological Systems Model

Microsystem: Structures with which the child has direct contact;

Mesosystem: Comprise the interrelations among microsystems, such as peers and family;

Macrosystem: While not being a specific framework, this layer is comprised of cultural values, customs, and laws. The effects of larger principles defined by the macrosystem have a cascading influence throughout the interactions of all other layers.

For example, if it is the belief of the culture that parents should be solely responsible for raising their children, that culture is less likely to provide resources to help parents.

The social-ecological model is ideal for addressing diversity-based bullying. Oppression does not appear in a vacuum and is influenced by each ecological system. Thus the prejudicial and discriminatory beliefs that underlie diversity-based bullying are insidious and difficult to combat. Effective prevention and intervention must target each ecological system.

Social Norming to Better Understand Bullying

While social ecological frameworks have been used in abundance to understand intervention approaches to bullying, the use of social norming theories are much less prevalent in the research. The idea of social norming related to bullying is that students' perceptions of others' bullying behavior and reactions to those behaviors will impact their own behavior. For those who are able to adapt themselves to social norms have better social life management. Those who stay outside of the norm or who cannot muster themselves to conform to the majority are marginalized; the attitudes of the non-marginalized toward the marginalized are essentially negative (Goffman, 1963).

The idea of social norming has been criticized for further isolating the target of the norming campaign (Kim and Shanahan, 2003; Yanovitzky and Stryker, 2001). Although social norming has not been applied to bullying in the literature, this may in fact be an advantage

as literature purports bullying behavior is supported by peers (Olweus, Limber, and Mihalic, 2000; Orpinas and Horne, 2006). In addition to focusing on bullying behavior being "out of the norm," social norming can also encourage joining the majority and intervening when others are being bullied. Social norming works by simply reframing the data that traditionally highlights the minority of students who are engaging in negative or "bad" behavior, and presenting it with a focus on the majority who are not acting in that manner (Haines, 2001). For example, social norming operates on this notion, if the general impression is that most kids do not bully others in school, then those who *do* bully will bully less, and fewer will start bullying in the first place. The key is to not over-report the incidences of dangerous bullying that occur, and to broadly promote the general good health and safety of students so that it is perceived as normal to *not* engage in bullying behavior.

From a diversity-based perspective, social norming can be utilized to create a more nurturing environment. An example of this type of social norming is promoting that the majority of students have friends that are racially/ethnically different from them, which can send the message that racist behavior is unusual and goes against the norms of the school. In addition, social norming can be used to point out that the majority of students celebrate and nurture differences in their friends and classmates.

MIXED-METHODS RESEARCH

Setting and Participants

The setting for this study was a medium-size urban city located in the Southwest of the United States. It is the second largest city in the state and has large white (non-Latino) and Hispanic/Latino populations. Additionally, over 51 percent of the residents in this city are female. The city is cushioned between a large public university and several military bases.

In this particular state, a state senator put forth a senate bill, which requires the public education department to establish guidelines for bullying prevention policies to be promulgated by local school boards. In collaboration with the local school board, every public school should have implemented an anti-bullying program by August 2012.

A total of 1,188 students, in two large middle schools in the Southwest, with relatively equal distributions of sixth, seventh, and eighth graders, and of boys (48.9 percent) and girls (49.1 percent) completed a school-wide questionnaire. Some respondents (0.8 percent) did not indicate their gender. The majority, 66.3 percent, of respondents self-identified as Hispanic/Latino(a)/ Mexican American. The remaining participants self-identified as White/Caucasian (17.5 percent), African American (3.5 percent), Native American (2.9 percent), or Asian (0.8 percent).

Measure and Procedures

A packaged, for-sale, bullying intervention program produced the questionnaire used for this study. The local school district adopted this specific bullying intervention program in accordance with a district-wide anti-bullying initiative. The packaged survey/questionnaire was used; the researchers added a demographic portion in order to further assess student perceptions of bullying in the middle schools of that district. The main questionnaire consists of twenty questions on bullying; the added demographic portions consists of thirteen questions; and there was one open-ended response question also added by the researchers that stated: "In the space below, feel free to write down anything you think teachers, administrators, or parents could do to stop bullying and make your school safer."

Students, from two large middle schools in the district, were given the questionnaire that assessed their experience with bullying, the environment of the school, their family, and their school climate related to bullying and diversity. Students were asked to complete the questionnaire during her or his first period class for the day. The students' teacher read aloud a definition of bullying before he/she asked the students to complete the questionnaire. The definition that was read aloud stated: "Bullying is the mistreatment of an individual or group characterized by a willful intent to cause harm and a perceived advantage in power. These acts can be socially, emotionally, or physically damaging in nature and can include, but are not limited to, teasing, name calling, rumor spreading, exclusion, intimidation, threats, damaging personal property, stealing, public humiliation, stalking, pushing, shoving, or other physical attacks, and sexual, religious, or racial/ethnic ha-

rassment. Any of these acts can also be committed via the Internet, e-mail, telephone, text messages, or other forms of electronic devices and is also considered bullying (known as cyberbullying)."

In addition to the survey, a total of five focus groups were conducted with students— students self-selected to participate in the focus groups. Three focus groups for sixth grade, one for seventh grade, and one for eighth grade were conducted. There were approximately twenty-nine sixth graders, ten seventh graders, and ten eighth graders for a total of forty-nine students who participated in the focus groups. Given the volume of discussion generated, each of the five focus groups was met with three times. The focus groups were led in a semi-structured manner by a facilitator who prompted the students with five questions. The questions that were asked included: (1) What do you think it means to be a bully or be bullied? (2) Why do you think kids in your school bully? (3) How well do you think your principals, teachers, and staff handle bullying at your school? (4) What differences (i.e., racial, religious, appearance, disability, and sexual orientation) do you notice in your school? (5) How accepting are others (students, teachers, and principals) about these differences?

DATA AND FINDINGS

Results from Surveys

Descriptive statistics were gathered on all results. Of all respondents, 33.3 percent reported being bullied in the prior year and 19.2 percent reported being bullied one or more times per week in the prior month. Of all respondents, 25.7 percent reported bullying others in the prior year and reported bullying others one or more times per week in the prior month. Based on respondents' self-reported ethnicity, 40.68 percent of White/ Caucasian, 40 percent of Native American, 39.02 percent of African-American, 30.93 percent of Hispanic/ Latino(a)/Mexican-American, and 20 percent of Asian respondents reported being bullied in the prior year.

Respondents at each school reported witnessing bullying related to specific constructs: appearance, 43 percent; ethnic/racial diversity, 42.3 percent; sexual orientation, 25.6 percent; disability, 25 percent; religion, 21.2 percent; and family income/wealth, 19.3 percent (see figure 14.1). We also found significant difference

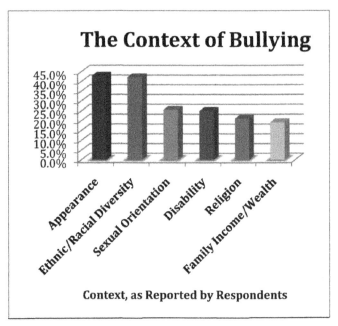

Figure 14.1. *The Context of Bullying*

among grade levels, with bullying decreasing from sixth to seventh to eighth grade with a significant difference in bullying between sixth and eighth grade.

Of all respondents, 12.5 percent reported not fitting in with their school community; of those reporting not fitting in, 54.7 percent reported being bullied. Of all respondents, 34.3 percent reported one or more instances per week of conflict in their home, defined as fighting or arguing. Of the respondents who reported conflict in their home, 36.3 percent reported bullying others.

A series of one-way ANOVAs were conducted using SPSS to analyze the questionnaire results. These ANOVAs examined the significance of a student's ethnicity, the existence of conflict in their home, and their "fit" within their school community in relation to either bullying others or being bullied in their current school setting. Ethnicity, conflict in their home, and "fit" within their school community were used as independent variables. Both bullying others and being bullied by others were used as dependent variables.

A one-way between subjects ANOVA was conducted to compare the effect of ethnicity on bullying others among the adolescent respondents. There was a significant effect of ethnicity on bullying others at the $p < .05$ level for the conditions, $F(6, 1079) = 2.86$, $p = .009$. Given that significant effect, a Tukey HSD post hoc was conducted, which found a significance difference between the respondents' self-reported ethnicity and

bullying of others, within the Hispanic/Latino(a)/Mexican-American and White/Caucasian groups, $p < .025$.

A one-way between subjects ANOVA was conducted to compare the effect of conflict within a student's home on bullying others among the adolescent respondents. There was a significant effect of conflict within a student's home on bullying others at the $p < .05$ level for the conditions, $F(2, 1038) = 4.21$, $p = .015$. Given that significant effect, a Tukey HSD post hoc was conducted finding a significance difference between the bullying and non-bullying students and conflict in the home, $p < .013$.

A one-way between subjects ANOVA was conducted to compare the effect of a student's self-report of "fit" within their school on being bullied among the adolescent respondents. There was a significant effect of a student's self-report of "fit" within their school on being bullied at the $p < .05$ level for the conditions, $F(2, 1126) = 4.60$, $p < .001$. Given that significant effect, a Tukey HSD post hoc was conducted finding a significance difference between the bullied and bullying students who reported that they "fit" within their school and those students who reported that they do not "fit" within their school, $p < .001$.

Given the results of our data, we determined a number of connections between bullying and diversity. The results indicate that there is an overall decrease in instances of bullying, from sixth grade to eighth grade, but we found that eighth-grade students more frequently perceived that bullying is related to ethnic/racial diversity. Additionally, while the ethnic composition of the majority of the sample population is Hispanic/Latino/Mexican-American and the next largest portion is white/Caucasian, the majority of the non-Hispanic/Latino/Mexican-American respondents reported being bullied at higher rates. Given the sum of the results we found, we believe there is some indication that a reasonably greater proportion of bullying in general is related to the larger issues of in-group versus out-group dynamics and not simply ethnic/racial diversity.

We also found indications of other factors that influence both being bullied and being a bully. We identified a relationship between conflict within a student's home and bullying of others, as students who identified one or more instances of fighting or arguing in their home per week were more likely to report bullying others. Further, we found that students who identify as not fitting in at their school are more likely to be bullied, which lends support to Flaspohler et al.'s study (2009), which looked at the impact of bullying on quality of life and well-being.

Additionally, some limitations to this study need to be considered. First, the questionnaire utilized was developed by the school district, and although the researchers revised it, measure of the reliability and validity the questions asked is unknown. Further, due to the fact that the majority of the respondents identified as Hispanic/Latino/Mexican-American and the study was conducted in middle schools in Southwestern United States, the results may not be generalizable.

Future research may want to examine either a more ethnically heterogeneous school setting, as well as a significantly more diverse school setting, in which larger numbers of more ethnicities are present, in order to better understand the intricacies behind students being bullied and identifying that they "fit" in their school environment. Examining elementary and high school students' behavior and experiences as well as their level of "fit" within their school may also add to our understanding of how bullying occurs within different grade and age levels.

Results from Open-Ended Survey Question

Three emergent themes presented from the one open-ended question on the survey. Nearly one-third of the 1,188 students completed the open-ended question. Again, the question asked: In the space below, feel free to write down anything you think teachers, administrators, or parents could do to stop bullying and make your school safer. The three themes were: (1) More Monitoring—Students strongly advocated for more school-based security guards, backpack inspections, metal detectors, drug tests, and hallway cameras; (2) Greater Adult Awareness and Responsibility—Students urged administrators, teachers, and parents to be more attentive, and to keep "better watch," stay "on top of things," and "do something" when they witness bullying as opposed to doing "nothing"; (3) Better and Clear Communication—Students asked for better information and documentation regarding bullying plans, interventions, consequences, reporting systems, and in general conversations aimed at understanding the dynamics of bullying.

Results from Focus Groups

The five focus groups produced a total of fifteen meetings. Four major themes developed from these meetings and over one hundred pages of transcripts. The transcripts were hand-coded for themes. For the purposes of achieving a holistic view of the focus groups, responses were not disaggregated based on middle school, grade, gender, or race. The question that sparked the most conversation was, "why are kids bullied at this school?" The four themes were: (1) Being Different; (2) Bullied Students are Overreacting; (3) Bullying for Fun; and (4) Bullying Starts at Home. Please note: transcripts were not altered for spelling, grammar, or punctuation. Only student names, when mentioned, were withheld.

Being different. When prompted with better understanding *why* bullying occurs at their schools, students responded:

I think it's them being different. I mean, being different isn't like something that is . . . it's not something bad but some people think of it as like the worst thing in the world! Everyone is different—your race, religion, how you look, if you're good at sports or in band, if you're gay or sound gay, if you're in special ed, if you're dad's in jail, if you get good grades. Anything can make you different.

I think that it really can be anything that separates us [students/adolescents]. If you want to be different or if someone wants to make you different than them then they can really choose anything about you to point out that you are different from them.

In elementary school, everyone was a lot more accepting of everyone else. You know, like, even if you were different, they still would include you. But in middle school, as the years progress, it gets more and more of "oh you're different, I don't want to talk to you" and whatever.

Yeah, because it might be you look different, you feel different, you talk different, you're raised different. It's just, everyone is different. You cannot have one person like another.

Take [name withheld], for example. He wears glasses because he's visually impaired. [laughter] And I don't because I have 20/40 vision. That's a flaw in him, that's different. His eyes are jittery, mine aren't. I have brown hair, he has brown hair. He's from a different race. And I'm from a different race. You can just point out so much but we're actually 99 percent alike.

I think there is a change at million dollars school because he will men tear we only have one class to is he see the sometime people everyday, in middle school we see more yeah we see a loft different people so, you know like it's just different I don't know.

There's so many different people, they're all so different. And you'd never expect them to be friends because the tallest kid in the sixth grade is like my best friend. And I have a friend, he's . . . he's finds his roots in Asia, he's Asian and Native American and there's just no prejudice at all. I don't want to be prejudice.

And . . . it's your . . . like . . . um . . . if there are a bunch much different things and everybody likes a different thing then everybody can have what he they want and nobody tells is going the care because they're like "okay, you have what you want, I have what I want, and we're good."

Say a new person comes, he's not exactly like you, he does some things different, he even collects insects, for some reason. And they just call you a nerd, or [inaudible], something like that, to make them feel good about themselves because they probably have something that they do that they don't like about themselves.

Bullied students are overreacting. Students did not always recognize potential bullying behavior as the result of the bully/victim relationship. Instead, students remarked openly that sometimes students who were being "bullied" were just in fact overreacting.

Ok, well, this isn't really on topic but I thought I should probably bring it up before, like, the end. It was on last week's topic, how people deal with it. I was saying that I don't think people really deal with it well. But then some kid was like, it wasn't really even bullying, it was kind playing around, but he got in big trouble just cause that kid took offense.

Choose your words with certain people. I know a certain person and if you, like, say something that like normally if I said to one of my other friends, they would just like laugh. But he'd be hurt and it's just that person's mental structure. And yeah if they're sensitive, you don't say that stuff.

Because you're not intending to hurt them, but it's hurting them. And if I said that to one of my friends, like "hey, that's stupid, man" when I'm playing a video game. He might be hurt, like, because he's very sensitive. And . . . but . . . yet my other friends might just laugh, you know, because it's just how they are.

Bullying for fun. Many students commented on the nonsense nature of bullying. That bullying happened because it was "fun" for some kids, while others wanted to maintain that "it" factor in junior high school.

I think people kind of want to bully just because sometimes they think it's fun. Like, I really, really love to read, like I've got four books right now, so I'm always sitting and reading or walking around reading and reading during lunch and sometimes when I'm sitting outside people will like throw the balls over my head and try to like get me . . . to see if I'll notice.

He is a bully for no reason. They just want to get to your head tell you that you're stupid the tell you that you look stupid and that you talk weird, that you walk weird, stuff like that.

I have a friend that was picked on and, I tried the him with it and I noticed one time when it was like maybe a month ago and I confront had the person who did it I told them that's not right you don't do that just because he's different from you don't have to be mean. He didn't look like he felt anything, just looked like he thought it was funny.

Bullying is like a business. A fun business.

Because if you wants to be like noticed like being popular you wanted to think that make someone else think that you're a creep like bullying you might wanted to that because it makes other people think oh hey look at how cool that person is.

Bullying starts at home. Many students drew parallels between home life, school life, and bullying. The juxtapositions were clear, poignant, and powerful. Most students who commented on this theme recognized that negative experiences at home can, and in fact may, translate to bullying behavior at school.

I think it starts at home mostly because maybe they're getting though don't get what they want at home or look maybe their parents aren't there for them and some people their parents are always there so they might make fun because there parent are always there able they feel bad.

Mostly, they feel that . . . mostly . . . at home they're treated not as well as they hope. So, at school they treat people not as well, either, to make themselves feel better.

I that it starts when people the talk about like how happy their families are because not every family is a happy family. The rest was us don't have that family life. Then it makes it harder for us to actually realize that. We then we get those feelings that we don't want.

I think bullying is basically they don't have any power at home, any say, anything any choices of their own, so here they have less restrictions than they do at home so they try abusing the power.

I'm going said I'm not a bully I don't think I am. I may tell somebody something every once in a while but doesn't make me a bully, I don't do it ever single day or the whole school year. But yes, I do not have a say at home. Yell at any stepdad mostly ever single day of my life. And sometimes I really just want to ignore everybody and do what I want but, no . . . my stepdad always has the last word and always has to tell me something to get me to do something. He tells me ever single day when he tells petition all this crap that I don't like and I just I'm not a bully I didn't turn out to be a bully. And I don't like the way that he gets into any mom's head and he tells her stuff that's wrong and he lies about our arguments, stuff like that.

Think it's basically because they want someone to feel how they feel. If they have a happy family life they want you to feel like they feel at home. And if they are being abused or if they're being mistreated then they want to another person to feel what it's like to be angry and frustrated and scared.

Also like self control because I don't think anybody really has the perfect sometimes families done get along they're in the perfect and I think what it is being able the control yourself instead of taking the out on is others. Like, being able the talk to your family about it what you don't feel is going on really well in the family.

RECOMMENDATIONS

These recommendations have been categorized into six different, yet interconnected, areas. These six categories highlight the inherent connectivity of these actions items and demonstrate that a comprehensive holistic approach is needed to successfully address bullying on a middle school campus.

1. *Structural school approaches are needed.* School-wide measures focus on the ongoing training of the entire school staff, which may include a coordinating committee whose work drives the anti-bullying program in the school. It is important to have student input and involvement on any anti-bullying committees or task forces that are developed. These groups should not be devoid of student participation. Moreover, school rules against bullying are posted throughout the school and students are surveyed yearly. Within this strat-

egy, it is imperative to establish clear, anonymous reporting systems as well as coherent and student-centered anti-bullying policies. Also, important is the identification of bullying "hotspots" in the school and to ensure those areas are consistently monitored for safety during passing periods. Overall, the goal is to create an inclusive, safe climate of belonging for everyone.

2. *Student education is needed.* It is important for students to understand the dynamics of bullying to be active participants in preventing it. From a diversity perspective, students should understand the seriousness and prevalence of hate-based bullying. Hate-based bullying is bullying targeted at a marginalized and oppressed population. Not only should schools treat this type of bullying differently, students should be aware of the seriousness of hate-based bullying and be prepared to take action to prevent it. Understanding the dynamics of hate-based bullying goes hand in hand with general education about diversity and the dynamics of discrimination. In general, students need to have a general knowledge of bullying, including the roles of bully and the victim. It is particularly important for students to understand the power dynamic inherent in bullying and how to differentiate between bullying and normal peer conflict. Students should be educated on the best way to intervene in a bullying situation, the ways to solicit help from school personnel, and how generally to discourage bullying. Finally, students need to be well versed on school policy related to bullying. They should expect follow-up meetings with the student who is bullied and the student who is bullying. Furthermore, students should understand how to view the school as an ally in stopping bullying and how to utilize school resources. Students should understand that they can (and should) be active in stopping bullying at their school.

3. *Administrators need transparent strategies.* First and foremost, school administrators need to conduct a bullying needs assessment of the school. This will also help uncover and examine the unique ecological climate of the school. From the needs assessment, administrators will be able to identify the unique challenges and strengths (i.e., diverse demographics, influential security personnel,

and highly involved parents) of the school, which will then highlight the potentially most effective approaches to disciplining bullies at her or his particular school. Once the needs assessment and ecological mapping are completed, administrators can spearhead a bullying intervention plan for the school. It is of the utmost importance that the school leader (1) supports teachers, counselors, and staff in their anti-bullying measures, (2) communicates with parents regarding bullying procedures, policies, and consequences, (3) communicates seriousness of policy to students, and (4) addresses all incidences of bullying at her or his school. Most important, the administrator must be the role model for the school.

4. *Teacher training is a nonnegotiable.* In the teacher's classroom anti-bullying measures should include follow-up discussions, class meetings, curriculum conversations, and enforcement of school rules against bullying. Dose and intensity of teacher training is important as well. Teachers must be trained in anti-bullying initiatives and policies consistently with major themes being addressed. Additionally, teachers should respond to any bullying incident that you witness and use the incidents as a possible "teachable moment." Teachers should never ignore a student who reports being victimized by peers and should not let the peer group "off the hook" that is doing the bullying. Moreover, as teachers often know her or his student on a more personal level than say the school administrators, it is important the teacher recognizes both the bully and victim as unique individuals. This means that teachers should not adopt a one-size-fits-all model for intervening in school bullying, whether it is to help the student who is being bullied or to address the bully's consequences. Lastly, and much like the recommendation offered school administrators, teachers must set an example with her or his own behavior.

5. *Family and community involvement is a key to success.* Integrate a prevention program that helps guide the school's response to bullying that is clear for all families. This may mean having literature that is in multiple languages. Consider allowing for parental involvement with the creation, maintenance, and dissemination of the school's anti-bullying policies. Parental involvement could come in the form of comprehensive PTA strategies as well as discussion that explores the safe home/safe school connection for parents. And as always, parents need to know that they are the best role models for their children. Community interest and involvement can be gauged by assessing the strengths and needs of your community as it relates to anti-bullying measures. For example, do store owners and proprietors know of any community bullying "hotspots"? How can these businesses become involved with issues of bullying? Community participation constitutes the involvement of local government, law enforcement, community agencies, faith-based organizations, media, and other community partners who may provide valuable time, resources, and information toward the success of the program. Spreading the anti-bullying message outside the walls of the school is an essential component. In this particular Southwest community, school sporting events are very popular. So, one strategy might be to spread anti-bullying messages and hand out anti-bullying flyers (with anti-bullying policy information) at school sporting events. This way, the conversation about this topic is being addressed in an informal manner and brought to family and community members on their terms.

6. *Capacity building in the area of diversity must happen.* As the data and the previous research demonstrates, building diversity skills is essential to better understand bullying behavior. Every school has a unique ecological context, thus the diversity climate of every school will also be unique. To prevent hate-based bullying, it is vital to address the diversity climate at each school. This can be conceptualized as a box of "normal" behavior, with any behavior that strays outside of the box becoming a target for bullying. Strategies for increasing the size of that "box" must be tailored to the school diversity climate. Some strategies for increasing diversity awareness and positively engaging with difference for students, teachers, and school administrators include, but are not limited to, holding diversity assemblies, adopting cultural sharing circles, hiring and training in social justice and multicultural leadership, programs designed

to promote ethnic identity, engaging in a school-wide "I Am From" writing project, and conducting a diversity audit of the school.

FINAL THOUGHTS

In general, a collaborative systemic approach is needed to combat middle school bullying. Each school is unique and has a specific context that bullying happens within. This includes a wide range of activities mentioned above including, but not limited to, developing strategies for understanding ecological systems impacts, ecological mapping, teacher training, family involvement, student engagement, and comprehensive community approaches. Hate-based bullying must be indentified and addressed as a unique and deleterious type of bullying. The response must be system wide to prevent and address hate-based bullying as it happens. Since discriminations and stereotypes do not happen in a vacuum, it is important to collaborate with all ecological contexts to prevent the impact of prejudice. In addition, students should be active participants in creating a safe nurturing environment at their school.

REFERENCES

American Association of University Women Educational Foundation. (1993). *Hostile Hallways: The AAUW survey on sexual harassment in America's schools* (No. 923012). Washington, DC: Harris/Scholastic Research.

American Association of University Women Educational Foundation. (2001). *Hostile Hallways: The AAUW survey on sexual harassment in America's schools*. Washington, DC: Harris/Scholastic Research.

Batsche, G. M. and Porter, L. J. (2006). Bullying. In G. G. Bear, K. M. Minke (Eds.), *Children's needs III: Development, prevention, and intervention* (pp. 135–148). Washington, DC: National Association of School Psychologists.

Bender, D. and Lösel, F. (2011). Bullying at school as a predictor of delinquency, violence, and other antisocial behaviour in adulthood. *Criminal Behaviour and Mental Health, 21*(2), 99–106.doi:10.1002/cbm.799.

Boyle, D. J. (2005). Youth Bullying: Incidence, Impact, and Interventions. *Journal of the New Jersey Psychological Association, 55*(3), 22–24.

Bronfenbrenner, U. (1979). *The ecology of human development*. Cambridge, MA: Harvard University Press.

Cohn, A. and Canter, A. (2003). Bullying: What schools and parents can do. (National Association of School Psychologists Fact Sheet). Retrieved February 22, 2005, from www.guidancechannel.com/default.aspx?M=aandindex=508andcat=50.

D'Augelli, A. R. (2003). Mental health problems among lesbian, gay and bisexual youth ages 14 to 21. *Clinical Child Psychiatry and Psychiatry, 7*, 1359–1045.

Espelage, D. L. and Holt, M. K. (2001). Bullying and Victimization During Early Adolescence: Peer Influences and Psychosocial Correlates. *Journal of Emotional Abuse, 2*(2/3), 123–142.

Farrington, D. P. and Ttofi, M. M. (2011). Bullying as a predictor of offending, violence and later life outcomes. *Criminal Behaviour and Mental Health, 21*(2), 90–98. doi:10.1002/cbm.801.

Flaspohler, P. D., Elfstrom, J. L., Vanderzee, K. L., Sink, H. E., and Birchmeier, Z. (2009). Stand by me: The effects of peer and teacher support in mitigating the impact of bullying on quality of life. *Psychology in the Schools, 46*(7), 636–649.

Garrity, C., Jens, K., Porter, W., Sager, N., and Short-Camilli, C. (2000). *Bully-Proofing Your School: A Comprehensive Approach for Elementary Schools*. Second edition. Longmont, CO: Sopris West.

Gay, Lesbian, and Straight Education Network (GLSEN). (2010). 2009 National School Climate Survey: Nearly 9 out of 10 LGBT Students Experience Harassment in School. Retrieved from www.glsen.org/cgi-bin/iowa/all/news/record/2624.html.

Hoover, J. H., Oliver, R. L., and Hazler, R. J. (1992). Bullying: perceptions of adolescent victims in the Midwestern USA. *School Psychology International 13*, 5–16.

Kim, S. H. and Shanahan, J. (2003). Stigmatizing smokers: Public sentiment toward cigarette smoking and its relationship to smoking behaviors. *Journal of Health Communication, 8*, 343–367.

Kimmel, M. S. and Mahler, M. (2003). Adolescent masculinity, homophobia, and violence. *American Behavioral Scientist, 465*, 1439–1458.

Nansel, T. R., Overpeck, M., Pilla, R. S., Ruan, W., Simons-Morton, B., and Scheidt, P. (2001). Bullying behaviors among US youth: Prevalence and association with psychosocial adjustment. *JAMA: Journal of the American Medical Association, 285*(16), 2094–2100. doi:10.1001/jama.285.16.2094.

National Education Association (2003). Parents' role in bullying: Prevention and intervention, What can parents do when a child complains of being bullied. Retrieved from www.nea.org/schoolsafety/bullying.html.

Olweus, D. (1993). *Bullying at School: What We Know and What We Can Do.* Cambridge, MA: Blackwell Publishers, Inc.

Olweus, D., Limber, S., and Mihalic, S. (1999). *Blueprints for Violence Prevention, Book Nine: Bullying Prevention Program.* Boulder, CO: Center for the Study and Prevention of Violence.

Orpinas, P. and Horne, A. M. (2006). *Bullying prevention: Creating a positive school climate and developing social competence.* Washington, DC: American Psychological Association.

Pilkington, N. W. and D' Augelli, A. R. (1995). Victimization of lesbian, gay, and bisexual youth in community settings. *Journal of Community Psychology, 23,* 34–56.

President and First Lady call for a united effort to address bullying. 2011. Retrieved from, www.whitehouse.gov/the-press-office/2011/03/10/president-and-first-lady-call-united-effort-address-bullying.

Swearer, S. M. and Espelage, D. L. (2004). Introduction: A social-ecological framework of bullying among youth. In D. L. Espalage and S. M. Swearer (Eds.), *Bullying in American schools: A social-ecological perspective on prevention and intervention* (pp. 1–12). Mahwah, NJ: Erlbaum.

Yanovitzky, I. and Stryker, J. (2001). Mass media, social norms, and health promotion efforts: A longitudinal study of media effects on youth binge drinking. *Communication Research, 28,* 208–239.

CHAPTER 15

Toward Community-Centric Educational Leadership in Addressing the School Discipline Disparity

Jacqueline Roebuck Sakho, Ronald W. Whitaker II, and Rodney Hopson

CHAPTER BACKGROUND AND PURPOSE

This chapter embraces Noblit and Pink's (2007) notions of urban education as a complex and complicated concept and that simplistic understandings and definitions about urban schooling and education deserve unpacking and critique. For instance, defining urban education limited by geographical, political, and socioeconomic realities or by mainstream discourses oftentimes neglects interactions and intersections that promote practices to support urban education, school, and community leaders. We are proposing a response to the persistent call for educational leadership to be community work, to be community-engaged as community-centric leadership in order to provide "site-specific" examples of problems of practice in urban school settings. We are also purposing that urban educational leaders as scholars in practice adopt a social justice identity that (1) "links the struggle for education with the struggle for social justice" and (2) demonstrates "nuances that embrace cultural and racial realities in the context of the larger social and political milieu" (Hopson et al, 2010, pp. 782, 783). Urban educational leaders' toolbox enriched with practices of teaching and learning must also include strategies to navigate and negotiate spatial, institutional, and knowledge politics as well as translating research into practice that can be absorbed and utilized effectively. Lipman (2011) in the main title of her book, *The New Political Economy of Urban Education*, describes the climate of urban education, as a climate that "situates urban education in the social, economic, political, and cultural contexts shaping the city" (p. 15).

In addressing and framing the notions of interest convergence, urban school leaders are placed in inviolable positions where race theories and historical discussions around inequities are front and center. Typically, the work of educational leaders, as Berliner (2006) and Anyon (1997, 2005a, 2005b) understand, requires a more nuanced understanding of theories, perspectives, and practices to respond to challenging conditions in the United States. However, as we authors understand in the challenging work of urban education and school leaders of the twenty-first century, even narrow and bounded conceptualizations of educational leadership are part of the problem which tend to be limited within school walls and carry with it uncritical displays of notions of being transformative, participative, collaborative, distributive, and liberatory.

This chapter problematizes urban education and schooling and the type of leader that seeks to address the myriad of challenges and interest convergences faced in the context of schools, communities, and higher education institutions. We demonstrate the challenges of urban educational leadership as (a) the urban politics of space and place; (b) public pedagogy of deficit thinking paradigms; and (c) the impact of the knowledge-practice gap in educational leadership through the example of systemic, racialized disciplinary practices in schools, including how the aforementioned intersect with matters pertaining to CRT and interest convergence in particular. We do so by illustrating the data, literature, and lived experience through a chronicle as a critical race methodology.

We are rendering an account of the problem of racially inequitable discipline practices as a system of individuals, processes, and procedures nested within the broader system of urban education. A system governed as an educational enterprise, a structure that is heavily influenced and bond to the performance of race, producing and reproducing actions of racism. We borrow

Solorzano's education-centered critical race framework to illustrate how the urban education system is heavily influenced by race performances and reproduces racist actions, built on five core elements: (1) the centrality of race and racism and their intersectionality with other forms of subordination in education; (2) the challenge to dominate ideology around school failure; (3) the commitment to social justice in education; (4) the centrality of experiential knowledge; and (5) the transdiciplinary perspective (Solorzano, 1997; Stovall, 2010).

A GRAVE MATTER: DISCIPLINE DISPARITY 1972–2010

It appears that the organization of education has a problem. A grave research-practice gap is contributing to racialized discipline practices occurring in PreK–12 schools nationally. Despite both literature and empirical studies within the education organization and across disciplines identifying the potentiality of racial disparity and disproportionality impacting African-American students (Gregory, Skiba, and Noguera, 2010; Losen, 2011; Losen and Gillespie, 2012; Losen and Skiba, 2010) along with recommendation to adjust policy and

practice, African-American students continue to outperform their white peers in out-of-school suspensions.

Figure 15.1 (Losen, 2011) below demonstrates a steady increase of the out-of-school suspensions as a discipline practice that appears to impact African-American students at a greater propensity and steady rate compared to their peers (Losen, 2011). Since the 1972–1973 school year African-American students as a group continue to outperform their peers in exclusionary discipline practices, representing 6 percent of the data and double their white peers during the 1972–1973 school year increasing to 15 percent in the 2006–2007 school year and three times the rate of their white peers (Losen, 2011).

EDUCATIONAL LEADERSHIP, DISCIPLINE PRACTICES, AND THE RESEARCH-PRACTICE GAP

Equally problematic is the practice of educational leadership impacting exclusionary discipline practices (Bireda, 2010; Children's Defense Fund, 1975; Losen, 2011; Losen and Skiba, 2010; Skiba, et al., 2011); however, the scholarship is not robust and requires further examination.

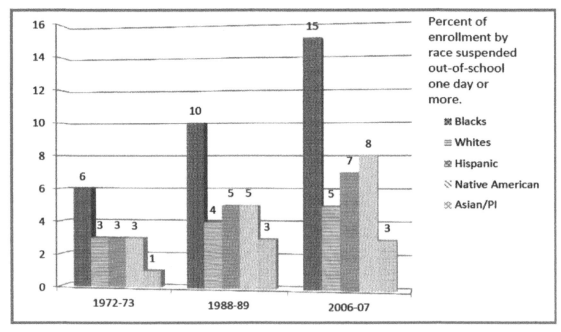

Figure 15.1. *Out-of-school Suspensions*

With vast amounts of research around racial impact on exclusionary practices and the consistent finding, I believe that the knowledge-practice gap in the organization of education is a substantial barrier. (Ball, 2012, p. 285)

On the ground, we still learn that educators look to meritocracy, deficit thinking paradigms, and low SES as primary and key drivers of racially inequitable discipline practices. Research as politics and as public pedagogy are added dimensions to the knowledge-practice gap in education. Viewing the problem from this vantage point offers a different reveal on why forty years of knowing that the potentiality of students' civil rights being violated through inequitable practices might not be enough; Robinson argues,

Narrowing the research-practice gap is not just a matter of disseminating research more effectively, or of using more powerful influence strategies. Such approaches assume that our research does speak to practice, if only the right people would listen. By taking a methodological perspective, I am making the more radical claim that research may be ignored regardless of how skillfully it is communicated . . . while researchers' criticisms may be grounded in numerous high-quality studies, such research may still be declared irrelevant if it ignores the factors that convince those who control the practice of the continuing value of the activity. (Robinson, 1998, p. 17)

Robinson unearths what we understand as the politics of place and the power of public pedagogy as influential interests of the dominant culture as significant drivers informing problems of practices unfolding in urban school settings. Stovall (2010, p. 410) describes "politics of place" as those "site-specific policies" acting as influencers both outside and inside the traditional school setting that raise voice in powerful ways that are interfering and interrupting the liberatory efforts of "community-engaged" research scholars (p. 410).

Although urban educational leaders understand the need to provide more critical educational leadership research (Giroux, 1992; Riehl and Firestone, 2005), there is a dearth of information about what educational leaders know and the ways in which they are making

sense of this phenomenon. The literature is very limited on the ways in which educational leadership is involved with the disparity crisis of discipline practices in schools nationally as an example. Additionally, the practice of educational leadership is not robust and requires further examination on how educational leaders can impact the disparity of discipline practices (Bireda, 2010; Children's Defense Fund, 1975; Skiba et al., 2011). Losen (2011) provides the following observation on the research around education leaders and disparate discipline practices:

Other kinds of research also suggest that suspensions are significantly influenced by factors other than student misbehavior. For example, researchers have concluded, after controlling for race and poverty that the attitude of a school's principal toward the use of suspension correlated highly with its use. Principals who believed frequent punishments helped improve behavior and those who tended to blame behavioral problems on poor parenting and poverty also tended to suspend more students than those principals who strongly believed in enforcing school rules but who regarded suspension as a measure to be used sparingly. This evidence suggests that factors other than student behavior (in this case, principals' beliefs) can influence suspension and expulsion rates. (p. 8)

Knowledge-practice gaps exist in educational leadership in the context of how race and racism are involved with how disciplinary practices are enacted, and research has demonstrated a correlative effect of education leaders' beliefs around exclusionary discipline practices and the rate of use for the practice. Skiba and colleagues (2011) identify race and ethnic differentials in disciplinary treatment of both "selection at the classroom level and processing at the administrative level" (p. 88) that contributes significantly to disproportionate racial disparity in discipline practices. Gregory and colleagues (2010) report, "no studies have been conducted on the implicit bias of teachers and how race may activate stereotypes" (p. 63). However, the research still indicates that we might not know enough about race in general and both as a factor in exclusionary discipline practices are informing the inequity of the practice (Skiba, Arrendondo, and Karega Rausch, 2014).

Skiba and colleagues (2002) raised awareness around the role of K–12 education leaders in disciplinary practices. The authors demonstrated in the study that African-American students were disproportionately referred for subjective violations—"disrespect" and "perceived threat"—resulting in a higher rate of suspensions, while white students were referred for objective violations—smoking, vandalism, and leaving school without permission (Skiba et al., 2002). This study concluded that the racial discipline disparity observed was due in large part to disproportionate discipline referrals of African-American students by school administration. The agenda of this project seeks to understand the role and preparation of education leadership in the context of discipline practices to inform learning in the field.

THE TIES THAT BIND: RACE, EDUCATION, AND DEFICIT THINKING

Our entire field was resting on a deficit paradigm that makes it difficult to uncouple the work we want to do from the centuries of work handed down from ideological positions that emerged from constitutive disciplines that insist on the inferiority of entire groups of people. (Ladson-Billings, 2012, pp. 117–118)

Ladson-Billings highlighting key historical observations in her 2012 American Educational Research Association annual *Brown v. Board of Education* lecture further solidifies the link between the organization of education and race, noting key social science scholarship and practices as drivers of contemporary inequitable practices in education settings. She names three key theoretical frameworks that have informed and influenced the organization of education and established a foundation to build a bond relationship between race and education. These frameworks are:

- The rise of Eugenics, establishing a conceived genetic inferiority based on race and ethnicity, Ladson-Billings quotes a Eugenics definition by Galton (1883), "Eugenics is the study of the agencies under social control that seek to improve or impair the racial qualities of future generations

either physically or mentally" (Ladson-Billings, 2012, p. 116);
- The development of the Stanford-Binet Intelligence test, a social assessment system for education or "a stratifying practice for providing or denying access to resources" (ibid), in this case a higher quality of education for students in the "gifted and talented" program and;
- The field of anthropology, key scholarship that "is so heavily implicated in forming our ideas and thinking about race . . . in the formation of race as a worldview," scholarship creating pseudoscientific classification for race and legitimizing systemic structures of inequity had become so heavily engrained and woven into belief systems that the American Anthropological Association launched a $4 million re-education campaign "debunking prevailing thinking about race" (p. 117).

Ladson-Billings (2012) specifically maps an observation of how racialized scholarship in social science disciplines have both influenced and informed education practice. Beginning with establishing the "social death" (Patterson, 1982) of the enslaved as a method to desensitize social worthiness then, criminalizing the act of education for enslaved children and finally, manipulating social science "product[s] of scientific investigation" (p. 117) to both legitimize and substantiate a permanent deficit space, a place to permanently locate the "othered" (Kumashiro, 2000; Ogbu, 1978; Valencia, 2010). A place and space fostered by "public pedagogy," defined by the editors of *The Handbook of Public Pedagogy: Education and Learning Beyond Schooling* as "spaces, sites, and languages of education and learning that exist outside of the walls of the institution of schools" (Sandlin, Schultz, and Burdick, 2010, p. 1). A place and space that is nested within inequitable structures of power and where education serves as the vehicle to produce, reproduce and legitimize inequity.

Ladson-Billings (2012), Valencia (1997, 2010), and others, demonstrate how systemic inequity becomes legitimated in education through research that is anchored on historical conditions and public pedagogies (Giroux et al., 1996; Sandlin, Schultz, and Burdick, 2010; Stovall, 2010; Zamudio et al., 2011). Ladson-

Billings (2012) informs that "[e]ducation research borrows psychology's notions of normal and exceptional individuals, sociology's notions of normal and exceptional groups such as families and communities, as well as institutions' and anthropology's notions of normal and exceptional cultures with implicit beliefs about the classification and ranking of cultural groups" (2012, p. 117). These historical conditions lay a sturdy foundation for building the deficit-thinking paradigm and further, by a strong argument of low socioeconomic status become the genuine culprit for inequitable educational practices and thus, explaining away the need or possibility of improvement.

The deficit-thinking paradigm can be understood as a process that explains away systemic inequity and gives credence and support to a "structure of hierarchy and inequality" (p. 117) in the organization of education.

CRITICAL RACE METHODOLOGY

Critical race theory (CRT) was born out of the struggle and agitation experienced by Derrick Bell and others at how slowly racial reform was unfolding during the 1970s. After great diligence and the legal achievement of moral rightness, Bell did not witness a swift generation of remedies to accompany the hard-won rights of the Civil Rights Movement (Ladson-Billings, 1998). Bell and his colleagues grew weary in regard to the expected impact of traditional civil rights strategies and legal approaches of "filing amicus briefs, conducting protests and marches, and appealing to the moral sensibilities of decent citizens" (Ladson-Billings, 1998, p. 10). Therefore, CRT has roots in a personal liberation cycle for Bell and a systemic liberation cycle of the critical legal studies movement. Both journeys sought to create new ways of critically thinking about and examining law that incorporates the impact of social and cultural narratives of individuals and groups. Specifically, critical race theory examines how racialized legal and social structures re-create and legitimate structural and systemic networks of power.

Utilizing CRT as a framework to analyze inequities in the organization of education was introduced in Ladson-Billings and Tate's (1995) work. The authors argue that because race and racism are interwoven in our societal belief system and thus normalizes dominant and subordinate communities, it is a safe assertion that racism is systemically embedded in the educational system. Gloria Ladson-Billings warns in the annual *Brown* lecture in Education Research that "[u]ntil we begin to carefully examine the way race and racialized thinking influence our work, we will continue to perpetuate destructive thinking about the capabilities of learners based on race" (Ladson-Billings, 2012, p. 115).

Critical race theory transcends disciplinary boundaries (B. Delgado, 1998; R. Delgado, 1989; Duncan, 2005; Solorzano and Yosso, 2002; Zamudio et al., 2011) to both understand that these systems are nested within a greater historical impact and to examine the historical impact of racism on these systems.

Examining racially inequitable discipline practices as a system then, like other systems it operates through implementing processes that are influenced by beliefs, policies, procedures, and practices and negatively impacts students and increasing their exposure to high risk factors. Within the system of urban education, there exists a problem of discipline practice as suspensions and expulsions, a practice that over the last forty years is found to produce racially inequitable outcomes. With that notion in mind, what is the system of discipline practices in urban schools designed to produce? And in what other systems is the system of discipline practices in urban school settings nested and how are those systems influencing and/or informing the inequity of the practice? How are urban educational leaders, both internal and external of the school settings, involved with the ways in which racially inequitable discipline practices are enacted? Finally, how might we bridge improvement specifically for this problem and broadly for urban educational leadership?

An invaluable asset of CRT is the recognition and authentication of the lived experiences of marginalized people as counter narratives. By centering their narratives as critical to developing a holistic ontology or deep understanding of how racialized policy and practices impact their situatedness within dominant and subordinate dimensions of power.

Solórzano and Yosso (2002) define critical race methodology as a theoretically grounded approach to research that . . . "uses the interdisciplinary knowledge base of ethnic studies, women's studies, sociology, history, humanities, and the law to better understand the experience of students of color" (p. 24). In this work, critical race research methodology translates research and data, and combines tacit theory or the lived experience of the practitioners with the art and imagination of storytelling to create counter-narratives as pedagogy. Creating counter-narratives as research methodologies to unearth and expose the ties that bind problems in education with notions of race and actions of racism is a way to unravel the rope by exposing data, and meta/grand narratives "majoritarian stories" (Solorano and Yosso, 2002, p. 28) that formulate and create theories that reproduce and produce inequity in practice. Such stories are deeply embedded in practices in ways that by simply examining and analyzing data sets and surface narratives could not be unearthed.

Zamudio et al. (2011) and colleagues explain critical race methodology this way, as a research process that utilizes counter narration to focus the scope of the examination on "who is telling which stories in what way, from what theoretical lens are they being explained and for what purpose are they being told" (p. 117).

Narratives and storytelling are qualitative tools utilized within critical race theory. Counter-narration, the telling of stories that "can open new windows into reality, showing us that there are possibilities for life (Delgado, 1989). Delgado shares how counterstories have the capacity to "enrich imagination and teach that by combining elements from story and current reality, we may construct a new world richer and either alone" (Delgado, 1989). Counter narratives serve as a process of critical analysis that is more than gaining a deeper understanding but more so exposing, unsettling, disrupting what has been sanctioned as the norm (Giroux et al., 1996; Solorzano and Yosso, 2002; Zamudio et al., 2011).

The counter-narrative as a methodology utilizes literature, historical context, data, and tacit knowledge through storytelling as a way to produce the human side of change necessary to document and thus create sustainable transformative change systemically and structurally (Delgado, 1989; Duncan, 2005; Ladson-Billings, 2012; Solorzano and Yosso, 2002; Zamudio, et al., 2011).

URBAN EDUCATIONAL LEADERS AND THE WAR OF NARRATIVES

A primary way individuals make sense of experiences is by casting it in narrative form (Kohler Riessman, 2002, p. 220).

Counter narratives are important for the way they help counteract stereotypes and expose the contingent nature of presumed universal truths. (Bridgeman, 2011, p. 145)

The above quotes are guideposts that lead to the purpose of utilizing the chronicle of Coach TJ to critically examine racialized discipline practices in schools and also to identify the processes within the system of discipline practices that are not contributing to equitable education opportunities for all students. We understand that storytelling as a design thinking process leads to strategic story making, an organic continuous process of designing, assessing, implementing, and evaluating simultaneously through a process of modeling tangible actions that assist education leaders.

What follows is a critical race chronicle, a fictitious account based on reality, constructed utilizing counter-methodology (Solorzano and Yosso, 2002). The chronicle serves to translate current research and data along with combining tacit theory and lived experience as a practitioner into the art and imagination of storytelling and story making (Guajardo and Guajardo, 2010) or the counterstory. The Chronicle of Coach TJ is the illustration of critical performative counterstory (Denzin, 2010) to demonstrate our desire for readers to go deeper than the data and normative practices, tying the public narrative, the historical narrative, and personal narrative together as a means to critically interrogate lived experiences and sense-making.

The Chronicle of Coach TJ and the War of the Narratives

Coach TJ's doctoral cohort has been invited by the Antebellum School District to assist with developing a strategic plan to address discipline practices flagged by the State with a high racial disparity ratio. Thomas Jefferson Accelerated Academy Middle School suspended 200 students in the month of February of 2012. The

Professor gives background on the problem and some information on key committee members.

The Professor: The Superintendent has asked our co-hort to partner with the Districts' school-turn-around Taskforce assembled as a requirement of a lawsuit which found that district violated the civil rights of students through racially inequitable discipline practices. In both the federal Annual Yearly Progress (AYP) report and the state Academic Excellence Indicator System (AEIS), Antebellum School District was among the top three school districts in the state with the highest rate of African-American students suspended and/or expelled in the previous school year. Thomas Jefferson K–8 Academy last school year in the month of February the rate of suspensions/expulsions for African-American students was three times the total number of African-American students enrolled in the district. The State is requiring an investigate of the discipline practices for potential Civil Rights violations. While ASD as a whole is being monitored by DOE Office of Civil Rights, Antebellum Middle has the largest disproportionate rate and racial disparity in the practice of discipline. Because of the success of our social justice learning and design collaboratory program model, the Superintendent of Antebellum School District has asked that practitioners from the cohort assist the Taskforce with designing a process for improvement.

We will all go over to Thomas Jefferson Academy today for our initial meeting. Coach TJ along with Emily and Robin will be the on-site support team for all other meetings and the rest of us will act as the external critical friends examining the issues and findings generated by the taskforce. So a little background on the Taskforce committee members:

Alison Parker is the Assistant Director of Federal Programs, Grants, and Compliance for the district, a 2009–2011 Millennium Foundation Urban Education Fellow. Ms. Parker holds a JD and worked in the District Attorney's Office under Juvenile Justice and Truancy before being accepted into the Conti Residency in Urban Education—a management development program. Conti Residency trains recent graduate students with at least two years work experience to be placed in management positions within the central offices of urban school districts. The other members are Dr. Linda Thomas, Director of Exceptional Children; Richard Stevenson, Chief of School Safety, Security and Emergency Management, who last year led the political battle

to acquire licensure for Antebellum School District Security to become an independent police force; Mrs. Catherine Matthews, State PTA Representative; Dr. Louisa Martinez, Director of English Language Learners Services; and Mrs. Khadijah Saleem, Executive Director of Urban Youth Empowerment. Khadijah Saleem is a scholar practitioner, a graduate of the predecessor of this very program. She is a proponent for urban school equity with very close ties to the Jefferson Academy community.

Coach, you have worked with Dr. Saleem, is that right?

Coach TJ: Yes, wow, I was in the first cohort of UYE Sankofa Fellows. The project was very successful, and short-lived . . .

The Professor: Yes, Dr. Saleem, in our many conversations, speaks of the various situations at Jefferson as the rug being pulled from under Jefferson Academy. Please, Coach, give us some background?

Coach TJ: The Sankofa Fellowship recruited teacher candidates from HBCU's historically black colleges and universities, placing candidates in urban schools. Jefferson was the flagship site and would serve as the model after the two-year pilot. The district designated Jefferson a "Teaching Academy" where teacher candidates could gain real-world teaching experience and culturally relevant strategies as professional development simultaneously. Dr. Saleem brought in veteran teachers and top-ranked scholars to participate in the program. While I was a fellow, Dr. Rosa Tubman, whose pivotal and seminal work cultivated what we know as urban educational leadership, spent her sabbatical at Jefferson Teaching Academy. At the end of year two, the school board pulled the funding for the pilot.

The Professor: Ok, colleagues, any questions? If not, we will adjourn and meet at Jefferson Academy

The cohort reconvenes in the conference room at Jefferson Academy. The deputy superintendent Mr. Lieber (who ironically served as the middle school principal when Coach TJ was in middle school and who in one year suspended Coach fifty-seven times) facilitates the meeting, makes introductions, and opens the floor for discussion. Coach and the superintendent have been engaged in several organic conversations about equity and place since Coach started the doctoral program.

Mr. Lieber makes introductions and opens the floor up.

Alison Parker: How does the federal government propose that we deal with this, that is clearly driven by cultural issues? Let's see, the Middle is designated Title 1; 81 percent of the students are recipients of Free and/or Reduced Lunch program and 92 percent come from families identified as low Socioeconomic Status who reside in Eastgate Public Housing Complex. Oh, and a third of those numbers are super subgroup kids receiving Special Education services.

The rest of the committee members are silent or nodding in agreement. Ms. Parker continues:

The Superintendent is fully aware of the cultural and social issues of these kids and the dysfunctional issues they bring with them from home and community. I mean honestly speaking, are we really expected to repair the social and culture deficits along with being accountable for their educational deficits? So tell us, what's the next new and dazzling methodology that you are proposing, and I'm sure you have factored in how teachers are going to squeeze whatever it is . . . in with the educational and effectiveness mandates?

Richard Stevenson: Right . . . I mean the district provides breakfast, lunch, and now dinner, and wellness exams, what are the parents responsible to provide? I understand, really I do, but I spend time with these kids and their parents, well usually just the mom or the grandmother because the father is not necessarily in the picture. A high percentage of these kids have at least one incarcerated parent. Some of them get in trouble on purpose because at juvenile detention they get a good meal, place to sleep, and structure. How are we supposed to fix that, which in my opinion is the real cause of why only certain kids are receiving referrals?

Khadijah Saleem: Are we suggesting black kids and their families are inherently problems?

It has been my experience that when Low SES is discussed it is code for . . . generational welfare black mothers (some drug addicted) breeding with absentee criminal black fathers who produce criminally prone black babies, who are destined to low achievement. Free/Reduced Lunch is code for . . . criminal black babies who come to school with intellectual deficits, developmental and socially bankrupt, and destined to develop into the black "super-predator" (for boys) or black aggressive and promiscuous teen mothers and restart the continuous Eugenics cycle grossly deficient and/or dysfunctional home social development.

We are here because ASD is currently being monitored for possible Civil Rights violations of students, disproportionately African-American male youth? This is not a situation that is only occurring in the ASD, it's a national problem that has been tracked since the first study conducted by CDF in the early 70s. While low SES and cultural misunderstanding are variables, these factors do not explain the intractability and longevity of the problem. This is a high leverage civil rights issue, which means we must investigate the inequity within the problem. I am challenging this committee to be courageous enough to investigate the social justice issues embedded in this problem and the systemic issues influencing the problem of race and discipline practices.

Alison Parker: Dr. Saleem, this is not a personal attack, the data is clear. And with regards to education, it doesn't appear that the attainment of education occupies the same meaning, drive, and/or ambition as it did for our families. This is quite a different generation.

Khadijah Saleem: Dr. Parker, I'm not quite clear on the data you are referencing; however, what we absolutely know empirically and experientially is that poor, hungry, neglected students can learn.

The assistant superintendent jumps in with nervous laughter; tension and discomfort is building.

Assistant Superintendent: Good stuff. I would like to set the foundation for our next meeting with a story. I was the Assistant Principal when Coach was in middle school in this district. Under my tenure, I personally suspended him, literally pushed him out of school fifty-seven times in one school year and failed that grade. He sits before you today as a colleague, respected community member, and a highly rated educational leader. I want this taskforce to reconvene prepared to engage in the hard work of relationship building first among one another at this table and then work to design a sustainably transformative response that weaves, mending the torn relationships between schools and community.

Coach, Emily, and Robin look at each other as if one gigantic light bulb just turned on.

Assistant Superintendent: We will pick these concerns up at our next meeting. Come prepared to engage in some critical dialogue to examine the issues that have surfaced in our discussion this morning. Please thank our guests and we hope to see you guys next week?

The Professor: Thank you for inviting us, a small group will continue to attend the meetings and act as support for your discussions.

CONCLUSIONS AND SUMMARY

Utilizing the chronicle of Coach TJ to critically examine racialized discipline practices in schools as a critical methodological tool exposes the need to expand the school knowledge to practice table in order to "develop thick critical descriptions of phenomena and to uncover how things are understood from the perspective of those who are mostly directly affected" (Zamudio et al., 2011, p. 118). To utilize literature, historical context, data, and tacit knowledge through storytelling as a way to produce the human side of change necessary to document and thus create sustainable transformative change systemically and structurally.

Because if the design must produce sustainable improvement (transformative change) that produces generative impacts then, the design must yield more than a deeper knowing and understanding of the practice and "conditions of the community engaged." The work must become a "critical stance, in which the researcher becomes a change agent who is collectively developing structures intended to critique and support the transformation of the communities being studied" (Barab et al., 2004, p. 255). Allow an organic space where the educational leader creates and cultivates an advocacy identity together with the researcher and other relevant voices in order to improve issues of systemic and structural inequity unfolding in urban schools and in the larger urban community.

It appears that for the scholar engaged in researching disparate discipline practices, it becomes problematic to understand that empirical research is not enough to disrupt normative practices that produce disparities and inequity. Research that should on its merit and guided by a standard or practice foster policy change and ensure the implementation of alternative approaches to improve the learning environment. For practitioners, it appears that simply knowing race influences and informs the inequity of exclusionary discipline practices is not enough to engage their resistance to normative practices.

Why is knowing that racial inequity exists in the system of discipline practices not enough to produce change? There also appears to be a gap not only in the knowledge-practice continuum but also in how education researchers understand how education leaders are making sense of the practice.

The work will require a type of educational leadership that expands beyond the current scope of leadership in schools described by Maxcy (1995) as "decentered and dispersed" (p. 473) to develop critically centric collectivist leadership. How can educational leaders become more involved in the research that occurs in practice settings? Are educational leaders equipped in their programs to engage and decode research? How does the educational leader prepare the community with the language and tools that activates their empowerment to become active participants in school research?

The aim here is to "speak back" to the research practice gap call to expand the research to practice process to include a "Critical Educational Leadership Collaboratory" (hereafter the CELC, a community-engaged research model informed by design-based implementation research (hereafter DBIR) that is centered within the community. Community-centric educational leadership facilitates the CELC.

We see the both the value in DBIR as a response to the research practice gap in educational leadership broadly and urban educational leadership specifically. We also see DBIR as a vehicle to respond to the call for more site-specific and critical analysis of traditional urban school environment. We are suggesting the need to expand the authors' DBIR "stakeholder perspective" to include community-centric urban educational leaders who are involved in community-engaged work as relevant stakeholders, whose voice might be missing and further, whose voice adds value to the collaborative, iterative design principle of DBIR.

Penuel, Fishman, Cheng, and Sabelli (2011) identify four primary principles that are emergent across projects structured as DBIR: (1) a focus on persistent problems of practice from multiple stakeholder perspectives; (2) commitment to iterative, collaborative design; (3) developing theory related both to classroom learning and implementation through systematic inquiry; and (4) developing the capacity of sustainable systems change. The authors stress the need to engage "learning scientists, policy researchers, and practitioners in a model of collaborative, iterative, and systematic research and development" (p. 331).

This call for extending the research practice table to include more innovative and forward thinking about educational leadership is perpetual within the organization of education (Firestone and Riehl, 2005) and specifically in urban education.

Called for by Giroux (1992) as an "emancipatory theory of leadership . . . that speaks a common language of critique and possibility" (1992, p. 18). To engage in emancipatory leadership (Cambron-McCabe, 2010; Giroux, 1992; Starratt, 2004) is to engage in this process of critical examination, critical inquiry, and critical understanding of problem of practices. By the coauthor of this chapter and his colleagues (Miller, Brown, and Hopson, 2011) to engage in Freirien Leadership, that recognizes social conditions, invites new actors, and transcends school-community boundaries (in both theory and practice)" (p. 1081) and a challenge by Ehrich and English (2012) for educational leadership to go and learn from the "grassroots leaders" whom the authors differentiated from community-based leadership. They are describing those folks in the community with "reverent power" whose followers work with [these] leaders not because they must, but because they identify with them and a common cause (p. 7).

In the edited volume, *The Sage Handbook of Educational Leadership: Advances in Theory, Research and Practice*, Young and Lopez (2005) are urging a leaping of educational leadership into the seventh moment of inquiry (Denzin and Lincoln, 1994) by substantiating social justice as a research competency. As proponents of expanding the scholarship of educational leadership

"to include a broader range of perspectives" in conducting research, the authors argue,

> To be certain, the research framework one uses dictates—to a large extent—the way one identifies and describes research problems, the way one researches these problems, the findings that are highlighted, the implications that one considers, and the approach(es) one takes to planning and implementation. (p. 339)

The theories of learning that support the need to expand the DBIR practitioner role to include community-engaged leaders and community-centric educational leaders is described by Russell and Jackson (2013) and colleagues as "cross-setting" learning and knowledge production. The authors examined four cases engaging DBIR as a response to problems of practice occurring in or in the community of education settings. One of the four cases organized stakeholders around transitioning underserved youth into college placement unearthing the possibility for DBIR to encompass processes for boundary spanners as facilitators, navigators, and translators who move between multiple settings. The authors argue, "theories that conceptualize learning as cross-setting phenomenon . . . suggest that an individual's participation in any particular event is shaped not only by what happens in that event or setting over time but also by the individual's participation in events in other settings and how resources and relationships are linked between events and settings" (p. 166).

The CELC can function as a third space for "community-engaged" research defined by Stovall as aligned to activist scholarship, engaged research, and participatory action research (PAR) methods; integrated with ". . . the day-to-day community work, [and] with research to address the issues and concerns expressed by those communities in relationship to education" (Stovall, 2010, p. 411). Routledge draws our attention to a notion of research practitioners who engage in matters of social justice and do so in a space of activist and a defined academic space, a "third space" as critical engagement to "live theory and as well as write about it" (Routledge, 1996, p. 403). He argues that the two spaces are interwoven and can influence one another in important ways"; however, there is a disconnect "between the academy and the people it professes to represent." Quoting Katz (1994). Routledge expounds further on the fragile relationship between community and academy, "we have theories about theory and practice, practice takes a beating in the stakes debates of academia" (p. 400).

How can urban educational leaders become more involved in the research that occurs in practice settings? Are educational leaders equipped in their programs to engage and decode research as a matter of social justice? What is the role of educational leadership in preparing the community to become active participants in school research? What tools, artifacts, and/or strategies are educational leaders in need of when engaging the political economy of urban education?

We leave the community of urban educational leadership with these questions as a way toward generative thinking. We also challenge our community to be disruptive of normative practices and to dance with notions of imaginative innovations that speak back to perpetual problems of practices. Lastly, we call to urban educators, practitioners, researchers, and scholars to erect collaborations "in a dynamic and changing urban, public school context" (Hopson et al., 2010, p. 790) that deepen the understanding of practice and discover thicker descriptions of phenomena.

We acknowledge Dr. Sonya Douglas Horsford for her support and commitment to facilitating premier educational leadership.

REFERENCES

Anyon, J. (1997). *Ghetto schooling: A political economy for urban school reform*. New York: Teachers College Press.

Anyon, J. (2005a). *Radical possibilities: Public policy, urban education, and a new social movement*. New York: Routledge.

Anyon, J. (2005b). What "counts" as educational policy? Notes toward a new paradigm. *Harvard Educational Review*, 75, 65–88.

Ball, A. F. (2012). To know is not enough: Knowledge, power, and the zone of generativity. *Educational Researcher*, *41*(8), 283–293.

Bell, D. A. (1979). *Brown v. board of education* and interest convergence dilemma. *Harvard Law Review*, *93*, 518–533.

Bell, D. (2004). *Silent covenants:* Brown v. board of education *and the unfulfilled hopes for racial reform*. New York: Oxford University Press.

Berliner, D. (2006). Our impoverished view of educational research. *Teachers College Record, 108*, 949–955.

Bireda, M. R. (2010). *Cultures of Conflict: Eliminating racial profiling in school discipline* (2nd ed.). Lanham, MD: Rowman and Littlefield Education.

Bridgeman, J. (2011). African American counter narratives: Telling one's story, finding one's place. In M. Zamudio, C. Russell, F. Rios, and J. Bridgeman, *Critical race theory matters: Education and ideology* (pp. 143–150). New York: Routledge.

Cambron-McCabe, N. (2010). Preparation and development of school leaders: Implications for social justice policies. In C. Marshall, and M. Oliva, *Leadership for social justice: Making revolutions in education* (2nd ed., pp. 35–54). Boston: Pearson Education, Inc.

Carter, P., Fine, M., and Russell, S. (2014). *Discipline disparities series: Overview*. Bloomington: The Equity Project, Indiana University.

Children's Defense Fund. (1975). *School Suspensions: Are They Helping Children*. Cambridge, MA: Washington Research Project.

Delgado, B. D. (1998). Using a chicano feminist epistomology in educational research. *Harvard Educational Review*, 555–582.

Delgado, R. (1989). Storytelling for oppositionists and others: A plea for narrative. *Michigan Law Review*, 2411–2441.

Denzin, N. (2010). A critical performance pedagogy that matters. In J. Sandlin, B. Schultz, and J. Burdick, *Handbook of public pedagogy: Education and learning beyond schooling* (pp. 56–70). New York: Routledge.

Department of Justice, Office of Public Affairs. (2012, October 24). *Justice News*. Retrieved October 26, 2012, from The United States Department of Justice: www.justice.gov/opa/pr/2012/October/12-crt-1281.html.

Duncan, A. (2005). Critical race ethnography in education: narrative, race, inequality, and the problem of epistemology. *Race Ethnicity and Education*, 93–114.

Ehrich, L. and English, F. (2012). What can grassroots leadership teach us about school leadership. *Halduskultuur—Administrative Culture*, 85–108.

Firestone, W. and Riehl, C. (2005). *A new agenda for research in educational leadership*. New York: Teachers College, Columbia University.

Giroux, H. (1984). Public philosophy and the crisis in education. *Harvard Educational Review, 54* (2), 186–195.

Giroux, H. (1992). *Educational leadership and the crisis of democratic culture*. University Park: University Council of Educational Administration.

Giroux, H., Lankshear, C., McLaren, P., and Peters, M. (1996). *Counternarratives: Cultural studies and critical pedagogies in postmodern spaces*. New York: Routledge.

Gregory, A., Skiba, R. J., and Noguera, P. (2010). The achievement gap and the discipline gap: Two sides of the same coin. *Educational Researcher, 39* (1), 59–68.

Guajardo, F. and Guajardo, M. (2010). Cultivating stories of change. In K. Ruder, *The collective leadership storybook: Weaving strong communities.* Seattle: The Center for Ethical Leadership.

Hopson, R. K., Hotep, U., Schneider, D. L., and Turene, I. G. (2010). What's educational leadership without an African-centered perspective: Explorations and extrapolations. *Urban Education,* 777–796.

Kohler Riessman, C. (2002). Narrative Analysis. In A. Huberman and M. Miles, *The qualitative researcher's companion* (pp. 217–270).

Kumashiro, K. (2000). Toward a theory of anti-oppressive education. *Review of Educational Research,* 25–53.

Ladson-Billings, G. (1998). Just what is critical race theory and what's it doing in a nice field like education? *International Journal of Qualitative Studies in Education, 11* (1), 7–24.

Ladson-Billings, G. (2006). From the achievement gap to the education debt. *Educational Researcher, 35* (7), 3–12.

Ladson-Billings, G. (2012). Through a glass darkly: The persistance of race in education research and scholarship. *Educational Researcher, 41* (4), 115–120.

Lipman, P. (2011). *The new political economy of urban education: Neoliberalism, race and the right to the city.* New York: Routledge.

Losen, D. (2011). *Discipline policies, successful schools, and racial justice.* Boulder: National Education Policy Center.

Losen, D. and Gillespie, J. (2012). *Opportunities suspended: The disparate impact of disciplinary exclusion from school.* The Center for Civil Rights Remedies at UCLA. Los Angeles: The Civil Rights Project.

Losen, D. and Skiba, R. (2010). *Suspended Education: Urban Middle Schools in Crisis.* Southern Poverty Law Center.

Miller, P., Brown, T., and Hopson, R. (2011). Centering love, hope, and trust in the community: Transformative urban leadership informed by Paulo Freire. *Urban Education,* 1079–1099.

Ogbu, J. (1978). *Minority education and caste: The American system in cross-cultural perspective.* New York: Academic Press.

Online Etymology Dictionary. (2012). *Online Etymology Dictionary* (D. Harper, Producer). Retrieved February 26, 2013, from Online Etymology Dictionary: www.etymonline.com/index.php?allowed_in_frame=0andsearch=forge andsearchmode=none.

Pink, W.T. and G. W. Noblit. (2007). (Eds.). *International handbook of urban education.* Dordrecht, The Netherlands: Springer.

Riehl, C. and Firestone, W. (2005). What research methods should be used to study educational leadership. In W. Firestone, and C. Riehl, *A new agenda for research in educational leadership* (pp. 156–170). New York: Teachers College Press.

Robinson, V. (1993). Current controversies in action research. *Public Adminstration Quarterly, 17* (3), 263–290.

Robinson, V. (1998). Methodology and the research-practice gap. *Educational Researcher, 27* (1), 17–26.

Shah, N. (2012, August 12). *News and Updates.* Retrieved October 26, 2012, from NoVo Foundation: novofoundation.org/newsfromthefield/groups-ask-districts-to-stop-using-out-of-school-suspensions/.

Skiba, R., Arrendondo, A., and Karega Rausch, M. (2014). *New and developing research on disparities in discipline.* Bloomington: The Equity Project, Indiana University.

Skiba, R., Eckes, S., and Brown, K. (2009–2010). African American disproportionality in school discipline: The divide between best evidence and legal remedy. *New York Law School Law Review, 54,* 1071–1112.

Skiba, R., Horner, R., Chung, C., and Rausch, M. (2011). Race is not neutral: A national investigation of African American and Latino disproportionality in school discipline. *School Psychology Review,* 85–107.

Skiba, R., Michael, R., Nardo, A., and Peterson, R. (2002). The color of discipline: Sources of racial and gender disproportionality in school punishment. *The Urban Review, 34,* 317–342.

Skiba, R., Reynolds, C., Graham, S., Sheras, P., C.J., C., and Garcia-Vazquez, E. (2006). *Are zero tolerance policies effective in schools? An evidentiary review and recommendations.* Indianapolis: APA.

Skiba, R. and Williams, N. (2014). *Are black kids worse? Myths and facts about racial differences in behavior.* Bloomington: The Equity Project, Indiana University.

Solorzano, D. (1997). Images and words that wound: Critical race theory, racial stereotyping and teacher education. *Teacher Education Quarterly,* 186–215.

Solorzano, D. and Yosso, T. (2002). Critical race methodology: Counter-storytelling as an analytical framework for education research. *Qualitative Inquiry, 8* (23), 23–44.

Starratt, R. J. (2004). *Ethical Leadership.* San Francisco: Jossey-Bass.

Stovall, D. (2010). A note on the politics of place and public pedagogy. In J. Sandlin, B. Schultz, and J. Burdick, *Handbook of public pedagogy: Education and learning beyond schooling* (pp. 409–419). New York: Routledge.

U.S. Department of Education, Office of Civil Rights. (2014). *Civil rights data collection: Data snapshot (school discipline).*

Valencia, R. R. (2010). *Dismantling contemporary deficit thinking.* New York: Routledge.

Young, M. and Lopez, G. (2005). The nature of inquiry in educational leadership. In F. English, *The sage handbook of educational leadership: Advances in theory, research,* *and practice* (pp. 337–361). Thousand Oaks: Sage Publications, Inc.

Zamudio, M., Russell, C., Rios, F., and Bridgeman, J. (2011). *Critical race theory matters: Education and Ideology.* New York: Routledge.

CHAPTER 16

Revisiting Black Feminist Thought and Home-School Relations in the U.S. South

Tondra L. Loder-Jackson, Andrew N. McKnight, Michael Brooks, and Tonya B. Perry

Relationships between urban families and schools have sparked considerable interest in the public discourse and research on the fate of urban education. Home-school relations are viewed as essential to improving and enhancing the academic achievement of urban students. The fact that many parents and school personnel in urban schools are predominantly African American and female tends to be taken for granted in much of the discussion about home-school relations. A shift in focus to foregrounding race and social class may unearth factors and dynamics that facilitate or undermine sincere efforts to promote affirmative home-school relations.

This chapter addresses relationships between predominantly African-American mothers and women school personnel (teachers, counselors, and administrators) in an urban school district in the Southeast by amplifying their voices through interviews. Given the predominance of African-American women across these three studies, it is important, and admittedly controversial, to revisit P. H. Collins's (2000) Black Feminist Thought perspectives on women's work, family, and intra-racial group dynamics within the context of national and local conversations about home-school relations. Specifically, this chapter is framed conceptually around P. H. Collins's (2000), along with other feminist writers', theories about how normative perspectives of motherhood, work, and family in the United States often adversely impact African-American women, particularly single, low-income mothers. Before revisiting these perspectives, the discussion segues to an illustration from African-American literature and popular culture as a narrative device for foregrounding the issues addressed in this chapter (Eisner, 1979).

An Illustration: The Women of Brewster Place

Gloria Naylor's critically acclaimed novel, *The Women of Brewster Place*, portrayed seven primary characters of African-American women from different walks of life whose lives intersected in a dilapidated tenement in an unnamed city reminiscent of the Northeast (Naylor, 1982). In the television adaptation of Naylor's novel (Naylor, Hall, and Deitch, 1989), there is a contentious scene between a young community activist attempting to escape her affluent family roots ("Kiswana Browne" played by actress Robin Givens), and a young, poor, single mother of several children allegedly conceived by different fathers ("Cora Lee" played by actress Phyllis Yvonne Stickney). Kiswana frantically alerts Cora that her oldest son is rummaging through the neighborhood dumpster for food, to which, Cora, simply brushes off as one of his antics to find sweets, which she has forbidden him to eat. The scene reveals Kiswana's sincere but patronizing efforts to "help" Cora and her children by trying to engage them in neighborhood life, particularly tenement housing meetings. Cora is put off by Kiswana's efforts and politely shows her to the door. However, the two later make a breakthrough after Kiswana's boyfriend ("Abshu" played by actor Leon Robinson) tries to help her empathize with Cora's plight. He tells her that Cora reminds him of the women in his family and former neighborhood, who were making it the best way they could, and then he challenges her to bridge the socioeconomic cultural gap that has estranged them. Cora eventually accepts Kiswana's invitation to attend a neighborhood Shakespeare play, and proudly parades her clean and well-dressed children to this special event. After an uncomfortable theatrical prologue, Cora is almost convinced her children will be bored and embarrass her with their misbehavior. However, she and her children eventually settle in and are pleasantly surprised by the culturally adapted rendition of this Shakespeare play.

The scene described above is, no doubt, played out frequently in urban schools across the country. Very well-meaning and well-intentioned urban school personnel and leaders desire to help mothers, who are sometimes young, unmarried, and low-income, make a better life for their children. They give them guidance on parenting, academic enrichment, social skills, and participating in school activities. These efforts to help may be initially shunned and viewed as patronizing. But when there is a "cultural translator" who plays a role similar to the one that Abshu did, then there may be an opportunity for a breakthrough that ultimately benefits the child.

Social class dynamics between parents and guardians and school personnel in urban schools are not often at the forefront of educational scholarship (Gorski, 2004; Loder, 2005; Rist, 1970; Rothstein, 2004). Speaking publicly or writing about these differences is viewed by some as taboo—an airing out of dirty laundry for mainstream audiences. However, given that urban school districts in the United States are comprised predominantly of low-income students of color (Institute for Education Statistics, 2013), and by association, their parents and families, social class and intra-racial group dynamics between parents and school personnel warrant closer attention.

CONCEPTUAL FRAMEWORK

Revisiting Black Feminist Thought

P. H. Collins (2000) reminded us that African-American mothers, especially low-income and unmarried ones, have been historically maligned in the United States. This perception is rooted in white supremacist and sexist views about race and gender, particularly in relation to the intersection of work and family roles. Historically, in the United States, there has been a paid/unpaid work binary that reflects the presumption that "real men work and real women take care of families" (P. H. Collins, 2000, p. 47). Consequently, African-American women who work outside of the home have been viewed as less "feminine" because of both their economic competition with men and their perceived dereliction in fulfilling motherhood duties (P. H. Collins, 2000, p. 47). Single, low-income African-American mothers who send their children to urban schools have been especially maligned by this stereotypical binary, which unfortunately, is sometimes perpetuated by African-American middle-class or upwardly mobile professional women who serve in teaching and leadership roles in urban schools. P. H. Collins (2000) also addressed a post–World War II political economy that has reified social class stratification in many African-American communities, which, in turn, has exacerbated social class tensions among working-class, new working poor (i.e., "black single mothers"), and middle-class African-American women (p. 47).

Social class differences have always existed within the African-American community to varying degrees (Frazier, 1957). The concern today is how these differences have increasingly alienated African Americans from each other, which undermines efforts to mobilize communities and schools for positive transformative change. According to Omolade (1994), "Unlike the slave plantation, which brought different kinds of workers together in an oppositional community of resistance, today's triple-tiered black female work site does not foster community" (p. 63). Referring to the segregated pre-mid-twentieth-century phase of a perpetual civil rights movement era, Omolade (1994) wrote: "Black school teachers, maids, and farm laborers shared the same vision of the power of education to expand opportunities for black children. Supported in their efforts by black men, poor black women, with great sacrifice and struggle, sent their children to the schools and institutions founded by better-educated and more 'middle-class' women" (p. 41). Omolade (1994) also credited working-class African-American women with raising millions of dollars in the early twentieth century to pay for black schools and the salaries of black educators. In their critical analysis of multicultural women's economic history in the United States, Amott and Matthaei (1996) credited primarily middle-class Colored Women's Clubs with assisting low-income and working-class women with improving their work conditions. But this kind of solidarity has been undermined since the mid-twentieth century "classical era" of the civil rights movement (Rustin, 1965, p. 25; Robinson, 2010). Drawing on insights from historian Elizabeth Higginbotham, Omolade (1994) described contemporary African-American professionals as being "colonized" because their employment relies upon the dependent relationship of the African-American poor to public institutions, which are supposed to serve their needs for education, health care, and government services (p. 51). Omolade described this relationship as "mammification," an enduring and demeaning legacy that transcends professional titles, statuses, and salaries of nearly all African-American women in the workforce (p. 51). Furthermore, Omolade (1994) observed:

> Black professionals are expected to fix systems which are in crisis because of underfunding, infrastructure deterioration, and demoralization of unskilled staffs. As "colonized" professionals black women are increasingly hired to repair the damage done to families and entire communities by social inequality and downturns in the economy. The work of these modern "mammies" is the care of the personal needs of the destitute and the weak in public institutions. These women teach and care for the children of workers of color; nurse the elderly and poor in public hospitals, nursing homes, and shelters; and counsel in public colleges. (p. 54)

In light of this context, African-American family dynamics should not be viewed or approached in a vacuum, but rather within a complex political, economic, social, and cultural context. Critical sociopolitical changes since the classical phase of the civil rights era, which transformed employment conditions and welfare policy, have exacerbated the persistent poverty that both one- and two-parent-headed black households have encountered historically (Amott and Matthaei, 1996; Brewer, 1988; P. H. Collins, 2000). However, even in the midst of these changes, African-American mothers have been found to be particularly resilient, somehow finding a way to maintain a positive personal outlook, which makes a tangible positive difference in their family's life experiences (Wallace, 2013). These complex changes and African-American families' resiliency must be conveyed in teacher education programs (TEPs) through critical course content, dialogues, field experiences, and more frequent and constructive home-school contact, which occurs as early as possible in the pre-service education experience (Loder-Jackson,

Voltz, and Froning, 2014). A review of the literature on school personnel's perspectives on parent social context and involvement indicates there is still much work to be done.

LITERATURE REVIEW

This review addresses three strands of scholarship: 1) relationships between African-American parents and school personnel; 2) deficit orientations of urban parents and their school involvement; and 3) efforts to recast parent involvement from being focused squarely on parents' involvement with their children in school to their involvement across school, home, and community.

Relationships Between African-American Parents and School Personnel

Relationships between African-American parents and predominantly African-American school personnel in urban schools across the United States, especially in the South, have altered dramatically since the classical phase of the civil rights era. Prior to and during this particular phase, most African-American teachers in the South "were single women who had limited opportunities in other professions" (Feldman, 1999, p. 129). Similar to single white teachers during that time (Carter, 2002), many single black women teachers roomed and boarded in the homes of their students' families, which placed them in intimate contact with their students as well as under the watchful eyes of parents and community members. Teachers and principals were viewed as important community leaders, often working side-by-side with community members to raise money for education (Feldman, 1999; Walker, 1996, 2000).

In contrast, today many affluent African Americans no longer reside in the same neighborhoods as working-class and poor residents (Fultz, 2004; Henig, Hula, Orr and Pedescleaux, 1999; Massey and Denton, 1993; Pattillo-McCoy, 1999; Robinson, 2010; W. J. Wilson, 1987). The racially homogeneous and relatively economically heterogeneous communities of yesteryear, where African-American educators, students, and families lived, worked, and attended religious and community events together (Davis, Gardner, and M. Gardner, 2009), are few and far between in the contemporary urban South (Robinson, 2010). Therefore, analyses of home-school relations in the contemporary urban South must take into account this transformed context (Fields-Smith, 2005, 2009; Loder-Jackson, 2011, 2012). Today's urban students and their relatively young parents are in some respects generationally distinctive from previous urban school clientele (Loder-Jackson, 2011, 2012). Contemporary urban family trends are characterized by intergenerational, condensed-age structures, which produce relatively younger familial networks of mothers, grandmothers, and great-grandmothers (Burton, 1996; Jarrett, 1994; Jarrett and Burton, 1999; Ladner and Gourdine, 1984; Slaughter-Defoe, 1993). Furthermore, unprecedented numbers of African-American children are being raised by a single parent (typically a mother), relative, or guardian and many are "school-dependent" for their academic learning (Annie E. Casey Foundation, 2011; E. J. Cooper, 2009, p. 441). This rapidly changing context necessitates that current and aspiring educators become more culturally competent about and responsive to urban students and families (C. W. Cooper, 2009; C. W. Cooper, Riehl, and Hasan, 2010; Loder-Jackson, McKnight, Brooks, McGrew, and Voltz, 2007; Milner, 2009). Yet far too many possess deficit-orientations about urban families.

Deficit-Orientations of Urban Parent Involvement

In a previous publication (Loder-Jackson et al., 2007), three of the authors featured here, along with their colleagues, reviewed literature that addressed deficit-orientations of urban parent involvement. The authors concluded that these deficit-orientations are rooted in narrow and rigidly defined normative conceptualizations of parent involvement that are school-sponsored and viewed as valuable to school personnel (for example, participation in parent-teacher organizations and parent-teacher conferences). From this perspective, within the context of high-poverty urban schools, parental involvement often has been characterized as "minimal, sporadic, or altogether nonexistent" (Lawson, 2003, p. 79). According to a report of the National Center for Educational Statistics, as poverty levels increase, parent participation in activities such as attending a general school or PTO/PTA meeting, attending parent-teacher conferences, attending a school event, participating in school fundraising, and serving on a school committee decreases (Planty et al., 2009). Along similar lines, in a national survey of principals and teachers in high-poverty urban schools, Voltz (1998) found that the majority of both groups of educators cited poor parental involvement as a major challenge they faced as educators. In a follow-up interview study, again involving educators in high-poverty schools, Voltz (2000) observed the same trend in responses. One participating principal reported: "Parent involvement in students' education is very, very low" (p. 46). Likewise, speaking of the parents of students at her school, a participating teacher noted: "They don't value education. To get them involved is a real challenge. The parents come from a totally different social background" (p. 46).

A number of factors reportedly contribute to the perceived paucity of parental involvement in urban schools. One of these factors is the manner in which school personnel define and categorize parental involvement. In an ethnographic study involving teachers and parents in a high-poverty urban school, Lawson (2003) found that often "teachers define parent involvement as a means for parents and families to cooperate and acquiesce to the needs of the school as defined by teachers" (p. 104). This implies that parents have little or no role in shaping what parental involvement should entail. Lawson (2003) has described this orientation to parent involvement as "schoolcentric" and limiting from the standpoint of developing truly collaborative relationships with parents (p. 79). It reflects what Smrekar and Cohen-Vogel (2001) have described as "highly defined, socially constructed scripts that institutionalize the relationships among parents, teachers, and school administrators" (p. 75). Voltz (1994) has cautioned that by rigidly adhering to these scripts, educators "are dictating unilaterally the nature of the relationship between themselves and parents. If parents feel uncomfortable with the school's conceptualization of parent involvement, they may be inclined to abstain" (p. 288). As social and cultural dissonance between parents and educators increases, the likelihood that parents will reject school conceptualizations of parent involvement also increases (Lawson, 2003).

Another important factor influencing the quantity and quality of parental involvement in urban schools is the manner in which educators view parents. Lightfoot (2004) conducted an analysis of scholarly texts addressing parental involvement. This analysis revealed middle-class parents in a positive light, that is, as "overflowing containers, whose involvement in schools is to be valued, but must be constrained in quantity" whereas low-income urban parents, some of whom spoke English as a second language, were portrayed as "empty containers, which need to be filled before they can give anything of value to the schools or to their own offspring" (Lightfoot, 2004, p. 93). Voltz (1994) referred to this "empty-full" dichotomy as the "tracking" of urban parents. According to Voltz (1994), "This occurs when school officials decide . . . that certain groups of parents are usually 'concerned parents' . . . who want to be involved in the education of their children, whereas other groups of parents are usually 'unconcerned parents' who do not care to be involved in the education of their children" (p. 289). These preconceived notions may then shape the interaction of educators with parents. Greater efforts may be exerted to involve those who are presumed to care. These parents' opinions may be more highly valued, and their concerns taken more seriously. As Lightfoot (2004) stated, "the more we talk or write of low-income or immigrant parents as empty of useful knowledge, the more difficult it becomes to imagine inviting them into schools to share their ideas or expertise with us" (pp. 94–95).

A related issue is the degree to which parents perceive schools to be receptive to their ideas. In a study involving interviews of low-income mothers, Overstreet, Devine, Bevans, and Efreom (2005) found that parent perceptions of school receptivity was the strongest predictor of parent involvement. According to these researchers, "the degree to which parents felt that the school listened to and sponsored activities for them significantly predicted their level of school involvement" (p. 109). This underscores the importance of listening to the voices of parents.

Recasting Parent Involvement

Some education scholars are calling for a recasting of parent involvement that takes into account how parents perceive and value their involvement in schools and in their children's lives. They note that previous literature on parent involvement has been understood largely in terms of what parents do and how their involvement does or does not fit the school agenda, that is, "school-centric" (Lawson, 2003, p. 79).

In her qualitative study of African-American parents from diverse socioeconomic backgrounds, Fields-Smith (2009) found that parents' definitions of their involvement transcended the school and encompassed their home, neighborhood, and civic life. According to Fields-Smith (2009), "Highly involved African-American parents in this study participated in the PTO to varying degrees, ranging from assuming leadership roles to avoiding PTO involvement altogether" (p. 161). Home-based involvement included conversations, monitoring and assisting with homework and "extrawork," visits to museums, providing books and other community resources (for example, church-based education, learning about history and heritage, especially among upper-income families). Fields-Smith (2009) found career stage and age to be important factors to consider. Some parents became more active in school activities after they secured their families' economic and social well-being through full-time employment and, sometimes, full-time parenting for stay-at-home mothers. Concerns about their children's negative behavior ("acting out") deterred some younger parents from getting involved. However, in spite of their previous negative encounters with schooling, low-income parents remained determined to be involved in their children's lives.

In a study of parental engagement in high-poverty urban communities, Barton, Drake, Perez, St Louis, and George (2004) proposed a paradigm shift from this view by introducing the Ecologies of Parental Engagement (EPE) framework. According to the authors,

> [EPE] marks a fundamental shift in how we understand parents' involvement in their children's education—a shift from focusing primarily on what parents do to engage with their children's schools and with other actors within those schools, to also considering how parents understand the hows and whys of their engagement, and how this engagement relates more broadly to parents' experiences and actions both inside and outside of the school community. (Barton et al., 2004, p. 3)

From this perspective, parental engagement is viewed as "the mediation between space and capital by parents in relation to others in school settings" (p. 11). The authors placed at the center of their model the efforts of urban parents to negotiate parent involvement in schools by activating nontraditional resources and leveraging relationships with school personnel as well as other parents and community members. Rather than to view parental engagement as an object or outcome, as it has been traditionally conceptualized, the EPE frames these concepts as a relationship among a network of actors.

However, egalitarian approaches to parent involvement necessitate a fundamental paradigm shift for school personnel and leaders, in particular (Spillane, 2006). As Bauch and Goldring (1996) found in their study of parent involvement and teacher decision making under different school choice models (Catholic schools, magnet public schools, and a single-focus or specialty public schools) in Washington, DC, Chicago, and Chattanooga, a more egalitarian approach to parent involvement may prove threatening to teachers and administrators "who may not wish to include parents' opinions and ideas in their decisions" (p. 425). School leaders must also contend with "how increased teacher decision making could mitigate the influence of parents in school matters" (Bauch and Goldring, 1996, p. 425). Ultimately, the success of new approaches is contingent upon school leaders' and teachers' willingness to share power, cultivate trust, and adapt to new roles in relation to their respective constituencies (Spillane, 2006). In turn, policymakers must also modify their assessment of parent involvement by shifting away from bean-counter approaches that enumerate parent participation in school meetings and pay closer attention to "the ways that deficit orientations shape schools' willingness to extend themselves to parents and children" (Flessa, 2008, p. 21). Furthermore, school personnel and parents must embrace rather than shun certain levels of conflict and tension as "an inevitable part of collaboration" (Flessa, 2008, p. 121).

The concepts and ideas addressed in this literature review provide a critical framework for understanding the approach to this inquiry, interpretation of the data, and implications for research and practice.

METHODOLOGY

Site

The three studies featured here were conducted in a mid-size urban school district in the Southeast. The school district is predominantly African American (96 percent) with white, Hispanic/Latino/a, Asian, and "other" students constituting the remaining 4 percent

of the population (Phi Delta Kappa International, 2011). Eighty-six percent of the students are in the federal free and reduced lunch program (Phi Delta Kappa International, 2011). The district is surrounded by a suburban ring of middle- to upper-middle-class, predominantly white, well-financed school districts (Alabama State Department of Education, 2012; Frankenberg, 2009). Similar to other school districts in the Southeast, once school desegregation mandates were finally under way, white parents withdrew their children from the city's public schools in droves and set in motion the widespread development of suburban school districts (Frankenberg, 2009). A number of African-American families that have remained vie desperately to enroll their children into a few coveted magnet public schools.

Studies

The objective of these three studies was to learn more about the perspectives of urban parents, P–12 educators, and university teacher educators on parent involvement and how to improve home-school relations and teacher preparation. Across these studies, thirty-four urban parents, forty-two P–12 school personnel (including teachers, counselors, administrators, central office, and afterschool enrichment personnel), and seven P–12 and university teacher education program (TEP) collaborating faculty (total N = 83) were interviewed individually or as a small team or *focus group* (Morgan, 1997). Ninety-four percent of the parents and 81 percent of the P–12 and university faculty across these three studies are African-American women. Participants were asked to respond to questions that probed their definitions and descriptions of parent involvement, their relationships with parent and school personnel, their perceptions of and experiences in urban schools, particularly as it related to parent-school personnel interactions, and their recommendations for improving home-school relations. Interviews were audiotaped and transcribed by a transcriber.

Data analysis took place during regular bimonthly face-to-face meetings coupled with e-mail and telephone correspondence; investigators also reviewed and coded data both independently and collectively to ensure audiotape-to-transcript accuracy and enhance data reliability and validity (Huberman and Miles, 1994;

Patton, 1990; Seidman, 1998). To maintain the agreement of anonymity, the participants are not identified by name.

The parent focus group study employed strategies to maximize parent engagement and establish trust (for example, partnering with local district parent organizations to advertise and co-facilitate interviews, providing dinners meals and on-site child care, convening meetings at the neighborhood school, reading Internal Review Board forms aloud and answering questions, reporting findings back to school personnel privately for their review and comment before public dissemination as well as to parents in a "parent-friendly" venue) (Loder-Jackson et al., 2007; Morgan, 1998; Smalley and Reyes-Blanes, 2001).

Dissemination

It is important to note that findings from these studies served a dual purpose at the outset: first, to inform the stakeholders in this study about the results so that they can improve and enhance parent involvement and home-school relations; and second, to enhance education scholars' and practitioners' knowledge and understanding of this topic, particularly in the unique context of the post-civil rights movement urban South. To fulfill the first dissemination purpose, the first author prepared a white paper for the former district school superintendent and family involvement personnel. In addition, three of the authors (Brooks, Perry, and Loder-Jackson, 2008) presented findings to parents and school personnel in a readers-theater format (Donmmoyer and Yenner-Donmoyer, 1995). In this format, the research was transformed from academic language to a practical, more useful form for parents. If the research had remained in academic journal language, parents outside of the field of research may have found the information inaccessible, stilted, and somewhat confusing. Through the creation of a readers' theater, several objectives were accomplished. First, parents from all professions and backgrounds had access to the findings of the research through performance. Education difference among parents was not necessarily a factor for understanding the research in this form. Second, parents could connect to the work because they could hear their voices and language through the research. The readers' theater allowed the participants to actually receive the message

through the authentic and collective albeit mediated voice of parents. Third, parents could use the readers' theater to spur ongoing conversation about issues raised in the performance. Fourth, and finally, school personnel could hear parents' perspectives from a third-party partner, which presented a unique set of challenges and opportunities that will be discussed in this chapter's conclusion.

DATA ANALYSIS AND DISCUSSION

The following analysis was organized around three major categories, which addressed school personnel's perceptions of home-school relations, parents' perceptions of home-school relations, and both school personnel's and parents' recommendations for improving and enhancing home-school relations. The quotes are most illustrative of the perspectives of African-American women participants across these studies.

School Personnel's Perceptions of Home-School Relations

P–12 school personnel were fairly unanimous about the importance of parental involvement and their desire to see increased participation from parents. The participation they sought ranged from parents helping with homework, making sure their children were fed and well-rested, showing up for PTA meetings, volunteering at the school, communicating with the teachers and administrators, assisting with behavioral discipline, and improving academic performance. Notably, some of these expectations are similar to those conveyed by parents in the focus group study; yet most expectations were "schoolcentric" (Lawson, 2003, p. 79).

The school personnel sometimes conveyed affirming perspectives on parent involvement. School personnel generally believed that it was the school's job to provide parents with a productive and safe space for their children. This view was illustrated by a K–8 principal, who stated: "What they want from the school, looking from the school outward[ly] is respect—[to] make sure their students are safe; make sure their kids are receiving proper quality instruction." Some school personnel emphasized the importance of creating a welcoming and nonjudgmental environment for parents. For example, another K–8 principal stated: "The openness of the school [is] to be willing to allow parents to come in as they are, and not expect something [from them] that they are not." In general, school personnel stated that they believed that parents mostly wanted what was best for their children and had confidence in their respective school's ability to help realize this aspiration. School personnel generally believed that it is the school's responsibility to establish a rapport with parents and convince them that the staff has their children's best interests at heart. For some this responsibility was shared between parents and school staff. For example, a middle school principal stated:

> If Johnny fails, then I fail. And I think that as teachers and as parents, we should all assume that particular philosophy . . . if the child fails, then we fail. Then we should look for solutions to make sure that doesn't happen.

However, this optimism and shared sense of responsibility was accompanied by another belief that parental involvement had declined dramatically compared to previous years. Even more disconcerting were the deficit-oriented perspectives, which surfaced in several of the interviews irrespective of race or gender. Views most typically verbalized were that urban parents did not care, had not been taught to care in their own upbringing, or were not in a socioeconomic position to care about parent involvement, due to work schedules, transportation, disability, and addiction. Additionally, some of the school personnel placed ultimate responsibility for parental involvement on the parents, and often lamented that parents do not utilize the resources available to them or visit the school on their own initiative. One participant described a generational cycle of poverty in this way:

> You know it's just a cycle. So your mama was on welfare, so your grandma was on welfare . . . and now you . . . It's what they see, and it's the environment that they're in. And if this is what you see then this is what you do. If you're out and you see seventeen- and eighteen-year-old boys standing on the corner selling crack, and they're walking around with two and three thousand dollars in their pocket driving Lexus and Cadillacs . . . then the first thing that pops into your mind as an eight-year-old and nine-year-old is, "Man I'm a be just like John." You know, instead of, "I need to be going to school and getting my education."

Another K–8 counselor and parental involvement coordinator at her school discussed a learned helplessness on the part of her students and added that extra-community influences, for example, popular culture, might be negatively affecting their expectations by giving them unrealistic aspirations. She stated:

> They feel that they are behind the eight ball and really can't compete . . . They usually act out and try to find a false sense of hope in videos or rappers, and . . . they try to identify with what they see television-wise rather than [with] reality.

In general, school personnel's attitudes toward parents and students trended toward deficit-oriented perspectives. However, this assertion does not imply a universal condemnation of the quality of parental involvement in the schools represented in this study. For instance, one principal reported being "pretty satisfied with the level of parental involvement here at our school." Others, such as an elementary school reading coach, expressed sympathy: "I don't want people to think that I just have a negative view of the parents of my students because I know that certain things come up to where they may not be able to be involved in the school." Yet, the overwhelming majority of school personnel in our studies expressed frustration with parents' perceived unwillingness to show up for school-sponsored programs such as afterschool enrichment programs, parenting seminars, or PTA meetings. The following complaint was voiced by a school personnel member who was not pleased with parents who did not respond to communication sent directly to the parents' homes. She stated, "They get notices about parent seminars and district-wide seminars that the city district is providing. It's just a matter of them taking it up." Similarly, another participant was disappointed about the great lengths she believed she had taken to get parents to attend PTA meetings. She stated, "We did everything to try to accommodate. We changed times [of PTA meeting] . . . that didn't do any good . . . it was just one thing after another."

Another notable perspective was a belief that the relationship between parents and school personnel was frequently adversarial. One participant laid most of the onus on the behavior of educators. She stated:

> We have a lot of educators, in my opinion, that are not sensitive to some of the needs of those students. . . . I

can see why a lot of parents don't want to be involved and are suspicious of administrators and are suspicious of teachers. Teachers a lot of times don't communicate with parents as they should . . . [and] I have seen administrators target students to get them kicked out of school. [Actually] target students to get them in detention! And every administrator isn't like that, and every teacher isn't like that. But a lot of kids that may just need someone to pull them aside and talk to them . . . so there's a lot of mistrust there between parents, students, teachers, and administrators.

Most of the participants, however, levied some type of indictment of student behavior on the attitudes of parents, although often with an acknowledgment that past experience may have undermined their current home-school relationships. One participant stated,

We have some angry parents. Parents that obviously had bad experiences in school and, and we need to dispel that anger somehow. We need to collaborate and partner in the education of children. It doesn't need to be adversarial.

Others were more one-sided in their criticism of parents' attitude as being expressly adversarial. For example, an elementary schools counselor stated:

I'm being biased on [the] educator viewpoint—but it is automatically assumed that we have done something wrong to the child, and *we* are the ones [at] fault, and *we* didn't do enough, or *we* didn't do what we should have.

An afterschool program coordinator at an elementary school shared her disappointment that it seemed that:

Parents show up when kids are in trouble. But they don't show up for conferences; or if they schedule a conference, they won't show up until it's too late to do something about the problem. . . . There's some who are defensive about what's happening with their kids . . . they're reactive instead of proactive.

Some of the participants viewed their students' attitudes in school as a direct reflection of their parents' attitudes. This was specifically the case for two participants. One stated that students "mimic the actions, the reactions that their parents take to certain situations, and they tend to follow those patterns and bring them to

school . . . . some parents don't realize how much of an effect those things have on children."

The last item of note with regard to school personnel's perceptions of home-school relations came from an African-American woman participant. She saw the schools as a site of intimidation for the parents due to the educational and socioeconomic gap between them and the school staff: "where the parents are middle class . . . they can come in and they can comprehend what is being discussed without feeling any type of intimidation."

Parent Perspectives on Home-School Relations

Consistent with the extant literature on parent involvement, the parents in this study held both "schoolcentric" (Lawson, 2003, p. 79) and parent-centered perspectives on their involvement in their children's academic lives. From the perspective of parents in our study,

parental involvement is inhibited (1) when parents do not feel that teachers and administrators are receptive to their meaningful involvement and concerns and (2) when teachers and administrators are not flexible regarding the schedules of parents who would like to be more involved but cannot be at the usual times or whose involvement would need to take new forms other than evening meetings. (Loder-Jackson et al., 2007, p. 371)

Parent focus group interviews also revealed that parents may be involved with their children's education, or would like to be, in ways that are not always recognized by schools as parental involvement, such as: helping with homework; checking in with teachers by phone; or providing for the emotional and physical needs of their children (Loder-Jackson et al., 2007).

Parents saw meaningful involvement as a shared responsibility between parents and teachers where both assume responsibility for monitoring the student's progress. Parents expressed a desire for two-way communication that is frequent, timely, and reliable. They also acknowledged their discomfort with the fact that teachers have more knowledge about their children's behavior during the day than they do. In their view, a teacher's perceived neglect to be transparent about their children's progress left some parents feeling like they were left out of the information loop. Parents conveyed that not receiving pertinent information about their child's progress in a timely manner hindered them from intervening at critical stages. For example, one parent lamented:

> Parents can't straighten out anything if we don't know what's wrong. I call the school [and inquire], "Well, what is Charles doing now? Is he acting up or is he sweet?" [Teacher's response]   called." [My response is] "No, you should have called me. I call all the time." (Loder-Jackson et al., 2007, p. 368)

Parents also commented that teachers should not presume that all parents do not care about their children simply because they encounter other parents who do not seem to care. One parent remarked that it is incumbent upon the teacher to inform her about her child's progress because she is more knowledgeable about what is going on with her child during the school day.

> I felt [like] the teacher should take time out of her personal schedule and call us as parents and say, "This is 'Miss Whatever,' your child has not turned in homework. We've sent notes home, [and] you have not responded." If that's a good parent then that parent it going to be at the school the following day. If that's a bad parent, I would give them the benefit of a couple of phone calls . . . There are parents that don't care. [But] the ones that do, we wanna know. (Loder-Jackson et al., 2007, p. 368)

Similar to the sentiment expressed by school personnel, overall, parents expressed a sincere desire to do the best for the children both at home and at school. But many parents felt like their best efforts were undermined by what they perceived as an unwelcoming school environment, the lack of, infrequent, or untimely communication about their children's progress, and a general disregard for their self-identification as being their children's "first" teachers. Parents viewed these barriers as hindering them from working collaboratively with teachers on their children's behalf (Loder-Jackson, et al., 2007).

School Personnel and Parent Recommendations

Both school personnel and parents were invited to share recommendations for improving and enhancing parent involvement and home-school relations. In summary, school personnel recommended several strate-gies, a number of which were already in practice. For instance, one participant reported having a very success-ful community building day with a high turnout from the surrounding neighborhood. An elementary school principal reported a "new beginning" for home-school relations when she established the policy of having teachers greet students and parents in the car line each morning. A teacher and parent liaison at the same school also reported some success with teaching parents to use educational games that they can then check out and use with their children. She also mentioned that food, also discussed later, seems to be a big draw for parents, and for her, led to at least one very successful PTA meeting. However, despite the description of a few successes, there was no shortage of suggestions concerning new programs and efforts the participants felt would help them to get parents more involved. When asked about other potential initiatives that might augment beneficial parental involvement, the responses ranged from an additional emphasis on sports to incentive programs for receiving tutoring, to various social events that the schools could host—seasonal celebrations, etc. Some wanted more school- and neighborhood-site specific programs for parents rather than those offered by the more central-site district family involvement program.

Parents' recommendations focused primarily on im-proving communication between home and school (Loder-Jackson et al., 2007). Parents suggested more frequent, timely, and consistent phone calls from their teachers. They also desired to make unannounced visits to the school to check on their children's behavior when they are not expecting to see them at school. Parents inferred they need more guidance helping their children with homework, especially with certain subjects in which they have become unacquainted or lack profi-ciency. However, even though they were not familiar with all of the content to assist their children, they con-veyed that they do not wish to be lumped together in the category of parents who do not care about their children.

In addition to these findings, the authors are also learning how to improve our practice as university teacher educators by examining results from a recent alumni evaluation of the CUE's signature program, the Urban Teacher Enhancement Program (UTEP). UTEP is designed to prepare university teacher education can-didates for careers in urban education. The program has graduated 140 pre-service teachers over the past five years. Some of the results are heartening in the sense that UTEP alumni, who are now teaching primarily in urban or high-poverty schools, appear to recognize their need for more knowledge about and preparation to work effectively with parents and families. UTEP alumni are very supportive of the program, and they believe it has yielded positive results. They attested to the importance of UTEP's emphasis on diversity, equity, culture, social class, and poverty. However, UTEP alumni call for a greater emphasis on parent involvement in TEPs and school district professional development workshops, particularly exposing teachers to real-life experiences with parents as early as possible and consistently throughout the TEP (for example, role playing, parent-teacher conferences, PTA). In addition, UTEP alumni would like to see more emphasis placed on sharpening their communication and conflict-resolution skills with parents (Lawrence-Lightfoot, 2004). These findings will help enhance UTEP as well as the school's overall TEP, and offer insights to TEPs nationally.

These studies point to a pressing need to engage UTEP candidates and urban school collaborators in deeper dialogues about the meaning of race, social class, and gender in the post-civil rights movement urban South. It cannot be taken for granted that school personnel, students, parents, families, and community members who share the same racial identification also share the same communal bonds that have characterized previous generations of African Americans in the urban South. In light of this new context, how might TEPs sensitize future school personnel and leaders to the unique dilemmas and struggles that low-income African-American mothers in urban areas are encountering, and in turn, parley this empathy into a viable plan of action? Faculty and administrators in TEPs and urban school districts must be more intentional about creating spaces, in collaboration with parents, guardians, and family members, that foster meaningful dialogue and strategic planning.

CONCLUSION AND IMPLICATIONS

In this chapter the authors reviewed conceptual and empirical writings on home-school relations, particularly as they relate to urban schools and families. They set the stage for interpreting these findings by examining African-American women within a broader sociopoliti-

cal and cultural context that has historically demeaned their personhood, work, and contributions to society. The authors also examined the extensive literature documenting the deficit-oriented perspectives that far too many school personnel and university TEP candidates espouse as it relates to urban parent involvement. Yet they also presented hopeful recommendations for recasting parent involvement from both the extant literature and the parents and school personnel featured in this study.

Lessons learned from the readers' theater point to the need for leaders in university TEPs and urban school districts to join ranks to create safer spaces conducive for university, school personnel, parents, and students to discuss their collective hopes, frustrations, and strategies for advancing urban education. The authors' attempt to convey the authentic voices of parents to an audience that included primarily parents and some school personnel was both welcomed and challenged. Parents were receptive to this forum whereas some school personnel leaders responsible for coordinating parent programs for the district were concerned about publicizing some of the less-than-flattering findings. Although the authors involved with this readers' theater (most notably the first author) worked closely with school personnel beforehand to co-facilitate the parent focus groups as a university/school district team, and then to discuss and review the findings and the readers' theater script in detail *prior* to public dissemination, actually hearing the script in a public venue was difficult for some school leaders. This reaction is understandable in light of the context discussed previously regarding the "mammification" of African-American women middle-class professionals who are expected to turn around struggling urban public school bureaucracies with very few resources and under lots of public scrutiny (Omolade, 1994, p. 51). But upon deeper reflection and empathy, especially considering the authors' own similar challenges as TEP faculty, who confront intensifying public scrutiny and critique, it is unlikely that anyone can escape experiencing this discomfort (Loder et al., 2007). As Flessa (2008) acknowledged, there is some level of interpersonal conflict and tension that schools, parents, and their organizational partners must contend with in order to ultimately improve and enhance home-school relations.

Findings reveal that school personnel and parents share a desire to create a positive educational experience for children. But in the context of a post-classical civil rights era where many of them are living "worlds apart" (Lawrence-Lightfoot, 1978, title page), TEPs and school districts will have to be more intentional about creating productive spaces for collaboration (Barton et al., 2004). Locally, some civic, community, and university groups have been surveying parents about desirable meeting spaces and topics of interest, and then planning parent initiatives accordingly (Loder-Jackson, Voltz, and Froning, 2014). As a result, there is a notable increase in parent attendance at educational events than has occurred in the past. But there is still a long way to go.

University TEP and urban school faculty and administrators must reexamine curricula and initiatives to determine how much content actually addresses social class dynamics (Gorski, 2008; Rothstein, 2008). They (and the authors included) can no longer implicitly presume that students, parents, families, and school personnel of the same race share the same worldview and life experiences. The authors have encountered TEP students who admit that although they share the same racial/ethnic identity of some of their future students, families, and clients, they sometimes feel alienated from their day-to-day experiences. Therefore, greater strides must be made to bridge this gap through curricular, programmatic, and even structural role changes (Bauch and Goldring, 1996; Lott, 2003; Spillane, 2006; Trotman, 2001). A few specific examples include convening meaningful service learning (Chavkin, 2005) and field experiences in settings where parents are actively involved (for example, school-sponsored parent events, neighborhood meetings, community, civic, and religious events). In fact, one of the coauthors has required his Counselor Education Program students to attend church and community meetings with their future clients as a part of their university training experience. Other ideas include enlisting parents and guardians as co-teachers and speakers in university courses (Chavkin, 2005; Norris, 2010; Trotman, 2001), and incorporating video case studies and modules that present authentic issues and actual questions raised by real parents (Roushias, Barton, and Drake, 2009). Finally, as modeled in this chapter, more connections should be made between the classroom and popular culture (for example, our previous illustration from *The Women of Brewster Place*) to help cultivate a younger generation of educators' cultural responsiveness to the students and families they will one day serve.

REFERENCES

Alabama State Department of Education. (2012, March). *Alabama's education report card, 2010–2011*. Montgomery, AL: Author.

Amott, T. and Matthaei, J. (1996). *Race, gender and work: A multi-cultural economic history of women in the United States*. Boston, MA: South End Press.

Annie E. Casey Foundation. (2011). *Kids Count*. Baltimore, MD: Author. Retrieved from www.kidscount.org.

Barton, A. C., Drake, C., Perez, J. G., St. Louis, K., and George, M. (2004). Ecologies of parental engagement in urban education. *Educational Researcher, 33*(4), 3–12.

Bauch, P. A. and Goldring, E. B. (1996). Parent involvement and teacher decision making in urban high schools of choice. *Urban Education, 31*(4), 403–431.

Brewer, R. M. (1988, Winter). Black women in poverty: Some comments on female-headed families. *Signs, 13*(2), 331–339.

Brooks, M., Perry, T., and Loder-Jackson, T. L. (2008, March). *Communities and Schools Together (CAST) Project reader's theater for parents and community members*.

Burton, L. M. (1996). Age norms, the timing of family role transitions, and intergenerational caregiving among aging African American women. *The Gerontologist 36*(2), 199–208.

Carter, P. A. (2002). *"Everybody's paid but the teacher": The teaching profession and the women's movement*. New York: Teachers College Press.

Chavkin, N. F. (2005). Strategies for preparing educators to enhance the involvement of diverse families in their children's education. *Multicultural Education, 13*(2), 16–20.

Collins, P. H. (2000). *Black feminist thought: Knowledge, consciousness, and the politics of empowerment*. (2nd ed). New York: Routledge.

Cooper, C. W. (2009). Parental involvement, African American mothers, and the politics of care. *Equity and Excellence in Education, 42*(4), 379–394.

Cooper, C. W., Riehl, C. J., and Hasan, A. L. (2010). Leading and learning with diverse families in schools: Critical epistemology and communities of practice. *Journal of School Leadership, 20*(6), 758–788.

Cooper, E. J. (2009). Realities and responsibilities in the education village. In L. C. Tillman (Ed.), *The Sage handbook* of African American education (pp. 435–449). Thousand Oaks, CA: Sage.

Davis, A. B., Gardner, B. G., and Gardner, M. (2009). *Deep South: A social anthropological study of caste and class.* Columbia: University of South Carolina Press.

Donmoyer, R. and Yennie-Donmoyer, J. (1995). Data as drama: Reflections on the use of readers' theater as a mode of qualitative data display. *Qualitative Inquiry, 1*(4), 402–428.

Eisner, E. (1979). *The educational imagination: On the design, and evaluation of school programs.* New York: Macmillan.

Feldman, L. B. (1999). *A sense of place: Birmingham's Black middle-class community, 1890–1930.* Tuscaloosa: University of Alabama Press.

Fields-Smith, C. (2005). African American parents before and after *Brown. Journal of Curriculum and Supervision, 20*(2), 129–135.

Fields-Smith, C. (2009). After "It takes a village": Mapping the terrain of Black parental involvement in the post-*Brown* era. In L. C. Tillman (Ed.), *The Sage handbook of African American education* (pp. 153–170). Thousand Oaks, CA: Sage.

Flessa, J. (2008). Parent involvement: What counts, who counts it, and does it help? *Education Canada, 48*(2), 18–21.

Frankenberg, E. (2009). Splintering school districts: Understanding the link between segregation and fragmentation. *Law and Social Inquiry, 34*(4), 869–909.

Frazier, E. F. (1957). *Black bourgeoisie.* New York: The Free Press.

Fultz, M. (2004). The displacement of Black educators post-*Brown*: An overview and analysis. *History of Education Quarterly, 44*(1), 11–45.

Gorski, P. (2008). The myth of the "culture of poverty." *Educational Leadership, 65*(7), 32–36.

Henig, J. R., Hula, R. C., Orr, M., and Pedescleaux, D. S. (1999). *The color of school reform: Race, politics and the challenge of urban education.* Princeton, NJ: Princeton University Press.

Huberman, M. and Miles, M. (1994). Data management and analysis methods. In N. K. Denzin and Y. S. Lincoln (Eds.), *Handbook of qualitative research* (pp. 428–444). Thousand Oaks, CA: Sage.

Institute for Education Statistics, National Center for Education Statistics. (2013). *Urban education in America* [Website]. Washington, DC: IES/NCES. Retrieved from nces.ed.gov/surveys/urbaned/.

Jarrett, R. L. (1994). Living poor: Family life among single parent, African-American women. *Social Problems, 41*(1), 30–49.

Jarrett, R. L. and Burton, L. M. (1999). Dynamic dimensions of family structure in low-income African American families: Emergent themes in qualitative research. *Journal of Comparative Family Studies, 30*, 177–187.

Ladner, J. A. and Gourdine, R. M. (1984). Intergenerational teenage motherhood: Some preliminary findings. *SAGE: A Scholarly Journal on Black Women, 1*(2), 22–24.

Lawrence-Lightfoot, S. (1978). *Worlds apart: Relationships between families and schools.* New York.

Lawrence-Lightfoot, S. (2004). *The essential conversation: What parents and teachers can learn from each other.* New York: Random House.

Lawson, M. A. (2003). School-family relations in context: Parent and teacher perceptions of parent involvement. *Urban Education, 38*(1), 77–133.

Lightfoot, D. (2004). "Some parents just don't care": Decoding the meanings of parental involvement in urban schools. *Urban Education, 39*(1), 91–107.

Loder, T. L. (2005). African American women principals' reflections on social change, community othermothering, and Chicago Public School reform. *Urban Education, 40*(3), 298–320.

Loder, T. L., Sims, M. J., Coker, A. D., Collins, L., Brooks, M., Voltz, D., and Calhoun, C. (2007, Winter). On becoming and being faculty-leaders in urban education and also being African American . . . Seems promising [Special issue]. *Advancing Women in Leadership, 23.* Retrieved from www.advancingwomen.com/awl/winter2007/Loder.htm.

Loder-Jackson, T. L. (2011). Bridging the legacy of activism across generations: Life stories of African American educators in post-civil rights Birmingham. *The Urban Review, 43*(2), 151–174.

Loder-Jackson, T. L. (2012). Hope and despair: Southern Black women educators across pre- and post-civil rights cohorts theorize about their activism. [Special Issue] *Educational Studies: The Journal of the American Educational Studies Association, 48*(3), 266–295. doi:10.1080/0013194 6.2012.660665.

Loder-Jackson, T. L., McKnight, A. N., Brooks, M., McGrew, K., and Voltz, D. (2007). Unmasking subtle and concealed aspects of parent involvement: Perspectives from African-American parents in the urban south. *Journal of School Public Relations, 28*(4), 350–379.

Loder-Jackson, T. L., Voltz, D. L., and Froning, M. (2014). New horizons for urban educators engaging families in the post-civil rights South. In C. Wilson and S. Horsford (Eds.), *A nation of students at risk: Advancing equity and achievement in America's diversifying schools* (pp. 186–199). New York: Routledge.

Lott, B. (2003). Recognizing and welcoming the standpoint of low-income parents in the public schools. *Diversity in Consultation, 14*, 91–104.

Massey, D. S. and Denton, N. A. (1993). *American apartheid: Segregation and the making of the underclass.* Boston, MA: President and Fellows of Harvard College.

Milner, H. R. (2009). Preparing teachers of African American students in urban schools. In L. C. Tillman (Ed.), *The Sage Handbook of African American Education* (pp. 123–139). Thousand Oaks, CA: Sage.

Morgan, D. L. (1997). *Focus groups as qualitative research* (2nd ed). Thousand Oaks, CA: Sage.

Naylor, G. (1982). *The women of Brewster Place.* New York: Viking Press.

Naylor, G. (Writer), Hall, K. (Writer), and Deitch, D. (Director). (1989). *The women of Brewster Place* [Television series]. In Winfrey, O. (Executive Producer) and Eisenberg, C. (Executive Producer). Chicago, IL: Harpo Production and King Phoenix Entertainment.

Norris, K. E. L. (2010). Beyond the textbook: Building relationships between teachers and diversely-structured families. *Multicultural Education, 18*(1), 48–50.

Omolade, B. (1994). *The rising song of African American women.* New York: Routledge.

Overstreet, S., Devine, J., Bevans, K., and Efreom, Y. (2005). Predicting parental involvement in children's schooling within an economically disadvantaged African American sample. *Psychology in the Schools, 42(1),* 101–111.

Pattillo-McCoy, M. (1999). *Black picket fences: Privilege and peril among the Black middle class.* Chicago, IL: University of Chicago Press.

Patton, M. Q. (1989). *Qualitative evaluation methods* (10th ed.). Beverly Hills, CA: Sage.

Phi Delta Kappa International. 2011. [Anonymous School District] *Curriculum Audit.* Bloomington, IN: International Curriculum Management Audit Center, Phi Delta Kappa.

Planty, M., Hussar, W., Snyder, T., Kena, G., Kwela Ramani, A., Kemp, J., Bianco, K., and Dinkes, R. (2009). *The Condition of Education 2009 (NCES 2009-081), Indicator 30: Parent and Family Involvement in Education.* National Center for Education Statistics, Institute of Education Sciences, U.S. Department of Education. Washington, DC.

Rist, R. (1970). Student social class and teacher expectations: The self-fulfilling prophecy of ghetto education. *Harvard Educational Review, 40*(3), 411–451.

Robinson, E. (2010). *Disintegration: The splintering of Black America.* New York: Anchor Books.

Rothstein, R. (2008, April). Whose problem is poverty? *Educational Leadership,* 8–13.

Roushias, C., Barton, A. C., and Drake, C. (2009). The design and development of a multimedia case-based environment on parental engagement. *Educational Media International, 46*(1), 37–52.

Rustin, B. (1965, February). From protest to politics: The future of the civil rights movement. *Commentary, 39,* 25–31.

Seidman, I. (1998). *Interviewing as qualitative research: A guide for researchers in education and the social sciences,* 2nd edition. New York: Teachers College Press.

Slaughter-Defoe, D. T. (1993, Winter). Home-visiting with families in poverty: Introducing the concept of culture. *The Future of Children* [Special issue], 3(3), 172–183.

Smalley, S. Y. and Reyes-Blanes, M. E. (2001). Reaching out to African American parents in an urban community: A community-university partnership. *Urban Education, 36*(4), 518–533.

Smrekar, C. and Cohen-Vogel, L. (2001). The voices of parents: Rethinking the intersection of family and school. *Peabody Journal of Education, 76*(2), 75–100.

Spillane, J. P. (2006). *Distributed leadership.* San Francisco, CA: Jossey-Bass.

Trotman, M. F. (2001). Involving the African American parent: Recommendations to increase the level of parent involvement within African American families. *The Journal of Negro Education, 70*(4), 275–285.

Voltz, D. L. (1994). Developing collaborative parent-teacher relationships with culturally diverse parents. *Intervention in School and Clinic, 29,* 288–291.

Voltz, D. L. (1998). Challenges and choices in urban education: The perceptions of teachers and principals. *Urban Review, 30,* 211–228.

Voltz, D. L. (2000). Challenges and choices in urban teaching: Voices of general and special educators. *Multiple Voices, 4*(1), 40–51.

Walker, V. S. (1996). *Their highest potential: An African American school community in the segregated South.* Chapel Hill: University of North Carolina Press.

Walker, V. S. (2000). Valued segregated schools for African American children in the South, 1935–1969: A review of common themes and characteristics. *Review of Educational Research, 70,* 253–285.

Wallace, G. (2013). African-American mothers, community social capital and parenting quality: Does personal outlook make a difference? *Sociological Perspectives, 56*(2), 261–285.

Wilson, W. J. (1987). *The truly disadvantaged: The inner city, the underclass, and public policy.* Chicago: The University of Chicago Press.

PARENTAL INVOLVEMENT AND COMMUNITY

In section 5, "Parental Involvement and Community," we explore the contextual importance of the community in urban educational leadership. We include this section since community support and parent involvement have been cited in literature as one of the top three issues in urban schooling and leadership. The authors in this section demonstrate that several important factors impact the relationships parents have with schools. Given the context within which urban educational leaders operate, it seems fitting that school-parents-community relationship is one of the areas requiring the most pressing attention. This research establishes important implications for school leaders concerning parental involvement and the communities in which they live.

In chapter 17, "'I Know Momma Didn't Have to Work This Hard': Leadership Implications of Intergenernational Differences in Engaging African-American Families," Cheryl Fields-Smith, Sheneka Williams, and Jaqueline Shoemaker examine the diversity of those who identify as parents within urban communities, and how these intergenerational differences present in schools when related to parental attitudes, beliefs, and customs, informing the practices of school leaders. Also highlighting the changes within a community, in chapter 18, "Where Has All of the Community Rage Gone? Neoliberalism, Community Encroachment, and Unconventional Resistance in Detroit," Muhammad Khalifa,

Elizabeth Gil, Stefanie Marshall, and Gregory White examine community responses and protest behaviors in one of our nation's most notorious sites for protest, Detroit, Michigan. Recognizing that protest has evolved, this group sought to locate the voices of protest to neoliberal reforms that have debilitated community and parental voices that once resisted hegemonic control, limiting the democratic rights of both the community and parents.

Lastly, in chapter 19, "A Spectrum of Parent and Community Engagement for Conceptualizing and Responding to the Institutional Complexity of Urban Schools," Sharon Watkins, Anika Ball Anthony, Christopher Shaffer, and Kirsten Smith recognize that the demands on school leaders to innovatively engage with parents and communities can be futile if such initiatives lack strategy, and therefore are ineffectively sustained. The authors present a spectrum of five urban school engagement models that can serve as a framework for school leaders when implementing parent and community initiatives in order to achieve chosen goals. These chapters inform how school leaders of the evolving nature of the parents and communities in urban contexts, informing practice and implementation of various initiatives. Overall, the chapters in this section confirm the importance of regular interaction between parents, schools, and communities.

CHAPTER 17

"I Know Momma Didn't Have to Work This Hard"

Leadership Implications of Intergenerational Differences in Engaging African-American Families

Cheryl Fields-Smith, Sheneka Williams, and Jaqueline Shoemaker

Given the long-standing and ever-growing research tradition, the association between student achievement and family engagement is undeniable. Family engagement plans are federally mandated through the No Child Left Behind, Head Start, and Title I legislation. Moreover, school districts require educational leaders to include family engagement in their School Improvement Plans. Even with these widespread calls for family engagement in children's schooling, tensions remain regarding definitions of involvement and in clarifying the boundaries between the roles of home, school, and community.

Epstein's (1995) theory of overlapping spheres assumes that the adults in the school, home, and community will share responsibility for educating their children. However, we have learned from research that parents' beliefs regarding their role in children's education will vary by ethnic, cultural, and sociological background (i.e., Chavkin, 1993; Fields-Smith, 2005, 2006, 2007, 2008; Lareau, 2000, 2003). For example, seminal research has demonstrated institutional structures and school personnel's perceptions of urban families can lead to inequities by social class and race or ethnicity, which result in disenfranchisement in participating in their children's learning (i.e., Abrams and Gibbs, 2002; Lareau and Horvat, 1999; McGrath and Kuriloff, 1999). Additionally, role construction theory supports the notion that some parents, perhaps low-income parents in particular, may limit their engagement because they lack confidence in their ability to make a difference in their children's education (Hoover-Dempsey and Sandler, 1997). Lawrence-Lightfoot (2003) also posits that parents who had negative experiences in school as a child tend to limit involvement in their children's learning at school.

However, family involvement researchers rarely consider that the parents within one school community can vary considerably by age, and therefore heads of families may represent multiple generations, each with diverse perspectives on when, how, and even if, to be engaged in their children's learning as well. During the first author's dissertation study, a community nomination process for participant selection yielded a relatively homogeneous participant pool in terms of age (forties and fifties) and educational level (undergraduate or graduate school level). When she attempted to replicate the study among younger parents (twenties and thirties) within the same school settings, community nomination could not be used because the older participants from the previous study reported that even though their children attended the same schools, they did not know any parents from the younger age group. This eye-opening experience has inspired the writing of this chapter.

Intergenerational diversity among parent populations in urban schools is likely to increase. Trends indicate that grandparents are increasingly raising their grandchildren (Bailey, 2012; Baker et al., 2008). U.S. Census data indicates that roughly five million American families consist of three or more generations living under the same roof and that multigenerational households have increased by 5 percent between 1980 and 2009 (Jensen, 2014). In addition, although reports suggest that the teen pregnancy rate has declined overall, the Center for Disease Control still indicates that even the new lower rate at thirty-one births for every thousand teens is still too high (Shah, 2013). These two trends suggest that schools are likely to have parents or guardians representing the Baby Boomer generation (persons born between 1946 and 1964), Generation X (persons born between 1965 and 1982), and the New Boomers (persons born between 1983 and 2001) as described by U.S. demographers (Rosenberg, 2013). The generalized characterizations of persons in each of these generations suggest tensions in cross-generational interactions. For example, Baby Boomers are described as valuing meaningfulness in one's work whereas Generation X has been depicted as working in order to live. Researchers have examined and developed best practices for resolving cross-generational conflicts in the workplace (Glass, 2007, for example).

Yet, the influence of intergenerational differences on family engagement within urban schools has rarely been examined. Understanding the intergenerational differences in family engagement will have considerable implications for urban school administrators' leadership practices. This chapter examines the ways in which parents' attitudes, beliefs, and practices can vary by age within the same urban school and the engagement experiences of grandparents who are serving as parents to their grandchildren. Moreover, the chapter explores how family engagement practices and attitudes may change from one generation to another within a family. These types of intergenerational differences are rarely captured in the literature.

The primary aim of this chapter is to demonstrate how family engagement has changed from one generation to the next among black families including households where grandparents are serving as parents again, and then to posit how school leaders can address the cross-generational differences within their schools. Based on three independently conducted studies situated in two distinct urban contexts, our chapter addresses the following research question: what intergenerational differences and similarities exists among parents' and grandparents' attitudes, beliefs, and practices related to engagement in their children's, or grandchildren's education?

REVIEW OF RELEVANT LITERATURE

Several databases (for example, JSTOR, Academic Search Complete, PsyInfo) and a variety of search terms for "cross-generational" and "parental involvement" were used to search for literature related to intergenerational differences in family involvement. The results of these searches led to mixed results. For example, research articles documenting the value of school programs designed to promote young and adolescent children to interact with elders provide evidence that cross-generational interaction in schools benefits both

the children and the seniors (see Kaplan, 2002, for example). However, the elders and young people in these studies tended to not be related, and therefore did not fit the parameters of this chapter, which aims to focus on intergenerational differences in family involvement in their children's education.

More closely related, several studies focused on intergenerational closure, which refers to connections among people within a network that cross generations. As described by Carbonaro (1998), intergeneration closure suggests that critical knowledge related to student success in school is passed on through interaction between children's parents and the parents of children's friends. Carbonaro explained the converse, "When social networks lack closure, parents lose an important resource for dealing with their children" (p. 296). Previous studies employing social capital theory have demonstrated that low-income and black families tend to not have social networks situated within the school (e.g., Lareau and Horvat, 1999; McGrafth and Kuriloff, 1999) and therefore, may be assumed to have limited intergenerational closure. Carbonaro's (1998) study of intergenerational closure among 16,489 families from the National Education Longitudinal Study in 1988 (NELS 88) demonstrated that regardless of background characteristics such as family structure, students' math achievement increased 13 percent yearly for each friend's parent who was known by the students' parents. Interestingly, the researcher did not find the same results with other subjects, which he attributed to differences in parental expectations. Although no association was found between intergenerational closure and overall GPA of a student, the study did provide evidence that as intergenerational closure increased then dropout, class skipping, absenteeism, and even suspension declined among high school students. More recently, Freeman and Condron (2011) queried the function of intergenerational closure among first graders. Their study provides further evidence that black parents tend to have fewer school-based relationships than Hispanic or white parents. Children of families with limited intergenerational closure or weak ties to school-based relationships tended to not achieve as well as those families who have strong relationships with other families at the school. None of these studies considered the age of participating parents in their studies.

METHODOLOGY AND FINDINGS

This chapter presents findings from three independently conducted studies related to intergenerational differences in parental engagement among families. The methodology and subsequent findings used for each of the studies has been described separately within this section. Methods used in all three studies represented culturally relevant processes as described by Tillman (2002). In addition, findings have been interpreted and conceptualized with a strength-based focus (that is, Funds of Knowledge) in order to avoid the pathological characterization often associated with research in urban settings. Within each of the three studies one parent has been highlighted as a representative of other participants in order to foster deeper understanding of the characteristics that differentiate perspectives across families in each of the groups (parents age thirty-five and older, younger parents, and grandparents as parents).

Study 1 Parents Age Thirty-Five and Older

Methods

The first author conducted this study of nineteen families, representing five elementary schools in DeKalb County, Georgia, which is part of Metro-Atlanta (Fields-Smith, 2004). This study took place from 2003 to 2004, as a dissertation focused on understanding the attitudes, beliefs, and practices of highly engaged black parents. According to U.S. Census data available at the time, DeKalb County, which was classified as an urban county, had experienced a 10 percent growth rate of the past decade. In addition, the racial composition had changed from majority white (71.3 percent) in 1980 to majority black (55.3 percent) in 2000. Rapid growth occurred in DeKalb County's student population as well. In 2000, the Georgia State Department of Education website reported 90,837 students attended DeKalb County schools. By 2003, DeKalb Public Schools served 97,284 students. Of these, 74,739 students identified as black and 10,372 identified as white.

Community nomination beginning with Parent Teacher Organization (PTO) leaders and educators resulted in a participant pool with similar ages, income levels, and educational levels. Data sources included two semi-structured interviews (one during the sum-

mer or at the start of the school year and the other toward the end of the school year). Interviews assumed a two-phased approach based on a modified version of Seidman's (1998) interviewing method. The first phase focused on parents' childhood and how their parents engaged in their schooling. The second phase of the interview queried their current motivations and practices related to participating in their children's education. Using this two-phased approach fostered intergenerational reflection on their beliefs and practices related to parental involvement. Participant observation in the schools provided additional data. Parents reviewed transcripts of their recorded interviews for accuracy. Data analysis involved multiple-level coding procedures resulting in thematic matrices as suggested by Bogdan and Biklen (2003).

Study 1 Findings

The community nomination process used in this Metro-Atlanta-based study resulted in a relatively homogeneous group of participating parents in terms of age and income, but diverse in their backgrounds. Parents represented in Study 1 ranged in age from thirty-four to fifty years old; the mean age of the group was forty-two years old. Participating families represented middle-income (twelve families) and upper-income households (seven families). Of the nineteen families, six people represented single-parent households. Parents reported growing up in urban communities (eight parents), suburban communities (four parents), rural communities (five parents), and military bases (two parents). Parents in this study enrolled their children in one of five schools located within the same Metro-Atlanta school district. Schools included two predominantly black traditional elementary schools, a predominantly black theme school, a predominantly black magnet school, and a predominantly white magnet school.

To report findings most relevant to the stated aims of this chapter, we focus on analysis of parents' self-reports reflecting on connections and disconnections between how their parents were involved in comparison to the ways in which they currently participate in their own children's learning. In addition, pertinent notes from the researcher's journal developed throughout Study 1 will be presented.

Reflecting on Generational Differences

Mrs. Howard, a forty-six-year-old mother of three children, summed up the intergenerational differences well when she stated, "I know my mother didn't have to work this hard." Older families expressed similar thoughts, indicating a belief that parental involvement today requires more thought and energy than when they were children, during the 1950s–1970s. Mrs. Howard reported that unlike her parents, she and her husband employed strategies that enabled them to be "in the loop," meaning they purposely positioned themselves to have access to decision-making at the school every year. This meant she and her husband rotated roles on the Executive Board of the Parent Teacher Organization and on the School Council each year. Mrs. Howard also expressed a belief in parents' need to manage the relationships with their children's teachers. Regarding the home-school relationship, Mrs. Howard stated, as a parent, "I am responsible for making sure that there is one [a relationship with the teacher]." The study further revealed that highly engaged families perceived their visibility in the school served as an essential component to managing relationships with their children's teachers with statements such as, "I try to put forth an effort at my son's school that I'm visible in there and in the classroom and in the halls at least once a week because I don't want there to be no mistakes mentally in the fact that I'm a highly proactive mom, highly involved mom."

Conversely, parents' beliefs of having to manage relationships with school staff and maintain visibility in their children's school marked a drastic divergence from the ways in which participating parents describe their own families' involvement when they were children themselves. Candice (age forty-four), a self-employed mother of two children, described her mother's engagement as simply, "Pretty much it was one of those things where my mom just said, Don't have me come to school for any foolishness." Arthur, a fifty-year-old father of two children (one who was an adult at the time of the interview and the other a nine-year-old), shared that his mother's primary engagement in his schooling included her admonition, "Boy, you better mount to something," meaning make something of yourself and do better than she did. Seldom did the parents of these older participants enter their schools beyond PTA meetings and school performances. These descriptions corroborated findings reported in seminal African-American

educational history research (for example, see Walker, 1996, 2000) where black parents were highly involved in their children's education, but not necessarily within the school. Relationships with teachers developed as a result of the close-knit community interactions experienced in the segregated South.

Interesting to note, older black parents (forties and fifties), who had Southern upbringings, reported that they, like the infamous Little Rock Nine, had integrated their schools at some point in their schooling. This experience left an undeniable passion for advocacy in children's schooling on the older parents as evidenced by several notations in the researcher's journal indicating a challenge to getting older black parents to consider their parental engagement roles on behalf of their own children instead of what they have done in terms of advocacy for the school overall, a particular classroom, or other people's children. Advocacy required older parents to share ideas and work together in order to obtain resolution to issues such as overcrowding on school buses and allocation of district funds to provide a gymnasium or increase the capacity of a school kitchen. In other cases, older black parents reported that they advocated on behalf of other families as well. For example, one fifty-year-old mother, who was serving as the PTO president at the time of the interview, shared that she publically criticized the school administration for requiring families to provide children with two recorders (flute-like musical instrument), one for home and one for school, because this policy assumed all families could afford to purchase two of the musical instruments. Though she was not successful in changing the policy immediately, she mitigated the policy's effect on lower-income families by rallying a group of parents to contribute funds to support them by purchasing the extra recorders for those families in need. In this way, older black parents demonstrated a strong value of communicating and advocating for each other and the larger school community as a whole. This overall sense of advocacy on behalf of others differed from the beliefs and practices described by younger black parents within the same schools.

Study 2 Parents, Ages Twenty to Thirty-Four

Methods

The first author conducted this study in the same urban district as Study 1. This study represented a follow-up to her dissertation as an attempt to replicate the study among younger parents (ages twenty to thirty-four) within the same school settings described in Study 1 above. Five African-American mothers and one single parent father participated in this qualitative study, which followed a methodology process similar to that described above for Study 1. In addition, three younger parents (under age thirty-five) from Study 1 have been included in this younger parent study. Therefore, eight families in total are represented in Study 2. Three of the eight parents represented had not completed their college education at the time of the interview; the remaining five parents held undergraduate degrees.

Study 2 Findings

Study 2 represented a replication of Study 1, but with younger parents within the same school settings. Fields-Smith (2007) describes economic differences among families in the dissertation study, which have implications for considering the context of studying younger parents. Specifically, unlike the older parents, who most likely achieved a particular status in their careers, younger parents tend to still be trying to establish themselves, or face pressures of excelling on their jobs and putting in face time in the office in order to obtain promotions. This, in part, may explain older black parents' descriptions of younger black parents in their schools as "dropping their children off at the curb" instead of taking time to come into the school. For example, Stephanie, a thirty-four-year-old single parent of one explained her lack of involvement on the PTA Executive Board, "I just don't have to, I'm not going to say that I don't have the motivation, I just don't have the time to do it because I have other things to do. You know, I'm getting off from work; I'm coming home, picking up my child and making sure her work's done; it's like I'm on a schedule so it's, I shouldn't use the term that I don't have time, which I can make time, but it's like I'm burnt out when I get home." Additional factors contributing to the aloof practices of younger black parents thematically emerged from the interviews.

Unlike the older black parents in these settings, when asked about their parental involvement practices, young black parents focused almost exclusively on the activities they did on behalf of their own children's learning. As an exemplar of their responses, Stephanie described

her engagement: "[I] continue to have communication with her teacher. She gives me feedback on her day-to-day, a weekly report of her, of her work flow. You know, if there are some areas where she's having problems, she'll address that with me and I'll try to nip that in the bud and/or help [her] with doing homework." Reminiscent of older black parents' belief in their need to manage the parent-teacher relationship, Stephanie further reported that she initiated the weekly communication process with the teacher and that they used primarily telephone or email communication. Owning the communication, she stated, "I check in with [the teacher] weekly to see how [daughter] is doing." Stephanie also shared that she relied on involvement from the After School Program to some extent to review her child's homework. This type of shared engagement with After School Programs was not frequently reported in Study 1 with older black parents; this is most likely due to the different job statuses. Older black moms tended to be stay-at-home moms, entrepreneurs, or in other careers that provided flexibility in their work hours such that after-school care was not needed. Stephanie, a single parent, worked eight a.m. to five p.m. as an administrative assistant in a major company. She reported to several executives, and her daily one-way commute was over an hour long, thus her child required after-school care. She described her at-home engagement, "You know, sometimes I look over it and sometimes I don't because the after school program does that, but if she has a problem where you know she feels as though it wasn't correct and after-school care didn't do a good job, then I'll correct it. I'll go back and look at it." When asked how she evaluated the after-school program's abilities with homework, Stephanie replied, "Well, because my child will dispute it. She'll dispute it and she'll say, 'That's not how we did it, dah-dah-dah.'"

Stephanie also differed from the older black parents in her predominantly black elementary school in that she did not develop relationships with the other parents in the school. She shared, "I don't have any relationships with any other parents. It's kind of hard because of the work schedule. Some people work night shift; some people work day shift. So it's kind of hard. I used to have a little network group, but we seemed to just fade away. Everyone has their own agenda, you know, it's just that it's hard, it's hard, it's hard," Similar to other parents under age thirty-five represented in this study,

Stephanie did not describe a sense of agency or community with other parents in the school and expressed an as-needed approach to engagement in her child's education. In comparison, older parents acknowledged that they believed they had to work harder to be engaged in their children's education compared to their own parents, and their conviction of advocacy, and their advanced economic development enabled them to form and maintain effective networks informally and formally within and outside of the school.

Stephanie's beliefs regarding her own neighborhood, including parents with children attending the same school as her daughter, contributed to her disconnect within the school community. When asked if she discussed school matters with her neighbors with children in the same school, Stephanie responded, "No, I don't get involved on a personal level like that with my neighbors, because they're wishy-washy . . . Wishy-washy means that they could be your neighbor one day and next day they won't be your neighbor so I tend to keep my personal business within myself, within my household, and not to discuss it with my neighbors and my community." Stephanie's work schedule enabled her to have every other Friday off. On these days she reported that she occasionally would "pop in" to the classroom. Describing these unannounced visits, she explained, "I just go look in the class, in my daughter's classroom and you know, see how she's doing and um just check up on her." When asked if teachers approved her spontaneous visits, Stephanie vehemently proclaimed, "Yes and regardless if they're not, I'm a taxpayer; I'm going to pop up." The purpose of the surprise visits she explained, "I don't need to be, I don't interfere with their school, their academics. But you know, I just peek in and look and observe; that's it. I try not to pull the teacher out and say, 'You know, I need to talk to you.' I'll schedule an appointment, but I just pop up to see how she's [her daughter] interacting and doing." Reflecting later in the interview, Stephanie revealed her belief that if she did not do her surprise visits, "[Her daughter] would probably be in detention every day. Well, not so much every day, but it's just, you know, it would be like she wouldn't have a care. She being my daughter, she would be like, 'Oh well, Mommy doesn't care so I can have an I don't care attitude.' And that's not good." By periodically coming to the school, Stephanie believed she was communi-

cating to her daughter, "That I am not playing. That I mean business." Older parents reported hearing similar motivational adages from their parents during their childhood. But, for Stephanie, saying "I mean business" was not enough; she had to follow up with monitoring pop-in visits to the school.

Yet, Stephanie rarely volunteered at the school most likely due to stresses of being a single working mother. She shared, "I don't volunteer up there. I used to at one point, but with work, I'm just burned out so I really don't do much volunteering, but I do try to, when I have a Friday off, I'll either take something for her classroom, or make some goodies or something like that, candy apples." Stephanie also reported that she refrains from interacting with other children in her daughter's classroom, "No, I don't. And the reason why I don't do that is because some parents may have funny feelings, mixed feelings about you know, another parent interacting with their child and/or if they're misbehaving and you try to correct them and they go home and say, 'Such and such mom said this and that.' It just creates too much controversy so I focus on my child and my child only unless it's a field trip and then if I have to have five other students with me, I'll keep them in my care, chaperone." This relatively isolated stance contrasts with older black parents in the school who shared numerous accounts of advocating on behalf of the school overall and particular families or children within the school. Moreover, using a longitudinal dataset and based on Social Capital Theory, Carbonaro (1998) studied intergenerational closure, or the extent to which parents know the parents of their children's friends, and found that the greater the contact parents had with their children's friends' parents, the greater the children's educational outcomes among over sixteen thousand students. Therefore, according to Carbonaro, Stephanie's self-segregating perspective with other people's children potentially limits student achievement.

Even within this isolating perspective on engagement at the school and with other families, similar to their older parent counterparts, younger parents reported that they had to work harder to be involved in their children's education more than their parents had to when they were children. Comparing her mom's parental involvement practices to her own, Stephanie shared, "It's different a little bit. I'm more active in my daughter's education. And not to say that my parents weren't; it's just back in the days, you had to work hard. It's just that I, um, what I do more is I monitor her homework more and I try to, um, if there's a problem, I address it right then and there and don't wait have to wait three months down the line. [pause] Oh, and go up to her classroom and stuff like that." Stephanie recounted that her parents did not have to do the check-ins or even monitor her homework and learning as closely as she felt she had to do, and she attributed the difference to "It's, our kids going up in this day and age are different than we were back in the day. It's a whole different breed; they're a lot more active. They're a lot more active and they, um, just busy, not focused, easy to get off track and you just have to put an army on them. It's just not like how we were brought up." The imagery of having to "put an army" on the children compared to the "it takes a village" concept of each one reaching one on behalf of children provided an interesting contradiction to consider. In Stephanie's engagement practice she is the army, but in the older families within the same school, the army is more of a collective. Stephanie's case suggests an overall lack of trust of most of the adults in and outside of the school. Her self-reported confidants and close friends included family and non-family members who for the most part did not reside in her neighborhood, but had children older or in the same grades as her own. The distance from her community seemed to provide a desired sense of anonymity within the school.

The other younger parents in the study reported attitudes and beliefs that would also lead to isolation from other parents. For example, when asked how often she visited her daughter's school, Katie, a twenty-eight-year-old single mother, and a schoolteacher within the same district, reported, "More often than I would like to." Specifying, she clarified that her desired frequency of visiting the school would be, "Let's see. If I had it my way, I probably would go to her school for the usual parent conferences, which I probably go to two to three times a year, and I probably would go for whatever special events or Honor's Day and things like that." Instead Katie reported,

> But I have to go because [child] has such unique personality and attitude. I'm called up to her school more than I think an average parent might be. It's always to do with [child]'s behavior. She's in first grade; she still has tantrums. She may be hitting someone else, screaming things like that. I think that in a way they may call a

little more than they need to, but on the other hand, I do understand. It is important to keep the parents involved, especially when the child is misbehaving. Of course with me having other responsibilities, it's an inconvenience for me to have to come up there in the school day or to things like that, but umm [pause]. I understand it, but you know, as a teacher and as a parent too, the school, in the school we do have to have a certain level of consequences within ourselves too, you know. You can't call a parent for everything.

Katie also shared that she did not have relationships with other parents in her child's school. As a teacher at another school in the district, Katie experienced tremendous challenges in going to her child's school during the daytime, which contributed to her inability to get to know children in her daughter's class as well as their parents. In addition, her daughter's negative behavior in school contributed to Katie's desire for anonymity. This even influenced her engagement in after-school outlets such as PTO as she disclosed, "I go, the only time to be honest with you I've ever gone to PTO is if they [the children] perform. Then I'd go. But you know what I think to tell you the truth, I'm not really involved a lot in the PTO and things like that. Another reason is because of [child]'s behavior. I kind of shy away from different things because of the type of child she is and I know that she's labeled. You know, so I think that kind of puts a barrier, not with the volunteering because I would do that anyway, but as far as getting real connected with a lot of the parents and things like that . . . You know, with [child] having some of the difficulties that she has [pause] hmmm [pause] it's like [pause] like I don't want to be seen as the bad child's mother."

Younger parents also tended to discuss their engagement practices in terms of what they did at home in order to be involved in their children's learning more so than what they did at the school. Younger black parents described their parental roles as reinforcing and supporting the learning at school through activities such as checking homework and helping with projects. Across all families represented, discussions around the dinner table served as both a check-in and an opportunity for parents to remind children of their expectations in terms of grades and behavior at school. Jennifer, a thirty-two-year-old married mother of five, stated, "A lot of times at the dinner table, that's when we usually are all together as a family also when the report cards come home. We are letting them know they are doing well you know if they are slipping, you know the . . . what the results of that could be if you don't education seriously you don't keep grades, work hard." Jennifer also shared that her engagement at the school had decreased considerably since having a baby (eighteen months old).

Other factors led parents who are in their twenties and thirties to restrict their engagement in children's learning at school as well. For example, several of the parents reported that they were taking classes working toward advanced degrees. Nancy, thirty-one-year-old single mother of two boys, also stated that she attended a PTO meeting and found it to be "kind of a waste of time." She explained, "There is a whole lot of talking and people complaining and whining but I don't think people got anything accomplished. It has been always how much money we have and how much money we need." It is important to note that older parents sometimes hold similar beliefs regarding PTO/PTA in schools, just like Barbara (Fields-Smith, 2006), a forty-seven-year-old parent from Study 1, who attended a PTO meeting and found that she was not needed in any way and therefore never returned. Other limitations on parental engagement at the school included school policies. When asked about her comfort level when entering her children's schools, Nancy responded, "I feel comfortable. I probably feel a little more welcome at the elementary school than I did at the middle school . . . At the middle school unless I had an appointment with the teacher they just made it very difficult, like she is not here or she is busy, you can't talk to her right now. And I understand that they are busy, but once I meet the teachers I feel welcome and I feel like they giving me the best for my children."

Overall, younger black parents in this setting demonstrated a decreased frequency of visits to the school with one or two times per month most common compared to older parents in the same settings reporting, who reported weekly or daily visits to their children's schools. Some of the factors for this limited at-school engagement included life factors such as inflexible work schedule, enrollment in evening college classes, or care for younger siblings. But some of the isolating factors included perspective and perceptions such as not seeing the value of PTO or not wanting to get involved with other people's children or their families.

Study 3 Grandparents as Parents, Again

Methods

The third author conducted this study as her dissertation, which focused on the growing trend of grandparents raising grandchildren, exploring the social and cultural factors that influence grandparents as they engage in their grandchild's learning and schooling (Shoemaker, 2012). The participants in this study were grandparents raising grandchildren who are in preK–twelfth grades in two public school systems in Georgia. Census data indicated that one of the school districts had a population of nearly 120,000 people, one-third of which live below the poverty line. African Americans represent one-fourth of the population in this urban school district while 62 percent were white and 10 percent Latino. Much smaller in comparison, the other district had a population of approximately thirty-three thousand people; roughly 90 percent of the population was white, 6 percent black, and 5 percent Latino, and only 7.4 percent of the population lived below poverty. Participating grandparents ranged in age from forty-two to seventy-two years old, and they represented both working-class (three families) and middle-class (five families) households. Half of the grandparents held a high school or equivalent education while the other half had undergraduate degrees.

Data collection included Seidman's (2006) three-phased interview model with eight grandparents. She also recorded the grandparent-grandchild interactions and conversations during a family collage-making activity. This case study was framed broadly in the interpretive paradigm using thematic analysis to arrive at the commonalities and differences pertaining to grandparents raising grandchildren. To explore and analyze the data, Jaqueline selected aspects of grounded theory—constant comparative analysis and, specifically, coding (Corbin and Strauss, 2007; Merriam, 2009), memo writing (Glaser, 1998), and theoretical sampling (Charmaz, 2006; Glaser and Strauss, 1967) to guide the data analysis and to help her make meaning of the grandparents' stories.

Study 3 Findings

Given the trend of grandparents increasingly assuming responsibility for their grandchildren, educators must remember that this phenomenon typically occurs for undesirable, frequently tragic reasons. The eight participating grandparents reported that incarceration, abandonment, drugs, and domestic violence led them to serve as their grandchildren's parent. Very sadly, eight of the grandparents reported that along with these maladies, the death of their child had caused them to be raising their grandchildren. Even though at least two years have passed since their children were killed, the pain was still raw, and each one of these grandparents became very emotional when they were talking about the deaths. *I felt like my whole world just came to an end and I was screaming. I was just there, alone with my brother, and I've never screamed that loud in my entire life. I questioned God at that point. I said, "God I do everything I can for you and I know, God, if I could get back," I said, "If I could get back and I could just lay hands on her and I could just pray and I know she'll come back. You just got to let me get back to her, just let me get back." And I didn't get back in time and when I got back they*

had already sent her to the crime lab. And I was upset about that because I felt like they could have at least let me see her before they took her off, but they didn't.

This narration from Mrs. Lee about when she found out about her daughter's death is an example of the pain the grandparents had to endure, and it foreshadows the struggles they faced henceforth.

The sudden occurrence of these events can present issues with legal status of grandparents' custody of their grandchildren as well. In this study, six grandparents had permanent custody or adopted their grandchildren while two grandparents had temporary custody; one of these grandparents reported she had only informal temporary custody. In some cases, grandparents also found themselves caring for their elderly parents while they raise their grandchildren as well. As an example, the oldest participant, Moon (seventy-two), was raising her ten-year-old great-grandchild and caring for her own mother at the time of the study.

A number of common themes emerged in the data obtained from the eight participants. The grandparents in this study can help demystify views of grandparents raising grandchildren in challenging circumstances by demonstrating that they are articulate, confident, and have high aspirations for their grandchildren, as most parents do. These findings reinforce the claim made

by other researchers (Fields-Smith, 2008; Gonzalez et al., 2005; Lareau, 2000) that families, including those led by grandparents, possess rich funds of knowledge and are invaluable resources that educators can tap to support children's learning. The themes outlined below illustrate the strengths and resilience of the grandparents in the study who strived to keep going despite the adversities they might face.

Support Networks

Study 3 participants, both white and African American, relied, in varying degrees, on others within their social networks to help them raise their grandchildren. Gibson (2005) and Ruiz and Zhu (2004) also found this to be true among the African-American grandmothers in their study. Their participants, along with the grandparents in Study 3, sought out extended family; teachers; church and other nonprofit organizations, such as CCA and Boy Scouts; and people at the local university for assistance. Moon talked about how she was willing to ask anybody for help, including calling other parents. "Me and the other parents, we get together on the phone and talking and if one of us don't know something, we'll call the other one. We'll eventually get it somewhere or another, so that helps when the kids are friends. Brooke has a friend, Sara, she is a big help with a lot of stuff, and the teachers are great too." They reciprocate and help each other, asking for assistance for a variety of reasons ranging from homework, to extracurricular activities, to advice about their grandchildren's relationships with their peers.

Barton et al. (2004) refers to this as building "sustaining relationships" (p. 3), and Grace reiterated how important it was that the teachers and parents, everybody kind of know each other on some level and we're not complete strangers and this is helpful to her because she trusts the people within her social network. In their study with African-American grandparents, Moore and Miller (2007) found that the informal support from their participants' social network was vital to them because the people in their social network—extended family, friends, neighbors, and church members—provide emotional and tangible support that enhances the grandparents' psychological well-being. Gibson (2005) pointed out that the extended family and social network of the seventeen African-American grandmothers in her study provided respite to her participants, and they were also positive role models for the grandchildren.

Reaching Out to Others

One of the findings of this study that is impressive is the way these grandparents reciprocate the support they receive from the community by helping others. Mrs. Lee showed great compassion by using the tragedy of her daughter's demise to help others. Her active contribution toward the wider community through her efforts to stop domestic violence is one worth mentioning because of the broad range of her outreach and the various methods she is using through her book, poems, preaching, school talks, and radio broadcast to spread her message. The fact that she is willing to repeatedly share the painful story of her daughter's murder speaks volumes for her willingness to give back to the community at large. Similarly, Party's hope of speaking to the black male prisoner population reflects how these grandparents are thinking beyond their own families. They have endured pain and loss beyond what most of us have experienced, and yet they are willing to give to others in the hopes of helping someone else. Party willingly welcomed friends' children and those from her neighborhood into her home, but she was also not afraid to chastise them as a parent would, if needed. Mrs. Lee too enjoyed being with children. "I am a magnet to kids. They are my first passion. I wanna make sure that they are protected at all times. I wanna make sure that they've learn at all times. You know, I check all of them." This idea of watching over everyone's children is much like the concept of "it takes a village to raise a child" and was mentioned by several of my participants. "Everyone, everybody that they [are] around [with] should be teaching them something." Party confidently acknowledged that teachers, family, church family, neighbors, and CCA were instrumental in helping her raise her four grandchildren. "You see I got to give everybody credit, cos it takes all of us. I can't do it by myself, the teachers can't do it by their selves, and most of it start at home. I thank my mom and dad for my raising, because not only did they help me with my child, they also help with my grandchildren, their great-grandchildren. My sister, my aunts, my uncles, cousins, I mean it takes everybody!"

Daisy and Hoke spoke about the village concept originating with black people. "That's the thing from the days of slavery. . . . Black people they come more together." And Boolie, their grandson, gave his example: "They still have that now, like if I fight somebody, his cousin gonna come at me and his brother going to be with him, you know, it's a big village thing, but it's with the black people." Fields-Smith (2008) also spoke about this village ideology with reference to older African-American parents reaching out to other younger parents, feeling responsibility for the school as a whole, for all the children, and not just for their own children.

As we had anticipated, we found many commonalities shared among our eight participants. The grandparents in this study experienced some type of significant event or trauma that propelled them into the position of being the custodial grandparent for their grandchild. As they raised their grandchildren, they also had to juggle this with the responsibility of being a parent and for some, it also included caring for an elderly parent. The participants acknowledged the value of their social network support, and they offered a few suggestions about how teachers and other school personnel can help them raise their grandchildren.

DISCUSSION AND IMPLICATIONS FOR URBAN SCHOOL LEADERSHIP

Data from this study reveal that parent and family engagement differs depending upon the parent's generation. Additionally, data from this study might also suggest that African-American families in urban contexts have come full circle in terms of which family member might engage with schools. That is to say that as grandparents play a more active role in their grandchildren's education, they find themselves communicating with a generation of teachers that are the same age as their children. In thinking about these interconnecting spheres of family engagement, how then do urban school leaders of today maintain and encourage parent engagement of families, regardless of generational differences?

Previous studies that focused on school-community relations prior to *Brown v. Board of Education* (1954) have shown that segregated schools for black students staffed by black teachers and principals exhibited strong school-family-community relations. Teachers provided academic support to the child, whereas parents provided economic support to the school (Siddle Walker, 1993). This type of symbiotic relationship between school and community ultimately enhanced the child's overall academic achievement.

Research has also suggested that African-American families were more engaged with schools prior to school desegregation. As schools became more racially integrated and African-American teachers and principals were demoted, African-American families felt their "ownership" in the school had been removed. This is not to say that African-American families abandoned the education of their children. However, it does mean that African-American families did not feel as welcome in school environments. Scholars have documented that the extensive histories of racial discrimination and exclusionary practices have, in some instances, made African-American parents feel disconnected with public schools (Diamond and Gomez, 2004; Lareau and Horvat, 1999). Ultimately, this is one reason family engagement began to look differently for African-American families over time.

Desegregated schools might also explain why research in the post-*Brown* era suggests that parental support often takes on different appearances and cultural patterns (Chang, Park, Singh, and Sung, 2009). Oftentimes white parents tend to be seen in the school volunteering, while parents of color participate by assisting with homework and encouraging children to do their best in order to have a more promising future (Patel and Stevens, 2010). Additionally, Msengi (2007) found that many African-American parents surveyed believed that as long their children were doing well in school, they did not need extra support at home. However, once parents were given specific information on how to support their children at home, they implemented the suggestions.

Msengi (2007) indicated that communication is the key to increased family engagement and student learning. This finding was also reiterated in a study of middle-class African-American parents conducted by Howard and Reynolds (2008). Parents emphasized the importance of keeping informed about what is happening in school, and claimed that the greater the amount of school information they accessed, the better they were equipped to advocate for their children (Howard and Reynolds, 2008).

In order for school leaders to foster African-American family engagement in the educational process of their children, school leaders must take ownership of the communication between the school and school community. The school leader is the driving force in the creation of a parent-friendly school environment (Epstein and Rodriguez-Jansorn, 2004); therefore, he or she needs to begin with a mind-set that focuses on a collaborative, democratic leadership style. To implement this leadership style, the principal should provide opportunities for ideas and opinions to be heard (Stelmach and Preston, 2007). Once an atmosphere of collaboration has been initiated, parents should see positive results from their involvement.

One way for today's urban school leader to foster family engagement among African-American parents is to gain an understanding of the context of their communities. That being said, the school leader should engage parents in their respective communities to understand the differences that exist across them. As Khalifa (2012) notes, principals, especially urban principals, must move beyond their school walls in order to gauge the social and cultural conditions of their neighborhood communities. In essence, principals who lead schools that constitute majority African-American students must hold without debilitating conflict multiple identities and multiple responsibilities particularly as it relates to family engagement (Fordham, 1996).

In an effort to engage African-American parents across multiple generations, the principal must also understand parenting styles of that particular generation. For example, Baby Boomers, who are more apt to physically visit the school, differ from the Generation X parents who support their children via technology. This means that while a Baby Boomer will visit the teacher in person, a Generation X parent might choose to call or email the teacher, and a New Boomer might communicate with the teacher and via social media. This does not necessarily mean that one parent from one generation is more involved and engaged than another parent. It simply means that involvement manifests itself differently across generations. Additionally, whereas parents in the Baby Boomer generation depend on social networks to provide them with information, parents of Generation X and the New Boomers rely less on information from individuals and more from websites and social media. These differences suggest that communication between the school and the community should be available via word of mouth, print media, and social media. This ensures that all generations of parents feel connected to the school, which ultimately might lead to more involvement and increased academic achievement for students. Hence, the role of the school leader is to understand how to communicate effectively with parents, regardless of generation. This adds another layer of skill for districts to consider when hiring principals of schools that have high African-American student enrollment.

African-American parents, as well as any other race, support their children's education. However, African-American family engagement is unique in that today's Baby Boomers might raise their children's children, which influences school-family communications and the way they engage with the school. Given that Baby Boomers tend to be advocates for their children's education, their advocacy might be beneficial for African-American student achievement. In the end, it could be that Baby Boomers restore the school-community relationships of yesteryear.

REFERENCES

Bailey, S. (2012). *Grandparents raising their grandchildren: Parenting the next generation.* Montana State University Extension. msuextension.org/publications/Home-HealthandFamily/MT200401HR.pdf.

Baker, L., Silverstein, M., and Putney, N. (2008). Grandparents raising grandchildren in the United States: Changing family forms, stagnant social policies. *Journal of Sociology and Social Policy, 7*, 53–69.

Barton, A., Drake, C., Perez, J., St. Louis, K., and George, M. (2004). Ecologies of parental engagement in urban education. *Educational Researcher, 33*, 3–12.

Bogdan, R. C and Biklen, S. K. (2003). *Qualitative research for education: An introduction to theories and methods* (4th ed.). New York: Pearson Education Group.

Cabarnaro, W. (1998). A little help from my friend's parents: Intergenerational closure and education outcomes. *Sociology of Education 71*, 295–313.

Chang, M., Park, B., Singh, K., and Sung, Y. Y. (2009). Parental involvement, parenting behaviors, and children's cognitive development in low-income and minority families. *Journal of Research in Childhood Education, 23*(3), 309–324.

Charmaz, K. (2006). *Constructing grounded theory: A practical guide through qualitative analysis.* Thousand Oaks, CA: Sage.

Chavkin, N. (1993). *Families and Schools in a Pluralistic Society.* Albany: State of New York University Press.

Corbin, J. and Strauss, A. (2007). *Basics of qualitative research: Techniques and procedures for developing grounded theory* (3rd ed.). Thousand Oaks, CA: Sage.

Diamond, J. and Gomez, K. (2004). African American parents' educational orientations: The importance of social class and parents' perceptions of school. *Education and Urban Society, 36*(4), 383–427.

Epstein, J. (2010). School/family/community partnerships: Caring for the children we share. *Kappan 92*, 81–96.

Epstein, J. L. and Jansorn, N. R. (2004). School, family and community partnerships link the plan. *Education Digest: Essential Readings Condensed for Quick Review, 69*(6), 19–23.

Fields-Smith, C. (2004). After 'It takes a village': The attitudes, beliefs, practices, and explanations for parental involvement among upper and middle income african american families in elementary school settings. Unpublished dissertation, Division of Educational Studies, Emory University.

Fields-Smith, C. (2005). African American parents before and after *Brown. Journal of Curriculum and Supervision, 20*, 129–135.

Fields-Smith, C. (2006). Motivation for participation: Why highly involved African American parents participate in their children's education. *Journal of School Public Relations, 27*, 234–257.

Fields-Smith, C. (2007). Social class and African American parental involvement. In J. Van Galen and G. Noblit (Eds.), *Late to class: Social class and schooling in the new economy* (pp. 167–202). Albany: State University of New York Press.

Fields-Smith, C. (2008). After "It takes a village": Mapping the terrain of Black parental involvement in the post-*Brown* era. In L. Tillman (Ed.), *The SAGE Handbook of African American education* (pp. 153–168). Thousand Oaks, CA: Sage Publications.

Fordham, S. (1996). *Blacked out: Dilemmas of race, identity, and success at Capital High.* Chicago: University of Chicago Press.

Glass, A. (2007). Understanding generational differences for competitive success. *Industrial and Commercial Training 39*(2), 98–103.

Glaser, B. (1998). *Doing Grounded Theory—Issues and Discussions.* Mill Valley, CA: Sociology.

Glaser, B. and Strauss, A. L. (1967). *The discovery of grounded theory: Strategies for qualitative research.* Chicago, IL: Aldine.

Gonzalez, N., Moll, L., and Amanti, C. (2005). *Funds of knowledge.* Mahwah, NJ: Lawrence Erlbaum Associates.

Howard, T. C. and Reynolds, R. (2008). Examining Parent Involvement in Reversing the Underachievement of African American Students in Middle-Class Schools. *Educational Foundations, 22*(1), 79–98.

Jensen, B. (2014, June/July). The new American family. *American Association of Retired People Magazine*, 36–42.

Kaplan, M. (2002). Intergenerational programs in schools: Consideration of form and function. *International Review of Education 48*(5), 305–334.

Khalifa, M. (2012). A re-new-ed paradigm in successful urban school leadership principal as community leader. *Educational Administration Quarterly, 48*(3), 424–467.

Lareau, A. (2000). *Home advantage: Social class and parental intervention in elementary education*. Lanham, MD: Rowman and Littlefield Publishers.

Lareau, A. (2003). *Unequal childhoods: Class, race, and family life*. Berkley: University of California Press.

Lareau, A. and Horvat, E. (1999). Moments of social inclusion and exclusion race, class, and cultural capital in family-school relationships. *Sociology of Education 72*, 37–53.

Lawrence-Lightfoot, S. (2003). *The essential conversation: What parents and teachers can learn from each other*. New York: Random House.

McGrath, D. and Kuriloff, P. (1999). "They're going to tear the doors off this place": Upper- middle-class parent school involvement and the educational opportunities of other people's children. *Education Policy, 13*, 603–629.

Merriam, S. (2009). *Qualitative research—A guide to design and implementation*. San Francisco, CA: Jossey-Bass.

Msengi, S. G. (2007). Family, child, and teacher perceptions of African American adult assistance to young readers. *School Community Journal, 17*(1), 33.

Patel, N. and Stevens, S. (2010). Parent-teacher-student discrepancies in academic ability beliefs: Influences on parent involvement. *School Community Journal, 20*(2), 115–136.

Rosenberg, M. (2013). Names of generations. *About.com Guide*. Retrieved June 16, 2013 from geography.about.com/od/populationgeography/qt/generations.htm.

Shah, N. (2013, May 23). Teen pregnancy rate at its lowest, again, CDC says. *Rules for engagement newsweek blog*. Available at blogs.edweek.org/edweek/rulesforengagement/2013/05/teen_pregnancy_rate_at_its_lowest_again_cdc_says.html.

Seidman, I. (1998). *Interviewing as qualitative research: A guide for researchers in education and the social sciences*. New York: Teachers College Press.

Seidman, I. (2006). *Interviewing as qualitative research* (3rd ed.). New York: Teachers College Press.

Shoemaker, J. (2012). Grandparents raising grandchildren: Family stories about schooling and learning. (Doctoral dissertation, University of Georgia.) Retrieved from grad-schoolforms.webapps.uga.edu/system/attachments/11819/Jaqueline_Shoemaker_Ho%20Hock%20Neo_201212_PhD.pdf?1354719061.

Siddle Walker, E. V. (1993). Caswell County training school, 1933–1969: Relationships between community and school. *Harvard Educational Review, 62*(3), 161–182.

Stelmach, B. L. and Preston, J. P. (2008). Cake or curriculum? Principal and parent views on transforming the parental role in Saskatchewan schools. *International Studies in Educational Administration, 36*(3), 59–74.

Tillman, L. (2002). Culturally sensitive research approaches: An African-American perspective. *Educational Researcher 31*(9), 3–12.

United Nations. (2003). Intergenerational relations. In World youth report, 397–409. New York: United Nations. Available at www.un.org/esa/socdev/unyin/documents/worldyouthreport.pdf.

U.S. Census Bureau. (2006). Selected characteristics of baby boomers 42–60 years old in 2006. Available online at www.census.gov/population/age/publications/files/2006babyboomers.pdf.

Walker, V. (1996). Their highest potential: An African American school community in the South. Chapel Hill: The University of North Carolina Press.

Walker, V. (2000). Valued segregation schools for African American children in the south, 1935–1969: A review of common themes and characteristics. *Review of Educational Research, 70*, 253–285.

CHAPTER 18

Where Has All of the Community Rage Gone?

Neoliberalism, Community Encroachment, and Unconventional Resistance in Detroit

Muhammad Khalifa, Elizabeth Gil, Stefanie Marshall, and Gregory J. White

INTRODUCTION

Few other cities have reputations of resistance more prominent than that of Detroit, Michigan. From some of the fiercest First Nation-colonialist battles, to the establishment of automobile unions in an industrialized Motor City, deindustrialization, and on to the 1967 riots, there has always been a rich tradition of protest in Detroit when the citizens have perceived threats to their democratic rights (Gabin, 1982; Shaw, 2009; Sugrue, 2005, Thomas, 1992; Widick, 1989). Yet, despite a sustained disproportionate economic crisis impacting city services, spiraling crime rates, and biased emergency manager laws being used to take over Detroit schools and government, the city residents seem ostensibly quiet. This paper examines community responses and protest behaviors toward school takeover/emergency manager laws that have a direct impact on Detroit. Given that protest performatives may look different, change based on period, or appear in unconventional places, the purpose of this paper is to locate these community voices in Detroit, to describe recent trends of protest voices, and to describe ways that such voices both perceive and resist an encroachment on their democratic rights.

We use a conceptual framework of neoliberalism to situate our discussion of protest around schooling in Detroit. Steeped in color-blind business/market theory from the 1960s (Burch, 2009), neoliberal school reforms claim a certain ahistoricity as they seek to describe current market conditions solely through lenses of objectivity and competition. In an educational context neoliberalism is purported to represent neutrality and meritocracy. But because neoliberal reforms often reproduce contexts of marginalization and reaffirm power relationships in society, and because such re-

forms have largely not helped minoritized Detroit, we challenge these claims of meritocratic neutrality.

In a snowball sampling, we utilized critical phenomenological research methodology (Guedes and Moreira, 2009; Reid, 1973; Willen, 2007). Our research rests on the assumption that protest is productive and useful for marginalized populations because it gives them a voice and a means to resist oppression in an imbalanced power relationship. This approach allowed us to identify and embrace our own positionalities as researchers. We sought to understand how protest has been subverted, if not altogether disrupted. We interviewed four community members and leaders about their impressions of takeover measures in Detroit. We also attended an event in which many of the participants and other key protesters took part. This meeting and all interview data was transcribed and coded (axial) based on a number of themes that we identified in the extant literature on protest and resistance.

We arrived at five basic findings. One, we found that participants generally felt that traditional forms of protest and resistance were diminishing in Detroit. Two, we found that participants felt that the once very palpable images and symbols of oppressive domination and control were obfuscated by neoliberal corporatization of schooling and shifting methods and locations of control of urban policies. This suggests an invisibilization and normalization of oppression for most Detroiters. Three, we found that the types of protest in Detroit, which might be described as "rustbelt protest"—such as picket lines, large union strikes, and rallies—were not most-compatible with modernized, technological forms of protest. Four, participants found that changing demographics of Detroiters influence the strength and solidarity of the protest. And finally, we found that State-level legislation prevented many forms of legal protest that were once available to those resisting hegemonic control. The rise in neoliberal reforms—as these findings help us to realize—is directly linked to the fall in the presence, reach, and intensity of the protest voice in Detroit. This has deep implications for democracy given that the voice of dissent, resistance, and protest has always been a part of educational (and more broadly, democratic) reform.

This research has implications for school leaders and policymakers who would benefit from hearing, elevating, and incorporating community-based voices. Indeed, when such voices are included in reforms, students and communities ultimately stand to benefit. It follows that if the very process of neoliberal reform serves to marginalize stakeholder voices, policymakers and school leaders must be aware that such reforms will likely be oppressive toward those marginalized voices.

LITERATURE REVIEW

Frame Analysis and Protest

Frame analysis is useful in understanding general notions of protest because it situates how participants view protests and their roles in it. Essentially, frame analysis allows researchers to understand how social experiences are understood, engaged, formed, and organized (Goffman, 1974). Frame analysis allows for a better understanding of how protesters view their places and roles within a movement. Bonded together by the beliefs and ideologies that are collectively held by group members, protest social movements are framed similarly by those involved in the cause (Snow and Benford, 1988).

Frame analysis (Goffman, 1974; Snow and Benford, 1988) is used here to understand how and why protestors become involved in Detroit's educational protest activities. It is particularly useful because it helps us to define who can and cannot be considered a protestor; if an individual is drawn to the beliefs and objectives of the protest movement, and acts accordingly, then that person can be considered as a protestor. As an analytical tool, frame analysis can shed light on how individuals understand their own involvement in the movement. Snow and Benford (1988, 2000) explain that when all protestors agree on these beliefs and objectives, "frame alignment" and then "frame resonance" occurs. This alignment, they argue, allows for primal success in the movement, and will eventually lead to major change in society.

We agree with Goffman (1974) and Snow and Benford (1988) that social movements have common activities, beliefs, and ideologies. But we also hope to explore the extent to which people protest for personal, and sometimes even divergent, reasons. For example, as we reflect on Goffman (1974) and subsequent research, we critically wonder if a collective history of racial oppression is enough to spur protest and resistance in protestors. Must all protestors have common "frames," we ask? Or is it possible that people are, to various degrees, involved in a movement, for personal or even spiritual reasons? Indeed, movements create their own cultures that may facilitate or impede mobilization, resistance, recruitment, and solidarity (Fine, 1985; Scott, 1990). Collective identities are relevant for understanding how groups define their boundaries, plans of action, determined goals, and what actions are "out of bounds" (Oliver, Cadena-Roa, and Strawn, 2003). Thus, while we find resonance with the importance of framing in analyzing protestor actions in a movement, we also leave room to find what some researchers may refer to as anarchy, others perhaps "agency," and others yet, spiritual, transcendence, or even moral epistemologies—all whilst having radically different frames for being involved in a movement.

A Reason to Protest? Neoliberalism and Community Voice in Education

> Neoliberalism is in the first instance a theory of political economic practices that proposes that human well-being can best be advanced by liberating individual entrepreneurial freedoms and skills within an institutional framework characterized by strong private property rights, free markets, and free trade.
>
> —Harvey, 2005, p. 2

Neoliberalism is intricately linked to globalizing policies that—based on specific business policies from the 1960s—seek to maintain order, prediction, and control. This has deeply impacted modern educational policy and reform (Burch, 2009). Globalization has set the tone for new forms of urban protest, community organizing, cooperation, and coalition-building (Shepard and Hayduk, 2002). From an educational perspective, regimes and policies of globalization are coterminous with corporate and governmental control, increased monitoring, intensified and high-stakes evaluation, sanctions, and other actions that are hostile toward personal and community democratic education. These intensifications of high-stakes, corporate observation and control are broadly referred to as "neoliberal" reforms in education. Neoliberal education is an extension of corporatized globalization, and because of the encroachment on democratic rights of individual and community, has a visceral resistance.

According to Hayduk (2002), "the new activism" has evolved out of four factors: globalization, shifting boundaries between public and private space, demographic change, and income inequality. Thus, one result of globalization is social displacement (Shepard and Hayduk, 2002). This leads to protest. The goal of these new forms of protest is to promote globalizing democracy, opposed to corporate rule. Many U.S. problems derive from economic inequality, which in turn can be converted into social inequality (Shepard and Hayduk, 2002). Global capitalism is causing the general public to be taken advantage of by transforming what we know to be "common" into private entities (e.g., seeds being genetically modified and patented, the "common areas" being turned into malls, children being tracked from birth) (Shepard and Hayduk, 2002).

Such encroachments on the rights of individuals and communities have extended to educational systems and educational reforms. Though public education was formally bureaucratized, and situated to benefit the common good (Dewey, 1900), neoliberal reforms often rebuff these earlier commitments in place of a far more controlled/ structured, punitive, post-political/ racial, and intangible understanding of schooling and reform (Burch, 2011; Hursh, 2005; Lipman, 2004). In fact, neoliberal reforms would tend to minimize, if not outright ignore, all historical considerations of how Detroit's student educational outcomes came to be at present. Scholarly historiographies that help explain this are rendered unimportant. Rather, neoliberal reforms only focus on high-stakes results at the expense of all other explanations. And finally, neoliberal reforms are generally disproportionately applied to poor, minoritized communities.

Emergent Protests. The Twenty-First Century and Beyond

Protest in Detroit has changed shape and form dependent on the backgrounds, frames, awareness, access-

sibility, and abilities of its residents to resist. There are also broader systems of reform and social protest that may impact the visibility and strengths of protest. For example, in the findings and conclusion of this paper, we explore the relationship between globalizing neoliberalism and twenty-first century forms of protest. Moreover, new forms of protest are taking place online in the form of news reports, video feeds, photos, and online diaries (Shepard and Hayduk, 2002). As Shepard and Hayduk (2002) note, "Over the last decade and a half, as activism has moved from ACT UP to the WTO, what has emerged is a series of competing urban narratives, embodying different views of reality and strategy" (p. 7).

Arguably, the most interesting form of twenty-first century protest was the Occupy Movement. The unique mixture of more traditional forms of protest, combined with the technological innovations of our present context, expanded the frame of who could become a protestor. Traditional facets of the movement included marches, sit-ins, and physically occupying public spaces. Technology expanded participation via cell phones and social media outlets that could not be readily silenced by an accommodating power structure, nor a media sympathetic to, or beholden to, neoliberal interests. The combination presented a disruptor variable that was previously unaccounted for.

Framing the movement as the 99 percent versus the one percent directly spoke to Hayduk's four factors of new activism. The one percent, as the primary champions of neoliberal activity, could be seen as representative of globalization and income inequality. The 99 percent can be seen as representative of a demographic change due to the way the framing numerically, racially, economically, and ideologically enlarged the class of protestors. The use of physical space, to create or revive political space, grabbed headlines. Physically occupying key public spaces en masse forced authorities to take notice. This often led to confrontations. Confrontations forced the power structure to physically meet the protestors wherever they were. This almost always ensured that media coverage would ensue, either through the traditional media outlets or through citizen-generated media, as images and activities were captured on devices from cell phones to video cameras. This surfaced the real and political ideas, activities, and aspirations of the protestors in a way that transfixed the global audience in way that is rarely observed. And that last act satisfied Hayduk's blending of public and private space.

As we explore the manifestations of protest in Detroit, we see that neoliberal efforts have had a particularly chilling effect through degradation of labor unions and severely restricted self-governance. More importantly, our exploration shows that some of the strengths of the Occupy Movement may not be available in Detroit. Occupy was successful in creating a movement that crossed the barriers of class and race. Detroit is over 80 percent black and largely poor. There is not much room for movement with such a starting point. In addition, a key dimension of Occupy was its horizontal leadership structure. Without a clearly identifiable leader, there was no particular person or group to be accountable to. As we saw in Detroit, this allows neoliberalism to flourish.

Once a bastion of union activity, union membership is in decline and Michigan is a right-to-work state. The governor has a corporate background (venture capitalist) and openly encouraged neoliberal right-to-work efforts. He further supported the strengthening of existing emergency manager laws. Such laws have removed democratically elected control over the city of Detroit and its related entity, the Detroit Public Schools. With the Detroit Public Schools under the control of a hand-picked agent of the state, the state has chosen to support the neoliberal agenda of privatization by legislatively making Michigan a state that is open to unlimited numbers of charter schools. The challenge of our protestors was to learn from the body of past protest work, to create an agenda broad enough for others to see themselves in such a frame, and yet narrow enough to achieve their desired end goals. Our paper explores the degree to which this reality was met.

Corporate (Neoliberal) Responses to Protest

Literature regarding the curtailing of protests expresses concern over how legislation and legal decisions affect the possibility, quality, and effectiveness of protest. Several of the participants in this study referenced the legal roadblocks to their protest. Despite its deep union and industrial past, Michigan is known to have passed earlier legislation making it illegal to participate in some forms of organized protest. Laws regarding collective bargaining and striking, as well as organiz-

ing around strike action, have an effect on how often and for how long this type of protest is undertaken as well as potential outcomes of strikes. Finally, research has also looked at the connections between protest and policymaking, including responses to protest and how issues get on the policy agenda.

The public space? Protests are often resisted through and around discourses pertaining to the "public space." Zick (2006) argues that public spaces are "increasingly subject to spatial tactics, the utilization of space for social and political control" (p. 651). Cages and "cocoons," restricted zones, and barricades near funerals, political national conventions, on campuses, and along parade routes are examples of these tactics. The law's consideration of "expressive rights in terms of . . . 'what' speech is being regulated and 'why'" (p. 581) is insufficient because "place is often critically associated" (p. 646) with protestors' "expressive message" (p. 646). Zick also asserts that face-to-face confrontation is now "treated as presumptively insidious and dangerous" and "public officials who travel in bubbles and appear in dissent-free zones are increasingly isolated and insulated from the public and its concerns" (p. 647). With the "rapidly diminishing resources" of public space, "opportunities for significant debate and expression are few, and dwindling" (p. 647).

McAllister (2007) states that any laws being considered in relation to funeral picketing should focus on the regulation of "several aspects of funeral protests, including intrusive noise, impeding access, trespassing on private property, crowd size, and actual threats" (p. 577). Under these conditions a constitutional funeral picketing law might be enacted. This all suggests that protest happens in contested spaces, and when the State or other powerful actors have interest, the activities of protest themselves become contested.

Anti-protest legislation. In blog posts regarding the overwhelming support for HR 347 and its companion Senate bill and its signing in by President Obama in March of 2012 (Camp, 2012; Molloff 2012) authors express concern over the law, which "makes protest of any type potentially a federal offense with anywhere from a year to ten years in federal prison, providing it occurs in the presence of elites brandishing Secret Service protection, or during an officially defined 'National Special Security Event' (NSSE)" (Molloff, 2012). Referred to by some as the "anti-Occupy law," "it could be a federal crime to protest near an event of, quote, 'national significance,'" events that are deemed to require the presence of the secret service (Camp, 2012). Moloff (2012) refers to the current climate as one of "increasing police militarization and shrinking civil liberties" and says that the legislature's action is an indication that "the political class has degraded to writing obviously illegitimate 'laws' in a desperate attempt to crush any dissent."

Turning to protest actions that public sector employees may take, in a study spanning a sixteen-year period, Currie and McConnell (1994) estimated the impact of collective bargaining legislation on disputes during labor negotiations. Results of the study suggest that "no legislation" is the "worst form of collective bargaining legislation" (p. 520). Strikes were least frequent and shortest in jurisdictions with arbitration. While in these jurisdictions arbitration use increases, arbitration may be a beneficial trade-off because it is much less costly than a strike. In an examination of six states with different public policies toward such strikes through 1980, Craig Olson (1986) finds that "public policies have had a significant impact on strike frequency in the six states" (p. 550). Strike penalties led to decreases in strike frequency in those states and unenforced laws did not show evidence of having an effect on strikes. The author finds that arbitration showed some evidence of decreased strike occurrence. In their discussion of the 2006 Detroit strike, posted on the *Solidarity* website, Regalado and Lare (2007) conclude that the union "had the leverage to win more than it did," citing the strike's outcome as "another long decade of UAW retreat, a slow response from labor to a mainly people-of-color union and student population, and the toll taken by assaults on labor and social services generally" (Regalado and Lare, 2007).

Studies have shown that protest and policymaking are not isolated from one another and actually have an interdependent relationship. King, Bentele, and Soule (2007) find that "protest plays a significant role in the agenda-setting stage of legislation" (p. 153), as political protest, brings to light issues not previously "part of the legitimate domain of government domain" (p. 152) and serves as an "external ignition to agenda setting" (p. 153). The authors find that competition among protest groups to get different issues on the agenda has an impact as well. Oliver and Maney (2000) note that a complex triangular relationship exists between pro-

test, political processes, and media coverage of protest. Protests are affected by electoral cycles, with elections presenting protestors an opportunity to have influence, but also results in competing for media time and attention. Protestors' relationships with politicians also play a role, with a "candidate's sympathizers sometimes refrain[ing] from protesting to avoid antagonizing potential voters" (p. 464). Protestors' responses to legislative issues tend to be considered more newsworthy than other reasons, and more coverage tends to take place when the legislature is in session.

METHODOLOGY

In a snowball sampling, we utilized critical phenomenological research methodology (Guedes and Moreira, 2009; Reid, 1973; Willen, 2007). Our research rests on the assumption that protest is a productive and useful means for marginalized populations because it gives them voice and a means to resist oppression in an imbalanced power relationship. This approach allowed us to identify and embrace our own positionalities as researchers. We sought to understand how protest has been subverted, if not altogether disrupted. We interviewed four community members and leaders about their impressions of takeover measures in Detroit. We also attended an event in which many of the participants and other key protestors took part. This meeting and all interview data was transcribed and coded (axial) based on a number of themes that we identified in the extant literature on protest and resistance.

In addition to the literature, however, a number of additional themes emerged after the first few interviews. The themes rested on protest for, protest against, frustration with protest movement, protest purpose/goals, unconventional forms of protest, location of protest, and inhibitors to protest.

Context of Study

Initially, we set out to identify, collect, and examine protest-oriented responses to legislation in Michigan most often referred to as the Emergency Manager Law (PA4). We focused on these voices in and around Detroit. We were also open to the possibility that these voices were diminished or nonexistent. The law was initially brought to Michigan under a Republican governor as PA72, which was exclusively intended to address school districts that were facing financial difficulty. But in 2011, the law, now referred to as PA4, was greatly strengthened as it was extended to include sweeping powers toward both educational and economic reform. In Michigan, the law is indeed controversial for a number of reasons, not the least of which that it has been exclusively applied to districts with black, brown, and otherwise minoritized students. This is true despite the fact that a number of predominantly white districts fall under the purview to be overtaken by the state-mandated law. In 2013, when the Republican-held state legislature attempted to expand the law in ways that would allow access to suburban districts, with whiter constituencies, there was state-wide fallout that inhibited such an expansion of the law into areas outside of minoritized areas.

Essentially, PA4 resulted in three drastic actions that would severely weaken Detroit Public Schools (DPS) and downgrade it from a Class A to a Class B district. This significantly reduced the level of democratic self-rule compared to what most other districts in the country have. For one, this downgrading alone meant that more independently run charter schools could be established within DPS boundaries and targeted specifically at DPS students. There is research suggesting that most parents who choose charter education for their children are uninformed. Some research even suggests that parents who left a public school for a charter school moved their child(ren) from a better-performing school for a worse-performing school. Secondly, the law gave the governor the ability to install an emergency manager (EM)—which he did—to lead DPS to financial health. Unlike in the past, the EM instituted sweeping changes that reached far beyond financial issues. Everything from curriculum to public campaigns were affected by his reform behaviors. Lastly, the new law led to the establishment of the Educational Achievement Authority, or EAA, which is a new and separate school authority that gained immediate control of fifteen DPS schools. This radical takeover of schools led to the professional dismissal of most of the teachers and administrators who were previously employed at these schools (and others, due to seniority practices within DPS).

Participants and Sources of Data

The participants for this study were interviewed for between one to two hours in semi-structured interviews. While we were initially interested in investigating the

perceptions of the emergency manager law, it became clear that participants were far more interested in one of the local results of the law—the EAA. With powers granted by the governor and state legislative body via PA4, this authority assumed control of fifteen "failing" schools. Legislation was also passed that prevented counter-legislation or litigation against the EAA. We sought participants from among the publically known voices that opposed or actually protested the takeover of schools. This led to the inclusion of a number of lesser known voices of protest as well. Additionally, we attended a panel discussion held at a local church in which several of the voices of protest participated. Each participant is described below.

Mari. Mari is an elected member to the DPS school board. Initially, Mari was placed on the school board in place of another board member who, abruptly, was no longer a member of the DPS school board. But when DPS was overtaken, and the EAA was given administrative power over DPS schools, Mari and other board members were deposed and removed from their elected leadership positions. In protest, several of the board members continue to meet in absentia as a way to continue to address the needs of Detroit children. She is a founding member of a task force with other protest-oriented allies. She and her colleagues meet regularly in protest to the EAA, EM, and other policies they see as unjust.

Faith. Faith is a parent who has been a vocal critic of the EAA and the EM at DPS. Her daughter attended a school that proactively catered to students with disabilities. The school was closed amid questionable claims made by DPS. She organized other parents to protest, met with the EM, and had several newspaper articles written about her protesting against the closing of the school. She has also protested against the EM, the EAA, and other takeover actions in general.

Mary. Mary is a former teacher with the EAA who resigned amid unfilled promises made by the EAA and her school principal at the time of hire. Mary was a new urban teacher, and felt that the class sizes, the promises around help in the school, and the technology promises were all unfilled and problematic. When the principal reprimanded her because one of her students was injured in a drastically oversized kindergarten classroom, she chose to resign in protest. In the two months she

WHERE HAS ALL OF THE COMMUNITY RAGE GONE? 261

worked at the EAA, she consistently protested her classroom conditions, but felt that no one was listening.

Jay. Jay is a professor at a local university in Detroit who is also a visible activist and vocal critic of the State's takeover measures. He has appeared in local print, radio, and TV media dozens of times, and has challenged DPS and EAA officials on a number of occasions in public forums. He has written about similar issues in his research for nearly ten years.

Community forum. This community forum included diverse voices representing the EAA, charter school organizations, protest voices, and experts in the field of education. They were there to talk about the purpose of various educational offerings for students in Michigan. During the panel discussion, a number of positions were presented by panelists regarding what is in the best interest of children in Michigan. Although the intent of the forum was not to target concerns toward the EAA, panel members and the community expressed their discontent with the EAA. Some of the area's most notable protest activists were in attendance or on the panel. The panel was held in a suburb just north of Detroit.

FINDINGS

Protest activism against state-level educational domination is present in Detroit. Yet the findings also suggest that what was traditionally known as protest is either in decline, changing shape, or is not as palpable as it once was. Participants expressed such a commitment to their own protest and activism, yet they also expressed disappointment at many of their fellow Detroiters and other professors who were not involved in the struggle. We arrived at five basic findings. One, we found that participants generally felt that traditional forms of protest and resistance were diminishing in Detroit. Two, we found that participants felt that the once very palpable images and symbols of oppressive domination and control were obfuscated by neoliberal corporatization of schooling and shifting methods and locations of control of urban resources. This suggests an invisibilization and normalization of oppression for most Detroiters. Three, we found that the types of protest in Detroit, which might be described as "rustbelt protest"—such as picket lines, large union strikes, and rallies—were not most compatible with modernized, technological forms of protest.

Four, participants found that changing demographics of Detroiters influence the strength and solidarity of the protest. And finally, we found that the State-level legislation prevented many forms of legal protest that were once available to those resisting hegemonic control. The rise in neoliberal reforms—as these findings help us to realize—is directly linked to the fall in the presence, reach, and intensity of the protest voice in Detroit. This has deep implications for democracy given that the voice of dissent, resistance, and protest has always been a part of educational (and more broadly, democratic) reform.

Decline of Protest in Detroit

> No. I'm going to say some of them don't know, some of them don't care, and some of them may not know how to get that information, even though we've had advocates that reach out to us that service and know the laws, and they won't call them back, or I'll give them the number and someone will call, and it's not consistent.
>
> —Parent activist, Faith

Education. The protest voices in this study indicate a small but focused group of protestors present in Detroit. This quote captures deep urgency and commitment that was so obvious from the actions and statements from participants in the study. Yet another message was also unmistakable: we need help in the battle. During the interviews, a number of participants indicated that we were welcome to join the fight against their democratic rights being taken. The group of protestors was committed but smaller than what the participants wanted, and this seemed to lead to immense frustration and disappointment. This all led to the question of protest capacity. The participants in this study suggested that changing demographics is a contributing factor to why protest is less now than it was forty years ago in Detroit. For example, Mari suggested a difference in levels of education is one possible reason. She thought that many Detroiters—unaware how the modern oppression is exhibited and of how dangerous it was to have democratic rights taken away—seemed less informed than Detroiters from earlier eras. Other protestors expressed frustration as well:

> This connects to my sense of frustration with some of your student researchers. And it's not fair to

them in some ways, or fair to you. But I have often thought, there is so much low-hanging fruit and with so little effort I have been able to help, and with others, to expose all this shit, that if I had ten more of me, can you imagine what can be exposed?

—Jay

Other obligations and fatigue. The participants also suggested that fatigue may play a role in why some parents may not have been involved in the struggle as intensely as the participants may have wanted. Research suggests (see Smith, 2004; Smith, Allen, and Danley, 2007) people who feel marginalized and oppressed can suffer from what is known as (racial) battle fatigue:

They either have other children, some of them have told me that, "you know I have other kids"; "I can't do this fight." I'm like, well hey, give me your information, give me your issues, and I'll fight for you. In actuality, I'm fighting for the parents too, but the main thing is these babies. I've seen them, I know them, it still makes me very upset.

—Faith

In addition to perceptions of battle fatigue, life commitments impacted the ability to engage in protest activities. Protest activism requires a certain level of time, ability of movement, and autonomy of one's schedule to attend various activities. People with children, professional obligations, or other commitments cannot as easily engage in protest activism, despite their strong beginning in activities.

Maybe people feel defeated; I wonder if there is internalization of the blame of what happened in Detroit.

—Jay

Protestors believed that state-level, neoliberal legislation likely contributed to a decline in protest. It contributed to a context that was preventing protestors from remaining optimistic that their efforts would yield tangible results. Mari complained a number of times that legislation had been passed that prevented them from using judicial, legal, or legislative means to protest:

The Emergency Manager replaces all the decision-making of the board, so there's no contracts

that go before the board . . . EAA [is a] separate district, self-governing schools, separate district. Separate districts. They have their own hiring, their own contracts for everything. Then there's the DPS charters and Detroit Public Schools—four districts in one. They broke up an economy of scale and gave everybody a little piece of it. This is what emergency manager means. They answer to no one.

—Mari

Moreover, even when the Emergency Manager legislation was voted down in the November 2012 election, the Republicans quickly passed another bill that not only re-legalized EM takeover, but it also illegalized any further attempts to disband the law. This did not thwart or derail the activities of the core protestors whom we interviewed, but it likely had an impact on the morale of non-core members and contributed to their lessened activities. The state-level legislation was a primary reason protestors felt they were not able to protest. A Republican governor and legislature had previously used this tactic, as they prevented public school teachers from striking by making it illegal.

Neoliberal Dominance and Protest

Participants in this study felt that the images and types of oppression had changed, and was less obvious than before. So in addition to the fact that the Detroit populace changed, now the oppression was not as identifiable as it had been in previous years. The symbols of tanks traversing Detroit streets, of angry mob-like white residents protesting black integration, or of brutal white police officers enacting open aggression on black youth were no longer visible. Instead, the participants perceived a newer, deeply systemic, hegemonic, yet often invisible type of dominance:

The whole idea of Emergency Management is that Detroiters cannot govern themselves.

—Jay

Jay's impressions were that districts and state officials oppressively controlled the discourses of reform in Detroit. He would continually challenge the narratives put out by the district officials who claimed that it was an economic necessity to close and merge schools:

That's bullshit! What I did was examined the data to challenge their claim.

—Jay

This suspicion of the administrative behaviors was held commonly by all of the participants in the study. They constantly challenged the official reasons for the reforms, and chose an alternate view than what administrators and policymakers claimed about schooling in Detroit. Jay's statement that "public education in American cities for low-income communities of color has not been a great thing" indicates a critique of the structures of current schooling in Detroit. The high-stakes models of schooling, focus on standardized test scores, and heavy emphasis on financial health of schools was unhealthy and often fabricated to oppress the people of Detroit. The protestors constantly called these narratives into question, as Mari notes:

> What it is, is a way of stripping away any kind of accountability. For example, the first emergency manager puts us $100 million more in debt . . . and closed 50 percent of the schools in Detroit . . . Robert Bobb; followed then by Roy Roberts, who continues his actions, closing the Detroit Day School for the Deaf . . . the Oakland Orthopedic School, with absolutely no alternative for the students who were in them. It's a human rights violation. There was nothing wrong. Detroit Day School for the Deaf is almost completely federally funded, so it wasn't for finances, if you even would. I have to say this too: This is really, really, important to people in education. Why do we accept that finances are the most important issue of education, that you don't do something . . . because you can't afford it? Why would we accept that, that narrative, that . . . it's just not feasible? There's no cost, no cost spared for war or these emergency managers' lifestyle.

—Mari

Jay also described an exclusive focus on incentivized education as problematic for minoritized, low-income families of Detroit. There were other things that should be considered even more. Faith weighed in on this too, as she contested the claims that anything was wrong with her daughter's school which was closed: "Even when I met with Covington, he admitted that it was a beautiful school."

The constant pressure that the participants placed on the EAA leaders and the Detroit Public School leaders all suggested that their protest activities offered pushback and alternative perspectives of high-stakes, neoliberal schooling:

> Neoliberal stuff is the status quo . . . I am interested in a liberatory vision of education . . . Look at how much the state is spending on these SIG grants, on incentive grants, to bring in industry, which they say will create all these jobs, which is the neoliberal model of trickle down—you bring in the industry and they bring in jobs to make everything better—and they say, how many jobs have they actually produced? It's always much less than what was claimed, for how much money? If you reallocated the money to schooling, you could fully fund schooling . . . That's where I want us to go.

—Jay

Essentially, Jay, Mari, and Faith were all challenging the claims that this form of schooling was healthy or right for Detroit. They brought up the fact that these types of reforms had not been successful, and they disseminated information to news outlets, to forums, and panel discussions across the city, and to legislative bodies, that this was not useful. Yet, neoliberalism, which was understood so well by protestors, was a type of oppression that was not well-understood by most Detroiters.

Finally, in addition to the inability to recognize neoliberalism as a threat, there are a number of other changes in Detroit that may have impacted protest activities. The hyperghettoization, use of drugs, the flight of the middle-class residents to areas outside of the city, and the loss of popularized resistance culture in general (such as the decline of the Black Panthers, protest civil rights, and the Nation of Islam in Detroit) may all have extraneously impacted the protest movement in Detroit.

New Methods of Protest?

The types of protest in Detroit looked unlike protest in other parts of the country, or the world, and it even looks starkly different from Detroit protests from earlier eras. While technology-based and takeover protest strategies (i.e., the Arab Spring and Occupy Wall Street) may have been used to some degree, that is not primarily what we found in Detroit protests. Rather, these findings suggest that the type of activism in Detroit is quite unique to Detroit, situated within a long historical trajectory of strikes and union-based protest. Traveling to a site to protest, picketing, walk-outs, and engaging media were all commonplace. The numbers of the protestors are considerably smaller, each protestor carries a much heavier responsibility of leadership, and the numbers appear to be much smaller than what may have been found in protests in other parts of the country, and world. Jay explains,

> Keep the vote, no takeover has regular meetings, and at least fifty people show up, which, for Detroit standards, is good.

—Jay

The Detroit protest activities looked different from other protests for other reasons as well. The first notable difference between these new age protests (i.e., Occupy Wall Street and the Arab Spring) was the difference in age. The age seemed to be slightly older for the Detroit protestors profiled for this study, and this is likely related to the observation that they used technology differently than other protestors around the world. Email, flyers, web blogs, and occasional videos seem to be the primary use of technology for the Detroit protestors. But uploading videos of oppression and control, using Facebook to organize impromptu rallies, or recording the resistance were all largely absent. In other words, the Detroit protestors used technology as part of their protest, but unlike the Arab Spring, it is not facilitated or organized via technology.

Goals of Protest

The goals of protestors seemed to be independent of why they were involved in their resistance activities. For Mary, it was the incompetence of the EAA officials:

> They virtually broke every single promise that they made when they hired me. Nothing was set up like they said it would be.

—Mary

But for the others, they had more goals to disrupt the state and local politics that they viewed as oppressive and marginalizing toward their interests. For their short-term goals, there was significant alignment—dismantle the State-appointed emergency manager, the EAA, and regain Detroit's democratic representation. Their long-term goals, however, seemed less clearly aligned. For Jay, it was to impact long-term educational opportunities and experiences for Detroit's children:

> I want to build a coalition that can fundamentally transform the way education happens in Detroit, if not nationally. I see the potential of building a coalition of people who are not on board with the Democrats for Educational Reform liberal agenda . . . militant or at least self-respecting African-American folks who are sorta conscious of things in Detroit, more progressive parts of unions, faculty, and grassroots organizations to sorta renovate an old coalition that was once there . . . progressive modernization.

—Jay

Mari suggested that her goals were all about the right to self-determination. All else would come after that:

> If we can't get rid of emergency managers, then it doesn't matter what we're doing. The board who didn't know me and didn't necessarily like me, appointed me . . . the only thing that matters in front of us right now is governance. Don't talk about education. Don't talk about children. Don't talk about anything until we can get the right to govern back . . . that board, who didn't like me, chose me.

—Mari

Like the others, Faith's short-term goals were to resist her child's school closing. But her long-term goals were to make sure that the students are provided appropriate services as required by the Americans with Disabilities Act, and each child's Individualized Education Plan at each of their new schools, and to continue to advocate for transparency:

> So I'm just going to focus on getting those babies what they need. Making sure the staff is at least equipped and getting the word out as much as possible that the school's closed on lies.

—Faith

CONCLUSION

Protest is present and visible in Detroit. The protest efforts that manifest are aligned with older, more traditional "rustbelt protest" actions and ideology. The results are not as robust as the actors would like. It is clear that the number of protestors are falling, but the intensity of those that remain is undeniable. The decrease in protestors, and the associated effectiveness of said protestors, is greatly impacted by increasing globalization and neoliberal policies articulated at the state level. The public media and the broader society seem to be more entertained with a certain type of protest and the newness of protest movements. For example, there were a number of newspaper stories, radio interviews, and even some TV presence about the protestors' resistance to current reform in Detroit. The small number of Detroit protestors and organizations were well-organized, quite vocal, and seemed to be organized and co-supportive of each other's activities. There is a possibility that Detroit protestors could expand their utilization of social media to encompass strategies and tactics used by more recent protest movements, like the Occupy movement and the Arab Spring.

Though the policies in Michigan are state-level in nature, and often proffered as race-neutral, objective, and designed to positively impact communities, their implementation runs counter to this narrative. State-level policies have had a disproportionate impact when compared to the rest of the state of Michigan. In fact, the emergency manager law has been particularly effective in disrupting the Detroit Public School system. Destroying economies of scale, closing schools under questionable circumstances, and taking over underperforming schools to create a new, yet unproven, educational authority are what happened to Detroit. Of note is the fact that the area of impact is largely comprised of a population that has been traditionally underrepresented, disenfranchised, and of low socioeconomic status.

Implications for Urban School Leaders

This research has implications for school leaders and policymakers who would benefit from hearing, elevating, and incorporating community-based voices. Indeed, when such voices are included in reforms, students and communities ultimately stand to benefit. Placed against the backdrop of desirable student outcomes, understanding and working with the community has been shown to positively impact this metric. The neoliberal activities that inspire protest do not work to support the very outcomes that are most desired by educators: improved student outcomes, increased parental involvement, and more consistent community involvement. Instead, the student will be increasingly marginalized and unsupported by policies that do not work to maintain inclusion or the democratic options of parents or other community stakeholders.

What this research reveals is that neoliberal reforms have stripped the democratic rights of the very people policymakers claim to serve. School leaders should understand that the population being oppressed may not have the capacity to recognize that they are being disserviced and targeted, as seen by the implementation of PA4. Current protestors in Detroit may never observe large numbers of people aligning until individuals take on the responsibility of informing school communities that they are being oppressed through these recognizable and seemingly harmless systematic changes: high-stakes models of schooling, standardized test scores, heavy emphasis on financial health of schools. The means of communication should also be considered so that the media is looking to the movement for the news rather than the opposite. Parents, community members, and other stakeholders must first have awareness in order to take a stance and reclaim their democratic rights.

Protest is brewing in Detroit; however, individual needs may take precedence over social needs. Protest in Detroit has taken on a new form, and school leaders may believe that they are in a losing battle. Where in past generations we saw movements of people that united for a specific cause, we question whether the current protestor's ideals are individualistic in nature, rather than social, which may explain the low number of protestors. Those interested in social change are willing to take on the fight for others, as Faith said, "I'll fight for you." Individualized agendas can yield protest, but researchers need to identify examples of how individual agendas align to bring about meaningful change. When one considers the time, effort, and consequences of protesting, individuals may not be willing to take on a social cause that may impede either their everyday life, or the lives of their immediate family.

According to Hirschman (1970):

For competition (exit) to work as a mechanism of recuperation from performance lapses, it is generally best for a firm to have a mixture of alert and inert customers. The alert customers provide the firm with a feedback mechanism which starts the effort at recuperation. (p. 24)

School leaders and policymakers need to be aware of this in order to create strategies and leverage resources in a way that allows them to mitigate, stall, or arrest the negative impact of neoliberal activities. School leaders must be willing to engage with their alert customers, the parents, in order to prevent exit. Ironically, if the very process of neoliberal reform serves to marginalize stakeholder voices, policymakers and school leaders must be aware that such reforms will likely be oppressive toward those marginalized voices.

REFERENCES

Benford, R. D. and Snow, D. A. (2000). Framing processes and social movements: An Overview and assessment. *Annual Review of Sociology, 26*, 611–639.

Burch, P. (2009). *Hidden markets: The New education privatization.* New York: Routledge.

Camp, L. (2012 March 14). Anti-protest law passes nearly unanimously and is signed by the president. Retrieved from www.huffingtonpost.com/lee-camp/anti-occupy-law-passes-nea_b_1343728.html.

Currie, J. and McConnell, S. (1994). The impact of collective-bargaining legislation on disputes in the U.S. public sector: No legislation may be the worst legislation. *Journal of Law and Economics, 37*(2), 519–547.

Fine, G. A. and Stoecker, R. (1985). Can the circle be unbroken: Small groups and social movements. *Advances in Group Processes, 2*, 1–28.

Gabin, N. (1982). "They have placed a penalty on womanhood": The Protest actions of women auto workers in Detroit-Area UAW locals, 1945–1947. *Feminist Studies, 8*(2), 373–398.

Goffman, E. (1974). *Frame analysis: An Essay on the organization of experience.* Cambridge, MA: Harvard University Press.

Guedes, D. and Moreira, V. (2009). The Critical phenomological research methodology based on Merleau-Ponty's Philosophy. *Terapia Psicológica, 27*(2), 247–257.

Harvey, D. (2005). *A Brief history of neoliberalism.* Oxford University Press.

Hayduk, R. (2002). From anti-globalization to global justice: A twenty-first-century movement. In J. Berg (Ed.), *Teamsters and turtles?: U.S. progressive political movements in the 21st century.* Lanham, MD: Rowman and Littlefield Publishers.

Hirschman, A.O. (1970). *Exit, voice, and loyalty: Responses to decline in firms, organizations, and states.* Cambridge, MA: Harvard University Press.

King, B. G., Bentele, K. G., and Soule, S. A. (2007). Protest and policymaking: Explaining fluctuation in congressional attention to rights issues, 1960–1986. *Social Forces, 86*(1), 137–163.

McAllister, S. R. (2007). Funeral picketing laws and free speech. *Kansas Law Review, 55*, 575–627.

Molloff, J. (2012, March 12). HR 347 "Trespass Bill" Criminalizes Protest. Retrieved from www.huffingtonpost.com/jeanine-molloff/trespass-bill_b_1328205.html.

Oliver, P. E., Cadena-Roa, J., and Strawn, K. D. (2003). Emerging trends in the study of protest and social movements. *Research in Political Sociology, 12*, 213–244. Retrieved from 60475889?accountid=12598.

Oliver, P. E. and Maney, G. M. (2000). Political processes and local newspaper coverage of protest events: From selection bias to triadic interactions. *American Journal of Sociology, 106*(2), 463–505.

Olson, C. A. (1986). Strikes, strike penalties, and arbitration in six states. *Industrial and Labor Relations Review, 39*(4).

Regalado, C. and Lare, R. (2007, January/February). The Detroit teachers' strike. *Solidarity.* Retrieved October 24, 2013 from www.solidarity-us.org/site/print/308.

Reid, H. (1973). American social science in the politics of time and the crisis of technocorporate society: Toward a critical phenomenology. *Politics and Society, 3*(2) 201–243.

Scott, J. C. (1990). *Domination and the arts of resistance: Hidden transcripts.* New Haven, CT: Yale University Press.

Shaw, T. C. (2009). *Now is the time!: Detroit black politics and grassroots activism.* Durham, NC: Duke University Press.

Shepard, B. and Hayduk, R. (2002). *From ACT UP to the WTO: Urban protest and community building in the era of globalization.* New York, NY: Verso.

Smith, W. A. (2004). Black faculty coping with racial battle fatigue: The Campus racial climate in a post-civil rights era. In D. Cleveland (Ed.), *A long way to go: Conversations about Race by African American faculty and graduate students* (pp. 171–190). New York: Peter Lang International Academic Publishers.

Smith, W. A., Allen, W. R., and Danley, L. L. (2007). "Assume the position . . . you fit the description": Psychosocial experiences and racial battle fatigue among African American male college students. *American Behavioral Scientist, 51*(4), 551–578.

Snow, D. A. and Benford, R. D. (1988). Ideology, frame resonance, and participant mobilization. *International Social Movement Research, 1*(1), 197–217.

Sugrue, T. (2005). *The Origins of the urban crisis: Race and inequality in postwar Detroit.* Princeton, NJ: Princeton University Press.

Thomas, R. W. (1992). *Life for us is what we make it: Building Black community in Detroit, 1915–1945.* Bloomington: Indiana University Press.

Widick, B. J. (1989). *Detroit: City of race and class violence.* Detroit, MI: Wayne State University Press.

Willen, S. (2007). Toward a critical phenomenology of "illegality": State power, criminalization, and abjectivity among undocumented migrant workers in Tel Aviv, Israel. *International Migration, 43*(3), 8–38.

Zick, T. (2006). Speech and spatial tactics. *Texas Law Review, 84*(3), 581–651.

CHAPTER 19

A Spectrum of Parent and Community Engagement for Conceptualizing and Responding to the Institutional Complexity of Urban Schools

Sharon Watkins, Anika Ball Anthony, Christopher Shaffer, and Kirsten J. Smith

INTRODUCTION

In recent years, there has been an increased interest in innovating education by reconsidering student outcomes, using new instructional resources and instructional strategies, and finding creative ways to engage families and communities in student learning (Christensen, Horn, and, Johnson, 2008; Johnson et al., 2013; Wagner and Compton, 2012). Such interests have been fueled by changes in the workplace and broader society, as well as by federal grant programs, philanthropists, and media attention given to schools that attempt novel solutions to persistent issues. Some school leaders may perceive innovative program development as a strategy to defund locally controlled public schools and redistribute tax dollars to for-profit entities such as instructional service providers and management organizations. However, others may view innovotive programs as means for combating hopelessness by reengaging families and communities who may feel demoralized when low achievement scores are used to characterize their local schools as failing. As the complexity of school leadership tasks increases, community school models and after-school programs are again gaining support and national attention as potential vehicles for energizing schools and supporting student learning (Weiss, Lopez, and Rosenberg, 2010).

Although parent and community engagement is often cited as critical to creating a school culture that strongly supports student achievement, many urban school leaders are dissatisfied with such engagement levels in their buildings. Despite what is known about the positive effects of parent and community engagement, there are concerns that in many schools, effective programs are not implemented (Hagelskamp and DiStasi, 2012) or poorly sustained (Speth, Saifer, and Forehand, 2008), thus resulting in "random acts" that are unlikely to

positively impact students' educational experiences (Weiss, et al., 2010). Such programs are not aligned with the academic mission of the district or school and are therefore disconnected from instructional practice. Others are scheduled to showcase student work and student success but little else. Although individual parents may interact with school staff to discuss particular academic or behavioral accommodations for their own student, most remain disconnected from the educational process, relegated to the role of observer or responder after the completion of successful or unsuccessful learning exercises.

The current expectation for innovative school improvement efforts, including in the area of parent and community engagement, can lead to additional launching of isolated and sporadic initiatives. Without an in-depth understanding of various forms of parent and community engagement, as well as supporting rationales, school leaders face challenges when attempting to develop and implement meaningful, effective, and sustainable engagement initiatives. Scholarship is needed that can suggest directions for emerging research and offer guidance to school leaders who seek inventive approaches to engaging families and communities. Much of the existing literature tends to be school-centric, focused on improving student achievement as an outcome of parent and community engagement. There is limited scholarship on participatory models that extend beyond an immediate goal of achievement gains. Through a review of the literature and drawing on experiences as urban school leaders, the authors suggest alternative parent and community engagement models.

This chapter presents a spectrum of parent and community engagement along with examples of common and unconventional engagement approaches. By considering the spectrum, leaders can map their school's engagement efforts to determine whether change is needed and how they may go about influencing change. Researchers can also benefit from examining this spectrum as they study the design, implementation, and effectiveness of parent and community engagement initiatives. The chapter presents several strategies for addressing the gap between where schools currently are and where they seek to move in light of parent and community engagement solutions under consideration.

This chapter begins with a review of the literature on urban school leadership as it relates to parent and community engagement. It then draws on institutional complexity to explain how the environment beyond the school has resulted in increased pressures for schools to devise innovative ideas, processes, and structures—including efforts to engage parents and communities. The authors explain how this state further complicates the already challenging work of urban school leadership. Next, an engagement spectrum is presented along with bridging strategies. The chapter concludes with ideas for practice and future research that can enhance the field's understanding of alternative approaches to parent and community engagement.

URBAN SCHOOLS' EFFORTS TO ENGAGE PARENTS AND COMMUNITIES

A number of scholars have offered insights on the importance of administrators and teachers actively engaging parents and communities. Despite what is presently known about parent and community engagement, there is little research that moves beyond what this chapter describes as a *Supporting* model, which seeks to extend responsibilities for teaching and fostering conditions for learning beyond the school staff to parents and volunteers to increase student achievement. The paucity of scholarship on alternate models is problematic because, in practice, the intent of parent and community engagement can extend beyond directly improving student achievement. Furthermore, existing literature does not adequately capture the range of potential principal, staff, parent, and community roles and power distribution during engagement efforts.

Importance of Parent and Community Engagement

Simply put, learning is central to a school's mission, and according to research literature, school leadership is second only to classroom instruction concerning factors known to influence student learning (Bryk, Sebring, Allensworth, Luppescu, and Easton, 2010; Hallinger and Heck, 1996; Witziers, Bosker, and Kruger, 2003). The literature commonly references three foci for leaders that are critical for student learning: (1) developing and advancing the school mission and goals, (2) fostering trust and collaboration, and (3) actively supporting instruction (Hallinger, 2005; Supovitz, Sirinides, and May, 2010). The educational leadership literature consistently mentions parent and community engagement as important elements of school success (Leithwood, Louis, Anderson, and Wahlstrom, 2004; Marzano, Waters, and McNulty, 2005). Although this work is demanding, it is even more challenging for urban school leaders who strive to unite a variety of constituents, including students, parents, educators, school boards, and business and community leaders in order to develop educational visions and initiatives (Cuban, 2001; Gooden, 2005; Spillane, Diamond, Walker, Halverson, and Jita, 2001).

Positive effects of schools' efforts to reach out to parents and community members have been well established, including improvement in areas such as parents' involvement (Jeynes, 2012), students' academic achievement (D'Agostino, Hedges, Wong, and Borman, 2001; Fan and Chen, 2001; Jeynes, 2005; Lee and Bowen, 2006), social development (El Nokali, Bachman, and Votruba-Drzal, 2010), participation in additional learning opportunities (Little and Lauver, 2005), graduation rates (Bridgeland, DiIulio, and Morrison, 2006), college and career readiness (Jeynes, 2007), school climate (Goldring and Hausman, 2001), availability of school resources (Weiss, et al., 2010), and community impact (Tillman, 2004).

Urban school leaders know they must partner with their largest clientele, parents and community members, to meet their complex missions (Mathews, 2009; Tough, 2008; Weiss, Lopez, and Rosenberg, 2010). Epstein (2009) identifies effective ways of partnering with parents including assisting with parenting skills, developing effective communication skills and strategies, encouraging volunteerism, helping families engage children in learning at home, empowering families to participate in school decision making, and collaborating with the community to remove barriers by providing supportive services and resources beyond the classroom.

Although some urban school leaders successfully engage parents and communities, many struggle in this regard. Challenges range from un-strategic "random acts" of parent and community involvement (Weiss et al., 2010) to "no acts" at all, examples of which include some leaders attempting to shield educators by "managing" parents, families, and communities rather than connecting with them in meaningful ways (Leithwood and Riehl, 2003). Other leaders state they do not have access to any parents or community resources that can be leveraged (Hagelskamp and DiStasi, 2012). Although families from all backgrounds report a desire to be involved in children's learning (Epstein, 1995; Henderson and Mapp, 2002), educators lack efficacy to actively engage parents and communities because they do not understand why families from affluent and underserved communities tend to engage with student learning differently. Parents belonging to groups that historically have been marginalized due to race and class are more likely to report that they have had negative prior experiences with school (Gordon, 2005), engage in few practices at home that are reinforced by schools (Grolnick and Slowiaczek, 1994; Keith et al., 1998; Kohl, Lengua, and McMahon, 2000), and experience difficulties connecting with schools (Diamond and Gomez, 2004; Lareau and Horvat, 1999; National Center for Education Statistics, 2006).

As explained in the next section, challenges school leaders experience with parent and community engagement are rooted in a number of issues, some of which include: (a) multiple definitions of parent and community engagement, (b) diversity and change in urban communities, and (c) growing expectations to engage parents and communities in innovative ways.

Environmental Pressures That Further Complicate Engagement Initiatives

The institutional environment of schools has become increasingly complex, further complicating urban school leaders' decisions about if and how to engage parents and community members. Within and across urban districts there is a great deal of social, academic, and cultural diversity. Previous reforms have attempted to cope with such diversity by standardizing teaching practices, outcomes, and measures of student learning and school

effectiveness (Cuban, 2001). Historically, the institutional environment of schools has been viewed as a source of normative, coercive, and imitative conformity that constrains operations (Meyer and Rowan, 1977) by narrowly defining the form, function, and operation of schools. While many sources of constraint still remain, the push and pull between pressures to conform to traditional notions of schools versus pressures to redefine goals, locations, and scheduling of schools can thwart or muddle efforts to engage parents and communities in ways that are strategic, systemic, and sustainable. Thus, what is needed is a reconsideration of the normative, coercive, and imitative conformity factors. In addition to influencing standardization across urban schools, they are also forces for change and variation.

Normative Pressures

Normative institutional pressures are those that guide action through cognitive frames that enable actors to know and interpret their environment. Actions are also informed by norms of acceptability, morality, and ethics (Scott, 1995). Examples include professional standards and expectations that are spread across organizations (Hoy and Miskel, 2013). Sadly, in many schools, there is a culture of educational expertise that fosters a sentiment that families in urban communities are not motivated or qualified to help students learn. This attitude, coupled with an expectation that the primary intent for parent and community engagement is increased student achievement, leads to school-centered efforts that discourage rather than encourage parent and community engagement. While potentially effective at raising student achievement scores, school-centered initiatives do not acknowledge that urban communities are not only characterized by poverty, population density, and social stress and dislocation, but a range of social, cultural, and economic assets often exist within and across urban communities and schools. Thus, families, politicians, businesses, and other community members may have a range of complementary and conflicting expectations for the purpose of schools and how they can work with schools to meet those goals.

Another normative pressure is that in an age of hyper-choice of education providers (for example, neighborhood and charter schools, magnet and themed schools for STEM or the arts, out-of-district schools, virtual schools, blended schools, and vouchers for use at private schools), "different" is often equated with "good." As questions surface concerning the relevance of traditional schools, there is a sentiment that schools that continue to reform, innovate, and abandon business as usual are moving in the right direction. In turn, many school leaders feel pressured to offer creative programming to satisfy community leaders and attract and retain families that value accessibility to an array of educational options. Leaders' urgency to respond to these pressures, combined with the perception of parents as unskilled clients, can result in confusion about how to simultaneously appease, manage, and engage them.

Coercive Pressures

Coercive pressures use regulations and threat of formal sanction to guide actions (Scott, 1995). In schools, examples include government mandates and inducements (Hoy and Miskle, 2013). Federal, as well as local, legal, and policy initiatives directly impact parent and community engagement, often imposing new, extensive, complex challenges for school leaders, challenges for which they are directly or indirectly held accountable. Occasionally, federal and local programs define and encourage parent and community engagement differently, even within the same agencies and programs (Weiss, Bouffard, Bridglall, and Gordon, 2009). This leads to unclear goals or strategies to guide school leaders. Additionally, there have been recent shifts away from promoting a standardized approach to school operations, toward active encouragement to innovate education at state and local levels (for example, state and district Race to the Top grants, i3 grants, NCLB waivers). Expanding the standards of success from academic achievement to also include evolving definitions of college and career-readiness has increased the scope of responsibilities for which school leaders are held accountable. Union policies regarding parent access to educators can further complicate engagement efforts. Finally, state policies that result in capricious measures and designations of local school effectiveness can further undermine efforts to engage communities in good faith with their local schools.

Imitative Pressures

Organizations tend to imitate other organizations in their institutional environment that are perceived as respected or successful. Less organizational diversity in an institution results in organizations that tend to adopt similar processes and structures (Meyer and Rowan, 1977; Scott and Davis, 2007). In schools, examples include efforts to adopt standard responses from other sources in order to reduce uncertainty and gain legitimacy (Hoy and Miskel, 2013). This is akin to sentiments such as, "This innovative program worked for another urban district. We should also consider doing the same thing." However, organizational literature also suggests that as the institutional environment increases in complexity, this introduces more choice and ideas for informing program design, as well as more organic forms of management (Burns and Stalker, 1966). The work of institutional entrepreneurs who seek to leverage resources to influence institutions and organizational processes (Garud, Hardy, and Maguire, 2007) contributes to the environmental complexity of schools. Such actors can mobilize politicians, think tanks, for-profit school providers, nonprofit organizations, philanthropists, families, and educators to paint a picture of crisis and scarcity that calls for market-driven approaches and strategies that change the institutional environment of schools. These shifts, coupled with increased access to rapidly emerging technologies, make innovation en vogue. Grant-supported partnerships for neighborhood-specific educational programming, the use of social media to connect with families, and contracts for parental involvement are a few examples of parent and community engagement that have received attention from national media and practitioner-oriented publications. Thus, leaders may elect to imitate elements of such initiatives in their own schools.

Change for the sake of change, or choice for the sake of choice, does not necessarily create high-quality schools. Instead, school leaders can build upon an integrated framework that is informed by practice, research, and theory to guide meaningful parent and community engagement. While there is no one factor that leads to increased engagement, and there is no one program that will work best in every building, urban school leaders can benefit from considering a spectrum of engagement models to identify both where their school community engagement locates and how it compares to other possible models.

SPECTRUM FOR PARENT AND COMMUNITY ENGAGEMENT

Given the aforementioned challenges that the institutional complexity of schools presents for urban school leaders' efforts to foster parent and community engagement, this section of the chapter presents a spectrum of five urban school engagement models: *Welcoming, Supporting, Engaging, Partnering,* and *Participatory.* These models are distinguished in regard to the extent to which they are (a) school- or community-centered, and (b) informed by school, parent, or community agendas. The models are informed by schools-community relations theory (Epstein, 2002) and school-centered, community-centered, and balanced approaches for engagement (Khalifa, 2012). The spectrum is not intended to prescribe or limit urban school leaders' options for parent and community engagement, but instead it can serve as a metacognitive tool to encourage reflection and inform discussions as leaders work with faculty, staff, and constituents to monitor existing programs and consider new ideas for engagement. Figure 19.1 displays the five models of parent and community en-

gagement and implications each model has for school leaders' administrative responsibilities. Moving left to right, the extent of parent and community engagement and responsibilities expands, as does the criteria of what constitutes a learner.

Welcoming

A Welcoming School provides opportunities for families to feel connected to the school and the schooling process. Factors that drive attempts to make the school climate more welcoming may stem from a number of causes such as a need to better understand family and community issues that influence interest in student success and school involvement patterns. Another cause may be to help families trust school administrators, particularly if the school has received negative attention for its academic achievement and has been constructed as a place that lacks a commitment to meeting the needs of all students. These schools invite parents to functions and seek to provide a pleasant atmosphere. They affirm a child's background and cultural capital, try to increase families' confidence in educational programming, and encourage home-school continuity.

Schools are not unified in their approach to interactions with families and communities. Unlike schools

Welcoming	Supporting	Engaging	Partnering	Participatory
Students		← Learner →		All Stakeholders
Schools seek to improve student achievement by helping families feel connected to the school	Schools share teaching and academic support responsibilities with families and volunteers	Schools seek to extend their resources, educational offerings, and reach	Schools aim to extend student learning opportunities and strengthen communities	Schools attempt to address community education needs for learners of all ages
Leaders and staff foster a welcoming climate and maintain positive communication with families and communities	Leaders work with staff to develop parent involvement programs and contracts and provide support to communicate expectations	Leaders recruit, train, and/or screen skilled parent and community volunteers. They develop policies and coordinate initiatives	Leaders develop contractual relationships with external organizations; They ensure school-partner alignment	Leaders, staff, and community collaboratively redesign learning systems; Administrators ensure space for community learning
School		← Accountability and Control →		Shared

Figure 19.1. *The Spectrum for Parent and Community Engagement displays five engagement models and indicates leadership responsibilities in light of (a) what constitutes a learner and (b) school-centric or shared accountability and control in the decision-making process.*

that view their relationship with the school and communities as interdependent, those that do not make an effort to foster a welcoming climate do so because they view the school as separate from families and society, and thus feel they do their best work without the distraction imposed by families, communities, and other influencers. These two reactions are due to what Leithwood and colleagues (2004) describe as either the independent producers view or the interdependent co-contributor view—two incompatible views of the family and community.

Leaders in Welcoming Schools view relationships as key to assisting students and families with committing to the work and follow-through that learning requires, as parents and community volunteers are more likely to be involved when administrators, teachers, and staff proactively reach out to them (Hoover-Dempsey and Sandler, 1997; Sheldon, 2005; Simon, 2004). Parents and volunteers may be asked to do very little in a Welcoming School as staff are busy learning about the difficulties community members have had connecting with schools (Diamond and Gomez, 2004) and learning how to effectively communicate with diverse groups (Epstein, 2009).

The Welcoming School, while making efforts to learn about students, families, and communities, tends to be school-centric in its perspective. Through making the school climate more inviting, schools hope to improve student attendance and academic motivation by encouraging home cultures to have views about education that are aligned with the school's. Additionally, such schools seek to share information by sending home newsletters, providing updates about students' test scores and what is being done to improve them, and communicating attempts to address parents' concerns.

Supporting

A Supporting School goes beyond the Welcoming School with specific expectations or agreements regarding parent involvement. Urban districts, typically larger and more diverse than suburban districts, require more resources to serve the needs of a heterogeneous school-aged population. Thus Supportive Schools, along with Engaging and Partnering Schools, attempt to share the burden of addressing factors likely to influence student learning through formal and informal contracts for la-

bor distribution. Explicit agreements can be articulated in a signed document that expresses the shared commitments of parents, teachers, and school administrators (Epstein, 2009; Mathews, 2009; Tableman, 2000; Tough, 2008). For example, parents may agree to volunteer in the classroom for a given number of hours or lead a school fundraising project several times a year. In both of these examples, primary responsibility for student achievement still rests with the school faculty and administrative team while parents and communities are largely left disengaged.

Supporting Schools are more deliberate than Welcoming Schools in their efforts to influence the culture and climates of homes to foster academic achievement (Leithwood et al., 2004). They attempt to help parents understand the significance of the work schools are engaged in and how parent support can lead to greater success. Such schools tend to sponsor what Jeynes (2012) describes as parental involvement programs that encourage or require parental participation. Jeynes's review of the literature revealed several programs that align with the Supporting model such as shared reading programs for parents and children to read together, parent partnership programs that encourage parents and teachers to work together to address children's behavior and improve academic outcomes, and checking homework programs that require parents to confirm that students have completed assignments. Other examples include encouraging parents to attend parent-teacher conferences, identifying room parents and volunteers (Weiss et al., 2010), giving parents explicit instructions, and holding them accountable for helping students learn academic skills beyond the school day (Epstein, 2009; Hagelskamp and DiStasi, 2012), as well as providing families access to electronic data resources that enable them to actively monitor their child's academic progress (Chen, 2010).

Similar to the Welcoming School, the Supporting School also has a school-centric perspective, thus leadership responsibilities may entail developing and enforcing policies about expectations for school staff to communicate with parents, as well as for parents to be actively engaged. Leaders ensure that teachers have forums and resources for explicitly communicating areas of needed help and associated responsibilities for parents and volunteers.

Engaging

The Engaging School moves into the community to develop relationships with community agencies and leaders—both formal and informal. The leader engages parents, community organizations, and business with school governance, thus cultivating a stronger climate of trust across the broader community by establishing bonds beyond the school doors. Unlike the Welcoming and Supportive Schools that have a more traditional culture that maintains clear distinctions between school professionals and community volunteers (Hargreaves, 1995) who may possess some skills for supporting student learning, the Engaging School views select parents, community members, and organizations as valued entities with specific assets and expertise for significantly extending the school's resources, educational offerings, and reach (Hagelskamp and DiStasi, 2012; Weiss et al., 2010). Engagement examples include parent associations, advisory councils, and community partners who help with program development (Epstein, 2009). Additional examples include guest speakers and consultants.

Because the Engaging School is primarily concerned with expanding the school's capacity, this model is still school-centric; however, it views individuals and groups who were once outsiders as potential insiders or boundary-spanners. The responsibilities for leaders in such a model include learning about the expertise that parents and community members have and considering how to engage them in targeted ways. Leaders must approve, coordinate, or provide resources for engagement. They help develop policies for operations, and as needed, formal screening procedures or contractual agreements.

Partnering

The Partnering School expands learning support systems by developing partnerships with community agencies and businesses. This may take the form of hosting medical clinics within the school, providing classes that address specific parenting concerns, or working with businesses to provide student internship opportunities. Unlike the Welcoming, Supporting, and Engaging models, the Partnering School seeks to be both school-centric and community-centric. Leaders of such schools understand that schools are expected to be accountable for student learning; however, they are also interested in helping to strengthen urban communities (Cuban, 2001). Partnering School administrators and staff feel that working alone, schools cannot improve the quality of life in urban communities. Thus, they attempt to focus on student learning, while enabling partners to attend to other aspects of student and community development. This allows the school to become a space for overlapping school and community spheres (Epstein, 2009; Khalifa, 2012) that have capacity to provide educational programs, health and social services, high-quality early childhood education, and after- or outside-of-school experiences (Tough, 2008; Weiss et al., 2010). The school can also be used as a space for community programming when the facility is not in use.

As with the Engaging School, leaders in the Partnering School actively take advantage of the larger community surrounding their schools (Portin et al., 2009), working with various entities, including the mayor's office, business leaders, community organizations, post-secondary institutions, and parents to mobilize and implement far-reaching, multi-thronged reform agendas (Cuban, 2001; Hagelskamp and DiStasi, 2012). School leaders also make necessary adjustments in space, scheduling, policies, and budgets to ensure that partnership barriers are identified and addressed.

Participatory

The Participatory School is more democratic and egalitarian than the three previously described models. Its collegial culture (Hargreaves, 1995) extends beyond teachers and administrators to also encompass students, families, and community members. In this model, *the entire community* is invited to *participate* in and contribute toward the development of an agile learning center that incorporates local expertise while being flexible enough to respond to the educational needs of the community. Multiple platforms of education delivery are employed, and innovative instructional practices are piloted while a community-wide learning culture emerges. Traditional instructional delivery is one of many choices available to learners of all ages, along with e-learning, apprenticeships, and other learning alternatives.

The model is built around the assumption that if parents and communities participate in the learning process rather than just supporting it, then learning will take on a new meaning for the community. In the Participatory School learning is viewed as an ongoing activity that continues throughout the life span. With increased involvement from the broader community, the student is no longer viewed as the sole learner where success is primarily measured by academic achievement scores. Instead, administrators, teachers, staff, families, and community members are all viewed as learners as they learn about one another and the world around them and seek to put that learning into practice.

Just as the learner in a Participatory School is broadly defined, what constitutes a leader is also broadly defined. Anyone who has ideas for how to advance learning and is willing to work with others to create a space for shared learning can be deemed a leader. Administrators ensure there is space for dialogue to develop values and assumptions about teaching, learning, and educational outcomes across the broader school community. Schools may use a range of shared decision-making strategies (Hoy and Tarter, 1993) to ensure that school processes and structures are adjusted in order to pursue the agreed-upon vision.

These five models are ideal types, which no one school or district may fully reflect at a given time. A specific program that a school develops or adopts may fit into one of the five previously described models, or it may intentionally entail aspects of multiple models. For example, when thinking of ways to make the school more welcoming, educators may use Engaging School tactics by reaching out to parents or community members who have expertise in this area or who can serve as informants about why other parents view the school as unwelcoming. In devising solutions to make the school more welcoming, a school may take a more Participatory School approach where a committee of parents, school employees, community members, and student representatives co-design efforts to foster learning about one another and the community. Furthermore, a school may experience multiple types of models of parent and community engagement over time. A strategy that worked in the past might need to change as the community and school changes.

BRIDGING STRATEGIES

The spectrum for parent and community engagement is presented as a continuum in regards to views of learners and the locus of school control. Despite this, the authors do not view schools' intents and strategies for engaging parents and communities as adhering to a developmental model in that a school needs to advance from Welcoming to Supporting, and so forth, before it can reach the Participatory Model. Schools are free to determine if and where their school and planned initiatives fit within this spectrum. Bridging strategies for advancing from one ideal type to another include the following: (1) taking time for goal-setting, (2) using data, (3) engaging in resource capacity-building, and (4) realigning organizational structure and culture.

Goal-Setting Strategies

Schools need to be intentionally reflective about what they intend to achieve. Thus, adopting and following a strategic goal-setting process is essential. Understanding existing goals and identifying goals that still need to be achieved requires thoughtful work on the part of school leaders. Without doing this, parent-community engagement has potential to become another random act.

Building stakeholder buy-in is essential to goal implementation. School leaders can use regularly scheduled formal and informal conversations with students, staff, parents, and the community at large to attentively listen to constituents. Leaders should deliberately utilize a variety of sources of local informants to help determine where the community is headed so that school goals are aligned with community signature needs. Leaders may find unique educational goals arise out of the need to support the local work force. For example in a school district where the shipping industry has a large presence in the local economy, preparing qualified workers to fill logistics positions could be a critical need. The engagement models would each have a distinct response, such that a Partnering School may work with shipping companies to establish high school internship experiences. However, a Participatory School may meet with shipping industry representatives to identify staff training needs, provide courses for their staff and high school students, and schedule courses for both groups of learners at locations within and outside the school building.

Bridging between one engagement model and another using goal-setting strategies will require leaders and their teams to first establish where their school falls on the spectrum and then determine where they want to go. Using a shared decision-making process, leaders and their teams can evaluate a range of school- and community-centric ideas and then identify necessary resources such as staffing, community support, and finances to put ideas into practice.

New Ways to Think About Data

Data-driven school change has become a mantra over the past two decades. Schools tend to rely on achievement scores to inform decisions about school-centric goals. A broader view of what constitutes data is required to move toward a Participatory School model. The data examined may include, but not be limited to, information about employment, wealth, health, attitudes, beliefs, population trends, housing statistics, and student motivation data. All of this data viewed by a community that is participating together in the learning process can paint quite a different picture than a school-centric approach where students are either passing or failing.

Bridging engagement categories using data will require leaders to think differently, not only about what data to use in decision making, but also about how to involve new stakeholders in gathering, interpreting, and setting data-informed goals for the community. For example, a Welcoming School, which previously may have only shared state grade cards with parents, may instead share information about the school's and classroom's assets and needs that contextualize achievement scores. Moving across the spectrum, schools can find ways to share more types of critical data and increase parent and community participation in decision-making. For example, a U.S. Department of Education website features a program that uses the teacher-parent conference to help parents become more knowledgeable about student data and what parents can do to help raise achievement. Giving parents the ability to understand the metrics being used to assess their schools' performance may lead to rich dialogue about academic achievement. Absent a critical framing of school performance, parents and community members rely on limited data sources, such as state report cards and media characterizations, to evaluate schools. Leaders can promote understandings among families about current state practices to identify failing schools, work with the community to articulate alternate outcomes and measures, explain what the school is doing in an effort to meet various expectations, and solicit assistance with advocacy messaging about the school and its community.

Resource Capacity Building

Resource and capacity building entail using existing and new resources to do more than focus just on student performance. When local experts, businesses, families, and learners collaborate to create a culture of learning where the entire community participates together in teaching and learning, resource and capacity building take on greater community significance. School leaders need to ask questions to identify new resources and to repurpose existing ones. For example, can existing resources be used in a different class? Grade level? Building? Can resources be extended beyond the typical school day? Can instruction take place in a new environment? While the Welcoming School may view its budget as its primary resource, the Participatory School utilizes local expertise to advance the community in meaningful ways. The possibilities of resources are as large as the community, limited only by the imagination of participating stakeholders.

Systemic and Structural Innovations

To remain relevant in a digital society, urban school leaders are going to have to think differently about their school buildings and the structures within which they operate. As technological developments continue to influence everyday practices, the look of school is likely to change drastically. One need look no further than courses being offered online by a variety of service providers to consider what may be coming in the near future. Leaders can work to move their schools from school-centric, Welcoming environments to Participatory Schools where people of multiple age groups can learn together in virtual and physical environments. School can become a space for family classes. Districts can partner with area businesses and nonprofit organizations to equip buildings with new laboratories that serve the needs of diverse learners. The length and times of the school day can also be re-imagined.

Systemic and structural innovations will look different as one moves across the spectrum. A Partnering School may rent out space to local business to recruit student interns and teach them skills not already covered in the academic curriculum. A Participatory School may have those same experts teach adults and students together. Building capacity in new ways is required as the community participates to identify and utilize a variety of resources for learning.

Adjusting School Culture

Although schools can be described as having either a more traditional or collegial culture (Hargreaves, 1995), as new technologies, globalization, and expectations for change shape schooling processes, broadening the definition of "school," school culture will also likely become more difficult to define and cultivate. For example, the culture of a completely online school may differ from that of a blended or a brick-and-mortar school. As leaders consider whether their approach to parent and community engagement will adhere more to a Welcoming versus a Participatory model, they will need to consider how to leverage data and leadership practices to influence school culture transformations that align with new structures, resource redeployment, and decision-making processes.

CONCLUSION

The literature on parent and family engagement predominantly discusses how parents can satisfactorily support traditional, brick-and-mortar schools. As school choice, personalized learning, and workplace needs proliferate, challenging the conceptions of when, where, and how students learn, parent and community engagement aims and strategies are also likely to change. Increased complexity in school environments may result in uncertainty about how to effectively and efficiently deliver customized learning experiences. To meet students' needs in a changing world, it is likely that many parents will assume new roles as they learn about and work with a range of education providers (for example, schools, content developers, nonprofit organizations, businesses) to ensure their children receive targeted and high-quality education. Urban school leaders will need a framework for navigating these new waters.

Research can contribute to this work by presenting alternates to school-centric models and outcomes for parent and community engagement. As practitioners and researchers gain familiarity with a variety of school configurations, research is needed that evaluates a range of parent and community engagement models. A logical step for future research is to examine the utility of the parent and community engagement spectrum for helping to ground discussions about creative ways to increase such engagement. Research is also needed that examines practices for selecting, designing, and implementing various efforts, highlighting nuances in organizational processes, structural arrangements, leadership practices, and power redistribution. Such research can spotlight issues and complications associated with parent and community engagement initiatives that otherwise would go unnoticed in academic circles, thus limiting the educational research community's ability to help conceptualize and evaluate alternative engagement models.

REFERENCES

Bridgeland, J. M., DiIulio, J. J., and Morrison, K. B. (2006). The silent epidemic: Perspectives of high school dropouts. Washington, DC: Civic Enterprises, LLC. Retrieved from www.gatesfoundation.org/united-states/Documents/TheSilentEpidemic3-06FINAL.pdf.

Bryk, A. S., Sebring, P. B., Allensworth, E., Luppescu, S., and Easton, J. Q. (2010). *Organizing schools for improvement: Lessons from Chicago*. Chicago, IL: University of Chicago Press.

Burns, T. and Stalker, G. M. (1966). *The management of innovation*. London: Tavistock.

Chen, M. (2010). *Education nation: Six leading edges of innovation in our schools*. San Francisco: Jossey-Bass.

Christensen, C. M., Horn, M. B., and Johnson, C. W. (2008). *Disrupting class: How disruptive innovation will change the way the world learns*. New York: McGraw-Hill.

Cuban, L. (2001). Leadership for student learning: Urban school leadership—different in kind and degree. Washington, DC: Institute for Educational Leadership. Retrieved from www.iel.org/pubs/sl21ci.html.

D'Agostino, J. V., Hedges, L. V., Wong, K. K., and Borman, G. D. (2001). Title I parent involvement programs: Effects on parenting practices and student achievement. In G. D. Borman, S. C. Stringfield, and R. E. Slavin (Eds.), *Title I: Compensatory education at the crossroads: Sociocultural, political and historical studies in education* (pp. 117–136). Mahwah, NJ: Lawrence Erlbaum Associates.

Diamond, J. B. and Gomez, K. (2004). African American parents' educational orientations: The importance of social class and parents' perceptions of school. *Education and Urban Society, 36*(4), 383–427.

El Nokali, N. E., Bachman, H. J., and Votruba-Drzal, E. (2010). Parent involvement and children's academic and social development in elementary school. *Child Development, 81,* 998–1005.

Epstein, J. L. (1995). School/family/community partnerships: Caring for the children we share. *Phi Delta Kappan, 76*(9), 701–712.

Epstein, J. L. (2002). *School, family, and community partnerships: Your handbook for action.* Thousand Oaks, CA: Corwin Press.

Epstein, J. L. (2009). *School, family, and community partnerships: Your handbook for action* (3rd ed.). Thousand Oaks, CA: Corwin Press.

Fan, X. and Chen, M. (2001). Parental involvement and students' academic achievement: A meta-analysis. *Educational Psychology Review, 13*(1), 1–22.

Garud, R., Hardy, C., and Maguire, S. (2007). Institutional entrepreneurship as embedded agency: An introduction to the special issue. *Organization Studies, 28*(7), 957–969.

Goldring, E. and Hausman, C. (2001). Civic capacity and school principals: The missing link in community development. In R. Crowson and B. Boyd (Eds.), *Community development and school reform.* Greenwich, CT: JAI Press.

Gooden, M. (2005). The role of African American principal in an urban information technology high school. *Education Administration Quarterly, 41*(4), 630–650.

Gordon, E. W. (2005). The idea of supplementary education. In E. W. Gordon, B. L. Bridglall and A. S. Meroe (Eds.), *Supplementary education: The hidden curriculum of high academic achievement* (pp. 320–334). New York: Rowman and Littlefield.

Grolnick, W. S. and Slowiaczek, M. L. (1994). Parents' involvement in children's schooling: A multidimensional conceptualization and motivational model. *Child Development, 65*(1), 237–252.

Hagelskamp, C. and DiStasi, C. (2012). Failure is not an option: How principals, teachers, students, and parents from Ohio's high-achieving, high-poverty schools explain their success. New York: Public Agenda. Retrieved from www.publicagenda.org/files/pdf/FailureIsNotAnOption_PublicAgenda_2012.pdf.

Hallinger, P. (2005). Instructional leadership and the school principal: A passing fancy that refuses to fade away. *Leadership and Policy in Schools, 4,* 221–239.

Hallinger, P. and Heck, R. H. (1996). Reassessing the principal's role in school effectiveness: A review of the empirical research, 1980–1995. *Educational Administration Quarterly, 32*(1), 5–44.

Hargreaves, D. H. (1995). School culture, school effectiveness and school improvement. *School Effectiveness and School Improvement, 6*(1), 23–46.

Henderson, A. T. and Mapp, K. L. (2002). A new wave of evidence: The impact of school, family, and community connections on student achievement. Annual Synthesis, 2002. Austin, TX: National Center for Family and Community Connections with Schools, Southwest Educational Development Laboratory (SEDL).

Hoover-Dempsey, K. V. and Sandler, H. M. (1997). Why do parents become involved in their children's education? *Review of Educational Research, 67*(1), 3–42.

Hoy, W. K. and Miskel, C. G. (2013). *Educational Administration: Theory, Research and Practice* (9th ed.). New York: McGraw-Hill.

Hoy, W. K. and Tarter, C. J. (1993). A normative model of shared decision making. *Journal of Educational Administration, 31,* 4–19.

Jeynes, W. H. (2005). A meta-analysis of the relation of parental involvement to urban elementary school student academic achievement. *Urban Education, 40*(3), 237–269.

Jeynes, W. H. (2007). The relationship between parental involvement and urban secondary school student academic achievement: A meta-analysis. *Urban Education, 42*(1), 82–110.

Jeynes, W. H. (2012). A meta-analysis of the efficacy of different types of parental involvement programs for urban students. *Urban Education, 47*(4), 706–742.

Johnson, L., Adams Becker, S., Cummins, M., Estrada, V., Freeman, A., and Ludgate, H. (2013). *NMC Horizon Report: 2013 K–12 Edition.* Austin, TX: The New Media Consortium.

Keith, T. Z., Keith, P. B., Quirk, K. J., Sperduto, J., Santillo, S., and Killings, S. (1998). Longitudinal effects of parent involvement on high school grades: Similarities and differences across gender and ethnic groups. *Journal of School Psychology, 36*(3), 335–363.

Khalifa, M. (2012). A *re*-new-*ed* paradigm in successful urban school leadership: Principal as community leader. *Educational Administration Quarterly, 48*(3), 424–467.

Kohl, G. O., Lengua, L. J., and McMahon, R. J. (2000). Parent involvement in school: Conceptualizing multiple dimensions and their relations with family and demographic risk factors. *Journal of School Psychology, 28*(6), 501–523.

Lareau, A. and Horvat, E. (1999). Moments of social inclusion and exclusion: Race, class, and cultural capital in family school relationships. *Sociology of Education, 72*(1), 37–53.

Lee, J.-S. and Bowen, N. K. (2006). Parent involvement, cultural capital, and the achievement gap among elementary school children. *American Educational Research Journal, 43,* 193–215.

Leithwood, K., Louis, K. S., Anderson, S., and Wahlstrom, K. (2004). Review of research: How leadership influences student learning: Center for Applied Research and Educational Improvement at the University of Minnesota and

Ontario Institute for Studies in Education at the University of Toronto. Retrieved from www.wallacefoundation.org/KnowledgeCenter/KnowledgeTopics/CurrentAreasofFocus/EducationLeadership/Pages/HowLeadershipInfluencesStudentLearning.aspx.

Leithwood, K. and Riehl, C. (2003). What do we already know about successful school leadership? Paper prepared for the American Educational Research Association Division A Task Force on Developing Research in Educational Leadership.

Little, P. M. D. and Lauver, S. (2005). Engaging adolescents in out-of-school time programs: Learning that works. *The Prevention Researcher, 12*(2), 7–10.

Marzano, R. J., Waters, T., and McNulty, B. A. (2005). School leadership that works: From research to results. Alexandria, VA: Association for Supervision and Curriculum Development.

Mathews, J. (2009). *Work hard. Be nice: How two inspired teachers created the most promising schools in America.* Chapel Hill, NC: Algonquin Books.

Meyer, J. W. and Rowan, B. (1977). Institutionalized organizations: Formal structure as myth and ceremony. *The American Journal of Sociology, 83*(2), 340–363.

National Center for Education Statistics. (2006). School and parent interaction by household language and poverty status: 2002-03. NCES Report No. 2006-086. Washington, DC: Author.

Portin, B. S., Knapp, M. S., Dareff, S., Feldman, S., Russell, F. A., Samuelson, C., and Theresa, Y. L. (2009). Leadership for learning improvement in urban schools: Center for the Study of Teaching and Policy, University of Washington. Retrieved from www.wallacefoundation.org/knowledge-center/school-leadership/district-policy-and-practice/Pages/Leadership-for-Learning-Improvement-in-Urban-Schools.aspx.

Scott, R. W. (1995). *Institutions and organizations.* Thousand Oaks, CA: Sage.

Scott, R. W. and Davis, G. F. (2007). *Organizations and organizing: Rational, natural, and open systems perspectives.* Upper Saddle River, NJ: Pearson Prentice Hall.

Sheldon, S. B. (2005). Testing a structural equation model of partnership program implementation and parent involvement. *Elementary School Journal, 106*(2), 171–187.

Simon, B. S. (2004). High school outreach and family involvement. *Social Psychology of Education, 7*(2), 18–209.

Speth, T., Saifer, S., and Forehand, G. (2008). Parent involvement activities in school improvement plans in the Northwest Region. Washington, DC: U.S. Department of Education, Institute of Education Sciences, National Center for Education Evaluation and Regional Assistance, Regional Educational Laboratory of Northwest. Retrieved from ies.ed.gov/ncee/edlabs/projects/project.asp?ProjectID=170.

Spillane, J. P., Diamond, J. B., Walker, L. J., Halverson, R., and Jita, L. (2001). Urban school leadership for elementary science instruction: Identifying and activating resources in an undervalued school subject. *Journal of Research in Science Teaching, 38*(8), 918–940.

Supovitz, J. A., Sirinides, P., and May, H. (2010). How principals and peers influence teaching and learning. *Educational Administration Quarterly, 46,* 31–56.

Tableman, B. (Ed.). (2000). *Full service schools–1 (Issue Brief No. 6).* Lansing: Board of Trustees of Michigan State University.

Tillman, L. C. (2004). African American principals and the legacy of *Brown. Review of Research in Education, 28,* 101–146.

Tough, P. (2008). *Whatever it takes: Geoffrey Canada's quest to change Harlem and America.* Boston: Houghton Mifflin.

Wagner, T. and Compton, R. A. (2012). *Creating innovators: The making of young people who will change the world.* New York: Scribner.

Weiss, H. B., Bouffard, S. M., Bridglall, B. L., and Gordon, E. W. (2009). Reframing family involvement in education: Supporting families to support educational equity. *Equity Matters: Research Review No. 5.* Retrieved from www.hfrp.org/family-involvement/publications-resources/reframing-family-involvement-in-education-supporting-families-to-support-educational-equity.

Weiss, H. B., Lopez, M. E., and Rosenberg, H. (2010). Beyond random acts: Family, school, and community engagement as an integral part of education reform. Retrieved from www.hfrp.org/content/download/3809/104680/file/PolicyForumPaper-120710-FINAL.pdf.

Witziers, B., Bosker, R. J., and Kruger, M. L. (2003). Educational leadership and student achievement: The elusive search for an association. *Educational Administration Quarterly, 39,* 398–425.

SOCIAL JUSTICE, EQUITY, ADVOCACY, AND ACTIVISM

In section 6, the authors both define and describe the practicalities of preparing and practicing school leaders for careers committed to social justice work. In this regard, advocacy and activism are integral to successful social justice leadership. The role of advocacy, activism, and social justice must take an increasingly central role in urban educational leadership and reform. Without emphasis of these areas, indeed, inequities will not only continue to exist, but will grow and become systemic. Urban school leaders must help lead the fight of social justice in schools. The section begins with a reflection by Ivory Berry and Adrienne Dixson.

In chapter 20, "AYP, Access, and Expectations: Superintendents' Legal, Distributive, and Transformative Approaches to Equity," Rachel Roegman and Thomas Hatch present a framework that incorporates three approaches: legal, distributive, and transformative. This framework empowers decision makers by unpacking the meanings of equity in order to be strategic and responsive to issues of equity. In chapter 21, "Learning to Lead for Social Justice: How Leadership Preparation Programs Can Improve Equity in Schools," Gaëtane Jean-Marie, Anthony Normore, and Jeffrey Brooks examine the literature in order to address if leadership preparation programs have both the capacity and have demonstrated commitment to prepare administrators for social justice.

Chapters 22 and 23 both provide explicit actions that school leaders for social justice have exemplified. In chapter 22, "Social Justice in Action: Urban School Leaders Address the School to Prison Pipeline via a Youth Court," Heather Cole, Julian Vasquez Heilig, Tina Fernandez, Meg Clifford, and Rey Garcia provide a case study of an urban middle school combatting students being tracked into the juvenile justice system. This chapter follows the school leaders that implemented this program, documenting their trials, and the actions required to challenge institutionalized oppression. In chapter 23, "Actions Matter: How School Leaders Enact Equity Principles," by Jessica Rigby and Lynda Tredway, the authors discuss a qualitative research study that provides insights as to how a school district developed and utilized a Principal Leadership Rubric that is grounded in practices of equity.

The authors found that the ways in which the principals enacted equity varied in three areas: the level of explicitness, the type of issue, and indicators toward change, providing implications for both research and practice of supporting principals and evaluations. These authors provide information to school leaders in order to make social justice work tangible and congruent with daily practice. Overall, all authors make a strong case of implementing social justice in their practice, and this will, in turn, improve the lives and educational experiences of children.

A Critical Race Theory Perspective on Urban School Leadership

Ivory Berry and Adrienne D. Dixson

As the racial demographics in U.S. public schools is becoming more diverse, according to a report produced by the National Center for Education Statistics (Hussar and Bailey, 2013), school districts and its leaders must consider and prepare for what it means to serve a culturally diverse constituency that is now the majority. Moreover, educational stakeholders, i.e., policy makers, educators, researchers, parents, students, and community advocates, must be attentive to how schools are designed and the ways they service and help students prepare for success. In both urban and suburban settings, too often, national, state, and local school policies—even those developed and implemented with good intention—have had adverse effects on students of color. Many of these policies contribute to disparities in discipline and curriculum placement, marginal gains in academic performance and achievement, and lower graduation and college-going rates compared to their white peers. Indeed, urban educational administration and leadership scholars, program leaders, practitioners, and social justice advocates, in particular, have contributed immensely to positively advancing schools to better serve and meet the needs of students of color. Nonetheless, the aforementioned racial disparities, and many other perplexing issues and outcomes, continue to persist or reappear. A Critical Race Theory (CRT) analysis can be useful for school leaders in understanding how school structures and policies, including reform, may contribute to or exacerbate unfavorable outcomes for students of color, and, in return, illuminate the need for interventions and solutions that redress racial disparities. In this way, school leaders would need to be thinking about how to frame race-conscious policies.

CRT defines racism as "not the acts of individuals, but the larger, systemic, structural conventions and customs that uphold and sustain oppressive group rela-

tionships, status, income, and educational attainment" (Taylor, 2009, p. 4). Educational scholars, in particular, use CRT to examine racial inequalities in schools (De-Cuir and Dixson, 2004; Dixson and Rousseau, 2005; Ladson-Billings and Tate, 1995). Like CRT legal scholars, CRT in education is not wedded to any particular doctrine (Ladson-Billings and Tate, 1995; Lawrence, Matsuda, Delgado, and Crenshaw, 1993); however, its scholarship (1) recognizes that racism is permanent and intersects with other forms of subordination; (2) challenges dominant claims of race neutrality (i.e., color-blindness); (3) offers a transformative response to oppression; (4) recognizes the experiential knowledge of people of color is critical to understanding racial subordination; and (5) insists the inclusion of both a contextual and historical analysis of race and racism. Further, CRT is useful for highlighting the ways whiteness is normalized, privileged, and used as a reference to assess students of color.

Often, educational stakeholders, even those advocating for students of color, may fail to acknowledge and critique the normalization of whiteness within school structures and, consequently, pursue policy changes or reform agendas that seek to "fix" students of color to perform and socialize them to behave like their white peers rather than attend to cultural differences (Dixson and Dingus, 2008). Additionally, educational stakeholders who are unaware of racialized educational inequality may support liberal visions of race reform in education, which promote color-blind racial ideologies (Rousseau and Tate, 2003). According to Kimberlé Crenshaw (2011), based on a color-blind or liberal ideology, laws, practices, policies, and institutions, and in many ways schools, are considered to be race-neutral; all persons are presumably treated as equal as possible with no regard to racial identities, thereby rendering racist acts as anomalous, unintentional incidences by otherwise un-biased individuals. Moreover, racial subordination and disparities are perceived as "merely opportunities yet to be realized by individuals disinclined to take advantage of them" (Crenshaw, 2011, p. 1318) rather than markers of exclusion. CRT offers a critique to this color-blind, liberal approach to antiracism, highlighting how it fails to recognize the institutional and structural reproduction of white racial power. Fundamental to CRT is the notion that white supremacy is maintained within laws, policies, and structures by way of systemically normalizing whiteness, or standards of white culture (Harris, 1993). In education, urban school leaders must attend to the ways in which school discipline policies are hyper-vigilant as it pertains to the behaviors of students of color and overly permissive of white students' behaviors. Concomitantly, urban school leaders must examine district and school policies that restrict the access for students of color to rigorous courses and extracurricular opportunities. In particular, urban school leaders must focus on outcomes rather than process. That is, creating an application process that is presumably open to "everyone" does not ensure an equitable outcome. Thus, from a CRT perspective, it is imperative that urban school leaders examine enrollment and admission outcomes to ensure that students of color are participating in rigorous courses and extracurricular activities and opportunities and to work with students of color to address and eradicate the obstacles regardless of origin.

The failure to recognize and understand the normalization of whiteness within school systems and/or the adoption of liberal visions of race reform in education positions educational stakeholders to be complicit, intentionally or not, in maintaining such systematic white racial power. Their complicity may undermine the very changes that they advocate for to better attend to the needs of students of color and address racial disparities and other undesired outcomes.

In order to obtain desired outcomes, educational stakeholders must become critical of how they may be complicit in the reproduction of white supremacy and be willing to pursue race-based solutions to race problems. The use of critical race theory tools, such as naming whiteness and property analysis, are two methods to help unveil racial oppression within educational structures. The use of these tools may also pave the way for the deconstruction, or transformation, of current

education systems and structures and the reconstruction of new ones that are designed with the intention of meeting the needs of all students, taking in to account varying cultural differences and experiences. To be sure, transforming current educational structures will be challenging in light of increasing opposition and aggressive push-back in a society that promotes post-racialism and color-blindness. Moreover, for some, racialized educational disparities are the by-product of "broken homes" and communities and advocate interventions that put the responsibility on families and students of color to essentially "clean up their own mess." For urban school leaders to effect equitable outcomes for students of color they may need to be strategic and pursue some reform that will build support for sustainable transformations to educational structures.

For us as critical race theorists and education scholars, we urge urban educational leadership and educational administration/leadership professors to educate themselves on racial inequity and transformative practices that they can deploy to redress it. Moreover, we urge these leaders to work with and train their pre-service teachers and graduate students and central administrators to name whiteness and perform property analyses to aid in unveiling oppression within educational structures. Further, professors should continue to challenge their students to be more culturally competent and to think critically about the normative beliefs on and what constitutes intelligence that they may hold about students of color. Professors should also encourage their students to explore and develop best practices, pedagogies, and curricula for engaging students of color in academic settings informed by theory, practice, and sound research specifically as it relates to racialized educational equity.

REFERENCES

Crenshaw, K. W. (2011). Twenty years of critical race theory: Looking back to move forward. *Connecticut Law Review*. *43*(5).

DeCuir, J. T. and Dixson, A. D. (2004). "So When It Comes Out, They Aren't That Surprised That It Is There": Using Critical Race Theory as a Tool of Analysis of Race and Racism in Education. *Educational Researcher*, 26–31.

Dixson, A. D. and Dingus, J. (2008). In search of our mothers' gardens: Black women teachers and professional socialization. *The Teachers College Record*, *110*(4), 805–837.

Dixson, A. D. and Rousseau, C. K. (2005). And we are still not saved: Critical race theory in education ten years later. *Race ethnicity and education*, 8(1), 7–27.

Harris, C. (1993). Whiteness as property. *Harvard Law Review*, 106(8).

Hussar, W. J. and Bailey, T. M. (2013). *Projections of Education Statistics to 2022 (NCES 2014-051)*. U.S. Department of Education, National Center for Education Statistics. Washington, DC: U.S. Government Printing Office.

Ladson-Billings, G. and Tate, W. (1995). Toward a critical race theory of education. *Teachers College Record, 97*, 47–68.

Lawrence, C. R., Matsuda, M., Delgado, R., and Crenshaw, K. W. (1993). *Words that wound: Critical race theory, assaultive speech, and the First Amendment*. Boulder, CO: Westview Press.

Rousseau, C. and Tate, W. F. (2003). No time like the present: Reflecting on equity in school mathematics. *Theory Into Practice, 42*(3), 210–216.

Taylor, E. (2009). Foundations of critical race theory in education: An introduction. In Taylor, E., Gillborn, D., and Ladson-Billings, G. (Eds.), *Foundations of critical race theory in education* (pp. 1–13). New York: Routledge Publishing.

CHAPTER 20

AYP, Access, and Expectations

Superintendents' Legal, Distributive, and Transformative Approaches to Equity

Rachel Roegman and Thomas Hatch

Once seen as instructional leaders and business managers, superintendents are now being called upon to be "equity warriors" and reduce disparate educational outcomes across student groups (Leverett, 2011). However, there is neither a shared understanding of what educational equity should look like nor a common sense of the specific steps districts need to take to achieve this vision. To some, educational equity means ensuring that resources are distributed according to need (Rebell, 2009). To others, equity means changing teachers' beliefs about different groups of children (Capper, 1993). Some conceptions of equity focus on outcomes, aimed at eliminating the predictability of achievement based on race or class. Other conceptions include families' sense that they are treated fairly by schools or perceptions that their children are not subjected to discriminatory curricula (Carnoy and McEwan, 2005; Froschle and Spring, 1988).

In order to help superintendents, researchers, and others to make sense of this diversity of conceptions and to develop responsive strategies for addressing equity, in this chapter we outline a framework for thinking about equity that we developed based on three different approaches—legal, distributive, and transformative—that highlight somewhat different conceptions of equity. The chapter then illustrates what these approaches look like when they are pursued by a diverse group of superintendents and examines the challenges they face as they do so.

UNDERLYING APPROACHES TO EQUITY-MINDED REFORM

Our review of the literature on approaches to equity began with broad reading of empirical studies and popular texts from several fields, including education, educational administration, law, and political theory. We began by using the term "educational equity" in several search engines, including JSTOR and Google Scholar, as well as soliciting recommendations for major works from colleagues working in these fields. As our search expanded, we used authors' reference lists and citations as further sources of literature to review. We deliberately sampled works across disciplines, paying particular attention to the background material the authors drew upon, the equity-related goals on which they focused, and the specific strategies for achieving equity that were discussed.

In organizing this literature, we began to look specifically at how different authors addressed the question of "Equity of what?" In so doing, we identified four distinct foci: equity in legal matters, equity of inputs, equity of outcomes, and equity in society at large. As we continued to refine these categories, we considered the source of the authors' different rationales for equity. It became quite clear, for example, in terms of equity in society at large, that authors drew on notions of social justice and changing society, while in terms of equity of inputs and outputs, the emphasis was on ensuring that something (varied inputs and/or outputs) were distributed in an equitable fashion. Through this, we developed our framework for equity based on three approaches to equity, identified in table 20.1.

Legal equity sees the Constitution and legislative and judicial decisions as defining equity; distributive equity focuses on resources, access, or outcomes; and transformative equity sees as its goal the end of all oppressions, thus societal change. Each approach is based on its own philosophy and has its own vision of equity and set of strategies to reach its vision. These approaches are evident in research, working as epistemological

Table 20.1. Three Approaches to Achieving Educational Equity

	Background	Overarching Goals	Strategies
Legal	• Constitution • 14th Amendment	• Protection from overt discrimination • Reduction of bias and stereotypes • Ensuring that laws are followed	• Litigation • Development of instructional materials
Distributive	• Rawls's theory of justice	• Allocation of resources, including teachers, curriculum, and access • Allocation of outcomes, including test scores	• Litigation • Legislation • Policy
Transformative	• Social justice • Freire • Civil Rights	• Changing school culture • Changing society • Changing people's beliefs	• Critical Friends Groups/self-inquiry • Mandates • Community activism

foundations (for example, Theoharis, 2004) that guide topics, research questions, and methodologies. They become apparent when researchers ask participants about equity (for example, Brantlinger, 2003) and when advocates use them to frame educational problems (for example, Reed, 2001). In table 20.1, these approaches are depicted as distinct categories that do not interact; in practice, they are fluid and overlapping, and work more to provide a foundation for analysis than a normative prescription or definition.

Legal Equity

From the legal approach, equity is defined by the laws that a society establishes and by the way the judicial system and other aspects of the system interpret and enforce (or fail to enforce) those laws. As such, strategies related to legal equity are most often pursued in the legal or legislative arena. The legal basis for equity was established with the Fourteenth Amendment to the U.S. Constitution, which protects individuals from discriminatory government laws and policies. How the law defines equity and different legal and legislative mechanisms for using the law to address equity has shifted over time, as society changes. As an example, changing notions of disability in the United States have led to an increase in the number of laws and protections for people with disabilities in general and for students with disabilities in educational settings, expanding notions of legal equity beyond the initial set of protected classes outlined in the Fourteenth Amendment, such as gender and race. Those who take a legal approach can focus on enforcing the laws, ensuring that laws are not broken in the first place, or trying to extend or change the laws.

The Texas school financing case, *San Antonio Independent School District v. Rodriguez* (1973), illustrates both the strategy of using the Fourteenth Amendment as well as the problems with doing so. In this case, plaintiffs demonstrated gross disparities in funding levels of local school districts in the San Antonio area and argued that children in low property-wealth neighborhoods were being discriminated against based on wealth (Rebell, 2009). However, because the legal understanding of equity derives from the Equal Protection Clause, and because social class is not a protected class in that clause, unlike gender or race, the Supreme Court found that even though the disparities existed, they were not a violation of the Constitution (Welner, 2001).

As a result of the plaintiffs' loss in this case and others, new legal strategy moved from relying on the U.S. Constitution to relying on education clauses of state constitutions that included a general expectation of providing education, such as the clause in the constitution of New Jersey that it provide a "thorough and efficient education" (Reed, 2001). In shifting from a focus on equity based in the Fourteenth Amendment to one based on education clauses in state constitutions, plaintiffs and their lawyers continue to use a legal approach to achieving equity, but draw on a different aspect of the law. At the same time, the shift from guaranteeing equal protection to guaranteeing equal distribution of resources reflects a distributive approach as well.

First's (2001) analysis of Supreme Court cases related to education offers some of the implications of a superintendent's legal approach to issues of equity. She found that superintendents who predominantly work out of this approach view ethical issues as legal issues, and only take action if a situation is illegal or unconstitutional, regardless of other potentially ethical or moral dimensions. For example, in the 1999 case of *Davis v. Monroe County Board of Education*, after repeated, unanswered complaints to school officials about their fifth grade daughter being sexually harassed by a peer, the parents chose to file a complaint with the court. The superintendent supported the principal and teachers' decision not to change the young girl's seat, based on a belief that, by law, they were not required to do so. (The family eventually won their legal case, though during the process, the student's grades dropped and she became depressed.) First also looks at cases related to molestation, racism, and discrimination based on disability or homelessness, in which superintendents supported site-level administrators' decisions to follow the law, even if it meant risking students' physical, educational, and/or emotional harm. It most of these cases, teachers or principals were those directly responsible, but their decisions were upheld by superintendents and school boards. Because most of the issues that First raised are protected classes in the Constitution, aside from homelessness, families were able to take their cases to the Supreme Court and win a favorable decision, but for unprotected classes, such redress is not possible.

Evidently, a clear limitation for those who take a legal approach is that laws are limited. Merely adhering to the Constitution and other laws does not ensure that students will be protected when ethical issues arise (First, 2001). Noticeably, the Fourteenth Amendment does not apply to many areas of potential discrimination in the United States, unprotected classes such as those who are economically disadvantaged. Further, instances of *de facto* segregation could be considered acceptable within a legal approach to equity, but many would argue that they are inequitable regardless (Oakes and Lipton, 2002). Therefore, a key part of the legal work on equity includes efforts to change the laws in response to changing views of equity, not just to enforce those in place at a given time.

Distributive Equity

Distributive approaches to equity focus on how resources, opportunities, and outcomes should be allocated among students. Key issues in these approaches include the basis for "fair" allocation and the extent to which the focus is on inputs, outcomes, or both. Rawls's (1971) theory of justice provides a foundation for this approach to equity as it focuses on inputs, with the implication that the additional resources enables all students to have similar outcomes. Based on the concept of justice as fairness, Rawls argued that resources should be distributed and decisions should be made in favor of society's weakest members, which aligns with the concept of "vertical equity"—that people should be treated differently based on their perceived needs (Welner, 2001). Braveman and Gruskin (2003) identify these members as belonging to "socially disadvantaged, marginalized, or disenfranchised groups . . . including but not limited to the poor" (p. 2). For Singleton and Linton (2006), decisions should be made in favor of the student groups who make up the "lowest achievement categories" (p. 46). Gordon (1999) sees the students in need of distributive equity as those labeled "at-risk" because they are in schools that are incapable of supporting their cognitive and noncognitive needs. Thus, while "weakest" itself carries multiple meanings, the idea behind distributive equity is that certain groups of students are at some sort of societal disadvantage and resources should be allocated in a way so as to support these groups first, so that they have similar educational outcomes to students from privileged backgrounds. In considering the distribution of resources and opportunities, people also may draw on the concept of "horizontal equity" as well, which refers to the idea that students with similar needs should receive similar resources and opportunities.

Educational inputs and outputs are a central point of discussion in distributive approaches to equity. Dimensions of equity in this sense include "the fair distribution of educational inputs—qualified teachers, per-pupil expenditures, school facilities, and materials—as well as educational outputs such as high academic achievement, high school graduation, college admissions, and college graduation" (Petrovich, 2005, p. 12). In addition to resources, this approach to equity considers the distribution of opportunities. Many proponents of distributive equity would argue, for example, that tracking and other forms of ability grouping are inequitable because they limit students' access to more demanding academic classes, among other deleterious effects (for example, Darling-Hammond, 2007; Murphy, 1991; Wells, Scott, Lopez, and Holme, 2005). An academic input would thus be what type of coursework that students have access to, such as AP or honors classes versus remedial curricula.

The "achievement gap" is another way of framing issues of equity through a distributive approach, with a primary focus on student scores on standardized tests, an educational outcome. According to the logic behind the "achievement gap," student scores should be proportionate to the makeup of the population being tested. Thus, if 50 percent of the students are white and 50 percent are black, in the results, half of the students who score advanced should be of each racial group. The outcome—in this case, the test score—should be distributed proportionally. For Ladson-Billings (2006), however, focusing on the distribution of academic outcomes carries a risk of blaming students, when the focus instead should be put on academic inputs; she argues "that the historical, economic, sociopolitical, and moral decisions and policies that characterize our society have created an education debt" (p. 5). From this standpoint, distributional equity is still the approach at play, but the emphasis has shifted to how schools and society in general allocate resources to different groups of children. In fact, Luke, Green, and Kelly (2010) have themselves renamed this gap, calling it the "equity gap" (p. viii), while Carter and Welner (2013) and Milner (2012) use the term "opportunity gap" to frame educational disparities.

The shift from equity litigation to adequacy litigation, mentioned above, exemplifies the way legal strategies can be used to advance distributive approaches to equity at the same time. In *Abbott v. Burke II* (1990), the New Jersey school finance case, for example, plaintiffs and their attorneys argued that children from property-poor districts were not receiving the resources, including teachers, facilities, and supplies, that they required to meet the state constitutional mandate of a "thorough and efficient education" (Tractenberg, 2008). The state could remedy this by either redistributing funds across its 603 school districts or by increasing overall levels of supports to plaintiff districts (Paris, 2010). This case demonstrates the distinction between legal and distributive approaches to equity: a legal approach says that whatever is in the law is what is equitable, whereas a distributive approach says that whatever is fair is what is equitable, whether it is in the law or not. The plaintiffs, focusing on their view of what was fair, searched for new laws to support their case when their initial approach failed.

One potential consequence of a distributive approach to equity is a focus on technical aspects of reform, to the neglect of the cultural, political, or normative. Focusing solely on distributing resources or ensuring equality of test scores may not be enough when students live in an unjust society (Welner, 2001). If all students gain access to AP classes, for example, but do not have the prerequisite cognitive and affective skills and knowledge to be successful, or have teachers in these classes that adhere to beliefs of certain students' inferiority, the distribution of access is irrelevant (Gordon, 1999). Similarly, if all students have similar outcomes on standardized tests, colleges and hiring committees may find different measures to make sure they admit certain types of students.

Another possible limitation with distributive approaches to equity is around competing views of what is fair. Just like competing views of what is legal or constitutional exist, competing views of fairness can be used to promote equity or preserve inequities. For example, parents in Welner's (2001) and Brantlinger's (2003) studies who identify their children as high-achieving rely on equity arguments about individual needs as a way to advocate for gifted and honors classes for their children, excluding those whom they do not see as deserving this type of education. While most academics in the field of gifted education make their claims on the basis of excellence—to provide "a quality education for the best and brightest" (Gallagher, 1991, p. 13), some, like the parents in the above studies, use the language of distributive equity in arguing to ensure that high-achieving students get their needs met, regardless of the consequences that may have for other students (Reis et al., 1998). Distributive approaches to equity can be co-opted by those with privilege as a way to preserve their privilege through the language of equity, further disadvantaging those already with less power in society.

Transformative Equity

Where a distributive approach focuses on ensuring a fair distribution of inputs and/or outputs and a legal approach focuses on ensuring the law is upheld, transformative equity involves ensuring that society as a whole becomes more equitable in a collective sense. In other words, this approach sees societal laws and current social structures that allocate resources as inherently unequal, and thus there is a need for society as a whole to change. Transformative equity is rooted in beliefs about social justice and the desire to make schools and society more just (Theoharis, 2004); for many educators, transformative equity comes out of Freire's (1970) *Pedagogy of the Oppressed* and his view of education as holding the purpose of transforming people and empowering them to educate themselves and then change the system they are in (Shields, 2010). "Transformative" here is derived from the literature on educational leadership, emphasizing not only individual student achievement but also collective achievement and societal transformation (for example, Capper, 1993; Shields, 2010). While our usage of the term is not synonymous with Capper's and Shield's uses, all of our usages share a mind-set that the school leader's role is to be a change agent. This applies to equity in that superintendents and other school leaders working within this approach take on responsibility for making their school systems more equitable places. Thus, if teachers, for example, believe that some students cannot learn, the distribution of resources is irrelevant to the ability for students in that class to receive an equitable education (Welner, 2001). Some of the critiques of *Brown v. Board* (1954) are related to its emphasis on distribution of access to school placement, based on an assumption that African Americans would receive an equitable education if they attended predominantly white schools, with no attention given to issues of curriculum and instruction, and instead an expectation for them to fit in or "act white." Instead of creating equity, this type of desegregation actually perpetuated educational inequity (Gay, 2004). Capper (1993) refers to educational equity as social-reconstructionist and multicultural because it explicitly challenges existing societal and educational oppressions, critiquing society and offering a new vision for the future.

Transformative approaches to equity are generally more explicitly political and often name the groups in school or society that are not being treated equitably, as opposed to a potentially "neutral" understanding of reform that advantaged parents can use to advocate for more advantages for their children. Many proponents of transformative equity focus on court decisions, not aligned with a legal approach for equity aimed at preventing discrimination or allocating resources, but as a legal strategy to support practitioners and activists at the local level. They argue that a combination of federal

mandates and grassroots efforts is necessary to create change (Oakes, Welner, Yonezawa, and Allen, 1998; Welner and Oakes, 2005). Oakes, Welner, Yonezawa, and Allen (1998) propose an approach to school reform that attempts to change people's core beliefs. Sirotnik and Oakes (1986) further argue that the current inequitable educational system exists because of society's need for a differentiated population that is willing to accept an uneven distribution of resources. Thus educational equity is about changing society as much as it is about changing educational opportunities and outcomes for students.

Much of the literature on leading for social justice or transformative leadership is normative or theory-building, expressing beliefs about what these leaders should learn in preparation programs or actions they should take as leaders. For example, Brown (2004) draws on three theoretical frameworks, adult learning, transformative learning, and critical social theories, to develop "a practical, process-oriented model that is responsive to the challenges of preparing educational leaders omitted to social justice and equity" (p. 77). Similarly, Frattura and Capper (2007) advise school leaders on how to conduct a formative analysis of their school districts that focuses on providing equitable education within an inclusive school framework in their book, *Leading for Social Justice: Transforming Schools for All Learners*. Lugg and Shoho (2006) draw connections between the current call for social justice and Counts's radical 1932 call to educators to build a new social order, highlighting the need for school leaders to have courage and vision in challenging the status quo, while Furman and Shields (2005) present a research agenda to investigate the links between educational leadership, social justice, and democratic community, using conversation as a primary research methodology.

Shields's (2010) study of transformative leadership offers one example of empirical research situated within the transformative approach. In this study, Shields first identified two principals who were part of a larger study of self-professed educators for social justice and who worked at schools with a high level of student achievement on statewide tests. Then she engaged in a backwards-mapping process and analyzed these principals' experiences through the tenets of transformative leadership that she had identified in a literature review.

Some of these tenets include balancing critique and power, acknowledging power and privilege, and focusing on liberation and democracy. This lens enabled Shields to operationalize the conceptual idea of transformative leadership through examining the practice of school leaders who identify as working for social justice. For Shields, this study also served her purpose of providing examples to practicing administrators of the possibilities of a transformative approach to equity: "The study does not indicate that the practice is widespread, only that transformative leadership is not simply a blue-sky theory too idealistic and too difficult to implement" (p. 583). Further, this equity framework allowed Shields to consider effects of schooling beyond academic outcomes, such as democratic citizenship and civic participation.

One potential complication of a transformative approach to equity is that those holding such a view choose to address inequitable aspects of society that may take them away from the school's purpose of educating students. At the same time, of course, there are contested ideas of what the purpose of schools should be, as well as differences over the extent to which schools, and superintendents, should be expected to critique and transform societal structures. In fact, the idea of superintendents working to transform American society runs counter to the mainstream belief in the role of school as ensuring stability. The role of American schools "has never been to promote social radicalism and create new orders" (Glass and Franceschini, 2007, p. xiv) and parents, school personnel, and other stakeholders often rally against changes to school that portend this type of change, from white parents protesting *Brown v. Board* in the 1950s (Gay, 2004) to teachers and parents fighting against inclusion and de-tracking initiatives at the turn of the twenty-first century (Perry, 1997; Welner, 1999). Another potential issue is in thinking about transforming to what. While there may be agreement among many groups about certain societal inequities, no uniform vision exists of what school and society should look like. When such critical issues are contested, students may become pawns in a political game, or the ensuing debates may take attention away from what is happening in the classroom. Of course, given the political nature of schooling in the United States, this risk has the potential to occur by school leaders using any of the equity approaches.

The legal, distributive, and transformative approaches that we outline here offer a framework for thinking about the multitude of understandings of equity. For any of these three approaches, one can imagine ways that it might be used to promote particular conceptions of equity but could also be used to reinforce the status quo. These approaches are not meant to be definitive or normative, nor are they strict categories. Instead, these approaches grow out of different conceptions of what equity is, raising different issues and limitations. What they do offer are ways of thinking about equity and implications in what it means to lead for equity, as well as what it means to research leading for equity.

DOCUMENTING LEADING FOR EQUITY IN PRACTICE

In order to illustrate the ways in which these different approaches might be manifested in superintendents' work, we draw on a project that documents the systemic leadership strategies of a superintendent network in a northeastern state. In the ensuing sections, we describe different ways that the superintendents in this network talk about equity, the different strategies they use, and the possibilities and challenges using each of the three approaches in leading for equity.

Launched in the fall of 2008 with fifteen superintendents, this network initially focused on improving outcomes for all students by having superintendents focus on instruction. The first two years focused on the development of relationships and observing instruction through instructional rounds (City, Elmore, Fiarman, and Teitel, 2009). Then, in the third through fifth year, the network focused on identification of issues of equity and strategies for addressing them, providing us with an opportunity to investigate practicing superintendents' approaches to equity in a range of districts.

Part of the design of the network included regular documentation to provide feedback to participants and facilitators as well as to share network learning with the field at large. This documentation includes transcription and analysis of the network's monthly meetings, annual surveys, and annual one-on-one interviews, all of which is part of the network's use of regular documentation to reflect on its development and impact. In this chapter, we draw on data directly related to superintendents' equity work within the network and within their districts. This includes excerpts of meetings and interview transcripts, which cover topics such as how superintendents are defining equity, how equity is talked about in their districts, and what strategies or initiatives they are pursuing. We also draw on documentation of network activities, such as "gallery walks." Held in December 2010 and October 2012, gallery walks were opportunities for network superintendents to bring in a data presentation related to an issue of equity they were experiencing. Superintendents examined each others' presentations and then met in small groups to ask questions and brainstorm possible next steps together.

As the network began to focus explicitly on equity in its third year, we look to network participants in years three, four, and five. In this time span, twenty-two superintendents took part in the network. They represent a range of contexts, including urban, rural, and suburban districts; K–8, K–12, 9–12, and county districts; racially and ethnically homogenous and heterogeneous districts; ranging from less than 1 percent of students in poverty to 84 percent of students qualifying for free and reduced lunch. The superintendents themselves are also diverse: six females and sixteen males; sixteen white, two Hispanic, three African American, and one Asian; starting out their career or considering retirement; and in the same district for one year or over twenty years.[1]

SUPERINTENDENTS' APPROACHES TO EQUITY

Literature and our own experiences with superintendents suggest that superintendents often show legal and distributive approaches to equity that involved references and reliance on the law, primarily No Child Left Behind (NCLB) and Adequate Yearly Progress (AYP) provisions, as a means of making sure that outcomes are achieved at proportions appropriate to students' representation in the population as a whole (which would indicate that students had received adequate/fair resources). Superintendents drew on legal and distributive approaches to equity in identifying two primary conceptions of equity: equity as proportionality as test scores and equity as access. In thinking about equity as test scores, superintendents drew on legal guidelines that dictate expected achievement levels of various subgroups and consider distributive notions around "achievement gaps" and proportionate test score al-

location. In conceiving of equity as access, superintendents drew on distributive notions of representation in upper-level coursework. Across both of these ways of thinking about equity, issues and limits are also evident, especially as superintendents' discussions and approach often suggested an individual orientation and focus.

Equity as Proportionality in Test Scores

Superintendents frequently used AYP and other indicators of student performance on standardized tests as a tool to identify issues of equity in their district that needed to be addressed. For a school to reach AYP, all subgroups must hit certain targets, determined by a federal formula based on the number of students in each subgroup that score proficient or higher on state tests. Looking at which subgroups did not make AYP in specific schools or the district at large served as a first step in identifying an issue of equity for superintendents and their leadership teams—a step that was often public, as school and district report cards have become widely distributed in the United States. From this approach, the performance of identified subgroups such as "economically disadvantaged," "African American," or "special education," becomes a central issue. Within our superintendents' network, all but one superintendent identified improving the performance of an AYP subgroup as a key focus for their work on equity. The role of AYP in determining accountability measures as well as in comparing districts to each other demonstrates an underlying attention to distributive equity, as the federal government and the districts themselves aim for student outcomes to be distributed proportionality to their backgrounds. At the same time, it demonstrates an underlying attention to legal equity, as the federal government has used regulation to define for school districts what equity should look like (each subgroup achieving certain test score results). Interestingly, the state in which these superintendents work received a waiver from NCLB requirements in early 2012, with the potential for the concept of AYP to be less relevant as this state, and others, develop new accountability measures with a different set of performance targets. Nonetheless, superintendents continued to refer to AYP as a key influence on the development of their equity work through the 2012–2013 school year, and the more recent conversations related to the new performance measures demonstrate similar themes in terms of state citations being a focus of their equity work.

Related to AYP, the idea of the "achievement gap" as disparities in test scores between subgroups is a common way to frame issues of equity. Superintendents frequently referred to achievement gaps and asserted a desire to have greater proportionality of all groups being ranked proficient (or advanced proficient) on state tests. One superintendent shared his district's equity focus in this way:

> While [the middle school] has students achieving extraordinarily high academically, [it] does have achievement gaps in excess of 44 percent and is currently working to ensure that all children achieve and demonstrate appropriate growth . . . We are disappointed that despite all of the initiatives that have taken place to raise the level of reading instruction in our building, an achievement gap still exists among our black, Hispanic, and special education subgroups.

This type of comment was typical across the superintendents' districts. Another superintendent explained the connection between achievement gaps, proportionality, and academic outcomes: "equity means there's no differences in measurable outcomes . . . that are correlated to demographics." While much of the achievement gap discussion focused on subgroups meeting AYP, superintendents also noted achievement gaps in relation to representation in AP courses and to persistence in college.

In addition to drawing on legal and distributive approaches in conceptualizing equity, superintendents often referred to subgroups, which referenced societal issues of racism, classism, and so on. There were also some instances when superintendents reframed the "achievement gap" as a "teaching gap," "assignment gap," or "belief gap" that highlighted the ways in which societal and systemic factors might contribute to equity issues. Thus, one superintendent asked, "Is equity narrowing the achievement gap . . . on this particular test, or is equity narrowing a different gap?" Like Ladson-Billings (2004), in these instances, superintendents reconceptualized the achievement gap as a gap about societal issues that led to students' performance that created inequitable outcomes.

Despite some references to the societal contributions to issues of equity, the superintendents often identified the reasons for students' difficulties as individual issues. For example, one superintendent of a mixed-wealth, suburban district, said: "There aren't any schools, even those with all so-called wealthy kids, where there's not unattended-to pain in kids that is affecting their academic progress." Here, the emphasis is on the internal emotional pain as a contributor to low academic performance rather than systemic poverty or racism. Similarly focusing on students as individuals, another superintendent, of an affluent, suburban district, saw equity as "being aware that different people learn differently, bring different things to the table . . . the better our structures are for knowing and learning about each individual student, the more we'll be able to address equity." Even in considering systemic factors, such as the impact of poverty on education, another superintendent saw the solution to low performance for poor students as "something . . . to change the pattern, either a teacher, an adult role model, somebody interjects into these lives to have people jump off of the track that would take them into the cycle of poverty and move into another channel." In this case, while poverty was viewed as a systemic issue, the solution proposed focused on responses and strategies that would address the needs of a particular individual.

Focusing on individuals, while ignoring race- or class-based patterns, "allows many of us to avoid the task of dismantling communally the racial patterns that actually exist" (Pollock, 2001, p. 3). This focus resonates with the prior research on school leaders and equity, particularly in studies of white school leaders (Alsbury and Whitaker, 2006; McMahon, 2007). Conceptions of equity focused on individuals may connect to several underlying beliefs, such as a view that racism or other institutional oppressions cannot be or do not need to be addressed, a fear that naming something like racism would create hostility, or a discomfort around discussing such issues, among others (Pollock, 2001).

Equity as Access

Where equity as proportionality in test scores focuses on distributive equity as a legal right to a certain proportion of outcomes, in conceptualizing equity as access, superintendents aim to ensure that all students have access to quality educational opportunities and that they are supported in these opportunities. Illustrating this conception, when asked to explicitly define equity, one superintendent reflected on her childhood experience of desegregation, in which school policy implicitly denied access to African-American students who lived "too close" to school by not providing transportation to school.

> Well, equity, to me, means access to all . . . I grew up in a black neighborhood. We weren't allowed to ride the bus to the high school, even though we lived two miles away from the high school. The bus went to pick up other [white] kids and drove right past us, but the ruling was that they lived two and a half miles away from the high school . . . We all got to the high school . . . but for those students that didn't have the motivation or drive that I had it was a thing of, "Well, maybe I won't go today 'cause it's too far away."

All students could attend the high school, but there was a lack of support around actually getting to school, especially for students who may not have had as much personal support from family members or teachers as she did. Thus, all students did not actually have access. Instead of "putting ceilings on kids," as one superintendent stated, equity as access and support involves providing educational experiences that would "open up doors that were locked" while providing "proper guidance and direction."

Equity as access can be seen as more than attending school, but as being involved in the types of educational experiences that will lead to college. Several superintendents are engaging in data analysis with the National Student Clearinghouse to identify which of their high school graduates completed college with a degree after six years, and then are looking at these students' course-taking patterns. One superintendent shared how his district drew on this data to begin to determine the "pathway" that students need to be on in order to be on track to earn a college diploma, as shown in figure 20.1.

Understandings of equity as access and opportunities to learn can also be made manifest in superintendents' conversations around classroom instruction. As superintendents observe classrooms and notice a range of expectations around cognitive demand, they become aware of different educational experiences in different "tracks": remedial, general, honors, and AP. For example, during an instructional rounds visit, superintendents demonstrated a conception of equity as access in sharing their observations of levels of student collaboration and cognitive demand of student activities across several high school classrooms. Three out of four small groups of superintendents raised a potentially inequitable pattern around the types of collaboration and the rigor in different levels of classes—in-class support classrooms (team taught with a general education and a special education teacher), general education classrooms, and honors classrooms. One small group noted that overall there was a high degree of collaboration in the visited classrooms, but that

Percent of Students Reaching a Benchmark and Achieving Future Success

- 80% of the students completing an honors level or higher language arts class in grade 11 with a B- or higher and scoring proficient or better on the Language Arts portion of the High School Exit Exam earned a college degree.
- 78% of the students completing an honors level or higher Math class in grade 11 with a B- or higher and scoring proficient or better on the Math portion of the High School Exit Exam earned a college degree.
- 77% of the students participating in one or more AP courses in Math, Science, Language Arts, Social Studies, World Language, Art, or Music earned a college degree.
- 77% of the students participating in Level 4 or higher courses in Math, Language Arts, Science, and Social Studies and earned a B- or better in all 4 courses earned a college degree.
- 65% of the students participating in all level 4 or higher courses in Math, Language Arts, Science, and Social Studies earned a college degree.

Figure 20.1. *Predictors on the Pathway to College in One Superintendent's District. Leadership responsibilities for relative degrees of learner definitions and control for parent and community engagement ideal types.*

the [classroom] that was an odd-man out was an in-class support environment, and we're not inferring anything on that, it was just that was the one that was the outlier for most of what we were seeing.

Superintendents expressed a concern that students in the in-class support classrooms might not have the access to similar curricula as students in other classrooms. Observing a range of classroom types and discussing their observations together, superintendents become aware of inequitable access to rigorous curricula, demonstrating a conception of equity as access.

SUPERINTENDENTS' STRATEGIES FOR ADDRESSING INEQUITIES

Legal, distributive, and transformative strategies can be used to support one another, but the challenges of addressing people's beliefs and of addressing societal issues that go far beyond the control of schools may mean that superintendents more often rely on legal and distributive approaches to equity.

Upholding the Law: Addressing Legalities

In terms of legal equity, federal and state laws and judicial decisions offer specific ways to think about equity and what schools and districts need to do in pursuit of equity. They guide what superintendents pay attention to, often raising awareness of issues that superintendents might otherwise overlook, such as the academic performance of English language learners or overrepresentation of African-American youth in special education, as well as providing legal standards, such as the definition of disproportionality.

The federal policy, No Child Left Behind (NCLB), points to specific data that superintendents need to use to determine inequities, including a reliance on data sets such as AYP and Safe Harbor. One superintendent noted that

> No Child Left Behind was the greatest impetus . . . if we hadn't done it, if we hadn't been forced to acknowledge some of that we'd be right back where we were . . . it kicked us in the tail and told us that we weren't doing it well before. So while we could have overall results that were very good, there were kids that were left on the outside and now it made us accountable for this kids.

For another superintendent, being cited by NCLB brought attention to poor performance by two subgroups—economically disadvantaged youth and English language learners, which led the district to "put together a pretty comprehensive action plan of what we were doing," including using Title 1 funds for "additional time especially in Language Arts and Mathematics."

When districts are cited by the state for not making AYP, for example, or by any government body, such as the Office of Civil Rights (OCR), the superintendents can use those legal proceedings as prompts, rationales, and incentives for undertaking equity-focused initiatives. For example, one superintendent, whose district was cited by OCR for a disproportion of African-American males classified as special education, responded immediately:

> we did a special ed. program review and are creating interventions there. The other place we're doing a lot of work is in the intervention and referral services (IRS) . . . We're doing a lot of work there too. And the teachers have toolkits and everything to try before they even bring a kid to IRS, so that it becomes a regular education intervention.

Superintendents shared similar strategies around ensuring that if their districts are cited, they fix the situation, including changing referral processes, providing additional learning time, working with parents, and restructuring schools.

Even if superintendents do not view legal strategies as the primary or ideal approach to addressing inequities, legal strategies can provide external clout that can be used if they face resistance in their districts. In one district, which was cited by the OCR for how classified students were placed in AP courses, the superintendent used the opportunity for a system-wide rethinking of selection criteria for advanced courses. The citation offered the necessary "jolt" to the system to create a change. Another superintendent saw the state's mandate around adopting a new method of teacher evaluation as a way for him to work with the teachers' association so that they can "develop what's important from those models together. We have the conversations from teaching and learning together and prioritize within that external mandate together on what our nonnegotiables are." Instead of seeing a citation or a mandate solely for the challenges it creates, superintendents can use these external events to support their district visions.

Legal approaches can also be pursued, however, in ways that might undermine equity.

One superintendent cautioned that legal equity encourages superintendents to focus more on "the regulatory side of it and the covering our tail so we don't get sued" than on engaging in reforms that actually help children. Another shared a rumor that some districts "fudge" the numbers to ensure that they do not have enough students to constitute a subgroup (thirty students), so that schools will not be at risk of not meeting their AYP targets. In addition, it is possible that the instructional strategies adopted do not support students. For example, if districts choose to lower the referral of African-American youth into special education, but do not change how teachers are working with those students in the general education classrooms, it is unlikely that these students' educational experiences will be equitable.

Furthermore, the legal expectation for schools to meet AYP means that students receive a score of proficient on state exams. However, for superintendents in the network, there was a growing understanding that AYP was too low of a standard to be the goal. One superintendent shared an "aha" moment: "The smack came from [the last group's presentation] because we were thinking all along, just by talking about the floor's not good enough, the ceiling's where we need." For this superintendent, AYP was the floor, and college-readiness was the ceiling that all students should be aiming for. Using AYP as the standard for defining equity issues was a problematic foundation if superintendents and districts set college completion as their goal.

Allocating Resources, Access, and Outcomes: Distributive Strategies

Distributive strategies include efforts to provide additional resources and/or opportunities that are intended to support improvements in learning. Consistent with their emphasis on individualistic and distributive approaches to equity, superintendents in our network provided numerous examples of distributive strategies. Some districts were reallocating support staff to schools with the highest numbers of students scoring below proficiency, while others have extended the school day or developed extended-day programs specifically for lower-performing subgroups. Several have implemented specific programs during the school day to help students who have been identified as lower-performing, including Read 180, AVID, or supplemental math. A few superintendents shared concerns around resource allocation and the belief that some of their constituents have "of equity and excellent being in competition, and whether there's a zero sum game relationship between the two or not." While superintendents create specific programs to target struggling students, they need to maintain a political awareness of whether they are distributing or redistributing, and the fear of parents or teachers that some programs might be cut in favor of others. Or they may choose to adopt initiatives that benefit the entire student body, such as one superintendent whose district began to pay for all sophomores to take the PSAT, increasing access to a gatekeeping test that was previously only accessible to more affluent students but providing the exam for all students, not just targeted populations.

In terms of access, issues of student placement in specialized programs are common strategies. One superintendent in the network, for example, expanded the AVID program in his middle school to ensure that all students have access to the instructional strategies and social-emotional benefits of the college-preparatory program. Other superintendents changed the selection process for honors and AP courses. In one district, the process had been based on teacher recommendation. The superintendent and district leadership team noticed that

a small percentage of students were recommended by the teachers and only the students whose parents advocated for them went against teacher recommendations. This parental override process was limiting students whose parents did not have the time and skills to navigate this process.

They developed a new process based on students' grades and common assessments. The purpose of these changes was to eliminate teacher bias—that teachers' low expectations for certain groups of students, especially African-American students, students with IEPs, and students who were perceived as "average," would not prevent them from advanced coursework of which they were capable. The superintendent had strong concerns about the faculty's belief systems and chose to use distributive strategies to try to limit opportunities for faculty beliefs to impact student learning. Other prominent strategies to increase underrepresented groups' access to specialized programs included having guidance counselors specifically recruit students for advanced classes and developing summer pre-AP programs to provide confidence and support for students who had never taken an AP course to do so in the upcoming year. One superintendent was doing this work with the support of the Minority Student Achievement Network. He found that "they have a methodology for finding kids, especially kids of color, who should be in AP classes but are not, and training the whole school environment to encourage and support the kids in the AP classes," which provided him and his district with support and specific strategies for opening up access.

Beyond considering how students are placed in different courses, superintendents and districts may also consider eliminating different levels of courses entirely, referred to as de-leveling or de-tracking. Two superintendents in our network were engaged in this type of initiative, trying to create greater heterogeneity in courses and provide students who may have had weaker academic backgrounds the opportunity to learn in classrooms with their peers, instead of continuing to stratify students, which generally leads to greater discrepancies in opportunities and outcomes. One of the superintendents, who was de-tracking the middle school by transitioning from three achievement levels into two achievement levels, said that "we've done a lot of work to dismantle structures that sort kids purportedly by prior academic performance but really end up with in-school segregation." For him, de-tracking is dismantling segregation and ensuring that students' prior academic performance, which in his district was strongly predicted by their race, does not limit their access to rigorous curriculum.

The other superintendent working on de-leveling has eliminated the lower levels in ninth grade language arts and social studies classes. This was accompanied by intense professional development for special education teachers, who began co-teaching with general education teachers in the 2011–2012 school year, along with revising of the district's curriculum to create differentiated units to support teachers in working with more heterogeneous groups of students. He had initially planned to eliminate the lower levels in math the following year. After considering the issue with his leadership team, the district decided to not

do anything in the immediacy with math because we think we would be putting a lot of our students at a disadvantage . . . we think we'd actually be hurting some of our students who don't have some basic skills.

For superintendents who engage in de-leveling initiatives, being aware of the potential avenues of resistance and preparing for the transition are keys to ensuring that students' access is real—that they and their teachers receive the supports needed to be successful.

Changing Beliefs? Transformative Strategies

Perhaps it should not be surprising that few transformative approaches to equity are reflected in the empirical literature on the superintendency, as having people consider underlying beliefs and structures around issues such as race and class that perpetuate systems of privilege and oppression are rife with potential discord and struggle. At the same time, the superintendents in our network saw a need to transform the beliefs of parents, teachers, district personnel, and the community around the potential for all students to achieve at high levels. For example, as one superintendent put it, "I find too often that our staff does approach kids from a sense of deficiencies as opposed to looking for where there are strengths." Despite the widespread agreement on the need to transform beliefs, the superintendents also expressed a number of concerns about whether and how to do so.

Raising issues of equity is a dangerous proposition likely to create resistance. In fact, the superintendents' discussions showed that they were all well aware of peers from other states who tried to redraw school boundaries or de-track one or more of their high schools and then lost their jobs. As one superintendent put it, "If your local context is that the haves get and the have-nots don't," raising issues of equity can be the "third rail that kills you." Another superintendent received hate mail and significant negative attention in the media and at board meetings, when he and the school board chose to allocate additional resources to students with greater needs, most of whom were African American. In one instance, he was confronted at a board meeting by a white community member who declared that when he moved to the district, he did not sign up "for reparations"; the community member went on to say that the superintendent's rhetoric and actions were working as a disincentive for affluent people to move to the community. Situations like these only begin to hint at the beliefs and issues that may require transformative work with community members as well as teachers and administrators.

Sharing of data with district staff and the community at large is one potential strategy for addressing beliefs; this strategy suggests that when people see data that reveal inequities, they will feel a sense of urgency and a need for change. However, the same deep-seated beliefs that reinforce inequities can also make it difficult to use data to reveal inequities. For example, after a presentation to staff showing that African-American and Latino students were underrepresented in higher-level academies, the superintendent was shocked to hear an administrator say that these patterns did not apply to her academy. In response, the superintendent, with his central office team, has begun to create an "opportunity index," which is a graphic representation of different subgroups' likelihood of being in advanced courses or academies. Their strategy is based on the hope that the graphic representation of inequity will be a motivating tactic to generate change. Another superintendent who tried to share data with principals and teachers was struggling about how to do so in a way that led to changes in practice:

> How can we go back and now personalize this in a positive way to help teachers understand the moral imperative of moving each kid up a notch, so when they all come together, the district is seeing that it is doing what it should be doing relative to supporting those kids?

Sharing data offers superintendents the possibilities of motivating staff, but doing so effectively remains a challenge. Furthermore, using data to try to expose inequities can also reinforce negative stereotypes and beliefs that make work on equity difficult. One former superintendent, and a network facilitator, experienced these negative consequences of publicizing achievement gaps when he served as a court monitor for federal desegregation cases:

> we kept reporting out on the achievement gap, and we realized we were our own worst enemy, that now everybody thought that every black kid in the district was a low-achieving kid, when there were literally hundreds of kids who were high-achievers, AP, the whole thing, good ACTs, good colleges.

In short, even the very efforts to address the underlying beliefs that support inequities can themselves be undermined by the depth and pervasiveness of those beliefs.

Another method of addressing beliefs is to focus on people's behaviors and hope that as behavior changes, beliefs will change as well. One superintendent explicitly pursued this strategy, focusing on developing "structures that change behaviors that change beliefs":

> For example, [Danielson's] Framework for Professional Practice, we're in the second year of having a district-wide way of observing. Evaluating and developing teachers. Changed the supervisory structure to provide the support for that to happen, having a curriculum based on the Common Core [State] Standards and developing common assessments . . . a strong, district-wide hiring process.

Developing structures aims to ensure that all students have access to a rigorous curriculum and that all teachers are responsible for teaching all students. This superintendent hoped that as teachers came to see that all students, including students with disabilities, were succeeding academically, then teachers would change their beliefs to actually believe that all children can learn to high levels and not set limits. She believed that changing structures to change beliefs was the most likely avenue to success in her district.

In considering transformative approaches to equity, superintendents may well differ in the extent to which they feel society needs to be transformed, whether it is the role of the school/superintendent to do that, and whether pursuing such strategies not only might create additional problems that they feel might limit their ability to have a positive impact on the students and schools, but also might still be unsuccessful. Superintendents may rely on distributive approaches to achieve transformative ends, and they may also find that their distributive approaches, such as reallocating resources, elicits strong feelings from constituents that raise the need to consider transformative approaches as well.

IMPLICATIONS AND RECOMMENDATIONS FOR FUTURE RESEARCH

This examination of superintendents' work on equity highlights both the variety of meanings of the term as well as different kinds of strategies that superintendents pursue in addressing issues of equity. In particular, this work illustrates the possibilities and limits that come with pursuing legal, distributive, and transformative approaches. Thus, when facing local resistance, superintendents may find legal strategies particularly helpful in pursuing their equity-minded initiatives. At the same time, simply complying with existing laws, and maintaining an adherence to legal notions of equity will not create more equitable experiences for all students, especially those who have been marginalized in school systems. Similarly, superintendents who take a distributive approach may find their efforts to create more equitable learning opportunities stymied if they do not also address the beliefs and societal issues that contributed to those inequities in the first place. However, pursuing the kinds of transformative strategies that can address underlying beliefs and assumptions involves the kind of community-building work that goes far beyond a superintendent's traditional purview.

Superintendents in urban districts, as well as those in suburban districts with changing demographics that include increasing numbers of African-American and Latino youth and youth living in poverty, face a unique set of challenges as well. For instance, the superintendents of urban districts in the network see issues of equity not only as problems *within* districts, but also as problems *between* districts. From their perspective, all of their students lack the kind of access to resources and opportunities that students enjoy in many of the surrounding suburban districts. As a consequence, much of their work on equity has to take place outside the district and beyond the educational system itself, fighting for advantages that they believe their students are often denied. In contrast, suburban superintendents in the network, especially in districts with changing demographics, are trying to address inequities within their districts between students of different income levels and from different racial and cultural backgrounds. These superintendents have to find ways to help their board members and their communities to understand the challenges of creating equitable opportunities without blaming the particular groups in their communities that are less successful, often within a context of privileged community members resisting change (Brantlinger, 2003; Oakes, Welner, Yonezawa, and Allen, 1998; Welner, 1999). In both cases, superintendents have to make the work on equity public without allowing their opponents and critics to

use that work to impede their progress or to force them to leave. On the whole, however, all the superintendents in this network, whether from urban, suburban, or rural contexts, drew primarily on legal and distributive strategies and talked about equity as proportionality in test scores and equity as access.

While these challenges are daunting, superintendents and those who prepare them may be able to draw on these three different approaches to develop, sequence, and link strategies that are mutually reinforcing. For example, superintendents who are engaged in strategies related to allocating resources or opening up access can consider which legal bodies support their work while at the same time developing a strategy to address underlying beliefs and taken-for-granted school structures that might be inhibiting greater equity. For strategies addressing beliefs to be successful, collaborative and community-oriented work is needed, and for superintendents to initiate and engage in that work, they will likely need more support from their local boards of education and state and federal policymakers.

As such, the creation of policies and regulations that define equity, such as subgroups meeting AYP or as a certain percentage being an indicator of disproportionality, may also need to include measures that look at multiple aspects of equitable educational experiences. For example, a district that was cited for the overrepresentation of African-American youth in special education may remedy this by decreasing referrals without changing classroom practice for those youth, leading to low academic outcomes. Those changes would mean the district is no longer under the watch of OCR, but continues to engage in inequitable practices. Furthermore, policymakers can work with equity-minded school leaders to craft policies that provide them with the institutional support needed to work for change against ideological forces in their communities that would prefer to maintain the status quo.

The framework for equity that we have developed supports future lines of inquiry into what it means to lead for equity. Understanding the different kinds of strategies that superintendents use, including how and when they adopt different approaches to equity, whether legal, distributive, or transformative, and how these approaches are linked or overlap in their work can further illuminate how school leaders can create more equitable systems. Future research may also investigate the specific types of equity issues faced by different districts, such as those that are more or less homogenous and those experiencing different degrees of changing demographics, to better understand how leaders tend to address those issues, and the degree of success that they find. This may inform more context-specific leadership preparation, as leaders may require different sets of skills and knowledge. This research may also demonstrate that it is not enough to prepare leaders for a type of district, such as "urban"—a term with many different connotations (Matsko and Hammerness 2014; Popkewitz, 1998; Watson, 2011), but to prepare leaders to investigate the unique issues of equity a specific district is facing. While all urban districts may experience political turmoil, for example, they do so in different way, with different populations, based on varied issues such as governance structures, demographic stability or change, history, and so on.

NOTE

1. In order to identify examples of different approaches to equity, we coded transcript excerpts related to equity, in particular where superintendents offered definitions of equity, gave examples of equitable or inequitable situations or practices, or shared strategies under way that aimed to increase equity. Data was coded by the three approaches to equity: legal, distributive, and transformative. Within each category, a second round of coding identified patterns or trends within each approach. For example, the "Office of Civil Rights (OCR)" and "citations" were codes in legal equity; "achievement gaps" and "resource allocation" were codes in distributive equity, and "beliefs" and "sense of urgency" were codes in transformative equity. After coding in this manner, we reread the data to ensure that the participants' ideas were accurately captured.

REFERENCES

Abbott v. Burke, 575 A.2d 359 C.F.R. (1990).

Alsbury, T. L. and Whitaker, K. S. (2006). Superintendent perspectives and practice of accountability, democratic voice, and social justice. *Journal of Educational Administration, 45*(2), 154–174.

Brantlinger, E. (2003). *Dividing classes: How the middle class negotiates and rationalizes school advantage.* New York: Routledge/Falmer.

Braveman, P. and Gruskin, S. (2003). Poverty, equity, human rights, and health. *Bulletin of the World Health Organization, 81*(7), 539–545.

Brown, K. M. (2004). Leadership for social justice and equity: Weaving a transformative framework and pedagogy. *Educational Administration Quarterly, 40*(1), 77–108.

Brown v. Board of Education, 347 U.S. 483 C.F.R. (1954).

Capper, C. A. (1993). Administrator practice and preparation for social reconstructionist schooling. In C. A. Capper (Ed.), *Educational administration in a pluralistic society* (pp. 288–315). Albany: State University of New York Press.

Carnoy, M. and McEwan, P. J. (2005). Do school vouchers lead to greater social equity? In J. Petrovich and A. S. Wells (Eds.), *Bringing equity back: Research for a new era in American educational policy* (pp. 263–290). New York: Teachers College Press.

Carter, P. L. and Welner, K. G. (Eds.) (2013). *Closing the opportunity gap: What America must do to give every child an even chance.* Oxford: Oxford University Press.

Counts, G. S. (1932). *Dare the school build a new social order?* New York: John Day Company.

Davis v. Monroe County Board of Education, 526 U.S. 629 C.F.R. (1999).

First, P. F. (2001). The new superintendency as guardian of justice and care. In C. C. Brunner and L. G. Björk (Eds.), *The new superintendency: Vol. 6. Advances in research and theories of school management and educational policy* (pp. 249–266). New York: Elsevier Science Ltd.

Frattura, E. and Capper, C. A. (2007). *Leading for social justice: Transforming schools for all learners.* Thousand Oaks, CA: Corwin Press.

Freire, P. (1970). *Pedagogy of the oppressed.* New York: Seabury Press.

Froschl, M. and Sprung, B. (1988). Introduction. In M. Froschl and B. Sprung (Eds.), *Resources for educational equity: A guide for grades pre-kindergarten–12* (pp. ix–xv). New York: Garland Publishing, Inc.

Furman, G. C. and Shields, C. M. (2005). How can educational leaders promote and support social justice and democratic community in schools? In W. A. Firestone and C. Riehl (Eds.), *A new agenda for research in educational leadership* (pp. 119–137). New York: Teachers College Press.

Gallagher, J. J. (1991). Educational reform, values, and gifted students. *Gifted Child Quarterly, 35*(1), 12–19.

Gay, G. (2004). Beyond *Brown*: Promoting Equality Through Multicultural Education. *Journal of Curriculum and Supervision, 19*(3), 193–216.

Glass, T. E. and Franceschini, L. A. (2007). *The state of the American school superintendency: A mid-decade study.* Lanham, MD: Rowman and Littlefield Education.

Gordon, E. W. (1999). *Education and justice: A view from the back of the bus.* New York: Teachers College Press.

Labaree, D. F. (1997). Public goods, private goods: The American struggle over educational goals. *American Educational Research Journal, 34*(1), 39–81.

Leverret, L. (2011). The Urban Superintendents Program leadership framework. In R. S. Peterkin, D. Jewell-Sherman, L. Kelley, and L. Boozer (Eds.), *Every child, every classroom, every day: School leaders who are making equity a reality* (pp. 1–15). San Francisco: Jossey-Bass.

Lugg, C. A. and Shoho, A. R. (2006). Dare public school administrators build a new social order? Social justice and the possibly perilous politics of educational leadership. *Journal of Educational Administration, 44*(3), 196–208.

Luke, A., Green, J., and Kelly, G. J. (2010). What counts as evidence and equity? *Review of Research in Education, 34*(1), vii–xvi.

Matsko, K. K. and Hammerness, K. (2014). Unpacking the "urban" in urban teacher education: Making a case for context-specific teacher preparation. *Journal of Teacher Education 65*(2), 128–144.

McMahon, B. (2007). Educational administrators' conceptions of whiteness, anti-racism, and social justice. *Journal of Educational Administration, 45*(6), 684–696.

Milner, H. R. (2012). Beyond a test score: Explaining opportunity gaps in educational practice. *Journal of Black Studies, 43*(6), 693–718.

Murphy, J. T. (1991). Superintendents as saviors: From the Terminator to Pogo. *Phi Delta Kappan, 72*(7), 507–515.

Oakes, J. and Lipton, M. (2002). Struggling for educational equity in diverse communities: School reform as social movement. *Journal of Educational Change, 3*(1), 383–406.

Oakes, J., Welner, K. G., Yonezawa, S., and Allen, R. L. (1998). Norms and politics of equity-minded change: Researching the "zone of mediation." In A. Hargreaves, A. Lieberman, M. Fullan, and D. Hopkins (Eds.), *International handbook of educational change* (pp. 952–972). Norwell, MA: Kluwer Academic Publishers.

Paris, M. (2010). *Framing equal opportunity: Law and the politics of school finance reform*. Stanford, CA: Stanford University Press.

Perry, E. A. (1997). Is equity always best? Educational stakeholders lash out. *Journal of Educational Administration, 35*(5), 451–465.

Petrovich, J. (2005). The shifting terrain of educational policy: Why we must bring equity back. In J. Petrovich and A. S. Wells (Eds.), *Bringing equity back: Research for a new era in American educational policy* (pp. 3–15). New York: Teachers College Press.

Pollock, M. (2001). How the question we ask most about race in education is the very question we most suppress. *Educational Researcher, 30*(9), 2–12.

Popkewitz, T. S. (1998). *Struggling for the soul: The politics of schooling and the construction of the teacher*. New York: Teachers College Press.

Rawls, J. (1971). *A theory of justice*. Cambridge, MA: Belknap Press of Harvard University Press.

Rebell, M. A. (2009). *Courts and kids: Pursuing educational equity through the state courts*. Chicago: The University of Chicago Press.

Reed, D. S. (2001). *On equal terms: The Constitutional politics of educational opportunity*. Princeton, NJ: Princeton University Press.

Reis, S. M., Kaplan, S. N., Tomlinson, C. A., Westberg, K. L., Callahan, C. M., and Cooper, C. R. (1998). A response: Equal does not mean identical. *Educational Leadership, 56*(3), 74–77.

San Antonio Independent School District v. Rodriquez, 444 U.S. 1 C.F.R. (1973).

Shields, C. M. (2010). Transformative leadership: Working for equity in diverse contexts. *Educational Administration Quarterly, 46*(4), 558–589.

Singleton, G. E. and Linton, C. (2006). *Courageous conversations about race: A field guide for achieving equity in schools*. Thousand Oaks, CA: Corwin Press.

Sirotnik, K. and Oakes, J. (1986). Critical inquiry for school renewal: Liberating theory and practice. In K. Sirotnik and J. Oakes (Eds.), *Critical perspectives on the organization and improvement of schooling* (pp. 3–93). Boston, MA: Kluwer-Nijhoff Publishing.

Theoharis, G. T. (2004). *At no small cost: Social justice leaders and their response to resistance*. Doctoral dissertation. Available from ProQuest Dissertations and Theses (AAT 3143016).

Tractenberg, P. L. (2008). Beyond educational adequacy: Looking backward and forward through the lens of New Jersey. *Stanford Journal of Civil Rights and Civil Liberties, 4*(2), 411–446.

Watson, D. (2011). What do you mean when you say "urban"? Speaking honestly about race and students. *Rethinking Schools, 26*(1), 48–50.

Wells, A. S., Scott, J., Lopez, A., and Holme, J. J. (2005). Charter school reform and the shifting meaning of education equity: Greater voice and greater inequality? In J. Petrovich and A. S. Wells (Eds.), *Bringing equity back: Research for a new era in American educational policy* (pp. 219–243). New York: Teachers College Press.

Welner, K. G. (1999). They retard what they cannot repel: Examining the role teachers sometimes play in subverting equity-minded reforms. *The Journal of Negro Education, 68*(2), 200–212.

Welner, K. G. (2001). *Legal rights, local wrongs: When community control collides with educational equity*. New York: University of New York Press.

Welner, K. G., and Oakes, J. (2005). Mandates still matter: Examining a key policy tool for promoting successful equity-minded reform. In J. Petrovich and A. S. Wells (Eds.), *Bringing equity back: Research for a new era in American educational policy* (pp. 77–102). New York: Teachers College Press.

CHAPTER 21

Learning to Lead for Social Justice

How Leadership Preparation Programs Can Improve Equity in Schools

Gaëtane Jean-Marie, Anthony H. Normore, and Jeffrey S. Brooks

There has been an increased focus on social justice in the field of educational leadership (Aiken and Gerstl-Pepin, 2012; Bogotch, Beachum, Blount, Brooks, and English, 2008; Boske and Diem, 2012; Marshall and Oliva, 2006; Normore and Brooks, 2014; Shoho, Merchang, and Lugg, 2005). This chapter explores and extends themes in contemporary educational research on leadership preparation in terms of social justice and its importance for both research and practice on a national and international level. In particular, we examine various considerations in the literature regarding whether leadership preparation programs are committed to, and capable of, preparing school leaders to think globally and act courageously about social justice to better serve the needs of students in high-poverty schools.

Although we have revised and updated the content, sections of this chapter are partially reprinted from: Jean-Marie, G., Normore, A. H., and Brooks, J. (2009). Leadership for social justice: Preparing 21st century school leaders for a new social order. *Journal of Research on Leadership and Education*, 4(1), 1–31. Permission for partial reprint was granted by Sage Publications.

INTRODUCTION

The primary purpose of this chapter is to explore and extend themes in contemporary educational research on leadership preparation and training in terms of social justice and its importance for both research and practice on a national and international level. In particular, we focus on leadership preparation programs that help schools and their leaders grapple with social justice issues and have implications for responding to the educational needs of students in high-poverty schools.

There has been an increased focus on social justice and educational leadership (Aiken and Gerstl-Pepin, 2012; Bogotch, Beachum, Blount, Brooks, and English, 2008; Boske and Diem, 2012; Marshall and Oliva, 2006; Normore and Brooks, 2014; Shoho, Merchang, and Lugg, 2005). Research indicates that social justice issues are often neglected and marginalized within educational leadership degree and certification programs, as such an orientation is considered "soft" in comparison to more traditional topics such as organizational theory, principalship, school law, school personnel management, and finance (Shoho, 2006). Other research contends that social justice as an educational intervention is a continuously relevant topic that should be infused into every aspect of leadership preparation, including the aforementioned subjects (Bogotch, 2005). In this era of increased standards, schools are thrust into a position in which they must prepare children and communities for participation in a multicultural, multiethnic, multireligious, and a multinational society (Capper, 1993). As a result, school leaders are under fierce accountability and fiscal pressures, while coping with a larger political environment that is polarized and apprehensive about the growing complexities of high-poverty schools (Lugg and Shoho, 2006; McMahon, 2007).

A growing concern among educators is whether emerging school leaders are prepared to face these pressures and create schools that advocate for education that advances the rights and education for all children (Spring, 2001). Furthermore, studies suggest that leadership training, development, and preparation programs need to better prepare school leaders to promote a broader and deeper understanding of social justice, democracy, and equity (Aiken and Gerstl-Pepin, 2012; Boske and Diem, 2012; Marshall and Oliva, 2006; Young and Mountford, 2006). This article examines various considerations as suggested in the literature regarding whether leadership preparation programs are committed to, and capable of, preparing school leaders to think globally and act courageously about social justice. Yet, while we ultimately advocate for a glocal (meaningful integration of local and global issues, imperatives, and concepts) approach to leadership preparation, it is important to note that the central context for this work is the United States. We understand that while we likely identify some issues and trends that may be relevant to scholars and educators in other national contexts, we do not pretend that this work is universally applicable. Instead, we offer a context-bound analysis from the perspective of three U.S.-based educational leadership scholars and issue an invitation to a multi-national dialogue rather than propose a definitive statement about leadership preparation, writ large.

Based on review of the literature, our analysis revealed four dominant issues between educational leadership and social justice that are essential for developing, training, and preparing school leaders with an orientation toward educational equity. These are: (a) conceptualizing social justice in leadership preparation programs, (b) expanding beyond traditional leadership preparation to leadership for social justice, (c) moving toward critical pedagogy: leadership for liberation and commitment to social justice, and (d) making connections between local and global research to extend leadership for social justice. The balance of this chapter is devoted to a discussion of each of these themes.

CONCEPTUALIZING SOCIAL JUSTICE IN LEADERSHIP PREPARATION PROGRAMS

The term *social justice* is an elusive construct, politically loaded, and subject to numerous interpretations (Shoho, Merchant, and Lugg, 2005). Its foundation is rooted in theology (Ahlstrom, 1972; Hudson, 1981), social work (Koerin, 2003), and it has deep roots in educational disciplines like curriculum and pedagogy (Apple, 1996; Freire, 1998b, 1996). Social justice has also been studied in law and criminal justice, philosophy, economics, political studies, sociology, psychology, interdisciplinary studies, black studies, anthropology, and public policy (Brooks, 2008a; Jean-Marie and Dancy, 2014; Normore and Brooks, 2014). However, it continues to evolve in the field of educational leader-

ship (Aiken and Gerstl-Pepin, 2012; Shoho, Merchant, and Lugg, 2005). Researchers (for example, Furman and Gruenewald, 2004; Shields, 2003) contend that social justice has become a major concern for educational scholars and practitioners at the beginning of the twenty-first century and is driven by many factors such as cultural transformation and demographic shift of Western society, increased achievement and economic gaps of underserved populations, and accountability pressures and high stakes testing.

Bogotch (2002) asserts that social justice has "no fixed or predictable meanings" (p. 153). However, other scholars in educational leadership (for example, Dantley and Tillman, 2006; Larson and Murtadha, 2002; Marshall and Oliva, 2006) identify common threads and shared understanding of social justice to include creating equitable schooling and education (Bredeson, 2004; Jean-Marie, 2008; Larson and Murtadha, 2002); examining issues of race, diversity, marginalization, gender, spirituality, age, ability, sexual orientation and identity (Dantley and Tillman, 2006); anti-oppressive education (Kumashiro, 2000); and conceptualizing the preparation of leaders for social justice (Capper, Theoharis, and Sebastian, 2006; Marshall and Oliva, 2006). When synthesizing the social justice discourse in educational leadership, Furman and Gruenewald (2004) offer three shared meanings of social justice embedded in various ways throughout contemporary literature: critical-humanist perspective, focus on school achievement and economic well-being, and the narratives and values of the Western Enlightenment (see also Brooks, 2008b). The increased attention given to social justice brings to the fore a focus on the moral purposes of leadership in schools and how to achieve these purposes (Furman, 2003). As Evans (2007) observed, "the scholarship of social justice supports the notion that educational leaders have a social, ethical, and moral obligation to foster equitable school practices, processes, and outcomes for learners of different racial, socioeconomic, gender, cultural, disability, and sexual orientations backgrounds" (p. 250).

Recognizing that the role of school leaders is at least in part to advocate on behalf of marginalized and poorly served students carries a corollary contention that traditional hierarchies and power structures must be deconstructed and reconfigured, in order to subvert a long-standing system that has privileged certain students while oppressing or neglecting others (Allen,

2006; Jean-Marie and Normore, 2010; Lugg and Shoho, 2006; Normore and Jean-Marie, 2008; Scheurich and Skrla, 2003). This means that school leaders must increase their awareness of various explicit and implicit forms of oppression, develop an intent to subvert the dominant paradigm, and finally act as a committed advocate for educational change that makes a meaningful and positive change in the education and lives of traditionally marginalized and oppressed students (Allen, 2006; Brooks and Arnold, 2013; Brooks and Tooms, 2008; Freire, 1998b; Jean-Marie and Mansfield, 2013; Leonard, Schilling, and Normore, 2014, in press; Theoharis and Brooks, 2012). If educational leaders with this perspective on their practice "can sufficiently increase their stock of courage, intelligence, and vision, [they] might become a social force of some magnitude" (Counts, 1978, p. 29) and extend their scope of influence well beyond the school's walls. Given this perspective, school leaders are potentially the architects and builders of socially just schools wherein traditionally disadvantaged peoples have the same educational opportunities, and by extension social opportunities, as traditionally advantaged people.

Beyond Traditional Leadership Preparation to Leadership for Social Justice

In considering the emergence of social justice in educational administration, two strands categorize the paradigmatic shift from indifference or ignorance toward issues of social justice by practitioners and scholars to an embracement of said issues. For the purpose of this article these strands are categorized as the *historic administrative practice in public schools* and *a social justice approach to leadership preparation*. Karpinski and Lugg (2006) drew from the historical work of other researchers (for example, Arnez, 1978; Blount, 1998; Cubberley, 1919; Nassaw, 1979) to examine the shift of traditional leadership preparation to the emergence of social justice in the field. Similarly, Capper, Theoharis, and Sebastian (2006) examined the scholarship—to name a few (for example, Bredeson, 1995; Littrell and Foster, 1995; Murphy, 1999, 2001; Murphy and Vriesenga, 2004) who have debated what makes up the knowledge base of educational administration. They further examined other scholarship (for example, Dantley, 2002; Gerwitz, 1998; Grogan and Andrews, 2002;

Larson and Murtadha, 2002; Marshall, 2004) to provide an analysis of the growing interest and body of scholarship on leadership for social justice. We likewise conducted further review of the literature, which included Brooks and Miles' (2008) retrospective on intellectual zeitgeist in educational leadership, English's (2005) edited handbook of educational leadership, Murphy's (2006) and Murphy and Vriesenga's (2006) examination of the education of school leaders through an historical context, Marshall and Oliva's (2006/2010) edited work on leadership for social justice, Boske and Diem's (2012) edited work on global leadership for social justice, Normore's (2008) edited work on leadership, social justice, equity and excellence, and special issues of journals devoted to leadership for social justice (i.e., *Educational Administration Quarterly*, 2004; *Journal of Educational Administration*, 2007; *International Electronic Journal for Leadership in Learning*, 2006; and *Journal of School Leadership*, 2007).

In the first categorization, *historic administrative practice in public schools,* the knowledge base of educational administration was premised on the traditional model of scholars such as Cubberly, Strayer, and Mort (Brooks and Miles, 2008; Karpinski and Lugg, 2006; Murphy, 2006). Karpinski and Lugg (2006) argue that the early history of educational administration as a profession and mode of inquiry drew heavily from hierarchical and simplistic business models that obscured the rich diversity of public schools in the early twentieth century. The promotion of standardization and regimentation of grade levels, teaching materials and curricula, and curricula tracking were the bases of preparing generations of administrators committed to a "one size fits all" (Callahan, 1962) approach to their work that Brooks and Miles (2008) characterized as a "first wave of scientific management" (pp. 101–102). According to Grogan and Andrews (2002), traditionally, university-based leadership preparation programs are best characterized as preparing aspiring administrators for the role of a top-down manager and are overloaded with courses on management and administration (i.e., planning, organizing, financing, supervising, budgeting, scheduling, etc.) rather than on the development of relationships and caring environments within schools to promote student learning (p. 238).

Murphy's (2006) and Murphy and Vriesenga's (2006) historical overview of the preparation of school leaders reveal the impact each era of the period—i.e., ideological (1820–1900), prescriptive (1900–1915), scientific (1947–1985) and dialectic (1986–present)—had on the field. The first three eras, in particular the ideological and prescriptive, were greatly influenced by the homogeneous scholars in educational administration (i.e., white male professors). A similar homogeneity characterized students of these periods in that nearly all were white males holding full-time positions as school administrators (Murphy, 2006, p. 5) whose training and professional socialization were grounded in technical and efficiency approaches and largely removed from the social and philosophical foundations of education (Karpinski and Lugg, 2006). Concerns with the social order of schools dominated in the 1930s and 1950s (Evans, 2007). As Karpinksi and Lugg (2006) conclude:

> Efficient administrators saw human differences in terms of deficiencies and frequently labeled these differences as genetic and moral failings. As a result, generations of mainstream educational administrators were simply not interested in broadly defined discussions of individualism, democracy, and community. (p. 281)

Conclusively, inclusiveness and diversity were overshadowed by the norms of dominant voices in American society (Karpinski and Lugg, 2006; Pounder, Reitzug, and Young, 2002) during these periods and permeated the preparation of school leaders.

A post-scientific management shift in the preparation of school leaders occurred during the dialectic era. It was fueled by an onslaught of criticism on the state of leadership preparation programs. As some have argued (e.g., Evans, 2007; Murphy; 2006), cultural and political shifts during the eras of educational administration greatly influenced the ideologies in educational leadership preparation (Brooks and Miles, 2008). However, as the field evolved in response to broader social movements, preparation of school leaders prompted new frameworks that included standards of performance guided by the Interstate School Leaders Licensure Consortium's (ISLLC). The standards address the school leader's role in developing a shared vision of learning; sustaining a school culture conducive to learning; ensuring appropriate management of school operations and resources; facilitating collaboration with families to respond to diverse needs; acting with integrity and fairness; and responding to the school's political, social, economic, legal, and cultural context (Cambron-McCabe, 2006, p. 112).

As Evans (2007) cogently asserts, prescriptive performance standards have weakened school leaders' responsibility and ability to respond to the social needs of children and families the public schools serve. Additionally, some (for example, Achilles and Price, 2001; Anderson, 2001; English, 2000; Cambron-McCabe, 2006) have criticized the ISLLC standards for its inadequacy in addressing social justice concerns despite the vast improvement of underlying assumptions that impacted earlier approaches to leadership preparation. Brooks and Miles (2008) went as far as to characterize the current standards movement, such as the 2002 No Child Left Behind legislation, ISLLC, as a "second wave of scientific management in educational administration" (p. 109). The current hot button standards issue—Common Core State Standards Initiative—is yet another U.S. education initiative that seeks to bring diverse state curricula into alignment with each other by following the principles of standards-based education reform (see Brooks, 2008; Normore and Brooks, 2012).

Moreover, embedded in the ISLLC standards is a culminating requirement, an internship that is viewed as the ultimate performance test or final rite of passage before gaining an initial license to practice. Principal interns have the opportunity to expand their knowledge and skills in authentic settings as they work on problems with real-world consequences (Southern Regional Education Board, 2007). However, the internship in many preparation programs is suffering from a number of blind spots on addressing social justice concerns schools and communities confront, and have failed to provide a robust, dynamic, and multifaceted description of leadership for schools. Quality internships require significant investments by university leadership preparation programs in order to fully prepare new principals to face the challenges of leadership (SREB, 2007). Furthermore, licensure standards must move beyond vague statements to specific actions to embody social justice (Cambron-McCabe, 2006; Marshall and Ward, 2004) in educational leadership.

The second categorization which depicts a shift in leadership preparation programs is a *social justice approach* that focuses on how to best educate school administrators and achieve "just" schools (Quantz, Cambron-McCabe, and Dantley, 1991). Scholars have paid considerable attention to practices and policies that marginalize students and pose challenging questions to school leaders, educational scholars, and the broader community to engage in discussions about leadership for social justice (Capper, Theoharis, and Sebastian, 2006; Fua, 2007; Marshall and Oliva, 2006; Moos, Moller, and Johanson, 2004; Normore, 2008). Hoff, Yoder, and Hoff (2006) conducted a study of pre-service administrators in three master's level certification programs at a state university in New England. Findings from this study support Shoho's (2006) assertion that educational leaders are not adequately prepared to lead public schools toward a greater understanding of diversity. These aspiring leaders claimed little responsibility for promoting social justice, especially when social change challenged local norms. According to Hoff et al. (2006), in order to prepare leaders to meet these responsibilities with skill and forethought (i.e., habits of hands and habits of mind), university leadership preparation programs must recognize they are in a key position to impact the practices and behaviors of future school leaders. As such, educators who prepare school leaders must question how well they are cultivating revolutionary educational leaders (Kezar and Carducci, 2007) to embrace the social responsibility for creating better schools and better educated students, while simultaneously serving the public good.

Schools today face shifting demands such as growing pressures for accountability, achieving higher levels of learning for all children, and an increase in public scrutiny (Jean-Marie, 2008). Expectations are escalating, and leadership preparation programs face fundamental questions in regard to their purposes, visions of excellence, and measures of programmatic quality. With the launching of a series of conversations in 1994 about the impact of leadership preparation programs and the numerous approaches used in universities around the country, the executive committee of the University Council of Educational Administration (UCEA) raised important questions about how well prepared were school leaders to respond to the demanding policy and cultural challenges schools have to contend with (Black and Murtadha, 2007). Leadership preparation programs are now challenged to provide curricula that shed light on and interrogate notions of social justice, democracy, equity, and diversity (Hafner, 2005; Young and Brooks, 2008). Among the challenges identified in the leadership preparation literature for meeting the new demands are a need for district financial commitment

for leadership development programs that will likely draw more candidates to fill the diminishing pipeline for school leadership positions (Jackson and Kelly, 2000; Kelley and Petersen, 2000; SREB, 2007). Also, there is a need to select texts and articles in educational leadership curricula that adequately address issues of how race, sexual orientation, ethnicity, and other characteristics create a climate which places some students at an educational disadvantage (Beyer and Apple, 1988; Furman and Starratt, 2002). Building on these factors, there is a need to adequately prepare educational leaders who will have experiences which affect their ability and desire to promote and practice social justice (Brooks and Arnold, 2013; Furman and Shields, 2005; Jean-Marie and Mansfield, 2013; Scheurich and Skrla, 2003). Young and Mountford (2006) assert that there will be an influx of leadership preparation programs seeking to infuse these issues in their program of study within the next decade that will "emphasize issues of diversity, ethics, and equity, and utilize transformational learning to train leaders who will be better able to advance social justice in their schools and districts as well as in their communities and society at large" (p. 265). In considering curricular revisions to orient aspiring leaders, consideration must be given to students' resistance to transformational learning around issues of diversity and social justice (Hoff et al., 2006; Young and Mountford, 2006). Preparation programs must also consider the issue that promoting diversity can be more daunting when the population of aspiring school leaders and their own experiences are themselves homogeneous (Capper et al., 2006; Hoff et al., 2006). Many aspiring leaders have too few opportunities to cross school boundaries and form close linkages with surrounding communities in "porous" relationships (Furman, 2002). Yet, preparation programs must seek to infuse curricula with multiple perspectives to broaden aspiring leaders' experiences beyond their familiarity or limited to their current school setting (Hafner, 2005).

Dimmock and Walker (2005) and Brooks and Normore (2010) are among scholars who argue that given the phenomenal and rapid spread of multiculturalism and globalization, there is a need for better understanding school leadership in multiple contexts. Their work in infusing culture and diversity in educational leadership seeks to inform how practitioner-leaders come to understand their immediate contexts better, while appreciating the contextual differences with their counterparts elsewhere. Challenging university educators in educational leadership, Allen (2006) asserts that professors need to reexamine how aspiring leaders are prepared to address the complexity of culture and schooling. They can be guided to reframe the issues surrounding education and develop the skills that will assist in exploring how they think about schools, as well as cultivate in them a more insightful understanding of social justice and equity. A 2004 special issue of *Educational Administration Quarterly* (EAQ) examined the issue of a broader curriculum in educational leadership, focusing specifically on the ways that social justice concepts could be integrated into existing curricula. The community of scholars and scholarship in educational leadership is increasingly global, as evident by the nationality of authors published in journals such as the *Journal of Educational Administration, Journal of School Leadership, Planning and Changing, Educational Administration Quarterly, International Journal for Leadership in Education, Journal of Research on Leadership Education, Educational Management, Administration and Leadership,* and *Values and Ethics in Educational Administration.* Social justice leadership is likewise receiving attention at conferences such as the annual New Democratic Ethical Educational Leadership (New DEEL), University Council of Educational Administration (UCEA), American Educational Research Association (AERA), Commonwealth Council for Educational Administration and Management (CCEAM), and UCEA Values, Ethics and Leadership conferences promulgating national and international perspectives about educational administration. Present in these professional publications and conferences are elusive themes that aim to include an increasingly broader range of perspectives. Through research and inquiry, leadership preparation programs can take a comparative perspective in regards to the influence of culture of leadership styles as well as the different world-views, values, and belief systems of our complex nation and world.

Young and Lopez (2005) maintain that the nature of inquiry in educational leadership scholarship is constrained by both its theoretical and methodological tools. They believe that broader frameworks for understanding leadership, organizational life, and the role and purpose of leaders in a changing social context are needed. They also propose that these frameworks are at-tainable by expanding our theoretical and methodological lenses through three theoretical approaches—critical race, queer, and feminist post-structural—that expose the field to different understandings of leadership and organizational phenomena. Critical race theory, queer theory, and feminist post-structural theory approaches have much to offer the educational leadership scholarship. *Critical race theory,* a mid-1970s movement that began in law but has spread broadly to other disciplines, examines the relationship among race, racism and power, and challenges the overt and hidden manifestation of racism in the political, legal and organizational, and social arenas that maintain beliefs about neutrality, equal opportunity, and democracy in popular U.S. ideology (Bell, 1992; Delgado and Stefancic, 2000). *Queer theory* as a cultural study field emerged in the 1990s. It examines sexual identities such as sex, sexuality, and gender and seeks to understand discourse, structures, behaviors, and actions that normalize the interlocking systems of power and sexuality (Foucault, 1980; Tierney, 1997; Tierney and Dilley, 1998). Canonical texts of queer studies by scholars like Foucault (1981, 1987) heavily influenced the modern discourse on the social construction of sexual identities. *Feminist post-structural* theory combines both feminist and post-structural perspectives and draws from post structural conceptions of discourse, subjectivity, power and knowledge, and resistance in relation to issues of gender roles, inequity, and oppression (Grogan, 2003; Ortiz and Marshall, 1988; Shakeshaft, 1989; Skrla, 2003; Young and Lopez, 2005).

Embedding critical theory, queer theory and feminist post-structural theory in the curriculum of educational leadership preparation programs provides deeper knowledge for exploring the historically neglected issues of race, ethnicity, gender, sexual orientation, ability and class and their impact on public school and the education of children. However, they cannot remain on the margins of mainstream educational leadership (Young and Lopez, 2005). The application of these theoretical roots of inquiry in conceptualizing leadership for social justice makes possible an agenda that strengthens research and practice, and enhances the possibility for constructing new thinking, methods, and tools for teaching and doing social justice (Marshall and Oliva, 2006). As Karpinski and Lugg (2006) contend, exploring these issues in educational administration has the potential to ensure better academic and social outcomes for all students. According to Young and Lopez (2005), these theories can disrupt our taken-for-granted assumptions of what leadership is, what it can be, and what purposes it ultimately serves (p. 351). Whether critical race theory, queer theory, or feminist post-structural theory, all of them, when applied to scholarship and research in educational leadership, have important contributions to make to the field. Also, when used in educational leadership, they can disrupt our taken-for-granted assumptions about the centrality of race, class, gender, and sexual orientation in schools and raise the social consciousness of school leaders (Brunner, Opsal, and Oliva, 2006). Researchers (for example, Bell, 1992; Delgado and Stefancic, 2000; Lind, 2004; Sandoval, 2000; Shohat, 2001) have suggested that while disruption is necessary and good, we also need to know how to reformulate assumptions that are more healthy and empowering to those oppressed by misguided educators and school leaders. Resistance to preparing leaders for social justice might be overcome when we are able to effectively move from the deconstruction phase to the reconstruction phase and beyond.

The renewed call for creating socially just schools suggests that it is incumbent upon leadership preparation programs to teach, model, and cultivate the necessary behaviors, attitudes, and knowledge to help shape the social justice value stances and skills of practicing and aspiring school leaders (Marshall, 2004) and for shaping their organizations in ways that are inclusive. Additionally, our analysis of the literature suggests that we may need to focus on ways for leadership preparation programs to move in the direction of a social constructivist approach to teaching and learning involving critical dialogue and pedagogy, and a concentrated effort to understand knowledge construction and social development.

Advancing Critical Pedagogy: Leadership for Liberation and Commitment to Social Justice

At a time when educators continue to deploy new strategies to confront the transformative and changing social and historical contexts, they struggle with a common definition for the term critical pedagogy. Researchers have defined critical pedagogy as educational theory, and teaching and learning practices that are designed to raise learners' critical consciousness concerning oppressive social conditions (Freire, 1998a, 1998b; Ladson-Billings, 1997; McLaren, 1998, 1993; McLauren and Torres, 1999). Freire (1998a, 1998b) argues that critical pedagogy focuses on personal liberatory education through the development of critical consciousness. He further argues that liberatory education "raises students' consciousness and prepares them to engage in larger social struggles for liberation" (1998b, p. 28). Serving as a catalyst to the commitment of social justice and to the advancement of critical pedagogy, liberatory education attempts to empower learners to engage in critical dialogue that critiques and challenges oppressive social conditions nationally and globally and to envision and work toward a more just society (Shields, 2002). The use of such a dialogical approach in leadership development programs is one strategy that can help current and future leaders to confront transformative and changing social conditions and historical contexts.

We propose that the dialogical approach to learning abandons the lecture format and the "banking approach" to education (Freire, 1998, p. 58) in favor of dialogue and open communication among students and instructor where everybody teaches and everybody learns. In preparation for social justice leadership, critical pedagogy is particularly concerned with:

reconfiguring the traditional student/teacher relationship, where the teacher is the active agent, the one who knows, and the students receive, memorize, and repeat information as the passive recipients of the instructor's knowledge. As we move toward a critical pedagogy and a commitment to social justice we envision the classroom as a site where new knowledge, grounded in the experiences of students and teachers alike, is produced through meaningful dialogue and experiences (Freire, 1998a, p. 58).

In promoting critical pedagogy and a more social constructivist approach to teaching for social justice, important concepts about knowledge and learning emerged from our analysis of the literature (Gredler and Shields, 2004; Hacking, 1999). Understanding how knowledge is constructed is critical. As Galloway (2007) asserts, knowledge is not something that exists outside of language and the social subjects who use it. In support of earlier research (for example, Vygotsky, 1978; Willard, 1992), Galloway suggests that knowledge is a process socially constructed and one that cannot be divorced from learners' social context. Knowledge is constructed by "doing" and from social development experience (2007). Students bring prior knowledge into a learning situation, which in turn forms the basis for their construction of new knowledge (Searle, 1995). Upon encountering something new, learners must first reconcile it in some way with their previous ideas and experiences. This may mean changing what they believe, expanding their understanding, or disregarding the new information as irrelevant (Gredler and Shields, 2004; Sernak, 2006; Shields, 2002). In a constructivist framework, learning is not a process of information transmission from instructor to student, but is instead a process that positions students to be actively involved in constructing meaning from a multiple stimuli (i.e., real-world examples, problem solving activities, dialogues). As Searle (1995) indicates, the instructor makes sure she understands the students' preexisting conceptions and guides activities to address and build on them. Constructivism also often utilizes collaboration and peer criticism as a way of facilitating students' abilities to reach a new level of understanding (Searle, 1995) and "coming to consciousness" (Freire, 1998b). Sernak (2006) adds that leadership preparation programs ought to prepare educational leaders who seek to liberate students to make social changes, create space and spaces for trust, and nurture participatory, equitable, and just relationships rather than simply managing programs, services, and facilities. Leadership preparation programs should also provide the opportunity for empowerment rather than "delivering it."

Educators of social justice leadership would be wise to adopt a constructivist approach to training, preparing, and developing twenty-first-century school leaders as the necessary first step of "praxis" configured as an ongoing, reflective approach to taking action. According to Freire (1998b), praxis involves "engaging in a cycle of theory, application, evaluation, reflection, and then back to theory. Social transformation is the product of praxis at the collective level" (p. 75). Researchers argue that critical pedagogy also has a more collective political component in that critical consciousness is positioned as the necessary first step of a larger collective political struggle to challenge and transform oppressive social conditions and to create a more egalitarian society (Apple, 1995; Apple and King, 1977; Broderick, 1997; Carlson and Apple, 1998; Giroux, 1996; 1998).

Although leadership preparation and development programs (as well as teacher education programs) have included curriculum topics focused on social justice as part of the prescribed curriculum, another important strategy for increased effective leadership development is to focus on the hidden curriculum (Eisner, 1994).

Hidden curriculum. Recognizing and acting on the "hidden curriculum" (Apple, 1990; Eisner, 1994) or the "unintentional ways of teaching" (Kumashiro, 2004) can be a powerful and influential tool for effective teaching and learning. According to Lea and Griggs (2005), this "implicit curriculum" in schools is often conducted in the hallways, lunchrooms, playgrounds, locker rooms, and at the back of classrooms. Ironically, in the hidden school curriculum, students often build a replica of the very power structures from which they are excluded in the larger social order. Within the culture of social and cultural oppression, students learn about competition, unequal self-worth, and psychological warfare. They also learn that covert relational aggression is a viable and useful strategy to take with them into the adult world. For example, bullying is a curriculum of dominance and oppression in which some students (both perpetrators and witnesses) have learned that bullying is an acceptable form of dehumanization, while other students (both victims and witnesses) have learned docility and silence (see SooHoo, 2004). SooHoo further asserts that an obvious issue perpetuated by educators at many levels in dealing with social issues such as racism, homophobia, and bullying is to simply ignore the issues. The age-old panacea doled out by adults to bully victims is "just ignore it" (p. 2004). The act of ignoring leads to indifference and "bystanderism."

Bystanderism and indifference. According to SooHoo (2004), bystanderism is the "response of people who observe something that demands intervention on their part, but they choose not to get involved" (p. 200). Indifference is heavily influenced by teachers' duty schedules and classroom geographic boundaries. A common code of conduct often expressed in the teacher's lounge is, "If it is not on my watch or in my classroom, I am not responsible." Responsibility for students' behavior in transit during passing periods, nutrition or lunch breaks, or in areas such as hallways, locker rooms, and lunch quads are relegated to other adult supervisors, leaving classroom teachers and school leaders not only duty-free but also absolved of any responsibility for incidences of oppressive behaviors and practices. The bystander effect is not new. Latane and Darley (1969) examined the factors that cause bystanderism. Theory findings indicated pluralistic ignorance to be a contributing factor. For example, when in a group, people often look to others to know how to react. They termed this as "informational social influence." Essentially, when people see that others are not reacting, then they will not react either. A second factor is the diffusion of responsibility when people expect that someone else more competent would help. A third factor is the proximity of distance. The smaller the distance between the bystander and the victim, the more directly responsible the bystander will feel—and thus they are more likely to help.

Given current research that indicates the critical need for new thinking, many educators and/or theorists refuse to rethink the role academics might play in defending teaching and learning institutions of higher education as a crucial democratic public sphere (Giroux, 1998). These institutions are in a position to serve as catalysts of opportunities that address what it means to make teaching and learning more critically and socially conscious and politically responsive in a time of growing conservatism, racism, and social injustices locally, nationally, and internationally. In the following section we discuss strategies for connecting social justice practice and the study of educational leadership in both national and global spheres by delving into other important arenas of study.

Making Connections between Local and Global Research to Extend Leadership for Social Justice

In this final section, we explore three separate strategies for connecting the local practice (again, in the case of our overarching context for this chapter, we mean the United States) and study of educational leadership to these activities at a global level and consider the reciprocal nature of these relationships. These strategies include: (a) broadening our conception of the knowledge base that undergirds educational leadership for social justice in order to deepen it; (b) reconsidering research designs and outcomes, and (c) realizing that local and global are parts of one interrelated whole.

Strategy One: Broadening our conception of the knowledge base that undergirds educational leader-ship for social justice in order to deepen it. Literature related to educational leadership for social justice has suffered by not connecting to extant lines of related inquiry in the social sciences and in other related disciplines. More specifically, fields such as sociology, anthropology, psychology, philosophy, peace studies, black studies, and comparative and international education have much to offer research in leadership for social justice (Jean-Marie and Dancy, 2014; Normore and Brooks, 2014). As Brooks (2008a) contends,

> a more deliberate and meaningful connection to the social sciences could ultimately help provide a foundation for radical innovation in both the research and practice of educational leadership—it could also be the intellectual scaffold on which a theory of social justice is ultimately built. (p. 1)

However, too often educational leadership scholars confine their perspectives on social justice to either: (a) a single powerful inspiration such as the works of Paulo Freire, Michael Eric Dyson, John Rawls, or Hannah Arendt, or (b) works published in the past two decades in the field of educational leadership, which have appeared as part of a relatively recent interest in social justice. To be fair, perspectives developed and collected in edited volumes (for example, Marshall and Oliva, 2006), in special issues and individual articles published of respected scholarly journals,[1] and scholarly books (Scheurich and Skrla, 2003) constitute important contributions to our understanding of the relationship between justice and educational leadership. It is important to recognize that the rising number of works grounded in recent educational leadership for social justice perspectives suggests a rise of the field's collective consciousness on issues of inequity. That being said, the field of educational leadership should consider taking a step back to consider what philosophers, sociologists, anthropologists, legal scholars, political scientists (Cohen, 1986), and others have done that might inform our contemporary work (Normore and Brooks, 2014). This is especially relevant when considering that many of these fields have been investigating different forms of justice, equity, and equality for decades, and in the cases of legal thought and philosophy, much longer. Further, in addition to being aware of historical and disciplinary discourses related to social justice in other academic fields, it is important to be aware of classic and cutting-edge conversations happening with regard to equity-related constructs such as race, gender, ethics, and many other sources from which leaders might learn lessons to guide their inquiry and practice (Grogan, 1999).

In addition to expanding our perspective on social justice to include and extend lines of inquiry born in other disciplines, it likewise is important to take into account research conducted on leadership development on a transnational level, and in the fields of international education, comparative education, and work on teaching for social justice. Moreover, there is increasing acknowledgment that it is important for instructional leaders to understand issues of both equity and excellence in specific content areas if they are to provide high-level support to teachers and students (Theoharis and Brooks, 2012). Connecting with and contributing to these disparate yet interrelated domains of inquiry will allow us much greater insight into international leadership (see Normore and Erbe, 2013), leadership for social justice, and help scholars and practitioners contextualize their work in a global context and in the context of multiple lines of theoretical and empirical inquiry.

Strategy Two: Reconsidering research designs and outcomes. Educational researchers have relied on a relatively limited number of research designs and methodologies to inform our understanding of justice-related phenomena. While educational leadership scholars have contributed a plethora of outstanding conceptual works (for example, Marshall and Oliva, 2006), case studies (for example, Gooden, 2005), state-level investigations (Fuller, Young, and Baker, 2011), and a few large-scale analyses of quantitative data (Gay, 1997), we have yet to expand our approaches into other designs. In particular, the dearth of quantitative, historical, cross-cultural comparative, international, and mixed-method studies of social justice are disappointing and limit our ability to understand leadership for social justice in its many forms. However, it is important to note that in suggesting that we explore these approaches more fully and use quantitative measures as a way to gain insight into issues related to social justice, we are emphatically not calling for a single-minded emphasis on aggregate standardized and/or norm-referenced test outcomes (Ravitch, 2010; 2013). It is troubling that discussions of mixed-method approaches in education tend to over-emphasize correlating outcomes and trends in student achievement data with other factors and phenomena when there are

so many potentially fruitful avenues for inquiry. For example, looking at various quantitative measures such as census data, researcher-generated measures of equitable and equal distribution of goods and services, school and district finance data, state-level educational and social service appropriations, and even biometric data all hold tremendous potential for explaining and helping us explore social justice issues as phenomena related directly to communities, both local and global.

In addition to reconsidering the design of educational leadership for social justice studies, it is also important to reassess the intended beneficiaries and audiences who might use the work. That is, considering that leadership for social justice suggests an active and possibly *activist* orientation toward issues of inequity, it seems obvious that the scholar of leadership for social justice cannot be content to write to a small and exclusive audience of fellow academics. If leadership for social justice scholars are to take their charge seriously, we must reconsider the manner in which we communicate, the people with whom we communicate, and the deliverables produced by our inquiry. This may mean, for example

1. writing policy/leadership briefs about salient local issues, OP-ED for mass print media, in international journals and/or brief articles in local and national practitioner newsletters,
2. creating free-access websites and multimedia materials that communicate important ideas in an accessible manner,
3. seeking out politicians and policymakers who will collaborate on various initiatives,
4. giving presentations to school boards, parent teacher organizations, nongovernmental organizations, and other stakeholders,
5. writing blogs or other forms of instant electronic communication as individual scholars or in collectives of scholars,
6. producing findings in multiple languages,
7. working with established foundations/think tanks who support leadership for social justice-related initiatives OR establishing new think tanks and initiatives.

Strategy Three: Realizing that local and global are parts of one interrelated whole. In the United States, where the three of us do the majority of our work, the federal political organization of education makes certain levels of education more important, in a policy-making sense, than others. This tends to urge educators to focus their attention on certain levels and de-emphasize others. In particular, the state is the most important level of educational policy implementation and interpretation in the United States. This is because states are legally empowered to interpret, and to a large part to implement, federal educational policy and legislation (Cambron-McCabe, McCarthy, and Thomas, 2004). After the state, educators in the United States must then look to their district to see how these decisions will be implemented before finally discovering and shaping how they will influence the daily practices of education in a school or classroom. As a result of this organizational structure, educators often develop a kind of educational myopia, wherein they focus most intently on their most immediate organizational level. Given this perspective, the scope of their vision ends at the national/federal level and they tend to think of the entire system as a hierarchical-linear system, meaning that they feel they cannot influence parts of the system much "higher" or "lower" than their level (see figure 21.1).

However, rather than continue this "leveled" vision of the system and of their work, educational leaders (and educational leadership researchers) might instead seek

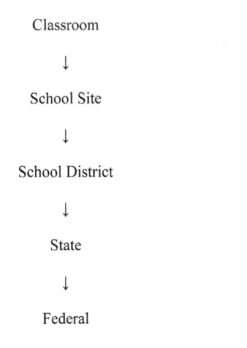

Figure 21.1.   Linear perspective on educational leadership practice and research

to understand that given technological, economic, and indeed educational trends over the last half-century, the local *is* the global; all *domains* of practice—not *levels*—are interrelated (Weber, 2007). We argue that rather than accepting the extant organizational vision of schooling often suggested by scholars in the United States (see figure 21.1), educational leadership practitioners and scholars should instead adopt a vision of schooling that conceives educational leadership research and practice as interrelated domains rather than levels of schooling (figure 21.2). This will allow and urge leaders to consider, for example, how their local labor markets, the prices of goods and services, and student achievement influence, and are influenced by, international events and trends in an ecological rather than isolated manner. This may allow leaders of nations to move beyond competing with other leaders over international and comparative measures of student performance such as the datasets from The Trends in International Mathematics and Science Study (TIMSS), Progress in International Reading Literacy Study (PIRLS), and the Program for International Student Assessment (PISA) and instead adopt the perspective that such tests can help us learn from one another at a global level. Imagine a world in which school leaders look not only to their peers in a neighboring school district or even another U.S. city for ideas and solutions that might help their students, but to a global community of leaders who understand that the success of the local should be informed by and contribute to the success of students around the globe.

CONCLUSIONS AND IMPLICATIONS

Based on our review of literature and subsequent analysis, a growing concern among educators is whether

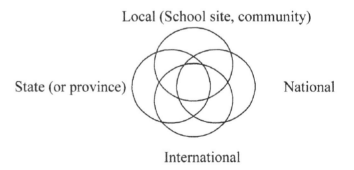

Figure 21.2.   An interrelated perspective on the relationship between local and global practice

emerging school leaders are prepared to face political, economic, cultural, and social pressures and create schools that advocate for education that advances all children. Research suggests that leadership preparation programs ought to engage in new ways of instruction that promote a broader and deeper understanding of issues such as social justice, democracy, and equity (Marshall and Oliva, 2005; Normore, 2008; Young and Mountford, 2006). In an effort to dialogue across local, national, and international boundaries, this chapter examined various propositions and considerations if leadership preparation programs are committed to preparing school leaders to think globally and act courageously about social justice.

As Bogotch (2005) reminds us, more discussions of educational leadership are in order to deliberately and continuously refocus our educational work (in theory and practice) on understanding and becoming more socially just. Leadership development and preparation programs have become the object of intensive scrutiny in the past few years, and again more recently with the Levine (2005) report that questioned the efficacy of educational leadership preparation programs. Local school districts, state departments of education, as well as local and national foundations have provided funds for programs that are focused on retraining current leaders and preparing future leaders for our schools. While there is much activity, less is known about the impact of this investment. As scholars and practitioners of educational leadership, we have an obligation to move beyond high-sounding abstractions and turn to research and action. In order to help school leaders become more successful in educational leadership roles, research topics, and other activities should be developed and implemented at the postsecondary level of preparation that help school district personnel examine how various policies, procedures, rules, and norms may limit the success of their leaders. This implies that leadership preparation programs should promote opportunities for critical reflection, leadership praxis, critical discourse, and develop critical pedagogy related to issues of ethics, inclusion, democratic schooling, and social justice. Coordinated efforts that provide opportunities for critical dialogue and liberatory education through strategies identified in this chapter (for example, appropriate field-based curricula, national and global collaborative research, alternative research designs) may lead to more

effective leadership development. It seems appropriate that efforts to increase the capacity of schools by broadening educators' work beyond conventional notions of teaching and administration would be improved by paying attention to how issues of social justice (for example, gender, race, ethnicity, sexual orientation) shape and influence possibilities and desires for a more harmonious society that transcends national and international boundaries.

An implication from this research focuses on the need to conduct further comparative studies of educational leadership and social justice in diverse countries outside the United States. While the knowledge base in educational leadership, leadership preparation, and social justice in North America continues to grow, we know much less about these issues in other countries and the importance of transcending cultural norms, national and international boundaries. In order to fully capture the impact of gender, sexuality, race, and culture on leadership, research must involve a greater number of organizations at extreme ends of the value dimensions for measuring leadership effectiveness. We need more comparative research studies that investigate the contexts, processes, leadership and work experiences, and attitudes of school leaders with particular reference to similarities and differences between countries that experience modernization and industrialization and poor countries. Such comparative studies may generate cross-fertilization of ideas and experiences that will provide insight into the social justice leadership orientation that, thus far, have not been illuminated in what Oplatka (2006) refers to as "current Anglo-American literature."

As noted earlier, schools are thrust into the realistic notion that they must prepare children and communities for participation in a multicultural, multilinguistic, multiethnic, multi-religious, multi-ability, and a multinational society. In support of previous research (for example, Jean-Marie, 2008; Jean-Marie and Normore, 2010; Lugg and Shoho, 2006; Normore and Jean-Marie, 2008; Walker and Dimmock, 2006), school leaders are held under fierce accountability and fiscal pressures, while coping with a larger political environment that is polarized and fearful about the growing complexities of this new social order. Given current conversations about increasing the diversity among leadership ranks, we need to provide authentic and relevant experiences pertaining to leadership and social justice. The literature related to educational leadership for social justice has suffered by not connecting to extant lines of related inquiry in the social sciences and in other related disciplines. Much can be shared and learned from other fields such as sociology, psychology, anthropology, law, and business that may well catapult into a whole new theory of social justice. It is time to join the conversation on effective leadership preparation and to take seriously the call to work in support of leadership success and to combat leadership failure for all educational leaders and other leaders in leadership preparation programs across continents.

NOTE

1. For example, see *Journal of Educational Administration, 45*(6); *International Electronic Journal for Leadership in Learning* (10).

REFERENCES

Achilles, C. M. and Price, W. J. (2001). What is missing in the current debate about education administration standards. *AASA Professor, 24*(2), 8–13.

Ahlstrom, S. E. (1972). *A religious history of the American people*. New Haven, CT: Yale University.

Aiken, J. and Gerstl-Pepin, C. (Eds.). (2012), *Social Justice Leadership for a Global World. Book series:* Educational Leadership for Social Justice. North Carolina: Information Age Publishing.

Allen, L. A. (2006). The moral life of schools revisited: Preparing educational leaders to "build a new social order" for social justice and democratic community. *International Journal of Urban Educational Leadership, 1*, 1–13.

Anderson, G. (2001). Disciplining leaders: A critical discourse analysis of the ISLLC national examination and performance standards in educational administration. *International Journal of Leadership in Education, 4*(3), 199–216.

Apple, M. W. (1990). *The hidden curriculum and the nature of conflict in ideology and curriculum*. New York: Routledge.

Apple, M. W. (1995). *Education and power*. New York: Routledge.

Apple, M. W. (1996). *Cultural politics and education*. London: Open University Press.

Apple, M. W. and King, N. R. (1977). What do schools teach? In A. Molnar and J. A. Zahorik (Eds.), *Curriculum Theory* (pp.108–126). Washington, DC: The Association for Supervision and Curriculum Development.

Arnez, N. L. (1978). Implementation of desegregation as a discriminatory process. *Journal of Negro Education, 47*(1), 28–45.

Bell, D. (1992). *Faces at the bottom of the well: The permanence of racism*. New York: Basic Books.

Beyer, L. E. and Apple, M. W. (Eds.). (1988). *The curriculum: problems, politics and possibilities*. Albany: State University of New York Press.

Black, W. R. and Murtadha, K. (2007). Toward a signature pedagogy in educational leadership preparation and program assessment. *Journal of Research on Leadership Education*. Retrieved from www.ucea.org/JRLE/pdf/v ol2/Black_Murtadha%20PDF.pdf.

Blount, J. M. (1998). *Destined to rule the schools*. Albany: State University of New York Press..

Bogotch, I. E. (2002). Leadership for socially just schooling: More substance and less style in high-risk, low-trust times. *Journal of School Leadership, 12*, 198–222.

Bogotch, I. E. (2005, November). Social justice as an educational construct: Problems and possibilities. Paper presented at the annual meeting of the University Council of Educational Administration, Nashville, TN.

Bogotch, I., Beachum, F. Blount, J., Brooks, J. S., and English, F. W. (2008). *Radicalizing educational leadership: Toward a theory of social justice*. Netherlands: Sense.

Boske, C. and Diem, S. (Eds.). (2012). *Global leadership for social justice: Taking it from the field to practice*. Bingley, United Kingdom: Emerald Group Publishing Limited.

Bredeson, P. V. (1995). Building a professional knowledge base in education administration: Opportunities and obstacles, In R. Donmoyer, M. Imber, and J. J. Scheurich (Eds.), *The knowledge base of educational administration: Multiple perspectives* (pp. 47–61). Albany: State University of New York Press.

Bredeson, P. V. (2004). Creating spaces for the development of democratic school leaders: A case of program redesign in the United States. *Journal of Educational Administration, 42*(6), 708–723.

Broderick, D. (1997). *Theory and its discontents*. Geelong: Deakin University.

Brooks, J. S. (2008a). Introduction part one: What can social justice educators learn from the social sciences? In I. Bogotch, F. Beachum, J. Blount, J. S. Brooks, and F. W. English, *Radicalizing educational leadership: Toward a theory of social justice* (pp. 1–10). Netherlands: Sense.

Brooks, J. S. (2008b). Freedom and justice: Conceptual and empirical possibilities for the study and practice of educational leadership. In I. Bogotch, F. Beachum, J. Blount, J. S. Brooks, and F. W. English, *Radicalizing educational leadership: Toward a theory of social justice* (pp. 61–78). Netherlands: Sense.

Brooks, J. S. and Arnold, N. (Eds.). (2013). *Educational leadership and racism: Preparation, pedagogy and practice.* Charlotte, NC: Information Age Publishing.

Brooks, J. S. and Miles, M. T. (2008). From scientific management to social justice . . . and back again? Pedagogical shifts in educational leadership. In A. H. Normore, (Ed.), *Leadership for social justice: Promoting equity and excellence through inquiry and reflective practice* (pp. 99–114). Charlotte, NC: Information Age.

Brooks, J. S. and Normore, A. H. (2010). Educational leadership and globalization: Toward a glocal perspective. *Educational Policy, 24*(1), 52–82.

Brooks, J. S. and Tooms, A. K. (2008). A dialectic of social justice: Learning to lead through reflection and dialogue. *Journal of School Leadership, 18*(2), 134–163.

Brunner, C. C., Opsal, C., and Oliva, M. (2006). Disrupting identity: Fertile pedagogy for raising social consciousness in educational leaders. In C. Marshall and M. Oliva (Eds.), *Leadership for social justice: Making revolutions in education* (pp. 214–231). New York: Pearson.

Callahan, R. E. (1962). *Education and the cult of efficiency.* Chicago, IL: University of Chicago Press.

Cambron-McCabe, N. (2006). Preparation and development of school leaders: Implications for social justice policies. In C. Marshall and M. Oliva (Eds.), *Leadership for social justice: Making revolutions in education* (pp. 110–129). New York: Pearson.

Cambron-McCabe, N. H., McCarthy, M. M., and Thomas, S. B. (2004). *Public school law: Teachers' and students' rights.* Boston, MA: Pearson Education.

Capper, C. (Ed.). (1993). *Educational administration in a pluralistic society.* Albany: State University of New York Press.

Capper, C. A., Theoharis, G., and Sebastian, J. (2006). Toward a framework for preparing leaders for social justice. *Journal of Educational Administration, 44*(3), 209–224.

Carlson, D. and Apple, M. W. (Eds.). (1998). *Power/knowledge/pedagogy.* Cresskill: Westview.

Cohen, R. L. (1986). *Justice: Views from the social sciences.* New York: Plenum.

Counts, G. S. (1978). *Dare the school build a new social order?* Originally published in 1932. Carbondale: Southern Illinois University.

Cubberley, E. P. (1919). *Education in the United States: A study and interpretation of American educational history.* Boston, MA: Houghton Mifflin.

Dantley, M. (2002). Uprooting and replacing positivism, the melting pot, multiculturalism, and other impotent notions in education leadership through an African American perspective. *Education and Urban Society, 34*(3), 334–352.

Dantley, M. E. and Tillman, L. C. (2006). Social justice and moral transformative leadership. In C. Marshall and M. Oliva (Eds.), *Leadership for social justice: Making revolutions in education* (pp. 16–30). New York: Pearson.

Daresh, J. C. (2000). *New principals: new induction programs.* Paper presented at the Annual Meeting of the American Educational Research Association, New Orleans.

Delgado, R. and Stefancic, J. (2000). *Critical race theory: The cutting edge.* Philadelphia: Temple University.

Dimmock, C. and Walker, A. (2005). *Educational leadership: Culture and diversity.* Thousand Oaks, CA: Sage.

Eisner, E. W. (1994). *The educational imagination: On design and evaluation of school programs.* New York: Macmilllan.

English, F. W. (2000, April). *The ghostbusters search for Frederick Taylor in the ISLLC standards.* Paper presented at the annual meeting of the American Educational Research Association, New Orleans, LA.

English, F. W. (2005). *The Sage handbook of educational leadership: Advances in theory, research, and practice.* Thousand, Oaks, CA: Sage.

Evans, A. E. (2007). Horton, Highlander, and leadership education: Lessons for preparing educational leaders for social justice. *Journal of School Leadership, 17,* 250–275.

Freire, P. (1998a). *Pedagogy of hope.* New York: Continuum.

Freire, P. (1998b). *Pedagogy of the oppressed.* (New rev. 20th anniv. ed.). New York: Continuum.

Freire, P. (1996). *Letters to Christina.* New York: Routledge.

Foucault, M. (1981). *The history of sexuality*: An introduction (vol. 1). London: Penguin.

Foucault, M. (1987). *The use of pleasure* (vol. 2). London: Penguin.

Foucault, M. (1980). *Power/knowledge: Selected interviews and other writings by Michel Foucault, 1972–1977* (C. Gordon, Ed.). New York: Pantheon.

Fua, S. J. (2007). Looking towards the source—social justice and leadership conceptualizations from Tonga. *Journal of Educational Administration, 45*(6), 672–683.

Fuller, E.J., Young, M.D., and Baker, B. (2011). Examining the impact of school leaders and their preparation on teacher quality and student achievement. *Educational Administration Quarterly, 47:* 173–216.

Furman, F. (2002). *School as community: From promise to practice.* Albany: State University of New York Press.

Furman, G. C. (2003). The 2002 UCEA presidential address: Toward a new scholarship of educational leadership? *UCEA Review, 45*(1), 1–6.

Furman, G. C. and Gruenewald, D. A. (2004). Expanding the landscape of social justice: A critical ecological analysis. *Educational Administration Quarterly, 40*(1), 47–76.

Furman, G. C. and Shields, C.M. (2005). How can educational leaders promote and support social justice and democratic community in schools? In W.A. Firestone and

C. Riehl (Eds.), *A new agenda for educational leadership* (pp. 119–137). New York: Teachers College.

Furman, G. C. and Starratt, R. J. (2002). Leadership for democratic community in schools. In J. Murphy (Ed.), *The educational leadership challenge: Redefining leadership for the 21st century* (pp. 105–133). Chicago: National Society for the Study of Education.

Galloway, C. (2007). *Vygotsky's constructivism*. Retrieved from projects.coe.uga.edu/epltt/in dex.php?title=Vygotsky's_constructivism.

Gay, G. (1997). Multicultural infusion in teacher education: Foundations and applications. *Peabody Journal of Education, 72*(1), 150–177.

Gewirtz, S. (1998). Conceptualizing social justice in education: mapping the territory. *Journal of Education Policy, 13*(4), 469–84.

Giroux, H. A. (1996). *Fugitive cultures: race, violence and youth*. New York: Routledge.

Giroux, H. A. (1998). *Channel surfing: racism, the media, and the destruction of today's youth*. New York: St. Martin's.

Gredler, M. and Shields, C. (2004). Does no one read Vygotsky's words? Commentary on Glassman. *Educational Researcher 33*(2), 22.

Gooden, M. A. (2005). The role of an African American principal in an urban information technology high school. *Educational Administration Quarterly, 10*(4), 630–650.

Grogan, M. (2003). Laying the groundwork for a reconception of the superintendency from feminist postmoderm perspectives. In M. D. Young and L. Skrla (Eds.), *Reconsidering feminist research in educational leadership* (pp. 9–34). Albany: State University of New York Press.

Grogan, M. (1999). Equity/equality issues of gender, race, and class. *Educational Administration Quarterly, 35*(4), 518–536.

Grogan, M. and Andrews, R. (2002). Defining preparation and professional development for the future. *Educational Administration Quarterly, 38*(2), 233–256.

Hacking, I. (1999). *The social construction of what?* Cambridge: Harvard University.

Hafner, M. M. (2005). Teaching strategies for developing leaders for social justice. In C. Marshall and M. Oliva (Eds.), *Leadership for social justice: Making revolutions in education* (pp. 167–193). Boston: Pearson.

Hoff, D. L., Yoder, N., and Hoff, P. S. (2006). Preparing educational leaders to embrace the "public" in schools. *Journal of Educational Administration, 44*(3), 239–249.

Hudson, W. S. (1981). *Religion in America* (3rd ed.). New York: Charles Scribner's Sons.

Jackson, B. L. and Kelley, C. (2002). Exceptional and innovative programs in educational leadership. *Educational Administration Quarterly, 38*(2), 192–212.

Jean-Marie, G. (2008). Leadership for social justice: An agenda for 21st century schools. *The Educational Forum, 72*, 340–354.

Jean-Marie, G. and Dancy, T. E. (2014). Pedagogy of the discipline: How Black Studies can influence educational leadership. In A. H. Normore, and J.S. Brooks, J. S. (Eds.), *Educational leadership for ethics and social justice: Views from the social sciences* (pp. 43–61). Charlotte, NC: Information Age Publishing.

Jean-Marie, G. and Mansfield, K. (2013). Race and racial discrimination in schools: School leaders' courageous conversations. In J. Brooks and N. Arnold, (Eds.), *Educational leadership and racism: Preparation, pedagogy and practice* (pp. 19–35). Charlotte, NC: Information Age Publishing.

Jean-Marie, G. and Normore, A. H. (2010). The impact of relational leadership, social justice, and spirituality among female secondary school leaders. *International Journal of Urban Educational Leadership, 4*(1), 22–43.

Karpinski, C. F. (2006). Social justice and educational administration: Mutually exclusive? *Journal of Educational Administration, 44*(3), 278–292.

Koerin, B. (2003). The settlement house tradition: Current trends and future concerns. *Journal of Sociology and Social Welfare, 30*(2), 53–68.

Kumashiro, K. K. (2000). Toward a theory of anti-oppressive education. *Review of Educational Research, 70*(1), 25–53.

Kumashiro, K. K. (2004). *Against common sense: teaching and learning toward social justice*. New York: Routledge Falmer.

Kelley, C. and Peterson, K. (2000, November). *The work of principals and their preparation: Addressing critical needs for the 21st century*. Paper presented at the annual meeting of the University Council for Educational Administration, Albuquerque, NM.

Kezar, A. and Carducci, R. (2007). Cultivating revolutionary educational leaders: Translating emerging theories into action. *Journal of Research on Leadership Education*. Retrieved from www.ucea.org/JRLE/pdf/v ol2/kezar.pdf.

Ladson-Billings, G. (1997). I know why this doesn't feel empowering: A critical race analysis of critical pedagogy. In P. Freire, J. W. Fraser, D. Macedo, T. McKinnon, and W. T. Stokes (Eds.), *Mentoring the mentor: A critical dialogue with Paulo Freire* (pp. 127–141). New York: Peter Lang.

Langer, E. J. (1989). *Mindfulness*. Boston: Da Capo.

Larson, C. and Murtadha, K. (2002). Leadership for social justice. In J. Murphy (Ed.), *The educational leadership challenge: Redefining leadership for the 21st century* (pp. 134–161). Chicago: University of Chicago.

Latane, B. and Darley, J. (1969). Bystander "Apathy." *American Scientist, 57*, 244–268.

Lea, V. and Griggs, T. (2005). Behind the mask and beneath the story: Enabling students-teachers to reflect critically on the socially-constructed nature of their "normal" practice. *Teacher Education Quarterly, 32*(1), 93–114.

Leonard, P., Schilling, T., and Normore, A.H. (in press, 2014). Toward a holistic approach to moral development of educational leaders. In Branson, C. and Gross, S. (Eds.), *An international handbook for the development of ethical educational leadership.* New York: Routledge/Taylor and Francis.

Lind, R. A. (2004). *Race/Gender/Media: Considering diversity across audiences, content, and producers.* Boston: Pearson Education.

Littrell, J. and Foster, W. (1995). The myth of a knowledge base in educational administration. In R. Donmoyer, M. Imber, and J. J. Scheurich (Eds.), *The knowledge base of educational administration: Multiple perspectives* (pp. 32–46). Albany: State University of New York Press.

Lugg, C. A. and Shoho, A. R. (2006). Dare public school administrators build a new social order?: Social justice and the possibly perilous politics of educational leadership. *Journal of Educational Administration, 44*(3), 196–208.

Marshall, C. (2004). Social justice challenges to educational administration: Introduction to a special issue. *Educational Administration Quarterly, 40*(1), 3–13.

Marshall, C. and Oliva, M. (2006). *Leadership for social justice: Making revolutions in education.* Boston, MA: Pearson Education.

Marshall, C. and Ward, M. (2004). Strategic policy for social justice training for leadership. *Journal of School Leadership, 14*(5), 530–563.

McLaren, P. (1998). *Life in schools: An introduction to critical pedagogy in the foundations of education.* New York: Longman.

McLaren, P. (1993). *Schooling as a ritual performance.* New York: Routledge.

McLaren, P. and Torres, R. (1999). Racism and multicultural education: Rethinking "race" and "whiteness" in late capitalism. *Critical Multiculturalism: Rethinking Multicultural and Antiracist Education.* Stephen May (Ed.). New York: Falmer.

McMahon, B. (2007). White educational administrators: Working towards antiracism and social justice. *Journal of Educational Administration, 45*(6), 684–696.

Moos, L., Moller, J., and Johansson, O. (2004). A Scandinavian perspective on educational leadership. *The Educational Forum, 68,* 201–210.

Murphy, J. (1999). Reconnecting teaching and school administration: A call for a unified profession. *UCEA Review, 40*(2), 1–3.

Murphy, J. (2001). The changing face of leadership preparation. *The School Administrator, 58*(10), 14–17.

Murphy, J. (2006). *Preparing school leaders: Defining a research and action agenda.* Lanham, MD: Rowman and Littlefield Education.

Murphy, J. and Vriesenga, M. (2004). *Research on preparation program in educational administration: An analysis.* University Council for Educational Administration, Columbia, MO: UCEA Monograph Series.

Murphy, J. and Vriesenga, M. (2006). Research on school leadership preparation in the United States: An analysis. *School Leadership and Management, 26*(2), 183–195.

Muth, R. and Barnett, B. (2001). Making the case for professional preparation: Using research for program improvement and political support. *Educational Leadership and Administration: Teaching and Program Development, 13,* 109–120.

Nasaw, D. (1979). *Schooled to order: A social history of public schooling in the United States.* New York: Oxford University.

Normore, A. H. (2008). *Leadership for social justice: Promoting equity and excellence through inquiry and reflective practice.* Charlotte, NC: Information Age.

Normore, A. H. and Brooks, J. S. (2012). Instructional leadership in the era of No Child Left Behind. In L. Volante (Ed.), *School leadership in the context of standards-based reform: International perspectives* (pp. 41–67). New York: Springer.

Normore, A. H. and Brooks, J. S. (Eds.). (2014). *Educational leadership for ethics and social justice: Views from the social sciences.* Charlotte, NC: Information Age Publishing.

Normore, A. H. and Erbe, N. (2013*). Collective efficacy: Interdisciplinary perspectives on international leadership.* Bingley, UK: Emerald Group Publishing Limited.

Normore, A. H. and Jean-Marie, G. (2008). Female secondary school leaders: At the helm of social justice, democratic schooling and equity. *Leadership and Organizational Development Journal, 29*(2), 182–205.

Oplatka, I. (2006). Women in educational administration within developing countries: Towards a new international research agenda. *Journal of Educational Administration, 44*(6), 604–624.

Ortiz, F. and Marshall, C. (1988). Women in educational administration. In N. Boyan (Ed.), *Handbook of research on educational administration* (pp. 123–141). New York: Longman.

Pounder, D., Reitzug, U., and Young, M. D. (2002). Preparing school leaders for school improvement, social justice, and community, In J. Murphy (Eds.), *The educational leadership challenge: Redefining leadership for the 21st century,* (pp. 261–288). Chicago: The University of Chicago Press.

Ravitch, D. (2010). *The death and life of the great american school system: How testing and choice are undermining education.* New York: Basic Books.

Ravitch, D. (2013). *Reign of error: the hoax of the privatization movement and the danger to America's public schools.* New York: Knopf.

Sandoval, C. (2000). *Methodology of the oppressed.* Minneapolis: University of Minnesota Press.

Scheurich, J.J. and Skrla, L. (2003). *Leadership for equity and excellence: Creating high-achievement classrooms, schools, and districts.* Thousand Oaks, CA: Corwin Press.

Searle, J. (1995). *The construction of social reality.* New York: Free Press.

Sernak, K. (2006, December). School reform and Freire's methodology of conscientization. *International Electronic Journal for Leadership in Learning, 10*(25). Retrieved from www.ucalgary.ca/~iejll.

Shakeshaft, C. (1989). The struggle to create a more gender inclusive profession. In J. Murphy and K. Seashore Louis (Eds.), *Handbook of research on educational administration* (2nd ed., pp. 99–118). San Francisco: Jossey-Bass.

Shields, C. M. (2002, October). *Towards a dialogic approach to understanding values.* An address presented at the 7th Annual Conference of Values and Leadership, Toronto, Ontario.

Shields, C. M. (2003). *Good intentions are not enough: Transformative leadership for communities of difference.* Lanham, MD: Scarecrow.

Shohat, E. (2001). *Talking visions: Multicultural feminism in a transnational age.* New York: MIT.

Shoho, A. R. (2006). Dare professors of educational administration build a new social order: Social justice within an American perspective. *Journal of Educational Administration, 44*(3).

Shoho, A. R., Merchant, B. M., and Lugg, C. A. (2005). Social justice: Seeking a common language. In F. W. English (Ed.), *The Sage handbook of educational leadership: Advances in theory, research, and practice*, pp. 47–67. Thousand Oaks, CA: Sage.

Skrla, L. (2003). Normalizing femininity: Reconsidering research on women in the superintendency. In M. D. Young and L. Skrla (Eds.), *Reconsidering feminist research in educational leadership* (pp. 247–264). Albany: State University of New York Press.

Social development theory (Vygotsky). (1978). Retrieved from www.learning-theories.com/vygotskys-social-learning-theory.html.

SooHoo, S. (2004). We change the world by doing nothing. *Teacher Education Quarterly, 31*(1), 199–211.

Southern Regional Education Board. (2007). *Good principals aren't born—they're mentored: Are we investing enough to get the school leaders we need?* Atlanta.

Spring, J. (2001). *Globalization and educational rights: An intercivilizational analysis.* Mahwah, NJ: Lawrence Erlbaum.

Theoharis, G. and Brooks, J. S. (Eds.) (2012). *What every principal needs to know to create equitable and excellent schools.* New York: Teachers College Press.

Tierney, W. G. (1997). *Academic outlaws: Queer theory and cultural studies in the academy.* Thousand Oaks, CA: Sage.

Tierney, W. G. and Dilley, P. (1998). Constructing knowledge: Educational research and gay and lesbian studies. In W. F. Pinar (Ed.), *Queer theory in education* (pp. 49–71). Mahwah, NJ: Lawrence Erlbaum Associates.

Walker, A. and Dimmock, C. (2005). Leading the multicthnic school: Research evidence on successful practice. *The Educational Forum, 69,* 291–304.

Weber, E. (2007). Globalization, "glocal" development, and teachers' work: A research agenda. *Review of Educational Research, 77*(3), 279–309.

Willard, C.A. (1992). *Liberalism and the social grounds of knowledge.* Chicago: University of Chicago Press.

Young, M. D. and Brooks, J. S. (2008). Supporting graduate students of color in educational administration preparation programs: Faculty perspectives on best practices, possibilities, and problems. *Educational Administration Quarterly, 44*(3), 391–423.

Young, M. and Lopez, G. R. (2005). The nature of inquiry in educational leadership. In F. W. English (Ed.), *The Sage handbook of educational leadership: Advances in theory, research, and practice* (pp. 337–361). Thousand Oaks, CA: Sage.

Young, M. and Mountford, M. (2006). Infusing gender and diversity issues into educational leadership programs: Transformational learning and resistance. *Journal of Educational Administration, 44*(3), 264–277.

CHAPTER 22

Social Justice in Action

Urban School Leaders Address the School-to-Prison Pipeline via a Youth Court

Heather Cole, Julian Vasquez Heilig, Tina Fernandez, Meg Clifford, and Rey Garcia

The purpose of this chapter is to utilize a case study of a unique peer-run youth court at an urban middle school to contextualize social justice in action. The youth court was developed through a collaborative partnership with the local university's law school and the administrators and teachers of a high-poverty, high-minority inner-city middle school in Texas. Social justice leaders from both institutions identified a troubling trend: students from the middle school were being increasingly tracked into the juvenile justice system. The proverbial school-to-prison pipeline was not just theoretical, it was a frightening reality.

Osterman and Hafner (2009) contend that a social justice-oriented curriculum views leaders as primary change agents, arguing that "preparation programs should develop skills and dispositions that will enable school leaders to recognize, critique, and change inequitable structures, policies, and practices within our nation's schools" (p. 176). Our case study explores how the school's administrators and teachers along with community partners took the initiative to transform their commitment to social justice into action, implementing a program to change the dismal trajectory of many urban, poor, minority public school students.

Building upon social justice leadership literature, this chapter begins with an overview of what it means to be a socially just leader. We then proceed to introduce our case study, explaining our choice to focus on this particular urban middle school's youth court and its participant leaders. This is followed by a brief accounting of traditional school discipline policy and Texas's heavy reliance on punitive approaches to provide background for the program. For context, existing empirical research on the youth court model is presented. The evolution of the youth court as an alternative to punitive school discipline is discussed along with the restorative

justice framework on which it is based. Using qualitative data collected from the principal, other administrators, teacher leaders, and the law school partners, we highlight the relevant actions of the members of this unique school leadership team to actively change and redirect the educational and social outcomes of students. The chapter concludes with implications for school leaders that want to foster a socially just school culture and how they can turn their commitment into action, specifically in the area of school discipline.

SOCIAL JUSTICE AND LEADERSHIP LITERATURE

McKenzie, Scheurich, and Skrla (2006) argue that part of being a socially just leader is embracing the idea of an "equity consciousness." This equity consciousness occurs when leaders understand that all children can achieve academic success, regardless of race, social class, gender, sexual orientation, learning difference, culture, language, religion, etc. Leaders must recognize that traditional school practices have failed to yield equitable results and may even perpetuate inequalities. For "equity consciousness" to occur, leaders must acknowledge that they are responsible for moving adults in their school community toward a common vision so that students can achieve their greatest success (McKenzie, Scheurich, and Skrla, 2006).

Shepherd and Hasazi (2008) define social justice in the context of the commitment that schools, as institutions, make to provide "access to equal opportunities and outcomes" which help students to achieve "full citizenship and actualization of their full potential" (p. 476). Schools committed to social justice "recognize, understand, and promote the cultural contributions of everyone in the community, including those who have been historically de-valued, marginalized, and under-represented in society" (p. 476).

Put into practice, socially just leaders take their beliefs into action. As Brown (2006) explains, social justice leadership is not just espousing a theory of social critique but entails an actual civic duty to "become active agents for political and social change" (p. 711). Brown (2006) continues that those practicing social justice leadership "challenge exclusion, isolation, and marginalization of the stranger; respond to oppression with courage; empower the powerless; and transform existing social inequalities and injustices" (p. 711).

Educational leaders can utilize the principles of social justice to transform their schools, to work against the wrongs of society rather than perpetuating them. As Dantley and Tillman (2005) explain the use of social justice in education, schools "become the arenas of struggle among multiple points of view, ideologies, and technology, and social justice leaders facilitate an environment where these perspectives are welcomed and are given free course to be voiced" (p. 22). Furman (2012) expands this idea, defining social justice leadership as "action oriented" and entailing "identifying and undoing these oppressive and unjust practices and replacing them with more equitable, culturally appropriate ones" (p. 194). A socially just leader cannot simply identify the problem; he/she must be able to offer solutions to be implemented in the midst of their leadership roles in schools.

WILSON MIDDLE SCHOOL YOUTH COURT: A CASE STUDY FOR CHANGE

According to Stake (1995), a case study has three main elements: description, issue, and interpretation. The purpose of a case study "is particularization, not generalization. We take a particular case and come to know it well, not primarily as to how it is different from others but what it is, what it does" (p. 8). Here, the case is educational leaders operating a peer-run youth court in a Texas urban middle school (hereinafter referred to by the pseudonym Wilson Middle School Youth Court). The practice of the school's leaders in Wilson offer a glimpse of social justice in action because they are actively engaged in trying to eradicate a persistent and sad reality for students in poor, majority minority urban schools—the school-to-prison pipeline. These schools often implement extreme, exclusionary discipline policies that drive students out of the classroom and eventually into the prison system (Cole and Vasquez-Heilig, 2011).

The leaders documented in this case study made a deliberate choice to actively combat the pipeline by creating an alternative to punitive discipline school policy. The youth court was carefully crafted to offer students involved both as volunteers and as referred offenders an option to suspension or expulsion from school. In the youth court process, students learn about acceptance and responsibility. There are consequences for behavior, but those consequences are intended to be restorative learning opportunities, teaching students how to replace their problematic behavior with more socially appropriate responses while keeping them in school and learning. Students help one another—rather than judging and dismissing one another—they seek to understand and uncover the reasons for the maladaptive behavior so that they can fully address its impact on the individual and the school community. The Youth Court is a restorative approach to school discipline that is not simply about punishment.

This chapter is an instrumental case study (Stake, 1995) because it is being used to understand the larger context of social justice leadership in urban majority minority schools. We examine and detail the challenges and successes of educational leaders trying to affect change in a system that often seems complacent in the criminalization of young people into the school-to-prison pipeline. We seek for this chapter to inform the field on how a properly executed youth court can foment socially just leadership in school discipline practice and how committed leaders can truly change what would otherwise be a dismal trajectory for many young people.

Site and Participants

As noted, the research site for this case study was Wilson Middle School (a pseudonym). An urban majority minority Texas middle school, Wilson is a public middle school in a large metropolitan city and part of the city's public school district. The district is one of the ten largest school districts in the state of Texas, enrolling over 100,000 students and comprising more than 120 schools including elementary, middle, high, and alternative schools. Wilson is located in the St. Thomas area (a pseudonym) in the central part of town along an interstate highway. The school opened in the late 1960s, a time when new apartment complexes and subdivisions had changed what was once a rural African-American neighborhood on the edge of the city into a thriving urban community. As the St. Thomas neighborhood grew between the 1970s and 1990s, the demographics of the area changed. In 1970, St. Thomas was a predominately African-American community with a population under one thousand. It is now home to more than twenty thousand people—of which the majority is now Latina/o.

Wilson Middle School currently serves predominately low-income minority students. In 2012–2013, the racial demographics of Wilson Middle School were about 89 percent Latina/o, 7 percent black, and less than 4 percent white, Native American, and Asian or Pacific Islander. Concurrently, 97 percent of the student population at Wilson was economically disadvantaged compared to 60 percent in Texas. About 15 percent of the student population was categorized as special education compared to 9 percent in Texas. English Language Learner (ELL) students were about 42 percent of the population at Wilson, which was more than the state average of 17 percent. Notably, around a third of Wilson students de-enroll during a typical school year, moving to other cities and neighborhoods.

After making strides in academic performance during the 1990s, Wilson Middle School was targeted by the state's education agency, Texas Education Agency (TEA), for school closure based upon multiple years of low student scores on the Texas Assessment of Knowledge and Skills (TAKS). In 2006, Shirley Neeley, then Texas Education Commissioner, placed a state intervention team at Wilson to observe student achievement. In 2007 the school district board of trustees, district administration, and local stakeholders sent a letter to TEA expressing that it was their desire that Wilson continue to serve students in the St. Thomas community and remain open. In 2009, Wilson made a "near miraculous turnaround" to clear state standards and stay open.

Being no stranger to change or interventions, Wilson Middle School leaders embraced the opportunity to be the local progenitor of a school-based youth court project. Wilson offered the perfect site to pilot the program as its middle school students continue to be at high risk for contact with the juvenile justice system in the school district. Despite modest success in recent years, police and local officials have identified the school as having a large gang presence. Understandably, many of its students have already had some kind of interaction with the criminal court system.

School leaders were not the initial creators of the youth court, but they did seize upon the opportunity when it presented itself. Students and a law professor from the local university's law school proposed the idea. The law professor had long been an advocate for young people in the juvenile justice system. She knew the St. Thomas area well and wanted to do something within the community to affect young people's lives. She had read about the success of other youth court programs around the country and felt the time was ripe to introduce something similar in her city. With interested law students from her juvenile justice seminar, she found an enthusiastic group of volunteers to help develop the program.

To combat the school-to-prison pipeline and offer an alternative means of addressing student misconduct in schools, a small contingent from the law school pitched the idea to Wilson's principal. When Wilson's principal was pitched the youth court model, he not only agreed to host the program, he also assigned a teacher to coordinate it in partnership with the law school.

From a law school course project, the students' and professor's original vision grew and became part of both the middle school's curriculum and the law school's pro bono program. What was originally an after-school program become a bona fide elective for students in their regular school day schedules. In three years, Wilson established a fully integrated and operationalized youth court program. The youth court program is now an integral and popular part of Wilson's curricular program and central to the school's student-centered culture.

Law students work with middle school students to run the youth court to address student disciplinary offenses and keep students in their classroom learning environments. As the program has developed, it has also expanded its programming to include a complementing mentoring program that assigns law students as mentors to students who are referred and complete the adjudication process in the youth court.

To uncover the insider commitment to the implementation and success of the youth court, participants in this case study were the school leaders, including the principal, assistant principals, and teacher leaders at Wilson Middle School. In addition, one of the early law student creators and the current faculty supervisor were also interviewed for a more comprehensive understanding of the implications of this collaborative approach to social justice in schools. In total, seven people were interviewed. Each interview lasted approximately one hour. Each interviewee was asked the same questions using a standard interview protocol.

SCHOOL DISCIPLINE BACKGROUND

Over the last several decades, youth crime has steadily declined (Butts and Mears, 2011), but public school approaches to discipline have become increasingly punitive (APA, 2008). With schools across the country continuing to rely on zero tolerance policies to address student behavior, growing numbers of children are finding themselves suspended and expelled from educational institutions as well as referred to the juvenile justice system (ACLU, 2009; Martinez, 2009). Imposing harsh sanctions on students has resulted in a systematic and pervasive "pushing out" of children from schools into the juvenile justice system. Researchers and advocates alike have questioned the punitive treatment of children in schools and argue that it lays the groundwork for a phenomenon called the school-to-prison pipeline (Leone, Christle, Nelson, Skiba, Frey, and Jolivette, 2003).

The "push-out" of children from schools strongly correlates with higher dropout rates and with increased involvement with juvenile court and the correction system (Texas Appleseed, 2007). Research undertaken within schools on students at risk confirms that poor academic and punitive behavioral practices are closely linked to juvenile delinquency (Justice Center, 2011; Texas Appleseed, 2007). Students in juvenile detention centers are likely to be several years behind their peers academically. Their time in school is often marked by persistent underachievement, unmet instructional needs, and disengagement (Leone et al., 2003). This pattern of behavior tends to escalate over time.

Maguin and Loeber (1996, as cited in Christle, Jolivette, and Nelson, 2005) in a meta-analysis of youth at risk found that low achievement has the strongest relationship to youth crime and that academic problems often bring about behavior problems resulting in the removal of students from academic instruction. These removals perpetuate a cycle of failure whereby students lose access to educational and social development op-

portunities, fall further behind, and become even greater behavioral concerns (Costenbader and Markson, 1998). As indicated in a recent report from the American Psychological Association,

> Schools with higher rates of school suspension and expulsion appear to have less satisfactory ratings of school climate, less satisfactory school governance structures, and to spend a disproportionate amount of time on disciplinary matters. Perhaps, more importantly, recent research indicates a negative relationship between the use of school suspension and expulsion and school-wide academic achievement, even when controlling for demographics such as socioeconomic status. (APA, 2008, p. 854)

For schools, there are some perverse incentives to push these students out and keep them out. Within the high-stakes testing accountability system, schools can suffer dire consequences if their students fail to meet certain academic standards (Cole and Vasquez-Heilig, 2011). Low-performing youth are an albatross for schools. When those youth bring with them real or perceived behavior problems, it is not surprising that schools are often hesitant to embrace them (Vasquez-Heilig and Darling-Hammond, 2008).

Often, students find themselves on a continuum of disciplinary action. That is, once a child has been labeled a "troublemaker," it is very hard for them to escape the stereotype. The cycle has begun and it is difficult, if not impossible, to stop it. Impediments to students successfully reentering school and completing their education magnify the school-to-prison pipeline, increasing the likelihood that students will find themselves back in the juvenile justice system or worse, graduating into the adult prison system (Greenwood, 2008).

Given the potential disastrous effect of current exclusionary discipline policy, educators and policymakers have been keen to seek out viable alternatives for the system. Many of these alternatives are based on a restorative justice model that attempts not to impose arbitrary consequences as a deterrent for misconduct but rather educate the offending student and discourage future misconduct through supportive services that teach and foster pro-social behavior (Hirschinger-Blank et al., 2009; Varnham, 2005). With increasing regularity, youth courts are being offered up as an alternative to exclusionary discipline policy. Youth courts have been in existence for thirty years, but during the last decade they have become the most replicated juvenile justice program for non-violent offenders (Schneider, 2008).

The Texas Context

Texas has the largest number of children subjected to corporal punishment in the United States. In 2006–2007, of the 223,190 students that received corporal punishment, 49,197 of those students attended Texas schools (Human Rights Watch and ACLU, 2008). The numbers show a strong preference for an overly punitive approach to discipline. This is exemplified by the statistics related to Texas' school-to-prison pipeline—Texas school districts suspend, expel, or refer at-risk minority students to alternative schools at disproportionately higher rates compared to the overall population.

In Texas, the likelihood of a child receiving a disciplinary referral depends more on the school attended (i.e., poor, minority) than the nature of any offensive behavior. For example, in 2007–2008, Texas public schools removed more than 100,000 students from school and sent them to alternative disciplinary placements; two-thirds of the 100,000 students were removed at the discretion of local school districts not for behavior for which removal was mandated by law (Hogg Foundation, 2008; Southern Poverty Law Center, 2007; Texas Appleseed, 2009).

The Youth Court Research and Model

The youth court model in many ways mirrors traditional adult courts. Teachers, school officials, or police can offer juveniles the option of youth court following their arrest, or after referrals. The model of the youth court described in this paper to a large extent follows that of youth courts around the country. To qualify for the youth court, juveniles must admit guilt. The youth court is responsible for determining the consequences of the action, taking into account any material put before it by the juvenile or other parties. The entire court, including judge, attorneys, jurors, bailiff, and clerk, are student peers. If a juvenile declines to go to youth court, he or she may be subject to a referral to juvenile court, a criminal record, and the penalties that may be imposed including fines and possible confinement to a juvenile detention center (Poch, 2000).

According to the research, the main goal of youth court and what distinguishes it from traditional courts is its attempt to prevent the criminalization of students by directing them away from the formal intake of the juvenile justice system. With youth court, they will not have a criminal record nor be subjected to the more constraining conditions imposed by a real court of justice. Youth courts create a different pathway for addressing student misconduct. In a sense, they reject traditionally held views about the management of student behavior and more importantly, the superiority of the teacher and administrator to determine appropriate consequences for students.

The youth court model is based on a restorative justice underpinning (Godwin, 2001). Restorative justice, in turn, is supported by core restoration values. These values reflect the underlying beliefs that: 1) children are rich resources who can benefit communities; 2) young people are educators' social equals; 3) children can develop problem-solving skills, pro-social character traits, and healthy self-concepts; 4) children's physical, educational, social, spiritual, and emotional needs must be met; 5) families are the best environments for healthy development of children, but everyone can help; and 6) every child succeeds; no child fails (Brendtro, Ness, and Mitchell, 2001, pp. 156–158).

The supporters of the peer-run youth court believe that a discipline model run by youth will be more effective in addressing problem behavior and deterring future misconduct. Students who do not necessarily represent the high-achieving and well-behaved contingents of the school population are encouraged to volunteer for the program. The idea is to have a mix of students running the court, from the natural leaders to the "troublemakers." In this way, students referred to the court will see those assisting and judging them as peers they can relate to from the honors students to those who have taken a more circuitous reformed approach. The architects of youth courts strongly design their programs in an effort to decrease referrals to the juvenile courts and ultimately decrease problem behavior as students take responsibility not only for their own actions, but also for those of their fellow students through their participation in a student-run system (Ashworth et al., 2008). As youth courts continue to take shape around the country, the assumptions of its advocates seem to be true. They are indeed, an alternative to the proverbial school-to-prison pipeline (Cole and Vasquez-Heilig, 2011).

In Their Own Words: Youth Court Leaders Articulate Social Justice

While there is little agreement on an exact definition of social justice (McKenzie et al., 2008), there are certain elements or principles of social justice leadership that the scholars universally acknowledge. To help illuminate the actions of those involved in the Wilson youth court, the authors have extrapolated from the social justice literature six principles for practice that seem to cut across the literature on social justice leadership: (1) social justice leaders are change agents; (2) social justice leaders share an equity consciousness; (3) social justice leaders believe all students can contribute to the community; (4) social justice leaders are political and social strategists; (5) social justice leaders see schools as arenas for change and; (6) social justice leaders offer solutions. Relying on these six principles, what follows are quotes and descriptions of actions taken from those involved in the Wilson Middle School Youth Court exemplifying how these individuals turned theory into reality.

Social justice leaders are change agents. The people behind the Wilson youth court truly believe that their program can make a difference in young people's lives. They understand that the students in their school may be perceived as having limited choices, but regardless of their income, the color of their skin, the language they speak, or their family history, anything is possible. As one vice principal explained,

> We have many kids from broken homes. We have kids that struggle with English. Half our kids, their second language is English. So, they are working hard. They come with a lot of stress . . . so positive things, like letting them know there are people here for them and there are ways to work through problems positively and that people can change and do better. They have hope. That is a big thing to have hope. And also, to change that paradigm. Youth court gives them a chance to visit the university and the legal system. They change that paradigm that is about I will always do what my parents have done. For many that is clean houses, construction . . . there is nothing wrong with that, it is just that they can open their minds to yes, I can go to college and yes, I will go to college. I can be an advocate for people and hopefully, that will be a grain in them to become better citizens. That is the end goal but the change is just the step by step of just being better, being better students, which will lead to more success.

There is no quiet acceptance on the part of the staff at Wilson that their students will simply be the failures in the statistics—the high-risk students who never graduate and too often populate our prisons. The principal, who has been involved with the youth court since its inception, railed against any blanket dismissal of his students or their abilities. He proudly claimed, "We have awesome students." Many would run away from leading a school that had been targeted for closure, but Wilson's principal faced that challenge head on and was able to raise test scores to meet federal standards. When he speaks about the challenges students face outside of school, he understands that those circumstances are hard to change but is quick to add that school can be different and that part of his job is to acknowledge that "so much is going on in our community." But, he notes, "we have a lot of services here to support our kids" and "those services are what make the difference."

Social justice leaders share an equity consciousness. The community leaders represented by the law school partners of the youth court were very aware from the beginning that schools did not treat all students equally and that injustices in the legal system were being mirrored in school disciplinary policy. When speaking about the youth court, the law faculty member who oversees the program stated, "We are presenting a whole new framework for dealing with conflict, breaking the rules. We need to create a whole new context." In explaining that statement, the supervisor noted that the students who are part of the youth court come from backgrounds in which the institutional responses of the education system are not familiar and may even conflict with the cultural backgrounds of the students. Being a member of a minority group herself, the supervisor could understand how students might perceive that they are not welcomed in a school and that their differences mean they can never meet the institution's expectations. She strongly disagrees with this approach and uses her own experience to inform the youth court. The youth court "teaches students new ways to act and to manage problems. It gives them the tools they need to succeed."

A Wilson vice principal spoke at length about the disconnect many students feel between their home and school experience.

> A lot of my kids are from families living with families. There are seven or eight people in a one-bedroom

apartment. It is extremely difficult. A lot of my kids become parents when they leave here. They have to take care of younger siblings. They come from single-parent homes. They leave here and they become Mom and Dad. They leave here and they are the adult in the family. It makes youth court a need. We have kids in youth court because out in the real world, they have to be grown-ups and then they come here [to school] and we don't want them to talk like that. It is really difficult for them to deal with this and when we have youth court, it helps them to realize their place in this school and have their peers help them and show them what they expect them to be; it is extremely helpful.

It was apparent in the interviews that the school leaders realized they must share an equity consciousness in school discipline practice rather than one of a deficit-orientation and punitive responses.

Social justice leaders believe all students can contribute to the community. Throughout the school and community leadership there is tremendous personal support for the students. As one school administrator simply stated, "People here are so invested in these kids." There is a strong-held belief that even kids making bad choices can turn things around and give back. A key component of the youth court program is to have students who were formerly referred to youth court for discipline problems come back and pay it forward by serving as volunteers for the court to help other students. They can serve in any capacity on the youth court. They may come back as jurors, attorneys, and even as judge.

Those involved with the youth court see the program as a second chance and a way to communicate to students that they have worth and that people do care about them. As the teacher leader of the youth court mapped out its purpose,

> I see youth court as a group of peers and adults surrounding the students to help pick them up, to put them where they need to be. If you are on the wrong path, youth court can, in a very positive way, edge you the other way.

Social justice leaders are political and social strategists. Trying to address a systemic problem like the school-to-prison pipeline is definitely a challenge. In Texas, where punitive discipline policies are the norm, going against accepted practice requires a strategic

mind. The principal at Wilson understands this. When he agreed to bring the youth court to his school, he made sure that his bosses would see it as a "win-win" situation. Relying on support from the law school through their students and staff, the first year of the program was offered after school using a teacher volunteer. Once the youth court gained popularity and began to show results with the students, he was able to include the program as an elective slot in the regular school day timetable.

From the law school's perspective, the leaders are pleased with the progress and acceptance of the youth court program. However, they are also realistic about its place and aware that other changes in schools still need to occur for true equity and fairness for students. As the former law student who now coordinates the program acknowledged,

> This is a problem of scale. Youth court can be a vehicle to help change things. [But], we can only do so much. I think youth court cannot be the sole mechanism for dealing with school discipline. It needs to be integrated into a more comprehensive system.

True to her words, the coordinator also volunteers her time to represent students in disciplinary matters, mentors at-risk youth, and continues to be involved with a number of agencies and advocacy groups that are lobbying for change in Texas' school discipline policy.

Social justice leaders see schools as arenas for change. While there may be limitations to how much the youth court can accomplish with respect to a complete reversal of the school-to-prison pipeline, those involved with youth court see the power that the school can have in redirecting children's lives. As the Wilson principal voiced in his description of what the school (and his staff) can do to assist students,

> We have to be sure we are meeting the needs of students both socially and academically. We know kids are coming to school with things that are part of their environment and we have a lot of kids that have a lot of situations that are beyond their control and that affects their behavior at school. We have a lot of services at our school that we can provide . . . we have a spectrum of scenarios but students with a lot of potential. With the right support, they can really excel.

The law school leaders who brought the youth court to Wilson understood the potential to affect change at the school level. Instead of taking traditional legal rights, such as civil rights complaints or court action, they chose to develop a school-based program that could engage and empower students to change their own pathways.

Social justice leaders offer solutions. The youth court was firmly established as an alternative to the school-to-prison pipeline. Most of the literature on this phenomenon has been largely descriptive, documenting the problems with the system but offering little by way of solutions. For the leaders of the Wilson youth court, action was the only solution. They developed youth court specifically as a tool to combat the school-to-prison pipeline, and every leader interviewed for this chapter articulated a clear connection between the program and the school-to-prison pipeline.

A number of the school administrators indicated how important youth court was as an alternative to traditional punitive options that are commonplace in the Lone Star State and elsewhere. The Wilson youth court truly is a solution for those struggling to find positive ways of dealing with problematic student behavior. As one vice principal honestly proffered, "I don't know what we would do without youth court. It gives us an option." The leaders who rely on youth court rely on it as a real mechanism for change. It is not just another program or silver bullet flying by—it is a restorative justice solution for so many students whose traditional options are far less than ideal.

CONCLUSION

When social justice is placed at the core of how school leaders operate and function, a paradigm shift must occur. The cultural and organizational aspects of schools and communities must also fundamentally change. This requires a strong sense of will and purpose. Paradigm shifts, such as limiting punitive disciplinary approaches, are not easy in the current "no excuses" educational policy environment. To facilitate the notion of restorative justice in disciplinary policy, school leaders need to identify not just their goals but the foundations of those goals. A surface understanding will not suffice. Change in school disciplinary policy requires a fully informed consciousness, a true equity consciousness. School leaders must serve as change agents, helping others to recognize, access, and buttress the abilities of each student and providing each one with the opportunity to succeed via school disciplinary policy.

Instigating a paradigm shift from punitive to restorative school disciplinary policy can be a slow and painful process, but important improvements can and do take place (Cole and Vasquez-Heilig, 2011). At the Wilson youth court, change is happening as the program evolves and expands. The positive school response from the teachers and students taking part in the program is paving the way for the court to be scaled up and operationalized at another school. This will provide important comparative data for the program and help substantiate what is already observed by school leaders at Wilson Middle School—students are staying in class and learning not being excluded from instruction and set on the path to dropping out or, worse, sitting in a county jail cell. Students are also learning about what it means to build relationships and how to foster trust and respect in the classroom—in their school and beyond.

The vision of Wilson's principal is having a ripple effect. Seeing the strengths of his students, rather than their deficits, he was determined to provide them with the tools they needed to succeed, to stay in school and to never head down the destructive path to prison. Thus, the youth court is not just an alternative discipline program—it is something much greater—a reflection, an inspiration to greater ideals of social justice in majority minority urban middle schools. The youth court is school reform in action and exemplifies how the tireless dedication of school and community leaders working together can lead to social justice in action.

REFERENCES

American Civil Liberties Union. (2009). *School to prison pipeline: Talking points.* Retrieved from www.aclu.org/print/racial-justice/school-prison-pipeline-talking-points.

American Psychological Association Zero Tolerance Task Force. (2008). Are zero tolerance policies effective in the schools? An evidentiary review and recommendations. *American Psychologist, 63*(9), 852–862.

Ashworth, J., Van Bokern, S., Ailts, J., Donnelly, J., Erikson, K., and Woltermann, J. (2008). The restorative justice center: An alternative to school detention. *Reclaiming Children and Youth, 17*(3), 22–26.

Brendtro, L., Mitchell, M., and Ness, A. (2001). *No disposable kids.* Bloomington, IN: Solution Tree.

Brown, K. M. (2006). Leadership for social justice and equity: Evaluating a transformative framework and andragogy. *Educational Administration Quarterly, 42*(5), 700–745.

Butts, Jeffrey A. and Mears, D. (2011). Trends in American Youth Crime. pp. 23–52 In Juvenile Justice and Delinquency, edited by David W. Springer and Albert R. Roberts. Sudbury, MA: Jones and Bartlett.

Christle, C. A., Jolivette, K., and Nelson, C. M. (2005). Breaking the school to prison pipeline: Identifying school risk and protective factors for youth delinquency. *Exceptionality, 13*(2), 69–88.

Cole, H. A. and Vasquez-Heilig, J. (2011). Developing a school-based youth court: A potential alternative to the school to prison pipeline. *Journal of Law and Education, 40*(2), 305–321.

Costenbader, V. and Markson, S. (1998). School suspension: A study with secondary school students. *Journal of School Psychology, 36*(1), 59–82.

Dantley, M. E. and Tillman, L. C. (2005). Social justice and moral transformative leadership. In C. Marshall and M. Oliva (Eds.), *Leadership for social justice: Making revolutions in education*. Boston: Allyn and Bacon Publishers.

Furman, G. (2012). Social justice leadership as praxis: Developing capacities through preparation programs. *Educational Administration Quarterly, 48*(2), 191–229.

Godwin, T. M. (2001). *The role of restorative justice in teen courts: A preliminary look*. Lexington, KY: American Probation and Parole Association.

Greenwood, P. (2008). Prevention and intervention programs for juvenile offenders. *The Future of Children, 18*(2), 185–210.

Hirschinger-Blank, N., Simons, L., Volz, G. L., Thompson, R., Finely, L., and Cleary, J. (2009). *Juvenile and Family Court Journal, 60*(2), 31–47.

Hogg Foundation for Mental Health. (2008). School discipline and children with serious emotional disturbances [Web page]. Retrieved from www.hogg.utexas.edu/programs_SpecialEd.html.

Human Rights Watch and American Civil Liberties Union. (2008). A violent education: Corporal punishment of children in US public schools. Retrieved from www.specialed-connection.com/.

Justice Center. (2011). *Breaking schools' rules: A statewide study on how school discipline relates to students' success and juvenile justice involvement*. New York: Council of State Governments.

Leone, P. E., Christle, C. A., Nelson, C. M., Skiba, R., Frey, A., and Jolivette, K. (2003). *School failure, race, and disability: Promoting positive outcomes, decreasing vulnerability for involvement with the juvenile delinquency system*. Washington, DC: National Center on Education, Disability and Juvenile Justice.

Martinez, S. (2009). A system gone berserk: How are zero-tolerance policies really affecting schools? *Preventing School Failure, 53*(3), 153–157.

McKenzie, K. B., Christman, D. E., Hernandez, F., Fierro, E., Capper, C. A., Dantley, M. E., Gonzalez, M. L., and Scheurich, J. J. (2008). From the field: A proposal for educating leaders for social justice. *Education Administration Quarterly, 44*, 111–138.

McKenzie, K.B., Skrla, L., and Scheurich, J. J. (2006). Preparing instructional leaders for social justice. *Journal of School Leadership, 16*(2), 158–170.

Osterman, K. and Hafner, M. (2009). Curriculum in leadership preparation: Understanding where we have been in order to know where we might go. In M.D. Young, G.M. Crow, J. Murphy, and R.T. Ogawa (Eds.), *Handbook of research on the education of school leaders* (pp. 269–317). New York: Routledge.

Poch, T. (2000). Alternative sentencing programs for teenagers. *Clearing House, 74*(2), 60–61.

Schneider, J. (2008). *Youth Courts: An empirical update and analysis of future organizational and research needs*. Washington, DC: The George Washington University, Hamilton Fish Institute. Retrieved from hamfish.org/Publications/Serial/HFI_Youth_Courts_Report.pdf.

Shepherd, K. and Hasazi, S.B. (2008). Leadership for social justice and inclusion. In L. Florian (Ed.), *The sage handbook of special education*, (pp. 475–485). Los Angeles: Sage.

Stake, R. (1995). *The art of case study research*. Thousand Oaks, CA: Sage Publications.

Southern Poverty Law Center. (2007, November 11). *SPLC launches 'school to prison reform project' to help at-risk children get special education services, avoid incarceration*. Retrieved from www.splcenter.org/news/item.jsp?aid=282.

Texas Appleseed. (2007). *Texas' School to Prison Pipeline: Dropout to Incarceration. The Impact of School Discipline and Zero Tolerance*. Austin: Texas Appleseed.

Texas Appleseed. (2009). *When my child is disciplined at school: A guide for families* [Report and slides]. Austin, TX: Author.

Varnham, S. (2005). Seeing things differently: restorative justice and school discipline. *Education and the Law, 17*(3), 87–104.

Vasquez-Heilig, J. and Darling-Hammond, L. (2008). Accountability Texas-style: The progress and learning of urban minority students in a high-stakes testing context. *Educational Policy and Evaluation, 30* (2), 75–110.

CHAPTER 23

Actions Matter

How School Leaders Enact Equity Principles

Jessica G. Rigby and Lynda Tredway

The education research and practice communities are in agreement: school leadership is of central importance for what happens in schools. Effective school leaders are the connective tissue in school reform, and substantial consensus among researchers verifies the importance of school leadership in influencing teacher practice to improve student outcomes (Branch, Hanushek, and Rivkin, 2012; Bryk, Sebring, Allensworth, Luppescu, and Easton, 2010; Darling-Hammond, LaPointe, Meyerson, Orr, and Cohen, 2007; Knapp et al., 2003; Knapp, Copland, Honig, Plecki, and Portin, 2010; Leithwood and Louis, 2012; Leithwood, Harris, and Strauss, 2010; Leithwood and Sun, 2012; Louis, Leithwood, Wahlstrom, and Anderson, 2010; Wallace Foundation, 2010; Waters, Marzano, and McNulty, 2003). Yet effectiveness of school leaders is not completely understood. In the policy arena and in district evaluations, school leader effectiveness is often conflated with value-added measures, which, like the teacher value-added measures, have limited validity and reliability (Loeb and Grissom, 2013).

Nationwide, in both schools of education and leadership standards and evaluation, the focus is on the principal as an instructional leader (see, for example, Bryk et al., 2010; Louis et al., 2010). However, the instructional leadership and accountability frames, while important, do not take into account the underlying or prerequisite leadership actions around equity. We argue this plays a significant role in a principal's ability to set the stage for and produce improvement in instruction and student achievement. This study examines how a group of urban principals (n = 10) enact an equity frame to promote and direct school change. We define "equity frame" as an intentional structure that a principal uses systematically and intentionally to guide decisions about leadership actions and professional interactions when he or she encounters inequities. An equity frame is the visible enactment of an equity perspective or vision and presumes that a principal understands and communicates structural elements that undergird and influence the conditions for effective leadership in instruction and management. We argue that using an explicit equity frame is a foundational element of effectiveness for urban principals. In this study, we explore what an equity frame looks like in effective leadership practice in the context of accountability mandates and requirements, and we make recommendations for how to make an equity vision more visible, tangible, and consistent. Specifically, we seek to understand how principals convey a commitment to a vision of equity in a complex urban school context. Our overarching question was: How do principals convey a commitment to equity at all times and reshape conversations about school direction, instruction, and accountability using an equity frame?

Multiple circumstances may intervene and redefine the direction of leaders who are not solidly situated in an equity frame. Urban principals, facing complex and often urgent situations, encounter multiple and conflicting expectations (Grubb and Flessa, 2006) and look for ways to reconceptualize their work and maintain their persistence. In 2013, a study of urban principals reported that their jobs are increasingly more complex and more stressful; principal job satisfaction decreased by 9 percent from 2008–2012; and they lead teachers whose job satisfaction decreased 23 percent in the same period (Markow, Macia, and Lee, 2013). Principals are pulled by school reform efforts to be instructional leaders without a clear understanding of what that means (Rigby, 2013b). Further, in spite of lack of research on using test scores as an effective way to evaluate principals, many districts, nonprofit leadership organizations, and states are crafting value-added measures to evaluate principals (Braun, Chudowsky, and Koenig, 2010; Loeb and Grissom, 2013). This focus on standardized tests inevitably narrows curriculum (for example, D. Berliner, 2011; Darling-Hammond, 2011; Milner, 2013) and focuses instruction toward one kind of success—that which is measurable on standardized tests.

We know that leaders in urban schools serve in increasingly vulnerable communities that face debilitating effects of economic disparity, structural racism, and spikes in urban violence that affect neighborhoods and schools. Ample research illustrates poverty's impact on multiple facets of individuals' lives, including health outcomes, food security, exposure to violence, and educational outcomes (for example, Lawrence, Sutton, Kubisch, Susi, and Fulbright-Anderson, 2010). Further, it is evident that poverty is not equitably distributed by race; rather, African-American and Latino communities face organizational and social structures that systematically differentiate access to goods, services, and opportunities. In turn, these out-of-school factors dramatically affect school outcomes. Principals in urban settings work with increasing numbers of families that are subject to the effects of intergenerational poverty and multiple other out-of-school factors (D. C. Berliner, 2009; Rothstein, 2004). And while bilingualism is an asset, learning a second language in many schools adds to the complexity of the instructional program, and principals must manage this. These complicate the task of schools and their leaders to deliver on their core educational mission. Yet, despite these prevailing conditions created in communities and districts, we know that all families and children bring significant cultural and personal assets to our schools and communities (for example, Hess, Lanig, and Vaughan, 2007; Kretzmann and McKnight, 1993; Lindsey, Karns, and Myatt, 2010).

At the same time, school districts set seemingly arbitrary expectations for instructional leadership actions, such as spending a minimum of two hours observing teachers per day. These expectations, however, are often ephemeral. One year, after reading one set of recommendations from researchers or reports, a district might shift their expectations from classroom observations to facilitating professional learning communities, or in the case of the principals in this district, a focus on academic conversations as the silver bullet for improvement. Yet,

we know that shifts in instructional leadership practice necessitate time and expertise to build teachers' capacity and see transfer to the classroom, which is often limited at best (Bransford, Brown, and Cocking, 2000; Cobb, Zhao, and Dean, 2009; Cuban, 1990; Kazemi and Hubbard, 2008). The shifting nature of expectations makes it nearly impossible for principals to dig in deeply with their staff and successfully contextualize district attempts at coherence to their schools.

Iterating school district agendas, while trying to create coherence, actually detract from alignment and successful implementation (i.e., Fuhrman, 1993; Honig and Coburn, 2008; Johnson and Chrispeels, 2010). School districts, often with changing leadership, modify vision statements and district plans; and, along with changes in the "reforming again and again" tradition we have come to expect, come strategies, programs, and efforts directed at improving student learning (Cuban, 1990; Grubb and Tredway, 2010). Without a clear and present equity frame, principals can easily get sidetracked by a changing district agenda, neglect the need for school context to be the driver of decisions, and lose touch with his or her principles.

Thus, urban leaders and the teachers who work to bring about substantial changes in student social-emotional, civic, and academic growth within the current accountability climate require a set of knowledge, skills, and dispositions that, while hard to quantify, are palpable, visible, and documentable. This set of knowledge, skills, and dispositions, girded by an equity frame, can support a principal in recognizing the assets and the significant challenges of their communities. As schools in our urban communities face increasingly untenable conditions without the financial and social supports from community agencies and nonprofits, cities, and states that were available a decade ago, we must look afresh at what it takes to be an effective as an urban leader who has and enacts a commitment to equity.

One approach to these formidable challenges is to take a strong and vocal stance on equity. Explicit and clear attention to equity serves as a foundational guide that fortifies and directs the underlying motivations and actions of leaders who make multiple daily and long-term choices to guide teachers in their mutual goals of improved student outcomes (Browne, 2012). We define equity as conditions for learning that interrupt historically discriminatory practices, support democratic schooling, and achieve fair, inclusive, and just outcomes. Further, leadership for equity is acting on those beliefs and understandings intentionally, regularly, and systematically. In this approach, equity needs to be the guiding light for the forty-plus leadership actions (i.e., school schedule, classroom observations, parent meetings, disciplinary meetings, teacher professional development, and providing supervision in halls and cafeterias) that principals enact each day (Horng, Klasik, and Loeb, 2009). Leverett (2002) describes this panoptic focus on equity as being an "equity warrior." He explains:

> Equity warriors are people who, regardless of their role in a school or district, passionately lead and embrace the mission of high levels of achievement for all students, regardless of race, social class, ethnicity, culture, disability, or language proficiency . . . Equity warriors often act outside their formally assigned roles; communicate effectively and persistently with diverse publics to influence the core business of schools and districts; participate successfully in cross-functional teams; work to improve their knowledge, skills, and disposition; engage in risk-taking; and model these values, beliefs, and behaviors for others to emulate in the quest for higher levels of learning for all groups of children and youth.

Given the set of circumstances of urban schools, principals must recognize the importance of equitable access and opportunity for students as a primary starting point for creating the conditions for improved student success, and they must act on this proposition in daily ways through their actions and words (Boykin and Noguera, 2011; Darling-Hammond, 2010).

In this study, we examine the practices of ten principals in an urban West Coast school district. As part of its strategic plan to offer a different approach to leadership professional learning and principal evaluation, the district created a Leadership Task Force (LTF) to create and pilot an administrator rubric to be used for both support and evaluation. The LTF chose to emphasize equity as an underlying dimension of the rubric for school leaders. The ten focal principals in this study were a part of the pilot program, self-selected to be members of the LTF, and, in general, voiced a strong commitment

to creating more equitable outcomes in their schools. By using a best-case logic in choosing our district and principals, or choosing a sample that is the most likely to demonstrate the phenomena we seek to understand (Horn, Kane, and Wilson, under review), we hope to shed light on how equity is actualized in leadership practice. In short, these principals were equity warriors. Here, we attempt to capture the range of practices they enacted. The following research questions guided our study: *How, if at all, did the equity dimension in the Principal Leadership Rubric show up in the leadership practices of the ten focal principals? What does equity look like in the leadership practices of the ten focal principals?*

In this chapter, we first define what it means to be a principal focused on equity and describe two key elements in the process of learning how to be an "equity warrior": first, understanding self, school community, and the intersection in-between; and second, connecting to a larger social justice leadership community. We then explain our methods including details about the school district's process to create the Principal Leadership Rubric. Then, we describe our key findings, both overall with counts and in-depth through qualitative excerpts from video transcripts. Finally, we discuss the implications of our findings as well as the limitations and make recommendations about how school leaders and the programs that prepare them can enhance their ability to be equity warriors.

DEFINING EQUITY FOR SCHOOL LEADERSHIP

Equity is a widely used term in school reform language, and has come to mean different things to different people. We conceptualize equity as a key lever to achieve educational opportunity that focuses on fairness, inclusion, and justice. School leaders who operate with an equity frame "advocate, lead, and keep at the center of their practice and vision issues of race, class, gender, disability, sexual orientation, and other historically and currently marginalizing conditions in the United States" (Theoharis, 2007, p. 222). We suggest two key levers that move from the rhetoric of equity to action: understanding self, school community, and the intersection in-between; and connecting to a larger community of like-minded leaders.

Understanding Self, School Community, and the Intersection In-Between

As leaders of diverse communities, principals must first examine the multiracial, multicultural, and class identities that often influence the ways they intersect with a multitude of different people (Kivel and Zinn, 2002; McIntosh, 1989; Page, 2007; Wise, 2009). Without a firm self-examination of his or her own role in historically inequitable structures, a school leader is not able to authentically engage with his or her school community (regardless of the level of sameness or difference in the principal's and school community's identities). Without examining self and developing the ability to engage others in conversation about their stories of self, a principal cannot hope to create the story of all school constituents (students, teachers, families, support providers, community nonprofit partners, etc.) or support others to examine structural issues once they emerge as the underlying causes of the instructional and achievement concerns (Ganz, 2011).

Second, school leaders must cultivate and maintain a deep knowledge and understanding of the history and culture of the constituents in the school community (Banks and McGee Banks, 2004). This includes a broad knowledge of history and literature, popular culture, youth culture, and specific knowledge of the community where the school is situated. This knowledge is essential for principals to support their teachers in broadening and deepening a common standard of most teacher rubrics—knowing their students as individuals and members of specific communities (Andrade-Duncan, 2009; Danielson and McGreal, 2000).

Third, principals must understand how issues around equity show up both in school structures and in classrooms themselves. They must have a deep sense of how race, class, stereotype threats, and cultural discontinuity both create inequity in discipline systems and classroom practices, and undercut the ability of students and families to engage in schools (Arum, 2003; Boykin and Noguera, 2011; Ferguson, 2000; Foucault, 1977; Lee, 2008; Steele, 1997, 2010; Valdés, 1996; Valenzuela, 1999). Further, in order to insist on equitable access and opportunity to learn in classrooms, a principal has to have an understanding of culturally responsive curriculum and pedagogy, including how home language impacts and supports learning (Banks and McGee Banks, 2004; Dutro and Moran, 2003; Gay, 2000; Hollie, 2012;

Jones and Vagle, 2013; G. Ladson-Billings, 1994, 2006; Menkart, Murray, and View, 2004). Finally, principals need experience in and ability to facilitate complex conversations in their school environment that simultaneously keep people in difficult conversations while also fostering diverse ideas and identities (Browne, 2012; Byrne-Jimenez and Thompson, 2012; Eubanks, Parish, and Smith, 1997; Gooden and O'Doherty, 2013; McKenzie and Scheurich, 2004; Singleton and Linton, 2006; Tredway and Maxis, forthcoming). This is especially true as principals must often serve as a broker between families and teachers who come from distinct cultural and educational backgrounds (Sleeter, 2001).

Connecting to a Larger Community of Like-Minded Leaders

The role of the principal is a lonely one (Whitaker, 1996). Explicitly using equity as a foundational value in leadership actions places principals as a part of a larger community of social justice leaders (for example, Furman, 2012; Theoharis, 2008). It is important for principals to be able to connect to something larger than the daily urgencies and exigencies of urban schools. Naming equity as a driving force behind leadership actions situates these actions as part of a larger concept, purpose, and social justice movement, thus allowing principals to take more risks, have difficult conversations, and hold themselves and others accountable for the outcomes not only at their schools, but also across the district and broader education community. It places them in an informal social network of equity warriors.

Beyond an abstract connection to like-minded principals, school leaders need interactions with other individuals in similar roles who face similar problems. Research on informal social networks points to the value that these types of connections can serve both to sustain emotional support as well as foster persistence in the implementation of a particular set of practices (Coburn, Choi, and Mata, 2010; Coburn and Russell, 2008; Daly, 2010; Keleher et al., 2010; Rigby, 2013a; Theoharis, 2010). To have input and develop the skills to interrupt typical organizational structures, principals need to hear and use stories of change from colleagues that support a "moving force for change" (Dewey, 1938, p. 38). Keleher et al. (2010) describe how participating in a network of like-minded leaders supports individuals:

Network weaving is a leadership strategy to intentionally introduce and link people together to strengthen their bonds and build bridges among groups that are not already connected, thereby expanding the network's reach, influence, and innovation. These connections also help people self- organize and experiment around common interests, forming many collaborative projects and initiatives.

Further, individual and collective successes are not based on a special or inherent set of skills; few principals are born equity warriors. Intentional efforts by school districts to foster their professional capital and create conditions for professional learning, combined with the right set of peer-to-peer relationships, can support their equity beliefs and practices (Hargreaves and Fullan, 2012). The next section describes the background of our study, including the intentional practices of the school district we studied to foster the types of networks and connections described above.

BACKGROUND CONTEXT

Conditions of income inequality were present in the school district in which this study was conducted. In addition, violent crimes increased by almost 20 percent from 2010–2011 (from 6,652 to 7,962); the number of homicides increased from ninety-five in 2010 to 131 murders in 2012. Further, youth were a substantial part of this violence. In 2007 (the most recent data available), the city was the third in the nation for youth firearm murder, with forty-two youth firearm homicides, or a rate of 47.7 (per 1,000,000 of ten- to nineteen-year-olds) (Gabrielson, 2011). Despite the collapse of social safety nets, the structural issues of inequality and racism that result in a growing education apartheid and re-segregation (Arum, 2003), urban principals are responsible for maintaining resilience in the face of daily tragedy and trauma, or what Jeff Andrade-Duncan (2009) calls perpetual traumatic stress.

It is within this context that the ten principals in this study participated in a Leadership Task Force (LTF) in an urban West Coast school district over a three-year period (varying years for each principal). The school district made a concerted effort to engage principals to investigate the multiple ways that their leadership work could be seen and categorized. In the first year, the LTF developed the first iteration of the Principal Leadership Rubric with eight dimensions of leadership practice and descriptions of those dimensions: equity, vision, relationships, resilience, partnerships, management, instruction, and accountability. In order to develop indicators of practice for each of the elements, in the second year the LTF conducted qualitative analysis of their "on-the-ground" leadership work, based on scripts from videotaping leadership work, in order to understand what these dimensions looked like both in authentic practice and in this particular context.

Some dimensions commonly appear in most leadership rubrics: vision, relationships, instruction, management, and accountability. However, others are either unique to or are more elaborated in this rubric: equity, partnership, and resilience. The Principal Leadership Rubric offers a theory of action about leadership support and evaluation that names equity, vision, relationships, and resilience as the foundational dimensions and posits that partnership, management, instruction, and accountability rely on the foundational dimensions for enactment. In this chapter, we analyze the cornerstone dimension that is used as a frame for the other seven rubric dimensions: equity. (See Appendix A for the Equity Dimension of the Principal Leadership Rubric.)

METHODS

As described above, each principal in the LTF (which included forty principals over three years) was videotaped for sixty to ninety minutes, typically once each in the fall and spring. To reiterate: the principals self-selected to participate in the LTF. The videotapes included a variety of leadership activities such as leading parent meetings, conducting post-observation conferences with teachers, leading teacher professional development, monitoring halls or recess, etc. These videotapes were transcribed and analyzed using codes from indicators of practice and names of practice from the existing Principal Leadership Rubric.

For this study, we randomly sampled ten principals (n = 10) from our larger best-case sample (n = 40) for deeper analysis. We labeled the principals P1–P10, and each of their transcripts a and b. Using NVivo, the authors coded the twenty transcripts just for the equity dimension of the rubric.

Using a modified version of the constant comparative method of qualitative analysis (Glaser and Strauss,

1967), two of the authors first compared their coding along the elements of the equity dimension on the Principal Leadership Rubric (see figure 23.3). Then, they determined trends and patterns in their coding, which they identified as three distinct analytical components: 1) explicit to implicit; 2) macro to micro; and 3) clear to unclear next steps. They used these analytical components to jointly recode the original codes, what Strauss and Corbin (1990) refer to as axial coding. Through discussion and collaboration, the authors created matrices to compare the leadership actions along the three analytical components (Miles and Huberman, 1994). Below are the definitions we used to classify the leadership actions:

- *Explicit leadership actions*: the principal verbalized the purpose of a leadership action as rooted in notions of equity
- *Implicit leadership actions*: the principal embodied notions of equity in action to some degree, but not unequivocally stating it as a central purpose for engaging in the task or action
- *Macro issues*: abstract, structural, and systemic, such as the importance of parental participation, the importance of having a diverse student body, or the structural nature of racism and classism
- *Micro issues*: concrete and actionable, such as how a teacher should re-teach a concept or which students should be tested for extra resources
- *Clear next steps:* individuals with whom the principal communicates appear to have explicit actions to enact following the communication
- *Unclear next steps:* individuals with whom the principal communicates do not appear to have explicit actionable next steps following the communication

From these matrices, the authors selected different sections of principals' leadership actions to highlight the various facets of and range within the frames.

Limitations

Our data present one main limitation: we only see a snapshot in time. While the scripts provide detail of leadership work not often analyzed in this depth, the video scripts remain moments in time and reflect only one slice of the complexities of leadership practice.

Given a different situation, would the principal "show up" differently? This challenge is particularly salient in scripts in which a more typical and equity-neutral narrative for having a conversation about practice is present and principals, who in other scripts demonstrate equity clearly and explicitly, fail to do so in certain circumstances. For example, in a meeting about a grant in which one principal (P10) participates, the grant meeting narrative follows a fairly routine agenda and does not indicate a clear message about equity. It could, but interrupting types of narratives that have such embedded scripts appear to be instances where the principal follows the traditional script, rather than imagining how that type of meeting could be different. Our data could represent the dominant narrative of our principals most of the time, or we could have captured an uncommon demonstration of the principals' approaches.

FINDINGS

The video transcripts of the leadership practices of the ten principals (P1–P10) in this study had varying degrees of evidence of a focus on equity; there was a range or continuum in how equity was addressed and represented in their practice. Our analysis indicates that the equity frame is exemplified in three components of leadership practice and indicate a range of expression of the equity frame: (1) *Explicit to implicit:* Was the equity explicit in the principal's words or actions? (2) *Macro to micro*: Was the leadership practice focused on a macro issue addressing broader systems and structures or a micro issue closer to practice? Does the leader cast the micro issue in a macro or structural context? and 3) *Clear to unclear next steps*: Were there clear or unclear next steps indicated by the response of the other person(s) in the script or the direction of the principal?

In the following section, we illustrate the variety of approaches to invoking equity in leadership practice in an effort to first, describe what "invoking equity in leadership practice" looks like; and second, to argue for the use of explicit equity language with clear next steps. While there is clearly a range within each component of the equity frame, we first describe each script as explicit or implicit, macro or micro, and clear or unclear. We then use the rich qualitative data to illustrate what these practices look like in action.

As discussed previously, the analysis uses a best-case sampling logic. That is, the ten focal principals work in a school district explicitly working to create more equitable structures, practices, and outcomes for their students. Each was a part of extensive and ongoing conversations about what it looks like to be an equity warrior. It is not surprising, then, that all principals in this study had a stated equity stance. Nonetheless, some of the principals demonstrated this more explicitly than others. Based on these analyses, we argue that it is more likely that principals who were explicit about the equity issue and clear about next steps, whether the issue was micro or macro, would be successful equity warriors. That is, they would be more likely to disrupt historical inequities and foster the conditions in which all students encounter more learning opportunities.

Looking across the data, several relationships between the three components of the equity frame emerged. First, all but one implicit invocation of equity was a micro issue, mainly focused on classroom instruction and specific school structures. Explicit invocations of equity were spread along the type of issue, more or less equally distributed along macro, micro, or a situation that addressed both types of issues.

Second, nearly all of the invocations of equity that had clear next steps addressed micro issues (seven of ten, two of the other three instances simultaneously addressed micro and macro issues, and the last instance addressed a macro issue). The opposite was not true in relation to unclear next steps. With respect to lack of clarity, the results were mixed between macro (four), micro (three), and both (two).

There were no discernible relationships between implicit/explicit invocations of equity and clear or unclear next steps.

Figure 23.1 illustrates how each transcript was coded along the three analytical components of the equity frame. While the descriptive data are illustrative of trends, they do not accurately represent the ranges within our dimensions nor do they describe what it

Principal	Explicit	Implicit	Micro or Macro	Next Steps
P1a		X	Micro	Unclear
P1b		X	Micro	Unclear
P2a	X		Micro	Clear
P2b		X	Macro	Unclear
P3a		X	Micro	Clear
P3b		X	Micro	Clear
P4a	X		Both	Unclear
P4b	X		Both	Unclear
P5a	X		Micro	Clear
P5b		X	Micro	Clear
P6a	X		Both	Clear
P6b	X		Both	Clear
P7a	X		Macro	Unclear
P7b		X	Micro	Clear
P8a	X		Micro	Clear
P8b		X	Micro	Unclear
P9a	X		Macro	Unclear
P9b	X		Macro	Clear
P10a		X	Micro	Unclear
P10b	X		Macro	Unclear

Figure 23.1 Explicitness, level of issue, and clarity of next steps

actually looked like to enact equity-focused leadership actions. To paint a more accurate picture of how individuals invoked equity in their speech and in their actions, we rely on the qualitative evidence itself.

Component I: Invoking Equity Explicitly to Implicitly

Of the twenty transcripts from the ten principals, eleven invoked issues of equity (as defined by the Principal Leadership Rubric) explicitly. The examples below show the range in explicitness evident in the leadership practice. To illustrate an implicit invocation of equity, we rely on the script from P3a that was based on a conversation with a school-based intervention team. The meeting addressed chronic absenteeism. First, the principal addressed why chronic absenteeism is an important issue for the school: "I think I have some information of how studies have shown if kids miss so much amount of school that it can really predict their outcomes later; whether they're going to graduate from high school or not." Then, she prepared her teachers and support personnel to have conversations with individual parents (including conducting home visits) to ensure that every child on the chronic absence list got individual attention.

Using the equity dimension on the Principal Leadership Rubric as a guide, this transcript was coded using the indicators of practice on the rubric (all indicators are in parentheses; see Appendix A for Equity rubric). These include: the principal used data to identify a problem (Inventory); framed the problem in the context of the larger context of educational opportunities for students (Framework); took specific actions to ensure educational opportunities for individual students (Equity Actions); engendered dialogue between the school and parents or caregivers (School Community Dialogues); and, finally, assigned specific actions for individual teachers and staff members to address the issue (Collective Action). While the principal never stated explicitly that equity was the driving force behind her leadership actions, designating explicit conditions and directions for the teachers that lead to creating equitable opportunities for all children offered clear and tangible next steps that promoted equity.

Representing a high degree of explicitness, P7's first script describes a meeting with the potential incom-

ing parents. P7 was a principal at one of the few high schools in this district that had a sizable white student population (according to the 2011–2012 demographics on the state's Department of Education website, this principal's school had around 20 percent white students whereas most high schools in the district range from 0.0 percent to 1.5 percent, with the exception of one other high school that had a little less than 10 percent). The meeting consisted of predominantly white parents with children in the eighth grade that attended private schools. The parents were choosing high schools for their children. The principal described her school to this group of parents:

> I strongly believe that [this city] deserves to have a school that meets all students' needs . . . It's a great place for folks interested in a public school . . . Our vision is that all students are involved in discourse, conversations, write, and present their work . . . We celebrate students who are successful with lunch and awards; we meet with parents of kids who are struggling.

A parent asked, "Why not have an academic school? Are kids going to be able to take all the classes they need?" and P7 responded, "I don't want to be a [magnet school] principal. I want to be a principal of a school that serves all students." Her personal commitment was evident through her use of an equity lens to guide the conversation with parents (Framework); she modeled a conversation that interrupted typical inequitable school systems to support an equitable learning environment (Individual Dialogue); and she engaged the parents as partners in the work to take co-responsibility for equitable structures (Collective Responsibility for Outcomes). Further, P7's value of equity was evident through her explicit language, such as her repeated use of "all students" as well as through her response to the parent question. She made it clear to the parents that her school not only served all students, but that it was the goal of the school to do so.

These examples illustrate a range of explicitness around issues of equity. Both examples highlight the principals' actions that were clearly driven by a focus on equity. They differ in how they direct the next steps, however. In the case of P3, she did not specifically use equity language, but equity framed everything she said and asked teachers to do. Her teachers left the meeting knowing exactly what actions they were asked to take, yet not necessarily understanding how their actions fit into a broader equity agenda. In contrast, P7 was completely explicit about her goal of creating an equitable school, although the next steps for parents included fewer directives and would be classified as unclear. While the principal's language indicates she wants parents who have children from more advantaged circumstances to know that tracking and privileging are not acceptable for the school's vision, the parents' next steps were more abstract: they could elect to send their children to the school or not. These examples illustrate the complexity of the intersections of these components of analysis, and, more broadly, of the implementation of equity actions as a school leader.

Yet, we argue that an explicit invocation of equity is more likely to lead to more just, inclusive, and fair opportunities for children, even in the case of implicit equity with clear next steps. For example, there are two potential benefits if P3 had been more explicit about why she was asking her team to take the specific actions she advocated. First, her staff would have had the opportunity to understand a bigger picture behind their micro actions, and potentially they could have connected this understanding to other actions in the future. In effect, she would have been bringing them into the equity loop. Second, she would have been connecting her own actions with that of the larger network. As discussed previously, this type of connection may have situated her as a part of something larger, thus supporting her in otherwise isolating and risky work.

On the other hand, P7 spoke explicitly, but about a macro issue that did not allow for specific direction for the parents. Yes, they had the choice to either send their children to the school or not, but in the realm of actions that work toward creating more equitable outcomes for all children, her call is less actionable than those for the individuals in P3's school. These examples speak at once to the limitations in our data in that we only capture small moments in the life of these principals, and to the complexity of these issues. Rather than ranking one principal's invocation of equity as "better" than another's, at least in this case we hope that the examples highlight the various ways in which the principals invoked equity in their practice along the explicitness component while concurrently illustrating that the components overlap.

Component II: Micro to Macro

School leaders engage with a wide variety of issues on a daily basis, such as classroom instruction, a fight in the hallway, allocating resources, and meeting with parents. These issues range from concrete and actionable, what we term "micro" to structural and systemic, or "macro." The data highlighted that the more micro the issue, the less likely a principal was to speak out about equity explicitly. Take the above example of P3 working to break patterns of chronic absenteeism. While a macro issue is at its core, achievement linked directly to attendance (Bryk et al., 2010), the script addresses a micro issue: the group wrote a list of individual children and families, discussed possible issues that caused the absenteeism, and created individual follow-up plans. As indicated, the principal did not explicitly link this to an equity platform or school vision. The role of the principal was to direct the technical follow-up actions of the teachers and herself to address the issue; she did not explicitly use this time to discuss how chronic absenteeism is directly linked to achievement for those students and for the school. She does not specifically support teachers in understanding that many out-of-school factors are at the root cause of the absenteeism and they are dealing with a symptom. The script, then, addresses a specific micro issue.

Another example of a micro incident with implicit notions of equity is a post-observation conference between P2 and a teacher. Below is part of the conversation:

Teacher: The makeup of the class is [not as strong as other classes]

P2: Low

Teacher: Low . . . still working on

P2: With that being said and watching other classes . . . those classes talk more to each other. This class doesn't really talk to each other like the other classes.

Teacher: Yah.

P2: In the other classes, I see you use the equity sticks and you did not do that with them. . . . what I would suggest . . . this notion called wait time, but even more than that, get in the habit of telling them to turn to partner and see if that gets them in the habit. Not jumping out of order, but there is this thing about how kids think about themselves as learners. This may be a low-skilled class, ten out of twelve said that they could get better by learning. . . . So there is something that gets them to believe they can get better at math.

This script focuses on a micro instructional issue on the surface: getting a teacher to use equity sticks, wait time, and turning to talk to a partner. Here, the principal does not state the shift in instruction as one explicitly about equity (i.e., "You do not give your low students equitable learning opportunities!"), yet his framing of the issue, "This class doesn't really talk to each other like the other classes" is one about equity. P2 addresses a macro issue, low expectations, through a specific and actionable micro instructional practice. He emphasized that the teacher should have similar practices with both classes (Framework); he facilitated and modeled in conversation the types of choices the teacher should be making to make his classroom more equitable (Individual Dialogue); and, later in the same conversation, he pressed the teacher to use a common strategy as the rest of the math department (students saying a second sentence for any answer they share in class) (Civic Capacity).

This script again illustrates the complexity in how principals invoke issues of equity in their practice. P2 explicitly addressed a micro issue, equitable participation of students in a particular teacher's classroom. He also implicitly addressed a macro issue, teachers' low expectations for lower-skilled students. Earlier, we argued that explicitly naming equity issues is preferable as it is more likely that others will take up the practices in their own work. Yet in this scenario, P2's tacit pushing on his teacher's inequitable practices was likely more effective than "calling him out," which may have led to defensiveness and an inability to hear the feedback at all. While we continue to press on the benefit of explicitly naming leadership actions and practices in schools as more likely to forward the equity frame, we also recognize the complexity surrounding issues of equity and that there are situations that may call for more subtlety. We wonder how this principal might have invoked an equity lens for this first-year teacher without personalizing his practice as inequitable so as to cast the dilemmas of practice in a larger equity frame.

Five of the scripts addressed what we call "macro" issues, or those that address larger school systems, values, or problems of practice. Like the micro issues, these offer a variety of enactments of macro issues. Some were presentations to constituents that voiced equitable values for the organization whereas others focused on

the general importance for parents' involvement in their children's daily work at school. An illustration of the macro-micro range of the equity frame is useful to highlight the depth that the principals' addressed issues of equity along the dimension of the level of issues. The script below (P4) is from the opening of school assembly with parents. The principal described the vision of the dual immersion school, speaking in both English and Spanish:

> our vision is really a vision that is focused on social justice. So what we try to do at [this school]—everything that we do—is really geared to prepare students to be able to take responsibility for their school, for their community, and for the world so that they can create a better world for our boundless. And that is what the work that we have, that we do together, is all about.

She goes on to say that the focus of the school is not on test scores, but on "preparing students to understand each other and to develop community." Here, the principal presents a school vision that is focused on empathy, curiosity, experience, and learning to live in community. Her statement supports democratic schooling for the public good (Element 3 of Equity Dimension), and given the context of an opening-day assembly, the principal positions herself as an advocate for social justice and equity. She sets up a framework of an equity lens to guide future conversations and decisions (Framework). Of course, it is hard to tell from these data if her remarks are rhetorical or if they authentically engage in structures and outcomes that would lead to more equitable practices and outcomes.

In contrast, P9's presentation to her new kindergarten parents both addressed a macro issue, parental participation, and went beyond the rhetorical by setting up conditions and structures that supported full constituent engagement. She spoke both in English and in Spanish. During the first part of the meeting, the principal set up an activity for parents to interact with each other:

> You are in groups where some of you speak only English, some speak English and Spanish, and some speak only Spanish. I would like you to introduce yourselves. And if you want a little support from English to Spanish we can use these frames [points to sentence frames on the board]. Tell the people at your table your name, and what is one hope you have for your child.

She then explained four different structures that the school used to keep parents informed about their children's activities at school. First she described academic expectations and how parents were able to see these in the work their children brought home: "You'll see [high-frequency words] on their homework packets, when we send the poem home every week. And they should be circling or coloring those same words." The parents also had to check their children's homework packets, which they got once a week to allow for families to complete the homework at different times based on their needs. She explained the behavior system and when the school would contact the parents: "If their card goes to red . . . we will let you know. We know that you would want to know if there is something like that going on with your child." Finally, she explained the report card that students received:

> Believe it or not, your kids will get a report card. This is what it looks like. We do, however, have the children come to the report card conference. They are going to sit with you, and they're going to show you what they can do and demonstrate their learning to you in both English and Spanish. We call it student-led conferences, and we're going to do it twice a year. So not only will you get the written report card, but your child will be demonstrating what they've learned and you'll have a chance to set goals with them as well. So this is a really great opportunity to support your children's learning.

P9 began by honoring home languages by speaking both in English and Spanish and by providing structures (sentence frames in Spanish) for all individuals to participate in the parent/caregiver community (School-Community Dialogue/Equity Actions). She publically shared collective processes and actions by explicating each of the systems that the school used for both academic and behavioral classroom expectations for their children, and how they communicated their children's progress with parents. These actions made often-tacit school structures explicit for all parents who might have otherwise not had experience or knowledge about the structures and expectations (Collective Action). Further, she brought parents into the process, thus creating a co-responsibility to maintain the structures (Collective Responsibility for Outcomes). Finally, the report card structure gave both parents *and* children an explicit voice in the education of the children and in the school's structures (Constituency Voice).

Again, when a principal is clear in the macro or micro frame, the next steps seem clearer. However, if a leader does not explicitly invoke equity language, even if he or she is clear about next steps, we posit that there is a missed opportunity to help teachers, parents, and students frame their actions and their conversations in schools as an explicit vision of equity.

An Equity Warrior

We use P6 as one model of a successful equity warrior. As illustrated in figure 23.1, her scripts were both explicit, addressed both macro and micro issues, and had clear next steps. One script is conversation that she had with her assistant principal in which they debriefed a faculty meeting about student discipline issues the school faced. We note that this type of meeting opened the door for more explicit language because it was a place where the principal and assistant principal could be explicit about their vision and equity frames. In the meeting they discussed, teachers stated that they wanted to use Student Study Teams (SSTs) to push students out of the school. Further, the teachers were using the referral system as their main disciplinary tool, sending up to ten students to the office per period. P6 and the AP discussed how to shift the faculty culture away from a behaviorist disciplinary culture that P6 believed undermined their efforts to create a more choice-oriented model and their commitment to use restorative justice that students considered fair and equitable (Amstutz and Mullet, 2005; Arum, 2003; Wolfgang, 2005). She concurrently addressed the macro issue of urban schools' discipline systems generally pushing children out of classrooms and away from learning (Ayers, Dohrn, and Ayers, 2001; Irby, 2013) and the micro issue of how and why these inequitable practices showed up at her school with her faculty. Below is an excerpt from their conversation:

> *P6:* The guiding question always has to be: How is this in the service of kids? The comment at the end about SST about documenting kids out . . . [We need to be] going into these things, we have to exert some control and influence over what happens. One of us has to be in these.

AP: Teachers are like children, and kids do not learn when they are tense . . . the staff is tense . . . I am never going to be able to get to them on [how to change their perspectives].

P6: I think if we do leading and planning about what an SST looks like and what it is we are looking for . . . We can keep doing restorative justice . . . [to teachers] you said these are things you agreed to, we did not impose this on you. I think the other thing it brought up is the leadership team . . . we need to do some reading and reflecting . . .

P6 named the macro problem: the work was not in service of children (Framework). Then, she set out the specific micro ways in which the work was not serving children, and that some teachers wanted to use the SST process to document students out of the school. She then set out next steps for how she and her assistant principal could lead the teachers toward using restorative justice rather than their current practices (Plan for Equity Actions). Further, her plan was focused on building teacher capacity and shifting their beliefs by modeling an SST meeting, building buy-in around restorative justice, and creating time for the teacher leaders to read and reflect on how to shift the culture of the school (Individual Dialogue, Collective Action). P6 laid out clear next steps: she and her AP would be present in SST meetings, model an SST for the staff, and would meet with the Leadership Team to read and reflect.

The principal's plan for a shift in the discipline structure was evident in the next script, from the fall that followed the spring conversation. It illustrates how P6 explicitly addresses issues of equity with students. The script shows the principal in the hallway, coaching students on how to show up differently in the classroom. Several students were kicked out of their classroom for disrupting the lesson. The principal had a twenty-minute discussion with students about how to reenter the class and what they might say to the teacher. She said to one student: "Because now I've got five kids out of one class, that there shouldn't be anyone out of that class. So let's just think about you. What's something that you could do that would help fix this situation?" She coached them and practiced with them what they could say: "Because it made a big disruption. It actually stopped learning and pulled me into it. A bunch of other students—it stopped their learning, too. It stopped your

learning. So we've got to fix it . . . So, Titana, what words would you say?" Her equity focus included the micro attention to how the students and teachers had to change their ways of acting and reacting if the disciplinary space was to become more fair and equitable.

The two scripts from P6 illustrate the principal's focus on equity frame on multiple component levels. She at once discussed the inequitable nature of her school's disciplinary practices on the macro level, "in service of children," and on the micro level by planning teacher learning through modeling and guidance. She was explicit about how issues of equity were important at both the macro and micro levels. She created structures to address inequitable actions for the faculty; she also explicitly described to the students the micro and macro implications of equity.

However, P6 did not become an equity warrior on her own. She was a part of a principal preparation program that taught both theoretical and practical approaches to equitable leadership; she worked in a school district that both had an explicit theory of action around equity and enacted processes and structures for individuals in the organization to design what that theory of action looked like in practice; and she was a part of the pilot project described earlier in this chapter.

DISCUSSION AND RECOMMENDATIONS AND IMPLICATIONS FOR PRACTICE

The findings from this analysis demonstrate the variety in approaches to enacting equitable leadership practices and the complex situations that urban principals face in doing so. We argue that the explicit naming of equity as a stated purpose of a leadership action is more likely to lead to an increase in equitable learning opportunities for students and communities. In addition, the use of explicit equity language could over time increase the likelihood that school constituents (teachers, staff, parents, and students) will develop a common language and framework for school actions. Our evidence indicates, however, that implicit equity language is necessary but not sufficient to move schools toward more equitable practices and outcomes. Rather, our findings suggest that implicit equity language paired with clarity in next steps may be more indicative of change than explicit equity language without clear next steps. At the school level, it is important for principals to set clear expectations for teachers and staff, motivate staff to achieve those expectations, and set up the conditions for instructional change (Little, 1982). Naming the purpose or moral imperative behind their leadership actions, however, is important for teachers, staff, and community to understand that equity is a key driver of school practices. If principals remember to invoke equity as the driver of change, they may, by consistently naming equity across a variety of leadership actions, establish coherency in purpose and vision. As Elmore (2000) states, "Organizational coherence on basic aims and values, then, is a precondition for the exercise of any effective leadership around instructional improvement" (p. 17). If principals name the underlying impact on equity behind any number of decisions, both macro and micro, the value of the equity is reinforced across all practices.

In our findings we provided a strong example of a principal's implicit push for equity tied to clear next steps, P2's case of maintaining high expectations across all classes of children. In that case, his implicit actions were likely more efficacious in the short run as next steps for the first-year teacher than if he had overtly named the teacher's practices as inequitable. However, using an explicit equity frame with the teacher could have connected what the teacher saw as strategies for engagement, which were largely technical or instrumental, to the larger structural issues that an equity emphasis undergirds. Full engagement and participation in classrooms serves an important purpose of schooling: to prepare students for full participation as citizens in a democratic society. Yet, this disconfirming evidence is important in that it illustrates the complexity of being a principal, in general, and specifically a principal in an urban school. When and how school leaders invoke an explicit equity lens is a judgment call in multiple contexts.

Our findings highlight how equity emerged in principals' leadership actions in a wide variety of situations; those that address historical issues of inequity in education, like tracking (Loveless, 1999; Oakes and Wells, 1998), and those that address specific needs of specific children and families, like chronic absenteeism. The examples also illustrate a range of perceived equity outcomes based on the principals' choices, language, and clarity of next steps. It was more likely that individuals would take actions toward creating more equitable schooling when a principal used implicit equity language combined with clarity about what the other school constituents are supposed to do next, rather than when a principal used explicit equity language that was less clear about what to do next. The polemical uses of equity as rhetorical without clear next steps are vague in terms of what the teachers, parents, or students are supposed to do. Figure 23.2 below illustrates the connections between how the principals in our study invoked equity and the potential strength of equity outcomes.

Another pattern emerged across our data: when principals discussed micro issues, they often engaged in a more mainstream frame of discussion. They moved away from an equity frame to one that is more typically used in schools, bureaucratic, and "value-free." Rather than connecting their daily, perhaps ordinary, work to a moral imperative, principals stayed close to the task at hand. This makes sense; principals are extremely busy and often just need to get things done in order to move on to the next task. Naming equity as driver behind actions is also risky, as we addressed earlier in this chapter. Principals must establish trust and a singleness of purpose with their staff and community if they are to

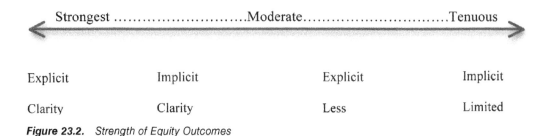

Figure 23.2. *Strength of Equity Outcomes*

connect their daily work with that of a moral impera-tive. This is hard work that requires ongoing support and development.

The following recommendations may support pro-spective and current leaders in invoking an explicit and clear equity frame with specific next steps that support equitable outcomes:

1. School leaders, in preparation and in professional learning, must engage in conversations about

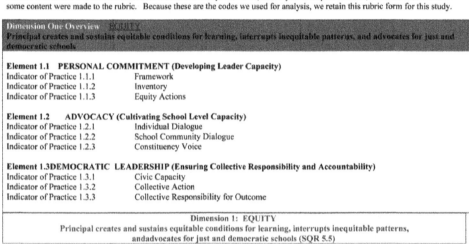

Figure 23.3. Equity Dimension of the Principal Leadership Rubric

identity so that they are comfortable with themselves and others. In order to facilitate conversations about race, class, and equity, they need tools, protocols, and practice. Many of the leaders in this study came from principal preparation programs that had such a focus.

2. Central Office leaders need to model an equity frame for their principals so that principals will do so for their teachers, students, and families. In this case, the district's vision was to interrupt the historical inequities that create lack of opportunity and access for students.

3. The Central Office should set up norms and protocols for equitable conversations that are used both in meetings and classrooms across the organization. In this case, the professional learning practices (the group norms) of the Leadership Task Force were developed with the equity emphasis and that authorized their input on the principal dimensions and supported their work as equity warriors.

4. These findings, and others from similar research, should be shared in digestible form for the principals. In this case, we created a one-page synopsis of the research findings and made recommendations.

There are principals who will maintain a focus on equity throughout their daily work, and receive support and impetus to do so. These are the equity warriors. This study not only examines the work of ten principals, it offers a road map for all principals who take up equity as a major tenet of their work to be more explicit about the equity frame, no matter the context or dilemma, offer clear next steps for others to follow, and remember to cast any micro issue in a larger macro context. These actions appear to help principals maintain a discernible emphasis on equity.

We view this chapter, and the project as a whole, as a beginning. We know that our principals and this school district are moving toward more equitable practices and outcomes, and we also know that it is not without individual and organizational challenges. Further, there are many districts, district leaders, and principals across the nation who are also either working toward becoming equity warriors or who want to engage in the practice, but are unclear about where to start or where to find support. We hope that this study helps to frame the work

while illustrating specific examples of what equity in leadership practice looks like; the study offers specific evidence for those conversations about how to enact equity as a framing tenet of their work.

In terms of research, while our findings indicate the range within the components of invoking equity in leadership practice, further research and analysis could determine more precise attributes of the frames and their interconnections. This research also points to an important and novel methodology used to capture principal leadership actions: video. The video allowed us to see the complexities and interconnections in quotidian principal leadership actions. Future research can further explore the use of video in conjunction with robust leadership rubrics. Finally, we believe it is important to discern the interactions between the formal organizational structures, such as the leadership rubric, the LTF, support for principals from their supervisors, professional development, support from principal preparation programs, etc. and the individual enactments of the equity frame. The exploration of when and under what conditions principals are able to lead with strong equity principles can lead to stronger research, policy, and practice.

REFERENCES

Amstutz, L. S. and Mullet, J. (2005). *The Little Book of Restorative Discipline for Schools: Teaching Responsibility; Creating Caring Climates*. Intercourse, PA: Good Books.

Andrade-Duncan, J. (2009). Note to educators: Hope required when growing roses in concrete. *Harvard Education Review, 79*(2).

Arum, R. (2003). *Judging school discipline: The crisis of moral authority*. Cambridge, MA: Harvard University Press.

Ayers, W., Dohrn, B., and Ayers, R. (Eds.). (2001). *Zero tolerance: Resisting the drive for punishment in our schools*. New York: The New Press.

Banks, J. and McGee Banks, C. (Eds.). (2004). *Handbook of research on multicultural education*. San Francisco, CA: Jossey-Bass.

Berliner, D. C. (2009). *Poverty and potential: Out-of-school factors and school success*. Boulder and Tempe: Education and the Public Interest Center and Education Policy Research Unit.

Berliner, D. (2011). Rational responses to high stakes testing: the case of curriculum narrowing and the harm that follows. *Cambridge Journal of Education, 41*(3), 287–302. doi: 10.1080/0305764x.2011.607151.

Boykin, A. W. and Noguera, P. (2011). *Creating the opportunity to learn: moving from research to practice to close the achievement gap.* Princeton, NJ: Association for Supervision and Curriculum Development.

Branch, G. F., Hanushek, E. A., and Rivkin, S. G. (2012). Estimating the effect of leaders on public sector productivity: The case of school principals. *NBER Working Paper No. 17803.* Washington, DC: National Bureau of Economic Research.

Bransford, J., Brown, A., and Cocking, R. (2000). *How people learn: Brain, mind, experience, and school.* Washington, DC: National Academy Press.

Braun, H., Chudowsky, N., and Koenig, J. (2010). Getting value out of value-added: Report of a Workshop Committee on Value-Added Methodology for Instructional Improvement, Program Evaluation, and Educational Accountability. Washington, D.C.

Browne, J. R. (2012). *Walking the equity talk: A Guide for Culturally Courageous Leadership in School Communities.* Thousand Oaks, CA: Sage Publications.

Bryk, A. S., Sebring, P. B., Allensworth, E., Luppescu, S., and Easton, J. (2010). *Organizing schools for improvement: Lessons from Chicago.* Chicago: The University of Chicago Press.

Byrne-Jimenez, M. and Thompson, E. (2012). Curriculum modules for leadership preparation: Leadership for English Language Learner (ELL) success. Retrieved from ucea.org/instructional-leadership-for-e/.

Cobb, P., Zhao, Q., and Dean, C. (2009). Conducting design experiments to support teachers' learning: A reflection from the field. *The Journal of the Learning Sciences, 18*(2), 165–199.

Coburn, C. E., Choi, L., and Mata, W. (2010). "I would go to her because her mind is math": Network formation in the context of a district-Based mathematics reform. In A. Daly (Ed.), *Social network theory and educational change* (pp. 33–50). Cambridge: Harvard Education Press.

Coburn, C. E. and Russell, J. L. (2008). District policy and teachers' social networks. *Educational Evaluation and Policy Analysis, 30*(3), 203–235. doi: 10.3102/0162373708321829.

Cuban, L. (1990). Reforming again, again, and again. *Educational Researcher, 19*(1), 3–13. doi: 10.3102/0013189x019001003.

Daly, A. (2010). *Social network theory and educational change.* Cambridge: Harvard Education Press.

Danielson, C. and McGreal, T. (2000). *Teacher evaluation to enhance professional practice.* Princeton, NJ: Association for Supervision and Curriculum Development.

Darling-Hammond, L. (2010). *The flat world and education: How America's commitment to equity will determine our future.* New York: Teacher's College Press.

Darling-Hammond, L. (2011). Testing, No Child Left Behind, and Educational Equity. In L. M. Stulberg and S. L. Weinberg (Eds.), *Diversity in American higher education: Toward a more comprehensive approach.* New York: Routledge.

Darling-Hammond, L., LaPointe, M., Meyerson, D., Orr, M. T., and Cohen, C. (2007). Preparing school leaders for a changing world: Lessons from exemplary leadership development programs *Stanford Educational Leadership Institute.* Stanford, CA: Stanford University.

Dewey, J. (1938). *Experience and education.* Indianapolis: Kappa Delta Pi.

Dutro, S. and Moran, C. (2003). Rethinking English language instruction: An architectural approach. In E. Garcia (Ed.), *English learners: Reaching the highest level of English literacy.* Newark, DE: International Reading Association.

Elmore, R. F. (2000). *Building a New Structure for School Leadership.* Washington, DC: The Albert Shanker Institute.

Eubanks, E., Parish, R., and Smith, D. (1997). Changing discourse in schools. In P. Hall (Ed.), *Race, ethnicity and multicultural policy and practice.* New York: Garland.

Ferguson, A. (2000). *Bad boys: Public schools in the making of Black masculinity.* Ann Arbor: University of Michigan.

Foucault, M. (1977). *Discipline and punish: The birth of the prison.* New York: Random House.

Fuhrman, S. (1993). *Designing coherent education policy: improving the system.* San Francisco: Jossey-Bass.

Furman, G. (2012). Social Justice Leadership as Praxis: Developing Capacities Through Preparation Programs. *Educational Administration Quarterly.* doi: 10.1177/0013161x11427394.

Gabrielson, R. (2011). 3rd in nation for youth firearm murder. *California Watch.*

Ganz, M. (2011). Public narrative, collective action, and power. In S. Odugbemi and T. Lee (Eds.), *Accountability through public opinion: From inertia to public action* (pp. 273–289). Washington, DC: The World Bank.

Gay, G. (2000). *Culturally responsive teaching: Theory, research, and practice.* New York: Teachers College Press.

Glaser, B. G. and Strauss, A. L. (1967). The constant comparative method of qualitative analysis. *The Discovery of Grounded Theory: Strategies for qualitative research.* New York: Aldine DeGruyter.

Gooden, M. and O'Doherty, A. (2013). Curriculum modules for leadership preparation: Building a community of trust through racial awareness of self. From ucea.org/building-a-community-of-trust/.

Grubb, W. N. and Flessa, J. J. (2006). "A job too big for one": Multiple principals and other nontraditional approaches to school leadership. *Educational Administration Quarterly, 42*(4), 518–550. doi: 10.1177/0013161x06290641.

Grubb, W. N. and Tredway, L. (2010). *Leading From the Inside Out: Expanded Roles for Teachers in Equitable Schools.* Boulder, CO: Paradigm Publishers.

Hargreaves, A. and Fullan, M. (2012). *Professional Capital: Transforming teaching in every school.* New York: Teachers College Press.

Hess, D. J., Lanig, H., and Vaughan, W. (2007). Educating for equity and social justice: A conceptual model for cultural engagement. *Multicultural Perspectives, 9*(1), 32–39. doi: 10.1080/15210960701334037.

Hollie, S. (2012). *Culturally and linguistically responsive teaching and learning: Classroom practices for student success.* Huntington Beach, CA: Shell Education.

Honig, M. I. and Coburn, C. (2008). Evidence-Based Decision Making in School District Central Offices: Toward a Policy and Research Agenda. *Educational Policy, 22*(4), 578–608. doi: 10.1177/0895904807307067.

Horn, I. S., Kane, B. D., and Wilson, J. (under review). Making sense of student performance data: Mathematics teachers' learning through conversations with assessment reports. *American Educational Research Journal.*

Horng, E., Klasik, D., and Loeb, S. (2009). Principal Time-Use and School Effectiveness. In Institute for Research on Education Policy and Practice (Ed.), *School Leadership Research Report* (Vol. 09-3). Stanford, CA: Stanford University.

Irby, D. (2013). Net-Deepening of School Discipline. *The Urban Review, 45*(2), 197–219.

Johnson, P. E. and Chrispeels, J. H. (2010). Linking the Central Office and Its Schools for Reform. *Educational Administration Quarterly, 46*(5), 738–775.

Jones, S. and Vagle, M. D. (2013). Living Contradictions and Working for Change: Toward a theory of social class–sensitive pedagogy. *Educational Researcher, 42*(3), 129–141.

Kazemi, E. and Hubbard, A. (2008). New directions for the design and study of professional development. *Journal of Teacher Education, 59*(5), 428–441.

Keleher, T., Leiderman, S., Meehan, D., Perry, E., Potapchuk, M., Powell, J., and Yu, H. C. (2010). Leadership and Race: How to develop and support leadership that contributes to racial justice. *Leadership for a new era series.* Oakland, CA: Leadership Learning Community.

Kivel, P. and Zinn, H. (2002). *Uprooting Racism: How White People Can Work for Racial Justice.* Vancouver, B.C.: Friesens.

Knapp, M., Copland, M., Ford, B., Markhold, A., McLaughlin, M., Milliken, M., and Talbert, J. (2003). *Leading for Learning Sourcebook: Concepts and examples.* Seattle, WA: Center for the Study of Teaching and Policy, University of Washington.

Knapp, M., Copland, M., Honig, M., Plecki, M., and Portin, B. (2010). *Learning-focused Leadership and Leadership Support: Meaning and practice in urban systems.* Seattle, WA: Center for the Study of Teaching and Policy, University of Washington.

Kretzmann, J. P. and McKnight, J. L. (1993). *Building Communities from the Inside Out: A path toward finding and mobilizing a community's assets.* Chicago, IL: ACTA Publications.

Ladson-Billings, G. (1994). *The Dreamkeepers: Successful Teachers of African American Children.* San Francisco: Jossey-Bass.

Ladson-Billings, G. (2006). From the achievement gap to the education debt: Understanding achievement in U.S. schools. *Educational Researcher, 35*(7), 3–12.

Lawrence, K., Sutton, S., Kubisch, A., Susi, G., and Fulbright-Anderson, K. (2010). Structural racism and community building. In R. Hofrichter and R. Bhatia (Eds.), *Tackling Health Inequities Through Public Health Practice: Theory to action* (2nd ed.). New York: Oxford University Press.

Lee, C. (2008). The centrality of culture to the scientific study of learning and development: How an ecological framework in education research facilitates civic responsibility. *Educational Researcher, 37*(5), 267–279.

Leithwood, K., Harris, A., and Strauss, T. (2010). *Leading School Turnaround: How successful leaders transform low-performing schools.* San Francisco: John Wiley and Sons.

Leithwood, K. and Louis, K. S. (2012). *Linking leadership to student progress.* San Francisco: Jossey-Bass.

Leithwood, K. and Sun, J. (2012). The nature and effects of transformational school leadership: A meta-analytic review of unpublished research. *Educational Administration Quarterly, 48,* 387–423.

Leverett, L. (2002). Warriors to advance equity: An argument for distributing leadership *Spotlight on student success* (Vol. 709). Calverton, MD: Mid-Atlantic Regional Educational Laboratory.

Lindsey, R. B., Karns, M. S., and Myatt, K. (2010). *Culturally Proficient Education: An asset-based response to conditions of poverty.* Thousand Oaks, CA: Corwin.

Little, J. W. (1982). Norms of Collegiality and Experimentation: Workplace Conditions of School Success. *American Educational Research Journal, 19*(3), 325–340. doi: 10.3102/00028312019003325.

Loeb, S. and Grissom, J. (2013). What do we know about the use of value-added measures for principal evaluation? *The Carnegie Knowledge Network.* Stanford, CA: Center for Education Policy Analysis.

Louis, K. S., Leithwood, K., Wahlstrom, K. L., and Anderson, S. E. (2010). Investigating the Links to Improved Student Learning: Final Report of Research Findings. *Learning from Leadership Project.* St. Paul, MN: University of Minnesota: Center for Applied Research and Educational Improvement.

Loveless, T. (1999). *The Tracking Wars: State reform meets school policy.* Washington, DC: Brookings Institution Press.

Markow, D., Macia, L., and Lee, H. (2013). *The MetLife Survey of the American Teacher: Challenges for school leadership.* New York: Metropolitan Life Insurance Company.

McIntosh, P. (1989). White privilege: Unpacking the invisible knapsack. *Peace and Freedom,* July/August.

McKenzie, K. B. and Scheurich, J. J. (2004). Equity Traps: A Useful Construct for Preparing Principals to Lead Schools That Are Successful With Racially Diverse Students. *Educational Administration Quarterly, 40*(5), 601–632. doi: 10.1177/0013161x04268839.

Menkart, D., Murray, A., and View, J. (2004). *Putting the movement back into civil rights teaching: A resource guide for classrooms and communities.* Washington, DC: Teaching for Change and Poverty and Race Research Action Council.

Miles, M. and Huberman, A. M. (1994). *Qualitative Data Analysis* (2nd edition). Thousand Oaks: Sage Publications.

Milner, H. R. (2013). Scripted and Narrowed Curriculum Reform in Urban Schools. *Urban Education, 48*(2), 163–170. doi: 10.1177/0042085913478022.

Oakes, J. and Wells, A. (1998). Detracking for High Student Achievement. *Educational Leadership, 55*(6), 38–41.

Page, S. E. (2007). *The difference: How the power of diversity creates better groups, firms, schools, and societies.* Princeton, NJ: Princeton University Press.

Rigby, J. G. (2013a). *Beliefs and Informal Social Networks: an exploration of the mechanisms of the meso level.* Paper presented at the American Educational Research Association, San Francisco.

Rigby, J. G. (2013b). Three Logics of Instructional Leadership. *Educational Administration Quarterly.* doi: 10.1177/0013161x13509379.

Rothstein, R. (2004). Class and schools: Using social, economic, and educational reform to close the black-white achievement gap. Washington, DC: Economic Policy Institute.

Singleton, G. E. and Linton, C. W. (2006). *Courageous Conversations About Race: A field guide for achieving equity in schools.* Thousand Oaks, CA: Corwin Press.

Sleeter, C. E. (2001). Preparing Teachers for Culturally Diverse Schools: Research and the Overwhelming Presence of Whiteness. *Journal of Teacher Education, 52*(94).

Steele, C. M. (1997). A threat in the air: How stereotypes shape the intellectual identities and performance of women and African-Americans. *American Psychologist, 52,* 613–629.

Steele, C. M. (2010). *Whistling Vivaldi and other clues to how stereotypes affect us.* New York: W.W. Norton.

Strauss, A. and Corbin, J. (1990). *Basics of Qualitative Research: Grounded Theory Procedures and Techniques.* Newbury Park, CA: Sage.

Theoharis, G. (2007). Social justice educational leaders and resistance: Toward a theory of social justice leadership. *Education Administration Quarterly, 43*(2), 221–258.

Theoharis, G. (2008). Woven in Deeply: Identity and Leadership of Urban Social Justice Principals. *Education and Urban Society, 41*(1), 3–25. doi: 10.1177/0013124508321372.

Theoharis, G. (2010). Disrupting injustice: Principals narrate the strategies they use to improve their schools and advance social justice. *Teachers College Record, 112*(1), 331–373.

Tredway, L. and Maxis, S. (forthcoming). Meaningful conversations. In F. Guajardo, M. Guajardo, C. Janson and M. Militello (Eds.), *Signature pedagogies of the Community Learning Exchange.*

Valdés, G. (1996). *Con respeto: Bridging the distances between culturally diverse families and schools: An ethnographic portrait.* New York: Teachers College Press.

Valenzuela, A. (1999). *Subtractive schooling: U.S.-Mexican youth and the politics of caring.* Albany: State University of New York Press.

Wallace Foundation. (2010). School principal as leader: Guiding schools to better teaching and learning. New York: Wallace Foundation.

Waters, T., Marzano, R. J., and McNulty, B. (2003). *Balanced leadership: What 30 years of research tells us about the effect of leadership on student achievement.* Aurora, CO: Mid-Continent Research for Education and Learning.

Whitaker, K. S. (1996). Exploring causes of principal burnout. *Journal of Educational Administration, 34*(1), 60–71.

Wise, T. (2009). The Pathology of Privilege: Racism, White Denial and the Costs of Inequity. *Challenging Media.* Northampton, MA: Media Education Foundation.

Wolfgang, C. (2005). *Solving discipline and classroom management problems.* San Francisco: Jossey-Bass.

PERSPECTIVES IN POLICY

The face of education is changing and reflecting the needs of the students. In the twenty-first century many educators are collaborating between education and government systems and connecting between research, reform, and sustainability. In these three chapters the authors reflect on the role and the interests of government; the contribution to the state of education and to educational leadership; and the external factors that are underwriting the resistance and reform movements in education.

Is the role of policymaker and the ideological free-market system of government to oversee the interests of the schools and implement reward and consequence system at the cost of student education? And will the deregulated market continue to be influenced by private-sector money? Chapter 24, "Urban Leadership, Neoliberalism, and New Policy Entrepreneurs: Merging Leadership with Resistance" by Gary L. Anderson, Michael I. Cohen, and Milagros Seraus, discusses how urban districts and their leaders face increasing policy shifts due to neoliberal market ideologies. How do educational leaders in the community leverage the power of policy and national organizations to bring to life their vision into historically segregated urban school districts? In chapter 25, "Destiny High School:

Redesigning Urban High Schools for Student Success," Frank Gaines, Ira Bogotch, and Omar Salaam provide the composite of Destiny High School which represents data from thirty-three urban public school educators and their vision of success for urban schooling. And how do leaders perceive government's role when implementing research supported reforms? As a leader connecting the opportunities to utilize government to move change is also an opportunity for sustainable and a base of support when implementing broad changes, such as personalized learning communities. In chapter 26, "Leaders of the New School(s): Reconceptualizing an Autonomy Framework for Urban Principals Implementing Small School Reform," April L. Peters, Jia Liang, and Rejer Finklin discuss framework autonomy to generate high levels of student achievement.

Policymaking plays one of the bigger roles in the reformation of school systems and the distribution of resources. There is a growing dissonance amongst educational leaders who feel that government is not hearing their voices and the voices of the students when making decisions that are meant to support quality education. In this section, the authors articulate the ideas and research to support these constructs.

CHAPTER 24

Urban Leadership, Neoliberalism, and New Policy Entrepreneurs

Merging Leadership with Resistance

Gary L. Anderson, Michael I. Cohen, and Milagros Seraus

INTRODUCTION

This chapter provides an overview of the challenges that urban districts and their leaders face as public policy shifts increasingly toward neoliberal, or free-market, ideology. The authors discuss broadly the evolution of the state's role over the course of the twentieth and early-twenty-first centuries: from providing public services and regulating private sector activities to presiding over a largely deregulated market of private interests. As the state governs public schools from a distance through systems of high-stakes accountability with rewards and consequences, private entities such as for-profit corporations and venture philanthropists enjoy greater influence over education policy and the day-to-day life of the classroom. This greater influence often comes at the expense of decreased input from local communities and a growing business ethic in the administration of public schools. Although neoliberal reforms continue to gain momentum, the authors cite a growing array of resistance efforts stemming from school leaders, teachers, parents, and students, suggesting that dissident voices are beginning to attract an audience. Invoking recent critical literature and a post-structural theory of power, the authors call for a reconceptualization of urban school leadership that entails the notion of productive resistance.

Urban school districts have become sites of experimentation with an array of neoliberal and managerialist reforms. These include high-stakes accountability, school choice, charter schools, mayoral control, data-driven management, public-private partnerships, school policing and surveillance, schools and districts as profit-centers, and digitalization of learning. While suburban and rural schools are also experiencing some of these reforms, their full weight is felt in low-income urban districts, with New York, Philadelphia, New Orleans, Detroit, Chicago, and Washington, D.C. leading the way. These changes have had a dramatic impact on what it means to be an urban school leader.

The system is increasingly controlled from a distance through high-stakes testing with punitive consequences and quasi-markets that are meant to discipline "failing" schools by closing them. Principals and teachers are "empowered" with greater autonomy over hiring and budgets in exchange for greater responsibility for outcomes, but real power is exercised from outside the system through markets and testing. Individual parents are given choices over a limited range of schools, while communities are largely disempowered in many urban districts through mayoral control.

There are signs, however, that growing numbers of teachers, principals, parents, communities, and students are beginning to push back against these reforms, even as they are often confused as to where to focus their dissent. We are seeing forms of resistance to some or all of these reforms at all levels: the classroom, the school, the district, the community, the municipality, state departments, and even at the federal and global levels. This resistance is coming from individuals and small groups, professional organizations, community organizations, advocacy organizations, unions, and bloggers. There have been some recent headline-grabbing events—the Chicago teachers strike, teachers in Seattle refusing to give the state exam, and teacher and principal revolts in Race to the Top states over the use of value-added student assessments to evaluate teachers. Nevertheless, resistance is largely diffuse and inchoate. While we will document more of this resistance below, we are particularly interested in this chapter in how leadership and the field that studies it might be redefined within the context of these increasingly contested reforms. As educational leaders or scholars, we may be approaching the uncomfortable necessity of resisting these top-down reforms. But what would resistance look like for school leaders?

There has been a long history of leaders who have worked against the grain of dominant views of education or in defense of oppressed groups. For instance, Johanek and Puckett (2007) have provided a detailed account of Leonard Covello's leadership in the 1940s and 1950s as principal of Benjamin Franklin High School in New York's East Harlem. His sweeping vision of a community school that honored students' cultural capital and provided a network of resources and civic engagement is exemplary. Like Covello, Deborah Meier and other Coalition of Essential Schools leaders also attempted to resist traditional notions of leadership by bringing a Deweyian democratic perspective to their schools. There are numerous historical and contemporary accounts of African-American leaders for whom leadership was a form of activism and resistance against unjust practices. (Dillard, 1995; Murtadha and Watts, 2005; Siddle Walker, 2003, 2005; Spencer, 2009). The reason that so many African-American school leaders link school leadership with resistance and activism no doubt has something to do with their traditional subaltern role and their view of school leadership as a legacy of the civil rights movement.

In order to understand the multilevel resistance required to challenge neoliberal reforms in education, it is necessary to understand how we arrived at this state of affairs. The following section will provide some historical background to how the neoliberal state came to be so dominant during the last thirty years and how the private sector has triumphed over the public.

THE EMERGENCE OF THE NEOLIBERAL STATE

The second half of the twentieth century in the United States was characterized by marked shifts in the relationship among state, market, and civil society. Post-Great Depression and World War II, there was a need to reconfigure the relationship among the three sectors for the sake of restoring domestic order. Restorative efforts were largely premised on the belief that "a blend of state, market, and democratic institutions [was needed] to guarantee peace, inclusion, well-being, and stability" (Harvey, 2005, p. 10) and that class compromise between capital and labor was necessary.

As a result, "embedded liberalism" emerged, both domestically and internationally, as a form of political-economic organization in which market processes and the activities of the private sector exist within a "web of social and political restraints and a regulatory environment" (Harvey, 2005, p. 11). Within what came to be known as the Welfare State, the State was made responsible for full employment, economic growth, and the welfare of its citizens, and it had the power to intervene or substitute market processes in order to achieve these aims. This interventionist State allowed for the creation of a distinct social and moral economy, one in which labor unions, the political left, and professional associations had significant influence. The initial institution of the interventionist state led to high rates of economic growth during the 1950s and 1960s.

However, by the 1970s, the U.S. and world economy were in crisis due to a mix of factors, including rising inflation and stagnant wages ("stagflation"), unemployment, plunging tax revenues and soaring social expenditures, failed monetary policies, and in the United States, growing military expenditures for the Vietnam War. The embedded liberalism model was under attack from the political left and right. One initial response to the crisis was to increase state control by introducing massive regulatory reforms on capital. The response led to a deepening polarization between those who favored an interventionist state and those who sought to increase market freedoms.

Neoliberalism freed the market from regulatory control and provided an alternative to embedded liberalism. Its discourse and policies became dominant. Harvey (2005) describes neoliberalism as

a theory of political economic practices that proposes that human well-being can best be advanced by liberating individual entrepreneurial freedoms and skills within an institutional framework characterized by strong private property rights, free markets, and free trade . . . [in which] the role of the state is to create and preserve an institutional framework appropriate to such practices. (p. 2)

Buoyed by a sense of economic crisis, partly real and partly manufactured, and the promotion of Milton Freidman's (1962) free market ideology by think tanks and the media, the neoliberal state was aggressively promoted under Margaret Thatcher in Great Britain and

Ronald Reagan in the United States. It spread globally in the 1980s, attacking labor unions and weakening or replacing welfare states that had been in place for three decades. Neoliberalism promotes a new role for the state as it shifts from provider of public services to steerer, referee, and contractor of multiple providers from the state, nonprofit, and for-profit sectors. In the U.S. context, this neoliberal state is made up of a new set of bipartisan policy networks and policy entrepreneurs in education (for example, venture philanthropists, think tanks, lobbyists, etc.) that have gained increasing importance, often eclipsing traditional policy actors, such as teachers' unions, school boards, and professional associations (Anderson and Montoro Donchik, 2014; Scott, 2009).

At the institutional and organizational levels, neoliberalism was manifested as new managerialism or New Public Management, which essentially meant that public bureaucracies should be run more like private sector businesses. Ward (2011) describes the relationship of neoliberalism to New Public Management (NPM):

> Key to the restructuring initiated by neoliberal governments over the past few decades . . . has been an attempt to bring the "bottom line" economic rationality of the marketplace into the public sector. In this transition NPM has become one of the mechanisms through which neoliberals have sought to reconfigure not just the political economy of states but the public institutions where people receive services and work. (p. 207)

School leaders, who have traditionally been viewed as delivering a public service and serving the common good, are now viewed as CEOs promoting a bottom line. And these trends are not limited to the United States; they are global.

NEW POLICY NETWORKS AND EDUCATIONAL LEADERSHIP

Networks of new policy entrepreneurs have influenced educational leadership in a number of ways. In this section, we will discuss several of the major strategies these new policy networks employ: (1) funding from venture philanthropy, (2) alternative pathways to teacher and principal certification, (3) public-private partnerships, (4) edubusinesses and contracting of services, (5) high-stakes testing and quasi-markets, and (6) a "what works" movement based on randomized experiments.

Ball (2008) refers to these networks as a *"global policy ensemble* that rests on a set of basic and common *policy technologies"* (p. 39). These technologies, according to Ball, are the market, management, and performativity, and together they "work to bring about new values, new relationships, and new subjectivities in public organizations—public schools, hospitals, universities, etc." (p. 40). New global policy actors, such as those listed above, in many countries have largely replaced traditional policy actors that were the product of grassroots social movements or professional organizations. These policy networks are creating new forms of governance that promote privatization, business models, and market principles as better ways to organize public education systems. These policy shifts create changes across institutional fields that are manifested at the organizational level and in classrooms as the everyday experience of teaching and leading undergoes dramatic changes. These changes include the ways teachers and leaders are trained, the ways they are evaluated, the curriculum they oversee, and the levels of professional autonomy they enjoy in schools. What follows is an overview of each of these new policy actors.

First, venture philanthropists have aggressively promoted privatization and the creation of quasi-markets in education to replace public bureaucracies (Scott, 2009). As part of this privatization effort, leaders' roles have been redefined from that of public servant to CEO. Among venture philanthropists, Eli Broad has probably had the most direct influence on educational leadership (Saltman, 2009). In fact, his retreats and workshops influenced so many urban superintendents that it is referred to as the "Broad effect." For well over two decades, Broad recruited non-educators into the superintendency and taught business principles such as Total Quality Management (TQM) (Bradley, 1993). In this way, the language of business found its way into the lexicon of urban superintendents, who were now referred to as district CEOs. The new business language, borrowed specifically from the TQM lexicon, included "statistical control of product quality," "empowerment," "outcomes-based accountability," "continuous improvement," "skill sets," and "transparency." This language brought with it a new common sense about teaching and leading, the goals of schooling, and what constitutes an educated person.

Many of the new urban policies implemented in the last twenty years have been supported by venture philanthropy. In the case of New York City, many of Mayor Bloomberg's market-based reforms would not have been feasible without the funding of venture philanthropists like Bill Gates and Wall Street hedge fund managers. With formal community input eliminated, these wealthy individuals became de facto policymakers.

Second, alternative programs of teacher and principal preparation have been created by policy entrepreneurs seeking a nontraditional route to certification. Most of the alternative training programs for principals are run by nonprofits, such as New Leaders for New Schools, or school districts, such as New York City's Leadership Academy. Many "fast track" leadership certification programs have gone entirely online. More recently, the state of New York created the Relay Graduate School of Education, which is a non-university-based graduate school created with the support of Charter Management Organizations in part to train teachers and principals. These alternative leadership preparation programs represent a career track for many young Teach for America alumni who do not see teaching as a career, and who will likely run charter schools or move directly to central office positions (Zeichner and Pena-Sandoval, 2014).

Third, there is a proliferation of partnerships with nonpublic organizations that sometimes function as management organizations (Ball, 2007; Scott, 2009). As a result of these developments, a "third space" in education is forming that combines elements of the public and private sectors, what Emmert and Crow (1988) referred to as "hybrid organizations." For example, with the encouragement of the Wallace Foundation, partnerships with business schools to prepare school leaders are currently gaining popularity (Haslam and Turnbull, 2011).

Fourth, a growing education industry has been promoted that aggressively markets its products to educational leaders. As traditional school districts are replaced by market-based systems of vendors, school and district leaders find themselves targeted by salespeople hawking their products. Principals and superintendents report being marketed to almost daily by vendors claiming to solve their problems of low-performing students, teacher supervision, student discipline, or classroom management. Their wares include cafeteria services, data management and warehousing, educational software, tutorial services, educational design and management, professional development, and transportation services (Burch, 2009; Koyama, 2011). Increasingly, administrators also feel pressured to divert funds from education to pay for private security guards, surveillance cameras, and metal detectors (Anderson, 2007).

Fifth, high-stakes testing and quasi-markets provide a new policy context in which all educational leaders must now work. In many schools, teachers "teach to the test" and leaders "lead to the test." This has placed educational leaders in the position of pitting their educational values against the pragmatism of raising test scores by any means necessary. The urgent need to improve scores has led to the promotion of questionable practices—from expending more energy on the kids on the "bubble" to, in some cases, outright cheating (Jones, Jones, and Hargrove, 2003). Quasi-markets and competition have led to similar forms of game-playing as some charter schools seek to attract "lower-maintenance" students, rejecting more behaviorally difficult students or those requiring special education or ELL services. This new policy represents a new form of governance in which accountability operates through both market mechanisms and placing high stakes on testing and other outcomes indicators (Anderson, 2009). This tendency is supported by a perceived need to "scale up" and quantify everything, which leads to the sixth way the new policy entrepreneurs have influenced leadership.

An evidence-based, "what works" movement promotes randomized experiments that provide the intellectual justification for one-size-fits-all standardized testing, scripted curricula, school design models, and the growth of an audit culture in schools (Ball, 2001; Biesta, 2007). While principals in some districts are given more autonomy over purchasing from vendors and hiring teachers, most curricular and instructional issues are determined from the outside and have to be implemented with fidelity. In this way school-based policy regarding instruction and curriculum is "steered from a distance" (Kickert, 1995; Marceau, 1993), essentially taking them out of the hands of school leaders. Teachers, with the tacit support of principals, used to be able to shut their doors and make their own professional judgments about what to cover and how to cover it within broad state guidelines. Today, these policies have reached behind the classroom door and discipline teachers and principals in ways that make resistance more difficult.

In this context, there are two key notions that might help educational leaders navigate this new reality. One is the notion of *authenticity* (Anderson, 2009) and the recovery of the life world of schools, which has been colonized by the system world described above (Sergiovanni, 2000; Habermas, 1987). This involves seeking ways that leaders might use post-bureaucratic forms of organization to empower students and teachers rather than incorporate them into broader neoliberal agendas. This means adapting or resisting reforms in ways that honor the public nature of schooling and seek the common good, rather than relying on markets to allocate values. While risky, some have even appropriated neoliberal reforms like charter schools toward more authentic, public affirming ends.

The other notion is that of *resistance*, or how, given the new discursive nature of what Foucault calls *governmentalities,* leaders might, through strategies of "irresponsibility," engage in forms of resistance that ultimately open up spaces for authentic knowledge and relations (Anderson and Grinberg, 1998; Ball and Olmedo, 2013). In the final section, we will explore how some of these new spaces might be opened up and used to promote more authentic and equitable social relations and a new research agenda for scholars in urban leadership.

POSSIBILITIES OF RESISTANCE

Neoliberal reforms, such as mandating quantitative measurement of student performance within primary and secondary schools and tying this performance to educator evaluation, has created what Ball (2001) calls an *audit culture* in schools. Moreover as private corporations seize opportunities to market their wares—curricula, assessments, evaluation instruments, data management systems—as indispensable solutions for struggling schools, one must begin to wonder: do possibilities of resistance remain? Is there a place for dissident voices?

In their analysis of teachers' and school leaders' experiences within the audit culture, Ball and Olmedo (2013) apply Foucault's theories of power and subjectivity to demonstrate the way neoliberal discourses have, in effect, produced new kinds of educators: because the "apparatuses of neoliberalism are seductive, enthralling,

and overbearingly necessary" (p. 88), teachers and leaders are inclined to become what the competitive market wants them to be. They push themselves and others toward high performance on standardized tests, strive for awards, and work tirelessly to construct and disseminate positive images of their schools. To do anything else, after all, is to put oneself "in danger of being seen as irresponsible," Ball and Olmedo argue (p. 88).

Foucault's work questions the more conventional understanding of power as a negative or repressive force. According to Foucault (1995), power is not a force that simply prohibits people from doing what they want to do. Power is more insidious in the sense that it circulates through discourses that, over time, become taken-for-granted as norms or truths. It is *productive* in the sense that it creates new subjectivities—that is, new kinds of individuals who readily accept certain discourses as true. Replete with technologies of surveillance, our postmodern society ensures that individuals will live up to the expectations of certain norms because they are aware that, at any given time, someone may be observing and judging them. Foucault (1995) explains:

> He who is subjected to a field of visibility, and who knows it, assumes responsibility for the constraints of power; he makes them play spontaneously upon himself; he inscribes in himself the power relation in which he simultaneously plays both roles; he becomes the principle of his own subjection. (pp. 202–203)

In what Foucault (1980) calls a *"society of normalisation"* (p. 107), individuals under surveillance police themselves to act in accordance with accepted norms or truths. Examples of norms within the discipline of school leadership and policy might include the following ideas: that quantitative measurements of teacher performance are inherently superior to other ways of determining the effectiveness of educators; that market-based competition among schools is needed in order to effect positive systemic changes; that the primary function of schools is to produce a competitive labor force for the economy; that "good" schools are the ones that rank highly in the local newspapers; or that an important competency of school principals is the ability to find the best products on the market for instruction and assessment. A Foucauldian critique would recognize these norms as culturally constructed, not as natural or commonsensical truths of school leadership. Such critique would, for example, question whether a principal should even go to the private market in the first place to seek solutions for local school problems.

Although the pressures to perform up to the expectations of the market are numerous and persistent, Ball and Olmedo (2013) suggest that Foucault's theory of power offers educators an opportunity to examine critically who they have become under neoliberal governance. This critical examination ultimately allows the principal subject to resist what have become taken-for-granted or commonsense notions of what a school leader and teacher ought to be (Hoyle and Wallace, 2007). Thomson (2008) points out that the notion of principal resistance is complex:

> Some take it to mean actions in opposition to policy (this might be called overt resistance), while others include actions that are intended to shift policy (these might be seen as reforming activities, some of which occur within quite rigid bureaucratic constraints) and actions that are critical of policy (such as speaking out). (p. 88)

Another way to think about resistance might be to classify it as internal and external. A school leader might work within his/her school to resist the exorbitant emphasis on test scores and competition, yet he/she might also take part in collective action with organizations and movements outside the school district. Because the new managerialism is not just a cultural shift, or a change in people's mind-sets—rather, it is legislated through new teacher and school evaluation systems, and then buttressed by an industry selling products that help schools meet the demands of new regulations—it is necessary for school leaders to engage in internal and external resistance simultaneously. Indeed, the political, legislative, and corporate forces outside the schools are formidable; they must be met with advocacy outside the school building.

New Resistance Movements?

In the era of President Obama's Race to the Top legislation, which has incentivized the development of new assessments and the evaluation of educators based on student achievement as measured by those assessments, the federal arm has reached so far into the daily life of the classroom that pockets of resistance and protest have begun to emerge—though arguably with

less media coverage and overall visibility than the supporters of performance accountability have enjoyed. For those who would resist the audit culture, these movements provide a modicum of hope. They have included teachers' and parents' boycotting of standardized tests, school principals' protests against new evaluation systems, student walkouts, movements organized through social media and the blogosphere, and independently produced documentary films. The movements have their limits, but they suggest a desire on the part of educators, students, and parents to take issue with the policy model of governing schools through rewards and sanctions based on students' academic achievement, rather than by providing the resources that underserved school systems need in order to be effective. As we noted above, since the economic downturn of the 1970s, the concept of the welfare state providing public goods has been eclipsed by the concept of the state as a distant referee presiding over a free market.

When, in November of 2011, over six hundred principals in the state of New York signed a letter of protest against the use of test scores to evaluate teachers and administrators, the *New York Times* marked the event as possibly "the first principals' revolt in history" (Winerip, 2011). Indeed, as one of the protesting principals observed, it was an unlikely action for school leaders, who tend to conform with the demands of the bureaucracy: "Principals want to go along with the system and do what they're told" (Winerip, 2011). However, when the principals attended a two-day conference to learn about the new testing and evaluation programs, they became frustrated by policies that had, in their view, reached a point of absurdity. The protesting principals pointed to a system that appeared to be "slapped together," and to training sessions that amounted to "two days of total nonsense," including a new requirement that they be trained by outside consultants to evaluate teachers—notwithstanding the principals' own certifications and, in many cases, doctoral degrees in administration (Winerip, 2011).

Teachers in Seattle have also made the national news in their resistance efforts. In early January of 2013, the teachers of Garfield High School voted unanimously to boycott the Measure of Academic Progress (MAP) test, spurring the Seattle superintendent, José Banda, to threaten them with suspension should they decide not to administer the exam (McCauley, 2013, February 5).

356 GARY L. ANDERSON, MICHAEL I. COHEN, MILAGROS SERAUS

Ultimately, Garfield teachers convinced colleagues in other schools to join their movement (Shaw, 2013) and won a somewhat favorable decision from the district: the test would no longer be required in high school as a graduation- or exit-exam (Strauss, 2013). Still, though, the *Washington Post* has reported that the MAP test would continue to be administered at the elementary and middle levels, leading one teacher to remark that the "fight is far from over" (Strauss, 2013).

Parents have also begun to organize in visible ways against the testing culture. In New York City, parent activist groups such as Change the Stakes, Parent Voices NY, and parent-teacher associations at local schools have joined educators in an effort to raise awareness of what they deem a corporate takeover of public education. These groups also use a web presence to provide parents with information on how they might "opt out" of having their children tested by the state. The anticorporate nature of the movements is, perhaps, best illustrated by a parodic version of the logo of Pearson, the publishing company that makes the tests, posted on the website of Change The Stakes ("Change the stakes," 2013). In the picture, the corporate tagline of Pearson, "Always Learning," has been amended to "Always earning," with the "l" cleverly crossed out in red pen. The *New York Times* reported that in June of 2012, parents of students at approximately fifty schools kept their children at home during the field-testing of the Pearson assessments (Sangha, 2012). But, the newspaper noted, the decision to boycott the actual testing is a riskier proposition as it endangers a student's chances of promotion considerably.

The opting out movement attempted to gain national attention two years in a row in 2012 and 2013 by rallying in front of the U.S. Department of Education (DOE) in Washington, DC. Protestors, which included activist parents and educators—Diane Ravitch and Deborah Meier among them—signified solidarity with the various Occupy movements across the country, referring to their rally as "Occupy DOE." Calling attention to the privatization of public education, the group's official name and tagline reads as follows: "United Opt Out National: The Movement to End Corporate Education Reform" ("United opt out, The movement to end corporate education reform," 2013).

When more than three hundred students in Chicago staged a walkout during standardized testing in April

of 2013, they focused on issues of discrimination. Their group, Chicago Students Organizing to Save Our Schools, uses its presence on multiple social networking sites to spread its message and connect with other student organizers, such as the long-standing Philadelphia Student Union, whose recent emphasis has been to protest drastic cuts to public school funding and the closing of schools due to low performance on state tests. The Chicago students referred boldly to Mayor Rahm Emanuel's accountability policies as "racist," since the district had planned the closing of fifty-four elementary schools in 2013, all of which were located in neighborhoods with predominantly black and Latino residents (McCauley, 2013, April 24). Similarly, the Philadelphia group has raised the point that school closings throughout the United States "have disproportionately impacted communities of color" (Philadelphia Student Union, 2013).

Some activists have turned to the art of filmmaking to make their point. Their work responds to the widely screened documentary *Waiting for Superman*, which depicts traditional public schools as failing, averse to change, and corrupt overall. While the film has gained much public attention and acclaim, some critics have accused its director, Davis Guggenheim, of disseminating a neoliberal agenda and a disingenuous portrait of the public schools, offering charter schools and the competition they present as the solution for public school failure (Ravitch, 2010; Sadovnik, 2011). Activists have been responding with their own documentaries, including *The Inconvenient Truth Behind Waiting for Superman* (playing on the title of Guggenheim's other film about global warming), produced by a parent and educator organization called The Grassroots Education Movement, and *Going Public*, a documentary produced by an organization of the same name and still in the funding and development stages at the time of this writing ("GoingPublic.org: A great education is priceless," 2013). Both films point to the school choice movement and neoliberal policy agenda as a boon for the private sector and a perpetrator of increased segregation between the haves and have-nots. *The Inconvenient Truth Behind Waiting for Superman*, for example, demonstrates how high-performing charter schools have been able to select only the types of students who would enhance their test scores and overall ratings.

School Leaders and Resistance

Whether activists are rallying in front of the Department of Education or producing films, the important point is that they are resisting the dominant narrative of market-based solutions as a cure-all for what has been called a failing public system. And yet, despite some isolated moments of protest by principals, school leaders are, for the most part, playing a minor role in the activist movements. In some cases, the very organizations that are designed to advocate for school leaders are actually providing a forum for corporations to sell products that enhance the audit culture of schools. When one of the authors of this chapter attended a workshop on teacher evaluation offered by his professional association in 2012, he found very quickly that the workshop was not really the professional development opportunity that it purported to be in its advertisement; rather, it was a series of sales pitches offered by four competing producers of teacher evaluation instruments—each of them on the state's list of approved providers. This association's focus has been to help principals work *within* the new accountability regime, not to critique its very foundation or offer better solutions.

So what is a resistant principal to do? It would be naïve to suggest that principals simply ought to speak out, or to stage protests in front of their state education departments. Such actions involve considerable professional risk, and it does not take any stretch of the imagination to recognize that principals have tended to conform because it is awfully dangerous not to. And yet, to suggest that principals can either conform or resist is to oversimplify their predicament.

Much research has demonstrated the ways in which school leaders have, in response to accountability standards that they deem unreachable, engaged in various forms of fabricated compliance (Ball, 2001; Cullen and Reback, 2006; Darling-Hammond, 2007). Some principals focus much of their attention on public relations and image management so as to attract students and funding, please their local communities, and put on a positive impression for visiting accountability monitors (Niesz, 2010; Cohen, 2014). Furthermore, many principals rely on explicit test-preparation curricula and materials in order to boost their students' examination performance without having to modify their core curricula too drastically (Thomson, 2008). Yet, as Ball (2001) has pointed out, these diverse forms of fabrication constitute an ironic combination of "resistance *and* capitulation" (p. 217). After all, the test-preparation, the public relations work, and any other strategies employed to satisfy the audit culture are time-consuming endeavors. Principals could be spending this valuable time on authentic curriculum leadership instead. Thus, the forms of resistance available to principals within the school are, to an extent, versions of conformity or compliance.

Some recent critical work, however, has introduced empirical evidence of the way school leaders have begun to resist the neoliberal agenda more productively. As noted above, a critical perspective toward the recent reform efforts is a necessary, albeit insufficient, precursor to such resistance. Foucault's (1990) theory of power as circulating within discourse helps us to see possibilities of resistance in the discourse itself. Arguing that the notion of discourse as an instrument of power is overly simplistic, and that we should avoid conceptualizing a binary model of one discourse conveying power and another speaking against power, Foucault (1990) tells us: "Discourse transmits and produces power; it reinforces it, but also undermines and exposes it, renders it fragile and makes it possible to thwart it" (p. 101). Thus, when we adopt a Foucauldian perspective, we may be able to disrupt, or at least problematize, modes of thinking that have become unquestioned common sense.

Although Ylimaki (2011) does not draw on the work of Foucault overtly, her case studies of resistant principals demonstrate the fruitfulness of his method. Two of the principals in Ylimaki's (2011) study use faculty and parent meetings to engage their teachers and communities in what might be called a rigorous discourse analysis of policy documents and scripted curricula designed for test preparation. One principal "became increasingly concerned when she noted a concurrent increase in use of decontextualized skills-based pedagogy and test preparation materials and a decrease in student engagement during her classroom observations" (Ylimaki, 2011, p. 336). In response to this concern, she began to help teachers and parents think critically about some of the conservative ideologies underlying curricular reforms.

Quite explicitly, the two resistant principals in Ylimaki's (2011) study "distributed policy documents and asked faculty members to reread the policies and related documents and write their questions about language (and assumptions and philosophies behind that language) in the margins" (p. 336). In this way, the principals were able to expose some of the taken-for-granted assumptions in recent reform efforts. Such assumptions included the need for a back-to-basics movement focused on repetitive drilling of skills, the validity of externally developed curricula to support this movement, and a view of education as chiefly about the production of human capital. A teacher who attended these meetings later noted that she could "see now how important it is for us to have policy reading skills. We need to be thoughtful educators in a political sense as well as a curricular sense and then we can show our students how to do the same" (p. 337). Speaking of her principal, Mr. Hughes, this teacher even said, "He's got me thinking things like, 'What do they mean by differentiated instruction? Whose knowledge is the norm to differentiate? What are we differentiating and to whom'?" (p. 337).

School principals are, through their formal leadership positions, uniquely situated to promote shifts in teachers' thinking about educational reforms. But they cannot do so if *they* are not inclined to think critically—not only with respect to neoliberal policy, but also with respect to the way the discourse of this policy constitutes them in the Foucauldian sense. This is why Ball and Olmedo (2013) emphasize the need for principals to resist the insidious ways in which discourse can come to define them. When educators take on a critical reflexivity, the authors argue, "it is then that [they] can begin to take an active role in their own self-definition as a 'teaching subject,' to think in terms of what they do not want to be, and do not want to *become*" (Ball and Olmedo, 2013, p. 86; italics in original). The critical principal, then, must determine what options are available as he/she works to construct, or reconstruct, a principal identity.

Writing about the way neoliberal discourse can define the principal subject, Niesche (2013) has also used Foucault to show how school leaders can engage in "counter-conduct" (p. 152). In a case study conducted in Australia, Niesche shows how a principal named Angela does more than speak openly against her government's narrow emphasis on quantitative indicators of performance. She engages candidly and boldly in discussions of the Queensland state government's neglect of her neediest students, but she has also formed

connections with political figures in order to advocate for her students' receipt of better health benefits and university scholarships. Here, the school leader resists subjectification by the neoliberal state and, instead, "constitutes herself as a political subject in seeking to improve the circumstances and opportunities for [her] students" (Niesche, 2013, p. 153). Crucially, Angela argues that when one "really start[s] to unravel and dig and think about and critique" the leadership framework and standards designed by the state agency, one finds that they are "quite removed from the day-to-day practice of a principal" (p. 154). Angela recognizes the need for ongoing critique of the discourses circulated by policy; she exemplifies the kind of "vigilance" that Ball and Olmedo (2013, p. 86) would have school leaders practice if they wish to disrupt neoliberal discourses and play a greater role in the construction of their own identities.

Ongoing critique requires a specific set of intellectual perspectives and tools, and school leadership preparation programs need to ensure that their pre-service principals are exposed to, and can apply, such tools. Foucault's work on power and discourse is but one of many perspectives that can enable leaders to critique and question the taken-for-granted. For example, the neoliberal policy environment that we currently inhabit is perpetuated by discourses that, on the surface, seem to speak of uncontroversial matters. The What Works Clearinghouse™, an important program within NCLB policy, claims to determine which teaching practices are based on "high-quality research" so that educators can make "evidence-based decisions" ("What Works Clearinghouse™: Evidence for what works in education," 2014). Race to the Top challenges states and local districts to find and use "the most effective" strategies to address their educational issues ("Race to the Top: Annual Performance Report," 2014). It is difficult to argue against notions such as *high-quality research* and *effective* strategies and still sound rational. Nevertheless, a critical perspective enables one to ask some deeper questions about these notions. For example, with whose definition of *high-quality research* are we working? With whose definition of *effective*? What methodological and ideological assumptions underlie these definitions? Are quasi-experimental methods assumed to be more valuable than, say, qualitative methods or practitioner action research? Is effectiveness defined only by scores on state-mandated or vendor assessments? School leaders' capacity to ask such questions for themselves would be a step toward engaging their communities in critical consumption of education policy, and possibly shifting toward an advocacy role.

Indeed, practicing principals know that critique can only bring them so far. It is just a beginning. They also know that in most cases, there is so little time for an individual principal to engage in the public advocacy work that Angela, above, has so admirably done. In a principal's day-to-day work, he/she must come to terms with policies that cannot simply be pushed aside in the name of what he/she deems more important work. Principals must find ways to appropriate policy sensibly—ways that will not hurt their students and teachers and schools. As noted above, fabrication and cynical compliance are time-consuming endeavors that might satisfy the next accountability check, but leave little room for sustainable school improvements. And yet an outright rejection of state mandates is a risky proposition, a realistic possibility only for those with many decades of experience, or for the principals of high-performing, affluent schools (Thomson, 2008).

Arguing that resistant principals should find strength in numbers, Thomson (2008) sees possibility in the "collective activities" (p. 93) of school leaders' professional associations. She argues that such associations have become narrowly concerned with issues such as salary and adversarial collective bargaining, and that they could, instead, attempt to play a more active role in policymaking at the state level. The National Association of Head Teachers (NAHT) in the UK, according to Thomson, provides its members with much more than advice and support for salary negotiations; it engages in research, produces publications for professional development, provides assistance with accountability inspections, and—perhaps most importantly—participates formally in government policymaking. Thomson (2008) notes, for example, that the NAHT has been directly involved in national-level decisions regarding the way schools are structured, organized, and governed. The association also works with policymakers to make the jobs of school leaders more manageable, especially as performance accountability systems increase their workload with bureaucratic requirements.

Leading Through Resistance

Those who are troubled by the market-based reforms we have described in this chapter might find some encouragement in the various forms of resistance we have discussed. The protests, student walkouts, activist blogs, documentary films, and strategies of resistance attempted by some principals are signs that parents, students, teachers, and administrators are pushing back against what appears to be an unstoppable wave of neoliberal reforms. And yet, as we have also noted, the corporate interests, bipartisan policy networks, fast-track pathways to school leadership, and shifts in political culture are so well-established and far-reaching that it would be naïve to think that speaking out, on its own, is capable of turning the tide.

What is needed, it seems, is a notion of school leadership that includes resistance as one of its chief dimensions. This means that school leaders must understand their roles not simply as agents of improvement in curriculum and instruction, but also as advocates for their schools and communities (Anderson, 2009). As advocates, school leaders bear the responsibility of empowering teachers and parents with the critical tools necessary to discern whose interests are served by the latest reforms, and of working with their professional associations—which, themselves, may need to be redefined and repurposed—to determine what kinds of counter-conduct are realistic and productive.

REFERENCES

Anderson, G. L. (2007). Media's impact on educational Policies and practices: Political spectacle and social control. *The Peabody Journal of Education, 82*(1), pp. 103–120.

Anderson, G. L. (2009) *Advocacy leadership: Toward a post-reform agenda in education.* New York: Routledge.

Anderson, G. L. and Grinberg, J. (1998). Educational administration as a disciplinary practice: Appropriating Foucault's view of power, discourse, and method. *Educational Administration Quarterly, 34*(3), 329–353.

Anderson, G. L. and Montoro Donchik, L. (2014). Privatizing schooling and policy-making: The American Legislative Exchange Council and new political and discursive strategies of education governance. *Education Policy,* 1–43.

Ball, S. (2001). Performativities and fabrications in the education economy: Towards the performative society. In D. Gleason and C. Husbands (Eds.) *The performing school:*

Managing, teaching and learning in a performance culture (pp. 210–226). London: Routledge/Falmer.

Ball, S. (2008). *The education debate*. Bristol: The Policy Press.

Ball, S. and Olmedo, A. (2013). Care of the self, resistance and subjectivity under neoliberal governmentalities. *Critical Studies in Education, 54*(1), 85–96.

Biesta, G. (2007). Why "what works" won't work: Evidence-based practice and the democratic deficit in educational research. *Educational Theory, 57*(1), 1–22.

Bradley, L. (1993). *Total Quality Management for schools*. Lancaster, PA: Technomic Pub.

Burch, P. (2009). *Hidden Markets: The new education privatization*. New York: Routledge.

Change the stakes. (2013). Retrieved from changethestakes.org.

Cohen, M. I. (2014). "In the back of our minds always": Reflexivity as resistance for the performing principal. *International Journal of Leadership in Education*, 1–22.

Cullen, J. B. and Reback, R. (2006). Tinkering toward accolades: School gaming under a performance accountability system. *The National Bureau of Economic Research*. Retrieved from www.nber.org/papers/w12286.

Darling-Hammond, L. (2007). Race, inequality and educational accountability: The irony of "No Child Left Behind." *Race Ethnicity and Education, 10*(3), 245–260. doi: 10.1080/13613320701503207.

Dillard, C. B. (1995). Leading with her life: An African American feminist (re)interpretation of leadership for an urban high school principal. *Educational Administration Quarterly, 31*(4), 539–563.

Emmert, M. and Crow, M. (1988). Public, private and hybrid organizations: An empirical examination of the role of publicness. *Administration and Society*, 20, 216–244.

Foucault, M. (1980). *Power/knowledge: Selected interviews and other writings, 1972–1977* (C. Gordon, Ed.). New York: Pantheon Books.

Foucault, M. (1990). *The history of sexuality*. New York: Vintage Books.

Foucault, M. (1995). *Discipline and punish: The birth of the prison*. New York: Vintage Books.

Friedman, M. (1962). *Capitalism and freedom*. Chicago: University of Chicago Press.

GoingPublic.org: A great education is priceless. (2013). Retrieved from www.goingpublic.org/.

Grassroots Education Movement. (2011). *The inconvenient truth behind Waiting for Superman*.

Guggenheim, D. (Director). (2010). *Waiting for superman* [Motion picture]. United States.

Habermas, J. (1987). The theory of communicative action: Vol. 2. Lifeworld and system: A critique of functionalist reason (Thomas McCarthy, Trans.). Boston: Beacon Press.

Harvey, D. (2005). *A brief history of neoliberalism*. London: Oxford University Press.

Haslam, B. and Turnbull, B. (2011). *Executive Education for Educators: A vehicle for improving K–12 systems?* Washington, DC: Policy Studies Associates, Inc.

Hoyle, E. and Wallace, M. 2007. Education Reform: An Ironic Perspective. *Educational Management Administration and Leadership 35*(1), 9–25.

Johanek, M. C. and Puckett, J. (2006). Leonard Covello and the making of Benjamin Franklin High School as if citizenship mattered. Philadelphia: Temple University Press.

Jones, G. M., Jones, B. D., and Hargrove, T. (2003). *The unintended consequences of high-stakes testing*. Lanham, MD: Rowman and Littlefield Publishers.

Kickert, W. (1995). Steering at a distance: A new paradigm of public governance in Dutch higher education. *Governance, 8*(1), 135–157. doi: 10.1111/j.1468-0491.1995.tb00202.x.

Koyama, J. (2011). Principals, power, and policy: Enacting "Supplemental Educational Services." *Anthropology and Education Quarterly, 42*(1), 20–36.

Marceau, J. (1993). *Steering from a distance: International trends in the financing and governance of higher education*. Canberra: Australian Department of Employment, Education, and Training.

McCauley, L. (2013, February 5). Seattle teachers lead day of action against standardized tests. *Common Dreams*. Retrieved from www.commondreams.org/headline/2013/02/05-3.

McCauley, L. (2013, April 24). Hundreds of Chicago students walk out of standardized test. *Common Dreams*. Retrieved from www.commondreams.org/headline/2013/04/24-8.

Murtadha, K. and Watts, D. M. (2005). Linking the struggle for education and social justice: Historical perspectives of African-American leadership in schools. *Educational Administration Quarterly, 41*(4), 591–608.

Niesche, R. (2013). Foucault, counter-conduct and school leadership as a form of political subjectivity. *Journal of Educational Administration and History, 45*(2), 144–158.

Niesz, T. (2010). "That school had become all about show": Image making and the ironies of constructing a good urban school. *Urban Education, 45*(3), 371–393.

Philadelphia student union. (n.d.). *Philadelphia Student Union*. Retrieved from www.phillystudentunion.org/.

Race to the Top. (n.d.). *The White House*. Retrieved from -www.whitehouse.gov/issues/education/k-12/race-to-the-top.

Race to the Top: Annual performance report. (2013). Retrieved from www.rtt-apr.us/.

Ravitch, D. (2010, November 11). The myth of charter schools. *The New York Review of Books*. Retrieved from www.nybooks.com/articles/archives/2010/nov/11/myth-charter-schools/?pagination=false.

Sadovnik, A. R. (2011). Waiting for school reform: Charter schools as the latest imperfect panacea. *Teachers College Record*. Retrieved from www.tcrecord.org/Content.asp?ContentId=16370.

Saltman, K. (2009). The rise of venture philanthropy and the ongoing neoliberal assault on public education: The case of the Eli and Edythe Broad Foundation. *Workplace, 16*, 53–72.

Sangha, S. (2012, October 12). Dear teacher, Johnny is skipping the test. *The New York Times.*

Scott, J. (2009). The politics of venture philanthropy in charter school policy and advocacy. *Educational Policy, 23*(1), 106–136.

Sergiovanni, T. (2000). *The life world of leadership: Creating culture, community, and personal meaning in our schools.* San Francisco: Jossey-Bass.

Shaw, L. (2013, April 29). Teachers at 2 more Seattle schools join MAP test boycott. *The Seattle Times.* Retrieved from seattletimes.com/html/localnews/2020888064_maptestxml.html.

Siddle Walker, V. (2003). The architects of Black schooling in the South. The case of one principal leader. *Journal of Curriculum and Supervision, 19*(1), 54–72.

Siddle Walker, V. (2005). Organized resistance and Black educators' quest for school equality, 1878–1938. *Teachers College Record, 107*(3), 355–388.

Spencer, J. (2009). A "new breed" of principal: Marcus Foster and urban school reform in the United States, 1966–1969. *Journal of Educational Administration and History, 41*:3, 285–300.

Strauss, V. (2013, May 16). Seattle teachers boycotting test score a victory. *Washington Post.* Retrieved from www.washingtonpost.com/blogs/answer-sheet/wp/2013/05/16/seattle-teachers-boycotting-test-score-a-victory/.

Thomson, P. (2008). Headteacher critique and resistance: a challenge for policy, and for leadership/management scholars. *Journal of Educational Administration and History, 40*(2), 85–100.

United opt out, The movement to end corporate education reform. (2013). *United Opt Out National.* Retrieved from unitedoptout.com/.

Ward, S. (2011). The machinations of managerialism: New public management and the diminishing power of professionals. *Journal of Cultural Economy, 4*(2), 205–215.

What Works Clearinghouse™: Evidence for what works in education. (2014). Retrieved from ies.ed.gov/ncee/wwc/.

Winerip, M. (2011, November 27). Principals protest role of testing in evaluations. *The New York Times.*

Ylimaki, R. M. (2011). Curriculum leadership in a conservative era *Educational Administration Quarterly, 48*(2), 304–346. doi: 10.1177/0013161X11427393.

Zeichner, K. and Pena-Sandoval, C. (2015). Venture philanthropy and teacher education policy in the U.S: The role of the new schools venture fund. *Teachers College Record, 117*(6), www.tcrecord.org ID Number: 17539.

CHAPTER 25

Destiny High School

Redesigning Urban High Schools for Student Success

Frank Gaines, Ira Bogotch, and Omar J. Salaam

INTRODUCTION

In this chapter, we focus on the urban high school through the eyes of thirty-three urban educators, who had 667 years of urban school experiences. What might these individuals know that others do not? They are not executives in multinational corporations, such as IBM. They do not run or write for philanthropic foundations, such as the Gates Foundation. To a person, they do not study urban high schools using theoretical frameworks or research methodologies. They are not those who make the laws and policies or write the regulations governing school curricula and programs. Their ideas do not make the cover of *Time* magazine (February 24, 2014). All they do is come to work with urban high school students, specifically segregated minority students, each day of their adult lives. Hence, we made a decision that those who work inside high-poverty, high-minority schools really do know what may be needed to successfully educate their students. As you read their ideas and take note of their visions for urban education, you will undoubtedly see similarities to existing policy reforms and proposed new programs presented through traditional research. In part, this is true because urban educators have been calling for radical reforms for decades, and their voices have been heard in many new reform proposals but not at critical mass levels. But what is different here is their agenda for school, student, and community success is not tied to a particular government policy or an industry's long-term employment needs. The success defined here is grounded in the freedom of individuals living in communities to choose how to engage in social, economic, and political actions to change their human condition without first getting the approval of mainstream society.

All of the thirty-three educators currently work in three "historically segregated" high schools serving students from segregated, disenfranchised neighborhoods, defined here as neighborhoods where poverty and unemployment rates far exceed city, state, and national averages and where low-wage service jobs predominate. Demographically, these three urban high schools mirror the six hundred high schools designated as "dropout factories" where "half of the African-American boys who veer off the path to high school graduation." (Balfanz, June 8, 2014). Geographically, these urban schools are located in major cities, smaller, decaying industrial cities, and southern cities in the United States.[1]

And yet, much of what happens inside segregated urban schools remains invisible to and misunderstood by the larger city-wide residents and elected officials. The dominant discourses of today have relentlessly "sold" the American public on the idea that accountability measures such as school letter grades and students' tests scores are the best and only indicators of student achievement and future economic success. What we found, however, are far more direct interventions into the everyday lives of urban high school students. At the same time, what we found were only "pockets" of success, often disconnected from the curriculum, but which when reconnected—at this stage conceptually only—transcended the social, economic, and human conditions in both the schools and communities in which the students lived. As educational practitioners and researchers ourselves, we trusted the caring concerns and programmatic ideas we heard expressed by the participants. We present, therefore, a systemic view of these "pockets of success" in order to overcome the current school structures and policies that obstruct pathways to student success. We call this model Destiny High School.

It was from our analysis of these now isolated pockets of success that we extracted the values and opportunities that reflected positive attitudes and ideas toward both students and communities. We then proceeded to combine and integrate these values and opportunities with initiatives, practices, and programs from the three urban high schools in our study. The composite result is a comprehensive urban high school model of success, Destiny High School, which became, for us, a counternarrative reflecting what urban high schools are currently doing well. In other words, these reforms are already present inside segregated urban schools and communities, only not at the critical mass levels needed to influence the minds of policymakers, multinational corporations, or philanthropic foundations (and our school leaders) to make systemic changes.

We do not ignore the social realities [of poverty] within the urban school crisis, although much of it is socially constructed (Miron, 1996). Yet, we deliberately foregrounded the many voices of committed urban educators who over their lifetimes have worked in segregated urban public schools. Our thesis, again, is that *these are the experts* whom we should be listening to.

THE PLACE OF RESEARCH

For readers expecting to see rigorous systematic analysis, our conceptual framework was grounded in the educative ideas of John Dewey (1909) and Alice Miel (1961) on the meanings of community and opportunity. We then appended these ideas to the appreciative aesthetic approach taken by Sara Lawrence-Lightfoot and Jessica Hoffman-Davis (1997), referred to as portraiture. From there, we conceptualized a redesign of the urban high school, operationalizing mission statements, job descriptions, curricular reforms and personnel processes. Unfortunately, the more our national educational reform processes have become standardized based on STEM curricula (that is, science, technology, engineering, and mathematics) and test score criteria of accountability, the more difficult it has become to design unique and culturally relevant within-school policies and programs (Vasquez-Heilig, Khalifa, and Tillman, 2014). While standardized practices may serve the needs of students who score high on standardized tests and satisfy the interests of those in power who control economic policies, the realities of students and

families living in low socioeconomic status communities mandates opportunity structures that allow them to transcend their social, economic, political, and human condition. Achievement measures inextricably linked to the success of families (today as well as tomorrow), and their neighborhoods and communities collectively must be given consideration. For too long we have maintained an arbitrary separation between schools and neighborhoods, expecting individual students to achieve and "escape" from their lives in neighborhoods of poverty (Miron, Bogotch, and Biesta, 2001). Connected schools and communities were historically a common practice (e.g., laboratory and settlement schools). Unless we are able to return to the more fundamental educational ideas grounded in social, economic, cultural, and human capital for urban schools and students, we cannot expect there to be meaningful urban school reform. Individual student success will not end poverty. Educating just one of four or five siblings in a family is not a strategy for success. Therefore, it is incumbent upon urban educational leadership researchers to offer counternarratives which are systemic and based on native voices in opposition to socially constructed "crises" (Miron, 1996).

Normore, Rodriguez, and Wynne (2007) warned that "silencing" the voices of critical and relevant stakeholders in disenfranchised community environments is counterproductive to building schools that can make a difference in the communities they are expected to serve and rebuild. Their silence limits the opportunities of minority students and communities to self-determine what is necessary in order to flourish in today's postindustrial society. Being told what to do by external groups from noneducational sectors of society as well as by those outside the urban communities that is, district and state level governing bodies, have perpetuated cycles of poverty in the very communities expected to be reformed. It has led to what Sergiovanni (1992, 2004) and others have labeled as "trained incapacity" which now applies to urban school administrators, teachers and staff as well as students and parents. Today's system of urban education has failed to bring generational change to communities, which is an indictment of public education as articulated a century and a half ago by the father of public schools, Horace Mann (1867–1891). Mann made it very clear that school could not in one generation change the socioeconomic status of parents, but through a viable public school system, communities could make a transformative difference for the children. And while Colin Greer (1972) and many other critics of public education refer to this American Dream as a myth, urban schools can provide tangible opportunities (e.g., jobs and quality of life) to students and their communities beyond earning a high school diploma.

Therefore, we see nothing nostalgic in referencing Horace Mann or John Dewey, individuals who made a difference in public education for their own generations. Unfortunately, not since Albert Shanker, a controversial teacher-union leader to be sure, has urban education had such a strong political voice. Neither of the last five U.S. secretaries of education, nor their respective presidents, will go down in history as progressive voices for public education, and especially urban schools. And yet, we remain hopeful because there are progressive educators working inside urban schools, if only we could hear and learn from them.

In conducting this study, what quickly became clear to us was the paradox that while most urban high school students have little or no idea of what success means or how they can achieve it, that role has to be assumed by urban educators. Therefore, urban school educators, unlike their counterparts in suburban or middle-class schools satisfied with maintaining the status quo, carry the added burden for educating urban youth, that is, working to rebuild communities and make our society as a whole more equitable. For many Americans, the notion of a common good as the purpose of public education has been overshadowed by voices that speak to special interests and private concerns. We have lost sight of the larger purpose of public education (Bogotch, Nesmith, Smith, and Gaines, 2014). In today's neoliberal era of individual and private self-interests, it is hard to argue persuasively that by helping public schools in disenfranchised communities, one is engaged in a moral responsibility and a public good. Doing so is an appeal to the common good and welfare of all members of society, given that by eliminating differences in opportunity between disparate groups, educators can facilitate greater cohesion and promote societal equity. Equity-based reforms are in the best interest of society as a whole, not just the disenfranchised. Today, urban high school practices do not move indigenous neighborhood students toward productive ends that include the development of the social, political, and economic

capacity to be functional citizens able to transcend their blighted urban surroundings. Instead, urban schools utilize complacency and conformity to maintain the status quo suited to perpetuate a subservient and attendant working class. Urban schools today provide a curriculum that is based on disconnected academic disciplines focusing on numeracy and literacy—essential foundational skills, but not the end goals of education in and of themselves. Indigenous neighborhood students with the help of urban educators need to develop and advance agendas on their own behalf which include the ability to read, write, and understand democratic principles that serve both larger society's interests as well as interests that meet students' own needs.

THE REALITIES OF URBAN SCHOOL LEADERSHIP

Urban school administrators' lives are not their own. The question repeatedly raised by Thomas Sergiovanni (1992, 1996, 2004) was whether the busy-ness of administrators (and teachers) is necessary or a deliberate strategy to prevent educators from prioritizing and collaborating. When the work consumes much of the practitioners' workloads which extends days far beyond contractual hours as well as working on weekends just to complete their expected duties and responsibilities, then supporting isolated "pockets of success" becomes more difficult—if not impossible. It is here where the personal becomes political, as we heard the pain in participants' voices when they recognized that it is humanly impossible to do what needs to be done under the current standardized, bureaucratic educational system that protects the status quo. Neither legislative decision-makers nor large urban system superintendents have successfully challenged the status quo by allowing urban educators to do "what needs to be done" as part of their professional judgments; therefore, the chapter's underlying message: urban educational change must be initiated by the participants themselves.

That said, urban school participants have been socialized to conform, thus limiting their abilities to work for socially just practices and programs. Nonconformity is quickly labeled as being ungrateful for entitlement programs and being "disloyal" to those in authority. For today's educators, this is a subtle form of social control, and participants openly talk about fear, intimidation, threats, blame, and distrust within

the systems they work. Nonconformists find career opportunities limited. In today's standardized schooling
environments, unique programs tailored to the needs of
disenfranchised students are not considered or valued
as they fit the needs of a "minority" (which has become
the majority) population.

Within this intimidating environment, a closed system is enacted whereby urban minority parents blame
teachers and schools for their performance rather than
their children, while others reference poverty and
lack of parental concern as the culprit. Students cite
boredom, not being challenged or cared for, and being
dismissed by adults. Educators bear the primary burden
of solving these problems, while educational leaders
bear the burden of charting the course that will remove
the barriers to enable urban teachers to be effective in
disenfranchised settings.

From federal, state, and district officials as well as
politicians and businesspeople alike, the purpose of
schooling in today's competitive global economy necessitates highly trained technicians (of technology) with
advanced degrees. This message from the U.S. Secretary of Education and the *New York Times* (editorial,
December 15, 2013) is continuously repeated throughout society. What we don't hear are counternarratives
describing service work as gainful employment; why
those working in retail, tourism, domestics, and food
service should not be paid a living wage for eight hours
a day and forty hours a week; why all heads of household should receive annual leave and affordable health
insurance. The resistance in society to not see all necessary hard work as respectable has contributed to the
income inequalities and the great divide in society (see
Krugman, 2014; Stiglitz, 2014). All gainful employment should provide for individuals and their families
not at subsistent wages and abusive working conditions.
The fact that educators are not on the forefront advocating for economic justice demonstrates how socially
just practices have been dichotomized into categories
of legal justice, political justice, and educational justice
as if procedural fairness (for example, school rules)
can transform education and society. It cannot. Educators need to think about their role in the larger society
in terms of how to promote socially just programs and
practices beyond being good teachers and moral administrators (Anyon, 2005; Bogotch, 2014).

DOING RESEARCH IN URBAN SETTINGS

Over their careers, urban educators have faced many
challenges ranging from a steady succession of building
leadership (Clark, Martorell, and Rockoff, 2009), the
lack of equitable and adequate resources (Kozol, 1991;
Orfield, Kucsera, and Siegel-Hawley, 2012), and the
influx of inexperienced teachers (Hanushek, Kain, and
Rivkin, 2004). They have also had to suffer from a combination of heavy-handed state supervisory restrictions
and personnel as well as educational researchers who
"study," "sell," and "profess" solutions that, however
well-intentioned, do not arise from the visions of urban
educators themselves.

Interviewing thirty-three participants with 667 years
of experience required skills and rapport to build trust
and overcome years of willful abuse and neglect. Rapport, trust, and collaboration needed to extend across
all the urban school participants of this study. The first
author was able to establish these relational bonds based
on his previous experiences working in these three urban
school settings and communities. The urban schools'
environmental conditions intensify participants' willingness to be open and honest with researchers. Urban
communities are deeply entrenched in the culture and
traditions of urban schools, especially in high schools. A
long history of researchers who have come to these participants with non-community-building agendas, deficit
perspectives, or seeking to document "disadvantages"
(often made in comparison to middle-class values, Eurocentric values) not only telegraphs a bias and lack of
understanding of traditions and cultures, but it also fails
to "speak truth to power" (AFSC, 1955).

Given the fact that the first author was perceived
by all thirty-three participants as an "inside-outsider"
(Foster, 1996), he was able to elicit truthful responses
to questions guided by the following themes:

- Participants' values for student success;
- Participants' actions for student success;
- Participants' promotion of programs for student
  success;
- Participants' roles in rebuilding the surrounding
  communities of families and students; and,
- The communities' highest priorities for its high
  school graduates

PARTICIPANTS' VOICES AS COUNTERNARRATIVES

There was an inextricable and affectionate link between the schools and their surrounding communities. These were not just schools, but rather integral, inseparable parts of the lives of those who live in the communities. Two of the three high schools in this study were built pre-*Brown* as segregated schools that ultimately transitioned into "integrated" schools. The other high school housed a student population that once attended a now-closed segregated school. It was this shared history of segregation, as both a legacy and an urban reality, which emerged significantly in the participants' narrations of values and actions needed for students' success and which was incorporated into the redesign as Destiny High School.

Any research study that is grounded in the voices of urban educators and which privileges the values and needs of indigenous, neighborhood students becomes, ipso facto, a counternarrative in today's environment of school reform. Bureaucratic standardization erases cultural narratives in the programmatic delivery of pre-scribed programs—all of which ignores the expertise of urban educators. And while some policymakers and educational researchers specialize in urban school reform, their views are not grounded in the perspective of those working daily in segregated urban schools. Therefore, in describing Destiny High School, we have attempted to capture the words and meanings of urban educators in the schools themselves.

In so doing, however, it became obvious that both words and concepts used by the thirty-three urban educators working inside these schools could not be reproduced verbatim without some explanations for readers. That is, the articulated values held by urban school educators challenge middle-class values which permeate schools and school systems. And when it becomes clear, as it was to us as educational leadership researchers, that approval from outsiders (i.e., external authorities) is not a value that is sought, acknowledged, or recognized in a subculture, then needed to better understand how those values derive their own contextual legitimacy. In other words, where compliance and obedience has been the norm of public school educators in the face of external mandates, the administrators, teachers, and staff in Destiny High School answer accountably to other values, notably the needs of communities and urban students. Subsequently, the significant values identified in this study included relationships, athletics, performing arts, and black educational and cultural experiences: all of which reflect the support and cohesiveness of students and their families. These values extend beyond school rules, societal definitions, traditional academic disciplines, and test score measures of success.

Language use and indigenous perspectives often depict a very different reality and meaning than that which is understood by authorities, including law enforcement, to conceptualize neighborhood dynamics. In the first narrative, consider an alternate perspective on "gangs" as described by one urban educator:

> look at the pride they [teenagers] have in the neighborhoods, because if that wasn't the case, they wouldn't have all these little groups. The Pride Boys and all that. They gather around and support each other. We call them gangs, but I think you can say more or less, teens, community teens, they are trying to protect each other and help each other, and show that they belong to a certain community. They are proud to be part of that community. Hey, this is my community. (C1-1)

This view may seem extreme as it connects the term "gangs" to a caring community of teens; but in the context of the disenfranchised neighborhoods that are bastions of generational poverty, housing, and racial discrimination, pride and respect are important values. "Groups" of young black males bonded together in the only way they know how: to fraternize, socialize, and prosper in accordance with value systems ingrained through their cultural development as opposed to those promoted through mainstream value systems that label black males as failures. On the one hand, this explains misunderstandings, isolation, and even invisibility of values; on the other hand, it speaks to the need for committed urban educators who can approach teens on their terms to build relationships that allow them to develop the capacity for success when these dynamics do not exist within mainstream America. At the same time, we again emphasize that bureaucratic rules and structures steal away the time and space so necessary for urban educators to succeed in their work, as they are unable to connect the pockets of excellence into systemic school and community reforms. Thus, as educational leadership researchers, we feel obligated to make those connections, if not in reality, then at least in print form. The problem is well articulated by the following quote:

> there's a wound inside of them [teens], and every now and then somebody touches a part of that wound and they get hurt and they act on that hurt what they have inside . . . [T]he question is trying to find out exactly, how to get inside of the kids. In this community, there's a lot of abuse, whether or not it be physical abuse or mental abuse or verbal abuse, a lack of a lot of things that these kids don't have in the community. I think, like I said, these kids go through so much that we don't know about. I think until we address these issues, . . . if you don't know what's happening inside these kids, you'll never solve the problem. (T3-6)

Moreover, given the public and its designated experts do not see what goes on inside a segregated urban school, the students themselves, who often lack the knowledge and skills to build healthy relationships, find that social skill development necessary for interaction with mainstream society is absent.

> We do not equip students with the proper relational skills. Like how to be able to have different relationships and be able to actually say okay, this is a relationship where I am a student, this is the teacher. And there is another relationship where I am the child and (this is) the parent. And (then) there is (a relationship with) my friends where I am the friend and be able to deal with those three different levels of relationships. Because the kids, their main thing is oh, this teacher doesn't like me. I didn't pass that class because they don't like me. And they don't know to say okay, even though this person doesn't like me doesn't mean that I have to fail the class. What is it that I can do so that I can still pass, even though that person and I don't see eye to eye. That's one of the main things that I see all the time. That the student and the teachers are not getting along because of their relational skills. (G1-2)

Social networking skills were an oft-mentioned roadblock to success for students when interacting with mainstream society. Due to the dynamics and stress of confrontation that exist in the urban school neighborhood, confrontation is often met with just that, confrontation. Consequently, the need to build capacity in this area is critical for student success.

The value of relationships is primary to urban children and is not what schools are known to cultivate, especially in this era of accountability based solely on academic skills. Here is how one urban school administrator describes his efforts to build capacity for student success.

> What I tell the teachers, we need to understand poverty, and understand the kids. And my, this is one of the sayings that I say in staff meetings quite a lot. Before you can teach me, you have to reach me; before you can reach me, you have to know me. They have to know what they're dealing with. They don't say it, but they talk about relationships a lot of times. That acceptance piece; all kids want to be accepted but I think coming from some of the homes, they don't know how to receive being accepted. A lot of times, all they've been coming through is conflict in the homes. There's a whole lot of inner turmoil going on at home. When you try to show them a different perspective of what's going on, they don't know how to receive that. (A3)

For these concrete reasons, urban educators work harder than their suburban peers trying to adhere to the values of academics as the only measures of student achievement amidst a backdrop that ascribes importance to athletics and performing arts as mainstays of cultural expression and pride in communities of color. Until urban educators convince policymakers to respect the values of hardworking indigenous [and immigrant] parents and families who support their children within their comfort zone, the dichotomy between schools and communities will persist alongside victimization and blame in urban settings, for these reflect the imposition of mainstream values.

The urban educators do not ignore the accomplishments of generations of students, the traditions, and the role these schools play as surrogate homes to indigenous youth; they do not marginalize or diminish urban schools' contributions to communities, regardless of the negative stereotypical images that subjugate their school's true value to the neighborhood and society.

The community significance is reflected upon by the third author, who shared his own memory of an urban high school:

> The connection I felt to my high school, which was known for producing some of the best basketball players in America and was the school she and each of her nine siblings graduated from, meant far more to me than the schools' academic standings or societal reputation. Through that connection I and the majority of my

classmates felt to our beloved high school, we were encouraged to do well in school, knowing that was the only way we'd be allowed to attend those sold-out basketball games. We did well in school knowing the pride we would feel being able to one day say not only did we attend F. H. S., but that we were graduates of the school . . . The connection we still feel to what was then known as a community high school created a bond that inspired us to send more students off to college/university than any other high school in my hometown during the 1980s. Our school, though once known for the race riots which occurred during its initial years, developed into a part of the community which tied us all closer to one another with support systems, making us aware of the positive things we were capable of and preparing us to become the leaders many of us have become today.

In countering the negative stereotypes, an administrator in this study (A2) pointed out the high percentage of students enrolled and successfully completing advanced placement classes as a promotional tool used to overcome negative social programming and send the message of "yes, we can succeed." He also identified the presence of black teacher leaders as an asset used to promote success. A guidance counselor (G2) highlighted the fact that all members of the guidance staff are graduates of HBCUs (Historically Black College or Universities): "I can't speak for the demographics of other high schools in Eagle County (pseudonym) . . . but every guidance counselor at this school is an HBCU grad. Every single one." The exposure and experience of faculty and staff of color who were HBCU graduates increases their capacity to sell the black college experience to students who need to consider more than just the traditional college options and variables to options that are often not within their reach, be it academically or otherwise:

the reality is that you need to consider more than academic programs when you are selecting a college. Because you are only going to be in class a certain portion of the day so it has to meet your social needs, it has to meet your financial ability; including travel home. (G2)

The urban educators' counter-narratives reinforced the value of the black student experience at a black high school. They underscored the inherent benefits created through education in an environment created for black students, educated in black schools, built by blacks, and taught by blacks. Inherent is the fact they could see, touch, witness, and live within a model of success every day through their direct participation in an educational experience in a school they viewed as their own. The urban high school provides stakeholders a unique opportunity to promote models of success not available to students of color educated in schools without a representative minority presence in faculty, staff, and the student body.

That they [students] should feel that comfortable, that at ease, that they should have that same relationship where if they have a problem, if something's wrong, even if something is not wrong; successes that they want to celebrate or whatever. They should be able to come to their teachers under any circumstances, whether it is class related or content related or not, they should be able to do that . . . the more the culture shifts in that area, the more the students will benefit and we'll see scores increase. My kids, they learn. I think a lot of it has to do with the fact that sometimes they do it for me. (T3-3)

The value of pride was also evident as influential alumni kept a close eye on the school and fought for the schools' success and reputation. This works in the school's favor because it creates a built-in recruiting mechanism for magnet programs and athletic programs in particular, in spite of the fiscal challenges the school faces.

All of the values identified here speak to the significance of relationships, in particular how students' academic achievement reflects their personal relationships with teachers (Gooden, 2012; Miron, Bogotch, and Biesta, 2001). Gooden (2012) writes, "These African-American principals also call upon an ethic of justice to challenge how they govern their schools with their staffs . . . have confidence in their students and consider developing more productive relationships with African-American children." (p.82) It is critical to guide these communities to define self-determination. This is fundamental to what is needed for African-American and all students of color as a whole to experience overall success in the K–12 schools.

The ethic of care is historically a major foundation for the success of educating African-American students. The care we heard expressed repeatedly and with passion in this study was not of the "let's pretend we care" (Barber, 1993) variety. It was not the rhetoric of care, but the value of care translated into opportunities which become programs. Unfortunately, the inability to distinguish between the ethic of care and pretend care is not easy as Americans have for too long played the pretend game (Barber, 1993). Not so in the voices of these urban educators.

FROM VALUES TO OPPORTUNITIES

Clearly, there are misunderstandings and an underappreciation for the core values inside the world of educational administration in relationship to urban education. The ghost of Frederick Taylor continues to haunt school leadership such that platitudes like "if a program can't show a measurable difference—aka quantification—then it's not worth doing or at least not a priority for education." And so, technical skills in teaching and managing, important to a point, continue to erase the socioemotional, aesthetic, and cultural dynamics at the heart of education. Recognizing that performances on stage or on the ball fields bring joy and meaning and that the black education experience matters as a recognition of historical and contemporary respect for African Americans allows us to see why and how values can be translated into opportunities for students to succeed.

Everything we do has an impact on everything else. It's going to impact something and somebody and they need to take personal responsibility for that. They can't be where it's about me and my. What happens when you just worry about me and my, is everyone around you starts having the same mind-set, and when that happens, there is no community. If there's no community, there is no togetherness. And where there is no togetherness we are setting ourselves up to be destroyed. Every generation, every kind of people that ever faced this earth, the moment you become divided, you are through.[2] Across the three historically black high schools, we identified ten integrated themes that create and promote student opportunities. As we listened, we heard the passion behind these themes—which are integrated into the counternarratives, not listed 1 to 10 as so many researcher and policy-driven documents prefer to do.

Many of the ideas presented, not surprisingly, revolved around the need to improve collaborations with church, civic, and community groups. In addition, vocational and trade opportunities for students were

recurring themes. Across each of the themes, we want readers to see an understanding for the need to build political capacity and the need to fight continuously for what is valued by stakeholders in these communities as paramount for success. In this sense, we agree with Scherrer (May, 2014) that a two-dimensional approach, resources and capacity, must be considered within each integrated theme. In the next two sections, the authors of this study will take a backseat to the urban educators who work every day in these settings. We ask readers to just listen.

The story of Destiny High School begins with connecting the Black Educational Experience as a Legacy central to all course subjects in the school's curriculum, and the necessity to have their "own" schools as opposed to assimilation into mainstream institutions.

Well, originally [the school] was the second center of community activity after the church. It was a place where people met, meetings were held, and things were discussed. That's when it was an all-black community. Now, when they desegregated the school, that went out the window. They had no place to go to. We were attending their schools, you see, that was the mentality that existed at the time, . . . Well, I worked real hard back in the early 70s to get the high school here because there were a lot of forces against (us) . . . We managed to rally the city commission to fight and advocate on behalf of the citizens here. (C3-1)

At the same time, consideration must be given to the deep-seated prejudice that manifests itself in the stereotyping of black males and hinders developing traditional and nontraditional pathways to student success, selfdetermination, and civic engagement.

They leave here with whatever we taught them, that's what they know when they get out into the world. And if they fail, sometimes it's because we didn't give them the proper tools. It's like going to war. If you don't give that soldier the proper tools to fight the war, if they get out in combat, if that other person has better equipment, they can't win that battle. The world is a battle out there. And I think that's what some of the things our kids may not understand; and the work of the black males is getting to be an endangered species; we definitely need to work with them so they can understand that they can be achievers. You know every time I would have a class just for males and people talk about that's being partial, but they still have some classes and you get to teach the males how to become men. How to dress, how to act, and how to go to job interviews; the ladies the same thing. (C1-1)

You know what I think? To me, they don't see enough men in positions as role models. I think that we are lacking that. Especially black African-American men. I really think that if we had some role models, male role models. (T1-3)

Participants suggest that if a school's message is expected to create, maintain, and effect change on a captive audience, then it must identify positive end goals for the school to promote. It underscores the value and importance of hard work as a both a way to create opportunities, and ingrain moral responsibility as foundational to student and community success.

We have to let our kids see black people in the light, with the neon lights on. I don't care if they are lawn service men because guess what? They are taking care of their business, they are doing a job, they look good, they are living good, and they get a salary from it. Before, when Mr. S was there, we started a program, Unsung Heroes. That means that there are some people here in the community these kids come out of; people that have their little businesses, Flowers by Ms. R, little people, not all of these is a child going to notice, you don't look at Flowers by Ms. R as being a successful business person. You don't look at Mrs. H as being a successful seamstress. You never see them. We need to let those kids see them. I don't care what they do. They can cut lawns, they can be the mower or the owner of the business. Because we want our children to see people working. These kids got to know that you can make an honest living. You don't have to sell drugs. You don't have to be a gangster. You don't have to go rob anybody. (C2)

As such, vocational job opportunities emphasize that not all high school students will or need to go to four-year colleges and universities, although these postsecondary options always need to be kept open. Initial access to postsecondary education is the high school diploma—as a means to an end, not as an end in itself.

Because if I look at the statistics, . . . the number of kids that actually do go on, it's maybe 20 percent, 25, 30 percent do go off (to college). So the question is,

what happens to the other 70 percent? Where are these graduates going? . . . First of all, I'm a big supporter of technical centers, because again, as we spoke about the business careers and all, those jobs just aren't there. Aren't out there, but the kid can maybe go in and learn refrigeration, learn air conditioning. I think one thing that I hear a lot . . . about going to college . . . They talk about it because that's what we teach. What are we doing for those 70 percent that aren't going off to college? (G3-2)

I make sure that every single student has a set plan that involves parents with it. That strategy has worked as a result of the success of my students. I have police officers and doctors out there right now. (T2-2)

High school graduation does not constitute the end of education, but rather a pathway to lifelong learning, which includes mentoring, as role models, counselors, advisors, etc. It does take a village to raise a child:

I have to be committed and dedicated to what I am doing. That's what I had [when I went to school]. I had those kinds of teachers. They didn't care if it was Saturday or Sunday. They didn't care if it was in the morning time or not. They did what they needed to do, to make sure that we passed. This comes from both board members all the way down. They've got to be committed, dedicated, and concerned. They have to put themselves in the place of those families. They've got to think about every parent. And if they come here and their child comes through those gates, comes on those campuses that child should get a quality education before he or she leaves. When they walk across that stage, (and) their diploma is given to them, there should not be what, that certificate of completion. That should not be given to any child. We know these types of things are happening so we need to have our kids ready. (C2)

Within and beyond the urban high school is the need for political and citizenship skills coupled with the capacity to engage in wider social, political and economic issues—all as a part of the school curriculum.

I'm going to call you and talk to you tonight and then I'm going to call you in the morning to see if you still remember what I said when you go to the meeting to make sure that you say this. Then I am going to go to the meeting to make sure you said it because many times when we get in audiences we don't fight for each other. And that's how I had a problem with some of our elected officials. When during that penny sales tax, and I know you remember that, and we had people saying we are going to float that penny sales tax and buy technology and put all the technology out west. The schools over here will have to wait until we get this done then we will come over here and do it. We said no, we won't (wait) to do that. So we fought the penny sales tax. This thing with them not taking care of (our needs), my main thing is quality schools and staff for every child . . . Do what you are supposed to do. . . . You can blindfold them and bring them in this community and stand them in front of any school in our community and ask them what area do you think you are in now? You can blindfold them out west and you can ask them what community are you in now? It's obvious . . . They've got to think about every parent. Where they come from and guess what? We have experts (locally). We know how they live, that means we know what they need. (C2)

If U.S. education is unique, it is because of the many second- and third-chance opportunities built into public education, not just for students themselves, but also for members of their family and the community.

And that's what we have to (do), knock down that wall. I don't care whether they are a prostitute, I don't care whether they are the president of the bank, in other words, you are just as important to me and just as deserving of my time because of who you are and what you are. I said many times as you said, they're intimidated and don't want to come to the school. We want to remove the intimidation. Come on, do you want to volunteer, or can you help me do this, or what, you mean you really made my day when you did this. We have to let parents know, hey listen, this is not my school, I'd tell them, this is our school. If you think you want to use my facility, by all means. Let's come in and let's clear it. This is our school and we need to use it 24/7. And we want you to come in whenever you feel comfortable, volunteer, whatever you think you can contribute. We can find something for you to do if you have the time. It has to be a joint effort and we have to make them feel it's not we and you, but it's us. (G3-1)

DESTINY HIGH SCHOOL: A REDESIGN

The urban school collective that has been discussed is a very unique grouping, not to be confused with the standard mainstream conceptualization of a high school, or the media depicted dysfunctional conceptualization of high schools serving predominantly black populations. Communities populated by people of color have a deep affection, attachment, and commitment to their "community high schools" as sources of hope, opportunity, optimism, and accomplishment to serve as beacons of light for their students. Destiny High School is conceptualized in that vein.

Overview: Among the faculty, staff, guidance, and administration, urban students see representatives of not only the indigenous community's population, but also members from every U.S. demographic possible. The world created at Destiny is no more all black than it is all white. Each member of the faculty and staff are acutely aware of their leadership responsibility to empathetically connect, understand, and serve the needs of the indigenous student population; keeping in mind that as adults, they must reach out to students through how students are greeted and engaged in conversation; appropriate body language, attitudes, as well as verbal and nonverbal cues are critical. In order for staff to meet these teaching objectives will likely require a rewriting of current job descriptions—which are grounded in a different school reality. Therefore, every individual employed at DHS understands that they have a leadership responsibility regardless of title and position, because every student should have a one-to-one connection with an adult at the school, whether that connection is to a custodian, clerk, teacher, counselor, assistant principal, or the principal. Every staff member is responsible for an informal "classroom" setting, not to be confused with traditional subject matter classroom teaching; rather, the school becomes a life classroom presenting alternate perspectives designed for students to transcend the lived experiences and dynamics of their community. It is up to school leadership to ensure that each student has access to an adult they can trust to guide them to connect to support networks which can address multiple urban challenges. This requires a knowledge base mastered by staff members versed in school resources, accommodations, and networks inside and outside the school. Everyone inside the school becomes a lifelong learner and educator, and that includes the students.

Student socialization must be grounded in ideology that accepts the notion that it's the adults who must change first to guide the students, because the world the students must navigate was created by adults.

Thus, urban high schools need to enact new structures of a school day. Destiny High features a nontraditional four-day schedule with extended hours. Students have four ninety-minute blocks of core classes each day, and one ninety-minute elective block. True on-the-job opportunities outside the school focused on placement in vocational apprenticeship programs would complement upper-class student options. It extends the current school day by one hour and forty-five minutes, but eliminates Friday as a regular school day. Friday would be used as an opportunity to build back in the creative opportunities that low socioeconomic students have seen replaced by a focus on testing. This may perhaps be idealistic from a financial standpoint, but certainly noteworthy to begin needed conversations for change.

Among the other structural and personnel changes needed, the following are highlighted:

- One of the systemic breakdowns in disenfranchised cultures is the lack of knowledge and accessibility to support-service networks. DHS will expand this by funding and locating wraparound services for students and their families at the school on a full time basis. DHS will have a full-time grant facilitator to accomplish this.
- Urban educators recognize the standardized testing process . . . as a detrimental and counterproductive aspect of the school process for students and staff. If the goal of testing is to assess college readiness, why not simplify the testing process by administering the two tests colleges and universities use in the admissions process; the Scholastic Aptitude Test (SAT), and the American College Test(ing) (ACT)? [It makes perfectly good sense that to] administer them early to students, during their first year, and continue at least twice annually through students' senior year of high school. This [would be to the advantage of not only minority students, but to the advantage of all students].
  - Testing provides challenges to school leaders in the high school setting. The standardized testing process takes place throughout the school year, commands huge amounts of human and time resources to execute, and virtually did not exist a decade ago. During the study, faculty and staff frequently identified testing as a detrimental and counterproductive aspect of the school process

for students and staff. Its focus to measure standardized output for what all students should know without consideration for input, or more importantly starting points, was a point of contention.

- Legislators who have no professional educational background by and large decide on the answers for urban schools. Yet, their lack of knowledge and expertise is evidenced by educational policy debates that have prompted constant changes and modifications to local, state, and federal policies that drive the testing machine in this country; a machine that has become a huge business unto itself in its association with high schools. Discontent and solutions in this area are perhaps the most perplexing and challenging problem for educators and lies beyond the scope of this conversation.
- The foundation of the discipline program will be behavior modification, not punitive. Referring to the findings presented, changing the perception of the vast majority of educators who do not connect or have an appreciation for the experiences that result in the perceptions of African-Americans/students of color, lack empathy and thus continue with punitive actions starting with removal from classrooms and eventual removal (even if temporary as in suspension) from school will remain a challenge.
- Athletics and performing arts have always been mainstays as forms of cultural expression and creativity in the black community, and that will not be suppressed at DHS, it will be celebrated and highlighted.
- Students will be introduced to ethnically diverse two-year and four-year institutions to enable students to observe higher learning executed en masse by people of color. This is an unfamiliar model to the typical student attending school in a disenfranchised setting. It could be the edge they need to create a positive attitude about school and postsecondary pursuits.
- The guidance counselor's responsibilities associated with test taking [will be] delegated to personnel hired specifically for that purpose as the design for this model school.
  - A guidance counselor articulated a strategy to engage the community and provide leadership

opportunities for civic organizations to serve as mentors. She talked about local chapters of fraternities and sororities being used as mentors for coaches of sports programs at local parks. These college-educated groups can help build a foundation for success that parents and/or coaches in park situations can't necessarily do. She went on to restate that "it takes a village to raise a child," noting partnerships with churches and the community to reach black students to provide programs outside the school are of critical importance. Networking and relationship-building with the business community, sororities, fraternities, churches, and national organizations were all identified as elements for success. These organizations have members that maintain a passionate affectionate relationship with the school, and have the ability to provide students with mentoring, internships, and glimpses into unimaginable real-world possibilities for success.

The above is not a complete picture of tomorrow's urban high school, but it represents a new beginning far superior to many of today's urban reforms based on ignoring communities and contexts, international rankings, self-interests, elite CEO visions for workforce productivity, separating student achievement and school improvement from neighborhood development, and privatization profits from education.

CONCLUSION

Bogotch, Nesmith, Smith, and Gaines (2014) contend that:

> The position we take here is that any school leadership policy or action that frustrates deep discussions, honest explanations, and transparent debates ultimately undermines the legitimacy of public education—urban or otherwise—from within. For urban educators to reposition themselves in a national debate, the future of urban schools would need to be perceived as a "public good," rather than as a reform that benefits special interests or minority students alone. (p. 306)

Some will continue to argue that it is not the schools' responsibility to address critical societal issues as they don't impact numeracy and literacy using short-term measures. But participants in this study asserted otherwise. Listening to their voices, but not tempering their messages, it is clear that their ideas differ from current federal, state, and district mandates regarding standardized testing, disciplinary policies, and delimited curricular offerings. It is also clear that while "historically" black signifies a leadership identity belonging to their indigenous neighbors and students, and that their larger identity is linked to opportunities for success in society. It is also clear that we documented a departure from traditional school improvement research. That is, we can no longer continue to delimit policy or research to coherent "within-school" rules and school improvement models (see Leithwood, 2009), as these, we believe, have effectively erased the role that communities need to play (Furman, 2002; Furman and Shields, 2003; Larson and Ovando, 2001; Warren, 2005) in transforming urban education.

As both educational leadership researchers and practitioners, we have worked in forgotten and abandoned schools in our nations' cities; therefore, like the urban educators in this study, we found no reason to temper our words. We are forever grateful to those men and women across this nation who continue every day to drive into rundown facilities with unmowed lawns, peeling paint, missing ceiling tiles, and broken water fountains. Educators who reach into their pockets for paper and materials while central office administrators dare to say to these dedicated individuals that unless test scores rise we will bring down sanctions and punishments. In our disenfranchised neighborhoods, educators have turned against other educators working with indigent and indigenous students. The result: decades of recycled generations of poverty.

What we are calling for is a cohesive national educational improvement agenda with districts in partnership with organizations such as the National Alliance of Black School Educators (NABSE), the NAACP, the Urban League, and the nine historically Black Greek letter service organizations. These groups possess the social and political capital that urban school leaders lack and need in order to redefine success measures and promote opportunities beyond school. It is up to them to invite the CEOs and Foundation Leaders to their urban reform tables, not vice versa. But even as the call here is for a national agenda, the specific reforms have to be translated into within-school practices aligned with an ethic of care and community needs. This agenda paints a different story than the one which expects individuals who work alone heroically to make changes.

> the first thing you need to do is teach your kid how to deal with society, about the everyday things of the world. Like we should come to class and talk about things before you start the lesson; we would talk about the news, what happened in the news; the effects the decisions of the president is making; the decisions that the governor is making, and how it's going to affect you later on. The decisions that the school board made or the county made, and how it's going to affect you. We look at what we saw in the news about this situation in the war, and how it's going to affect you. . . . And it's our job here to prepare those kids to go out into the world and be productive. (C1-1)

We end our chapter with one more urban educator's voice:

> if we can't get the ["historically"] black schools to really talk about their past as a reminder of how we got here and also remind them it took the strength of these people to persist, to overcome some obstacles and [if we don't] paint a clear picture of what these obstacles and the consequences are, if we don't rise to the occasion; if YOU don't rise to the occasion, [then] we don't understand [that] we are under attack, and YOU won't know how to ready yourself.

You can't go to a black community and find a common thread that connects all black people. You can't even find a superficial connection. So I think that when I look at the big picture and look at our school and look at our kids, it's not the kids that are really failing, it's the system. The system is failing. The system is broken and has become disconnected. There are people who are driving the system. They think they are still in charge of the system, but the system is starting to break down in levels and in ways that the people that think they are driving have not anticipated. What is about to happen, I feel is that the society as a whole, and I really feel that the black community is a microcosm of the whole United States. Eventually what happens in the black community will happen in the whole United States . . . because we've been the backbone for years and years and years. (T2-1)

NOTES

1. According to the Broad Foundation's criteria, seventy-nine school districts have high poverty urban schools (alphabetical order):

Albuquerque Public Schools, New Mexico; Aldine Independent School District, Texas; Arlington Independent School District, Texas; Atlanta Public Schools, Georgia; Austin Independent School District, Texas; Baltimore City Public School System, Maryland; Baltimore County Public Schools, Maryland; Boston Public Schools, Massachusetts; Broward County School District, Florida; Charleston County School District, South Carolina; Charlotte-Mecklenburg Schools; Chicago Public Schools, Illinois; Clark County School District, Nevada; Clayton County School System, Georgia; Cleveland Metropolitan School District, Ohio; Cobb County School District, Georgia; Columbus Public Schools, Ohio; Corona-Norco Unified School District, California; Cumberland County Schools, North Carolina; Cypress-Fairbanks Independent School District, Texas; Dallas Independent School District, Texas; DeKalb County Public Schools, Georgia; Denver Public Schools, Colorado; Des Moines Public Schools, Iowa; Detroit Public Schools, Michigan; District of Columbia Public Schools, Washington, DC; Duval County Public Schools, Florida; East Baton Rouge Parish School System, Louisiana; El Paso Independent School District, Texas; Elk Grove Unified School District, California; Forsyth County Schools, North Carolina; Fort Worth Independent School District, Texas; Fresno Unified School District, California; Fulton County Schools, Georgia; Garden Grove Unified School District, California; Granite School District, Utah; Greenville County Schools, South Carolina; Guilford County Schools, North Carolina; Gwinnett County Public Schools, Georgia; Hamilton County Schools, Tennessee; Houston Independent School District, Texas; Indianapolis Public Schools, Indiana; Jefferson County Public Schools, Kentucky; Jefferson Parish Public Schools, Louisiana; Lee County Public Schools, Florida; Long Beach Unified School District, California; Los Angeles Unified School District, California; Manatee County School District, Florida; Memphis City Schools, Tennessee; Mesa Unified School District, Arizona; Metropolitan Nashville Public Schools, Tennessee; Miami-Dade County Public Schools, Florida; Milwaukee Public Schools, Wisconsin; Mobile County Public Schools, Alabama; Newark Public Schools, New Jersey; New York City Department of Education, New York; Norfolk Public Schools, Virginia; North East Independent School District, Texas; Northside Independent School District, Texas; Oklahoma City Public Schools, Oklahoma; Omaha Public Schools, Nebraska; Orange County Public Schools, Florida; Palm Beach County School District, Florida; Pinellas County Schools, Florida; Portland Public Schools, Oregon; Prince George's County Public Schools, Maryland; Saint Paul Public Schools, Minnesota; San Bernardino City Unified School District, California; San Diego Unified School District, California; San Francisco Unified School District, California; Santa Ana Unified School District, California; School District of Hillsborough County, Florida; School District of Philadelphia, Pennsylvania; Seattle Public Schools, Washington; Seminole County Public Schools, Florida; Tucson Unified School District #1, Arizona; Washoe County Public Schools, Nevada; Wichita Public Schools, Kansas. www.broadprize.org/about/eligible_school_districts.htmld political dynamics.

2. Some quotes cannot be attributed to only one participant and so there is no codebook i.d. for some of them.

REFERENCES

American Friends Service Committee. (1955). Speak truth to power: A Quaker search for the alternative to violence. AFSC.

Anyon, J. (2005). *Radical possibilities: Public policy, urban education and a new social movement.* New York: Routledge.

Balfanz, R. (2014, June 8). Stop holding us back. *The New York Times,* New in Review. page 5.

Barber, B. (1993). America skips school: Why we talk so much about education and do so little. *Harpers Magazine,* 39–47.

Bogotch, I., Nesmith, L., Smith, and Gaines, F. (2014). Urban school leadership and fit. In R. Milner and K. Lomoty (Eds.). *Handbook of urban education,* Chapter 17 305–324. New York: Routledge.

Clark, D., Martorell, P., and Rockoff, J. (2009). School Principals and School Performance: Working Paper 38. National Center for the Analysis of Longitudinal Data in Education Research (CALDER), The Urban Institute.

Dewey, J. (1909). *Moral principles in education.* Boston: Houghton Mifflin.

Foster, M. (1996). Like Us but Not One of Us: Reflections on a Life History Study of African American Teachers. In G. Etter-Lewis and M. Foster (Eds.), *Unrelated Kin: Race and Gender in Women's Personal Narratives* (pp. 215–224). London: Routledge.

Furman, G. (Ed.). (2002). *School as Community: From Promise to Practice.* Albany: State University of New York Press.

Furman, G. and Shields, C. (2003, April). *How can educational leaders promote and support social justice and democratic community in schools.* Paper presented at the American Educational Research Association Annual Meeting, Chicago.

Gooden, M. A. (2012). What does racism have to do with leadership? Countering the idea of color-blind leadership: A reflection on race and the growing pressures of the urban principalship. *Educational Foundations, 26*(1), 67–84.

Greer, C. (1972). *The great school legend: A revisionist interpretation of American public education.* New York: Penguin Books.

Hanushek, Eric A., John F. Kain, and Steven G. Rivkin. 2004. Why Public Schools Lose Teachers. *Journal of Human Resources, 39*(2): 326–54.

Krugman, P. (2013, January 20). Inequality and recovery. krugman.blogs.nytimes.com/2013/01/20/inequality-and-recovery/?smid=tw-NytimesKrugmanandseid=auto.

Kozol, J. (1991). *Savage inequalities.* New York: HarperCollins.

Larson, C. and Ovando, C. (2001). *The color of bureaucracy.* Belmont, CA: Wadsworth Press.

Lawrence-Lightfoot, S. and Hoffman-Davis, J. (1997). The art and science of portraiture. San Francisco: John Wiley

Mann, H. (1867/91). Annual Reports on Education. *Life and works of Horace Mann, Volume 3.* Boston: Lee and Shepard Publishers.

Miel, A. (1961). *Creativity in teaching: Invitations and instances.* Belmont, CA: Wadsworth Publishing Co.

Miron, L. (1996). *The Social Construction of Urban Schooling Situating the Crisis.* New York: Hampton Press.

Miron, L., Bogotch, I., and Biesta, G. (2001). In Pursuit of the Good Life: High School Students' Constructions of Morality and the Implications for Educational Leadership. *Cultural Studies <=> Critical Methodologies* November 1, 490–516.

Normore, A. H., Rodriguez, L., and Wynne, J. (2007). Making all children winners: Confronting social justice issues to redeem America's soul. *Journal of Educational Administration, 45*(6), 653–671.

Orfield, G., Kuscera, J., and Siegel-Hawley, G. (2012). *E pluribus . . . Separation deepening double segregation for more students.* Los Angeles: UCLA Civil Rights Project.

Scherrer, J. (May, 2014). The role of the intellectual in eliminating the effects of poverty: A response to Tierney. *Educational Researcher, 43*(4), pp, 201–207.

Sergiovanni, T. (1992). *Moral Leadership.* San Francisco: Jossey-Bass Inc., Publishers.

Sergiovanni, T. (1996). *Leadership for the Schoolhouse.* San Francisco, CA: Jossey-Bass Inc., Publishers.

Sergiovanni, T. (2004). Balance individual autonomy and collaboration to center on students. *Education Digest, 70*(3), 17–22.

Stiglitz, J. (2013, January 19). Inequality is holding back the recovery. opinionator.blogs.nytimes.com/2013/01/19/inequality-is-holding-back-the-recovery/?_r=0.

Time. (2014, February 24). The diploma that works: Inside the six-year high school (pp. 22–29).

Vasquez-Heilig, J., Khalifa, M., and Tillman, L. (2014). High stakes reform and urban education. In R. Milner and K. Lomoty (Eds.), *Handbook of urban education*, 523–538. New York: Routledge.

Warren, M. (2005). Communities and Schools: A New View of Urban Education Reform. *Harvard Educational Review*, *75*(2), 133–139.

CHAPTER 26

Leaders of the New School(s)

Reconceptualizing an Autonomy Framework for Urban Principals Implementing Small School Reform

April L. Peters, Jia Liang, and Rejer Finklin

The current context of education is characterized by accountability and change. In an effort to meet the challenges of accountability, several states and districts have implemented various reform models to assist schools in increasing student achievement. In particular, urban school districts have engaged in myriad reform efforts to address the many challenges of educating at-risk students, including comprehensive school reform, charter school reform, charter school districts, innovative programs, small school reform, and so on. The success of each of these reform efforts has been mixed at best (American Federation of Teachers, 2004; Fink and Silverman, 2007; Hill, Angel, and Christenson, 2006; Hoxby, 2004; Iatarola, Schwartz, Stiefel, and Chellman, 2008; Lee, Ready, and Johnson, 2001; U.S. Department of Education, 2004; Wyse, Keesler, and Schneider, 2008).

Small school reform is an initiative implemented in urban districts to aid large failing comprehensive high schools to restructure in order to facilitate targeted professional learning, rigorous instructional practice, healthy student and faculty relationships, increased student support, and improved student achievement outcomes (Ancess, 1997; Cotton, 2001; Raywid, 1998). Small school reform is frequently an intervention initiated as district policy and implemented at the school level. Several large, urban cities currently implement small school reform in their metropolitan districts in an effort to increase student achievement and turn around failing schools, including Atlanta, Baltimore, Chicago, Detroit, New York City, and Seattle.

Research indicates that in addition to classroom instruction, school leadership has a significant impact on student achievement outcomes (Leithwood, Seashore Louis, Anderson, and Wahlstrom, 2004). Naturally, reform efforts and other efforts to improve school and student achievement rely largely on the effectiveness of the leader. Often the school leader is responsible for reform implementation, as well as some stage of the actual development of the new (reforming) school. Therefore, in addition to adequate resource allocation and district (and community) support, the success of many school reforms is dependent on the leader's ability to implement with fidelity the elements of the reform within his or her school. A leader's agency to implement reform is equally important in determining his or her effectiveness.

Autonomy here is defined as the leader's power, or agency, to implement district, state, or national policies while simultaneously empowering local school-level independence. This definition is advanced to capture the leader's agency to make and share decisions along several dimensions (personnel, budget, curriculum, etc.) within the scope of his or her position. This chapter examines the concept of autonomy and the influence on a school leader's ability to implement an urban school reform model effectively and with fidelity given the expectation of student achievement and within the context of accountability that pervades the educational context on a federal, state, and local level. More specifically, this chapter investigates the ways in which urban school leaders perceive their agency to exercise autonomy in implementing the small school reform model.

DEFINING SMALL SCHOOL REFORM

Small school reform is not a new phenomenon. This movement traces its origin back to the *A Nation at Risk* (1983) report, which criticized traditional comprehensive high schools for being large and impersonal. The current wave of small school reform exists largely in high-poverty, urban school districts (Cotton, 2001; Darling-Hammond, Ancess, and Ort, 2002; Peters, 2011). The goal of most small school reform is to create a more personalized school environment where students can be known and be provided the supports that they need to be successful academically and socially.

Several characteristics typify small schools. The term "small schools" is used to capture the idea that these schools differ most obviously from their comprehensive school counterparts in enrollment. In addition, they differ in that the design and intent of the small school reform is to offer "historically underserved populations an opportunity to flourish and grow in settings where teachers know and care about them" (Copland and Boatright, 2004). Thus, the intent of small schools is to change the culture of a failing comprehensive high school from despair and neglect, to success and engagement (Antrop-Gonzalez and DeJesus, 2006). Being deliberate in instituting such changes to culture and outcomes suggests several benefits to small schools including increased student engagement, increased (physical and emotional) safety, greater staff morale, and increased student achievement (Cotton, 2001; Lee and Loeb, 2000; Wasley and Lear, 2001).

Small schools are not without challenges, however. Wasley and Lear (2001) outline the following barriers to starting small schools and converting large high schools into small schools:

- Cultural expectations about what an American high school should be are deeply embedded. Americans hold high schools as a nostalgic place of "sacred cow" (p. 24) activities such as extracurricular activities and large selections of courses.
- Schools attempting to become small do too little too slowly. Many pilot programs do not succeed because the entire faculty is not committed to the mission and goal of the small school. They seek to wait out the research to verify the evidence for implementation. By this time the enthusiasm for the innovation has died down and the program or school has failed.
- Small schools are not small enough and continue to act as large comprehensive high schools. The research suggests small schools have no more than four hundred students, but most actually have between five hundred and eight hundred students.

As such it is much more likely that the school will maintain its larger comprehensive structure and organization but with fewer students.
- Decision makers and legislators focus mainly on short-term results. Seeking reelection, results are requested by small schools much quicker in order to justify the decision to support the reform. This pressure to produce student performance improvements causes teachers to revert back to traditional pedagogy and abandon the innovative curriculum of the new small school.
- Many funding mandates are actually promoting the consolidation of small schools into larger schools particularly in regards to funding formulas for resource allocations and construction.
- Leaders try to make reform "educator-proof" (p. 25) by creating cookie-cutter small-school packages that everyone in a district must adopt and implement in the same manner essentially eliminating the necessary autonomy and creativity for small schools to be successful.

The research is mixed in terms of small schools and student academic achievement (Hammack, 2008). There are several reasons for this fact. Often, districts implement small school reform without maintaining fidelity to the small school reform paradigm, including limiting schools' autonomy (Raywid, 1996, 1998). However, some literature suggests that the small school paradigm has been successful in some districts' reform efforts. Specifically, there is research that suggests that when schools are able to personalize the learning environment for their students these schools experience gains in student achievement and engagement including increased attendance, decreased dropout rates, increased graduation rates, and improved student achievement as measured by state assessments (Cotton, 1996; Gladden, 1998; Meier, 1996).

While early categorization of small schools into freestanding small schools, schools-within-a-building (SWB), and schools-within-a-school (SWS) has been more focused on physical arrangement (Husband and Beese, 2001; Lee et al., 2001; Legsters and Kerr, 2001; Ready, Lee, and Welner, 2004), a more recent and relevant categorization came from Peters' (2011) distinction between *conversion* schools and *creation* schools (see also Feldman and O'Dwyer, 2010). Conversion schools are those essentially emanate from the "parent school," which is the original failing comprehensive high school, and are typically located on the same campus as the parent school (Peters, 2011; see also Feldman, Lopez, and Simon, 2005; Feldman and O'Dwyer, 2010). It is not uncommon for several small conversion schools to coexist within the same campus, along with the parent, or "phase out" school. They are "established by the district and the charge and challenge to the leadership and faculty is to clean up the school by changing the culture, structure, and student achievement outcomes" (Peters, 2011, p. 90). Creation schools, also known as the start-up schools (Benitez, Davidson, and Flaxman, 2009; Feldman and O'Dwyer, 2010; French, Atkinson, and Rugen, 2007; Lake, Winger, and Petty, 2002), on the other hand, though share structures and intended outcomes, differ from conversion schools as they are "developed by a visionary leader or a group of stakeholders" (Peters, 2011, p. 91). Although creation schools and conversion schools both originate from districts' intentional reform measures focused on addressing issues like high dropout rates, low student achievement, low student engagement, high absenteeism, and lack of parental involvement (Ancess, 2003; Cotton, 2001; Darling-Hammond, Ross, and Milliken, 2007; Feldman and O'Dwyer, 2010; Iatarola, Schwartz, Stiefel, and Chellman, 2008; Smerdon and Cohen, 2009; Wallach, 2010; Wallach and Lear, 2005), creation schools offer an opportunity for creating a new school culture rather than changing a preexisting, negative culture inherited from the previous school, a task prevalent in the work of conversion schools.

Small urban schools, created or converted, potentially suffer from uncertainty and ambiguity (though they are unavoidable in any types of change); lack of district support (financially, technically, and politically); the absence of committed and/or veteran staff; unsustainable funding; unsafe and overcrowded facilities; conflicting institutional demands; and lack of autonomy, albeit with variation in scope and extent depending on the district and school contexts (American Institutes for Research and SRI International, 2004, 2006; Nehring and Lohmeier, 2010; Nehring, Lohmeier, and Colombo, 2009; Noguera, 2002; Quint, 2006; Ready et al., 2004; Shaw, 2006; Wallach and Lear, 2005; Wasley and Lear, 2001). Nonetheless, the conversion school leaders are more susceptible to lack of critical decision-making authority on issues like staffing and budgeting because of tighter district macro- and micromanagement from

the district office (Fouts, Baker, Brown, and Riley, 2006; Peters, 2012; Wallach and Lear, 2005). In many ways this translates into a lack of autonomy. Research also demonstrates that particularly for those created or converted small schools who share buildings (though mostly conversion schools), the violation of implementation fidelity is more prominent as conflicts over funding, faculty tensions, space constraints, scheduling conflicts for shared facilities, and lack of communication between administrations have made it unlikely for these small schools to increase student achievement despite the positive effect on improving the climate of schools (Oxley, Croninger, and DeGroot, 2000; Quint, 2006; Supovitz, 2002). Furthermore, the positive changes in the level of personalization and sense of community the conversion small schools experience are not at the same extent as those found in creation small schools (American Institutes for Research and SRI International, 2006). Researchers warn that without autonomy and flexibility for creativity, the cultural changes needed to bring about personalization, assessment based on deep understanding (rather than achievement purely measured by standardized tests), and cross-disciplinary instruction is insufficient to bring about improvements in student outcomes (Bryk and Driscoll, 1998; Cleary and English, 2005; Cotton, 2001; Davidson, 2002; Feldman and O'Dwyer, 2010; Feldman, O'Dwyer, and Kleigman, 2009; Hantzopoulos, 2009; Lee, Smith, and Croninger, 1995; Nehring et al., 2009; Nehring and Lohmeier, 2010; Oxley et al., 2000; Raywid, 1996, 1998; Stevens, 2008; Strike, 2008; Tung and Ouimette, 2007).

Small school reform is initiated at the district level and implemented at the school level. That is, although school building principals are responsible to execute small school reform, often they are subject to the district vision relative to the support and resources provided to accomplish such tremendous responsibilities. The role of the school leader in this context is expanded, and necessarily, more entrepreneurial (Peters, 2011). However, there is no research in this area that suggests a reconsideration of the district's role in such reform implementation. Thus, although small school reform requires a reconceptualization of the principal's role and responsibilities, urban districts do not necessarily conduct themselves differently in terms of relating to small reforming high schools in ways that are distinctly different from large, comprehensive high schools.

MAKING A CASE FOR LEADER AUTONOMY

In the literature autonomous schools have been defined as those that are self-determining but are nested in district or state authority (Wohlstetter, Wenning, and Briggs, 1995). While past research has examined school autonomy in terms of personnel, budget, and curricular decisions, few, if any, studies have focused specifically on the perspective of the principal in implementing reform models. The majority of studies on school autonomy have focused on the impacts of decentralized schools and improved instruction. These studies, at best, have found limited or indirect impacts on improved instruction. More often, these studies have found increased decision-making on the part of parents and teachers, as reported by Malen, Ogawa, and Kranz (1990).

A small number of studies found a direct correlation between school autonomy and instruction. For example, Smylie, Lazarus, and Brownlee-Conyers (1996) found that school-based participative decision-making was related positively to instructional improvement and student achievement. Again, results did not speak to the principal's role in improving instruction or student achievement. Additionally, researchers investigated the effects of teacher empowerment in decentralized schools on instruction (Marks and Louis, 1997, 1999; Newmann, Marks, and Gamoran, 1996). These studies suggested that not all forms of teacher empowerment have the same effects on instruction.

Since there is a paucity of research on school leader autonomy in the implementation of school reform models, this chapter adds to the literature base examining how school leaders' autonomy might lead to improved instruction and increased student achievement in small school reform. Reform often carries with it specific mandates for implementation and expectations for outcomes; small school reform is no exception. In order for leaders to facilitate successful implementation, they must be empowered to be innovative within their school contexts. However, schools and districts often operate within certain levels of constraint. In order to lead effectively within their contexts, leaders must understand where the district and school are situated with respect to autonomy and constraint.

In a study examining autonomy and American charter schools, Wohlstetter and colleagues (1995) define autonomy along the following three dimensions: autonomy from higher levels of government, local autonomy, and consumer sovereignty. Autonomy from higher levels of government is defined as self-management. Self-management suggests, "decisions at the school level are being made within a framework of local, state or national policies and guidelines" (Caldwell and Spinks, 1992, p. 4). Thus, although the school organization has the agency to self-manage, it is still subject to district, local and state policies and regulations. The second dimension, local autonomy, suggests that at the school level, the leader and faculty are empowered to make personnel, policy, instructional, and curricular decisions and set organizational goals according to the needs and preferences of those at the school level (Wohlstetter et al., 1995). This autonomy is extended to teachers at the classroom level as well.

Finally, consumer sovereignty, the third dimension, refers to the level of agency, or choice that parents (consumers) have in selecting the appropriate school for their children. Wohlstetter et al. (1995) suggest that consumer autonomy is linked to accountability. That is parents choose the best schools for their children, indirectly applying pressure for schools to perform well. These schools are then accountable to parents for student achievement outcomes. Wohlstetter et al. (1995) indicate, "the effect of this accountability is to establish autonomy at several levels and among various entities, that is, the school, the parents and the students."

The Small School Autonomy Framework (see table 26.1) offered in this chapter as a means to examine small schools is adapted from the framework Wohlstetter et al. (2005) applied to examine the impact of autonomy on charter schools. It is used here to examine the agency of two principals of small schools established under the auspices of district-initiated small school reform. Although this framework has been invoked to understand autonomy in charter schools, small school reform is a phenomenon not unlike charters in many ways, except that small (conversion) schools are established by the district, and the district sanctions/approves any small schools that are established therein. Like charters, small schools are established to increase student achievement and engagement and to personalize the learning environment. Other similarities between small schools and charters include innovative instructional techniques and themed academic programs. There is, however, a significant difference between charters and small school reform in that small schools are established under the auspices of the district. Thus, this framework is being adapted to frame the leader's behavior as "agency," defined as the leader's power to act or operate in the interest of his or her school. Small schools themselves are autonomous from other schools, and provide a context in which a leader has the power to exercise his or her agency.

METHODOLOGY

This qualitative cross-case study (Yin, 2009) examined the differences between the founding principal of a "conversion" small school and that of a founding principal of a "creation" small school. The cross-case analysis "provides opportunities to learn from different cases and gather critical evidence to modify policy" (Khan and VanWynsberhe, 2008). Further, this kind of analysis allowed the researchers to compare and contrast cases across contexts, groups, and communities (Khan and VanWynsberhe, 2008). The analysis is undertaken to compare the findings from two earlier case studies of principals leading small school reform in urban contexts.[1] The current analysis was conducted in order to understand the similarities and differences between two types of small schools, conversion and creation. Yin (1994) suggests that the purpose of cross-case analysis is to "to build a general explanation that fits each of the individual cases, even though the cases will vary in their details" (p. 112). Although the literature about small schools is rich (Copland and Boatright, 2004; Cotton, 2001; Darling-Hammond et al., 2002; Fink and Silverman, 2007; Gladden, 1998; Hammack, 2008; Iatarola et al., 2008; Peters, 2011; Smerdon and Cohen, 2009) the comparison between conversion and creation (Peters, 2011) has not been previously conducted in the literature. Because small school reform is prevalent in many urban contexts across the United States, analysis of the different methods of implementation may suggest implications for policy, leadership, districts, and so forth.

Data collection consisted of site visits and in-depth interviews with both principals, in order to gain a rich, thick description (Glesne, 2011) of their experiences in implementing such a reform. Further, school documents (such as evaluation reports and school report cards data) and field notes were analyzed in order to gain contex-

tual and historical information about the districts, the schools, and the leadership (Glesne, 2011; Merriam, 1998; Yin, 2009). Several research questions guided this cross-case study: (a) How is the small school reform model implemented in creation and conversion schools? What are the similarities and differences?; and (b) How is a leader's autonomy to implement small school reform influenced by district involvement?

SCHOOL AND DISTRICT PROFILES

This section compares and contrasts a conversion and creation small school in two different urban districts. The idea is not that the findings are generalizable to all small schools, nor that the findings can be used in other comparisons between creation and conversion schools in urban districts. The purpose is to develop a depth of understanding of two specific small schools that came to existence by two very distinct paradigms of urban small school reform. There were many demographic similarities between the districts, the principals, and the student body from each school. The following sections examine these similarities and differences.

The districts. Both schools were located in large, urban, public school districts that serve in excess of fifty thousand students. Both districts served a majority (over 70 percent) of children of color and students with low socioeconomic status. Both districts face challenges typical of urban high schools: high dropout rates; low student attendance; school violence; gangs; low socioeconomic status of students and families; and so forth.

The creation school district (Emerson City School District) serves a student body that is racially diverse, whereas the majority of children served in the conversion school district (Sheridan Area School District) are African American. While the Emerson City School District has a number of creation high schools, the district has embraced both the creation and conversion small school paradigms. However, in the conversion district (SASD), all of the small schools participating in this reform are conversion schools.

The leaders. There are some striking similarities between the two principals in this study. Both are male and in their mid-thirties. Both served as assistant principals prior to being named principal. Both earned doctorates in educational leadership. Further, the small school reform setting served both as their first principalship and they were the first principals of their schools. They assumed this leadership role early in their careers, as both became principals before they turned forty. In both cases they taught less than seven years before moving into administration. Neither had previously worked in small reforming schools. Dr. Richards (Technology Conversion High School) taught four years and Dr. Mathers (Creative Arts High School) taught for six years prior to becoming an administrator. Both had some input into the design of their schools, but Dr. Mathers had far more input and involvement as the founding principal of a creation school. Dr. Richards was the principal of a conversion school and so he was appointed largely to implement the district's vision of his school, rather than his own. It must be noted that Dr. Mathers is Caucasian, while Dr. Richards is African American.

The Purpose of Small Schools

Something old: Converting Technology Conversion High School. Technology Conversion High School (TCHS) is located in Sheridan Area School District (SASD). Sheridan Area is a large, urban city in the south. Sheridan Area School District enrolls over fifty thousand students. SASD has been engaged in small school reform since 2004. All of the schools involved in small school reform in SASD are conversion schools. That is, the district reconstituted large, failing, comprehensive high schools by converting them into small schools. The former large schools house several small schools on a campus, each with a different curricular theme. District support for small schools does not particularly differ from the support offered to large high schools, with the exception that the district has partnered with an agency that provides support in a few ways: (a) each of the small schools is staffed with an instructional coach who works with the principal and staff specifically to implement the small school reform model, (b) small school principals attend an annual leadership conference, and (c) small school principals and their teachers attend two annual workshops where they receive support in implementing curricular objectives, student social support, and support in implementing small school reform.

TCHS is a conversion school established by the district. Dr. Richards was the inaugural principal appointed to implement the small school reform. TCHS started in 2007 with the ninth and tenth grade and a total of three hundred students. Enrollments have fluctuated over the years, but the current enrollment is 347 students. In general, enrollment at TCHS has either declined or been low since its inception. TCHS shares a campus with two other small (conversion) schools.

Something new: Creating Creative Arts High School. Creative Arts High School (CAHS) is located in Emerson City School District (ECSD). Emerson City is a large, metropolitan city in the north. The district enrolls over eighty thousand students. ECSD has been engaged in small school reform for over the past twenty years. The majority of small schools in ECSD are creation schools. That is, most small schools have come to be as a result of strategic planning and vision development done by a leader and a small design team, rather than converted from a large, comprehensive school. The district has created a sophisticated network designed to support small schools and their leaders, called the Small School Network (SSN). The SSN is designed specifically to function as a small "area" or unit within the district. Several SSNs exist in small clusters throughout the ECSD. The network is organized as a system that grants schools a great deal of flexibility in terms of decision making, budgeting, staffing, and structure, while requiring a high level of principal accountability (Peters, 2011). In spite of the increased principal accountability, there are several advantages to participation in the SSN, including sharing a cadre of potential school partners; engagement with other similar small schools; and providing extracurricular activities for students within the same network cluster. An additional layer of support is provided by the district via a partnership with an outside operator that provides a coach to provide instructional, curricular, and leadership support to the small school principals, counselors, and teachers. This partnership also features an annual professional learning seminar for principals to support their leadership practice and two annual professional learning seminars for the entire faculty.

CAHS is a creation school that was started by its visionary principal, Dr. Mathers. Dr. Mathers developed the design plan for CAHS. CAHS is a small intensive college preparatory school that has a media arts theme. CAHS opened its doors in 2006 to one hundred freshmen and has added a grade each year. Presently, the school has four hundred students in grades nine though twelve. Although enrollment is open throughout the city and there are no enrollment criteria, CAHS serves the local community in which it exists. That is, preference is given to students who live in the community. There is a tremendous interest in CAHS and annually the school receives 750–850 applications for admission for about one hundred slots. Although it is a "creation" school, CAHS shares a building with several other schools.

LEADER AUTONOMY

Wohlstetter et al. (1995) suggest that schools' autonomy can be expressed along a continuum. That is, autonomy is not an all or nothing condition. The data in this study indicates that there are some areas in which each principal had more autonomy than others. This section presents the data along the three dimensions of autonomy adapted from the Wohlstetter et al. (1995) framework for the purpose of analyzing the ways in which both principals were empowered to exercise agency in implementing the reform.

Autonomy from Higher Levels of Government

For the purposes of this study, "autonomy from higher levels of government" is regarded as freedom from traditional school restraints (e.g., state and district mandates imposed on traditional schools). The Emerson City School District and Sheridan Area School District both established small schools as a way of addressing student achievement issues. The purpose of the small school reform was to create more personalized school environments for students in order to provide needed academic, social and emotional supports that promote student achievement. The way in which the district supported or interfered with implementation became a significant factor for both schools.

Creative Arts High School. ECSD created opportunities for interested leaders to develop their design plan for establishing a new school. Principals in this district choose their focus related to the kind of school they lead. Dr. Jackson related:

> That was more attractive to me, to try to create a vision and create a model that was from scratch and build our own culture as opposed to [taking over another culture].

School leaders who design their schools have the autonomy (granted by the district office) to choose the theme of their school and their clientele, to some degree. That is, the schools are a part of the larger school district; however, in the case of Creative Arts High, the design team led by the principal deliberately chose to design a school that drew clientele from the local neighborhood. Dr. Mathers shared:

> So we really wanted to . . . start a school that was a community-based school that served students and families in the general community . . . but also partnered with community-based organizations and educators and entities to try to fulfill the dream of a [school that is a] hub in the community.

In addition, the principal and the design team had the opportunity to determine the thematic focus of the school. In the case of Arts High, the principal chose a media arts focus as the school's curricular theme.

Although ECSD principals who establish their own small schools have autonomy in terms of theme and curriculum, they are still bound by district and state regulations regarding state and district exit exams.

In addition, the district has established a structure for small schools who wish to be included. This structure, referred to in this study as the Small School Network, provides additional autonomy for small schools but at a higher standard of accountability. Dr. Mathers clarified:

> It's an accountability structure that puts the principals' job on the line . . . but in exchange for that we have a lot more freedom and a lot more flexibility to make decisions . . . we budget the way we want. And . . . the old regions where they were dominant about holding you accountable and managing, now these centers more support you in carrying out your stuff.

The Emerson City School District created the Small Schools Network as a means to provide support to small school leaders and faculty. As a member of the Small Schools Network, the principal of Arts High was given autonomy from district mandates to implement the reform as he saw fit. As a condition of increased autonomy he was subject to more strenuous accountability, which meant he was assessed by a quality assurance team from the Office of Accountability in addition to the regular district-established school and leader assessment measures.

Technology Conversion High School. The Sheridan Area School District developed a model for small school reform in which large, failing comprehensive high schools were converting into small schools. The district determined the thematic focus of each school and then set about to find a principal to lead each school. For each large, comprehensive school that was a part of this reform, three to four conversion schools were established in a building.

The district model was to establish small schools with a ninth and tenth grade. Dr. Richards did not have any say in this configuration. When he was hired, there was already a design team in place working on the school's design plan. This team was selected by the district. Thus, Dr. Richards did not have an opportunity to select them nor did he have an opportunity to have much input into the design plan for the school he was to lead.

The Sheridan Area School District was less experienced than Emerson City Schools in implementing small school reform. There were several other conversion schools within SASD, but the district was still learning how to implement this reform when Dr. Richards became principal. As a result of the district's inexperience in implementing small school reform, Dr. Richards felt that there was an extreme lack of support for him and other principals like him. He intimated that this lack of knowledge and resultant support from the central office made the job of implementation even more difficult:

> [Principals] can't get resources [or] . . . phone calls [returned], the communication is nonexistent . . . it carries over to the school and makes the job of the principal and the school leadership that much more stressful when you cannot get effective communication or efficient means of support from the central office.

Dr. Richards had little autonomy over the organizational structure of his "new" school. He was hired to assist in changing the culture of the campus where his school was located. The expectation at the district level was that he would lead his school toward cultural and academic change. However, the district provided little support to, or agency for, the principal in accomplishing such a challenge. Further, as will be discussed later in this chapter, in the section on *Accountability and Achievement*, although TCHS was a new school converted from a large, failing comprehensive high school,

the state required the school to assume the same failing (underperforming) designation that the comprehensive high school had with regard to student achievement on state assessments. Thus, TCHS was not recognized by the state as a "new" school with a clean student achievement slate. Dr. Richards articulated the following rationale to explain this decision:

> Brand new school, brand new everything else, but because you have repeat [returning] students, you carry the status of the previous school from the previous year.

Dr. Richards felt penalized from the start for assuming the leadership of TCHS. While becoming a small school principal offered the opportunity to lead a new school, the rationale of superimposing the previous school's state report card designation penalized this school and placed Dr. Richards and his students in a deficit before they even got started.

Local Autonomy

The adapted conceptual framework employed in this research defines local autonomy as the agency that the leader has at the school level to implement policy, hire personnel, and make decisions that impact curriculum and instruction (see table 26.1). Small school reform offers new opportunities to conceptualize teaching and learning in urban contexts. In light of the disparate ways in which large urban districts conceptualize small school reform, local autonomy varies from district to district as well. Given that this school level reform was implemented by the district, the school is not truly an independent operator here, and there are implications for higher levels of government (that include the district and, at times, the state as well). There are many ways in which local autonomy for the small school is intricately connected to higher levels of government (i.e., staffing, assessment, curriculum). This section specifically examines these issues of local autonomy from the perspective of the principal and the impact on the school.

Creative Arts High School. By virtue of his school's participation in the Small School Network, Dr. Mathers had the opportunity to experience a great deal of autonomy at the local level. As a result of this increased level of autonomy, Dr. Mathers was able to make some key decisions that were tailored to the needs of his school and freed from the impositions of certain district

Table 26.1.

Charter School Autonomy Framework	*Adapted Small School Autonomy Framework*	*Creation (start up) School*	*Conversion School*
Autonomy from Higher Levels of Government	Freedom from Traditional School Restraints (e.g. State and District Mandates)	Leader (and team) develops a school plan based on leader vision and is granted district permission to implement	Leader is hired to carry out district mission
Local Autonomy	Administrator Discretion (with regard to curriculum, instruction and staffing)	Leader has the autonomy to select staff Leader has autonomy to make curricular decisions with respect to content and delivery Leader determines what advisory will look like	Leader may select staff, but staffing needs are determined by a central office formula rather than in consultation with principal or based on school need Leader is told to implement advisory without support and without district permission to implement as he deems fit
Consumer Sovereignty	Parent and Student Participation, Interest and Choice	Students and parents want to attend the school There is a waiting list each year to get in to the school	Small school enrollment declines Without district and state support, the reputation of the school remains unchanged and unappealing as a choice for parents and students Student school choice is limited based upon parity amongst the other small schools on the campus

*Wohlstetter, et al (2005)

mandates. Most notably, he was able to make decisions regarding staffing based upon the individualized needs of his school. Increased autonomy included autonomy over budget. For Mathers, the most important line item was staff. He stated:

> I hired much more staff . . . I spend the lion's share of our budget on people. I'd rather have good people in places to support students than any amount of technology and materials.

Mathers used his autonomy to hire staff in order to meet his goals and vision for the school. It was more important to him to have the people in place who could actually help to personalize the school environment and engage students than to use his district budget for equipment, technology, and materials. In this way, he didn't just add staff, but was purposeful in his decision about how many and which staff to hire. He conceptualized the responsibilities of additional staff in a way that utilized their talents in a multiplicity of ways that facilitated the personalization of the school environment. He informed:

> Every staff member is responsible for a small group of students as an advisor . . . meeting four times a week, so

they really get to know each other and it creates a safe space and an atmosphere where every student is known by a specific staff member and has a safe staff member they can trust . . . is their advocate and their connector to their family and knows them well.

In addition, Dr. Mathers used his autonomy to make some curricular decisions with regard to course offerings. Mathers selected his school theme, and built a program around that thematic focus. Given that the theme of Creative Arts High was media arts, Dr. Mathers made art a core academic subject and hired two full-time art teachers to ensure that all students received two full years of media arts. Further, he hired community-based educators and artists to teach some of the art classes. In addition, his teachers were committed to engaging inquiry-based instructional strategies for which they had additional professional development and a coach who worked with them weekly.

Dr. Mathers had a great deal of local autonomy related to curriculum and instruction in his school. However, he did not have a choice regarding whether students are required to take state-administered high stakes testing. Each public school in the district, irrespective of type (traditional, small school, etc.) was required to administer state tests.

The Small School Network was a fairly new entity for the district and to that end, Dr. Mathers and his colleagues were new participants. However, while as a fairly new principal and a member of the (fairly) newly created SSN, Mathers felt like "guinea pigs" at times, he has been empowered with the autonomy to create and support the schools he envisioned.

Technology Conversion High School. The principal of the creation school had far less local autonomy to implement the reform than did his creation school counterpart. While he (and the other small schools in his district) had an external coach to provide professional learning for administrators and teachers, there was no formal structure to provide support to the small reforming schools, as the SSN did in Dr. Mathers's district.

Further, Dr. Richards was hired after the school was already established as an entity. That is, the district created the small school in which Dr. Richards served as principal before he was hired. He had no influence over school theme or staffing as these issues had been decided prior to his hiring. Nor did he have agency over the organizational structure related to the student body. Dr. Richards intimated that it wasn't until he accepted the position that he learned the school would not just open with ninth grade students only. He stated, "It wasn't until school started that I was made aware there would be ninth *and* tenth graders."

Dr. Richards conceptualized his role as one in which he was to be a cultural change agent. That is, his role was to drastically change the culture that pervaded the building prior to the reconstitution. Dr. Richards spent a great deal of time focused on breaking up fights, increasing student attendance, and maintaining order in a space that was not renovated to meet the needs of the four schools housed there. With the amount of chaos that converting a large comprehensive high school into three small schools created, Dr. Richards had little time or agency to be thoughtful about implementing his vision of this urban reform. However, Dr. Richards was successful in addressing the immediate cultural needs in his school. He prioritized his work in the school such that he placed changing culture as the most important priority, realizing that if culture changed, he could improve teaching and learning. Changing the culture took some time. He implemented regular town hall meetings with students in order to communicate his vision and to give students a voice. He stated:

[T]hese meetings provided the opportunity to know me and articulate the vision with the teachers and the students . . . in addition, in the second year as we got new students from inside and outside the district, [older] students really bought into what we were trying to do . . . they would take ownership in the school and they were quick to say, "We don't do that here. We don't do that fighting and stuff here anymore."

Further, Dr. Richards's hands were tied with respect to matters of staffing. Unlike Dr. Mathers, who had the agency to select the staffing model that worked best for the school that he envisioned and implemented, Dr. Richards was limited to a district model of staffing. Dr. Richards had very little local autonomy in this way. The Sheridan Area School District followed a strict model for staffing schools. This model applied to traditional schools as well as the reform schools. However, this model negatively impacted Dr. Richards's ability to implement the small schools model at CAHS. Richards had some freedom in selecting the actual individuals hired to fill specific vacancies, but not how many. This caused a hardship when his student enrollment declined. As a result of declining enrollment, he lost teachers (which were assigned based on enrollment) in spite of continued need for these staff. He stated:

I think that one thing that caused some of the greatest grief and heartache was the staffing model that was used . . . and how as a small school we didn't meet our enrollment and we lost teachers . . . I had to reschedule students and class sizes were still above twenty-five. It just shot a hole in advisory . . . and everything we were trying to do.

Specifically, advisory proved to be a challenge for Dr. Richards to implement without autonomy or district support. Advisory was mandated (as is often the case in small schools) to meet the goal of a more personalized learning and developmental environment for students. However, the mandate came without the autonomy needed to implement such an initiative. Richards was thoughtful about the necessary elements for a successful advisory program, but was not allowed to implement such a plan. He shared:

If [the district] is going to value my insight as a principal, then I should have the entitlement to build and advisory program that benefits my students . . . I know what my school's needs are. If [the district] told me, "Okay, this is what the expectations are for advisory," I would have met those. I would have done it in a way which would have been more conducive to my school.

For Dr. Richards, the district's use of this staffing model sent a contradictory message to him regarding the importance of personalizing the small school. He stated, "I would say the transformation lost a lot of integrity in that decision to staff (the schools) in that way . . . one thing that was communicated to me was that small schools don't mean small classes."

In addition to agency (or lack thereof) regarding staffing, Dr. Richards attempted to make some changes in the instructional program at TCHS as well. In some ways he seemed to have some agency in shaping this aspect of the instructional program. Specifically, he was interested in increasing curricular options available to students. His focus was college readiness for his students. One way in which he was deliberate in addressing this focus was to increase the number of Advanced Placement (AP) courses he offered. When he first became principal, Dr. Richards's school only offered one AP course. Under his leadership, this increased to four AP courses.

Dr. Mathers seemed to have a great deal more autonomy in implementing decisions around staffing, curriculum, and instruction. His school was really the product of his vision, and the district allowed him a great deal of agency in implementing this vision. Conversely, as the principal of a conversion school, Dr. Richards's autonomy seemed much more limited. He was not able to execute his own plans for selecting staff and personalization of the school context (via advisory). With respect to increasing academic achievement he seemed to have more agency to increase the number of AP courses offered, but this particular goal was likely very much aligned with district expectations around course rigor. The number of AP courses a school offers provides a metric of assessing rigor that is more overt, as opposed to Dr. Mathers's curricular initiatives which were focused on instructional strategies and strategies for engaging students at a high level. As a result of differences in leadership autonomy and district expectations, Mathers seemed more focused on the instructional process, whereas Dr. Richards was more focused on the achievement outcomes

Consumer Sovereignty

This concept is used by Wohlstetter et al. (1995) to convey the agency of choice residing with parents regarding school selection. This in turn creates pressure for the schools to continue to attract students and their families. Similar to the Wohlstetter et al. (1995) concept of parental choice, the Small School Autonomy framework considers parent and student participation, interest, and choice (see table 26.1). Although small school reform is implemented in public schools that are part of large, urban districts, one intention of some small reform is to offer parents and their children choice. The notion of choice played out very differently in the conversion and creation schools in this study.

Creative Arts High School. In the case of Arts High, Dr. Mathers was intentional in creating a school that students from the neighborhood would want to attend, and designed a proposal to start a school that would serve the students in the neighborhood. He offered:

Half of our staff lives within a mile of [the school] and we purposely wanted to serve this community of [City], original community, not the gentrifying community.

Within the ECSD students traveled widely across the city to attend schools. They did not necessarily attend a neighborhood high school, and as in many communities with poor students of color, the neighborhood high school was an unattractive option for parents. Mathers's intent was to provide parents with a palatable choice so that students could opt to remain in their own local neighborhood to attend school. In addition, he engaged members of the local arts community to partner with his school so that students had exposure to these individuals in school. This option increased the visibility of the school and the desire for parents to send their students to the school. As a result, as the school continued to grow, interest in the school grew as evidenced by the fact that there were regularly seven hundred to eight hundred applicants yearly for one hundred available slots.

This indicated that as the school continued to grow, parents in the neighborhood (as well as others) had a strong desire for their students to attend Creative Arts High. In addition, the academic program was tailored to student interest in order to maintain their engagement and participation. Mathers described the ways in which the curricular program facilitates student interest, "They enjoy it more because we try to tailor classes with students in mind, not just with material [and curriculum] in mind."

Dr. Mathers created a school where a personalized culture and a curriculum tailored to student interest spurred interest as evidenced by the number of student applications for the one hundred spaces open each year. At the high school level students are as much vocal consumers as are their parents. Choice impacted student engagement in that if a student chose the school based on the curricular theme, they were more likely to attend and do well because they are taking courses in a content area of interest. The environment of this school facilitated greater engagement and interest in the school. In addition, consumer (parent and student) interest coupled with membership in the Small School Network increased the school's accountability to the district as well as parents and students.

Technology Conversion High School. In TCHS there were many constraints that limited student and parent choice. Unlike Emerson City Schools, the Sheridan Area District Schools did not have nearly as much experience with the small schools model. Largely, students attending small schools were assigned to a building (which housed several small schools) and within that building, in theory, they were allowed to choose which school they would like to attend based on curricular theme (i.e., performing arts, sciences, liberal arts, etc.). In theory, given that each small school operated with a particular theme, students were to have a great deal of agency with respect to school choice *on a campus*. Thus, the district initiative would provide a means for students, while zoned to a building, to choose the small school they wanted to attend.

Dr. Richards' school started with ninth and tenth grade students, unlike many creation (and some conversion) schools who start only with ninth grade students and add a grade each year. The ninth graders were new high schoolers, the tenth graders were returning students who had previously attended the (pre-reform) large, failing high school. So, at its inception, TCHS was serving two different student groups, one who was new, and therefore needed to be socialized to the small school model, and the other that had to be re-acculturated from the experience they had in the large failing comprehensive high school prior to the reorganization. Given that Dr. Richards's mission (handed down by the district

office) was to change the culture of the school, this was a complicated task and obviously significantly impaired consumer sovereignty.

Notably consumer sovereignty was impaired due to the negative reputation that the school (prior to conversion) had in the community. Dr. Richards complained of low parental interest and involvement with his school, mainly attributable to the previous negative reputation of the school. Many of the most savvy parents with children zoned to the pre-conversion campus sent their children elsewhere. This left the campus in an intellectual and cultural deficit and increased the challenge of creating small schools that would attract parents and their children back to a space where they had historically been fleeing.

Further, in an effort to maintain some semblance of parity among the small schools in the SASD, although there was some student choice, it was limited. For example, there were three small schools sharing a building on Dr. Richards's campus. If a student chose Technology Conversion High, but TCHS had significantly more students than the other small schools on the campus, then the student's choice was summarily overlooked and the student was placed wherever the powers-that-be decided the student should be. As a result, this structure negatively impacted the opportunity for Dr. Richards (and his small school leader colleagues) to recruit and advertise the unique programs contained in their individual schools.

Accountability and Achievement

In the current educational landscape, accountability for student achievement is the currency that determines success. The differences between the conversion and creation schools being compared here are vast. The leader's agency to implement the reform aligned with his or her own mission has the potential to significantly affect student achievement outcomes as well. Given the disparate levels of autonomy between the creation and conversion school principals, and the unique challenges in each context, student achievement outcomes seem to reflect the leader's ability to implement his vision.

Creative Arts High School. At Creative Arts High, accountability is established both by district assessment of the reforming schools within the Small Schools Network as well as by student achievement measures on state outcomes. To that end, under Dr. Mathers's leadership Creative Arts High performed very well on state accountability measures, making Adequate Yearly Progress (AYP) for the 2008 through 2012 academic years. In addition, the Office of Accountability conducted an assessment during the 2008–2009 academic year in which Arts High scored in the proficient range for nearly every category assessed. In addition, qualitative feedback from the report noted:

- The principal makes informed and effective organizational decisions across all aspects of the school to support improvements in learning
- Teachers work collaboratively to collect and share data, ideas, and good practice to continually improve student learning, and
- This small school is supportive of students, staff, and families with a sound understanding of its strengths, areas for continued development, and a clear vision and commitment for its future growth.

In the current context of schools, success is often measured by student achievement and obtained through the vehicle of accountability. The stipulation for autonomy in ECSD is that schools join the SSN and principals of the schools within the network be subject to additional scrutiny via accountability assessments, in additional to the regular district assessments of leaders, on an annual basis (particularly in the first four years of a school's existence/leader's principalship). Per Dr. Mathers's leadership, the emphasis at Arts High is laser-focused on student achievement. This is accomplished via the triumvirate of intense academics, student social support, and the message of college readiness.

Technology Conversion High School. At the conversion school, student achievement was viewed from the vantage point of a deficit rather than an appreciative model. Dr. Richards conceptualized achievement in terms of lack rather than in terms of strength. This approach does not seem surprising considering all of the areas in which he felt there was a lack or he was left unsupported in implementing this reform.

Unlike Dr. Mathers, Dr. Richards did not have the freedom to articulate his own definition of student achievement. Rather, his definition was the definition that was given to him by the district, and for that matter, the state as well. Dr. Richards' school was assigned the pre-conversion school's state report card status. Given that the previous school was labeled low performing, this designation hurt TCHS which was essentially a "new" school. An analysis of the school report card indicated that the school did not make adequate yearly progress during any academic year from 2008 through 2011. Further, the graduation rate was 64 percent in 2010 and rose only to 69 percent in 2011. Finally, during this time period there was a turnover in faculty, including the principal, who left the district for another position elsewhere.

As a new school the challenge was not just to build an effective learning program, but to combat the unearned failing status of the previous pre-transformation school. The state district approach to supporting the implementation of the small school reform was punitive in nature rather than appreciative and supportive. This limited autonomy and negative culture colored the way in which achievement was viewed in TCHS.

DISCUSSION

Perhaps one of the most important foundational understandings for small schools is the philosophy of its purpose. In general, in urban contexts the purpose of reform is to create more positive opportunities for students who have not had access, through increased personalization and curricular engagement. However, the manner in which these opportunities come to be creates the foundation of the purpose. This comparison is clearly not an "apples to apples" comparison of two schools. They are in different districts and different states with different requirements and disparate understandings of small school reform.

Although the two small schools here have similar purposes, the execution of the small philosophy is qualitatively different. The creation school principal (Dr. Mathers) clearly had time and space to develop a paradigm for schooling. The conversion school principal (Dr. Richards) did not have this opportunity and was given a different set of marching orders. Dr. Richards understood his purpose as that of cultural change insurgent, whereas Dr. Mathers was chief implementer, or, visionary, responsible for leading the creation of opportunity. These divergent understandings of purpose ultimately influenced every aspect of the reform implementation.

What is clear is that the creation school presented here had a great deal more autonomy in implementing the reform. As a result, the principal felt more agency and connectedness to the school and the community. With less autonomy, implementing the reform was much more difficult, due to unclear goals and lack of support and resources. What makes the creation school leader's experience different? There are several potential reasons: the district had more experience implementing small school reform in the creation district, giving them time to learn what works and doesn't work in reform implementation; in addition to having more experience with the reform the creation district had both kinds of small schools paradigms (conversion and creation), which may have provided unique insights into how these reforms are different; the conversion school district had much experience with reform and much more tumult in the central office—the culture of the central office in the conversion district was much more top-down and less participatory relative to the ways in which district leaders interacted with school leaders. All of these ideas need to be explored further in examining the importance of autonomy in implementing small school reform in urban settings.

In summary, the different methods of reform implementation, creation versus conversion, pose qualitatively distinctive challenges for leaders in these two types of schools. The differences manifested themselves in the districts' understanding of the reform, their support for the school leader, and their evaluation of student achievement which ultimately affect the scope, extent, and results of the changes (culturally and academically) the school leaders could achieve in those small schools.

Implications for Future Research and Policy

As revealed in this study, in addition to those common challenges coming with the small school reform, the leaders in creation and conversion schools face distinct challenges associated with the creation or conversion model respectively. Should the leadership requirements differ between creation and conversion small schools? What are the strategies small school leaders utilize to exercise agency to lead their schools with respect to: communicating with the central office, negotiating and garnering support, and buffering unsupportive influence, and implementing the small schools model tailored to the needs of their schools and communities? How are these strategies played out differently under creation and conversion schools? What are the opportunities and challenges for small schools facing dual accountabilities resulting from involvement of external agencies (as the creation school in this study)? How do districts work differently (if any) with external agencies to support creation versus conversion small schools? How can the district tailor support to better serve the different needs of the creation and conversion school leaders? What are the districts' expectations and support for implementing small school reform and how do the two small school paradigms complement (or disconnect) with each other? What are the driving and restraining forces behind the districts' decision of implementing small school reform as a creation paradigm or the conversion paradigm? Future research should engage in close comparisons between these two small school paradigms for the purpose of informing the literature on effective models of reform in urban contexts.

Implications for policymakers point to the contextualized policy implementation. Rather than demanding a program (or policy) to be executed uniformly, policymakers need to take into consideration of state and district constraints; the local school context; the community and student needs and be willing to keep open dialogue and ready to learn from building level leaders, and understand "deviation" is inevitable and sometime even necessary. As was evident in this study, at times urban reform initiatives stumble over old policies (such as the conventional way of staffing and requiring a "new" school to assume the prior state designation of the large, comprehensive high school from which it "emerged"). In policy contexts such as this, how can the central office engage, educate, and work with state policymakers to smooth the transition and assist in changing broader policy context in which these schools must exist?

Implications for Leadership Preparation

Findings from this study may also provide insight into leadership preparation. New knowledge and skill sets may be considered and added into curriculum of university leadership programs helping future leaders (or current leaders) better understand the complex roles associated with distinctive urban school contexts, such as their roles as liaisons between their schools and surrounding communities, as visionaries in developing and designing a school model, as advocates for their schools, and as public relations representatives when engaging and soliciting support from various social agencies and organizations. More beneficial programs are those that emphasize problem-based learning and curriculum with immediate challenges-relevancy (Dunbar and Monson, 2011) and social justice leadership in urban contexts (Marshal and Oliva, 2009; Theoharis, 2009). Moreover, meaningful professional development is not a unidirectional endeavor from the university or the central office to the school, but rather, a partnership co-constructed with expertise from both sides (Gooden, Bell, Gonzales, and Lippa, 2011; Houle, 2006; Kaimal, Barber, Schulman, and Reed, 2012; Orr, 2006). Some urban school districts (such as Hartford, Connecticut; San Diego, California; Gwinnett County, Georgia, and New York City, New York) are collaborating with universities or establishing their own programs on leadership preparation and professional development for implementing district reforms and improving schools, focusing on the development of leaders' capacity for creating and implementing a school's vision, facilitating instructional quality and faculty development, and engaging parents and communities (Corcoran, Schwartz, and Weinstein, 2012; Darling-Hammond, LaPointe, Meyerson, Orr, and Cohen, 2007; Orr, King, and LaPointe, 2009).

Nevertheless, the literature is silent in terms of integrating the knowledge associated with small school reforms into the leadership preparation curriculum. On the other hand, since the central office personnel are the ones who have the most direct interactions with school leaders, their capacity to understand contexts and facilitate reform implementation is critical. A more beneficial format for professional development may be a cohort involving both the central office personnel and building level leaders where close contact disrupts a power disparity, breaks a bureaucratic wall, and allows more authentic learning and mutual consideration (Beaumont, 1997; McIver and Farley-Ripple, 2008; Nelson, 2010), particularly in the implementation of specialized policies like small school reform.

NOTE

1. One of the cases is published in Peters (2011).

REFERENCES

American Federation of Teachers. (2004). *Charter school achievement on the 2003 National Assessment of Educational Progress.* Washington, DC: American Federation of Teachers.

American Institutes for Research and SRI International (2004). *The National school district and network grants program: Year 2 evaluation report.* Washington, DC: AIR.

American Institutes for Research and SRI International (2006). *The National school district and network grants program: Year 4 evaluation report.* Washington, DC: AIR.

Ancess, J. (1997). *Urban dreamcatchers: Launching and leading new small schools.* The National Center for Restructuring Education, Schools, and Teaching. Teacher's College, Columbia University.

Ancess, J. (2003). *Beating the odds: High Schools as communities of commitment.* New York: Teachers College Press.

Antrop-Gonzalez, R., and DeJesus, A. (2006). Toward a theory of critical care in urban small school reform: examining structures and pedagogies of caring in two Latino community-based schools. *International Journal of Qualitative Studies in Education, 19*(4), 409–433.

Beaumont, J. J. (1997). Issues in urban school district leadership: Professional development. *Urban Education, 31*(5), 564–581.

Benitez, M., Davidson, J., and Flaxman, L. (2009). *Small schools, big ideas: The essential guide to successful school transformation.* San Francisco, CA: Jossey-Bass.

Bryk, A. S., and Driscoll, M. (1998). *The high school as community: Contextual influences and consequences for students and teachers.* Madison, Wisconsin: National Center on Effective Secondary Schools.

Caldwell, B. J. and Spinks, J. M. (1992). *Leading the self-managing school.* Washington, DC: Falmer.

Cleary, M., and English, G. (2005). The small schools movement: Implications for health education. *Journal of School Health, 75*(7), 243–247.

Copland, M. A. and Boatright, E. E. (2004). Leading small: Eight lessons for leaders in transforming large comprehensive high schools. *Phi Delta Kappan, 85*(10), 762–770.

Corcoran, S. P., Schwartz, A. E., and Weinstein, M. (2012). Training your own the impact of New York City's Aspiring Principals Program on student achievement. *Educational Evaluation and Policy Analysis, 34*(2), 232–253.

Cotton, K. (1996). *School size, school climate, and student performance.* Seattle: Northwest Regional Education Laboratory.

Cotton, K. (2001). *New small learning communities: Findings from recent literature.* Northwest Regional Educational Laboratory.

Darling-Hammond, L., Ancess, J., and Ort, S. W. (2002). Re-inventing high schools: Outcomes of the coalition campus schools project. *American Educational Research Journal, 39*, 639–673.

Darling-Hammond, L., LaPointe, M., Meyerson, D., Orr, M. T., and Cohen, C. (2007). *Preparing school leaders for a changing world: Lessons from exemplary leadership development programs* (Vol. 6). Stanford, CA: Stanford Educational Leadership Institute.

Darling-Hammond, L., Ross, P., and Milliken, M. (2007). High school size, organization, and content: What matters for student success? In T. Loveless and F. Hess (Eds.), *Brookings papers on education policy: 2006–2007* (pp. 163–203). Washington, DC: Brookings Institution Press.

Davidson, J. (2002). Elements of smallness create conditions for success. *Horace, 19*(1). Retrieved from ERIC database (EJ672065).

Dunbar, K., and Monson, R. J. (2011). Fellowship connects principal learning to student achievement. *Journal of Staff Development, 32*(1), 40–43.

Feldman, J., Lopez, M. L., and Simon, K. (2005). *Choosing small: The essential guide to high school conversion.* San Francisco: Jossey-Bass.

Feldman, J. and O'Dwyer, A. (2010). Patterns in student perceptions of start-up and conversion small high schools. *Peabody Journal of Education, 85*(3), 313–332.

Feldman, J., O'Dwyer, A., and Kleigman, R. (2009, April*). Authentic intellectual achievement and CES small schools.* Paper presented at the 90th annual meeting of the American Educational Research Association, San Diego.

Fink, S. and Silverman, M. (2007).The not-so-inevitable failure of high school conversions. *Education Week, 27*(9), 29.

Fouts, J. T., Baker, D. B., Brown, C. J., and Riley, S. C. (2006). *Leading the conversion process: Lessons learned and recommendations for converting to small learning communities.* Tucson, AZ: Fouts and Associates.

French, D., Atkinson, M., and Rugen, L. (2007). *Creating small schools: A handbook for raising equity and achievement.* Thousand Oaks, CA: Corwin Press.

Gladden, R. (1998). The small school movement: A review of the literature. In M. Fine and J. I. Somerville (Eds.), *Small schools, big imaginations: A creative look at urban public schools* (pp. 113–137). Chicago: Cross City Campaign for Urban School Reform.

Gooden, M. A., Bell, C. M., Gonzales, R. M., and Lippa, A. P. (2011). Planning University-Urban District Partnerships: Implications for Principal Preparation Programs. *Educational Planning, 20*(2), 1–13.

Hammack, F. M. (2008). Off the record—something old, something new, something borrowed, something blue: Observations on the small schools movement. *Teachers College Record, 110*(9), 2067–2072.

Hantzopoulos, M. (2009). Transformative teaching in restric-tive times: Engaging teacher participation in small school reform during an era of standardization. In F. Vavrusand L. Bartlett (Eds.), *Comparatively knowing: Vertical case study research in comparative and developmental educa-tion* (pp. 111–126). New York: Palgrave.

Hill, P., Angel, L., and Christensen, J. (2006). Charter School Achievement Studies. *Education Finance and Policy, 1*(1), 139–150.

Houle, J. C. (2006). Professional development for urban principals in underperforming schools. *Education & Urban Society, 38*(2), 142–159.

Hoxby, C. (2004). *Achievement in charter schools and regu-lar public schools in the United States: Understanding the differences.* Cambridge: Harvard University, National Bu-reau of Economic Research.

Husbands, J. and Beese, S. (July, 2001). *Review of selected high school reform strategies.* Paper presented at the meet-ing of the Aspen Program on Education, Aspen, CO.

Iatarola, P., Schwartz, A. E., Stiefel, L., and Chellman, C. C. (2008). Small schools, large districts: Small school reform and New York City's students. *Teachers College Record, 110* (9), 1837–1878.

Kaimal, G., Barber, M., Schulman, M., and Reed, P. (2012). Preparation of urban high school leaders in Philadel-phia through multiorganizational partnerships. *Journal of School Leadership, 22*(5), 902–921.

Khan, S., and VanWynsberhe, R. (2009). Cultivating the under-mined: Cross-case analysis as knowledge mobiliza-tion. *Forum: Qualitative Social Research, 9*(1). Retrieved from www.qualitative-research.net/index.php/fqs/article/view/334/730.

Lake, R., Winger, A., and Petty, J. (2002). *The new schools handbook.* Seattle, WA: Center on Reinventing Public Education.

Lee, V.E. and Loeb, S. (2000). School size in Chicago elementary schools: Effects on teachers' attitudes and students' achievement. *American Educational Research Journal, 37*, 3–31.

Lee, V. E., Ready, D. D., and Johnson, D. T. (2001). The difficulty of identifying rare samples to study: The case of high schools divided into schools-within-schools. *Edu-cational Evaluation and Policy Analysis, 23*(4), 365–379.

Lee, V. E., Smith, J. B., and Croninger, R. G. (1995). Another look at high school restructuring: More evidence that it improves student achievement, and more insight into why. *Issues in Restructuring Schools, 7*, 1–10.

Leithwood, K., Seashore Louis, K., Anderson, S., and Wahl-strom, K. (2004). How leadership influences student learning. Learning from Leadership Project. Wallace Foundation Report.

Legters, N. and Kerr, K. (2001). *Easing the transition to high school: An investigation of reform practices to promote ninth grade success.* Cambridge, MA: Center for Social Organization of Schools. Retrieved from www.civilrightsproject.ucla.edu/research/dropouts/legters.pdf.

MacIver, M. A., and Farley-Ripple, E. N. (2008). *Bringing the district back in: the role of the central office in instruction and achievement.* Alexandria, VA: Educational Research Service.

Malen, B., Ogawa, R.T., and Kranz, J. (1990). What do we know about school basedmanagement? A case study of the literature—A call for research. In W.H. Clune and J.F. White (Eds.), *Choice and control in American education. The practice of choice, decentralization, and school restructuring* (vol. 2, pp. 289–342). London: Falmer.

Marks, H. and Louis, K.S. (1997). Does teacher empowerment affect the classroom? The implication of teacher empowerment for instructional practice and student academic performance. *Educational Evaluation and Policy Analysis, 19,* 245–275.

Marks, H. and Louis, K.S. (1999).Teacher empowerment and the capacity for organizational learning. *Educational Administration Quarterly, 35* (Supplement, December).

Marshall, C. and Oliva, M. (2009). *Leadership for social justice: Making revolutions in education* (2nd ed.). Boston: Allyn and Bacon.

Meier, D. W. (1996). The big benefits of smallness. *Educational Leadership, 54,* 12–15.

A Nation at Risk: The imperative for educational reform (1983). The National Commission on Excellence in Education.

Nehring, J. H. and Lohmeier, J. H. (2010). Leadership challenges converting a large high school to small schools: A follow-up study. *NASSP Bulletin, 94*(3), 184–212.

Nehring, J. H., Lohmeier, J. H., and Colombo, M. (2009). Conversion of a large, urban high school to small schools: Leadership challenges and opportunities. *NASSP Bulletin, 93*(1), 5–26.

Nelson, E. A. (2010). *Get out of the rut and into a circle-cycle of inquiry professional development for central office leaders.* Retrieved from ProQuest Digital Dissertations. (AAI3406026)

Newmann, F., Marks, H.M., and Gamoran, A. (1996). Authentic pedagogy and student performance. *American Journal of Education, 104*(4), 280–312.

Noguera, P. A. (2002). Beyond size: The challenge of high school reform. *Educational Leadership, 59*(5), 60–63.

Orr, M. T. (2006). Mapping innovation in leadership preparation in our nation's schools of education. *Phi Delta Kappan, 87*(7), 492–499.

Oxley, D., Croninger, R. G., and DeGroot, E. (2000). *Considerations for entry level students in schools-within-schools: The interplay of social capital and student identity formation.* Retrieved from ERIC database (ED443143).

Peters, A. L. (2011). Small urban high school success: A case study. *Journal of Education for Students Placed at Risk, 16*(2), 89–99.

Peters, A. L. (2012). Leading through the challenge of change: African-American women principals on small school reform. *International Journal of Qualitative Studies in Education, 25*(1), 23–38.

Quint, J. (2006). Meeting five critical challenges of high school reform: Lessons from research on three reform models. Retrieved from Manpower Demonstration Research Corporation website: www.mdrc.org/publications/428/execsum.pdf.

Raywid, M. A. (1996). *Taking stock: The movement to create mini-schools, schools-within-schools, and separate small schools. Urban Diversity series No. 108.* Retrieved from ERIC database (ED393958).

Raywid, M. A. (1998). Small schools: A reform that works. *Educational Leadership, 55*(4), 34–39.

Ready, D. D., Lee, V. E., and Welner, K. G. (2004). Education equity and school structure: School size, overcrowding, and schools-within-schools. *Teachers College Record, 106*(10), 1989–2014.

Shaw, L. (2006, November 5). Foundation's small schools experiment has yet to yield big results. *Seattle Times.* Retrieved from seattletimes.nwsource.com/html/education/2003348701_gates05m.html.

Smerdon, B. and Cohen, J. (2009). Evaluation findings from high school reform efforts in Baltimore. *Journal of Education for Students Placed at Risk, 14*(3), 238–255.

Smylie, M., Lazarus, V., and Brownlee-Conyers, J. (1996). Instructional outcomes of school-based participative decision making. *Educational Evaluation and Policy Analysis, 18*(3), 181–198.

Stevens, W. D. (2008). *If small is not enough . . . ?: The characteristics of successful small high schools in Chicago.* Retrieved from ERIC database (ED501458).

Strike, K. A. (2008). Small schools: Size or community? *American Journal of Education, 114*(3), 169–190.

Supovitz, J. A. (2002). Developing communities of instructional practice. *Teachers College Record, 104*(8), 1151–1626.

Theoharis, G. (2009). *The school leaders our children deserve: Seven keys to equity, social justice and school reform.* New York: Teachers College Press.

Tung, R. and Ouimette, M. (2007). *Strong results, high demand: A four-year study of Boston's Pilot high schools.* Boston: Center for Collaborative Education. Retrieved from cceobs.org/Pilot_School_Study_11.07.pdf.

U.S. Department of Education. (2004). *America's Charter Schools: Results from the NAEP 2003 Pilot Study.* Washington, DC: U.S. Department of Education, National Center for Education Statistics, 2005-456.

Walker, A. and Qian, H. (2006). Beginning principals: Balancing at the top of the greasy pole. *Journal of Educational Administration, 44,* 297–309.

Wallach, C. A. (2010). The complexities of operating multiple small schools in a high school conversion. *Peabody Journal of Education, 85*(3), 264–275.

Wallach, C. A. and Lear, R. (2005). *A foot in two worlds: The second report on comprehensive high school conversions.* Seattle: Small School Project.

Wasley, P. A. and Lear, R. J. (2001). Small schools real gains. *Educational Leadership, 58* (6), pp. 22–27.

Wohlstetter, P., Wenning, R., and Briggs, K.L. (1995). Charter schools in the United States: A question of autonomy. *Educational Policy, 9*(4), 331–358.

Wyse, A. E., Keesler, V., and Schneider, B. (2008). Assessing the effects of small school size on mathematics achievement: A propensity score-matching approach. *Teachers College Record, 110*(9), 1878–1900.

Yin, R. K. (2009). *Case study research design and methods* (4th ed.). Los Angeles, CA: Sage.

LEADERSHIP PREPARTION, DEVELOPMENT, AND SUPPORT

Section 8 Introduction

Jennifer Haan

This section explores urban leadership through the lens of policies at various levels: district, community, state, and federal. Through a critical policy lens we examine how educational policies influence urban communities, schools, and urban leadership. However we also examine urban leaders' role in educational policy negotiation, creation, and articulation. Not only do we need to attract the right people to assume educational leadership roles in an urban setting, we need to prepare them with the stamina and skill sets to overcome the injustices they will face as social justice leaders. The researchers in this section expose some of these barriers and highlight the efforts to overcome them.

In chapter 27, "Turnaround, School Choice, and the Hidden Discourses of Race in Leadership Preparation," Sarah Diem and Bradley W. Carpenter illustrate the barrier is bureaucratic reform efforts that result in the re-segregation of schools, and how leadership programs must assume antiracist stances to prepare leaders who become advocates for communities of color. In chapter 28, "The Urban School Leaders Collaborative: An Alternative and Effective Model for Leadership Preparation and Practice," Encarnacion Garza illustrates how educational leadership programs fail to take into account an urban student population that is predominantly Latino, and how one award-winning leadership preparation program placed social justice front and center. The barrier in chapter 29, "School Leadership in Urban Schools: How Social-Relational Leadership Shapes Teacher Engagement," is traditional quantitative research methods that fail to capture the lived experiences of its subjects as author Heather E. Price articulates. Along with quantitative data, network theory is utilized along with the rich perspectives of leaders to reveal how principals can become more effective leaders. In chapter 30, "Preparing Leaders to Support the Education of Diverse Learners," Michelle D. Young, Mark A. Gooden, and Ann O'Doherty share how an innovative leadership preparation model infuses criticalist perspectives to develop the potential of traditionally marginalized students who represent the students they will serve. Lastly, in chapter 31, "Lessons from a District-Based Doctoral Cohort: Faculty Stories of Challenge, Opportunity, and Impact" by Monica Byrne-Jimenez, Catherine DiMartino, and Eustace Thompson, we hear the perspective of faculty who struggle to build a cohort-like model with a local school district. Although the project failed in its goal to form a collaborative relationship between the two institutions, the cohort members emerged as empowered leaders who continue to improve the schools in which they serve.

A Theory of Emancipatory Leadership

Juanita M. Simmons

The original philosophy of neoliberalism, according to Boas and Gans-Morse (2009), was more moderate than classical liberalism and promoted the use of state policy to balance social inequality and prevent excessive monopoly. Neoliberalism has shifted to currently denote the transfer of public sector to private sector control, with limited government protection, and the promotion of privatized businesses that may have previously been under state or federal control.

This shift is thought to have enhanced privatization, and is often characterized by its influence over standards-driven, test-oriented educational policies and practices, state takeovers (and the reassignment of PK–12 student enrollment and other factors). These actions challenge educators who desire to broaden their PK–20 students with instruction and experiences beyond the whip of punitive accountability tactics. But current test-centered curricula provide little opportunities for holistic development, human interaction and development, and for development of democratic citizenship (e.g., equity training). Worse, containment structures imposed by the current neoliberal climate reduce knowledge-making opportunities that might otherwise enable participants to discern the political and institutionalized inequalities governing their lives. One brings one to wonder whether education will remain a democratic right.

Freire might refer to the current climate as a "cultural invasion" (Freire, cited in Torres, 2014, p. 5) described such restrictive actions as strategic means to transform "specialized knowledge" and "techniques into something static, materialized, and mechanically extends them to the persons, indisputably invading their culture, their view of the world" (Freire, cited Torres, 2014, p. 5). Even though some will disagree, there are many similarities between Freire's oppressed participants to that of oppressed groups in America, especially in our educational system. A historical chronology of the education of minorities in America might help one to better align the similarities. Sadly, this rings true especially for the most vulnerable populations in public education—the racially and socially marginalized populations who are fast becoming the majority in PK–12 public education. Although it may appear that only oppressed populations are debilitated by cultural invasions, Americans must be alerted that the overall shifting culture of public education.

How, then, can we help to prepare educational leaders to counteract these conditions? What measures might aspiring and appointed educational leaders take in designing and preparing their leadership platforms to navigate these changes? Should preparation programs promote and encourage accommodation and acceptance of these changes or should they form alliances to create new leadership pedagogy?

That asked, I argue that there is a need for a specifically pointed style of leadership which is aimed at deliberately exposing and challenging these issues. Not excluding or discrediting the importance of social justice leadership, transformative leadership, spiritual leadership, or other styles and leadership theories. Rather, I argue for the need to create a new pedagogy of leadership that includes these, along with a deeper infusion of Freire's tenet of *education for development*. In other words, a reinvention of Freire's tenets with an objective to "provide students with the necessary instruments to resist the deracinating powers of an industrial civilization"—and "education that makes it possible for people to fearlessly discuss their problems"—"situated in dialogue" (Freire, cited in Torres, 2014, p. xxiii). As an example of this rare combination of leadership skills and disposition, I offer this narrative as an example of this type of leadership:

My mentor, the late Dr. Napoleon B. Lewis, was the former principal of Lincoln High School in Dallas, Texas. I was fortunate to have had the experience of teaching and serving as dean of instruction under his leadership for a decade. Dr. Lewis earned a reputation for strong nurturing leadership, acts of social justice, uncompromising spirituality, and high expectations for social and academic excellence of his students, teachers, parents, and staff. His years as principal of this economically challenged, South Dallas, predominately African-American, urban high school brought national and international recognition for consistent excellence in academics and athletics. Such academic recognition as "America's Ten Best Schools," reported in the 1999 review by *U.S. News and World Report* and *Good Morning America* national talk show, The National Alliance of Black School Educator's Demonstration School, and other awards and accomplishments adorned the school's highly decorated Wall of Fame.

Few, if any, studies ever reveal when or how Dr. Lewis gained the knowledge to successfully navigate in the midst of historical and contemporary sociopolitical barriers. Under his leadership, racism, poverty, community graft, and other conditions were confronted and mediated through successful collaboration with community. Rather than allow these conditions to control the outcomes of these, Dr. Lewis instituted decades of success in excelling in high school completion indices, diffusing and eradicating in-school gangs and rivalry groups, enrolling unprecedented numbers of students into college-track classes, producing high numbers of National Merit and National Commended Scholars, and record-breaking ratings in UIL scholarship and athletics. Most important, Dr. Lewis instituted a system for promoting and helping to produce generations of wholesome, productive, confident citizens of Lincoln students.

He was most known for his weekly lyceums which were held in the Lincoln auditorium—a place which he referred to as his "classroom." In his auditorium platform, students were taught about international, national, and local issues. His lyceum platform often included lectures from such conscious-raising guests as Rev. Jesse Jackson, Coretta Scott King, Yolanda King, Martin Luther King III, Jawanza Kunjufu, Asa Hilliard, Na'im Akbar, Joseph Lowry, Montel Williams, Tom Joyner, Steve Harvey, Mirimba Ani, Ivan Van Sertima,

successful graduates, and countless other speakers, writers, entertainers, and politicians who added to the seventy-year legacy of this historic black school.

He had as many idioms and words of wisdom for his staff as he did for students. He voiced these idioms in his bimonthly faculty meetings where his lectures revealed his observations and thoughts about policies, teaching practices, and other subtle structures that perpetuate social and economic inequities. He was careful to surround himself with strong teachers, caring counselors, supportive parents, and community stakeholders. He involved many in decision-making and empowered them to assist in supporting students.

Volumes should and could be written about Dr. Lewis's wisdom and his strategic instructional leadership. I'm sure that there are hundreds of similar stories. But what do we learn from these successes that might transfer into our leadership preparation programs? How do we allow these stories to add new meaning to conversations surrounding leadership development for aspiring leaders, especially in urban schools and communities? How can these experiences empower leaders in the midst of neoliberal climate?

My experiences with Dr. Lewis and other courageous leaders cause me to believe that there is a need to reinvent the tenets of Freire, to model the passion and activism of Dr. Lewis, and to create a new pedagogy of leadership. This new pedagogy demands broader leadership preparation curricula to include qualities, tenets, and strategies outlining the successes of leaders who dare to go beyond the practice of "going along to get alone." Telling this story and reviewing the tenets of Freire provide a framework of skills, dispositions, and actions needed to redefine leadership. Together, the qualities and actions of Dr. Lewis's leadership platform and the tenets upheld by Freire promote emancipation. Therefore, I call this pedagogy EMANCIPATORY LEADERSHIP (EL). And in an effort to articulate its meaning, I define it as *the intentional design of one's leadership platform which includes his/her vision and agenda for liberation education. The agenda includes a means to inform, educate, and strategize for the purpose of challenging, and eradicating oppression. EL includes the delivery and instruction of liberation education; promotes an inquiry into moral concepts, opposition of oppression; uncovers myths and injustices of the dominant culture; promotes transformation, injustice, and inequality; and empowers oppressed individuals.* Tenets of emancipatory leadership include four major components: 1) Cognitive skills, 2) Interpersonal skills, 3) Intrapersonal skills, and 4) Language.

EL Tenet #1 Cognitive Skills. Included in the pedagogy of Emancipatory Leadership is the need for strong cognitive skills. Leaders must be aware of historical cultural truths that serve as counter-narratives (particularly that of the leaders' service constituents and connected others). An effective EL understands the processes of institutionalized inequality (Larson and Ovando, 2001), and readily identifies and acknowledges oppressive barriers by communicating inequities to the constituents. This enables him/her to assist with the development of "conscientization" for furthering the process of "education for development" (Freire, 1970). Additional to the needed cognitive skills must be knowledge, skills, and disposition to support, advocate, promote, and further liberation education as critical pedagogy. Of course, high professional content knowledge in management and leadership skills are critical to this process.

EL Tenet #2 Interpersonal Skills. In earning influence and power with others, the EL masters the skill of mobilizing and globalizing issues, and strategically interacts with social and political organizations to help build support and advocacy for the agenda. In furthering the agenda, the EL establishes strategic mentoring and sponsorship. The EL has a clear understanding of how leadership influences the social and cultural climate of institutions.

EL Tenet #3 Intrapersonal Skills. It should be evident that high moral and ethical standards are the foundation of this leadership platform. He/she is an intercessor and a mediator for others. The EL must be a reflective leader who possesses the ability to self-assess, self-correct, include and hear all voices, and to be skilled at analyzing and detecting his and other's personal motives. This includes courage, conviction, and compassion, and the ability to form and follow a clear mission which includes hope, and flourishing lives for others. The EL has uncompromising values and beliefs.

EL Tenet #4 Language. Last by important are the communication skills of the EL. He/she is skilled in the use of language to express passion and hope, demands, and to motivate. This includes appropriate audience analysis and border crossing alliances in communication.

What if this becomes the new norm for leadership in PK–20 educational institutions? What if leadership preparation curricula includes these tenets as a major focus of instruction and teaching? What if credentialing institutions, evaluation processes, and hiring requirements demand evidence of these tenets in its applicants? My answer—the production of hope, confidence, academic excellence, and the return of education as a democratic right!

REFERENCES

Boas, T. C., and Gans-Morse, J. (2009). Neoliberalism: From New Liberal Philosophy to Anti-Liberal Slogan. *Studies in Comparative International Development 44*(2), 145, 146, doi:10.1007/s12116-009-9040-5.

Freire, P. (1968/1970). *Pedagogy of the oppressed.* New York: Bloomsbury Press.

Freire, P. (1970). Cultural action and conscientization. *Harvard Educational Review*, 40(3), 457–477.

Freire, P. (1998). *Politics and education.* Los Angeles: Latin American Center, University of California–Los Angeles.

Larson, C. L. and Ovando, C. J. (2001). *The color of bureaucracy: The politics of equity in multicultural communities.* Belmont, CA: Wadsworth Press.

Paulo Freire: dialogue, praxis and education. Retrieved from infed.org/mobi/paulo-freire-dialogue-praxis-and-education/.

Torres, C. A. (2014). *First Freire: Early writings in social justice education.* New York: Teachers College Press, Columbia University.

CHAPTER 27

Turnaround, School Choice, and the Hidden Discourses of Race in Leadership Preparation

Sarah Diem and Bradley W. Carpenter

INTRODUCTION

Almost immediately after being selected to serve as the U.S. Secretary of Education, Arne Duncan began to unveil a policy agenda focused on "turning around" the nation's lowest performing schools. One of the central policy priorities within this agenda was to revise the Title I School Improvement Grant (SIG) program policy, a set of reforms intended to address the burgeoning number of schools labeled as persistently low-achieving (PLA). Efforts targeting PLA schools were largely deemed as necessary due to the fact that approximately five thousand public schools—5 percent of the nation's total—were labeled as PLA in 2009, the year Duncan was appointed. Additionally, in the four years prior to Duncan's appointment, the number of schools categorized as in need of improvement rose 30 percent (from 9,699 to 12,608), and the number of schools needing to be completely restructured tripled (from 1,180 to 5,017; Planty et al., 2009).

While one of the primary purposes of the revised Title I SIG program policy is to close the achievement gaps between "minority and nonminority students" (U.S. Department of Education, 2009, para. 6), embedding school choice language within the policy creates a number of issues that potentially hinder its intended goals. For instance, research has shown school choice policies, and those who benefit from them, are overwhelmingly connected to race-related factors. Indeed, school choice policies date back to the days of *Brown v. Board of Education* (1954). It was during this era that districts struggled to implement policies intended to provide black children with more access to a higher quality of education as proponents of segregation initiated choice plans maintaining segregation, allowing white families to avoid integration all together (Orfield, 2013). Today, as school choice options and competition for students grow, critics of school choice believe an expansion of these programs will lead to increased racial and socioeconomic segregation and isolation of the most disadvantaged students in the worst schools (Chingos, 2013). Further, choice plans may result in only some families (those of higher incomes) being able to choose which schools their children will attend (Frankenberg and Siegel-Hawley, 2008; Holme, 2002).

With such policy implications as a contextual backdrop, it is important to understand the current state of educational leadership preparation, especially as it relates to the preparation of leaders able to realize their identities as antiracist educators and social justice advocates for the communities they are called to serve. First, as noted in the Hawley and James (2010) study of leadership preparation programs, many programs are failing to equip their students with the skills and knowledge necessary to address race-related issues. Specifically, leadership preparation programs frequently neglect to provide their students with pedagogies that critically examine the multifaceted issues surrounding race and racism (Dantley, 2002; Herrity and Glasman, 1999; López, 2003; Parker and Hood, 1995; Parker and Shapiro, 1992; Rusch, 2004; Rusch and Horsford, 2009; Tillman, 2004; Young and Laible, 2000). This is particularly disturbing as preparatory classrooms should be the place where professors are educating students to participate in the development of a more tolerant and culturally diverse citizenry. While a number of leadership programs have included a social justice component within their curricula, aspiring leaders are ill-prepared when it comes to engaging in the complex social and cultural realities within the communities they are called to serve, particularly when these issues focus on race (Gooden and Dantley, 2012). Therefore, the question must be asked, how can these leaders be expected to advocate for the very school communities most frequently shaped by the school choice emphasis embedded within the Title I SIG program?

We begin this chapter by discussing the current state of educational reform policy as it pertains to the turnaround of PLA schools and the impetus to continue to push districts toward school choice. Next, after highlighting the racial and political aspects of such policies, we discuss the need for preparation programs to explicitly address the antiracist underpinnings of a social justice curriculum, and the resurgent focus on developing the political identity and skill sets of educational leaders. Within this conversation, we discuss the conceptual and practice-specific constructs we believe should be embedded within the curricula of leadership preparation programs. It is our belief that antiracist and political concepts must be woven throughout the entire preparatory curricula in order to develop the school leaders our diverse communities deserve. We conclude the chapter by charting a course for further recommendations and by offering implications as to the ways in which preparation programs should re-think how they prepare aspiring school leaders for urban school communities.

TURNAROUND, CHOICE, AND THE IMPACT ON URBAN SCHOOL COMMUNITIES

Turnaround. Beginning in earnest with No Child Left Behind, and continuing with Race to The Top, the values underlying educational policies created as a categorical lever for the procurement of general welfare (i.e., The Elementary and Secondary Education Act) have been replaced by neoliberal values suggesting the well-being of democratic citizens (students) should be placed in the care of the competitive marketplace. Accordingly, the federal educational policymaking in this era sought to expand the educational reform marketplace via policies such as school choice, vouchers for supplemental educational services, and competitive subgrants. A primary example of this shift in values are the set of educational reform efforts targeting the turnaround of the nation's persistently low-achieving (PLA) schools, the majority of which are populated by students of color and students living amidst conditions of poverty (Noguera and Wells, 2011). Hence, the shift in values shaping today's educational policies have contributed

to a situation where communities of color are being disproportionately targeted by reform efforts promoting: (a) the removal of "ineffective" school personnel, (b) the exclusion of site-based and community-led decision making, and (c) the closure of low-performing schools. This has not gone without notice, as those who advocate for historically marginalized communities are questioning whether turnaround-specific policies worsen the already present inequalities endured by school communities of color (Cucchiara, 2008; Karp, 2010), while others argue against such policies due to the lack of empirically based research available to support turnaround efforts (Ravitch and Mathis, 2010).

Initially, Section 1003(g) of Title I was authored by the G.W. Bush Administration to provide a separate program which would provide states with monies earmarked for low-performing districts and schools. The Bush/Spellings version of the Title I SIG program provided assistance to schools that had failed to meet Adequately Yearly Progress (AYP) for two consecutive years. The financial assistance provided to such schools was intended to facilitate the rapid improvement of student proficiency on standardized test measures (NCLB, 2002). Differing from the Obama/Duncan revision of the Title I SIG program, SIG under the Bush Administration provided states and local school districts with a significant amount of autonomy, allowing local and state policymakers to spend SIG monies on the research-based reform efforts they believed to be appropriate for their low-performing campuses. While providing a certain level of autonomy to local decision makers, NCLB and the Title I SIG program privatized supplemental education services, allowing governmental funds to be used for faith-based initiatives (via supplemental educational services), and promoted new options for parents such as potential private and charter school selection.

When the Obama Administration assumed office, it abruptly revised the Bush Administration's version of the SIG program, appropriated $546 million to the Title I SIG program overall, and then provided an additional $3 billion to the SIG program via the passage of the American Recovery and Reinvestment Act (2009). The regulatory constructs determining the issuance of SIG monies under the Obama/Duncan plan signaled a major shift from the Bush/Spellings SIG program. Specifically, the decision-making authority of state and local education actors was significantly diminished through three primary measures. First, in order for schools to receive SIG monies, they were forced to choose from four prescribed school-improvement strategies ("Obama Administration Announces," 2009):

1. *Turnaround* means districts must replace the school principal, at least 50 percent of the school's staff, and adopt a new governance structure while implementing a reshaped instructional program.
2. *Restart* means districts must close failing schools and reopen them under the management of a charter school operator (which could be a private entity).
3. *School closure* requires districts to close failing schools, sending all students to high-achieving campuses in the district.
4. *Transformation* means districts must provide a massive professional development effort that addresses teacher and leader effectiveness, comprehensive instructional reform strategies, extended learning, teacher planning time, and operating flexibility.

Second, state education agencies were forced to craft a formula meant to separate low-performing schools into three separate tiers. The intended outcome of this scaffolding was meant to ensure SIG funds reached schools considered to have the greatest need, yet there were a number of struggling schools under these formulas that would no longer be eligible for SIG funding.

Third, in an attempt to keep schools from choosing what reformers considered the least rigorous strategy for school improvement (transformation), the Department of Education authored a new amendment to SIG, the "Rule of 9." The Rule of 9 stated that any district with nine or more Tier I and II schools would not be allowed to implement the transformation model in more than 50 percent of its schools (U.S. Department of Education, 2009).

While the Obama/Duncan Title I SIG program appears to offer communities a certain level of autonomy by allowing them to choose from four reform models—turnaround, restart, transformation, and school closure—the reaction to this reform has been complicated and even controversial, as the majority of the options promote school closure and the removal of ineffective teachers and administrators. Therefore, when considering that the majority of SIG turnaround efforts occur in communities populated by low-income persons of color, questions about whether such policies should be viewed as racially discriminatory continue to lurk.

Choice. Often thought of as a contemporary idea, a number of different types of school choice policies have been adopted in the United States over the past half-century. These policies differ both in structure and goals depending on the historical contexts from which they were developed (Holme, Frankenberg, Diem, and Welton, 2013). School choice was originally advocated for by both liberals and conservatives in Southern states that struggled with civil rights and the enforcement of *Brown v. Board of Education* (1954). Some school districts were trying to respond to demands made by black families for access to higher quality schools provided only for white students. Conversely, those who wished to keep school segregation intact initiated choice plans that would allow white families to avoid integration all together (Fuller, Elmore, and Orfield, 1996; Orfield, 2013). Indeed, it took over a decade for the federal government to establish minimal standards for choice that provided every family the opportunity to make choices, fulfill those choices, and ensure that students were treated fairly in their new schools (Orfield, 2013). Although these guidelines resulted in more desegregated schools, black schools remained highly segregated. As a result, the federal government began to focus more on requiring the actual desegregation of schools as opposed to choice plans (*Green v. New Kent County*, 1968).

In the 1970s, school choice began to be viewed by liberals as a means to empower poor and working-class families by allowing them to challenge paternalistic bureaucracies. Magnet schools, a school choice option first accepted by the courts as a method of desegregation in 1975, were widely supported and increased dramatically over time in the number of students they served (Smrekar and Goldring, 1999). Indeed, in just over fifteen years from inception, 1.2 million students were enrolled in magnet schools in 230 school districts in the 1991–1992 school year (Yu and Taylor, 1997, as cited in Smrekar and Goldring, 1999). In the 2008–2009 school year, more than two and a half million students were enrolled in magnet schools in the United States (Siegel-Hawley and Frankenberg, 2013). Typically established in urban school districts with large student populations, magnet schools work to improve academic standards, promote socioeconomic and racial diversity, and provide a range of programs that may meet the needs and talents of individual students (Smrekar and Goldring, 1999). While the original goals of magnets have evolved over time as federal law and politics have changed (Siegel-Hawley and Frankenberg, 2013), they still constitute the nation's largest system of school choice.

In the 1980s, school choice was expanded and welcomed by political conservatives interested in subjecting schools to competitive market forces (Levin, 1991). Additionally, people falling in the middle of the political spectrum supported allowing parents to leave their neighborhood school for other public schools (Fuller et al., 1996). During this time, intra- and inter-district open enrollment policies were adopted by many school districts as a way to promote school improvement through competition (Lubienski, 2005).

School choice efforts expanded in the 1990s through voucher and charter school legislation. Charter schools and vouchers have been the leading forms of school choice for the past three decades. Charter schools have increased under federal education policy by every president since George H. W. Bush. Indeed, a major reason for the expansion of school choice in the form of charter schools is due to broad bipartisan support (Orfield, 2013). Advocates of the charter school movement argue that by forcing all schools to compete for students, better student outcomes will occur. Further, the autonomy of charter schools also attracts many supporters. Yet, although the number of charter schools has expanded exponentially and are the most rapidly growing sector of school choice, they still only make up a small fraction of public school enrollment (Frankenberg and Siegel-Hawley, 2013).

Following the passage of No Child Left Behind in 2001 (NCLB), school choice became the core of federal education policy (Holme, Frankenberg, Diem, and Welton, 2013). NCLB helped to further the dominant ideology surrounding school choice, which espouses that by definition any type of school choice is better than regular public schools and "good" or "bad" schools are determined almost exclusively based on test scores (Holme and Wells, 2008; Orfield, 2013). Today, school choice has been further expanded through the Obama/

Duncan administration via Race to The Top and Title I SIG. Indeed, the adoption and expansion of charter schools is encouraged by school districts if they wish to be competitive in acquiring federal funding.

Regardless of their structure and objectives, all school choice programs share the common goal of trying to improve the opportunities of students by breaking free from the traditional model of neighborhood schools. However, the overall impact of school choice all too often depends on which parents and students take advantage of school choice, the types of options these students have, parental knowledge about school choice, and most importantly, what happens to the students who get left behind (Cullen, Jacob, and Levitt, 2005; Holme and Wells, 2008). The ability for choice policies to increase or reduce racial integration can depend on the design of the policy. Deregulated policies, which establish a free, market-based, competitive environment, tend to lead to more stratification, whereas regulated policies, with more equity-minded goals, lead to more diversity and equitable outcomes (Blank, Levine, and Steel, 1996; Frankenberg and Siegel-Hawley, 2008). Further, the kind of choice offered and made available to families matters.

RETHINKING THE SOCIALLY JUST PREPARATION OF ANTIRACIST EDUCATIONAL LEADERS

In light of how the Title I SIG program and its embedded emphasis on school choice may disproportionately and negatively affect school communities of color, the field of educational leadership must re-think the ways in which preparing socially just educational leaders takes place. The preparation of leaders oriented to issues of social justice has become a growing concern among U.S. scholars and practitioners, particularly given the rapidly shifting demographics of PK–12 public schools and the inequities that continue to exist between affluent white students and low-income students of color. It is our belief that in order for principals to realize their positions as leaders of social-justice-oriented communities of teachers, they must be better prepared to address issues specific to students of color. This belief is supported by Evans' (2007) concern that U.S. classrooms are led by a predominately white teaching force lacking the experiences necessary to realize their role as effective instructional leaders for diverse student populations, and by Darling-Hammond's (2006) research, which asserts that the current teaching population will likely enter classrooms where 25 percent of students will be from households living in poverty; 10 percent to 20 percent of the students will exhibit major learning struggles; 15 percent of the students will be identified as English language learners; and 40 percent of the students will identify as members of racial/ethnic groups (p. 301).

While many scholars within the field of educational leadership have recognized such realities, and are thus exploring the role of social justice in leadership preparation programs and what it means to be regarded as a socially just leader (for example, Blackmore, 2009; Brown, 2004, 2006; Jean-Marie, Normore, and Brooks, 2009; Marshall and Oliva, 2006; McKenzie et al., 2008; Theoharis, 2007, 2009, 2010), the social justice leadership literature still lacks sufficient information as to the actual practice of social justice leadership within public schools and what capacities may be needed for such action to occur (Furman, 2012). Moreover, as scholars have long called attention to the failure of leadership preparation programs to adequately focus on race within their coursework and extra classroom practices (Dantley, 2002; hooks, 1994; López, 2003; Parker and Shapiro, 1992; Rusch, 2004; Rusch and Horsford, 2009; Tillman, 2004; Young and Laible, 2000), these programs continue to marginalize race and/or relegate race-related issues to special topics or stand-alone courses (Hawley and James, 2010). Consequently, many programs are shortchanging race-related issues in an "effort to couch the preparation of school leaders in a larger social justice context" (Gooden and Dantley, 2012, p. 238). Indeed, in our own research (Carpenter and Diem, 2013; Diem and Carpenter, 2013a) we have found how difficult it can be for professors in leadership preparation programs to facilitate candid conversations about race with their students. Further, when these conversations do occur, how race is defined and deconstructed may look very different depending on who is included in the discussion.

Excluding race within leadership preparation programs contributes to what Rusch and Horsford (2009) define as a culture of "silence and fear" among professors. Preparatory programs choosing to endorse such a culture are more likely to graduate public school leaders without the skills needed to address the "challenging,

but necessary, conversations" connecting to issues of race (Rusch and Horsford, 2009, p. 303). Further, by remaining "color-mute" (Pollock, 2004) or excluding "race language" (Gooden and Dantley, 2012) as part of a social justice framework within leadership programs, the ability for genuine conversations to occur about the racial discrepancies existent within schools fails to materialize. Additionally, as the current school leader population remains predominately white during an era when public schools are rapidly becoming more demographically diverse, it is perhaps more important than ever for preparation programs to provide aspiring leaders with the communicative skills necessary to address race-related issues within their increasingly diverse school communities.

(Un)Muting Issues of Race

Although we have become a more racially diverse society, when it comes to talking about issues related to race, there is often a struggle to engage in meaningful conversations. There are a number of reasons why such conversations become divisive and polarizing and leave of us "virtually incapable of talking about or thinking about race in a transformative way" (Rudd et al., 2009, p. 1). Indeed, our inability to fully grasp the history of race in the United States and the structures and systems of power put in place that continue to result in insurmountable inequities among different racial groups has left us paralyzed in challenging a discourse that prefers to color-mute, color-blind, or avoid race issues all together.

Within the field of educational leadership preparation, the findings that leadership programs frequently relegate issues of social justice, race, and diversity to singular courses offerings are cause for great alarm (Hawley and James, 2010). Subsequently, via a reexamination of our previous studies, and an extensive reading of the literature addressing the preparation of educational leaders for issues of social justice and equity, we previously outlined five critical concepts— color-blind ideology, misconceptions of human difference, merit-based achievement, critical self-reflection, interrogation of race-related silences—we believe must be embedded throughout the curricular scope and sequence of all leadership programs focused on preparing leaders for diverse settings (Diem and Carpenter, 2012,

2013b). The development of the five critical concepts was encouraged by the teaching and learning scholar Milner (2010), who several years earlier unveiled what he terms as the "repertoires of diversity"—issues he believes must be included within all curriculum guiding teacher preparatory programs. Milner (2010) outlined these concepts—color-blindness, cultural conflicts, myth of meritocracy, deficit conceptions, and expectations—with the idea that through his call to action regarding the status of diversity studies within teacher education curricula, teacher educators from across the country would engage in conversations focusing on how to help create a diversity studies curriculum for teacher education programs.

We echo Milner's thoughts on diversity within teacher preparation and believe by highlighting critical concepts that warrant more attention in leadership preparation program curricula, the field may better recognize the need to reform the ways in which future leaders are being prepared to serve and engage in race-related conversations in diverse communities. Alternatively, if we continue following the current path in leadership preparation, avoiding a meaningful dialogue around issues related to race, we will further diminish its continued significance in society and how it impacts the lives of those in our schools and communities. Rudd et al. (2009) state:

> We need to talk about race because we are often thinking about race in ways that profoundly impact our decisions and understandings. Race has also been an important factor in the way that institutions are designed and the work that they do. It has been a principal force in building, sustaining, and shifting the social and political structures and organizational arrangements that control the distribution of opportunity and resources across all populations. Race also plays a significant role—either explicitly or implicitly—in many of the most important decisions that we make in our personal, professional, and social lives: where we live, who our children's friends are, who our friends are, which political candidates we vote for, what social programs we support, etc. For most Americans, all of these issues include some consideration of race and while these considerations are often very subtle, they have the power to shape and control individual attitudes, values, and behaviors. It is not possible to talk coherently or truthfully about the history of our democracy or the future well-being of the American people without talking about race. The process of

racialization continues to depress our aspirations as a nation as well as our economic and civic well-being, and while this process impacts racially marginalized and non-marginalized groups differently, it impacts us all. (p. 2)

We highlight this statement above as it supports our belief that race can no longer be subsumed via the implicit and sporadic addressing of race-related issues within social justice curricula. Instead, issues of race must be brought to the forefront, explicitly addressed within each and every course taken by aspiring leaders.

RETHINKING THE PREPARATION OF SCHOOL LEADERS AS POLITICAL AGENTS

The political nature of school leadership became a renewed topic of intense interest in the late 1980s and early 1990s. During this period a number of scholars brought attention to the political and micropolitical aspects of school building leadership and school organizations (Ball, 1987; Blasé, 1989, Iannaccone, 1991; Marshall and Scribner, 1991; Mawhinney, 1999). In addition, critically oriented scholars (Apple, 2008; Giroux, 1992) argued the political aspects of education and educational leadership should be one of the field's foremost concerns due to the continued presence of inequitable and historically defined power relations that negatively influence all educational stakeholders. In fact, Giroux (1992), believing the identity of an educational leader must be developed to foster a democratic society, challenged the entire field of educational leadership by asking preparatory programs to "refashion" their practices so the everyday experiences of school leaders could be viewed "through a language of critique and possibility that expands and deepens the possibility for cultural and political democracy" (p. 1).

Comments such as this encourage leadership preparatory faculty to reconsider the educational system as a politically oriented institution, one that must be interpreted via the sociopolitical context of a diverse and complex society.

While each of the previously cited scholars agree that schools are absolutely essential for democracy, the ways in which educational policies are crafted and implemented often define how democracy can be pursued within local school districts. As previously highlighted, the Title I SIG program and its school choice priorities certainly help define the roles practitioners are able to inhabit on a daily basis. Fortunately, the recent re-authoring of national school leadership standards—Interstate School Leaders Licensure Consortium (ISLLC) standards and the Educational Leadership Constituent Council (ELCC) standards—are pushing educational leadership preparation programs to recognize the political identity of the school leader can be an effective political advocate for their community at the local, state, and federal levels. Specifically, the most recent revision of the ISLLC standards, asks programs to prepare leaders able to advocate for all students by "understanding, responding to, and influencing the political, social, economic, legal, and cultural context" (CCSSO, 2008). In addition, the latest ELCC standards suggest all principals must be prepared in a way that allows them to realize their role as an advocate who promotes "equitable learning opportunities and success for all students" (www.npbea.org/ELCC). Subsequently, while today's school leaders are being asked to realize their role as advocates at the local, state, and federal levels, it is imperative that leadership preparatory programs help define what in fact this advocacy looks like in practice.

(Un)Muting the Political

The recent shift to include advocacy-oriented language within leadership preparation standards offers hope. Certainly, the purposeful embedding explicit advocacy language into national leadership standards should be viewed as a positive. Yet, while advocacy-related language and expectations now exists, those left to interpret how exactly such standards should be enacted are left with the difficult job of having to realize their politically savvy identity, while also having to negotiate the political nature of school building leadership, dutifully implementing centralized and standards-based accountability systems. Subsequently, while today's school leaders are expected to embrace the role of the instructional leader, and embrace their role as political advocate for their broader educational community, they may, via the mandatory implementation of high-stakes accountability reforms, potentially exacerbate the very inequalities such reforms are designed to ameliorate (Carpenter and Brewer, 2012).

If leadership preparation programs are to develop school building leaders who can realize their identities as savvy participants in a complex political context, educational leadership scholars must investigate which practices, levers, and/or vehicles allow leaders to promote community-based needs, while also protecting their vulnerable position as a middle manager in the hierarchy of a school district. However, much like the preparation of leaders about issues pertaining to race, there are a number of critical concepts that must be brought to the surface during the preparation of school leaders. First, educational leadership courses must acknowledge the literature suggesting that educational purposes have been reshaped by global economic interests (Apple and Beane, 1995; Ball, 2007, 2008; Blackmore, 2007; Rivzi and Lingard, 2010). Specifically, students in leadership preparation classes must be able to deconstruct the authoring of policies, paying specific attention to how the discourses of market and choice, management and surveillance, and performativity and accountability determine the expected outcomes of educational policy measures (Carpenter, 2011).

Considering the unequal ramifications of policies such as turnaround and school choice, it is our argument that leadership students must be given the skill set necessary to critically evaluate the intent and potential effect of educational policies. Specifically, aspiring leaders must be able to decipher the ways in which educational reforms have been shaped by economic rationalities focused on the preparation of a globally competitive workforce (Levin, 1998)—market/choice. They must also question the intentionality behind policies that "empower" local authorities and parents, while closely monitoring how their actions will meet the centralized objectives of state and federal government agencies (Dean, 1999)—management/surveillance. Finally, tomorrow's school leaders administrators must be able to critically interrogate the values supporting policies which legislate the standardized ideal of proficiency, the prescribed reconfiguration of school governance, and the performance driven evaluation of student, teacher, and administrator success (Jensen and Walker, 2008)—performativity/accountability.

When asking how critical practitioners can realize their role as a political advocate for school communities, perhaps the field should look toward the work of critical policy scholars. Hajer (2003) challenges policy scholars to "renew" their investigatory methods to better unveil the ways in which "meaning is hidden in policymaking discourse and thus be able to anticipate political controversies" (p. 110). Should we expect less of practitioners? If a critical mass of educational practitioners is to become a reality, our future leaders must be equipped with the skills needed to recognize the discourses shaping educational policymaking so they can, in a politically sophisticated manner, work with and through varied interests and differences to address the continued persistence of educational and social inequalities.

DISCUSSION AND IMPLICATIONS FOR THE FIELD

Evans (2013) states,

> While issues of equity and diversity have long been central themes in education policy and law, they have not always been acknowledged as such in practice or in research. . . . We know that the study of educational leadership is in a relative infancy but in its short history, it too has failed to recognize or acknowledge how race, class, and diversity have been addressed in practice and in research. (p. 3)

The persistent and profound discrepancies that still exist among students of differing backgrounds should serve as an impetus for educational scholars and leaders to leverage what we already know about race, social justice, diversity, and equity in school leadership so that we can make meaningful and long-lasting changes in the education that is provided in schools. We know that principals today work within a context defined by the continued emphasis on high-stakes accountability and the inequitable distribution of chronically low-performing schools. Therefore, it is extremely important that educational leadership preparation programs include the pursuit of equity and social justice as a central priority. Scholars responsible for preparing PK–12 administrators must better evaluate their programs' ability to offer adequate exposure to curricula focused on issues of race and racism. Specifically, educational leaders called to serve diverse populations must be more informed about the important role race plays in education reform efforts—specifically, those pertaining to school turnaround and school choice.

"School leaders must give voice, dialogue, and conversation to the issue of educational equity . . . School leaders who fail to promote equity via discourse, dialogue, and the appropriate productive action continue to legitimize inequitable systems and differential educational outcomes and life chances for poor children and children of color" (Evans, 2013, p. 463). Gooden and Dantley (2012) offer a leadership preparation framework centered on race that we believe can better assist leaders in recognizing the role of race in education. Further, the framework can also teach leaders how to become better advocates for racial equity within their schools and communities. By centering race "within a broader context of social justice," Gooden and Dantley (2012) argue that this framework "holds all players in the educational process accountable for creating equitable spaces for children and youth to learn" (p. 241). This critically grounded theoretical framework suggests race language must be included throughout the curricula and practices in preparation programs so that leaders can locate race within a historical context and link them to current economic, cultural, and political contexts, all of which will help them better realize how discrepancies in schools came about and still exist. Further, the framework states that educational leaders should learn how to develop prophetic and pragmatic voices and become self-reflective so that they can engage in transformative actions within their schools and communities. Utilizing such a framework can develop leaders who are able to better understand the role of race in education reform policies and better decode the masked narratives of race. Moreover, future school leaders may be more adequately prepared to communicate with community stakeholders about the benefits of enrolling their children in diverse school communities.

While scholars have historically focused on how the shifting policy context has impacted educational stakeholders such as teachers, students, and even parents, little work has been done to clarify how such shifts in policy affect the everyday work of school building leaders. As Evans (2013) states, "Clearly, a policy environment shaped by a federal mandate can and does influence the work of local leaders and teachers." (p. 464). The ramifications of working as a school leader in this environment cannot be overlooked, as even prior to the latest wave of school accountability measures such as those embedded within the Obama/Duncan Title I SIG program, Portin, Shen, and Williams (1998) highlighted the ways in which educational leaders were quickly becoming overwhelmed due to the abundance of external priorities and the limited amount of time they can allot to the job required of an instructional leader.

The information presented in this chapter acknowledges these pressures by highlighting the need for educational leadership programs to more purposefully equip aspiring leaders with the skill sets necessary to address issues of race, deconstruct the political intentionality of mandated policies, and thus better advocate for their school community. While equipping leaders with such skill sets will not necessarily ease the pressures associated with serving as a principal in a low-performing school, it may help principals better connect with a broader range of educational stakeholders, altering the composition of school improvement/turnaround from a within building pursuit, to a collective effort involving a diverse group of motivated stakeholders.

REFERENCES

Apple, M. W. (2008). Can schooling contribute to a more just society? *Education, citizenship, and social justice, 3*(3), 239–261.

Apple, M. W. and Beane, J. A. (Eds.). (1995). *Democratic schools* (2nd ed.). Alexandria, VA: Association for Supervision and Curriculum Development.

Ball, S. J. (1987). *The Micropolitics of the school: Towards a Theory of School Organization.* London: Methuen.

Ball, S. J. (2007). *Education PLC: Understanding private sector participation in public sector education.* New York: Routledge.

Blackmore, J. (2007). Localization/globalization and the midwife state: Strategic dilemmas for state feminism in education? In S. Ball, I.F. Goodson, and M. Maguire (Eds.), *Education, globalisation and new times* (pp. 21–46). New York: Routledge.

Blackmore, J. (2009). Leadership for social justice: A transnational dialogue. *Journal of Research on Leadership Education, 4*(1), 1–10.

Blank, R. K., Levine, R. E., and Steel, L. (1996). After 15 years: Magnet schools in urban education. In B. Fuller, R. F. Elmore, and G. Orfield (Eds.), *Who chooses? Who loses? Culture, institutions, and the unequal effects of school choice.* New York: Teachers College Press.

Blasé, J. J. (1989). The micropolitics of the school: The everyday political orientation of teachers toward open

principals. *Educational Administration Quarterly, 25*(4), 377–407.

Brown v. Board of Education of Topeka, 347 U.S. 483 (1954).

Brown, K. M. (2004). Leadership for social justice and equity: Weaving a transformative framework and pedagogy. *Educational Administration Quarterly, 40*(1), 77–108.

Brown, K. M. (2006). Leadership for social justice and equity: Evaluating a transformative framework and andragogy. *Educational Administration Quarterly, 42*(5), 700–745.

Carpenter, B. W. (2011). *(Re)Framing the politics of educational discourse: An investigation of the Title I School Improvement Grant Program of 2009.* (Unpublished doctoral dissertation.) The University of Texas at Austin, Austin, TX.

Carpenter, B. W. and Brewer, C. (2012). The implicated advocate: The discursive construction of the democratic practices of school principals in the USA. *Discourse: Studies in the Cultural Politics of Education, 35*(2), 299–306.

Carpenter, B. W. and Diem, S. (2013). Talking race: Facilitating critical conversations in educational leadership preparation programs. *Journal of School Leadership, 23*(6), 902–931.

Chief Council of State School Officers (CCSSO). (2008). *Educational Leadership Policy Standards: ISLLC 2008 as adopted by the National Policy Board for Educational Administration.* Retrieved from www.ccsso.org/projects/education_leadership_initiatives/ISLLC_Standards/.

Chingos, M. M. (2013, May 15). *Does expanding school choice increase segregation?* Washington, DC: The Brookings Institution.

Cucchiara, M. (2008). Re-branding urban schools: urban revitalization, social status, and marketing public schools to the upper middle class. *Journal of Education Policy, 23*(2), 165–179.

Cullen, J. B., Jacob, B. A., and Levitt, S. D. (2005). The impact of school choice on student outcomes: An analysis of the Chicago Public Schools. *Journal of Public Economics, 89*(5/6), 729–760.

Dantley, M. E. (2002). Uprooting and replacing positivism, the melting pot, multiculturalism, and other impotent notions in educational leadership through an African American perspective. *Education and Urban Society, 34,* 334–352.

Darling-Hammond, L. (2006). Constructing 21st-century teacher education. *Journal of Teacher Education, 57*(3), 300–314.

Dean, M. (1999). *Governmentality: Power and rule in a modern society.* Thousand Oaks, CA: Sage.

Diem, S. and Carpenter, B. W. (2012). Social justice and leadership preparation: Developing a transformative curriculum. *Planning and Changing, 43*(1/2), 96–112.

Diem, S. and Carpenter, B. W. (2013a). Examining race-related silences: Interrogating the education of tomorrow's educational leaders. *Journal of Research in Leadership Education, 8*(1), 56–76.

Diem, S. and Carpenter, B. W. (2013b). Exploring the blockages of race-related Conversations in the classroom: Obstacles or opportunity? In J. S. Brooks and N. W. Arnold (Eds.), *Confronting racism in higher education: Problems and possibilities for fighting ignorance, bigotry and isolation* (pp. 1–20). Charlotte, NC: Information Age Publishing.

Evans, A. E. (2007). School leaders and their sensemaking about race and demographic change. *Educational Administration Quarterly, 43*(2), 159–188.

Evans, A. E. (2013). Educational leaders as policy actors and equity advocates. In L. C. Tillman and J. J. Scheurich (Eds.), *Handbook of research on educational leadership for equity and diversity* (pp. 459–475). New York: Routledge.

Frankenberg, E. and Siegel-Hawley, G. (2008). The forgotten choice? Rethinking magnet schools in a changing landscape. Los Angeles: University of California, The Civil Rights Project.

Frankenberg, E. and Siegel-Hawley, G. (2013). A segregating choice? An overview of charter school policy, enrollment trends, and segregation. In G. Orfield and E. Frankenberg (Eds.), *Educational delusions?: Why choice can deepen inequality and how to make schools fair* (pp. 129–144). Berkeley: University of California Press.

Fuller, B., Elmore, R. F., and Orfield, G. (Eds.). (1996). *Who chooses? Who loses? Culture, institutions, and the unequal effects of school choice.* New York: Teachers College Press.

Furman, G. (2012). Social justice leadership as praxis: Developing capacities through preparation programs. *Educational Administration Quarterly, 48*(2), 191–229.

Giroux, H. A. (1992). Educational leadership and the crisis of democratic government. *Educational Researcher, 21*(4), 4–11.

Gooden, M. A. and Dantley, M. E. (2012). Centering race in a framework for leadership preparation. *Journal of Research in Leadership Education, 7*(2), 237–253.

Green v. County School Board of New Kent County, 391 U.S. 430 (1968).

Hajer, M. A. (2003). A frame in the fields: Policymaking and the reinvention of politics. In M. A. Hajer and H. Wagenaar (Eds.), *Deliberative policy analysis: Understanding governance in the network society* (pp. 88–112). Cambridge, England: Cambridge University Press.

Hawley, W. and James, R. (2010). Diversity-responsive school leadership. *UCEA Review, 52*, 1–5.

Herrity, V. and Glasman, N. S. (1999). Training administrators for culturally and linguistically diverse school populations: Opinions of expert practitioners. *Journal of School Leadership, 9*, 235–253.

Holme, J .J. (2002). Buying homes, buying schools: School choice and the social construction of school quality. *Harvard Educational Review, 72*(2), 177–205.

Holme, J. J., Frankenberg, E., Diem, S., and Welton, A. D. (2013). School choice in suburbia: The impact of choice policies on the potential for suburban integration. *Journal of School Choice: International Research and Reform, 7*(2), 113–141.

Holme, J. J. and Wells, A.S. (2008). School choice beyond district borders: Lessons for the reauthorization of NCLB from interdistrict desegregation and open enrollment plans. In R. Kahlenberg (Ed.), *Improving on No Child Left Behind: Getting education reform back on track* (pp. 139–215). New York: Century Foundation Press.

hooks, b. (1994). *Teaching to transgress: Education as the practice of freedom.* New York: Routledge.

Iannacone, L. (1991). Micropolitics of education: What and why. *Education and Urban Society, 23*(4), 465–471.

Jean-Marie, G., Normore, A., and Brooks, J. S. (2009). Leadership for social justice: Preparing 21st-century school leaders for a new social order. *Journal of Research on Leadership in Education, 4*(1), 1–31.

Jensen, K. and Walker, S. (2008). *Education, democracy and discourse.* New York: Continuum International Publishing Group.

Karp, S. (2010). School reform we can't believe in. *Rethinking Schools, 24*(3), 48–53.

Levin, B. (1998). An epidemic of education policy: (what) can we learn from each other? *Comparative education, 34*(2), 131–141.

Levin, H. (1991). The economics of educational choice. *Economics of Education Review, 10*, 137–158.

López, G. R. (2003). The (racially neutral) politics of education: A critical race theory perspective. *Educational Administration Quarterly, 39*, 68–94.

Lubienski, C. (2005). Public schools in marketized environments: Shifting incentives and unintended consequences of competition-based educational reforms. *American Journal of Education, 111*(4), 464–486.

Marshall, C. and Oliva, M. (2006). *Leadership for social justice: Making revolutions in education.* Boston: Pearson.

Marshall, C. and Scribner, J. (1991). It's all political. *Education and Urban Society, 23*(4), 347–355.

Mawhinney, H. B. (Ed.). (1999). Special feature: What can the study of micropolitics contribute to the practice of leadership in school reform? Introduction to a collection of reflections onmicropolitics. *School Leadership and Management, 19*(2).

McKenzie, K., Christman, D., Hernandez, F., Fierro, E., Capper, C., Dantley, M., Gonzalez, M., Cambron-McCabe, N., and Scheurich, J. (2008). Educating Leaders for social justice: A design for a comprehensive, social justice leadership preparation program. *Educational Administration Quarterly, 44*(1), 111–138.

Milner IV, H. R. (2010). What does teacher education have to do with teaching? Implications for diversity studies? *Journal of Teacher Education, 61*(1–2), 118–131.

Noguera, P.A. and Wells, L. (2011). The politics of school reform: A broader and bolder approach to Newark. *Berkeley Review of Education, 2*(1), 5–25.

Obama Administration announces historic opportunity to turn around nation's lowest-achieving public schools [Press release]. (2009). Retrieved from the U.S. Department of Education website: www2.ed.gov/news/ pressreleases/2009/08/08262009.html.

Orfield, G. (2013). Choice theories and schools. In G. Orfield and E. Frankenberg (Eds.), *Educational delusions?: Why choice can deepen inequality and how to make schools fair* (pp. 37–68). Berkeley: University of California Press.

Parker, L. and Hood, S. (1995). Minority students vs. majority faculty and administrators in teacher education: Perspectives on the clash of cultures. *Urban Review, 27*, 159–174.

Parker, L. and Shapiro, J. (1992). Where is the discussion of diversity in educational administration programs? Graduate student voices addressing an omission in their preparation. *Journal of School Leadership, 2*, 7–33.

Planty, M., Kena, G., and Hannes, G. (2009). *The condition of education 2009 in brief.* Washington, DC: National Center for Education Statistics.

Pollock, M. (2004). *Colormute: Race talk dilemmas in an American school.* Princeton, NJ: Princeton University Press.

Portin, B. S., Shen, J., and Williams, R. C. (1998). The changing principalship and its impact: Voices from principals. *NASSP Bulletin, 82*(602), 1–8.

Ravitch, D. and Mathis, W. J. (2010). A review of college- and career-ready students. In W. J. Mathis and K. G. Welner (Eds.), *The Obama education blueprint: Researchers examine the evidence* (pp. 9–22). Charlotte, NC: Information Age.

Rivzi, F. and Lingard, B. (2010). *Globalizing education policy.* New York: Routledge.

Rudd, T., Johnson, A., Staats, C., powell, j.a., and Grant-Thomas, A. (2009). *Talking about race: Toward a transformative agenda.* Columbus: The Ohio State University Kirwan Institute for the Study of Race and Ethnicity.

Rusch, E. A. (2004). Gender and race in leadership preparation: A constrained discourse. *Educational Administration Quarterly, 40*, 14–46.

Rusch, E. A. and Horsford, S. D. (2009). Changing hearts and minds: The quest for open talk about race in educational leadership. *International Journal of Educational Management, 23*, 302–313.

Siegel-Hawley, G. and Frankenberg, E. (2013). Designing choice: Magnet school structures and racial diversity. In G. Orfield and E. Frankenberg (Eds.), *Educational delusions?: Why choice can deepen inequality and how to make schools fair* (pp. 107–128). Berkeley: University of California Press.

Smrekar, C. and Goldring, E. (1999). *School choice in urban America: Magnet schools and the pursuit of equity.* New York: Teachers College Press.

Theoharis, G. (2007). Social justice educational leaders and resistance: Toward a theory of social justice leadership. *Educational Administration Quarterly, 43*(2), 221.

Theoharis, G. (2009). *The school leaders our children deserve: Seven keys to equity, social justice, and school reform.* New York: Teachers College Press.

Theoharis, G. (2010). Sustaining social justice: Strategies urban principals develop to advance justice and equity while facing resistance. *International Journal of Urban Educational Leadership, 4*(1), 92–110.

Tillman, L. C. (2004). (Un)Intendend consequences? The impact of the *Brown v. Board of Education* decision on the employment status of Black educators. *Education and Urban Society, 36*, 280–303.

U.S. Department of Education (2009). *Title I: Improving the Academic Achievement of the Disadvantaged.* Retrieved from www2.ed.gov/policy/elsec/leg/esea02/pg1.html.

Young, M. D and Laible, J. (2000). White racism, antiracism, and school leader preparation. *Journal of School Leadership, 10*, 374–415.

Yu, C. M. and Taylor, W. L. (1997). *Difficult choices: Do magnet schools serve children in need?* Washington, DC: Citizens' Commission on Civil Rights.

CHAPTER 28

The Urban School Leaders Collaborative

An Alternative and Effective Model for Leadership Preparation and Practice

Encarnacion Garza Jr.

INTRODUCTION

The purpose of this chapter was to analyze and report on a "different" model of leadership preparation that was designed and customized to prepare school leaders to practice in schools where the student population is predominantly Latino and in an urban school setting. It is a preparation program designed to advance interactive collaboration between students, professors, and school district administrators. As researcher and coordinator, I have been involved with the Urban School Leaders Collaborative (USLC) since the planning and inception of the program.

With the rapidly changing demographics, this chapter will serve as a framework for practitioners and scholars seeking an alternative way to prepare school leaders who will serve a growing number of students in urban school settings. This chapter will be useful to educators who want to develop and establish programs that have a social justice focus.

BACKGROUND OF URBAN SCHOOL LEADERS COLLABORATIVE (USLC)

The USLC is a partnership between the University of Texas at San Antonio (UTSA) and the San Antonio Independent School District (SAISD). The USLC was established eleven years ago by Dr. Betty Merchant, department chair; Dr. Blandina Cardenas, dean of the College of Education and Human Development (COEHD); and Dr. Ruben Olivarez, the superintendent of SAISD. The founding superintendent believed that the USLC would help the district "identify the brightest and the best and prepare them to lead toward equity and social justice." Both superintendent and assistant superintendent partnered with UTSA and the department of Edu-

cational Leadership and Policy Studies (ELPS) to build a needs-based pre-service program that strongly focused on the sustainability of inner-city students and their families. In 2002, UTSA and SAISD jointly designed a two-year program to prepare emerging leaders in the district, preparing them with both a master's degree and principal certification.

The context—inner city urban school district

San Antonio, Texas, is one of the fastest growing cities in the nation. The city of 1.5 million inhabitants is located in south Texas and two hours away from the Mexico border in a culturally rich community composed of a 58 percent Latino population (U.S. Census, 2010). In this visitor-friendly city, English and Spanish are often culturally blended in the language and customs, through the city's festivities, printed and visual media, and general public services. Not all people of Mexican descent speak Spanish. The city has also received a new influx of migrants and refugees from economically depressed states.

The city's growth pairs up with other large cities, where societal changes common to urban centers can be identified, such as the exodus of affluent families to the suburbs. In 2008, for example, SAISD began the difficult task of closing some of the schools due to the decreasing enrollment of students moving out to nearby suburban districts. The enrollment in the inner-city SAISD is approximately fifty-four thousand students. Through a careful demographic analysis of the district, differences with surrounding districts are noticeable. When comparing SAISD with the demographics of the state of Texas, the district has close to 90 percent Latinos in its ethnic composition (compared to 48 percent in the state) (Texas Education Agency, 2009).

The SAISD is a public, urban school district in the heart of the city's urban center. SAISD is one of fifteen districts in Bexar County. The school district has a high percentage of students classified as at-risk (67 percent) as well as a large group with limited English proficiency (17 percent). SAISD also serves a significant number of economically disadvantaged students (90 percent) (Texas Education Agency, 2009). SAISD deserves particular attention because it shows an authentic need for investment in children in terms of societal improvement and sustainability. The need for educational leaders committed to the district, acting as social justice agents, is significant when national evidence suggests that public schools where English language learner test-takers are concentrated have, on average, a substantially greater proportion of students qualifying for free or reduced-price school lunches and are significantly more likely to be designated Title I schools (Fry, 2008).

The USLC was therefore developed from a strong partnership between the district and the university. The superintendent voiced his interest in advancing the preparation of strong leaders that would partner in his mission to actively support this community. Among the superintendent's concerns was the critical shortage of qualified candidates for principal preparation programs (Davis, Darling-Hammond, LaPointe, and Meyerson, 2005). Similar patterns existed at SAISD, especially the departure of qualified educators and educational leaders to more affluent areas of the city.

The program has been in existence since 2002, currently preparing the sixth cohort of aspiring leaders. A total of eighty-three students were admitted in the first five cohorts and seventy-six students have graduated from the USLC.

ONGOING STUDY OF THE USLC

Our research clearly indicates that the USLC has had significant success in its mission to develop leaders prepared to assume leadership in an urban inner-city setting. Since its inception, the coordinator and other faculty have studied the USLC and published several articles and chapters that reflect and confirm the effectiveness of the program. A 2006 article, "The urban school leaders collaborative: A school-university partnership emphasizing instructional leadership and student and community assets" (Garza, Barnett, Merchant, Shoho,

and Smith, 2006, describes the early stages of the development of the Urban School Leaders Collaborative and examines the experiences of the first cohort of master's students. Throughout the program students, as well as faculty members, engage in critical self-reflection and evaluation about their program, their professional practice, and their interpersonal interactions. Faculty and student collaboration in the early stages of this collaboration led to the generation of a framework for what has resulted in an ongoing study of the USLC. The major findings of this study indicate that there are three main factors that are critical to a successful school-university partnership: (1) Establishment of a clear need to identify and prepare quality school leaders; (2) Sanction of the collaborative from top-level leaders; and (3) Trust between the two organizations' leaders. It is important to note that an unintended, but significant, consequence of engaging students as researchers in the systemic investigation of their experiences in the collaborative has been the enrollment of several of these students in the university's doctoral program in educational leadership.

The book chapter, "American Culture: Latino Realties" (Garza and Merchant, 2009), presents the findings of a two-year longitudinal study of the USLC. In contrast to the 2006 article that focused on the structure and implementation of the collaborative, this piece examines the data from the first two student cohorts in the USLC for the purposes of critically examining our programmatic efforts to prepare school leaders to practice in schools where the student population is predominantly Latino. Our findings indicate that this leadership program differs from traditional models of leadership preparation in several distinct ways. First, this program is driven by a philosophy of social justice advocacy. The focus of preparation is initially on attitudes and mind-sets, and then on the development of professional skills. Second, this is a truly collaborative partnership; both entities (school district and university) are actively involved in the selection, planning, teaching, and evaluation processes. Third, this is a closed cohort model, only for employees of the partnering school district, and the leadership preparation is intentionally customized to meet the needs of the children in this school district. Fourth, professors have moved away from their home campus into the field; all classes taught by department faculty are held in campuses throughout the school district. And fifth, support continues through the mechanism of the collaborative even after the students graduate and assume leadership positions.

Another article, "Lessons from country borders: Preparing leaders for social justice and diversity through a district and university partnership" (Murakami, Garza, and Merchant, 2009), the researchers explore the preparation of educators as school leaders in a master's degree program focused on diversity and social justice. The program's proximity to the Mexican border provides an opportunity to examine permeable exchanges and accommodations where schools exist at the intersection of geography, culture, politics, and diversity (racial/ethnic and linguistic). This study asked, "To what degree were the educators in this program being prepared as emerging leaders for social justice?" The cultural relevancy of who they are, as part of a distinct cultural fabric, is captured in the narratives of the educators as they prepare to become future educational leaders in this district–university partnership.

The lessons in this study included concrete examples of a district–university partnership that prepares educators to embrace a mission and actively engage in promoting social justice in schools. Once in the cohort, these educators are charged to mentor the next generation of leaders, creating an ongoing cycle of professional development, reflective practices, and collaboration. The connection between the emerging leaders' experience and their mission was significant.

The latest book chapter published about the USLC is titled "Lessons from a principal preparation program: Creating support through social justice practices" (Murakami-Ramalho, Garza, and Merchant, 2012). In this chapter, we focus on some of the important reflections that the emerging leaders in the USLC program have shared. Many reflections relate to how they learned about social justice and advocacy. Important to any program is to examine whether the emerging leaders are taking with them applicable concepts. Through the study of these reflections, we observed their transformational journeys. An important lesson that can be transferred to other educators is that social justice advocacy will in most cases be confronted by the same forces that once convinced these emerging leaders in their childhood that they were different and lacking, and were therefore unworthy of academic investments. The literature about effective schools indicates that principals play a major role in the academic success or

failure of students (Garza et al., 2004; Gonzales, 2002; Marshall and Oliva, 2006). Therefore, given the critical role of the principal, it is crucial that school leaders be prepared to meet the needs of Latino students (Gonzales, Huerta-Macias, and Tinajero, 2002; Lomotey, 1989). The importance of sustaining programs that develop social justice through critical consciousness, and culturally relevant practices, is of utmost importance in developing effective practices and in creating social agendas conducive to student learning. We carry a similar duty while coordinating this program: we need to continuously reexamine our pedagogy, and the field of education, if we want to prepare professionals as social justice advocates.

METHODOLOGY

The main sources of data for this project are the voices of the cohort members. I rely heavily on the experiences of the members of all six cohorts to share the transformational experiences of the students and describe the collaboration between UTSA and SAISD. Additional data for this chapter was drawn from the history and record of the program and the experiences of cohort members who have graduated from the USLC and are practicing administrators in an urban school district. Given the impact and remarkable sustainability of this principalship preparation program, it was important to bring together the existing published research about the USLC, extend the research, and document the success of the program.

URBAN SCHOOL LEADERS COLLABORATIVE (USLC)

The USLC is a principalship preparation program that prepares educators to become transformational leaders committed to social justice who can work effectively in diverse, ambiguous, and challenging contexts. By design, this is a "different" model of leadership preparation customized to prepare school leaders to practice in schools where the student population is predominantly Latino. The majority of educators in the program are Latino or African American, serving a population with a majority of Latino children.

Students in USLC program collaborate with the school district to practice and reflect on the issues facing the students and administrators, particularly with respect to advocating for students and ensuring equal access to educational opportunities for all students. The cohort experience is meant to establish mentorship networks, provide students with a curriculum with leadership skills needed to execute a collective vision of social justice, and prepare them to be leaders within their districts.

The USLC program is designed to advance interactive collaboration among students, professors, and school district administrators. This partnership (Martin and Papa, 2008) between UTSA and SAISD has helped to facilitate and enhance opportunities for practitioners and scholars to work collaboratively in a meaningful and effective manner in the preparation of aspiring school leaders.

The USLC has been nurtured, sustained, and studied for the past eleven years. As coordinator of the USLC, I have facilitated the successful completion of five cohorts; a total of seventy-six students have graduated from the USLC and about 60 percent of students have been promoted to positions of leadership within the district. Currently, forty-six out of seventy-six total students are in official leadership positions and two are in the UTSA doctoral program. The program continues to thrive; twenty-one new students were recruited for Cohort 6 that started the program in spring 2013. In addition to the UCEA Exemplary Educational Leadership Preparation Program Award, the USLC was nationally recognized as an innovative leadership preparation program in the University Council for Educational Administration (UCEA) Review and on the UCEA website (Hollingsworth, 2009).

Social Justice as a Mission

Social justice is significant in the preparation of emerging leaders, especially in the examination of schools operating within culturally deficient models (Murakami, Garza, and Merchant, 2010). Social justice as a theory relates to building a new social order (Capper et al., 2006; Lugg and Shoho, 2006; Merchant and Shoho, 2006). For school administrators, the focus on social justice relates to advocacy and mentorship: the drive to change culturally deficient paradigms, and mentoring teachers and other stakeholders in supporting programs and practices that disrupt hegemonic prac-

tices. Such practices are revealed through the development of critical consciousness and culturally relevant practices. As professors, it was our responsibility to set the stage for critical thinking about social justice. Students in cohort 1, for example, cited how one of the program coordinators facilitated critical reflection about social justice advocacy. The emerging leaders reflected, "We must know ourselves before we can lead a group of students in a school. The main idea is that social injustice is an uncomfortable area of discussion, but the program coordinator had a way of addressing it in a way that was thought-provoking" (Karen, cohort 1).

The mission of the Urban School Leaders Collaborative is to prepare aspiring school leaders who are committed to social justice advocacy to practice in schools where the student population is predominantly Latino. The purpose of the USLC is to prepare educators to become transformational leaders who work effectively in diverse and challenging contexts. The focus of the program includes equity, excellence, social justice, democracy, risk-taking, and responsiveness to community needs, tenets included in the mission of the department of ELPS (elps.utsa.edu/admin/mission.htm). Such strong commitment is important in the development of collaborative and responsive relationships with area schools and communities.

Students in the USLC acknowledge that being part of a principal preparation program that is focused on social justice was significant in their future career plans. Carrying on a mission that "advances equity within schools," and guided by a critical need to improve the students' opportunities in the district is paramount in the USLC. Their mission toward social justice permeated the educators associations from theory to practice. "When I heard that the program focused on social justice, my antennae wiggled," stated Donnie (cohort 1), who decided to join the cohort mainly due to its focus on social justice. Another participant stated, "As an African American, I grew up living social justice, but that terminology is uncommon outside of conversations with my father. So that really had my interest" (Etta, cohort 1).

In the USLC program interactions are safe places for students to reflect on their own experiences. These opportunities were critical in equipping the educators with the tools to bridge (Merchant and Shoho, 2006) "who they were" and their decision to adopt social justice as a mission toward equity and social justice efforts. Facing discrimination and translating it into social agency, for example, was harder when the educators had to confront their own racial identity. One of the students stated:

> I had already come to the realization that schools were tools for assimilation into the mainstream society. My own experiences working in schools awakened me to the notion that education is packaged as a one size fits all, and if it is too little or too big it is the student's fault. As a female, trying on a garment of a one size fits all; I can say that it feels awful when the garment does not fit. This same concept applied to education can have devastating effects on students. (Etta, cohort 1)

The coursework for the USLC is grounded in theoretically sound and empirically tested models of instructional reform, particularly as these apply to the education of Latinos and the socioeconomically disadvantaged. The portion of the coursework in the "Cultural Core" is what makes the program significantly different from the other educational leadership master's program at UTSA. Students take two courses that differ from the core, which are culturally relevant and teach methodological and theoretical approaches to education in a linguistically diverse society. The difference is the transformational focus, the delivery of the content, and the engagement of students into looking deeply into their nonnegotiables. How are they going to be courageous principals who will make a difference? Most importantly, the courses are taught in the field; professors travel to classrooms in the SAISD where they meet the cohort of students for class. Additionally, UTSA hires SAISD staff as adjunct professors to teach some of the courses.

Unique Features of the USLC

The USLC is distinguished by three prominent and unique features: (1) student recruitment, (2) selection, and (3) collaborative support. These features are discussed briefly in this section.

Student recruitment. The school district, in collaboration with department faculty, is deeply involved in identifying a particular set of students who have the predisposition for social justice. The principals in the district and graduates of the USLC nominate teachers or staff who have demonstrated the potential to become

district leaders. There are over one hundred schools in the district, which serves approximately fifty-four thousand students. Students are admitted to the USLC as a cohort each January and graduate in December two years later. Five cohorts have graduated; the sixth cohort (twenty-one students) just started in January 2013.

Since the inception of the USLC, nomination has been the main recruitment strategy and it has been very effective. The process begins with the superintendent:

1. All principals are directed by the superintendent to nominate two to three teachers or staff they believe have demonstrated leadership potential and a predisposition for social justice.
2. All former cohort members are asked by the coordinator to nominate one or two teachers/staff that have demonstrated leadership potential and a predisposition for social justice (beginning with cohort 4).
3. When all the nominations are compiled, the district forwards the list of potential candidates to the coordinator (Dr. Garza) of the USLC.
4. The coordinator informs (via email) each nominee that they have been highly recommended as potential candidates for the USLC and they are asked to confirm their interest.
5. An orientation session is held on a designated school district campus to explain the USLC model and discuss the expectations, admission criteria, application process, and to answer any questions they may have.
6. The coordinator stays in constant contact with all nominees, helping them navigate through the challenges of the application process and encouraging them to remain persistent.

The relationship with the eventual candidates begins during the recruiting process. As coordinator, I am in constant communication with all interested nominees. Upon their admission, the department chair and I meet with all the candidates in an orientation session to congratulate them, discuss the course plan, and explain what their commitment for the next two years means.

This recruitment model has been effective because there is a high level of support from the superintendent of the school district. The deputy superintendent provides support by collecting the nominations from the principals. On the university side, there is a designated coordinator of the USLC. The coordinator works closely with the deputy superintendent to make sure that principals submit their nominations. The coordinator has been involved with the district in many projects and has developed a strong relationship with the principals. Principals know about the USLC and they encourage their nominees to apply. Faculty who teach in the USLC also participate in the orientation session/s. It is an opportunity for prospective students to meet the professors from whom they will take classes.

When the fourth cohort was recruited, we involved members of the first three cohorts to be part of the nomination process. They were asked to nominate one to two teachers/staff for cohort 4. Together with the principal's nominations, the number of nominations increased dramatically and the number of students admitted increased as well. Table 28.1 below illustrates the enrollment per cohort:

We learned that former cohort members were more responsive to the nominations than the principals. They were also more diligent and selective with their nominations. They felt it was their responsibility to maintain the reputation of the USLC by nominating students that demonstrated a predisposition for social justice. Doug (cohort 5) shared why the nomination process is so critical. "We know what type of candidate will do well in the USLC and we are very selective. We want to maintain the integrity and reputation of the UCLC cohort. It is a reflection on us." Cynthia (cohort 5) added: "The USLC is certainly open to all who may be interested, but it definitely encompasses an approach that not everyone may be open to or comfortable to engage in. Those prospects would likely be better suited for a traditional leadership program." Recruitment for cohorts 5 and 6 has been easier with the participation of former cohort members as nominators. Cohort member nominations were critical to the increase in enrollment in the last two cohorts.

Candidate selection. Selection begins with the nomination process. Principals and former cohort members are asked to nominate teachers/staff that have demonstrated leadership potential and a strong predisposition for social justice. The USLC recruits students who are:

1. Willing to engage in deep reflection for the purpose of self-discovery and to establish a strong sense of self, learn who they are, and what they stand for as they prepare to become leaders for social justice.
2. Competent to work in diverse and increasingly complex cultural contexts.
3. Committed to aggressive reform and improvement.
4. Committed to understanding organizational cultures, how they operate, and how to create dynamic learning and working environments.
5. Skilled in the management of innovation and change.

Applicants are expected to demonstrate evidence of these criteria in their statement of purpose and their supervisor/nominator letters of recommendation.

All applicants must be admitted to the regular program before they are considered for admission to the USLC. Regular program applicants must meet the first three criteria listed below for admission. For consideration to the USLC candidates must submit a letter of recommendation and a statement of purpose (items #4 and #5).

1. Conferral of a baccalaureate degree from a regionally accredited college or university in the United States or proof of equivalent training at a foreign institution;
2. At least two years of teaching experience as **documented by a resume**; or a satisfactory letter of endorsement from a person who holds administrator certification and who has immediately supervised and evaluated the applicant and (2) engaged in leadership activities outside the classroom;
3. A grade point average of at least 3.0 (on a 4.0 scale) in the last sixty semester credit hours of

Table 28.1.

Cohort 1	Cohort 2	Cohort 3	Cohort 4	Cohort 5	Cohort 6
14	12	9	23	18	21

coursework for the baccalaureate degree, as well as in all graduate-level work taken. If an applicant's GPA is between 2.7 and 2.99, probationary admission may be granted and the student must maintain a minimum of a 3.0 GPA during the first twelve hours of coursework. Applicants with a GPA below 2.7 are denied admission;

4. **One letter of recommendation** addressing the applicant's administrative leadership capabilities from the principal of the school at which the applicant currently teaches or most recently taught;

5. A **statement of purpose** which outlines: (1) the applicant's reasons for pursuing the master's degree and principal certification; (2) a biographical sketch of the applicant's experiences relevant to the field of education, including the leadership roles the applicant has held in his/her teaching position(s), (3) the applicant's career plans, and (4) the applicant's views on one current educational or future educational reform effort.

Candidate selection is three-tiered. The first screening is the nomination process. The first participants in the selection process are the nominators—principals and former cohort members. The second stage of selection is at the university admissions level. The graduate school reviews all applications and clears qualified applicants for admission. During the third stage, the USLC coordinator and co-coordinator review the statements of purpose and letters of recommendation.

It has been the philosophy and practice of the USLC, to admit all applicants who have complied with the submission of the additional required items for admission to the USLC. If students go above and beyond to be considered for the USLC, we acknowledge this effort as a positive indicator of their commitment. More importantly, if we, the program faculty, are truly social justice advocates, it is our obligation to create space for students who have historically been excluded and denied access to programs such as the USLC.

Our method of selection has proven to be very effective. We have admitted eighty-three students in the first five cohorts and seventy-six have graduated. Of the seven who did not finish, three self-selected out, one withdrew for financial hardship, one for medical reasons, one married and relocated, and one was accepted to law school.

To date, all but four of the seventy-six graduates from the USLC have remained in the school district; that is about a 95 percent retention rate. The "grow your own" program has been very effective. USLC graduates continue to serve the children of SAISD as leaders for social justice—that is what they were prepared and trained to do.

Collaborative support. The ELPS department at UTSA, and SAISD, have been generous in their support of graduate students in the cohort to travel to the annual University Council of Educational Administration (UCEA) meeting for paper presentations. These presentations are often celebrations of the innovative work that has come out of the cohort groups and reports from the field. Dean Betty Merchant has been involved deeply as one of the founders of this program and continues to be involved by teaching classes and mentoring the emerging leaders. She provides financial support through travel grants made available to graduate students and is sensitive to requests such as extensions on admissions deadlines because of recruitment issues within the district. In addition, SAISD administration supports USLC students through internships and release time to attend principals' meetings and other administrative functions.

Pedagogical Framework

Constructivist approach. Teaching and learning are simultaneous activities that are integrated through a process of facilitation. The instructional methods of teaching and learning are driven by a constructivist theoretical approach. Students are engaged as learners as well as teachers. They are expected to participate in activities that allow them to be co-constructors of knowledge, theory, and alternative epistemological ways of understanding. In the USLC courses, students are always given the time and opportunity to engage in critical, personal, and professional reflection. Self-reflection is a means to transformation and this is accomplished through a well-crafted process to engage students in a critical analysis and development of their core beliefs and philosophy.

In a constructivist classroom students are in constant interaction with each other. It is important to develop a climate of trust and strong positive relationships in order to create an environment of genuine and meaningful dialogue. Thus, we believe students must be treated with dignity, respect, and empathy. They must be challenged with high expectations, expected to produce quality work, and they must be exposed to relevant, meaningful, and productive learning. All classroom activities, readings, and projects are carefully designed to encourage and compel students to engage in high levels of inquiry.

Learning Experiences

The USLC curriculum provides for many types of learning experiences; most of them are transformational in nature. Through a constructivist pedagogical approach coursework is designed to engage students in continuous self-inquiry and self-discovery. The major assignments to facilitate these types of learning experiences are reflection, community projects, and autoethnographies.

Reflection. The learning experiences of this program are reflective in nature. Students are challenged to delve into their own lived experiences. They are products of the current system and are now educators in the same system. The reflective piece invites/requires each student to engage in reflection from the initial class meeting until the very last course meeting. Reflecting requires students to share concerns, fears, celebrations, comments from readings, reactions to readings, and anything they feel compelled to share. There is only one rule for the exercise of reflection; there is no interactive discussion until all students have shared their reflection. There are no interruptions whatsoever. After each student has participated, others may react, follow-up or reflect. Reflection is always conducted at the start of class. As reflected in the following quote,

> Students struggle and sometimes even resist reflection. Initially this activity seemed to be overwhelming, time-consuming, even intrusive, but in time it soon became the most vital part of the program. Learning that we share similar fears or views helps with the bonding that takes place over the first few weeks in our first semester in the program. This new relationship is what creates the success of the cohort model. In fact, it illustrates the very belief in community that our cohort strives to promote. The USLC becomes a community within itself and the outcome is invaluable. (Hugo, cohort 5)

Community projects. Another challenging but priceless learning experience is that of the community project

assignment. The assignment has two components, a micro-ethnography and a video documentary. Each student begins this assignment by identifying a family that is willing to participate in a micro-ethnography and is also willing to host a parent/community meeting in their home. The micro-ethnography serves two purposes: to get to know the family and to build a relationship before they open their home for the meeting. Students are instructed to study a common school concern from the perspective of the parents and organize a community meeting to address the concern. Ana (cohort 5) shared:

> As part of our work in the cohort, we conducted community-meeting projects. This was an effective way to connect with our community and be more aware and sensitive to our communities' concerns and needs. The cohort challenges us to utilize research-based information in making social justice decisions.

To document the community meeting, each student is required to produce a ten-minute video documentary. Students are encouraged involve the parents, students, and their colleagues in the production of the documentary. At the end of the semester, students share their documentary with the rest of the class and participate in a critical analysis of each other's work.

Autoethnographies. At the beginning of the two-year leadership program, students were assigned initial autoethnographies in which they are to give personal accounts of their lives, describing any significant moment they cared to share. Students were to recall their lives and their educational journeys during this time period. As the semesters passed, students added an additional section to their autoethnographies; the *professional moments* recalled each member's experiences regarding their previous professions and educational professions and their views toward schooling throughout these periods. During the final semester, after thirty-three graduate hours and eleven courses especially designed with the social justice model as the foundation, students added the final *transformational* piece describing their evolving philosophies in education. Consequently, the assigned papers were not only intended to stimulate the students' reflections about formative educational incidents, but to document the experiences that shaped their viewpoints, led them to work in inner-city schools, and made them amenable to advocating for and implementing equitable educational practices. Although the students wrote and refined their autoethnographies over the course of the two-year graduate program, in the first semester, their papers primarily grappled with issues dating back to their personal lives prior to their careers as educators.

Praxis: Connecting Theory with Practice

Students are expected to connect the readings to real-life experiences through hands-on class projects and assignments. Students have the opportunity to work with their respective principals/mentors to apply their learning to leadership practice. One good example is the community project assignment students conduct in their School and Community Relations course. Informed by Freire's (2000) work of critical consciousness and praxis, students work closely with their principals/ mentors to connect theory with practice. Students apply Freire's (2000) notion of "conscientização" in their work with parents. They focus on developing a critical awareness of their social reality through reflection and action. Action is fundamental because it is the process of changing the reality. According to Freire (2000), people bring their own knowledge and experience into the process. Training is typically undertaken in small groups with lively interaction.

Most of the courses have an internship component. For example, students conduct an equity audit in EDL 5503, a community project in EDL 5302, an action research project in CandI 5003, attend and reflect on school board meetings in EDL 5703, and they shadow the principal (the whole day) in several courses. In their last semester, they take the internship as a capstone course. In most cases, their principals at their respective campuses are their internship sponsors, mentors, and supervisors. The professor of record for the students serves as a co-supervisor with the principal.

Leadership development is organized around the seven major functions of the principal: 1) campus improvement plan, 2) the campus budget, 3) staffing, 4) professional development, 5) facilities maintenance and operations, 6) food services, and 7) special programs. Students work closely with their principals/mentors to learn and gain experience in each of these functions.

Given the model of the internship, there is no special internal or external funding to relieve students of their teaching duties to participate in a full-time internship. However, SAISD and UTSA are committed to support

their participation in several important ways. The school district and the university have consistently supported USLC students in the following ways:

SAISD Support

1. Superintendent is personally committed to the success of the USLC-SAISD program.
2. Principals engage candidates in leadership and internship experiences each semester throughout the duration of the program.
3. Principals support candidates with flextime when they need to attend/observe activities and conduct assignments required for classes.
4. Principals support candidates with funding and time to attend the annual national University Council of Educational Administrators Conference.
5. Principals and SAISD administrators will be invited to mentor USLC-SAISD students.
6. Principals and SAISD administrators participate as guest speakers to selected classes to share their expertise with the aspiring leaders.

UTSA Support

1. Provide an opportunity for SAISD candidates to earn a Master's in Educational Leadership and the Texas Principal Certificate.
2. Design a customized program of study to meet the unique needs of the school district.
3. Offer an innovative program to prepare educators to become transformational leaders who can work effectively in diverse, ambiguous, and challenging contexts.
4. Provide faculty that are strongly committed to developing collaborative and responsive relationships with area schools and communities.
5. Hold all courses at designated school campus in SAISD.

In their final semester, students enroll in the internship as a capstone course. The purpose and goal of this course is to bring together all the roles and functions of the principalship through intensive and structured fieldwork. To gain an understanding of the roles and responsibilities associated with the principalship, students spend a minimum of sixty clock hours interacting with a principal/mentor throughout the semester. This interaction is a combination of shadowing/observation, interviewing/discussion, co-leading, assigned projects, etc. The field journal entry includes a reflection about the activity or observation and documented evidence of dates and times of internship activities.

Advocacy for Social Justice

The USLC is driven by a philosophy of social justice. The mission of the USLC is to prepare aspiring school leaders who are committed to social justice advocacy who will practice in schools where the student population is predominantly Latino. In their positions as teachers, USLC students serve a population of students that are predominantly Latino and from low socioeconomic backgrounds.

Issues related to their commitment to serve marginalized children are addressed during reflection at the beginning of each class. Students are constantly engaged in deep critical reflection throughout the program. Identifying personal experiences, voicing them in reflective practice in class discussions, and transforming these into agency is one of the ways in which cohort members have acknowledged that the mission of social justice was already embedded in their experiences. Their lived experiences were strongly connected to their commitment to social justice; their potential for social justice advocacy was evident in their reflections. "I know the meaning of suffering, and do whatever I can to help end it. Students misbehave in classes because they are dealing with issues no child or adult should have to experience," stated Emerald (cohort 3). "The program helped me to stand up for the people who are unable to speak for themselves," affirmed Jennifer (cohort 2), "especially children who are unable to verbalize their troubles—that's why I want to be a voice for them." However, some cohort members were becoming aware that advocating for social justice was uncomfortable, difficult, and solitary. They knew that maintaining their commitment to social justice would be under constant challenge, but they also knew that they could not turn back. This was evident when a student (Donnie, cohort 5) speaking on behalf of the group expressed the following:

> We kind of came to the conclusion that we knew too much to go back . . . and that kind of stemmed from the fact that administrators go into the position ideal-

istic and then all of a sudden something happens. We couldn't define it, but we understood that because there were fourteen of us and we are all working in the same district, there was no way that we could actually stray away from our vision or stray away from what's right for kids without somebody calling us on it later on down the line. During reflection and some of the topics that we covered, there was always an opportunity to share what it was we believed in, but there is just no way that we can stray from doing what's right.

Systems of Support

The USLC is a closed cohort model, only for employees of the SAISD. When students graduate, they become mentors for the next cohort of students. Mentors often attend class with their mentees and participate in class activities and reflection. The mentorship has continued throughout the five generations of cohorts, especially by means of continuous promotion of mentor-mentee interactions, including workplace visitations, internship opportunities, formal and informal forums, presentations at national conferences, and informal gatherings. These interactions promote not only a solid social network, but also an opportunity to create a trustworthy environment in which open and candid experiences can be shared. The majority of interactions have proven to be conducive to personal and professional development.

Engaging USLC graduates as mentors is reciprocally beneficial. By involving them as mentors, we stay connected with our students beyond completion of their program. We support them in their job search and we promote them through our own network including the superintendent, deputy superintendent, assistant superintendent for human resources, area superintendents, and principals. Beginning with cohort 5, which graduated in fall 2012, the assistant superintendent for human resources and her staff agreed to conduct an interview and resume workshop. This is critically important because it gives them significant visibility as future candidates for administrative positions.

Professors build relationships and provide unconditional support to students. Cynthia (cohort 5) wrote in her autoethnography:

> The support created in the cohort is tremendously vital to its success. The professors provide the academic and emotional support to be able to physically make it through the oftentimes, grueling requirements. The

academic aspect of our studies is time-consuming, difficult, and overwhelming, but with the organization and timelines required from each professor, it becomes clear that it can be completed successfully. Our professors take no shortcuts and do not allow excuses to hinder our learning. Although they are flexible with specific parameters and open to other perspectives, they push us to comprehend the importance of each and every requirement. Emotionally, they became the shoulders we leaned on through trying times by creating this connection with each student. Nothing was off limits, there was nothing that couldn't be worked through in their eyes and this understanding and bond was something that cannot be manufactured. This relationship was sincere and continues to this day. We were held in high regard by our professors and always expected to lean on each other for support. If one was lagging, it was our duty to fix the situation and bring that member back up where he/she was needed to be successful. Our discussions and journey were always OUR struggles. The cohort is the structure of support. Students' rapport with professors maintains a high level of accountability via constant reflection and challenging of perceptions. This creates a sense of safety and in turn encourages growth. The professors not only provide a huge amount of valuable learning but also encourage, inspire, and mentor the students within the first cohort to the very latest cohort.

Students often say: "We might graduate but we are never finished." This is true because they are always involved as mentors for the new cohorts. This keeps them connected to the USLC network. As coordinator, I am always in contact with students as practitioners. They know they can depend on me for letters of recommendation and for support. Likewise, when I call them for meetings or to participate in cohort activities, they are always willing to help out.

Student Assessment

The manner in which the USLC assesses whether students have met the criteria is non-traditional. By design, we do not want to use the traditional rubric or checklist because we believe it is too restrictive and one-directional. Instead, we engage students in sustained self-assessment from the beginning of the program to the end. We encourage and expect them to direct their own learning. Using a constructivist pedagogical approach,

students are both learners and teachers and teachers and learners. It is through this approach that students, in collaboration with their professors, identify their own professional and personal areas of growth.

Assessment is formative and ongoing in several ways. First, students engage in critical reflection in most of their courses. Second, they begin writing their autoethnographies at the beginning of the program. Third, students analyze autoethnographies collectively, write papers, present them at UCEA, and submit for publication. And fourth, students produce a video documentary about their transformational journey in the USLC and present it at UCEA.

Reflection. Students engage in critical reflection in most of their courses. I (Dr. Garza) teach three courses in the program, one at beginning, in the middle, and the internship at the end. This gives him the opportunity to gauge their commitment and progress toward becoming leaders for social justice. Other faculty members team-teach with the coordinator at least three semesters (eighteen credit hours).

Reflection is introduced to the cohort in their first semester. For many members the process of openly reflecting in a group is a new process but quickly becomes a vital part of their transformation throughout the program. Gilbert (cohort 5) states, "Something that began very intimidating became something that brought us together as a group . . . I know my fellow cohort members more than I ever thought that I would and this has helped me." The process of open reflection, though new, helped participants not to feel alone in their journey as becoming educational leaders. The reflection process provided a space for community to grow amongst the participants. As community grew so did participants. Vanessa (cohort 5): "This behavior of reflection was natural and allowed me to grow as a person and in turn a professional." Participants' reflections as a group help facilitate reflection within themselves that began to affect how they behaved in the workplace. Vanessa's growth as a professional came from the reflection of her own personal views and how those were being carried out in the workplace. Reflection in class has set the cohort apart from other programs. Lessons are not solely empty discussions of theory and practice but real-world relations and collaboratively discussed and examined. Ana (cohort 5) shares, "The process of reflection itself was, for me, transformative. I gained not only insight about my own thinking but had the most valuable experience of hearing out colleagues within the class which have proven invaluable to me." It was a process for many that took lessons and attached meaningful experiences with them. Maria (cohort 5) explains, "One person can effect change if it comes from the heart." This was one of Maria's ultimate lessons from the process of reflection. She was able to understand how multicultural understanding and social justice advocacy with the elimination of deficit thinking could have saved students in her past. Actually looking into her professional day she was able to add impact into everything she not only did but also would now do.

Autoethnography. All students write an autoethnography that focuses on their personal, professional, and transformational journeys. This is a two-year project; students begin writing their autoethnographies during the first semester under the direction of their professor, Dr. Garza. Their first paper focuses on their personal ethnographic moments. The second section of the autoethnography focuses on their professional ethnographic moments, which they submit at the end of their first year of coursework when they take their second class with Dr. Garza. The final section of their autoethnography, transformational ethnographic moments, is due during the final semester when they are enrolled in the internship with Dr. Garza. As a final manuscript, students integrate all three sections into one paper for final submission. The autoethnography is a two-year exercise of self-reflection and self-assessment.

Autoethnography papers. A deeper reflection of their growth and transformation was evident when the students in cohort 5 compiled and analyzed each of the sections of their autoethnographies. The analysis yielded three papers they presented at the annual 2012 UCEA conference in Denver, Colorado.

1. USLC Cohort Paper 1: Personal Ethnographic Moments
2. USLC Cohort Paper 2: Professional Ethnographic Moments
3. USLC Cohort Paper 3: Transformational Ethnographic Moments

This is an activity we will continue with future cohorts. Cohort 6 is in its first semester of coursework and they have already written the first section for submission.

Video documentary. Students produce a video documentary for the purpose of telling their story of transformation in the USLC program. Students interview and video record each other, analyze the data, interpret their stories, and document their story of transformation through a video documentary. They do this during the last semester (always fall semester). In conjunction with their autoethnography papers, they present their video documentary at the annual UCEA conference. Four of the five cohorts that have graduated from the USLC program have presented this video documentary at UCEA.

Systems for Improvement

We have learned that feedback from students about their progress and experience in the cohort is critical. It is important to meet with students early and throughout the program to discuss their progress. This has been useful because students are asked to assess themselves individually and as members of the cohort. Although this is done in an informal and non-threatening way, the information has been useful because it helped us make changes to improve the program.

We strongly believe that unless we formally include our former students in our teaching and preparation programs, they will not feel connected to the university beyond the completion of their program. Their involvement and feedback is invaluable in the continuous improvement process of the USLC. One student offered the following reflection about his mentor: "Requiring us to meet and log our experiences was difficult, but necessary. If we weren't forced to do it, the likelihood of our getting together would be minimal. I intend to maintain our friendship for as long as possible and only hope that I in turn can provide something of value in return."

It is evident that collaboration has been crucial for both institutions; both the school district and the university manifest a mutual commitment to the students and their success. This partnership approach has helped to facilitate and support students through the program and beyond. Students have expressed their appreciation for the opportunity to learn from each other and their professors. Equally important is the support and recognition from the school district. Student persistence and success is the product of the genuine collaboration of the partnership.

The principal ingredients of a successful partnership are in place to maintain credibility with district leaders and cohort members. The knowledge gained from the cohort experience has not only contributed to the individual development of each aspiring school leader, but it has provided us with important insights into the value of reflective practice as a tool for training school leaders to recognize how their racial identity intersects with their position as leaders for social justice.

USLC PROGRAM EFFECTIVENESS

One of the major strengths of this program has been its sustainability. It is self-sustainable because it does not depend on any dedicated funding that may expire. Students assume total responsibility for tuition and fees, and the school district supports them with flexible time for class, assignments, and internship activities. Every cohort has been supported financially (by the district and UTSA) for travel to present papers at the annual UCEA conference.

According to the data, the USLC has been very successful. A total of eighty-three students have been admitted to the USLC in the first five cohorts and seventy-six have graduated. Of the seven who did not finish, three self-selected out, one withdrew for financial hardship, one for medical reasons, one married and relocated, and one was accepted to law school. The first five cohorts consisted of enrollments of fourteen, twelve, nine, twenty-three, and eighteen students respectively. Cohort 6, which started in spring 2013, consists of twenty-one students.

Forty-eight of the seventy-six (60 percent) students in the first five cohorts who have graduated have been promoted to leadership positions. USLC graduates currently serve in the following leadership capacities: seven principals, twenty-two vice-principals, two academic deans, and the others serve as curriculum specialists, program coordinators, and administrative assistants. Cohort 5 graduated in December 2012, and already eight students have been promoted to leadership positions. A critical benefit of this "grow your own" program for the SAISD is that the superintendent considers the USLC graduates when there are leadership vacancies. This is particularly important when nearby districts will pay more to try to recruit the best talent away from San Antonio public schools.

Program effectiveness can be qualitatively measured through the voices and work of the students. Students

evaluate the program through shared critical reflections, autoethnographies papers presented at conferences, and video documentaries.

SUMMARY AND CONCLUSION

Perhaps the most important component for program sustainability, effectiveness, and success is that the USLC has been under the direction of the same coordinator since its inception in 2003. This stability is especially important because the school district has had three different superintendents during the life of the USLC. In spite of the change in district leadership, the partnership has been maintained and continues to get stronger. As coordinator, I have developed a strong relationship with the district through my work not only as the coordinator of the USLC, but also with my work with district leadership, school principals, and other staff in SAISD. The USLC has been institutionalized and not externally funded, which has extended the life beyond each cohort.

REFERENCES

Capper, C. A., Theoharis, G., and Sebastian, J. (2006). Toward a framework for preparing leaders for social justice. *Journal of Educational Administration, 44(3)*, 209–224.

Davis, S., Darling-Hammond, L., LaPointe, M., and Meyerson, D. (2005). *School leadership study: Developing successful principals.* Stanford, CA: Stanford Educational Leadership Institute.

Freire, P. (2000). *Pedagogy of the Oppressed.* New York: Continuum International Publishing Group.

Fry, R. (2008). The role of school in the English Language Learner achievement gap. Pew Hispanic Center Report. Retrieved March 23, 2010, from pewhis panic.org/files/reports/89.pdf.

Garza, E., Barnett, B., Merchant, B., Shoho, A., and Smith, P. (2006). The urban school leaders collaborative: A school-university partnership emphasizing instructional leadership and student and community assets. *International Journal of Urban Educational Leadership*, 1, 14–30.

Garza, E. and Merchant, B. (2009). American culture: Latino realities. In J. Collard A. and Normore (Eds.), *Leadership and Intercultural Dynamics* (pp. 131–149). Charlotte, NC: Information Age Publishing Inc.

Gonzales, M. L. (2002). The pivotal role of the principal. In M. Gonzales, A. Huerta-Macias, and J. Tinajero (Eds.),

Educating Latino students: A guide to successful practice. Lanham, MD: Scarecrow Press.

Gonzales, M., Huerta-Macias, A., and Tinajero, J. (Eds.). (2002). *Educating Latino students: A guide to successful practice.* Lanham, MD: Scarecrow Press.

Hollingsworth, L. (2009). Innovative programs: The University of Texas at San Antonio. In *University Council of Educational Administration Review 50*(2), 22–23.

Lomotey, K. (1989). Cultural diversity in the urban school: Implications for principals. *NASSP Bulletin, 73,* 81–85.

Lugg, C. A. and Shoho, A. R. (2006). Dare public school administrators build a new social order? Social justice and the possibly perilous politics of educational leadership. *Journal of Educational Administration, 44(33),* 196–208.

Marshall, C. and Oliva, M. (2006). *Leadership for social justice: Making revolutions in education.* Boston: Pearson.

Martin, G. E. and Papa, R. (2008). Examining the principal preparation and practice gap. *Principal, 88*(1), 12–16.

Merchant, B. and Shoho, A. (2006). Bridge people: Civic and educational leaders for social justice. In C. Marshall and M. Oliva (Eds), *Leadership for social justice: Making revolutions in education* (pp. 85–109). Boston: Pearson.

Murakami-Ramalho, E., Garza, E., and Merchant, B. (2009). Lessons from country borders: Preparing leaders for social justice and diversity through a district and university partnership. *Journal of School-University Partnerships, 3*(2), 80–97.

Murakami-Ramalho, E., Garza, E., and Merchant, B. (2010). Successful school leadership in socioeconomically challenging contexts: School principals creating and sustaining successful school improvement. *International Studies in Educational Administration, 32(2).*

Murakami-Ramalho, E., Garza, E., and Merchant, B. (2012). Lessons from a principal preparation program: Creating support through social justice practices. In E. Murakami-Ramalho and A. Pancake. *Educational leaders encouraging the intellectual and professional capacity of others: A social justice agenda* (pp. 163–174). Charlotte, NC: Information Age Publishers.

Texas Education Agency. (2009). 2008–9 Academic Excellence Indicator System, State Report. Retrieved April, 2, 2010, from www.tea.state.tx.us/perfre-port/aeis/2007/state.html.

U.S. Census Bureau. (2010). www.census.gov/Press-Release/www/2010/.dp.comptables.html.

CHAPTER 29

School Leadership in Urban Schools

How Social-Relational Leadership Shapes Teacher Engagement

Heather E. Price

There is often a disconnection between scholarly research and the on-the-ground reality of school functioning. Part of this disconnect is due to the "tidiness" of research and the "messiness" of the real school world. When scholars research, there is a preference to theoretically drill down to one narrow issue and investigate it extensively, controlling for everything else. This is good practice, as it simulates experimental treatment effects in either natural- or quasi-experimental contexts. But, as practitioners find, isolating treatments can lead to policy implementation and scaling-up of programs that lead to disappointing or deflated results. This is in part due to the interactions of isolated treatments in the context of the whole school. The nature of schools as a formal institution as well as a social community makes understanding school context especially significant.

One crucial actor in the school community, whose role is much more complex on-the-ground than many of our theories account for, is the principal. On one hand, principals are in the position to shape the school culture, and on the other hand, principals are placed in schools with prefabricated structures and established teacher cultures. They may enter schools with no administrative assistance where they are expected to "steer the ship" on their own or they may be introduced to a band of administrative faculty where they are expected to "captain" the entire ship of administrators with the teachers far removed from their everyday interactions. In these different contexts, principals can choose, to the extent of their personality and training, how they will adapt their leadership style and roles to this predefined arrangement. These contexts are known to be even more complex in urban schools (Crow and Scribner, 2013) with a particular pull from the external community (Honig, 2009).

In order to conceptualize principal effectiveness within the context of how schools work, statistical models need to allow theoretical realities to coexist within the context of the school, rather than mutually exclude or control-out the context. This study shows how the principals' social characteristics—their disposition type and relational position—work within the structural context of schools to influence teacher engagement and overall school community. To do this, a methodological process is used that selects a sample with a wide range of contexts, conducts fieldwork data on the lived realities of principals, collects survey and network data from the school staff, and then applies network methods and fixed effect regression modeling to test core ideas of leadership theories within the context of each school. This case will demonstrate how introducing network theory and methods into education scholarship offers a promising new approach to accommodate the complex issues associated with urban schools and urban school leadership.

REVIEW OF RESEARCH

The last two decades of empirical research sheds light on how, and to what degree, principals influence their schools. Scholars provide ample evidence that effective principals enhance teacher success and quality when they authentically involve school staff in school goal and improvement decision-making (Bryk et al., 2010; Goddard, Goddard, and Tschannen-Moran, 2007; Lee, Dedrick, and Smith, 1991; Leithwood and Jantzi, 1990, 1999, 2008; Louis et al., 2010; Robinson, Lloyd, and Rowe, 2008; Tschannen-Moran and Hoy, 2000). Most of this research concludes that principals directly influence teacher attitudes and behaviors and then indirectly influence student achievement and engagement by way of the teachers (Brewer, 1993; Goddard et al., 2010; Hallinger, 2003, 2005; Louis and Leithwood, 2010; Louis et al., 2010; Newmann, Smith, Allensworth, and Bryk, 2001; Robinson, Lloyd, and Rowe, 2008; Wahlstrom and Louis, 2008). Given the mobility and quality deficits among urban school teachers, the importance of principal influence holds even more weight (Lackford, Loeb, and Wyckoff, 2002).

It is the supportive workspace that principals propagate for teachers which provides a successful schooling environment (Bryk et al., 2010; Hallinger, 2003; Honig et al., 2010; Knapp et al., 2010; Portin et al., 2009). Supportive administrators enhance collegial support and cohesion among staff, a process that feeds back to form even stronger professional relationships (Bryk et al., 2010; Leithwood and Jantzi, 1990). It is thus important to focus on the social-relational characteristics of principals within the school context to gauge variation in teacher engagement and school community. Although technocratic skills of principals have been the focus of urban leadership, the social-relational aspect of the role cannot be overlooked (Crow and Scribner, 2013). Below, the leadership literature is organized by its core ideas on the social-relational characteristics of

the principal: their dispositional type, their accessibility, and their formal structural position. These core ideas conceptually frame the model tested in this analysis, as figure 29.1 shows: To what extent do the various social-relational characteristics of principals explain teacher engagement?

Social-Relational Characteristics of the Principal

The duties of principals are diverse and many. Unlike schoolteachers and district administrators, principals are not confined to a single stage of the classroom, a central office, or a boardroom. Principals bridge the district to the schoolroom and the community to the district, school, and schoolroom. The expectations of principals vary in each of these contexts. The manners in which principals choose to handle these different duties are expressed in their leadership approaches.

Dispositional type. The different demands of students, teachers, parents, and administrations make for principals who act as liaisons, facilitators, and representatives to all and between all of these groups (Bidwell, 1957, 1965; Barr and Dreeban, 1983). Mitigating these roles often involves bridging and buffering the different domains (Honig and Hatch, 2004). Although principals

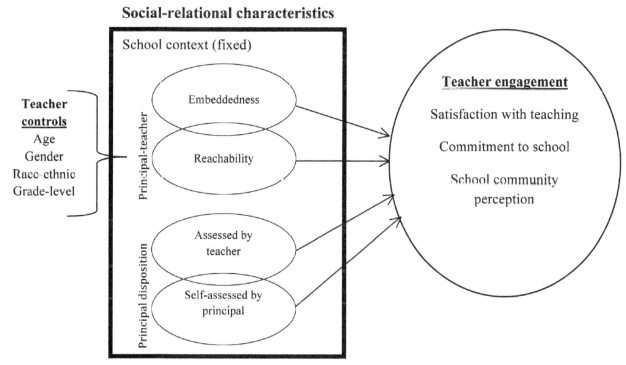

Figure 29.1. *Principals' social-relational characteristics on teacher engagement*

need to attend to all of these domains, they inevitably find themselves favoring one group over the other. Instructional leaders, for example, favor responsibility toward teachers and students, given their internal, curriculum, and instruction focus (Coldren and Spillane, 2007; Hallinger, 2007; Hallinger and Murphy, 1986).

In their study of urban Chicago schools, Bryk and Schneider find that principals tend to become identified as "teachers' principals," "students' principals," or "parents' principals" (2002). The dominant role of the school principal implicitly reflects to the school members the dispositional preference of the principal as to who is the most important stakeholder in the school community. The corresponding stakeholders—teachers, parents, and students—appear to behave and trust the intentions of principals differently depending on the dominant role type of their principal (Bryk and Schneider, 2002).

Bryk and Schneider do not identify one additional principal type, the "administrators' principal." This type of principal puts the needs of the state education officers, central office administration, school board members, and other principals in the preferential position among the school community. Urban school leaders commonly need to attend to the demands of these external stakeholders more so than other principals (Honig, 2009). Following the Bryk and Schneider (2002) line of thinking, the corresponding schools' teachers, students, and parents would be likely to respond differently to this type of principal as well.[1]

Accessibility. Wahlstrom and Louis (2008) find that embedded and reachable principals improve teaching. Most of the rest of the literature, however, strays from directly discussing embeddedness and reachability of principals. That is, embeddedness refers to how centrally principals involve themselves in the school functioning and decision-making while reachability refers to how directly teachers can access their principals.

The instructional leadership literature does concentrate on leaders who are deeply embedded and immediately reachable to all teachers, as it is endemic to the headmaster role associated with instructional leaders. The high embeddedness and high reachability occurs as a direct result of the hands-on, direct involvement of principals in the classroom teachings, school mission, and instructional program (Hallinger, 2003). This embeddedness and reachability, however, is tradition-

ally limited in scope to only those areas related to curriculum and instruction (Hallinger, 2003; Hallinger and Murphy, 1986).[2] This excludes the broader school functioning of the organization and management included in other school leadership theories (Hopkins, 2003).

Much of the rest of the research morphs into discussions about the level of power that principals do or do not distribute to their teachers as main characteristic of effective leadership. Although somewhat off the theoretical mark, the findings in this research do offer ideas about the importance of principals' accessibility (embeddedness and reachability) for teachers.

Principals who manage in a traditional, top-down, hierarchical manner are found to engage in frequent professional interactions with their staff (embedded) but in a more distant manner (less reachable) (Wahlstrom and Louis, 2008). Meaning, these principals are closely embedded in the professional lives of teachers, but are more socially distant (see figure 29.2). The organizational structure places these principals in a different social realm than the teachers. In a hierarchical, vertical structure, the principal occupies the top of the structure where few have direct access. In some studies, these hierarchical principals correlate with higher teachers' job satisfaction (Hulpia, Devos, and Rosseel, 2009) and increased innovation, commitment, and performance among teachers (Hulpia, 2009; Moolenaar, Daly, and Sleegers, 2010; Rosenholtz, 1985; Somech, 2005).

Non-hierarchic leadership, the focus of the distributed leadership literature, shows that peripheral principals who allow teachers to become the central decision-makers benefit teachers (Firestone and Pennell, 1993; Hillard, 2003; Leithwood and Jantzi, 1990; Smith and O'Day, 1991; Robinson, Lloyd, and Rowe, 2008). Distributing leadership moves principals to the outside of a horizontal structure of school decision-making and, hence, they have fewer social interactions with teachers (less embedded) in the social structure of the school.

In some cases, this structure of distributing power among teachers increases innovative teaching (Leithwood and Jantz, 1990; Somech, 2005) and increases teacher empowerment (Somech, 2005). But a Dutch study finds teacher commitment levels depleting in schools with distributed administrative duties (Hulpia, Devos, and Rosseel, 2009). These differences in findings may be due to the lack of distinction in the distributed leadership literature regarding the reach-

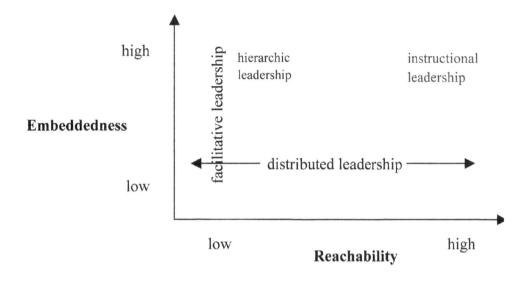

Figure 29.2. *Variation in principal accessibility on leadership type*

ability of principals. Principals could, in theory, cede embeddedness while their level of social distance (being more or less reachable to staff) could vary, as figure 29.2 shows.

Another set of studies find that principals who undertake facilitative personas are more effective than authoritarian ones (Bryk, Camburn, and Louis, 1999; Bryk et al., 2010; Firestone and Wilson, 1985; Goldring and Pasternack, 1994; Leithwood and Jantzi, 2008; Louis et al., 2010; Spillane and Healey, 2010). Facilitative leaders are low on reachability, as their approach promotes coaching rather than direct involvement, but can vary on the level of embeddedness with their teachers. This contrasts to instructional leaders who are much more direct than facilitative, at least as it pertains to the teaching portion (Hallinger 2003; Hallinger and Murphy, 1986). It is assumed that the rest of the school community develops indirectly through the instructional focus under the instructional leadership model.

How can these findings all be correct? Do different contexts explain the variation? Many of these studies use large databases, so that is likely not the case. Instead, the assumptions of accessibility in the conceptual frameworks of these theories are likely causing confusion. Variation on the two dimensions of accessibility—reachability and embeddedness—may explain these differences. Figure 29.2 shows how the variation on reachability and embeddedness could constitute different discussions in the leadership literature.

This study parses teachers' accessibility characteristics into two conceptually distinct measures. Namely, this analysis uses network measures to capture the embeddedness and reachability of principals to investigate how they relate to teachers' engagement levels, as measured by teacher commitment, satisfaction, and perception of school community. By taking this approach, these ideas can be teased apart so that principals can vary on both measures within accounting for dispositional type of the principal within the context of the school, in order to better understand what it is about principals' leadership that influences teacher engagement. This is especially important in urban schools, as the disengagement of teachers leads to high rates of teacher attrition and these rates are often two-times greater in urban schools than suburban schools (NCTAF, 2007).

DATA AND METHOD

To test the differences in principal accessibility in relation to principal type and the school context, a longitudinal survey of teachers and principals in fifteen Indianapolis charter schools was conducted in the spring of 2010.[3] These surveys collected data on the self-reported commitment and satisfaction of staff and their perceptions of the overall school community. Additionally, the social network data of the school staff members were collected on the surveys. In all, 302 school staff and

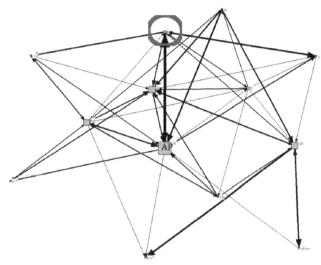

Liatris high school with assistant principal as broker

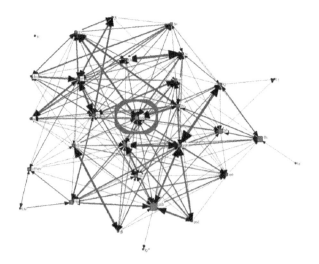

Fuschia K-8 with no assistant principal as broker

Figure 29.3. *Network configuration with and without an assistant principal in the broker position.* **Key:** *Grey lines indicate two-way reciprocal ties. Black lines indicate one-way ties. Circled node indicates the principal of the school.*

450 social network matrices were collected over three time points. Table 29.1 shows the descriptive statistics about the respondents and their schools who completed the survey.

From the network matrices, the principal position can be mapped within the social structure of the school to determine the embeddedness and reachability scores of the principals. The schools' social web structures are then used in conjunction with the regular survey data to understand how the social aspects of principals interact with the dispositional type of the principal and the school role structure. This analysis pools the responses

of the 268 teachers across the three time points to reduce error on any one score and uses these averaged scores to model principal effectiveness.

Sample

Indianapolis charter schools were selected for this study for several reasons. The consolidation of these schools in one city (1) reduces possible unexplained error due to resource allocation differences from the tax base; (2) reduces error from possible spatial and regional differences in normative school culture; and (3) levels the playing field with respect to access and information about local resources available to these schools due to the orientation of these schools to the Indianapolis mayoral office.[4] Alleviating these three concerns reduces the error term associated with external heterogeneity that can muddle results in school studies. Clustering on school identifier in fixed effects regression modeling additionally controls for any remaining extraneous between-schools variation that could bias the results so that a clear, within-schools generalized process can be tested.

In general, the representativeness of this sample is similar to most other urban public schools, with the main exceptions being that they are smaller in size and have a smaller student: full-time teacher ratio than most other schools. Using the Common Core of Data database, table 29.2 compares the fifteen Indianapolis charter schools used for this study to other U.S. public schools, other U.S. urban public schools, other Indiana schools, Indianapolis schools, other charter schools, and the seven other Indianapolis charter schools. Table 29.2 summarizes the differences in means on the selected student body and school characteristics for these comparison groups. (For complete T-test statistical test information, contact author.)

In general, these fifteen schools have significantly smaller enrollments, lower proportions of Hispanic/ Latino and higher proportions of white, non-Hispanic students than urban public schools. The proportion of white, non-Hispanic students in these fifteen schools, however, is not different from other Indianapolis public schools. All but one of the fifteen schools receives Title 1 funding, a characteristic not commonly found in other charter schools, but common in other urban public schools.

Table 29.1. Descriptive statistics of selected staff and school characteristics

	Individual				Schools			
	Obs	Proportion	Min	Max	Obs	Proportion	Min	Max
Position								
Teachers	302	0.709	0	1	15	0.700	0.250	0.952
Staff, non-teaching	302	0.132	0	1	15	0.168	0.000	0.750
Administrators	302	0.050	0	1	15	0.041	0.000	0.115
Admin w/teaching	302	0.109	0	1	15	0.091	0.000	0.269
Education								
BA degree	283	0.558	0	1	15	0.595	0.167	1.000
More than BA	283	0.369	0	1	15	0.404	0.130	0.603
Grades served								
Kindergarten	247	0.146	0	1	15	0.115	0.000	0.500
1st gr	247	0.162	0	1	15	0.127	0.000	0.500
2nd gr	247	0.162	0	1	15	0.127	0.000	0.444
3rd gr	247	0.158	0	1	15	0.126	0.000	0.444
4th gr	248	0.169	0	1	15	0.133	0.000	0.438
5th gr	247	0.174	0	1	15	0.149	0.000	0.500
6th gr	247	0.190	0	1	15	0.165	0.000	0.500
7th gr	247	0.223	0	1	15	0.241	0.000	0.769
8th gr	247	0.190	0	1	15	0.239	0.000	1.000
9th gr	247	0.368	0	1	15	0.425	0.000	1.000
10th gr	247	0.360	0	1	15	0.420	0.000	1.000
11th gr	247	0.381	0	1	15	0.444	0.000	1.000
12th gr	247	0.372	0	1	15	0.439	0.000	1.000
Individual Controls								
Female	280	0.690	0	1				
Non-white, non-anglo	277	0.217	0	1				
18–24	280	0.100	0	1				
25–34	280	0.479	0	1				
35–44	280	0.239	0	1				
45–54	280	0.121	0	1				
55–64	280	0.057	0	.				

Source: SSNSCS, Spring 2010.

Using charter schools in one urban area allows for a maximization of school contexts that could otherwise be truncated if only the local urban district was sampled. The independent nature of charter schools does allow within-school networks to operate nearer to an isolated, within-organization research design. This structure is helpful for theoretical development of how social-relational principal characteristics relate to teacher engagement since it isolates network effects, but this structure is not necessary for policy implications, generalization purposes, or future research.

Data

This study combines survey data with interview and field work data to identify the type, accessibility, and formal role of the fifteen principals. Data from the School Social Network and School Community Survey (SSNSCS) is used to investigate the premise that the underlying social-relational characteristics of principals contribute to teacher engagement. The survey data assesses the school staff perceptions of their school leadership, commitment, satisfaction, and school community. For validity and comparison, nearly all of the survey questions mimic the *Schools and Staffing Survey* from the National Center on Educational Statistics.

In addition to this survey data, the SSNSCS collected two-way social network data on all school staff. This method of two-way social network data is unique to education research, as the few studies that do use social network data only collect one-way data on teachers' outgoing ties by naming who a teacher goes to for information and/or help. These surveyed social data continue to ask for this information, but additionally asks teachers and other school staff about their incoming ties. Adding the information about who comes to the respondent for information and/or help overcome three limitations of the one-way studies. First, this type of two-way social

Table 29.2. Student demographic and other select school characteristics compared to sampled schools[a]

	Sample Schools		other Indianapolis charter schools		Other Public charter schools		Other Urban public schools		Other Indianapolis public schools		Other Indianapolis public schools		Other US public schools	
	Mean	s.d.	Mean	s.d.	Mean	s.d.	Mean	s.d.	Mean	s.d.	Mean	s.d.	Mean	s.d.
Enrollment	303.71	153.62	401.71	175.23	325.28	418.62	620.36	512.19	685.90	561.94	555.79	392.67	546.31	443.31
Student Body														
% Male	0.483	0.073	0.488	0.034	0.496	0.085	0.505	0.063	0.480	0.050	0.493	0.044	0.509	0.050
% Amer Ind	0.003	0.005	0.002	0.003	0.022	0.101	0.010	0.032	0.002	0.002	0.003	0.004	0.020	0.091
% Hispanic	0.037	0.045	0.081	0.095	**0.232**	0.286	**0.356**	0.322	**0.125**	0.119	0.064	0.099	**0.179**	0.251
% Blk, nonH	0.502	0.383	0.673	0.364	**0.295**	0.355	0.357	0.345	0.409	0.273	**0.112**	0.209	**0.161**	0.252
%Wht,nonH	0.414	0.352	0.200	0.283	0.394	0.351	**0.198**	0.240	0.391	0.270	**0.767**	0.266	0.587	0.340
% AsnPIAmr	0.002	0.004	0.003	0.006	0.037	0.097	0.067	0.128	**0.014**	0.021	0.012	0.022	0.039	0.084
% FRL	0.604	0.238	0.736	0.249	0.515	0.321	0.666	0.279	0.644	0.216	**0.446**	0.226	0.469	0.274
School traits														
Pupil:T ratio	17.014	4.717	20.286	5.636	22.725	56.597	16.780	13.777	16.767	3.574	17.374	3.192	16.224	18.196
Pupil:FT Tratio	18.293	9.627	19.886	6.735	19.135	18.494	**38.533**	26.698	**40.172**	28.508	**31.620**	20.296	**34.802**	25.556
Title I school	0.929	0.267	1.000	0.000	**0.670**	0.470	0.811	0.391	0.868	0.340	0.714	0.452	0.689	0.463
Charter	1.000	0.000	1.000	0.000	1.000	0.000	**0.143**	0.350	**0.037**	0.014	**0.020**	0.139	**0.054**	0.226
Large Urban	1.000	0.000	0.857	0.378	0.376	0.484	1.000	0.000	0.847	0.361	**0.116**	0.320	**0.132**	0.338

[a] significant differences from sampled Indianapolis charter schools bold faced.

Source: Common Core of Data, 2008-09.

network data collection allows for relationship reciprocity to be analyzed. Second, two-way data increases the validity of the social data collected. Third, it allows for non-respondents, who are otherwise missing data in one-way studies, to be captured and mapped within the school social network.

Surveys were distributed to staff at similar organizational time points in order to maximally reduce error on responses due to anomalistic sampling points and to capture the variation in the flow of relationship interactions over the course of a semester. In order to try to capture the breadth of school networks for teachers and staff, respondents were surveyed at times which could induce respondents to call upon different personnel in the school network. The first survey was collected over the spring (Easter) break holiday during a switch in the grading period. The duties of staff and teachers likely took on a more administrative role during this time. The second survey was collected over the spring Indiana state testing (ISTEP) period of which all Indianapolis charter schools participate. Uniform teaching duties of staff during this time likely called upon a different set of norms and expectations as well as different school personnel that faculty might not regularly use during non-testing classroom days. The third and final survey was collected at the end of each school's year. This final survey time point was designed to identify how teachers and other staff utilize their social resources in times where more collaboration may be needed. Due to various school calendars, this last survey fluctuated in dissemination per school.

To map the school-wide social network, these individual social network data from individual respondent matrices data are combined into one school-wide matrix. The network characteristics are measured, coded, and stored to generate theoretically and empirically appropriate social resource measures. The five network matrices are added together per survey time point using the consensus structure matrices in UCINET network software (see Krackhardt, 1988). From the school matrix, measures of the principals' accessibility are quantified.

The network characteristics are measured, coded, and stored to generate theoretically appropriate social-relational measures. To code the social-relational measures, the network matrices are averaged across the three time points using the consensus structure matrices

in UCINET network software (see Krackhardt, 1988). The threshold function for this consensus matrix is set to 0.33, which ultimately tags any identified relationship in the three time points as relevant. For respondents who participated in all three surveys, identifying a direct interaction with the principal would be coded as a 0.33; relationships named in all three of the surveys receive a score of 1 in the matrix.

This method of appending the three sets of matrices more adequately represents the full web of relationships that respondents access in their schools, as it identifies persistent relationships (those relationships that are consistently named in each of the three surveys by respondents) and identifies fluctuating relationships that vary by the organizational need at the time such as those relationships that are only named during the ISTEP testing period. Pooling the 268 teacher survey responses across the three time points also reduces error on any one score.

Measures

Teacher engagement is assessed with three measures: teacher satisfaction with teaching, commitment to the school, and overall perception of the school community. **Teacher satisfaction** is a scale, $\alpha = 0.798$, that combines the scores from the SSNSCS on the degree to which the staff members rate overall job and career satisfaction, how much they like how their school is run, the influence of state standards on satisfaction, and their satisfaction with the amount of support they receive for special needs students and from parents. **Teacher commitment** is created from staff members' answers to questions about their likeliness to return to the school the next year, the likeliness that they would leave this job for one with better pay, whether they would become a teacher again if they started college over again, and the degree of stress, thoughts of transferring, wanting to stay home, and worries about job security, $\alpha = 0.762$.

The teachers' perceptions of the **overall school community** assesses the level of relational trust, shared values and norms, shared activities, and diffuse roles in the school community.[5] These four variables load onto one factor and correlate at $\alpha = 0.503$. The overall school community scale is weighted by the factor loading scores of these four dimensions; trust is weighted at 0.652, shared values and norms is weighted at 0.644, diffuse roles is weighted at 0.092, and shared activities is weighted at 0.240.

Principals' social-relational characteristics are categorized by their principal dispositional type, accessibility, and formal structural position in the school. Dispositional type is directly derived from the survey question from the SSNSCS. Teachers are asked to choose whether they think of their principal mostly as a **teachers' principal**, a **students' principal**, a **parents' principal**, an **administrators' principal**, or as something other than those choices. Of the 15 percent of teachers that named their principal as something other than the four types, the vast majority wrote explanations that they perceived their principal as a combination of several types. Very few teachers listed their principals as parents' principals (see table 29.3).

There is no school where all staff members rated their principal as one single dispositional type. In fact, all schools demonstrate great variation in identifying their principal type; all schools match a minimum of three different "types" to their principal. In addition, over the three surveys, teachers alter their identification of their principal's type. This variation on dispositional type demonstrates the dynamic nature of the roles of principals, confirming that certain school time points

(grading vs. testing vs. end-of-year) or perhaps certain individual situations warrant principals to attend to their duties differently.

Principals are also asked about the type of principal they perceived themselves to be—the self-identified disposition. These responses of a **self-perceived student, teacher, parent, administrator,** or **other** type of principal are triangulated with the same question during the interviews to gauge the reliability. In seven of the fifteen instances, principals listed more than one principal type. For example, one principal stated that she was "mostly a students' principal, but [the school] needs an administrators' principal to keep us going" (Monarda, interview 7/2/10).[6] This occurrence of multiple identifications by the principals reiterates the complex task nature of the principal position. In the cases where principals ranked a primary and secondary principal type for themselves, the first type is coded as a 1 and the second type is coded as a 0.5 in order to maintain the variation in principal roles in schools. As table 29.3 shows, the distribution across the principal types is quite the same, with the exception of the low occurrence of the parents' principal type. Only one principal mentioned that he thought of his secondary role of principal as attending to the parents. No other principals self-identified as a parents' principal.

Table 29.3.   Descriptive statistics of outcomes and principal characteristics

	Obs	Mean	s.d.	Min	Max
Outcomes					
Teacher commitment	297	−1.550	0.801	−.262	0.200
Teacher satisfaction	297	3.966	0.828	1.268	5.750
Overall school community	297	2.201	0.407	0	3.338
Principal type					
Teachers' principal	297	0.313	0.394	0	1
Students' principal	297	0.186	0.346	0	1
Administrators' principal	297	0.284	0.397	0	1
Parents' principal	297	0.067	0.216	0	1
Other principal type	297	0.150	0.307	0	1
Self-perceived principal type					
P: Teachers' principal	15	0.313	0.443	0	1
P: Students' principal	15	0.375	0.500	0	1
P: Administrators' principal	15	0.313	0.403	0	1
P: Parents' principal	15	0.031	0.125	0	1
P: Other principal type	15	0.188	0.359	0	1
Principal Accessibility					
Embeddedness	15	1.201	0.613	0.248	2.656
Reachability	15	−2.247	1.844	−8.857	−1.417
Formal role of principal					
Strong CMO	15	0.267	0.458	0	1
Assistant principal	15	0.533	0.442	0	1

Source: SSNSCS, Spring 2010.

The accessibility of principals is distinguished with two network position measures: embeddedness and reachability. **Embeddedness** measures how nested the principal is within the social web of their school community network. The coreness measure (nearness to the center of the network configuration with respect to popularity), in-degree (nearness to the center of the network when only looking at incoming ties), and out-degree (nearness to the center of the network configuration when only looking at the outgoing ties) are all quite similar, $\alpha = 0.921$, but capture slightly different aspects of embeddedness. To reduce error and increase reliability, principal components factor analysis informs the embeddedness scale. Each component is weighted by its factor loading coefficient—coreness at 0.906, out-degree at 0.947, and in-degree at 0.938—to create the embeddedness measure. Most principals have embeddedness scores between 0.60–1.80 on a 0–3 scale (see table 29.3). It is important to remember that principals, no matter their "type" or the schools' organization, can vary on how central they are to the myriad of interactions in their school.[7]

Reachability is a measure about how immediately accessible someone is to a person. In this case, the accessibility of the principal for the teacher is of primary interest. Therefore, a measure that calculates the distance between a teacher and her principal—the number links before a teacher can reach her principal—is what is measured. If a teacher is only one link away, it signals that a direct correspondence between the teacher and principal has appeared in the network data. One link therefore indicates the nearest possible distance between two persons. More links mean a person is less reachable. If a teacher is more than one link away, that means that the teacher goes through a broker-like person to interact with the principal. For example, the teacher could be connected to her principal through an assistant principal. Longer distances signal less reachability. In these data, the distance to the principal measure ranges from one to twenty path lengths. For ease of interpretation, the distance measure is reversed so that a positive coefficient indicates a person is closer to the principal (more reachable) instead of farther away; see table 29.3.

It is also necessary to account for formal position of the principal in the school. Principals' interaction with their teachers can be mediated by the presence of **assistant principal/s** (as the previous reachability example

illustrates). In addition, schools with charter management organizations (CMO) that are involved with the functioning of the school also need to be accounted in the models. Like school districts and school boards, CMOs can exogenously contribute to the type and degree of interaction between principal and teachers. From the field site visits, it was evident in a few schools that strong CMO executives can create tensions between the principal and teachers with respect to the decisions made on discipline, curriculum, and other school issues (Fuscia, Fern, Kildeer). Thus, in order to fully account for the importance of the principal on teacher engagement, **strong CMOs** need to be accounted in the models.[8]

FINDINGS

Mixing methods to include field site and interviews allows researchers to confirm or reject assumptions that underlie the theory that they are trying to demonstrate in their study. In this case, if the principals did not discuss the diversity of their role and the wider range of their influence on the school context, the justification of the sample would not hold and the network theory testing would hold no more weight than if the study was conducted in traditional schools. If that was the case, that would not nullify the results; rather, it would put more conditions on the findings. Using data from interviews and field site visits helps to make tangible the lived reality of principals and the multidimensionality of the principal job.

Interviews with principals confirm the assumption regarding charter schools as a least restrictive space for their leadership. In these schools, every principal interviewed discussed that their roles are much more expansive and powerful than traditional school principals. All principals had previously been administrators (principals, assistant principals, or assistant superintendents) prior to this current charter school. Except for one principal, all had previously worked for Indianapolis or another urban public school district. As one principal stated, "My job is really a combination of what a principal would do and [what] a superintendent would do" (Huechara, interview July 2, 10). In all but two of the principal interviews (Centaurea, Iris), principals discussed their position as a combination of duties similar to a superintendent, principal, Title I coordinator, facilities manager, community liaison, fundraiser, and school board (Huechara, Monarda, Hibiscus, Daisy, Liatris, Shasta, Trillium, Fuscia, Pulmonaria). Two principals referred to the charter school principal role as "a hybrid role" (Pulmonaria, Trillium). These principals do the hiring, firing, and most of the other decision-making for the school. These principals decide how much power they would like to share with their faculty. These principals have more power than most principals. This less restrictive context allows for a more diverse range of principal types and styles of leadership to be tested and helps to robustly support the findings.

Fixed effect regression results in table 29.4 show that principals' social-relational leadership characteristics are related to teacher engagement. Internally focused principal dispositions—those principals who focus on students and/or teachers as compared to principals who attend to the needs of administrators or parents—correlate with higher levels of teacher commitment, teacher satisfaction, and overall school community levels. Moreover, through the interviews with principals, it was apparent that they thought it important for their own perception of their dispositional type to be accounted in the models. Indeed, principals who perceive themselves as internally focused on the students' needs impact teacher satisfaction and perception of school community. This highlights the importance of the type of principal disposition, as there is an additive effect of student-focused principals on teacher satisfaction and school community.

The accessibility of the principal does not significantly correlate with teacher commitment levels, but does impact teacher satisfaction and overall school community perceptions. The embeddedness of the prin-

Table 29.4. Teacher engagement and school community as a function of principal leadership[a]

	(1) Teacher commitment	(2) Teacher satisfaction	(3) Overall school community
Principal Accessibility			
Embeddedness	0.061	0.228+	0.135**
	(0.149)	(0.110)	(0.042)
Reachability	0.013	0.026	0.022*
	(0.023)	(0.021)	(0.010)
Principal type			
Teachers' principal	0.559***	0.748***	0.255**
	(0.127)	(0.128)	(0.079)
Students' principal	0.633***	0.648***	0.245***
	(0.149)	(0.094)	(0.041)
Teacher & Student principal	0.689*	0.823**	0.343***
	(0.243)	(0.242)	(0.076)
Formal school structure			
Strong CMO	0.001	0.029	-0.024
	(0.296)	(0.161)	(0.057)
Assistant Principal	-0.017	0.470***	0.249***
	(0.153)	(0.105)	(0.051)
Self-perceived principal type			
P: Teachers' principal	0.092	0.306+	0.072
	(0.162)	(0.160)	(0.082)
P: Students' principal	0.150	0.328***	0.121**
	(0.134)	(0.073)	(0.037)
P: Teacher & Student principal	0.030	0.208	-0.079
	(0.385)	(0.197)	(0.063)
Constant	-1.896***	2.762***	1.740***
	(0.304)	(0.226)	(0.110)
Observations	268	268	268
R-squared	0.182	0.221	0.222

Robust standard errors in parentheses   *** $p<0.001$, ** $p<0.01$, * $p<0.05$, + $p<0.10$

[a] Models run fixed effects for schools and control for teacher age, gender, race-ethnicity, and grade level.

cipal is positively correlated with higher staff satisfaction and school community while reachability is only slightly correlated with school community. This shows that teachers respond more positively to principals who are core to schools' web of relationships (high on embeddedness, see figure 29.1), not peripheral. And, for the intents and purposes measured here, the level of reachability of a principal matters little to none.

Teachers also respond positively when the formal structure of the administration in the school has an assistant principal. The presence of this assistant principal imputes distance (less reachability) between the principal and the teacher, as the assistant principal would act as a broker between the teacher and the principal, as figure 29.2 shows. However, as these results show twice over—the presence of an assistant principal correlates with higher teacher satisfaction and better school community perceptions and the reachability to the principal matters little to none.

In sum, within the natural context of schools' social web, the embeddedness of the principal matters for teacher satisfaction and school community perceptions. Teachers respond more positively when principals are more socially embedded with staff. Teachers also respond more positively when there is an assistant principal broker who operates between the teacher and principal. Lastly, the relational context works in conjunction with the social dispositional type of principals—teachers positively respond to principals who are internally focused on the needs of the student and teacher stakeholders.

DISCUSSION

These results reframe the ways in which scholars can interpret school leadership effects in prior research. It is not sufficient to assess leadership of principals without accounting for the relational-social aspects of leadership. Teachers may interpret principals distributing leadership as anything from principals' concerted effort to encourage teachers to "own" the school to a "punting-off" of responsibilities onto their teachers so that they can attend to external school stakeholders.[9] Similarly, instructional leaders may be perceived as overstepping school-classroom boundaries or deeply engaging in the school learning process. The core idea here is not which interpretation is correct, but rather to bring to the

forefront that internally focused and embedded leaders are important to gain or maintain teachers' engagement with their school.

Distributed leadership assumes a low level of principal embeddedness—a "stand back and let the teachers decide it and own it" leadership style. The results here do not support this leadership approach as preferable, at least in relation to teacher satisfaction, commitment, and overall perception of the school community. The association of embeddedness to instructional leadership is not invalidated with this analysis, but future research would have to tease apart principals who are embedded in classroom instruction apart from the general network embeddedness, as was tested here, in order to test that hypothesis.

These results do emphasize that an internally focused principal is beneficial to teacher engagement. The idea that the principal is disposed toward the needs of the teacher and student stakeholders is an assumption associated with distributed leadership and instructional leadership. With distributed leadership, the principal would let the teachers decide what is best for the school to do since the teachers are the most embedded with the students. With instructional leadership, the principal acts as the decision-maker for the teachers and students. Either way, these models support the premises that teachers respond well to principals who put the needs of the teachers and students first. Urban principals may more effectively engage teachers if they do not focus their primary relational energies on the external stakeholders.

Lastly, direct access to the principal (reachability) is not a necessary characteristic of principals for the health of the teacher community. Having an intermediary broker, like an assistant principal, positively correlates with teacher satisfaction and school community perceptions. Given the nature of teachers' work, this indirect access to the principal may signal professional trust. This explanation is post-hoc, however, and warrants further exploration.

These results do help to resolve some conflicting conclusions regarding leadership that exist in the literature. For example, it makes more sense now to understand studies concluding that teachers don't experience positive engagement when they are assigned non-teaching duties in conjunction with studies that find that principals who distribute leadership to their teachers show increased levels of teacher satisfaction. The direct level of access to the principal in relation to the teachers needs to be accounted among these qualities of role structure and disposition of the principal. Teachers appear to respond more positively to "hands-on" principals when they perceive the intentions of the principal to be internally focused on the students and teachers. With this analysis, we can now imagine that these conclusions from other studies might depend on whether or not the teachers perceive a distribution of leadership as internally focused for the betterment of the teachers and students or as externally focused and self-serving for the principal.

IMPLICATIONS

This study demonstrates how a rich, mixed-methods dataset can be used to better understand the multidimensional, complex nature of urban school principals in relation to their duties, roles, and relationships with teachers. Findings from the field act as theoretical springboards to reconceptualize theories surrounding principals, their roles, and their duties in their school. From data like these, scholars can begin to analyze principal leadership effectiveness within the realities and contexts in which that learning occurs in order to produce research that better matches the lived realities in schools.

Orienting to these teacher engagement outcomes is important for the discussion of urban school leadership. Not only did the school community concept develop in the context of Chicago schools (Bryk and Driscoll, 1988), but it appears important to drive teacher and student successes (Bryk, et al., 2010; Crow and Scriber, 2013; Young, 2012). Sharpening our theoretical understanding of the multidimensionality of principal leadership, including its relational-social aspects, and connecting it to teacher engagement could lead to lower rates of teacher attrition and improvements in school communities. This is especially important in urban schools where "urban school leaders are challenged by high rates of teacher turnover that compromise the development of instructional quality, organizational trust, teacher leaders, and school climate and culture that foster authentic engagement of the school community" (Crow and Scribner, 2013, 291).

In leadership programs, there is little distinction between general leaders and urban leaders (Young, 2012). The additional complexity of the urban school context—from school size to number of external stakeholders—provides a dynamic environment that commands

different types of personalities and charisma. The findings regarding these relational-social leadership characteristics can provide some fixed attributes with which to foster in principal preparation programs. Principal management trainings could focus on the importance of leaders' dispositions, styles, personas, and interactions with their staff to directly influence the school space. "Leaders in urban contexts deal with uniquely challenging issues" which are frequently in flux (Beachum and Obiakor, 2005). These relational-social characteristics are aspects of urban school leadership that can be taught, fostered, and maintained to sustain teacher engagement in schools.

The social-relational structure is important to attend to if change is to take hold. If principals are not internally focused or have a level of embeddedness with their teachers, teacher engagement will suffer.

RECOMMENDATIONS FOR FUTURE RESEARCH

Future research will want to investigate how these findings resonate with educators and principals in a broader context. This research was based on data from fifteen Indianapolis charter schools for a variety of theoretical and statistical reasons. Network data was critical to map in the naturally occurring social and structural context of the school. Collecting more data such as these in other contexts would be crucial to do before policies and programs are implemented.

Knowing which key social concepts are important to the school context can lead future studies to draft survey questions that tease apart these same concepts. Survey data is easier to collect and analyze on a grander, more representative scale than network data and so could expedite the testing of these ideas among a variety of grade levels, school types, or even international comparisons. In these cases, field site visits and interviews would be critical to then integrate into the research in the development phase in order to confirm or deny the assumptions embedded in the theoretical assumptions framing the survey data collection.

NOTES

1. Some studies do find that the type of principal matters less if the principal is a charismatic leader (Bryk and Schneider, 2002). Strong principals positively influence the school climate in such a way that teacher attitudes and behaviors

toward teaching improve (Ingersoll, 2003). This leadership type directly and indirectly extends to the students as well, increasing their enthusiasm for school (McCloskey, 2008).

2. Hallinger (2007) does propose an expansion of instructional leader beyond the curriculum and instruction focus.

3. This study limits its time frame to within one school year, 2009–2010. It is necessary for the student body and faculty contexts to be as stable as possible in order to isolate the network effects on their perceptions of engagement and school community. On average, charter schools have higher rates of student mobility between school years (Ballou, Teasley, and Zeidner, 2008; Booker et al., 2007). In addition, approximately two thirds of these Indianapolis charter schools are still "growing," meaning that are still working toward achieving the building enrollment capacity on size and/or grade levels served. Consequently, the school staff grows every year to accommodate increases in capacity. A one-year, contained school year therefore helps to isolate the staff network effects on the school community independent of these structural changes which take place between school years. Similarly, the year-to-year contract of teachers in charter schools creates an environment where teacher turnover between years could also be high. In order to avoid conflating effects from changing staff demographics, a within school year analysis is preferred.

4. The mayor's office does not serve as a pseudo-district administrative office. Rather, it is the chartering authority whose main responsibility is to keep the schools within paperwork compliance according to Indiana law.

5. For a complete explanation of the questions from the SSNSCS, see Price (2012).

6. All school names are pseudonyms.

7. There are no isolated principals in these data, so none are coded.

8. Strong CMOs are defined as CMOs that are involved with individual schools' decisions. Schools that paid an annual due to a CMO simply for national affiliation are not included in the "strong CMO" coding. With these weak CMO schools, there are no retributions for noncompliance. In strong CMOs, the executive has the power to fire the principal. Strong CMOs therefore create a tension for these principals not experienced by other Indianapolis charter school principals.

9. Interviews with teachers and principals, not presented here, corroborate this conclusion.

REFERENCES

Barr, R. and Dreeben, R. 1983. *How Schools Work*. Chicago: The University of Chicago Press.

Beachum, F. D. and Obiakor, F. E. (2005). Educational leadership in urban schools. In F. E. Obiakor and F. D. Beachum (Eds.), *Urban education for the 21st century: Research, issues, and perspectives* (pp. 83–99).

Bidwell, C.E. (1957). Some Effects Of Administrative Behavior—A Study In Role-Theory. *Administrative Science Quarterly 2*:163–181.

Bidwell, C.E. (1965). The School as a Formal Organization. In *Handbook of Organizations*, edited by J. G. March. Chicago: Rand McNally.

Bryk, A.S., Bender Sebring, P., Allensworth, E., Luppescu, S., and Easton, J.Q. (2010). *Organizing schools for improvement: Lessons from Chicago*. Chicago: The University of Chicago Press.

Bryk, A.S., Camburn, E., and Seashore Louis, K. (1999). Professional Community in Chicago Elementary Schools: Facilitating Factors and Organizational Consequences. *Educational Administrative Quarterly 35*:751–781.

Bryk, A. S. and Driscoll, M. (1988). *The high school as community: Contextual influences and consequences for students and teachers*. Madison: University of Wisconsin: National Center on Effective Secondary Schools.

Bryk, A.S. and Schneider, B.L. (2002). *Trust in schools: a core resource for improvement*. New York: Russell Sage Foundation.

Coldren, A. F. and Spillane, J. P. (2007). Making Connections to Teaching Practice The Role of Boundary Practices in Instructional Leadership. *Educational Policy, 21*(2), 369–396.

Crow, G. M. and Scribner, S. P. (2013). Professional Identities of Urban School Principals. *Handbook of Urban Education*, 287.

Firestone, W. A. and Pennell, J. R. (1993). Teacher commitment, working conditions, and differential incentive policies. *Review of Educational Research 63*:489–525.

Goddard, Y. L., Goddard, R. D., and Tschannen-Moran, M. (2007). A theoretical and empirical investigation of teacher collaboration for school improvement and student achievement in public elementary schools. *Teachers College Record 109*:877–896.

Goldring, E.B. and Pasternack, R. (1994). Principals coordinating strategies and school effectiveness. *School Effectiveness and School Improvement 5*(3):239–253.

Hallinger, P. (2003). Leading educational change: Reflections on the practice of instructional and transformational leadership. *Cambridge Journal of Education, 33*(3), 329–352.

Hallinger, P. (2005). Instructional leadership and the school principal: A passing fancy that refuses to fade away. *Leadership and Policy in Schools, 4*(3), 221–239.

Hallinger, P. (2007). *Research on the practice of instructional and transformational leadership: Retrospect and prospect*. research.acer.edu.au/research_conference_2007/7.

Hallinger, P. and Murphy, J. F. (1986). The social context of effective schools. *American Journal of Education*, 328–355.

Hillard III, A. (2004). No Mystery: Closing the Achievement Gap Between African-Americans an Excellence. In *Young, Gifted, and Black: Promoting High Achievement Among African American Students*. Boston: Beacon Press.

Honig, M.I. (2009). "External" organizations and the politics of urban educational leadership: The case of new small autonomous schools initiatives. *Peabody Journal of Education, 84*(3), 394–413.

Honig, M.I., Copland, M.A., Lorton, J.A., and Newton, M. (2010). "Central Office Transformation for District-wide Teaching and Learning Improvement." Center for the Study of Teaching and Policy, Seattle.

Honig, M.I. and Hatch, T.C. (2004). Crafting Coherence: How Schools Strategically Manage Multiple, External Demands. *Educational Researcher 33*(8):16–30.

Hulpia, H. (2009). Distributed Leadership and Organizational Outcomes in Secondary Schools. Doctoral dissertation.

Hulpia, H., Devos, G., and Rosseel, Y. (2009). The relationship between the perception of distributed leadership in secondary schools and teachers' and teacher leaders' job satisfaction and organizational commitment. *School Effectiveness and School Improvement* 20:291–317.

Knapp, M.S., Copland, M.A., Honig, M.I., Piecki, M.J., and Portin, B.S. (2010). "Learning-focused Leadership and Leadership Support: Meaning and Practice in Urban Systems." Center for the Study of Teaching and Policy, Seattle.

Lankford, H., Loeb, S., and Wyckoff, J. (2002). Teacher sorting and the plight of urban schools: A descriptive analysis. *Educational Evaluation and Policy Analysis, 24*(1), 37–62.

Lee, V.E., Dedrick, R.F., and Smith, J.B. (1991). The Effect of the Social Organization of Schools on Teachers' Efficacy and Satisfaction. *Sociology of Education 64*:190–208.

Leithwood, K. and Jantzi, D. (1990). Transformational Leadership: How Principals Can Help Reform School Cultures. *School effectiveness and school improvement 1*(4): 249–280.

Leithwood, K. and Jantzi, D. (1999). The relative effects of principal and teacher sources of leadership on student engagement with school. *Educational Administration Quarterly 35*:679–706.

Leithwood, K. and Jantzi, D. (2008). Linking leadership to student learning: The contributions of leader efficacy. *Educational Administration Quarterly 44*:496–528.

Louis, K.S., Leithwood, K., Wahlstrom, K.L., Anderson, S.E., Michlin, M., Mascall, B., Gordon, M., Strauss, T., Thomas, E., and Moore, S. (2010). "Learning from Leadership: Investigating the Links to Improved Student Learning." University of Minnesota, Minneapolis.

Moolenaar, N.M., A.J. Daly, and P.J.C. Sleegers. (2011). "Ties with Potential: Social Network Structure and Innovative Climate in Dutch Schools." *Teachers College Record*.

National Commission on Teaching and America's Future (NCTAF). (2007). "The High Cost of Teacher Turnover." Policy Brief, Washington, DC.

Portin, B.S., Knapp, M.S., Dareff, S., Feldman, S., Russell, F.A., Samuelson, C., and Ling Yeh, T. (2009). "Leadership for Learning Improvement in Urban Schools." Center for the Study of Teaching and Policy, Seattle.

Robinson, V.M. J., Lloyd, C.A., and Rowe, K.J. (2008). The Impact of Leadership on Student Outcomes: An Analysis of the Differential Effects of Leadership Types. *Educational Administration Quarterly 44*:635–674.

Rosenholtz, S.J. (1985). Effective Schools: Interpreting the Evidence. *American Journal of Education 93*:352–388.

Smith, M.S. and O'Day, J. (1991). Systematic School Reform. In *The Politics of Curriculum and Testing*, edited by S. H. Fuhrman and B. Malen. Philadelphia: Falmer Press.

Somech, A. (2005). Directive versus participative leadership: Two complementary approaches to managing school effectiveness. *Educational Administration Quarterly* 41:777–800.

Spillane, J.P. (2006). *Distributed leadership*. San Francisco: Jossey-Bass.

Tschannen-Moran, M. (2004). *Trust matters: leadership for successful schools*. San Francisco: Jossey-Bass.

Tschannen-Moran, M. and W. K. Hoy. (2000). A multidisciplinary analysis of the nature, meaning, and measurement of trust. *Review of Educational Research* 70:547–593.

Wahlstrom, K. L. and K. S. Louis. 2008. How teachers experience principal leadership: The roles of professional community, trust, efficacy, and shared responsibility. *Educational Administration Quarterly 44*:458–495.

Young, M. D. (2012). The UCEA Urban Leadership Development Initiative. *Urban Education: A Model for Leadership and Policy*, 105.

CHAPTER 30

Preparing Leaders to Support the Education of Diverse Learners

Michelle D. Young, Mark A. Gooden, and Ann P. O'Doherty

Education has changed significantly over the decades. Although critics like to claim that education is stuck in the past, this simply isn't the case. How could it be, given the rapid pace of change in education policy, state and national standards, school technology, and expectations for educator practice as well as the significant demographic shifts in the school age population? Like other areas of education, leadership has changed as well. However, it isn't clear whether leadership has changed enough or in ways that will ensure high quality and equitable educational opportunities for all of the students that schools serve today.

This chapter emerges from an understanding that the majority of school leaders in the United States are not adequately prepared to support the education of diverse student populations. Although most educational leadership preparation programs are aligned to national and state educational leadership standards and many have engaged in program redesign and improvement efforts, we argue that it is not enough to have a high-quality educational leadership preparation programs. Programs must ensure that the learning experiences they provide enable leadership candidates the opportunity to build the knowledge, skills, and experiences they will need to effectively lead the learning of diverse student populations.

The 2010 U.S. Census analysis reveals a significant shift in the nation's racial makeup, a shift that has been reshaping public schools for years. In fact fourteen states, including California, Delaware, Florida, Georgia, Hawaii, Washington DC, Maryland, Mississippi, Nevada, New Jersey, New Mexico, New York, and Texas, have been "majority-minority" states for several years (Frey, 2013). As these states and their public schools have become increasingly diverse, the racial achievement gap in schools has increased (Hemphill,

Vanneman, and Rahman, 2011; Vanneman, Hamilton, Baldwin Anderson, and Rahman, 2009).

Given the essential role educational leaders play in fostering positive school culture, supporting teacher effectiveness and supporting student learning, addressing the achievement gap must be a chief concern of educational leaders and those that prepare them. As Hawley and Wolf (2011) assert "opportunities to learn will not become more equitable until this becomes a priority for school leaders and school leaders have the knowledge and skills they need to respond effectively to the needs of students of color" (p. 1). Eliminating the achievement gap and ensuring high-quality education for diverse student populations depends upon the capacity of local educational leaders to be highly effective at enabling schools in all contexts to prepare all students effectively. It also depends upon the capacity of local universities to prepare and support educational leaders who can achieve these results, even in the most daunting school contexts.

This chapter describes the efforts of faculty from University Council for Educational Administration (UCEA) member institutions to develop, pilot, distribute, and support the use of a set of innovative instructional modules, the Leaders Supporting Diverse Learners (*LSDL*) instructional modules.[1] The modules were designed to infuse critical content knowledge and learning experiences aimed at strengthening a leader's ability to support the education and development of traditionally marginalized student populations such as racially diverse and/or low income, into the core curriculum of educational leadership preparation programs. The chapter begins with an overview of recent research relevant to the preparation of educational leaders to support diverse student populations. Subsequently, we review the LSDL module development effort and provide examples from these efforts. We conclude with a call to action to our leadership colleagues to embrace the goal of preparing leaders to support the learning of diverse learners by making effective use of the LSDL modules and other high-quality leadership development materials.

RESEARCH INFORMING THE PREPARATION OF EDUCATIONAL LEADERS TO SUPPORT DIVERSE LEARNERS

There are essentially two key areas of research from which we draw for this section. The first is research on the importance of high-quality leadership development for effective leadership practice. This research has mapped the connection between leadership preparation and leadership practice. The second is research focused specifically on the development of leaders to support diverse student populations. Importantly, it is not our intent to provide a comprehensive review of these two areas of research within this chapter; rather, we present the research that informed the development of the LSDL initiative.

Preparation to Practice

Effective school leaders are critical to the transformation of our nation's schools into twenty-first-century learning communities where the potential of all students to learn at high levels can be maximized. Indeed, with the introduction of improved research designs and statistical methods, a growing body of empirical evidence demonstrates that principals have an important impact on schools, teachers, and student achievement (Hallinger and Heck, 1996; Leithwood and Jantzi, 2000, 2005, 2008; Robinson, Lloyd, and Rowe, 2008; Waters, Marzano, and McNulty, 2003). Specifically, research has found that principals positively influence student achievement through several key "avenues of influence": people, purposes, and goals of the school; structure of the school and social networks; and organizational culture (Hallinger and Heck, 1996, p.171; Leithwood, Seashore, Anderson, and Wahlstrom, 2004; Supovitz, Sirinides, and May, 2010).

Importantly, many universities have redesigned their leadership preparation programs, but only in the last ten years has there been enough research to demonstrate the effectiveness of program models or to foster agree-

ment on appropriate outcome measures to assess their effectiveness. Specifically, in programs with a strong instructional leadership focus, research shows a positive relationship between the program content and learning experiences and graduates' career-related knowledge, leadership positions and practices, and school improvement work (Darling-Hammond, Meyerson, LaPointe, and Orr, 2009; Young, Crow, Murphy, and Ogawa, 2009). Similarly, research indicates that educational leaders are best prepared through curriculum and learning experiences that are well-defined, purposeful, and coherent, that have a leadership-for-learning focus, challenging and reflective content and candidate-centered instructional practices, and include curriculum and learning experiences developed to address both their individual needs as well as the needs of the learners, communities, and schools they will serve (Darling-Hammond, Meyerson, LaPointe, and Orr, 2009; Young, Crow, Murphy, and Ogawa, 2009). These and similar findings have fostered the understanding that more strategically designed and focused preparation can yield improvement in leader practices.

Preparing Leaders to Support Diverse Learners

With growing recognition of the importance of school leadership has come increased concern regarding how leaders are prepared, particularly for schools that serve students representing low-income and diverse student populations (Young, Peterson, and Short, 2002). Developing leaders who can work within challenging contexts to promote quality teaching and learning for all students is central to many state and local reform agendas (Bottoms and O'Neill, 2001). However, the empirical research base documenting how leaders are, or should be, prepared for this important work is quite thin.

It is not that scholars in the area of educational leadership are ignoring issues of diversity. On the contrary, scholarship in this area has increased significantly since the late 1990s. However, most of this work focuses on the practice of leaders within the K–12 school or district setting, typically take an organizational view, such as restructuring schools or providing integrated social services (Astuto, 1990; Roberts, 1990; Thompson, 1990). As Young and Laible (2000) noted, while some of this scholarship has stressed the importance of facilitating the development of "a general appreciation for cultural diversity" (for example, Thompson, 1990, p. 164), of including or "mainstreaming" diversity in educational administration courses and /or creating discrete courses that focus on issues of difference (for example, Parker and Shapiro, 1992, p. 24), of recruiting and supporting more students of color in educational administration programs (for example, Allen et al., 1995), and of faculty development (Parker and Shapiro, 1992). (p. 387)

Less attention has been given to the actual content of learning experiences provided through higher education leadership preparation programs.

In an effort to ascertain the practices used in higher education to prepare leaders to support diverse learners, UCEA[2] collaborated with several research teams. Teams have examined preparation practices in a number of areas, from broad preparation activities to preparation around more specific foci, including special education, diversity, and lesbian, gay, bisexual, and transgendered issues. For example, Hawley and Wolf (2011) surveyed sixty-two universities affiliated with UCEA. The survey contained open-ended questions asking faculty to list the courses, resources, and strategies they used to prepare educational leaders to ensure that students of diverse races and ethnicities learn at high levels. The results indicated that while issues of diversity are being addressed, the way they are addressed may not result in the adequate preparation of educational leaders to support diverse student populations. First, they found that most diversity-related education for educational leaders occurs in a single course. On average, universities reported offering only one course in which diversity is the main focus and between four and five courses (including internship courses) in which diversity was a minor element of the course. Moreover, these courses tended to focus on the sociological and economic conditions faced by students of color, the persistence and damages of discrimination, inequities in learning resources, and the responsibilities leaders have to pursue social justice. They found little evidence of curricular content focused on the diversity issues that school leaders confront in their schools on a daily basis. Second, their results found a minimal amount of correspondence among the course readings, films, and tools regarding racial and ethnic diversity used to prepare educational leaders across university programs. Third, "despite the priority given in most educational leadership programs to 'in-structional leadership,' only two of the listed readings used to educate leaders about diversity deal with teaching and learning" (p. 2). Thus, while many leadership preparation programs do address issues of diversity, they tend to focus on causes, conditions, and impact of different social, cultural, historical, and political conditions and racial, ethnic, class, and gender discrimination, but not the leader actions to redress or reform these conditions and directly improve academic outcomes for diverse students

Without question there is a critical need for high-quality, innovative curriculum materials for educational leadership preparation, particularly materials designed to prepare leaders to narrow achievement gaps and support the success of all students (Hawley and Wolf, 2011; Rusch, 2005; Young and Laible, 2000).

A CURRICULUM FOR DEVELOPING LEADERS TO SUPPORT DIVERSE LEARNERS

Although a number of past efforts at program reform have been quite successful (Leithwood, Jantzi, Coffin, and Wilson, 1996; Milstein, 1992; Orr, King, and La Pointe, 2010), too little attention has been invested in dissemination and replication of efficacious curriculum and program components. Furthermore, many past efforts have involved whole program redesign, which requires a significant investment of time and other precious resources—resources that few programs can easily access—as well as the navigation of state and institutional approval processes. Thus, rather than promote whole program redesign, the LSDL project focused on developing and disseminating relevant and promising new strategies through highly impactful curriculum modules that can be incorporated into a wide range of preparation (and district development) programs, facilitating implementation.

The LSDL project built on the work of the University Council for Educational Administration's Urban Leadership Development Project (UCEA ULDP), a 2007 UCEA initiative that involved faculty from public and private urban leadership preparation programs in the United States[3] to rethink and redesign the preparation of urban leaders. Specifically, the LSDL developers and project leaders[4] designed an overarching theory of action for the development of leaders to support diverse learners, surveyed practicing educational leaders regarding their expertise and knowledge needs in this area, designed a signature pedagogy for the preparation of leaders called Powerful Learning Experiences (PLE), and developed seven curriculum modules. These are each shared in the following subsections.

Theory of Action

Those who prepare educational leaders usually have a series of implicit and explicit beliefs about what they teach, how they teach it, and why they teach it (Young, 2011). These beliefs, according to Argyris and Schon (1996) are their "theories of action" about leadership preparation. ULDP participants worked together to develop a theory of action for the LSDL Module Development Project, making the goals and beliefs of the development team explicit. This was a two-phase process that involved: 1) the identification of important outcomes of preparation and, subsequently, 2) the backward-mapping of preparation experiences that would lead to such outcomes. The final version of the LSDL theory of action states:

> If we intentionally design comprehensive and connected learning experiences situated in authentic contexts that provide graduate students the opportunities to explore and apply leadership knowledge and skills and disseminate these modules to leadership faculty, then together, we will develop leaders who can address increasingly complex challenges so that all children do learn. (UCEA, 2014)

This theory of action played an important role in the LSDL project, anchoring the development work as well as discussions about that work to a clear, overarching vision. The process used to develop this theory of action was repeated later by each development team prior to designing their individual curriculum modules.

Module Focus

Although the Interstate School Leadership Licensure Standards ISLLC (1996, 2008) standards have been adopted or adapted by the majority of states in the United States, disagreements still exist regarding the appropriate foundation for administrator preparation (Murphy, 2002; Young, Crow, Murphy, and Ogawa; 2009). Specifically, the ISLLC standards specify the general

nature of leadership need in schools today—in vision building, curriculum and instruction, management and operations, parent and community involvement, ethics, and policy. Faculty who work with diverse student populations have found the 2008 ISLLC standards to lack the specificity around issues like equity and diversity, needed to provide appropriate guidance for curriculum.

LSDL developers addressed this challenge in several key ways. First, developers examined several sources of information about preparation: 1) survey findings gathered through the Hawley and Wolf (2011) survey of how diversity was addressed in programs; data provided by the UCEA-LTEL Evaluation Research Taskforce on the most commonly offered courses in educational leadership preparation programs; and 3) a framework designed by Hawley and Wolf (2011) that identified diversity-related school leadership challenges. Second, based on these sources of information, developers identified a number of areas in which curriculum modules would be most helpful. Third, developers designed a survey for their program graduates and district partners seeking input on their areas of greatest need with regard to knowledge and skill gaps concerning leading the education of diverse student populations. Based on these activities, the LSDL developers identified the following areas for their curriculum development work: (1) Building a Community of Trust Through Racial Awareness of Self; (2) Developing Advocacy Leadership; (3) Family and Community Engagement; (4) Leadership for English Language Learner Success; (5) Organizing Learning and the Learning Environment; (6) Culturally Relevant Teaching; and (7) Marshaling and Using Resources Based on Data and Student Needs.

Just as participants had identified their theories of action at the program level, subsequent to the development of the curriculum themes, participants developed theories of action for each curriculum area. A sample theory of action for the developing trust through racial awareness module[5] is:

> If we provide graduate student/participants with multiple opportunities to reflect on how race plays a personal and professional role in their lives and in the lives of the students they serve, then our participants will develop a keen awareness of inequities and beliefs that may enable them to actively fight institutional racism in schools and society.

Similarly, a theory of action for the leadership and advocacy module[6] is:

If participants work together to apply the concepts and steps of advocacy engagement (identifying an issue, analyzing the policy levers and decision-making process, analyzing interest group and coalition opportunities, creating a persuasive argument, taking action or advocating, and conducting an after action review) around issues or problems of concern to them, then they will gain an understanding of advocacy engagement generally, evaluate its application to a variety of issues, and develop an actionable advocacy plan for engaging others or acting on a problem or issue.

Following the identification of curriculum module areas and the development of module theories of action, the team turned its attention to pedagogy. Specifically, developers designed a pedagogical approach that they believed would support their theories of action in each of the six theme areas.

Powerful Learning Experiences

Starting from the foundational work of the UDLP, LSDL developers refined an innovative pedagogy for the development of leaders working in diverse communities, called Powerful Learning Experiences (PLE). The PLE framework is designed to engage learners in authentic problems of practice, problems they are likely to face when they assume leadership positions (Young, 2011). This pedagogical approach develops collaborative skills, is highly motivating, and facilitates the transfer of research-based knowledge to practice.

Powerful learning experiences have the following nine features: 1) they are authentic, meaningful, relevant, problem-finding activities; 2) they involve sense-making around critical problems of practice; 3) they involve exploration, critique, and deconstruction from an equity perspective (for example, race, culture, language); 4) they require collaboration and interdependence; 5) they develop confidence in leadership; 6) they place both the professor and the student in a learning situation; 7) they empower learners and make them responsible for their own learning; 8) they shift the perspective from classroom to school, district, or state level; and 9) they have a reflective component. The PLE framework reflects research on adult learning,

particularly research on the learning of adults with rich experiential backgrounds (Edelman and Tononi, 2000; Kolb, 1984; Lehrer, 2009).

Although it was not be possible for every PLE to include all nine of the above features, LSDL developers were committed to intentionally incorporating as many of the nine features as feasible. To illustrate this point, we draw from the family and community engagement module.[7] This module, which is available in full on the UCEA website (www.ucea.org) has the following four overarching learning objectives:

1. Continue to examine their own beliefs about race, particularly as it connects to, or potentially impacts, their relationships with diverse students and families in their school's community.
2. Assess the physical environment and the culture of the school from the perspective of diverse students and their families.
3. Explore the school's neighborhood, identifying the strengths and potential needs of diverse students and families living in the community.
4. Scan the community for organizations that partner with, or could partner with, the school to better serve diverse students and families.

Based on these overarching the objectives, the developers designed three PLEs that each incorporate multiple learning activities and between seven and nine of the above characteristics (UCEA, 2014). This is reflected in table 30.1 below.

The first PLE, the neighborhood walk, is a multistep learning experience that involves pre-readings, class discussion, the identification of a "cultural broker" within the community, the identification of key elements to attend to during the walk and questions to ask, the actual neighborhood walk, reflection on the walk and the walker's positionality, class discussion, and a presentation of how the experience informed their learning and leadership perspective. The PLE also includes additional supplementary activities, such as the development of a digital story, photo essay, or slideshow.

The techniques included in this and other PLEs offer situated learning and the means to think through problems of practice from a variety of perspectives (Hart, 1993; Holyoak and Thagard, 1999; Kolb, 1984). Research on adult learning and on educational leader-

Table 30.1.   Family and Community Involvement PLEs

PLE 1: Neighborhood Walk	PLE 2: Engaging Families	PLE 3: Engaging a Community Organization
Five individual learning activities. Two that occur in the classroom and three that occur outside the classroom. Features included: 1) authentic; 2) involves sense-making; 3) equity perspective; 4) collaboration; 5) both professor and students engage in learning; 6) learners are responsible for own learning; 7) expands perspectives; and 8) reflective component.	Five individual learning activities. Three that occur in the classroom and two that occur outside the classroom. Features included: 1) authentic; 2) involves sense-making; 3) equity perspective; 4) collaboration; 5) develops confidence in leadership; 6) both professor and students engage in learning; 7) learners are responsible for own learning; 8) expands perspective; and 9) reflective component.	Five individual learning activities. Two that occur in the classroom and three that occur outside the classroom. Features included: 1) authentic; 2) involves sense-making; 3) equity perspective; 4) collaboration; 5) develops confidence in leadership; 6) both professor and students engage in learning; 7) learners are responsible for own learning; and 8) reflective component.

ship preparation indicates that leadership candidates perceive that they benefit more from authentic, problem-based pedagogies than the typical lecture-and-discussion formats of coursework (Young, Crow, Murphy, and Ogawa, 2009).

Like the developers of the family and community involvement module, all of the LSDL developers agreed that each module would be comprised of one or more powerful learning experiences designed to build core leadership knowledge and expertise. The number of PLEs incorporated into the modules depended on the complexity of the issues addressed in each of the modules. For example, the marshaling resources module includes eight PLEs, the leadership for English language learners module includes five PLEs, and the developing trust through racial awareness module includes three PLEs.

THE MODULES

Today's school leaders must be able to apply theory to practice in order to lead schools to improve achievement for all students. Whether they are designing professional development for teachers and staff or attempting to develop positive and productive learning environments, leaders must be able to apply their diversity-responsive expertise to ensure their decisions and actions support the learning of all children. Thus, the LSDL curriculum modules were designed with three key goals in mind:

1. Modules strengthen leaders' ability to support the education and development of students from low-income and diverse populations.

2. Modules incorporate critical content knowledge, powerful learning experiences, learning assessments, and teaching guidance.
3. Module format enables ease of incorporation into a wide range of preparation (and district development) program models and delivery approaches.

In order to ensure ease of use and consistency between and among the different modules, the modules were developed using a common format. Developers were required to include at a minimum the following six elements:

1. Overview of the Content/Thematic Area
2. Learning Goals and Theory of Action
3. Alignment to National Standards
4. Learning Experiences, Resources, Instructional Materials, and a Reflection Component
5. Candidate Assessment Exercises and Evaluation Rubrics
6. Teaching and Evaluation Notes

Furthermore, the content of the LSDL modules are aligned to national leadership standards and address identified diversity challenges associated with core leadership roles.

Importantly, virtually every basic role of school leaders has diversity implications (Hawley and Wolf, 2011), including efforts to foster school improvement, to ensure quality teaching, to foster and sustain a positive learning-centered environment, to maximize opportunities to learn, and to engage stakeholders in student success. To illustrate, the LSDL module focused on marshaling resources, which incorporates an equity audit, requires students to engage in an analysis of data on student learning, to explore literature that documents the over-identification of students of color for special education programs and services, to raise questions about the reasons for such disparities, and to examine and challenge inappropriate remedies. Importantly, student work is scaffolded and guided by peers and the course instructor.

Furthermore, each curriculum module includes an instructor's guide detailing the theory of action, module objectives, an outline of learning experiences, materials and reference lists, suggested timelines, learning assessment rubrics, and evaluation protocols. Developing the modules with a common protocol has many advantages including support for uniform implementation of the modules and replication. Finally, not only are the modules aligned with the Interstate School Leadership Licensure Consortium (ISLLC) and the Educational Leadership Constituent Council (ELCC) standards, which serve as the national standards for school leadership and leadership preparation respectively, but they were also designed to supplement the six most commonly offered courses in building-level educational leadership preparation.

A CALL TO ACTION

The achievement gap cannot be substantially narrowed unless we eliminate the gap in opportunities to learn. This requires school leaders who have the knowledge and skills to enhance the opportunities to learn for all students, but especially students of color, students from low-income families, students who are English language learners, and students with disabilities. To develop such leaders on a broad scale requires expanding the capacity of universities to provide relevant and effective leadership content, instructional resources, and scaffolded practice.

Through the LSDL project, UCEA faculty developed purposeful, accessible, and high-quality curriculum modules, designed specifically to align with and enhance the preparation provided through the six most commonly offered courses in building-level educational leadership preparation. By strengthening university-based educational leadership preparation programs' ability to deliver learning experiences that build leaders' knowledge of and skills for supporting the education of low-income and diverse student populations, we expect

program graduates will have the capacity to improve their own leadership practices and build the capacity of their school communities to positively impact student achievement and narrow achievement gaps.

The LSDL curriculum modules were designed to benefit all programs that prepare educational leaders in the United States, and the resources are available free of charge through the UCEA website (www.ucea.org). We invite readers to explore these curriculum materials, to use them in their courses and programs, and to share their experiences with UCEA. Additionally, we invite faculty to work with UCEA as we build additional program materials for this important curriculum project.

As increasing numbers of institutions adopt these modules into their leadership preparation programs, aspiring leaders will be better prepared to lead schools that effectively serve diverse and low-income students. Perhaps more importantly, by strengthening educational leaders' knowledge of and skills for supporting the education of diverse student populations, we anticipate significant and positive changes in our nation's school system.

NOTES

1. The LSDL initiative was supported by a grant from the Fund for the Improvement of Post Secondary Education and with funding from the University Council for Educational Administration.
2. UCEA, a consortium of just under one hundred major research universities with strong educational leadership programs, has a sixty-year history of working with university faculty to develop and implement innovative instructional materials, such as cases and simulations, designed to prepare highly effective school leaders.
3. Programs included Temple University, University of Texas-Austin, University at Buffalo, Bank Street College, Duquesne University, New Mexico State University, New York University, University of Wisconsin-Milwaukee, the University of Cincinnati, the University of Massachusetts-Boston, Lehigh University, the University of Texas-San Antonio, the University of Utah, and Claremont Graduate School of Education.
4. The LSDL project was led by Michelle Young, Ann O'Doherty, Mark Gooden, and Bill Hawley. The project was managed by Scott Blackshire. The development team consisted of Ann O'Doherty, Mark Gooden, Rick McCowan, Gretchen Generett, Eustace Thompson, Monica Byrne Jimenez, Charol Shakeshaft, Whitney Sherman, Floyd

Beachum, Goerge White, Adafo Austin, Ann Marie Fitzgerald, Betsy Wolf, Bill Hawley, Margaret Terry Orr, Denise Armstrong, and Marcia Springer. Technical assistance and evaluation expertise were provided by Matt Militello and Chris Jansen. A number of other faculty served as critical friends and early adopters.

5. This module was developed by Mark Gooden, University of Texas-Austin, and Ann O'Doherty, University of Washington.

6. This module was developed by Denise Armstrong, Marcia Springer, and Margaret Terry Orr, Bank Street College.

7. This module was developed by Floyd Beachum; George White and Adafo Austin, Lehigh University; and Anne Marie Fitzgerald, Duquesne University.

REFERENCES

Argyris, C. and Schon, D. (1996). *Organizational Learning II*. Reading, MA: Addison-Wesley.

Astuto, T. (1990, September). *Reinventing school leadership* (pp. 2–5) [Memo prepared for the Reinventing School Leadership Conference]. Cambridge, MA: National Center for Educational Leadership.

Baker, B., Orr, M. T., and Young, M. D. (2007). Academic drift, institutional production, and professional distribution of graduate degrees in educational administration. *Educational Administration Quarterly, 43*(3), 279–318.

Bottoms, G. and O'Neill, K. (2001). *Preparing a new breed of school principals: It's time for action*. Atlanta: Southern Regional Education Board.

Darling-Hammond, L., LaPointe, M., Meyerson, D., and Orr, M. (2007). *Preparing school leaders for a changing world: Lessons from exemplary leadership development programs*. Stanford, CA; Stanford University.

Edelman, G.M. and Tononi, G. (2000). *A universe of consciousness: How matter becomes imagination*. New York: Basic Books.

Frey, W. H. (2013, June 19). Shift to majority-minority population in the U.S. happening faster than expected. Brookings Up Front. Retrieved from: www.brookings.edu/blogs/up-front/posts/2013/06/19-us-majority-minority-population-census-frey.

Hallinger, P. and Heck, R. (1996). Reassessing the principal's role in school effectiveness: A review of empirical research, 1980–1995. *Educational Administration Quarterly, 32*(1), 5–44.

Hart, A. W. (1993). Reflection: An instructional strategy in educational administration. *Educational Administration Quarterly, 29*(3), 323–338.

Hawley, W. and Wolf, R. (2011). Diversity responsive school leadership. *UCEA Review*. Charlottesville, VA: UCEA.

Hemphill, F., Vanneman, A., and Rahman, T. (2011). How Hispanic and White Students in Public Schools Perform in Mathematics and Reading on the National Assessment of Educational Progress. NCES.

Holyoak, K., and Thagard, P. (1999). *Mental leaps: Analogy in creative thought*. Cambridge, MA: MIT Press.

Kolb, D. (1984). *Experiential learning: Experiences as the source of learning and development*. Englewood Cliffs: Prentice Hall.

Lehrer, J. (2009). *How we decide*. New York: Houghton Mifflin Harcourt.

Leithwood, K., Harris, A., and Hopkins, D. (2008). Seven strong claims about successful school leadership. *School Leadership and Management, 28*(1), 27–42.

Leithwood, K., Jantzi, D., Coffin, G., and Wilson, P. (1996). Preparing school leaders: What works? *Journal of School Leadership, 6*(3), 316–342.

Leithwood, K., Louis, K. S., Anderson, S., and Wahlstrom, K. (2004). *How leadership influences student learning*. New York: Wallace Foundation.

Milstein, M. M. (1992). *The Danforth Program for the preparation of school principals. Six Years Later: What we have learned*. Paper presented at the annual meeting of the University Council of Educational Administration, Minneapolis, MN.

Orr, M. T., King, C., and La Pointe, M. M. (2010). *Districts developing leaders: Eight districts' lessons on strategy, program approach and organization to improve the quality of leaders for local schools*. A Wallace Foundation Report. Newton, MA: EDC.

Orr, M. T. and Orphanos, S. (2010, forthcoming). How preparation impacts school leaders and their school improvement: comparing exemplary and conventionally prepared principals. *Educational Administration Quarterly*.

Parker, L. and Shapiro, J. P. (1992). Where is the discussion of diversity in educational administration programs? Graduate students' voices addressing an omission in their preparation. *Journal of School Leadership, 2*(1), 7–33.

Roberts, L. (1990, September). *Reinventing school leadership* (pp. 132–136) [Memo prepared for the Reinventing School Leadership Conference]. Cambridge, MA: National Center for Educational Leadership.

Robinson, V. M. J, Lloyd, C. A., and Rowe, K. J. (2008). The impact of leadership on student outcomes: An analysis of the differential effects of leadership types. *Educational Administration Quarterly, 44*(5), 635–674.

Rogers, E. M. (1995). *Diffusion of Innovations* (4th ed.). New York: The Free Press.

Rusch, E. (2004). Gender ad race in leadership preparation: A constrained discourse. *Educational Administration Quarterly, 40*(1), 14–46.

Supovitz, J., Sirinides, P., and May, H. (2010). How principals and peers influence teaching and learning. *Educational Administration Quarterly, 46*(1), 31–56.

Thompson, T. E. (1990, September). *Reinventing school leadership.* Cambridge, MA: National Center for Educational Leadership.

UCEA. (2014). *Preparing leaders to support diverse learners: Curriculum Modules for Leadership Preparation.* Charlottesville, VA: Author. Retrieved from: ucea.org/lsdl-preparation-modules-new/.

Vanneman, A., Hamilton, L., Baldwin Anderson, J., and Rahman, T. (2009). *Achievement Gaps: How Black and White Students in Public Schools Perform in Mathematics and Reading on the National Assessment of Educational Progress.* NCES.

Waters, T., Marzano, R. J., and McNulty, B. (2003). *Balanced leadership: What 30 years of research tells us about the effect of leadership on student achievement.* Retrieved February 21, 2009, from www.mcrel.org.

Weiss, C. H. (1998). *Evaluation.* Upper Saddle River, NJ: Prentice Hall.

Young, M. D. (2011). Leadership for Urban Schools. In K. Gallagher, D. Brewer, and R. Goodyear (Eds.), *An Introduction to Urban Education.* New York: Routledge.

Young, M. D., Crow, G., Orr, T., Ogawa, R., Creighton, T. (2005). An educative look to educating school leaders. *UCEA Review, 47*(2), 1–5.

Young, M. D. and Laible, J. (2000). White racism, anti-racism, and school leadership preparation. *Journal of School Leadership, 10*(5) 374–415.

Young, M. D., Petersen, G. J., and Short, P. M. (2002). The complexity of substantive reform: A call for interdependence among key stakeholders. *Educational Administration Quarterly, 38*(2), 137–175.

CHAPTER 31

Lessons from a District-Based Doctoral Cohort

Faculty Stories of Challenge, Opportunity, and Impact

Mónica Byrne-Jiménez, Catherine DiMartino, and Eustace Thompson

The reform of urban school districts continues to be of interest to researchers and policymakers alike. In the past decade the use of vouchers and the charter school movement have made inroads into both the practice and discourse of reform. The growth of educational management organizations and increased efforts at privatization influences much of the policy discussions on how to improve urban districts. Additionally, the role of state departments in district takeovers and the number of districts under mayoral control also indicate that district leadership and improvement continue to be an intractable problem.

According to the National Center of Educational Statistics, the largest one hundred urban districts educate 22 percent of the school-age population in public schools (Sable, Plotts, and Mitchell, 2010). The five hundred largest urban districts represent 43 percent of school-age children. Sixty-three percent of students in these districts are Latino or African American. New York City, with close to one million students, is the largest district in the nation. And while urban districts dominate the landscape of reform and improvement policy, issues of race, class, and achievement do not stop at city borders. Inner or first-tier suburbs, those communities that surround large cities, have been experiencing increased poverty and suburban decline since the late 1990s (Cooke, 2010; Jargowsky, 2003). Furthermore,

[S]mall, fiscally constrained inner-ring suburbs are not in a good position to address any increase in poverty. Indeed, inner-ring suburbs face a unique set of circumstances. They must cope with aging housing, school systems, and infrastructures along with declining incomes and an over-reliance on property taxes. (Cooke, 2010, p. 181)

Despite the dramatic shifts occurring in suburbs, educational policy and research continues, to a large degree, to ignore the needs of increasingly diverse suburban schools and districts. Suburban school districts, and not just those in the first tier, are coming to understand the need to address the increasing racial achievement gap (Ferguson, 2002). The need to explore the issues of district reform in the suburbs looms and warrants more attention. As these districts grapple with significant demographic shifts and seek help in developing equitable responses, universities, schools of education, and researchers located in those suburbs must be prepared to offer their support.

As faculty in educational leadership, we are concerned with the development of leadership and systems for sustained improvement. The main vehicle for strengthening school and district leadership is most often through research. We, however, decided to partner with a local district to develop a doctoral cohort with the intent of fostering system-wide improvement. This district, located in a first-tier suburb, had experienced decades of turmoil and decline under both local and state control. This chapter relates our experiences as faculty in the development and implementation of that doctoral cohort. As the cohort completed the doctoral program, we reflected on the program structures and our assumptions that prevented a true partnership between the university and the district and, in some instances, undermined the success of the cohort while doing little to effect district improvement. Organized around three "critical incidents" which highlight our learnings, the chapter identifies important discussions and decisions that faculty must make in conjunction with district personnel. As we, and others, move forward to further develop district relations, we offer our experiences as a starting point for laying the necessary groundwork and understanding for effective university-community relationships.

ROLE OF UNIVERSITIES

As centers of research and knowledge production, universities have long held a privileged position in the educational pipeline. Traditional relationships between universities and local public schools have served to maintain the distance between community needs and university goals (Maurrasse, 2001). These relationships are, at best, cool and, at worst, asymmetrical, where the university interacts with the community as a way to enhance its own reputation. There have been many calls for universities, particularly in urban centers, to renew their commitment to social justice and strengthen their engagement with local communities and schools (e.g., Astin and Astin, 2000; Butcher, Bezzina, Moran, 2010; Goldring and Sims, 2005). And while universities' administrators may encourage outreach efforts, the actual point of contact between universities and communities occur at the individual faculty or academic program level. Any collaboration between universities and schools rely on the relationships among the people involved. Organizational structures and resources are important, to be sure, but relationships matter just as much.

The literature is replete with studies and commentary on effective university-school partnerships (Barnett, Anderson, Houle, Higginbotham, and Gatling, 2010; Butcher, Bezzina, Moran, 2010). Miller and Hafner (2008) identify key elements of successful partnerships, "mutuality, supportive and strategic leadership, assets-based building, and sound processes" (p. 71). Others highlight the numerous obstacles to authentic partnerships (i.e., Coburn, Bae, and Turner, 2008; Maurasse, 2001). These studies also emphasize the importance of joint goals and agreement on processes. What is often overlooked, however, is that these partnerships are also a manifestation of how universities approach communities. Discussions of university-school partnership need to be embedded in larger conceptualizations of the *engaged university*.

Engaged universities are those that enact the moral dimensions (Starrat, 2004) of their work and approach communities from a social justice stance in which knowledge, resources, and relationships are equal (Brin-

gle and Hatcher, 2002). As a result, engaged universities are active participants in "an interactive process in which all partners apply critical thinking skills to complex community problems" (Brown, Reed, Bates, Knaggs, Casey, and Barnes, 2006, p. 10). Relationships with local communities take on a new dimension,

> Genuine engagement moves beyond the level of mere service and allows the opportunity for societal response to help redefine the nature of the problem itself and perhaps forge new solutions. (Sheehan, 2006 in Butcher et al., p. 30)

Engaged universities do not just simply use their expertise and resources for the benefit of the community, they understand that they themselves will be transformed through the process. The mutuality is more than problem-solving; it is an opportunity to build the capacity of both organizations and to evolve as learning organizations.

The framework of an *engaged university* provides a useful tool for understanding and enacting social justice at the institutional level. It allows individuals to question the assumptions that underlie their work within their institution and with partner institutions.

METHODOLOGICAL APPROACH

This chapter is a result of a decision we made, as faculty, to share our experiences developing this doctoral cohort. Over several years we accumulated knowledge about how the program worked, challenges, successes, and how we grew as faculty. We wanted to share these experiences as a way to help us make sense of them, but also to engage others in an open and honest evaluation of our program. Unlike most program evaluations, we did not want to highlight the strengths of our model, but rather use it as an opportunity to analyze and uncover where we had gone wrong and why.

To do so we began to tell each other "stories" of what was happening in our classrooms and with our students. The use of narratives and storytelling as a method of inquiry and learning is widely accepted (Clandinin, Murphy, Huber, and Orr, 2009; Connelly and Clandinin, 1990; Guajardo and Guajardo, 2010). We embraced the concept of narrative as a "mode of knowing" (Connelly and Clandinin, 1990, p. 45), rather than as a strict methodology. The process of telling and retelling our stories provided the opportunity to relive the experiences and draw meaning from the analysis. It also allowed us to develop a joint narrative of the experience and to identify collective learnings over the duration of the program.

We had many stories.

In order to help us communicate some of the threads that appeared in many of our stories, we identified critical incidents that encapsulated some of the larger learnings of our experiences. Critical incidents have long been used in teacher development (Angelides, 2002; Tripp, 1994) and developing reflective practice (Francis, 1997). According to Tripp (1994), critical incidents are "straightforward accounts of very commonplace events that occur in routine professional practice which are critical in the rather different sense that they are indicative of underlying trends, motives, and structures" (pp. 24–25). We wanted to uncover these underlying trends, motives, and structures, and so each of us identified a critical incident that allowed us to explore these issues.

While writing these critical incidents, we focused on the elements we found interesting, both positive and negative, of the incident. We also discussed other "possible" critical incidents and how they were not rich enough to allow for the in-depth exploration we wanted. Lastly, we explored, and pushed each other to explore, alternate interpretations of each incident. This final step truly gave us the opportunity to uncover our own assumptions and allowed us to write more freely about the incident. Through this process we developed the three critical incidents presented written by one of us in consultation with the other two. Each critical incident includes a detailed description followed by a reflection on the meaning of the incident and an attempt to uncover individual and faculty assumptions.

DEVELOPMENT OF DISTRICT-BASED PROGRAM

The leadership faculty conceived the District Cohort Initiative following a meeting between the then department chair, the director of the principal certification program, and the Provost. The Provost posed the questions: "What can we do to help the district? Do you have any ideas?" Further, the Provost explained that although there were some university linkages with the district,

they were narrow in focus, sporadic, and faculty specific. In other words, one or two faculty might provide a limited professional development activity or pursue the district's teachers to participate in research studies, but nothing that was long-term or systemic.

The district has long been targeted by the state education department, local media, and community organizers. Since the mid-1990s the district saw rapid superintendent turnover, budget deficits, school board politics, and declining student achievement. In 2002 the state moved to take over the district and replaced the district leadership with a team of state-appointed trustees. The district serves almost three thousand students of whom 92 percent are African American or Latino, 56 percent receive free or reduced lunch, and 21 percent are English Language Learners. Sixty-eight percent of high school seniors graduate, well above the rate at the beginning of the state takeover but below the state average. Of the three elementary schools, two are designated as "in good standing" and one is in the midst of "improvement." The middle school is in "corrective action" and the high school is designated as "persistently low achieving." In 2013 the state officially ended the takeover, and while most of the financial and management issues have been resolved, many are left wondering about how to address the academic issues that continue to plague the schools.

Because of its label as a perpetually underperforming district, the district is perceived as an unattractive university-community partnership site. The relatively small size of the district, with fewer teachers and students, allows it to be frequently overlooked or ignored as sites for research or professional development. Other local school districts with similar ethnic and racial characteristics offered much larger participant pools. In addition, there are other local districts that were practically "majority-minority," African American and Latino students, with a high percentage of low socioeconomic status families that were better resourced and do not have the stigma of being the lowest performing district in the region. Researchers seeking successful outcomes for their work seek high leverage sites.

When the questions of service to the district were posed to the faculty, they were received enthusiastically as a worthy challenge. Aligned to our social justice program strand, it seemed natural to brainstorm a service plan for the district. We began our inquiry with a discussion of what we thought the district might need in terms of leadership development. This was followed by a frank discussion of what we as a program do best. The alignments of these inquiries led to the creation modification of the district model. The model was presented to the Provost, who approved the offsite cohort. It is important to note that this district-based cohort was being developed *in addition* to our regular campus cohort.

The plan for the doctoral cohort was then shared with the district Superintendent who enthusiastically embraced the concept. The agreement with the district included a cohort of district leaders at the school and district levels, approval for district-based research, and space for class meetings. The district initiative was the first university-conceived effort to address the needs of a local distressed school district at a program level. It was only one of two local districts with majority African-American and Latino students and high poverty rates with which the leadership programs had formal partnerships.

We also developed an in-depth admissions process. The admissions process included the regular application, transcript review, letters of recommendation, a personal statement, and a sample of academic writing. We waived the GRE requirement. We added three other requirements that were organized during one day. The first was a group task in which the applicants were divided into two groups and had to engage in a team-building problem. Once each team resolved the problem, they then had to negotiate with the other group for the needed resources. This exercise allowed us to observe group dynamics, communication styles, and creative thinking. The second activity was an "in-time" writing exercise. Applicants were sent a leadership article in advance for them to study. Once on campus, and after the group activity, students were asked to respond to two of four questions (the last of which was to offer their own response) within a set time limit. We had access to a computer lab and so students worked on these to complete their essays. This exercise allowed us to assess students' writing and thinking skills, as well as how they responded to a high-pressure task. Lastly, each applicant was interviewed by a member of the faculty with the same interview protocol. This allowed us to speak with each student individually and get to know his/her interests and motivations for doctoral work. We developed rubrics for each of these exercises and used these and our observations to make admissions decisions.

Cohort members were recruited through two meetings at the district, one attended by the superintendent and one not. In these meetings the faculty presented the program plan and addressed general questions regarding doctoral-level work. The university also offered a tuition "discount" to members of the cohort. The district leadership invited specific administrators to apply.

The cohort consisted, initially, of seventeen established and emerging leaders (i.e., assistant superintendents, curriculum coordinators, assistant principals, deans) from the partner district and one neighboring district. All cohort members held at least one master's, and advanced certificate in leadership, and were state certified as school or district leaders. All but two of the original cohort members were African American. Of the remaining two cohort members, one was Latina/o (with English as her second language) and one was white. Thirteen members of the cohort were women. Years of experience in leadership positions ranged from three to fifteen. Over the course of the program we lost four students due to job mobility and personal demands.

The faculty was 50 percent white and 50 percent color (one African American and one Latina). Three of the faculty were women, one male. Years at the university ranged from two to twenty-seven. One of us had worked several years as a bilingual urban educator and another had spent almost two decades as a school and district leader in a first-tier suburban district.

FACULTY STORIES

Our experiences in implementing this district-based doctoral program partnership are divided into three "critical incidents." These stories relate the faculty experiences at three key junctures in the process of implementing our partnership that represent our "learning" during implementation. These incidents highlight when our assumptions or expectations were challenged in unexpected ways.

The first incident highlights the dual challenges of implementing a new curriculum without a common understanding of the outcomes. While the curriculum was modified as the faculty reflected on student learning, the lack of clarity on the final product, in this case the action research dissertation, continued to plague long-term planning. While the second focuses on cohort interaction and perceptions. This incident addresses how the faculty neglected to plan for intergroup interactive outcomes within the doctoral program. The final incident chronicles and explains the challenge of accessing district and school-based data. It highlights how unclear expectations regarding access to data, administrator turnover, and mistrust within the cohort precluded the students from conducting in-depth analyses of the district's data.

Critical Incident One: *Curriculum Responsiveness*

I looked over to the Smartboard in frustration. It was the third or fourth meeting and still no resolution on what to do with the qualitative research class. The four of us had been talking about this for a long time. Three things had me worried: (1) preparing them for an "action research dissertation," (2) my belief that students needed a solid grounding in qualitative research before focusing on action research, and (3) our lack of agreement on what an "action research dissertation" would look like. Add to that feedback that we were getting from our students that we were going "too fast" (i.e., our curriculum had them graduating in four years as compared to five in our university-based cohort), and we needed to make a decision soon. I had less than a semester to figure out what to do with the class.

I was pleased with the way we retooled our doctoral curriculum. After a year of planning, we came up with a focused, systems approach that we thought would meet our cohort's needs and ours. Thinking in terms of four full years of study, we came up with the following plan of study:

Essentially we took our existing courses and *repurposed* them specifically to the needs of our partner district.

I took a breath and tried again, "Our campus-based program takes the whole year to develop and implement a pilot study, right? During the first semester we look at foundations of qualitative research, elements of design, and developing data collection protocols. Then during the second semester they collect their data, analyze their data, and write it up. And we still seem to run short on time!"

"If we break this up into two independent semesters like we planned and like we did with the intro and quant course," I continued, "I'm not sure whether to focus the first semester on the foundations stuff broadly or just dive in to the action research stuff? I get how they come out of *Intro to Doc Studies* having identified an issue to research. I even get how I can use action research as a form of professional development in the professional growth class. But what are we trying to do here? Do we even know what we want them to do for the action research dissertations? I'm struggling with getting them ready for something that I'm not clear on. And if I skip over the foundations stuff, what are we saying about becoming critical researchers?"

A colleague nodded. "And you know they've been telling me that they're having a hard time keeping up with everything we've been throwing at them. So we're getting the breadth, but losing the depth."

Table 31.1.   Original Program Plan

	Summer	Fall	Winter	Spring
Year 1 *System-wide Assessment/ Development of Priorities (2009–2010)*	Retreat: Vision Building	Intro to Doctoral Studies: Leadership for Learning	Reflective Administrator	Quantitative Inquiry: Data Collection and Analysis
Year 2 *Finding Leverage: Organizational Learning to Improve Student Learning (2010–2011)*	Curriculum Management & Children of Color	Intro to Doctoral Studies: Student Learning	Naturalistic Inquiry in School Leadership I	Facilitating Professional Growth
Year 3 *Finding Leverage: Working More Effectively with the Community (2011–2012)*	Community Leadership	Quantitative Inquiry: Data Collection and Analysis	Issues in Educational Policy	Naturalistic Inquiry in School Leadership II
Year 4 *Leading Change (2012– 2013)*	Dissertation Advising: Action Research	Dissertation Advising: Action Research		Dissertation Advising: Action Research

"Yes and we haven't been keeping up with our process of doctoral exams at the end of each course," added another colleague. "We are a year and a half into this and I still don't have a good sense of their strengths and weaknesses. That's becoming a problem for us."

"So, ah, we are back to the same place. What do we do?" I said.

We all looked at the plan of study that was projected on the Smartboard and remained silent.

Finally, one of us said, "What if we switch the second half of the qualitative class and the PD class this summer?"

"You mean, they will take the yearlong sequence in spring and summer?" I asked.

"Yeees," was the tentative response.

"So what's the relationship between the policy course and the PD course?" someone asked, "There isn't one, right?"

"Maybe not," I said, "but if we switched the policy and the quant class and the way you've been thinking about doing that course with a focus on a gap analysis, I can use the PD class to have them use action research to work with teachers on those gaps."

"And that could actually get them doing some sort of preliminary work on their dissertations in terms of conducting action research," said another.

"Right, and they would still come into that with the full qual class and having had experience understanding data collection and analysis, which you've been worried about," another commented.

"Not to mention this gives us some time to figure out how we want the action research dissertation to go and how we want to advise them," I said.

We all nodded in agreement and set to work on reorganizing and aligning the curriculum in the remaining the courses.

Reflection

From the beginning we knew that working with our partner district would be challenging. Historically, the district had experienced high turnover rates at the superintendent level and among many of the principals. Community relations had deteriorated over time, and there was a deeply entrenched culture that maintained the status quo. Many had tried to impose school reform and many had failed.

To try to address these leadership issues and build district capacity, our thinking was twofold:

- *Action Research*: If all the students engaged in action research dissertations, then we would have instructional/leadership change occurring at different levels of the organization. This, we hoped, would lead to district improvement.
- *System-Wide Approach*: We developed each year "thematically" to address one element of systemic improvement. In the first year the focus was on developing a set of priorities. Year Two focused on internal structures and processes and Year Three focused on external ones. Year Four was the development of the action research project and dissertation. By seeing the doctoral curriculum as one way to address and explore the district, we believed that we could help doctoral students develop a systems lens as both emerging researchers and leaders.

The courses were the same as those offered in our campus-based program, but they were reorganized (rather than using the year-long approach as we did on campus, we used the more traditional semester approach that allowed us flexibility as to when the courses were offered and their content) and refocused.

As part of our ongoing discussions, it became clear midway through year one that our students were struggling with the pace and demands of the courses. In our regular yearlong approach, students explore issues in depth and have a longer timeframe for acquiring the necessary skills. The semester-long courses were proving to be "too fast." Also, we were coming to the realization that many of our students, based on their past educational experiences, did not have strong academic skills or high levels of confidence in their own abilities. We had students in other cohorts who had the same academic gaps in their preparation, but never so many in one cohort. Our program support structures were being taxed to their limits. It also became clear that faculty were struggling with the implications of both modifying their expectations (from a yearly to a semester perspective) and the action research dissertation. We had been engaging in discussions around action research, understanding the participative research paradigm, and questioning the role of the advisor/chair in the process, yet could not come to agreement on

Table 30.2.   Revised Program Plan

	Summer	Fall	Winter	Spring
Year 1 System-wide Assessment/ Development of Priorities (2009–2010)	Retreat: Vision Building	Intro to Doc Studies: Leadership for Learning	Reflective Administrator	Quantitative Inquiry: Data Collection and Analysis
Year 2 Finding Leverage: Organizational Learning to Improve Student Learning (2010–2011)	Curriculum Management & Children of Color	Intro to Doc Studies: Student Learning	Naturalistic Inquiry in School Leadership I	Naturalistic Inquiry in School Leadership II
Year 3 Finding Leverage: Working More Effectively with the Community (2011–2012)		Issues in Educational Policy)	Quantitative Inquiry: Data-Driven Decision-Making	Professional Growth
Year 4 Constructing Change (2012–2013)	Dissertation Advising/ Action Research	Dissertation Advising	Dissertation Advising	Dissertation Advising

what a satisfactory product (aka dissertation) would be. This caused tension within the faculty, which led to indecision.

To a large degree these conversations came to a head early in the second year when we were forced to think about not just the qualitative course but how to prepare them for action research. As a result, our final curriculum ended up looking more like this:

Not only did we "move" courses around in years two and three, but we also ended up with an additional dissertation advising course.

In the process of revision we gained some things and we lost others. One loss was that our yearly "themes" were diluted over time. We did not refer to them in our planning or in the courses. As a result we deleted the "community relations" course in Year Three. This happened because our students were exhausted from the heavy course load in Year Two. It did, however, allow us to increase the dissertation advising in Year Four in order to provide focused, small-group work on the action research projects. Our focus throughout was on student learning and being responsive to what we were learning about this new curriculum over time.

It is also important to note that while all but one of the faculty were involved in the design of this district-based doctoral program, it became difficult to change *our* pedagogy. While my concerns were grounded in the needs of our students, I must also confess that reconceptualizing my yearlong course into two separate semesters over two years proved daunting. Innovation requires extended support and clarity. I needed more support and clarity from my colleagues, and when this did not

happen, I simply relied on my past practice and pushed back on our "innovation." It became clear that we were not as skilled as we thought in having extended conversations about our practice. As a result, we ignored an opportunity to strengthen our learning community.

Lastly, our curriculum modifications, in the name of responsiveness, allowed us to continue to avoid the harder discussion regarding research expectations and processes. We believed that an action research dissertation would help reform "bubble up" across the district, but we did not have the internal capacity to advise action research. Nor were we able to foresee the difficulties that some students would face implementing an action research project either because of their roles in the district or because they did not develop the necessary skills or dispositions. It was difficult for us to come to this realization and have an extended conversation about other options. In the end, only a small number of students implemented an action research project, and our hopes for school and district improvement were lost.

Critical Incident Two: *Managing Student and Faculty Perceptions*

I was the instructor for the summer elective doctoral course titled Curriculum Management. Two sections of the course were offered on two different evening, Mondays and Tuesdays. The Monday course was designed for the partner cohort and the Tuesday course for the on-campus cohort. Courses were designated by cohort so that the district-based cohort could receive the 25 percent discount for off-site programs. The district-based section was originally scheduled at the local middle school, but had to be relocated to campus because of renovations to the middle school building. This schedule change brought the cohort to campus for the first time. During the first class meeting, several students from both classes indicated preferences for specific days, citing professional development activities, family commitments, etc. By accommodating these request the resulting class rosters indicated a mixture of district-based and on-campus students. The Monday course had a total of thirteen students, seven from the partner district and six from the on-campus cohort. The Tuesday class had a total of ten students, six from the district cohort and four from the on-campus cohort. A large portion of the class sessions was devoted to group presentations and focused class discussions.

Details of the Incident

It was during the third of our six sessions when a group was reporting on an article by Jean Anyon, *Social Class and the Hidden Curriculum of Work*. Following the group's presentation of the major "take aways" from the reading, a full class discussion ensued focusing in on the relevance of Anyon's findings. Of the five or six students from both cohorts to comment, all agreed that socioeconomic status, race, and gender remained significant factors for educational attainment.

One of the district-based students then stated that she felt their cohort program had many of the same attributes described in the reading as a hidden curriculum. She cited that the doctoral curriculum experiences for the district-based cohort were different for the on-campus cohort. She used the admission criteria as an example, indicating that her cohort did not have to take the GRE exam required of on-site candidates. I highlighted, I am sure somewhat defensively, the commonalities of the curricula taught and the consistency of full-time faculty teaching all the doctoral course offerings. Following my defense of the equality of the doctoral experience for both cohorts, another district-based cohort member said she felt the way the courses were rearranged for them was an indication that faculty felt that the ability of the cohort as a group was inferior and therefore the material had to be "chunked," making it easier for the members to comprehend.

This perception of faculty attitudes of the cohort's insecurity was reinforced by another district-based member who stated that one professor strongly suggested that the class take University of Chicago's Little Red School writing program courses geared toward the needs of writers who are experts in scholarly, research, and professional fields. A university-based cohort member jotted down the program, saying he had the same professor who had not made this suggestion to his class.

Another district-based cohort member indicated that the narrowness of perspectives in their cohort was a disadvantage. She indicated that the on-campus cohort offered members a greater diversity of experiences. Another student indicated that the only time he felt truly a part of the on-site doctoral program was at full doctoral events. One on-campus cohort member nodded, citing the annual potluck event at a faculty member's home and the end-of-year celebration honoring doctoral graduates as events that he termed "equalizers" between the two cohorts. The conversation ended with general agreement that combining the cohorts was positive for both cohorts.

Reflections

This incident was very disturbing to me on several levels despite only a few students were contributors to the conversation. It caused me to reflect on my own motives and assumptions regarding the development of the cohort, and secondly it forced me and then enabled me to view the doctoral cohort members in a different way. I have been a full-time faculty member of the Educational Leadership department for over ten years. As an African American and the only male in our doctoral program, the development of a doctoral cohort based in a historically troubled school district to appealed to my equity lens. Introducing and navigating the group of minority African-American men and women through our program with my thoughtful and equally committed colleagues was a worthy endeavor that gave evidence of our social justice mission.

What the incident demonstrated for me was that in the doctoral setting, although I did not view the cohort members as "damaged," they viewed themselves as inferior as individuals and as a group when compared to the on-site prevalently white cohort. The curriculum in leadership programs places a heavy emphasis on race and poverty variables related to student success. Our cohort participants as products of primarily minority schools in suburban and urban areas viewed themselves as denied resources such as advanced placement courses and college placement seminars. This was particularly true in the highly racialized geographic area of the school district where the cohort was based.

This perception of *inferiority* arose in part from our failure to explain our rationales for the structural changes in the program. I also wonder if this is an example of "internalized oppression" or buying in to a hegemonic system. For example, *they* believe in the validity (symbolic of otherwise) of the GRE as a measure of "intelligence" in spite of research that clearly states that it does not. Perhaps they accept these racial constructs and are unable to be critical of their own role in them.

In addition, we failed to predict how the doctoral faculty were viewed by this cohort. The cohort interaction with this cohort was very different from our interaction with our onsite cohort. From the very beginning of the process the entire doctoral faculty met with the cohort as a group. This started with the first introductory meeting and proceeded through the application process. For the onsite cohort, students meet individually with the doctoral director and were formally introduced to faculty as they proceeded from course to course through the program. The way faculty viewed the cohort as a group and the way the cohort viewed faculty as a cohesive group created cohort group anxiety. The cohort's feelings that faculty viewed them as inferior was reinforced by the syllabi focus on failing school literature and by their work in a district identified as failing. The anxiety produced made the cohort hypersensitive to differences between the two cohorts and to interpretations of comments from faculty. This was an unanticipated outcome of bringing together a group that already had established group norms in their work setting with a united faculty with a targeted objective. We did not anticipate their internal dynamics and the overall lack of trust (in themselves or their cohort). Because of that we didn't really create a "safe space" for them (even though that was the purpose of the initial orientation). This could contribute to how they "externalized" their feelings and/or "blamed" us for their *perception* of inferiority

The faculty failed to take into account the intragroup versus the intergroup relationship of the two cohorts. The implications from the mostly minority cohort and the majority white cohort was revealed by statements made during the critical incident. There is a notable

relationship between intergroup anxiety and prejudice. The cohort attributed prejudicial attitudes to the faculty and had negative stereotypes of themselves as scholars compared to the on-site cohort. The vastly different course schedules and sites reinforced the cohort's feelings of isolation.

A larger question for us as faculty and program designers is did we, in our enthusiasm to support a district and the district's administrators, fail to understand the impact of race on the perceptions of our cohorts. Did we design a doctoral program within a racialized institution using racialized structure? Some might suggest we fell prey to "epistemological racism." Epistemological racism means that our current range of research epistemologies—positivism to postmodernism/poststructuralism—arise out of the social history and culture of the dominant race, that these epistemologies logically reflect and reinforce that social history and that racial group (while excluding the epistemologies of other races/cultures), and that this has negative results for people of color in general and scholars of color in particular. In other words, our "logics of inquiry" (Stanfield, 1993a) are the social products and practices of the social, historical experiences of whites, and, therefore, these products and practices carry forward the social history of that group and exclude the epistemologies of other social groups. Perhaps we just moved the structural program, pieces around without reconceptualizing the program.

The incident also brought up the specter of the affirmative action debate for our students. The change in the admission standards for the district-based cohort appeared to be troubling to the students. Although the faculty felt strongly that we had developed a more rigorous and realistic admissions protocol, we were unaware of the symbolism of the GREs and the assumptions they held that the GREs were a determining factor for program acceptance. They falsely assumed that those onsite cohort members excelled on the exam and thus were more prepared for doctoral work. They viewed their acceptance as akin to the affirmative action acceptances. Aligned to the notion of affirmative action for the cohort member entered the concerns about curriculum "dumbing down," and inherent feelings of whiteness as a symbol of academic superiority.

Given the feedback that we received from our district cohort, it is clear that we did not think carefully enough about how the cohort perceived itself (intragroup dynamics), how the two cohorts perceived each other (intergroup dynamics), or how differences in the curriculum would be perceived. We believed that the district-based cohort was *more* rigorous, from the admissions process (that included group interviews and an in-time writing exercise) to program completion in four years. Our inability to predict and manage these varying perceptions undermined the learning and confidence of some of our cohort members.

Critical Incident Three: *Unexpected Barriers*

As mentioned earlier, we imagined a program tailored to the needs of the district with the goals of systemic improvement. A prerequisite to building a tailored program is empirical knowledge about the district, most often in the form of data. In partnering with the district, we assumed that there would be a free flow of data—demographic, attendance, and achievement—available for students and faculty to review so as to be fully informed of the strengths of and challenges facing the district. With agreements, however, concerning data being left to informal discussions or word-of-mouth agreements, rather than delineated stipulations of a formal contract, the acquisition and use of data become a source of contention. Leadership turnover, mistrust, and communication become key themes around which this critical incident involving data unfolds. It is also important to note that the planning and organization of the course sequence occurred before I joined the program. Therefore, I learned from the students about the issues in the first quantitative course from the cohort members.

Stage 1: Access with Push-Back

A key series of courses in the doctoral curriculum is the Quantitative Inquiry sequence. This course teaches students to use data to develop a culture of high standards and equity in learning organizations and monitor student achievement and learning. Students in this class build a student database; use data to describe institutional processes, practices, and progress; and examine institutional belief systems, underlying assumptions, and behaviors. In November 2009, the adjunct instructor teaching the course and the assistant superintendent in the partner district met with the district superintendent to discuss what types of data might be available for the course.

The superintendent, a member of the doctoral cohort, "gave" the instructor access to the district's achievement, demographics, and attendance data. The director of data, also a member of the cohort, downloaded the data from the district's Data Warehouse system and gave the data to the instructor in Excel. The data would be used to conduct an equity analysis across the district as a whole and use data to pinpoint the major issues and challenges in terms of schools, grades, and subgroups. Additionally, the instructor together with the superintendent decided to administer a survey across the district to teachers. This teacher survey was modified from the work of Silins, Mulford, and Zarins (2002) on organizational learning and school change. Also included are four sets of questions from a teacher sense of efficacy scale. As this part of the story illustrates in the beginning of the partnership, the district provided open access to its data with the goal of driving systemic reform.

Members of the cohort conducted the equity analysis, created preliminary action plans, but did not, as had been planned, present them to the individual schools. Over the course of the semester, one of the principals learned about the use of school-level data by cohort members and voiced concerns over data security, especially the confidentiality of student and teacher level data. This principal did not like that the cohort members had access to her school's data—neither the achievement data nor the survey results. These issues of confidentiality changed the nature of the final project. As a result, the instructor decided that students would no longer present their action plans to the individual schools, thereby weakening the link between what cohort members were doing in the Hofstra courses and what they were doing in the district. Additionally, the principal's push-back raised questions about limits and dangers of sharing data and revealed that the necessary conditions for sharing data did not exist. It is interesting to note that just one of the seven principals complained, yet the one voice was a powerful deterrent to sharing the results of the students' data analyses. It also foreshadowed future issues around data access and usage.

Stage 2: A Data-Based Plan to Drive Instructional Change

The second half of the course began in winter 2012 taught by me, a new, full-time faculty. Given that time had lapsed between the first and second parts of the course, I discussed with my colleagues various possibilities for the course content. From these exchanges we decided to build an integrated two-course sequence that would use data to increase organizational learning, and, in turn, improve educational outcomes. In my class, students would focus on conducting analyses by school, grade, and teacher to identify areas in which teachers needed professional growth and development. Cohort members would use achievement and demographic data as well as conduct in-depth item level analyses of state tests and other formative assessments. The hope being that a shift would take place from teachers focusing on what they are teaching to what students actually are learning. The results of these analyses would be used in the following course, Professional Growth, which was referenced earlier in the first critical incident. In this course, the cohort would learn about the role of action research in teacher professional growth. Then, for their action research dissertation, cohort members would engage a group of teachers in an analysis of the data, develop a plan for changing their practice, and implement it.

Excited about this plan, I asked the director of data about the accessibility of this data. Specifically, I wanted the students' actual test answers, not just the final scores, so that an item analysis could be conducted. The director of data invited me to come to her office and look through the data with her. Together we found and downloaded the appropriate data. The director of data shared that she was glad that the class was focusing on this work because it was something that she had been struggling to implement across the schools in the district. She felt that taking the class would teach her how to do item-level analyses and give her more tools with which to work with principals.

Stage 3: Access Denied

After the above-mentioned data meeting with the director of data, I received a letter from the assistant superintendent in the district, also a student in the cohort, saying that district data could not be used and that it was inappropriate for me to be working independently with the director of data without having submitted a formal data request. This development surprised me as I was under the impression that access to the data had already

been granted. It should also be noted that the superintendent had dropped out of the program by this point and that tension began to emerge within the district leadership team.

I wrote a formal letter of request for data to the superintendent and assistant superintendent in which I explained how the data would be used. An excerpt from my letter follows:

> I would like to formally request the use of district data for the quantitative inquiry course to be offered to the district-based doctoral cohort during the January Session. Following an inquiry model, this course will use data to drive school improvement. Students in the course will learn how to "drill down" the data to individual testing items. Uncovering these insights will allow students to build professional development plans to drive improvement, which will be the focus Professional Growth to be taught in Spring 2012.

The district superintendent and assistant superintendent denied me access to the data.

The assistant superintendent, who was also a member of the cohort, shared that she did not trust her cohort peers to keep the data confidential. She felt that it was too political to share the data. Interestingly, unlike with the first half of the quantitative inquiry sequence, in which the superintendent managed data, now all interactions around data involved the assistant superintendent. As a result of this decision by the district official, the students conducted their data analyses using data from another, anonymous district. This also meant that the subsequent course, professional growth, would no longer be viable as the data needed to identify the root problem was unavailable. This decision by the district to withhold data not only prevented rigorous data analyses from being performed on their behalf, but also it prevented members of the doctoral cohort from finding key issues within the district on which to focus their dissertation research.

Reflections

The turnover by key administrators, mistrust, and unclear communication regarding the availability of data greatly impacted the cohort experience. The loss of the superintendent as a member of the cohort drastically changed our ability to work with and in the district. Rather than fostering an open and transparent partnership, it created a closed one. Further, the transition from the superintendent to the assistant superintendent being the key point person on data issues resulted in different norms. For example an unwritten agreement to share data by the superintendent was not supported by the assistant superintendent. Though here, it should be noted that we do not know exactly who blocked the accessibility to data. It is important to also remember that personnel change occurred within the program as well. The district community knew the original instructor as he was a local assistant superintendent and was active in local professional development organizations. In contrast, the new professor had no prior ties to the district and community except for a previous semester of teaching. These personnel changes—on both sides—made it challenging to establish a lasting, strong, and trusting relationship around which the exchange of data could occur.

The political context in which the district functions exacerbated mistrust. It was simultaneously being scrutinized by the state for consistent low performance as well as implementing a new state-wide teacher evaluation system. It is not surprising then that the assistant superintendent shared that during this time of increased data scrutiny, she feared that the school board would have issues with the sharing of school-level data, especially if the data was linked to individual teachers.

The assistant superintendent's perceptions regarding her cohort peers is also important. The assistant superintendent felt that she could not trust them to keep the data and the information gleaned from the data confidential. This issue raised an important question about district doctoral cohorts, namely: How does one ensure confidentiality within the cohort, especially when the cohort consists of individuals spanning numerous positions including teachers, guidance counselors, principals, and superintendents? Further, is confidentiality necessarily beneficial when the results of the data could be instrumental to driving district and school reform?

Better communication would have improved some of these relationships. I could have set up a meeting with the central office administrators instead of assuming access. A conversation could have been set up with the class regarding confidentiality of data in which the assistant superintendent shared her concerns. Further, the professors could have done a better job of conveying

their vision of the final project and the need for data from the start. Specifically, open access to data could have been a stipulation of the original agreement with the district. It could have been written into the formal agreement with the district. Given the important role that data play in understanding a district, its limited access, especially in a struggling district was counterproductive and ultimately stymied progress.

DISCUSSION

The first critical incident tells the story of structures and support—or the lack thereof. Specifically clear curricular structures and supports were missing from both the students' and faculty's experiences. Referring to the later group, faculty's indecision about the type of action research to be enacted by the students and the scope of the final product made it very difficult for the individual program faculty to plan their courses. This experience is akin to flying a plane while building it. In an effort to be "responsive," the faculty created more uncertainty. As a result not only were faculty frustrated and left feeling unsupported, but students were confused about what was expected. Ultimately, it was hard to implement the proposed program as all those involved lost the clarity around program scope and sequence.

The second critical incident highlights themes of poor communication and limited foresight. The off-site cohort's perception that they were "inferior" to the on-site cohort as illustrated by admissions standards and the coursework was troublesome. Given that the two cohorts co-existed—one predominantly white and the other predominantly African-American—faculty should have realized that issues of race and identity would emerge. Rather than allowing the cohorts to function as two separate groups from the beginning, steps should have been taken to facilitate inter-cohort dialogue and learning. Further, the program's vision for each cohort should have been clearly articulated to ensure that all students understood the rigor embedded in the overall cohort structures. Such actions would have encouraged transparency, fostered understanding, and also challenged students' own perceptions and biases about these very structures.

The third critical incident surfaced issues of planning and mistrust at the heart of the relationship between the district and the program. The district's decision to grant access to data followed by its decision to rescind that access dramatically impacted the partnership, richness of the students' learning experiences, and the ability to drive systemic reform. Open access to district data became a vehicle for the exercise of power that clearly undermined the learning of the cohort. Unbeknownst to us, expectations regarding the type, access, and use of data needed to be formally outlined in a memo of understanding between our university and the district. However, even if stipulations around data had existed, a culture of trust also needed to be present in order for candid conversations around data to occur. Unfortunately mistrust occurred on numerous levels: district-level officials did not trust members of the cohort to keep the data confidential, and at the same time, principals expressed concerns about their schools' data being scrutinized by cohort members. Rather than seeing the sharing of data as a means to understanding, growth, and development, access to data became a threat, and in the end did not occur.

Planning and Structures

Planning, vision and commitment, and missed opportunities are themes that emerge across these three critical incidents. Each incident highlighted how additional "pre-partnership" planning would have improved the experiences of both students and faculty. A more detailed plan of the study with a clear understanding of the final outcome for the cohort would have significantly improved the scope and sequence of coursework. It would have given program faculty enough time to fully re-imagine their courses, and it would have provided students with a firmer understanding of the program's expectations. Additional planning around cohort inter- and intra-personal dynamics would have built stronger and more transparent understands across cohort groups. This planning, for example, could have involved writing and sharing the program's faculty's vision for each cohort prior to the start of the school year. It also could have built in time for cohorts to both learn from and network with each other. Lastly, pre-planning around data would have greatly enhanced access to it. As mentioned earlier, if stipulations had been built into the original MOU regarding data, its usage would be an expected and a fully integrated aspect of the cohort experience.

Vision and Commitment

All of these incidents reveal confusion or lack of knowledge of stakeholders' vision for the cohort—both the faculty's and the districts. Without a universally shared vision, participants commitment or buy-in to the partnership was weak and in some cases nonexistent. Critical incident one and two reveal how students did not have fully integrated understandings of the faculty's vision for their learning. As critical incident one showed students did not know what their final deliverable would be. This resulted in students not understanding what they were working toward. Similarly, in critical incident two students did not have a clear grasp of the mission and goals of the cohort—a situation that made them wonder if they were inferior to other cohorts in the program. In critical incident three, the district chose not to give the cohort access to data—a necessary ingredient to driving school improvement. This reveals a lack of commitment to the learning of cohort members themselves and to the vision of driving systemic reform in the district. As these examples illustrate, all of the stakeholders did not fully integrate and own the vision for the partnership.

Missed Opportunities

The incidents reveal areas of missed opportunities. In critical incident one there was the potential to build a new action research focused doctoral cohort. However, lack of agreement about the type of action research to be used precluded this from happening. Similarly, as described in critical incident two, potential existed for an exchange of ideas and networking to take place across cohorts. This cross-pollination would have allowed each group to be challenged and grow in new ways. However, a limited structure for this type of sharing existed. Lastly, as critical incident three showed, there was potential for cohort members to manage and analyze district data; however, district politics prevented such an analysis. While good intentions were at the core of this relationship, various factors made its implementation challenging and ultimately left both faculty and students frustrated.

Implications for "Engaged" Program Faculty

The initial outreach to the district reflected the faculty's lack of experience in developing a true community partnership. In the deliberations leading up to the beginning of the doctoral program, faculty met with district personnel to outline the plan of study but did not include the district in decisions regarding program goals or individual outcomes. From the faculty perspective, the expertise and resources lay in the university. This approach, and the assumptions embedded in it, undermined that "partnership" from the beginning.

Through collective reflection, however, both the faculty and program developed in unexpected ways. The program curriculum has been redesigned again, and faculty are in agreement that alternate dissertation models must be fully explored. Beyond these structural changes, the faculty are addressing assumptions about the role of districts in the learning and research process. As faculty committed to social justice, the need to develop as an engaged *program*, not just university, and be aware of the need to continue our transformation and district transformation is at the forefront of our work.

CONCLUSION

Our experiences contribute to the ongoing discussions of district-university partnerships in several ways. First, it addresses the delicate relationship between universities and communities (as represented by the school district). These relationships while forged out of common goals are precarious to navigate over time. The exploration of these relationships must continue. Second, by offering a faculty perspective, this chapter provides insight into program and faculty-level experiences in the development and implementation of a district-based program. In addition, the use of reflection and storytelling allows for a more in-depth exploration of these experiences. Third, the district in this chapter reflects a recent demographic trend in which suburban areas are confronting many of the same issues as large, urban districts. This "story," therefore, pushes our understanding and definitions of urban schools/districts. Fourth, this chapter addresses a little studied effort: district-based programs at the doctoral level. Many district-based leadership programs focus on aspiring leadership. This program focused on existing leadership structures and developing district-based dissertation research. Fifth, this chapter highlights the need for ongoing faculty and program development as an important element of any district-university partnership. By

positioning faculty as learners, it is possible that future partnerships may be more equitable and collaborative.

Of equal importance is the need for faculty, university administrators, and community/school leaders to engage in discussions of the role of higher education in "improving, in a very intentional way, the human condition" (Goldring and Sim, 2005, p. 223). The days in which universities, particularly in urban contexts, could remain apart from local communities are over. More and more, in an era of increasing accountability throughout the K–20 pipeline, universities must actively engage with local communities. Maurasse (2001) also emphasizes that increasing the interdependency between institutions of higher education and communities, partnerships can only improve colleges and universities" (p. 138). Schools of education and education faculty are perfectly positioned to convene these disparate groups and create opportunities for school and university improvement. Faculty, however, must be highly skilled and reflective in order to "embrace significant changes in our curricula, teaching practices, reward system, and governance process and, most importantly, in our institutional practices, values, and beliefs" (Astin and Astin, 2000, p. 4). The critical incidents highlighted here are focused on classroom experiences, but there is significant overlap with assumptions, structures, and processes that emerge in any relationship between universities and communities. This chapter is one attempt to help faculty prepare as they begin similar work and develop true community collaborations.

REFERENCES

Angelides, P. (2001). The development of an efficient technique for collecting and analyzing qualitative data: The analysis of critical incidents. *International Journal of Qualitative Studies in Education, 14*(3), 429–442.

Astin, A. W. and Astin, H. S. (2000). *Leadership reconsidered: Engaging higher education in social change.* Battle Creek, MI: W. K. Kellogg Foundation.

Barnett, M., Anderson, J., Houle, M., Higginbotham, T., and Gatling, A. (2010). The Process of Trust Building Between University Researchers and Urban School Personnel. *Urban Education, 45*(5), 630–660.

Bernardo, M. A. C., Butcher, J., and Howard, P. Conceptualizing University Community Engagement Leadership: Weaving Theory and Story.

Bringle, R. G. and Hatcher, J. A. (2002). Campus community partnerships: The terms of engagement. *Journal of Social Issues, 58*(3), 503–516.

Brown, R. E., Reed, C. S., Bates, L. V., Knaggs, D., Casey, K. M., and Barnes, J. V. (2007). The transformative engagement process: Foundations and supports for university-community partnerships. *Journal of Higher Education Outreach and Engagement, 11*(1), 9–23.

Butcher, J., Bezzina, M., and Moran, W. (2011). Transformational partnerships: A new agenda for higher education. *Innovative Higher Education, 36*(1), 29–40.

Clandinin, D. J., Murphy, M. S., Huber, J., and Orr, A. M. (2009). Negotiating narrative inquiries: Living in a tension-filled midst. *The Journal of Educational Research, 103*(2), 81–90.

Coburn, C. E., Bae, S., and Turner, E. O. (2008). Authority, Status, and the Dynamics of Insider–Outsider Partnerships at the District Level. *Peabody Journal of Education, 83*(3), 364–399.

Connelly, F. M. and Clandinin, D. J. (1990). Stories of experience and narrative inquiry. *Educational researcher, 19*(5), 2–14.

Driscoll, A., Holland, B., Gelmon, S., and Kerrigan, S. (1996). An assessment model for service learning: Comprehensive case studies of impact on faculty, students, community, and institution. *Michigan Journal of Community Service Learning, 3*, 66–71.

Evans, A. and Chun, E. B. (2007). *Are the walls really down?: Behavioral and organizational barriers to faculty and staff diversity.* ASHE Higher Education report, *33*(1). San Francisco: Jossey-Bass.

Ferguson, R. F. (2002). What Doesn't Meet the Eye: Understanding and Addressing Racial Disparities in High-Achieving Suburban Schools.

Francis, D. (1997). Critical incident analysis: a strategy for developing reflective practice. *Teachers and Teaching: theory and practice, 3*(2), 169–188.

Goldring, E. and Sims, P. (2005). Modeling creative and courageous school leadership through district-community-university partnerships. *Educational Policy, 19*(1), 223–249.

Guajardo, F. and Guajardo, M.A. (2010). Cultivating stories of change. In Ruder, K., Nienow, D., Guajardo, F., Guajardo, M., and Fields, C. (Eds.), *Weaving Strong Communities: The Collective Leadership Storybook* (pp. 85–103). Battle Creek, MI: W.K. Kellogg Foundation and Seattle, WA: Center for Ethical Leadership.

Hanlon, B. (2008). Fixing inner-ring suburbs in the USA: A policy retrospective. *International Journal of Neighbourhood Renewal, 1*(3), 1–30.

Hanlon, B. (2009). A typology of inner-ring suburbs: Class, race, and ethnicity in US suburbia. *City and Community, 8*(3), 221–246.

Hanlon, B., Vicino, T., and Short, J. R. (2006). The new metropolitan reality in the US: Rethinking the traditional model. *Urban Studies, 43*(12), 2129–2143.

Hendry, P. M. (2009). Narrative as inquiry. *The Journal of Educational Research, 103*(2), 72–80.

Holland, B. A. (2001). *Characteristics of engaged institutions and sustainable partnerships, and effective strategies for change.* Indianapolis: Office of University Partnerships, HUD, at Indiana University Purdue University at Indianapolis.

Jacoby, B. (2003). *Building partnerships for service-learning.* San Francisco: Jossey-Bass.

Jargowsky, P. (2003). Stunning progress, hidden problems. Washington: Brookings institution.

Kim, J. H. and Latta, M. M. (2009). Narrative inquiry: Seeking relations as modes of interactions. *The Journal of Educational Research, 103*(2), 69–71.

Latta, M. M. and Kim, J. H. (2009). Narrative inquiry invites professional development: Educators claim the creative space of praxis. *The Journal of Educational Research, 103*(2), 137–148.

Maurrasse, D. J. (2001). *Beyond the campus: How colleges and universities form partnerships with their communities.* New York: Routledge.

Maurrasse, D. J. (2002). Higher education/community partnerships: Assessing progress in the field. *Nonprofit and Voluntary Sector Quarterly, 31*(1), 131–139.

Miller, P. M. and Hafner, M. M. (2008). Moving Toward Dialogical Collaboration: A Critical Examination of a University—School—Community Partnership. *Educational Administration Quarterly, 44*(1), 66–110.

Orfield, M. and Luce, T. F. (2013). America's racially diverse suburbs: Opportunities and challenges. *Housing Policy Debate, 23*(2), 395–430.

Paletta, A., Candal, C. S., and Vidoni, D. (2009). Networking for the Turnaround of a School District The Boston University—Chelsea Partnership. *Education and Urban Society, 41*(4), 469–488.

Perkins, D. D., Crim, B., Silberman, P., and Brown, B. (2001). Community development as a response to community-level adversity: Ecological theory and research and strength-based policy. *American Psychological Association*, pp. 1–14.

Sable, J., Plotts, C., and Mitchell, L. (2010). Characteristics of the 100 Largest Public Elementary and Secondary School Districts in the United States: 2008–09 (NCES 2011-301). U.S. Department of Education, National Center for Education Statistics. Washington, DC: U.S. Government Printing Office.

Sanzo, K. L., Myran, S., and Clayton, J. K. (2011). Building bridges between knowledge and practice: A university-school district leadership preparation program partnership. *Journal of Educational Administration, 49*(3), 292–312.

Tripp, D. (1994). Teachers' lives, critical incidents, and professional practice. *Qualitative Studies in Education, 7*(1), 65–76.

Ward, K. (2003). Faculty service roles and the scholarship of engagement. *ASHE-ERIC Higher Education Report. Jossey-Bass Higher and Adult Education Series.* San Francisco: Jossey-Bass.

Ziebarth, T. (2002). State Takeovers and Reconstitutions. Policy Brief. Education Commission of the States. Denver, CO.

CRITICAL FOUNDATIONS IN URBAN EDUCATIONAL LEADERSHIP

In order to meet the educational needs of our youth, school leaders require critical skills and knowledge to respond to the challenges facing our nation's schools. Section 9 identifies the problems school leaders encounter in urban communities as well as the issues with school leadership preparation programs.

College readiness requires more than academic preparedness. Researchers recognize the importance of social support from parents and their community members on student achievement. Urban schools are at a distinct disadvantage as they serve a high population of students who have low social capital. In chapter 32, "College Readiness and Urban Schools: Challenges and Opportunities" by Lindsay R. Granger and Pedro A. Noguera, the authors introduce a theoretical framework that will support urban school leaders in their quest to create higher education opportunities for their urban students.

Through the experience of one school leader preparation program, chapter 33, "Change Agency in Our Own Backyards: Meeting the Challenges of Next-Generation Programs in School Leader Preparation," authors Steve Tozer, Paul Zavitkovsky, Sam Whalen, and Peter Martinez shed light on the tensions that continue to persist, for over a decade, and as a result, stifle the educational potential of our nation's children. These tensions not only stem from the lack of cultural alignment within and between institutions (i.e., university and school district), but moreover, within the nation's beliefs and values about education. The collaborative efforts of our institutions have created a complex foundation for principal preparation and new challenges. In order to begin exploring solutions for our preparation programs nationwide, we must begin confronting these issues in our own backyards. Lastly, Eric J. Cooper discusses the historical context of social, economic, and educational disparities for students of color and the hope in reclaiming these communities. Cooper's chapter 34, "Our Fierce Urgency of Now: Obstacles and Solutions for Improving the Promise of America," dispels the "myths" of schooling in favor of ones that are culturally responsive, antiracist, and socially just.

CHAPTER 32

College Readiness and Urban Schools

Challenges and Opportunities

Lindsay R. Granger and Pedro A. Noguera

INTRODUCTION

Preparing students for a productive life after high school has become the priority of the latest round of education reform efforts (Conley, 2012; Gewertz, 2012). President Obama and the U.S. Department of Education have implored schools to do more to get students to be "college or career ready" (Conley et al., 2011; Maruyama, 2012). As a result of this charge, school and district leaders are looking for ways to significantly increase the number of students who graduate from high school genuinely prepared to succeed in college.

Traditionally, college-related efforts for urban students have focused primarily on providing access to college. This is particularly true for efforts aimed at assisting groups that have historically been underrepresented in colleges and universities, namely, students from low-income backgrounds, as well as racial and ethnic minorities (Roderick, Nagoaka, and Coca, 2009). However, there is growing awareness that while providing access is essential, it is not sufficient. The success of past efforts to increase college enrollment, particularly among historically underrepresented groups, has convinced many advocates and policymakers that with further attention and focus it will also be possible to increase their rates of college readiness.

Figuring out how to prepare such students for postsecondary education has proven to be far more complex than many of these stakeholders may have envisioned. Much of the literature on this topic has emphasized the academic knowledge that students must have to be successful after high school, which implies that such knowledge is all that is necessary for students to be ready for learning (and life) after college (Conley et al., 2011; Gamm et al., 2012). Researchers of college retention and success, however, have pointed out that, while

academic skill development is important, it is only one aspect of preparation that is critical to achievement (Maruyama, 2012; Savitz-Romer and Bouffard, 2012). By excluding these important aspects of postsecondary readiness in favor of knowledge that can easily be tested for, stakeholders are providing the public with an incomplete picture of what it takes for students to be ready for the future. And, without an acknowledgment of such nonacademic skills and an explicit emphasis on developing them, students will continue to be unprepared for college.

More attention needs to be paid to the interaction between academic, individual, and social factors that influence college readiness for urban public school students. A growing body of research points to the need to teach a variety of noncognitive skills—the behavioral and/or character-based traits that are not directly tied to the act of doing academic work but contribute to one's ability to successfully complete such tasks—that are essential to academic and social success (Savitz-Romer and Bouffard, 2012; Tough, 2012). Helping students to acquire skills such as intrinsic motivation, goal setting, time management, and an ability to overcome unforeseen obstacles is a different process than the mastery of the content of core subjects or mastery of fundamental academic skills. Moreover, determining whether students have acquired such skills is not readily discernible on traditional standardized tests employed by the current educational environment.

In this chapter we analyze this important dimension of college readiness, placing particular attention on the contextual factors that influence the outcomes of urban school students. Following a review of relevant research literature on college readiness and related social and psychological theories, we will present recommendations on what urban schools can do to provide their students with academic and social experiences that will lead to greater likelihood of success in college

LITERATURE REVIEW

Testing, the Common Core, and College Readiness

The responsibility of preparing students for college has traditionally been assigned to high schools; however, it is only in recent years that college has become the standard post-graduation expectation. In fact, prior to the enactment of No Child Left Behind, secondary schools serving low-income students in urban and rural areas were under relatively little pressure to boost college enrollment or lower dropout rates (Payne, 2011). The majority of these institutions operated on a model developed during the manufacturing economy of the early twentieth century, when a college education was not a requirement for a comfortable career at a unionized job that could last a lifetime (Conley, 2012; Lehmann, 1999). Back then, college was perceived as largely for middle class and affluent students, who often navigated the process of obtaining admission with the support of their college-educated parents. Support from school counselors was minimal and unexpected, and while schools took great pride in sending students to college, they felt little pressure to expand access for those thought of as not being "college material" (Arbona, 2005; Kinzie et al., 2004).

With the adoption of affirmative action policies during the 1970s, many colleges and universities began to diversify their student bodies (Bok and Bowen, 1998). As racial and ethnic minority students began to apply to college in large numbers, an increasing number of working-class white students also began applying to college, causing a higher level of competition for a small number of seats. Some of this increase for white students has been explained by changes in the economy related to deindustrialization, which reduced the number of jobs that required only a high school diploma or training (Kinzie et al., 2004). In addition, there was a more general tendency toward "credential inflation," as a growing number of jobs that never required college degrees before—police officers, healthcare workers, civil servants, etc.—increased their credential requirements for new employees (Bankston III, 2011). Whatever the reason for it, colleges and universities saw this increased enroll-

ment as an effective way to raise revenue and actively encouraged greater numbers of high school students to apply (Stulburg and Weinberg, 2011). All of these factors combined to create an environment where college became the social norm for high school graduates.

The enactment of No Child Left Behind (NCLB), with its requirement that schools be held accountable for student test scores, and the adoption of similar policies in many states that required schools to accurately report dropout rates and the number of students enrolling in college (Boykin and Noguera, 2011), significantly increased the pressure on and expectation that high schools would have to do more to prepare students for both college access and college success. The requirement for schools to disaggregate their data based on race also showed discrepancies along these lines. In their annual study on the state of college and career readiness in the United States, for example, the ACT (2012) reported that none of their benchmarks in English, reading, mathematics, and science were met by at least 50 percent of African-American, American Indian, or Hispanic students. Likewise, while the percentage of Asian/Asian-American and white students who met at least three of the four benchmarks is above 50 percent, there remained considerable room for further improvement (ACT, 2012).

To many educators and policymakers, these low numbers make it clear that there must be an across-the-board focus on the pervasive problem of college readiness (Conley, 2012; Farmer-Hinton, 2008; Roderick, Nagoaka, and Coca, 2009). With the U.S. population in the midst of a major demographic shift that will result in racial minorities constituting the majority of the population by 2041 (Kinzie et al., 2004), the need for sustained attention on this issue has never been greater. However, it is also clear that to achieve sustainable improvement policymakers will have to do more than simply pressure schools to do a better job.

One of the solutions that has been offered to address the problem of college readiness is the implementation of the Common Core State Standards (CCSS). With support and encouragement from the federal government, already forty-five states and the District of Columbia have adopted CCSS. The aim of these standards is to "define the knowledge and skills students should achieve in order to graduate from high school ready to succeed in entry-level, credit-bearing academic college courses and in workforce training programs" (Conley et al., 2011a). Advocates of CCSS have argued that they could be a vehicle for significantly increasing college readiness and advancing educational equity in schools throughout the country (Gamm et al., 2012).

The definition of college readiness employed by the writers of the CCSS is almost identical to that of the ACT—"the knowledge and skills a student needs to enroll and succeed in credit-bearing first-year courses at a postsecondary institution . . . without the need for remediation" (ACT, 2012, p. v)—and relies heavily on the importance of academic preparation. Testing groups like the ACT, Partnership for Assessment of Readiness for College and Careers (PARCC), the Smarter Balanced Assessment Consortium (SBAC), for example, have created measures designed to predict a precollege student's ability to tackle college-level work at every grade level (Gewertz, 2012). These tests are not without their detractors. Maruyama (2012), for example, wrote that they "do not adequately assess college readiness" because they "provide imprecise and often misleading information" (p. 253). Still, as the CCSS becomes implemented across the country, more and more states are likely to adopt these new tests as a way to prove that their high school graduates are indeed ready for college.

Social Capital as a Lens for Understanding College Readiness

For some students, these new standards will not be a problem. As recent data from New York State reveals, the majority of the students who have met or exceeded the state's tougher graduation and college readiness requirements are white students who attend schools in affluent areas (Strauss, 2013). English language learners actually experienced a drop in their college graduation rate to a low of 21 percent, and similar drops were experienced by African-American, Latino, and low-income students (Strauss 2013). The successful students generally have access to the support and resources outside of school and are therefore able to make it to college with limited institutional intervention. In academic terms, they have the social capital necessary to fill in the information that they are not getting from school.

Traditionally, studies of college access and preparation for underrepresented populations have looked at the lack of social capital as the explanation for differ-

ential outcomes between these students and those with majority status. Social capital can be defined as the norms and information channels available through social relationships (Bryan, Moore-Thomas, Day-Vines, and Holcomb-McCoy, 2011; Farmer-Hinton and McCullough, 2008; Holland and Farmer-Hinton, 2009; Stanton-Salazar, 1997, 2011). In terms of access to and success in higher education and beyond, having such social capital means that these students are exposed to more life options, opportunities, and general guidance than the school provides. Their future plans are not dependent on what their high schools either have time to tell them or, as is the case with many schools that serve students of color, deem appropriate for their lives.

Several studies have shown that students from urban schools tend to lack the social capital that is essential for obtaining access to college and being ready for the experience. To some degree, this is because they have parents who lack both college degrees and experience with the admissions process (McDonough and Calderone, 2006). It is also because many low-income students, especially racial minorities in urban areas, grow up in communities where the college-educated role models are few and far between (Bryan, Moore-Thomas, and Holcomb-McCoy, 2011; Farmer-Hinton, 2008), and there are often widely held perceptions of limited possibilities for upward mobility which produces a glass ceiling effect on their aspirations (Mickelson, 1990). Because such students are more likely to attend schools that do not have time or resources to invest in the type of intensive advising that would counter these negative contextual factors (Farmer-Hinton and McCullough, 2008; McClafferty, McDonough, and Nunez, 2002), they are substantially less likely to be able to take advantage of the opportunities that may exist to change their circumstances.

Using social capital as a lens, it is easy to understand how the lack of resources and connections in these schools contributes to differential access to opportunities. Indeed, "due to racial and socioeconomic segregation, inequality in social capital exists because people of color tend to reside among other people of color who have also experienced limited educational and economic opportunities" (Farmer-Hinton and McCullough, 2009, p. 79), which then leads to a limited amount of information and influence. While students whose family members have gone to college or who have outside role models for postsecondary educational success may not have the social capital necessary to navigate this process entirely on their own, they at least have an idea about how the process works. Many urban students lack this capital, however, and are dependent on their high schools and other college-related programs for this information (Bryan et al., 2011; Holland and Farmer-Hinton, 2009; Roderick, Coca, and Nagoaka, 2011). This can prove to be problematic.

In his discussions of the importance of social networks for socially marginalized students, Stanton-Salazar (1997, 2011) spoke directly to the need for school-based support from "institutional agents" (Stanton-Salazar, 1997, p. 6). He defined institutional agents as "those individuals who have the capacity and commitment to transmit directly, or negotiate the transmission of, institutional resources and opportunities" and believed that "through relationships with institutional agents, a segment of society gains the resources, privileges, and support necessary to advance and maintain their economic and political position in society" (Stanton-Salazar, 1997, p. 6). In other words, students who are lacking in social capital can benefit greatly from the bonds they form with faculty and staff members of their schools because these people can provide them with the information, resources, and norms necessary to become socially mobile. These relationships, however, are "fundamentally conditional" because "the construction of authentically supportive relationships is subject to the forces of institutionalized exclusion" (Stanton-Salazar, 1997, p. 18).

This "institutionalized exclusion" usually comes in the form of the gatekeeper role that teachers and school counselors in schools that serve vulnerable populations often play. According to Stanton-Salazar (1997, 2011), since teachers are tasked with picking educational winners and losers, and school counselors then use these distinctions to differentially provide access to resources, only a small percentage of students are ever in the position to have relationships with institutional agents that translate into social gains. These students tend to be the ones who are, comparatively speaking, easiest to build relationships with because they are the ones who actively seek them out. Their behavior is then rewarded because it mirrors the behaviors that many teachers and school counselors were trained to see as positive, such as the ability to self-advocate and ask for help (Savitz-Romer and Bouffard, 2012).

Throughout the literature related to college readiness for urban students, there is recognition of the importance associated with educators and school leaders providing the resources and time that all students require in the college readiness process. However, there is simultaneously a resignation that most urban schools lack the capacity to make this happen (Holland and Farmer-Hinton, 2008; Roderick, Nagoaka, and Coca, 2009). As stated above, many urban students do not have parents or role models who attended or successfully completed college, and they will need more direct support from their schools than students who have these external resources. While this information is widely known, the structural constraints facing many urban schools are often a barrier to making social capital-based college readiness efforts happen on a large scale. School counselors in urban schools typically have large caseloads (often several hundred students per one counselor), making it difficult to work closely with more than a handful of students (Farmer-Hinton, 2008).

Moreover, many urban high schools lack an accountability culture focused on student outcomes related to college. Instead, preference is given to preparing students for the standardized tests required by the state as opposed to ensuring that they are building the knowledge and skills that will serve them well after graduation (Darling-Hammond, 2001; Estevez, 2008). Additionally, the policies and practices governing many low-income urban schools make it almost impossible to provide the levels of support that have been shown to be successful with students from these environments. The subpar academic outcomes and related low college readiness rates that are seen in many urban schools are a by-product of these constraints. It is unlikely that these challenges will be overcome prior to the implementation of the CCSS.

Noncognitive Skill Development as a Tool for College Readiness

A growing segment of educational research is looking beyond the lesson plans and course maps schools use to prepare students for college, for new ways to boost both student achievement and college readiness. Evidence of this shift can be found in the current academic and popular literature surrounding noncognitive skills which, as stated above, are skills and traits that impact an individual's ability to successfully accomplish a goal (Adams, 2012; Farrington et al., 2012; Tough, 2012). In terms of college readiness, the noncognitive skills associated with task assessment, goal setting, motivation, and outcome expectations have become increasingly valuable as researchers and practitioners aim to create better academic and behavioral interventions for students (Blackwell, Trzesnieski, and Dweck, 2007; Savitz-Romer and Bouffard, 2012).

One theory that is especially helpful for understanding how to make students more prepared for future challenges is Albert Bandura's Social Cognitive Theory (SCT) (Bandura, 1995, 2006). As opposed to stage-based psychological theories that assign age ranges to individual skills and behaviors, SCT posits that individuals and their behaviors are influenced by the interactions between self and social context (Muuss, 1996). The explicit consideration of external factors is not common among psychological theories, but Bandura wrote that "human behavior cannot be fully understood solely in terms of sociostructural factors or psychological factors" (Bandura, 2006, p. 5). Rather, Bandura suggested that it is only by understanding the interactions between the two that any insights can be made.

The key component of SCT is the explanatory value of an individual's self-efficacy and related outcome expectations on their behaviors. Self-efficacy beliefs "are concerned with an individual's capabilities" while outcome expectations involve "imagined consequences of particular courses of action" (Lent, 2005, p. 104). These perceptions of the relationship between skill and result are built up over time through an individual's experiences, both direct and indirect, and have a profound influence on the choices students make, the goals they set, and the amount of effort they put into achieving these goals (Chemers, Hu, and Garcia, 2001; Choi, 2005; Phan, 2012). In short, if a person believes they are good at something and that engaging in this activity will bring about a positive consequence, they are more likely to do it. And, the more they do it and achieve the same (positive) result, the more confident they become in this ability and more likely they are to continue to engage in it (Komarraju and Nadler, 2013). In SCT, this is called a "feedback loop," and it is widely regarded as essential for keeping an individual motivated toward the completion of a desired task (Lent, 2005).

Since self-efficacy is the most important aspect of SCT and informs outcome expectations, motivation, persistence on task, and a whole host of other noncognitive skills necessary for academic success (Komarraju and Nadler, 2013), it is important to understand how it is developed. There are four primary factors that influence self-efficacy: mastery of experience, vicarious learning, social persuasion, and affective states (Savitz-Romer and Bouffard, 2012).

- *Mastery of experience* means that an individual has had a positive experience in a particular domain, thus building their self-efficacy in that area.
- *Vicarious learning* refers to the messages that an individual receives by seeing people to whom they relate either succeed or fail in a domain, and extrapolating their own ability in the same domain from this person's outcome.
- *Social persuasion* is the influence of another party's perceptions of an individual's ability to be successful.
- *Affective states* are the emotional states that allow an individual to accurately self-assess and draw conclusions about their abilities.

This combination of factors is where the "social" and the "cognitive" parts of SCT meet. The research on noncognitive skill acquisition suggests that while "people's beliefs about themselves and their future possibilities are internal processes, they are strongly influenced by social contexts and experiences and the meaning that people make of them" (Savitz-Romer and Bouffard, 2012, p. 104).

The links between SCT and academic performance are very well documented and illustrate why this construct is important for college readiness efforts. The literature reviewed below provides evidence of self-efficacy's importance in the academic domain, and describes self-efficacy's relationship with other noncognitive skills and metacognitive strategies that have been shown to contribute to student success.

In their study of academic self-efficacy and first-year college student performance and transition, Chemers, Hu, and Garcia (2001) found that confidence and high expectations of self (evidence of high self-efficacy) were highly correlated with greater academic performance and a better adjustment to college. The reason for this connection is that students with high self-efficacy viewed the increased workload associated with college as a challenge that could be conquered rather than as a threat that should be feared. According to the authors, "Such students hold higher expectations for themselves in part because they trust in their capabilities and in part because they see the world, and their ability to respond to it, as less threatening" (Chemers, Hu, and Garcia, 2001, p. 62). As a result, these students performed significantly better on their academic tasks than their less confident and less efficacious peers. The authors also found that having high academic self-efficacy resulted in students being less stressed and generally healthier than others with lower academic self-efficacy.

A related study on the relationship between academic self-efficacy and stress by Zajacova, Lynch, and Espenshade (2005) explored the importance of these factors on academic performance and retention among college freshmen. The authors reported similar findings to Chemers, Hu, and Garcia (2001) regarding the difference in how students appraised a task: as a challenge as opposed to a threat. When a task is seen as the former, "one is more likely to select an effective coping strategy and to persist at managing the task" (Zajacova, Lynch, and Espenshade, 2005, p. 680). When appraised as the latter, students were more likely to be stressed by the situation, make inappropriate choices, and have negative performance outcomes. Self-efficacy's role here is as the mediator of the response to the external demands, with the highly efficacious students being less likely to become overwhelmed by the activity at hand. This resulted in a better ability to remain rational and make the choices appropriate for the achievement of a positive outcome.

High self-efficacy of self-regulation, or an individual's confidence in their capability to control their task orientation, has also been shown to positively impact student academic achievement. In their attempt to develop a theory of procrastination, Klassen, Krawchuk, and Rajani (2008) explored the link between academic procrastination and self-efficacy via perceptions of self-regulation. The authors found that the ability to self-regulate was less important than a student's self-efficacy to self-regulate. They wrote: "Skills in self-regulation are not sufficient to ensure that academic tasks get started or completed; self-efficacy to structure the learning environment . . . leads to timely task completion and successful academic achievement" (p. 922). This finding echoes that of Zimmerman and Kitsantas (2005), who found that students with high self-efficacy for self-regulation were more likely to consistently and successfully complete homework assignment than those with low self-efficacy in this domain.

Komarraju and Nadler (2012) examined the relationship between self-efficacy and theories of intelligence, and found that "students who have high self-efficacy and confidence in their academic performance are also more likely to believe that intelligence is changeable and determined by effort" (p. 4). The importance of a student's perceptions of the malleability of intelligence have been consistently shown to influence their effort on academic tasks, as students who believe that they can get smarter often work harder and perform better in school than students who believe that intelligence is fixed (Savitz-Romer and Bouffard, 2012; Yaeger and Dweck, 2012). Similarly, Komarraju and Nadler (2012) found a strong connection between high self-efficacy and the metacognitive strategies that students utilized to maintain high academic achievement. The authors found that "training students to strengthen their self-efficacy and their belief that they have the ability to determine their performance can facilitate valuing effort and hard work" (Komarraju and Nadler, 2012, p. 4).

While none of these studies are focused exclusively on urban students, the overarching message of the importance of self-efficacy is strong enough to be translated to a variety of settings. Taken together, they show the positive role that high self-efficacy can play in the college readiness process. From helping students perform the academic tasks necessary to get the grades to qualify for the competitive applicant pools of highly selective institutions, to giving them the confidence necessary to complete the nonacademic tasks associated with the stressors of college life, high self-efficacy in college readiness related domains can mean the difference in the success or failure of a student's postsecondary aspirations. Perhaps most importantly, these studies of self-efficacy also show that it can be developed in students. This provides a starting point for school leaders who are interested in helping their students develop this and related noncognitive skills.

RECOMMENDATIONS FOR PRACTICE
AND POLICY

Knowledge of social capital and Social Cognitive Theory (SCT) can inform how urban school leaders approach issues of college readiness within the testing constraints of the Common Core State Standards (CCSS). Understanding the ways that lacking social capital contributes to the negative outcomes of urban students can provide a jumping-off point for the creation of programming and practices, while understanding the development of self-efficacy can serve as a roadmap for these interventions. By using these theories together, urban school leaders can find ways to create opportunities to address the needs of their students while working under the curricular constraints of the CCSS.

In order to significantly increase college readiness for students in urban schools, their school leaders must place greater emphasis on forging relationships between students and supportive institutional agents who are crucial in providing the basic knowledge that they will need to make the choices that are right for their lives (Stanton-Salazar, 2011). School counselors, who often have had explicit training in noncognitive skill development and are often the point person for future-focused activities, should be called upon to lead such efforts (Farmer-Hinton and Adams, 2006). Through these relationships, students can be provided with access to the information and norms necessary for college readiness, as well as the support necessary for students to see themselves as college ready. And with an explicit focus on the development self-efficacy (Komarraju and Nadler, 2012), these institutional agents can also provide students the opportunity to build up this crucial set of skills that will be of use to them in college and beyond.

When practitioners are mindful of what it takes to build up positive self-efficacy among students, the noncognitive skills that are predictive of college success can be taught to students without much adjustment of the standard curriculum. School leaders should encourage the creation of lesson plans that build students' positive self-efficacy in the domain of that particular subject. By sticking with the four ways that self-efficacy is built—mastery experiences, vicarious learning, social persuasion, and affective states—school leaders can ensure that their teachers are imparting this message in everything they do. Providing students with activities and assignments that allow them to grow and develop confidence in their abilities as learners can help build the academic self-efficacy that will enable them to be more prepared to overcome the obstacles they will face in college.

In addition to these institutional supports and curricular changes, school leaders should work to actively address the gaps in social capital through activities that connect their students to colleges and college students to whom they can relate. In their study of Glenn Hills College Preparatory Charter High School, a community charter school in Chicago, Farmer-Hinton and Adams (2006) described the college-related programming that the school's counselors use to give their predominately low-income African-American students multiple opportunities to "see themselves, in the future, on a college campus" (p. 112). In the previous professional experience that one of the authors had as a school counselor in an urban public high school, she found that having recent alums of the school return and talk to students about their experiences in college often inspired the current students to pursue higher education for themselves. Since the returning visitors were in the same seats (literally) as the current ones, they served as valuable role models for postsecondary success. Such programs also serve to build self-efficacy, as they are both mastery and vicarious learning experiences.

While many urban schools may claim to lack the resources to reduce student-to-counselor ratios or to expand curricular add-ons, it is important to note that a small but significant number of urban schools have found ways to do these things. For example, thirty-eight high schools in New York City have formed a performance-based consortium that has been in existence for many years. The schools in the consortium have had a waiver from the state of New York that allows them to utilize their own performance-based assessments instead of the state's standardized tests in every subject with the exception of math. A recent longitudinal study of these schools found that they have substantially higher graduation rates and significantly better college readiness rates (as measured by lower percentages of their graduates being required to take remedial courses) than students of similar demographic backgrounds at traditional public schools (Performance Consortium Report, 2011). Schools like these show us what might be possible on a larger scale if schools and, more importantly, policymakers, were to embrace a framework that incorporates social capital and noncognitive skill development into their strategies and frameworks.

The ideal policy recommendation for increasing rates of college readiness for urban students would be to modify the current content-focused state assessments so that schools can focus more broadly on educating students for life rather than test taking. A more realistic policy change would be to give equal weight to both the academic and noncognitive skills associated with college readiness, while actively addressing the gaps in support that urban school students face. This holistic approach to student development would mean allowing time for them to grow as people as well as learners. Unfortunately, many urban districts have pressures and constraints that do not allow for anything but academic preparation. For real strides to be made in college readiness for urban students, policies must be in place at the state and federal level that reinforce the importance of a more comprehensive approach to college readiness.

CONCLUSION

Focusing on self-efficacy and social capital can serve as strategies that expand college readiness for a greater number of students in urban public schools. However, such strategies should not come at the expense of addressing the very real social, economic, and structural barriers that they face. Instead, they should be used as tools for school leaders to create opportunities to help students to overcome these barriers so that they can be as prepared as possible for a successful future in college and beyond. Social capital theory provides urban school leaders with a lens through which to view the contextual factors that impact their students' outcomes. And, with a holistic focus on the individual, Social Cognitive Theory provides a way for education practitioners in urban public schools to build the noncognitive skills necessary for urban students to overcome these barriers and be successful in college and beyond.

College readiness must not be treated as simply an academic matter. Any effort to increase college readiness must also include a focus on preparing students to acquire the noncognitive skills that make it possible for them to adapt to new situations and face down challenges with self-confidence. Urban school leaders should work to create spaces for their students to build

up the skills necessary for them to be ready for life after high school.

REFERENCES

ACT (2012). *The Condition of College and Career Readiness—National.* Retrieved from www.act.org/readiness/2012.

Adams, C. (2012, November). "Soft-skills" pushed as part of college readiness. *Education Week, 32(12)*, 1–14.

Arbona, C. (2005). Promoting the career development and academic achievement of at-risk youth: College access programs. In Brown, S.D. and Lent, R.W. (Eds.), *Career Development and Counseling: Putting Theory and Research to Work.* Hoboken, NJ: John Wiley and Sons, Inc.

Bandura, A. (1995). Exercise of personal and collective efficacy in changing societies. In Bandura, A. (Ed.), *Self-Efficacy in Changing Societies.* Cambridge, UK: Cambridge University Press.

Bandura, A. (2006). Adolescent development from an agentic perspective. In Pajares, F. and Urdan, T. (Eds.), *Self-efficacy Beliefs of Adolescents.* Greenwich, CT: Information Age Publishing.

Bankston III, C. L. (2011). The mass production of credentials: subsidies and the rise of the higher education industry. *Independent Review, 15(3)*, 325–349.

Blackwell, L. S., Trzesniewski, K. H., and Dweck, C. S. (2007). Implicit theories of intelligence predict achievement across an adolescent transition: A longitudinal study and an intervention. *Child Development, 78(1)*, 246–263.

Bok, D. and Bowen, W. G. (1998). "Affirmative action has worked at the nation's top colleges." *Boston Globe*, September.

Boykin, A. W. and Noguera, P. (2011). *Creating the Opportunity to Learn: Moving from Research to Practice to Close the Achievement Gap.* Alexandria, VA: ASCD.

Bryan, J., Moore-Thomas, C., Day-Vines, N., and Holcomb-McCoy, C. (2011). School counselors as social capital: The effects of high school college counseling on college application rates. *Journal of Counseling and Development, 89*, 90–100.

Chemers, M., Hu, L., and Garcia, B. F. (2001). Academic self-efficacy and first-year college student performance and adjustment. *Journal of Educational Psychology, 91(3)*, 66–64.

Choi, N. (2005). Self efficacy and self-concept as predictors of college students academic performance. *Psychology in the Schools, 42(2)*, 197–207.

Conley, D. T. (2012). *College and Career Ready.* San Francisco: Jossey-Bass.

Conley, D. T., Drummond, K. V., de Gonzalez, A., Rooseboom, J., and Stout, O. (2011). *Reaching the goal: The applicability and importance of the Common Core State Standards to college and career readiness.* Eugene, OR: Educational Policy Improvement Center.

Darling-Hammond, L. (2001). *The Right to Learn: A Blueprint for Creating Schools that Work.* San Francisco: Jossey-Bass.

Estevez, E. (2008, May). College readiness: A different mirror. *The Hispanic Outlook in Higher Education, 18(16),* 60.

Farmer-Hinton, R. (2008). Creating opportunities for college access: Examining a school model designed to prepare students of color for college. *Multicultural Perspective, 10(2),* 73–81.

Farmer-Hinton, R. and Adams, T. (2006). Social capital and college preparation: Exploring the role of counselors in a college prep school for Black students. *The Negro Educational Review, 57(1-2),* 101–116.

Farmer-Hinton, R. and Garth McCullough, R. (2008). College counseling in charter high schools: Examining the opportunities and challenges. *The High School Journal, April/May,* 77–90.

Farrington, C. A., Roderick, M., Allensworth, E., Nagoaka, J., Keyes, T. S., Johnson, D. W., and Beechum, N. O. (2012). *Teaching adolescents to become learners: The role of noncognitive factors in shaping school performance: A critical literature review.* Chicago: University of Chicago Consortium on Chicago School Research.

Gamm, S., Elliott, J., Wright Halbert, J., Price-Baugh, R., Hall, R., Walston, D., Uro, G., and Casserly, M. (2012). *Common Core State Standards and diverse urban students: Using multi-tiered systems of support.* Washington, DC: The Council of the Great City Schools.

Gewertz, C. (2012, November 27). Testing consortium crafts college-readiness definition. [Web log post]. Retrieved from blogs.edweek.org/edweek curriculum/2012/11/testing_consortium_crafts_coll.html?intc=es.

Holland, N. and Farmer-Hinton, R. (2009). Leave no schools behind: The importance of a college culture in urban public high schools. *The High School Journal, Feb Mar,* 24–43.

Kinzie, J., Palmer, M., Hayek, J., Hossler, D., Jacob, S. A., and Cummings, H. (2004). *Fifty Years of College Choice: Social, Political, and Institutional Influences on the Decision-Making Process.* Indianapolis, IN: The Lumina Foundation.

Klassen, R. M., Krawchuk, L. L., and Rajani, S. (2008). Academic procrastination of undergraduates: Low self-efficacy to self-regulate predicts higher levels of procrastination. *Contemporary Educational Psychology, 33,* 915–931.

Komarraju M. and Nadler, D. (2013). Self-efficacy and academic achievement: Why do implicit beliefs, goals, and effort regulation matter? *Learning and Individual Differences.* dx.dio.org/10/1016/j.lindif.2013.01.005.

Lehmann, N. (1999). *The Big Test: The Secret History of American Meritocracy.* New York: Farrar, Straus and Giroux.

Lent, R. (2005). A social cognitive view of career development and counseling. In Brown, S.D. and Lent, R.W. (Eds.) *Career Development and Counseling: Putting Theory and Research to Work.* Hoboken, NJ: John Wiley and Sons, Inc.

Maruyama, G. (2012). Assessing college readiness: Should we be satisfied with ACT or other threshold scores? *Educational Researcher, 41,* 252–264.

McClafferty, K., McDonough, P., and Nunez, A. (2002). *What is a college culture? Facilitating college preparation through organizational change.* Paper presented at the Annual Meeting of the American Educational Research Association, New Orleans, LA.

McDonough, P. and Calderone, S. (2006). The meaning of money: Perpetual differences between college counselors and low-income families about college costs and financial aid. *The American Behavioral Scientists, 49(12),* 1703–1718.

Mickelson, R. (1990). The attitude-achievement paradox among Black adolescents. *Sociology of Education, 63 (1),* 44–61.

Muuss, R. (1996). *Theories of Adolescence,* 6th edition. New York: McGraw-Hill.

Payne, C. (2011). *So Much Reform, So Little Change: The Persistence of Failure in Urban Schools.* Cambridge, MA: Harvard Education Press.

Performance-based Consortium (2011). Educating Students for the 21st Century: Data Report on the Performance Standard Consortium. New York. www.nyclu.org/files/releases/testing_consortium_report.pdf.

Phan, H. P. (2012). Informational sources, self-efficacy, and achievement: A temporally displaced approach. *Educational Psychology: An International Journal of Experimental Educational Psychology, 32(6),* 699–726.

Roderick, M., Nagoaka, J., and Coca, V. (2009). College readiness for all: The challenge for urban high schools. *The Future of Children, 19(1),* 185–210.

Savitz-Romer, M. and Bouffard, S. (2012). *Ready, Willing, and Able: A Developmental Approach to College Access and Success.* Cambridge, MA: Harvard Education Press.

Stanton-Salazar, R. (1997). A social capital framework for understanding the socialization of racial minority children and youths. *Harvard Education Review, 67(1),* 1–40.

Stanton-Salazar, R. (2011). A social capital framework for the study of institutional agents and their role in the empowerment of low-status students and youth. *Youth and Society, 43(3),* 1066–1109.

Strausss, V. (2013, July 1). "New York's Graduation Gap Widens." *Washington Post*.

Stulburg, L. and S. Weinberg (2011). *Diversity in American Higher Education*. New York: Routledge.

Tough, P. (2012). *How Children Succeed: Grit, Curiosity, and the Hidden Power of Character*. New York: Houghton Mifflin Harcourt Publishing.

Yaeger, D. S. and Dweck, C. S. (2012). Mindsets that promote resilience: When students believe that personal characteristics can be developed. *Educational Psychologist, 47(4)*, 302–314.

Zajacova, A., Lynch, S. M., and Espenshade, T. J. (2005). Self-efficacy, stress, and academic success in college. *Research in Higher Education, 46*, 677–706.

Zimmerman, B. J. and Kitsantas, A. (2005). Homework practices and academic achievement: The mediating role of self-efficacy and perceived responsibility beliefs. *Contemporary Educational Psychology, 30*, 397–417.

CHAPTER 33

Change Agency in Our Own Backyards

Meeting the Challenges of Next-Generation Programs in School Leader Preparation

Steve Tozer, Paul Zavitkovsky, Sam Whalen, and Peter Martinez[1]

Although its origin is debated, the expression is familiar: "Your system, any system, is perfectly designed to produce the results you are getting" (Carr, 2008). This insight frames the challenge of preparing principals to lead urban schools to significantly improved student learning. The current system has evolved effectively to produce the learning outcomes that we are getting in urban schools. That "system" is made up not just of urban schools and districts but also of their municipal and state political and economic settings, national policies, and an inequitable national and international maldistribution of wealth and power, among many other system components (Watkins, 2011).

A key part of that system is the higher education institutions that produce teachers and leaders for schools. That is, higher education is a part of a system that is perfectly designed to produce the results we are getting in urban schools. There are those in higher education who might be inclined to say, "Now wait a minute: I have been critiquing the system for a long time and offering alternatives to boot. If the schools would do as I have been recommending, we would have very different outcomes." That response, too, is part of a system that works as it is designed to. What is needed is something that actually disrupts the system.

In this chapter, we describe a school leadership preparation program that shows promise for disrupting the system of inequitable educational outcomes in necessary but still insufficient ways. We use this program to illustrate fundamental institutional challenges that arise in efforts to disrupt systemic inequity, and how even an award-winning principal preparation program is still struggling with these challenges after twelve years of continuous development. We identify how university efforts to work collaboratively and intensively with an urban school district can create tensions in institutional norms that must be addressed if the goal of producing principals as change agents is to be achieved.

Principal preparation programs seem to be unlikely candidates for disrupting the entrenched, inequitable outcomes of urban schools. In fact, in the influential, bipartisan No Child Left Behind legislation that expressly sought to address educational inequities, school principals are barely mentioned (U.S. Department of Education, 2001). Of course, principal preparation is not going to challenge the fundamental social inequities of post-industrial global capitalism, or disrupt racist housing segregation in the nation's cities.

Yet we have known since the Effective Schools research of the 1970s that an outstanding principal can lead a high-need school to greatly improved, life-changing outcomes in student learning (Lezotte, 1984). In other words, we have known for some time that despite structured inequalities in the social and economic context, at least some schools have been successful in supporting low-income and other traditionally marginalized students' academic success (Bryk et al., 2010; Chenoweth, 2011; Marzano, 2003; Newmann et al. 1996). Moreover, we have known that such schools share a number of features in common, among which are school principals who know how to lead the school organization to successful learning outcomes (Borko, Wolf, Simone, and Uchiyama, and Theokas, 2003; Bryk et al., 2010; Chenoweth, 2011; Wallace Foundation 2006, 2008). What has been missing has been a theory and practice for producing such principals at scale.

The last two decades have produced a number of studies sharply critical of principal preparation programs and their failure to produce school leaders of the quality our schools deserve (Bottoms and O'Neill, 2001; Finn and Broad, 2003; Levine, 2005; Milstein, 1992). At the same time, a number of principal preparation and development programs nationwide have received attention in recent years for innovative practices that in some cases produce promising early results on indicators of student learning outcomes in schools. Some of these programs are led by not-for-profits (e.g., New York City Leadership Academy, or New Leaders), some by school districts (e.g., Gwinnett County, Georgia), others by charter organizations (e.g., KIPP), and some by institutions of higher education in close partnership with districts (e.g., Delta State University, University of San Diego, University of Illinois Chicago) (Cheney, Davis, Garrett, and Holleran, 2010; Davis and Darling-Hammond, 2012).

A first observation here is that school leader preparation is clearly no longer the province of higher education alone. Second, as others have pointed out, whether in higher education or not, these programs tend to have a number of design features in common (Cheney et al., 2010; Darling-Hammond et al., 2007; Davis and Darling-Hammond, 2012; Orr and Orphanos, 2011). Although the following formulation of these design features is informed by these sources, it is our own amalgam rather than a direct reference to any single source. It is informed also by our own work, often in collaboration with next-generation programs that demonstrate all or most of these features. These features include:

- a results-oriented commitment to demonstrating principal impact on schools, however that impact may be measured;
- close working partnerships with school districts that invest resources in program success;
- highly selective admissions to structured cohorts of students;
- full-time, intensively coached, yearlong paid residencies as an integral part of the program;
- integration of academic learning and practical experience to address the relevance of research and theory to leadership practice;
- post-licensure support, taking such forms as continued study in cohorts, or direct coaching, or structured networking—or all of these—to accelerate early-career development and success.

Most of the programs with these characteristics got their start early in the first decade of the twenty-first century, and the list of such next-generation programs

is growing, but slowly. These design features sharply challenge how we have conducted school leadership preparation in the past, both by introducing new institutional players into the landscape of school leadership preparation (districts, not-for-profits, charter organizations) and by introducing new models of principal development that most of the traditional players in higher education are not yet prepared to adopt. These innovative program design features have not swept the nation and at this writing are found in only a relatively few districts, largely urban centers of some size, and even then rarely district-wide (Zubrzycki, 2012). The reasons for this slow adoption of innovation are understandable. Part of the answer is simply that higher education is still the dominant producer of principals in the United States, and higher education is notoriously slow to change.

But the reasons go further than that. If each of the six innovations listed above has face-value for improving the preparation of principals who can improve learning outcomes in schools, why is there little evidence of adoption of these components in higher education (Cheney and Davis, 2011; Levine, 2005)? It is reasonable to believe, for example, that principal preparation would benefit from highly selective admissions to results-oriented cohorts of students who spend at least a year in full-time paid leadership posts in high-need schools.

But while small-cohort, highly selective programs may be effective, they are also costly, compared to low-intensity, traditional programs that may enroll hundreds of school leadership candidates in a single year. In-depth collaborations with school districts may provide intensive school-based practical experiences, but at what cost to university autonomy? And what university faculty, particularly in research universities, are eager (or qualified) to provide field supervision in schools? For every attractive feature that can be identified in next-generation school leader preparation programs, an institutional challenge lurks not far behind.

A different way to frame this may be to say that next-generation programs encounter a number of serious tensions. The tensions persist *within* institutional cultures, *between* institutional cultures (e.g., university and school district), and *throughout* the wider culture's beliefs and values about education (e.g., what is good teaching, what are good schools, and how are they achieved?). How a program negotiates these tensions is likely going to define much about the character of the program—and its impact on schools.

Our purpose in the remainder of this chapter is to explore those tensions through the experience of one program that has been discovering and struggling with these tensions for more than a decade. Next generation, practice-intensive, principal preparation programs do not offer easy solutions to the well-documented weaknesses of principal preparation nationwide. Instead, these new programs give us a new set of challenges that must be met if we are to unlock the learning potential of the nation's children and youth (Waters et al., 2003).

THE UNIVERSITY OF ILLINOIS-CHICAGO EDD IN URBAN EDUCATION LEADERSHIP

In 2002, the Urban Education Leadership Program at the University of Illinois-Chicago (UIC) began to organize our practice around one guiding question: *What would it take to produce principals who could lead schools to significantly improved learning outcomes in low-income, urban communities—and to do so as a rule, rather than as rare exceptions to the rule?* Our efforts to answer this question through an intentional combination of theory and practice would lead us to understand that we could not simply be educators, but institutional "change agents," as Kenneth Benne coined that term in the early post-war organizational change literature (Bennis, 2001).

Kegan and Lahey capture the need for change agency with a complementary theoretical insight: "a process of change initiated with an eye to effectiveness under existing norms turns out to yield a conflict in the norms themselves" (Kegan and Lahey, 2009, p. 26). We would find that our effort to produce principals who could lead schools to improved student learning would run afoul of institutional norms—and that these norms would create challenges and tensions that we are still addressing, and expect to continue to address for some time to come. Simply designing a new professional preparation program is analogous to writing an article for publication: it has a defined end point after which the work is finished. To commit to changing seemingly intractable institutional norms to accommodate a program that actually produces sustained results in schools, however, is more analogous to having a robust research agenda: it defines and directs the work for years to come.

Program structure

We have elsewhere discussed in considerable detail our program structure, and we will not repeat that here (Cosner, Tozer, Smylie, 2012; Cosner et al. in press; Shoho, Barnett, and Martinez, 2012). It is useful, however, to summarize the main elements and rationale as presented in these earlier publications.

Degree structure. By 2003, we had replaced our traditional, master's level school administration certificate program with a highly selective, cohort-based, field-intensive program embedded in an EdD structure that allowed us to conduct ongoing school-based work with students before and after licensure. We did not begin with the assumption that school leaders need a doctoral degree to be good principals. We believed, however, that creating a new generation of highly effective principals at scale would require more than the one- or two-year experience of a typical master's degree. We also knew that our selection criteria, which emphasized deep teaching experience and a clear record of teacher leadership, were highly likely to favor candidates who already had master's degrees. Practically speaking, a second master's was a weak incentive to support the extensive program we envisioned. From the beginning, the EdD structure was designed so candidates could achieve state licensure and district eligibility in the first eighteen months of the program, then continue their professional development in the program for at least another two years, and typically longer. Ginsberg, Knapp, and Farrington (2014) have made an important recent contribution to the field's thinking about the learning opportunities provided by an EdD structure for principal preparation and development.

They identify, for example, how the EdD can position principals to engage in the ongoing work of practice-scholarship within their schools and communities, as well as within broader networks of "learning-focused" leaders who strive for long-term trajectories of improvement.

Program design features. While the program has gone through a number of key modifications since 2003 (Cosner et al., 2012): (1) We remain a selective, cohort-based EdD program dedicated to the preparation and ongoing support of principals whose goal is to improve student learning in high-need urban schools. (2) The Chicago Public Schools (CPS) has partnered with us since the beginning by funding salaries for, and helping us structure, yearlong, full-time, leadership residencies for every candidate. (3) Students admitted to the EdD program attend a semester of coursework before entering the full-year residency experience under the supervision of a mentor principal and with the critical support of a UIC leadership coach, a former CPS principal who has a demonstrated record of significant impact on school transformation and improved student learning outcomes. (4) Coursework continues during the internship, integrating the thematic strands of instructional leadership, organizational leadership, and practitioner inquiry, with particular attention to the social contexts of schools and the essential need for adult learning within schools. (5) After eighteen months of coursework and a year's supervised residency, students are expected to have passed the state licensure assessments and the CPS Principal Eligibility Assessments, a district "bar exam" with an annual failure rate that approaches or exceeds 60 percent. (6) After passing the state and local principal assessments, 99 percent of candidates take leadership positions in urban schools, all but a few of them in Chicago, and continue their coursework and coaching until they complete the Certificate of Advanced Study or the more demanding EdD degree, which requires a capstone case study of their organizational change theory and practice. Because coaching and academic study may continue for as much as three years beyond initial licensure, UIC effectively becomes a working partner in helping each school leader improve school culture, climate, and learning outcomes.

Indicators of Early Program Impact

In trying to answer our founding question about how to produce transformative principals at scale, we have produced over one hundred principals for urban schools, nearly all of them in Chicago. We have forged and sustained a working partnership with Chicago Public Schools through the tenures of five district CEOs. We have won continuous funding from philanthropic and government sources since the beginning of the program. Our university has supported our work with the establishment and funding of a Center for Urban Education Leadership, committing three clinical faculty lines on university funding to provide field-based leadership coaching during and after the residency year.

Our principals have won numerous local, state, and national awards for their impact on student learning, as measured by a range of indicators from increased attendance and graduation rates to increased standardized test scores. UIC's program is the only one in the nation to receive exemplary performance awards from the University Council on Education Administration, the Council of Great City Schools, and the Bush Institute Alliance to Reform Education Leadership. On the strength of the program's work, UIC faculty chaired a state Legislative Task Force that led to now-implemented legislation making principal preparation programs in Illinois documentably more selective, more practice-based, and more results-oriented (Cheney and Davis, 2011).

Finally, the UIC program is a founding partner in the new Chicago Leadership Collaborative, a consortium of higher education and not-for-profit residency-based principal preparation programs that work collaboratively with CPS to produce outstanding principals for every principal vacancy in Chicago—that is, highly selective, residency-based principal preparation at scale (Zubrzycki, 2012).

Key Tensions in Program Theory and Practice

And yet we have so far to go, if we are to produce transformative principals "as a rule." It is with considerable disquietude that we report the early successes of the UIC program, because we do not want to give the impression that we think we "have it right" when we know we do not. The satisfaction we take in seeing some of our principals transform school cultures is countered by the concern that not all of our principals are doing so.

With the assistance of external funding, we are now attempting to investigate the candidate and program variables that seem to have the greatest impact on whether a principal will genuinely succeed by the transformative standards that we have set for ourselves and our graduates. It is not enough to obtain a principalship; it is not enough to keep the position; we expect our graduates to demonstrate a significant impact on the kinds of academic success indicators that can be life-changing for urban children and youth.

Such an aspiration carries within it a central tension: what does it mean to "transform" a school? What counts as success in an age of accountability and in a partnership with a public school district? Clearly, there is a danger of reducing the work of the principal to creating systems and structures that lead to improved standardized test scores and improved college attendance rates. Such measures may limit our educational horizons and narrow our aspirations, as the Chicago Teacher's Union argued in recently passing a resolution in opposition to CPS adoption of Common Core State Standards for student learning (Chicago Teachers Union, 2014).

Before attempting to address these questions that arise from a tension over program goals and aspirations, it is worth noting that this is but one of several tensions we have encountered in our work. In the remainder of the chapter, we describe but do not resolve examples of these tensions in an effort to contribute to the discourse on bringing transformative principal preparation to scale.

It is our view that these tensions can effectively be addressed only through a *praxis* that marries theory and practice with institutional change. The concept of praxis has many origins, from the Classical Greeks to Karl Marx to Hanna Arendt. Our relatively straightforward take on praxis is informed by Freire's notion of the unity of change theory and change practice that derive from, and inform, one another (Freire, 1986).

FIVE KEY TENSIONS IN DEVELOPING PRINCIPALS FOR URBAN SCHOOLS

We have selected five key tensions for examination because they represent a range of different kinds of significant challenges that next-generation programs in urban school leadership preparation are likely to face, as we are facing them now. These are all features of conflicts within the university culture, between university and school district culture, and between program goals and the wider culture's discourse on education. We will introduce these tensions in list form, then discuss each:

- The social justice vs. neoliberal educational agendas
- University culture vs. needs of schools
- Partnership with urban school districts vs. academic autonomy and program control
- Individual vs. organizational locus of high-quality instruction
- National and local challenges vs. state authority

Social justice vs. neoliberal educational agenda. The first of these tensions might be described as the tension between a social justice orientation to school leadership and a neoliberal results orientation to school leadership. As Swanson has pointed out in a recent review of the social justice leadership literature, what counts as social justice leadership is itself contested terrain, as is the centrality of improved academic performance to such leadership (2013). To produce principals who can lead schools to student learning outcomes such as improved test scores and graduation rates seems to play right into the hands of a neoliberal agenda that reinforces unequal power and privilege (Lipman, 2004).

But not to improve the literacy and other academic skills that typically result in improve student test performance, and not to improve graduation rates for traditionally marginalized children and youth serves such students poorly in any future now foreseeable for them and serves to reproduce social stratification (Delpit, 1995; Pathways to Prosperity Project, 2011).

To an important extent it would be difficult to justify support for school leadership programs today without appealing to some of the values and measures also represented in neoliberal discourse in a climate of accountability. These include improved standardized test scores, reduced dropout rates, improved college attendance rates, and so on: the kinds of measures on which neoliberal charter school advocates, for example, base their claims (Civic Committee of the Commercial Club of Chicago, 2009).

When we assess the success of our principals partly by these measures, then we run the risk of simply replicating and reinforcing a neoliberal accountability discourse, or of treating the symptoms of an inequitable social structure rather than going to root causes. Failure to address these tensions can undermine any possibility of faculty working together effectively with a common vision for improving schools through redesigned principal preparation programs. It can also derail any attempts to build state-wide and nation-wide attempts to build coalitions of those who advocate social justice in education and those who advocate reform in school leader preparation—often very different professional communities.

Our response to this tension is, first, to recognize that it is reductionist to think that because two different systems of thought share some elements in common (in this case leadership for social justice and neoliberal educational reform), they are essentially the same, or that one necessarily reinforces the other. Both communism and capitalism, for example, value something called a "work ethic." But to think that this common commitment to work ethic cancels out the fundamental differences in these two systems of thought is a mistake that few would make. Similarly, a number of very different religions are monotheistic, but we have little difficulty telling these religious systems apart.

What is essential in distinguishing systems of thought, or educational orientations, from one another, is to articulate the differences as well as the similarities. While there are strong social justice reasons to advocate that schools develop marginalized students' academic skills, for example, both the means and the justifications by which these ends are achieved may be very different from the neoliberal justifications and means.

Advocating increases in attendance, achievement scores, and high school graduation rates through proliferation of charter schools in service of global economic competition is one orientation. It is a very different orientation, with different means and justifications, to advocate the same academic success indicators in service of increasing the life opportunities and empowerment for traditionally marginalized children and youth systemically in every neighborhood school in urban environments. The latter orientation makes clear that all such children, and not just those who may sometimes benefit from market-model competition among schools, deserve the opportunity to master the "codes of power" (Delpit, 1995) that will enable them to exercise greater autonomy and collective action in their lives—and that a just society puts the systems in place to ensure such a goal.

Moreover, it must be recognized that social injustice resides in institutions, and that any good theory of social justice education must have a strong theory of institutional change. Social justice talk that lacks a plausible, evidence-based theory of change has little promise of making a difference in institutional injustice. School leaders can be powerful institutional change agents at a scale that is potentially achievable district-wide in urban centers (Weast, 2010). This is a different theory of change than that which is signaled by the competitive market model of charter schools, or the unsupported faith that standards and accountability will produce

dramatic school improvement (Elmore, 2005). Such otherwise neoliberal metrics as improved test scores and graduation rates can in fact be used effectively in service of improving the impact of school leadership programs on public schools (Bambrick-Santoyo, 2010; Fielding et al., 2007)—and can also be used to bolster arguments for why it is more cost-effective for states and districts to invest in system-wide school improvement through school leadership than not to (Belfield and Levin, 2007).

School leadership is highly influential, and may prove be the strongest factor, in the promotion and realization of school success, particularly in championing students of poverty and color (Mckenzie and Scheurich, 2004, 2007). Although Leithwood's finding—that school leadership is second only to teaching quality in improving student learning outcomes (Leithwood et al., 2004; Leithwood and Jantzi, 2008)—is regularly cited, McKenzie and Scheurich's work reminds us that without strong school leaders, it will be difficult to attract, retain, and develop teachers who can rise to the challenge of improving learning outcomes for traditionally marginalized students (Gamoran et al, 2000). Because high quality instruction is essential for such students' learning, school leaders are essential to any vision of significant learning improvements at scale.

To produce change agents who can transform schools into fulfilling workplaces for teachers and students, the status quo in higher education will be insufficient; and higher education is not likely to change in the directions needed unless higher education faculty become change agents within their own institutions. Otherwise higher education as a system will continue to be perfectly designed to produce the results that we are now getting. In our experience, for example, simply collecting the data on program graduates' impact on standard measures of school improvement, is a step most leadership programs have not yet taken and that requires institutional commitment to support (Davis and Darling Hammond, 2012).

University culture vs. needs of schools. The second key tension to address is the culture of the university versus the needs of school systems. Peterman's (2008) outstanding edited volume on partnerships in teacher education identifies a range of tensions in district/university collaborations to prepare and develop teachers. We have found tensions of our own in our efforts to

486 STEVE TOZER, PAUL ZAVITKOVSKY, SAM WHALEN, AND PETER MARTINEZ

produce principals who will meet the learning needs of teachers and students in schools.

If the university culture, for example, values as its primary client the graduate student who seeks an advanced degree, then the program commitment and design is likely to be very different from an orientation in which the primary client is the K–12 student who needs a transformational principal. The former orientation can lead to a university master's program that is essentially open admissions, because graduating large numbers of credentialed professionals is itself a sign of success as well as a source of valuable tuition revenue. That orientation has led to individual programs enrolling hundreds of students annually, in IHEs in Illinois and elsewhere (including online programs), while the latter orientation tends to lead to small-batch, high-intensity programs (Davis and Darling- Hammond, 2012).

A clearly related institutional tension here is the tension between tuition income and strategic impact on student learning outcomes schools. Small-batch, high-intensity programs are more expensive then massive programs in which the chief added university expense is an adjunct professor standing in front of a large class of students. At UIC and elsewhere, faculty are demonstrating that universities can at least begin to successfully overcome some of these seemingly intractable priorities in service of demonstrated impact on schools.

It can even be argued that it is in the university's interest to take whatever institutional change steps are necessary to demonstrate such impact. As programs grow in reputation and demand, it is good for the university in multiple ways. For example, our university administration has for over a decade welcomed a program initiative that: a) brings in a steady stream of philanthropic funds to develop a new program model that is highly regarded by the Chicago Public Schools and by the State Board of Education; b) secures funds from the local school district to provide high-end administrative salaries for each aspiring school leader's yearlong internship; and c) secures a steady stream of research dollars to support inquiry into the value of the program and to support faculty publications that are part of the coin of the realm for research institutions.

State governments can play a significant role here. In the long run, it will be far less expensive for states to support high-quality principal preparation than to pay the otherwise inevitable price of educational failure

(Belfield and Levin, 2007). It has been fifteen years now since Harvard's Richard Elmore (1999) first published a path-breaking analysis of why the standards movement was not appreciably changing, nor could be expected to change, student learning outcomes in schools without rethinking school leadership altogether. Elmore's was not a pessimistic analysis; it was just the opposite. He argued that if we look in the right place—namely school leaders who know how to improve student learning—we will see the results at scale that we have long known can be achieved in even the most struggling schools.

The sobering but instructive corollary to Elmore's argument is that none of the potentially valuable, high-cost reforms that have been promoted over the past thirty years since *A Nation At Risk*—neither the professional standards movement, nor increased testing and accountability, nor Teach For America and other alternative routes to teacher certification, nor teacher education reform, nor charter schools—has much of a chance of success at scale unless we improve how schools are led.

Nationwide, relatively flat achievement growth over the past quarter-century and the stubborn persistance of differential outcomes for different population groups appear to confirm that corollary (IES, 2013). Normal, everyday school leadership unwittingly undermines all of these reforms, systemically and inevitably. The evidence for this is old news, yet we continue to invest extraordinary sums in reforms unlikely to succeed until we begin to invest significantly in school leader preparation. Such investment will likely have to be undertaken by state governments, not borne simply by tuition-dependent universities.

The culture of the large research university and the small-college school of education alike have historically rewarded academic faculty not for improving the learning outcomes in public schools but for doing the work of the university or the small college—the classic triad of teaching, research, and service frames the incentive structure that leads regularly to faculty promotion, tenure, and status (Shils, 2008) without any need to show results in PreK–12 student learning. As we will later argue, the fortunes of academic faculty are untethered, in any direct way, to the fortunes of public school districts—except perhaps in limited state budgets in which a zero-sum financing means that greater resources for the university may mean reduced resources for the public schools.

In addition to the incentives for colleges and schools of education to privilege tuition income over selective, small-batch, results-oriented principal preparation programs, and in addition to the incentive structures which frame faculty productivity in ways that are not directly linked to public school outcomes, there are other cultural tensions within a college or university seeking to serve the interests of children in public schools more effectively. One of these is the tension between faculty autonomy and the individual faculty reward structure versus programmatic excellence, which requires collaboration for coherence and continuous improvement.

We have found that excellence in preparing transformational principals is a time-consuming problem for faculty who are feeling the responsibility, if not the absolute necessity, to spend more time on research and publication. In research, the academy more readily supports a scholarship of critique then it does an applied praxis of demonstration. In teaching, the academy more readily supports teaching academic content than producing change agents who produce demonstrated impact on institutional change.

To challenge these institutional norms requires rethinking the staffing and reward structures of departments, schools, and colleges of education. As a point of contrast, one can compare the staffing pattern of a typical department in the liberal arts and sciences such as philosophy or history of mathematics with a department that produces physicians in the medical school.

The structure of the LAS department is flat and undifferentiated, typically comprised of a department chair, secretary, and academic faculty. Medical school staffing structure is far more complicated, with a greater variety of staff and administrative rules to support the professional preparation responsibilities shared between the medical school and sites of practice such as clinics and hospitals. Today's education departments preparing school leaders are staffed like LAS departments, not like medical schools. It may be reassuring to note that one hundred years ago medical schools, too, were nonselective in their admissions and lacked clinical experience in sites of practice, until a massive reform in medical preparation was launched (Flexner, 1910; Starr, 1982).

Higher education has demonstrated that it is capable of fairly profound structural change in professional education, although the most well-documented example (medicine) is now a century old. Our experience tells us that such change is necessary in school leadership preparation. In medicine, as expectations of medical treatment increased, so increased the demands on medical education Starr, 1982). In education, as our expectations of schools have elevated, so have the expectations of the school leader—and consequently our expectations of school leader preparation. That the job description of the principal has changed is not much in doubt.

Prior to 1990, it would have been difficult for Marks and Printy to synthesize the literature on principal as instructional leader vs. transformational leader as they did in 2003, because principals were expected to be neither (Marks and Printy, 2003). If principals are not yet the change agents we need, it would be hard to have expected otherwise: there is little evidence to be found that the discourse—scholarly and practical—on preparing principals as change agents has yet to penetrate widespread practice.

There is similarly little evidence that faculty now joining schools and colleges of education are themselves prepared to be change agents in their institutions. Assistant professors are ill-positioned to challenge the university reward structure. Yet, given the structures of colleges and department of education, there is no strong reason to believe that teaching courses better or publishing in refereed journals will by themselves dramatically improve the impact principals have on student learning in schools. It is highly likely, however, that if we are to work effectively with school districts, higher education will have to support that work by making changes in staffing and reward structures to do so—as the medical field has done with the heavy infusion of clinical faculty.

Most academic faculty in education are neither interested in, nor qualified to, spend large proportions of their time in schools coaching aspiring and novice principals, yet without such support, it is not reasonable to expect the clinical experience to be as fruitful for leadership development (Shoho, Barnett, and Martinez, 2012; Wallace Foundation, 2007b). UIC has for over a decade employed the district's highest-performing retiring principals as leadership coaches. We insist on high-performing principals as coaches because we do not confuse experience with expertise, and our aspiring and novice principals need to learn from the latter. Statistically, principals who lead schools to dramatically elevate student learning above socioeconomic status predictors remain a relatively rare breed (hence, SES remains a powerful predictor of student learning outcomes)—but they are there to be found. Making such practitioners full members of the academic team, sharing in decision-making on all phases of the program, has been a learning experience for all of us—and has benefited the learning of our principal candidates.

Partnership with urban school districts vs. academic autonomy and program control. The third major tension is a specific sub-problem of the university/district cultural mismatch, and we treat it separately to emphasize its importance. The university culture and the urban district culture make for a relatively comfortable relationship at a distance, but a formal partnership is more like a marriage. It takes sustained and often creative effort on both sides to make it work, and each side sometimes suspects that the other is not doing its share (Peterman, 2008; Walsh and Backe, 2013).

Many academics are attracted to research universities because of the considerable autonomy that the research environment affords, and we have found that working closely with a school district constrains that autonomy considerably. We hasten to add that such constraints are a price that we are willing to pay for the access and leverage that the district provides us through the partnership, but it is a price that must be acknowledged.

University faculty cherish control over their daily and weekly schedules, in part because serious scholarship and conscientious preparation for teaching require such control, in part because for most people, greater autonomy is a good in itself. But urban school districts run according to a different tempo, with decision-making that in the massive context of the of the district is more bureaucratic, top-down, crisis-driven, and erratic than higher education faculty are accustomed to—and that provides much less autonomy to its employees than university faculty expect in their work. The difference in scale is itself significant. Our College of Education, for example, has about sixty faculty, while the district has over six hundred school principals and over twenty thousand teachers. Our college budget is under $10 million, somewhat higher with grant money, while the district budget is about $6 billion, somewhat higher with grant money.

But the differences in institutional culture go beyond scale. The school district has to respond to public pressure and protests from various constituencies, rich and poor, powerful and marginalized, over any number of matters. It must respond to budget shortfalls that exceed the entire budget of any college of education in the nation. It must provide meals to almost 400,000 children and youth, and transportation to a large subset of them. It must respond on a weekly and often daily basis to violence and death that touches children in their neighborhoods.

Higher education faculty rarely have to confront such things so urgently and directly, and for the most part we did not enter academe with the expectation that our schedules would be much affected by the urgencies and schedule-reversals that are common to urban school systems. And we certainly did not expect that our control over the quality of our programs might at times be ceded, in a partnership agreement, to an urban district that is fighting battles that most of us are not called upon to fight (Chou and Tozer, 2008).

This is partly why the fortunes of higher education are largely untethered, at least in the long term, to the fortunes of urban public schools systems. The greatest universities in the nation, boasting well-paid and honored faculty, can and often do reside in urban districts in whose schools these same faculty would not enroll their own children. The political economy of higher education in the United States is in important ways divorced from the political economy of urban schools.

To engage with the public schools as joint problem-solvers is difficult for both sides. The district has reason to believe that its needs are not a priority for the university, and higher education faculty typically do not want districts making any decisions that might affect the quality of our programs—such as, for example, where resident principals might be placed, or what local standards will be used to judge program candidates at admission or at graduation. We have found that it is much easier to write articles about what the public schools should do than to join with them shoulder-to-shoulder to do it. As the division of labors fall out, most higher education faculty have chosen the former as their contribution. A key question, then, is how does the university leverage its resources in a way that truly disrupts the systemic nature of school failure without being swallowed up in it?

One way to respond to that question is to throw up one's hands and say that the urban district is simply too bureaucratic, too resource-starved, too chaotic, or too driven by a neoliberal agenda to work with directly, and that higher education faculty are best equipped to teach classes and publish research anyway; so we should stick to what we know how to do. But we also know how that stance works. And millions of students are still in those school districts that many higher education faculty find so dysfunctional.

Our experience is that building the capacity to partner well with the school system means, at the least, clear and unambiguous institutional change in four main areas: goals, personnel, time, and money. In our context, partnering with the district to produce transformational principals has meant:

1. making a clear, public, long-term commitment to joining with the school district in a shared, focused initiative with a clear and compelling theory of action for improving learning outcomes in schools, and being willing to share accountability to that goal with the district;
2. hiring high-quality non-research staff with the knowledge and skill to forge and sustain district relationships, show respect for the district, and earn district respect in turn;
3. persisting collaboratively year in and year out no matter what obstacles arise, affirming by word and deed that neither the district nor IHEs can achieve the transformative goals alone and that joint problem-solving work over time is necessary if genuine institutional change is to be achieved; and
4. continuously seeking external funding, just as we would for research, to support this all-important effort.

This is a short and inadequate list, but these represent some of the essentials that have served us well. In its broader categories, this list—goals, people, time, and money—is little different from the requirements of ambitious research in the university environment. One key difference, however, is the commitment to demonstrated impact on student earning outcomes. Consequently, a second key difference is that this is not a partnership project within a finite funding opportunity. Rather, it is a long-term commitment to changing how we do business: in this case the business of preparing and developing principals who demonstrate significant impact on student learning in PreK–12 schools, and

finding the resources to support that. It is a promise that carefully constructed school leader development programs can keep.

Individual vs. organizational locus of high-quality instruction. If the first cultural tension above is largely ideological (social justice vs. neoliberal) and the second and third are largely inter-institutional (IHEs and school districts), the fourth is a combination of both: colleges of education are at once victims of, and institutional contributors to, the ideology of the individual teacher as the locus of high-quality instruction. Concerns about the quality of teachers in the United States have a long history, going back to Washington Irving's Ichabod Crane and the Annual Reports of Horace Mann in Massachusetts (Tozer and Senese, 2012).

These long-standing concerns are punctuated periodically, such as during the Conant era reforms of the early 1960s and the national response to *A Nation at Risk* after 1983 (Tozer and Senese, 2012). Schools and colleges of education are routinely taken to task for accepting poorly prepared teacher education candidates and for producing inadequately prepared graduates. Teach for America, in contrast, is regularly lauded for the academic strength of its teachers, and by the U.S. Secretary of Education, for bringing "more talented" teachers into the profession (Ardinger, 2012).

The problem with such thinking is that it locates instructional quality in individual teachers instead of in schools as organizations. Given that it is widely acknowledged that novice teachers from even academically strong institutions have only learned a small portion of what they need to learn to meet the needs of marginalized children, it may well be that teacher education programs are relatively weak levers for improving the quality of teaching in low-income neighborhoods—though they can provide important foundations for such work (Murrell, 2001). That is, what beginning teachers can do is limited, compared with what they can be expected to do several years later—if they stay in the field and function in an environment that enables professional learning to progress (Borman and Dowling, 2008; Hargreaves and Fullan, 2012).

To illustrate, high teacher turnover would not matter if beginning teachers were just as effective as experienced teachers at working with traditionally marginalized kids (Kane, Rockoff, and Staiger, 2008). All school districts, wealthy and poor alike, would embrace teacher turnover as a way to save money because beginning teachers are so much less expensive to employ than experienced teachers, and the learning outcomes would be the same. School principals and school district superintendents know, however, that a steady influx of novice teachers is an obstacle to bringing high-quality instruction to children who need high-quality instruction the most. In teaching, as in other complex human endeavors, experience matters a lot (Day et al., 2009).

Consequently, the majority of teacher learning takes place on the job in schools; there just is not enough time-on-task in a teacher education program to develop the complex knowledge and skills necessary for the challenges of teaching in urban classrooms. The best school principals not only retain teachers, they also provide the conditions in which adult learning can take place most effectively (Hargreaves and Fullan, 2012). Teachers need time, support, and systems of shared learning if they are to effectively learn how to meet the learning needs of marginalized children and youth whose cultural capital may be quite different from their own. When schools are led in this way, quality of instruction develops as a property of school organization, not simply as a result of "teacher talent."

It is not that "teacher talent" and teacher education don't matter; there is every reason to believe they do. One simply needs to conduct a thought experiment: compare the expected teacher impact of randomly selected new graduates of teacher education programs with randomly selected twenty-two-year-olds at large—or even randomly selected new college graduates across all disciplines (and Teach for America is not a good proxy for that second group, as they reject nine out of ten candidates [Ardinger, 2012]). But acknowledging that teacher education matters, novice teachers are, at best, still novices—and colleges of education should not be attacked for producing them. Under the supervision of the right school leader it could be that most beginning teachers are in fact right where they need to be in terms of their development—we won't know until we see more examples of school leaders who systematically support the success and growth of new teachers.

Unfortunately, schools of education have traditionally invested far less per candidate in principal preparation programs then teacher preparation programs. Unlike in principal preparation, it is standard practice in teacher education to invest considerable resources in field-based supervision of student teachers and early field experiences. Ironically, the surest route to producing more effective teachers from teacher education programs may well be to produce more effective principals who can retain and nurture the talents of teacher education program graduates to have a far greater impact of students in high-need schools.

Ultimately, schools of education have failed to challenge the ideology of "teacher talent" with an argument that instructional quality must ultimately reside in schools as organizations. In other words, "teacher talent" is something that is neither innate nor produced through a brief preparation program—but something that can be developed effectively over a period of years.

We cannot resist adding that the instructional development of academic faculty in IHEs can and should also be a product of such thinking. Through intensive program collaboration, shared examination of student work, consideration of relevant data, and collaborative redesign of courses, academic faculty can grow their own ability to produce principals of a quality that these same faculty would not be able to produce as isolated individuals. This observation is made in service of underscoring instructional quality as an organizational property, and underscoring as well the prevalence of private practice in university academic culture.

National and local challenges vs. state authority. The final tension is that the problem of school leadership preparation in the United States is a national problem, but the solutions are located primarily in local and state agencies. New Leaders is a good example of an organization that has tried to work at a national scale, and a recent Rand study shows that much positive has been achieved (Gates, Hamilton, et al., 2014). But New Leaders has to forge individualized relationships in each district and state in which it offers leadership preparation, and in the larger cities, it can supply only a fraction of the principals needed.

In education reform efforts, districts and states have considerable authority. Because of the difference in scale, states have much deeper resources than districts do, and federal dollars are typically channeled through state agencies to local districts, as well. Districts can engage local initiatives to improve school leadership, but if school leadership preparation is to make a full-scale shift as medical preparation did a century ago, states are going to have to play key roles.

The good news is that the scale of change needed is relatively modest, by state standards. While the ranks of teachers nationwide are so overwhelming as to make high selectivity of teachers a distant dream (educational philosopher Harry Broudy used to say that "no profession of three million anything will ever be selective," and now the field is nearly four million strong), there are fewer than 100,000 principals in K–12 schools today. This is about one-third the number of practicing physicians—all of America's principals would all fit into a single university football stadium. As one of the most populous states, Illinois has four thousand schools, meaning an average annual principal vacancy rate of about four hundred—smaller than the senior class of many high schools in Illinois. If the state were to finance full-year residencies of four hundred potential principals a year, it would barely show up on the state education budget. In fact, in Tennessee the State Coalition on Educational Reform is proposing to the governor to fund full-year residencies and the university tuition as well (Woodson, 2014).

State governments are the great enabler and the great obstacle here, because even if this victory is won in Tennessee, the battle will have to be re-fought in Illinois and forty-eight other states, one at a time, across a broad spectrum of state-level political and ideological climates (Shelton, 2010). The reason this is a tension for faculty in principal preparation programs is that state agencies—including the governor's office, the board of education, and the legislature—are indispensable allies if we are to change principal preparation at scale in the United States. Neither local districts nor the federal government have the resources nor the constitutional clout to achieve such change at scale. Nor is it likely that IHEs can make the necessary shifts without resources that only the state can provide. But where will the political energy come from to move these state agencies? In Illinois, that political energy has come partly from faculty in higher education, partly from national and state philanthropic foundations, and partly from leaders in state agencies who had begun to recognize how much difference school leadership can make.

The philanthropic groups and state agencies are quick to remind us, as Giroux once wrote, that a "scholarship of critique" is not enough: it is well established that our schools are inequitable, and we have good scholarship to tell us why. Nor is a "scholarship of possibility" or "politics of hope" enough, as we have long been able to describe a better state of affairs for our schools (Dewey, 1916; Giroux, 2006). We have been learning instead to conduct a scholarship of *demonstration*. In committing to a praxis that demonstrates empirically what schools and kids are capable of, we are trying to provide the most powerful tool we have to bring about change at the state level: compelling evidence. But that praxis will likely have to develop from the ground up before the evidence becomes compelling enough for most states to act. And ground-up initiatives require change agents on the ground.

CONCLUSION

We began this chapter with the familiar observation, "Your system, any system, is perfectly designed to produce the results you are getting" (Carr, 2008). Over the past thirty years, the educational and political landscape has changed considerably at the national, state, and local levels. The "Reagan Revolution" produced a new era of conservatism, digital technology exploded into every aspect of daily life, university degrees became obtainable without leaving one's living room, charter schools were established in cities throughout the nation, the United States was attacked on its own soil and became embroiled in two foreign wars, and the nation elected an African-American president. Despite these and other events that could scarcely have been predicted thirty years ago, the reproduction of educational inequity in public school has remained virtually unchanged. The system that produced inequitable educational outcomes when *A Nation at Risk* was released in 1983 continues to operate today, and higher education is a major part of the system. It continues to produce the teachers and the principals who are the key educators in the public schools.

A recurrent theme in this paper is that the problem of preparing principals who can lead schools to significantly improved learning outcomes is fundamentally a problem of institutional and organizational change. Twelve years into our work, our results tell us that principals cannot produce markedly better outcomes in schools without learning to be change agents able to alter school culture, climate, organization, and instructional practices. Because principals have not sufficiently learned to be change agents in schools and colleges of education as we know them, we believe that IHEs will have to change.

Our experience to date strongly suggests a model in which IHEs will have to alter their vision and justifications for what they are seeking to accomplish, their understanding of instructional quality as a property of organizations and not simply of individuals, their internal staffing and reward structures, their relationships to school districts, and their relationships to state agencies. We have argued that there are five consequential tensions, among others that could be examined, that will require adept change by university faculty if they are to produce transformational principals with any kind of fidelity. These tensions are:

- The social justice vs. neoliberal educational agendas
- University culture vs. needs of schools
- Partnership with urban school districts vs. academic autonomy and program control
- Individual vs. organizational locus of high-quality instruction
- The national challenge vs. state authority

Unfortunately, few university faculty are professionally prepared to be change agents in these diverse arenas. It's not what we signed up for. To succeed on all of these fronts is to assume roles for which we were not trained, working with people with whom we were not trained to work, and within a reward structure that does not support such role re-definition. It will be important for us in higher education to form and sustain our own professional learning communities, sharing strong evidence on what is working and what is not working for children and youth in schools, if we are to support each other in becoming the kinds of scholar-activists needed if we are to produce the principals our schools need. We may then be able to convert traditional expectations into a new set of professional norms with corresponding incentive systems that support the practices described here. Only then is it likely that next-generation programs will come to define our field.

NOTE

1. The authors thank our colleagues Shelby Cosner, Margery Ginsberg, and Jason Swanson for their critical comments in the preparation of this chapter. The recurrent use of first person plural ("we" and "our") in this chapter is intended to represent the authors only, not the views of all faculty participating on the UIC program that is described herein. While the program has been for many years so deeply collaborative that all faculty have contributed to the authors' thinking, and although perspectives in this article may be widely shared among our faculty, we cannot assume that all faculty would agree with <u>all</u> points of view expressed here.

REFERENCES

Ardinger, E. N. (2012). "Unlikely Triumph"? A Critical Discourse Analysis of Press Coverage of Teach for America. Unpublished doctoral dissertation. Chicago: University of Illinois.

Bambrick-Santoyo, P. (2010). *Driven by Data: A Practical Guide to Improve Instruction*. San Francisco: Jossey-Bass.

Belfield, C. R. and Levin, H. M. eds. (2007). *The Price We Pay: Economic and Social Consequences of Inadequate Education*. Washington, DC: Brookings Institution.

Bennis, W. (2001). An intellectual memoir. In Bennis, W., Spreitzer, G.M., Cummings, T.G. (eds.), *The Future of Leadership*. San Francisco: Jossey-Bass.

Bottoms, G. and O'Neill, K. (2001). *Preparing a new breed of school principals: It's time for action*. Atlanta: Southern Regional Education Board.

Borko, H., Wolf, S., Simone, G., and Uchiyama, K. (2003). Schools in transition: Reform efforts and school capacity in Washington state. *Educational Evaluation and Policy Analysis*, 25(2), 171–201.

Borman, D. B. and Dowling, N. M. (2008). Teacher Attrition and Retention: A Meta-Analytic and Narrative Review of the Research. *Review of Educational Research*. 78(3), 467–409.

Brown, Emma. (2014, May 7). Math, reading performance is stagnant among U.S. 12-graders, assessment finds. *Washington Post*. www.washingtonpost.com/local/education/math-reading-performance-is-stagnant-among-us-12th-graders-assessment-finds/2014/05/07/6a5e743e-d47a-11e3-aae8-c2d44bd79778_story.html.

Bryk, S., Sebring, P., Allensworth, E., Luppescu, and Easton J., (2010). *Organizing Schools for Improvement: Lessons from Chicago*. Chicago: University of Chicago Press.

Carr, Susan (2008). A quotation with a life of its own: Editor's notebook. *Patient Safety and Quality Healthcare*. July. August. Downloaded 2/13/14. www.psqh.com/july-august-2008/1864-editor-s-notebook-a-quotation-with-a-life-of-its-own.

Cheney, G. R., Davis, J., et al. (2010). *A New Approach to Principal Preparation: Innovative Programs Share Their*

Practices and Lessons Learned. Fort Worth, TX: Rainwater Charitable Foundation.

Cheney, G. R., Davis, J., et al. (2011). *Gateways to the Principalship: State Power to Improve the Quality of School Leaders*. Washington, DC: Center for American Progress.

Chenoweth, K. (2009). *How It's Being Done: Urgent Lessons from Unexpected Schools*. Cambridge, MA: Harvard Education Press.

Chenoweth, K. and Theokas, C. (2011). *Getting It Done: Leading Academic Success in Unexpected Schools*. Cambridge, MA: Harvard Education Press.

Chicago Teachers Union: Media Press Release (2014). Chicago Teachers Union joins growing national opposition to Common Core State Standards. Chicago Teachers Union: Media Press Release. May 7. Retrieved August 15, 2014, from www.ctunet.com/media/press-releases/chicago-teachers-union-joins-opposition-to-common-core.

Chou, V. and S. Tozer (2008). What's urban got to do with it? In Peterman, Francine (ed.), *Partnering to Prepare Urban Teachers: A Call to Activism*. Washington DC: AACTE.

Civic Committee of the Commercial Club of Chicago (2009). *Still Left Behind*. Chicago: The Commercial Club of Chicago.

Cosner, S. (2005). High school principals and school capacity: An exploratory study of capacity building from a social and human capital perspective. Unpublished doctoral dissertation.

Cosner, S. A., Tozer, S., and Smylie, M. (2012). The EdD program at the University of Illinois at Chicago: Using continuous improvement to promote school leadership preparation. *Planning and Changing, 43*(1/2), 127–148.

Cosner, S. A., Tozer, S. T., Whalen, S. W., and Zavitkovsky (in press). Cultivating exemplary school leadership preparation at a research intensive university, *Journal of Research in Leadership Education*.

Davis, S., and Darling-Hammond, L. (2012). Innovative principal preparation programs: What works and how we know. *Planning and Changing, 43*(1/2), 25–45.

Day, D. V., Harrison, M. M., and Halpin, S. M. (2009). *An Integrative Approach to Leader Development*. New York: Psychology Press.

Delpit, Lisa. (1995). *Other People's Children: Cultural Conflict in the Classroom*. New York: New Press.

Dewey, J. (1916, 2009). *Democracy and Education*. Radford, WA: Wilder Publishing.

Elmore, R.F. (1999). Building a new structure for school leadership. *American Educator*, Winter, 1–9.

Elmore, R. (2005). *School Reform from the Inside Out: Policy, Practice and Performance*. Boston: Harvard Education Press.

Fielding, L., Kerry, N., Rosier, P. (2007). *Annual Growth, Catch-up Growth*. Kennewick, WA: The New Foundation Press.

Finn, C. E. and Broad, E. (2003). *Better leaders for America's schools: A manifesto*. Washington, DC: The Broad Foundation and The Fordham Foundation.

Flexner, A. (1910). Medical Education in the United States and Canada. *Carnegie Foundation Bulletin Number Four*. New York: Carnegie Foundation.

Freire, P. (1986). *Pedagogy of the Oppressed*. New York: Continuum.

Gamoran, A., Secada, W., and Marrett, C. (2000). The organizational context of teaching and learning: Changing theoretical perspectives. In M. Hallinan (Ed.), *Handbook of the Sociology of Education* (pp. 37–63). New York: Kluwer Academic/Plenum Publishers.

Gates, S. M., Hamilton, L. S., et al. (2014). *Preparing Principals to Raise Student Achievement: Implementation and Effects of the New Leaders Program in Ten Districts*. Washington, DC: Rand Corporation.

Gavin, L. (2011, May 24). Setting targets for grades 3–12 linked to the ACTs college readiness benchmarks. *Evanston Roundtable*, pp. 1–10.

Ginsberg, M. B., Knapp, M. S., and Farrington, C. A. (2014). Using transformative experiences to prepare instructional leaders through doctoral education. *Journal of Research on Leadership Education, 9*(2), 168–194.

Giroux, Henry A. (2006). *The Giroux Reader*. Edited by Christopher Robbins. Boulder, CO: Paradigm Publishers.

Hallinger, P. and Heck, R. (1996). Reassessing the principal's role in school effectiveness: A review of the empirical research, 1980–1995. *Educational Administration Quarterly, 32*(1), 5–44.

Hallinger, P. and Heck, R. H. (1998). Exploring the principal's contribution to school effectiveness: 1980–1995. *School Effectiveness and School Improvement, 9*(2), 157–191.

Hargreaves, A. and Fullan, M. (2012). *Professional Capital: Transforming Teaching in Every School*. New York: Teachers College Press.

IES National Center for Educational Statistics (2012). Trends in Academic Progress: NAEP 2012. Washington, DC: U.S. Department of Education NCES2013-456. nces.ed.gov/nationsreportcard/subject/publications/main2012/pdf/2013456.pdf.

Kane, I. Rockoff, J., and Staiger, D. (2008). What does teacher certification tell us about teacher effectiveness? Evidence from New York City. *Economics of Education Review, 27*(6) 615–31.

Leithwood, K., Louis, K. S., Anderson, S., and Wahlstrom, K. (2004). *How Leadership Influences Student Learning*. New York: The Wallace Foundation.

Levine, A.L. (2005). *Educating School Leaders*. Washington, DC: The Education School Project.

Lezotte, L. W. (1984) School Effective Research: A Tribute to Ron Edmonds. "One Perspective on an Effective Schools Research Agenda." ERIC Clearinghouse. www.eric.ed.gov/ERICWebPortal/search/detailmini.jsp?_nfpb=trueand_andERICExtSearch_SearchValue_0=ED252961andERICExtSearch_SearchType_0=noandaccno=ED252961.

Lipman, Pauline (2004). *High Stakes Education: Inequality, Globalization, and Urban School Reform*. New York: Routledge Falmer.

Marzano, R. J. (2003). *What Works in Schools*. Alexandria, VA: Association for Supervision and Curriculum Development.

Murrell, P. (2001). *The Community Teacher: A New Framework for Effective Urban Teaching*. New York: Teachers College Press.

Leithwood, K. and Jantzi, D. (2008). Linking leadership to student learning: the contribution of leader efficacy. *Education Administration Quarterly*, 44(4), 496–528.

Leithwood, K., Seashore Louis, K., Anderson, S., and Wahlstrom, K. (2004). *How Leadership Influences Student Learning*. Toronto, Ontario: Center for Applied Research and Educational Improvement and Ontario Institute for Studies in Education.

Marks, H. and Printy, S. (2003). Principal leadership and school performance: an integration of transformational and instructional leadership. *Education Administration Quarterly* 34(3), 370–397.

McKenzie, K. B. and Scheurich, J. J. (2004). Equity traps: a useful construct for preparing principals to lead schools that are successful with racially diverse students. *Education Administration Quarterly* 40(5) 601–632.

McLester, Susan (2011). Turnaround principals: New training models have emerged for preparing school leaders to transform low-achieving schools. In *District Administration: Solutions for School District Management*, pp. 1–5.

Mead, Sara (2011). PreK–3rd: Principals as crucial instructional leaders. *Foundation for Child Development Policy to Action Brief*, p. 5

Milstein, M. M. (1992). *The Danforth program for the preparation of school principals (DPPSP) six years later: What we have learned*. Paper presented at Danforth Principal Preparation Network and University Council for Educational Administration.

Mitgang. L. (2012). The Making of the Principal: Five Lessons in Leadership Training. The Wallace Foundation.

National Commission on Excellence in Education. (1983). *A Nation at Risk: The Imperative for Educational Reform*. Washington, DC: U.S. Government Printing Office.

Newmann, F. and Associates. (1996). *Authentic achievement: Restructuring schools for intellectual quality*. San Francisco: Jossey-Bass.

Orr, M. T., King, C., and LaPointe, M. (2010). Districts Developing Leaders. Education Development Center, Inc. Funded by the Wallace Foundation.

Orr, M. T. and Orphanos, S. (2011). Graduate level preparation influences the effectiveness of school leaders: a comparison of the outcomes of exemplary and conventional leadership preparation programs for principals. *Education Administration Quarterly*, 47(1), 18–70.

Pathways to Prosperity Project. (2011). *Pathways to Prosperity*. Cambridge: Harvard Graduate School of Education.

Payne, C. M. (2008). *So Much Reform, So Little Change: The Persistence of Failure in Urban Schools*. Cambridge, MA: Harvard Education Press.

Peterman, F. P. (ed.). (2008). *Partnering to Prepare Urban Teachers: A Call to Activism*. Washington, DC: AACTE.

Sahlberg (2012). *Finnish Lessons: What Can the World Learn from Educational Change in Finland?* New York: Teachers College Press.

Shelton, S. (2010). *Strong Leaders, Strong Schools: 2010 State Leadership Laws*. Denver, CO: National Conference of State Legislatures.

Shils, E. (2008). *The Calling of Education: Academic Ethic and Other Essays*. Chicago: University of Chicago Press.

Shoho, A. R., Barnett, B. G, and Martinez, P. (2012). Enhancing "OJT" internships with interactive coaching. *Planning and Changing, 43*(1/2), 161–182.

Smylie, M. (2010). *Continuous School Improvement*. Thousand Oaks, CA: Corwin Press.

Starr, Paul. (1982). *The Social Transformation of American Medicine*. Basic Books.

Swanson, J. A. (2013). *Transformative Dialogue: The Principal's Role in Raising Issues of Difference*. Unpublished doctoral dissertation. University of Illinois.

Ujifusa, A. (2012). State ballot measures include hot K–12 issues. *Education Week*, September 25, 1–5. www.edweek.org/ew/articles/2012/09/26/05ballot.h32.html?tkn=WVLF45mtSBj2iPUxD3KmSW8G3aYp5Atlr2vSandamp;cmp=clp-edweekandprint=1.

Ujifusa, A. and Klein, A. (2012). Education issues underscore election stakes at all levels. *Education Week*, 2012, 1–5. www.edweek.org/ew/articles/2012/10/31/10guide.h32.html?tkn=VQSF4QdC8jybShfS6yqtjq2tArxHVt2pPjGbandcmp=ENL-EU-NEWS1.

U.S. Department of Education. (2001). PL107-110 No Child Left Behind Act of 2001. www2.ed.gov/policy/elsec/leg/esea02/index.html.

Wallace Foundation. (2006). *Leadership for Learning: Making the Connections Among State, District, and School Policies and Practices*. New York: The Wallace Foundation.

Wallace Foundation. (2007a). *A Bridge to School Reform*. New York: The Wallace Foundation.

Wallace Foundation. (2007b). *Getting Principal Mentoring Right: Lessons from the Field*. New York: Wallace Foundation. www.wallacefoundation.org.

Walsh, M. E. and Backe, S. (2013). School-university partnerships: reflections and opportunities. *Peabody Journal of Education, 88*(5), 594–607.

Waters, J. T., Marzano, R. J., and McNulty, B. A. (2003). *Balanced leadership: What 30 years of research tells us about the effect of leadership on student achievement*. Aurora, CO: Mid-continent Research for Education and Learning.

Watkins, W. (2011). Globalization, the new social and political architecture. In Tozer, S., Gallegos, B., and Henry, A., *Handbook of Research in the Social Foundations of Education* (327–228). New York: Routledge.

Weast, J. (2010). Deliberate excellence: Five stages to school system maturity leading to college-ready graduates. *School Administrator, 67*(6), 25–29. www.aasa.org/SchoolAdministratorArticle.aspx?id=13650.

Woodson, J. (2014). School leadership: tapping the power of potential. State Collaborative on Reforming Education. May 12 SCORE web posting: tnscore.org/school-leadership-tapping-the-power-of-potential/.

Zubrzycki, Jaclyn. (2012). Training programs connect principals to district realities. *Education Week*, December 5, p. 1.

CHAPTER 34

Our Fierce Urgency of Now

Obstacles and Solutions for Improving the Promise of America

Eric J. Cooper

THE ARC AND THE LONG PATH

I was a young boy when my parents and other members of the Peekskill, New York, Unitarian Church congregation organized a bus trip to the March on Washington. I was on board—a witness to history—when the buses left Peekskill in the early morning of August 28, 1963, part of a huge national caravan that headed to the nation's capital for the march, led by A. Philip Randolph, John Lewis, the Rev. Martin Luther King Jr., and other civil rights leaders.

As we entered Maryland, I noticed with growing discomfort the water fountains, restaurants, and restrooms labeled "for whites" and "for coloreds." Though our bus was filled with both "majority" and "minority" Americans, we who were black had to learn to curtail our impulses to drink, eat, or refresh where we pleased. We also had to increasingly steel ourselves against the hardened stares of whites as we moved deeper into the South. Television brought images of the Civil Rights movement into our living rooms, but it was quite a different experience that day for the black Americans on the bus who were born in the North and now experienced the Southern realities of "separate but equal."

But it is a measure of the promise of America that I also remember the thousands and thousands of blacks who waved white handkerchiefs at us from their homes, apartments, and streets in Washington on that hot August day, buoyed by the hope our arrival portended.

It was an uplifting experience, framed by the deep hope of many in a nation that was inextricably moving forward to address its challenges. It was as if the crowd felt Dr. King's "fierce urgency of now"—the need to change policies that segregated and isolated all too many Americans in schools, restaurants, housing, jobs, swimming pools, and even cemeteries, denying them

the promise of America "until justice rolls down like waters and righteousness like a mighty stream." He often thundered that black civil rights devotees would not be satisfied until "police brutality, disenfranchisement, lodging and [job discrimination], black ghettoization, and attacks on black self-esteem were abolished" (Dyson, 2000, p. 19).

Fifty years have passed. I write this chapter in the aftermath of the golden-anniversary observance of the March on Washington. Amid the many interviews and reminisces I've heard, the various polls and other assessments of the state of race relations in this country, and the discussion of what many feel has been progress, many commentators referred to this sentence, part of the "I Have a Dream" keynote speech Dr. King delivered on that fateful day:

"The moral arc of the universe is long but it bends towards justice."

For me, that sentence also is relevant to the state of K–12 public education in our nation, especially for low-income and poor children of color living in urban areas. The challenges are many and long-standing, and some seem overwhelming, just as they were for those who stood with Dr. King in Washington. But when I close my eyes, I see handkerchiefs waving, just as they did fifty years ago, buoyed by all we have learned about what works and what doesn't in public education.

The challenges ahead are enormous, as they were then. By 2019—in five short years—children of color will be the new majority in this country, and in thirty-plus years there will no longer be a demographic majority in America (U.S. Census Bureau, 2013). Given the current state of "minorities" and those challenged by poverty, that could be a sobering prospect. Today, too many people of color are in prison, on parole, or caught up in the court system—primarily caused by an ill-advised and mostly ineffective "war on drugs" that began with former president Ronald Reagan, intensified with Bill Clinton, and remains in force under President Obama (Alexander, 2010; Wise, 2010). Too many people of color remain disproportionately out of work, out of school, and out of hope (Alexander, 2010).

Recognizing the persistence of racism in America, the U.S. government recently reported to the United Nations that, as a country, "we could do better," citing the following data:

- In the 2009–2010 school year, 74 percent of African-American students and 80 percent of Latino students attended majority-minority schools, where most of their classmates were nonwhite. An outcome of the deeply segregated and racially and economically isolated American education system is severe "achievement gaps" between students of color and white students.
- Indigenous peoples, African Americans, and Latinos are disproportionately incarcerated in the United States. Two-thirds of the two million prisoners in the United States are African American or Latino. The disparities can be linked to improper policing practices like racial profiling. Drug policy and drug sentencing also contribute by disproportionately targeting African Americans and Latinos.
- People of color and indigenous peoples are also more likely to live near hazardous waste facilities, accounting for nearly half of all people of color in the United States living less than two miles from these facilities (colorlines.com/archives/2013/06/us_reports_to_un_on_ending_racial_discrimination_without_a_national_plan_for).

To this list, I would add the following for consideration:

Income inequality continues to rise to levels not seen since the Great Depression (www.nytimes.com/2012/10/17/business/economy/income-inequality-may-take-toll-on-growth.html?pagewanted=alland_r=0). The wealth gap between the haves and the have-nots continues to grow. CEOs of major companies were paid about twenty-five to thirty times more than typical American workers in the 1950s and 60s. In 1980, the CEO took home roughly forty times more; by 1990, it was one hundred times. But in 2005, the CEO of Walmart took home nine hundred times the pay and benefits of the typical Walmart worker, and in 2007 (right before the Great Recession), pay packages for executives ballooned from about 350 to an extreme of two thousand times typical earnings in this country (Krugman, 2013; Wilkinson and Pickett, 2010).

America is thirty-fifth out of forty industrial nations in the dropout rate, with approximately six thousand-plus students choosing to quit school every day (Ripley, 2013). Across racial and ethnic demographics, approximately 30 percent of our K–12 students are not succeeding. But disaggregate the data by race and ethnicity, and it gets uglier: On average, 55 percent of black and brown Americans graduate from high school, while the graduation rate for white Americans is approximately 78 percent (nces.ed.gov/pubs2012/2012006.pdf).

Students in urban school communities continue to drop out at unprecedented rates, ranging from 40 to nearly 50 percent in many cities and localities (Cooper, 2009; www.jrre.psu.edu/articles/27-12.pdf).

More than 30 percent of African- and Hispanic-American men who do not graduate from high school are in prison, on parole, or somewhere else in the criminal justice system (Alexander, 2010).

Approximately 72 percent of black American children were born to unwed mothers in 2010 (www.theroot.com/buzz/72-percent-african-american-children-born-unwed-mothers), and almost two million children in the United States have a parent who is incarcerated (www.acf.hhs.gov/blog/2013/06/improving-the-future-for-children-of-incarcerated-parents).

More than three-quarters of black men do not have the education increasingly required for middle-class life. Just 12 percent of black men have bachelor's degrees and 5 percent have graduate degrees. These are, respectively, just over one-third and less than half of the attainment rates for non-Hispanic white men. (Holzman, 2013, p. 3)

Cases of racism and overt discrimination in schools, housing, the workplace, and penal institutions may trigger legal responses, but as we have seen recently, there is no guarantee that the U.S. Supreme Court will rule against policies and practices that continue to marginalize people of color (Alexander, 2010; Holzman, 2013; Wilson, 2009; Williams, 2010; Wise, 2010; www.huffingtonpost.com/2014/03/21/schools-discrimination_n_5002954.html?ir=Black%20Voic-esandutm_hp_ref=black-voices).

THE OPPORTUNITIES AND DISADVANTAGES OF BIRTH

The lingering effects of racism are exacerbated by the effects of poverty. Coincidences of birth and geography shape children from the beginning. Children from wealthier families are nourished through diet, exercise, exposure to arts and literature, and the time and attention of parents, family members, and tutors when high content and standards demand additional help.

These children live in more expensive neighborhoods, with access to cultural resources and schools that expect and enable academic excellence through, among others, student-generated projects and real-world applications (Duncan and Murname, 2011).

But the child challenged by what Robert Walker of Oxford University calls the "shame of poverty" is not so lucky (www.guardian.co.uk/society/2010/aug/24/research-poverty-shame-links). More often than not, that child is born to a household led by a single parent—usually a mother—who holds two or three jobs just to scratch out a meager existence.

There may be no shortage of love, but time and attention are lacking. Mom is out the door before the child gets up in the morning and isn't home in time to read a book before bedtime. More often than not during the day, she is forced to think about where the family's next meal may be coming from, let alone finding the time to think about the education of her children. And if the family is not bouncing from one homeless shelter to another, and is fortunate to have an apartment or home, the home environment may not be healthy, with a physical space often constructed with inferior materials, remnants of lead paint peeling off the walls, and the living structure in constant disrepair. "Junk food," high in carbohydrates and sugar and low in nutrients, may anchor the child's diet, because that is what the family's time and finances can afford.

If this reality were not enough, reminders of what poverty does *not* provide are on television, billboards—everywhere. The message is that those in poverty are not "getting it right." Poor children internalize this shame, negatively affecting their sense of self and threatening their achievement trajectory (Nelson and Sheridan,

2011). There may even be a chemical reaction. Feelings of stress, threat, and helplessness can cause adrenal glands to emit the hormone cortisol into the body, inhibiting thinking and memory—two obvious and essential intellectual processes for the classroom.

The news is doubly bad for poor children who happen to be black. Society teaches that the black race is less attractive and less intelligent. Little wonder that long-standing research on racial preferences by young black children and a CNN study suggest that black children often make white bias choices because they have learned from the wider society that these are the "right" choices (Banks and Banks, 2004; ac360.blogs.cnn.com/2010/08/11/kids-on-race-doll-study-revisited/).

Thanks to recent neuroscience research, Wilkinson and Pickett (2009) point out, "When we feel threatened, helpless, and stressed, our bodies are flooded by the hormone cortisol which inhibits our thinking and memory . . . [and inequalities] . . . in our society and in our schools have a direct and demonstrable effect on our brains, on our learning and educational achievement" (p. 115).

The consequences of this research should be obvious; that is, if we ignore the impact poverty has on children, we may limit the life trajectory of American schoolchildren. Yet there is hope if we devise national policies, to support the form and function of effective early-childhood programs. The need is clearly stated below:

> During childhood, the plastic brain receives inputs and quickly adapts to the environment it is in. These adaptations become permanent differences in neural structure and function, altering the opportunities of children as they grow into adulthood. By ensuring that early environments are more positive and more equitably distributed, we increase the chance of success that all children have. By ignoring early inequality, we risk permanently altering the chances that some children have to succeed. These early differences in environment are etched into the structure of the brains; the way we think, react, and feel in adulthood is necessarily related to the environmental exposures we did and did not experience in our childhood. (Nelson III and Sheridan, 2011, p. 41)

ATTRIBUTIONAL AMBIGUITIES AND NEUROSCIENCE RESEARCH

Many urban and increasingly for some suburban students challenged by poverty as well, have, in effect, been left by family circumstances feeling helpless and threatened and fearful, and it's in that state that they come to school (Kneebone and Berube, 2013; Wilson, 1978). Because of this, they become overly school dependent (Cooper, 2004). They come relying on school to identify and engage their strengths, provide them with enrichment (often lacking during their preschool years), teach them how to learn skills, develop strength in character, and gain opportunities to apply their learning so they are equipped, motivated, and self-directed to be college and career ready.

However, programs and instruction designed for school-dependent urban and suburban students of color frequently are driven by the pernicious focus on weaknesses. Activities that should enrich education are replaced with policies that marginalize it, halting innovation and steering teachers away from student-centered instruction (Jackson, 2011). As a consequence, the strengths of these students often are ignored and undervalued, which may give rise to what Dweck (2004) calls the "entity theory": the belief that their intelligence is fixed and unchangeable. This theory affects what they believe they are capable and not capable of learning, influencing their self-concept, motivation, goal setting, and tenacity in school. Rarely are they taught that "within each race, prior knowledge predict[s] learning and reasoning, but between the races it [is] only prior knowledge that differ[s], not learning or reasoning ability" (Nisbett, 2007, p. 99).

I have written that "the challenge that a student of color may face when receiving feedback about his or her performance, is determinative whether it is accurate and particular to his or her performance, or is reflective of general racial bias on the part of the one giving the feedback" (Cooper, 2009, pp. 435–450).

Misperceptions about identity are compounded during adolescence, a developmental stage that used to occur during middle school, but now is starting earlier and lasting into the twenties (Jackson, 2011; Noguera, 2008; Sylvester, 2007). This is when the inextricable interrelation between emotion and cognitive development is most affected.

Cognitive and neuroscience research about this interrelationship and its impact on learning and achievement largely has been ignored in the design of pedagogy for secondary-school students. During this developmental state, self-esteem and self-confidence are concretized in the frontal lobes, which are responsible for self-perception associated with social acceptance and affirmation of strengths and recognition mature (Sylvester, 2007).

This is a significant factor for adolescents of color. They are keenly aware of the realities that accompany the stereotypical perceptions attributed to their race or ethnicity (Steele, 2010). They are acutely aware of labels used for them, including the designation related to the "achievement gap." As Jackson has written, students "astutely infer what the labels and designations imply about their intelligence. Consistent perception of stereotype threat in school can reduce the degree to which school is valued. Inhibitions and low expectations caused by inferiority complexes [may] curb a wide range of assertive acts, most of which are required for confidence-building, goal-setting, self-directed learning, inquiry, communication, problem solving, and self-actualization" (Jackson, 2011, pp. 47–48).

Violence also critically impacts the learning and achievement of school-dependent students. Research suggests that experience with excessive violence can actually distort the brain, causing test scores to deflate dramatically (Nelson and Sheridan, 2011; Smith, 2010). Stress associated with prejudice, stereotype threat, feelings of failure, ambiguity attributes, inability to succeed, positional or marginalizing language, and feelings of low self-esteem can cause, as mentioned earlier, the emission of cortisol.

This hormone can inhibit comprehension, resulting in underachievement and rewiring the brain to cognitively predispose an individual to repeat the same things over and over, including patterns of poor performance and self-sabotaging behaviors (Angier, 2009). Stress is insidious and often hidden in the impact it has on "poor learning ability and [the] ability to solve novel problems as it can damage pathways between the limbic lobe and the prefrontal cortex" (Nisbett, 2007, pp. 182–183).

But there is evidence that the influences of negative stereotyping and violence can be reversed. Neuroscience provides further reason for soul searching. It reveals the miraculous workings of the brain: how memory is stored and where; how to retrieve it; how to grow brain cells through physical activity and mental stimulation. It also explains how neurotransmitters work by sending signals that engage the left and right hemispheres, the prefrontal cortex of the brain along with the hippocampus.

Brain cells build on what is known (prior knowledge) and connect with new information, concepts, and ideas. So important is prior knowledge to learning, that it is suggested "Within each race, prior knowledge predicted learning and reasoning, but *between* the races it was only prior knowledge that differed, not learning or reasoning ability" (Nisbett, 2009, p. 99).

Neural integration occurs when neurotransmitters and their receptors stimulate neighboring cells. Information from one neuron flows to another neuron across a synapse. The synapse contains a pre-synaptic ending that contains neurotransmitters and a post-synaptic ending that contains receptor sites for neurotransmitters.

Neurotransmitters such as the dopamine pathways (affect cognitive ability), oxytocins (affects our capacity to love and our ability to socially engage), norepinephrine (is a part of our fight-or-flight reflex and is central to motivation), and serotonin are what helps with executive functioning (that is, the mental processes that help us connect past experience with present, appropriate action, and good decision-making), prefrontal lobes and also helps to regulate mood (for a deeper exploration please see Colvin, 2008; Coyle, 2009; Doidge, 2007; Kahneman, 2011; Nisbett, 2009; Shenk, 2010; Siegel, 2007).

We know the brain is flexible, with a neural plasticity that "refers to the process whereby the structure of experience weaves its way into the structure of the brain" (Nelson and Sheridan, 2011, p. 30). The brain is built during childhood, but it's important to recognize that with appropriate interventions, it can be remolded or modified in adulthood, enabling the brain to adapt to any number of circumstances, grow new neural pathways, or even develop bi-laterality in one hemisphere when the left, for an example, is removed to control for epilepsy (Doidge, 2007; Feuerstein, 1979, 2007; Feuerstein, Falik, and Feuerstein, 2013; Siegel, 2007; Vincent and Lledo, 2014.) In particular, the regeneration of cells in the hippocampus area of the brain, which was felt to be impossible by medical research several years ago, has been found possible when other cells are destroyed (www.ncbi.nlm.nih.gov/pubmed/12202033). As indicated, the hippocampus plays an important role in learning and memory for children and adults, as does the prefrontal cortex, which is the seat of where executive functions and self-concepts are engaged, accelerated, and deepened through the aforementioned

neurotransmitter serotonin (Nelson and Sheridan, 2011; Siegel, 2007).

Neuroscience research also suggests that when students are provided with pedagogy that is student-centered, with challenging content, guided reflection, outlets for self-expression, feedback, and contextualized instruction that connect to their frame of reference and prior knowledge, cognitive dysfunctions can be mitigated and intellectual development optimized (Delpit, 1995, 2012; Feuerstein, 1980; Feuerstein, Feuerstein, and Falik, 2010; Jackson, 2011; Ladson-Billings, 1994; Nisbett, 2009; Smith, 2010).

Learning is propelled when students have enrichment, opportunities to demonstrate strengths and apply learning in meaningful ways, support to address weaknesses and guidance which helps the student learn from their mistakes, strategies for developing critical thinking, and experiences that encourage them to be focused, engaged, vocal, tenacious, self-confident, and eventually self-actualized (Feuerstein, 1978; Feuerstein, Falik, and Feuerstein, 2013; Renzulli, 1975; Renzulli, Reis, 2007; Sternberg, 1998).

With education applications in mind, what we are gaining from neuroscience is understanding the role effort, deliberative, and guided practice plays in learning and ultimately the development of expertise (Colvin, 2008; Coyle, 2009). By gaining the knowledge of how the brain works, as simple as it may sound, can unleash the love of learning and a resilience required for a "growth mind-set" to emerge.

Siegel, 2007, has written that:

> a focus on the self, and in particular on the mind, is often absent from those thousands of hours we spend in the classroom [with a potential detrimental impact on learning] . . . if teachers were also aware of the scientific finding that how a person reflects internally will shape how he treats both himself and others . . . [then teachers might become] aware that attuning to the self—being mindful—can alter the brain's ability to create flexibility and self-observation, empathy, and morality. (p. 261)

A focus on "mindfulness" and a growth mind-set may enable the learner to power through the challenge and fear of failure, enabling skills to develop and great accomplishments to emerge (Dweck, 2006).

With the brain in mind, skills can be defined in neurological terms as "insulation that wraps neural circuits and grows according to certain signals" (Coyle, 2009, p. 58). In this definition, the insulation is what is called myelin, "a microscopic fatty substance . . . that wraps . . . nerve fibers and increases signal strength, speed, and accuracy" (ibid., p. 32), and signals are stimulated by techniques such as chunking (that is, ". . . break[ing] a skill into its component pieces, memoriz[ing] those pieces individually, then link[ing] them together in progressively larger groups [which result in] new interconnected circuits" (ibid., p. 84), which allows slowing down the cognitive processing demanded by the task. The author explains the process in this quote:

> Why does slowing down work so well? The myelin model offers two reasons. First, going slow allows you to attend more closely to errors, creating a higher degree of precision with each firing—and when it comes to growing myelin, precision is everything . . . Second, going slow helps the practice to develop something even more important: a working perception of the skill's internal blueprints—the shape and rhythm of the interlocking skill circuits. (ibid., p. 85)

We have found that the sharing of this understanding with students often facilitates a sense of trust that they are in control of their skill development. Belief in their ability to learn can lead to a "mindful" state of hopefulness, and the determination which comes from hope can develop the confidence required for accelerating their academic, occupational, and civic trajectories (Cooper, 2009; Groopman, 2004; Siegel, 2007; siatech.org/schools/pdf/SIATech_overall_2012results.pdf). Daniel Kahenman (2011) responding to a question about his favorite equation shared that "success = talent + luck" and that "great success = a little more talent + a lot of luck" (p. 177).

Yet based on a review of the literature, the thousands of narratives on people who have excelled due to hard effort, Kahenman may have slightly missed the proverbial bull's-eye in his equation by leaving out guided practice and effort, for example, success = effort + talent + luck (Gladwell, 2008; thisibelieve.org/essay/16583/). For instance, the oft-cited research of Anders Ericcson and his colleagues suggests that a 10,000 hours rule of deliberative practice may be required for expert performance (Ericcson, Krampe, and Tesch-Romer, 1993).

In summary, student engagement may be maximized through 1) educator intervention which fosters the irrefutable belief that the gap between student potential and actual achievement can be eliminated, and that with deliberative practice and sustained student effort, will enable the cognitive agility they are capable at all stages of development; and 2) the relationships that teachers cultivate with their students so that they learn to "observe, judge, and strategize their own performance—[where] they in essence, [learn] to coach themselves" (Coyle, 2009, p. 85).

THE INFLUENCE OF CORPORATE REFORM

Based on research and experience in school districts, there are a number of factors that can contribute to the "achievement gap" and point to the need for reform of pre-K–12 education:

- Lack of access to high-quality full-day preschool where cognitive, social, and personal development attributes such as self-control, resilience, and perseverance are taught (Campbell, Ramey, Pungello, Sparling, and Miller-Johnson, 2002; Kirp, 2013; Ravitch, 2010; www.sfi.dk/graphics/Campbell/Dokumenter/Farrington%20marts08/The%20HighScope%20Perry%20Preschool%20Project.pdf).
- The failure to set high expectations and standards for all students and an intractable belief that some students are born smart and others are not (Cooper, 2004).
- The need for more effective teachers and school leaders—especially in low-income areas (Darling-Hammond, 2010).
- Lack of coherence in curriculum and teaching (Cooper, 2009; Levine and Cooper, 1991).
- Teacher and administrative mobility within and among urban schools and the districts which serve them (Cooper, 2009; Rothstein, 2004).
- Inefficient and opaque funding formulas for education (Darling-Hammond, 2010).
- Complacency with chronically low-achieving schools (Ravitch, 2010).
- Segregated schooling which denies at times access to funding, good teachers and may cause a diminished sense of self-worth which has students asking "why don't we have any white students?" (www.nytimes.com/2012/05/13/education/at-explore-charter-school-a-portrait-of-segregated-education.html?pagewanted=alland_r=0; Ravitch, 2013).

- The mismatch between expectations driven by state and district standards and an environment where text complexity and readability assessments often suggest student difficulty with grade level comprehension (Pearson, 2013).
- A singularity of focus on private and corporate reforms rather than those interventions that have been proven to be sustainable by research (Darling-Hammond, 2010; Ravitch, 2013; Shyamalan, 2013).

There are 98,706 public schools in this nation, serving approximately fifty million students (Center for Education Reform, www.edreform.com/2012/k-12-facts/#schools). While about 14 percent of all students are enrolled in urban districts, 30 percent of those attending urban schools are students of color (CGCS, 2013). One-third of children of color attend schools in smaller suburban cities (Cooper and Orfield, 2011).

As discussed earlier, urban districts face remarkable challenges, not the least of which is the need to overcome poverty, racism, and segregation while promoting human values such as equality and respect. I won't deny the magnitude of the task. But what I *will* question are assumptions that "corporate" education reform, in the form of vouchers and charter schools rooted in the private sector, are public education's salvation (Kirp, 2013; Ravitch, 2013).

Many in this country seem to want to enable poor urban students to flee—either to private schools through the use of vouchers, or to existing schools that are essentially privatized and repurposed as charter schools (Kirp, 2013; Ravitch, 2013; Thernstrom, Thernstrom, 2003; www.redefinedonline.org/2012/11/what-does-privatization-in-public-education-really-mean/). Approximately 2.3 million children in this country attend six thousand charter schools (www.forbes.com/sites/greatspeculations/2013/09/10/charter-school-gravy-train-runs-express-to-fat-city/).

Among the tenets of "corporate" reform are: increased test-based evaluation of students, teachers, and schools of education; elimination or weakening of tenure and seniority rights; an end to pay for experience or advanced degrees; closing schools deemed low performing and their replacement by publicly funded but privately run charters; replacing governance by local school boards with various forms of mayoral and state takeover or private management; vouchers and tax-credit subsidies for private school tuition; increases in class size, often tied to the firing of 5 to 10 percent of the teaching staff; implementation of common core standards and adoption of college and career readiness as a standard for high school graduation (Ravitch, 2013).

Charter schools are no sure bet. Some research suggests they perform no better than existing public schools, with public schools doing slightly better on state achievement tests: "A new report issued by the Center for Research on Education Outcomes (CREDO) at Stanford University found that there is a wide variance in the quality of the nation's several thousand charter schools with, in the aggregate, students in charter schools not faring as well as students in traditional public schools (credo.stanford.edu/reports/National_Release.pdf).

There is another point of view: that achievement and opportunity gaps are significantly reduced when poverty decreases, schools become more integrated, significant new investments in economic growth occur, and research becomes the driving engine for national policy (Darling-Hammond, 2012; Kirp, 2013; Ravitch, 2013).

From my perspective, attempting to corral leaders into one of the two camps is problematic. The broad generalizations one has to make may or may not be appropriate. Each group seems to seek the policies it believes supports underserved people in our country.

For that reason, I find Siddhartha Mitter, writing in a Teachers College, Columbia University article, instructive: "There's no single solution to the achievement gap, but a lot of solutions, together, just might do the trick" ("Building The Village It Takes," Spring/Summer 2013). It is in our self-interest to devise policies and implementation strategies to meet the needs of all children. The policies cannot be considered in isolation, nor can they be framed by a belief that schools alone can address society's problems.

We can transform urban education in this country, given a broader, more strategic approach that is based on (a) the leadership of the estimated 3.2 million educators in America, (b) successful programs, practices, policies, and structural change that are rooted not in ideology, but rather in research, and (c) a sustained national effort to reduce poverty and the need to mitigate the pernicious impact it has on learning.

It is the reduction and elimination of poverty that remains a formidable obstacle if we are to live up to the promise of our nation. And though education is a major factor in working toward the reduction of poverty in our country, it is obvious social programs such as the earned-income tax credit, Supplemental Nutrition Assistance Program (known as food stamps), and addressing the inequality of economic outcomes cited earlier are critical policies that can and do help those who remain poor (Danziger, 2013).

When combined with new policies, and teamed with improvements in education and school reform, we may be able to avoid the shaming and debilitating Hobson Choice those challenged by poverty continue to face in their lives. It is here that I challenge those voices which state that poverty does not impact achievement—that the improvement of urban schools are the sine qua non of how we eliminate poverty (www.usnews.com/opinion/articles/2009/05/04/urban-schools-need-better-teachers-not-excuses-to-close-the-education-gap).

The answer research continues to suggest seems to be that a two-prong approach focused on improving schools, in combination with maintaining and devising anti-poverty programs, may well provide the policy roadmap that leads to enabling families challenged by poverty to write themselves a better future.

INVESTING IN SCHOOL COMMUNITY SUPPORTS

Along with his colleagues, the late John Ogbu, in his highly regarded *Black American Students in an Affluent Suburb: A Study of Academic Disengagement* (2003), first attracted national attention in the 1980s with a study that raised the issue of "community factors" in underperformance of black students.

In 1997 Ogbu and his associates were invited to Shaker Heights, Ohio, to study and suggest strategies to improve scholastic opportunities for African-American students. Parents wanted to know why their children were underperforming (the average grade point average for African-American high school students was about 1.9, as compared to 3.45 for whites).

In the resulting analysis, Ogbu and his associates reviewed the causes of the achievement gap and ended with a series of recommendations with potentially far-reaching implications:

- Enhance academic orientation with supplementary education programs;
- Develop a cultural context to increase the value of academic success and the visibility of academically successful blacks as role models;
- Distinguish the effective from pragmatic value of education;
- Develop and institutionalize appropriate and effective parental educational strategies;
- Teach children how to work hard and persevere to improve grades.

Ogbu addressed this by citing teacher expectations and programmatic interventions, as well as parent involvement in his recommendations for improvement.

This is not a pipe dream. The following has been reported in Union City, New Jersey, a school district with a large Hispanic student body:

Union City—with a population that is one-fourth undocumented immigrants and with nearly all its students eligible for free or reduced-price school lunch—boasts a 90 percent high-school graduation rate. That's 15 percent higher than the national average. . . . The story how this place succeeded is one that any educator with a pulse will understand. . . .

The "well-proven ideas" include two years of full-day preschool for all students, a bilingual program for younger kids that grounds them in Spanish and transitions them to English: "port-of-entry" classes for older, non-English-speaking children that immerses them in Spanish and English as a Second Language before bringing them into mainstream English literature courses by their senior year; low-stakes assessments are used "to pinpoint places where students and teachers need help"; and an intensive parent-engagement program that distributes materials in Spanish and employs Spanish-speaking community liaisons . . . similar strategies are employed in varying forms, in other successful school systems. Still, (he concedes that) Union City enjoys two unique advantages. One is New Jersey's thirty-year education finance lawsuit, *Abbott v Burke*, which has brought billions of additional dollars to the state's poorer schools and established court-ordered universal preschool. (Mitter, 2013; for extended research and discussion, see Kirp, 2013)

With the understanding that a confluence of factors, ranging from the positive political "calculus" between the Mayor of Union City and the Governor of New Jersey, to court directions that "the private-for-profits, the churches, the babysitting places" in the community each have college-educated staff who are steeped in child development, Union City provides a framework for other districts to follow (Kirp, 2013).

Connecticut provides another example. In her award-winning 2010 publication "The Flat World and Education: How America's Commitment to Equity Will Determine Our Future," Linda Darling-Hammond cites the improving trends of fourth-grade reading achievement on the National Assessment for Educational Progress (NAEP) in the state of Connecticut during the years of 1992–1998 and again in 2007:

> Connecticut fourth graders ranked first in the nation in reading and math on the NAEP by 1998, despite increasing numbers of low-income, minority, and new immigrant students in the state's public schools during that time. More eighth graders in Connecticut were proficient in reading and writing than in any other state, and, in the world, only top-ranked Singapore outscored Connecticut students in science. The achievement gap between white and minority students decreased, and the more than 25 percent of Connecticut's students who were black or Hispanic substantially outperformed their counterparts nationally.
>
> In 2007, among the states that ranked in the top five in reading, writing, and mathematics on the NAEP, Connecticut and New Jersey were the only two that had African-American and Latino students comprising more than 30 percent of their public school populations. (p. 133)

Darling-Hammond (2010) discusses some of what worked in Connecticut during those years:

> Connecticut's reforms followed the 1977 *Horton v. Meskill* decision, in which the Connecticut Supreme Court became one of the first of the state high courts, along with California's and New Jersey's, to invalidate a state education finance system because its reliance on local property taxes generated greatly unequal spending. Later reforms were prodded by the filing of the *Sheff v. O'Neill* lawsuit in 1989, challenging racially segregated schools . . . [the state] . . . raised standards for teacher education and licensing, while also raising and equalizing teacher salaries and creating subsidies for preparing teachers who would work in high-need fields and high-need locations . . . [the state also] . . . funded professional development school initiatives for improving teacher training . . . instituted mentoring for beginning teachers, and . . . created an infrastructure for ongoing professional development . . . [the state also] . . . instituted new learning standards for both students and teachers, and created assessment to evaluate progress . . . Connecticut created performance assessments that engaged students in writing extensively and solving open-ended problems . . . Most notably, [Connecticut] held to the course of these reforms over a sustained period—more than fifteen years in each case . . . In explaining Connecticut's strong achievement gains, the National Education Goals Panel cited the state's teacher policies as a crucial element. (p. 136)

Additionally Darling-Hammond suggests the willingness of the state of Connecticut to invest $300 million to "boost minimum beginning teacher salaries in an equalizing fashion that made it possible for low-wealth districts to compete in the market for qualified teachers" (p. 136) was also an important factor in the achievement.

What Connecticut did in support of teaching and learning was both laudable and strategic. In essence, the state recognized that teachers matter in achievement (Sanders and Rivers, 1996), and that standards, assessments, as well as increased funding, were vital for gains in achievement (Darling-Hammond, 2010).

THE NEED FOR LEADERSHIP

Conversation about K–12 improvement has done a remarkable job of reducing complex issues to simple choices. Failed traditional public schools or successful charter schools? Ineffective union teachers or excellent nonunion teachers? The truth, as I have written with a colleague, "is that these conversations are the easy ones and not the ones that will solve the real challenges in underperforming schools [and communities. Besides the many cited in the literature], just below the surface [reside] perplexing issues of race, white entitlement, and culture that continue to leave students of color behind academically and economically" (Cooper and Jackson, 2011).

Yet in spite of these obstacles, educators—teachers, principals, and administrators—are uniquely positioned to become the advocates and activists students of color need. They are, for the most part, trusted by students and parents (Anyon, 2005). When provided sustained, coherent, and timely professional development, educators have or can obtain the knowledge and the strategies that may accelerate learning in the classroom. Teachers also are that connection between school and home that ultimately may lead to partnerships between families, businesses, universities, policymakers, and politicians (Comer, Haynes, Joyner, and Ben-Avie, 1996). That in turn might prompt sustained education reform and actually improve and repair shattered lives.

Among others described here and elsewhere, the research implications are clear: Teacher quality remains the single most important in-school factor related to student achievement (Darling-Hammond, 2012; Darling-Hammond and Bransford, 2005; Nisbett, 2009; Sanders and Rivers, 1996). In a significant contribution to the field, Darling-Hammond and Bransford (2005), state:

The differential allocation of skillful teachers appears to play a particularly important role in . . . disparate outcomes [between affluent students and those challenged by poverty]. For example, a number of studies have found teacher expertise (as measured by certification status and test scores, education, and experience levels) to be a significant determination of student outcomes (Betts, Rueben, and Dannenberg, 2000; Ferguson, 1991a; Ferguson and Ladd, 1996; Fetler, 1999; Goldhaber and Brewer, 2000; Strauss and Sawyer, 1986).

These and other studies have suggested that much of the difference in school achievement found between more and less advantaged students is due to the effects of substantially different school opportunities, in particular great disparate access to high-quality teachers and teaching (Barr and Dreeben, 1983; Dreeben and Gamoran, 1986; Dreeben and Barr, 1987; Oakes, 1990). However, teachers alone do not account for all of the educational opportunities that make a difference to students' learning. The ways schools are organized for instruction, what curriculum they offer to whom, what teachers are assigned to which students, how families are involved, and whether and how teachers are encouraged to collaborate all matter for the quality of opportunity different students receive. (pp. 238–239)

To this end, educators and leaders must believe in the potential of all students to achieve at levels that advance them to the next grade, so they can tackle postsecondary education or get a job that requires postsecondary literacy and the ability to think critically. This belief should apply whether a student wants to be an auto mechanic or a technology engineer. Educators must believe in their ability to engage and educate students, and in their own ability to gain the needed professional knowledge and skills to do so. It is here that universities hopefully will continue to seek interventions which recruit, prepare, and retain urban teachers (Froning, 2006).

Educators working with families, students, stakeholders, faith-based and business leaders, and politicians might begin a national embrace of the African proverb "Unbuntu"—I am because We are. It is as much a family and student responsibility for learning as it is a community responsibility.

The question is: Do we, as a nation, have the will to eliminate the achievement gap between white and nonwhite students?

In *Young, Gifted, and Black* (Perry, Steele, and Hilliard III, 2003), the late Asa Hilliard offered a perspective on this fundamental question by quoting Ronald Edmonds of Harvard University: "We can, whenever and wherever we wish, teach successfully all children whose education is of interest to us. Whether we do or do not do it depends in the final analysis on how we feel about the fact that we have not done so thus far" (p. 165).

To Edmonds, who died in 1983, the fact that poor children of color had succeeded in some school circumstances proved that success in all similar circumstances was possible. He asserted that the nation, states, school districts, schools, and educators—those at home and in the community—lack the will [at the time of his writing and, based on the prevailing data thirty-plus years later, the lack of will still exists] to bring the achievement distribution of black, brown, and impoverished children in line with that of white middle- and upper-class students (Perry, Steele, and Hilliard, 2003).

The challenge is a broad one. Martin Haberman (2002) wrote: "Schools, rather than functioning as the great equalizer, tend to both reflect and replicate social-class structures and societal biases . . . the end result: families in the top 25 percent of income send 86 percent of their children to college; while families in bottom 20 percent send 4 percent of their children to college" (p. 1).

Developing the will to enable the "promise of America" for all of the nation's citizens, that is, for those struggling with poverty, for those who feel the sting of institutional racism and bias on a daily basis, will require renewed beliefs, actions, and policies that reflect and enable a greater national determination from what we have seen to-date. And for the most part, education remains the primary pathway for improving the life trajectories of schoolchildren and youth.

FROM "JUST AN EDUCATOR" TO JUSTICE IN TEACHING

Mindful of the challenges, some courageous teachers trade the notion of "aptitude" for flexibility, or "plasticity" of the brain and its influence on ability and performance. Achievement becomes a function of how well the student learns to persevere in the face of academic and life challenges (Jackson, 2011; Siegel, 2007).

Wise (2010) tells the narrative of a Colorado math teacher who helped provoke substantial improvements by telling his black students " . . . in no uncertain terms the system is an unjust racist one, and there are people prepared to make you statistics. You can either collaborate with your own destruction or blow up the statistics and prove everyone wrong" (p. 183). The teacher's honesty, coupled with his belief in his students, enabled black students' scores to soar and "inspired the creation of a mentoring group, set up by the black students themselves, to encourage one another to strive for excellence" (p. 183).

Instructors like these use teaching to enable social justice. They work to substantiate in urban schools an irrefutable belief in the capacity of all children to reach the highest levels of learning and thinking. All students can succeed when educators are armed with strategies to achieve this. By improving classroom instruction and schooling through professional development, and engaging the entire community—parents, stakeholders, and students—in conversations and advocacy, the self-interest of a community is expressed in renewed belief and hope, not despair and sustained failure.

I have met many educators across this country who relish the opportunity to advocate for young people and recognize that the responsibility for improving the life trajectory of their students is shared by all members of the community. International leaders such as Hillary Clinton have recognized the African proverb "It takes a village to raise a child" an appropriate reminder and calculus for broad success to be sustained (Clinton, 1996).

As educators, parents, and stakeholders work to motivate their community's children, they are banding together as agents for justice in teaching by presenting at board meetings and community forums, writing letters and opinion pieces for commentary pages in local newspapers and blogs, about the success they are leading in classrooms and school communities, and the need for change. This is not new. As has been written and researched over the years, "There has never been a time in American education when there have not been 'gap closers,' that is, teachers and school leaders who demonstrate their capability to move students who typically perform in the lower quartile by standardized tests measures even into the top quartile, indeed in some cases into the lead position within their schools and districts" (Perry, Steele, and Hilliard III, 2003, p. 141).

Clearly teachers and for that matter students on their own cannot be held responsible for writing a better future. School districts across America suffer a lack of adequate funding, which can create and add to pockets of cynicism and foster criticism that the victims of poverty are to blame for their problems. Despite this, like-minded community members, dedicated administrators, and forward-thinking faculty are forging ahead with a new vision for the children—a vision fueled by a strong belief in the potential of every child and a relentless will to uncover ways to tap that potential (Jackson, 2011; Jensen, 2013).

This brand of leadership leaves no room for whining or blaming sessions, close-ended discussions that dead-end children's lives. Rather, during professional development sessions, teachers, administrators, and communities enjoy addressing deep and intransigent obstacles—together (Perry, Steele, and Hilliard III, 2003). They ponder and practice content and renewed pedagogies and watch—wide-eyed and excited—as their students engage in animated discussions, write extensive essays, think critically, creatively, and reflectively, improve their grades, reveal their thinking, demonstrate their comprehension, and otherwise display their learning and creativity with confidence and competence (Duncan and Murnane, 2014; Jackson 2011; Jackson, McDermott, 2012).

What follows are five examples of transformative leadership in a Midwestern district, two urban middle schools in Connecticut, and a high school and a middle school on the West Coast. I selected these due to my firsthand knowledge of the schools and their communities. Each should be viewed as broadly representative of the hundreds of other schools across America that are succeeding in the education of all their students (Perry, Steele, and Hilliard III, 2003; Shyamalan, 2013). The scope and broad principles that follow are wide, ranging from highly specific and targeted to learning-teaching approaches, to broad ones that have implications for policy. They are: strong school community leadership; an irrefutable belief in the capacity of all children to learn sufficiently to graduate from high school, and/or attend a college or secure an occupation of their choice; systemic and coherent professional development which enables high expectations to be applied in a culturally responsive pedagogy; academic rigor, high standards, and cohesive curriculum and instruction; improved teacher quality; instructional leadership; parent outreach and engagement; a student-centered school climate extended into summer school when needed; data analysis used to provide markers for intervention and support of learning; community and parental engagement and advocacy; and the applications of cognitive and neuroscience research. (Cooper, 2004; Perry, Steele, and Hilliard III, 2003; Cooper, 2009; Shyamalan, 2013; Duncan and Murnane, 2014)

Case Study: Eden Prairie, Minnesota

When Melissa Krull took over in 2002 as superintendent of the Eden Prairie Schools, she knew as a longtime special education teacher within the Minnesota system that dramatic change was needed to bolster academic excellence for all students.

Similar to countless communities across the country, Eden Prairie was on the cusp of a seismic shift in its demographics as more children of color and more low-income students filled its classrooms. Recognizing the importance of integrated and culturally diverse schools for accelerating achievement and social learning, Dr. Krull advocated against the resegregation of "minority" students into one or two of her school buildings (Wells, 2014). With this demographic shift, Krull says, the school system's leaders and board of education recognized a pressing need to address each child based on his or her individual academic and cultural backgrounds: "Gradually, we started noticing the achievement gaps

as the population shift began to occur, and we knew we wouldn't be able to meet our students' needs unless we made systemic changes," said Krull, who served as Eden Prairie's superintendent until October 2011. "We needed to change our approach to teaching and change our programming."

Since the 2003–2004 school year, Eden Prairie has partnered with the National Urban Alliance for Effective Education (NUA), where I serve as its president to:

- Give principals and teachers professional development to help break down barriers to high expectations and help them better understand the strengths of incoming students from different racial, cultural, and socioeconomic backgrounds.
- Develop curriculum and instruction that acknowledge students' culture rather than ignore it and its relevance to how students learn.
- Engage cognitive and neuroscience research in all classrooms through strategies that are typically used in gifted and talented programs—and focus on higher-order thinking skills as captured in common core state standards.
- Conduct community outreach and advocacy to build support for new instructional strategies and embrace an increasingly diverse student population.

Krull has reported that "ten years ago, we used certain strategies for all kids because they were from similar backgrounds," Krull added. "We weren't culturally competent as a system, and we needed to change that." Working directly with schools' staff, NUA has been training teachers and principals in how to differentiate instruction; learn the uses and applications of common core state standards; apply culturally responsive teaching; and integrate students into the professional development process with their teachers.

Over the course of several years the "gap" between students of color and white students has been reduced by nearly 60 percent while white students continued to improve 5 percentage points each year as well. Gains were not reached by lowering standards for higher-achieving students; rather, they were gained by raising standards for ALL students. "To eliminate achievement gaps, you have to use strategies that teach to the kids, that reach the kids in your classroom in diverse ways.

One approach does not work for everyone," Krull said. "We discovered that one of the best ways to differentiate instruction was to develop a deeper understanding of racial and economic differences among our students, and then teach with that knowledge. We needed to make all teaching as relevant as possible for each child" (http://nuatc.org/wp-content/uploads/2012/01/EdenPrairieCaseStudy.pdf).

Bridgeport, Connecticut

In her previous school district, Aliana was in special education and told by a teacher (more than likely out of frustration) that she had no future. Then Aliana came to Blackham Middle School in Bridgeport, Connecticut, where the principal and teachers were part of a multi-year professional development school reform initiative—focused on culturally responsive pedagogy as well as applications gained from neuroscience research. Teachers learned to become "fearless leaders," where affirmation, inspiration, and pedagogical practices aimed to enable students to succeed with higher-order thinking, develop a "growth mind-set," and where they worked to bridge the gap between student potential and actual achievement.

In a videotaped interview, Aliana provided deep insight into how trust, technique, instructional strategies her teachers learned through an outside education group, along with time, enabled her to earn top scores on the statewide Connecticut Mastery Tests (CMTs) and reverse her fortunes. She knows what it's like to work with teachers who "feel like they are wasting their time" with the very students who need them the most. Her conclusion and use of academic language are uplifting and hopeful for those working toward student transformation: "Without reading," she says, "Where are you? What can you do in life?" She also provides a short course on various vocabulary-learning techniques central to her academic success, as well as strategies for thinking critically, reflectively, and which deepened her reading comprehension skills. Her advice to teachers: "Don't underestimate your students" (Jackson, 2011; Jackson, McDermott, 2012).

The Beardsley School, a National Urban Alliance for Effective Education (NUA) Demonstration School, is a success story as well. The student body is 98 per-

cent minority, and 100 percent qualify for federal free lunch programs. It also was one of the first schools to be labeled a school in need of improvement before the advent of the federal No Child Left Behind Act. Today, Beardsley boasts of many accomplishments and impressive gains in academic performance. In grade six, for example, during the 2010–2011 school year, 94 percent of students scored at or above proficiency in math and 85 percent scored at or above proficiency in writing. In 2011, it was also named a Success Story School by the Connecticut Coalition for Achievement Now, a statewide education reform and advocacy group better known as ConnCAN.

The interventions brought to the school by the NUA focused on administration leadership, student engagement, culturally responsive teaching, and practices that elicit high intellectual performance such as including students with their teachers in the professional development workshops and classroom demonstrations. The school leadership team and NUA chose instructional practices gleaned from cognitive and neuroscience research, for example, spaced "interleaving" of content so that the new was connected to what was previously studied; creation of anticipation guides to help students come to understand they knew more than they thought they did prior to introduction of a new concept; the use of "dancing definitions," which used rhythm and rhyming to learn new vocabulary; a focus on student-generated instruction as well as high expectations and standards for ALL students (Jackson, 2011).

San Francisco, California

For years, George Washington High School in San Francisco has enjoyed a reputation as a high-performing school. But this status belied an uncomfortable truth—a widening achievement gap among racial, ethnic, and socioeconomic differences.

Early in her tenure as the school's principal, Ericka Lovrin set her sights on reducing, and ultimately eliminating, that achievement gap and enlisted the support of the NUA to help her meet this goal during the 2009–2010 school year. "In our ever-changing society, I saw that we needed to focus on an instructional strategy that would be culturally relevant and help us ensure that what we were teaching, the students were learning," Lovrin said.

Specifically, Lovrin praised the use of techniques such as "thinking maps" and "community builders," and a leadership component that trained the administrative team in walk-throughs, instructional rounds, and the Pedagogy of Confidence. The goal was to strengthen the school from all areas—student, teacher, parent, community, and administrator.

Lovrin indicated that the focus on neuroscience applications in the classroom and how that affects student learning has been instructive and inspiring for her and her teaching staff.

To help tackle the achievement gap, Lovrin and her staff decided to focus on students of color and other historically underachieving students. "We had an achievement gap," Lovrin said, noting as an example a 30 percentage point difference in the number of Asian-American students and African-American students.

The results of the work resulted in a 20 percentage point gain for her African-American students during the period of the work (Cooper, 2012).

Visitacion Valley Middle School in San Francisco is another example of what can happen with the right leadership, teamwork, consistency, and blend of student-focused programs.

In 1999 Visitacion Valley was designated the lowest-performing middle school in the district. That was also the year James Dierke became the principal and began to turn things around, eventually building a solid team of educators who worked to assist in making a change.

Not only has academic performance improved, but suspensions have decreased significantly. An average of ninety suspensions per year was normal until 2009, when the suspension rate dropped to just over a dozen in fall 2010. Teachers and students are assigned to academic families that use a variety of technology, cross-curricular writing programs, project-based and standards-based instructional programs, and use meditation before school starts every morning to set a tone and to focus attention.

Professional development engaged higher-order thinking practices applied to social studies, math, and language arts. Those practices—designed based on cognitive and neuroscience research—provide approaches that work with underachieving students of color and address the impact of culture on cognition, language, and motivation (Jackson, 2011). With teachers' guidance,

students use visual tools, storyboards, and journals to learn and to demonstrate progress in learning.

The results include a sixteen-point gain in sixth-grade math and an eighteen-point gain in eighth-grade social studies, while the school made a forty-point gain on the California Standards Test (CTS). "All subgroups made double-digit improvements, not just the top kids," Dierke said (Cooper, 2012, www.nuatc.org/case-study-san-francisco/).

School improvement success stories are growing but remain scattered throughout the nation. As colleagues have written in this volume, there is a need for an urban pedagogy to integrate neuroscience, culturally responsive teaching, and administrative interventions that allow them to be sustained and taken to scale. Led by educators and community stakeholders, it is my hope the broad principles outlined above and described in the case studies are recognized as transferable to a variety of school community circumstances.

COMMON PATHWAY FOR THE PUBLIC GOOD

Yet nothing less than long-term and total commitment to the "promise" of this country is required. Poverty must be dramatically reduced and, as people gain access to knowledge, work, housing, and transportation, eventually eliminated across generations. Educators for the most part will continue to work to meet their responsibilities, but so must the nation in developing policies and legislation that can help all Americans reach their potential. The goal is not a handout but a hand-up, if you will, stemming from the recognition that the individual and broader community are integral to success.

This, then, is our challenge. The research base is clear and focused; it has been for some time. Teaching is the intersection where policies, programs, practices, and beliefs meet. Good teaching lifts and accelerates student achievement. Educators' professional skills and behavior, and the beliefs that undergird and guide that behavior, are targeted and fine-tuned by professional development activities, before and during their service. We have so many young teachers currently in our classrooms, with so much of their careers ahead of them. In-service professional development delivered by universities, nonprofit agencies, and membership groups will be a critical support for them. It has a great mission and can become the binding agent for most reforms.

Nothing in this formulation or in nature denies that this can take place simultaneously with many places and people. This combination of efforts is demanding, but it is doable and long overdue. The urgency for change is obvious and captured in part by what Linda Darling-Hammond (2010) has written:

> Now more than ever, high-quality education for all is a public good that is essential for the good of the public. Smart, equitable investments will, in the long run, save far more than they cost . . . [and] as the fate of individuals and nations is increasingly interdependent, the quest for access to an equitable, empowering education for all people has become a critical issue for the American nation as a whole. As a country, we can and must enter a new era. No society can thrive in a technological, knowledge-based economy by depriving large segment of its population of learning. The path to our mutual well-being is built on educational opportunity. Central to our collective future is the recognition that our capacity to survive and thrive ultimately depends on ensuring to all of our people what should be an unquestioned entitlement—a rich and inalienable right to learn. (p. 328)

It is in our nation's self-interest to come to understand and embrace the supposition that each child's life trajectory is important to all Americans. To act on this requires individual, societal, and institutional commitment focused relentlessly and unapologetically on, for, and with the public good in mind. Public education must remain the bedrock for our American democracy: one nation, indivisible—as in, divided by none.

REFERENCES

Alexander, Michelle. (2010). *The New Jim Crow: Mass Incarceration in the Age of Colorblindness.* New York: The New Press, 2010.

Angier, Natalie. (2009, August 18). "Brain is a co-conspirator in a vicious stress loop." *The New York Times.*

Anyon, Jean. (2005). *Radical Possibilities: Public Policy, Urban Education, and a New Social Movement.* New York: Routledge.

Banks, J. A. (2004). "Multicultural Education: Historical Development, Dimensions, and Practice," in *Handbook of Research on Multicultural Education, second edition.*

Berube, Alan, and Kneebone, Elizabeth. (August 6, 2013). "Suburban Poverty Traverses the Red/Blue Divide." Retrieved from www.brookings.edu/research/reports/2013/08/06-suburban-poverty-berube-kneebone-williams.

Campbell, F.A., Ramey, C.T., Pungello, E.P., Sparling, J., and Miller-Johnson, S. (2002). Early Childhood Education: Young Adult Outcomes from the Abecedarian Project. *Applied Developmental Science,* 6, pp. 42–57. The Perry Preschool Project, Retrieved October 2000, from U.S. Department of Justice/Office of Justice Program, www.sfi.dk/graphics/Campbell/Dokumenter/Farrington%20marts08/The%20High-Scope%20Perry%20Preschool%20Project.pdf.

Casserly, Michael. (2013). *CGCS ebook: A Call for Change: Providing Solutions for Black Male Achievement.* Boston: Houghton Mifflin.

Clinton, Hillary. (1996). *It Takes A Village.* New York: Simon and Schuster.

Colvin, Geoff. (2008). *Talent Is Overrated: What Really Separates World-Class Performers from Everybody Else.* New York: Penguin Books.

Cooper, Eric J. (2004). "The Pursuit of Equity and Excellence in Educational Opportunity." In *Teaching All The Children: Strategies for Developing Literacy in an Urban Setting,* edited by Lapp, Diane, Collins, Cathy, Cooper, Eric J., Flood, James, Roser, Nancy, and Tinajero, Josefina V. New York: Guilford Press.

Cooper, Eric J. (2009). "Just a Teacher" to Justice in Teaching—Working in the Service of Education, the New Civil Right. In *Handbook of Research on Literacy and Diversity,* edited by Morrow, Lesley, M., Rueda, Robert, and Lapp, Diane. New York: The Guilford Press.

Cooper, E. J. (2009). "Realities and Responsibilities in the Education Village." *The Sage Handbook on African American Education,* 435–450.

Cooper, Eric, J. (2011). Eden Prairie Case Study. Retrieved from nuatc.org/wp-content/uploads/2012/01/EdenPrairieCaseStudy.pdf; www.nytimes.com/2011/03/25/opinion/l25herbert.html?_r=0.)

Cooper, Eric, J. (2012) San Francisco's George Washington High Schools. Retrieved from nuatc.org/wp-content/uploads/2012/03/san_francisco_case_study.pdf.

Cooper, Eric J., and Jackson, Yvette, F. (2011). "The 'Fierce Urgency of Now': It's Time to Close the Gap." *Education Week Commentary,* January 26, 2011.

Cooper, Eric J. and Orfield, Myron. (November 18, 2011). "Suburban schools: The next integration battleground." *Connecticut Post.*

Cooper, Eric, J. (2012). San Francisco's Visitacion Middle School. Retrieved from www.nuatc.org/case-study-san-francisco/.

Coyle, Daniel. (2009). *The Talent Code: Greatness Isn't Born. It's Grown. Here's How.* New York: Bantam Books.

Darling-Hammond, Linda. (2010). *The Flat World and Education: How America's Commitment to Equity Will Determine Our Future*. New York: Teachers College Press.

Darling-Hammond, Linda, and Bransford, John, (Eds.). *Preparing Teachers For A Changing World: What Teachers Should Learn and Be Able To Do*. San Francisco: John Wiley and Sons, Inc.

Danziger, Sheldon, H. (2013). "The Mismeasure of Poverty." *New York Times*, September 18, p. A23.

Doidge, Norman. (2007). *The Brain That Changes Itself: Stories of Personal Triumph from the Frontiers of Brain Science*. New York: Penguin Group.

Delpit, Lisa. (1995). *Other People's Children*. New York: New Press, Inc.

Delpit, Lisa. (2012). *"Multiplication Is for White People": Raising Expectations for Other People's Children*. New York: New Press, Inc.

Duncan, G. J., and Murnane, R. J. (2014). "Growing Income Inequality Threatens American Education." *Education Week*.

Duncan, Greg, J. and Murnane, Richard, J. (2014). *Restoring Opportunity: The Crisis of Inequality and the Challenge for American Education*. Cambridge, MA: Harvard University Press.

Dyson, Michael Eric. (2000). *I May Not Get There With You: The True Martin Luther King Jr*. New York: Touchstone.

Dweck, Carol, S. (2006). *Mindset: The New Psychology of Success: How We Can Learn to Fulfill Our Potential*. New York: Ballantine Books.

Ericcson, Anders K., Krampe, Ralf T., and Tesch-Romer, Clemens (1993). "The role of deliberate practice in the acquisition of expert performance." *Psychological Review*, 100(3), pp. 363–406.

Feuerstein, Reuven. (1979). Cognitive modifiability in retarded adolescents: Effects of instrumental enrichment. *American Journal of Mental Deficiency*, 83(6), 88–96.

Feuerstein, Reuven (1980). *Instrumental Enrichment: An Intervention Program for Cognitive Modifiability*. Baltimore: University Park Press.

Feuerstein, Reuven, Falik, Louis II., and Feuerstein, Rafi S. (2013). "The Cognitive Elements of Neural Plasticity." Retrieved from www.neuropsychotherapist.com/wp-content/uploads/2013/03/CognitiveElements.pdf.

Feuerstein, Reuven, Feuerstein, Rafi S., and Falik, Louis H. (2010). *Beyond Smarter: Mediated Learning and the Brain's Capacity for Change*. New York: Teachers College Press.

Froning, Michael J. (2006). "Recruiting, Preparing, and Retaining Urban Teachers: One Person's View from Many Angles," edited by Howey, Kenneth, R., Post, Linda M., and Zimpher, and Nancy L. In *Recruiting, Preparing, and Retaining Teachers for Urban Schools*. Washington, DC: AACTE Publications.

Gallup Student Poll. (2012). Retrieved from siatech.org/schools/pdf/SIATech_overall_2012results.pdf.

Gladwell, Malcolm. (2008). *Outliers: The Story of Success*. New York: Little, Brown and Company. An Athlete of God. (October 9, 2009). Retrieved from thisibelieve.org/essay/16583/.

Groopman, Jerome. (2004). *The Anatomy of Hope: How People Prevail in the Face of Illness*. New York: Random House.

Haberman, Martin. (2002, April). "Can teacher education close the achievement gap?" Paper presented at the symposium of The American Educational Research Association, New Orleans, LA.

Holtzman, Michael. (2013). *The Black Poverty Cycle and How to End It*. Briarcliff Manor, NY: Chelmsford Press.

Jackson, Yvette. (2011). *The Pedagogy of Confidence: Inspiring High Intellectual Performance in Urban Schools*. New York: Teachers College Press.

Jackson, Yvette, and McDermott, Veronica. (2012). *Aim High, Achieve More: How to Transform Urban Schools Through Fearless Leadership*. Alexandria, VA: ASCD.

Jensen, Eric. (2009). *Teaching with Poverty in Mind: What Being Poor Does to Kids' Brains and What Schools Can Do about It*. Alexandria, VA: ASCD.

K–12 Facts-The Center for Education Reform (2014, March 22). Retrieved from www.edreform.com/2012/k-12-facts/# schools.

Kahneman, Daniel. (2011). *Thinking, Fast and Slow*. New York: Farrar, Straus and Giroux.

Kirp, David L. *Improbable Scholars: The Rebirth of Great American School System and a Strategy for America's Schools*. New York: Oxford University Press.

Klein, Joel. (2004, May 4). "Urban schools need better teachers not excuses to close the education gap." *U.S. News and World Report*. Retrieved from www.usnews.com/opinion/articles/2009/05/04/urban-schools-need-better-teachers-not-excuses-to-close-the-education-gap.

Kleinfield, N.R. (2012, May 11). "A System Divided: 'Why Don't We Have Any White Kids?'" Retrieved from www.nytimes.com/2012/05/13/education/at-explore-charter-school-a-portrait-of-segregated-education.html?pagewanted=all and _r=0.

Krugman, Paul. (2013, September 13). "Rich Man's Recovery." *New York Times*. Trends in High School Dropout and Completion Rates in United States: 1972–2009. Retrieved October 2011, National Center for Education Statistics/IES from nces.ed.gov/pubs2012/2012006.pdf.

Ladson-Billings, Gloria. (1994). *Dreamkeepers: Successful Teachers of African-American Children*. San Francisco: Jossey-Bass.

Levine, Daniel U., and Cooper, Eric J. (1991). "The Change Process and Its Implications in Teaching Thinking." In *Educational Values and Cognitive Instruction: Implications for Reform*. Hillsdale, NJ: Lawrence Erlbaum Associates.

Lowrey, A. (2012). *Business Economy and Income Inequality May Take Toll on Growth*. www.nytimes.com/2012/10/17/business/economy/income-inequalitymay-take-toll-on-growth.html?pagewanted=alland_r=O.

Mitter, Siddhartha. (Spring/Summer, 2013). "Building the Village It Takes: There's No Single Solution to the Achievement Gap but a Lot of Solutions, Together Just Might Do the Trick." New York: "TC Today."

Mock, B. (2013). *U.S. Reports to U.N. on Ending Racial Bias, With No Plan of Its Own*. http://colorlines.com/archives/2013/06/us_reports_to_un_on_ending_racial_discrimination_without_a_national_plan_for_racial_justice.html.

Nakatomi, H., Kuriu, T., Okabe, S., Yamamoto, S. I., Hatano, O., Kawahara, N., . . . and Nakafuku, M. (2002). "Regeneration of Hippocampal Pyramidal Neurons After Ischemic Brain Injury by Recruitment of Endogenous Neural Progenitors." *Cell, 110*(4), 429–441.

Nelson, Charles A. and Sheridan, Margaret A. (2011). "Lessons from Neuroscience Research for Understanding Causal Links Between Family and Neighborhood Characteristics and Educational Outcomes." In *Whither Opportunity?: Rising Inequality, Schools, and Children's Life Chances*. New York: Russell Sage Foundation.

New Stanford Report Finds Serious Quality Challenge in National Charter School Sector. (2009, June 15). Retrieved from credo.stanford.edu/reports/National_Release.pdf.

Nisbett, Richard E. (2009). *Intelligence and How to Get It: Why Schools and Cultures Count*. New York: W.W. Norton and Company.

Noguera, Pedro. (2008, March). "Creating conditions that promote student achievement." Speech delivered at the Teaching for Intelligence Conference, Albany, NY.

Pearson, David P. "Research Foundations of the Common Core State Standards in English Language Arts." In Newman, Susan and Gambrell, Linda (eds.), *Quality Reading Instruction in the Age of Common Core State Standards*, pp. 237–262. Newark, DE: International Reading Association.

Perry, Theresa, Steele, Claude, and Hilliard III, Asa. (2003). *Young, Gifted, and Black: Promoting High Achievement among African-American Students*. Boston: Beacon Press.

Ravitch, Diane. (2010). *The Death and Life of the Great American School System*. New York: Basic Books.

Ravitch, Diane. (2013). *Reign of Error: The Hoax of the Privatization Movement and the Danger to America's Public Schools*. New York: Alfred A. Knopf.

Renzulli, Joseph S. (1975). Talent potential in minority group students. In W. Barbe and J. Renzulli (eds.), *Psychology and Education of the Gifted*. New York: Irvington.

Renzulli, Joseph S. and Reis, Sally M. (2007). A technology-based program that matches enrichment resources with student strengths. *iJET International Journal of Emerging Technologies in Learning, 3*(2).

Resmovitas, Joy. (2014, March 21). "American Schools Are Still Racist, Government Report Finds." Retrieved from www.huffingtonpost.com/2014/03/21/schools-discrimination_n_5002954.html?ir=Black%20Voicesandutm_hp_ref=black-voices.

Ripley, Amanda. (2013). *The Smartest Kids in the World and How They Got That Way*. New York: Simon and Schuster.

Rothstein, Richard. (2004). *Class And Schools: Using Social, Economic, and Educational Reform to Close the Black-White Achievement Gap*. New York: Teachers College Press.

Sanders, William L., and Rivers, June C. (1996). "Cumulative and residual effects of teaching on future student achievement: Value-added research and assessment." Knoxville, TN: University of Tennessee.

Shenk, Daniel. (2010). *The Genius in All of Us: Why Everything You've Been Told About Genetics, Talent, and IQ Is Wrong*. New York: Doubleday.

Shyamalan, M. Night. (2013). *I Got Schooled: The Unlikely Story of How a Moonlighting Movie Maker Learned the Five Keys to Closing America's Education Gap*. New York: Simon and Schuster. K–12 Facts-The Center for Education Reform (March 22, 2014). Retrieved from www.edreform.com/2012/k-12-facts/#schools.

Siegel, Daniel J. (2007). *The Mindful Brain: Reflection and Attunement in the Cultivation of Well-Being*. New York: W.W. Norton and Company, Inc.

Smith, Stephanie. (2010). "Violence weighs heavy on a child's mind." Retrieved from pagingdrgupta.blogs.cnn.com/2010/06/14/embargoed-Monday-614-3pm-violence-weighs-heavy on-a-childs-mind/.

Steele, Claude M. (2010). *Whistling Vivaldi and Other Clues to How Stereotypes Affect Us*. New York: W.W. Norton and Company, Inc.

Sternberg, Robert. (1998). "All intelligence testing is 'cross-cultural': Constructing intelligence tests to meet the demands of person x task x situation interactions. In R. Samuda (Ed.), *Advances in cross-cultural assessment* (pp. 197–217). Thousand Oaks, CA: Corwin Press.

Sylwester, Robert. (2007). *The Adolescent Brain: Reading for Autonomy*. Thousand Oaks, CA: Corwin Press.

Thernstrom, Abigail, and Thernstrom, Stephan. (2003). *No Excuses: Closing the Racial Gap in Learning*. New York: Simon and Schuster.

Tillman, Linda, C. (2009). In *The Sage Handbook of African American Education*. Thousand Oaks, CA: Sage Publications.

U.S. Department of Health and Human Services. Improving the Future for Children of Incarcerated Parents. Retrieved June 13, 2013 from www.acf.hhs.gov/glog/2013/06/improving-the-future-for-children-of-incarcerated-parents.

Vincent, Jean D., and Lledo, Pierre M. (2014). *The Custom Made Brain: Cerebral Plasticity, Regeneration, and Enhancement*. New York: Columbia University Press.

Wells-Stuart, Amy. (2014, March). "Seeing Past the 'Color-Blind' Myth of Education Policy: Addressing Racial and Ethnic Inequality and Supporting Culturally Diverse Schools." Retrieved from National Education Policy Center, nepc.colorado.edu/files/pb-colorblind_0.pdf.

What are the links between shame and poverty? Retrieved August 24, 2010, from www.guardian.co.uk/society/2010/aug/24/research-poverty-shame-links.

Wiggin, Addison (2013, October 10). Charter School Gravy Train Runs Express to Fat City. Retrieved from www.forbes.com/sites/greatspeculations/2013/09/10/charter-school-gravy-train-runs-express-to-fat-city./.

Wilkinson, Richard, and Pickett, Kate. (2010). *The Spirit Level: Why Greater Equality Makes Societies Stronger*. New York: Bloomsbury Press.

Williams, Juan. (2006). *Enough: The Phony Leaders, Dead-End Movements, and Culture of Failure That Are Undermining Black America—and What We Can Do About It*. New York: Random House.

Wilson, Amos, N. (1978). *The Developmental Psychology of the Black child*. New York: Africana Research Publications.

Wise, Tim. (2010). *Color-Blind: The Rise of Post-Racial Politics and the Retreat from Racial Equity*. San Francisco: City Lights Books.

International and Global Perspectives in Urban Education and Leadership

The chapters in this section offer readers a unique perspective about urban education and leadership from an international and global context. The section aims to shed light on how international and global research about urban education and leadership can be utilized to increase or refine the understanding of cultivating successful educational leaders for urban schools. Multiple international research studies are exposed in this section that focus on the contributions that educational leaders can gain by engaging in discourse that includes the voices and experiences of urban leaders from diverse societies. Specifically, the authors include international research that merges leadership for social justice and urban education leadership, framing a more robust approach to identifying effective urban education leadership practices. The three chapters in the section promote the identification of effective leadership practices by utilizing a multifaceted cultural lens, with the hopes of having a positive impact on current and aspiring urban school leaders.

In chapter 35, "International Perspectives in Urban Educational Leadership: Social Justice Leadership in High-Need Schools," Bruce Barnett and Howard Stevenson expand research findings derived from an international school leadership research project and its interrelationship to urban school leadership. And in chapter 36, "Indigenous School Leadership in New Zealand: Cultural Responsivity for Diverse Learners in Urban Schools," Lorri J. Santamaría, Andrés P. Santamaría, Melinda Webber, and Hoana Pearson discuss a cross-cultural research model aimed at reinforcing the value of examining culturally diverse leadership practices to improve leadership in urban schools. Special attention is also given in both chapters to social justice leadership from an international context and its influence on urban education leadership practices. This section ends with chapter 37, "Crises, Critical Incidents, and Community and Educational Leadership" by Noelle Witherspoon Arnold, Ty-Ron M. O. Douglas, and Tirza Wilbon-White. This chapter takes a unique examination of leadership in urban settings after community disaster and crisis.

CHAPTER 35

International Perspectives in Urban Educational Leadership

Social Justice Leadership and High-Need Schools

Bruce Barnett and Howard Stevenson

Urban school systems around the world serve economically disadvantaged communities that are plagued with inequitable resources and experience high teacher and student mobility (Alexander, Entwisle, and Dauber, 1996; Kerbow, 1996; National Center for Education Statistics, 2006). As large concentrations of people have moved into urban centers, these cities are characterized by intense concentrations of poverty; wide economic, social, and linguistic disparity; and high mobility (Ahram, Stembridge, Fergus, and Noguera, n.d.; Gordon and Armous-Thomas, 1992; McClafferty, Torres, and Mitchell, 2000). As a result, urban school systems, their teachers, and leaders face enormous challenges not experienced to the same degree as their suburban and rural counterparts. Moreover, a particular feature of urban schools is the way in which questions of race and class collide (Halford, 1996), layering additional complexity on already complex problems. In addition to the social and economic effects of poverty, there is the widespread misconception that children and adolescents living in poverty cannot be held to the same academic and social expectations as students from more affluent neighborhoods. The biggest danger of this type of "deficit thinking" is that students are viewed as being helpless and hopeless, with little chance of succeeding in the classroom, workforce, or society (Halford, 1996; NCES, 2006). Often, these dismal expectations lead students and families to feel isolated, neglected, and alienated within and from their local communities.

This chapter focuses on educational leadership in urban schools in a broad range of international contexts and focuses on findings from the International School Leadership Development Network (ISLDN), a collaborative international research project sponsored by the British Educational Leadership Management and Administration Society and the University Council for Educational Administration. The chapter begins by describing how global discourses are dominating the field of education, particularly at the school or campus level, and we present a framework developed by ISLDN to help connect the macro and micro-contexts of schooling that shape the experiences of school leaders in urban schools. Next, the research findings are presented from ISLDN team members who are exploring two interrelated topics germane to urban schools—leadership for social justice and leadership in high-need schools. By focusing on school leaders who seek to overcome economic and social disadvantage and challenge social injustice, the chapter explores how these issues are framed in a variety of different national contexts. In particular, the interface between policy at the macrolevel in different international settings and leadership practices at the institutional level are examined. We conclude by discussing the lessons that can be learned from international comparisons about urban leadership and examining the implications for preparing and developing leaders for urban schools.

THE GLOBAL DISCOURSE IN EDUCATION

A project that seeks to develop an international understanding of the challenges facing school leaders in urban contexts must necessarily adopt a global perspective in relation to its methodological approach. However, within the ISLDN there is a clear understanding that a "global perspective" is about much more than the development of comparative case studies drawn from around the world, but is one that recognizes that the actions and experiences of school leaders in their urban communities take place in a globalized context, and one shaped by global discourses. As Stevenson and Tooms (2010) have argued, what happens "down here" cannot be disconnected from "up there," and the challenge is not only to understand how global discourses frame local contexts, but also to appreciate how such contexts are mediated by myriad national, regional, and community factors that ensure that local contexts are unique and highly contingent.

Globalized pressures continue to intensify, and whether globalization is defined in economic, political, or cultural terms (Olssen, Codd, and O'Neill, 2004), it is possible to identify a clear trend to a concentration of power in globalized networks and institutions. This is increasingly evident in terms of education. Institutions such as the World Bank, IMF, and the OECD have long since had a substantial influence on education policy (Robertson and Dale, 2009). Hence, the globalization of education experienced in the form of the flow of discourses and policies across national borders has probably never been more pronounced. These pressures appear to intensify as economic success becomes more closely linked to educational achievement, and therefore globalized economic competition becomes intimately linked to globalized education competition. As

international league tables of educational performance, whether relating to schools or higher education, become ever more significant, so too do the globalized policy discourses that promise rising standards and student performance outcomes.

However, despite all these developments, what we know is that nation-states remain an enduring feature within the context of global governance. Individual nation-states retain considerable power and independence and consequently there continues to be considerable diversity in the face of what is sometimes presented as global homogeneity (Held and McGrew, 2007). National governments retain considerable power, and within nation-states more localized cultural traditions often reinforce the sense of difference and diversity. Therefore, there is a pressing need to understand how local experiences are shaped by global and national discourses, but this must also reflect how those working in individual institutions are able to assert their independence and agency.

ISLDN colleagues have developed a framework within which individual cases of school leadership can be situated (see figure 35.1). The framework draws on

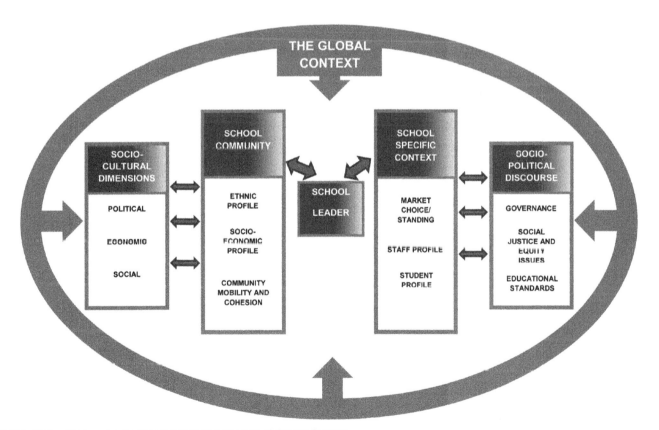

Figure 35.1. *Framework for Macro-Micro Examination of School Content*

previous work by Dimmock, Stevenson, Bignold, Shah, and Middlewood (2005) that located schools in a local (micro) context, but seeks to develop the micro-context and nest that within a national (macro) context. The framework identifies a range of key macro and micro factors that illuminate the context within which school leaders work. Individual agency is clearly critical when seeking to understand what it is that leaders do, and the ISLDN research is centrally concerned with this. But there also is recognition that this cannot be disconnected from the wider context that shapes those actions—reflecting the immediate context of the school, through to broader global discourses. The framework captures these features by identifying the factors at a micro and macro level that shape the context within which schools function.

The framework is located within a wider global context that recognizes there are discourses that frame educational debate and policy at a transnational and global level. The global hegemony of neoliberalism ensures that much of the educational discourse within individual countries is framed by wider debates about the knowledge economy, human capital development, and the drive for international competitiveness. However, within this global discourse the framework identifies a number of macro-level factors that help develop a better understanding of the context that is unique to each nation-state. One starting point is to identify the key political, economic, and social characteristics that are helpful in understanding the defining features of individual nation-states' context. Within each heading multiple descriptors are used, where relevant to individual nations, to highlight specific characteristics. For example, in *political terms*, might a nation's dominant culture be described as broadly neoliberal or social democratic? Recognizing the extent to which these terms reflect a westernized context, how else might political cultures be described? Furthermore, in relation to *economic factors*, can the country in question be considered affluent or otherwise? Is its economy growing or declining? Is the trend short-term or long-term? Finally, in *social terms*, to what extent is society divided by race and class? What role does religion play? These examples serve to illustrate some of the factors that might be used to frame a national context, but from our work to date we have seen how these factors can all contribute to explaining how what happens in individual schools in one country looks different to another. Set alongside these sociocultural dimensions the framework identifies a number of sociopolitical discourses that frame education policy. Such discourses are inevitably linked to the wider sociocultural dimensions, and have a specific focus on the way education policy debates are framed within individual national contexts. For example, the framework encourages an analysis of debates about accountability, equity, and "standards" within individual countries and how these are articulated at a national level, and then reflected in policy mandates.

Within these macro factors, the framework nests a micro-context that allows for an understanding of the specific contextual features that are unique to each school and that frame the experiences of those who study and work in the school. As with the macro-context, the starting point of this analysis is the wider local context of the school's community, framed largely in demographic terms. The framework therefore is concerned with the socioeconomic and ethnic profile of the school's community, but within this the inclusion of a category identifying "community mobility and cohesion" is a reflection of the need to recognize the specific challenges that can flow from considerable community turbulence (e.g., rapid population movements, conflicts, and tensions within communities). However, the framework also recognizes the school itself is a community, and that the specificity of the school's own context and community must be acknowledged and understood. For example, under the heading "School Specific Context" there is a sub-category of "Market Choice and Standing." This element seeks to establish to what extent a particular school can be said to function in a local market, in which significant choice and competition is experienced. In some school systems, such marketization is discouraged, while in others it may be encouraged in official discourses, but does not materialize in practical terms. In yet other contexts, individual schools may face vigorous contested local markets in which considerable parental choice is exercised. These different experiences can have a powerful influence on the experience of school principals and their latitude to pursue particular policies. It is important therefore to understand the extent to which local markets function, and the school's location within that market, not least because the existence of vigorous local markets can result in a school's own student population looking distinctly different to that of its immediate community. In these circumstances, the school's own internal community (its students) might not align with the school's immediate external community (those who live in its environs). Within the school's specific context, the framework also seeks to recognize that the staff profile can have a significant influence on any school's capacity to develop, which needs to be taken into consideration when understanding an individual school's circumstances.

The framework represents a practical response by ISLDN members to connect "up there" with "down here." In particular, it highlights two issues that are central to the Network's research. First, it recognizes that those leading schools in urban contexts face many common issues, but that individual leaders in urban schools face a particular set of circumstances that are unique to their schools. Understanding the relative importance of global, national, and local contexts is critical to understanding the experiences and actions of urban school leaders. Second, the framework recognizes that contextual factors are important, but that they provide no more than a background against which leadership is exercised. The importance of external factors does not mitigate against agency and therefore the framework seeks to help understand how agency is shaped, but not denied, by contextual factors.

THE CHALLENGES OF URBAN EDUCATION

The problems facing urban schools around the world are monumental. On one hand, various social and structural challenges pose significant problems for school systems. For instance, students in urban schools tend to have low achievement scores, recurring health problems, high teenage pregnancy rates, low secondary school graduation rates, high absenteeism and disciplinary problems, and high unemployment upon leaving school (Ahram et al., n.d.; National Center for Education Statistics, 1996, 2006). In addition, the educational infrastructure of urban education can be problematic. In comparison to other schools, many urban systems are plagued by incoherent instructional practices, inadequate data management systems and resources, decaying buildings, large student enrollments, and difficulty hiring and retaining high-quality teachers (Jacob, 2007; NCES, 2006).

On the other hand, cultural challenges compound the problems facing urban school educators. As noted earlier, deficit thinking reinforces the notion that urban students are incapable of learning academic content and social skills. In many instances, educators believe the prevailing norms in urban communities and households impede their efforts to educate their children. They sense parents not only are less likely to support the school's efforts to educate their children, but they also are not motivated to provide assistance at home (O'Conner and Fernandez, 2006). Many of these beliefs are rooted in negative stereotypes about race and class, leading teachers and administrators to unwittingly perceive that these students have learning deficiencies as well as behavioral and emotional problems. If urban educators do not have an "asset-based" view of students and communities, then their students may not see curriculum and instructional practices as being culturally responsive or relevant, resulting in mistrust, disengagement, and rebellion (Steele, 2010). Examples of an "asset" perspective are illustrated in the guiding principles of the National Institute for Urban School Improvement (2004–2005), which underscore that urban schools should value the knowledge and experience of children and families, use community resources, produce high-achieving students, and provide an education based on care and respect.

To typecast all urban education systems, teachers, and administrators as insensitive and non-responsive to the educational and emotional needs of their students would be a great mistake. For example, a host of major reform efforts have been launched in the United States to help improve and strengthen high-poverty urban schools, including the Coalition of Essential Schools (Brown University), School Development Project (Yale University), Communities in Schools (headquartered in Arlington, Virginia), Institute for Urban School Improvement (University of Connecticut), and National Institute for Urban School Improvement (Arizona State University). In addition, governmental policies, such as Getting It Right for Every Child in Scotland (Scottish Government, 2012) and massive efforts to direct resources to disadvantaged schools in China (Chinese Ministry of Education, 2005), have attempted to integrate services for children regardless of their social and economic standing. Furthermore, leaders who have achieved success in high-poverty schools have an unwavering belief in students' learning capabilities, maximize instruction time, develop the problem-solving capacities of their teachers, and use empirical evidence to monitor results (Chenoweth and Theokas, 2013). Other promising examples include restructuring school governance to foster greater local community involvement and ownership; reducing the size of schools and classrooms to personalize the schooling experience; and revising professional development to be teacher-directed, site-based, and collaborative (Halford, 1996).

Research and development in school leadership also acknowledges the importance of leading schools experiencing high poverty, low student achievement, and inadequate resources and facilities. Two prominent areas have captured the attention of researchers and practitioners: (a) social justice and (b) high-need schools. These areas reflect the central focus of the research being conducted by the members of the ISLDN, to which we now direct our attention.

THE INTERNATIONAL SCHOOL LEADERSHIP DEVELOPMENT NETWORK

Background

The globalization of educational policies and practices has affected the formation of regional and international networks of nations, international and nongovernmental organizations, and multinational companies (Pashiardis, 2008). The field of educational leadership preparation and development is becoming more engaged in international collaboration (Lumby, Crow, and Pashiardis, 2008); however, creating these networks poses substantial challenges, including the tendency for pro-Western views to dominate projects and the lack of financial and organizational support (Brown and Conrad, 2007; Walker and Dimmock, 2000). To counteract these problems, Walker and Townsend (2010) have discovered successful cross-national partnerships: (a) congregate a small group of individuals who are able to locate funding, create a vision, and establish political support, (b) rely on linkages with existing professional networks, (c) embrace and encourage diversity and differences, (d) establish high-profile events in different locations, and (e) promote activities, events, and products that support colleagues from different countries who otherwise would not be able to participate.

Guided by these principles of effective cross-national partnerships, in 2010 the University Council for Educational Administration (UCEA) and the British Educational Leadership Management and Administration Society (BELMAS) launched an international comparative study examining the preparation and development of school leaders, referred to as the International School Leadership Development Network (ISLDN). Two research strands of the ISLDN have emerged: (1) preparing and developing leaders who advocate for social justice and (2) preparing and developing leaders for high-need, low-performing schools. A description of the work being done in each of these strands is summarized below.

The Significance of Social Justice

A growing body of work focuses on social justice, which examines the equitable distribution of resources and the elimination of marginalization and exploitation (Woods, 2005). Cribb and Gewirtz's (2003) conceptualization of social justice captures the range of issues leaders can attend to: (a) distributive justice examines how social and economic resources are distributed and withheld from certain socioeconomic groups, (b) cultural justice refers to how certain cultures dominate others, leading to disrespect, exploitation, and nonrecognition, and (c) associational justice is concerned with how groups and individuals are prevented from participating in the decision-making process. Another depiction of social justice is advanced by Goldfarb and Grinberg (2002), who claim it is "actively engaging in reclaiming, appropriating, sustaining, and advancing inherent human rights of equity, equality, and fairness in social, economic, educational, and personal dimensions" (p. 162).

School leaders are central to advancing social justice, particularly in urban settings where resources are scarce and local citizens and communities have little power or influence regarding their social, economic, and educational standing (Scheurich and Skrla, 2003). Theoharis (2007) acknowledges that principals who openly confront issues of race, class, gender, disability, and sexual orientation are social justice advocates. Principals who tackle these issues are adamant about raising student achievement for marginalized students, eliminating school structures that segregate students, enhancing teachers' capacities to work successfully with high-need learners, and strengthening the school culture to be more inviting to marginalized groups and individuals (Theoharis, 2007).

Social Justice Leadership Studies in the ISLDN

The concept of "social justice" is inherently problematic—the term is used widely, and often imprecisely. It is used by those who reflect a broad range of philosophical and political traditions, some of which might be considered directly contradictory. For a group that was constituted within the ISLDN as focused on "social justice leadership," this inevitably posed an early problem—how could we identify "social justice leaders" without first reaching agreement between us about what we meant by "social justice"? This generated considerable debate, as might be expected. Of particular note was the assertion that the term "social justice" as an identifier or descriptor had little or no purchase in some cultural contexts. It is important to recognize therefore that the term itself reflects particular views of the world, and this in turn can reinforce various power relations in terms of how problems are framed, and by whom. This is an issue the group continues to be aware of, and to reflect on.

The group decided that its research approach was to be essentially inductive, in which the voices of principals were the key focus. They recognized the importance of viewing school leadership more widely, but for largely pragmatic reasons, the focus has been on the principalship. Being deliberately broad and inclusive, the group examined social justice leaders in two ways. First, they identified social justice school leaders as those for whom a commitment to reducing inequalities, in some form, was a high priority in their work. This could intentionally be across a broad range of issues— class, race, gender, sexuality, and (dis)ability—and might be expressed in a range of ways—reduction in achievement gaps or increases in student participation and engagement provide just two examples. As stated, this definition is deliberately broad—but it is not wide open. A commitment to reducing inequalities does frame social justice in specific ways, and it does rule out those who argue that the promotion of social justice is not incompatible with, and may involve, a widening of inequalities.

This led to the second element of the sampling strategy whereby we asked principals to self-identify them-

selves as social justice leaders in the terms identified in the project. In keeping with this broad approach, the group then determined a set of research questions that enabled the participants' own views of their values, motivations, and actions to set the agenda for the research. The questions were deliberately open-ended, and sought to start from the premise that social justice as a concept expressed in policy is often unclear, incoherent, and open to multiple interpretations. The group therefore sought to seek as its starting point an understanding of how principals "made sense" of social justice for themselves, before exploring in more detail how they sought to operationalize this, and how their values, motivations, and actions might be framed within the wider context in which they functioned. This pointed to a study focused on four, deliberately straightforward, research questions:

1. How do social justice leaders *make sense* of "social justice"?
2. What do social justice leaders *do*?
3. What factors *help and hinder* the work of social justice leaders?
4. How did social justice leaders *learn* to become social justice leaders?

The Social Justice Leadership strand of ISLDN now involves twenty-eight researchers, and to date, cases have been selected and interviews with principals conducted in fifteen different countries. The research is clearly at an early stage, with initial interviews conducted with school principals using a common interview schedule related to the four research questions presented here. What follows are some provisional findings from this research in relation to each of the four research questions.

How do social justice leaders *make sense* of "social justice"? The most common response from school principals was to articulate social justice as a type of "fairness for all," recognizing that social injustice meant unequal life chances, based on poverty and discrimination (Risku, 2012; Tian, 2012). As leaders of educational institutions, there was a strong emphasis on casting social justice in terms of supporting students to overcome disadvantage and be able to take on a role as full participants in society. Social justice was often framed in terms of the individual students within the school's local community. Principals' concerns tended to be immediate and practical with little sense of principals "theorizing" social justice, or locating their critique of social injustice within a wider structural critique of societal arrangements. One view that stood out as particularly distinct was that of a principal from Latin America who asserted, "There is no social justice if there is no active participation of the people." This approach emphasized principles of solidarity, cooperation, and respect for human rights as the basis of social justice—from which a critique of poverty followed (Torres, Cerdas Montano, and Slater, 2012). In this sense, associational justice was privileged over distributive justice (Cribb and Gewirtz, 2003). This was the exception when considered in the context of other interviewees.

What do social justice leaders *do*? As might be expected, the range of responses to this question was extremely broad, with much depending on the specificities of local context. For instance, there was an interesting mix between principals who advocated "equal treatment" approaches (based on holding everyone to common standards and expectations) and those who relied more heavily on varying approaches according to the needs and circumstances of students. One school principal from China (Wilson, 2012) talked about children having "the same life but different excellences" and therefore the need to "celebrate diversity and difference in terms of equality of value." Common across many of the principals' approaches was a strong ethic of care—to not only care, but to make care visible (Duncan, 2012). Principals were very aware of the precariousness and vulnerabilities of many of their students' lives, and the need therefore for school to provide an environment that offered stability and security. Another school principal from England (Potter, 2012), who had previously stated, "I take into my school the kids other schools don't want to teach," drew an analogy between her relationship to students and her experience as a mother:

> I came at being a social justice leader as I did as a mother . . . I run the school as I run my family . . . I believe in the young people . . . they come first . . . They are not scared of me . . . they are scared of me disapproving of what they have done.

A further feature of school principals' actions that emerged strongly from the data was a sense of "active principalship" (Norberg and Arlestig, 2012) whereby these school leaders felt the need to be highly visible within both their schools and their communities. Issues of social injustice were more acute in challenging environments and the principals in this study recognized the need to be seen and to be available to both students and their wider community. Several principals described their role in terms of being activists for their school's community, and advocating for their community's collective interests. This was perceived to be an important aspect of their work, and points to the high levels of demand placed on school leaders in challenging contexts and the difficulties of sustaining leadership practices in a context where boundaries of time and space are much more porous.

What factors *help and hinder* the work of social justice leaders? There were clearly a range of factors that both supported principals in their social justice mission, and undermined their activities. Within the scope of this summary, we will identify what emerged as the most supportive and most obstructive factors. Policies at a national level intended to support equity initiatives were identified as a considerable help to school principals in their work—although this needs some qualification. What appeared to be particularly significant was the way in which principals were able to work creatively with policies to mobilize the opportunities they provided to support their social justice efforts. This itself required considerable leadership skills. It is also important to recognize that policies could frequently undermine social justice work, and in some cases these were the unintended consequences of policies formed to support equity aspirations. In these cases, principals could be presented with difficult moral dilemmas as they juggled the needs of individual students with the wider needs of their school (Stevenson, 2007). Navigating policy, by exploiting positive outcomes from policy, while mitigating for negative ones, was a key leadership skill for these school leaders.

The factor that hindered school leaders most was identified as the sheer scale of the challenges students faced in their lives. Although not a universal experience, there was a common view that both short- and long-term factors were adding greater insecurity to the lives of students in their schools.

How did social justice leaders *learn* to become social justice leaders? Many of the principals interviewed made deliberate career choices to work in particular types of schools, in which their commitment to social justice could have correspondingly more impact. In these cases, their commitment to social justice was seen to be the product of a complex web of life experiences and influences. Several cited religious influences and/or their own personal experiences of living with disadvantage (Angelle, 2012). This was summarized by a Chinese principal who attributed his social justice convictions to "a whole-life experience of unfairness and social injustice in society" and therefore a commitment to challenge that (Wilson, 2012). Within these responses it is interesting to note that interviewees focused on their own acquisition of social justice values, rather than on the acquisition of the skills they required to be an effective social justice leader, and it is this gap in our understanding that now guides the future work of the project. How do leaders committed to social justice learn to be effective in their mission?

The Proliferation of High-Need Schools

Accountability trends in multiple international contexts have begun to focus on schools that have unique student and community characteristics and low student performance (Duke, 2012b; Leithwood, Harris, and Strauss, 2010). These so-called high-need schools mirror many of the characteristics associated with urban education settings, as noted by Duke (2008, 2012b):

- High levels of ethnic minorities, immigrants, mobility, homeless families, children in foster care, incarcerated students, drug abusers, and English Language Learners (ELLs);
- Large percentages of students not achieving expected levels of achievement;
- High numbers of student truancies, suspensions, and dropouts coupled with low attendance and graduation rates; and
- Significant problems with the learning environment, including high teacher and leader turnover, high teacher absenteeism, low staff morale, and financial problems.

In the 1990s, efforts to improve high-need, low-performing schools spawned the school turnaround movement (Duke, 2012b). Although there are few empirical studies of turnaround leadership, preliminary results highlighting how these leaders can attempt to alleviate their schools' low performance are emerging. Oftentimes, these leaders challenge the status quo, demand teachers embrace the school's new direction, or force them to find employment elsewhere (Hollar, 2004). Principals and teachers in turnaround schools understand the need to improve their literacy programs, increase parental involvement, provide timely data on student progress, focus interventions on low-achieving students, and develop new approaches to school discipline (Duke, 2008). Finally, because turnaround schools need "quick and dramatic" results (Duke, 2012b, p. 9), school leaders direct their initial focus on literacy programs, daily schedules, targeted intervention and staff development, and teacher teams responsible for data analysis and curriculum alignment (Duke, 2008).

High-Need Schools Studies of the ISLDN

The initial discussions among the high-need schools ISLDN team members raised several important issues that have guided their work: (a) determining how high-need schools are defined in different countries, (b) identifying local and national policies aimed at high-need schools, (c) completing case studies revealing the strategies leaders in high-need schools employ, and (d) determining ways in which high-need school leaders are prepared and supported. Initially, the countries represented were Australia, Italy, New Zealand, Mexico, Sweden, and the United States. Recently, members from Canada, China, Malaysia, and the Republic of Georgia have joined the project. Presently, there are sixteen researchers who have conducted twenty-two studies in eight countries.

Because of the lack of studies examining how leaders of high-need schools attempt to turn around and sustain changes to these environments (Duke, 2012b), the group identified factors that affect conditions in high-need schools in their countries: (a) student and community characteristics (e.g., ethnic minorities, mobility, poverty, nonnative language speakers), (b) student performance (e.g., math and reading scores, graduation rates, attendance), and (c) other contributing factors (e.g., teacher and leader turnover, staff morale, student engagement). Despite the relative infancy of the ISLDN, research team members have collected data about school leaders working in urban, suburban, and rural communities; national policies affecting high-need schools and their leaders; and professional development programs for turnaround school specialists. These include:

- Early childhood centers (Mexico)
- Elementary/primary schools (China, Mexico, USA)
- Middle schools (Mexico)
- Secondary schools (Australia, New Zealand, Sweden)
- PreK–12 schools (Australia, Republic of Georgia, New Zealand)
- State-level policies and preparation (USA)
- National policies (Republic of Georgia, Sweden)

As a result of these investigations, insights have emerged about how principals in a variety of national contexts sought to turn around high-need, low-performing schools as well as how policymakers have attempted to address the needs of these schools and their leaders.

Leadership at the school level. ISLDN researchers have conducted two types of case studies of school leaders across a variety of national contexts. First, they have observed and interviewed principals and teachers, capturing snapshots of the leadership strategies principals are using in high-need, low-performing schools in urban, suburban, and rural communities. Second, one of the studies followed a turnaround leader over the course of three years, capturing the dynamic nature of conditions over time. Both of these types of studies have revealed important information about the realities of turnaround leadership.

The short-term case studies demonstrated the strategies principals used to confront challenging aspects of their schools, including low staff morale; poor student academic performance, attendance, and graduation; high mobility rates of students and teachers; and community apathy. These studies demonstrated principals intervened at different levels, oftentimes using multiple strategies simultaneously. First, school leaders took a macro view by attempting to alter the school's vision and culture. Examples included developing an integrated intervention plan using comprehensive data collection and decision-making processes (Drysdale, Gurr, and Villalobos, 2012), being organized and planning thoughtfully (Notman, 2012), and constantly clarifying and communicating desired values and performance

expectations (Gu and Johansson, 2012; Hipp and Baran, 2013). Teachers who were unable or unwilling to meet new performance expectations were relocated to other schools (Wildy and Clarke, 2012). In some instances, improving the school's grounds and facilities gave communities a renewed sense of hope that a more productive school learning environment was occurring for their children (Sharvashidze and Bryant, in press).

Second, realizing the importance of human potential to effect change, principals possessed strong communication skills (Notman, 2012), especially in developing the expertise and capacity of teachers and other campus leaders. This occurred by investing in external leadership development programs, ensuring leadership team meetings provide opportunities for professional learning and sharing, and conducting leadership development sessions for teachers and staff members (Drysdale et al., 2012). Other high-need school principals recognized the value of involving staff members in determining areas for improvement, planning and implementing goals, and reviewing progress (Hipp and Baran, 2013). Understanding the importance of relationship building, a principal in a remote Australian Aboriginal village commented, "I am best at getting along with people. I think my greatest success here has been to build good relationships among teachers, throughout the community, and between all the students" (Wildy and Clarke, 2012, p. 26).

Third, gaining an understanding of the factors affecting the community context, especially the values and assets of parents and community organizations, was an important aspect of these principals' actions. They were well aware of the chronic problems facing families living in poverty, such as lack of food and health care services. Attempting to overcome these challenges, principals utilized school resources to purchase food for students and worked with local agencies to provide services (Wildy and Clarke, 2012). In an attempt to gain greater parental involvement, some schools entered into formal agreements with parents, requiring them to attend conferences with teachers, monitor their children's homework assignments, and provide transportation (Hipp and Baran, 2013). To regain community trust, principals confronted their past history of ineffectiveness in order to convince parents of the school's current efficacy (Drysdale et al., 2012; Qian, 2013). In extreme cases, principals and teachers were forced to deal with episodic traumatic events that disrupt their local communities, such as student suicides and natural disasters (Notman, 2012).

Finally, these short-term case studies revealed concentrated efforts to improve and monitor the teaching and learning process in their schools (Gu and Johansson, 2012; Hipp and Baran, 2013; Notman, 2012). In some instances, they utilized externally mandated resources, as demonstrated by Mexican principals who used the government's distribution of new textbooks and demand for new teaching practices to stimulate reform in their schools (Rincones, 2012). Despite resistance from teachers to these new reforms, principals realized these governmental resources allowed them to provide instructional support beyond what their local communities could afford. In other cases, they took advantage of local needs and interests in designing curriculum. One example of this approach was a principal who used the students' and community's love of art by displaying murals and pictures around the school, designing math lessons to incorporate artistic drawings, and creating an art gallery to display student work (Wildy and Clarke, 2012).

Another way to capture high-need school principals' leadership was to examine their actions over several years. Duke (2012a) determined how a turnaround school principal sought to sustain student improvement efforts over three years. Rather than a stagnant linear process, school improvement was dynamic. On one hand, the findings revealed the school maintained some efforts throughout the three years, including several literacy programs and teacher teams. On the other hand, new initiatives were begun and others were changed or replaced. For instance, efforts to increase parental choice, teacher-led committees, and assessment "for" learning activities were introduced (Stiggins, 2002). In addition, changes to existing processes emerged, such as teachers setting their own improvement goals, increasing cross-grade ability grouping, reducing "pull-out" programs in favor of "push-in" programs, and modifying end-of-year reviews. This study clearly demonstrated the iterative nature of school improvement, especially in low-performing schools striving to maintain and turn around student and teacher performance over time.

Policy and program implementation. Besides creating sanctions for under-performing schools and

systems, federal and state governments have created policies and provided resources intended to support high-need schools. While many of these policies and resource allocations are well intended, shifts in government leadership have created inconsistencies in reform implementation. For instance, unstable political leadership in the Republic of Georgia's Ministry of Education and Sciences has affected the implementation of reforms in teacher licensing, English language education, and programs for non-ethnic learners (Sharvashidze and Bryant, in press). In recent years, the Mexican government launched a host of reforms, such as competency-based teaching practices, extended-day programs, site-based/community participatory decision making, and programs to reduce school violence (Rincones, 2012). State-level politicians in America have instituted a number of incentives to improve working conditions in low-performing schools. Examples include grants to high-need school districts that create partnerships with universities and colleges focusing on math and science instruction, revisions to teacher licensing requirements, site-based committees for teacher hiring, and bonuses for teachers working in low-performing schools (Baran, 2012).

Recently, a variety of leadership development programs in the United States have been established to support school leaders working in high-need, low-performing schools. In general, university leadership preparation programs have been bypassed as potential sources of support (Duke, in press); however, a notable exception is the Virginia School Turnaround Specialist Program (VSTSP) operating at the University of Virginia since 2004. Sponsored by the Virginia State Department of Education, each year the program provides professional learning experiences and coaching for ten Virginia principals in high-need schools (Duke, 2012b). Based on the successes of the VSTSP, other programs aimed at developing school turnaround specialists have emerged. For instance, Microsoft, Carnegie Corporation, and Mass Insight have contributed funding to support principals serving in low-performing schools across the country. In addition, educational agencies have taken up the charge to support and prepare school turnaround specialists. The Texas Education Agency (2013) established the Texas Turnaround Leadership Academy (TTLA) to build the capacities of schools and districts to identify qualified turnaround specialists, establish improvement strategies for underperforming campuses, and collaborate with other schools engaged in turnaround initiatives.

One of the most ambitious state-wide turnaround specialist programs has been created by the Southern Educational Research Board in collaboration with the Florida Department of Education, referred to as the Florida Turnaround Leaders Program (FTLP) (Duke, in press). Rather than working with practicing school administrators, this program identified teacher leaders with the potential to become turnaround specialists. Aimed at improving the performance of Florida's middle, secondary, and charter schools, the first cohort of 118 teachers began the two-and-a-half-year program in the spring of 2012. The major components of the program include a six-month practicum with four-person teams assigned to a low-performing school in their district followed by a one-semester internship, where participants work in an underachieving school.

DISCUSSION AND CONCLUSIONS

The work of ISLDN highlights the importance of analyzing contemporary developments in education policy from an international perspective, and this is particularly the case with regard to an issue such as urban school leadership. (See Bryant, Notman, and Cheng [in press] for a synopsis of recent studies conducted by ISLDN team members.) Experiences of urban education, and the very specific challenges they pose for school leaders, are part of a global experience. This is in part because the experiences in urban areas are increasingly shaped by global developments. Economic policy, the jobs that flow from it (inward and outward), and the population movements that in turn follow have a profound effect on local communities. Therefore, it is important to recognize that the challenges faced by urban school leaders, whether in Chicago or Shanghai, are in part a result of the same global pressures. However, these pressures are mediated in very different ways as global trends collide with local cultures and contexts. The rich multi-country case studies from within the ISLDN project emphasize both the similarities, and the differences, that are the reality of urban school leadership in many contexts. While there are common pressures of uniformity, it is also important to recognize that each school faces its own unique context.

Overall, the studies conducted by the ISLDN teams reveal several themes regarding the realities school leaders face in striving to improve the learning conditions for their students, teachers, and communities. First, these school leaders realize the restrictions and problems associated with external state and federal policies; however, they are quite savvy about using policy to their advantage, realizing how these types of resources can support their intended reform initiatives beyond what is available at the local level. Second, they work tirelessly to learn more about the values and challenges of the parents and citizens in their communities. They are highly visible in order to better understand the physical, economic, social, and cultural aspects of the environment. This firsthand knowledge allows them to re-connect with communities that may have lost confidence in the school, seek additional resources to address the community's needs, and advocate community values within the school environment and curriculum. They view community values and culture as an asset, rather than a liability to the school. Finally, the commitment to leading urban school reform is based on a host of life experiences. Being a social justice advocate is not something that can be easily taught to school leaders, but is based on other significant life experiences, including their religious upbringing and having lived in disadvantaged conditions. However, we contend that sensitizing leaders to the realities of urban schools, especially those needing to turn around performance, can be enhanced through preparation activities, including concentrated practicum and internships experiences.

Although the ISLDN project emphasizes that we can learn a great deal from experiences elsewhere, there can be no globalized "one size fits all" that fails to take account of how local contexts shape experience. This has important implications for those who seek to support school leaders take on challenging roles in urban contexts. It is important to create the conditions in which we can learn from each other, within and between different national contexts, but at the same time our analyses, and leadership development strategies, need to be sufficiently nuanced to recognize that the work of school leaders committed to social justice, and working in high needs school environments, must be similarly fine-tuned. This can only be achieved when there is a rich understanding of the particularity of the factors that comprise the macro and micro contexts of schooling, and how school leaders in different urban contexts are able to successfully challenge the social injustices that arise from poverty and discrimination.

NOTE

The ISLDN is a collaborative project, and its outputs represent the collective efforts of its members. Several contributors are indicated in the sources referenced in this chapter, but we would like to acknowledge the contribution of all our colleagues in the Network. Full details of ISLDN's work, including a list of members, are available at isldn.wordpress.com/.

REFERENCES

Ahram, R., Stembridge, A., Fergus, E., and Noguera, P. (n.d.). Framing urban school challenges: The problems to examine when implementing response to intervention. *RTI Action Network*. Washington, DC: National Center for Learning Disabilities.

Alexander, K. L., Entwisle, D. R., and Dauber, S. L. (1996). Children in motion: School transfers and elementary school performance. *Journal of Educational Research, 90*(1), 3–12.

Angelle, P. (2012). *ISLDN project on social justice leadership: USA case study findings*. Paper presented at the annual convention of the University Council for Educational Administration, Denver, CO.

Baran, M. (2012). *Defining high needs schools in Milwaukee, Wisconsin*. Paper presented at the annual convention of the University Council for Educational Administration, Denver, CO.

Brown, L. and Conrad, D. A. (2007). School leadership in Trinidad and Tobago: The challenge of context. *Comparative Education Review, 51*(2), 181–201.

Bryant, M., Notman, R., and Cheng, A., (Eds.). (in press). Exploring high need and social justice leadership in schools around the globe. *Management in Education, 28*(3).

Chenoweth, K. and Theokas, C. (2013). How high-poverty schools are getting it done. *Educational Leadership, 70*(7), 56–59.

Chinese Ministry of Education. (2005, May 31). Further promoting the even development in nine-year compulsory education. *China Education Daily*.

Cribb, A. and Gewirtz, S. (2003). Towards sociology of just practices: An analysis of plural conceptions of justice. In C. Vincent (Ed.), *Social justice, education and identity* (pp. 15–29). London: RoutledgeFalmer.

Dimmock, C., Stevenson, H., Bignold, B., Shah, S., and Middlewood, D. (2005). School community perspectives and their leadership implications. In *Effective leadership in multi-ethnic schools* (pp. 26–40). Nottingham, United Kingdom: National College for School Leadership.

Drysdale, L., Gurr, D., and Villalobos, M. H. (2012). *Leading the formation and transformation of Hume Secondary College*. Paper presented at the annual convention of the University Council for Educational Administration, Denver, CO.

Duke, D. L. (2008). *The little school system that could: Transforming a city school district*. Albany: State University of New York Press.

Duke, D. L. (2012a). *"Raising test scores was the easy part": A case study of the third year of school turnaround*. Paper presented at the annual convention of the University Council for Educational Administration, Denver, CO.

Duke, D. L. (2012b). Tinkering and turnarounds: Understanding the contemporary campaign to improve low-performing schools. *Journal of Education for Students Placed at Risk, 17*, 9–24.

Duke, D. L. (in press). A bold approach to developing leaders for low-performing schools. *Management in Education, 28*(3).

Duncan, H. (2012). *ISLDN project on social justice leadership: USA case study findings*. Paper presented at the annual convention of the University Council for Educational Administration, Denver, CO.

Goldfarb, K. P. and Grinberg, J. (2002). Leadership for social justice: Authentic participation in the case of a community center in Caracas, Venezuela. *Journal of School Leadership, 12*, 157–173.

Gordon, E. W. and Armous-Thomas, E. (1992). Urban education. *Encyclopedia of educational research* (5th edition). New York: Macmillan.

Gu, Q. and Johansson, O. (2012). *Sustaining school performance: School contexts matter*. Paper presented at the annual convention of the University Council for Educational Administration, Denver, CO.

Halford, J. M. (1996, Summer). Policies of promise. *ASCD Information Brief, 5*, 1–6.

Held, D. and McGrew, A. (2007). *Globalisation/anti-globalisation: Beyond the great divide*. Oxford: Polity Press.

Hipp, K. K. and Baran, M. L. (2013). *Leadership for new schools: A glimmer of hope in urban schools*. Paper presented at the annual meeting of the American Educational Research Association, San Francisco, CA.

Hollar, C. (2004). The principal as CEO. *Principal, 84*(1), 42–44.

Jacob, B. A. (2007). The challenge of staffing urban schools with effective teachers. *The Future of Children, 17*(1), 129–153.

Kerbow, D. (1996). Patterns of urban student mobility and local school reform. *Journal of Education of Students Placed at Risk, 1*(2), 147–169.

Leithwood, K., Harris, A., and Strauss, T. (2010). *Leading school turnaround*. San Francisco: Jossey-Bass.

Lumby, J., Crow, G., and Pashiardis, P. (2008) (Eds.). *International handbook on the preparation and development of school leaders*. New York: Routledge.

McClafferty, K. A., Torres, C. A., and Mitchell, T. R. (2000). *Challenges of urban education: Sociological perspectives for the next century*. Albany: State University of New York Press.

National Center for Education Statistics. (1996). Urban schools: The challenge of location and poverty. Washington, DC: United States Department of Education.

National Center for Education Statistics. (2006). Characteristics of schools, districts, teachers, principals, and school libraries in the United States, 2003–04, schools and staffing report. Washington, DC: United States Department of Education.

National Institute for Urban School Improvement. (2004–2005). Great urban schools: Learning together builds strong communities. Retrieved from www.urbanschools.org/about_us/values_and_beliefs.html.

Norberg, K. and Arlestig, H. (2012). *ISLDN project on social justice leadership: Sweden case study findings*. Paper presented at the annual convention of the University Council for Educational Administration, Denver, CO.

Notman, R. (2012). *ISLDN project on high-need schools: New Zealand case study findings*. Paper presented at the annual convention of the University Council for Educational Administration, Denver, CO.

O'Conner, C. and Fernandez, S. D. (2006). Race, class, and disproportionality: Reevaluating the relationship between poverty and school education placement. *Educational Researcher, 35*(6), 6–11.

Olssen, M., Codd, J. A., and O'Neill, A. M. (2004). *Education policy: Globalization, citizenship and democracy*. London: SAGE Publications Limited.

Pashiardis, P. (2008). *The dark side of the moon: Being locally responsive to global issues*. Keynote presentation at the Commonwealth Council for Educational Administration and Management Conference, Durban, South Africa.

Potter, I. (2012). *ISLDN project on social justice leadership: England case study findings*. Paper presented at the annual convention of the University Council for Educational Administration, Denver, CO.

Qian, H. (2013). *"Ordinary" schools in Shanghai: How principals make a difference*. Paper presented at the annual conference of the British Educational Leadership, Management and Administration Society, Edinburgh, Scotland.

Rincones, R. (2012). *International perspectives on "high need schools": Implications for leadership preparation and development*. Paper presented at the annual convention of the University Council for Educational Administration, Denver, CO.

Risku, M. (2012). *ISLDN project on social justice leadership: Finland case study findings*. Paper presented at the annual convention of the University Council for Educational Administration, Denver, CO.

Robertson, S. L., and Dale, R. (2009). The World Bank, the IMF and the possibilities of critical education. In M. Apple, W. Au, and L. Gandin (Eds.), *International handbook of critical education*. (pp. 23–35). New York: Routledge.

Scheurich, J., and Skrla, L. (2003). *Leadership for equity and excellence: Creating high achievement classrooms, schools, and districts*. Thousand Oaks, CA: Corwin Press.

Scottish Government (2012). What is GIRFEC? Retrieved from www.scotland.gov.uk/Topics/People/Young-People/gettingitright/background.

Sharvashidze, N. and Bryant, M. (in press). A high need Azeri school: A Georgian perspective. *Management in Education, 28*(3).

Steele, C. (2010). *Whistling Vivaldi: And other clues to how stereotypes affect us*. New York: Norton.

Stevenson, H. (2007). A case study in leading schools for social justice: When morals and markets collide. *Journal of Educational Administration, 4*(6), 769–781.

Stevenson, H. and Tooms, A. (2010). Connecting 'up there' with "down here"—Thoughts on globalisation, neoliberalism, and leadership praxis. In A. Normore (Ed.), *Global perspectives on educational leadership reform: The development and preparation of leaders of learning and learners of leadership* (pp. 3–21). Bingley, United Kingdom: Emerald.

Stiggins, R. J. (2002). Assessment crisis: The absence of assessment for learning. *Phi Delta Kappan, 83*(10), 758–765.

Texas Education Agency. (2013). Texas Turnaround Leadership Academy. Retrieved from www.texasturnaround.net/about-us.html.

Theoharis, G. (2007). Social justice educational leaders and resistance: Toward a theory of social justice leadership. *Educational Administration Quarterly, 43*(2), 221–258.

Tian, M. (2012). *ISLDN project on social justice leadership: China case study findings*. Paper presented at the annual convention of the University Council for Educational Administration, Denver, CO.

Torres, N., Cerdas Montano, V., and Slater, C. (2012). *ISLDN project on social justice leadership: Costa Rica case study findings*. Paper presented at the annual convention of the University Council for Educational Administration, Denver, CO.

Walker, A. and Dimmock, C. (2000). Mapping the way ahead: Leading educational leadership into a globalised world. *School Leadership and Management, 20*(2), 227–233.

Walker, A. and Townsend, A. (2010). On school management—International Council on School Effectiveness and Improvement, Commonwealth Council on Educational Administration and Management (pp. 681–697). In P. Peterson, E. Baker, and B. McGaw (Eds.), *International encyclopedia of education*. Oxford, United Kingdom: Elsevier.

Wildy, H. and Clarke, S. (2012). *At the edge of the silent centre: An Australian principal's reflections on leading an isolated school.* Paper presented at the annual convention of the University Council for Educational Administration, Denver, CO.

Wilson, M. (2012). *ISLDN project preliminary research report.* Unpublished manuscript.

Woods, P. A. (2005). *Democratic leadership in education.* London: Sage.

CHAPTER 36

Indigenous School Leadership in New Zealand

Cultural Responsivity for Diverse Learners in Urban Schools

Lorri J. Santamaría, Andrés P. Santamaría, Melinda Webber, and Hoana Pearson

STUDY RATIONALE AND OVERVIEW

Because of their growing presence, it is wrongly assumed that indigenous or First Nations students in urban cities in the world are engaged meaningfully in the mainstream education system. In the United States these students are American Indian and Alaska Native and make up 3 percent of the total student population, when including those who identify with one or more other races (U.S. Census Bureau, 2013). Educational research, demographics, and statistical data reveal that even though the majority of these students are present in large numbers in our urban schools, they disproportionately comprise the bulk of academic achievement gaps separating them from their mainstream and often white or European descent peers.

New Zealand (NZ) is a unique country, in that indigenous Māori learners make up 14 percent of the total student population (New Zealand Government, 2013). Many schools in urban areas, similar to urban areas in the United States, have significant numbers of Māori students in attendance. The largest of these is Auckland city, home of approximately 1.4 million people, of which 11 percent are Māori. Like similar gaps separating learners in U.S. schools, the achievement gap between Māori and Pākehā (European/White) students remains a serious issue in the New Zealand school system. In 2013, approximately 88.3 percent of Pākehā students in Year 11 achieved Level 1 of the National Certificate of Educational Achievement (NCEA, New Zealand's standards' based national testing system), while only 70.7 percent of Māori students achieved this same qualification (NZQA, 2014). Additionally, in 2012 approximately one in ten Māori students left school without achieving any qualifications which is three times higher than for Pākehā students (Ministry of Education, 2014).

Despite an improvement in the achievement levels of both ethnic groups between 2009 and 2013, the achievement gap has persisted (NZQA, 2014).

Schools where diversity is most prevalent are likely to be urban in nature and tend to be schools where students who have been historically disenfranchised and traditionally marginalized by systems of inequality based primarily on race, ethnicity, culture, gender, social class, language, and/or disability are taught. Although underrepresented in educational leadership research and practice, there exist a small number of Māori principals working in urban schools in NZ (Bishop and Glynn, 1999).

This strengths-based comparative case study considers one Māori educational leader as an exemplar of leadership and urban education for indigenous multicultural multilingual learners whose leadership practice may be relevant to urban school leadership in the United States and like countries, and compares her leadership practices to those of culturally and linguistically diverse leaders in the United States. Ngaire,[1] a Māori urban school principal and member of the *Aka Tamaki* (regional) group of Māori principals, deputy principals and teacher leaders within the wider Auckland area, serves as an informant for consumers of the Urban School Leadership Handbook who struggle with ways to lead and positively impact indigenous learner outcomes in urban school settings in NZ, Australasia, the United Kingdom, the United States, Canada, and other countries challenged with the prospect of diversity. In this study as an urban primary school leader of color, Ngaire shares her challenges, experiences, and lessons learned in an effort to inform leadership practice in urban settings where indigenous students are being educated. Her experience is compared to similar experiences of other leaders of color[2] in the United States to gain insight on alternative ways of thinking about leadership in urban educational contexts in NZ, the United States, and abroad.

Further, this comparative study serves as an exemplar for culturally responsive ways in which research in parity can be accomplished with a cross-cultural team of two culturally and linguistically diverse researchers (African-American, Choctaw Nation of Oklahoma, and Mexican/Irish/Italian-American) from the United States and two Māori (Ngāti Whakaue, Ngāpuhi; Ngāti Rangiwewehi, Ngāti Raukawa) researchers, one of whom is also a school site leader. As such, this study is aligned with and complements components of the Treaty of Waitangi in 1840, the founding document of New Zealand as a nation, in that it recognizes Māori ownership of land and other properties and, in the contemporary context, the assumption that schools in New Zealand should be culturally responsive (New Zealand History, 2012). This research endeavor also reflects the reality that Māori leaders and scholars should be in partnership at every level of knowledge creation, policymaking, power sharing and decision-making with regard to the education of Māori and all learners.

The underlying research foundations for this study come from four core areas: Kaupapa Māori and critical race methodologies, culturally responsive educational leadership, Māori Leadership, and leadership practices that promote diversity and culturally responsive pedagogy in schools where educational inequities feature. To this end, literature will be briefly reviewed on Kaupapa Māori and critical race methodologies (Bishop and Glynn, 1999; Brayboy, 2006; Solórzano and Yosso, 2002; Tuhiwai Smith, 2012); Māori Educational Leadership (NZ Ministry of Education, 2010b); culturally responsive educational leadership (Gay, 2010; Gooden, 2005; Johnson, 2006; Khalifa, 2012; NZ Ministry of Education, 2010a); and applied critical leadership (ACL) (Santamaría, 2013; Santamaría and Santamaría, 2012). It is the authors' shared hope and vision that as a result of this work, a new model or theory of urban school leadership for indigenous learners is developed.

The research question guiding this chapter is: In what ways can indigenous school leadership inform culturally responsive education in urban school settings? This question is answered in the following review of related literature, methodology featured, findings, discussion including limitations, and conclusion with implications for practice and future study.

REVIEW OF SCHOLARLY AND EMPIRICAL RESEARCH LITERATURE

Kaupapa Māori and Critical Race Methodologies

Because this chapter is deliberately designed to contribute to international and global perspectives, we ground it in the epistemologies of Kaupapa Māori methodology first, complemented by critical race methodologies. Making these theoretical connections explicit is important in making the case that Ngaire's indigenous leadership practices are relevant to educational leaders in urban schools in the United States and other countries.

Kaupapa Māori. In the New Zealand context, there has been a proliferation of writing about Māori research theory and praxis (Bishop, 1996; Moewaka Barnes, 2000; Pihama, Cram, and Walker, 2002; Tuhiwai Smith, 2012; Walker, Eketone, and Gibbs, 2006). By far the most prominent research strategy to have emerged on the heels of the Māori Renaissance is Kaupapa Māori. In its broadest usage, Kaupapa Māori research refers to research that is "by Māori, for Māori, and with Māori" (Tuhiwai Smith, 2012; Walker et al., 2006, p. 333). Kaupapa Māori research developed as part of a broader movement by Māori to question "Westernized notions of knowledge, culture, and research" (Walker et al., 2006, p. 331), and shares the emancipatory goal of other post-colonial movements such as those developed by Freire (1985) and Gibson (1986). Kaupapa Māori challenges the raised status of Western knowledge systems and research methodologies and contests the exploitative nature of much research on Māori (Teariki and Spoonley, 1992). Kaupapa Māori also challenges the way in which research undertaken on Māori often results in few positive outcomes for Māori and selectively and unfavorably compares Māori with non-Māori, thus resulting in deficit-based approaches to viewing Māori people (Bishop, 1996).

Kaupapa Māori methodology has shown itself as a radical, emancipatory, empowerment-oriented strategy and collaborative-based process, and when it is used systematically it can produce excellent research which can lead to improved policy, practice, and outcomes for Māori people; including Māori academic achievement gains (Wearmouth, Berryman, Bishop, Peter and Clapham, 2011) and increased Maori parent participation in educational governance (Hoskins, 2010). According to Walker et al. (2006), the key principles underpinning Kaupapa Māori approaches to research are: *tino rangatiratanga* (self-determination, autonomy); social justice; Māori worldview; *te reo*/language; and *whakawhanaungatanga* (kinship/relationships). These features speak to Māori aspirations, philosophies, processes and pedagogies, which are consistently found within successful Māori interventions (e.g., academic achievement, increased parent participation). The term intervention is used in this sense to relate to the need, to bring about specific positive transformation in the experiences and positioning of Māori.

It is important to note that even though Kaupapa Māori research methods are specific for use and application in Māori communities, the methodology provides an example of a rigorous, relevant, culturally embedded, grounded, and responsive research framework for indigenous researchers to consider or build from. Researchers serving indigenous communities may well resonate with these principles and find them operational in their own struggles for decolonization. Tuhiwai Smith (2012), a prominent NZ Māori scholar, maintains that due to the focus on empowerment and emancipation of oppressed peoples, Kaupapa Māori research is localized critical theory. Building on this premise, though contentious in NZ, a country where the dominant European mainstream prefers to discuss settler relations as opposed to race relations; critical race paradigms are considered to further frame this chapter.

Critical race perspective. A critical race theory perspective is taken for this chapter for several reasons. First, prominent and progressive educational leadership scholars in NZ (Bishop, 2003; Pihama, 1993; Smith, 1997) and the United States (Gooden and Dantley, 2012; Jean-Marie and Normore, 2008; Ladson-Billings, 1999) employ these frameworks in their educational research. Second, this theory is centered on notions of critique and change versus understanding or explaining social phenomena (Horkheimer, 1972), as is this inquiry. Third, a critical race perspective functions optimally when it is explanatory, practical, and normative (Calhoun, 1995), as are the aspirations of this research.

Although they originate from race and racism in U.S. contexts, critical race methodologies, as theoretical frameworks, are used to complement this work carried out in NZ where systems of ignorance, exploitation, and power are used to oppress Māori and Pacific people on the basis of ethnicity, culture, mannerisms, and color

(Marable, 1992). Here, as do U.S. scholars of color who research leadership in diverse societies (e.g., Gooden and Dantley, 2012; Khalifa, 2012), the authors challenge traditional ways of thinking about educational leadership by using critical race theory (CRT) as a means of linking antiracist, anti-subordinate, social justice and transformation inquiry in the United States to the kinds of decolonized counter-narratives that Tuhiwai Smith (2006) exemplifies in her research. In her work, Tuhiwai Smith (2012) suggests conditions for the ongoing Māori struggle for decolonization. These conditions include having a shared critical consciousness; Māori reimagination of the present world and Māori world positionality; intersectionality;[3] challenge of the status quo; and opposition against imperialist structures. The present study operates under these conditions as they inform and contribute to a critical race approach to this study, while at the same time supporting established CRT methods and frames of reference bridging and engaging activist scholarship resulting in what authors intend to be transformation of leadership practice in urban schools. To this end, we purposively consider the intersectionality inherent to a Māori principal's reality as pertaining to race, class, and gender with the intent of bringing her indigenous-centric leadership practice in an urban school setting into "mainstream" educational discourse in order to confront more popular approaches to critical research (e.g., ethnography, autoethnography) (Bishop and Glynn, 1999; Brayboy, 2006).

In this instance, considering both Kaupapa Māori and critical race perspectives, Ngaire's counter-stories are collected, developed, and shared in order to accolade new and positive stories about Māori leadership. The intent is to disrupt racism and negative race relations in NZ with regard to educational leadership and education in general. Kaupapa Māori and critical race research methodologies that interrogate old paradigms while seeking solutions is not without its challenges. The authors acknowledge contradictory adherence to recognizable modes of research practice (e.g., methods, findings, discussion) employed in the present study run counter to the argument for rejecting Westernized research paradigms noted by Walker et al. (2006). This is done purposefully in a well-read space in order to underscore the point that mainstream ways of knowing can be adapted by researchers with "marginalized" experiences to disrupt dominant paradigms and to voice, retell, re-story, and revise traditional research paradigms, when given the opportunity. This is the spirit of emancipation and empowerment referenced by Tuhiwai Smith (2012). Ngaire's counter-stories as related to urban school leadership were collected by way of interviews, observation, and document analysis with the school leader as she engaged in her practice to benefit the Māori learners in an urban primary school (Solórzano and Yosso, 2002). These counter-stories were then collated and analyzed to create a record that serves to challenge and interrupt the deficit stories about Māori learners and Māori leadership, similar to that of other indigenous populations in the world, for the purpose of adding a new perspective and developing a model to promote and improve leadership practices for marginalized learners in urban settings. An understanding of Māori leadership is warranted.

Culturally Responsive Māori Educational Leadership

Culturally responsive educational leadership. Culturally responsive educational leadership to improve academic experiences and outcomes for learners of color in mainstream schools essentially grounded in multicultural education is a topic that is increasingly discussed and debated as a remedy for universal academic achievement gaps (Bishop, 2003; Gooden and Dantley, 2012; Khalifa, 2012; Santamaría, 2013). Māori educational leadership, in its various guises, is not immune to this as attempts are made to define and categorize the features or attributes of an effective Māori leader and good school leadership practice. According to Hohepa and Robinson (2008), there are a number of features of Māori leadership that are unique. The aforementioned authors have argued that, "the distinctiveness of Māori leadership lies in the duties and associated accountabilities that are bestowed upon Māori educational leaders by the communities they serve" (p. 36). Hohepa and Robinson (2008) have also argued that Māori communities see their school leaders as an important vehicle through which Māori community aspirations are met. Traditionally, and in contemporary society, leadership continues to be important to the welfare and well-being of Māori as indicated in the well-known Māori proverb, *He toka tūmoana he ākinga nā ngā tai* (A standing rock in the sea, lashed by the tides) (Kawharu, 2008). This proverb describes the role of a leader in traditional

Māori society as staunch and wise and an important buffer between their people and any external pressures and issues.

In the New Zealand context there are two key documents that inform professional development programs associated with growing culturally responsive educational leadership: *Tū Rangatira*: Māori Medium Educational Leadership and *He Kākano* (NZ Ministry of Education, 2010a, 2010b). Both documents are premised on the notion that projected demographic and ethnic population changes are likely to impact the school-age population, and specifically, Māori within that population. This has implications for the nation's educational leadership, including the need for greater Māori representation.

***Tū Rangatira*: Māori medium educational leadership.** *Tū Rangatira* (NZ Ministry of Education, 2010b) presents a model of leadership that describes some of the key leadership roles and practices that contribute to high-quality educational outcomes for Maori learners. *Tū Rangatira* focuses on growing effective leadership practices, providing insights into how effective professional development programs can work toward strengthening leaders' capabilities, growing capacity, and sustaining exemplary leadership in the Māori medium education sector. Within the perspective of *Tū Rangatira*, Māori leaders make a positive impact on Māori achievement when they focus on duties and tasks that center on the development and expansion of the whole community, and interests associated with the wider community. The *Tū Rangatira* model identifies seven key roles of an effective Māori school leader. These include: (1) *The Guardian*: to protect and nurture a caring environment where people and ideas are valued; health, safety, and well-being are enhanced; and relationships are strong; (2) *The Manager*: to ensure the effective and efficient management of people, environments, and education to transform teaching and learning communities; (3) *The Visionary*: to have innovative and visionary leadership to equip learners with the knowledge, skills, and values to succeed in the twenty-first century as Māori and as citizens of the world; (4) *The Teacher and Learner*: to use reciprocal learning and exemplary modeling of innovation that leads to the effective creation, development, and delivery of high-quality authentic learning contexts and practice; (5) *The Worker*: to be seen to be "leading by doing," upholding collegial practices that build capability in others in pursuit of the goals of the school; (6) *The Networker*: to network, broker, and facilitate relationships that contribute toward achieving school goals; and (7) *The Advocate*: to promote the development and implementation of strategies, plans, and policies to realize learners' potential and their educational success as Māori (NZ Ministry of Education, 2010b).

This method of educational leadership is explored as a model for culturally responsive leadership reflecting some of the key leadership roles and practices contributing to high-quality educational outcomes for Māori learners. The leadership practices reflected in this approach are juxtaposed to the ways in which Ngaire expresses exemplary leadership in her urban school setting.

***He Kākano*: Culturally responsive leadership.**
He Kākano (NZ Ministry of Education, 2010a) is a professional learning program for high school leadership teams. The program focuses on growing culturally responsive pedagogical school leadership—leadership that actively takes account of the identity, language, and culture of Māori learners to build relationships that result in achievement success. *He Kākano* is an approach that incorporates the culture of Māori learners to build relationships that result in their achievement success. The program is designed to strengthen pedagogical leadership and teachers' capability to: (1) Analyze their leadership and wider school capability to lead and implement culturally responsive pedagogical leadership practices and school processes (including governance) that build Māori achievement and success; (2) Lead and manage change within their professional practices that responds to the needs of culturally located Māori learners; (3) Build relationships, partnerships, and networks that include *whānau* (family and extended family), *hāpu* (clan, sub-tribe), and *iwi* (tribe) to support ongoing improvement in leadership, teacher, learner, and school performance; (4) Gather, interpret, and use a range of data and other evidence to develop a comprehensive profile of their Māori learners' achievements; and (5) Establish targets and tailored plans for sustainable improvement in the schools' performance for and with Māori learners (NZ Ministry of Education, 2010a).

Both of these Māori-centered educational leadership approaches require a shift in leadership styles, dispositions, and school-community relations. The ability of school leaders to engage in the culturally responsive leadership approaches advocated in *Tū Rangatira* (NZ Ministry of Education, 2010b) and/or *He Kākano* (NZ Ministry of Education, 2010a) requires that leaders are culturally competent themselves. Becoming a culturally competent leader is a constant learning process that requires flexibility and adaptability on the part of the leader depending on the particular students and contexts with which they are working. Finally, the two approaches also illustrate how the knowledge, norms, values, resources, and epistemologies of local communities must be viewed as legitimate and valuable and intimately integrated into schools. A U.S.-based consideration of culturally responsive leadership, applied critical leadership, will also be reviewed as an alternative appropriate point of reference.

Applied Critical Leadership

Applied Critical Leadership (ACL) is grounded in research on educational leadership promoting social justice and educational equity that considers leadership as both a professional practice and a lived experience (Santamaría and Santamaría, 2012). The approach has hybrid foundations including transformative leadership (Bass, 1985; Burns, 1978; Kouzes and Posner, 2007), critical pedagogy (Freire, 1970; Giroux, 1983; McLaren, 2003), and critical race theory (Delgado and Stefancic, 2001; Ladson-Billings, 1999; Parker and Villalpando, 2007). Specifically, ACL research explores the ways in which educational leaders from historically marginalized frames of reference are able to use positive aspects of their identity to guide their leadership practice (Santamaría, 2013; Santamaría and Santamaría, 2012). Findings from a study of eleven leaders of color who also drew their practice largely from their raced, gendered, and cultured experiences, indicated shared characteristics, or ways of leading. These leaders engaged emancipatory leadership practices resulting in the *choice* to actively address educational issues and challenges using a critical race perspective to enact context specific changes. These changes were considered critical when responsive to power, domination, access, or achievement disparities. These leaders all reported that, while focused on more critical aspects of leadership, they concentrated on improving the academic achievement of learners at every level in the schooling process. When thinking about the ways in which an indigenous educational leader in an urban school in NZ and leaders of color in the United States lead for diversity, educational equity, and cultural responsivity; it is useful to consider how approaches like *Tū Rangatira* and the key roles of an effective Māori school leader, and pedagogical leadership capabilities associated with *He Kākano* compare with characteristics of ACL. Table 36.1 illustrates these approaches for complementary features and possible alignment to strengthen and frame the premise of this inquiry.

Comparative analysis of *Tū Rangatira, He Kākano,* and findings from ACL inquiry confirm theoretical alignment and overlap. All three approaches serve to impact negative racialized relations in the sociocultural context where leadership innovations and research are undertaken to promote leadership practices of Māori and indigenous leaders and leaders of color in NZ, the United States, and other countries. Like Kaupapa Māori methodology, the underlying theoretical frame behind *Tū Rangatira* and *He Kākano*, ACL research findings, with critical underpinnings, challenge negative, racialized relations by providing alternative ways of thinking about people of color in urban educational contexts as highly educated, competent, and capable leaders. Research reveals these individuals as holders of valuable experiential knowledge and ways of relating based on the positive attributes of their ethnicity, culture, and lived experiences in educational systems. A closer consideration of leaders of color in ACL research, juxtaposed with Ngaire's experience, provides

Table 36.1. Roles of Effective Māori Leaders and Characteristics of Applied Critical Leadership (ACL)

He Kākano—Culturally responsive pedagogical school leadership	Tū Rangatira—Key roles of Māori leadership	ACL Characteristics
Lead and manage change within their professional practices that responds to the needs of culturally located Māori learners.	The Advocate: to promote the development and implementation of strategies, plans and policies to realize learners' potential and their educational success as Māori.	Leaders' willingness to initiate and ongage in critical conversations—often regarding race, language, culture, difference, access, and/or educational equity. Leaders' ability to choose or assume a CRT lens for decision-making.
Build relationships, partnerships, and networks that include whānau (family), hāpu (clan, sub-tribe) and iwi (tribe) to support on-going improvement in leadership, teacher, learner and school performance.	The Networker: to network, broker and facilitate relationships that contribute towards achieving school goals.	Leaders' use of consensus as the preferred strategy for decision-making.
	The Guardian: to protect and nurture a caring environment where people and ideas are valued; health, safety and well-being are enhanced; and relationships are strong.	Leaders feeling the need to build trust when working with mainstream constituents or partners or others who do not share an affinity toward issues related to educational equity.
	The Manager: to ensure the effective and efficient management of people, environments and education to transform teaching and learning communities.	Leaders feeling the need to honor all members of their constituencies.
Gather, interpret, and use a range of data and other evidence to develop a comprehensive profile of their Māori learners' achievements.	The Teacher and Learner: to use reciprocal learning and exemplary modeling of innovation that leads to the effective creation, development and delivery of high-quality authentic learning contexts and practice.	Leaders making empirical or research-based contributions to educational contexts, adding authentic research based information to academic discourse regarding educational equity issues.
Analyze their leadership and wider school capability to lead and implement culturally responsive pedagogical leadership practices and school processes (including governance) that build Māori achievement success.	The Worker: to be seen to be "leading by doing," upholding collegial practices that build capability in others in pursuit of the goals of the school.	Leading by example to meet unresolved educational needs or challenges.
Establish targets and tailored plans for sustainable improvement in the schools' performance for and with Māori learners.	The Visionary: to have innovative and visionary leadership to equip learners with the knowledge, skills and values to succeed in the 21st century as Māori and as citizens of the world.	Leaders describing themselves as transformative, servant leaders who work ultimately to serve the greater good.

a relevant and informative context on which to further expand this chapter.

INQUIRY METHODOLOGY

Case study research was chosen for the research design to build upon previous leadership studies that feature leadership in diverse societies and contexts (Gooden and Dantley, 2012; Hohepa and Robinson, 2008; Jean-Marie and Normore, 2008; Khalifa, 2012). As such, this inquiry serves to emphasize detailed contextual analysis of a limited number of events, conditions, and relationships (Yin, 1994). Further, this method was chosen to provide an in-depth profile for Ngaire, multifaceted enough to create a narrative counter-story of her leadership practice and experience to "counter deficit storytelling," while addressing the research question posed (Solórzano and Yosso, 2002, p. 23).

Counter-stories expose, analyze, and replace mainstream majority stories steeped in privilege in order to "challenge the dominant discourse" on difference (Solórzano and Yosso, 2002, p. 32). The selected method and design provided a comparison of findings to the literature framing the inquiry. Data sources included natural observations of Ngaire at school board meetings (three two-hour-long school board meetings over the course of six months), two one-hour formal interviews, supporting documents available in the public domain (e.g., ERO reports), and two academic narratives written by Ngaire reflecting her journey as a Māori urban primary school principal in fulfillment of a postgraduate degree study. The range of data collected ensured appropriate data triangulation for the purposes of theory corroboration, adding depth, texture, and multiple insights as a result of the study (Johnson and Christensen, 2012).

Participant

Ngaire, the participant[4] known by all researchers and purposefully selected for this study, is a Māori urban primary school principal who races herself outside of whiteness by identifying with people of color as an indigenous woman with multicultural experiences growing up in *Aotearoa*,[5] NZ (Haney Lopez, 1998). Ngaire's leadership practice inspired the researchers to consider taking a closer look at leadership practice in NZ, result-

ing in culturally responsive pedagogy, increased academic achievement, and well-being of Māori, Pasifika, and other students of color at the school. Ngaire was selected to participate because of her self-proclaimed practices coupled with researchers' informal observations of her leadership practices perceived as promoting social justice and educational equity (Santamaría and Santamaría, 2012). Ngaire's participation represented a purposeful convenience sample of an individual working as an urban primary school principal known by the researchers. These facts may be considered limitations or strengths to the study, depending on the perspective taken. Because the researchers' children attend the urban elementary school where Ngaire is principal, there were regular and authentic access opportunities including personal and professional rapport between researchers and the participant, which may also be perceived inquiry limitations.

Setting

Te Kura o Te Uru Karaka (Karaka Grove School) primary school is a small inner-city primary school. The school roll is currently at 304. At present there are sixteen nationalities in the school, although Pākehā/European descent (33 percent), Māori (47 percent), and Pacific Island students (7 percent) make 87 percent of the total. The community is diverse not only by ethnicity, but in the range of socioeconomic groups and family structures as well.

Currently, *Te Kura o Te Uru Karaka* has nineteen Ministry of Education Funded Teaching Positions. This is inclusive of Ngaire (Principal), the Special Needs Program, Reading Recovery, Māori Literacy Intervention, Sports Coordination, and classroom release time for beginning teachers and full-time classroom teachers. The Board of Trustees through the Māori medium funding employs a Director of Māori Medium Education responsible for the management and development of all Māori Medium Education. The Board also funds a role of student advocate to ensure that students' well-being, both physical and emotional, is given high priority.

Te Kura o Te Uru Karaka offers a safe, nurturing, and stimulating learning environment for children. It is an inner-city oasis, nestled between warehouses, car dealerships, repair stations, a residential block, and the freeway. The school provides education that reflects a deep commitment to biculturalism and the principles of the Treaty of Waitangi.[6] The school offers three learning pathways: English medium, Māori medium, bilingual English/ *te reo* Māori. *Te Kura o Te Uru Karaka* is a creative and visionary school, celebrating the diversity of its urban multicultural, multiethnic, and multi-socio-economic status community. Here, social background and culture are not obstacles to learning; rather, the school capitalizes on the diversity of its learners, taking learning to the learner by allowing students to engage in ways that are most conducive to their progress. The school values diversity and welcomes children, parents and caregivers from every background. The rich character of this metropolitan school proudly reflects the multicultural nature of its surrounding city.

Data Collection

Two informal hour-long interviews took place at the school, followed by three natural observations of Ngaire at two-hour long school board meetings over the course of six months. There was also a review of supporting documents available in the public domain (e.g., Educational Review Office reports, school Charter, Mission Statement), and two academic narratives written by Ngaire reflecting her educational leadership journey as an indigenous urban primary school principal were considered. Most of the data collection took place on site at *Te Kura o Te Uru Karaka*. Regular informal visits to the school and email communications allowed Ngaire to elaborate on her leadership practice over time and at her convenience. During the course of the inquiry and with Ngaire's ongoing permission during follow-up contacts, member checking, and other planned and unplanned meetings over the course of the year, along with formal and informal observations were made of Ngaire at the school or at school or community gatherings.

Data Analysis

Data was analyzed using a modified constant comparative analysis in two phases (Bogdan and Biklen, 1998). The first relied on the theoretical propositions for the study based on the core literature reviewed (Bishop, 1996; Hohepa and Robinson, 2008; Santamaría, 2013; Santamaría and Santamaría, 2012; Tuhiwai Smith, 2012). Table 36.1 shows the result of this analysis.

There, evidence for shared elements of *Tū Rangatira*, *He Kākano* and ACL were identified suggesting indicators for culturally responsive leadership in urban school settings. Additionally, answers to the research question were sought as part of the later analysis. Data was identified in combinations of more than one participant instance or utterance, to confirm ways in which Ngaire practiced culturally responsive educational leadership. Further, extant data from ACL research featuring individuals of color who were also school site leaders was also considered in order to check for shared leadership practices among the group and Ngaire to suggest global applications for this study's research findings. Following theoretical alignment, frequency analyses, and a comparison of Ngaire's practices to leaders in the United States, a detailed case study write-up was developed for Ngaire in the form of a counter-story (Solórzano and Yosso, 2002). Interview responses were then organized as related to the research question. Ngaire member-checked the original case study. Follow-up contacts were made when needed for clarity.

Data presented in the results section are organized by ways in which common characteristics across *Tū Rangatira*, *He Kākano* and ACL intersect with Ngaire's indigenous urban leadership practice and the ways in which her leadership practices align with those of urban leaders in the United States. Findings are presented as a counter-story case featuring a blend of a personal story in Ngaire's voice based on data gathered that recounted her more racialized or classed experiences as relevant to this study (Solórzano and Yosso, 2002). These findings are then presented in a discussion against the literature reviewed. The research question frames the discussion and is further addressed in the conclusion.

Findings

Data revealed that Ngaire is a dedicated and committed urban school principal. She defines the world through relationships; for her there is no bridge too far, no stakeholder too distant, or any dispute that cannot be resolved through consultation, dialogue, and collaboration. She welcomes all with a warm hug and a genuine smile. On any given day, Ngaire proudly escorts visitors throughout the school grounds where vegetable and flower gardens in raised beds are sprinkled throughout. She is most proud of the forest of native trees planted behind the school separating classrooms from sounds of the adjacent freeway below. Walking from one lavishly decorated classroom to the next, *Whaea* (Auntie) Ngaire, as the children call her, greets each student by name. She picks up pieces of trash to maintain the meticulous order of the premises on her walk. All this is built on the kind of culturally responsive, instructional, shared leadership that Ngaire nurtures and supports. Her number one focus is on reinforcing, evaluating, and developing teacher quality at *Te Kura o Te Uru Karaka*. At the school, teachers collaborate to design, lead, and manage innovative learning environments. Ngaire works collaboratively alongside individual teachers to become aware of any weaknesses in their practices. This ongoing professional development means not merely creating awareness of what they do but shifting their underlying attitudes and dispositions as they relate to culturally responsive pedagogy for the diverse student and community body at *Te Kura o Te Uru Karaka*. Ngaire scaffolds her teachers, assisting them in grasping deep understanding of specific best practices (e.g., incorporating students' culture and Māori culture into lessons) through experiencing such practices in the authentic setting of other classrooms. Ngaire motivates teachers at *Te Kura o Te Uru Karaka* to make the necessary changes through high expectations, a shared sense of purpose, and a collective belief in their common ability to make a difference for every child.

Further data analysis indicates close alignment with Ngaire's leadership practices and those shared by leaders of color in the United States featured in ACL research as well as alignment with *Tū Rangatira* and *He Kākano*. Data analyzed revealed ways in which Ngaire's practices resonated with and exemplified *Tū Rangatira, He Kākano*, and ACL in her context. Data from ACL research suggested ways in which U.S. leaders of color in urban contexts practice these characteristics similarly.

Ngaire's case study provides a brief summary of observations and reflections that further corroborate evidence of her practice of *Tū Rangatira, He Kākano*, and ACL as well as the rich literature and critical theory research base in which ACL is rooted. ACL research findings align with these practices as clearly evidenced in the examples provided (Santamaría, 2013). There are strong connections between the ways in which urban leadership practices and leadership that may promote,

support, and sustain culturally responsive educational leadership manifest in New Zealand and the United States.

Specifically, with regard to indigenous urban school leadership, Ngaire shares that when it comes to initiating and engaging in "critical conversations" like the ones cited in ACL findings (Santamaría and Santamaría, 2012; Singleton and Linton, 2006), her peers are quiet:

I frequently attend meetings and gatherings of principals in the Metro region as well as national conferences and workshops. On these occasions, the issue of Māori achievement often engenders a defensive reaction from some of those present. I have experienced this on many occasions and yet have never heard a conversation that involves the question: What are we going to do about improving educational outcomes for Māori?

In terms of her ability to choose or assume a CRT lens for decision-making, she adds:

Schooling will not become more equitable until paradigm shifts happen in the way we think about Māori, engage with Māori, and how we define achievement. I agree with Smith (2009) in that placing indigenous language, knowledge, and culture at the center of indigenous educational leadership is important so that emotional and moral energy related to identity may be harnessed to enhance learning more generally.

Data also indicate that like applied critical leaders in the U.S., Ngaire prefers to use consensus in her day-to-day leadership tasks (Santamaría and Santamaría, 2012). Reflecting on consensus, she stated, "Today the concept of *whānau* has evolved to include people who come together under a common purpose or effort." Along these lines, she also shared, "Leadership that is committed to relationships and to collaboration with *whānau* (family) in the development, design and implementation of strategies to improve outcomes for students is critical."

As do applied critical leaders in the United States (Santamaría and Santamaría, 2012), Ngaire reported feeling the need to honor all members of her constituencies. This is evidenced by her belief that leadership needs to trigger change in a school's collective culture in order to partner more effectively with the cultures of *whānau* (family) and communities. Similarly, data indicate that Ngaire led by example to meet unresolved educational needs or challenges. Ngaire's beliefs align with Durie (2001), who signaled that the most vibrant platform for Māori educational reform may not lie with the state, but with Māori, working toward the fulfillment of a range of objectives while committed to collective goals and the harnessing of collective energies.

As in the U.S. case studies, trust played an important role in Ngaire's urban educational leadership practice. On building trust with mainstream stakeholders, she reflects, "Integrity, identified by Bryk and Schneider (2002) as a determinant of relational trust, is important to Māori. For Māori, integrity is about values and authenticity. It means walking the talk and doing what you say you are going to—*he tangata kī tahi* (person of a single word)" (as cited in Robinson et al., 2009, p.185). Finally, applied critical leaders have a leadership for the greater good "calling" on their practice. Ngaire expresses some elements of this as well, as she supports and pushes all of the learners in her school Māori, Pasifika, *Pākehā* (White European), and international toward fulfillment, academic achievement, and a sense of value in their learning community. The realization of social justice and educational equity rings as true for the students at *Te Kura o Te Uru Karaka* in *Aotearoa*, NZ as it did in the schools and universities in the original ACL research studies that took place with leaders of color in the United States. If findings are further corroborated by the literature reviewed and provide an answer to the research question posed, they may suggest an emergent model for Indigenous Urban School Leadership or International Indigenous Urban School Leadership. This possibility follows here.

DISCUSSION

This inquiry explored the ways in which indigenous school leadership might inform culturally responsive education in urban school settings. Although there is a "call" for comparative cross-cultural studies of leadership in international contexts (Dimmock and Walker, 2000), here, authors situated the inquiry within another study comprised of educational leaders of color in the United States in urban settings (e.g., where diversity is most prevalent and where students who have been historically disenfranchised and traditionally marginal-

ized by systems of inequality based primarily on race, ethnicity, culture, gender, social class, language, and/ or disability are taught). In this instance, indigenous urban leadership and leadership practices of leaders of color provide the core focus of the study and are not compared to leadership in mainstream contexts at all. Self-determination, kinship, and relationships were cultivated in this inquiry, firmly grounded and placed within a primarily Māori context with Māori researchers and colleagues of color based on mutual *mana* (honor/ respect) and relationships built and established over time (Tuhiwai Smith, 2012; Walker et al., 2012).

Five key findings were revealed, which may be useful to leaders in both countries and similar contexts in Australasia and the world (See figure 36.1). These findings, which were gleaned from a culturally responsive critical research approach employed by a cross-cultural team of NZ and U.S. researchers and leadership practitioners and were based on relationships and time spent with a Māori primary urban school principal, aligned with the literature reviewed in this study.

First, it is important that educational leaders in urban educational settings know and understand their contexts well enough to identify a theoretical framework to ground their practice. For Ngaire, this was her deep knowledge of *tikanga* (general cultural behavior guidelines) and Kaupapa Māori (Bishop and Berryman, 2006; Walker et al., 2006). Second, when educational leaders are indigenous or otherwise representative of the diversity in their schools and communities or leaders of color, it is imperative they also have knowledge of critical race perspectives, particularly as they relate to decolonization, understanding lived oppression, and unequal racial stratifications impacting urban students and communities where power systematically disenfranchises oppressed people (Brayboy, 2006; Hylton, 2012; Tyson, 2003).

Third, Ngaire as compared to the other U.S. leaders of color, reveal educational leaders in urban contexts tend to embrace and support instructional leadership that is culturally responsive, inclusive, and relevant in nature (Gay, 2010; Gooden, 2005; Johnson, 2006; Khalifa, 2012; Santamaría, 2013). This type of instructional leadership that is empowering and emancipatory, participatory and traceable to a clear political position, further exemplifies Tuhiwai Smith's (2012) notion of

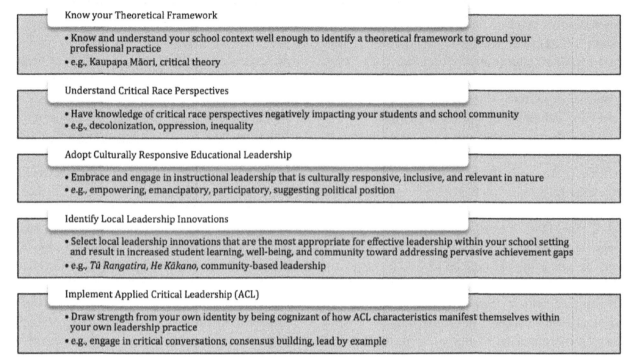

Figure 36.1.   *Model for Indigenous Urban School Leadership*

localized critical theory (Walker et al., 2006). Fourth, and expanding the last point, Ngaire's leadership practice emphasizes the importance of applying local leadership innovations that are the most appropriate for effective leadership in an urban school setting (e.g., Khalifa, 2012). In her case, beyond the more universal promotion and support of culturally responsive instruction at *Te Kura o Te Uru Karaka,* it was the use of *Tū Rangatira* and *He Kākano* leadership guidelines that were developed by Māori for use in Māori contexts (Hohepa and Robinson, 2008). These findings strongly suggest leaders of color in urban settings in the United States and the world adopt and use specific community-generated leadership practices in order to attain leadership practices that result in increased student learning, well-being, and community involvement toward addressing pervasive achievement gaps.

Finally, applied critical leadership, as a localized U.S. leader of color generated strategy, further corroborates this idea. The approach is based on shared characteristics of leaders of color in a variety of positions in the United States, yet the leaders' practice reiterated elements of strength inherent to their identities, as do *Tū Rangatira* and *He Kākano* in Ngaire's case (Santamaría,

2013; Santamaría and Santamaría, 2012). The cross-case analysis of the leadership practices, focusing on theory to practice, suggests similarities across the board in New Zealand and the United States. This final answer to what educational leaders in urban school settings might learn from Ngaire's indigenous urban school leadership is most valuable.

This chapter strongly suggests there are shared leadership practices employed by at least one indigenous educational leader in an urban school in New Zealand and at least nine leaders of color in the United States. Although this study shows promise for identifying best leadership practices for leaders of color and leaders who lead in diverse educational settings in global contexts, additional research and scholarship is needed in the area of urban educational leadership to strengthen the present findings.

CONCLUSION AND RECOMMENDATIONS FOR FUTURE RESEARCH

This chapter complements Kaupapa Māori research in that the inquiry process and subsequent findings were emancipatory and empowering (Freire, 1985; Gibson, 1986). Rather than comparing the Māori leadership practices of one Māori leader to non-Māori in unfavorable circumstances or, worse, in a deficit proposition, this chapter privileges Māori leadership in a largely indigenous urban school context as the center of the study in order to disrupt negatively held, erroneous, or absent assumptions about Māori and indigenous leadership (Bishop and Berryman, 2006; Walker et al., 2006). As with all case study research, the study has limitations with regard to generalizeability and this case comparison of two culturally different samples. We acknowledge these empirical shortcomings and others (e.g., convenience sample), and ask readers to keep them in mind as implications are suggested.

As a cross-cultural community of scholars, researchers, and practicing educational leaders, our recommendations for future research include a line of inquiry that identifies ways in which educational leaders can build relationships with families and community members in urban communities where education has served as an oppressive force in the lives of people. Inquiry findings bring up some concern that there should be some global or international work around healing and changing the perceptions of indigenous groups with regard to learning, coupled with treaty (in the case of New Zealand) responsiveness.

Authors note that in urban New Zealand and U.S. contexts, in response to increased diversity and attention to educational equity, many aspects related to schooling including curriculum, professional development, pedagogy, and teacher training have evolved. But one aspect, which authors have agreed has not changed is the way in which educational leaders are prepared. Findings from this inquiry suggest preparation and training can provide a strong critical theoretical foundation when it is directly linked to practical applications within the context of the populations leaders serve. Based on these findings, the authors believe that there is some work to be done in this particular area.

Finally, the authors maintain there should be some improvement in helping principals and school site leaders to understand ways in which to purposefully engage with families and community members (Khalifa, 2012). There are two components to this exploration. One is convincing leaders that they need to understand why educational leaders need to engage with family and community members in urban school settings, while the second component is providing leaders the strategies on how to engage with families and community members in urban school settings. Ngaire's indigenous urban school leadership example might be far from the United States on the globe, but our shared student and community characteristics make her practice relevant as we all strive to "walk the talk" for our students and their families. Indeed it takes a village.

NOTES

1. All proper names in this chapter are pseudonyms to ensure confidentiality and anonymity of participants.

2. People of color is a term used primarily in the United States to describe any person who is not white (e.g., African American, Latino/a, American Indian/Indigenous). The term is meant to be inclusive among non-white groups, emphasizing common experiences of racism.

3. Overlapping and lived axes of oppression (e.g., race, ethnicity, gender) (see Hankivsky & Christoffersen, 2008).

4. Participant name is a pseudonym to maintain anonymity.

5. *Aotearoa* is commonly given as the Māori name for New Zealand. Literally, ao – cloud, tea = white, pale, roa – long. This could be translated as (the) long white cloud.

6. New Zealand's founding document. It takes its name from the place in the Bay of Islands where it was first signed, on 6 February 1840. The Treaty is an agreement, in Māori and English, that was made between the British Crown and about 540 Māori *Rangatira* (chiefs).

REFERENCES

Bass, B. M. (1985). *Leadership and performance beyond expectation.* New York: Free Press.

Bishop, R. (1996). *Collaborative research stories: Whakawhanaungatanga.* Palmerston North, New Zealand: Dunmore Print Company.

Bishop, R. (2003). Changing power relations in education: Kaupapa Māori messages for "mainstream" education in Aotearoa/New Zealand. *Comparative Education, 39*(2), 221–238.

Bishop, R. and Berryman, M. (2006). *Culture speaks: Cultural relationships and classroom learning.* Wellington: Huia Press.

Bishop, R. and Glynn, T. (1999). *Culture counts: Changing power relations in education.* Palmerston North, New Zealand: Dunmore.

Bogdan, R. C. and Biklen, S. K. (1998). *Qualitative research in education: An introduction to theory and methods.* Needham, MA: Allyn and Bacon.

Brayboy, B. M. J. (2006). Toward a tribal critical race theory in education. *The Urban Review, 37*(5), 425–445.

Bryk, A. S. and Schneider, B. (2002). *Trust in schools: A core resource for improvement.* New York: Russell Sage Foundation.

Burns, J. M. (1978). *Leadership.* New York: Harper & Row.

Calhoun, C. (1995). *Critical social theory: Culture, history, and the challenge of difference.* Oxford: Wiley-Blackwell.

Delgado, R., and Stefancic, J. (2001). *Critical race theory: An introduction.* New York: New York University Press.

Dimmock, C. and Walker, A. (2000). Developing comparative and international educational leadership and management: A cross-cultural model. *School Leadership and Management, 20*(2), 143–160.

Durie, M. (2001). *A framework for considering Māori educational advancement.* Paper presented at the *Hui Taumata* conference. Turangi and Taupo, New Zealand.

Freire, P. (1970). *Pedagogy of the oppressed.* New York: Continuum.

Freire, P. (1985). *The politics of education: Culture, power and liberation.* London: Macmillan.

Gay, G. (2010). *Culturally responsive teaching* (2nd ed). New York: Teachers College Press.

Gibson, R. (1986). *Critical theory and education.* London: Hodder and Stoughton.

Giroux, H. A. (1983). *Theory and resistance in education: A pedagogy for the oppression.* South Hadley, MA: Bergin & Garvey Publishers.

Gooden, M. (2005). The role of African American principal in an urban information technology high school. *Education Administration Quarterly, 41*(4), 630–650.

Gooden, M. A. and Dantley, M. (2012). Centering race in a framework for leadership preparation. *Journal of Research on Leadership Education, 7*(2), 237–253.

Haney Lopez, I. (1998). *White by law: The legal construction of race.* New York: New York University Press.

Hankivsky, H. and Christoffersen, A. (2008). Intersectionality and the determinants of health: A Canadian perspective. *Critical Public Health, 18*(3), 271–283.

Hohepa, M. K. and Robinson, V. (2008). Māori and educational leadership: *Tū Rangatira. ALTERNATIVE, 4*(2), 20–38.

Horkheimer, M. (1972). *Critical theory: Selected essays* (Vol. 1). New York: Continuum International Publishing Group.

Hoskins, T. K. (2010). *Māori and Levinas: Kanohi ki te kanohi for an ethical politics.* Doctoral Thesis. Auckland, New Zealand: The University of Auckland.

Howard, T. C. (2008). Who really cares? The disenfranchisement of African American males in pre-K–12 schools: A critical race theory perspective. *Teachers College Record, 110*(5), 954–985.

Hylton, K. (2012). Talk the talk, walk the walk: defining Critical Race Theory in research. *Race Ethnicity and Education, 15*(1), 23–41.

Jean-Marie, G. and Normore, A. H. (2008). A repository of hope for social justice: Black women leaders at historically Black colleges and universities. In A. H. Normore (Ed.), *Leadership for social justice: Promoting equity and excellence through inquiry and reflective practice* (pp. 3–36). Charlotte, NC; Information Age.

Johnson, L. (2006). "Making her community a better place to live": Culturally responsive urban school leadership in historical context. *Leadership and Policy in Schools, 5*(1), 19–36.

Johnson, B. and Christensen, L. (2012). *Educational research: Quantitative, qualitative, and mixed approaches* (4th ed.). Los Angeles: Sage.

Kawharu, M. (2008). *Tāhuhu kōrero. The sayings of Taitokerau.* Auckland: Auckland University Press.

Khalifa, M. (2012). A re-new-ed paradigm in successful urban school leadership principal as community leader. *Education Administration Quarterly, 48*(3), 424–467.

Kouzes, J. M., and Posner, B. Z. (2007). *The leadership challenge.* San Francisco: Jossey-Bass.

Ladson-Billings, G. (1999). Preparing teachers for diverse student populations: A critical race theory perspective. *Review of Research in Education, 24*, 211–247.

Lee, J. (2005). *Māori cultural regeneration: Pūrākau as pedagogy.* Paper presented Centre for Research in Lifelong Learning International Conference. Stirling, Scotland.

Macfarlane, A. (1997). The Hikairo rationale teaching students with emotional and behavioural difficulties: A bicultural approach. *Waikato Journal of Education, 3*, 153–168.

Macfarlane, A. H. (2004). *Kia hiwa ra!—Listen to culture—Māori students' plea to educators.* Wellington: New Zealand Council for Educational Research.

Marable, M. (1992). *Black America.* Westfield, NJ: Open Media.

McLaren, P. (2003). *Life in schools: An introduction to critical pedagogy in the foundations of education* (4th ed). Boston: Allyn and Bacon.

Milne, A. (2009). *Colouring in the white spaces: Cultural identity and learning in school.* Auckland, New Zealand: ASB/APPA Travelling Fellowship.

Ministry of Education. (2014). Education Counts. *Highest Attainment Numbers 2009–2012*, 2014, from www.educationcounts.govt.nz/statistics/schooling/senior-student-attainment/school_leavers2/highest-attainment-numbers.

Moewaka Barnes, H. (2000). *Kaupapa* Māori: Explaining the ordinary. Auckland, New Zealand: Whariki Research Group, Auckland University.

New Zealand Government. (2013). Statistics New Zealand. Retrieved from www.stats.govt.nz/Census.aspx.

New Zealand History. (2012). *Treaty of Waitangi*. Retrieved from www.nzhistory.net.nz/politics/treaty/read-the-treaty/maori-text (Ministry for Culture and Heritage), updated 20-Dec-2012.

New Zealand Ministry of Education. (2010a). *He Kākano: Culturally Responsive Leadership*. Retrieved from www.educationalleaders.govt.nz/Leadership-development/Leadership-programmes/He-kakano.

New Zealand Ministry of Education. (2010b). *Tū rangatira: Māori medium educational leadership*. Retrieved from www.educationalleaders.govt.nz/Leadership-development/Key-leadership-documents/Tu-rangatira-English.

NZQA. (2014). *New Zealand Qualifications Authority Annual Report on NCEA and New Zealand Scholarship Data and Statistics (2013)*. Wellington, NZ: New Zealand Government, Retrieved from www.nzqa.govt.nz/assets/About-us/Publications/stats-reports/ncea-annualreport-2013.pdf.

Parker, L., and Villalpando, O. (2007). A race(ialized) perspective on education leadership: Critical race theory in educational administration. *Educational Administration Quarterly, 43*(5), 519–524.

Pihama, L. (1993). *Tungia te ururua, kia tupu whakaritorito te tupu o te harakeke: A critical analysis of parents as first teachers*. (Unpublished master's thesis). The University of Auckland, New Zealand.

Pihama, L., Cram, F., and Walker, S. (2002). Creating methodological space: A literature review of Kaupapa Māori research. *Canadian Journal of Native Education, 25*(1), 30–44.

Rigney, L. (1999). Internationalisation of an indigenous anti-colonial cultural critique of research methodologies: A guide to Indigenist research methodology and its principles. Reprinted in WICAZO SA review: *Journal of Indigenous American Studies, 14*(2), 109–122.

Robinson, V., Hohepa, M., and Lloyd, C. (2009). School leadership and student outcomes. Identifying what works and why. *Best Evidence Synthesis*. Wellington: Ministry of Education.

Santamaría, L. J. (2013). Critical change for the greater good: Multicultural perceptions in educational leadership toward social justice and educational equity. *Educational Administration Quarterly (EAQ)*. doi: 10.1177/0013161X13505287.

Santamaría, L. J. and Santamaría, A. P. (2012). *Applied critical leadership: Choosing change*. New York: Routledge Books.

Singleton, G. E. and Linton, C. (2006). *Courageous conversations about race*. Thousand Oaks, CA: Corwin.

Smith, G. H. (1997). *The development of kaupapa Māori: Theory and praxis*. (Unpublished doctoral dissertation.) The University of Auckland.

Smith, G. (2009). Transforming leadership: A discussion paper presented at the 2009 Simon Fraser University Summer Institute Lecture Series: Leading change in education, Surrey, B.C., Canada.

Solórzano, D. G. and Yosso, T. J. (2002). Critical race methodology: Counter storytelling as an analytical framework for educational research. *Qualitative Inquiry, 8*(1), 23–44.

Teariki, C. and Spoonley, P. (1992). *The politics and process of research for Māori*. Palmerston North, New Zealand: Massey University Press.

Tuhiwai Smith, L. (2006). Choosing the margins: The role of research in indigenous struggles for social justice. In N. K. Denzin and M. D. Giardina (Eds.), *Qualitative inquiry and the conservative challenge* (pp. 151–174). Walnut Creek, CA: Left Coast Press.

Tuhiwai Smith, L. (2012). *Decolonizing methodologies: Research and indigenous peoples*. Dunedin, New Zealand: University of Otago Press.

Tyson, C. (2003). Research, race and an epistemology of emancipation. *Mid-Western Educational Researcher, 16*(1), 2–5.

U.S. Census Bureau. (2013). *American FactFinder*. Retrieved from factfinder2.census.gov/faces/nav/jsf/pages/index.xhtml.

Walker, S., Eketone, A., and Gibbs, A. (2006). An exploration of Kaupapa Māori research, its principles, processes and applications. *International Journal of Social Research Methodology, 9*(4), 331–344.

Wearmouth, J., Berryman, M., Bishop, A. R., Peter, M., and Clapham, S. (2011). in Te Kotahitanga: Improving the educational achievement of Māori students in English medium schools. Report for Phase 3 and Phase 4: 2008–2010.

Yin, R. K. (1994). *Case study design research: Design and methods*. Thousand Oaks, CA: Sage.

CHAPTER 37

Crises, Critical Incidents, and Community and Educational Leadership

Noelle Witherspoon Arnold, Ty-Ron M. O. Douglas, and Tirza Wilbon-White

Leadership is not linear—it is circular and inter-connected.

—Angela Cole

In crises and disaster settings, institutional stability such as those of schools and communities are considerably interrupted. After a crisis, there remain deep emotional, psychosocial, economic, health, and achievement degeneration in youth and communities. In many of these communities, after a crisis, schools can be closed for considerable amounts of time or indefinitely. Even after a school re-opening, there remain deep emotional, psychosocial, economic, health, and achievement degeneration in youth and communities. In addition, school is rarely considered an ecology of its own in disaster and crisis management, instead focusing on the community structures alone in response to a crisis event

Despite popular belief, crises and disasters are not natural (Levitt and Whitaker, 2009). Incidents such as these often expose the fragile relations and tensions that exist between the natural, human, and built environments (Gonzalo, 2009). While crises can occur in any area of the world at any time, the towns and cities with limited resources, high vulnerability, and where people needs are great are the areas impacted the most in times of crisis. When crises are "man-made," there is often less confidence in any technical or external preparedness or how we view crisis. While tragedies often can rip existing structures apart, these situations also provide opportunity for overhaul and reform. These states of emergency present the need to challenge mere surface reforms and systems overhauls in favor of thoughtful, sustainable responses within communities and schools (Witherspoon, 2010).

Crisis and disaster have been critiqued as "convenient clichés, but very useful words in the age of mass media since they create emotion without reflection" (Starn, 1976, p. 13). Granatt (2011) recently concluded that "crisis has replaced emergency just because it is shorter" (Haeckel, 1877). Notably, there is a need to replace linear approaches to crisis management with a more robust one that includes the unique role of "school ecology" in examining the preparedness, impact, and response of disaster and crisis on youth and families. This paper highlights community and educational leadership after "critical incidents" in communities in Bermuda and the United States. *Critical incidents* are used to describe turning points or changes in a community, person, or social phenomenon (Tripp, 1993). Angelides (2001) clarifies that it is the justification, significance, or meaning one gives to these incidents that makes them "critical"—rather than any discourse, drama, or sensationalism in examining studies of how educational leaders in communities and school-based settings have responded to and been impacted by tragedy and natural disaster.

The U.S. Census Bureau identifies urban in two ways. Urbanized Areas (UAs) are those of fifty thousand or more people and Urban Clusters (UCs) of at least twenty-five hundred and less than fifty thousand people (2013). Despite official definitions that distinguish urban from rural, and metropolitan from nonmetropolitan, the realities of communities are far more complicated and exhibit a great deal of diversity (Dabson, 2007). International research has recognized the complicated human, market, environmental, and functional interactions that link urban to rural areas, but especially the linkage among global communities of the same kind. Heightening this focus is the recent United Nations finding that for the first time, more than half the world's population lives in what are classified as urban areas (United Nations Population Division, 2005).

Even in the international context, however, global urban connections remain understudied. A wide-ranging literature review by Simon Snoxell (2005) concludes there is a truncated body of research specifically focused on linkages between international urban communities, and no prevailing analytical framework for understanding these linkages. Thus, globalization provides motivation for researchers and policymakers to further probe the complexities and correlations of the world's urban contexts to unpacking problems and possibilities in these communities.

CRISIS AND URBAN RISK

According to the International Federation of Red Cross and Red Crescent Societies (IFRC), there is an "urban risk divide" between urban and those communities with different classifications (2010). In other words, urban cities worldwide are more susceptible to crises and risk than other types of cities. In fact, urban cities are affected by a wide range of crisis events, which extend beyond our conception of disaster. There are natural crises such as urban drought, earthquakes, windstorms, floods, and extreme temperatures; technological hazards such as aircraft crashes, fires, and explosions; social hazards such as violent crime, riots, and terrorism; as well as public health hazards such as epidemics, poor water quality, and inadequate sanitation and flooding. Urban food insecurity is another type of crisis event that is now recognized as seriously affecting urban dwellers globally.

In these areas, institutional stability is considerably interrupted such as those of schools and communities. According to the IFRC, community and school are two institutions that are among the most important in leadership and *adaptation*—re/building and/or adjustment—in natural or human systems after a crisis. How well we understand and the extent to which we explore crises will determine and is integral to dealing with roles and responses after crises. Watershed moments such as these are examined through the lens of *psychology of narrative* which (Witherspoon Arnold, 2012) centers on "extended experiences and/or speech acts about or compelling life aspects—relationships, work, illness, trauma, or conflict" (Holstein and Gubrium, 2012, p.1).

The analysis represented in this article involved a re-analysis of data of two larger research projects related to the aftermath of social crisis (gang-related violence) in Bermuda and a natural disaster (tornado) in the United States. One of the larger studies utilized an ecological approach in examining crisis in disaster which we then applied in this re-analysis. For this article in particular, we explore the micro-systems within our ecological framework related to the micro-processes of educational leadership. As illustrated further in this paper, educational leadership has been considered broadly, such as teacher leaders, shared governance, essential functions of leadership, and community-school relations. Simply put, leadership is characterized as encompassing responsibility—assuming, X, X, and X. In this re-analysis, data narrative "plots" were extracted and composed to highlight critical "episodes" in the original research. These episodes provided small, sub-story parts for analysis. This analysis focused on critical incidents highlighting turning points or changes related to 1) how people construct and internalize stories, 2) the psychosocial meaning of critical incidents, and 3) the tensions and negotiations occurring in these contexts (Holstein and Gubrium, 2012, p. 15). Major turning points or changes were identified by the actors in each study as significant, and then examined for themes related to community and leadership response.

Crisis management often extends beyond the disaster or crisis itself. Furthermore, the disaster or crisis often magnifies existing systemic problems in communities, leadership, schools, and districts. In fact, leadership processes often extend beyond those merely of the individual or organization. Often informal and more communal relationships and leadership processes take precedence and once-thought private or personal processes took precedence over public or professional processes.

The natures of crisis and disaster make it difficult to study these phenomena in a comprehensive and systematic manner because crisis and disaster are so complex in their cause and impact (Dinkin, 2007). In spite of educational leadership literature that outline how to write a school crisis plan or things a principal should do if a crisis hits, there is still little research on the complex processes that take place in the leadership of the school. Gaps in the literature contain inconsistent terminology and few theoretical models. Much of the dialogue concerning educational leadership in times of crisis and disaster has only focused on the individuals in formal, authoritative leadership roles and has not examined a broader view of leadership, advocacy, social justice, and a re-framing of crisis and crisis management. In particular, analyses of the two crises situations revealed themes such as: (re)visionary leadership systems and paradigms, breaking and interrogating the margins of traditional leadership, what constitutes as crisis, and advocacy.

In the next sections, we discuss the traditional emergency and crisis management in schools. Next, we discuss the psychology of narrative approach used in one of the larger studies and in article. We then discuss the theories that allowed us to focus on contextual aspects surrounding crisis.

CRISIS STUDIES

In the 1960s and 1970s, sociological studies devoted to communities confronted with natural disasters (Quarantelli and Dynes, 1977) and studies of international crises were prolific (Allison, 1971; Hermann, 1972). In the late 1970s, and increasingly in the 1980s and 1990s, the field of crisis theory began to examine new crises impact beyond natural disasters alone, such as riots, financial crises, community shootings, and terrorist threats (Topper and Lagadec, 2013). In all of these crises, the predominant theme was to find the "best practices to deal with these events and their ripple effects" (Topper and Lagadec, 2013, p. 5).

"From time to time, some big storm, disaster, or 'situation' rears its ugly head to disturb, for a moment, the so-called normal world. A dominant tendency is just to ignore such improper outbreaks and to concentrate on the 'normal' game plans" (Topper and Lagadec, p. 4). Crises appear to have taken on an entirely new makeup. They are no longer isolated accidents and require a new paradigm. In traditional crisis management, an organizational structure most often is created to establish a chain of command and responsibilities of staff members (Gullat and Long, 1996). In organizations such as schools, crisis management plans have been created to portray the notion of "ideal preparedness" (McConnell and Drennan, 2006). In many ways, these plans represent routine survival in routine situations. These management plans can be extensive; however, they are "add-ons" to the organizational structure and practice.

One of the driving factors of traditional crisis management in schools is related to Rittel and Webber's (1973) concept of *wicked problems*. Yet the operational toolkit for crises in schools is based on tame problems that presuppose precise definitions of crisis, the causes of the crisis, and providing remedial techniques for an event (Camillus, 2008). In fact, crisis management in schools begins as an event-focused plan that rests in "the emergency domain, which has been the original niche for crisis analyses and practices" (Topper and Lagadec, 2013, p. 7).

TRADITIONAL EMERGENCY AND CRISIS MANAGEMENT IN SCHOOLS

In understanding how schools respond to critical incidents, it is important to further explicate how crisis and emergency responses differ. An emergency plan usually involves procedures in the immediate aftermath or a crisis or disaster, and a crisis plan involves the procedures after an emergency situation is under control (Trump, 2009). Most school districts maintain two types of emergency plans: district emergency plans and building-level emergency plans. However, district-level plans are often not well-communicated to individual school sites, and the schools have little guidelines in how to coordinate services beyond the school site. While school sites are unique contexts that should maintain their own emergency and crisis procedures, there is often a breakdown in providing service due to a narrow focus of the plans and procedures. For example, Trump states, plans should reflect an "all hazards" approach to school emergency planning. Potential events should include situations such as weather, natural disasters, hazardous material spills, and power outages, as well as man-made acts of crime and violence such as suicides, stabbings, hostage situations, shootings, and other worst-case scenarios. Roles of administrators, teachers, support staff, and others should be clearly delineated in the plans (p. 13). In spite of this, many schools' crisis plans often only focus on weather and drills; are not developed with community emergency officials; and do not even focus on adequate training (Tripp, 2009).

PSYCHOLOGY OF NARRATIVE

"Narrative approaches have emerged as important research over the last decade . . . and offer exciting alternatives for connecting the lives and stories of individuals to the understanding of larger human social phenomena" (Hatch and Wisniewski, 1995, p. 113). If one were to ask different researchers to define narrative, one will likely receive varied responses based upon different interpretations and purposes. For the purposes of this chapter, narrative is regarded as "an autobiography, with one person having guided another through the telling of the story" (Atkinson, 1998, p. 2) and as a story that "revolves around questions pertaining to one's life" (Tierney, 1993, p. 1). Narrative has also been described as "the history of a life, a single life, told from a particular vantage point" (Lincoln, 1985, p. 115). In addition, the discussion of narrative also highlights those master narratives that presume a set identity and those that result in labels or branding of the individual. In the same way, narration indicates how individuals order, make sense of, live their experiences, and write their own lives. A psychological approach to narrative was applied and served as a foundation for this inquiry. "This approach takes as foundational the propositions that (1) People construct and internalize stories, (2) These stories have psychological meaning and staying power, (3) These psychological accounts can be co-examined for negotiation of and in the contexts most salient to them" (Golstein and Gubrium, 2012, p. 15). A psychology of narrative (Witherspoon Arnold, 2012) is one centered on "extended speech acts about or compelling life aspects—relationships, work, illness, trauma, or conflict" (Golstein and Gubrium, 2012, p. 1). This particular approach privileges how individuals re/write understandings and "examines the ways that narratives take therapeutic turns through the stories people tell in relation to how they understand events" (Golstein and Gubrium, p. 8).

There are psychological meanings to the stories we live by (McAdams, 2012). Individuals grapple with life realities by constructing experiences of their lives into sense-making stories. Through these stories they construct and redefine their roles, identities, and meanings both for themselves and others (McAdams, 1993; Ricoeur, 1992). From experiences, they create certain schemas. These schemas provide new spaces in which the teller can claim, reject, and experiment with identities and circumstances (Nelson, 2001).

ECOLOGY

Ecology studies interactions between individual organisms and their environments, including interactions with both conspecifics and members of other species (Haeckel, 1877). Though ecology includes a wide variety of sub-fields, philosophical analysis of ecology has so far been restricted to population, community, and ecosystem ecology. Contemporary ecology consists of a patchwork of sub-disciplines including population ecology, community ecology, conservation ecology, ecosystem ecology, meta-population ecology, meta-community ecology, spatial ecology, landscape ecology, physiological ecology, evolutionary ecology, functional ecology, and behavioral ecology (Sakhar, 2005). "Ecological philosophies" concentrates more on foundational and interpretive issues.

Bronfenbrenner's (1994) Human Ecology Theory notes that human development is influenced by different types of environmental systems. In Bronfenbrenner's theory, ecology is a makeup of systems that influence human development (Figure 1). The five systems of his theory that explain the ecosystem are:

- the microsystem—the immediate environment in which a person is operating, such as the family, classroom, peer group, neighborhood, etc.
- the mesosystem—the interaction of two microsystem environments, such as the connection between a child's home and school
- the exosystem—the environment in which an individual is not directly involved, which is external to his or her experience, but nonetheless affects him or her, i.e., parental work environment
- the macrosystem—the larger cultural context, including roles, values, and expectations
- the chronosystem—events occurring in the context of passing time

Context

Taguiri's (1968) concept of context typically is viewed as consisting of two dimensions: ecology and culture (Figure 2). In the case of my research, Bronfenbrenner and Taguiri's frameworks have been combined and reconceptualized to consider the goals of this chapter and our ongoing research (Figure 3). This new model allows us to consider the context or contextual factors that represent the interrelatedness and interdependence of all facets of the school ecology, including those that are traditionally considered out-of-school components with the students at the center. In this model, the school ecology is made up all systems and facets such as family background and the school context and how they all interact to create certain conditions through "ecology (physical and material aspects); milieu (social dimension created by the characteristics of groups of persons); culture (social dimension created by belief systems, values, cognitive structures, and meaning); and social system (social dimension created by the relationships of persons and groups)" over time.

This paper focus takes an ecological approach with two major parameters: *complexity* and *uniqueness* (Sakhar, 2005). Examining *complexity* allows the researcher to examine how systems of behavior and organization are not merely complicated (difficult to understand or "pin down"), they are "complex." Complexity highlights the multi-organizational, multi-service, and multi-level processes that inform certain behaviors. In general, "complex systems exhibit *emergent* properties that resist reductionist explanation" (Sakhar, 2005. p. 1) such as those definitions such as *crisis, leadership, community*, and *rebuilding* which we discuss further in the paper. *Uniqueness* requires an examination of contingent epistemologies and structures (both historical and current) and contexts of the organization being studied that make them special.

METHODS

The analysis represented in this article involved a re-analysis of data from two studies. The first larger study centers on educational leadership in disaster areas. This study focuses on education issues in the aftermath of natural disasters in four areas in the United States: Tuscaloosa City, Alabama; Joplin, Missouri; East Baton Rouge Parish, Louisiana; and Lafourche, Louisiana. For this paper, data from Tuscaloosa study is presented.

Research Contexts

Tuscaloosa, Alabama. The 2011 *Tuscaloosa–Birmingham tornado* was a large and violent EF4 multiple-vortex tornado that devastated portions of Tuscaloosa and Birmingham, Alabama, as well as smaller communities and rural areas between the two cities, during the late afternoon and early evening of Wednesday, April 27, 2011. It was one of the 358 tornadoes in the April 25–28, 2011 tornado outbreak, the largest tornado outbreak in U.S. history. The tornado reached a maximum path width of 1.5 mi (2.4 km) during its path through Tuscaloosa, and once again when it crossed Interstate 65 north of Birmingham, and reached estimated maximum sustained winds of 190 mph (310 km/h) shortly after passing through the city. It then went on to impact parts of Birmingham, Alabama, as a high-end EF4 before dissipating. The final rating of this tornado was a source of controversy, as some survey teams concluded EF5 damage, while others did not. Officially, an EF4 rating was decided on. This was the third tornado to strike the city of Tuscaloosa in the past decade.

When the tornado reached Tuscaloosa, several stores and restaurants in a business district at the intersection of McFarland Boulevard and Fifteenth Street, near the DCH Regional Medical Center and University Mall (both of which sustained some damage), were reduced to rubble by the tornado. Buildings were also reported destroyed on Thirty-fifth Street, between Interstate 359 and Martin Luther King Jr. Boulevard. As the tornado traveled east to Thirty-fifth Street and Kauloosa Avenue, the Tuscaloosa Environmental Services and Cintas facilities suffered severe damage. Numerous homes in the Rosedale and Forest Lake neighborhoods, as well as a PandP Grocery store in Rosedale, were devastated. Numerous fatalities occurred in this area. The tornado was caught on camera by ABC 33/40's Skycam, which is on top of the Tuscaloosa County Courthouse, as it was going down Skyland Boulevard and McFarland Boulevard. The tornado plowed through the east side of Tuscaloosa, leveling many homes, schools, and businesses before exiting the city limits.

Two elementary schools in the Tuscaloosa City School district were completely destroyed during the tornado. Both schools were located in neighborhoods with 50 percent or more of the population at the poverty level. Alberta Elementary will become the Alberta School of Performing Arts, a Pre-K–8 magnet school that school officials said will offer new opportunities for children in the community and throughout the city. The school, set to open in August 2014, will feature programs for instrumental music, vocal music, theater, dance, visual art, and piano in addition to a normal curriculum. Classrooms will be joined by technology labs, music rooms, a theater classroom, a dance studio, a multipurpose performance space, an outdoor theater, as well as sports fields and playgrounds on the 12.5-acre site off University Boulevard East.

University Place Elementary School STEAM stands for Science and Technology interpreted through Engineering and the Arts, all based in Mathematical elements. It's a holistic, hands-on, project-based learning curriculum that focuses on science and technology that's taught through engineering, arts, and math. University Place is serving as a pilot program for the STEAM curriculum and will be the first and only accredited STEAM school in the world once it finishes meeting all of the curriculum's requirements, such as successfully completing STEAM projects and lesson plans this school year.

Bermuda. The second study is a case study of a black Bermudian female urban elementary school principal, Mrs. Theresa Stevens. Mrs. Stevens was chosen because she has led Carver Elementary School through a period of unprecedented incidents of gang-related violence in the community surrounding her school and, in particular, the shooting death of the parent of one of her students on the school premises. This study draws on a larger study in which author 2 spent two months collecting approximately forty hours of data toward the better understanding of culturally relevant leadership in the practices of sixteen Bermudian school principals and assistant principals. The primary research methods included semi-structured interviews, informal observations, and collecting various school-related documents (i.e., school demographic information). Interviews were typically conducted in offices of the school leaders or in another mutually agreed upon location between the researcher and the participants, with each interview lasting approximately two to three hours. Author 2 spent two full days directly observing and interviewing Stevens, as her leadership and school contexts became centered units of study in my work in Bermuda.

Consistent with qualitative research and the "(re)interpretation of the culture and . . . the constructed meanings of leadership" within the unique significance of each sociocultural contexts and geopolitical space (Dillard, 1995; Douglas, 2013), we offer a brief description of the recent proliferation of gang violence in Bermuda and the *situatedness* of Carver Elementary as contested and complex terrain in this context.

Crisis in paradise. While gang violence is an all-too-common phenomenon that has plagued communities in the United States and other Western nations for decades, the emergence of gang violence in Bermuda is relatively new. For this reason, the plight of black males in Bermuda has become a pressing national issue that is the subject of government and media attention. Concomitantly, the Bermuda government has invested heavily in the services of overseas experts in an effort to repair a public educational system that has undergone significant structural changes in the last twenty-five years. In fact, many Bermudians have attributed the recent upsurge in gang violence amidst black males in Bermuda to the alleged deterioration of the educational system (Christopher, 2009; Douglas and Gause, 2009; Douglas and Peck, 2013; Pearman, 2009). Although black people in Bermuda account for 54 percent of the national population, black children make up over 90 percent of the population in what some describe as a troubled public school system (Bermuda Department of Statistics 2010 Census of Population and Housing, 2010; Social and Demographic Division, Department of Statistics, Bermuda, 2006).

The irony is that much like gang violence has only recently been acknowledged as a national issue, the term *urban schooling* in Bermuda is relatively foreign language even though it has certainly been a local reality for decades (Smith and Douglas, in progress). Nevertheless, these issues exist and the disproportionalities in Bermuda certainly mirror those found in the United States. For example, at the time of this writing, nearly thirty black males have been shot and killed since 2009 in Bermuda and every victim (and alleged perpetrator) has been a black male even though black males represent approximately 25 percent of the 65,000 population[1] (Bermuda Department of Statistics, 2000). This represents a sharp increase in gun-related murders in Bermuda, a country where gun possession is illegal and, until recently, it was presumed by many that guns were not even present on the island.

Carver Elementary School is a borderland space (Anzaldua, 2007). Three predominate gangs are known to be rivals on the twenty-two square miles that make up Bermuda, and two of these gangs sit on opposite hills above Carver Elementary. Exemplifying the complexity of space and crisis, Carver Elementary literally sits in the valley between the territories of two rival gangs. Exacerbating the complex work of Mrs. Stevens and her staff, Carver Elementary serves the relatives (fathers, uncles, cousins, etc.) of Bermudian males who have been traumatized (as victims and perhaps villains) by the realities of gang warfare. This is a new crisis for Bermudian educators. Mrs. Stevens and her colleagues at other urban schools are leading the first generation of Bermudian children who cannot only identify the squeak of a tree frog[2] in the night but many of them can also describe—from firsthand experience—the disturbing bang of a gunshot.

At the time of this writing, as many as seven children at Carver have lost their fathers to gang violence in the last three years, and countless other students have lost uncles, cousins, and older neighborhood friends. Teachers have lost husbands, and Mrs. Stevens herself had a man gunned down on the porch of her parents' home. While these events have been traumatic, the events of Good Friday 2011 were particularly hard. Good Friday is a family day in Bermuda where children frolic on fields flying kites and families gather to enjoy fish cakes and hot crossed buns. It is a national holiday, and community members often host various social events on school fields in their neighborhood. As a central fixture in the Carver community, Carver Elementary School field is a regular gathering spot for many in the community to come together for fun, food, and fellowship. Good Friday 2011 was one of those events; however, this particular year would be far different than any other. It was on this day that Bermuda's social history changed forever, as a young father was gunned down on Carver's field in front of a large crowd while he was flying a kite with his son and daughter. Bermuda changed that day. The requirements of Mrs. Stevens's leadership also changed that day and have continued to evolve since that time. Clearly, crisis has encroached on paradise, and the premises, students, and leadership of Carver Elementary have certainly been specifically affected.

Data Analysis

In re-analysis, data narrative "plots" were extracted and composed to highlight critical "episodes" in the af-

termath of crises. Doing this provided small, sub-story parts for analysis. This analysis focused on *critical incidents* highlighting the crisis event itself and turning points or changes related to the event (Tripp, 1993). It is important to note that critical incidents, similar to narratives, are not always linear, chronological, or cohesive; however, they can still provide a picture of the processes and provide cohesive themes. Major turning points or changes were identified as significant by the participants, and then coded for themes. Four major themes emerged across the studies: (re)visionary leadership systems and paradigms, breaking and interrogating the margins of traditional leadership, what constitutes as crisis, and advocacy.

FINDINGS

Like many educational leaders, the administrators in this paper spend many hours dealing with the complexities of leadership (Hanson, 2003; Henkin, Cistone, and Dee, 2000; Riehl, 2000). While the task of dealing with complexity is a daily, draining requirement that is the status quo in the work of school leaders, there is variance as to what, when, where, why, and how school leaders are exposed to crises. As such, what makes dealing with crises so challenging is its inherent variability and suddenness, coupled with the requisite immediacy in how leaders must respond; specifically, crises comes in many unexpected forms and times in school contexts.

Data from the projects in this paper reveal important intersections as it relates to the realities of and responses to crises. Across time and space, there is some semblance of symmetry in the challenges faced and lessons learned by school leaders as they sought to tend to the environmental and ecological ruptures caused by communities' crises. In what follows in this section, we highlight the four major themes that emerged across the two studies.

(Re)visionary Leadership: Rethinking Systems and Paradigms

During a crisis, individuals did not work or lead in isolation. Collectively, as the situation demanded, they made sense of what was around them, adjusted, and readjusted to meet the demands of the crisis. As one principal said in the first study,

It doesn't matter at that point who is in charge. I needed everybody. I delegated to people. When you are faced with students and families who were basically homeless after the tornado, everyone becomes a leader as the situation requires.

A teacher echoed this statement,

We all pitched in. I was already the grade level chair but I took on responsibilities that were far outside the duties of that position.

In the Bermuda study, Mrs. Stevens is intentional about drawing on her staff to handle crises. As the gang-related issues became more frequent, she was able to identify her school guidance counselor—Ms. Gibbs—as a key point person on her leadership team in dealing with these issues. Mrs. Stevens notes,

We have a very committed school counselor; she is phenomenal! And, I rely on her a lot. She handles the situations and if she needs to include me then I'm included. But most times, she will handle the situation if a student comes in having had something traumatic happen over the weekend then she will be first hand to deal with that.

Mrs. Stevens demonstrated a high level of trust in Ms. Gibbs to not only meet the needs of the students but to decide what information needed to be shared with her as the principal. Mrs. Stevens was intentional about creating an environment where students could share confidential information with the guidance counselor, without administrative interference that may hinder the counselor's capacity to develop trust with students. Stevens explains,

We had a little boy last year whose house was broken into . . . and it ended up with the boyfriend jumping up and beating up the guy (the intruder). He (the boy) came in here and he said to me "have you heard?" and I said "no" and he said "Ms. Gibbs didn't tell you?" and I said "no" because I want them to know that Ms. Gibbs' office is a safe space.
I want them to really have that full trust.

In this regard, the guidance counselor is not merely a reporting member of the general staff or a nominal member of the leadership team; she is one of the school leaders whose discretionary prerogative is trusted to make decisions that are in the best interest of all school stakeholders.

Data from both studies suggest that it took individual leaders and collective leadership to respond to the crisis. The static idea of traditional leaders and followers can be too restrictive when responding to crises. When a natural disaster or community crisis occurs, these incidents negate the normal influence structure. It forces people into more of a peer context without a strict vertical, hierarchical leadership structure.

Expanded View of Crisis

Crisis is often confused with emergency. According to McConnell and Drennan (2006), conventional crises plans are often little more than emergency plans to deal with immediate coping issues after a crisis event. These emergency plans are usually designed to maintain customs, habits, and procedures, whereas a crisis plan should not only address short-term issues but long-term sustainable plans as well. One principal in the U.S.-based study indicated,

Our crisis plan was terribly inadequate. Beyond the immediate procedures, there was no plan to address the weeks and months after the disaster. There are indeed tensions between the ideals of crisis preparedness and the actual realities of crisis. Emergency preparedness rarely prepares organizations of communities for the widespread impact of the crisis. Mrs. Stevens was sensitive to this reality as she sought to stabilize her school community and account for the shock of the Good Friday murder that occurred on her school field. Stevens explains how she dealt with the aftermath of the shooting this way:

Well, first of all I prayed. I am a Christian. So that helps me in a lot of these situations and you know . . . God just told me to reach out and to go out and find them (students and their families), just to let them know that they are not alone [and] we are here for them if they need help or if they need to talk to someone. To let them, to show them that we weren't afraid even though, you know, you did have some...a little bit of fear inside you. But first of all we had to model that yes, we can walk out on their field. I walked out there the very next morning and so I wanted them to realize there is nothing to be afraid of. That they are safe. That school has to be a safe haven for them so we have to claim back that safety. So that's why I wanted to reach out in that way the whole week because I didn't know what they were hearing in the community. I didn't know what people would be saying. So that's what prompted me to go and look for them that very next morning.

In the hours and days following the Good Friday shooting, Principal Stevens embraced her expanded role as a community leader helping the people through a community crisis. Having preexisting relationships with the surrounding community was helpful in this process, and maintaining these relationships has been an intentional leadership strategy she has employed in the weeks and months since the watershed moment. The transcendence of her spirituality is also noteworthy. We further discuss the implications of spirituality in leadership below in our consideration of *New Leadership*.

While emergency preparedness can provide some immediate order, crisis planning after a disaster requires an ongoing, integrated approach to managing disaster among communities and organizations such as funding efforts, health and mental wellness care, rebuilding efforts, education, law enforcement, and transportation. A community member in the Louisiana study stated,

> It is amazing how unprepared we were for the aftermath. I know that no one can plan for each contingency and there are some things you can never plan for. But I don't even think hospitals and morgues were ready for the sick and dead. Some people weren't even buried until much later. Emergency sessions of City Hall and State Government had to be convened just to get funding where it needed to be. Why wasn't there a pot of "contingency" money for disasters? It's not like we didn't have Katrina and 9/11 to warn us about stuff like this. Data affirms the reality that each crisis comes with its own set of unique contextual factors that must be accounted for if any semblance of normalcy is to be regained after crises. School leadership in times of crises extends beyond the school grounds. Effective school leaders in these contexts are not only touched by the infirmities that impact their students but they also extend their hands and hearts far enough to touch the lives of the families and neighborhoods—the village—that is raising their students.

Advocacy

It is not unusual for *advocacy coalitions* to form after crisis (McConnell and Drennan, 2006). While many of

these coalitions can take the form of institutional agendas, these coalitions also form for the "public good." In particular, principals and teachers in both studies became vocal advocates for the socially just and equitable treatment of students and families in the community. In particular they advocated for redistribution of goods and services in ways they may not have done before. A principal in the Louisiana study shared the following:

> I am a pretty low-key, quiet person, but I spoke up in ways that I never would have when this happened. Sure I was advocating for my school, for my kids, but a disaster means you always have to be thinking about equity throughout, not just in your building. (Principal)

> I always knew there was poverty and unequal resources in the community and district. But when the tornado happened . . . WHEW! You really see the differences in resources and the haves and have-nots. Middle- and upper-class folks got help really quickly because they had families that could help or they could get attorneys, insurance. Poor folks had to get help for housing and just basic necessities. Many of them also needed help to fill out federal funds. It was really a mess for them. I knew I had to do something. It puts it all in perspective. You can't just fight for your family. You have to fight for everyone. (Teacher and Parent)

In the Bermuda study, Principal Stevens donned many hats in order to advocate for the needs of her students in response to the crisis. Ensuring the safety of her students and teachers became a priority, especially when it became apparent that her campus was far too accessible to loiterers and her school field could be used as an escape route for criminals. Stevens explains:

> We actually had the incident where two guys shot at [a man] and then . . . used our school field as their escape route and the police were chasing them. This was during the school day! So that's what made us realize and we had to lock the school down right away. That's what made us realize that we did need a policy right away. Since then, we have established a lock-down policy. We have regular drills, at least once a term, so that students know what will happen . . . . We have bought some cameras but they keep saying they're coming, but they're not here yet.

Advocacy also took on the form of providing access to resources—in particular, helping her urban school students tap into opportunities they may not have been exposed to without intentional efforts on the part of her school. These activities included music lessons, gardening, youth clubs, sailing, mentorship, and other community-based initiatives.

Consistent across the two studies was an understanding of the difference between equality and equity on the part of the school leaders. These leaders recognized that the social conditions in which their students were being nurtured required that they provide additional support mechanisms that may not be as necessary in more affluent school and community contexts. Similarly, these leaders understood the power of positive exposure in the educational journey of students who are equality gifted to students in less challenging school contexts but who are often marginalized by inequitable access to opportunities. The sentiments of Principal Stevens capture this ideology expertly: "The message I want students to get is their destiny is not based on their circumstances." Moreover, Stevens not only sought to account for the complexities and crises of students' lived experiences, but she also embraced a multi-organizational, multi-service, and multi-level process-based approach to serving her constituents.

New Leadership

During research, the stories we encountered demonstrated that there are no viable fixed, unitary ideas regarding educational leadership. In fact teacher and leader actions challenged current descriptive criteria, conceptual categories, and taxonomies of leadership. One such challenge was in the area of spirituality. After the crises, we found that individuals' beliefs about faith and their spiritual discourses coping strategies after the crises, yet also provided a foundation for advocacy in often hostile environments. Principal Stevens' approach is worthy of extended consideration here, not just because it demonstrates how she utilizes spirituality, but because it exemplifies practical faith—radical love even (Darder, 2002, 2009; Douglas and Nganga, in press; Freire, 1993)—to operationalize genuine care for people while drawing strength for herself in the most difficult of circumstances:

> Now, after the murder, that was a challenge, but what we did, myself and our MP from the area and my school

educational therapist, we came here the next day and we walked the neighborhood. We found some of the students and some of their parents and they were like, you know, "we're so glad you came." We reached out to them and we reached out to the young men because many of them, because the incident happened on our field, we're here grieving. So they had their little grieving party off in the corner. So we just reached out to the community and then luckily we were off school for that week so that gave students time, a bit of time, to get over some of their fears. But our first day back, we had a large assembly. We invited parents. We invited clergy from the neighborhood. We had my pastor, Bishop Bean; he came and we had prayer and after the assembly, we went out on the field. I think that was the really powerful piece. We went out on the field. We formed a large circle and we had the students recite our school creed that says, "This is our school. Let Peace dwell here." And then Bishop prayed for us and I think that is what really what broke the ice because many of the students did say that they were afraid to go on the field again. But because we had that prayer, we had that covering, and we just claimed back our field. They were able to begin the healing process.

Clearly, *spiritual leadership* went beyond solitary leadership in favor of an "adaptive, relational, and interactive models of leadership" (Fluker, 1998, p. 11). To this point, a principal in the Louisiana study stated,

> My faith got me through this crisis but it also convicted me to really help others. I became a spiritual figure to many of my teachers, students, and families. I was responsible for soothing fears and letting everyone know it would be all right. I was also able to infuse my faith in a different way than I had before the crisis. I wasn't worried about offending anyone or anything. Even if folks were not spiritual, they appreciated it and needed it at the time.

In both studies, we found that leaders were able to successfully navigate the thin line between promoting *relationships* and preaching *religion* (Dantley, 2005; Douglas and Peck, 2013). Spirituality, as enacted by the leaders in our studies, did not include the promotion of doctrines or edicts: these leaders understood the difference (Dantley, 2005; Douglas, 2012). Yet, they also understood how to leverage the inner recess of their faith in relevant, respectful, and culturally responsive ways. In each instance, spirituality meant *love as an action word* and faith meant reclaiming threatened territory and mending broken hearts. While we are still in the process of conceptualizing a theoretical framework that fully accounts for the intersections between crises and spirituality as demonstrated in this study, we also believe a possible example of this spiritual leadership style is grounded in a spiritual tradition theorized by Riggs (1998). We found that these leaders exhibited the following characteristics:

1. These leaders will be interpreters who exhibit moral courage. They will be social-analytical interpreters of the context and knowledgeable about counter-hegemonic narratives and traditions as resources for interpretation. They will be morally courageous in that they know that moral life is an act of imagination, depending upon which images are presented as central to it.

2. These leaders will be facilitators who are guiding a process of mediating differing ethical positions so as to engender creative moral responses. The leadership style will be more that of consensus building (educating, persuading, seeking to mediate the tension and conflicts) than that of crusader or commanders. They desire participatory democracy.

3. These leaders have committed but not absolutist morals, leaving themselves open to transformation in and through the very process of mediating the moral debate and agency that they are seeking to facilitate (p. 43).

DISCUSSION AND CONCLUSION

Solid school emergency and crisis plans provide good vehicles responses to critical incidents in schools and communities. Well-developed and exercised plans in the hands of trained faculty and staff can help school administrators build teams for crisis. However, as this paper has demonstrated, the school ecology and the nature of the crisis can also render these plans ineffectual. Post-crisis dialogue indicates that leadership in crises requires a systemic response that extends beyond the leadership capabilities of any individual or single organization. The leadership response often required individuals to pull in different—and sometimes opposing—directions: planning and improvisation . . . top-down and bottom-up leadership . . . individual leadership and collective ca-

pabilities . . . critical short-term crisis response and sustained long-term capabilities were the ones who worked collectively to improvise a response as physical and human systems collapsed. One question formed from the discussion is how we can enhance a more inclusive and adaptive leadership capability in more individuals, organizations, and communities so that we may be more effective in the face of future crises.

The millennium has issued a host of new challenges to address. "What we learn about the development and management of past crises may have limited value for improving the management of tomorrow's crises" (Rosenthal, Boin, and Comfort, 2001, vii). The recent bombings at the Boston Marathon that claimed the life of an eight-year-old schoolboy attest to this point. Crises are persistent realities of the human lived and leadership experience that will continue to rear their ugly heads in disturbing forms and unexpected places. Urban schools seem to be particularly vulnerable. School leaders must continue to prepare and respond to these moments with resolve and resilience, understanding that the occupants of our classrooms and communities are not just our future . . . they are our present.

NOTES

1. Comparatively, there were only two gun-related murders in 2007 in Bermuda.

2. The incessant whistling of tree frogs provides unique background music in the air of a Bermuda night.

REFERENCES

Angelides, P. (2001). The development of an efficient technique for collecting and analyzing qualitative data: The analysis of critical incidents. *Qualitative Studies in Education, 14*(3), 429–442.

Anzaldúa, G. (2007). *Borderlands la frontera: The new mestiza* (3rd ed.). San Francisco: Aunt Lute Books.

Bermuda Department of Statistics. (2010). *Report on the 2010 census of population and housing.* Bermuda: Bermuda Press.

Bermuda Department of Statistics. (2006). *Characteristics of Bermuda's Families.* Bermuda: Bermuda Press.

Christopher, J. T. (2009). *A random walk through the forest: Reflections on the history of education in Bermuda from the middle of the 20th century.* Winnipeg, Manitoba: Hignell's Book Printing.

Dabson, B. (2007). Rural-Urban interdependence: Why metropolitan and rural American need each other. Washington DC: The Brookings Institution.

Dantley, M. E. (2005). African American spirituality and Cornell West's notions of prophetic pragmatism: Restructuring educational leadership in American urban schools. *Educational Administration Quarterly, 41*, 651–674.

Darder, A. (2002). *Reinventing Paulo Freire: A pedagogy of love.* Boulder, Colorado: Westview.

Darder, A. (2009). Teaching as an act of love: Reflections on Paulo Freire and his contribution to our lives and our work. In A. Darder, M. P. Barltodano, and R. D. Torres (Eds.), *The critical pedagogy reader* (pp. 567–578). New York: Routledge.

Dillard, C. B. (1995). Leading with her life: An African American feminist (re)interpretation of leadership for an urban high school principal. *Educational Administration Quarterly, 31*(4), 539–563.

Dinkin, D. R. (2007). *Crisis in literature: Stepping into the void.* Greensboro, NC: Center for Creative Leadership.

Douglas, T. M. O. (2012). Resisting idol worship at HBCUs. The malignity of materialism, Western masculinity, and spiritual malefaction. *The Urban Review, 44*(3), 378–400.

Douglas, T. M. O. and Gause, C. P. (2009) Beacons of light in oceans of darkness: Exploring Black Bermudian masculinity. *Learning for Democracy, 3*(2).

Douglas, T. M. O. and Nganga, C. (in press). What's radical love got to do with it? Navigating identity, pedagogy, and positionality in pre-service education. *International Journal of Critical Pedagogy.*

Douglas, T. M. O. and Peck, C. M. (2013). Education by any means necessary: An historical exploration of community-based pedagogical spaces for peoples of African descent. *Educational Studies, 49*(1), 67–91.

Freire, P. (1993). *Pedagogy of the city.* New York: Continuum.

Gonzalo, R. (2009). *Rebuilding after disasters: From emergency to sustainability.* New York: SponPress.

Gullat, D. E. and Long, D. (1996). Components of a crisis management plan. *American Secondary Education 24*(2), 26–30.

Haeckel. E. H. P. A. (1877). On the evolution theory at the present time. *Nature, 16*, 492–496.

Hanson, M. E. (2003). *Educational administration and organizational behavior.* (5th ed.). New York: Allyn and Bacon/Longman Publishing.

Henkin, A. B., Cistone, P. J., and Dee, J. R. (2000). Conflict management strategies of principals in site-based managed schools, *Journal of Educational Administration, 38*(2), 142–158.

Holstein, J. A. and Gubrium, J. F. (2012). *Varieties of narrative analysis.* Thousand Oaks, CA: Sage.

Levitt, J. I. and Whitaker, M. C. (2009). *Hurricane Katrina: America's unnatural disaster.* Lincoln: University of Nebraska Press.

Pearman, M. (2009, September 14). Room for improvement in Bermuda's education system. *The Royal Gazette.*

Rosenthal, U., Boin, A., and Comfort, L. (eds). (2001). *Managing crises—Threat, dilemmas, opportunities.* Springfield, IL: Charles C. Thomas Publishing

Sarkar, S. (2009). In E. N. Zalta., U. Nodelman, C. Allen, and J. Perry, *Stanford encyclopedia of philosophy*, pp. 1–20. Stanford, CA: Stanford University.

Snoxell, S. 2005. "An Overview of the Literature on Linkages Between Communities." Paper presented at Aspen Institute conference, *Building, Connecting and Sharing Knowledge: A Dialogue on Linkages between Communities*, Aspen, CO, March 3.

Topper, B., and Lagadec, P. (2013). Fractal crises—A new path for crisis theory and management. *Journal of Contingencies and Crisis Management, 21*(1), 4–16.

Tripp, D. (1993). *Critical incidents in teaching.* London: Routledge.

Trump, K. S. (2009). School emergency planning: Back to the basics, "Nuts-and-bolts" details make or break schools in a crisis. *Student Assistance Journal*, 12–17. Retrieved October 7, 2014 from www.schoolsecurity.org/resources/School%20Emergency%20Planning%20Back%20to%20the%20Basics%20SAJ%20Spring%202009.pdf.

United Nations Population Division. (2005). World Urbanization Prospects: The 2005 Revision. New York and Geneva.

Witherspoon, N. (2010). *Leading after the Levees: Perspectives on Disaster, Crisis, and Educational Leadership.* College of Education Research Roundtable.

DIRECTIONS IN URBAN LEADERSHIP

Challenges and Solutions

The title of section 11, "Directions in Urban Leadership: Challenges and Solutions," underscores the importance of how leaders conceptualize their worldview, work, and direction. In school leadership, the word "problem" is the descriptor used versus "challenge." The difference in the intention behind each word can potentially affect how one internalizes the work that needs to be done. Choosing to view the work a challenge to be met, versus a problem to be solved, is a resolute and positive and reminder of how vital it is to take a strengths-based approach in leadership.

Chapter 38, "Urban Education Leadership in the Counseling Profession" by Cirecie West-Olatunji, engages in the discussion surrounding the untapped capital that school counselors carry with them to their school communities. They often encounter institutional barriers that prevent them fully sharing their skills, training, and ability that could assist in effect positive outcomes. The chapter offers insight into the skill set school counselors bring, as well as ways they can maximize their skills and be effective leaders in their schools. Chapter 39, "Principal Professional Identity and the Cultivation of Trust in Urban Schools" by Rodney S. Whiteman, Samantha Paredes Scribner, and Gary M. Crow, introduces a conceptual framework linking professional identities of school leaders and the cultivation of trust. It highlights relevant data on identity, trust, and urban school settings and how these can assist in understanding and cultivating school trust. Also included is a discussion of this framework and its potential use in practice, preparation and future research. Chapter 40, "Exemplary Leadership in Challenging Urban Public School Settings. It's the Principal of the Thing" by Harry Gutelius, answers the oft-asked challenge of how to improve schools in underprivileged areas. Chapter 41, "School Turnaround: The Meaning of Capacity in Practice for African-American Women," by Cosette M. Grant provides a fitting ending to this section. In this chapter, Grant demonstrates how improved student achievement is sustained in low-performing schools in urban districts which serve critically disadvantaged communities, and relies heavily upon the quality and skills of their educational leaders.

Urban School Leadership in Neoliberal Times

Critical Race Theory Reflection Perspectives

Laurence Parker

The neoliberal agenda for education policy has had a dramatic impact on urban schools as organizations, curriculum and instruction, and relations with parents and students. Since the passage of No Child Left Behind (NCLB) in 2001 by President Bush and the U.S. Congress, there has been a steady stream of policy edicts and mandates for accountability of administrators and teachers, and the punishment of schools that consistently fail to meet benchmark standardized test score standards. The urban school landscape has changed now to emphasize parents as consumers who can choose in the educational marketplace, in the form of charters and other avenues of the delivery of education as a product to improve the U.S. future workforce to compete in a global economy. This political agenda has worked its way into the daily operations of school leadership and practice. Furthermore, while the rhetoric of laws such as NCLB has been to target academic achievement for all students, particularly low-income African-American, Latino/a students, Asian-Pacific Island students, racialized immigrant students, and American Indian students, the reality has been that the neoliberal agenda has not served these students well. This failure is mainly due to institutional racism embedded in school policies and practices, coupled with structural/societal inequalities that have been difficult for most schools in low-income communities of color to overcome (Lipman, 2012).

I would argue that urban school leaders in the twenty-first century have to apply critical leadership in education (Santamaría and Santamaría, 2012). Anderson (2009) provided us with a working definition of this type of leadership by articulating a type of advocacy embodied by those who link with community movements inside and outside of schools to push for major structural change in the way schools are organized. Advocacy leaders also rely on parents and community leaders to organize for change and inclusion in the participation of shaping school policies for the benefit of social class and racial groups who have been typically marginalized by the administrative process of schooling. Anderson (2009) and Lipman (2011) argued that this type of leadership is even more important now in that the neoliberal education policy agenda has redefined the policy discourse in education.

This type of advocacy leadership links to the central themes of African American educational change among principals and superintendents that was documented by Lomotey (1989), Alston (2005), Murtadha and Watts (2005), and Tillman (2005), in that advocacy was a central component of what comprised critical and effective school leadership within the context of African-American schooling. In his study of leadership styles of successful urban African-American principals, Lomotey (1989) found that while the principals in his study exhibited different ways of leading (e.g., assertive, indirect), each administrator exemplified a commitment to the education of African-American students, and understanding of their neighborhoods, and confidence in the abilities of these students to learn. Alston's (2005) research looked specifically at African-American female superintendents and how they linked their activism with the agenda for success for African-American students. Alston found a theme of "tempered radical/ servant leadership" style that was firmly rooted in the African-American community. The advocacy displayed by these superintendents emerged from a sense of caring for the welfare of all segments of the African-American community, and these leaders were determined to push for change as hard as politically possible within the public school system in order for it to meet the needs of African-American students. Murtadha and Watts (2005) documented the historical role of African-American educational leadership for social justice. Their historical tracing of African-American education leaders and trends in African-American education leadership highlighted the link between education and social justice with a moral imperative to fight the racial injustice of poverty, social class exploitation, and legalized institutional racism. This type of advocacy leadership meant that community engagement was critical to African-American educational leadership to bring about change. Tillman (2005) summarized the research on African-American male and female school leaders in the pre-and post-*Brown* era, and she concluded that one of the major cross-cutting themes which emerged from the literature was a commitment to the academic and social development of African-American students, a resistance to the ideologies of individual achievement, and an advocacy based on concern for all African-American students.

The themes of African-American educational leadership and advocacy leadership described are in direct contrast to the tough urban "turnaround school" principal that is now characteristic of what is expected of school leaders of color in the neoliberal era (Zirkel et al., 2011). Gooden (2012) outlines how the popular media has linked the "tough black principal" who can get test score results and enforce discipline, as the expected way urban schools should be led. These models of school leadership also emphasize learning standards in close alignment with global market forces that delivers technically skilled managerial elites, and train urban youth for the service industries in globalized cities. The previous emphasis on desegregation and equal educational opportunity now gives way to a neoliberal policy agenda of school choice, and accountability control of teachers and students through standardized testing (Anderson, 2009). Increased measures of security and surveillance happen under the neoliberal agenda, and the rhetoric of color-blindness in everyday race relations masks the problems of structural racism that has resulted in housing gentrification in urban areas, the loss of well-paying jobs for minority youth and young adults, poor health care, and the control and regulation of the poor (Wacquant, 2009).

Critical race theory (CRT) can be brought to bear on applied critical leadership in education in the form of deeper racial understanding and seeing the links to the broader neoliberal economy agenda. CRT in urban education leadership can also be of use in challenging racial

neutrality and color-blindness regarding the impact of policy implementation, ranging from the common core to discipline to school organization. For example, tracking and ability grouping, special education classifications such as emotionally disturbed or intellectual disability, are often justified as a color-blind means to foster school achievement and create good schools in urban areas. To be sure, this is what we all as parents and students and community members want, but CRT school leaders can and should question underlying psychological and ideological assumptions based on race and racism and push for alternative ways of thinking that lead to action. We can use works by Harris (1993) and her article "Whiteness as Property" to address some of the bigger issues going on in urban schools around who is disciplined and why, how students are treated on a differential racial basis that has a deleterious impact on their education. CRT urban school leaders can and should also question embedded organizational assumptions, rules, and operational procedures in the public, private, and charter school sectors regarding an investment some of these schools have in promoting a "working identity" (Carbado and Gulati, 2013) that reinforces a certain type of African-American model of the good student—and if one does not conform to that racial prototype, they will be disciplined and denied a high-quality education. As an urban principal or superintendent who wants to utilize CRT, a set of questions you could begin to ask could for instance focus on the under-representation of students in the gifted programs, and over-representation in special education that leads to the school-to-prison pipeline and the general school racial climate. How can we use Bell's (2004) racial realism and other CRT tenets he articulated to address the short-term and long-term problems in urban schools? Is Bell right: maybe we should not put hope or faith in the judicial and political institutions to address these issues? From a leadership /policy standpoint, if you were conducting a racial equity audit, how would you describe what you see as a school leader from a CRT lens, how would you code your data from the audit and then use elements of CRT such as color-blindness ideology or racial realism to organize and code your data and interpret your data (Scheurich and McKenzie, 2004)? Finally, what sorts of policy actions would you recommend to your staff and parents and students to apply critical leadership in education?

REFERENCES

Alston, J. (2005). Tempered radicals and servant leaders: Black females perservering in the superintendency. *Educational Administration Quarterly, 41*(4), 675–688.

Anderson, G. (2009). *Advocacy leadership.* New York: Routledge.

Bell, D. A. (2004). *Silent Covenants:* Brown v. Board of Education *and the unfulfilled hopes for racial reform.* New York: Oxford Press.

Carbado, D. W. and Gulati, M. (2013). *Acting white? Rethinking race in post-racial America.* New York: Oxford University Press.

Gooden, M. A. (2012). What does racism have to do with leadership? Countering the idea of color-blind leadership: A reflection on race and the growing pressures of the urban principalship. *Educational Foundations, 26*(1–2), 67–84.

Harris, C. I. (1993). Whiteness as property. *Harvard Law Review, 106*(8), 1701–1791.

Lipman, P. (2011). *The new political economy of urban education: Neoliberalism, race, and the right to the city.* New York: Routledge.

Lomotey, K. (1989). *African-American principals: School leadership and success.* Westport, CT: Greenwood Press.

McKenzie, K. B. and Scheurich, J. J. (2004). Equity traps: A useful construct for preparing principals to lead schools with racially diverse students. *Educational Administration Quarterly, 40*(5), 601–632.

Murtada, K. and Watts Malik, D. (2005). Linking the struggle for education and social justice: Historical perspectives of African American leadership in schools. *Educational Administration Quarterly, 41*(4), 591–608.

Santamaría, L. J. and Santamaría, A. P. (2012). *Applied critical leadership in education: Choosing change.* New York: Routledge.

Tillman, L. (ed). (2005). Pushing back resistance: African-American discourses on school leadership. *Educational Administration Quarterly, 41*(4).

Wacquant, L. (2009). *Punishing the poor: The neoliberal government of social insecurity.* Durham, NC: Duke University Press.

Zirkel, S., Bailey, F., Bathey, S., Hawley, R., Lewis, U., Long, D., Pollack, T., Roberts, Z., Stanback Stroud, R., and Winful, A. (2011). "Isn't that what 'those kids' need?" Urban schools and the master narrative of the "tough urban principal." *Race Ethnicity and Education, 14*(2), 137–158.

CHAPTER 38

Urban Education Leadership in the Counseling Profession

Cirecie West-Olatunji

Urban schools within the public sector are beset with problems from within as well as from outside of the classroom that have influenced the crisis of pervasive underachievement for culturally and socially marginalized students (National Center for Children in Poverty, 2006; National Center for Education Statistics [NCES], 2003). In particular, education scholars have long asserted that, for children living in poverty, educational experiences are inadequate to support expected academic outcomes (Lamont and Small, 2006; Peske and Haycock, 2006). Urban schools that serve children in impoverished and disadvantaged neighborhoods often have: (a) underqualified and underpaid teachers, (b) low resources, (c) overcrowded conditions, (d) high teacher turnover rates, and (e) lower parental involvement (Frankenberg, Lee, and Orfield, 2003). Current and past efforts, such as compensatory programs, pre-referral intervention strategies, alternative education programs, professional development schools, and home-school collaboration initiatives, have focused on these issues without long-term success. However, educators have seldom included school counselors as a useful resource and partner in the school reform efforts.

As a profession, school counseling emerged, and continues to evolve, in response to the social-political, educational, and economic challenges faced by students (Wingfield, Reese, and West-Olatunji, 2010). Although the evolutionary shifts in the development of school counseling may be viewed as inevitable reactions to societal demands, each shift has brought about increased ambiguity regarding school counselors' purpose within schools, particularly those in urban settings. Consequently, school counselors have often been marginalized in school communities. Further, despite their training for cultural competence, school counselors are often overlooked as leaders or cultural brokers in school communities (Amatea and West-Olatunji, 2007).

The literature on leadership, regardless of tradition, has focused primarily on those in formal leadership positions, such as principals, directors, and superintendents (Spillane, Halverson, and Diamond, 2004). However, research on effective schools has suggested that leadership is not within the sole purview of the school principal and other traditional school administrators. Rather, other educators play vital roles in leading instructional innovation (Heller and Firestone, 1995; Spillane et al., 2004; Wingfield et al., 2010). Following a brief overview of the issues confronting urban schools, I describe the evolution of school counseling by outlining the vocational guidance, mental health, and developmental guidance eras. Additionally, I provide key points that inform the current direction of school counselors as leaders within urban schools. Finally, I offer recommendations for principals, school counselors, teachers, and parents that support the transformation of school counselors as leaders in urban schools.

ISSUES CONFRONTING URBAN SCHOOLS

Urban schools are besieged with issues that primarily relate to racial and economic inequities. National data shows that white students remain the most racially segregated of all student groups (Kozol, 2005). On average, white students account for approximately 80 percent of students in public schools and increases for private schools (Frankenberg et al., 2003). Additionally, this socially constructed backdrop to urban schooling has created what some authors call *apartheid* schools (Grant, 2006; Kozol, 2005) with virtually all non-white students. These schools are composed of about one sixth of the nation's African-American students and one ninth of Latino-American students (Frankenberg et al., 2003). These are schools where the majority of students are economically disadvantaged, thus creating a situation of concentrated poverty. As a result, these schools have few resources available and face many social and health disparities (Darling-Hammond, 2007). According to the U.S. Department of Education (NCES, 2006, 2007) and the National Assessment of Educational Progress (NAEP) (Grigg, Donahue, and Dion, 2007; Lee, Grigg, and Dion, 2007; Lee, Grigg, and Donahue, 2007), African-American and Latino students continue to lag behind their white peers in reading and mathematics at the fourth, eighth, and twelfth grade levels. Further, the U.S. Department of Education (Office of Special Education [OSEP], 2006) reported that African-American students are disproportionately represented in the mental retardation (MR), emotional disturbance (ED) categories, and Native American students are overrepresented in the category of learning disabilities (LD). As solutions to urban school achievement issues, compensatory programs, pre-referral intervention strategies, alternative education programs, professional development schools, and home-school collaboration initiatives have been implemented but, to date, demonstrate mixed results.

Previous and Current Approaches. As previously stated, intensive efforts by educational researchers to improve academic outcomes for low-income and culturally diverse students have been made. Early initiatives, such as compensatory programs, pre-referral intervention strategies, and alternative education programs, have been proven to lack sufficient empirical evidence regarding their value in changing academic performance for certain segments of the student population (Bullis, Walker, and Sprague, 2001; Trachtman, 2007). However, recent approaches, including professional development schools, home-school-community collaboration, and school leadership initiatives, have shown some success when incorporating culturally informed school-wide interventions (Lefever-Davis, Johnson, and Pearman, 2007).

Stemming from the education reform movement, professional development schools (PDS) link universities to K–12 schools and are designed to impact teacher training by connecting practice to applied research and student learning (Carey, 2004). Unfortunately, the success of this approach has been compromised by a climate of: (a) high stakes testing that often distracts teachers' inquiry efforts (West-Olatunji and Behar-Horenstein, 2005), and (b) positioned perceptions of who can construct knowledge (practitioner or scholar) (Trachtman, 2007).

Home-school-community collaborations vary in design and can include out-of-school time (OST) programs (e.g., after-school and weekend) or full-service delivery schools. Such programs often provide non-educational services, such as medical and social care, within the school setting (McMahon, Ward, Pruett, Davison, and Griffith, 2000). The limited success of OST programs is due, in part, to the confluence between student learning and environmental influences. This attention toward environmental influences spawned increased interest in social, economic, and political context by educational researchers. As a result, scholars in the area of educational leadership began to develop innovative leadership models, particularly for urban school communities (Jackson and Kelley, 2002).

School leadership models have focused on various stakeholders, including principals (Eilers and Camacho, 2007; Theoharis, 2008), teachers (Beachum and Dentith, 2004; Tillman, 2005), and parents (Barton, Drake, Perez, St. Louis, and George, 2004; Noguera, 2001). These leadership models have often focused on transforming the culture of schools by focusing on social justice, culturally relevant knowledge, and community engagement. Yet few of these approaches have included a discussion of the role of school counselors as key agents in the school transformation process. Perhaps the lack of inclusion of school counselors within the urban school leadership discourse can be partially attributed to principals', teachers', and parents' limited understanding of who school counselors are and how they can serve as leaders in urban schools. Additionally, the role of school counselors has changed over time.

SCHOOL COUNSELING: A HISTORICAL OVERVIEW

Three significant eras mark the evolution of the school guidance movement: vocational guidance, mental health, and developmental guidance. Each of these eras has contributed its own characteristics to the current framework of leadership that the American School

Counselor Association (ASCA) promotes in its *ASCA National Model* (ASCA, 2005) for twenty-first-century school counselors. The vocational guidance era shaped the notion that school counselors assisted students in finding career avenues relevant to their interests and passions. The mental health movement expanded the career focus of the school counselor to include responding to the personal and social aspects of students and their families in the form of remedial services. This movement encouraged school counselors to consider the unique developmental circumstances their diverse students face in reaching quality education. Finally, the developmental guidance era ushered in Comprehensive Competency Based School Counseling Guidance Programs (CCBSCGP) that focused more on how school counselors can serve as leaders to meet the academic, vocational, and personal/social needs of students while collaborating with school stakeholders. These eras are discussed below and presented in table 38.1.

Vocational Guidance Era. The history of counselors in school settings can be traced back to the industrial era in the latter part of the nineteenth century in response to child labor abuses (Kromboltz and Kolpin, 2003). With the social advocacy works of Frank Parsons, profes-

sionals were trained to assist children in finding occupations that would allow them to become contributing members of society (Gysbers and Henderson, 2000). Additionally, vocational guidance personnel focused on character development and problem behavior assessment. Both aspects of school counseling remain evident in today's school counseling programs. Influencing the guidance movement during this era was the need following World Wars I and II to provide vocational assessment for military personnel (Myrick, 2003). The U.S. government needed to expeditiously determine soldiers' skills and talents in order to judiciously deploy a workforce during wartime. Vocational specialists served this need, allowing the government to focus its attention on military strategy rather than assessment. It was not until the mid-1990s that guidance personnel were trained to address the psychological and emotional needs of schoolchildren, thus initiating a major transformation of school counseling.

Mental Health Era. There were two main concerns that emerged in urban schools that fueled the need for guidance personnel to focus more on the mental health needs of students. First, early vocational guidance efforts did not incorporate an understanding of students'

Table 38.1. Models of School Counseling, Era, Roles, and Training

Major Models of School Counseling Period	Vocational Guidance 1900–1940s	Mental Health Movement in School Counseling 1950s–1960s	Developmental Guidance 1960s–1980s	Comprehensive Competency-Based School Counseling Guidance Programs 1990s–2000s
Role	Match a student's personal characteristics with an occupation. Goals include: assist students in finding a career	Provide remedial services. Goals include: help close achievement gaps, especially culturally diverse, low- income, English language learners, and differing ability children	Primary prevention focus. Integrate guidance and counseling program within the larger educational program. Goals include: increase student achievement, provide more equitable services to students, broader impact on student development and career decision-making, student satisfaction, & safe, orderly, connected school climate	Integral to students' daily educational environment. Goals include: partner and leader in student achievement with school stakeholders, providing vocational, remedial, and developmental interventions based on student data
Training	Training in assessment of occupational selection and placement for all students	Training in prevention & intervention skills to close achievement gaps	Training focuses on identifying the developmental needs of students to meet the diverse needs of students	Multicultural training that encourages school counselors to advocate for the academic achievement of all students

Taken from, "Counselors as Leaders in Schools," by R. Wingfield, C. West-Olatunji, & R. Reese (2010), *Florida Journal of Educational Administration & Policy*, Copyright (2010) by R. Wingfield, C. West-Olatunji, & R. Reese. Reprinted with permission.

personal needs and experiences that influenced their academic achievement and job choice. Second, little attention had been paid to diversity issues for schoolchildren. With the influence of Carl Rogers's nondirective approach to counseling, guidance counselors began to take a more individualized, remedial approach to meeting the needs of students (Schmidt, 1999). School counselors focused on: (a) assuming leadership roles in schools, (b) providing consultative services for school stakeholders, and (c) offering small group and individual counseling with students. However, over time, this remedial approach was criticized for not reaching a sufficient number of students and school counselors were encouraged to involve themselves more in curriculum development and mental health service delivery (Dollarhide and Saginak, 2008; Myrick, 2003).

The second concern that spurred the mental health movement in school counseling was the advent of the U.S. civil rights era in the mid-1950s and early 1960s. Segregated schools, primarily in the southern states, served as barriers to educational attainment for most African Americans as well as other culturally marginalized student populations, such as Native American Indians and Latinos. Overturning the nineteenth-century Dredd Scott decision that established segregated schools as "separate but equal," the Supreme Court issued the *Brown v. Board of Education* 1954 decision that served as a precursor to the Civil Rights Movement (Smith, 2005). This led Congress to form the Civil Rights Acts of 1964, the Federal Commission on Civil Rights, and the Elementary and Secondary Education Act (ESEA) of 1965. The purpose of ESEA was to fuel equal education for all by providing funding to local education agencies serving low-income areas. The intent was to meet the needs of more specialized at-risk groups, such as English language learners (Bilingual Act of 1967), women (Women's Educational Equity Act 1972), Native American students (Improvement of Educational Opportunities for Indian Students Act), children with disabilities (Education of All Handicapped Children Act of 1975), and immigrants (Thomas and Brady, 2005). As a result, the ESEA supported the hiring of more school counseling professionals. Unfortunately, recent research evaluating the effects of desegregation has suggested that integration has had little effect on improving academic outcomes for culturally and economically marginalized students (Hanushek, Kain, and Rivkin, 2009).

Another significant factor in the development of school counseling during the middle of the twentieth century was the passing of the National Defense Education Act (NDEA) in response to the 1957 launching of Sputnik, the Soviet spaceship, that spurred a nationwide focus on mathematics and science achievement. The NDEA initiated a massive training and hiring initiative that reemphasized assessment and vocational guidance (Baker, 2000). More importantly, this thrust toward academic achievement instigated school counselors to create counseling programs that addressed the developmental needs of all students rather than solely those needing remediation. Thus, rather than focusing on vocational guidance primarily at the high school level, funds were now available to train elementary and middle school counselors to focus on developmental, preventative, and proactive approaches (Myrick, 2003; Wittmer, 2000). An early pioneer of the developmental guidance movement was Robert Mathewson, who asserted that effective guidance involved the facilitation of human development (Aubrey, 1982). Mathewson challenged the belief that only teachers could provide students with the socio-emotional support needed for academic achievement and advocated for guidance as a significant factor in advancing students' maturation. Within this paradigm, the developmental guidance movement attempted to integrate vocational guidance with human development and emphasized the use of interventions that matched students' everyday realities and lifelong learning. Thus, guidance was reconceptualized within a broader framework.

Developmental Guidance Era. By the late 1960s, more concentrated evaluation of school counseling programs emerged with the passing of the Education for All Handicapped Children Act in 1975, the Americans with Disabilities Act in 1990, and the No Child Left Behind Act of 2001 (Gysbers, 2004). All of these legislative mandates have had a significant impact on the school counseling profession and required school counselors to deliver evidence-based and accountable services to address persistent underachievement for certain segments of the school population. Additionally, these mandates placed tremendous pressure on school personnel to promote the academic achievement of all students (West-Olatunji and Behar-Horenstein, 2005). Urban schools that were unable to promote achievement now risked losing their students, teachers, and funding. In response to such legislation, ASCA developed the National Standards for Students (2004) and the ASCA National Model (2005) that address the academic, career, and personal/social needs of students. According to ASCA, all school counseling programs should meet these student standards. Embedded in these standards is an assertion that school counselors need to become leaders in schools.

SCHOOL COUNSELORS AS LEADERS

Contemporary counselor educators assert that the primary role of the twenty-first-century school counselor should be one of school-wide leader (Amatea and West-Olatunji, 2007; Stone and Clark, 2001). As such, school counselors should work to develop a climate of appreciation for diverse worldviews and maintain strong home-school collaborations (ASCA, 2005; House and Martin, 1998; Martin, 2002). This concept is particularly relevant given the changes that have transpired in urban public education wherein assessment has become a salient feature of the school climate (Bemak, 2000; West-Olatunji and Behar-Horenstein, 2005). Additionally, the mandate that all students have access to rigorous academic preparation and support has heavily influenced how schools are run (House and Martin). Within these contexts, school counselors are uniquely positioned to assume leadership in urban schools because of their knowledge, awareness, and skills related to multicultural and diversity concerns. Additionally, school counselors employ leadership skills through augmented collaboration and consultation interventions with principals, teachers, and parents; all of whom are essential to the health and welfare of students (Stone and Clark; Cooper and Sheffield, 1994). Moreover, school counselors are capable of leading program design and advocacy (Dollarhide, 2003; Hatch and Bowers, 2002; Herr, 2001), engaging in school reform (Dollarhide; Adelman and Taylor, 2002; Bemak, 2000), and embracing certain organizational roles in the school (Dollarhide). In particular, school counselors are especially well situated to play proactive, catalytic roles in defining the future for programs that augment education for all students (Adelman and Taylor, 2002). Galassi and Akos (2004) proposed a developmental advocate role for the school counselor of the twenty-first century, suggesting that the school counselor's main duty is to promote the optimal development of all students.

School Counselors as Leaders With Principals. The idea that school counselors should partner with principals is not new (Worzbyt and Zook, 1992). Further, research has shown that many school counselors already take on leadership roles because their principals have invited them to do so or because they advocate for those kinds of roles (Clemens, Milsom, and Cashwell, 2009).

When investigating perceptions of school counselors by principals, several studies have found that counselors and principals have diverse perceptions of school counselors' duties (Monteiro-Leitner, Asner-Self, Milde, Leitner, and Skelton, 2006; Perusse, Goodnough, Donegan, and Jones, 2004). Despite recent efforts to educate principals and other school personnel about the training and usefulness of school counselors in urban school settings, the majority of principals persist in believing that suitable responsibilities for school counselors include clerical duties (registration and scheduling of all new students), administration of various cognitive, aptitude, and achievement tests, and the maintenance of student records. Hence, it is not surprising that principals might have difficulty in conceptualizing school counselors as leaders (McMahon, Mason, and Paisley, 2009).

However, school counselor educators assert that principals and school counselors can become powerful allies in addressing persistent underachievement in urban schools in several ways. First, counselor-principal teams can employ district-wide data to identify system-wide phenomena that correlate to unfair conditions for certain segments of the student population (Stone and Clark, 2001) and then compare the district data to the school under investigation. West-Olatunji and colleagues have initiated several studies in partnership with a school district in Florida to explore district-wide phenomena for low-income African-American (West-Olatunji, Sanders, Mehta, and Behar-Horenstein, 2010) and Latino (Ojeda, West-Olatunji, Wolfgang, and Varney, 2012) elementary schoolchildren. The findings of these studies were used to develop interventions at the individual school level, such as whole classroom guidance activities for students, multicultural education teacher training, advanced multicultural supervision training for school counselors, and parenting workshops.

Second, counselor-principal teams can design projects to improve educational outcomes for low-performing groups of students that focus on the multicultural competence of teachers and other school personnel. Studies have shown that the application of culturally appropriate pedagogy (CAP) by teachers (Foster, Lewis, and Onafowora, 2003, 2005) and demonstration of multicultural counseling competence by school counselors (Constantine, 2001) are correlative to academic success for low-income, culturally diverse students, particularly those in urban school communities. CAP theory attributes academic challenges for certain segments of the student population to structural aspects of schools, such as culturally insensitive curricula, instructional methods, and classroom environments (Ojeda et al., 2014). Projects co-designed by a counselor-principal team can begin by establishing the baseline for academic performance among the targeted student group using indicators, such as attendance, standardized test scores, psychosocial indicators, and teacher assessments. Then, the team could assess the level of multicultural competence among the school faculty and subsequently develop an intervention plan for the entire school, including teachers, students, and parents as well as other school personnel. Interventions should be followed by continuous assessment of outcomes for students to determine the effectiveness of any project. Central to the success of any school reform endeavor involving school counselors is teacher engagement and their perceptions of the role of school counselors.

School Counselors as Leaders With Teachers. Traditionally, teachers have viewed counselors as resource brokers to access needed vocational or psychological resources for individual children and their families or to facilitate the identification and placement of individual children into special education categories (Amatea and West-Olatunji, 2007). While this role may be a necessary one, there are other roles that counselors can play within culturally diverse and low-resourced schools. Serving as a resource to teachers, counselors can: (a) serve as a cultural bridge between teachers and students to impede the blaming that often derails efforts to work with low-income and culturally diverse students and their families and (b) function as a pedagogical partner with teachers to localize the curriculum and connect instructional content to students' lives.

Counselors in urban public schools can assist teachers to develop or enhance their cultural competence by serving as a *cultural* broker. In this role, school counselors serve as a bridge between the school and home communities. Counselors in the role of cultural broker serve as advocate, mediator, and community liaison. As advocates, counselors are aware of those macro-systemic factors that shape the presenting problems brought into the counseling arena (West-Olatunji, 2012; West-Olatunji and Watson, 1999). Thus, they can conceptualize children within the context of their families, communities, as well as their social, cultural, and religious systems. As mediator, counselors model and facilitate two skills central to cultural reciprocity: mediation and recovery skills. Mediation skills are needed to bridge between two or more cultural systems to communicate effectively. Recovery skills are needed to overcome the anxieties that surface when acquiring a new skill when working with unfamiliar communities and cultural contexts. In the role of community liaison, counselors can provide referrals to key stakeholders in the broader community. Community resource organizations and individuals can provide complementary interventions and support to families and children in urban communities. Moreover, by incorporating community resources, counselors can utilize more sociocentric and group-oriented interventions that are more likely to be consistent with the expectations of culturally diverse families. Additionally, family members are often more familiar with resources in their community where they have previously developed relationships.

Counselors in urban public schools can serve as pedagogical partners to teachers and educational support personnel by providing professional development workshops during pre-service and in-service trainings (Pedersen and Carey, 2003). Prior to the beginning of the school year, teachers can benefit from extended workshops and seminars that provide information and teaching techniques useful in working with the student population at the school. During the school year, in-service trainings conducted by counselors can be responsive to the dynamic needs of teachers who are experiencing challenges on a daily basis. Whether these are strategies for collaborating with culturally diverse families, classroom management, or localizing the curriculum to include culturally specific content into instruction, counselors in schools can assist teachers in becoming more effective in culturally diverse and low-resourced classrooms.

Counselors in urban public schools can serve as professional coaches to teachers by providing one-on-one training and in-class demonstrations. Current research suggests that teachers, particularly those within their first five years of placement, experience more success with their students, have more job satisfaction, and remain in the profession longer when they receive continuous support and mentoring throughout the year (Darling-Hammond, 2007). By allowing teachers to approach counselors in urban public schools with various issues that occur in their classrooms and parent interactions, teachers can receive technical assistance immediately in order to respond expeditiously and prevent interpersonal conflicts. School counselors in urban settings can process critical incidents and provide support, encouragement, and recommendations for next steps, such as referrals to outside experts, if necessary.

Finally, school counselors can serve as partners to teachers by facilitating movement from a school-centric paradigm to a family-centric one in which parents are active agents in the decision-making process of school policy and procedures (West-Olatunji, 2012). As in-house consultants, school counselors can aide other school personnel in decreasing judgments and criticisms directed toward culturally diverse and low-income families. In this role, school counselors can increase cultural competency to minimize the cultural discontinuity between home and school that often exists when working with culturally diverse students. One of the most significant correlates to student success is teacher expectations (Garrahy, 2001; Skiba, Michael, Nardo, and Peterson, 2002). When teachers perceive students as engaged and motivated learners, student achievement is higher. Additionally, when teachers perceive parents as involved in their child's education, student achievement is higher (Belgrave and Allison, 2006). Thus, counselors are critical in assisting teachers in altering their sometimes pejorative views toward culturally diverse and low-income families in urban communities.

School Counselors as Leaders With Parents. In asserting that school counselors should serve as cultural mediators between schools and culturally marginalized families, scholars have suggested that an ecosystemic framework is useful to investigate the context in which children are positioned and enhance collaboration between low-income families and schools (Amatea and West-Olatunji, 2007; Chung and Pardeck, 1997). School counselors working from an ecosystemic perspective can incorporate factors outside of the typical individually focused, microsystemic interventions (Bailey and Paisley, 2004). Instead of conceptualizing students' problems resulting from individual failing alone, school counselors can examine macrosystemic factors, such as poverty and cultural hegemony as contributing influences on children's behaviors and dispositions.

Today, school counselors in urban schools are shifting away from interventions that focus exclusively on the individual and toward those interventions designed for parents/caregivers and families. For example, Mullis and Chapman (2000) found that, for African-American youth, the availability of the extended family may provide African-American children with a mechanism for positive emotional development despite other hardships, such as poverty and racism. Supportive family members provide an important outlet for urban youth who frequently deal with an abundance of societal and familial stressors.

Another macrosystemic approach is wraparound counseling that emphasizes normative developmental themes applied to all families, including parents who identify no specific parenting problems and have no issues of concern (West-Olatunji, Frazier, and Kelley, 2011). Wraparound counseling addresses not only the presenting child but also microsystems present in the child's environment, such as parents and caregivers, teachers, and other school personnel. As a secondary outcome, wraparound counseling addresses non-symptomatic children by serving as a prevention tool for the school community. Wraparound counseling facilitates communication between the school and the home, giving voice to parents' concerns and thereby permitting bidirectional input and collaboration. Parents possess information and resources that are often outside of the perception of traditional counseling activity. By linking with adults in the student's family system, school counselors can minimize the time needed to assess and treat problems evidenced in the school setting.

As advocates, school counselors exemplify the humanistic foundations of the discipline of counseling: a belief that all individuals inherently seek self-actualization. This positivistic approach to mental health service delivery relies on a number of basic assumptions: social empathy, respect, and authenticity (Adams and Juhnke, 2001). *Social empathy* is exemplified within the context of pervasive underachievement due to socio-historical oppression that serves as an obstacle to self-actualization. This type of empathy is viewed as more comprehensive than conventional dyadic empathy that is evident in individualized service provision. Social empathy extends the traditional microlevel of empathy to incorporate macrolevel or sociopolitical context (Segal, 2007). Unfortunately, research has shown that counselors in urban schools have often served as gatekeepers to learning opportunities for culturally and socially marginalized students (West-Olatunji, Shure, Pringle, Adams, Lewis, and Cholewa, 2010). Thus, counselors are encouraged to use their social empathy skills to consider how persistent underachievement of some segments of the student population can ultimately impact society as a whole.

IMPLICATIONS FOR URBAN SCHOOL LEADERSHIP

By acknowledging and utilizing school counselors as leaders in urban schools, the entire community can benefit. Principals and teachers can acquire a new partner in addressing persistent underachievement. Additionally, parents can discover an advocate within the school environment who encourages bidirectional communication about their children. As leaders, school counselors can integrate more school-wide interventions and encourage teachers to utilize more culturally responsive instructional methods grounded in the worldviews and values of diverse families and communities. Culturally responsive system-wide interventions should include both micro- and macrosystemic interventions. For instance, microsystemic interventions, such as the use of culturally based games and the use of folk tales as narratives, have been shown to be effective. Additionally, interventions at the macrosystemic level could include investigating the history of racism and discrimination in the local community that focuses on understanding the relationship between historic discrimination and community residents' use of social services, health care and education.

School counselors can also help to remove systemic barriers resulting from historical marginalization by helping students to articulate and share their difficulties in environments that often do not validate their realities. Thus, students can overcome obstacles and reposition themselves within socially constructed classrooms and schools. By incorporating interventions, such as the use of cultural artifacts, school counselors can foster a deeper understanding of how low-income, culturally diverse students see themselves and provide an opportunity for students to link their similarities while acknowledging their differences. This leadership role as a change agent can include engaging students in critical conversations about the environmental context that frames their own positioning. This conversation can facilitate serve as a platform to encourage students to challenge and eventually change their positioning (Harley, Jolivette, McCormick, and Tice, 2002).

Recommendations for Principals. Urban school principals can take several steps to foster leadership among school counselors within the school setting. First, they can educate themselves about the current role of school counselors (Stone and Clark, 2001; Wingfield et al., 2010). This can be accomplished by attending local, regional, or national counseling and educational leadership conferences. Additionally, it would be more beneficial if principals co-presented with their school counselors at these conferences. This would be an excellent opportunity for them to disseminate the outcomes of their collaborative work. Co-presenting at counseling conferences can serve multiple purposes; it would: (a) model for other schools how principals and counselors partner and (b) share information about the success of the partnering initiatives and the impact on low-performing students.

Further, principals can seek opportunities to employ school counselors as part of their school reform initiatives. As has been stated previously, school counselors' and principals' perceptions of school counselors' responsibilities differ significantly (Monteiro-Leitner et al., 2006; Perusse et al., 2004). By including school counselors within school reform efforts, principals can further educate other members of the school community about the current role that school counselors play in school communities (Wingfield et al., 2010). Third, principals can view counselors as leaders in urban schools who have the capacity to initiate interventions and coordinate efforts among teachers, parents, and community stakeholders. However, school counselors must also see themselves differently and serve as active change agents in urban schools (Stone and Clark, 2001).

Recommendations for School Counselors. There are several key steps that school counselors can take to develop leadership skills. First, school counselors must see themselves as advocates for schoolchildren and their families. Therefore, they need to educate teachers and other school personnel about the environmental factors that influence academic achievement. Second, counselors need to enhance their collaboration skills and focus on strengthening their partnerships with principals, in particular. Research further indicates that the support of the school principal in the implementation and maintenance of a school counseling program is critical (Beale, 1995; Coll and Freeman, 1997; Lambie and Williamson, 2004; Ribak-Rosenthal, 1994). Niebuhr, Nieubuhr, and Cleveland (1999) found that many tasks that principals sometimes ask school counselors to perform, although related to the operation of schools, take school counselors away from the tasks and roles for which they were trained. In order to move beyond merely citing the lack of leadership observed in schools, school counselors must take an active approach in attaining the leadership status that is well needed and deserved.

According to Spillane et al. (2004), leadership involves mobilizing school personnel and clients to notice, face, and take on the tasks of changing instruction as well as harnessing and mobilizing the resources needed to support the transformation of teaching and learning. To implant, refine, and maintain leadership skills, school counselors should take part in activities, such as professional conferences, on-site in-service training, collaborative projects with counseling education faculty as investigative researchers, and continuing education courses and seminars. To promote a change in how they are perceived, school counselors will need more than principals as partners in the transformation of their role. Teachers can serve as strong allies in urban school settings.

Recommendations for teachers. Teachers can embrace counselors as leaders in urban school settings in several ways. First, they can solicit individual consultation and professional development training from school counselors regarding culturally diverse student concerns. Given school counselors' training in the area of multicultural counseling, they have knowledge of structural bias and the role cultural identity in preserving self-actualization and self-esteem among culturally marginalized students. Additionally school counselors have undergone training that has facilitated an awareness of their own embedded biases about various individuals who at least initially appear to be different from

them. Finally, school counselors have been trained to acquire the necessary multicultural counseling skills that are uniquely appropriate for the student body.

Second, teachers can incorporate school counselors into regularly scheduled teacher meetings as partners who can aid in the conceptualization of culturally diverse students' educational and psychosocial concerns. Often times, teachers gather to discuss symptomatic students who are experiencing academic or behavioral challenges. However, teachers may not think to invite school counselors to those meetings unless there's a request for a parent-teacher meeting to be scheduled. Thus, school counselors miss out on opportunities to participate in prevention-oriented activities and instead are primarily employed for remediation interventions. By integrating school counselors in teacher meetings, school counselors can: (a) provide useful information about children's development from a cultural perspective, (b) supplement any professional development training by providing consultation in response to a particular topic or phenomenon, and (c) innately educate school personnel about their roles as leaders in school settings. However, the task of re-visioning the role of school counselors in urban schools is not solely under the purview of school personnel. Parents can also assist school counselors in assuming leadership roles in urban school communities.

Recommendations for parents. Parents and caretakers of culturally diverse students, particularly those in low-income communities, can seek out school counselors to exchange information about their child's academic needs and talents. Research has shown that African-American and Latino parent knowledge, in particular, is often overlooked within urban school communities. It is most often educators providing information to parents without considering that parents have knowledge that is of value to them (West-Olatunji, Frazier, Baker, and Garrett, 2014).

Parents can also demand that counseling services are provided for their children in order to prevent problems or complement educational services. For example, given the current discussion regarding the overrepresentation of African-American students in special education, especially in the mental retardation and emotional disturbance categories (West-Olatunji et al., 2014), school counselors can be of particular assistance in reconceptualizing culture-bound behaviors and misperceptions about African-American children's expectations of the schooling experience.

CONCLUSION

In sum, I have outlined the myriad of challenges that urban schools face, especially when addressing the academic and psychosocial needs of low-income, culturally diverse students. However, school counselors have not been a salient feature in urban school reform efforts, partially due to educational leaders' misperceptions about school counselors' role in school settings. Additionally, school counselors may themselves struggle with assuming more prominent roles as leaders in urban schools. Following an overview of the developmental history of school counseling programs, I have highlighted what multicultural knowledge, awareness, and skills that school counselors bring to urban schools. Additionally, I have articulated specific areas where school counselors can make meaningful contributions as leaders and offered recommendations for how principals, teachers, and parents can serve as partners in re-visioning the role of school counselors as leaders in urban schools. The issue of persistent underachievement for low-income, culturally diverse students is complex with multilayered influences. Thus, it will necessitate an integrated approach to transform the educational experiences of African-American, Latino, and other marginalized students so that there is equity in academic outcomes for children in urban school communities. By facilitating leadership roles for school counselors in urban schools, educators take a giant step toward social justice for the entire school community.

REFERENCES

Adams, J. R. and Juhnke, G. A. (2001). Using the systems of care philosophy within counseling to promote human potential. *Journal of Humanistic Counseling, Education and Development, 40,* 225–232.

Adelman, H. S. and Taylor, L. (2002). School counselors and school reform: New directions. *Professional School Counseling, 5,* 235–248. Retrieved from www.schoolcounselor.org/content.asp?contentid=235.

Amatea, E. S. and West-Olatunji, C. (2007). Joining the conversation about educating our poorest children:

Emerging leadership roles for school counselors in high-poverty schools. *Professional School Counseling, 11,* 81–89. Retrieved from www.schoolcounselor.org/content.asp?contentid=235.

American School Counselor Association. (2005). *The ASCA national model for school counseling programs.* Alexandria, VA: Author. Retrieved from www.ascanationalmodel.org/.

Aubrey, R. F. (1982). A house divided: Guidance and counseling in 20th-Century America. *Personnel and Guidance Journal, 61*(4), 198–204.

Bailey, D. F. and Paisley, P. O. (2004). Developing and nurturing excellence in African American male adolescents. *Journal of Counseling and Development, 82,* 108–115.

Baker, S. B. (2000). *School counseling for the twenty-first century* (3rd ed.). Upper Saddle River, NJ: Merrill.

Barton, A. C., Drake, C., Perez, J. G., St. Louis, K., and George, M. (2004). Ecologies of parental engagement in urban education. *Educational Researcher, 33*(4), 3–12.

Beachum, F. and Dentith, A. M. (2004, September). Teacher leaders creating cultures of school renewal and transformation. In *The Educational Forum* (Vol. 68, No. 3, pp. 276–286). New York: Taylor and Francis Group.

Beale, A.V. (1995). Selecting school counselors: The principal's perspective. *The School Counselor, 42*(3), 211–217.

Belgrave, F.Z. and Allison, K.W. (2006). *African American psychology: From Africa to America.* Thousand Oaks, CA: Sage.

Bemak, F. (2000). Transforming the role of the counselor to provide leadership in educational reform through collaboration. *Professional School Counseling, 3,* 323–331. Retrieved from www.schoolcounselor.org/content.asp?contentid=235.

Bullis, M., Walker, H. M., and Sprague, J. R. (2001). A promise unfulfilled: Social skills training with at-risk and antisocial children and youth. *Exceptionality, 9,* 67–90.

Carey, L. (2004). The professional development school model: Unpacking knowledge. *International Journal of Leadership in Education, 7,* 319–337.

Chung, W. S. and Pardeck, J. T. (1997). Treating powerless minorities through an ecosystem approach. *Adolescence, 32,* 625–634.

Clemens, E.V., Milsom, A., and Cashwell, C.S. (2009). Using leader-member exchange theory to examine principal-school counselor relationships, school counselors' roles, job satisfaction, and turnover intentions. *Professional School Counseling, 13,* 75–85.

Coll, K. M. and Freeman, B. (1997). Role conflict among elementary school counselors: A national comparison with middle and secondary school counselors. *Elementary School Guidance and Counseling, 31*(4), 251–261.

Constantine, M. G. (2001). Multiculturally focused counseling supervision: Its relationship to trainees' multicultural counseling self-efficacy. *The Clinical Supervisor, 20,* 87–98.

Cooper, D. E. and S. B. Sheffield. (1994). The principal-counselor relationship in a quality high school. In D. G. Burgess and R. M. Dedmond (Eds.), *Quality Leadership and the Professional School Counselor* (pp. 101–114). Alexandria, VA: American Counseling Association.

Darling-Hammond, L. (2007). Race, inequality and educational accountability: The irony of "no child left behind." *Race, Ethnicity and Education, 10*(3), 245–260.

de la Garza, R. O., DeSipio, L., Garcia, F. C., Garcia, J., and Falcon, A. (1992). *Latino voices: Mexican, Puerto Rican, and Cuban perspectives on American politics.* San Francisco: Westview Press.

Dollarhide, C. T. (2003). School counselors as program leaders: applying leadership contexts to school counseling. *Professional School Counseling, 6,* 304–308. Retrieved from www.schoolcounselor.org/content.asp?contentid=235.

Dollarhide, C. T. and Sağınak, K. A. (2008). *Comprehensive school counseling programs: K–12 delivery systems in action.* Boston: Pearson Education, Inc.

Dotson-Blake, K. P. (2010). Learning from each other: A portrait of family-school-community' partnerships in the United States and Mexico. *Professional School Counseling, 14*(1), 101–114.

Eilers, A. M. and Camacho, A. (2007). School culture change in the making leadership factors that matter. *Urban Education, 42*(6), 616–637.

Foster, M., Lewis, J., and Onafowora, L. (2003). Anthropology, culture, and research on teaching and learning: Applying what we have learned to improve practice. *Teachers College Record, 105,* 261–277.

Foster, M., Lewis, J., and Onafowora L. (2005). Grooming great urban teachers. *Educational Leadership, 62,* 28–32.

Frankenberg, E., Lee, C., and Orfield, G. (2003). A multiracial society with segregated schools: Are we losing the dream? Retrieved February 19, 2007 from The Civil Rights Project, Harvard University website, www.civilrightsproject.harvard.edu/research/reseg03/reseg03_full.php.

Galassi, J. P. and Akos, P. (2004). Developmental advocacy: The twenty-first century school counselor. *Journal of Counseling and Development, 82,* 146–157.

Garrahy, D.A. (2001). Three third-grade teachers' gender-related beliefs and behavior. *The Elementary School Journal, 102,* 81–94.

Grant, C. A. (2006). Multiculturalism, race, and the public interest: Hanging on to great-great-grandaddy's legacy. In G. Ladson-Billings, and W. F. Tate (Eds.), *Education research in the public interest* (pp. 158–172). New York: Teachers College Press.

Grigg, W., Donahue, P., and Dion, G. (2007). *The Nation's Report Card: 12th-Grade Reading and Mathematics 2005* (NCES 2007.468). U.S. Department of Education, National Center for Education Statistics. Washington, DC: U.S. Government Printing Office.

Gysbers, N. C. (2004). Comprehensive guidance and counseling programs: The evolution of accountability. *Professional School Counseling, 8,* 1–14.

Gysbers, N. C. and Henderson, P. (2000). *Developing and managing your school guidance program* (3rd ed.). Alexandria, VA: American Counseling Association.

Hanushek, E. A., Kain, J. F., and Rivkin, S. G. (2009). New evidence about *Brown v. Board of Education*: The complex effects of school racial composition on achievement. *Journal of Labor Economics, 27*(3), 349–383.

Harley, D. A., Jolivette, K., McCormick, K., and Tice, K. (2002). Race, class, and gender: A constellation of positionalities with implications for counseling. *Multicultural Counseling and Development, 30,* 216–238.

Hatch, T. and Bowers, J. (2002). The block to build on. *ASCA School Counselor, 39,* 12–21.

Heller, M. F. and Firestone, W. A. (1995). Who's in charge here? Sources of leadership for change in eight schools. *Elementary School Journal, 96,* 65–86. doi: 10.1086/461815.

Herr, E. L. (2001). The impact of national policies, economics, and school reform on comprehensive guidance programs. *Professional School Counseling, 4,* 236–245. Retrieved from www.schoolcounselor.org/content.asp?contentid=235.

House, R. M. and Martin, P. J. (1998). Advocating for better futures for all students: A new vision for school counselors. *Education, 119,* 284–291.

Jackson, B. L. and Kelley, C. (2002). Exceptional and innovative programs in educational leadership. *Educational administration quarterly, 38*(2), 192–212.

Kozol, J. (2005). Still separate, still unequal. *Harper's Magazine, 311*(1864), 41–54.

Krumboltz, J. D. and Kolpin, T. G. (2003). Guidance and counseling, school. In J. W. Guthrie (Ed.), *Encyclopedia of Education* (2nd ed., Vol. 3, pp. 975–980). New York: Macmillan.

Lambie, G. W. and Williamson, L. L. (2004). The challenge to change from guidance counseling to professional school counseling: A historical proposition. *Professional School Counseling, 8,* 124–131.

Lamont, M. and Small, M. L. (2006). How culture matters for poverty: Thickening our understanding. *National Poverty Center Working Paper Series.*

Lee, J., Grigg, W., and Dion, G. (2007). *The Nation's Report Card: Mathematics 2007* (NCES 2007–494). National Center for Education Statistics, Institute of Education Sciences, U.S. Department of Education, Washington, D.C. Retrieved November 4, 2007 from nces.ed.gov/nationsreportcard/pdf/main2007/2007494.pdf.

Lee, J., Grigg, W., and Donahue, P. (2007). *The Nation's Report Card: Reading 2007* (NCES 2007-496). National Center for Education Statistics, Institute of Education Sciences, U.S. Department of Education, Washington, D.C. Retrieved October 17, 2007 from nces.ed.gov/nationsreportcard/pdf/main2007/2007496.pdf.

Lefever-Davis, S., Johnson, C., and Pearman, C. (2007). Two sides of a partnership: egalitarianism and empowerment in school-university partnerships. *The Journal of Educational Research, 100(4)*, 204–211.

Martin, P. J. (2002). Transforming school counseling: A national perspective. *Theory to Practice, 41*, 148–153.

McMahon, H. G., Mason, E. C. M., and Paisley, P. O. (2009). School counselor educator as educational leaders promoting systemic change. *Professional School Counseling, 13*, 116–124. doi:10.5330/PSC.n.2010-13.116.

McMahon, T., Ward, N. L., Pruett, M. K., Davidson, L., and Griffith, E. H. (2000). Building full-service schools: Lessons learned in the development of interagency collaborations. *Journal of Educational and Psychological Consultation, 11*, 65–92.

Monteiro-Leitner, J., Asner-Self, K. K., Milde, C., Leitner, D. W., and Skelton, D. (2006). The role of the rural school counselor: Counselor, counselor-in-training, and principal perceptions. *Professional School Counseling, 9(3)*, 248–251.

Mullis, R. L. and Chapman, P. (2000). Age, gender, and self-esteem differences in adolescent coping styles. *Journal of Social Psychology, 140*, 539–541.

Myrick, R. D. (2003). *Developmental guidance and counseling: A practical approach* (4th ed.). Minneapolis, MN: Educational Media Corporation.

National Center for Children in Poverty. (2006). *Basic facts about low-income children: Birth to age 18*. Retrieved from the National Center for Children in Poverty website: www. nccp.org/pub_lic06b.html.

National Center for Education Statistics. (2003). *The condition of education 2003* (NCES 2003-067). Washington, DC: Author.

Niebuhr, K. E., Niebuhr, R. E., and Cleveland, W. T. (1999). Principal and counselor collaboration. *Education, 119*, 674–678.

Noguera, P. A. (2001). Transforming urban schools through investments in the social capital of parents. *Social capital and poor communities*, 189–212.

Ojeda, K., West-Olatunji, C., Wolfgang, J., and Varney, M. (2014). Parenting practices articulated by a Latina parent that relate to her children's academic success. *Journal of Undergraduate Research, 15(2)*, 1–5. Retrieved August 14, 2014, from ufdc.ufl.edu/UF00091523/00694.

Pedersen, P. B. and Carey, J. C. (Eds.). (2003). *Multicultural counseling in schools: A practical handbook* (2nd Ed.). Boston: Allyn and Bacon.

Perusse, R., Goodnough, G. E., Donegan, J., and Jones, C. (2004). Perceptions of school counselors and school principals about the national standards for school counseling programs and the transforming school counseling initiative. *Professional School Counseling, 7*, 152–161.

Peske, H. and Haycock, K. (2006). *Teaching inequality: How poor and minority students are shortchanged on teacher quality*. Washington, DC: The Education Trust.

Ribak-Rosenthal, N. (1994). Reasons individuals become school administrators, school counselors, and teachers. *The School Counselor, 41*, 158–164.

Schmidt, J. J. (1999). *Counseling in schools: Essential services and comprehensive programs* (3rd ed.). Boston: Allyn and Bacon.

Segal, E. A. (2007). Social empathy: A tool to address the contradiction of working but still poor. *Families in Society: The Journal of Contemporary Social Services, 88*, 333–337.

Skiba, R. J., Michael, R. S., Nardo, A. C., and Peterson, R. L. (2002). The color of discipline: Sources of racial and gender disproportionality in school punishment. *The Urban Review, 34*, 317–342.

Smith, C. U. (2005). Observing the fiftieth anniversary of the 1954 United States Supreme Court school desegregation decision in *Brown v the Board of Education of Topeka, Kansas. Negro Educational Review, 56(1)*, 19–32.

Spillane, J. P., Halverson, R., and Diamond, J. B. (2004). Towards a theory of leadership practice: a distributed perspective. *Journal of Curriculum Studies, 1*, 3–34. Retrieved from www.eric.ed.gov.

Stone, C. B. and Clark, M. A. (2001). School counselors and principals: Partners in support of academic achievement. *National Association of Secondary School Principals Bulletin, 85*, 46–53.

Theoharis, G. (2008). Woven in Deeply Identity and Leadership of Urban Social Justice Principals. *Education and Urban Society, 41(1)*, 3–25.

Thomas, J. and Brady, K. (2005). The Elementary and Secondary Education Act at 40: Equity, Accountability, and Evolving Federal Role in Public Education. *Review of Research in Education, 29*, 51–67.

Tillman, L. (2005). Mentoring new teachers: Implications for leadership practice in an urban school. *Educational Administration Quarterly, 41(4)*, 609–629.

Trachtman, R. (2007). Inquiry and accountability in professional development schools. *Journal of Educational Research, 100,* 197–203.

U.S. Department of Education, National Center for Education Statistics. (2006). *The Condition of Education 2006,* NCES 2006-071, Washington, DC: U.S. Government Printing Office. Retrieved August 14, 2014, from nces.ed.gov/pubs2006/2006071.pdf.

U.S. Department of Education, National Center for Education Statistics. (2007). *The Condition of Education 2007* (NCES 2007-064). Washington, DC: U.S. Government Printing Office. Retrieved November 4, 2007, from nces.ed.gov/pubs2007/2007064.pdf.

U.S. Department of Education, Office of Special Education (2006). 26th annual report to Congress on the implementation of the Individuals with Disabilities Education Act, 2004. Washington, DC: Westat. Retrieved August 14, 2014 from www2.ed.gov/about/reports/annual/osep/2004/index.html.

West-Olatunji, C. (2012). Equal Access, Unequal resources: Appreciating cultural, social, and economic diversity in families. In E. Amatea, *Building culturally responsive family-school partnerships* (2nd ed., pp. 143–166). Upper Saddle River, NJ: Pearson.

West-Olatunji, C. and Behar-Horenstein, L. (2005). *Teaching and learning in fact-based pedagogy.* (ASCD), Alexandria, VA: Association for Supervision and Curriculum Development.

West-Olatunji, C., Frazier, K. N., Baker, J., Garrett, M. (2014). Using a rite of passage program to address the overrepresentation of African American boys in special education. In M. Garrett (Ed.), *Youth and adversity: Psychology and influences of child and adolescent resilience and coping* (pp. 263–276). New York: Nova Publishers.

West-Olatunji, C., Frazier, K. N., and Kelley, E. (2011). Wraparound counseling as a systemic intervention tool in school communities with non-symptomatic and symptomatic children. *Journal of Humanistic Counseling, Education and Development, 50,* 222–237.

West-Olatunji, C., Sanders, T., Mehta, S., and Behar-Horenstein, L. (2010). Parenting practices among low-income parents/guardians of academically successful fifth grade African American children. *Multicultural Perspectives, 12,* 138–144.

West-Olatunji, C., Shure, L., Pringle, R., Adams, T. L., Lewis, D. R., and Cholewa, B. (2010). Exploring how school counselors position low-income African American girls as mathematics and science learners. *Professional School Counseling, 13,* 184–195.

West-Olatunji, C. A. and Watson, Z. E. (1999). Community-as-client mental health needs assess- ment: Use of culture-centered theory and research. *The Community Psychologist, 2,* 36–38.

Wingfield, R., Reese, R., and West-Olatunji, C. (2010). Counselors as leaders. *Florida Journal of Educational Administration and Policy, 4*(1), 114–130. Retrieved August 14, 2014, from education.ufl.edu/fjeap/files/2011/01/FJEAP_2010 Fall_Winter_Wingfield_Reese_WestOlatunji.pdf.

Wittmer, J. (2000). Section one: Developmental school counseling: History, reconceptualization, and implantation strategies. In J. Witter (Ed.), *Managing your school counseling program: K–12 developmental strategies* (2nd ed., pp. 1–34). Minneapolis, MN: Educational Media.

Worzbyt, J.C. and Zook, T. (1992). Counselors who make a difference: Small schools and rural settings. *The School Counselor, 39,* 344–350.

CHAPTER 39

Principal Professional Identity and the Cultivation of Trust in Urban Schools

Rodney S. Whiteman, Samantha Paredes Scribner, and Gary M. Crow

Urban schools are under significant pressure to change. Pressures to reduce dropout rates and improve student achievement, increase graduation and college eligibility rates, and revamp curricular offerings have intensified amid threats of closure, state takeover, and competition for enrollments created by school choice policies. Add to these, state and federal policies inducing teacher merit pay and effectiveness measures, and budget cuts that have significantly hampered district financing, urban schools (and many other schools) face increased uncertainty and instability. The intensification of such vulnerability and uncertainty produce a context within which teachers and principals make decisions that are more or less risky—and can enhance or compromise their trust in each other.

This chapter examines trust amid the diverse urban settings in which vulnerabilities figure heavily into the daily operation of schools. We use professional identity as a lens through which we examine the salience of threats and risks that reflect vulnerabilities in these settings. Specifically, we develop a conceptual exploration of how principals' professional identities influence the cultivation of trust in the context of relationships between principals and teachers, given uncertainties related to major reform, accountability policies, threats of school closure, and students and families who navigate stressful living conditions associated with poverty.

The chapter begins with a review of the three major bodies of literature, professional identities, trust, and elements of contemporary urban school settings, which inform our conceptual discussion and formulations of how identity is a lens for understanding and cultivating school trust. We next present this formulation of the interaction between professional identity and trust, considering three specific elements of trust and the role of emotions in the identity-trust relationship. We end the chapter with a discussion of the implications for practice, preparation, and future research.

LITERATURE REVIEW

Three primary bodies of literature inform our conceptual formulation of how identity provides a lens for understanding and cultivating trust in diverse, urban school settings: professional identity, trust, and features of contemporary urban school contexts.

Professional Identity

Literature from social psychology, sociology, and education (Burke and Stets, 2009; Day and Leithwood, 2007; Gee, 2001; Stryker and Burke, 2000) suggests the importance of and nature of professional identity that are useful for understanding how principals make sense of their roles and position themselves in response to the demands and vulnerabilities of their urban setting. Role or professional identity "is the internalized meanings of a role that individuals apply to themselves" (Burke and Stets, 2009, p. 114). This definition highlights the fact that roles and identities are not synonymous. According to Ryan (2007), roles tend to be scripted, deterministic, and static, but identities are more improvisational, emphasize human agency, and are dynamic. He noted that frequently "people take on different and sometimes contradictory identities in different social contexts" (p. 345). In this particular case, we examine urban school settings in which relationships, especially those involving trust, are critical and potentially problematic, given varied and sometimes contradictory pressures and vulnerabilities amid often volatile political dynamics.

The exploration and use of professional identities as a lens for understanding principals' roles are important because of the relationship between identity and practice. "An identity is the set of meanings that define who one is when one is an occupant of a particular role in society, a member of a particular group, or claims particular characteristics that identify him or her as a unique person" (Burke and Stets, 2009, p. 3). This sense-making function of identity allows us to organize and direct our practices. Wenger (1998) referred to identity as developing out of our "lived experience" within a community. "Identity is not merely a category, a personality trait, a role, or a label; it is more fundamentally an experience that involves participation and reification" (p. 163). Identity is not a label we or others place on us, for example, an instructional leader. Rather it shapes and molds our practices. Identity also provides the motivation for our actions in the role. "The energy, motivation, drive that makes roles actually work require that individuals identify with, internalize, and become the role" (Burke and Stets, 2009, p. 38). The sense making, participation, and motivation necessary to perform the work of urban principals is embedded in relationships—in communities of practice—in which trust becomes enhanced or diminished.

Professional identities, as described in the literature, have several elements; they are dynamic, multiple, socially negotiated, contextual, and developmental. In contrast to the notion of a single self-concept, identities are not static. Rather they change as the context, role expectations, and individual change. For example, several researchers have noted how the role of principal has changed in the last twenty years (Goldring and Schuermann, 2009; Young et al., 2009). Such change creates the need for different ways to make sense of the job, respond to others, and motivate practice. However, as Burke and Stets (2009) noted, identity is not in constant flux. Because there is some degree of constancy in social groups, individuals tend to lean toward focus rather than fragmentation.

Principals manage multiple identities to respond to the role expectations of different school constituents, i.e., they engage in impression management (Goffman, 1959). Urban schools are nested within an environment in which multiple stakeholders become important. Obviously, students, their families, teachers, district administrators, community leaders, and state and federal policymakers influence the role expectations of principals. Moreover, these groups are not necessarily uniform in their expectations and influences. As Møller (2005) noted, these cultural and political influences impact identities. One implication of this is that some identities become more salient than others. These multiple identities complicate the principal's identity formation due to the need to negotiate with multiple audiences and stakeholders—a negotiation based on the need for trust-building.

Professional identities are socially negotiated with the audiences whom one encounters. Identity can only be understood within a cultural practice (Wenger, 1998). Møller (2005) further developed this perspective by explaining, "We define who we are within the activities and institutions and we negotiate who we are" (p. 43). Møller acknowledged that the negotiation processes are not exclusively cognitive but also involve the emotional and political, as individuals negotiate issues of power. Thus, a school principal has specific images of the job, which may challenge the expectations of teachers. These reciprocal social, cultural, emotional, and political processes result in some identities being confirmed, while others are rejected or perhaps revised—a process Burke and Stets (1999) refer to as identity verification. Confirming, rejecting, or revising identities may relate to the development and/or denial of trust (Burke and Stets, 1999). This social negotiation, however, involves a reciprocal relationship. A principal's identities are not merely a reflection of constituent demands or interests but also involve the active reflection, exploration, and commitment of the individual principal to a set of identities.

Negotiation of identity is understood within contexts in which the identities are relevant. Smulyan (2000) categorized four types of contexts: personal (family and educational background); community (teachers and families served by school); institutional (positions of power and structural regularities that influence principal's actions); and the historical and social context (larger patterns, hierarchies, and norms). Although our analysis of trust through the lens of identity will focus primarily on the community contexts, in which the principal's relationship with teachers is most salient, these other contexts influence the negotiation of identities through the principal's personal and cultural background, the larger district and community partners, and the social forces emphasizing reform. These identity contexts can introduce vulnerabilities that complicate the job of principal in various ways. For example, diverse urban communities can produce contradictory expectations of the principal, thereby creating vulnerabilities in how different stakeholders view the principal and his/her identities. A principal's response to such situations involves interactions with others that involve the negotiation of identities. This process presents its own vulnerable positions, since in negotiating identities with others, a principal risks the possibility that these others may reject the identity(ies) s/he is enacting. We argue that the affirmation or rejection of identities in interactions with teachers is central to the process of negotiation that contributes to (or detracts from) the cultivation of trust within these relationships.

A final element of professional identities is that their construction is developmental. Researchers have noted that this identity construction involves a kind of learning trajectory in which identities are adjusted, revised, eliminated, etc. (Møller, 2005; Ryan, 2007). Wenger (1998, p. 154) referred to this process as one in which individual identities are constantly becoming. Møller (2005) reflected this process when she said, "Identity is temporally constructed in the process of shaping a learning trajectory consisting of both convergent and divergent trajectories . . . It is not like a path that can be charted or foreseen. It is like a continuous motion—one that has a momentum of its own, but also opens to a field of influence" (p. 43). For urban principals, this "becoming" can be complex and intense as reform agendas, environmental pressures, and other changes occur in a context in which trust becomes essential.

Burke and Stets (2009, pp. 180–186) listed four sources of change: change in situation, identity conflicts, identity standard and behavior conflicts, and negotiation and the presence of others. For urban principals any of these sources are possible. For example, an urban principal's identity may change in response to new accountability reforms from the state or changing neighborhood power relationships. Trust becomes critical in each of these as the principal shields teachers from unwarranted intrusions into their teaching practices (Scribner and Crow, 2012) or maintains openness with different neighborhood power blocs.

Trust

Diverse organizations dependent upon teamwork and participative decision-making are increasingly dependent upon trust as a resource (Mayer, Davis, and Schoorman, 1995). Schools, particularly urban schools, are diverse organizations. Consequently, they introduce the possibility that participants do not share personal and cultural experiences that "contribute to mutual attraction and enhance the willingness to work together" (Mayer et al., 1995, p. 710). Yet, trust has been identified as an important factor linked to school effectiveness (Bryk and Schneider, 2002; Forsyth, Adams, and Hoy, 2011).

There is an extensive and diverse literature on trust (Lewicki and Bunker, 1996). Here we highlight the disciplinary perspective that informs this chapter. We begin by exploring various definitions and constructs of trust and their theorized antecedents. Finally, we will begin to construct a framework that links trust to meaning- and sense-making in professional identities and identity negotiation.

Definitions of trust. As implied above, different disciplinary perspectives lend themselves to distinct, yet overlapping definitions and conceptions of trust. Lewicki and Bunker (1995, 1996) citing Worchel (1979) suggest a typology that can help organize the diverse literature: views of personality theorists, views of sociologists and economists, and views of social psychologists (Lewicki and Bunker, 1996, pp. 115–116). In this typology, personality theorists tend to view trust as a belief or feeling connected to personality and psychosocial development. Sociologists and economists view trust as an institutional phenomenon in which individuals trust within and across institutions or trust the institutions themselves. Social psychologists focus on interpersonal relationships and the interactions that produce or erode trust. In this perspective, "trust can be defined as the expectation of the other party in a transaction, the risks associated with assuming and acting on such expectations, and the contextual factors that serve to either enhance or inhibit the development and maintenance of that trust" (Lewicki and Bunker, 1996, p. 116). In this chapter, we embrace the social psychologist perspective and use it as a lens to illumine the relationship between professional identity and trust.

Even within this social psychologist perspective, variations on how trust is conceptualized exist. For example, Bryk and Schneider (2002) emphasize *relational trust*. Relational trust emerges from social exchanges organized around role relationships (p. 20). Teachers interact with students, with other teachers, with principals, with parents, etc. Of course, individuals inhabiting those other roles (student, parent, principal, etc.) all interact with each other, as well. Drawing from a combination of interactions and norms embedded in cultural scripts, individuals develop expectations of behaviors within those roles. A battery of antecedent lenses (respect, competence, personal regard for others, and integrity; see also Mishra, 1996) are applied to interpret the behaviors of individuals inhabiting those roles, thus allowing trust to emerge or be eroded. Bryk and Schneider suggest their framework is applicable at intrapersonal, interpersonal, and organizational levels.

Forsyth and his colleagues (2011) suggest that interpersonal trust, like the Bryk and Schneider model, is insufficient to understand trust in school organizations. They argue for *collective trust*, and distinguish it from interpersonal (i.e., relational) trust by claiming that collective trust is an organizational property that can serve as a predictor for organizational outcomes. They define this property as "a stable group property rooted in the shared perceptions and affect about the trustworthiness of another group or individual that emerges over time out of multiple social exchanges within the group" (p. 22). Perceptions of trustworthiness come from a variety of antecedents (openness, honesty, benevolence, reliability, and competence; see also Tschannen-Moran, 2014) employed to interpret behaviors. Forsyth et al. (see also Tschannen-Moran and Hoy, 1998) have developed scales to measure collective trust, but those scales are based on the relationship between individuals inhabiting specified roles (e.g., student, teacher, parent) and aggregated roles of others (e.g., faculty, the school). So Forsyth et al. are still interested in expected behaviors for organizationally defined roles, just at a different unit of analysis than Bryk and Schneider.

Mayer, Davis, and Schoorman (1995) also examine trust from a social psychological perspective. Their definition of trust is "the willingness of a party to be vulnerable to the actions of another party based on the expectation that the other will perform a particular action important to the trustor, irrespective of the ability to monitor or control that other party" (p. 712). This definition is used as the foundation for a model that emphasizes both the relational aspect of trust, that is the expected behaviors between individuals inhabiting social roles, but also a personality trait of the trustor—a propensity to trust (see also Tschannen-Moran, 2014). Some individuals are just more likely to be trusting of others, influencing their willingness to make themselves vulnerable to others. They theorize that propensity to trust mediates the perceived trustworthiness of an individual and the act of trusting. The definition proposed by Mayer et al. is also useful because it suggests a political element. An individual cannot be forced into a trusting situation. If a principal can force certain actions to occur, then these interactions are based on power, not on trust. Though Mayer et al. do not explicitly connect the trustor's expectations of the trustee's actions in organizationally defined roles, that grounding is implied by situating the trust model within organizational contexts.

Antecedents to trust. As might be expected, different constructs of trust have different ideas of how trust emerges. In their *relational trust* framework, Bryk and Schneider (2002) identify four "lenses" (p. 23) through which individuals observe, interpret, and analyze the actions of others: respect, competence, personal regard for others, and integrity (pp. 23–26). Respect is a fundamental condition for having productive interactions between individuals, and it involves an individual's perception that others recognize that individual's importance in the organization and sincerely listens to the individual. Competence is the individual's perception that others can successfully execute their role responsibilities and are able to meet goals and achieve intended outcomes. Personal regard for others is the individual's perception that others will not take advantage of mutual dependence within organizations and will take actions to reduce the individual's sense of personal vulnerability. Finally integrity is the perception that others have consistency between what they say and what they do.

In their *collective trust* model, Forsyth and his colleagues (2011) identify similar antecedents: benevolence, reliability, competence, honesty, and openness (p. 18–19). These antecedents are criteria used to compare expected and observed behaviors within a set of nested external, internal, and task contexts. Benevolence is the belief that others will act in the individual's best interests. Reliability is the extent to which an individual can predict others' actions to meet the individual's needs. As Forsyth et al. describe it, "reliability implies a sense of confidence that one's needs will be met in positive ways," and that the individual need not "invest energy worrying about whether the person will come through nor make alternative plans" (pp. 18–19). The authors link reliability to benevolence in ways that suggest the two may not be conceptually distinct, as they are mutually reinforcing. Both benevolence and reliability seem to be related to the perception of others' intentions when acting. Competence is the belief that others have the ability to successfully complete tasks. Honesty encompasses character, integrity, and authenticity (p. 19). It is both the belief that others will accept responsibility for their actions, and not distort the truth (Tschannen-Moran and Hoy, 1998), and also the belief that others' words and actions are consistent. Collective trust is dependent upon a sense of openness, the extent to which information is shared and plans are made transparent. In Forsyth et al.'s view, openness creates vulnerabilities.

Mayer et al. (1995) propose three antecedents: ability, benevolence, and integrity. Ability is a combination of skills and characteristics that allow an individual to influence some domain (p. 717). A principal may have the technical skills required for instructional leadership of the faculty, but not the interpersonal skills to communicate with parents and community. So she would be trusted in one domain of the principalship, but perhaps not another. Benevolence is the extent to which an individual believes others want to do good for that individual, beyond those others' own personal gains. For Mayer et al., integrity is "the trustor's perception that the trustee adheres to a set of principles that the trustor finds acceptable" (p. 719). Note that this definition differs from Bryk and Schneider and from Forsyth et al. in that those definitions of integrity focus on correspondence between the trustee's words and deeds, rather than adherence to the trustor's principles. The more flexible definition provided by Mayer and his colleagues injects a conversation about individuals' values into the conversation regarding trust. Given the diverse, dynamic, and often conflictual nature of schools, it is reasonable to assume that value incongruences do exist, and these incongruences likely have an influence on trust.

Synthesis of definitions and antecedents. We focus on the trust construct offered by Mayer et al. (1995), who define trust as "the willingness of a party to be vulnerable to the actions of another party based on the expectation that the other will perform a particular action important to the trustor, irrespective of the ability to monitor or control that other party" (p. 712). This definition has the individual as the level of analysis, it suggests that characteristics of both the trustor and the trustee are related to the act of trusting, it introduces individuals' values, and it suggests that power dynamics influence trust. However, we also emphasize that organizationally constructed roles influence expectations of behaviors (Bryk and Schneider, 2002). When an individual inhabits a principal role, parents, student, teachers, and other administrators have expectations of how that principal should act. Those expectations are based on each individual's history with schools, personal and cultural beliefs connected to family or community of origin, (Bryk and Schneider, 2002, pp. 21–22) and, we will argue, each individual's own identity. Enactment of roles and interpretation of those enactments carry meaning (Mead, 1934), linking expectations and intentionality of trust to the understanding of self and others.

Regarding antecedents, we again borrow from Mayer et al. (1995) who theorized that perceptions of ability, benevolence, and integrity influence the perceived trustworthiness of the trustee, while also mediated by the trustor's own propensity to trust. We find these factors to be flexible enough to describe trustworthiness, while remaining conceptually distinct for purposes of analysis and empirical investigation. Though respect, as Bryk and Schneider (2002) conceptualize it, can be reasonably expected to be an antecedent to trust, the construct is so broad that it may be an antecedent to any number of social phenomena. Furthermore, respect can be included in the Mayer et al. concept of integrity, as the trustor's perception that the trustee treats her with respect arguably is one of the trustor's principles.

Trust in context. It is important to note that these trusting relationships are interpersonal, but they exist within various nested contexts. These are task, internal, and environmental contexts (Forsyth et al., 2011, p. 24). The task context is a set of constraints inherent in an individual or group's specialties. We might compare this to various domains within the assessment of ability (Mayer et al., 1995). Certain tasks require certain skills to complete, and different individuals can be positioned to be successful or unsuccessful based on the matching of task requirements and the individual's ability (Mayer et al., 1995). We contend that professional identity influences both task definition, via a sense-making process (Weick, 1995), and the repertoire of skills and dispositions brought to bear on the task. The internal context is a set of intra-organizational conditions, such as structure or culture, that influence definition of roles, and expected behaviors within those roles. Roles may be structurally defined, but interpretation of those roles and how those roles are enacted are socially and culturally defined. We contend that professional identity influences how individuals understand their roles, and thus, how they enact them. Finally, the external context includes all extra-organizational influences (e.g., laws and regulations, culture, personal histories outside of the specific organization's context, etc.) on attitudes, beliefs, and expectations of group members.

The introduction of these various contexts is important. The social situation and the nature of the risk being assumed inform the trajectory of trusting relationships (Cook, 2005; Hardin, 2002, 2006). We trust each other in different situations, depending on the unique influences defining that situation in space and time. Trust placed in context may be formulated as "actor A trusts actor B with respect to x in situation S" (Cook, 2005, p. 9).

Trust, risk, and vulnerability. Risk is a central theme in the social psychologist view of trust (Lewicki and Bunker, 1996). Trust emerges as confidence in the face of risk (Lewis and Weigert, 1985) and the willingness to be vulnerable to others (Mishra, 1996; Tschannen-Moran, 2014; Tschannen-Moran and Hoy, 1998). Indeed, without risk of suffering some kind of loss in a relationship, the concept of trust becomes pointless (Hardin, 2006). However, in the interactionist-focused framework we employ, risk is more than the willingness to be vulnerable; it is the actual *behavioral manifestation* of the willingness to be vulnerable" (Mayer et al., 1995, p. 724). A cannot be said to trust B if A never puts herself in a position of vulnerability to B. So risk-taking behavior is an outcome of trust, and the trustor's perceived outcomes of the risk-taking behavior feedback into the perceived trustworthiness of the trustee.

However, all social interactions involve some amount of risk of vulnerability, particularly emotional vulnerability. Enactment of social or professional roles is a presentation of identity, and identities can be verified or challenged by others. Challenging or rejecting particularly important identities results in negative emotions

(Burke and Stets, 2009; McCall and Simmons, 1978). Furthermore, meeting expectations in organizationally defined roles makes individuals feel good about themselves, and others feel good about them (Stryker, 2004). Indeed, meeting role expectations in organizational settings is consistent with the model of trust we propose here. A school principal whose behaviors are consistent with expected behaviors is perceived to be trustworthy.

Contemporary Urban School Contexts

Schools situated in urban contexts face a number of factors that enhance the vulnerability and the risks perceived and experienced by their constituents. Organizational complexity, policy and politics, and a multiplicity of institutional, community, and individual histories intertwine to produce uncertain and threatening environments for leaders, teachers, students, and families. As such, the negotiation of trust and professional identity becomes critical to understanding urban school leadership. The propensity to trust and the assessment of competence, benevolence, and integrity are very likely influenced by contextual characteristics that tend to be concentrated in urban spaces.

First, urban schools are situated in spaces characterized by intersecting histories of racial and ethnic difference and discrimination. Media representations of urban schools as violent, unsafe places have resulted in increased use of surveillance technologies, security guards, and disciplinary policies (Fine et al., 2003). Zero-tolerance policies are linked to the funneling of students into juvenile justice systems via a school-to-prison pipeline, further casting urban youth, particularly youth of color as "untrustworthy, suspicious, and potential criminals" (Fine et al., 2003, p. 144). Urban schools, thus, become constructed as dangerous spaces requiring surveillance in need of structure, surveillance, and civility (Vasquez Heilig, Khalifa, and Tillman, 2014). These and other "micro-aggressions" aimed at youth and adults of color accumulate in a school community, and urban educators and scholars are remiss to assume that best intentions are informed or attuned to these dynamics. The situation is made worse by the cultural and ethnic mismatch between urban educators, who are majority white, and their students of color, often resulting in deficit views of these students and their families (Flessa, 2009). The ways racism can influence constructions (and assessments) of integrity, benevolence and competence—i.e., the propensity to trust (students, teachers, parents, or administrators) must be central to any discussion of cultivating trust and developing professional identity in an urban school setting.

Scholars in education have long argued that the normalizing of racism is a mechanism by which claims of racism can be perpetually denied, diminished, or resisted by those who benefit from its effects (Ladson-Billings, 2014; Ladson-Billings and Tate IV, 1995). Without accounting for the counter stories of students, families, educators, and scholars of color, as well as critical white practitioners and scholars, urban leaders cannot accurately assess their own and others' positions in these narratives/counter-narratives associated with urban school life or the related vulnerabilities in the context of forging authentic trusting cross-cultural relationships in these settings. One cannot separate the mechanisms by which racism is perpetrated and the voices *and* identities of those who suffer its consequences.

Add to these dynamics, high-stakes accountability policy and its application in urban settings through school closures and turnarounds. Urban schools often respond to this press by narrowing curricula and delegitimizing knowledge and competencies that are not part of the official standardized curriculum, thereby invalidating knowledge indigenous to communities from which students come to school (Khalifa, 2010). At the same time, turnover and turnaround practices cause turbulence within schools and neighborhoods. School closures, staff reconstitution, and student mobility fueled by market-based reforms and open enrollment policies that are increasingly prevalent in urban centers create uncertainty and introduce threats to professional staff, increasing vulnerabilities and contributing to adversarial relations between and among teachers and administrators. In addition, in many urban centers, the stakeholders have multiplied to include representatives from sectors including social and human services, private corporations, faith-based organizations and other nonprofits, and education management organizations, among others. The vast array of interests and agendas can also complicate propensities to trust and the constant reevaluation of one's assessment of competence, benevolence and integrity—as well as their own vulnerability. Urban schools are complex places in which

policies, organizations, histories, and cultures intersect, complicating the negotiation of authentic relations among multiple constituents (Scribner, 2013). The examples discussed in this section highlight some salient dynamics common in urban schools that make the cultivation of trust, as informed by leaders' professional identities, a complex endeavor with ethical, political, and organizational implications.

IDENTITY AND TRUST: A CONCEPTUAL FORMULATION

Burke and Stets (1999, 2009) explain that trust emerges from iterations of identity verification; yet they do not explicate trust, nor do they refer to any construct of trust. Instead, they simply link trust to social exchange theories (i.e., Lawler and Yoon, 1996). We agree that trust emerges from identity verification, but we hope to connect the trust construct developed by Mayer et al. to identity theory. We do this by applying identity theory to three components of Mayer and his colleagues' model: perception of trustworthiness, propensity to trust, and assessment of outcomes. In this framework, both the trustor and the trustee bring their identities into the social exchange that may or may not yield trust. We will then consider the role that emotion plays in our conceptual formulation.

Trustworthiness. Recall that trustworthiness is an appraisal of the trustee's ability, benevolence, and integrity. When inhabiting a social role, like a school principal, the inhabitant makes sense and meaning of the role by using her or his identity as an interpretive lens. If a social situation carries signals that are interpreted through a father identity, then a principal may make sense of the situation as a father might, and thus inhabit the principal role by acting in ways a father might. These actions are perceived and interpreted by the trustor, who may accept or reject them. Acceptance signals verification. Trust emerges when the identities a trustee carries influence the trustee's actions in social situation, and when those identities lead the trustee to act with what the trustor perceives as desirable ability, benevolence, and integrity. If, in the example above, the principal acts in ways a father might, but the trustor determines the actions taken draw on the wrong skill set (calling ability into question), are actually harmful to the trustor (calling benevolence into question), and/

or may be paternalistic and inconsistent with her values (calling integrity into question), then the trustor may reject those actions, thus the father identity in that situation, and trust will not be formed.

Note in the brief example above, the trustor's identity is part of the social interaction. The teacher interprets the principal's actions through her own socially constructed identity. This teacher's willingness to accept or reject the principal-as-father interaction is dependent upon her own identity and willingness to be positioned in relation to the principal's father identity (Harré and Langenhove, 1999). A teacher may positively respond to a paternal principal-as-father if she feels it makes sense of her own professional role as a daughter seeking the wisdom of a father; she may negatively respond if her role includes rejecting all forms of paternalism. However, influencing perceptions of the potential trustee is not the only way in which identity influences trusting. As we will see, it also influences a general willingness, or propensity to trust.

Propensity to trust. An individual's identity is shaped by interactions with cultural, social, and personal contexts. These contexts correspond to the propensity to trust, as conceptualized in the Mayer et al. (1995) trust model. In that model, the propensity to trust is a general willingness to trust others prior to having an opportunity to perceive others' trustworthiness. Such a propensity is shaped by individuals' different cultural backgrounds, developmental experiences, and personality types (Mayer et al., 1995, p. 715, citing Hofstede, 1980). Though Mayer and his colleagues mention these three influences on the propensity to trust, they do not explain exactly why culture, socialization, and personality are influences. In our view, identity theory provides an explanation.

As stated before, identity is closely linked to ways in which we interpret the world, and that interpretation is co-constructed and intersubjective. Furthermore, that interpretive scheme involves communicatively differentiated cultural, social, and personality structures (Habermas, 1984, 1987). These structures inform identity; and meaningful communicative expressions include identity claims (Carspecken, 2003). As humans, we have a desire to have our inner selves recognized. So when one expresses identity, one is not only making a claim about the world but also is making a claim to existential needs (Carspecken, 2003).

An individual may make explicit identity claims about his or her propensity to trust. For example, she may claim in conversation that she is generally a trusting person, or generally not a trusting person. However, identity claims are often expressed much more covertly through communicative interactions (Carspecken, 1996, 2003). It seems likely then that propensity to trust, informed by culture, society, and personality, is often expressed through covert identity claims.

An example of an identity claim can help illustrate the link between identity and propensity to trust. Suppose a veteran teacher is talking to her colleagues about a new principal assigned to her school. She may quip, "I'm like Reagan with Gorbachev . . . trust but verify." Such a claim is a symbolic expression about the teacher's general willingness to trust a new principal before having a chance to see the principal in action. The identity claim and its embedded meaning is, "As a teacher, I am cautious of new administrators." Such a claim is built on the teacher's own cultural background, social development, and/or personality. Perhaps the teacher and principal come from different cultural backgrounds, and the teacher's cultural background leads her to be cautions in trusting administrators from a different background. Perhaps the teacher has been "burned" by trusting administrators of all manner of cultural backgrounds throughout her career, prompting her to shape her identity as a teacher around her perceived general untrustworthiness of all administrators. Or perhaps the teacher has a particular dimension of her personality, such as a level of agreeableness,[1] that may lead her to be hesitant to trust a new acquaintance or colleague in any situation.

The question of source of the propensity to trust is ultimately an empirical one, and a researcher would have to meet the methodological challenge of gaining access to the cultural, social, and personality aspects of the teacher's identity shaping that propensity to trust.

Assessment of outcomes. Trust involves taking risks in relationships. After committing to an act of trust, the trustor is then subject to the outcomes of that risk. As Mayer et al. (1995) suggest, these outcomes feedback into the trustor's perceptions of the trustee's trustworthiness. However, not everyone observing the outcomes of a trusting act would necessarily interpret those outcomes in the same way. We argue that identity, an expression of the self that includes cultural, social, and personality structures is linked to the interpretation and assessment of these outcomes through a process of sense-making (Weick, 2005).

Interpreting others' actions as outcomes of social exchanges is, broadly speaking, sense-making. Weick (2005) cites several scholars who refer to this process as putting observations into a frame of reference (Cantril, 1941), thus allowing them to "comprehend, understand, explain, attribute, extrapolate, and predict" (Starbuck and Milliken, 1988, p. 51, as cited in Weick, 2005, p. 4). Weick further explains that sense-making is grounded in identity construction, is retrospective, is enactive of sensible environments, is social, ongoing, focused on and by extracted cues, and is driven by plausibility rather than accuracy (p. 17).

The identity component of sense-making is key. Recall that identity is a means of interpreting the social world and understanding our place in it. This happens, as Burke and Stets (2009) explain, when perceptions of the social world are compared to an internalized referent attached to identity. Identity, then, functions as a lens "through which various kinds of information pass and take on meaning" (Smith, 2011, p. 62). An individual makes sense of the social world, the interactions within it, and the outcomes of those interactions by asking himself or herself what the implications have for who the individual is and who the individual wants to be (Weick, 2005, pp. 23–24).

An example may be illustrative of this point. Consider a young, female teacher who is having periodic difficulties managing the males in her tenth grade English class. One day, a male student walks up to the teacher and places his hand on her backside. The teacher is shocked and does not know how to handle this situation. She turns to her principal for guidance. Her principal, a male, can respond in many ways. He chooses to respond by pulling the student out into the hall and yelling at him for disrespecting a woman, that men shouldn't treat women in this way, and asked how the student would feel if he had a daughter that was treated how the student treated his teacher. Note that the teacher, turning to the principal for help, was acting in trust that the principal had the ability, benevolence, and integrity (i.e., was trustworthy) to respond in a way that the teacher would find appropriate. As a young female professional (all intersecting identity claims forming her understanding of herself as an educator), the teacher

observed the outcomes of that trust, and interpreted the outcome as paternalistic and further disrespecting her. The principal acted in a manner expressive of a "father" identity. However, as a novice educator who may face such challenges in the future, the teacher really wanted a response steeped in instructional leadership, in the principal's experience as a successful classroom teacher with excellent classroom management skills. She expected coaching and guidance but got paternalistic protection instead. In the future, the teacher may not trust the principal with similar situations because she now thinks he lacks the integrity and benevolence to act in a way that cares for her as a professional or from a set of values she holds.

It is also important to note that taking risks to trust others is a means of better understanding ourselves. As Weick (2005) explains, "people learn about their identities by projecting them into an environment and observing the consequences" (p. 23). Identity claims linked to being a trusting person, at least a trusting person of certain others in certain contexts, are developed by how the trustor perceives outcomes as care or betrayal of that trust. Betrayal may be emotionally painful, but we learn about ourselves through that process.

The role of emotion. Thus far, we have described our conceptual framework as if determining trustworthiness and evaluating outcomes of trust enactment is a kind of rational calculus in which individuals are completely self-aware of their identities and the role these identities play in guiding actions and interpretations within the social world. This is not the case. Here we wish to explore the role of affect and emotion in the development and maintenance of trust.

Emotions play a critical role in the construction of identity in part because the personal, professional, and situational dimensions of work are linked (Day et al., 2007). The role of principal in urban school settings clearly involves emotional investments. Policy changes that disrupt the way principals have come to view themselves, the intensity of the job created by major events that influence the everyday school life of teachers, students, parents, and administrators, and the possibilities of failure increased by factors not always under the principal's control create vulnerabilities with emotional consequences. These consequences influence the identity verification process and thereby the antecedents of trust, the propensity to trust, and the outcomes of trust.

Solomon (2005), in his discussion of leadership ethics and emotional integrity, argues that definitions of trust relying primarily on "expectations" are insufficient.

> Trust also involves decisions and the dynamics of a relationship. Trust involves self-confidence and a judicious balance between suspicion and trust, and no doubt other emotions too. Trust entails not only a risk but also a "leap of faith," and this involves all of those emotions having to do with courage, possibly friendship, and good management. (p. 41)

Trust (or distrust) can reveal itself in various emotions, as in the cases of betrayal, through fear, suspicion, anger, or resentment. In the positive manifestation, one may feel comfort, openness, or emotionally relaxed in the context of a relationship. In this way, "[t]rust is the framework within which emotions appear, their precondition, the structure of the world they operate" (Solomon, 2005, p. 42).

> Emotions are a systemic set of judgments, and trust, by way of this perspective, is a certain *conception* of the world and other people. It is a way of seeing, a way of estimating and valuing. Trust establishes a framework for expectations and agreements (explicit or not) in which actions conform or fail to conform. (p. 42)

One's "conception of the world" does not emerge out of thin air, of course. It is constructed throughout one's personal and social history and with cultural resources drawn from experiences in and around institutions. If, as Solomon argues, trust is "the structure of the world in which [emotions] operate" (p. 42), then propensity to trust is necessarily informed by one's cultural, social and political histories—histories that influence one's interpretations and expectations of situations, institutions, and individuals. These are both personal and shared histories that are invoked, revised, and retold in conversations with others in ways that constitute (and sometimes challenge) identities. Thus, the relationship between identity and trust rests in emotions that infuse interactions and relationships.

Identity verification occurs through a set of judgments that inform propensity to trust, the decision to give trust, and the parameters within which that trust is given. These judgments are influenced by contextual factors and emotions that manifest in the negotiation of these factors—whether it be fear, courage, vulnerability, safety, indignation, etc. The manifestation of these emotions both draws from and feeds one's view of oneself in a given situation, whereby identity(ies) become a lens through which the conception of the world is viewed, and the assessment of risk is filtered through the emotions that are most salient.

Take the case of a school official interacting with an undocumented child. The school official may view the child as "good student," even as "good Latino student." However, due to the local political context, the child's family history, and recent events resulting in a parent being detained and the threat of family separation and an increasingly hostile community environment, the child's citizenship status and the fear and trauma of family separation trump his view of himself as "good student," and inform his decision *not* to share information with the school official when asked. For him, at this particular point, membership in a tightly knit, Spanish-speaking network of supportive family and community members trumps his membership in the school community. A school official who does not understand the complex framework from which families make judgments about trusting school officials and institutions fails to recognize the overlapping spheres within which identities intersect and trust can be cultivated. On the other hand, a school official who encounters such a situation and can *trust* that the student's judgment to distrust is warranted may be more a promising act of *seeing* the student (or parent, teacher, community member, etc.) and cultivating trust in the long run.

IMPLICATIONS FOR PRACTICE, PREPARATION, AND FUTURE RESEARCH

Previously in this chapter we emphasized the pressure and vulnerabilities of urban school settings and the importance of building and maintaining trust in these contexts. The role of identities in developing this trust raises important implications for practice, leader preparation, and future research.

Implications for Practice

Our framework for understanding the relationship between the principal's identities and the cultivation of trust emphasizes the importance of critical reflection in the everyday practice of school leaders and staff. This reflection needs to occur both at the principal level and in dialogue among educators in the school. The principal's own reflection can benefit from considering his/her identities as an interpretive lens for self-assessing ability, benevolence, and integrity. But as we pointed out, this appraisal of the three components of trustworthiness does not occur in a self-induced vacuum but rather occurs as the principal and other staff members together interpret trustworthiness.

In developing the propensity to trust, principals and teachers must also critically reflect on how cultural, social, and personal contexts influence trust building and maintaining. As we noted, urban schools in particular exists in a context in which the diversity of cultural, social, and personal factors inherent in identities is intense and can foster the development of trust or, if ignored, can hinder the development of trust. Having critical conversations among principals and teachers that acknowledge these factors and their influence on sense-making can facilitate the trust-building process.

The assessment of trust outcomes is also critical for urban principals and teachers. The importance of taking risks for the sake of urban students does not always come easily, and the interpretation of the willingness to take those risks is not uniform among those in the urban school setting. Critical reflections by principals and teachers contribute to the sense-making around identities that permit an authentic and honest appraisal of trust outcomes.

Our inclusion of the role of emotions in this framework constitutes a reminder to principals and teachers that identities and identity verification are not completely cognitive or rational processes but also include emotions. The critical reflections we recommend are likely to be fraught with a variety of emotions, especially in the pressure cooker of urban educational reform. Acknowledging the existence of the emotional side of the identity-trust relationship and valuing the role of emotions can facilitate the trust-building process.

Preparation

In addition to implications for practice, our discussion of the identity–trust relationship between principals and teachers also has implications for how we prepare future leaders. In the previous section, we encouraged

critical reflections around identities to understand trustworthiness, the propensity to trust, and the assessment of trust outcomes. Such critical reflection seldom comes naturally. Leadership preparation programs should consider the development of skills for critical reflection and dialogue as a required part of coursework and program experiences. Engaging in critical reflection through the use of case studies, role plays, and other simulations can help the aspiring administrator understand her/his own identities and develop skills in assessing how these identities can be employed in building trust. In addition, preparation programs should help students develop skills in promoting authentic dialogue among teachers and other school constituents. If, as we claim, building and maintaining trust is critical, especially in urban schools, then preparation must focus on those skills—both personal assessment and facilitating dialogue among staff.

Future Research

A better understanding of professional identities can provide insights into how urban schools navigate the uncertainty and manage vulnerabilities of stakeholders, including teachers, school leaders, parents, and other community members. We have discussed how professional identities provide a lens through which vulnerabilities are interpreted as threats to the status quo and how these facilitate or hinder trust building. Future research should address how principals employ identities to navigate the trust relationship with stakeholders and whether this process is different in various types of urban contexts. For example, principals in urban schools that have experienced the extreme vulnerabilities of state takeovers may navigate the identity–trust relationship very differently than principals in other urban schools.

In the immediate future, research is necessary to more completely link professional identity to trust building among other stakeholders in urban school reform settings. Urban principals must interact with parents in a variety of contexts, from sharing a vision for the school's future to intervening in parent-to-parent conflicts that overflow into the school environment. Other stakeholders include the school's partners on campus, across the school district, and in the urban community. Professional identities will influence each of these interactions and the assessment by stakeholders of the level of trust.

We have emphasized how cultural, social, and personal contexts influence identities and the verification by others of those identities, and thus, the propensity to trust in urban schools. Future research should examine the specific role that these various factors play in identity construction and verification. For example, how do differences in race, ethnicity, or gender between principals and teachers influence the identity construction process and how identities are employed in establishing and maintaining trust?

NOTE

1. Agreeableness is one of the "Big Five" personality dimensions; the other four are extraversion, emotional stability, conscientiousness, and openness to experience. Barrick and Mount (1991) list being cooperative, forgiving, soft-hearted, tolerant, and trusting as traits associated with agreeableness (p. 4). The Big Five have received a great deal of attention in the organizational behavior literature, in which personality is linked to job performance (Barrick and Mount, 1991) and job satisfaction (Judge, Heller, and Mount, 2002), among other workplace outcomes.

REFERENCES

Barrick, M. R. and Mount, M. K. (1991). The big five personality dimensions and job performance: A meta-analysis. *Personnel Psychology, 44*, 1–26.

Bryk, A. S. and Schneider, B. (2002). *Trust in schools: A core resource for improvement.* New York: Russell Sage Foundation.

Burke, P. J. and Stets, J. E. (2009). *Identity theory.* New York: Oxford University Press.

Cantril, H. (1941). *The psychology of social movements.* New York: John Wiley.

Carspecken, P. F. (1996). *Critical ethnography in educational research.* New York: Routledge.

Carspecken, P. F. (2003). Ocularcentrism, phonocentrism and the counter Enlightenment problematic: Clarifying contested terrain in our schools of education. *Teachers College Record, 105*(6), 978–1047.

Cook, K. S. (2005). Networks, norms, and trust: The social psychology of social capital. *Social Psychology Quarterly, 68*(1), 4–14.

Day, C. and Leithwood, K. (2007). *Successful principal leadership in times of change.* Dordrecht, The Netherlands: Springer.

Day, C., Stobart, G., Sammons, P., Kington, A., and Gu, Q. (2007). *Teachers matter: Connecting variations in teachers' work, lives, and effectiveness.* Buckingham, England: Open University Press.

Fine, M., Freudenberg, N., Payne, Y., Perkins, T, Smith, K., Wanzer, K. (2003). "Anything can happen with the police around": Urban youth evaluate strategies of surveillance in public spaces. *Journal of Social Issues, 59*, 1, 141–158.

Flessa, J. (2009). Urban school principals, deficit frameworks, and implications for leadership. *Journal of School Leadership, 19*, 334–370.

Forsyth, P. B., Adams, C. M., and Hoy, W. K. (2011). *Collective trust: Why schools can't improve without it.* New York: Teachers College Press.

Gee, J.P. (2001). Identity as an analytic lens for research in education. In W.G. Secada (Ed.). *Review of Research in Education* (Vol. 25, pp. 99–125). Washington, DC: American Educational Research Association.

Goffman, E. (1959). *The presentation of self in everyday life.* New York: Doubleday.

Goldring, E. and Schuermann, P. (2009). The changing context of K–12 education administration: Consequences for EdD program design and delivery. *Peabody Journal of Education, 84*(1), 9–43.

Hardin, R. (2002) *Trust and trustworthiness.* New York: Russell Sage Foundation.

Hardin, R. (2006) *Trust.* Cambridge, UK: Polity Press.

Harré, R. and van Langenhove, L. (1999). Reflexive positioning: Autobiography. In R. Harré and L. van Langenhove (Eds.), *Positioning Theory.* Oxford: Blackwell.

Hofstede, G. (1980). Motivation, leadership, and organization: Do American theories apply abroad? *Organizational Dynamics, 9*(1): 42–63.

Judge, T. A., Heller, D., and Mount, M. K. (2002). Five-factor model of personality and job satisfaction: A meta-analysis. *Journal of Applied Psychology, 87*(3), 530–541.

Khalifa, M. (2010). Validating social and cultural capital of hyperghettoized at-risk students. *Education and Urban Society, 42*(5), 620–646.

Ladson-Billings, G. (2014). Race, research and urban education. In H.R. Milner and K. Lomotey (Eds.), *Handbook of urban education.* New York: Routledge.

Ladson-Billings, G., and Tate, W. (1995). Toward a critical race theory of education. Teachers College Record, *97*, 47–68.

Lawler, E. J. and Yoon, J. (1996). Commitment in exchange relations: Test of a theory of relational cohesion. *American Sociological Review, 61*(1), 89–108.

Lewicki, R. J. and Bunker, B. B. (1996). Developing and maintain trust in work relationships. In R. M. Kramer and T. R. Tyler (Eds.), *Trust in organizations: Frontiers of theory and research* (pp. 114–139). Thousand Oaks, CA: Sage.

Lewis, J. D. and Weiger, A. (1985). Trust as a social reality. *Social Forces, 63*(4), 967–985.

Mayer, R.C., Davis, J.G., and Schoorman, F.D. (1995). An integrative model of organizational trust. *Academy of Management Review, 20*(3), 709–734.

McCall, G. J. and Simmons, J. L. (1978). *Identities and interactions: An examination of human associations in everyday life* (Rev. ed.). New York: Free Press.

Mead, J. (1934). *Mind, self, and society*. Chicago: University of Chicago Press.

Mishra, A. (1996). Organizational responses to crisis: The centrality of trust. In R. M. Kramer and T. R. Tyler (Eds.), *Trust in organizations: Frontiers of theory and research* (pp. 261–287). Thousand Oaks, CA: Sage.

Møller, J. (2005). Old metaphors, new meanings: Being a woman principal. In C. Sugrue (Ed.), *Passionate principalship: Learning from life histories of school leaders* (chapter 6). London: Routledge Falmer.

Ryan, J. (2007). Dialogue, identity, and inclusion: Administrators as mediators in diverse school contexts. *Journal of School Leadership, 17*(3), 340–369.

Scribner, S. M. P. (2013). Beyond bridging and buffering: Cases of leadership perspective and practice at the nexus of school-community relations. *Journal of Cases in Educational Leadership, 16* (3), 3–6.

Scribner, S. M. P and Crow, G.M. (2012). Employing professional identities: Case study of a high school principal in a reform setting. *Leadership and Policy in Schools, 11*(3): 243–274

Smith, E. B. (2011). Identities as lenses: How organizational identity affects audiences' evaluation of organizational performance. *Administrative Science Quarterly, 56*(1), 61–94.

Smulyan, L. (2000). *Balancing acts. Women principals at work*. Albany: State University of New York Press.

Starbuck, W. H. and Milliken, F. J. (1988). Executives' perceptual filters: What they notice and how they make sense. In D. C. Hambrick (Ed.), *The executive effect: Concepts and methods for studying top managers* (pp. 35–65). Greenwich, CT: JAI.

Stryker, S. (2004). Integrating emotion into identity theory. *Advances in Group Processes, 21*, 1–23.

Stryker, S. and Burke, P. J. (2000). The past, present, and future of an identity theory. *Social Psychology Quarterly, 63*: 284–297.

Tschannen-Moran, M. (2014). *Trust matters: Leadership for successful schools* (2nd ed.). San Francisco: Jossey-Bass.

Tschannen-Moran, M. and Hoy, W. K. (1998). A conceptual and empirical analysis of trust in schools. *Journal of Educational Administration, 36*, 334–352.

Vasquez Heilig, J., Khalifa, M., and Tillman, L. (2014). High-stakes reform and urban education. In H. R. Milner and K. Lomotey (Eds.), *Handbook of urban education*. New York: Routledge.

Weick, K. E. (2005). *Sensemaking in organizations*. Thousand Oaks, CA: Sage.

Wenger, R. (1998). *Communities of practice: Learning, meaning, and identity*. Cambridge, England: Cambridge University Press.

Worchel, P. (1979). Trust in distrust. In W. G. Austin and S. Worchel (Eds.), *The social psychology of intergroup relations*. Belmont, CA: Wadsworth.

Young, M. D., Crow, G. M., Murphy, J., and Ogawa, R. T. (Eds.). (2009). *Handbook of research on the education of school leaders*. New York: Routledge.

CHAPTER 40

Exemplary Leadership in Challenging Urban Public School Settings

It's the Principal of the Thing

Harry Gutelius

BACKGROUND AND PURPOSE

Unfortunately, it has become more and more difficult to provide quality education in schools that serve students in poor urban environments. This premise played a major role in the No Child Left Behind (NCLB) legislation signed into effect by President George W. Bush on January 8, 2002 (New Jersey State Department of Education, 2011). With the election of a new president in 2008, this focus only intensified; Barack Obama's Education Secretary, Arne Duncan, dedicated an unprecedented $5 billion in federal funding to help reform America's most troubled schools, the vast majority of which are urban public schools (Ramirez, 2009).

"Is it possible for schools to help children who face the substantial obstacles of poverty and discrimination to learn to read, write, compute, and generally become educated citizens?" (Chenoweth, 2007, p. 1) This difficult question was asked in response to whether the challenge of NCLB could be met. Chenoweth's answer to her own question is "yes," which she explains in the preface of her book, *It's Being Done* (Chenoweth, pp. xi–xii). Indeed, not to say "yes" and thus to reject this challenge as unreachable simply has too many negative consequences, so to seek to provide all students, including those in poor urban communities, with a quality education must be our nation's goal.

NCLB notwithstanding, providing poor urban students with sufficient educational benefits is not happening, as evidenced by the fact that resources are unequal for lower- and upper-class students. An example of this can be seen in Southeastern Pennsylvania. In 2007, in the wealthy Philadelphia suburban communities of Lower Merion and Radnor, per-pupil spending was $21,399 and $17,105 respectively; meanwhile, in the nearby poorer urban areas of Philadelphia and Chester, the per-pupil spending was approximately $8,000 (Pennsylvania School Boards Association, 2008).

This disparity in resources has existed for a long time, and the political system required to address it seemed unlikely to change until the goal stated by Secretary Duncan "to rehabilitate the nation's five thousand lowest performing schools in the next five years" gave some hope (Ramirez, 2009, p. 1). However, until Duncan's goal can be attained, the challenge to help students in poor schools will remain, and will require those involved to use what little they have available to achieve success.

It has been my personal experience that this can be done. I worked in the School District of Philadelphia for thirty-two years, the final twelve being spent as principal of that city's largest school. Since my retirement from that system, I have done extensive work in schools located in other poor urban areas such as Harrisburg, Reading, Allentown, and Baltimore. It is my belief that schools do succeed despite negative conditions, and that there "are schools that demonstrate that successful change efforts are within our reach" (Smith, 2008). Effectively improving America's failing schools is the problem my research considered, and the purpose of my study was to show that effective leadership is a key, if not *the* key, to making this happen; moreover, it is both the fastest and the least expensive way to create effective change in challenging urban schools.

SCOPE OF THE RESEARCH

In order to accomplish my research, I needed to focus on a few specific questions. The first of these was as follows: what are the characteristics of both a "challenging" urban public school and of a school within that category that is considered to be a "success story"? In order to examine this question it was essential to define some key terms. First, what is a "challenging urban public school"? For purposes of my study, I defined "public school" as one that is under the control of the school board of the city in which it is located. Whereas charter schools are technically public schools, I was not considering those in my research. My career has been spent working in education in Philadelphia and its suburbs, including being employed for two years by a large nonprofit corporation that designs and operates charters, and I am well aware of how these schools operate through my personal experiences. In Pennsylvania charters operate free of the many local and state requirements that apply to traditional public schools, have their own boards of trustees, and are separate, independent educational institutions (Pennsylvania Charter School Law Act 22, 1997). As such, they often have specific advantages, including student selection and funding sources, which can give administrators distinct advantages that their counterparts in traditional school settings do not have. Pennsylvania's charters share characteristics with charters in other states, for the principles behind their formation are the same as on a national level.

My focus on public schools, then, also meant that I did not include private schools of any kind; once again the issue of advantages over traditional public schools is an obvious problem when trying to compare leaders. Other types of public schools excluded from my study were specially designed public schools under control of a city's district. For example, U.S. Department of Education Secretary Duncan was previously Superintendent of Schools in Chicago, and under his leadership that district established "turnaround" schools, of which there are presently eight in operation. All these schools have entirely new staffs and are run by a nonprofit group (Ramirez, 2009). Simply stated, any urban school that has special advantages was not considered. As such, when examining challenging urban public schools, I would visit only schools that could have no special advantages over other similar schools. In that way, if I was able to show the impact that the principal has had in the success of a school, I did not want there to be any factors attributing to the success of that school that would invalidate my points concerning the impact of the leadership.

Other factors also helped to further define the terms and parameters of my study. First, while I realize that challenging school situations can exist in other than urban settings, in the interest of consistency and validity of conclusions I limited my school visitations to those in urban areas. Also, as to the term "challenging," I defined this in my examination of objective data concerning poverty level, where the free/reduced-lunch percentage was the key indicator. In addition, other factors contributing to a challenging setting were identified. The "success story" was defined by referring to higher relevant measures such as test scores as well as by conducting a qualitative, in-depth exploration of schools.

As to which urban areas I visited to explore my sample schools, I needed to limit locations to places within a reasonable distance of my home and accessible by automobile. Philadelphia was a logical place to start, and I used that school system as a place where I was able to study some excellent samples; however, I wanted this research to be about urban principals, not just Philadelphia principals. Another important consideration in this process was that I wished to stay at least a full day at each school for my basic assessment.

CRITERIA FOR IDENTIFYING "SUCCESSFUL" SCHOOLS

After the initial task of establishing parameters for the kinds of schools to visit, the next step was to determine which schools and principals were, indeed, "successful." I developed a set of likely criteria upon which I was able to base my selection of successful urban models for education and for my study:

- Challenges: The profile of the principal's school indicates that there are distinct and vital challenges that were met and overcome.
- Data: Data such as state tests, district examinations, and in-house instruments show the school as above proficient.
- School Records: Other important data such as attendance, punctuality, graduation rates, and relevant school safety records demonstrate a school that is achieving.
- Assessments: At least one positive assessment by someone who supervises the principal is helpful.

In addition, positive comments from members of the school community were gathered and considered.

- School Climate: The observable school climate must be exemplary. In other words, hallways, classrooms, assemblies, cafeteria, bathrooms, and the exterior campus must all be clean, pleasant, graffiti-free, and orderly.
- Innovation: There are examples of positive innovative programs that have been established in the school under the principal's direction, some of which include components such as excellent use of technology and effective instructional delivery models.
- Student Engagement: The student body should be engaged in a positive fashion as shown by their attentiveness to the instructional program during the school day.
- Faculty Presence: Faculty attendance should be excellent and their active participation in a meaningful program of professional development verifiable.
- Awards: Awards for the school, portions of the school, and/or for the principal are desirable.
- Achievements: Any special achievements, including overcoming any unique and/or major problems in order to achieve a successful school, were given consideration.

Given all these criteria, following schools were selected for visits. Names of schools and principals are altered to protect confidentiality; however, all reported findings are factual and accurate.

DATA COLLECTION

The following describes how I incorporated criteria that have just been delineated in the context of visits to the above schools.

The profile of the principal's school took into account data that were indicative of a challenging setting, with the percentage of students eligible for free lunch being the primary indicator of the school's poverty level.

In the states where I studied a school and its leadership, I examined results of the respective standardized tests including the PSSA in Pennsylvania, the DSTP (Delaware Student Testing Program) in Delaware, the testing system for grades 3–8 and the Regents Examinations and Regency Competency Tests in New York State, and the Kentucky Core Content Tests. Where available, I also studied state test results for English language learners and/or students with disabilities (table 40.1).

While state test data were obtainable from each state, data such as attendance, punctuality, graduation rates, and school safety were obtainable at individual schools and/or from the districts in which they were located.

As to the observable school climate, that was obviously something that I viewed personally as I extensively toured through all areas of a school during my visitation. During the visitation, I sought written and/or oral comments from those to whom the principal reported as well as from those who taught, learned, or served in some other capacity in the school. It was during these visitations that I assessed students' involvement in instruction and extracurricular life, faculty professional development, and awards and special achievements of each school. I also endeavored to learn

Table 40.1. List of Schools Visited, Principal Names, and Locations

SCHOOL	PRINCIPAL	STATE
Baldwin Elementary	Mr. Moritz	Pennsylvania
Betsy Ross High	Mrs. Brown/ Mrs. Palmer	Pennsylvania
Boone Academy	Dr. Frazer	Kentucky
Brooks Middle	Dr. Peterson	New York
Central Elementary	Ms. Wilson	Pennsylvania
Cherokee High	Dr. Bray	Kentucky
Lincoln Elementary	Mrs. Boyer	Pennsylvania
Penn Elementary	Dr. Hiscott	Pennsylvania
Shaw Elementary	Mr. Aviola	Pennsylvania
Truman Elementary	Mr. Hayman	Delaware

as much information as possible about these areas in pre- and post-visitation communications.

As a result of the visits and the other related research, I produced detailed explanations that showed why the principal of each school was an effective leader. Thus, my examination was not cursory; moreover, my own background as an urban educator strengthened my analysis by adding credibility to any personal assessments that I made as part of my evaluations. Using state tests and other objective data combined with my qualitative research gathered from interviews and personal observations, I was able to form a strong body of convincing evidence to support the positive worth of each school leader.

At the close of my report on each school, I prepared a summary table to highlight major contributions of each principal's leadership and why they were such essential components for success. Two tables were developed for each school in order to summarize the dominant responses about each leader, and to offer a clear view as to how each principal was perceived. As examples, the tables from one school are shown below (tables 40.2 and 40.3).

EMERGING THEMES: LEADERSHIP—TEN PRINCIPLES FOR PRINCIPALS

The key result of all the research is that a conclusion can be reached as to common qualities that make the principals exemplary leaders and, as such, contributors to school success. In total, there are ten key emerging themes that were observed and explained below. These ten qualities represent the analysis of all the data gathered, as they form a guideline for defining leadership practices of exemplary leaders in challenging urban public school settings. It should be noted that these ten emerging themes are not presented according to any level of importance.

Theme One: Passion

It is obvious from reading the account of each school that in every instance the principal is an individual who truly seems to care about his/her school as well as the responsibilities and opportunities of leadership. The statement can be made that for each of these ten princi-

Table 40.2.   Prototypical Table Summarizing Responses About a School's Principal

SCHOOL NAME: Boone Academy (Parentheses indicate number of individual responses)		
DESCRIBE THE PRINCIPAL'S STYLE	GREATEST STRENGTHS	COMPARE TO OTHER PRINCIPAL(S)
Hard to label(1)	Ability to build an incredible team(4)	No one really compares to him(4)
An instructional coach(2)	Love of the kids(4)	Most caring person imaginable(3)
Ultimate team builder(4)	His passion/caring(4)	He has to be the best leader anywhere(5)
Awesome(1)	Kids and parents all know him and respect him and love having him as their principal(3)	Most visible by far(5)
Totally caring and committed leader(4)	Focus on learning(3)	Created a safe school(2)
Completely visible and dynamic(4)	Total visibility(5)	Best team builder ever(5)
Leads by example(5)	Has a complete belief in his staff(2)	Most dynamic(3)
Simply wonderful(2)	Leadership by example(4)	Most innovative leader I have ever seen(2)
Kid-focused and achievement oriented(4)	Super-supportive individual . . . loves and reassures everyone(3)	Most personable and sincere
Just a model principal	Strong leader who believes in discipline, yet does so with compassion	Easily the most passionate(2)
A dynamo(1)	Will not accept failure(2)	Strongest leader I have ever known(2)
Loving, caring, supportive(3)	Sees the big picture and plans accordingly(1)	Hard to think of anyone who could do as well as he has done in leading this school(3)
Focused on instruction(3)	A truly fabulous instructional leader(3)	Most kid focused(4)
Attention to every detail yet he is definitely not a micro-manager(3)	Ultimate teacher himself(4)	The very best at leading by example(3)
Totally passionate(2)	Creative yet knowledge based(1)	He has to be city's finest principal(3)

Table 40.3.   Prototypical Table Summarizing Responses About a School

SCHOOL NAME: Boone Academy
(Parentheses indicate number of individual responses)

WHY IS THE PRINCIPAL A GOOD FIT FOR THE SCHOOL?	HOW WOULD YOU DESCRIBE YOUR SCHOOL?	SCHOOL'S GREATEST STRENGTHS-ANYTHING TO CHANGE?
He is the school(2)	Warmest place imaginable(2)	Most team-oriented place imaginable(4)
He is the perfect fit(3)	An amazing success story for all to see(2)	Best leadership anywhere(4)
He knows everyone(4)	Most caring school anywhere(4)	Caring by principal and staff is awesome(3)
His background lets him understand our kids(5)	A true family(5)	More support from district would help(2)
No one else would have his passion(3)	Just a great place(2)	Number one strength is the principal(3)
He knows the community so well(3)	Where kids come first(4)	Family atmosphere is tremendous(3)
He has built a great team(4)	Product of incredible leadership(2)	Perceptions of us because kids are poor is wrong(1)
He relates to kids in poverty(4)	Comfortable place yet super busy(1)	Could use a longer school day and school year that would help kids in so many ways(1)
He wants every kid to learn(3)	Totally organized and structured(2)	Staff never gives up trying to do what is best to have the kids succeed(3)
He has empathy for the children(2)	Place where kids achieve(3)	School with unconditional love for kids(2)
He is the ultimate organizer who has every aspect of the school organized(2)	Good things go on here(2)	Only the best is accepted(2)
Has built the school to what it is(3)	We are really like a family(4)	Organization is awesome(1)
Inspiration for the school(2)	Truly, this is a wonderful school(3)	A truly safe haven for kids(2)
No one could do it as well(3)	Achievement-centered place for kids(3)	Teamwork and leadership are tops(3)
He leads by example(4)	Best an elementary school can be(2)	Student motivation is outstanding(2)

pals, his/her role is not merely a j-o-b; it is definitely a j-o-y. During the site visits and interviews, the passion for the position was constantly evident through both direct observation and interaction with others from the school community. While each principal displays an obvious passion for the work to be done, it manifests itself in a variety of ways.

At Betsy Ross High, Mrs. Brown rose to the principal's position from her background growing up in that neighborhood, and it was continually noted by those interviewed that she has a special feeling for her neighborhood school. Betsy Ross High is an important piece of where she has lived, and her passion for serving its students and the community was a logical extension. Dr. Hiscott, on the other hand, has never lived in the community where she serves as principal of Penn Elementary. Yet, after serving there for over a decade and immersing herself within the school and its community, she has become an integral part of that small society. Meanwhile, Dr. Frazer at the Boone Academy for Excellence was viewed by all who were interviewed as a person who has a complete passion for his job. Dr. Frazer's enthusiasm and caring are constantly apparent, and the sincerity of what he views as a calling to serve his school and its community was obvious.

This passion to work, lead, and serve is an attribute that is invaluable for these leaders. Leading schools in challenging settings is a difficult role, and when the leader is obviously committed to the task and exudes an attitude that is caring, optimistic, and sincere, that task of having the school succeed through effective leadership is more likely to occur. In each school, all members of the school community felt positively about the passion shown by their principal, and this was an important step for leading in the right direction. At each school the teachers expressed overwhelming sentiment that their leader is a person who truly cares about them and the school as a whole, and it makes their work a pleasing situation. Many parents were interviewed, and almost every one of them made it a point to state how much they appreciate their principal's caring about their children and their school. Likewise, the students continually demonstrate a truly positive attitude toward their principal that is reflective of the love that they feel from the one leading their school. Last, but not least, direct interviews with each principal yielded the type of comments and the sense of committed passion that showed how much each cares. Overall, there is no doubt that this passion for the position is evident and can be considered as a definite attribute for urban school leaders.

Theme Two: MBWA (Manage by Walking Around)

At each of the ten schools visited, the same thing could be said about the principal's office: it was a place where the principal would most likely not be found. These urban leaders spend most of their days in classrooms, hallways, cafeterias, bathrooms, playgrounds, gymnasiums, and any other location where their students might be engaged in activities. This is because each leader practices the principle of MBWA (Management by Walking Around) as a staple of his/her leadership style.

At the Baldwin Elementary School, the statement made about the prospect of touring the building with principal, Dale Moritz, is that anyone doing so had better wear roller skates. This was in actuality not much of an exaggeration. Mr. Moritz seemed like a man in perpetual motion gliding from room to room and throughout the hallways for hours. Perhaps even more important than his doing this, however, was the fact that he genuinely seemed to enjoy doing it. On both visits to the school Mr. Moritz was observed as the same continually moving person, a man determined to get into every room every day, and more than once at that, to see firsthand that instruction was taking place in the classrooms and that order was being maintained throughout the building.

At Lincoln Elementary School the principal, Mrs. Diane Boyer, might not have been as fast on her feet as Mr. Moritz but she was no less visible. The fact that the weather outside was extremely cold did not prevent her from being outside her building at the beginning and end of the day to greet and dismiss her children. Inside the building, she also made her way into every room, a routine that she has followed on a daily basis for many years. The teachers and children expect to see her continually, and it is thus no surprise when that is precisely what transpires. The boys and girls are totally accustomed to her presence, and they react with full respect; they all know who she is.

At Truman Elementary School Mr. George Hayman conducts his daily routine just as his principal counterparts at Baldwin and Lincoln do: he goes throughout his building continually. His style is a bit different from Moritz and Boyer. Whereas Moritz is very fast moving, Boyer is more deliberate; both of them are very business-like. Hayman, on the other hand, proceeds throughout the building more slowly than Moritz and more rapidly than Boyer, and he does so in a more relaxed fashion and is very likely to tell jokes and funny stories to children and teachers as he goes about. Yet, while each has his/her own style when utilizing MBWA, all three practice it fully and effectively. Indeed, they share this principle in common with all the principals in this study. It was obvious at each school that every student and every teacher know the principal well, for the leader is continually throughout the building and the campus to be certain that the school is operating in the most effective way possible. It is no wonder that so many of the teachers interviewed stated that an outstanding attribute of their principal is their leader's presence throughout the school.

Theme Three: Avoid Micromanaging

A continual theme that emerged among the teachers during their interviews was that they truly appreciate the fact that their principal allows them to do their jobs free from micromanaging. The leaders were cited as individuals who place their staff members into various positions, give clear directions as to what is expected, and support and evaluate as necessary; however, in terms of doing their jobs, the staff feel as though they are empowered to do what they are supposed to do without someone constantly "looking over our shoulders." The ten principals were all lauded for having enough trust in the people who had been placed into positions of responsibility to let those staff members have the freedom to work with a proper degree of autonomy.

At the Brooks Middle School Dr. Lois Peterson is extremely gifted in assigning roles to members of her staff and then giving them the freedom to just do their jobs. She engages in regular small group meetings with her assistant principals and teachers to let them know what she expects from them, and then she figuratively steps aside so they can do those jobs. A significant example of this leadership style was shown in an assignment she gave to one of her assistant principals. Dr. Peterson wrote a grant that enabled the school to obtain a great deal of technology, most of it connected to interactive whiteboards. Since she needed someone to manage this technology, she assigned the task to her assistant principal, who proceeded to organize all the necessary steps to get the technology into each room, to train the staff, and to provide necessary support. Everything Dr. Peterson wanted in terms of effectively using the technology her grant had brought to her school was accomplished, and it happened simply by her giving someone she selected the responsibility and accompanying freedom to do it.

At Cherokee High School, Dr. Kevin Bray was hailed by his staff as a master of delegating and permitting autonomy. Dr. Bray plans a schedule of small weekly meetings in which he meets with various staff members to review their responsibilities. Meetings are designed to be a cooperative effort, not just top-down directed. The expected end result of each such meeting is the same: everyone should depart understanding what his/her responsibility is; moreover, it is likely not until the next meeting that a progress evaluation takes place. Between the time of those two meetings, staff members are expected to do their jobs without direct supervision from the principal; they operate independently.

Dr. Bray has a highly complex organization where students receive traditional academic offerings but also have unique opportunities such as pilot training, jet engine repair courses, and even a Challenger space station. Obviously the principal cannot directly manage all of these effectively, so Dr. Bray does not attempt to do so. Instead, he delegates responsibilities as needed. In addition, the principal has divided the school into Small Learning Communities (SLCs) and has given the leadership of each SLC to a staff member. He depends on these teachers to run their SLCs effectively, and they stated that they respect the fact that Dr. Bray does not micromanage them.

Mr. Joe Aviola at Shaw Elementary School has a much different organization from that of either Dr. Peterson or Dr. Bray. In his mid-size elementary school he has very few support staff, including no administrative assistants. As a result, the greatest challenge that he faces is dealing with disciplinary issues, for all of these fall to him. In order to cope with this difficult task, Mr. Aviola has come to depend on several teachers to assist him during some time that he has managed to provide for them during the day. Several teachers stated that they enjoy supporting his efforts to provide a quality school climate because he has faith in them to do what he has asked and thus does not micromanage their work. Indeed, throughout the building, teachers continually praised Mr. Aviola for his style—while he provides support and is clearly in control, he gives them a feeling of autonomy in doing their jobs. They reported deep appreciation for their principal's respect for them as professionals by having faith in their ability to do their jobs without being micromanaged.

Theme Four: Know the Students

The reason that schools exist is actually quite simple: to serve their students. It stands to reason then that students should be the focus of everyone who works in the school, and that would include, of course, the principal. A principal's job is certainly quite complex and involves the necessities of doing much paperwork, attending many meetings, and interacting with staff, parents, superiors, and community. Yet, with all there is to do, it is essential that a principal not forget his/her students. In fact, it is invaluable to know them. The principals of these ten schools share a remarkable ability to know their students by name and, moreover, to actually learn so much about so many of them.

Ms. Janice Wilson, principal at Central Elementary, displays a remarkable facility for knowing her children. Her school runs from kindergarten through grade eight, and it is inconceivable that any students could attend Central for the full nine years and not be known by Ms. Wilson. As she goes about the building, Ms. Wilson not only continually greets students by name, but she asks relevant questions about them. "Is your leg feeling better?" "How's your mother doing now?" "Did everything go all right with your repairs to your home?" During the visit to Ms. Wilson's school, these were three actual questions that she was heard to ask as she interacted with her students. Not only did she know them by name, she also displayed an interest and a caring attitude. These qualities have an obvious positive impact, for all the children treated her warmly and with respect, and this certainly provides a good school climate. Indeed, the teachers repeatedly praised Ms. Wilson for her interaction with the students and their parents, and believe that it is one of the most significant reasons for the school's success.

Mrs. Jennifer Palmer ascended from vice principal to principal at Betsy Ross High School when the principal, Mrs. Brown, was promoted to a school district leadership position. A major reason given for Mrs. Palmer's selection was her rapport with the students. Mrs. Palmer knows every girl in this single-sex school by name, and that individualized relationship with each student is invaluable in setting a positive tone for the building. It is evident that Mrs. Palmer enjoys getting to know her students, and they respond by behaving and working in an exemplary fashion. Teachers gave high praise to Mrs. Palmer for her rapport with the girls, and they definitely feel that it is a leadership quality that helps make her such an outstanding person to lead their school.

Mrs. Boyer was another principal who displayed marvelous rapport with her students as she moved about Lincoln Elementary. During the visit to the school, she was seen to know each student by name and also be aware of relevant information about many of them. It was commonplace to hear her ask a student a question about a situation specifically related to that child. She displayed an obvious love and concern for each one, and she received the respect from each one in return. The teachers marveled at their principal's facility with the names of all the students and also praised her individualized attention for the children. Mrs. Boyer, as with all of the ten principals, knows her students, and the students know her. The fact that the principal is not some anonymous person in some office who somehow runs the school, but rather is an individual who knows the students personally and by name, is a significant factor in providing the type of exemplary leadership required to effectively run challenging urban schools. These urban students especially benefit from such individual attention.

Theme Five: Be the Principal Teacher

When public schools first emerged in America, they began as small units normally staffed by a single teacher. As schools grew over time and teaching staffs became larger, eventually a principal teacher position was initiated in order to have one person to oversee administrative tasks and other important non-teaching duties within the school. The released time from teaching to compensate for the completion of those responsibilities grew to the point where eventually the principal teacher no longer taught, and the role of school principal was created.

In the ten schools that were visited, teachers continually stated how pleased they are to have the head of their organization be a person who can lead by example; in other words, they appreciate having a principal who is able to model excellent teaching. Of all the principals observed, no one performs more capably as a principal teacher than Dr. Frazer at Daniel Boone. He begins

each day at his school by personally teaching the entire student body in a large group instruction format in the building's large multipurpose room. His observed presentation was dynamic, organized, and effective; in short, he is a model teacher. Through this daily routine, Dr. Frazer exhibits the type of enthusiastic, genuine instruction he expects from his staff, and he also sets a completely positive tone for the start of the day. When interviewed, the teachers praised Dr. Frazer as a principal teacher for his daily lessons as well as for the annual event where he releases the whole faculty for an extended appreciation luncheon while he personally teaches the entire student body. At Boone, all teachers know that their principal is credible when he challenges them to reach lofty instructional goals.

Mr. Moritz at Baldwin is another highly effective principal teacher. He also starts each day by meeting with the student body, and his work in the auditorium accomplishes its purpose of setting a proper tone for the day's outset. Moreover, as he travels throughout the building on his daily classroom visits, he continually participates in the instructional process by injecting himself into lessons that are presented. His enthusiastic participation is not resented by his staff; on the contrary, he received continual praise for his ability to join in and to lead instruction by example. He displays a thorough understanding of what is being taught and is also able to illustrate that he has the ability to deliver that instruction as well.

Not all of the principals are as overt in their display of being a principal teacher as were Dr. Frazer and Mr. Moritz; however, they are all seen as possessing this ability. For example, both Dr. Hiscott at William Penn and Ms. Wilson at Central are held in high esteem by their faculty for their previous accomplishments as classroom teachers. Each of these women came to be a principal with reputations as outstanding classroom teachers, and they often exhibit that past success in classroom visits and conversations with staff by relating their teaching background to issues at hand. As with all the leaders in this study, Dr. Hiscott and Ms. Wilson are viewed as excellent teachers as well as exemplary principals.

Theme Six: Be a Leader, Not Just a Manager

While it is certainly true that the principal must be a person who is able to manage the day-to-day routine of the school, school visits and interview responses made it apparent that in order to be a truly exemplary leader in a challenging urban public school setting, the principal must do more than just manage: he/she needs to be a leader as well. In order for each school to excel, it is essential that the person in charge must possess and exhibit definite leadership qualities.

At the Brooks Middle School Dr. Peterson was continually praised for her exceptional leadership. She was called "a transformational leader" as well as "visionary." It was said that "she is quick to analyze a problem and then deal with it effectively," and she was also hailed as someone "willing to try something with risk in order to improve." In addition, she "knows how to attract grants and other resources that have helped so much." And she was described as one who "never loses her 'cool'" and is "calm under fire." Moreover, she was described as being "approachable," as one who "encourages people to be creative," and as "an extremely skilled communicator." All of these qualities are those of one who does more than just manage an organization. While Dr. Peterson actually did receive high grades from her staff as one who is organized and, in effect, is a good manager, she was seen more as a resourceful leader who truly has a vision for what she wants to accomplish at her school.

Mrs. Brown was definitely viewed as a powerful and effective leader at her high school. Indeed, when asked to give qualities that describe Mrs. Brown, the teachers and other staff members repeatedly spoke of her leadership. They said that she was a "truly exemplary leader," "the most visible leader imaginable," "the model for a school leader," one who has "strong leadership," and a person who displays a "genuine sense of direction for staff and students." While Mrs. Brown was characterized as being "highly organized," which is certainly a solid managerial skill, she was also hailed as being extremely "student-oriented," "committed to excellence," "strong," and "charismatic." Indeed, she was often referred to be this latter quality, for she is viewed as a very charismatic individual whose personality resonated throughout her building. It is because of these combined leadership qualities that Mrs. Brown is viewed as much more than the manager of Betsy Ross High School; in fact, her leadership is so widely recognized that she was promoted to lead all of the secondary principals in the Philadelphia School System.

Dr. Bray is another principal who has skill at managing his organization, yet is viewed as doing so much more that he could be considered to be a dynamic leader, a man who is a "true visionary." Dr. Bray was described in interviews as a man who is a very intelligent, articulate leader, as one "not afraid to take chances," as an "'out of the box' thinker," and as an "intelligent, thoughtful leader who inspires the staff." One of the most colorful descriptions of Dr. Bray was that he is "a 'cowboy' . . . an extremely innovative and creative person." He was also praised for his ability to "lead by example" and to truly "understand the future."

Dr. Peterson, Mrs. Brown, and Dr. Bray all exhibit true leadership qualities that extend beyond the role of just managing a school. While their schools, as well as schools of the other seven principals, all certainly reflect solid management, it is the exceptional leadership of each of these educators—leadership that transcends just managing—that has been so important in having their respective organizations attain status as highly successful schools in challenging urban public school settings.

Theme Seven: Understand and Implement Best Practices

Since the primary purpose of a school is to educate its youngsters, it stands to reason that using best instructional practices is a good thing. At the ten schools visited for this study, the principals were repeatedly cited by their teachers as being leaders who both understand and implement best practices for use by their schools, and this is viewed as an important part of the success of each school.

Mrs. Palmer was highly respected at her Betsy Ross High for being a principal who has a solid knowledge of best instructional practices. She was said to have "knowledge of best practices and research," "to be a highly skilled trainer of teachers who presents outstanding professional development," and as one who "is open to new ideas." It was repeatedly said that Mrs. Palmer "understands the school's needs," which translates into her acquiring the best materials and staff development personnel she can find. She works very closely with her two curriculum specialists whose job it is to make certain that every teacher in the building has all materials they need as well as support for using them. Because of this focus on instructional practices, teachers described

Mrs. Palmer as running "a solid educational program" and Betsy Ross School as "a place focused on achievement," and "a school where teachers meet high demands placed on them by the principal."

The fact that Mr. Hayman, principal of Truman School, runs a school that is focused on achievement is evidenced by its receiving a Blue Ribbon Award. This distinction is given only to schools where academic achievement is apparent, and Mr. Hayman's leadership, which includes a focus on instructional practices, is viewed as a primary ingredient for this success. In the interviews, it was said of Mr. Hayman that "his knowledge of teaching and best practices is exemplary" and that he is "the strongest leader at focusing on achievement that I have ever known." He was continually hailed as one who uses data extremely well for achievement purposes. In addition, since he has been at Truman so long, almost every teacher has been personally hired and trained by Mr. Hayman, so the continuity of instructional practices is outstanding.

At Lincoln Elementary School, teachers have come to expect an occasional gift from their principal, Mrs. Boyer. As an educational leader who enjoys immersing herself in reading about innovative and successful teaching strategies, Mrs. Boyer often selects a book she has read and purchases a copy of it for each of her teachers. She expects each teacher to read the book within a reasonable period of time, and then follows up on what has been learned from that book during a future professional development opportunity. This is one reason that in the interviews, her teachers described Mrs. Boyer as "one who is able to utilize best practices every day" and that "her standards are so high and she knows how to have them met." It was repeatedly said that the principal's expectations are high and are what "drives the school to succeed." The fact that she is so focused on best practices and has them used by her faculty is invaluable in having the lofty expectations realized.

Mrs. Palmer, Mr. Hayman, and Mrs. Boyer share a common focus in the use of best instructional practices at their schools. All ten of the leaders share a belief that their schools can and must achieve educationally, and all realize that an important piece in that endeavor is providing their teachers with the knowledge of best instructional practices and then supporting their implementation.

Theme Eight: Be Supportive of the Staff

A common thread in many interviews at the ten schools was the teachers' knowledge that they are supported by their principals. This support can take many forms, such as backing in dealings with students and parents, supplying needed supplies and equipment for the job, providing quality professional development, or simply being an understanding and caring leader who makes each teacher feel wanted and important. The bottom line is that teachers feel that they need the support of their leaders, and at these ten schools it was readily apparent that they believe they have just that.

At the William Penn School, Dr. Hiscott was continually lauded for her support. Various comments included that she "truly cares about the students, staff, and community," "has built a committed staff," "is 'super' supportive," and is a "team player." Dr. Hiscott was praised for creating a collaborative, team approach in the school that has been made possible through her supportive presence. She was said to "lead by example and with humility," "be willing to listen and be flexible," and to be "kind and understanding, yet a strong disciplinarian." It was said of her that she is a "quality listener" and that if she "disagrees, she will do so without being disagreeable." There was a continual expression of appreciation among the staff for Dr. Hiscott's supportive leadership style.

At Shaw Elementary, Mr. Aviola was continually praised for his support for the staff and the school in general. He was described as being "a good listener," "flexible," "caring," and "people oriented." It was said that he "treats all of the staff members in a totally professional manner" and that "his respect for people is really great." Because Mr. Aviola possesses these qualities, it is not surprising to find that his staff believes that he "has their back" when it comes to any problems they might encounter in their school. It was said that his support and demeanor has "created a family atmosphere" and "a fabulous school."

Dr. Peterson at Brooks was described as "a very open and supportive person" who "enjoys working collaboratively." It is through these collaborative efforts that the staff finds their principal to be a highly supportive individual. She is viewed as especially supportive in terms of securing advanced technology for the school. An avid grant seeker and writer, Dr. Peterson has been able to secure interactive whiteboards for all classrooms as well as other hardware and software purchases that have placed Brooks in a position of technological leadership among schools in its city. The staff views this as a prime example of Dr. Peterson's support of their efforts. In addition, she was also praised for building "a genuine positive atmosphere in the school" and for fostering "collaboration among the staff."

Dr. Hiscott, Mr. Aviola, and Dr. Peterson all earn respect at their schools for the support that they provide to the staff and school at large. The same is true of the other seven principals cited in this research. Indeed, every one of them received high marks during interviews for the supportive nature of their leadership.

Theme Nine: Be a Team Builder

The principals in this research are not only supportive of their staff members, but also excel at building teams within their schools. An oft-repeated theme among those interviewed was that there is a sense of teamwork and togetherness where they work, and that their leaders do an outstanding job of team building and creating a family atmosphere.

Mr. Moritz at Baldwin was described as being "the ultimate team builder." To that end it was said that "teamwork abounds," that "the caring and cohesive teaching staff is a key to the school's success," and that there is "a family atmosphere" at Baldwin. Moritz was hailed as being "highly visible and genuinely supportive" and as being "the finest at caring for his staff." These are qualities that assist him in his team-building endeavors. Baldwin was described as a "place where everyone works together" and as "one big, happy family." In such an atmosphere it is not surprising that teamwork would abound.

Dr. Frazer at Boone was also described as being "the ultimate team builder." Indeed, responses about him yielded "best team builder ever," "ability to lead an incredible team," and "super-supportive individual . . . loves and reassures everyone." Corroboration of his strengths as a team builder included statements saying that he "leads by example" and "knows everyone" and is thus able to wisely direct people into the teams that are best for them and the organization. Partially as a result of the team spirit among the staff, Boone has become "a true family" and "just a great place" to be and to work. It was further said that Boone is the "most team-oriented place imaginable" and that in a school "where kids come first" the teams who design and operate the school's functions "never give up trying to do what is best to have the kids succeed." From the day's outset, when Dr. Frazer gathers his entire staff together as one large team to inspire the children, to the day's end, which often is marked by small team meetings that he attends to discuss student needs, this principal is truly an exceptional team builder.

Dr. Bray, at a school located not far from Dr. Frazer's, has a similar team building style, although his is accomplished at a complex high school organization that is very different from Dr. Frazer's elementary school. In interviews it was said Dr. Bray is "the best team builder," a "true team builder," and one who has fostered a "strong sense of teamwork." He is respected for being someone who "lets people take ownership" and for being the "finest at empowering his staff to do their best." It was also stated that part of his success as a team builder is that "he has recruited good people" and that individuals and groups find it "easy to follow his leadership because of his style and attitude that helps us do our jobs." Cherokee was described as a place where a "tremendous spirit of togetherness exists," and this was attributed in part to the team building that has taken place during Dr. Frazer's time as principal.

Mr. Moritz, Dr. Frazer, and Dr. Bray are clearly seen to be strong team builders, a trait common among all ten principals in this research. This willingness to work together seems to foster a spirit that is especially positive when dealing with the challenges that educators in urban public schools can face. Working together closely and cooperatively, principals, teachers, and others can better meet the challenges before them.

Theme Ten: Understand That the Little Things Are Not Little

While the leaders in this study are unanimously seen as not being micromanagers, it is interesting to note, however, they are also viewed as principals who pay attention to the "little things." By giving proactive attention to small details that can become large problems, these leaders are able to prevent many of the difficulties that can face any school, perhaps especially one situated in a challenging setting.

It seems as if no detail is inconsequential to Mrs. Boyer at Lincoln Elementary. Indeed, one of the responses made concerning her leadership was, "She is the best at details of any leader I have seen—nothing escapes her attention." This has resulted in an organization that is viewed as being highly organized. "A highly organized place," "This is one incredibly well run organization," and "This school is perfectly organized" were some of the comments made. The specific way that students enter the building and the way that lines have to be formed as students proceed in a highly structured fashion demonstrate the attention to detail concerning student movement. Indeed, Lincoln is a place where the children move about with purpose and under effective control.

Mrs. Boyer is meticulous with regard to the way everything in the building is arranged and presented. The banners outside each teacher's room showing where they had gone to college and graduate school, the total organization of everything in the lobby at the entrance to the school, and the neatness and cleanliness that had to be apparent in each room and in all hallways reflect an "attention to detail" that make Lincoln "a school where everyone dresses and behaves properly and learning happens."

Ms. Wilson at Central is also committed to giving small details the proper attention. It is partly due to this fact that Central is called "a complex organization (K–8) that works." Ms. Wilson was said to be a leader who "truly understands the total K–8 organization" and a "hands-on leader" who "provides the staff with whatever they need." All the items that appear on the walls of the office and in the hallway outside are important to her as she tries to set a tone from the time one enters the school. Once in the school, students pass throughout the building in highly prescribed ways, and extreme attention is paid to matters such as how food is distributed in the large cafeteria. The use of school uniforms that vary slightly by age group is effective in establishing a sense of togetherness. It should also be noted that the principal takes direct ownership of matters such as student and faculty scheduling as well as utilization of the budget to be certain that these school services operate to maximum effectiveness. While these are certainly not "little things" in an organization, it should be noted that by failing to give each "little detail" in these processes its proper attention, significant difficulties and confusion can result. By being proactive in these matters, Ms. Wilson is able to run a highly organized and effective school where the climate is actually enhanced as a result.

Mr. Aviola was described in the interviews as being "the best at organization" and as being "a highly organized principal." His attention to detail is evident throughout the building and also in programs such as the Backpack Program, which helps disadvantaged youngsters with free supplies, food, and clothing. Mr. Aviola developed a highly organized method for collecting, warehousing, and distributing these goods, including the recruitment of the individuals necessary to make this happen. It was said that "The Backpack Program is an example of his caring," and it is also an example of his attention to detail. It was also stated that Mr. Aviola is "supportive of all worthwhile endeavors" and that this includes his attention to the "little things that make it work." In order to provide Shaw School with a positive climate, Mr. Aviola developed a "discipline code that is fair and efficient and is enforced in a consistent manner." When interviewed about discipline in his school, Mr. Aviola was quick to point to all the attention to detail, to the "little things," as he calls them, that help to make the policy successful.

Mrs. Boyer, Ms. Wilson, and Mr. Aviola each exhibit a desire to be certain that all the details of the school are given proper attention. For each of them, and for the seven other subjects of this research, little things are not little if failure to address them might result in something very unwanted for the organization. This attitude is consistent with their overall desire to have a successful school and their passion they display for wanting to make that happen.

EMERGING THEMES: CONCLUSION

In summary, ten common themes emerged that characterize the leadership of the principals of the schools that were examined. It can be stated confidently that each of the leaders possesses these ten qualities and that each of these traits is a distinctive aspect of their exemplary leadership. Therefore, it is the conclusion of this research that for exemplary leaders in challenging urban public school settings, the following practices are critical to success:

1. Passion
2. MBWA (Manage by Walking Around)
3. Avoid Micromanaging
4. Know the Students
5. Be the Principal Teacher
6. Be a Leader, Not Just a Manager
7. Understand and Implement Best Practices
8. Be Supportive of the Staff
9. Be a Team Builder
10. Understand That the Little Things Are Not Little

CLOSING COMMENTS

Since the assumption is that exemplary leadership in challenging urban public school settings has at least to some extent been defined, it is the sincere goal of this research that there are indeed practical applications for what has been learned.

I have been blessed to serve in education for more than four decades, with thirty-two years of that time in urban public education. Throughout my career I have taken great joy in seeing and/or being a part of good things happening to students in their schools. For me, the bottom line has always been this: schools exist to serve their students. It has always been my personal goal to do whatever I could, whether as a teacher or an administrator, to help students receive the best educational and related services possible. It is my sincere hope that this research will be read and appreciated, and as a result some principals will be influenced in such a way that their students' lives will benefit.

REFERENCES

Chenoweth, K. (2007). *It's being done.* Cambridge, MA: Harvard Education Press.

New Jersey State Department of Education. (2011). *New Jersey No Child Left Behind.* Trenton, NJ.

Pennsylvania Charter School Law, Act 22 of the State Legislature of the Commonwealth of Pennsylvania. (1997).

Pennsylvania School Boards Association. (2008). *Annual report on per pupil spending by district in the state of Pennsylvania.* Harrisburg, PA.

Ramirez, E. (2009, May 27). Turning around troubled schools: Signs of how Education Secretary Arne Duncan plans to fix failing schools via his work in Chicago. *U.S. News and World Report,* 2–3.

Smith, L. (2008). *Schools that change.* Thousand Oaks, CA: Corwin Press.

CHAPTER 41

School Turnaround

The Meaning of Capacity in Practice for African-American Women Principals

Cosette M. Grant

INTRODUCTION

Evidenced in the literature base on student achievement are discussions replete with strategies and recommendations for change for the purpose of improvement that cannot be mandated (yet policymakers continue to do so); best practices must be modeled by educational leaders (yet it often is not); existing, unprecedented standards, structures, and processes must be dismantled and replaced by precedents that more accurately reflect the school's mission and operation (difficult to achieve, especially in low-performing schools); system change needs to be supported (while sustainable); behavioral change is essential (yet difficult to provoke, unless relatable). And the list of actions are unending.

America can no longer afford to continue with the status quo of our current education system, and in order for successful systemic change to occur, there is a need to "reframe our entire reform strategy so that it focuses relentlessly and deeply on capacity building and accountability" (Fullan, 2006, p. 28). This and similar charges emphasize the need to bring about internal and external support as the process of sustaining real change. It takes everyone; it is an extensive process; and the principal is centrifugal to the practice. That said, for the principal to be successful in the change process, it takes buy-in from all factions and without such, change for the purpose of sustainable improvement will be difficult to achieve.

However, we must turn around our lowest-performing schools with reform efforts that are innovative for turning around America's lowest-performing schools, asserts President Barack Obama (U.S. DOE, 2010a). To this end, the Obama administration has focused national attention on improving the academic achievement of all students. In response to this federal legisla-

tion, educators, policymakers, and others have sought remedies to turn around chronically low-performing schools. But, there are a number of conditions associated with turning around schools—appointing a new principal, infusing additional resources (Ansell, 2004), and built-in support mechanisms (Grant, 2014). There are also a number of conditions to overcome. School districts, especially in urban areas that serve disadvantaged communities, are challenged to meet the increasing requirements of ensuring learner proficiency and creating high performing schools. School districts acknowledge the need to recruit, hire, train, and sustain high-performing school leaders (Hall, 2008). The new educational leader, hence principals' agenda may be too daunting; 'quick-fix' changes may lead to a temporary save, which cannot be sustained over the long haul. These said changes often result in a burned-out and overwhelmed principal, rather than motivated (Hargreaves and Fink, 2006; Kanter, 2004). This may be the case, especially when change processes fail to provide the training and development opportunities and ongoing support necessary for principals as well as their staff to learn new skills and acquire new knowledge; in other words, when they fail to build the individual and/or collective power to improve student achievement—"capacity building" (Day, 2014).

Despite the profusion of empirical research and experience-generated opinions if we observe studies regarding the impact of newly trained and deployed educational leaders in low-performing schools, it would appear that we know little about their impact on performance of "turnaround" schools in the longer term (National Audit Office, 2006). Nor can the skills and talents necessary to bring about the sustained improvement of low-performing schools be clearly identified. This especially holds true as this study intends to look at African-American women principals turning around low-performing schools—an understudied area. Yet, what we do know is that African-American women tend to be notably placed in these tenuous positions at a much larger rate than any other group and with little to no support or guidance. African-American women principals in low-performing schools receive limited support or resources that hinder their leadership success (Bloom and Erlandson, 2003). There is limited empirical evidence on African-American women urban school principals' experiences effectively leading in school turnaround in low-performing schools. Even more, scant literature exists that have identified ways in which African-American women principals are mentored toward this success (Grant, 2014).

Therefore, this study attempts to fill a void by presenting the lived experiences of two African-American women principals from two separate low-performing schools. The findings featured narrative experiences reflecting their participation in a formal mentoring initiative for newly minted principals who eventually went on to effectively lead in school turnaround in an urban school district. It explores how, over a six-year period, both principals turned around their schools which were under threat of closure upon entry and appointment to the role of principal. The needs and challenges commonly identified by these women was a call for diversity in urban school leadership, mentoring support and resources in order to empower principals serving in low-performing schools, structured mentoring to aid newly minted principals to effectively improving student achievement in low-performing schools are addressed, and include issues of race, gender, and class dynamics. Therefore, the following research question was created to guide this study: What specific mentoring activities (if any) were effective in turning around your school?

CONTEXT

In an age of rigorous school accountability, the role of the principal is critical in predicting whether students will achieve at high levels (Marzano, Waters, and McNulty, 2005). Traditional examinations of principal effectiveness have included assessments of principal responsibilities and job tasks or have focused on the competencies, knowledge, and skills that principals should possess (Goldring, Cravens, Murphy, Elliott, and

Carson, 2008). While these studies have been useful in exploring principal leadership in general, they have not adequately explored how principals influence improved learning results for the diverse populations of learners served in urban schools throughout the United States.

In particular, there has been insufficient study of leadership in schools that generate sustained levels of high achievement for low-performing students. For the purposes of this study, the focus is on African-American students in low-performing schools. Principals, especially African-American women principals in urban schools, maintain that very little support exists as they embark on the challenges of being a new principal post-No Child Left Behind (NCLB), not to mention the difficulties and challenges that new principals face. In this regard, Murtadha and Larson (1999) contend that "principals of color, especially African-American women, typically emerge as the leaders of urban schools that are under-supported and economically depleted" (p. 6). They also assert, "they [women of color] are expected to establish and carry out educational agendas that clash with what they and the community see as vital to the education of African American children" (p. 6).

As both urban communities across the United States experience changing racial and ethnic demographics, school leaders are confronted with the needs, perspectives, and "funds of knowledge" that students from diverse backgrounds and their families bring to the school (Johnson, 2007). Yet, the myth remains that the ideal leader for most schools conforms to a white, masculine stereotype, particularly at the secondary level (Brunner and Peyton-Caire, 2000; Murtadha and Larson, 1999; Shakeshaft, 1989). For example, in 2003–2004, ethnic minorities, both men and women, represented only 24 percent of principals in the United States (Strizek, Pittsonberger, Riordan, Lyter, and Orlofsky, 2006). The numbers are more dismal for African-American women principals when categories are disaggregated to gender and race as well. Furthermore, African-American women principals are disproportionately found in urban school environments that have been exhausted of resources and lack support (Bloom and Erlandson, 2003).

Moreover, educational literature offers limited knowledge construction regarding African-American women principals (Alston, 2000; K. W. Collins and Lightsey, 2001; Henry, 2001; Lomotey, 1989). Because African-American women in leadership positions are scarce, their voices are rarely heard (Alston, 1999, 2000; Jackson 1999). And because they have been so few in number, there is little research about African-American women in educational leadership, their professional aspirations, the obstacles they face as they pursue their goals, and the roles of mentors and sponsors in advancing their careers (Allen, Jacobsen, and Lomotey, 1995). There is even less in the literature that provides leadership strategies that support African-American women principals' efforts to turn around low-performing schools. Further, misogynistic notions constrain the advancement of African-American women into leadership positions (Bloom and Erlandson, 2003) and advancement tools for them to be effective in leading toward student achievement. These limitations include difficulty in usurping the male dominance position, stereotyping, self-imposed barriers, circuitous pathways with lack of mentors, and inadequate training or coaching in managing issues of power and control (Blakemore, 1999; P. H. Collins, 1991; Grogan, 1999; Hill and Ragland, 1995; Shakeshaft, 1989), often bestowing unique challenges on African-American women principals, especially in low-performing schools, unlike that of their white counterparts, in leading toward effective student achievement outcomes.

In response to mounting pressure stemming from the federal NCLB, school districts across the United States have been confronted with the challenge of developing effective training programs provided to accommodate African-American women educational leaders' resource deficits in low-performing urban schools, while assisting all principals with trying to sustain success with all of their students. To support these efforts, school districts strive to find effective models to build the leadership capacity of school leaders to turn around low-performing schools (Petzko, 2008). Subsequently, mentoring has emerged as a professional development tool for building effective educational leaders. An important avenue to preparing newly minted principals, for instance, is through a mentor program, as the mentoring process is seen as a way to improve how school leaders are prepared to carry out their craft in the "real world" (Daresh, 1995, p. 7).

Historically, mentoring has played some part in the training and development of novice principals (Crow and Matthews, 1998; Daresh, 1986; Hobson, 2003; Weingartner, 2009). Mentoring has been a known

strategy for building leadership capacity as part of professional development and training (Bloom, Castagna, Moir, and Warren, 2005; Browne-Ferrigno and Muth, 2004; Daresh and Playko, 1990), yet we still know little about successful mentoring models effective in developing more African-American women principals. There is little empirical evidence identifying how such a knowledge base is enacted. Further, it is unclear what strategies, techniques, training, and other inherent qualities make for a successful African-American women principals with regard to turning around low-performing schools. These areas of research presently remain limited in the education literature.

REVIEW OF LITERATURE

Schools across the nation are expected to focus on delivering a high-quality educational product as evidenced by No Child Left Behind (NCLB, 2001). Still plagued by the widening achievement gap, the lack of equity amongst schools, our nation continues to seek innovative solutions that will provide a turnaround of our current educational crisis. Competent principals (Marzano, Waters, and McNulty, 2005) are major contributors in the success of a school. Since principals can have major impact on student learning outcomes, their professional development and competence has become a very important focus in the mission to improve U.S. schools and is integral to student achievement outcomes.

This review of literature provides a foundation for the current inquiry. The review acknowledged the current state of academic achievement for African-American students in low-performing schools in urban areas listed earlier in this chapter, and then explored key factors (capacity building, mentoring and training of two African-American women principals in these schools) that have influenced the success of schools that generate high-achieving African-American students. The literature review also examined leadership factors that influence achievement in low-performing schools that serve African-American students as well. This study examined systems and structures that leaders implemented and that were perceived to lead to school-wide effective pedagogy and learning, hence turning around two low-performing into high performing schools.

Public Education in the United States

Before, we examine the leadership and capacity of African-American women principals' efforts in turning around low-performing schools, we must reference the status of public education in the United States, in which these principals find themselves. These challenges point to the competitive disadvantages and subpar conditions that often times present challenges to transforming the school environment into higher performing standards, hence bring about student achievement. These challenges must be recognized and challenged in order to provide the necessary preparation for principals working in these settings.

That said, the National Commission on Excellence in Education (1988) examined the quality of the American public school education and identified many deficiencies within and between public school systems. The report revealed that 13 percent of seventeen-year-olds in the United States were functionally illiterate; however, the percentage was as high as 40 percent among students of color. The Commission made apparent that achievement levels among students of color, especially African-American students, were often much lower than their white counterparts. Provisions of the NCLB held school districts, site administrators, and teachers accountable for ensuring that students make adequate yearly progress (AYP) in specific curricular areas through the monitoring of annual standardized tests (California Department of Education [CDE], 2009). As a result of this increased accountability and deliberate focus on instruction, state assessments revealed measurable achievement gains for all demographic groups since the implementation of NCLB in 2001 (CDE, 2009). However, a significant achievement gap still remains between African-American students and white students (National Center for Educational Statistics, 2013). The achievement gap is prevalent throughout all levels of education beginning in elementary school and is evidenced in high school as well (Ferguson, 2010).

Student Achievement Gap

According to Gay (2010), a substantial body of evidence supports the notion that poor urban children can be very successful academically when trained and mentored leaders, for example, that foster improvement are in place. We already know that African-American students tend to perform significantly lower than white students and other higher-performing population groups. Existing research offers various explanations for many barriers that may slow success for African-American students, ultimately contributing to the gap. Social, cultural, historical, economic, and racial barriers that impact the daily lives of African-American students tend to be the lens by which we look at performance impediments (Ogbu, 2003), but equally, it is also important to focus research on the preparation of our educational leaders, especially African-American women principals to successfully lead on turning around, hence transforming low-performing schools into higher-performing schools.

New Principal's Challenges Leading School Turnaround

Research on educational leadership supports the claim that leadership matters when considering the achievement of African-American students. Experts assert that leadership remains pivotal in advancing school improvement efforts (Day, 2007; Griffith, 2001; Hines, 2007; Leithwood, 2005; Muijs, 2004). Many studies have been conducted on the correlation between leadership and academic growth. In fact, Marzano et al. (2005) conducted a meta-analysis of studies that looked at the linkages between school leadership and student achievement outcomes.

However, turnaround leadership concerns the kind of leadership needed for turning around a persistently low-performing school to one that is performing acceptably as measured by student achievement (Fullan, 2005). "Assessing the roles of strong interventions for failing schools is quite complicated," even in the narrow sense, because the combination of intended and unintended consequences is difficult to sort out (p. 174). With the knowledge that principals play an important role in school turnaround (Carter, 2000), school districts are faced with the challenge of finding ways to build the skills, knowledge, and abilities of their school leaders.

Moreover, as newly minted principals enter the ranks of this multifaceted position from preparation programs, most have emerged with beginners' skill sets, and they are left to figure out how to effectively meet the wide range of complex challenges faced by school leaders, especially in low-performing urban schools (Farkas, Johnson, Duffett, and Foleno, 2001; Perez, Uline, Johnson, James-Ward, and Basom, 2011; Sanders and Kearney, 2008; Searby, 2010). They enter the position prepared to be competent; however, the position of principal requires that they take on so much more. In reality, most novice principals enter the position feeling unsupported, and without the guidance and coaching necessary to effectively lead a school (Grissom and Harrington, 2010; Searby, 2010).

In the case of new principals, they are being asked to do something that they are not necessarily prepared to do (Elmore, 2005; Ladd, 1996). In fact, school principals feel enormous pressure to keep up with NCLB requirements despite the fact that many urban schools across the country have multiple factors thwarting principals' good intentions. For example, urban schools have inherent social, economic, and cultural conditions that perpetuate their competitive disadvantage. The changing role of a principal has brought new challenges that deal with influencing the social, economic, and political context of a school. Goodwin (2003) suggested that in essence, the role of a school leader is being transformed from that of a building manager to that of the leader of a community organization. Goodwin et al. (2005) indicated that new principals are not fully prepared to take on the responsibilities of their jobs. Principals are spending more time on the job, have increased responsibilities, but are held responsible for meeting or exceeding goals established by NCLB (2002). Goodwin et al. (2005) suggested that the quality of prospective principals should improve by having better preparation, recruitment, and professional development. Accordingly, the key lies with preparation before and after someone decides to take on the role of principal (Goodwin, 2003). However, it is unclear what strategies, techniques, training, and other inherent qualities make for a successful African-American woman principal, particularly in a low-performing school setting. This area of research presently appears scant in education literature.

New Principal's Role in Turning Around Low-Achieving Schools

It is evident that school principals play an integral role in increasing academic achievement. In fact, re-

search reveals that effective school leaders can raise a low-performing school's overall student achievement (Waters, Marzano, and McNulty, 2005). Despite the political changes that have transformed education as a result of NCLB, this research indicates that effective principals can make positive changes. The work of Marzano et al. (2005) is referred to here because it suggested twenty-one characteristics and behaviors that a new leader might use during his/her earlier tenure as a principal. These characteristics and behaviors were positively correlated with student achievement. For the purposes of this study, however, the focus is on mentoring as a strategy for African-American women principals, who make up the majority of educational leaders situated in low-performing schools.

Illusionary Opportunities for African-American Women Principals in Urban Schools

Dillard (1995) posited that when caring for students, African-American women principals who serve marginalized urban communities do not engage in traditional leadership activities "as they have been traditionally conceptualized" (p. 542). They consider culture and community context and focus beyond the school. Furthermore, some African-American women principals lead differently than their white colleagues, in part because they have been excluded from established power structures. Restricted access to resources and frustration with exclusionary bureaucracies prompted creativity and risk-taking in their leadership roles. Yet, African-American women principals have become adept at uniting and engaging stakeholders in marginalized school settings into action (Brooks, 2009; Johnson, 2007).

Increasingly complex and demanding, the role of an African-American woman urban school principal continues to evolve around a leader, not only in an educational institution context, but as a social agent as well. Over the years, educational researchers have tried to explain why patterns of social chaos and inequity tend to surface in poor, underserved schools (Anyon, 1997; Kozol, 1991; Noguera, 1996; Oakes, 1985). Agreement exists about the key role of the principal in urban schools, although conditions of professional practice often tend to be characterized by "situational and contextual variables that determine the appropriate application of professional skills" (Cistone and Stevenson, 2000, p.

435). Similarly, African-American principals perceive responsibilities toward African-American children emanating from their own experiences relating to race and class (Pollard, 1997).

Moreover, urban school leadership requires the principal to understand the long-range effects of poverty, the disparities widespread in local school funding procedures, the impact of neighborhood unemployment on crime within the school, the necessity of interagency collaborations, and causal factors for low parental involvement (Bloom and Erlandson, 2003). Also, African-American women principals especially in these settings face additional challenges with lack of infrastructural support and mechanisms to help them lead in the school turnaround. To add, Portin (2000), has conducted studies on the urban school principal and lists three challenges to leadership in the urban principals:

> The urban principals may be more challenging along characteristics of entrepreneurial requirements, managing social complexity, and political skill . . . [relying] more on political leadership skills . . . to make a case for the interests of their schools in a system of competing needs for limited resources . . . Urban principals will need to develop expertise in communicating the unique characteristics of their school that suffer when schools are ranked and compared against criteria that fail to account for the unique challenges of their community. (p. 503)

Additionally, these challenges for African-American women principals in the aforementioned are inherent conditions in urban schools that further impede their capacity to be effective. Murtadha and Larson (1999) contend that despite their credentials and abilities, African-American women principals, or urban schools in particular, lack support and are economically deprived. Moreover, they [women of color] are expected to establish and carry out educational agendas despite these overwhelming challenges within the schools and community. Yeakey, Johnston, and Adkison (1986, cited in Hill and Ragland, 1995, p. 20) refer to those souls who accept such challenges as taking on the role of a "messiah" or eventually becoming a "scapegoat" (p. 21). Oftentimes, leadership placement of African-American women in low-performing schools is the only opportunity African-American women will have to become a leader of a school.

Developing African-American Female Principals as Leaders to Implement School Turnaround

Few research-based sources exist regarding the application of turnaround efforts in schools (Boyne, 2006; Leithwood and Strauss, 2008; Murphy and Meyers, 2008). However, the research on successful turnaround initiatives in schools affirms the critical importance of leadership (Public Impact, 2008). The complexity of school turnaround precludes a simple approach. Effective turnaround requires competent leaders skilled at solving problems and influencing others to support and participate in the change initiative.

However, successful student achievement attributable to effective leadership in urban schools is difficult to measure because of the limited research in this area. The irony is that from these dismal portraits of abandonment and neglect emerge African-American women principals, who tackled these critically ill schools and over time created schools that became "beacons of light within the darkness of their communities" (Bloom and Erlandson, 2003, p. 347). Telling their stories can inform and enlighten our current theoretical formulations about what it feels like to be an invisible change agent who works "on the inside," yet with only illusionary career opportunities in the future (p. 347).

CONTEXTUALIZING MENTORING

As the faces of urban public school students in America become more diverse, the faces of leadership in America's urban schools should also reflect similar demographic changes. In fact, "women and minority candidates are certified in much larger numbers than they are chosen for administrative positions" (Shakeshaft, 1999, p. 100). Yet, few African-American women principals receive the necessary mentoring once they assume educational leadership roles (Grogan and Brunner, 2005). To address this, educational systems must deliberately mentor more women and especially more African-American women (Grant, 2014). Although mentoring is referenced in the context of women superintendents in Grogan and Brunner's (2005) study, the same recommendation is applicable to African-American women principals in low-performing schools in urban districts.

Accordingly, with the emergence of more formalized mentoring programs for school leaders, this study at-

610 COSETTE M. GRANT

tempts to fill a need by analyzing mentoring of African-American women principals in low-performing schools. Additional empirical research is needed to identify determinants of mentoring components that are most salient in African-American women principals' successes on student achievement outcomes in low-performing schools. Only a few studies have examined protégé-mentor relationships in school settings and even fewer for African-American women leaders in urban schools. Noe (1988) studied protégé-mentor similarity for participants in a short-term aspiring principal program, finding that protégés in heterogeneous gender mentor pairing used mentors more effectively than those in homogeneous mentor pairing.

For the purposes of this study, a *mentor* is a person who initiates assistance, helps, provides supports, or teaches skills necessary to successfully perform in a job (Mendez-Morse, 2004). Sheehy (1976) described a mentor as "one who takes an active interest in the career development of another person—one who actively provides guidance, support, and opportunities for the protégé" (p. 36). Also in this study, *mentoring* refers to the relationship in which a more experienced person takes under their tutelage a less-experienced person in order to provide career and psychosocial development is referred to as mentoring. Mentoring is further defined as "the establishment of a personal relationship for the purpose of professional instruction and guidance" (Ashburn, Mann, and Purdue, 1987).

Mentoring Principals

With regard to principals, Daresh and Playko (1990) contend that "mentoring to assist present and future leaders is a powerful tool that may be used to bring about more effective school practice" (p. 44). The use of mentoring, especially in urban schools, has potential value in creating highly effective principals as these first-time leaders engage in learning innumerable school tasks, procedures, policies, and practices that are designed to produce positive student achievement results (Daresh and Playko, 1990; McCreary-King, 1992; McGough, 2003; Mendez-Morse, 2004).

Mentoring of Principals in Low-Performing Schools

Many urban school districts across the United States are currently following the reform movement of turnaround schools. These turnaround programs are a result of the No Child Left Behind mandate, that requires that a school that has continuously been in academic emergency for five years even after interventions have been set in place, will be restructured by the state or district (NCLB, 2002). There are many options of how to do this process, and one is the turnaround program where the school is re-staffed and a new leader is appointed or hired to come in and "fix" the problem. Herein lies the problem that there are a large number of low-achieving schools and a smaller number of effective principals in low-income districts (Darden, 2011). However, there is literature that supports low-income districts going through reforms and becoming successful, but it takes time (Scribner, 2011). Moreover, the federal government and states are looking for effective models that will help their districts flourish. For example, the University of Virginia Darden School funded by the U.S. Department of Education has been working with Cincinnati Public Schools (CPS) on such turnaround issues (Darden, 2011) and trying to determine what is making the mentoring program work in some of the low-performing schools in CPS.

Mentoring Support of African-American Principals in Low-Performing Schools

In addressing equity and diversity in mentoring, mentors need a focus on both the needs of the students, particularly those currently under-served in schools, and the needs and support of diverse new principals. Such work means focusing on the specific needs of new principals in turning around low-achieving schools (Achinstein, 2010). In particular, the Achinstein and Ogawa (2011a) study focused on new principals of color as a potentially promising population in terms of diversifying the leadership in urban schools and in impacting urban high-need schools where students of color are schooled. Moreover, principals play key roles in improving student achievement (Gurr et al., 2006; Hallinger and Heck, 1996; Mullen, 2002; Spillane, 2005), so mentoring African-American women principals toward that end should be important to the purpose of improving student achievement in low-performing schools.

METHOD AND DESIGN

Qualitative research was chosen as the design for this study because it provides a means for exploring and understanding the meaning individuals or groups ascribe to a social or human problem (Cresswell, 2009, p. 179). In this study, the actions and beliefs individuals ascribed to the improvement of academic achievement for students in low-performing schools, especially African-American students. Gay and Airasian (2001) explained that qualitative research is exceptionally suited for establishing a foundation of understanding a group or phenomenon and can address questions that cannot be answered by quantitative methods. This study sought to establish a foundation for understanding high academic achievement for African-American students at two particular schools. The study addressed questions that could be best addressed by gathering descriptive data revealing how changes happened and how these two principals were able to influence and sustain changes that led to improved achievement of students.

To this end, the investigation in this study of the principals' perception of the effects of mentoring and its impact on their ability to improve schools in this study uses Erlandson et al.'s (1993) naturalistic inquiry methodology as a means for increasing knowledge for practice using narrative storytelling to design explanatory questions about the subjects' social setting (Erlandson et al., 1993). Naturalistic inquiry, conducted to understand human experience and to interpret the perceived realities of the research participants, allows the participants to construct reality within their social settings. Harrison (1995) uses this methodology to reduce the invisibility and silences of women of color in the world by concluding, "In the process of redefining educational administration's critical project[s] and of reconstituting education authority, we must offset the persistent pattern of relegating the work of women—and that of women of color in particular—to the discipline's periphery" (p. 242). The use of the naturalistic inquiry design sought "a deep understanding and explication of social phenomena as they are observed in their own contexts" (Erlandson et al., 1993, p. 16). Bounded by these positions, the

research questions emerged to investigate the realities about the role of mentoring in building leader capacity, race and gender in leadership, thoughts about the urban low-performing schools that were turned around, and training and mentoring options for the participants that supported their capacity and ability to lead, hence transform their respective schools.

Participants

The participants were identified and selected using purposeful sampling based on established criteria (Patton 2002). The participants were African-American female principals formerly in an urban low-performing school who: self-identified as African-American female; were within three years of a new principal position when assigned to a low-performing school; who participated in a mentoring program as part of the turnaround initiative; and who were mentored as newly minted principals. The participants' ages ranged from fifty to sixty-five years old (see table 41.1). Richness of professional background and willingness to participate in a series of personal in-depth interviews were the primary considerations in identifying participants for the study. This study included two African-American women who were new principals in schools that began turning around under their leadership within a three- to six-year period that were in the same urban school district.

Interviews

A qualitative methodology utilizing individual interviews and content analysis of documents was selected for this study (Bogdan and Biklen, 1998; Hakim, 2000; Marshall and Rossman, 1999; Miles and Huberman, 1994; Shavelson and Towne, 2002). Through a qualitative approach, the researcher gathered descriptive data revealing how changes happened in their school and how support and training through mentoring helped

Table 41.1.

Pseudonym Name	Discipline	New Principal (3 Yrs.)	Mentored Type	School Age Range
Principal Johnson	Principal	Yes	Yes	Urban 50–65
Principal Lovett	Principal	Yes	Yes	Urban 50–65

them lead, influenced their capacity to transform their schools into higher-performing schools, and sustained changes that led to improved achievement of African-American students.

The interviews consisted of three focal areas: participants' background in education with emphasis on their experiences being mentored in the mentoring program; their personal reflections on the constructed meaning of leadership in the context of a new principal in an urban low-performing school setting, and their perceptions of success in turning around a school. Each interview was approximately one hour. Plus, included face-to-face interviews that included observations in classrooms and attending principal leadership planning meetings using observation protocols. The observation helped illuminate issues that relate to school climate and culture, curricula, and instruction, as well as support mechanisms for the principals.

Further, the interview questions encouraged participants to tell their stories about specific mentoring experiences, during their early stages as principal in an urban turnaround school. The interviews were audiotaped. Interview questions focused on concern with the lack of mentoring of African-American women principals as a mechanism for diversifying leadership in urban school districts and as a catalyst for school improvement, hence student achievement in urban school settings.

Analysis

This qualitative study relied upon an analysis of the participants' perceptions of mentoring in order to gain knowledge of what they deemed as supportive in creating the leadership practices associated with effective school turnaround as well as diversifying leadership in urban school districts. The use of principal interviews, field observations, and documents from the mentoring program provided data to inform meaning, find emerging patterns and themes, and support a theory about the use of coaching and mentoring as a strategy to build principal capacity and impact student achievement (Creswell, 2009a, 2000b; Glaser and Strauss, 1967).

Using Erlandson et al.'s (1993) interactive process of data analysis, themes emerged from the transcriptions of the interviews. The data analysis followed Lincoln and Guba's (1985) techniques of unitizing data, creat-

ing and deleting categories as the researcher reads and rereads each unit, developing descriptive sentences that distinguish each category from the others, and starting over with each unit to refocus and refine category placement (Erlandson et al., 1993). The findings presented in this study are not monolithic; therefore, they are not the view of all African-American women principals or women in general. The findings are representative of the two women studied and interviewed.

Theoretical Framework: Black Feminist Thought

As the suppression of the ideas of African-American women in research and epistemological knowledge construction remains a force that undermines the economic, political, and social revitalization within the African-American woman's world, black feminist thought (BFT) is a theory that centralizes and validates the intersecting dimensions of race and gender uniquely experienced in the lives of African-American women. As an emerging number of African-American women are assuming leadership positions in challenging school settings, it is helpful to deconstruct their daily lives as leaders to provide direction for future leaders who may find themselves in similar circumstances.

To this end, one framework that is useful in understanding the experiences of African-American women principals in turnaround schools within the BFT context is standpoint theory. Standpoint theory provides legitimacy and rationale to how African-American women principals lead their schools, especially schools with low-performing circumstances. In this regard, some African-American women principals lead differently than their white colleagues, in part because they have been excluded from established power structures. Restricted access to resources commonplace in schools where African-American women principals lead compounded with frustration from exclusionary bureaucracies in many cases prompts creativity and risk-taking in their leadership roles. Standpoint theory uses language and stories to produce alternative realities. Yonezawa (2000) explains that:

> standpoint theory proposes that people gain knowledge through their positions or social locations. They use the term *positionality* to capture how people's positions in the larger social structure (e.g., race, class, gender, and sexuality) influence what they are aware of and their interpretations of events. (p. 111)

Therefore, African-American women would view the world from discrete perspectives based on their social positions, or positionality, within the confines of the larger social structures of race and gender (Collins, 1991; Guy-Sheftall, 1995; Scott, 1982). However, in this study, how African-American women principals view themselves and their work helps one to understand more comprehensively why principals "behave, respond, and act the way they do in specific situations in essence creates new knowledge and understanding that clarify an African-American woman's standpoint for African-American women" (Collins, 2002, p. 469). Furthermore, what is important to note with regard to standpoint theory is to recognize that African-American women leaders demonstrate difference in regard to class, sexuality, background, experience, and school environment, but they hold similarities as a "category."

FINDINGS: NARRATIVES

This section delineates how the two women principals operated in the world of work, constrained by race, gender, and class. This exploration depends on the words and verbal recitations of both participants, to fully dislodge the perspectives that created their personal philosophies regarding self, schools, and community. By presenting counter hegemonic African-American feminist discourses such as these, the findings of this study accommodate its activist aim—to unmask and scrutinize the power of racist and sexist practices operating within public school systems. Others' listening to the underrepresented, yet significant voices of African-American women principals, as leaders in turning around schools may begin to change minds and social constructs about the "Others" in America's urban school districts.

The findings were organized in individual narratives addressing the overarching research question while informing the conceptual framework. Each narrative was unique; however, there were common themes across the two study participants that was the focus. The stories of both participants did not follow the predicted path of survival to comfort in their roles as principal. They alluded to their preparation as a key factor in their success as new principals. This confirms the importance of mentoring, while transitioning into the role of a new principal in a challenging school environment.

Findings also confirm the literature on African-American women principal placements in challenging urban schools. These principals addressed student performance challenges as a competing priority to leadership training and development. This order of action is also present in the literature on successful urban principals in challenging schools. Findings confirm the effectiveness of mentoring. Support, training, and formal mentoring were important factors for successful school turnarounds for the two principals.

Finally, the narratives highlight the similarities between the two principals' experiences as it pertains to the research question. To this end, there are three common themes specific to mentoring experiences and activities for the study participants that were findings claimed to be effective in turning around their schools: supporting new principals in urban turnaround schools; mentoring activities focused on student achievement in low-performing schools; and mentoring African-American women principals as a catalyst for diversifying school leadership.

Theme 1: Findings Related to Mentoring New Principals in Low-Performing Schools

Both principals attended an orientation program that trained them in leadership. Both principals commented that new principal orientation was a valuable support provider to the new principals. Both principals indicated that they had a formal mentoring system in place for new principals, where the novice principals could work with and be guided by more experienced administrator/principal. They were assigned a mentor at different stages. For Principal Johnson, she was assigned a mentor in her first year as principal, whereas Principal Lovett was assigned a mentor in her third year as principal. Accordingly, Browne-Ferrigno and Muth (2004) contend that principals' training, in order to be most effective, should now consist of collegial-peer relationships that are left upon "conditions of trust, openness, risk taking, problem identification, problem solving, and goal setting" (p. 490). Based upon this idea, it was the goal of this research to determine the principals' perception of their participation in their mentoring training program initiative and how the program supported changes that helped them develop effective school leadership behaviors. The research examined data to determine what principals felt worked or did not work in this professional development model and their suggestions for future leadership training models.

In terms of encouraging and supporting additional professional development, Principal Lovett and Principal Johnson both indicated the value of mentoring early on in their assignments as principals. Not surprisingly, they were placed in two of the lowest performing schools in the district; there was leadership transition, moving from a history of experiencing an authoritarian leadership style to two that were more participatory. The needs assessment process was, as *Principal Lovett* noted, "an evolving piece," because professional development (PD) planning had previously been a more top-down process. Both principals indicated that they had relied more on administrators/mentors to identify and develop training activities, specific to improving instruction. For the purpose of this, both Principal Johnson and Principal Lovett noted that their knowledge of curriculum and assessment was central to their turn-around work, "because a solid curriculum and aligned assessments are the backbone in making meaningful changes and improvements to instruction."

As leaders in low-performing schools in the same school district, possessing a strong self-image and cultural understanding of their own personal histories allowed the study participants to recognize that the origin of problems in urban schools were not solely caused by the students' and parents' lack of resources or unwillingness to participate. Rather, low academic achievement must be viewed within the larger structural context of public education's bureaucratic and exclusionary practices. Both women reflected on their upbringings on the heels of *Brown vs. Board of Education* practices. It was apparent to the two study participants that a collective consciousness of identity supplied the educational movement the energy necessary to produce transformation. Building on this collective consciousness, they used their awareness of the bureaucratic culture and the political processes present in their school district to market a vision for their school. For all their differences, these two principals share certain traits and beliefs. Most notably, they are strong principals who hold their students and their teachers to the highest standards. Both believe that children of all races and income levels can meet high academic standards (Carter, 2000).

A U.S. Department of Education report on nine urban success stories, including schools in Milwaukee, Detroit, Chicago, and East St. Louis, also cited school leadership and accountability as key ingredients (Dana Center, 1999). The report indicated that the school leaders created a collective sense of responsibility for school improvement. Accordingly, in terms of accountability, Principal Lovett asserts:

The way I originally saw things is that we are in these difficult schools, the kids are poor, the parents are not committed. However, mentoring on specific accountability has shifted this notion . . . We are all accountable for student achievement and so we need to work through these factors instead of using them as excuses.

Further stated:

One of the first things I said when I came here as principal is that these children can learn—they will learn. You've got to give it to them. That's my continuing message, although it's not always highly accepted, but it's getting better. My mentor provided resources for me to obtain funding some infrastructural challenges to make for better learning conditions. I was glad to have access to mentor to share these issues.

In her new role as principal, Principal Johnson spent time planning staff development activities to raise the consciousness level of the teachers about racist teaching practices. According to Principal Johnson:

Many teachers refused to openly participate, but that did not stop my mission . . . However, I was clear about how we needed to change the rate of achievement for my students—African-American students.

Moreover, the factors that characterize student achievement did not occur by coincidence. Both principals were mentored as new principals, which played a major role in influencing improvements at their school. The principals represented in this study were provided with support and financial and in-kind resources to promote high-quality teacher collaboration, job-embedded professional development, and via monitoring classroom instruction and offering feedback. These findings coincide with findings from other studies of high-performing schools.

Many theoretical formulations of successful leadership nourish the development of an individualistic style.

In schools, the competitive American culture promotes and cherishes the individualistic style for academic success. This notion of individuality clashes with the African-American cultural group dynamic of racial uplift and equal opportunity and access in education. Being and becoming number one pales in comparison and importance when juxtaposed against other issues within the African-American community. It is within this dichotomous environment that African-American women must carve out their place. Principal Johnson's story supports this claim. In her case, she shared how the preceding principal tried to maintain the status quo, which made things worse. She further indicated how she almost made that mistake. Consequently Principal Johnson was placed in her school as part of her district's plan to provide competent leaders in low-performing schools while diversifying the leadership in response to the rapidly transforming demographics in the school system.

After being named principal of a large, inner-city school in 2006, Principal Johnson was astonished about the opportunity to improve a school in her community. Entering with a vision for improvement, Principal Johnson describes why she accepted the position of principal at a high school with a history of student failure and district neglect. One of her ardent philosophical beliefs is that "I will always work in a community where I live." Working hard, she tried to turn around the tide of indifference and despair. She shares:

> The school was looking for a leader. There was a feeling of hopelessness and helplessness at that school. There was a high turnover of principals for some time. The school was one of the lowest performing schools in the district and the challenge was to turn it around. The entire school was considered at risk, and it was located in a high poverty area. The building was in poor condition. When I started, there were eight teaching vacancies to fill before school began. It was a challenge. But I knew I could turn things around. I knew that one component of my leadership was change for the sake of school improvement.

In this regard, Principal Lovett shared, that she was also located in one of the lowest performing schools in the district as well. She indicated that when she was asked to take on this new role, she shared with central administration, "I don't mind being asked to do things if I am being supported." Accordingly:

For consequent years, Principal Lovett did her best to use her clout, charisma, servant leadership style, and community connections to restructure the school instructionally, organizationally, and fiscally.

Several studies have acknowledged the role that school leaders played in promoting high-quality professional development opportunities (Barth, 1999; Izumi, 2002; Johnson and Asera, 1999). In both instances here, rich professional development opportunities for the principals were supported. The professional development provided gave the principals practical tools they need in order to teach critical concepts or utilize important strategies to move their schools into higher performance. In this regard, Principals Lovett indicated:

> Working long hours, building new programs within the schools, while trying to maintain a stable staff in the school seemed like an overwhelming task.

Principal Johnson added:

> Despite the inherent challenges early on in my position, mentoring has enabled me to learn effective strategies to apply to school turnaround.

However, a variety of studies emphasized how effective principals of high-performing schools provide leadership by monitoring teaching and providing feedback toward enhancing instructional leadership for student achievement outcomes (Carter, 2000; Cawelti, 1999; Izumi, 2002; Johnson and Asera, 1999; Reeves, 2000). Accordingly, Principal Lovett indicated that at her school, she expended large percentages of each day in classrooms observing instruction and providing feedback. Nevertheless, these two women expected that they could do the job. This case in point speaks to what the ability to make change despite the odds (Hill and Ragland, 1995). In recalling her fierce determination to overhaul the failing school, Principal Lovett's voice reflects the unmistakable sound of defeat.

Theme 2: Findings Related to Mentoring Activities Focused on Leading Efforts on Student Achievement in Low-Performing Schools

Experts contend that principal leadership remains pivotal in advancing school improvement efforts and increasing school effectiveness (Day, 2007; Griffith, 2001; Hines, 2007; Leithwood, 2005; Muijs, 2004). For decades, researchers have sought empirical evidence of the connection between leadership and achievement (Hallinger and Heck, 1996; Leithwood, 2005; Marks and Printy, 2003). Marzano et al. (2005) meta-analysis of studies mentioned earlier, further linkage school leadership and student achievement. In studies of effective schools, leadership (e.g., an effective principal) is frequently a prominent factor in descriptions of influential factors (Firestone, 1991; Reynolds et al., 2002; Teddlie and Reynolds, 2000). A growing body of research demonstrates that the leadership of a school principal plays a critical role in closing achievement gaps and increasing overall student performance (Chance and Segura, 2009; Cotton, 2003; Marzano et al., 2005).

Regarding goals focused on student learning, both principals received follow-up and support on mentoring activities from their individual mentors. More evidence for adequate time for learning, integration, and reflection in their PD in this regard was found at both schools. "Each Thursday, students were released early from school so that new principals could engage in professional development and dialogue activities," states Principal Lovett and Principal Johnson. These sessions were structured and organized by central administration. Further, to support the effective implementation of school improvement and provide school-leaders with leadership and instructional expertise, and better capacity, Principal Lovett and Principal Johnson were provided with biweekly structured activities around capacity building. Principal Johnson exclaimed: "I don't mind being required to do more if I am being supported."

Both principals maintain a different level of investment in their schools and them as African-American women principals. Principal Johnson further described the difference relative to prior reform efforts in the following manner:

> I feel more supported now than ever. In my first year, I felt more out there on my own, left to my own devices, even though I had a support team. I thought I was grasping at straws and trying to figure it all out. I feel 110 percent more supported now.

Referred to as "getting the big yes" in the turnaround literature (Hassel and Hassel, 2009), providing support to principals and altering policies that may impede school turnaround efforts is critical to effective turnaround initiative. Both Principals Lovett and Johnson indicate:

> As it relates to this particular urban district, the sentiments regarding district investment and support reflect a paradigm shift for the central office. Rather than functioning as a bureaucratic organization charged with procedures and compliance as was the case previously, there is seemingly a concerted effort in working to create the right conditions for all principals in turnaround schools to succeed.

That said, many factors contribute to poor performance, but the key means of improving performance is professional development and the commitment by central administration of principals in turnaround initiatives, ensuring that students are consistently provided high-quality instruction. Principal Lovett noted:

Since then I have learned to focus on instruction and getting into classrooms, I have reflected on the prioritization of student learning for the purpose of achievement . . .

Turning around schools are one of the only proven strategies for quickly achieving success in very low-performing schools (Duke, 2008). And finally, according to Johnson, Uline, and Perez (2011), the following was evidenced on research regarding principal leadership and student performance: A growing body of evidence underscores a significant and positive relationship between effective principal leadership and student learning and achievement. Recent research included qualitative case studies of highly challenged, high-performing schools (Johnson, Lein, and Ragland, 1998; Scheurich, 1998) and quantitative studies examining indirect leadership effects on student outcomes (Hallinger, Bickman, and Davis, 1998; Heck, 2000; Heck, Larsen, and Marcoulides, 1990; Leithwood, Jantzi, and Steinbach, 1999; Marks and Printy, 2003). In fact, an extensive review of evidence related to the nature and size of these efforts concluded that, among school-related factors, leadership is second only to classroom instruction in its contribution to student learning (Leithwood, Louis, Anderson, and Wahlstrom, 2005). Further, these effects are greatest within contexts where they are most needed, that is, "the greater the challenge the greater the impact of [leader] actions on learning" (p. 31).

Theme 3: Findings Related to Mentoring African-American Women Principals as a Catalyst for Diversifying School Leadership

Diverse educational leaders should be reflected among school leaders (Brown, 2005). The setting for this is more imperative given the ending of the desegregation era and changing demographics, reflecting diversity in our urban schools. Indeed, fifty years after *Brown*, Orfield and Lee (2004) reported that K–12 schooling in the United States has experienced a "substantial slippage toward segregation in most of the states that were highly desegregated in 1991" (p. 2). Orfield and Lee also noted that:

> The vast majority of intensely segregated minority schools face conditions of concentrated poverty, which are powerfully related to unequal educational opportunity. Students in segregated minority schools face conditions that students in segregated white schools seldom experience. (p. 2)

Therefore, African-Americans must establish the agenda for the education of their children. This agenda must include increasing the number of African-American teachers, principals, and superintendents who interact with, nurture, guide, and protect African-American children (Tillman, 2010). In this regard, Principal Lovett shared in her experience that she modeled this notion as a holistic approach to encouraging her environment:

> I demanded much from my teachers, and I demanded much from myself. That is the only way you can get people to follow you. They have to know that you are working just as hard as they are . . . It's all about the care and development of our children, our future.

The African-American woman principal in Dillard's study viewed caring for children as "a lifelong responsibility" (p. 552) and, thus, behaved, Similarly, Principal Lovett based her belief on that same view—that she needed to change the system to work on behalf of the students. To add, Mills (1998) acknowledges the dual positions that African-American women confront

because of the "devastating interaction of the double hegemony" (p. 16). African-American women deal with sexist and racist norms that values women for their bodies and their beauty and seldom values their minds or thoughts. Further stated:

> African-American women feel the tugs of both sisterhood and African American-ness, and adjudicating between them in times of conflict can be a difficult task indeed. (Mills, 1998, p. 17)

Both women's stories suggest that sexism as the only two appointed to the role of principal during the time the district was undergoing changes in sixteen of the schools in the district, which is probably a more powerful and personal agent of discrimination in the school environment than racism. Although Principal Lovett and Principal Johnson understood how racist practices functioned to constrain and maintain their career advancement, they did not regard in the interview the sexist discriminatory practices operated in their workplace.

CONNECTIONS BETWEEN KEY FINDINGS AND THE RESEARCH LITERATURE

The findings described in this chapter suggest that both schools that attained strong academic results for African-American students found ways to avoid the pitfalls described in research literature as common among low-performing schools. As well, these schools developed strengths through mentoring their principals that enabled them both to exude many of the strengths described in studies of high-performing urban schools. This study may have added depth to our understanding of how leaders influence the development of these strengths. The connections between this study's key findings and the research literature are evident in the particular area of mentoring support, and the role leaders play in influencing improvements in those areas.

DISCUSSION AND CONCLUSION

The purpose for this study was to illuminate commonalities of African-American women principals as leaders of urban school environments and understand how they make sense of their leadership roles. The narratives that emerged during the interviews provided perspective and a voice that is absent in the education literature, that which pertains to the dual role of African-American women as leaders and social agents answering the call to action to improve, thus transform urban schools and communities therein. The section summarizes the similarities in the lived experiences of the two African-American women principals with regard to the overarching research inquiry, specific to mentoring activities that were acclaimed as most salient to their leadership success and school turnaround.

As the narratives unfolded, I found myself as an African-American woman educational leader inclined to identify with "truth" in each shared experience. What was found was that there were multiple truths from both women. Some of their experiences overlapped in theme and delineation, and similar to Dillard's (1995) findings, the women participants certainly incorporated culture and community contexts into their leadership priorities and strategies. BFT enabled that situation of experiences. However, we did not get a sense from the participants of how the community was embracing or not the turnaround initiative. Further study is warranted to learn of instances of responsiveness from the communities of African-American women principals, as leaders of urban schools transforming schools thus communities.

Accordingly, African-American women principals in urban schools develop strength, identity, and a sense of community consciousness that drives them to work in low-performing schools (Bloom and Erlandson, 2003). The women participants of this study had developed similar identities as leaders and social agents who operated from their own experiences past and present of forces of marginalization in schools and communities that led them to serve urban school communities. Coincidentally, that force of marginalization in a culture that expects centeredness and assimilation produced women who have followed their dreams and lived up to visions of excellence for them. These women were not deterred by the political exigencies of the dominant culture. Both women indicated that culture, experiences, with emphasis on mentoring positively influenced their leadership styles.

Delimitations

The delimitations here include the following: (a) the research site is located in a specific geographical region and district, (b) research subjects are African-American

women principals who have led the same school site for the past six years, and (c) study did not look at longer-term student achievement as a result of principals' leadership.

Conclusion

As noted in previous research on African-American women principals in turnaround schools, there remains a paucity of research. This article focused on African-American female principals' persistence in their positions in relation to the concepts of leadership in turnaround schools. This analysis of the role mentoring of aspiring principals contributes to the scant literature, removing another layer of educational research and lack of social justice embedded practices in turnaround school literature that has clouded the importance of the lived experience to our understanding of the imperative to develop more African-American principals in low-performing schools as a model for diversifying leadership and policy in schools.

Given this, the findings of this study have significant implications for leadership preparation and practice for African-American women. First, if African-American women leading urban schools are experiencing success with nontraditional notions of leadership, how can we explore alternate ways of theorizing and understanding black feminist thought to construct new interpretations of realities for African-American women in education. The framework can be an important lens through which to examine the formation and structure of lived realities for any group of color. More research using standpoint theory to create knowledge construction that is emancipatory, anti-oppressive, and politically active can add power and dimension to those working within racialized environments. Researching within one's own community may add value to the current scholarship on African-American women and other women of color.

Finally, given the powerful influence that self-identity and cultural consciousness (Collins, 1991) are believed to have on the lives of African Americans as a whole and as demonstrated by the two women principals–study participants, researchers must explore methodologies that will permit increasingly sophisticated studies of the meanings and interpretive effects of racism, sexism, and classism in the identity and cultural development of African-American women. If the task of politically active scholarship is to counter the European-derived cultural and social perspectives and versions of history associated with white dominance, then using any and all alternative means of deconstruction of this privileged epistemology is required for future scholarship development of researchers.

REFERENCES

Achinstein, P. (2010). *Evidence, explanation, and realism: essays in philosophy of science*. Oxford: Oxford University Press.

Achinstein, B. and Ogawa, R. T. (2011a). Change(d) agents: New teachers of color in urban schools. New York: Teachers College Press.

Achinstein, B. and Ogawa, R. T. (2011b). Change(d) agents: School contexts and the cultural/professional roles of teachers of Mexican descent. *Teachers College Record, 113*(11).

Aiken, J. A. (2002). The socialization of new principals: Another perspective on principal retention. *Education Leadership Review, 3*(1), 32–40.

Alston, J. (2000). Missing in action: Where are the African American female school superintendents? *Urban Education, 35*(5), 525–531.

Ansell, D. (2004). *Improving schools facing challenging circumstances*. Nottingham: National College for School Leadership.

Ashburn, E. A., Mann, M., and Purdue, P. A. (1987). Teacher mentoring. ERIC Clearinghouse on Teacher Education. Paper presented at the Annual Meeting of the American Educational Research Association, Washington, DC. Retrieved from www.ericdigests.org/pre-924/mentoring.htm.

Bennis, W. and Nanus, B. (1985). *Leaders: Strategies for taking charge*. New York: Harper and Row.

Blakemore, J. (1999). *Troubling women: Feminism, leadership, and educational change*. Buckingham, UK: Open University Press.

Blankenstein, A. M. (2004). *Failure is not an option: 6 principles that guide student achievement in high performing schools*. Thousand Oaks, CA: Corwin Press.

Bloom, G. (1999). One-on-one support for new principals: Sink or swim no more. *Thrust for Educational Leadership, 29*(1), 14–17.

Bloom, G., Castagna, C., Moir, E., and Warren, B. (2005). *Blended coaching: Skills and strategies to support principal development*. Thousand Oaks, CA: Corwin.

Bloom, G. and Kravetz, M. (2001). A step into the principalship. *Leadership, 30*(3), 12–13.

Bolman, L. and Deal, T. (1995). *Leading with soul: An uncommon journey of spirit*. San Francisco: Jossey-Bass.

Bolman, L. and Deal, T. (1997). *Reframing organizations: Artistry, choice and leadership* (2nd ed.). San Francisco: Jossey-Bass.

Bolman, L. and Deal, T. E. (2002). *Reframing the path to school leadership*. Thousand Oaks, CA: Corwin Press.

Bolman, L. G. and Deal, T. E. (2003). *Reframing organizations: Artistry, choice, and leadership* (2nd ed.). San Francisco: Jossey-Bass.

Brooks, S. M. (2009). A case study of school-community alliances that rebuilt a community. *School Community Journal, 19*(2), 59.

Browne-Ferrigno T. and Muth, R. (2004). Leadership mentoring in clinical practice: Role socialization, professional development and capacity building. *Educational Administration Quarterly, 40*(4), 468–494.

Brunner, C. C. and Peyton-Caire, L. (2000). Seeking representation: Supporting African American female graduate students who aspire to the superintendency. *Urban Education, 31*(5), 532–548.

California Department of Education [CDE]. (2009). Fact book 2009: Handbook of education information. Sacramento, CA: Author.

Carter, S. (2000). No excuses: Lessons from 21 high-performing, high poverty schools. Washington, DC. Heritage Foundation.

Cawelti, G. (1999). Improving achievement. Retrieved from www.educate.ece.govt.nz/Programmes/CentresofInnovation.aspx.

Chance, P. and Segura, S. (2009). A rural high school's collaborative approach to school improvement. *Journal of Research in Rural Education, 24*(5), 1–12.

Cincinnati Public Schools. (2009). *Quick wins put school success on fast track*. Retrieved April 14, 2010 from www.cps-12.org/academics/AcadInitiatives/QuickWins/QuickWinEx.pdf.

Cistone, P. J. and Stevenson, J. M. (2000, August). Perspectives on the urban school principalship. *Education and Urban Society, 32*(4), 435–442.

Clark, D. C. and Clark, S. N. (1996). Better preparation of educational leaders. *Educational Researcher, 25*(8), 18–20.

Collins, P. H. (1991). *African American feminist thought: Knowledge, consciousness, and the politics of empowerment*. New York: Routledge.

Collins, P. H. (2002). Learning from the outsider within: The sociological significance of African- American feminist thought. In *Racial and ethnic diversity in higher education*, ed. C.S. Turner, A.L. Antonio, M. Garcia, B.V. Laden, A. Nora, and C. Presley. Boston: Pearson Custom.

Collins, K. W. and Lightsey, O. R., Jr. (2001, August). Racial identity, generalized self-efficacy, and self-esteem: A pilot study of a mediation model for African American women. *Journal of African American Psychology, 27*(3), 272–287.

Cotton, K. (2003). Principals and student achievement: What the research says. Alexandria, VA: Association for Supervision and Curriculum Development.

Cowan, K. T., Manasevit, L. M., Edwards, C. J., and Sattler, C. L. (2002). *The new Title I: Balancing flexibility with accountability.* Tampa: Thompson.

Creswell, J. W. (2009a). *Qualitative inquiry and research design: Choosing among five approaches.* Thousand Oaks, CA: Sage Publications.

Creswell, J. W. (2009b). *Research design: Qualitative, quantitative, and mixed methods.* Los Angeles: Sage.

Crow, G. M. and Mathews, L. J. (1998). *Finding one's way: How mentoring can lead to dynamic leadership.* Thousand Oaks, CA: Corwin Press.

Dana Center. (1999). Hope for urban education: A study of nine high-performing, high-poverty, urban elementary schools. Austin: University of Texas at Austin, Charles A.

Dana Center. Retrieved June 4, 2002, from www.ed.gov/pub/urbanhope/.

Darden, G. W. (2011). *A Study of the Views and Positions of School Administrators Toward Professional Development.* Doctoral dissertation, University of Georgia.

Daresh, J. C. (1986). Support for beginning principals: First handles are highest. *Theory Into Practice, 25,* 168–173.

Daresh, J. C. (1992). *The professional development of school administrators: Preserves, induction, and in service applications.* Needham Heights, MA: Allyn and Bacon.

Daresh, J. C. (1995). Research base on mentoring for educational leaders: what do we know? *Journal of Educational Administration, 33*(5), 7–16.

Daresh, J. C. (2001). *Leaders helping leaders: A practical guide to administrative mentoring.* Thousand Oaks, CA: Corwin Press.

Daresh, J. C. (2004). *Helping leaders: A practical guide to administrative mentoring* (2nd ed.). Thousand Oaks, CA: Corwin Press.

Daresh, J. C. (2006). *Beginning the principalship: A practical guide for new school leaders.* Thousand Oaks, CA: Corwin Press.

Daresh, J. C. and Playko, M. A. (1990). Mentoring for effective school administration. *Urban Education, 25* (1), 43–53.

Daresh, J. C. and Playko, M. A. (1994). Aspiring and practicing principals' perceptions of critical skills for beginning leaders. *Journal of Educational Administration, 32*(3), 35–45.

Day, C. (2014). Sustaining the turnaround: What capacity building means in practice. *REICE. Revista Iberoamericana sobre Calidad, Eficacia y Cambio en Educación, 12*(1), 9–20.

Dillard, C. (1995). Leading with her life: An African American feminist (re)interpretation of leadership for an urban high school principal. *Educational Administration Quarterly, 31*(4), 539–563.

Dufour, R. and Marzano, R. J. (2011). *Leaders of learning: How district, school, and classroom leaders improve student achievement.* Bloomington, IN: Solution Tree Press.

Duke, D. (2006). What we know and don't know about improving low-performing schools. *Phi Delta Kappan, 87,* 729–734.

Eisner, E. W. (2002). The kind of schools we need. *Phi Delta Kappan, 83,* 576–583.

Erlandson, D., E. Harris, B. Skipper, and S. Allen. (1993). *Doing naturalistic inquiry: A guide to methods.* Newbury Park, CA: Sage.

Farkas, S., Johnson, J., Duffett, A., and Foleno, T. (2001). Trying to stay ahead of the game: Superintendents and principals talk about school leadership. New York: Public Agenda. Retrieved from www.publicagenda.org/files/pdf/ahead_of_the_game.pdf.

Ferguson, R. (2010). *Toward excellence with equity: An emerging vision for closing the achievement gap.* Cambridge, MA: Harvard Education Press.

Firestone, W. A. (1991). Introduction. In J. R. Bliss, W. A. Firestone, and C. E. Richards (Eds.), *Rethinking effective schools; Research and practice* (pp. 1–11). Englewood Cliffs, NJ: Prentice Hall.

Fullan, M. G. (1991). *The new meaning of educational change* (2nd ed.) New York: Teachers College Press.

Fullan, M. (2005). *Leadership and sustainability: System thinkers in action.* Thousand Oaks, CA: Corwin Press

Fullan, M. (2006). *Turnaround leadership.* San Francisco: Jossey-Bass.

Gay, G. (2010). *Culturally responsive teaching: Theory, research, and practice.* New York: Teachers College Press.

Gay, G. and Airasian, P. W. (2001). *Motivation, language learning, and course performance.* Boca Raton, FL: Lynn University.

Gitlin, A. (1994). *Power and method: Political activism and educational research.* New York: Routledge.

Goldberg, M. F. (2001). Leadership in education: Five commonalities. *Phi Delta Kappan, 82,* 757–761.

Goldberg, M. and Traiman, S. L. (2001). Why business backs education standards. In D. Ravitch (Ed.), *Brookings papers on education policy 2001* (pp. 75–129). Washington, DC: Brookings Institution Press.

Goldring, E., Cravens, X. C., Murphy, J., Elliott, S. N., and Carson, B. (2008). *The evaluation of principals: What and how do states and districts assess leadership?* New York: American Educational Research Association.

Grant, C. (2014). African-American Women Educational Leaders in Turnaround Schools: Narrative Perspectives on Transforming Urban School Communities. In W. Sherman and K. Mansfield (Eds.). *Women Interrupting, Disrupting and Revolutionizing Educational Policy and Practice.* Educational Leadership for Social Justice Series. Charlotte, NC: Information Age.

Griffith, A. (2001). *Parent participation in school improvement processes.* Ottawa, Canada: Canadian Research Association.

Grogan, M. (1999). Equity/equality issues of gender, race, and class. *Education Administration Quarterly, 35*(4), 518–536.

Grogan, M. and Andrews, R. (2002). Defining preparation and professional development for the future. *Educational Administration Quarterly, 38*(2), 233–256.

Gurr, D., Dysdale, L., and Mulford, B. (2006). Models of successful principal leadership. *School Leadership and Management, 26*(4), 371–295.

Guy-Sheftall, B., ed. (1995). *Words of Fire: An Anthology of African American Feminist Thought.* New York: The New Press.

Hall, P. A. (2004). *The first-year principal.* Lanham, MD: Scarecrow Press.

Hall, P. (2008). Building bridges: Strengthening the principal induction process through intentional mentoring. *Phi Delta Kappan, 89*(6), 449–452.

Hallinger, P., Bickman, L., and Davis, K. (1998). School context: Principal leadership and student achievement. *Elementary School Journal, 96*(5), 498–518.

Hallinger, P. and Heck, R. (1996). Reassessing the principal's role in school effectiveness: A review of empirical research, 1980–1995. *Educational Administration Quarterly, 32*, 5–44.

Hargreaves, A. (1998). The emotional practice of teaching. *Teaching and Teacher Education, 14*(8), 835–54.

Hassel, E. A. and Hassel, B. C. (2009). The big u-turn: How to bring schools from the brink of failure to stellar success. *Education Next, 9*(1), 21–27. Retrieved August 30, 2009 from educationnext.org/the-big-uturn/.

Heck, R. H. (2000). The study of educational leadership and management. *Educational Management Administration and Leadership, 33*, 229–244.

Heck, R. H., Larsen, M., and Marcoulides, N. (1990). Student transition to high school and persistence: Highlighting the influences of social divisions and school 185 contingencies. *American Journal of Education, 112*(3), 418–446.

Henry, A. (2001). Looking two ways: Identity, research, and praxis in the Caribbean community. In B. M. Merchant and A. I. Willis (Eds.), *Multiple and intersecting identities in qualitative research* (pp. 61–68). Mahwah, NJ: Lawrence Erlbaum.

Hill, M. S. and Ragland, J. C. (1995). *Women as educational leaders: Opening windows, pushing ceilings.* Thousand Oaks, CA: Corwin Press.

Hines, D. A. (2007). *Cultural competency for public administrators.* Armonk, NY: M.E. Sharpe.

Izumi, F. (2002). *Implicit and explicit knowledge in second language learning, testing and teaching.* London, UK: Short Run Press.

Johnson, L. (2007). Rethinking successful school leadership in challenging U.S. schools: Culturally responsive practices in school-community relationships. *International Studies in Educational Administration (Commonwealth Council for Educational Administration and Management [CCEAM]), 35*(3), 49–57. Retrieved from search.ebscohost.com/login.aspx?direct=trueandAuthType=ip,url,cookie,uidanddb=a9 handAN=32512777andsite=ehost-liveandscope=site.

Johnson, J. F., Lein L., and Ragland, M. (1998). *Successful Texas school-wide programs.* Austin: University of Texas Charles A Dana Center.

Johnson, J. F., Uline, C., and Perez, L. (2011). Expert noticing and principals of high performing urban schools. *Journal of Education for Students Placed at Risk, 16*(2), 122–136.

Kanter, R. (1983). *The change masters: Innovation and entrepreneurship in the American corporation.* New York: Simon and Schuster.

Kanter, R.M. (2004). *Confidence: how winning and losing streaks begin and end.* New York: Crown Business.

Kotter, J. P. (1996). *Leading change.* Boston: Harvard Business School Press.

Kotter, J. P. (2007). Winning at change. *Leader to Leader, 10*, 27–33.

Kvale, S. (1996). The 1,000-page question. *Qualitative Inquiry, 2*, 275–284.

Jackson, B. L. (1999). Getting inside history—against all odds: African American women school superintendents. In C. C. Brunner (Ed.), *Sacred Dreams: Women and the superintendency.* Albany: State University of New York Press.

Leithwood, K. (2005). *Understanding leadership effects on pupil learning.* Toronto, Canada: UK Department of Skills and Education.

Leithwood, K., Louis, K. S., Anderson, S., and Wahlstrom, K. (2005). *How leadership influences student learning.* Toronto, Canada: Center for Applied Research and Educational Improvement and Ontario Institute for Studies in Education.

Lomotey, K. (1989). *African American principals: School leadership and success: Contributions in Afro-American and African studies* (No. 124). New York: Greenwood.

Marks, M. and Printy, T. (2003). Qualities of effective principals. *Human Resource Administration, 6,* 65–70.

Marshall, C. and Rossman, G. B. (1999). Designing qualitative research (3rd ed.). Thousand Oaks, CA: Sage.

Marzano, R. J. (2003). *What works in schools: Translating research into action.* Alexandria, VA: Association for Supervision and Curriculum Development.

Marzano, R. J. and McNulty, B. (2005). *Balanced leadership: What 30 years of research tells us about the effect of leadership on student achievement.* Aurora, CO: Mid-continent Research for Education and Learning (McREL).

Marzano, R. J., Pickering, D. J., and Pollock, J. E. (2001). *Classroom instruction that works: Research-based strategies for increasing student achievement.* Alexandria, VA: Association for Supervision and Curriculum Development.

Marzano, R., Waters, T., and McNulty, B. (2005). *School leadership that works: From research to results.* Alexandria, VA: McREL.

McCreary-King, K. (1992). Mentoring principals: Who does it and when? *National Association of Secondary School Principals, 76,* 116–120.

McEwan, E. K. (2003). *Ten traits of highly effective principals: From good to great performance.* Thousand Oaks, CA: Corwin Press.

McGough, D. (2003). Leaders as learners: An inquiry into the formation and transformation of principals' professional perspectives. *Educational Evaluation and Policy Analysis, 25*(4), 449–471.

Mendez-Morse, S. (2004). Constructing mentors: Latina educational leaders' role models and mentors. *Educational Administration Quarterly, 40*(4), 561–590.

Miles, K. H. and Frank, S. (2008). *The Strategic School: Making the Most of People, Time, and Money.* Thousand Oaks, CA: Corwin Press.

Miles, M. B. and Huberman, A. M. (1994). *Qualitative data analysis.* Thousand Oaks, CA: Sage.

Mitchell, C. and Sackney, L. (2000). *Profound improvement: building capacity for a learning community.* Lisse: Zeitlinger.

Muijs, D. (2004). *Measuring teacher effectiveness: The learning level.* London, UK: Routledge Falmer

Mullen, L. (2002). Resources for educating children with diverse abilities. *Journal of Education, 5*(4), 238–251.

Murphy, J. and Meyers, C. V. (2008). *Turning Around Failing Schools: Leadership Lessons from the Organizational Sciences.* Thousand Oaks, CA: Corwin Press.

Murtadha, K. and Larson, C. (1999, April). *Toward a socially critical, womanist, theory of leadership in urban schools.* Paper presented at the annual meeting of the American Educational Research Association, Montreal, Canada.

National Audit Office. (2006). *Improving poorly reforming schools in England.* London: Department for Education and Skills.

National Center for Education Statistics. (2003). *The nation's report card: Reading highlights 2003.* Washington, DC: U.S. Department of Education.

National Commission on Excellence in Education. (1988). A nation at risk: The imperative for educational reform. Retrieved from http://datacenter.spps.org/uploads/sotw_a_nation_at_risk_1983.pdf.

No Child Left Behind Act of 2001. (2001, December 13). Title I: Improving the academic achievement of the disadvantaged [107th Congress, 1st Session]. Washington, DC: George Washington University, National Clearinghouse for Bilingual Education.

No Child Left Behind Act, 20 U.S.C. Sections 6301 et seq. U.S.C. (2002).

Noe, R. A. (1988). An investigation of the determinants of successful assigned mentoring relationships. *Personnel psychology, 41*(3), 457–479.

Ogbu, J. (2003). School ethnography: A multilevel approach. *Anthropology and Education Quarterly, 12*(10), 3–29.

Orfield, G. and Lee, C. (2004). *Brown* at 50: King's dream or Plessy's nightmare? The Civil Rights Project, Harvard University. Retrieved January 26, 2004, from www.civilrightsproject.harvard.edu.

Perez, L., Uline, C., Johnson, J., James-Ward, C., and Basom, M. (2011). Foregrounding fieldwork in leadership preparation: The transformative capacity of authentic inquiry. *Educational Administration Quarterly, 47*(1), 217–257.

Peterson, K. (2002). The professional development of principals: Innovations and opportunities. *Educational Administration Quarterly, 38*(2), 213–232.

Petzko, V. (2008). The perceptions of new principals regarding the knowledge and skills important to their success. *NASSP Bulletin, 92*(3), 224–250.

Pinkerton, E. (Ed.). (2002). The CAASFEP handbook: The ABC's of categorical program Principal. Auburn, CA: California Association of Administrators of State and Federal Education Program.

Pollard, D. S. (1997). Race, gender, and educational leadership: Perspectives from African American principals. *Educational Policy, 11*(3), 353–374.

Public Impact. (2008). *School Turnarounds: Actions and Results.* Lincoln, IL: Center on Innovation and Improvement. Retrieved February 1, 2011, from www.centerii.org/survey/downloads/Turnaround%20Actions%20and%20Results%203%2 024%2008%20with%20covers.pdf.

Reeves, D. (2000). *The learning leader: How to focus school improvement for better results.* Alexandria, VA: Association of Curriculum and Development.

Reynolds, D., Creemers, B., Stringfield, S., Teddlie, C., and Schaffer, G. (Eds.). (2002). *World class schools: International perspectives on school effectiveness.* New York: Routledge Falmer.

Santamaría, L. J. and Santamaría2, A. P. (in press). Black women scholars "talking mentoring story" with African American women elementary school principals. *Mentor and Tutor* Special Issue.

Saphier, J. and Gower, R. (1997). *The skillful teacher: Building your teaching skills.* Acton, MA: Research for Better Teaching.

Scribner, J. P. (1999). Creating professional learning communities in schools with organizational learning: An evaluation of the school improvement process. *Education Administration Quarterly, 35*(1), 130–160.

Scheurich, J. J. (1993). Toward a White Discourse on White Racism Author(s). *Educational Researcher, 22*(8), 5–10.

Scheurich, J. (1998). Thinking carefully about equity and accountability. *Phi Delta Kappan, 82*(4), 293–299.

Scott, P. B. (1982). Debunking Sapphire: Toward a non-racist, non-sexist social science. In G. T. Hull, P. B. Scott, and B. Smith (Eds.), *But some of us are brave: African American women's studies* (pp. 85–92). Old Westbury, NY: Feminist Press.

Searby, L. (2010). Preparing future principals: Facilitating the development of a mentoring mindset through graduate coursework. *Mentoring and Tutoring: Partnership in Learning, 18*(1), 5–22.

Sheehy, G. (1976, April 5). The mentor connection: The secret link in the successful woman's life. *New York Magazine,* 33–39.

Sockett, H. (1993). *The moral base for teacher professionalism.* New York: Teachers College Press.

Spillane, J. (2005). *Distributed leadership.* San Francisco: Jossey-Bass.

Strauss, A. and Corbin, J. (1998). *Basics of qualitative research: Techniques and procedures for developing grounded theory* (2nd ed.). Thousand Oaks, CA: Sage.

Teddlie, C. and Reynolds, D. (Eds.). (2000). *The international handbook on school effectiveness research.* New York: Falmer Press.

Tillman, L. C. (2007). Halls of Anger: The (Mis)representation of African American Principals in Film. In D. Carlson and C.P. Gause (Eds.), *Keeping the Promise: Essays in Leadership, Democracy and Education,* vol. 305. New York: Lang Publishing.

U.S. Department of Education (USDOE). (2009). Race to the Top Program: Executive summary. Washington, DC. Retrieved from www2.ed.gov/programs/ racetothetop/executive-summary.pdf.

U.S. Department of Education (USDOE). (2010a). A blueprint for reform: The reauthorization of the Elementary and Secondary Education Act. Washington, DC. Retrieved from www2.ed.gov/policy/elsec/leg/blueprint/blueprint.pdf.

U.S. Department of Education (USDOE). (2010b). Nine states and the District of Columbia win second round race to the top grants. Retrieved from www.ed. gov/news/press-releases/nine-states-and-district-columbia-win-second-round-race-top-grants.

Waters, T. and Watkins, M. (2003). *The first 90 days: Critical success strategies for new leaders at all levels.* Boston: Harvard Business School.

Weingartner, C. J. (2001). Albuquerque principals have ESP. *Principal, 80*(4), 40–42.

Wildman, L. (2001, August). *Research on the preparation of school administrators.* Paper prepared for the Board of the National Council of Professors of Educational Administration, Bakersfield, CA.

Wilmore, E. L. (2004). *Principal induction: A standards-based model for administrator development.* Thousand Oaks, CA: Corwin Press.

Wilmore, E. L. and Thomas, C. (2001). The new century: Is it too late for transformational leadership? *Educational Horizons, 79*(3), 115–123.

Yeakey, C. C., Johnston, G. S., and Adkison, J. A. (1986). In pursuit of equity: A review of research on minorities and women in educational administration. *Educational Administration Quarterly, 22*(3), 110–149.

Yonezawa, S. (2000). Unpacking the African American box of tracking decisions: Critical tales of families navigating the course placement process. In M. G. Sanders (Ed.), *Schooling students placed at risk: Research, policy, and practice in the education of poor and minority adolescents* (pp. 109–137). Mahwah, NJ: Lawrence Erlbaum.

Urban Educational Leadership for the Twenty-First Century

Michael E. Dantley

So much continues to be written focusing on urban education. Milner and Lomotey (2014) have edited a volume totally committed to exploring the nature of urban education. The late Jean Anyon (2014) completed a text that focused on what she called radical possibilities with particular attention given to public policy, urban education, and a new social movement. No doubt, some of the most prodigious, intellectually astute, and prolific scholars of our time have tackled the concept of urban education. And now, the text that holds this epilogue is one of the latest scholarly volumes to define and deconstruct the notions of urban education. This one, however, pays close attention to the leadership of schools in urban spaces. The pinpointing of this work graciously affords the articulation of a discussion that takes urban education to a dimension that I believe to be most efficacious and helpful.

Let me begin by arguing that scholarship in urban education and specifically urban educational leadership must have undergirding it a prophetic and subversive agenda. Allow me to explain just why the prophetic is a useful lens through which to view the work of urban educational leadership. The notion of the prophetic emanates from the Old Canon of the Judeo-Christian tradition. It was the prophet, in the Old Testament, who not only foretold the future of the people but the prophet also loudly proclaimed whatever was out of order. The prophet would denounce unjust and whatever behaviors, routines, and ways of thinking that were oppressing the people. The prophet's job was to establish the moral standard. The prophet's obsession was to command lifestyles from the people that were ethical and righteous. Finally, the prophet's role was to hold the people accountable for any malfeasance or immoral compromise of the holy expectations they were commanded to meet. The prophet was the moral barometer for the Old

Testament people. The prophets of the Old Testament announced such messages as loosing the chains of injustice and untying the cords of the yoke as well as the demand to set the oppressed free. Further, the prophet proclaimed that the people were to share their food with the hungry, to provide shelter for the wanderer, and to clothe the naked. The voice of the prophet heralded a return to justice. It called for the people to see themselves in what Martin Buber much later called the I-Thou perspective. The goal of the prophet was to uproot an unjust status quo with all of its appurtenances and to replace it with a radical, fundamental shift that shook the very foundation of society writ large.

Because of the poignant role the Old Testament prophet played, I maintain that such a historic model of forthrightly speaking truth to power is essential in a contemporary prophetic voice. I further contend that such a prophetic voice ought to be embraced by those who prepare school leaders and those practicing school leaders who are determined to cause a genuine discourse on urban educational leadership to be an expedient one. Allow me to explain why this should be the case.

The issues that are inherent in most urban environments are so significant, i.e., high levels of poverty, weighty concentrations of residents for whom English is not their native language, the ubiquity of race-based politics and legislation, and the monumental structural concerns of PK–12 education, that generic, homogenized versions of leadership that lack a poignant, subversive edge, leave these issues untouched and thriving. A prophetic discourse uncovers the multitude of euphemisms that serve as politically correct obfuscations for the realities of race and class bias. Additionally, a prophetic discourse uncovers the discrimination and inequities that are deeply embedded in the pervasive grammar of the traditional treatise on urban education and its reform.

The prolific urban philosopher Cornel West (2014, 1999) helps us to understand not only the prophetic tradition but also, more significantly, why wrapping our minds around how the prophetic tradition can and must undergird the discourse that attends to matters of urban education will lead to significant positive results. It is West's thinking, on what he has coined prophetic pragmatism, that provides the fodder for my aligning the notions of the prophet with urban educational school leadership. bell hooks (West, 1999), in an interview with West, restates his definition of prophetic pragmatism. She reminds him that his explanation of this concept is "a form of third-wave left romanticism that tempers its utopian impulse with the profound sense of the tragic character of life in history" (p. 544). In response to hooks' reminder by West of his definition of prophetic pragmatism, he retorts,

> And the fact that when you look closely at jazz, the blues, for example, we see a sense of the tragic, a profound sense of the tragic linked to human agency. So that it does not wallow in a cynicism or a paralyzing pessimism, but it also is realistic enough not to project excessive utopia. It's a matter of responding in an improvisational, undogmatic, creative way to circumstances in such a way that people still survive and thrive. This is a great tradition intellectually; in fact, it has tremendous impact on the way in which Americans as a whole respond to the human condition, respond to their circumstances. (p. 544)

That prophetic edge, that uses West's prophetic pragmatism as its foundation, unashamedly denudes the heinous machinations systemically inherent in urban systems of education. Those collusions celebrate processes and policies that profile especially black students, for academic failure. The agenda of the prophetic is an unmasking of the realities that perpetuate mass numbers of African-American male students enrolled in special education classes. Further, the agenda calls much needed attention to the egregious numbers of African-American males among the ranks of suspended and expelled students. Further, the prophetic voice situates the issues of education in a much broader context. It sees urban education in a racially divided Ferguson, Missouri, Southside and Westside, Chicago, Staten Island, New York, Millennial Activists United, St. Louis, Missouri, Monroe and Cleveland, Ohio, im-

migration reform, the Ebola crisis, and other societal complexities. Such a perspective compels the leader to comprehend the multifaceted nexus within which the educational process resides. It is the prophetic voice that demands that educators see what it is that happens in schoolhouses as being deeply entrenched in the exigencies of the home, the affairs of the community, the issues of the city, the concerns of the state, and the matters of the nation. Indeed, the prophetic voice positions the work of urban education within the global context that is clearly calling for transformation and progression. The required transformation and progression are in hopes of activating education to a position of serving as one of the essential vehicles for ordaining radical societal change. In fact, the call, from a prophetic perspective, on education, is to become a subversive medium, to bring about radical change to not only the system of education but also to the multiple, hegemonic systems in which it is embedded. It is the responsibility of the prophetic voice to critique assiduously, especially in the face of opposition and resistance, the status quo existence of the educational system. The prophetic voice remains attentive to that which is unscrupulous and immoral and unremittingly calls for reform, reconstruction, and a complete reestablishment, at the roots, of the educative process in urban spaces. The prophetic voice is not politically correct or polite. Again, West (1999) provides much needed insight where the prophetic is concerned. He writes, "The mark of the prophet is to speak the truth in love with courage-come what may" (p. 171). The prophetic is ignited through an amalgamation of love and anger. It is a type of righteous indignation that is motivated through compassion and an axiological commitment to right that which is so wrong in the system. Once again, let us look to West for further clarification on the role of the prophetic. He proffers,

> The prophetic . . . much like C. Wright Mills's activist intellectual, puts a premium on educating and being educated by struggling peoples, organizing and being organized by resisting groups. This political dimension of prophetic pragmatism as practiced within the Christian tradition impels one to be an organic intellectual, that is one who revels in the life of the mind, yet relates ideas to collective praxis. An organic intellectual, in contrast to traditional intellectuals, who often remain comfortably nested in the academy, attempts to be entrenched

in and affiliated with organizations, associations and possible, movements of grassroots folk. (pp. 171–172)

That is how the scholarship on urban education must be carried out. Urban educational leadership scholarship that is influenced by the prophetic will demonstrate not only an expose of the multiple areas of pathology that exist in many urban educational systems but will also offer strategies and critical practices that will bring about radical systemic change under the auspices of hope. The prophetic message is not simply one of social criticism. Rather it is one of Freirean praxis where the incisive deconstruction of realities receives appropriate reflection, and critical action steps are soon to follow. It cannot be overly emphasized that the agenda for change that emanates from a prophetic lens is grounded in a deep sense of hope and expectation. The irony of possessing hope is its inevitable alignment to despair. The words of West (1999) again give us food for thought. He offers on this matter,

> Despair and hope are inseparable. One can never understand what hope is really about unless one wrestles with despair. The same is true with faith. There has to be some serious doubt; otherwise, faith becomes merely a dogmatic formula, an orthodoxy, a way of evading the complexity of life rather than a way of engaging honestly with life . . . You have to be willing to look at the worst to push for the best . . . It means wrestling with despair and doubt but never allowing them to have the last word. (p. 554)

While I agree with West's assertions about embracing both hope and despair as an essential coupling, I would offer additionally that both the powerful emotions of love and anger must undergird the work of the urban school leader simultaneously. It is love, not patrimony that inspires the anger in the school leader. Love for the students, a high regard and respect for their personhood, and a commitment to their overall well-being are the motivators for anger. Impactful urban school leaders must be angry. In fact, I would argue that unless urban school leaders are angry, they will do the schools they lead a terrible injustice. Without rage, whose genesis is love, these urban school leaders will adopt status quo institutional behaviors sans critique. They will follow the traditional plans for leading a school without consciousness. They will accept the stereotypical typecast-ing of black students as intellectually deficient. Without anger, these school leaders will lack the fire to advocate for their students against a tide that washes away any notion of the strengths and assets urban students inherently possess. Both love and anger were foundational to the prophets' message. It was because of their love that they became angry with the ways the people were being oppressed by their enemies and therefore announced strategies to relinquish themselves from the hands of their oppressors. In like manner, the prophetic, and the emotions of love and anger, situate the urban school leaders in a position to engage projects that have substantive meaning to the life of their schools.

PROPHETIC, PRAGMATIC PROJECTS

So what the prophetic voice means practically for the urban school leader is that she/he must provide critical leadership in three areas or what I will call three projects. These three projects include the organizational structure of urban schools, administrative decision-making, and curriculum/pedagogy assessment in urban spaces. We will explore each of these in this section of the chapter.

When one examines the organizational structure of the urban school, the leader who is grounded in a prophetic paradigm will engage in creating an environment that sets high expectations for the leadership, faculty, staff, students, parents, and the community and sees the work of the schoolhouse in a broader social and cultural context. That is, the urban school leader embraces the community as a significant resource in the educative process and is therefore in a mutual partnership, a symbiotic relationship that is built upon the commutative understanding that both existences and ultimate success are reciprocal. So while the school leader practices proactive leadership endeavors such as creating vision, allocating resources, coalescing constituents around mission, setting direction, building alliances, partnerships, and positive professional relationships, all of this is done under the auspices of preparing an organizational structure that is nimble enough to entertain multiple voices, nuances of lived experiences, and the multifaceted complexities of urban community life. Deep and substantive conversations with community leaders, faculty, parents, and student groups all assist in creating the project that contextualizes the intellectual or academic project of the school. The organizational structure must lend itself to such inclusion. It is through this structure, which, by the way, is a permeable one, that substantive conversations regarding the realities of urban life and the hope for the resolution of the quotidian dilemmas that students, faculty, and members of the community bring with them to the schoolhouse doors can be facilitated. Such a leader must see and readily embrace the duality of his/her work. The work includes motivating positive movement toward the achievement of a goal while also celebrating differentiated participation, that is multiple gradations and degrees of participation, levels of commitment, and the articulation of the varieties of dreams and aspirations that exist in the stakeholders of an urban school community.

Leadership in an urban space must possess a kind of paradoxical nature. What this means is that there must be a combination of directive and non-directive leadership practices that can lead to the success of the urban school. Directive leadership practices include the work of the prophetic that pronounces direction, vision, and mission. The prophetic also underpins the directive behavior of the urban school leader to denude and denounce the inequitable and marginalizing practices lodged particularly against African-American, Latino and students of poverty that have a systemic existence in urban school systems.

Urban school leadership also has a non-directive component. I call this non-directive because the leadership practices that are included in this component do not require predictability, uniformity of thought, or standardization of behavior. Rather, the non-directive side of leadership organization takes as a priori the messiness and unpredictability of human beings, the inevitable vagaries of the human condition, and yet, strangely enough, strongly believes that some cohesion of thought, some synthesis of strategies for the school can come from this collection of perspectives. This aspect of leadership engages the school community, writ large, in a futuristic discourse that emanates from the strategies voiced by the constituents in the school community. This is non-directive leadership because it involves the school leader's commitment to dialogue. A dialogue that is inclusive of multiple and at times grossly divergent voices. The commitment to dialogue is one for which the Brazilian activist Paulo Freire (1970) outlined its essential components. These

components include love, faith, mutual trust, hope, and critical thinking. These are not the kinds of traditional leadership behaviors and perspectives touted as the ones that lead to leadership effectiveness. The urban school organization, however, cannot afford to placate a historicity that has been grounded in absenting the work of the schoolhouse from the intentions and agendas of all who hold a stake in its efficacy.

The decision-making project for an urban school leader is one that is not solely founded on the policies and sedimented formulas and edicts pronounced by the guardians of the institution's status quo. Decision-making, much like the organizational structure, has to be intentional in its vision to see academic achievement intimately aligned with community advancement. Decisions regarding prospective faculty, for instance, to fill vacancies in urban schools need to be made through answers to the following questions:

- Does the candidate have former experiences in urban schools?
- Have those experiences been positive for the students, the parents, and the community?
- Is the candidate aware of his/her personal biases and dispositions that may negatively impact performance in an urban setting?
- Does the candidate see teaching in the urban setting as also requiring the development of a vibrant relationship with parents and community?
- Is the candidate's motivation messianic or missionary or does it emanate from a desire to build upon the assets and strengths urban children bring with them through the schoolhouse doors?

Often the decision-making in an urban school, where the leader adopts the prophetic paradigm, will be grounded in disclosing those practices and policies that prolong the marginalization of students. Where both anger and love are present, decisions are made based upon a critical optimism (Freire, 2005), that is one that, "requires a strong sense of social responsibility and of engagement in the task of transforming society; it cannot mean simply letting things run on" (p. 10). Literally, every decision has the potential to impact hundreds of lives both internally and externally to the school. So the decision-making project therefore has to include the labor of a critical consciousness, courage to disclose practices and policies that marginalize, and a commitment to a moral vision fully cognizant of the unfinishedness of all human encounters.

Some may argue that this heightened sensitivity when making decisions should become the practice of all school leaders everywhere. I certainly would not lodge a counterargument against such a statement. However, in defense of such sensitivity being active in urban school leaders' decision making, it is not everywhere where economic resources to support academic endeavors are woefully lacking. It is not everywhere where racism is a motivation for purposeful disenfranchisement. It is not everywhere where the sanctity, especially of black male life, has to be called for. It is not everywhere where "the least qualified teachers are more often found in the lowest performing schools in the United States" (Lomotey and Lowery, 2014, p. 326). It is not everywhere where the expectation for black and brown children to succeed academically simply does not exist. So with these very powerful exigencies, the need for a heightened sensitivity to the decision-making process in an urban school setting is a must. The final project for urban school leadership is one grounded in pedagogy and curriculum.

The project that focuses on pedagogy and curriculum may, at first glance, appear to be ensconced in the domain of the classroom teacher. Such thinking is not incorrect. But urban school leaders must take special interest in what is delivered in the classroom and indeed how it is delivered. The prophetic edge requires that school leaders concern themselves with not only the academic messages the curriculum and pedagogy engender but also the sociocultural pronouncements that they make. Indeed, the urban school leader is actually demanded to ensure that cultural knowledge is used to dictate some of the pedagogical decisions that get enacted in urban classrooms (Gay, 2014). Additionally, "establishing congruency between classroom instructional techniques and the learning styles of different ethnic groups" (Gay, 2014, p. 365) has to play a prominent role on the daily agenda of the urban school leader. The monitoring of the curriculum and pedagogy becomes an academic/civil rights activist project that clearly understands the power of this kind of alignment.

It is important to assert that when the classroom is a place where intellectual challenge is carried out within an atmosphere of care, then academic achievement is bound to be a result and the incidences of disciplinary issues are bound to decrease. It is through this prophetic attention given to what happens in the classroom that the urban school leader monitors how urban school students' intellectual self-images are being shaped. Further, leaders are able to assess which teachers are genuinely committed to the social justice mission of the school and in what ways the powerful exchange between students and teachers can be enhanced. Urban school leaders do not have the luxury to enjoy simply the role of a manager. Indeed, it is often the managerial role that maintains the status quo and bristles against any form of transformation and particularly transformation grounded in a civil rights, social justice agenda. But the prophetic leader embraces the charge to lead and not simply manage the school. The prophetic leader acknowledges that some of the sedimented policies and procedures that have traditionally undergirded administrative structure, decision-making, and curriculum development have maintained the inequities and disenfranchisement that have accompanied the daily journeys of black children in urban schools. So while management has to be a concern, it cannot take the place of leading the urban school, and the curriculum and pedagogy project is one of the major areas of leadership urban school leaders must embrace.

The curriculum and pedagogy project requires the urban school leaders' style to be a peripatetic one, that is one that has the schoolhouse, writ large, rather than the school office as their base. They are required to know what is happening in every corner of the building. They are called upon to be cognizant of every nuance that has the possibility of negatively impacting the positive and culturally conscious learning environment that has to be in place in the urban space. Therefore, there is no doubt that the projects of administrative structure and decision-making not only influence the curriculum/pedagogy project but are also heavily influenced by this third project.

CONCLUSION

Throughout this epilogue, I have argued that a more substantive form of leadership has to undergird the professional practices of leaders in urban schools. No doubt, too much is at stake to simply rely upon the tried-and-true strategies for leading schools and to then believe that those practices and routines will achieve what has to occur in school in urban spaces. The fact that this volume focuses on urban leadership implies that there are very special, distinctive markers that characterize urban schools, and therefore the leadership of these institutions must also be unique and distinctive. It is for this reason that I have asserted that urban school leadership must be a prophetic and indeed subversive one. The plethora of complexities that contextualize urban schools requires that leadership in these spaces captures not only the mind but also the heart of the students and the community they serve. This prophetic leadership must see the community not only as a resource but also as a part of the learning environment whose issues are fodder for a relevant curriculum that guides urban school pedagogy.

So with this prophetic edge, urban school leaders set a moral standard whose goal is to prepare students to engage the issues of an urban context as matters to be resolved through the assistance of the educative process. It is a leadership of disclosure, critique, and transformation. Urban school leadership is subsumed in a commitment to civil rights and social justice and an agenda to engage the multiple ways children and adolescents are marginalized through traditional institutional practices.

This volume sheds light on the imperatives that contour urban school leadership. It richly demonstrates how this genre of leadership castigates a traditional model and endorses one with societal transformative motivations. It not only critiques but it also generously pronounces solutions. This volume represents the academic rigor and the intellectual acumen of the scholars who have contributed to its completion. Beyond this, however, this volume represents a demand for substantive changes to take place in those spaces where mostly black and brown students go to school. It calls for a prophetic fire (West, 2014) to undergird the daily practices of school leaders and promises that through this added dimension to leadership, schools in urban spaces will be physically and emotionally safe, challenging, and societally transforming spaces.

REFERENCES

Freire, P. (2000/1970). *Pedagogy of the oppressed* (M. R. Ramos, Translator). (30th anniversary edition.). New York: Continuum Publishing.

Freire, P. (2011). *Education for critical consciousness.* New York: Continuum International Publishing Group.

Gay, G. (2014). Culturally responsive teaching principles, practices, and effects. In H. R. Milner and K. Lomotey (Eds.), *Handbook of urban education.* New York: Routledge.

Lomotey, K. and Lowery, K. (2014). Black students, urban schools, and black principals. In H. R. Milner and K. Lomotey (Eds.), *Handbook of urban education.* New York: Routledge

West, C. (1999). *The Cornel West reader.* New York: Civitas Books.

West, C. (2014). *Black prophetic fire.* Boston: Beacon Press.

integrated intervention plan, 526

intellectual self-image, 628

internalized oppression, 458

International Federation of Red Cross and Red Crescent Societies (IFRC), 547

International School Leadership Development Network (ISLDN), 518–21, 529; background of, 522; high-need schools studies of, 525–26; social justice in, 522–23

interpersonal skills, 400

intersectionality, 179

Interstate School Leaders Licensure Consortium (ISLLC), 150, 168, 306, 407, 444, 447

Interstate Teacher Assessment and Support Consortium (InTASC), 168

intrapersonal skills, 400

Irvine, J. J., 7

Irvine, R. W., 7

Isaacson, L. E., 106

ISLDN. *See* International School Leadership Development Network

ISLLC. *See* Interstate School Leaders Licensure Consortium

isolation, 46

iterative reflections, 91

I-Thou perspective, 624

Jackson, 220

Jackson, Y., 67–68, 499

James, R., 401

JCPS. *See* Jefferson County Public Schools

Jeanes, Anna T., 22

Jeanes teachers, 22–24

Jean-Marie, G., 303

Jefferson County Public Schools (JCPS), 74–82

Jeynes, W. H., 273

Jia Liang, 349

Jiangang Xia, 3

Jianping Shen, 3

Johanek, M. C., 351

Johannesen-Schmidt, M. C., 29

Johnson, (principal), 614–16

Johnson, D., 94

Johnson, J. F., 616

Johnson, L., 132

Johnson, Lyndon, 8

Johnston, G. S., 609

journal writing, 95

Jupp, J. C., 138

juvenile justice system, 322–24

Kaagan, S. S., 87

Kahenman, Daniel, 501

Kantor, H., 50, 195–96

Karaka Grove School, 538–40

Karpinski, C. F., 23–24, 305–6, 308

Katzenmeyer, M., 87, 93

Kaupapa Māori, 533–35, 542–43

Kegan, 482

Keleher, T., 332–33

Kelly, G. J., 290

Kentor, 50

Kerr, K. A., 73

Khaja, M. A., 12

Khalifa, M. A., 125–26, 139, 241

Killion, J. P., 95, 104

King, B. G., 259

King, J. E., 148, 159, 169, 171–72

King, Martin Luther, Jr., 496, 550

kinships, 534, 541

Kitsantas, A., 475

Klaf, S., 66

Klassen, R. M., 475

Knapp, M. S., 482

Knobel, D. J., 118

Knoff, H., 165

knowledge: construction of, 309–10; educational leadership and base of, 311–12; tikanga, 541

knowledge-practicing gaps, 213

Komarraju, M., 475

Korabik, K., 28

Kotter, J., 16

Krajewski, B., 12

Kranz, J., 380

Krawchuk, L. L., 475

Krull, Melissa, 507

Kubrin, C. E., 5–6

Kusmer, Kenneth, 46–47, 48, 56

Kwan, M. P., 66

Labaree, D. F., 10, 56

Ladson-Billings, G., 131, 138, 148, 214, 284, 290, 294; culturally relevant teachings and, 119; dialogue for success and, 129; education debt from, 163

Lahey, 482

Laible, J., 442

Landsman, J., 131

language, 400; advocacy-oriented, 407–8; race, 405; racism perpetuated through, 194–95; of urban public schools, 366

Lare, R., 259

Larner, W., 65

Larson, C., 605, 609

Latane, B., 311

Dr. **Muhammad Khalifa** is an assistant professor in the Department of Educational Administration at Michigan State University. He has worked as a public school teacher and administrator in Detroit. His research focuses on culturally responsive leadership in urban schools, and demonstrates the necessity of school leaders to enact a nuanced school leadership unique to the sensibilities and histories of the local community. He also has prepared school leaders in a number of international locations in Asia, the Middle East, and Africa. He argues that principals must be culturally responsive in not only promoting school culture, but in how they even enact instructional, transformational, and other types of leadership. His research has been published in *Teachers College Record, Educational Administration Quarterly*, the *Urban Review*, the *Journal of School Leadership, Race Ethnicity and Education, Urban Education*, and *Education and Urban Society*. He is editor of the forthcoming book, *Becoming Critical*.

He has recently been helping school leaders and state-level education officials with conducting equity audits in local school districts, as it is one of the only tools that effectively confronts achievement and discipline gaps in school. The demand has been so great that he developed an online equity audit tool that principals can use to conduct equity audits in their buildings.

Noelle Witherspoon Arnold, PhD, is an associate professor and former Program PK12 educational leadership coordinator in the Department of Educational Leadership and Policy Analysis at the University of Missouri-Columbia. A former administrator at the district and state level, Dr. Arnold also currently serves as consultant throughout the United States, advising districts in analyzing data for school improvement, cultural mediation, STEM leadership for education, and teaching and leading in urban and rural contexts. Dr. Arnold is president and executive committee member of the University Council for Educational Administration (UCEA). Dr. Arnold is the first African-American female to serve as president for UCEA.

Dr. Arnold's articles have appeared in the *Teacher's College Record, International Journal of Leadership in Education, International Journal of Qualitative Studies in Education, The Journal of Educational Administration History, Equity and Excellence in Education, The Journal of Negro Education, International Journal of Educational Reform*, and the *Journal of Educational Administration*. Dr. Arnold has nine books published or in press including *Ordinary Theologies: Religio-spirituality and the Leadership of Black Female Principals*. Dr. Arnold is currently the series editor of *New Directions in Educational Leadership: Innovation in Research, Teaching and Learning* for Information Age Publishing, and assistant editor of the *International Journal of Leadership in Education*. Dr. Arnold is currently conducting two studies on the role of urban principals and student health disparities and educational leadership in crisis and disaster areas.

Dr. Arnold is a two-time nominee for both the Jack Culbertson Award for the University Council for Educational Administration (UCEA) and Division–A Emerging Scholar Award American Educational Research Association (AERA). She is the recipient of the Outstanding Reviewer of the Year for 2009–2010 for the *Journal of School Leadership* and Honorable Mention in *New Digest International* "Who's Who in Academia" in 2013. Dr. Arnold has served as expert on issues in urban schooling and religion and education for NPR and other news outlets.

Before joining the faculty of the Department of Educational Leadership and Administration at NMSU, Dr. **Azadeh F. Osanloo** received her doctorate in the Educational Leadership and Policy studies Program, specializing in the social and philosophical foundations of education at Arizona State University. Her research addressed civic education in a post–9/11 climate, focusing on the concepts of democracy, cosmopolitanism, human rights, and citizenship from theory to praxis. She has merged her work in civics and human rights with her new research agenda on collaborative systemic diversity-based interventions for bullying for middle schools. Prior to being in Arizona, she taught in the New York City public schools, working primarily with junior high school students in the South Bronx, and jointly was a program director at the Harlem Educational Activities Fund, a not-for-profit that specialized in closing the gap between educational attainment and disenfranchised students. While in New York City she obtained her master's in public administration from New York University's Robert F. Wagner School. In general, her research agenda focuses on issues of educational equity; educational leadership, and policy; the philosophical foundations of education; diversity, multiculturalism, and human rights; bullying interventions; and social justice. Her research agenda is underscored by the four edited books she is currently working on which cover the topics of urban school leadership, diversity-based bullying interventions, student and parent perceptions of bullying, and international and national social justice work. She is currently the Stan Fulton Endowed Chair for the Improvement of Border and Rural Schools and has won the Dean's Awards for her teaching and service.

Cosette M. Grant is an educational advisor and consultant in government. She serves as liaison to the White House, U.S. Department of Education, the National League of Cities, and the Pennsylvania Department of Education. She is an affiliate faculty member of Educational Leadership and Policy Reform at the University of Cincinnati. She is a recent tenure-track assistant professor, member of the graduate faculty and Director of the Center for the Study of Leadership in Urban Schools (CSLUS) at the University of Cincinnati. She also served as the editor of the *International Journal of Educational Leadership*. She serves on the advisory board of CSLUS and on the Barbara Jackson Scholars Program of the University Council for Educational Administration (UCEA). She is a Barbara L. Jackson Scholars Mentor. Dr. Grant's research focuses on culturally relevant pedagogy in leadership preparation programs that might inform equity and access to enhance learning outcomes for underrepresented populations. Her work also includes emergent work on effective leadership for educational equity in P–12 schools and the inclusion of social justice in leadership development and preparation programs for educators and educational leaders. Dr. Grant holds a doctorate degree in educational foundations and leadership. Dr. Grant has convened National Student Symposia centered on doctoral students engaged in action research on fast-breaking urban educational issues. She is a leader, scholar, and mentor.

Judy A. Alston, PhD, is chair/professor of the Department of Leadership Studies at Ashland University. Her research foci include black female school superintendents; the exploration of how the intersections of class, race, ethnicity, gender, sexuality, and ability affect leaders; tempered radicals; and servant leadership. She holds a PhD in educational administration from the Pennsylvania State University and two master's of education degrees from the University of South Carolina. She is author of numerous articles and books, including *School Leadership and Administration: Important Concepts, Case Studies, and Simulations*, 7th–9th editions, and *Herstories: Leading with the Lessons of the Lives of Black Women Activists*.

Gary L. Anderson, professor at New York University, has written widely on issues of neoliberalism and educational leadership. His 2009 book *Advocacy Leadership: Toward a Post Reform Agenda* provides an analysis of how neoliberal policies are shaping what it means to be a school leader.

Anika Ball Anthony is an associate professor of educational administration in the Department of Educational Studies at the Ohio State University. Her research focuses on technology implementation, technology leadership, and the systemic nature of school organizations. Her experiences include designing and evaluating online learning environments, studying technology integration in urban mathematics and science classrooms, and supporting educational leaders in their efforts to implement technology for system-wide improvements. Anthony teaches courses on educational administration, technology leadership, and technology integration.

Amanda Askin is a doctoral student in educational leadership at New Mexico State University.

Glenn Baete was a former high school principal in Jefferson County Public Schools, where he serves as the evaluation and transition coordinator. He earned his EdD from the University of Louisville.

Bruce Barnett is a professor in the educational leadership and Policy Studies Department at the University of Texas at San Antonio. Previously, he has worked at the Far West Laboratory, Indiana University, and the University of Northern Colorado. Besides developing and delivering master's, certification, and doctoral programs, his professional interests include: educational leadership preparation programs, particularly cohort-based learning and school-university partnerships; mentoring and coaching; reflective practice; leadership for school improvement; realities of beginning principals and assistant principals; and international trends in leadership preparation and development. Bruce's work in these areas appears in a variety of books, book chapters, and journals including *Educational Administration Quarterly, Journal of Educational Administration, International Journal of Urban Educational Leadership, Journal of Research on Leadership Education, Journal of School Leadership, Journal of Staff Development*, and *Leading and Managing*. For well over a decade, he has become involved in international research and program development, coauthoring books on school improvement; researching mentoring and coaching programs operating around the world; and presenting workshops in Australia, New Zealand, England,

Hong Kong, Ireland, and Canada. From 2008–2013, Bruce served as the associate director of international affairs for the University Council for Educational Administration. One of the current projects being implemented is the International School Leadership Development Network, a collaboration of colleagues around the world examining leadership preparation and development in different cultural contexts.

Dr. Ivory M. Berry is the associate director of retention and student success in the College of Science and Mathematics at Wright State University in Dayton, Ohio. Dr. Berry earned his PhD (2014) and master of arts (2008) in educational policy studies from the University of Illinois at Urbana-Champaign and a bachelor of science (2007) in mathematics from Southern University and A&M College in Baton Rouge, Louisiana. In his professional role at Wright State University, Dr. Berry develops and evaluates student success initiatives for science and math majors; directs a living-learning community for students pursuing undergraduate degrees in science, technology, engineering, mathematics, and medicine (STEMM); teaches student success classes; advises and monitors students on academic probation; and collects, analyzes, and reports college enrollment, retention, attrition, and graduation data. In addition to researching the effectiveness of high impact retention practices on underprepared and underperforming undergraduate science and math majors, Dr. Berry's research also focuses on students' perceptions and experiences of racial educational equity reform in the Champaign Unit #4 School District high schools (Champaign, Illinois)—a project that stems from his 2014 dissertation study.

Dr. Brian J. Boggs is an outreach specialist in the Office of K–12 Outreach at Michigan State University. He received his dual-major PhD in educational policy and administration from MSU with an Urban Education endorsement. Brian is an EPFP alumnus. After obtaining his bachelor's in English and history and master's in English language and literature, he returned to his alma mater to teach college rhetoric in the Department of English at the University of Michigan–Flint. Brian's research interests include organizational theory, policymaking, sociology of education, experimental design, school improvement, and the history and politics of U.S. education.

Ira Bogotch is a professor of school leadership at Florida Atlantic University. He co-edited (with Carolyn Shields) an international handbook on social justice published by Springer in 2014. Ira is also the associate editor for the *International Journal of Leadership and Education* and for the *Journal of Cases in Educational Leadership*, where he will promote the publishing of international school leadership case studies. In addition to his many editing responsibilities, Ira has coauthored and co-edited two books *Radicalizing Educational Leadership: Dimensions of Social Justice* (2008) and *The Elusive What and the Problematic How: The Essential Leadership Questions for School Leaders and Educational Researchers* (2008). He has also written many published journal articles in *Educational Administration Quarterly*, the *Journal of School, Teaching and Teacher Education, Urban Education, Urban Review*, and *Intercultural Education*, among other journals. Internationally, Ira has worked in Guatemala, Honduras, Ecuador, Malaysia, Scotland, and Queensland, Australia.

Jeffrey S. Brooks, PhD is professor of educational leadership in the Faculty of Education at Monash University. He is a J. William Fulbright Senior Scholar alumnus who has conducted studies in the United States and the Philippines. His research focuses broadly on educational leadership, and he examines the way leaders influence (and are influenced by) dynamics such as racism, globalization, distributed leadership, social justice, and school reform. He is the author of two full-length books based on his research: *The Dark Side of School Reform: Teaching in the Space between Reality and Utopia* and *Black School, White School: Racism and Educational (Mis)leadership*. He is also co-editor of the volumes *What Every Principal Needs to Know to Create Equitable and Excellent Schools* (with George Theoharis), *Confronting Racism in Higher Education: Problems and Possibilities for Fighting Ignorance, Bigotry and Isolation* and *Anti-Racist School Leadership: Toward Equity in Education for America's Students* (both with Noelle Witherspoon Arnold). Dr. Brooks has written articles in leading educational research journals, including *Teachers College Record, Educational Administration Quarterly, Educational Policy, Journal of Educational Administration, Science Education, Journal of Research on Leadership in Education,* and the *Jour-*

nal of Values and Ethics in Educational Administration. He has also contributed many chapters to scholarly edited volumes and written several entries for reference works. Dr. Brooks is series editor for the Educational Leadership for Social Justice book series. He has served in several leadership positions in universities and educational research organizations, including AERA Division A (Administration, Organizations and Leadership) and the AERA Leadership for Social Justice Special Interest Group.

Michael Brooks is an associate professor of counselor education at North Carolina A&T State University. His teaching interests include theories of counseling, career counseling, and social and cultural diversity. Dr. Brooks is a graduate of Morehouse College in Atlanta, Georgia, and he received his MA and PhD in counselor education and supervision from the University of Central Florida. His research and service interests include African-American male achievement and postsecondary education attainment. He is a former faculty member at The University of Alabama at Birmingham where he served as a Center for Urban Education faculty liaison and director of the Blazer Male Excellence Network (B-MEN).

Dr. Monica Wills Brown earned a PhD from Clemson University with a P–12 concentration in educational leadership. Her research interests include culturally responsive educational practices, educational leadership preparation programs, high-performing minority schools, Christian-based education, differentiated leadership issues, and charter school management. Her work includes coordinating federal school programs and charter school advising.

Beth E. Bukoski, PhD, is a clinical assistant professor at The University of Texas at Austin in the Department of Educational Administration, where she serves as assistant coordinator for the Program in Higher Education Leadership. Her teaching experience encompasses secondary as well as postsecondary undergraduate and graduate coursework, and she teaches courses in diversity, leadership, organization and administration, and qualitative methods. Beth has authored articles and book chapters related to the persistence of students from underserved populations, social justice leadership in P–12 and postsecondary contexts, and gender in higher education.

Joe Burks served thirty-seven years in the Jefferson County Public Schools (JCPS), Louisville, Kentucky, as a secondary school teacher, principal, and assistant superintendent. In 2010–2011, he guided the development and implementation of Project Proficiency.

Dr. Mónica Byrne-Jiménez is an associate professor and director of the Educational and Policy Leadership Doctoral Program in the School of Education at Hofstra University. Her research focuses on Latina/o identity and school leadership, the role of faculty diversity on doctoral student experiences, and effectiveness of a special education leader preparation program. Before joining the faculty, she worked in a number of urban settings, including as a K–6 bilingual teacher, Even Start coordinator, literacy instructional specialist, and trainer for the Accelerated Schools Project. She is coauthor of *Developing Effective Principals Through Collaborative Inquiry*. Her other work has appeared in *the Leadership and Policy in Schools Journal, Journal of Cases in Educational Leadership, Handbook of Research on Educational Leadership for Diversity and Equity*, and *Voices in Urban Education*. Dr. Byrne-Jiménez holds a BA in Latin American Studies/Sociology from Columbia University, an MA in Educational Studies from the University of Michigan, and an EdD in Education Leadership from Teachers College, Columbia University.

Bradley W. Carpenter, PhD, is a former principal, assistant principal, and public school teacher. As an assistant professor in the University of Louisville's Department of Leadership, Foundations, and Human Resource Education, Dr. Carpenter's research focuses on the politics of educational reform and school turnaround, paying particular attention to how issues of social justice, equity, race, and diversity intersect with school-level leadership. Bradley earned his PhD in educational policy and planning from the University of Texas at Austin.

Joshua Childs is a doctoral student in learning sciences and policy at the University of Pittsburgh. His research examines the role of interorganizational networks for educational improvement, urban education policy, and efforts to address chronic absenteeism.

Meg Clifford is a graduate of the University of Texas School of Law and currently works as an attorney for the Educational Equity Project based at the William Wayne Justice Center for Public Interest Law at The University of Texas School of Law.

Michael I. Cohen recently earned his doctoral degree in educational leadership, management and policy at Seton Hall University. He has served in public schools as a high school English teacher, a K–12 supervisor of English Language Arts curriculum and instruction, and a high school assistant principal. Currently he serves as manager of assessment support in the district offices of the Denver Public Schools. His dissertation examined the influence of performance accountability culture on the work of high school principals.

Heather Cole received her PhD in special education from the University of Texas at Austin. She is a former policy advisor and attorney, practicing for more than a decade in the areas of education and public law. In addition to her law degree, she also holds graduate degrees in public administration and education (learning disabilities and behavioral disorders). Heather's research interests include educational policy and reform, law and ethics, special education, school discipline and juvenile justice. She recently relocated to Toronto, Canada, where she works for the Law Foundation of Ontario.

Eric J. Cooper is founder of the New York-based National Urban Alliance for Effective Education. He obtained his doctorate in Interdisciplinary Studies from Columbia University's Teachers College. His experience includes: keynoter at the Aspen Ideas Festival (2005/2006); Huffington Post Commentator for black issues and education pages; thought leader for Huffington/TedTalk.Com; NCEBC Talk Radio host; recipient of a MacArthur Foundation award for producing a series of PBS documentaries; interviewed for PBS, CNN, ABC, NBC, CBS, and BBC features; first American educator to be selected for the 2008 Dr. Martin Luther King Jr. award by the state of Israel and the NY Israeli Consulate; and 2002 First for Kids Community Advocacy Award by Connecticut Voices for Children.

Gary M. Crow is professor and Department Chair in the Department of Educational Leadership and Policy Studies at Indiana University. Crow is currently conducting research on successful school principals and professional identities of urban school leaders in reform contexts. His most recent book is *The Principalship: New Roles in a Professional Learning Community* with Joe Matthews (2009). He is also a co-editor of the *International Handbook on the Preparation and Development of School Leaders* and the *Handbook of Research on the Education of School Leaders*. Crow is a past president of the University Council for Educational Administration.

Dr. Michael Dantley has more than twenty years of experience in higher education, including academic appointments in the School of Education, Health and Society at Miami University and, more recently, university leadership positions at Miami. From 2004 to 2008 Dr. Dantley served as interim associate dean and, subsequently, associate dean of Miami's School of Education, Health and Society. From 2008 to 2011 he served as Miami University's associate provost and associate vice president for academic affairs. Dr. Dantley also served as the chair of the Department of Educational Leadership in Miami's School of Education, Health and Society. In addition, Dr. Dantley's professional experience includes more than a decade of both teaching and administrative appointments, including principalships, in the Cincinnati public school system. As associate provost and associate vice president for academic affairs, Dr. Dantley had responsibility for the supervision of student academic services, including admission, advising, and retention. He also co-directed a university-wide initiative on undergraduate retention, developed an evaluation process for departmental program reviews, and served on both the University's

Council of Academic Deans and its Senate. As associate dean, Dr. Dantley directed processes for faculty searches and hiring, faculty promotion and tenure, and faculty development. He also served on the school's NCATE Steering Committee and directed graduate programs for the division. Dr. Dantley holds a BA in history and education from the University of Pennsylvania, an MEd in educational leadership from Miami University in Ohio, and an EdD in educational administration from the University of Cincinnati. An accomplished scholar, Dr. Dantley currently serves on the editorial boards of a number of educational journals, including the *Journal of School Leadership and Education* and *Urban Society*. His research interests focus on leadership, spirituality, and social justice, and he is currently pursuing research that explores new ways to conduct qualitative research and spirituality and the link between principals' moral development and the ways these principals define and demonstrate their commitment to social justice.

Sarah Diem is an assistant professor in the Department of Educational Leadership and Policy Analysis at the University of Missouri. Her research focuses on the social and cultural contexts of education, paying particular attention to how the politics and implementation of educational policy affect diversity outcomes. Dr. Diem is also interested in how conversations surrounding race and race relations are facilitated in the classroom and whether these discussions are preparing future school leaders to be able to address critical issues that may impact the students and communities they will oversee. She received her PhD in educational policy and planning from the University of Texas at Austin.

Dr. Catherine DiMartino, assistant professor, received her BA in anthropology from Haverford College, an MA in social studies education from Teachers College, Columbia University, and a PhD in Education Leadership from New York University. She teaches courses in applied data analysis and politics of education. Her dissertation, titled *Public-Private Partnerships and the Small Schools Movement: A New Form of Education Management*, won the 2008–2009 Politics of Education Associations' Outstanding Dissertation Award. Prior to joining the Hofstra community, she taught middle and high school social studies, had a fellowship at the Educational Testing Service, and, most recently, worked for the RAND Corporation. At RAND, her projects included evaluations of New York City's promotion policy and New York City's Schoolwide Bonus Performance Program. Her current research focuses on the politics of public-private partnerships, the implications of marketization and privatization for school leaders, and the role of foundations in public education. Most recently, her work appeared in the *Peabody Journal of Education* and *Teachers College Record*.

Dr. Adrienne Dixson is associate professor of education policy, organization, and leadership at the University of Illinois College of Education. Her primary research interest focuses on educational equity in urban schooling contexts, applying a Critical Race Theory framework. She is interested in how educational equity is mediated by school reform policies in the urban south and is examining school reform in post-Katrina New Orleans, how local actors make sense of and experience those reform policies and how those policies become or are "racialized."

Ty-Ron M. O. Douglas is an assistant professor in the Educational Leadership and Policy Analysis Department at the University of Missouri-Columbia. His research explores the intersections between identity, community/geopolitical space, and the social and cultural foundations of leadership and education, with an emphasis on black masculinity/families, spirituality, and community-based pedagogical spaces. Dr. Douglas's work has appeared in outlets such as the *Urban Review, Educational Studies, Teachers College Record*, and *Race, Ethnicity, and Education*.

Dr. Chris Dunbar is a professor of K–12 educational administration. He received his PhD from the University of Illinois Urbana Champaign. His research has focused on alternative education for students who have been unable to successfully matriculate through traditional public school. He has authored scholarly journal articles and studies. His book *Alternative Schooling for African American Youth* (2001) examines an alternative school designated for students perceived as disruptive. His current research examines the intersection between school choice and educational opportunities for disruptive students, zero tolerance policy, and its impact on school administrators.

Tina Fernandez is a partner with Bellwether Education Partners in the Talent Services practice area. Tina joined Bellwether in the Spring of 2014 as co-director of the Talent Readiness Pilot and Senior Advisor to the organization. Tina was a Bellwether founding board member and served as chair of the board in 2013–2014. Prior to joining Bellwether, Tina was a clinical professor at the University of Texas School of Law and the founding director of the school's Pro Bono Program. Tina earned her JD from Columbia University School of Law and her BA from Harvard College and is from the Rio Grande Valley. Before attending law school, Tina was a Teach for America 1994 corps member and spent two years as a bilingual elementary teacher in the South Bronx.

Dr. Cheryl Fields-Smith is an associate professor of elementary education in the College of Education at the University of Georgia in Athens, Georgia. She earned her doctorate from Emory University in 2004 under the direction of Dr. Vanessa Siddle Walker. Her research interests include family engagement and homeschooling among black families. Dr. Fields-Smith is also a founding board member of the International Center for Home Education Research (ICHER). She is the 2014 recipient of the University of Georgia, College of Education's Carl Glickman Faculty Fellow Award for distinction in research, teaching, and service.

Rejer Finklin is a doctoral candidate in educational administration at the University of Georgia. She earned her master's degree in educational administration and policy at the University of Georgia. Her research interests include school leadership and the experiences of teachers in rural school settings.

Dr. Leena Furtado is a professor at the Graduate School of Education at California State University, Dominguez Hills, Carson, California. She is the program coordinator and primary instructor of the MA: Curriculum and Instruction and the MA: CURR (Science Emphasis) program options. At the institutional level she directs the Title V-PPOHA grant to Promote Excellence in Graduate Studies (PEGS) in all twenty-four Masters and Credential programs for students and faculty and the HP Catalyst-STEM grant conducted through a national and international consortia partnership. Her research interests include teacher leadership, action research, language acquisition, critical and cultural pedagogy, and elementary-interdisciplinary STEM education.

Frank Gaines has been an urban middle and high school math teacher and basketball coach, serving the last twelve years as a middle and high school administrator. His doctoral thesis, "An Exploratory Examination of 'Pockets of Success' in Creating Urban High Schools of Opportunity for LSES Students" (2013), was a finalist for the 2014 Florida Atlantic University College of Education's Dissertation of the Year Award. Frank coauthored (with Bogotch, Nesmith, and Smith) a chapter titled "Urban School Leadership and Fit" in the *Handbook of Urban Education* (2014) edited by Milner and Lomotey.

Xingyuan Gao is a PhD candidate in educational leadership program with a concentration in organizational analysis. Mr. Gao has published one book chapter, and presented several studies in national conference in the area of K–12 educational leadership.

Rey Garcia earned his PhD in educational administration from the University of Texas at Austin. He currently works as the director of Operations for Middle Schools for the Austin Independent School District.

Encarnacion Garza is an associate professor at the University of Texas at San Antonio in the Department of Educational Leadership and Policy Studies. As a scholar-practitioner whose scholarship employs a critical theory perspective, his research focuses on three themes: (1) the study of minority student success, (2) the preparation of principals as leaders for social justice, and (3) the exploration of school district/university partnerships with respect to preparing principals as social justice advocates. Dr. Garza is active in the international study of leadership as a researcher and participant in the International Successful School Principals Project (ISSPP).

Elizabeth Gil is a doctoral student in K–12 educational administration at Michigan State University. Her research interests include family involvement in education, culturally responsive educational practices, and college access and completion and post-high school educational success. She taught in New York City public schools for over ten years, working with children, parents, and teachers.

Mark A. Gooden, PhD, serves as an associate professor in the Department of Educational Administration. He is also director of The University of Texas at Austin Principalship Program (UTAPP). His research interests include the principalship, antiracist leadership, urban educational leadership, and legal issues in education. His research has appeared in *Educational Administration Quarterly*, *The Journal of School Leadership*, *The Journal of Research on Leadership Education*, *The Journal of Negro Education*, *Brigham Young University Education and Law Journal*, *Education and Urban Society*, and other outlets. He currently serves as President of the University Council for Educational Administration (UCEA), a consortium of over one hundred higher education institutions committed to advancing the preparation and practice of educational leaders for the benefit of schools and children. Mark also serves as Associate Editor of *Urban Education* and on the editorial boards of *Journal of Cases of Educational Leadership*, *Journal of Research on Leadership Education* and *Leadership and Policy in Schools*. Mark earned his PhD in policy and leadership from the Ohio State University in 2001.

Lindsay R. Granger, is a doctoral candidate in educational leadership at New York University's Steinhardt School of Culture, Education, and Human Development. Previous experiences as a high school counselor in the School District of Philadelphia, an academic advisor at New York University, and an undergraduate career counselor at Columbia University have influenced her current research focus on the development of the non-cognitive skills associated with college readiness and career choice processes for underrepresented student populations.

Harry Gutelius, EdD (Wilmington University), is the associate dean of education at Eastern University in St. David's, Pennsylvania, a suburb of Philadelphia. Previously Dr. Gutelius served for thirty-two years in the School District of Philadelphia. He was an English teacher, a Department Head, a Vice Principal, and from 1987–1999 Principal of Washington High, the city's largest school at the time. He was honored as a Lindenbaum winner of the Principal of the Year Award, and his school was recognized by *Business Week* magazine for superior preparation of students for college and careers.

Jennifer Haan is a doctoral student in educational leadership at New Mexico State University.

Thomas Hatch is an associate professor at Teachers College, Columbia University and co-director of the National Center for Restructuring Education, Schools, and Teaching (NCREST). He previously served as a senior scholar at the Carnegie Foundation for the Advancement of Teaching. His research includes studies of a variety of school reform efforts at the school, district, and national levels. His current work includes a comparative study of school improvement policies in Singapore, Finland, the Netherlands, the United States, and Norway. His latest book is *Managing to Change: How Schools can Survive (and Sometimes Thrive) in Turbulent Times* (2009).

Julian Vasquez Heilig is an award-winning researcher and teacher. He is currently a professor of educational leadership and policy studies and the director of the Doctorate in Educational Leadership at California State University Sacramento. In addition to educational accomplishments, Julian Vasquez Heilig has held a variety of research and practitioner positions in organizations from Boston to Beijing. He blogs at Cloaking Inequity, consistently rated one of the top fifty education websites in the world by Teach100. You can also follow him on Twitter.

Craig Hochbein is an assistant professor of educational leadership at Lehigh University. His research utilizes quantitative analyses to examine the longitudinal development of school performance, specifically investigating factors associated with declining academic achievement and the effectiveness of policies intended to improve school performance.

Rodney Hopson is a professor in the Division of Educational Psychology, Research Methods, Education Policy, George Mason University. Dr. Hopson's research interests lie in social politics and policies, foundations of education, sociolinguistics, ethnography, and evaluation. Relative to his research interests, Hopson raises questions that (1) analyze and address the differential impact of education and schooling on marginalized and underrepresented groups in diverse global nation-states and (2) seek solutions to social and educational conditions in the form of alternative paradigms, epistemologies, and methods for the way the oppressed and marginalized succeed and thrive despite circumstances and opportunities that suggest otherwise.

Yvette Jackson is recognized for work in assessing and capitalizing on the learning potential of disenfranchised students, the cognitive mediation theory of Dr. Reuven Feurestein, and the impact of neurobiology and culture on intellectual development, learning, and achievement. She is author of *Pedagogy of Confidence, Inspiring High Intellectual Performance in Urban Schools* and *Aim High, Achieve More: How to Transform Urban Schools Through Fearless Leadership* (co-author Veronica McDermott), CEO of the National Urban Alliance for Effective Education, adjunct professor or Teachers College, Columbia University, and fequent presenter. Formerly director of Gifted Programs and director of Instruction and Professional Development (NYC Public Schools), Dr. Jackson received a Doctorate from Teachers' College, Columbia University.

Gaëtane Jean-Marie, PhD, is professor of educational leadership and chair of the Department of Leadership, Foundations and Human Resource Education at the University of Louisville. Her research focuses on leadership preparation and development in the United States and global context, women and educational leadership in P–20 system, and urban school reform through educational equity/social justice. Her recent co-edited books include *Cross Cultural Women Scholars in Academe: Intergenerational Voices* (2014), and *The Duality of Women Scholars of Color: Transforming and Being Transformed in the Academy* (2014). She is the editor of the *Journal of School Leadership*, former book review editor of the *Journal of Educational Administration*, and is an advisory board member for the Center for Educational Leadership and Social Justice at Duquesne University. She also serves on the editorial boards of the *Journal of Research on Leadership Education*, and *the Journal of Educational Administration*, former board of program reviewer for educational leadership programs for the Council for Higher Education Accreditation (CAEP), past program chair of AERA-SIG Confluent Education, and chair of the AERA-SIG Leadership for Social Justice. She is the co-founder of Advancing Women of Color in the Academy (AWOCA), a scholarly interethnic, transdisciplinary, and cross-institutional network linked by research in the field of education and higher education dedicated to the advancement of women of color in the academy. Additionally, she is co-founder and former Chief Information Officer of Women's Work Foundation, a national advocacy group that provides support and works with organizations in underserved communities to enhance the lives of women and girls.

Joyce E. King, PhD, holds the Benjamin E. Mays chair of Urban Teaching, Learning, and Leadership in the College of Education at Georgia State University. She is a graduate of Stanford University where she received a doctor of philosophy in the Social Foundations of Education and a Bachelor of Arts degree in Sociology. Dr. King also serves on the board of directors of Our Developing World and the international women's peace and justice organization, Women and Life on Earth. Dr. King's influential publication, *Dysconscious Racism: Ideology, Identity, and the Mis-Education of Teachers*, details how "dysconciousness" informed the epistemology of her pre-service teacher candidates. Dr. King's highly original research on and conceptualization of dysconsciousness has impacted the works of numerous scholars and has been reprinted in several anthologies. Additional publications by Dr. King include the books *Black Education: A Transformative Research and Action Agenda for the New Century*;

Preparing Teachers for Diversity; *Teaching Diverse Populations*; and *Black Mothers to Sons: Juxtaposing African American Literature with Social Practice*.

Judson Laughter is an assistant professor of English education at the University of Tennessee, Knoxville. His research interests include critical multicultural teacher education, dialogic pedagogy, and critical literacy. He teaches courses on ELA methods and action research and prepares teachers to be effective in diverse classrooms.

Jia Liang is a doctoral candidate in educational administration and policy at the University of Georgia. She earned her master's degree in adult and technical education from Marshall University. Jia earned her BA from Hunan University in China. Her research interests include school leadership, women in leadership, and race and gender in leadership.

Tondra L. Loder-Jackson is an associate professor of educational foundations at the University of Alabama at Birmingham. She received a master of public policy with a concentration in urban policy from the Irving B. Harris School of Public Policy at the University of Chicago, and a PhD in Human Development and Social Policy from the School of Education and Social Policy at Northwestern University. She was also a Constance E. Clayton Postdoctoral Fellow in Urban Education at the University of Pennsylvania. Dr. Loder-Jackson's research interests include urban education, life course perspectives on African-American education, and social movements and education, particularly, the impact of the Birmingham Civil Rights Movement on contemporary education. She formerly served as the Director of the UAB Center for Urban Education.

Kofi Lomotey has taught at SUNY-Buffalo and LSU. He was provost at Medgar Evers College-CUNY and at Fisk University. He served as Chancellor at Southern University and president at Fort Valley State University. Kofi has published several books, journal articles, and book chapters, including the *Handbook on Urban Education* (with H. Richard Milner), the *Encyclopedia of African American Education*, and *Going to School: The African American Experience*. He served as the editor of the journal *Urban Education* for nineteen years, and currently serves on the editorial boards of the *Journal of Negro Education* and *Educational Researcher*. He is also a member of the AERA Journals Publication Committee. Lomotey earned a BA degree in economics (Oberlin College), his MEd degree in elementary curriculum and instruction (Cleveland State University), an MA degree in educational administration and policy analysis (Stanford University), and his PhD degree in educational administration and policy analysis (Stanford University).

Kendra Lowery is an assistant professor in the Department of Educational Leadership at the University of Arkansas–Little Rock. She received her PhD from the Department of Educational Leadership and Policy Analysis at the University of Wisconsin–Madison. She spent seventeen years in P–12 education as a teacher and administrator. Kendra's research interests include the history of African-American education; school de/segregation and urban education; the principalship and black administrators; leadership practices that result in increased student achievement and decreased racial disparities; and organizational inclusion and diversity.

Roberto Lozano is a doctoral student in educational leadership at New Mexico State University.

Stefanie Marshall is a doctoral student at Michigan State University studying educational policy. Her research interest involves school leadership, science education, and equity. Stefanie earned a bachelor of science from Oakland University and a master of arts from the University of Michigan in Educational Studies with a concentration in leadership and policy.

Peter Martinez is the founding director of Leadership Coaching in the University of Illinois Chicago EdD Program in Urban Education Leadership. Martinez was formerly a Senior Program Officer at the John D. and Catherine

T. MacArthur Foundation where he managed the $40 million Chicago Education Initiative portfolio that funded research and dissemination, school restructuring, teacher and principal professional development and union reform, and parent and community involvement. In 1999 he was named by *Catalyst Magazine* as one of the ten most influential people in Chicago School Reform. For forty years he has worked in the field of leadership development and currently focuses on the development of school leaders in multiple areas: teacher leaders, principals, system leaders, and parent and community leaders working in urban areas. He has presented widely to national audiences on the professional development of school leaders through supervised clinical experiences and is coauthor of Shoho, Barnett, and Martinez, "Enhancing On the Job Internships with Interactive Coaching" (2012).

Judy Jackson May is an associate professor of educational administration and coordinator of the Doctoral Program in Leadership Studies at Bowling Green State University. Dr. May's research interests include organizational leadership and student achievement.

Mairi McDermott is a PhD candidate in the Department of Sociology and Equity Studies at the Ontario Institute for Studies in Education, University of Toronto. A former New York City public school teacher, her present work focuses on student voice and subjectivity in educational settings, marginalization in urban educational spaces, and the relationships and socio-historical contexts that frame urban schooling. She has published the following: *The Pedagogy of Uncertainty: Paths to Personally Meaningful Homework* and *Avoiding the Missionary (Dis)Position: Research Relations and (Re)Presentation*, coauthored with Athena Madan.

Veronica McDermott is regional director of the National Urban Alliance, retired superintendent of schools, and former assistant superintendent, principal, and teacher. Her interests in literacy, learning, and leadership have expanded to organizational studies and school transformation, the influence of leadership on learning and teaching, and the influence of educational policies on equity and social justice. Dr. McDermott, coauthor with Yvette Jackson of *Aim High, Achieve More: How to Transform Urban Schools Through Fearless Leadership*, has written articles and opinion pieces published nationally and internationally. Veronica McDermott received her PhD from New York University (Department of Educational Leadership and Organizational Studies).

Andrew N. McKnight is an associate professor of educational foundations at the University of Alabama at Birmingham. He earned his PhD in curriculum and teaching with a specialization in cultural studies from the University of North Carolina at Greensboro. His primary research concerns the application of philosophical, historical, and qualitative research methods to contemporary educational and cultural issues. Dr. McKnight has done extensive research on urban youth who have dropped out of high school and are seeking ways to reengage with formal education through alternative community education pathways. He currently serves on the advisory board of the UAB Center for Urban Education.

Rhodesia McMillian is a graduate assistant in the Department of Educational Leadership and Policy Analysis at the University of Missouri-Columbia.

Syreeta A. McTier is a doctoral student majoring in educational policy studies with a concentration in Social Foundations of Education in the College of Education at Georgia State University and an elementary school assistant principal in an urban school district in metro Atlanta, Georgia. Ms. McTier's research interests include urban education, media stereotypes as a form of institutionalized racism, pre-service teachers' perceptions of media stereotypes, and minority students and disproportionate school suspension rates.

Marlene Melendez is a doctoral student in educational leadership at New Mexico State University.

H. Richard Milner IV is professor of education, Helen Faison Endowed Chair of Urban Education, and director of the Center for Urban Education at the University of Pittsburgh. Professor Milner's research, teaching, and policy interests are urban teacher education, African-American literature, and the sociology of education. His most recent book is *Start Where You Are, But Don't Stay There: Understanding Diversity, Opportunity Gaps, and Teaching in Today's Classroom*. He is editor-in-chief of *Urban Education*.

Pedro A. Noguera, PhD, is the Peter L. Agnew Professor of Education and the executive director of the Metropolitan Center for Urban Education at New York University. He is the author of nine books and over 150 articles and monographs. Dr. Noguera serves on the boards of numerous national and local organizations including the Economic Policy Institute, the Young Women's Leadership Institute, the After School Corporation, and *The Nation Magazine*. He is also a member of the National Academy of Education.

Anthony H. Normore (Tony) holds a PhD from University of Toronto. He is professor of educational leadership, and department chair of special needs at California State University Dominguez Hills (CSUDH) in Los Angeles. Dr. Normore has been a visiting professor of ethics and leadership at Seoul National University, a visiting professor in the Department of Criminal Justice Studies at University of Guelph/Humber, and a graduate professor of law, ethics, and leadership for the Summer Leadership Academy at Teachers College-Columbia University. His thirty-plus years of professional education experiences has taken him throughout North America, South Central Asia, Eastern Asia, UK, Continental Europe, and South Pacific. Tony's research focuses on urban leadership growth and development in the context of ethics and social justice. He is the author or coauthor of several books including *What the Social Sciences Tell us about Leadership for Social Justice and Ethics* (2014), *Moral Compass for Law Enforcement Professional* (2014), and *Collective Efficacy: An Interdisciplinary Approach to International Leadership Development* (2013), and numerous scholarly articles and book chapters. Dr. Normore was recently appointed as chief leadership and ethics officer, and the chairman of the Criminal Justice Commission on Credible Leadership Development with the International Academy of Public Safety.

Dr. Laurence Parker is a professor in the Department of Educational Leadership and Policy at the University of Utah. He has developed and taught classes on critical race theory and education policy issues and has concentrated his research and teaching in this area as it relates to equity and education, both K–12 and higher education. His most recent publication is a co-authored book chapter that appears in *Facing Accountability in Education: Democracy & Equity at Risk* (edited by Christine Sleeter, 2007), and he recently edited vols. 29 and 31 of the *Review of Research in Education* for AERA. Parker is associated with the Utah Education Policy Center.

Ann P. O'Doherty, EID serves as Director of the Danforth Educational Leadership Program at the University of Washington where she develops educational leaders to serve as principals and program administrators. Ann has contributed to the University Council for Educational Administration's Leaders Supporting Diverse Learners FIPSE grant and has co-developed a leadership curriculum module, Building a Community of Trust through Racial Awareness. She also serves as a consultant to school districts and leads professional learning on culturally responsive leadership and engaging student voice. Along with her colleague Mark A. Gooden, she has presented at the Equity Diversity and Inclusion Conferences held in Munich, Germany and Athens, Greece. Prior to joining the University of Washington, Ann directed the University of Texas Collaborative Urban Leadership Project in Austin. Through this project, funded in part by a U.S. Department of Education School Leadership Program grant, she co-designed a preparation program to develop effective secondary school leaders for Dallas, Houston, and Austin-area school districts. Before serving in higher education, Ann devoted eighteen years to PreK–12 public schools as a principal at elementary, middle, and high school levels and special education teacher. Her ongoing research interests include program evaluation, coaching, leadership development, and district-level influence on school success.

Hoana Pearson has served as primary school principal for Newton Central School in central Auckland, New Zealand since 1998. Newton Central is multicultural with sixteen diverse ethnic groups and a large percentage of indigenous (Māori) students. She has worked with the changing school community and the wider Auckland community to establish bilingual and bicultural pathways in education. She is currently working toward her master's in educational leadership and management and leads Aka Tamaki, the Auckland Māori Principal and Leadership group. Ms. Pearson is a champion for social justice and sees her leadership practice as an opportunity to inform research and create change on a national level.

Tonya B. Perry is an associate professor of Secondary English Language Arts in the Department of Curriculum and Instruction. She teaches secondary methods, young adult literature, and classes in curriculum. Dr. Perry is a graduate of the University of North Carolina at Chapel Hill, and received her MA from the University of Alabama at Birmingham, and her PhD from a joint program from both the University of Alabama in Tuscaloosa and the University of Alabama at Birmingham. Her research and service interests include urban education, teaching writing, and teacher preparation. Dr. Perry is the Director and Principal Investigator for the UAB Red Mountain Writing Project, and she was recently appointed as Director of the UAB Center for Urban Education.

April L. Peters-Hawkins is an associate professor at the University of Georgia. She earned a PhD in educational policy and leadership from The Ohio State University, an MSW from Columbia University, and a BSEd from Northwestern University. She has worked as a teacher, school social worker, dean of students, and principal. Dr. Peters served as a consultant for the Institute for Student Achievement (ISA) in the Atlanta Public Schools, assisting school leaders and teachers in implementing small school reform in select high schools. Dr. Peters's research interests include: (a) women in school leadership; (b) mentoring for early career administrators; and (c) leadership and small school reform.

Marty Pollio is the principal at Jeffersontown High School in Louisville, Kentucky. His research interests include high school reform and educational policy. He earned his EdD from the University of Louisville.

Heather E. Price is senior associate at Basis Policy Research, LLC, an affiliate of the Center for Research on Educational Opportunities, and a consultant for the Teaching and Learning International Survey division of the OECD. Her dissertation investigated the influence of social resources, as measured with social network data of school staff, on school community and teacher and student engagement. She has published in *EAQ, Educational Policy, Social Science Research, AERJ*, and others volumes on topics of principal leadership, teacher engagement, and school policy. Her interests are primarily in the sociology of education, school organization, and urban schooling.

Richard J. Reddick, EdD, is an associate professor of educational administration at the University of Texas at Austin, where he also serves as faculty director for campus diversity initiatives in the Division of Diversity and Community Engagement (DDCE) and assistant director of the Plan II Honors Program. Dr. Reddick's research expertise encompasses the mentoring experiences of faculty and the impact on the trajectory of African-American students. Dr. Reddick's work has been published in leading educational journals, such as the *American Educational Research Journal* and the *Harvard Educational Review*, featured in the national news media, and he has authored and edited a number of scholarly volumes and chapters.

Jessica G. Rigby has worked in urban public schools since she was sixteen years old, including teaching English and history in urban middle and high schools for seven years. She received her PhD from the University of California, Berkeley in education policy and is an assistant professor in the College of Education at the University of Washington.

Jacqueline Roebuck Sakho, EID is a voice called on nationally to provide innovative perspectives in the field of restorative justice approaches and practices in urban settings and in response to historical inequities. She has consulted with the Thelton E. Henderson Center for Social Justice at Berkeley Law School and The National Association for the Advancement of Colored People (NAACP) Legal Defense Fund in partnership with Atlantic

Philanthropies. Further, Ms. Jacqueline Roebuck Sakho has also assisted in developing transformative tools for community-based organizations and organizers serving in vulnerable communities in the United States.

Adelina Rodriguez is a doctoral student in educational leadership at New Mexico State University.

Rachel Roegman is an assistant professor of educational leadership in the Department of Educational Studies at Purdue University. A former teacher in traditional and alternative schools, Rachel Roegman comes to education and research from a social justice perspective and a desire to create schools that serve all students well. Her research interests center on the interconnections between equity, contexts, and leadership.

Omar Salaam was born and raised in an urban environment and attended urban schools as well as graduating from an HBCU in teacher education. Omar has twenty years of urban experience as an educator in public and private schools as both a teacher and school administrator. He has also worked abroad in education. He is currently working toward his PhD in Educational Leadership at the University of South Florida while serving as a public school assistant principal.

Eugene Sanders is superintendent and CEO of the Sandusky City Schools in Sandusky, Ohio. Dr. Sanders is nationally recognized for his leadership in transformation and innovative instructional design and served as superintendent in Cleveland and Toledo, Ohio and is a former tenured professor at Bowling Green State University.

Dr. Andrés P. Santamaría is a lecturer for the School of Education in Educational Leadership at Auckland University of Technology, New Zealand. His area of expertise is leadership for diversity, and his research interests range from leadership for social justice and educational equity to principal efficacy in underperforming schools. Andrés' research agenda is currently focused on school site leadership that is responsive to the multicultural multilingual needs of Māori, Pasifika, and international communities. He is the author of *Applied Critical Leadership in Education: Choosing Change*, with Dr. Lorri J. Santamaría (2012). Prior to his academic appointment, Dr. Santamaría was an elementary school principal serving schools with high populations of culturally and linguistic diverse learners as well as learners from low socioeconomic backgrounds in Southern California.

Dr. Lorri J. Santamaría is associate professor of the Faculty of Education at the University of Auckland, New Zealand. Prior to this appointment she was a full professor of multicultural multilingual education and the director of the Educational Leadership Joint Doctoral Program with the University of California San Diego at California State University San Marcos. At the University of Auckland Dr. Santamaría continues her scholarly writing and research in the areas of leadership for social justice and educational equity and diversity. Her work explores the roles and intersectionalities of race, sexuality, language, gender, and exceptionality in leadership and learning. In New Zealand her work has expanded to be responsive to the needs of Māori and Pasifika communities in the Auckland Metro area as well as the global needs of the region. She is the author of *Applied Critical Leadership in Education: Choosing Change*, with Dr. Andrés P. Santamaría (2012) and Editor of *Cross Cultural Women Scholars in Academe: Intergenerational Voices*, with Gaëtane Jean-Marie and Cosette Grant (2014).

Jonathan P. Schwartz, Department of Counseling and Educational Psychology, New Mexico State University.

Samantha Paredes Scribner is an associate professor of educational leadership and policy studies at Indiana University–Indianapolis. Her research and teaching focuses on the organizational and political dynamics within and around urban K–12 schools, the policy contexts of these dynamics, and the consequences of leadership practices within and around such schools for various constituents of urban school communities. She is currently investigating the professional identities of leaders in urban settings, as well as how Latino/a community members navigate school-community relations to advocate for their students and families.

Milagros Seraus is a master's student in the educational leadership program at New York University. She is also a fourth grade special education teacher at P.S. 102 Jacques Cartier Elementary School in East Harlem. She is a member of Teachers Unite, a teacher-led advocacy program, and is currently working on a study of the declining numbers of Latino and black teachers in New York City.

Christopher Shaffer has over thirty-five years' experience working in urban schools. He is known as a turnaround principal, leading a variety of economically disadvantaged urban high schools to improved culture, climate, and student achievement. He is a leader in the effort to develop ways to engage families and communities in learning together, most recently with the development of an innovative Race To the Top grant-funded Family Academy. He is developing community models of transformation that integrate participatory learning into the fabric of the community. Shaffer holds a PhD in educational administration from The Ohio State University. He currently serves as an educational consultant and Executive Director of High Schools with Reynoldsburg City Schools.

Dr. Jianping Shen is the John E. Sandberg Professor of Education and the Gwen Frostic Endowed Chair for Research and Innovation in the Department of Educational Leadership, Research and Technology at Western Michigan University. He and his colleagues conducted numerous studies on principalship and published three books. In addition, Dr. Shen and his colleagues published about twenty-five articles on principalship.

Jaqueline Shoemaker is a National Board Certified Teacher with twenty-one years of teaching experience. She currently teaches first grade at Oconee County Primary School in Watkinsville, Georgia. She obtained her PhD from the University of Georgia, and her research interests include grandparents raising grandchildren and family engagement. She is the recipient of several professional and academic scholarships and is seeking educational leadership endorsement from UGA.

Juanita M. Simmons is an associate professor at the University of Missouri Columbia, where she has served for twelve years in the Educational Leadership and Policy Analysis division of the College of Education. Her research agenda focuses on race, gender, class, and equity in public school leadership development. She is the author of numerous publications and is currently under contract for an upcoming book on Emancipatory Leadership with Information Age Publishers (Witherspoon Arnold, Editor). As a former public school teacher and administrator, she continues to work with urban school leaders and to advocate for children and their communities.

Marlon Simmons holds a PhD in sociology of education from the University of Toronto. His current research interests include diaspora and transnational studies, race and ethnicity, and issues of governance of the self in the context of schooling and education. His publications include: *The Indigenous as a Site of Decolonizing Knowledge for Conventional Development* and the *Link with Education: The African Case*, coauthored with George J. Sefa Dei; and two co-edited texts, *Fanon and Education: Thinking Through Pedagogical Possibilities* (with George J. Sefa Dei) and *The Politics of Cultural Knowledge* (with Njoki Wane and Arlo Kempf).

Christine E. Sleeter, PhD, is professor emerita in the College of Professional Studies at California State University Monterey Bay, where she was a founding faculty member. Formerly a high school learning disabilities teacher in Seattle, she previously served as a faculty member at Ripon College in Wisconsin and at the University of Wisconsin-Parkside. She has been a visiting professor or lecturer at several universities, including University of Colorado Boulder, Victoria University of Wellington in New Zealand, San Francisco State University, University of Washington Seattle, Universidad Nacional de Education a Distancia in Madrid, Spain, and Høgskolen i Oslo og Akershus in Oslo, Norway. Currently she is consultant to a project for teacher education improvement at Pontificia Universidad Católica de Valparaíso. She is a past president of the National Association for Multicultural Education, and a past Vice President of Division K (Teaching and Teacher Education) of the American Educational

Research Association. Her research focuses on antiracist multicultural education and teacher education. Dr. Sleeter has published over one hundred articles in journals and edited books, such as *Educational Researcher, Multicultural Review, Urban Education,* and *Teaching and Teacher Education.* Her recent books include *Diversifying the Teacher Workforce* (2015, with L. I. Neal and K. K. Kumashiro), *Power, Teaching and Teacher Education* (2013), and *Professional Development for Culturally Responsive and Relationship-based Pedagogy* (2013). Her work has been translated into Spanish, Korean, French, and Portuguese. Recent awards for her work include the American Educational Research Association Social Justice in Education Award, the Chapman University Paulo Freire Education Project Social Justice Award, the American Educational Research Association Division K Legacy Award, and the American Educational Research Association Special Interest Group on Multicultural and Multiethnic Lifetime Achievement Award.

Kirsten J. Smith has eighteen years' experience working in urban districts. For the past thirteen years, she has worked as a gifted education coordinator with an emphasis on minority issues in the field of gifted education. She has also brought awareness to the underrepresentation of gifted, minority students in urban districts. As a result, she has analyzed data and helped to develop initiatives to improve gifted programming for minority students. She has also supported gifted students with social-emotional barriers that impact their interests and academic achievements. Smith is a doctoral candidate in educational administration at the Ohio State University.

Dr. Stella L. Smith is a postdoctoral fellow in the Division of Diversity and Community Engagement (DDCE) at the University of Texas at Austin, and has more than fifteen years of experience in higher education administration. Recognized with a 2014 Dissertation Award from the American Association of Blacks in Higher Education, her dissertation study was a phenomenological inquiry to investigate the experiences, challenges, and strategies for success of African-American females in senior-level executive positions in higher education at predominately white institutions. A qualitative researcher, her scholarly interests focus on African-American faculty and administrators in higher education, access to higher education for underserved populations, and P–20 educational pipeline alignment.

Howard Stevenson is a professor of educational leadership and policy studies at the University of Nottingham. He has extensive experience directing doctoral programs and collaborative action research projects in schools. In addition to published papers and books, Howard has presented his research to a range of bodies including the Department for Education and a range of teacher union bodies. He appears in the media regularly, mostly in the educational press, but he has also appeared on radio and TV.

Howard is a member of a number of research-based networks and societies. He is a committee member of the American Educational Research Association Teachers' Work/Teacher Unions Special Interest Group (including past program chair), and he currently chairs the SIG's Best Thesis Award Panel. Howard is also an elected member of BELMAS National Council. He is co-convenor (with Professors Helen Gunter and Pat Thomson) of the BELMAS Critical Educational Policy and Leadership Studies Research Interest Group, and co-convenor (with Professor Bruce Barnett) of the International School Leadership Development Network. This network involves researchers from over twenty countries engaging in a common project and is co-sponsored by BELMAS and UCEA.

Howard is co-editor of *Forum: For promoting 3–19 comprehensive education,* the journal that was originally founded by Professor Brian Simon over fifty years ago. The journal continues to challenge the (re-emerging) orthodoxy of fixed ability thinking and practice, while also making the case for the democratic control of education and education as a public good. Howard is an associate editor of *Professional Development in Education,* and (in the dim and distant past) he was editor of *Education Today and Tomorrow.* He is currently on the editorial board of *Education Administration Quarterly, Journal of Educational Administration and History,* and the *International Journal of Education Management.*

He blogs intermittently and Tweets erratically.

Corrie Stone-Johnson is an assistant professor of educational leadership and policy at the University at Buffalo. Her research uses the lens of micropolitics to view the impact of educational change on schools and those who work in them, focusing on the various protective actions that people in schools at all levels take when they are either participants in or agents of change and how structures in school, particularly organizational culture and demographics, lead to the need for these micropolitical actions. She previously taught middle school English in New York City through the Teach for America program.

Dr. Eustace Thompson is currently chair of the Department of Teacher Education Programs at Hofstra University. He also serves as the Graduate Director of the Certification of Advanced Studies program in Educational Leadership. He received his BA from the City College of New York, his MS from Long Island University, and his MA and PhD from New York University. He was formerly the Deputy Superintendent of the Uniondale Public Schools, located on Long Island, New York. He has thirty-seven years of experience in urban and suburban public schools settings and has held the positions of deputy superintendent for curriculum and instruction, high school principal, and middle school principal. He is certified in the areas of Walk-Through Supervision and Curriculum Deep Alignment. In addition to curriculum issues, Dr. Thompson's research interests include instructional leadership in urban suburban areas and structural barriers to African-American students' academic success.

Steven Tozer is professor in educational policy studies, founding director of the Center for Urban Education Leadership, and University Scholar at the University of Illinois at Chicago. Initiated as UIC's first professional doctorate in Education (EdD) in 2003, the Urban Education Leadership program has received national awards for exemplary practice from leading academic and policy organizations such as University Council of Education Administration, the Council of the Great City Schools, and the Bush Institute's Alliance to Reform Education Leadership. Steve is Associate Editor of *Educational Theory*; lead author of *School and Society, Historical and Contemporary Perspectives*, 7th edition (2012); lead editor of *The Handbook of Research in Social Foundations of Education* (2011); and author or editor of four other books. He has served as head of Curriculum and Instruction at University of Illinois Urbana-Champaign; chair of policy studies at UIC; and President of the American Educational Studies Association.

Lynda Tredway was the founding coordinator of the Principal Leadership Institute (PLI) at UC Berkeley's Graduate School of Education (2000–2012) where she designed the course of study, taught multiple courses, and provided professional development to principals and assistant principals in urban districts. At the Institute of Educational Leadership, she is senior associate on the Leaders for Today and Tomorrow Project, a catalyst for engaging IHEs, school districts, and nonprofits in uncovering and coordinating their efforts in social justice preparation and support of urban and rural leaders in our most vulnerable schools.

Sharon Watkins has thirty-five years' experience as an educator, having worked with students K–12, college, and adult. Throughout her career she designed new structures and programs to respond to local educational needs. Her work includes developing curriculum, student learning environments, and teacher professional learning communities. Her interests are in arts integration, educational technology, and innovative school design. She was co-designer and coordinator of the Family Academy model titled the Learning Café, which was funded by a Race to the Top Innovation Grant. Currently she is the administrator and lead concept architect for a program focused on high school students and community families that provides alternative learning environments to meet diverse needs and foster a shared culture of learning. Watkins is a doctoral candidate in educational administration at The Ohio State University.

Dr. Melinda Webber is a tenured senior lecturer and faculty member in the Faculty of Education in the School of Learning, Development, and Professional Practice at the University of Auckland, New Zealand. Dr. Webber is also a qualitative researcher on the Starpath Project. Her research interests focus on racial-ethnic identity development and Māori student success. She is a Principal-Investigator on a large research project, funded by Nga Pae o te

Maramatanga, which focuses on Māori student success within her tribal region of Rotorua. She is also the author of *Walking the Space Between: Identity and Māori/Pakeha* (2008).

Cirecie A. West-Olatunji serves as associate professor and director of the Center for Traumatic Stress Research at the University of Cincinnati. She is immediate past president of the American Counseling Association (ACA) and secretary of Division E: Counseling and Human Development in the American Educational Research Association (AERA). Dr. West-Olatunji specializes in traumatic stress and multicultural counseling with a focus on marginalized communities. Dr. West-Olatunji has provided over one hundred presentations and is the author of over forty peer-reviewed journal articles, numerous book chapters, and coauthor of three books. Internationally, Dr. West-Olatunji has provided consultation and training in southern Africa, the Pacific Rim, and Europe. She is also a past president of the Association for Multicultural Counseling and Development, a division of ACA. A graduate of Dartmouth College, Dr. West-Olatunji received her master's and doctoral degrees in counselor education from the University of New Orleans.

Samuel Whalen is research director in the Center for Urban Education Leadership, University of Illinois–Chicago, where he has engaged in obtaining federal and philanthropic grants to support the development of a an implementation science approach to developing programming and research in urban school leadership preparation. At the Center, he is responsible for developing a research agenda and performance management infrastructure for a nationally recognized university doctoral program to produce high-performance principals for underserved, urban elementary and high schools. He was formerly Chapin Hall Center for Children at the University of Chicago, where he was funded by John D. and Catherine T. MacArthur Foundation to study policy issues and opportunities to improve the workforce readiness of youth in the Chicago region, and where he was lead author on publications addressing public libraries and youth development. With M. Csikszentmihalyi (1993), Whalen published *Talented Teenagers: The Roots of Success and Failure*, followed later by Whalen, S. P. (1998), "Flow and the engagement of talent: Implications for secondary schooling" in the *Bulletin of the National Association of Secondary School Principals*.

Ronald W. Whitaker II is a recent 2014 graduate in the Professional Doctorate in Educational Leadership (ProDEL) program at Duquesne University. Further he is also a mental health clinician, diversity professional, subject matter specialist on issues pertaining to black males, and 2012–2014 UCEA Barbara L. Jackson Scholar. His dissertation problem of practice focuses on how African-American male student athletes who compete in revenue sports at predominately white institutions (PWIs) experience and perceive the climate on their campus and team. Past professional accomplishments include: (1) adjunct teaching for Princeton University's (PBC) social emotional program, (2) working with student athletes at the University of Delaware, (3) working on two research projects at the University of Pennsylvania, (4) serving as coordinator and instructor for the Trio program at Montgomery County Community College, (5) serving as a leadership educator and clinician for nonprofits who serviced the Philadelphia School District, and (6) providing committee leadership to both the National Association of Diversity Officers in Higher Education (NADOHE) and the National Association of African Americans in Human Resources (NAAHR).

Gregory White is a Detroit native and graduate of Detroit Public Schools. After earning a bachelor of education at the University of Michigan and a master of education at Harvard University, he came back to teach in Detroit Public Schools. At present he is a PhD student dual majoring in the Education Policy and K–12 Educational Administration programs at Michigan State University.

Rodney S. Whiteman is a doctoral candidate, studying educational policy and leadership at Indiana University. His research applies critical social theories to the investigation of education politics, educational policy formation and enactment, leadership, and leadership preparation, particularly within organizational contexts. He also conducts research on professional identity formation and methods of educational inquiry. Rod Whiteman is the corresponding author.

Dr. Frankie K. Williams is a full professor in the Department of Leadership and Foundations at Mississippi State University. Dr. Williams earned her PhD at the University of South Carolina in the area of educational leadership. Her work experiences include P–16 teaching and administrative positions. Dr. Williams's research interests include leadership preparation and practices, diversity issues, curriculum and teaching issues, and contemporary P–16 practices and policy issues.

Dr. Sheneka Williams is currently an associate professor in the Department of Lifelong Education, Administration, and Policy at the University of Georgia. Dr. Williams is an active member in her department, where she is currently co-leading an effort to revise the program's Education Doctorate in Educational Leadership. Dr. Williams has also conducted workshops at the university and in Metro Atlanta school districts concerning school-community relations. Dr. Williams is also an active member in the University Council of Educational Administration, where she currently serves as an associate director for policy and advocacy.

Camille M. Wilson is an associate professor in the Department of Educational Studies at the University of Michigan. Her research is interdisciplinary in nature and chiefly explores school-family-community engagement, urban education reform, school choice, and transformative leadership from holistic, critical, and culturally relevant perspectives. Dr. Wilson is co-editor of *Advancing Equity and Achievement in America's Diverse Schools: Inclusive Theories, Policies, and Practices*, which was published in 2014. Her work has also been published in outlets such as *Teachers College Record*, the *International Journal of Qualitative Studies in Education, Educational Administration Quarterly, Equity and Excellence in Education*, and in numerous scholarly books. Dr. Wilson serves as a member of the executive committee of the American Educational Research Association's Division A and as co-chair of Division A's Affirmative Action Committee. She received her Ph.D. in Urban Schooling from the University of California, Los Angeles.

Dr. Jiangang Xia is an assistant professor of educational administration in the Department of Educational Administration at University of Nebraska-Lincoln. His research focuses on both K–12 leadership/policy and quantitative research. Dr. Xia has published three articles and two book chapters, and presented several studies in national conferences in the area of K–12 educational leadership.

Michelle D. Young, PhD, is the executive director of the University Council for Educational Administration (UCEA) and a professor of educational leadership at the University of Virginia. Through her work with UCEA, an international consortium of research universities with programs in educational leadership, Young has fostered research on leadership preparation and brought that research to bear on the work of policymakers. Young's scholarship focuses on how university programs, educational policies, and school leaders can support equitable and quality experiences for all students and adults who learn and work in schools. She is the recipient of the William J. Davis Award for the most outstanding article published in a volume of the *Educational Administration Quarterly*. Her work has also been published in the *Review of Educational Research*, the *Educational Researcher*, the *American Educational Research Journal*, the *Journal of School Leadership*, the *Journal of Educational Administration*, and *Leadership and Policy in Schools*, among other publications. She recently edited, with Murphy, Crow, and Ogawa, the first *Handbook of Research on the Education of School Leaders*.

Paul Zavitkovsky is an instructor and leadership coach in the Urban School Leadership Program, University of Illinois–Chicago. There he is responsible for annually coaching up to fifteen practicing principals, principal interns, and district leaders on-site on a weekly basis, designing and conducting research-in-practice seminars and workshops, and conducting basic research on generating/formatting teacher-friendly data in real time to inform school-improvement conversations at the grade/departmental and school-wide level. Paul has thirty-five years of experience as a public school administrator, classroom teacher, and consultant to public and private organizations, and was nationally awarded for his work as principal in a Chicago elementary school. Prior to his UIC work, Paul was senior policy analyst civic committee, the Commercial Club of Chicago, Chicago, Illinois, where he provided data analysis and editorial support for Left Behind, an analysis of student achievement trends in Chicago and the six-county Chicagoland region.